UNIVERSITY CASEBOOK SERIES®

BUSINESS ASSOCIATIONS

A MODERN APPROACH

CATHY HWANG
University of Virginia School of Law

PAOLO SAGUATO
George Mason University Antonin Scalia Law School

FOUNDATION PRESS

University Casebook Series is a trademark registered in the U.S. Patent and Trademark Office.

© 2023 LEG, Inc. d/b/a West Academic
    860 Blue Gentian Road, Suite 350
    Eagan, MN 55121
    1-877-888-1330

Printed in the United States of America

ISBN: 978-1-63659-778-2

For my great-grandmother, Mei Cheng.
And for Tom and Angela.

Cathy

A Eva, Dalia, e Giulio, amori della mia vita
A Fabio, Gianna, e Giorgio, mio porto sicuro

Paolo

PREFACE

In the picture book *Glasses: Who Needs 'Em?*, a young boy declares confidently that nobody wears glasses—after all, *he* has never seen anybody wearing glasses. But as soon as the boy puts on his first pair of glasses, he realizes he's been wrong all along. *Everybody* wears glasses. The boy had just never noticed before because he couldn't see very well.

Many students approach a basic business law course like it's a side of badly cooked broccoli: something to choke down for the bar exam. But business law is more than that: it interacts with just about every aspect of the law. Through business law, one can, of course, vindicate the interests of business parties. But one can also protect students from predatory loans, dive into family dramas, prevent discriminatory housing practices, and protect the rights of migrant workers.

This book aims to show how business law interacts with the economy and with society—it aims to help readers put on the glasses, so to speak.

While this book includes well-edited versions of business law's greatest hits, it also introduces new cases that showcase the field's effects on family law, housing discrimination, workers' rights, and more.

The book also mimics real practice: its focus is on primary sources (cases and statutes) and on selected secondary sources (restatements). Like a practicing attorney, readers examine the primary sources to learn the law. Many chapters also feature self-study questions based on real cases, so readers can look up cases to review the courts' actual opinions.

When you finish this course, we hope you will believe, as we do, that business law really is all around us.

Some notes on how to use this book: You'll see that we've edited cases, footnotes, and in-line case citations to make the text more readable. The real cases are often pretty fun, and we encourage you to look up the full case if you're curious about the context and procedural background. The problems in the book are inspired by real cases or examples from the Restatement. Those inspired by real cases or examples are accompanied by a citation so that you can look up how a court approached the issue.

A few words of thanks. We're grateful to our families, who supported us and gave us the time to complete this project. We also thank the excellent staff at Foundation Press that have enthusiastically supported us, and our copy editor, Claire Haley. Special thanks to our early adopters: George Mason University Antonin Scalia Law School Business Associations students from Spring 2021, Spring 2022, and Fall 2023; University of Virginia School of Law Corporations students from Fall 2021; and our intrepid early-adopting colleagues Samuel Brunson and Benjamin Means and their students, who provided valuable user feedback.

And finally, a very special thank you to our hardworking research assistants:

Justin Angotti	Mahlon Mower
Nicole Banton	Doriane S. Nguenang Tchenga
Sean Michael Blochberger	Melissa Privette
Lauren Burns	Odett Alvarez Rodriguez
Joseph Camano	Tristan Deering
Sandra Castaneda	Claire Song
Michael Castrovilla	Jolena Sun
Christina Del Rosso	Shinae Yoon
Katiuska D. Moya Duran	Sawyer Linde
Channing Gatewood	Stephen Huie
Nathan Gonzalez	Regina Zeng
Timothy Miles	

CATHY HWANG

PAOLO SAGUATO

July 2023

SUMMARY OF CONTENTS

TABLE OF CONTENTS

TABLE OF CASES

The principal cases are in bold type.

UNIVERSITY CASEBOOK SERIES®

BUSINESS ASSOCIATIONS

A MODERN APPROACH

CHAPTER I

AGENCY LAW

Agency law is the DNA of any business association. Agency law concerns the extent to which one party (*the principal*) can be held liable for the actions of another (*the agent*) who acts on the principal's behalf, as well as the rights and obligations between the principal and her agent. Agency law likewise serves as the foundation for this course, and agency relationships and their principles apply to all forms of business associations: partnerships, corporations, and limited liability companies.

The Restatement of Agency provides a highly influential summary of agency law.

A. AGENCY DEFINED

The existence of a principal-agent relationship triggers certain legal consequences: fiduciary duties, authority, and liability. But when does a principal-agent relationship exist?

Restatement (Third) of Agency
Section 1.01—Agency Defined

Agency is the fiduciary relationship that arises when one person (a "principal") manifests assent to another person (an "agent") that the agent shall act on the principal's behalf and subject to the principal's control, and the agent manifests assent or otherwise consents so to act.

Section 1.02—Parties' Labeling and Popular Usage Not Controlling

An agency relationship arises only when the elements stated in § 1.01 are present. Whether a relationship is characterized as agency in an agreement between parties or in the context of industry or popular usage is not controlling.

Section 1.03—Manifestation

A person manifests assent or intention through written or spoken words or other conduct.

Section 1.04(5)—Person

A person is (a) an individual; (b) an organization or association that has legal capacity to possess rights and incur obligations; (c) a government, political subdivision, or instrumentality or entity created by government; or (d) any other entity that has legal capacity to possess rights and incur obligations.

Section 3.02—Formal Requirements

If the law requires a writing or record signed by the principal to evidence an agent's authority to bind a principal to a contract or other transaction, the principal is not bound in the absence of such a writing or record. A principal may be estopped to assert the lack of such a writing or record when a third party has been induced to make a detrimental change in position by the reasonable belief that an agent has authority to bind the principal that is traceable to a manifestation made by the principal.

Section 3.04—Capacity to Act as Principal

(1) An individual has capacity to act as principal in a relationship of agency as defined in § 1.01 if, at the time the agent takes action, the individual would have capacity if acting in person.

(2) The law applicable to a person that is not an individual governs whether the person has capacity to be a principal in a relationship of agency as defined in § 1.01, as well as the effect of the person's lack or loss of capacity on those who interact with it.

(3) If performance of an act is not delegable, its performance by an agent does not constitute performance by the principal.

Section 3.05—Capacity to Act as Agent

Any person may ordinarily be empowered to act so as to affect the legal relations of another. The actor's capacity governs the extent to which, by so acting, the actor becomes subject to duties and liabilities to the person whose legal relations are affected or to third parties.

Marya v. Slakey

190 F.Supp.2d 95 (D. Mass. 2001)

[. . .] Defendant Slakey owns a six-bedroom residential property at 83 Prospect Street, Amherst, Massachusetts. Throughout the time she has owned the residence, Slakey leased the residence to six unrelated individuals, one of whom occupied each of the six bedrooms, and who collectively shared the common areas within the house. [. . .] Whenever a tenant moved out of the premises and a new tenant moved in, Slakey entered into a new lease with the reconstituted group of tenants, or simply modified the old lease to include the name of the new resident.

Historically, Slakey's role in the selection of new tenants was limited. Indeed, she neither interjected herself into the tenant selection process nor rejected any applicant who had been accepted by her tenants. Nevertheless, the express terms of the lease reposed in Slakey the authority to either accept or reject the candidates who had been chosen by her tenants. In addition, Slakey was responsible for checking the references of prospective tenants, although she rarely exercised this prerogative.

In August 1998, a tenant notified Slakey that she would be terminating her tenancy at the end of the following month. Shortly thereafter, plaintiff Arora applied to fill the vacancy. Arora is a citizen and native of India who came to the United States in August 1995 to pursue graduate studies at the University of Massachusetts. At the time she applied to fill the vacancy, she satisfied the traditional criteria applied by the tenants in evaluating applicants: she was enrolled at UMass, and she is a vegetarian and non-smoker. However, Arora's application was rejected by two tenants: Suzanne Castello and defendant Paul Norris. [EDS.— Marya also applied, was rejected for similar reasons, and sued, but Marya's case did not proceed to trial.]

Castello explained her decision to vote against Arora as rooted in a personality conflict. Norris, who also voted against Arora, indicated that he rejected Arora's application because she is an Indian woman. Specifically, he stated on three separate occasions that he did not want to live with three Indian women; at the time of the vote, two Indian women already lived in the residence. [. . .] Arora filed a complaint with this Court, alleging that Norris, acting as Slakey's agent, denied them housing in violation of the Fair Housing Act [. . .] on the basis of her race, color, national origin, and/or sex. [. . .] The defendants now move for summary judgment on the ground that Norris was not acting as Slakey's agent for the purposes of renting vacant rooms in the premises. [. . .]

It is well established that a principal is liable for the wrongful acts of his or her agent in [Fair Housing Act] housing discrimination claims. To ascertain whether an agency relationship exists, the federal courts look to the Restatement (Second) of Agency (1958) [EDS.—This same language is found in § 1.01 of the Restatement (Third) of Agency]. [. . .]

Under the Restatement, agency results from "the manifestation of consent by one person to another that the other shall act on his behalf and subject to his control, and consent by the other so to act." To satisfy this definition, Arora must show that: (a) defendant Slakey, the alleged principal, manifested that Norris shall act for her; (b) Norris, the alleged agent, manifested his acceptance of such authority; and (c) both parties understood that Slakey was to exercise a degree of control over Norris's activities while he was acting as Slakey's agent. [. . .] [A]n agency [relationship] may be established "through actual conduct of the parties and regardless of written or other specific authority negativing or limiting the existence or extent of an agency." *Barefoot v. Int'l B'hood of Teamsters, Chauffeurs, Warehousemen and Helpers of Am.*

At least two federal courts have found property owners liable for the discriminatory actions of tenants who assisted in the rental of vacant apartments, but were not professional agents or property managers, based solely on the conduct of the parties. In *Harris v. Itzhaki,* for instance, the court denied the defendant's motion for summary judgment on the question of agency between the defendant property owners and an elderly tenant who assisted the owners in the operation of their

apartment building by receiving rent checks and showing vacant apartments to prospective tenants. Although the tenant did not receive a salary or any discount in rent in exchange for her assistance, the court held that there were sufficient facts from which the jury could find an agency [relationship].

Similarly, in *Wright v. Owen,* the court found the property owner liable [. . .] for the discriminatory actions of a tenant, Mrs. Stein, who showed a vacant apartment to black applicants, discouraged their application, but encouraged the application of a white applicant, Mrs. Epstein. Mrs. Stein advised the landlord of Mrs. Epstein's interest, and the landlord stated that Mrs. Epstein could rent the apartment. The court concluded: "Although Mrs. Stein was not the designated agent of [the] defendant . . . to rent her apartment, defendant's apparent acceptance of Mrs. Epstein as a tenant is sufficient to establish an agency relationship by conduct."

In this case, the Court concludes that there is sufficient evidence of the conduct of Slakey and Norris from which a reasonable jury could find the existence of an agency under Arora's FHA [. . .] claim [. . .]. The record reflects that a vacancy arose in the residence on approximately twenty occasions between 1993 and 1998. On each occasion, Norris and the other tenants were actively involved in posting the advertisements, and selecting each new tenant who moved into the residence. Like the tenants in *Harris* and *Wright,* therefore, Norris assisted his landlord by facilitating the process by which vacancies were filled. Moreover, no candidate was selected without the express approval of each tenant, and Slakey never rejected any of her tenants' selections, although the lease expressly reserved her right to do so. [. . .] In the case of Arora's application, Slakey acquiesced in Norris's decision to reject the application after speaking with many of her tenants, including Norris, regarding the origin of the dispute surrounding her rejection. Slakey's acceptance of her tenants' decisions to accept or reject applicants, like that of the landlord in *Wright,* is sufficient to establish an agency relationship by conduct. [. . .]

The defendants challenge the existence of an agency relationship between Norris and Slakey on two fronts. First, the defendants assert that there is no evidence of "continuous control and direction exercised by Slakey over Norris . . . such as would support a finding of agency." It is true that the right of control by the principal over the agent is an irreducible element of an agency relationship. However, the defendants exaggerate the quantum of control necessary to establish an agency. "The control of the principal does not . . . include control at every moment; its exercise may be very attenuated and, as where the principal is physically absent, may be ineffective." Restatement (Second) of Agency at § 1. In this case, the lease clearly reposes the ultimate decision-making authority for the selection of tenants in Slakey, as owner of the residence. In her deposition testimony, moreover, Slakey stated that she felt that she would have been within her rights as owner of the premises to reject candidates whose names were presented to her by her tenants. In addition, Slakey had the power, although rarely exercised, to check the references of candidates selected by her tenants. This is sufficient to establish control as an element of the agency relationship.

Second, the defendants suggest that Slakey did not benefit from the efforts of Norris, and the other tenants, to fill vacancies in the residence. Specifically, the defendants point out that, under the joint and several lease, the tenants were required to satisfy the entire rent obligation. Therefore, the defendants asseverate, the actions of the tenants were taken solely for their own benefit, not for the benefit of Slakey. The record evidence, however, belies this contention. As Arora persuasively argues, Slakey benefits from the efforts of her tenants in that she is relieved of the burden and expense of advertising the vacancies, showing the premises to prospective tenants, and interviewing applicants. [. . .] Thus, the Court concludes that Slakey benefitted from the efforts of Norris in facilitating the rental of vacant rooms in the residence.

Accordingly, the Court denies the defendants' motion for summary judgment. [. . .]

B. AGENCY FORMATION

A. Gay Jenson Farms Co. v. Cargill, Inc.
309 N.W.2d 285 (Minn. 1981)

Plaintiffs, 86 individual, partnership or corporate farmers, brought this action against defendant Cargill, Inc. (Cargill) and defendant Warren Grain & Seed Co. (Warren) to recover losses sustained when Warren defaulted on the contracts made with plaintiffs for the sale of grain. After a trial by jury, judgment was entered in favor of plaintiffs, and Cargill brought this appeal. We affirm.

This case arose out of the financial collapse of defendant Warren, and its failure to satisfy its indebtedness to plaintiffs. Warren, which was located in Warren, Minnesota, was operated by Lloyd Hill and his son, Gary Hill. Warren operated a grain elevator and as a result was involved in the purchase of cash or market grain from local farmers. The cash grain would be resold through the Minneapolis Grain Exchange or to the terminal grain companies directly. Warren also stored grain for farmers and sold chemicals, fertilizer and steel storage bins. In addition, it operated a seed business which involved buying seed grain from farmers, processing it and reselling it for seed to farmers and local elevators.

Lloyd Hill decided in 1964 to apply for financing from Cargill. Cargill's officials from the Moorhead regional office investigated Warren's operations and recommended that Cargill finance Warren.

Warren and Cargill thereafter entered into a security agreement which provided that Cargill would loan money for working capital to Warren on "open account" financing up to a stated limit, which was originally set as $175,000. Under this contract, Warren would receive funds and pay its expenses by issuing drafts drawn on Cargill through Minneapolis banks. The drafts were imprinted with both Warren's and Cargill's names. Proceeds from Warren's sales would be deposited with Cargill and credited to its account. In return for this financing, Warren appointed Cargill as its grain agent for transaction with the Commodity Credit Corporation. Cargill was also given a right of first refusal to purchase market grain sold by Warren to the terminal market.

A new contract was negotiated in 1967, extending Warren's credit line to $300,000 and incorporating the provisions of the original contract. It was also stated in the contract that Warren would provide Cargill with annual financial statements and that either Cargill would keep the books for Warren or an audit would be conducted by an independent firm. Cargill was given the right of access to Warren's books for inspection.

In addition, the agreement provided that Warren was not to make capital improvements or repairs in excess of $5,000 without Cargill's prior consent. Further, it was not to become liable as guarantor on another's indebtedness, or encumber its assets except with Cargill's permission. Consent by Cargill was required before Warren would be allowed to declare a dividend or sell and purchase stock.

Officials from Cargill's regional office made a brief visit to Warren shortly after the agreement was executed. They examined the annual statement and the accounts receivable, expenses, inventory, seed, machinery and other financial matters. Warren was informed that it would be reminded periodically to make the improvements recommended by Cargill. At approximately this time, a memo was given to the Cargill official in charge of the Warren account, Erhart Becker, which stated in part: "This organization [Warren] needs very strong paternal guidance."

In 1970, Cargill contracted with Warren and other elevators to act as its agent to seek growers for a new type of wheat called Bounty 208. Warren, as Cargill's agent for this project, entered into contracts for the growing of the wheat seed, with Cargill named as the contracting party. Farmers were paid directly by Cargill for the seed and all contracts were performed in full. In 1971, pursuant to an agency contract, Warren contracted on Cargill's behalf with various farmers for the growing of sunflower seeds for Cargill. The arrangements were similar to those made in the Bounty 208 contracts, and all those contracts were also completed. Both these agreements were unrelated to the open account financing contract. In addition, Warren, as Cargill's agent in the sunflower seed business, cleaned and packaged the seed in Cargill bags.

During this period, Cargill continued to review Warren's operations and expenses and recommend that certain actions should be taken. Warren purchased from Cargill various business forms printed by Cargill and received sample forms from Cargill which Warren used to develop its own business forms.

Cargill wrote to its regional office in 1970 expressing its concern that the pattern of increased use of funds allowed to develop at Warren was similar to that involved in two other cases in which Cargill experienced severe losses. Cargill did not refuse to honor drafts or call the loan, however. A new security agreement which increased the credit line to $750,000 was executed in 1972, and a subsequent agreement which raised the limit to $1,250,000 was entered into in 1976.

Warren was at that time shipping Cargill 90% of its cash grain. When Cargill's facilities were full, Warren shipped its grain to other companies. Approximately 25% of Warren's total sales was seed grain which was sold directly by Warren to its customers.

As Warren's indebtedness continued to be in excess of its credit line, Cargill began to contact Warren daily regarding its financial affairs. Cargill headquarters informed its regional office in 1973 that, since Cargill money was being used, Warren should realize that Cargill had the right to make some critical decisions regarding the use of the funds. Cargill headquarters also told Warren that a regional manager would be working with Warren on a day-to-day basis as well as in monthly planning meetings. In 1975, Cargill's regional office began to keep a daily debit position on Warren. A bank account was opened in Warren's name on which Warren could draw checks in 1976. The account was to be funded by drafts drawn on Cargill by the local bank.

In early 1977, it became evident that Warren had serious financial problems. Several farmers, who had heard that Warren's checks were not being paid, inquired or had their agents inquire at Cargill regarding Warren's status and were initially told that there would be no problem with payment. In April 1977, an audit of Warren revealed that Warren was $4 million in debt. After Cargill was informed that Warren's financial statements had been deliberately falsified, Warren's request for additional financing was refused. In the final days of Warren's operation, Cargill sent an official to supervise the elevator, including disbursement of funds and income generated by the elevator.

After Warren ceased operations, it was found to be indebted to Cargill in the amount of $3.6 million. Warren was also determined to be indebted to plaintiffs in the amount of $2 million, and plaintiffs brought this action in 1977 to seek recovery of that sum. Plaintiffs alleged that Cargill was jointly liable for Warren's indebtedness as it had acted as principal for the grain elevator. [. . .]

The jury found that Cargill's conduct between 1973 and 1977 had made it Warren's principal. Warren was found to be the agent of Cargill with regard to contracts for:

1.   The purchase and sale of grain for market.
2.   The purchase and sale of seed grain.
3.   The storage of grain.

The court determined that Cargill was the disclosed principal of Warren. It was concluded that Cargill was jointly liable with Warren for plaintiffs' losses, and judgment was entered for plaintiffs.

Cargill seeks a reversal of the jury's findings. [. . .]

The major issue in this case is whether Cargill, by its course of dealing with Warren, became liable as a principal on contracts made by Warren with plaintiffs. Cargill contends that no agency relationship was established with Warren, notwithstanding its financing of Warren's operation and its purchase of the majority of Warren's grain. However, we conclude that Cargill, by its control and influence over Warren, became a principal with liability for the transactions entered into by its agent Warren.

Agency is the fiduciary relationship that results from the manifestation of consent by one person to another that the other shall act on his behalf and subject to his control, and consent by the other so to act. [. . .] In order to create an agency there must be an agreement, but not necessarily a contract between the parties. Restatement (Second) of Agency § 1, comment b (1958) [EDS.—same language as § 1.01 of the Restatement (Third) of Agency]. An agreement may result in the creation of an agency relationship although the parties did not call it an agency and did not intend the legal consequences of the relation to follow [. . .]. The existence of the agency may be proved by circumstantial evidence which shows a course of dealing between the two parties. [. . .] When an agency relationship is to be proven by circumstantial evidence, the principal must be shown to have consented to the agency since one cannot be the agent of another except by consent of the latter. [. . .]

Cargill contends that the prerequisites of an agency relationship did not exist because Cargill never consented to the agency, Warren did not act on behalf of Cargill, and Cargill did not exercise control over Warren. We hold that all three elements of agency could be found in the particular circumstances of this case. By directing Warren to implement its recommendations, Cargill manifested its consent that Warren would be its agent. Warren acted on Cargill's behalf in procuring grain for Cargill as the part of its normal operations which were totally financed by Cargill. Further, an agency relationship was established by Cargill's interference with the internal affairs of Warren, which constituted *de facto* control of the elevator.

A creditor who assumes control of his debtor's business may become liable as principal for the acts of the debtor in connection with the business. Restatement (Second) of Agency § 14O (1958) [EDS.—This same language is found in § 1.01 of the Restatement (Third) of Agency]. It is noted in the Restatement (Second) of Agency that:

> A security holder who merely exercises a veto power over the business acts of his debtor by preventing purchases or sales above specified amounts does not thereby become a principal.

However, if he takes over the management of the debtor's business either in person or through an agent, and directs what contracts may or may not be made, he becomes a principal, liable as a principal for the obligations incurred thereafter in the normal course of business by the debtor who has now become his general agent. The point at which the creditor becomes a principal is that at which he assumes *de facto* control over the conduct of his debtor, whatever the terms of the formal contract with his debtor may be.*

A number of factors indicate Cargill's control over Warren, including the following:

(1) Cargill's constant recommendations to Warren by telephone;

(2) Cargill's right of first refusal on grain;

(3) Warren's inability to enter into mortgages, to purchase stock or to pay dividends without Cargill's approval;

(4) Cargill's right of entry onto Warren's premises to carry on periodic checks and audits;

(5) Cargill's correspondence and criticism regarding Warren's finances, officers salaries and inventory;

(6) Cargill's determination that Warren needed "strong paternal guidance";

(7) Provision of drafts and forms to Warren upon which Cargill's name was imprinted;

(8) Financing of all Warren's purchases of grain and operating expenses; and

(9) Cargill's power to discontinue the financing of Warren's operations.

We recognize that some of these elements, as Cargill contends, are found in an ordinary debtor-creditor relationship. However, these factors cannot be considered in isolation, but, rather, they must be viewed in light of all the circumstances surrounding Cargill's aggressive financing of Warren.

[Here,] Cargill furnished substantially all funds received by the elevator. Cargill did have a right of entry on Warren's premises, and it [. . .] required maintenance of insurance against hazards of operation. Warren's activities [. . .] formed a substantial part of Cargill's business that was developed in that area. In addition, Cargill did not think of Warren as an operator who was free to become Cargill's competitor, but rather conceded that it believed that Warren owed a duty of loyalty to

* EDS.—Restatement (Third) of Agency § 1.01 states "Agency is the fiduciary relationship that arises when one person (a "principal") manifests assent to another person (an "agent") that the agent shall act on the principal's behalf and subject to the principal's control, and the agent manifests assent or otherwise consents so to act."

Cargill. The decisions made by Warren were not independent of Cargill's interest or its control.

Further, [. . .] [t]he Warren operation [. . .] was financially dependent on Cargill's continual infusion of capital. [. . .] Cargill became, in essence, the owner of the operation without the accompanying legal indicia.

The *amici curiae* assert that, if the jury verdict is upheld, firms and banks which have provided business loans to county elevators will decline to make further loans. The decision in this case should give no cause for such concern. We deal here with a business enterprise markedly different from an ordinary bank financing, since Cargill was an active participant in Warren's operations rather than simply a financier. Cargill's course of dealing with Warren was, by its own admission, a paternalistic relationship in which Cargill made the key economic decisions and kept Warren in existence.

Although considerable interest was paid by Warren on the loan, the reason for Cargill's financing of Warren was not to make money as a lender but, rather, to establish a source of market grain for its business. As one Cargill manager noted, "We were staying in there because we wanted the grain." For this reason, Cargill was willing to extend the credit line far beyond the amount originally allocated to Warren. It is noteworthy that Cargill was receiving significant amounts of grain and that, notwithstanding the risk that was recognized by Cargill, the operation was considered profitable.

On the whole, there was a unique fabric in the relationship between Cargill and Warren which varies from that found in normal debtor-creditor situations. We conclude that, on the facts of this case, there was sufficient evidence from which the jury could find that Cargill was the principal of Warren within the definitions of agency set forth in Restatement (Second) of Agency §§ 1 and 140. [. . .]

C. FIDUCIARY DUTIES

A fiduciary is someone who stands in a position of trust, confidence, or responsibility in certain obligations to others. Agents are their principals' fiduciaries and have a fiduciary duty to act loyally for the principals' benefit when acting within the scope of the agency relationship. This section concerns the contours of the fiduciary duty of loyalty in the context of agency.

Restatement (Third) of Agency
Section 8.01—General Fiduciary Principle

An agent has a fiduciary duty to act loyally for the principal's benefit in all matters connected with the agency relationship.

Section 8.02—Material Benefit Arising Out of Position

An agent has a duty not to acquire a material benefit from a third party in connection with transactions conducted or other actions taken on behalf of the principal or otherwise through the agent's use of the agent's position.

Section 8.03—Acting as or on Behalf of an Adverse Party

An agent has a duty not to deal with the principal as or on behalf of an adverse party in a transaction connected with the agency relationship.

Section 8.04—Competition

Throughout the duration of an agency relationship, an agent has a duty to refrain from competing with the principal and from taking action on behalf of or otherwise assisting the principal's competitors. During that time, an agent may take action, not otherwise wrongful, to prepare for competition following termination of the agency relationship.

Section 8.05—Use of Principal's Property, Use of Confidential Information

An agent has a duty

(1) not to use property of the principal for the agent's own purposes or those of a third party; and

(2) not to use or communicate confidential information of the principal for the agent's own purposes or those of a third party.

Section 8.08—Duties of Care, Competence, and Diligence

Subject to any agreement with the principal, an agent has a duty to the principal to act with the care, competence, and diligence normally exercised by agents in similar circumstances. Special skills or knowledge possessed by an agent are circumstances to be taken into account in determining whether the agent acted with due care and diligence. If an agent claims to possess special skills or knowledge, the agent has a duty to the principal to act with the care, competence, and diligence normally exercised by agents with such skills or knowledge.

Section 8.09—Duty to Act Only Within Scope of Actual Authority and to Comply with Principal's Lawful Instructions

(1) An agent has a duty to take action only within the scope of the agent's actual authority.

(2) An agent has a duty to comply with all lawful instructions received from the principal and persons designated by the principal concerning the agent's actions on behalf of the principal.

Section 8.10—Duty of Good Conduct

An agent has a duty, within the scope of the agency relationship, to act reasonably and to refrain from conduct that is likely to damage the principal's enterprise.

Section 8.11—Duty to Provide Information

An agent has a duty to use reasonable efforts to provide the principal with facts that the agent knows, has reason to know, or should know when

(1)   subject to any manifestation by the principal, the agent knows or has reason to know that the principal would wish to have the facts or the facts are material to the agent's duties to the principal; and

(2)   the facts can be provided to the principal without violating a superior duty owed by the agent to another person.

Section 8.15—Principal's Duty to Deal Fairly and in Good Faith

A principal has a duty to deal with the agent fairly and in good faith, including a duty to provide the agent with information about risks of physical harm or pecuniary loss that the principal knows, has reason to know, or should know are present in the agent's work but unknown to the agent.

1.   DUTY OF LOYALTY

a.   OBLIGATION NOT TO COMPETE

Prince, Yeates & Geldzahler v. Young
94 P.3d 179 (Utah 2004)

[. . .] Factual and Procedural History

In April 1995, Prince Yeates hired Young as an associate attorney. Previously, Young had spent the majority of his twelve-year legal career as general counsel for Rocky Mountain Helicopters, where he acquired considerable experience in helicopter crash litigation. Prior to joining Prince Yeates, Young met with John Ashton, the firm's then-president, to discuss compensation. Under the terms of his original employment agreement, which was never reduced to writing, Young accepted a starting salary of $70,000 per year. [. . .]

In 1996, Young agreed to represent Charles Krause, who had sustained serious injuries in a helicopter crash, in a personal injury action in Texas. At approximately the same time, Young also undertook the representation of Mountain West Helicopters, the owner of the helicopter involved in Krause's accident, in a related lawsuit filed in federal court in Utah. As well as being the originating attorney, Young was the only lawyer at Prince Yeates who performed any work on either case.

For the next two years, Young spent considerable time on these two contingent fee cases, which resulted in lower collections and higher work-in-process figures compared to other Prince Yeates attorneys. As a result, some members of the firm began to question Young's overall profitability and readiness to become a shareholder. In September 1998, perhaps sensing this tension, Young inquired as to how the contingent fee in the

Krause case (assuming a successful outcome) would be divided between himself and Prince Yeates. The firm's Board of Directors ("the Board") responded by assigning Ashton and John Chindlund, Prince Yeates' then-president, to explore the possibility of reaching an agreement with Young on the Krause fee.

[. . .] Ultimately, the [. . .] parties reached a tentative verbal agreement under which Young would take one-third of the Krause fee, with the remaining two-thirds going to the firm. On May 5, 1999, Chindlund memorialized this proposal in writing and requested that Young sign it to acknowledge his acceptance. Young did not sign.

On June 14, 1999, Young learned that the Krause case had settled three days earlier at a mediation in Texas, which he did not attend, and that the contingent fee recovery would be nearly $650,000. The following day, June 15, without disclosing his knowledge of the settlement to his employer, Young made a counteroffer to the firm's May 5 proposal. In his counteroffer, Young agreed to divide the Krause fee one-third to himself and two-thirds to the firm, provided Prince Yeates made him a shareholder, allowed him a voice in that year's bonus distribution, and guaranteed an increased salary for the next two years. According to Young, over the course of their numerous meetings, Ashton and Chindlund promised him that the firm would fulfill these additional conditions upon the successful resolution of the Krause case. Ashton and Chindlund denied making such promises, and the firm did not respond to Young's proposal. Finally, on July 2, Young wrote a memo to the Board, informing them that he would leave Prince Yeates in two weeks if an agreement could not be reached on his counteroffer. The firm accepted Young's resignation on July 7.

After his departure, Prince Yeates learned that Young had represented certain clients during 1998 and 1999 without disclosing the representation to the firm, while simultaneously using firm resources and filing pleadings in the firm's name in connection with these matters. In addition, Young retained all fees derived from these cases for himself. Prince Yeates then filed suit against Young for breach of fiduciary duty, and Young counterclaimed alleging, among other causes of action, breach of oral contract. [. . .] [EDS.—The district court granted partial summary judgment to Young and denied partial summary judgment to the firm on the firm's breach of fiduciary duty claim. Prince Yeates now appeals.] [. . .]

Analysis

[. . .] Prince Yeates [. . .] argues that Young breached his fiduciary duty of loyalty—specifically, a duty of non-competition—when he represented clients in the firm's name without disclosing the representation to the firm, expended firm resources and filed pleadings in the firm's name in connection with these matters, and retained all fees derived from these cases for himself.[1] The district court denied Prince Yeates' motion for partial summary judgment on the issue of liability and granted Young's cross-motion, reasoning that, as a mere employee, he owed no fiduciary duty of non-competition to the firm. [. . .] [W]e disagree.

As a general matter, the second Restatement of Agency provides that "[u]nless otherwise agreed, an agent is subject to a duty not to compete with the principal concerning the subject matter of his agency." Restatement (Second) of Agency § 393. Furthermore, "[t]he rules as to the duties and liabilities to the principal of agents who are not servants [also] apply to servants." *Id.* at § 429. While the Restatement does not specifically include "employees" as "agents," it does refer to "servants," a term synonymous with "employees." *See* Black's Law Dictionary (defining "servant" by pointing to the definition of "employee").

Although this court has not directly addressed the issue of whether "mere employees" owe their employers a fiduciary duty of non-competition, other jurisdictions have. In *Fryetech, Inc. v. Harris*, the defendants argued that the fiduciary duties of good faith and loyalty did not apply to "mere employees." The court rejected this contention, emphasizing that "[w]hile most of the cases which have addressed the fiduciary responsibilities of agents . . . have involved corporate directors or officers, there is no basis for concluding these are the only types of agents subject to fiduciary duties." *Id.* Rather, "the cases speak of the duties of agents without respect to their exact status." *Id.* [. . .].

In response, Young cites *Microbiological Research Corp. v. Muna* ostensibly for the proposition that, under Utah law, "mere employees" owe no fiduciary duties to their employers. Young misreads *Muna*. This court in *Muna* noted that when a corporate officer no longer serves in that capacity due to resignation or removal, but remains as an employee, the fiduciary relationship may cease, depending on the factual circumstances. However, it is incorrect to conclude, as Young does, that this observation somehow inevitably leads to the conclusion that employees necessarily have no fiduciary duties to their employers. That is not the case. Moreover, Young cites no additional applicable law from this or any other jurisdiction.

In the relationship of a lawyer and his or her employer, there does exist a duty of honest and ethical behavior. Because of the privilege granted to engage in the practice of law, we impose upon members of our bar a fiduciary duty that encompasses the obligation to not compete with their employer, which we define as any law firm or legal services provider who may employ them in a legal capacity, without the employer's prior knowledge and agreement.

We therefore hold, as a matter of law, that the district court erred in denying Prince Yeates' motion for partial summary judgment on its

---

[1]   In addition, by invoking Prince Yeates' name, Young also effectively made the firm liable for any professional liability arising from the representation.

breach of fiduciary duty claim and in granting Young's cross-motion. To hold otherwise would imply that attorneys are free to join law firms, derive benefits from that association, and essentially operate as sole practitioners while simultaneously receiving a salary and using firm resources for their independent legal activities. If Young was unhappy at Prince Yeates, he was free, as an at-will employee, to leave at any time and presumably take those clients who wished to follow him. Merely because he was afraid that his interest in the Krause fee would be jeopardized does not justify his non-disclosure of representation and subsequent retention of fees. He had a higher duty to Prince Yeates than that. With that in mind, we now turn to the question of the firm's remedy.

Remedy

Regarding an appropriate remedy, Prince Yeates urges us to require the forfeiture of both Young's share of the Krause fee (determined by the jury to be $280,000) and all compensation paid by the firm to Young from January 26, 1998 through July 7, 1999—the time period during which Young breached his fiduciary duty of non-competition. [. . .] [W]e remand this issue to the district court, with instructions to determine the amount of those fees and order their payment to the firm forthwith.

Conclusion

[. . .] We reverse and remand for proceedings consistent with this opinion.

Pure Power Boot Camp, Inc. v. Warrior Fitness Boot Camp, LLC

813 F. Supp. 2d 489 (S.D.N.Y. 2011)

Plaintiffs Pure Power Boot Camp, Inc., brought this action against Defendants accusing Defendants of stealing their business model, customers, and confidential and commercially sensitive documents, breaching contractual and employee fiduciary duties, and infringing Plaintiffs' trade-dress. Defendants filed counterclaims asserting violations of the New York Labor Law, violations of the Stored Communications Act, and unauthorized use of Defendants' images in violation of New York Civil Rights Law. [. . .]

I.   Factual Background

While working as a trader on Wall Street in 2002, Plaintiff Lauren Brenner ("Brenner") decided to start her own physical fitness business, based upon the concept of a military boot camp. Investing substantial time and all of her savings, on or about December 17, 2003, Brenner opened Pure Power Boot Camp, Inc. ("Pure Power Boot Camp"), a facility located at 38 West 21st Street in Manhattan. Pure Power Boot Camp is modeled, in part, after United States Marine Corps training facilities. It is designed in military camouflage colors and decor and, unlike traditional gyms, does not have a membership fee; instead, clients sign renewable contracts for "tours of duty," meaning that "recruits"—as Pure

Power clients are called—sign up for a program to attend a certain number of sessions per week for a set number of weeks. If a recruit does not show up for a scheduled class, Pure Power personnel contacts them directly.

An important part of Brenner's concept is to use physical objects as part of an indoor obstacle course, modeled after a Marine Corps outdoor obstacle course at Fort Knox, to build confidence, physical fitness, and self-empowerment in her clients. To construct this obstacle course, Brenner contacted a company that built high rope courses. The owner of that company arranged for Brenner to visit Fort Knox and inspect the outdoor obstacle course there, in order to assess whether any of the individual obstacles were suitable for use in a smaller, indoor facility to be used by civilians. Brenner did so and adapted some of the Marine Corps' obstacles to her concept. One of Brenner's insights was that people will stick to an exercise regime if they work out in a group. She thus concluded that classes should be limited to 16 people who go through "training" together, and are called "recruits." [. . .]

Brenner employed former marines as "drill instructors," viewing it as an opportunity to provide jobs to veterans returning from combat in Iraq. In addition, Brenner felt that the hiring of military personnel would lead to good press coverage for her business. [. . .]

After the Pure Power facility was constructed according to her design, Brenner traveled to the Marines' Garden City Reserve Base to make a presentation to marines who had recently returned from combat service. Shortly following that presentation, a number of marines came to Pure Power to experience the program. One of those marines was Defendant Ruben Dario Belliard ("Belliard").

Belliard started working at Pure Power Boot Camp as an independent contractor in April 2005, and was hired as a full-time Pure Power drill instructor in or about July 2006. On Belliard's recommendation, Brenner hired Defendant Alexander Kenneth Fell ("Fell"), another marine, in or about August 2005. Fell started working as a full-time Pure Power drill instructor in or about September 2006. Both Belliard and Fell were well-liked and sought-after instructors. Indeed, Belliard eventually became Pure Power's head drill instructor. Brenner placed great trust in Belliard and, at least from her perspective, came to view him as a close friend.

Pure Power was a unique concept and unlike most other exercise facilities. It was an immediate success, garnering attention from a variety of media outlets, including MSNBC and Inside Edition. Brenner personally appeared on a variety of television shows, including NBC's The Today Show, the Donny Deutsch Show, and the Anderson Cooper Show on CNN. Brenner's intent when she created Pure Power was not to have one location, but to develop a business plan that could be rolled out as a national franchise. [. . .]

In preparation for Pure Power's franchising roll-out, Brenner had the drill instructors sign an Employment Agreement as a condition of continued employment. With the exception of Fell, every drill instructor, Belliard included, admits to having signed an Employment Agreement. Fell, however, disputes having signed such an Employment Agreement, while Brenner insists that he did. [. . .]

Around July 2007, while they were still working at Pure Power, Defendants Belliard and Fell began planning their own military-themed gym—Warrior Fitness Boot Camp, LLC ("Warrior Fitness").

[. . .] Defendants' efforts went beyond merely promoting and planning Warrior Fitness. As part of Defendants' combined efforts to open Warrior Fitness, Defendant Belliard stole documents from Brenner's private office and personal computer, including Pure Power's business plan, start-up manual, and operations manual. Belliard also stole a folder with Employment Agreements of Pure Power employees, including his own, and destroyed those agreements. In addition, Belliard, without permission, downloaded a copy of Pure Power's confidential customer list onto a thumb-drive. [. . .]

Belliard shared the stolen materials, including Pure Power's client list, with Defendants Fell and Baynard. [. . .]

On April 28, 2008, Brenner found out about Defendants' plan to open Warrior Fitness and the fact that confidential materials had been stolen from her office at Pure Power. Elizabeth Lorenzi ("Lorenzi"), who was an employee of Pure Power, knew that Fell had used the Pure Power computer. [. . .]

Belliard and Fell, along with their girlfriends at the time, Lee and Baynard, opened Warrior Fitness on or about May 12, 2008. [. . .]

DISCUSSION

[. . .]

II. Breach of the Duty of Loyalty

Plaintiffs contend that Defendants Belliard and Fell breached the common law duty of loyalty owed to Pure Power as employees of Pure Power.

A. Liability

"New York law with respect to disloyal or faithless performance of employment duties is grounded in the law of agency, and has developed for well over a century." *Phansalkar v. Andersen Weinroth & Co., L.P.* An agent is obligated under New York law to be loyal to his employer and is "prohibited from acting in any manner inconsistent with his agency or trust and is at all times bound to exercise the utmost good faith and loyalty in the performance of his duties." *Id.* This duty is not dependent upon an express contractual relationship, but exists even where the employment relationship is at-will. [. . .]

When an employee uses an employer's proprietary or confidential information when establishing a competing business, the employee breaches his or her fiduciary duty to the employer. [. . .] Although an employee may, of course, make preparations to compete with his employer while still working for the employer, he or she may not do so at the employer's expense, and may not use the employer's resources, time, facilities, or confidential information; specifically, whether or not the employee has signed an agreement not-to-compete, the employee, while still employed by the employer, may not solicit clients of his employer, may not copy his employer's business records for his own use, may not charge expenses to his employer, which were incurred while acting on behalf of his own interest, and may not actively divert the employer's business for his own personal benefit or the benefit of others. [. . .] In addition, even in the absence of trade secret protection, employees are not permitted to copy their employer's client list, and such acts have been deemed to be an "egregious breach of trust and confidence."

Here, the preponderance of the evidence establishes numerous breaches by Defendants Belliard and Fell of their duty of loyalty to Pure Power. Defendant Belliard stole Pure Power documents, including Pure Power's business plan, start-up manual, and operations manual. Belliard also stole personnel files from Brenner's private office, and destroyed his and other employees' signed Employment Agreements. After Belliard destroyed the original Employment Agreements, he sent an email to Fell, boasting that the "cat is in the bag," to which Fell responded "hallelujah." Belliard shared the other stolen materials with Fell, who did not return them to Pure Power, but, instead, destroyed them. Belliard also provided a copy of Pure Power's business plan, operations manual, and start-up manual to Lee, who referred to these documents in drafting business documents for Warrior Fitness. Belliard and Fell were also aware that, on their behalf, Lee was soliciting current Pure Power clients to join Warrior Fitness, while she was still a member of Pure Power.

Both Belliard and Fell collected and maintained Pure Power client contact information, while on Pure Power's payroll and at the Pure Power facility, in anticipation of opening Warrior Fitness. In addition, Belliard, without permission, downloaded a copy of Pure Power's customer list onto a thumb-drive and disclosed the confidential contact information contained therein to, at a minimum, Baynard, with the intention that this information be used to solicit Pure Power customers to join Warrior Fitness. The theft of the customer list, the theft of Pure Power's business documents, and the theft of the Pure Power files all took place on different dates and times, and within the Pure Power facility, either by logging on to Pure Power computers or by accessing Brenner's private office at Pure Power.

Finally, Belliard and Fell took deliberate steps to leave Pure Power understaffed just as Warrior Fitness was opening. Belliard provided information to Brenner about alleged problems that he was having with another Pure Power employee. Belliard recommended that this employee be fired, and Brenner, who placed a great deal of trust and confidence in Belliard, took his advice and did so. Falsely claiming that they wanted to work more hours at Pure Power, Belliard and Fell persuaded Brenner not to hire a new fitness instructor. Likewise, Fell, as part of Defendants' ill-intentioned scheme to hamstring Pure Power, brought about his own termination from Pure Power in refusing to comply with Brenner's explicit instructions, which led to a heated exchange in which Fell repeatedly screamed at Brenner, daring Brenner to fire him. Left with no choice, Brenner terminated Fell. Approximately two weeks later, Belliard quit Pure Power, on the basis of an admittedly fabricated story and without providing notice, knowing full well that the loss of three senior full-time employees, in such close succession, would leave Pure Power under-staffed and in a vulnerable position. In fact, when Belliard quit, other than Brenner, there was only one other drill instructor left to help her run the two Pure Power facilities. This ongoing and deliberate conduct, transpiring over the course of several months, constitutes a clear breach of the duty of loyalty owed by employees, Belliard and Fell, to their employer, Pure Power. [. . .]

[EDS.—The court concludes that Belliard must forfeit $55,196.70 in total compensation and Fell must forfeit $40,177.00 in total compensation during their "time period of disloyalty." The court also finds both Belliard and Fell liable for punitive damages for breach of the duty of loyalty owed to Pure Power. From Belliard, the Plaintiffs are entitled to punitive damages equivalent to two times the compensatory damages awarded to them for Belliard's breach of the duty of loyalty, in the amount of $150,570.40. And from Fell, the Plaintiffs are entitled to punitive damages in an amount equivalent to the compensatory damages awarded to the Plaintiffs from Fell's breach, in the amount of $40,177.00. Lee is also found to have aided and abetted Belliard and Fell's breach of the duty of loyalty and is thus jointly and severally liable for the total compensatory damages awarded for Belliard and Fell's breach of the duty of loyalty, in the amount of $95,373.70.]

b.   BUSINESS OPPORTUNITY

Advantage Marketing Group v. Keane
2019 Il App (1st) 181126

[. . .] [Advantage Marketing Group ("AMG")], an Illinois corporation, is a marketing services company that provides letter-shop and fulfillment services for its clients. AMG creates and administers print and mailing programs for its clients from its facility in Elk Grove Village. Keane had formerly served as a director, officer, and employee of AMG. He was an original founder of AMG and maintains a 35% shareholding stake in the company.

The amended complaint alleges that for several years prior to his resignation, Keane served as a "principal employee of AMG with wide-ranging responsibilities equivalent to those of an officer." For example, Keane consistently held himself out to third parties as an AMG owner when developing customer relationships. Keane had substantial responsibility for AMG employment decisions, including hiring and termination of staff. He had access to all AMG books and records, including client lists, employee records, tax documents, vendor information, and billing data. Keane received a bonus equal to that of Patty Hermann, AMG's director and majority shareholder. He was responsible for developing and maintaining AMG's financial records and had full access to the company's accounting system. Throughout his tenure with AMG, Keane's job duties included exploring strategic acquisitions, including the purchase of competing letter-shop businesses, their equipment, and customer lists. The amended complaint detailed instances when Keane participated in the negotiation and acquisition of related businesses, stating that he was "a key point of contact throughout 2013 regarding AMG's opportunity to move or acquire property to conduct business operations."

On July 10, 2013, Keane's son, James Jr., also an AMG employee, sent an email to Keane and Hermann with the subject line, "Mailhouse—Rebranded Website—Is that the same ownership group as before?" The body of the e-mail included a website link for The Mail House, a competing business located a few blocks away from AMG's office. The amended complaint alleged that during the summer and fall of 2013, Keane and Hermann discussed The Mail House and whether it was a viable acquisition target. The amended complaint stated, "Though Hermann is unaware of when Keane ultimately began his own discussions about buying The Mail House, the business was one that AMG had explored acquiring."

The amended complaint alleged that at some point before Keane's departure from AMG on September 4, 2015, he started to withhold information for himself and communicated outside AMG channels using his personal e-mail account while failing to forward information that would have benefitted AMG. On March 10, 2014, Keane transferred his assigned corporate cell phone number to his own personal account, outside the view of AMG. The amended complaint alleged that this action allowed him to retain and use the same phone number following his resignation from AMG and further prevented AMG from controlling communications that he had during his employment with AMG.

The amended complaint also alleged that Keane began preparations to acquire The Mail House before his September 4, 2015 resignation. For instance, on August 3, 2015, he registered a new internet domain name, "mailhousedm.com," along with seven other domain names that each contained the word, "mail house." On August 12, 2015, he formed Keane, Inc. d/b/a The Mail House. The alleged complaint stated that "Upon information and belief, Keane formed this corporation to acquire The Mail House," and that "[a]t all times, The Mail House has conducted letter-shop and fulfillment services similar to, and competitive with, those offered by AMG."

During the week before his resignation, Keane failed to disclose and tender to AMG a referral he received from another company, JD Graphics. James Jr., forwarded the referral from JD Graphics to Keane's personal e-mail account. The amended complaint alleged that Keane exploited this referral after he began operating The Mail House. In addition, Keane approached and told clients and vendors of AMG that AMG was in danger of closing its business due to financial issues.

On September 5, 2015, the day after Keane resigned, AMG discovered its security cameras were turned off and that its security tapes were missing. On September 9, 2015, Keane allegedly disabled AMG's website. He refused to transfer AMG's website materials back to the company for more than one week. Out of business necessity, AMG established an entirely new website. The day before Keane transferred the website content back to AMG, James, Jr. registered a new website domain, "amgltd.co," which differed by only one letter from AMG's domain name. The amended complaint alleged that Keane either was aware of or actively encouraged James, Jr. to disable AMG's website and then register a substantially similar domain name. During Keane's employment with AMG, James, Jr. reported directly to Keane. James, Jr. tendered his resignation to AMG on September 7, 2015.

The amended complaint alleged that Keane solicited James, Jr. to leave AMG and join him at The Mail House. Keane did not seek AMG's consent before soliciting James, Jr. to leave AMG and join a direct competitor. Further, Keane never sought AMG's consent to appropriate the JD Graphics referral or to interfere with AMG's website operation. Additionally, before his resignation, James, Jr. had obtained samples of confidential client material that belonged to AMG. Keane kept the samples for himself, resigned, and then returned the client materials after AMG's then-counsel demanded their return. Since his acquisition of The Mail House, Keane has continued to perform lettershop and print work for this particular client.

The amended complaint alleged that "At all times before Keane's resignation, The Mail House was known to AMG as a competitor. The Mail House provided comparable products and services to the same type of clientele that AMG had serviced and cultivated. Accordingly, The Mail House was, and remains, in the same line of business as AMG." Further, "[a]t no point in 2015 did Keane disclose to Hermann or AMG that he sought to acquire The Mail House. Nor did Keane ever advise Hermann or AMG that the prior owners of The Mail House were interested in selling their business to a third party." Finally, the amended complaint alleged that "[h]ad Keane brought The Mail House acquisition opportunity to AMG, AMG would have been interested in pursuing it."

keane

[T]he amended complaint alleged breach of fiduciary duty, stating that "[a]s a key AMG employee with responsibility equivalent to those of an officer, Keane owed a fiduciary duty of loyalty, fidelity, rectitude, candor, and good faith." This fiduciary duty prohibited Keane "from actively exploiting his position within AMG for his own personal benefit and from hindering the ability of AMG to continue the business for which it was developed." The amended complaint alleged that Keane owed AMG a fiduciary duty to disclose and tender all [business] opportunities, including all material facts to AMG. Keane allegedly breached this duty by secretly negotiating and purchasing a directly competing business, The Mail House, while still employed by AMG as "a key AMG employee." Keane failed to disclose and tender a corporate opportunity—the potential acquisition of The Mail House—to AMG for its full and complete consideration. In addition, Keane allegedly breached his fiduciary duty to AMG by: (1) soliciting James, Jr. to leave AMG and join The Mail House; (2) misappropriating referrals for existing lettershop work sent to AMG; (3) misappropriating client samples; and (4) disabling or otherwise interfering with AMG's website. AMG sought the imposition of a constructive trust on The Mail House business to be held for the benefit of AMG, and other relief.

facts

[. . .] On May 1, 2018, the circuit court granted Keane's motion to dismiss. [. . .] This appeal followed.

[On appeal,] AMG claimed that Keane breached his fiduciary duty when he misappropriated a corporate opportunity to acquire The Mail House. Keane argues that he was not an officer or director subject to the corporate opportunity doctrine. Keane contends that he was permitted under Illinois law to take the preparatory steps of outfitting a competing business. He also argues that he disclosed the potential acquisition of The Mail House and that AMG failed to allege in its amended complaint that it took any further action with regard to The Mail House.

rule

A claim for breach of fiduciary duty must allege: "(1) that a fiduciary duty exists; (2) that the fiduciary duty was breached; and (3) that such breach proximately caused the injury of which the party complains." *Lawlor v. North American Corp. of Illinois.* A duty of loyalty to the employer extends to officers, directors, and employees. "Accordingly, a fiduciary cannot act inconsistently with his agency or trust and cannot solicit his employer's customers for himself."

rule

The corporate opportunity doctrine prohibits a corporation's fiduciary from misappropriating corporate property and from taking advantage of business opportunities belonging to the corporation. "A corporate opportunity exists when a proposed activity is reasonably incident to the corporation's present or prospective business and is one in which the corporation has the capacity to engage." *Lindenhurst Drugs, Inc. v. Becker.* Our supreme court has held that it is a breach of fiduciary obligation for a person to seize for his own advantage a business opportunity which rightfully belongs to the corporation by which he is employed.

In contrast, "corporate competition" occurs when the corporate employer by definition already has an existing business relationship with a third party or is actively seeking to establish such a relationship, only to have its efforts thwarted by its own employees seeking the same third party relationship for themselves. [. . .] In corporate competition cases, an employee or agent may legitimately take certain preparatory steps during the agency relationship so long as they do not directly conflict with the employer or principal. [. . .]

Here, taking AMG's allegations as true, the amended complaint alleged that Keane "was a principal employee of AMG with wide-ranging responsibilities to those of an officer," and that he misappropriated for himself a corporate opportunity, the acquisition of The Mail House, a company that competed directly with AMG. In short, this case involves an alleged usurpation of a corporate opportunity to obtain a competing business so that the defendant could enter into direct competition with his former employer. This case does not only involve corporate competition, as Keane would prefer to characterize it. Here, the allegations of corporate opportunity and corporate competition are intertwined and, thus, we examine both accordingly in the context of the breach of fiduciary duty claim.

We first consider whether the amended complaint properly pled that a fiduciary duty between Keane and AMG existed at the time in question. Generally, "[e]very person who accepts the responsibility of acting on behalf of another is a fiduciary." *Graham v. Mimms*. "An agency is 'a consensual fiduciary relationship between two legal entities' whereby 'the principal has the right to control the conduct of the agent, and the agent has the power to effect [*sic*] the legal relations of the principal.' " *State Security Insurance Co. v. Frank B. Hall & Co.* [. . .] "An employee need not be an officer or a director to be accountable since an agent must act solely for the principal in all matters related to the agency and refrain from competing with the principal." *E.J. McKernan*. Indeed, "[w]hen a principal-agent relationship is present, a fiduciary relationship arises as a matter of law." *Stathis v. Geldermann, Inc*. The fiduciary owes a duty of loyalty to the entity for whom the fiduciary is acting. *Graham*. "Among other factors, the precise nature and intensity of the duty of loyalty depends upon the degree of independent authority exercised by the fiduciary [citation] and the reasonable expectations of the parties at the beginning of the relationship." *Id*.

In this case, AMG pled that Keane served as a key employee upon his resignation. Keane allegedly "held himself out to third parties as an AMG owner when developing customer relationships." He "had substantial responsibility for AMG employment decisions, including hiring and termination of staff." AMG alleged that Keane had access to all AMG books and records, including client lists, employee records, tax documents, and vendor information. He received a compensation bonus equivalent to the director and majority shareholder of the company. He was responsible for developing and maintaining AMG's financial records. In addition, Keane was expected to research and develop strategic acquisitions, including the purchase of competing lettershop businesses, their equipment, and customer lists. Finally, AMG alleged that at the time of his resignation, Keane owned a 35% shareholder stake in the company.

Even if Keane is not considered to be an officer or director of AMG, his considerable duties and responsibilities as an employee, his compensation, and his status as a minority shareholder put him in the position to act solely for the benefit of the principal in all matters connected with his agency. [. . .] [W]hen "employees continue to receive substantial salaries and continue to take part in top-level management meetings, negotiations and strategy discussions, their employer is entitled to their undivided loyalty and their utmost good faith." *Regal-Beloit Corp. v. Drecoll*. [EDS.—The court concludes that the amended complaint properly pled the existence of a fiduciary duty between AMG and Keane, both because Keane is a "mere employee" and because he is an employee who has duties similar to that of an officer or a director. The corporate opportunity doctrine also applies to Keane for those reasons.]

Next, we determine whether AMG properly pled a breach of fiduciary duty under the [business] opportunity doctrine. First, we consider whether AMG sufficiently pled the existence of a corporate opportunity, because if no opportunity existed, the fiduciary cannot commit a breach of duty in availing himself of the opportunity. [. . .] "A corporate opportunity exists when a proposed activity is reasonably incident to the corporation's present or prospective business and is one in which the corporation has the capacity to engage." *Dremco, Inc. v. South Chapel Hill Gardens, Inc.*. In determining whether the fiduciary may take advantage of a business opportunity in which a corporation is interested, "courts consider whether the corporation had an interest, actual or in expectancy, in the opportunity and whether the acquisition thereof by the [fiduciary] would hinder or defeat plans and purposes of the corporation in carrying on or developing the legitimate business for which it was created." *Id.* Significantly, "[w]hen a corporation's fiduciary wants to take advantage of a business opportunity which is in the corporation's line of business, the fiduciary must first disclose and tender the opportunity to the corporation, notwithstanding the fact that the fiduciary may have believed that the corporation was legally or financially incapable of taking advantage of the opportunity." *Id.* [. . .]

The amended complaint alleged that Keane and Hermann discussed The Mail House in the summer and fall of 2013 "and whether it was a viable acquisition target." The amended complaint alleged that The Mail House "was known to AMG as a competitor," and that it "provided comparable products and services to the same type of clientele that AMG had serviced and cultivated." AMG alleged, "[t]hough Hermann is unaware of when Keane ultimately began his own discussions about buying The Mail House, the business was one that AMG had explored acquiring." The amended complaint alleged that "[a]t no point in 2015 did Keane disclose to Hermann or AMG that he sought to acquire The Mail House. Nor did Keane ever advise Hermann or AMG that the prior owners of The Mail House were interested in selling their business to a third party." Finally, the amended complaint pled that "[h]ad Keane brought The Mail House acquisition opportunity to AMG, AMG would have been interested in pursuing it."

Taking the pleadings as true, as we must, AMG has sufficiently pled the existence of a corporate opportunity, namely, the acquisition of The Mail House, a competing business. AMG properly pled that The Mail House was in the same "line of business" as AMG because it provided comparable products and services to the same clientele as AMG. *Id.*

Under *Kerrigan v. Unity Savings Ass'n*, when a corporate opportunity within the same line of business arises, the corporate fiduciary must fully disclose and timely tender the opportunity to the corporation. *Id.* Keane argues that AMG "has pleaded itself out of court by expressly alleging that Keane disclosed and discussed The Mail House acquisition opportunity" with AMG. According to Keane, those allegations establish that he satisfied any possible duty owed to AMG. Further, Keane contends that because he informed AMG of the alleged opportunity and AMG declined to pursue it, he was free to pursue the opportunity himself. *See id.* ("It may be conceded that if a corporation has been informed by a director of a business opportunity, which it declines, the director may then be free to pursue the opportunity himself.").

In this case, however, AMG did not allege in its amended complaint that it declined to pursue the acquisition of The Mail House. Instead, AMG specifically claimed that it would have pursued the acquisition of The Mail House if Keane had disclosed the opportunity. The amended complaint alleged that Keane and Hermann discussed whether The Mail House was a viable acquisition target in 2013. AMG alleged that Keane never disclosed that he sought to acquire The Mail House. He also purportedly failed to disclose that the prior owners of The Mail House were interested in selling their business to a third party. In short, the pleadings reveal that Keane allegedly failed to fully disclose the pertinent facts involving the corporate opportunity to acquire The Mail House, a business that was reasonably incident to AMG's present operations.

Moreover, Illinois law requires more than disclosure and tender of the corporate opportunity. The Mullaney court specifically held that a fiduciary cannot begin to act on his own "without the consent" of the principal because otherwise, the fiduciary places himself "in a position where his personal interests will conflict with his duties to his principal." [. . .] Based on these findings, we reject Keane's argument that his disclosure of the potential acquisition of The Mail House excused him from his fiduciary duty.

[. . .] We find AMG sufficiently pled a breach of fiduciary duty. [. . .] We reverse the judgment of the circuit court and remand the cause for further proceedings.

D. PRINCIPAL'S LIABILITY IN CONTRACT

In an agency relationship, the agent acts on the principal's behalf. When the agent has the authority to act on behalf of the principal, the agent may bind the principal in contracts. This section discusses the different types of authority, which are different ways that allow an agent to cause a principal to be bound by a contract.

1. ACTUAL AUTHORITY

Restatement (Third) of Agency
Section 2.01—Actual Authority

An agent acts with actual authority when, at the time of taking action that has legal consequences for the principal, the agent reasonably believes, in accordance with the principal's manifestations to the agent, that the principal wishes the agent so to act.

Section 3.01—Creation of Actual Authority

Actual authority, as defined in § 2.01, is created by a principal's manifestation to an agent that, as reasonably understood by the agent, expresses the principal's assent that the agent takes action on the principal's behalf.

Section 2.02—Scope of Actual Authority

(1) An agent has actual authority to take action designated or implied in the principal's manifestations to the agent and acts necessary or incidental to achieving the principal's objectives, as the agent reasonably understands the principal's manifestations and objectives when the agent determines how to act.

(2) An agent's interpretation of the principal's manifestations is reasonable if it reflects any meaning known by the agent to be ascribed by the principal and, in the absence of any meaning known to the agent, as a reasonable person in the agent's position would interpret the manifestations in light of the context, including circumstances of which the agent has notice and the agent's fiduciary duty to the principal.

(3) An agent's understanding of the principal's objectives is reasonable if it accords with the principal's manifestations and the inferences that a reasonable person in the agent's position would draw from the circumstances creating the agency.

Castillo v. Case Farms of Ohio, Inc.

96 F.Supp.2d 578 (W.D. Tex. 1999)

Defendant Case Farms of Ohio, Inc. ("Case Farms"), is a chicken processing plant in Winesburg, Ohio. [. . .] Case Farms actively recruited workers for its processing plant during 1996 and 1997. Andy Cilona, primarily responsible for recruiting workers for Case Farms, served as Case Farms' Human Resources Director from his date of hire until February 1996, and as Case Farms' Director of Corporate Development, from February 1996 until mid-1997. During one of his recruiting trips in Florida, Cilona initiated contact with a labor agency for temporary employees, America's Tempcorps ("ATC"). In conformity with an unwritten agreement with Case Farms, ATC worked in Texas, recruiting and hiring a number of people to work at Case Farms' chicken processing plant in Ohio. [. . .] ATC also usually gave its recruits a free bus ticket or other free transportation to Ohio, as well as $20.00 each in traveling expenses. [. . .]

[. . .] [P]laintiffs generally claim that they were recruited in Texas to work at Case Farms' Winesburg facility, and that, upon arriving at Case Farms, they discovered that the actual terms and conditions of their employment, transportation, and housing in Ohio did not coincide with the promises made to them in Texas. At the trial of this case, plaintiffs testified to the inadequate housing conditions and transportation provisions they encountered upon arrival in Ohio.

[. . .] Plaintiffs contend that defendants violated a number of the statutory rights of employees created by the Migrant and Seasonal Agricultural Worker Protection Act ("AWPA") and the Fair Labor Standards Act ("FLSA"). [. . .]

The Migrant and Seasonal Agricultural Worker Protection Act is a broad-ranging network of migrant and seasonal worker protections that requires, in part, written and forthright disclosures, in the workers' language, of working conditions at the time of recruitment. It prohibits false and misleading representations concerning employment policies and practices, housing conditions, and transportation arrangements for workers. It also regulates housing and transportation standards for covered workers. [. . .]

In the event of violation of these provisions, the AWPA provides for statutory or actual damages, or equitable relief, at the discretion of the court. [. . .]

The distressing and deplorable conditions allegedly encountered and endured by [. . .] plaintiffs upon arriving in Ohio stand largely unrefuted. Often with little more than the $20.00 they were given for food during the three day bus ride from the Rio Grande Valley, the majority of the plaintiffs left behind their homes and families in Texas for the promise of suitable work in Ohio. Once there, many of the plaintiffs found themselves sleeping on floors in bare houses or apartments, often with a dozen or more other workers. One young woman described the frightening experience of sleeping in a unfurnished, one-bathroom house with approximately seventeen other people, mostly men. From the stand, she expressed her gratitude to several other male recruits, whom she had met just days before living with them in Ohio, for their willingness to allow her to sleep between them and the wall for protection. Another plaintiff testified that he and his sister were forced to sleep outside their apartment on concrete steps to escape the stench of the raw sewage that was seeping into their apartment. Other plaintiffs described their unremitting encounters with cockroaches and rats. With harrowing detail, plaintiffs related the discomfort and dangerousness of traveling to work in an overcrowded van that not only had only boards laid on cement blocks in lieu of seats, but which also was filled with exhaust fumes. For the most part, these disturbing and unsettling accounts were uncontested by Case Farms.

There can be no doubt that such living and transportation conditions were appalling, and would be, in many contexts, illegal. The plaintiffs' express challenge in this civil action, however, was to establish Case Farms' liability for such conditions. That is, before considering each of the many statutory violations alleged by the plaintiffs, an important threshold issue must be resolved. Does the law allow the plaintiffs to recover for their maltreatment from Case Farms? Can [. . .] plaintiffs, recruited and purportedly "employed" by ATC, recover from Case Farms? [. . .]

The fact that Congress has created a statutory framework of protections for migrant workers in no way exempts agricultural employers, recruiters, and overseers from common law agency principles. Rather, the protections afforded by the AWPA are designed to supplement traditional common law principles. [. . .]

Plaintiffs argue that an agency relationship existed between ATC and Case Farms, and that the scope of that relationship included both the *express authority* to recruit and hire people to work at Case Farms' plant, and the *implied authority* to do all things proper, usual, and necessary to exercise that authority. Case Farms responds that to the extent any agency relationship existed between ATC and Case Farms, the scope of that agency was limited solely to informing recruits about the availability of work in Ohio at Case Farms' processing plant.

The fundamental precepts of the law of agency are well settled. At common law, a principal may be held liable for the acts of its purported agent based on an actual agency relationship created by the principal's express or implied delegation of authority to the agent. Both forms of agency are at issue here. *Express actual authority* exists "where the principal has made it clear to the agent that he [or she] wants the act under scrutiny to be done." *Pasant v. Jackson Nat'l Life Ins. Co.* Further, giving an agent express authority to undertake a certain act also includes the *implied authority* to do all things proper, usual, and necessary to exercise that express authority.

Applying these principles, the plaintiffs assert that the scope of the agency relationship between Case Farms and ATC expressly authorized ATC to recruit and hire people to work at Case Farms' Ohio plant. Such a contention is certainly well-supported by the evidence. Former Case Farms' Director of Corporate Development, Andy Cilona, among others, testified that "the arrangement with ATC was for it to hire workers for Case Farms' production." Based on Case Farms' explicit agreement with ATC, it is found, by a preponderance of the evidence, that such an express agency relationship, the scope of which included recruiting and hiring migrant workers to perform jobs at Case Farms' plant, did exist between Case Farms and ATC.

A principal is liable for the actions of an agent only if those actions are taken in the scope of the agent's employment. While Case Farms acknowledges that ATC was expressly authorized to recruit and hire workers for its plant, the chicken processing company maintains that the *scope* of that relationship was extremely narrow, and that the vagueness of the plaintiffs' claim that ATC was Case Farms' agent glosses over the exact nature of the relationship between ATC and Case Farms. The plaintiffs, on the other hand, argue that the scope of ATC's express authority to recruit and hire people to work at Case Farms' plant included the implied authority to do all things proper, usual, and necessary to exercise that authority.

A preponderance of the evidence supports the plaintiffs' contention. Credible evidence, adduced at trial, reveals that housing and transportation issues were well within the class of activities proper, usual, and necessary to recruit and hire workers for Case Farms' Ohio processing plant. It is uncontested that the combination of its high turnover rate, and relative isolation from metropolitan areas, complicates Case Farms' recruitment process. For Case Farms, recruitment was, at all relevant times, an on-going, virtually nation-wide undertaking. The very fact that this Ohio chicken processing plant was recruiting workers in Florida and Texas attests to the difficulties it faces finding workers. Furthermore, once the workers arrived in Ohio, it was difficult for workers to find housing on their own because of language barriers, lack of personal transportation, and their unfamiliarity with the area. So, it was essential to the success of Case Farms' hiring practices to assist out-of-state workers with housing. Case Farms, before any relationship with ATC, actually did assist incoming workers with housing and transportation in Ohio. Furthermore, it was clear from the evidence adduced at trial that Case Farms meant for ATC to perform these duties. Thus, it is found that Case Farms knew that these duties were proper, usual, and necessary in order to recruit and retain a workforce primarily migrating from out-of-state.

Case Farms points out, and places much weight on the fact, that its representatives Cilona and Kohli both testified that ATC was not authorized to hire workers and make them full fledged "Case Farms" employees. Rather, under the arrangement with ATC, the workers would supposedly remain "ATC employees," despite the fact that they worked in the Case Farms plant, doing the same work, at the same rate of pay, under the supervision of the same supervisors, as Case Farms workers.

Whether or not a plaintiff would become a "full-fledged" Case Farms employee, however, cannot be dispositive of the agency issue at hand. At issue in this civil action is precisely the question of whether superficial differences (such as which company's name appeared on a plaintiff's pay stub) somehow immunize the company that owns and operates the plant from liability. Given the fact that housing and transportation were necessary components of Case Farms' recruitment process, ATC's actions in those arenas were within the scope of its relationship as an agent of Case Farms.

For the foregoing reasons, it is found that the ATC defendants were clearly acting as Case Farms' agent in all of their actions relating to the recruitment and hiring of workers for Case Farms' chicken processing plant in Winesburg, Ohio. And, under the AWPA, recruitment by an agricultural employer includes recruitment through an agent. Hence, ATC's interactions with the [. . .] plaintiffs may be attributed to Case Farms for the purpose of assessing compliance with AWPA. [. . .]

Case Farms' deplorable treatment of the plaintiffs in this civil action represents precisely the mistreatment that the AWPA was enacted to prevent and punish. It is found, based on the evidence presented to this court, by a preponderance of the evidence, that Case Farms violated the law in its treatment of the plaintiffs, in the manners and ways set forth herein, and that plaintiffs should be awarded judgment therefor.

2.   APPARENT AUTHORITY

Restatement (Third) of Agency
Section 2.03—Apparent Authority

Apparent authority is the power held by an agent or other actor to affect a principal's legal relations with third parties when a third party reasonably believes the actor has authority to act on behalf of the principal and that belief is traceable to the principal's manifestations.

Section 3.03—Creation of Apparent Authority

Apparent authority, as defined in § 2.03, is created by a person's manifestation that another has authority to act with legal consequences for the person who makes the manifestation, when a third party reasonably believes the actor to be authorized and the belief is traceable to the manifestation.

Tanner Co., Inc. v. WIOO, Inc.

528 F.2d 262 (3d Cir. 1975)

[Plaintiff Tanner alleges that it entered into five contracts with the ostensible general manager of radio station WIOO, F. Eugene Waite. After that, Tanner prepared and sent to WIOO highly personalized radio jingles and introductory tapes stylized with the WIOO logo. After Tanner performed, a WIOO officer refused to acknowledge the contract and Tanner filed suit.]

The district court concluded that ". . . the defendant WIOO created in F. Eugene Waite apparent authority to act as general manager of the station . . . ." WIOO argues here that the district court improperly looked to the actions of Waite rather than to the actions of WIOO in determining the existence of apparent authority.

Under Pennsylvania law, apparent authority flows from the conduct of the principal and not that of the agent. In *Revere Press, Inc. v. Blumberg*, the Pennsylvania Supreme Court stated:

> Apparent authority is power to bind a principal which the principal has not actually granted but which he leads persons with whom his agent deals to believe that he has granted. Persons with whom the agent deals can reasonably believe that the agent has power to bind his principal if, for instance, the principal knowingly permits the agent to exercise such power or if the principal holds the agent out as possessing such power.

The district court found that Waite held himself out to the public as the general manager of WIOO and that the owners of the station acquiesced in this conduct. Waite identified himself in four of the five contracts as the "general manager." Moreover, the industry-wide publications of the Standard Rate Data Service (SRDS) from February, 1967 to February, 1971 listed Waite as the general manager of WIOO, thereby creating in Waite apparent authority with respect to third parties.

Both owners of WIOO testified that they knew Waite used the title "general manager" and that they did not object. Furthermore, the court found that the owners of WIOO signed numerous checks payable to the order of Tanner without ever inquiring as to the reason for payment.

These findings of fact, supported as they are by the testimony, are not "clearly erroneous" and therefore may not be disturbed. Based upon these facts, we conclude, as did the district court, that the owners of WIOO through their actions "knowingly permit(ted)" Waite to hold himself out to the public as the 'general manager' of the station, *Revere Press, Inc. v. Blumberg*, thereby creating in Waite apparent authority with respect to third parties.

The district court determined that WIOO created in Waite apparent authority and that ". . . a general manager under like circumstances is empowered to enter into contracts binding the corporation . . . ." WIOO argues that contracts providing for spots that were "to be valid until used" represented so unusual an agreement as to exceed the scope of whatever apparent authority was created.

Under Pennsylvania law, an agent may bind his principal to third persons where "his acts are within the scope of the authority which the principal has caused or permitted him to possess." *Edwards v. Heralds of Liberty*.

The district court's finding that a general manager may contractually bind a radio station is supported in the evidence. Mr. E. D. Elmore, credit manager of Tanner, testified on direct examination (rebuttal) as follows:

> **Q.** Are you familiar or not with who normally signs such contracts with the radio station?
>
> **A.** Yes sir. It would be the general manager—I would say 95 percent of them, at least, are by the general manager.

This testimony was uncontroverted.

Elmore also testified concerning the usual nature of these contracts:

> **Q.** Have you ever put out a contract that didn't mention anything about the time element at all, whether it was for an indefinite period, or is this the sort of thing that is important to you and you always have a stipulation?
>
> **A.** That is the standard contract. It says, "valid until used" unless by agreement of the parties the contract is changed, and then it is subject to home office approval.

[. . .] We also agree with the district court that these contracts granting spots for an unlimited time are not so extraordinary as to exceed the authority of a general manager or to constitute reasonable notice to a third party of the inadequacy of the general manager's power.

The district court found [. . .] that Tanner entered into five contracts with the ostensible general manager of WIOO; that thereafter Tanner prepared and sent to WIOO highly personalized radio jingles and introductory tapes stylized with the WIOO logo. Moreover, the contracts all contain a clause which specifically attests that the party signing on behalf of the radio station is authorized to contractually bind the station. By a preponderance of the evidence the plaintiff established that its conduct was in response to a contract entered into by the apparent general manager of WIOO. No further evidence of reliance need to be shown.

WIOO argues that Tanner failed to establish its reliance upon the apparent authority of Waite. Here too, we may independently review the district court's finding as a mixed question of fact and law.

Pennsylvania law provides that a principal who has invested an agent with apparent authority is bound to "third persons who have relied thereon in good faith." *Edwards v. Heralds of Liberty*.

Each of the five contracts signed by Tanner and Waite contained a statement that the "(s)tation official signing this agreement certifies that he has the authority to make the agreement." Indeed, as we previously noted, Elmore, credit manager of Tanner, testified that 95% of the contracts entered into with radio stations were signed by "the general manager." These findings of fact by the district court are not "clearly erroneous." We agree with the district court that Tanner, in good faith, relied upon the apparent authority of Waite.

Having concluded that WIOO's actions created apparent authority in Waite as general manager authorizing him to execute contracts such as those here in dispute and that Tanner reasonably relied on such authority, we hold, as did the district court, that WIOO is contractually bound to Tanner. [. . .]

We hold, as did the district court, that Waite had apparent authority to contractually bind WIOO.

3. INHERENT AUTHORITY

Watteau v. Fenwick
[1893] 1 Q.B. 346 (1892)

From the evidence, it appeared that Humble had carried on business at a beerhouse called the Victoria Hotel, which he had transferred to [Fenwick], a firm of brewers, some years before the present action. After the transfer, Humble remained [Fenwick's] manager; but the license was always taken out in Humble's name, and his name was painted over the door. Under the terms of the agreement made between Humble and [Fenwick], [Humble] had no authority to buy any goods for the business except bottled ales and mineral waters; all other goods required were to be supplied by [Fenwick]. The action was brought to recover the price of goods delivered to the Victoria Hotel over some years, for which it is admitted that [Watteau gave to Humble on credit]: they consisted of cigars, bovril, and other articles.

[The county court judge awarded judgment for Watteau, the plaintiff. Fenwick appealed. At oral argument, Fenwick's counsel argued the county court judge erred:

> The liability of a principal for the acts of his agent, done contrary to his secret instructions, depends upon holding him out as his agent—that is, upon the agent being clothed with an apparent authority to act for his principal. Where, therefore, a man carries on business in his own name through a manager, he holds out his own credit, and would be liable for goods supplied even where the manager exceeded his authority. But where, as in the present case, there is no holding out by the principal, but the business is carried on in the agent's name and the good are

supplied on his credit, a person wishing to go behind the agent and make the principal liable must show an agency in fact.

When asked by Lord Coleridge, Chief Justice, whether a plaintiff could sue an undisclosed principal upon discovering him, Fenwick's counsel argued:

> Only where the act done by the agent is within the scope of his agency; not where there has been an excess of authority. Where any one has been held out by the principal as his agent, there is a contract with the principal by estoppel, however much the agent may have exceeded his authority; where there has been no holding out, proof must be given of an agency in fact in order to make the principal liable.

Watteau's counsel argued that Fenwick was an undisclosed principal who employed Humble to carry out its business with the authority necessary to run the hotel. He continued:

> All that the plaintiff has to do, therefore, in order to charge the principals, is show that the good supplied were such as were ordinarily used in the business—that is to say, that they were within the reasonable scope of the agent's authority.]

■ JUSTICE WILLS, with whom LORD COLERIDGE, CHIEF JUSTICE, joins.

[. . .] The [Victoria Hotel] was kept, not by the defendants, but by a person named Humble, whose name was over the door. The plaintiff gave credit to Humble, and to him alone, and had never heard of the defendants. The business, however, was really the defendants', and they had put Humble into it to manage it for them, and had forbidden him to buy cigars on credit. The cigars, however, were such as would usually be supplied to and dealt in at such an establishment. The learned county court judge held the defendants were liable. I am of opinion that he was right.

Once it is established that the defendant was the real principal, the ordinary doctrine as to principal and agent applies—that the principal is liable for all the acts of the agent which are within the authority usually confided to an agent of that character, notwithstanding limitations, as between the principal and the agent, put upon that authority. It is said that only so where there has been a holding out of authority—which cannot be said of a case where the person supplying the goods knew nothing of the existence of a principal. But I do not think so. Otherwise, in every case of undisclosed principal, or at least in every case where the fact of there being a principal was undisclosed, the secret limitation of authority would prevail and defeat the action of the person dealing with the agent and then discovering that he was an agent and had a principal.

But in the case of a dormant partner it is clear law that no limitation of authority as between the dormant and active partner will avail the dormant partner as to things within the ordinary authority of a partner.

NOTE: WATTEAU & RESTATEMENT (THIRD) OF AGENCY

The legal doctrine of inherent authority that emerged from *Watteau* was incorporated into the Restatement (Second) of Agency, Section 8A—Inherent Agent Power. However, when the Restatement was updated and redrafted, the concept of *inherent authority* was substituted with the doctrine of the "undisclosed principal's liability"—Restatement (Third) of Agency, § 2.06.

Restatement (Second) of Agency

Section 8A—Inherent Agent Power

Inherent agency power is a term used in the restatement of this subject to indicate the power of an agent which is derived not from authority, apparent authority or estoppel, but solely from the agency relation and exists for the protection of persons harmed by or dealing with a servant or other agent.

Section 194—Acts of General Agents

A general agent for an undisclosed principal authorized to conduct transactions subjects his principal to liability for acts done on his account, if usual or necessary in such transactions, although forbidden by the principal to do them.

Section 195—Acts of Manager Appearing to be Owner

An undisclosed principal who entrusts an agent with the management of his business is subject to liability to third persons with whom the agent enters into transactions usual in such businesses and on the principal's account, although contrary to the directions of the principal.

Restatement (Third) of Agency

Section 2.06—Liability of Undisclosed Principal

(1) An undisclosed principal is subject to liability to a third party who is justifiably induced to make a detrimental change in position by an agent acting on the principal's behalf and without actual authority if the principal, having notice of the agent's conduct and that it might induce others to change their positions, did not take reasonable steps to notify them of the facts.

(2) An undisclosed principal may not rely on instructions given an agent that qualify or reduce the agent's authority to less than the authority a third party would reasonably believe the agent to have under the same circumstances if the principal had been disclosed.

4. RATIFICATION

Restatement (Third) of Agency
Section 4.01—Ratification Defined

(1) Ratification is the affirmance of a prior act done by another, whereby the act is given effect as if done by an agent acting with actual authority

(2) A person ratifies an act by

(a) manifesting assent that the act shall affect the person's legal relations, or

(b) conduct that justifies a reasonable assumption that the person so consents.

(3) Ratification does not occur unless

(a) the act is ratifiable as stated in § 4.03,

(b) the person ratifying has capacity as stated in § 4.04,

(c) the ratification is timely as stated in § 4.05, and

(d) the ratification encompasses the act in its entirety as stated in § 4.07.

Section 4.02—Effect of Ratification

(1) Subject to the exceptions stated in subsection (2), ratification retroactively creates the effects of actual authority.

(2) Ratification is not effective:

(a) in favor of a person who causes it by misrepresentation or other conduct that would make a contract voidable

(b) in favor of an agent against a principal when the principal ratifies to avoid a loss; or

(c) to diminish the rights or other interests of persons, not parties to the transaction.

Section 4.03—Acts That May Be Ratified

A person may ratify an act if the actor acted or purported to act as an agent on the person's behalf.

Section 4.04—Capacity to Ratify

(1) A person may ratify an act if

(a) the person existed at the time of the act, and

(b) the person has capacity as defined in § 3.04 at the time of ratifying the act.

(2) At a later time, a principal may avoid a ratification made earlier when the principal lacked capacity as defined in § 3.04.

Section 4.06—Knowledge Requisite to Ratification

A person is not bound by a ratification made without knowledge of material facts involved in the original act when the person was unaware of such lack of knowledge.

Section 4.07—No Partial Ratification

A ratification is not effective unless it encompasses the entirety of an act, contract, or other single transaction.

Keams v. Tempe Technical Institute, Inc.

993 F.Supp. 714 (D. Ariz. 1997)

Plaintiffs are a class of former students at Tempe Technical Institute ("TTI"), a for-profit vocational school that operated from September, 1988 to April, 1990. Defendant Carl Forsberg owned TTI and served as its President; C. Colleen Forsberg, his wife, was the corporation's Secretary. Defendant Zions National Bank ("Zions") issued many of the federal student loans obtained by the Plaintiffs in order to finance their education at TTI. Defendant Student Loan Marketing Corporation ("Sallie Mae") purchased Plaintiffs' student loans from Zions.

TTI was incorporated in 1988 by Carl Forsberg, a former employee and part-owner of the Phoenix Institute of Technology, another Phoenix vocational school. TTI purchased the assets of the Southwestern Medical Society Academy, an accredited vocational school specializing in the training of nonphysician medical personnel, and renamed the school. The school continued to offer medical training and expanded its offerings to include courses in drafting, computers, and automotive technology. TTI was in financial trouble for most of its short life due to Carl Forsberg's inability to obtain sufficient financing to operate the school. Upon discovering financial irregularities, a guaranty agency withdrew its accreditation of TTI in March, 1990. TTI soon closed, and later that year both TTI and the Forsbergs filed for bankruptcy pursuant to Chapter 7 of the United States Bankruptcy Code.

Plaintiffs, who are primarily Native Americans, claim that they were recruited from Northern Arizona and New Mexico to attend school in Phoenix and Tempe with promises of practical training, financial aid, guaranteed housing, and job placement assistance. The former students contend that after taking out student loans they discovered that the school was "a sham, incapable financially, administratively and qualitatively of providing the services it marketed." Plaintiffs contend that TTI provided an inferior education, failed to provide housing, and did not assist them with job placement.

[. . .] Plaintiffs' Amended Complaint and Responses allege that Defendant Zions is [. . .] vicariously liable because TTI was acting as an agent for Zions when it injured the Plaintiffs. [. . .] Zions moved for summary judgment on all counts. [. . .]

Plaintiffs first contend that Zions is liable for TTI's alleged wrongdoings because Zions designated TTI as its agent by ratifying its actions. Ratification creates an agency relationship where "the affirmance by a person of a prior act which did not bind him but which was done or professedly done on his account, whereby the act, as to some or all persons, is given effect as if originally authorized by him." Restatement (Second) of Agency § 82 (1958). Plaintiffs assert that the act at issue was the assistance that TTI gave to students by providing them with student loan applications and by helping the students complete the forms. Zions then "affirmed" this act by processing the applications and issuing the loans. According to Plaintiffs, because Zions realized the benefits associated with processing the loans, it also "assumed responsibility for the concomitant burdens and liabilities as it would have for any authorized agent's act." In its Motion for Summary Judgment, Zions argues that its actions in extending student loans to Plaintiffs did not constitute an affirmance of any of TTI's actions.

The Restatement is clear that "[r]atification does not result from the affirmance of a transaction with a third person unless the one acting purported to be acting for the ratifier." Restatement (Second) of Agency § 85(1). In order for Plaintiffs to sustain a ratification theory of agency, they must show that TTI purported to act for Zions. The allegations of Plaintiffs show only that TTI made representations to the contrary. According to Plaintiffs, they "only dealt with and relied on school personnel as the source of [the] student loans," "TTI certainly held itself out to borrowers as the source of tuition and subsistence funds," and TTI "did not distinguish itself from the bank." These statements support the conclusion that TTI was acting for itself, not purporting to act for Zions.

Plaintiffs note that a comment in the Restatement provides that "an unauthorized agent need not expressly hold himself out as the principal's agent; it is enough that he undertakes a transaction for the other." The accepted majority view, however, is that the purported agent must disclose to the third party that he is acting as an agent. This view also prevails in Arizona, where the ratification can occur only when someone is "claiming to act as an agent." *Fuqua Homes Inc. v. Grosvenor.* Evidence provided by Plaintiffs shows that TTI claimed that it did not act as an agent. Accordingly, there can be no genuine issue of material fact that this essential element of ratification is present. [. . .]

IT IS ORDERED granting Defendant Zions First National Bank's Motion for Summary Judgment.

NOTE: THE EQUAL DIGNITY RULE & RATIFICATION

Under the equal dignity rule, if the Statute of Frauds requires a signed writing, the principal must also give her consent in writing for the agent to bind her to the transaction.[1] Similarly, if the Statute of Frauds requires a signed writing, ratification must also be in writing.[2]

5. AGENCY BY ESTOPPEL

Restatement (Third) of Agency

Section 2.05—Estoppel to Deny Existence of Agency Relationship

A person who has not made a manifestation that an actor has authority as an agent and who is not otherwise liable as a party to a transaction purportedly done by the actor on that person's account is subject to liability to a third party who justifiably is induced to make a detrimental change in position because the transaction is believed to be on the person's account, if

(1) the person intentionally or carelessly caused such belief, or

(2) having notice of such belief and that it might induce others to change their positions, the person did not take reasonable steps to notify them of the facts.

Hoddeson v. Koos Bros.

135 A.2d 702 (N.J. Super. Ct. App. Div. 1957)

The plaintiff Mrs. Hoddeson was acquainted with the spacious furniture store conducted by the defendant, Koos Bros., a corporation. On a previous observational visit, her eyes had fallen upon certain articles of bedroom furniture which she ardently desired to acquire for her home. It has been said that "the sea hath bounds but deep desire hath none." Her sympathetic mother liberated her from the grasp of despair and bestowed upon her a gift of $165 with which to consummate the purchase.

It was in the forenoon of August 22, 1956 that Mrs. Hoddeson, accompanied by her aunt and four children, happily journeyed from her home to the defendant's store to attain her objective. Upon entering, she was greeted by a tall man with dark hair frosted at the temples and clad in a light gray suit. He inquired if he could be of assistance, and she informed him specifically of her mission. Whereupon he immediately guided her, her aunt, and the flock to the mirror then on display and priced at $29 which Mrs. Hoddeson identified, and next to the location of the designated bedroom furniture which she had described.

Upon confirming her selections the man withdrew from his pocket a small pad of paper upon which he presumably recorded her order and calculated the total purchase price to be $168.50. Mrs. Hoddeson handed to him the $168.50 in cash. He informed her the articles other than those

---

[1]   *See id.* Restatement (Third) of Agency § 3.02.

[2]   *See, e.g.,* Rickerson v. Berkshire-Hudson Cap. XI, LLC, No. 4:11–CV–0068–HML, 2012 WL 13028178, at *14–15 (N.D. Ga. Mar. 9, 2012) (requiring a signed writing to ratify a real estate contract).

on display were not in stock, and that reproductions would upon notice be delivered to her in September. Alas, she omitted to request from him a receipt for her cash disbursement. The transaction consumed in time a period from 30 to 40 minutes.

Mrs. Hoddeson impatiently awaited the delivery of the articles of furniture, but a span of time beyond the assured date of delivery elapsed, which motivated her to inquire of the defendant the cause of the unexpected delay. Sorrowful, indeed, was she to learn from the defendant that its records failed to disclose any such sale to her and any such monetary credit in payment.

It eventuated that Mrs. Hoddeson and her aunt were subsequently unable positively to recognize among the defendant's regularly employed salesmen the individual with whom Mrs. Hoddeson had arranged for the purchase, although when she and her aunt were afforded the opportunities to gaze intently at one of the five salesmen assigned to that department of the store, both indicated a resemblance of one of them to the purported salesman, but frankly acknowledged the incertitude of their identification. The defendant's records revealed that the salesman bearing the alleged resemblance was on vacation and hence presumably absent from the store during the week of August 22, 1956.

As you will at this point surmise, the insistence of the defendant at the trial was that the person who served Mrs. Hoddeson was an impostor deceitfully impersonating a salesman of the defendant without the latter's knowledge.

It was additionally disclosed by the testimony that a relatively large number of salesmen were employed at the defendant's store, and that since they were remunerated in part on a sales commission basis, there existed considerable rivalry among them to serve incoming customers; hence the improbability of the unnoticed intrusion of an impersonator. [. . .]

The ground now asserted on behalf of the defendant for a reversal of the judgment is that there was a deficit of evidence to support the conclusion that a relationship of master and servant existed between the man who served and received the money from Mrs. Hoddeson and the defendant company. [. . .]

Where a party seeks to impose liability upon an alleged principal on a contract made by an alleged agent, as here, the party must assume the obligation of proving the agency relationship. It is not the burden of the alleged principal to disprove it.

Concisely stated, the liability of a principal to third parties for the acts of an agent may be shown by proof disclosing (1) express or real authority which has been definitely granted; (2) implied authority, that is, to do all that is proper, customarily incidental and reasonably appropriate to the exercise of the authority granted; and (3) apparent authority, such as where the principal by words, conduct, or other indicative manifestations has 'held out' the person to be his agent.

Obviously the plaintiffs' evidence in the present action does not substantiate the existence of any basic express authority or project any question implicating implied authority. The point here debated is whether or not the evidence circumstantiates the presence of apparent authority, and it is at this very point we come face to face with the general rule of law that the apparency and appearance of authority must be shown to have been created by the manifestations of the alleged principal, and not alone and solely by proof of those of the supposed agent. Assuredly the law cannot permit apparent authority to be established by the mere proof that a mountebank in fact exercised it.

Let us hypothesize for the purposes of our present comments that the acting salesman was not in fact an employee of the defendant, yet he behaved and deported himself during the stated period in the business establishment of the defendant in the manner described by the evidence adduced on behalf of the plaintiffs, would the defendant be immune as a matter of law from liability for the plaintiffs' loss? The tincture of estoppel that gives color to instances of apparent authority might in the law operate likewise to preclude a defendant's denial of liability. Broadly stated, the duty of the proprietor also encircles the exercise of reasonable care and vigilance to protect the customer from loss occasioned by the deceptions of an apparent salesman.

Our concept of the modern law is that where a proprietor of a place of business by his dereliction of duty enables one who is not his agent conspicuously to act as such and ostensibly to transact the proprietor's business with a patron in the establishment, the appearances being of such a character as to lead a person of ordinary prudence and circumspection to believe that the impostor was in truth the proprietor's agent, in such circumstances the law will not permit the proprietor defensively to avail himself of the impostor's lack of authority and thus escape liability for the consequential loss thereby sustained by the customer.

[EDS.—The Court reversed the judgment below and ordered a new trial based on the theory of agency by estoppel outlined in the opinion.]

NOTE: APPARENT AUTHORITY VERSUS AGENCY BY ESTOPPEL

The Restatement (Third) of Agency draws a distinction between apparent authority and agency by estoppel.[3] Some courts, however, do not distinguish between the two concepts.[4]

---

[3] *Compare* RESTATEMENT (THIRD) OF AGENCY § 2.03 (requiring the third party's reasonable belief about the agent's authority flowing from the principal's manifestations for apparent agency), *with id.* § 2.05 (estopping a principal from denying an agency relationship, even when the principal did not make any manifestation).

[4] *Id.* § 2.05, cmt. d.

E. AGENT'S LIABILITY IN CONTRACT

So far, we have considered how agents can cause their principals to be
bound by contracts. In limited circumstances, agents themselves can also
be bound by contracts they intend to enter into on behalf of the principals.

Restatement (Third) of Agency

Section 1.04—Terminology

[. . .] (2) Disclosed, Undisclosed, and Unidentified Principals

(a) **Disclosed principal.** A principal is disclosed if, when an agent and
a third party interact, the third party has notice that the agent is acting
for a principal and has notice of the principal's identity.

(b) **Undisclosed principal.** A principal is undisclosed if, when an
agent and a third party interact, the third party has no notice that the
agent is acting for a principal.

(c) **Unidentified principal.** A principal is unidentified if, when an
agent and a third party interact, the third party has notice that the agent
is acting for a principal but does not have notice of the principal's
identity.

Section 6.01—Agent for Disclosed Principal

When an agent acting with actual or apparent authority makes a
contract on behalf of a disclosed principal.

(1) the principal and the third party are parties to the contract; and

(2) the agent is not a party to the contract unless the agent and third
party agree otherwise.

Section 6.02—Agent for Unidentified Principal

When an agent acting with actual or apparent authority makes a
contract on behalf of an unidentified principal,

(1) the principal and the third party are parties to the contract; and

(2) the agent is a party to the contract unless the agent and the third
party agree otherwise.

Section 6.03—Agent for Undisclosed Principal

When an agent acting with actual authority makes a contract on behalf
of an undisclosed principal,

(1) unless excluded by the contract, the principal is a party to the
contract;

(2) the agent and the third party are parties to the contract; and

(3) the principal, if a party to the contract, and the third party have the
same rights, liabilities, and defenses against each other as if the principal
made the contract personally, subject to § 6.05–6.09.

Section 6.04—Principal Does Not Exist or Lacks Capacity

Unless the third party agrees otherwise, a person who makes a contract with a third party purportedly as an agent on behalf of a principal becomes a party to the contract if the purported agent knows or has reason to know that the purported principal does not exist or lacks capacity to be a party to a contract.

Section 6.10—Agent's Implied Warranty of Authority

A person who purports to make a contract, representation, or conveyance to or with a third party on behalf of another person, lacking power to bind that person, gives an implied warranty of authority to the third party and is subject to liability to the third party for damages for loss caused by breach of that warranty, including loss of the benefit expected from performance by the principal, unless

(1) the principal or purported principal ratifies the act as stated in § 4.01; or

(2) the person who purports to make the contract, representation, or conveyance gives notice to the third party that no warranty of authority is given; or

(3) the third party knows that the person who purports to make the contract, representation, or conveyance acts without actual authority.

F. PRINCIPAL'S LIABILITY IN TORT

A principal may be vicariously liable for an agent's tortious conduct if (1) an employer-employee relationship exists, and (2) the tortious conduct falls within the agent's scope of employment. As you will see in this section, however, those two elements are not always easy to determine.

Restatement (Third) of Agency

Section 2.04—Respondeat Superior

An employer is subject to liability for torts committed by employees while acting within the scope of their employment.

Section 7.01—Agent's Liability to Third Party

An agent is subject to liability to a third party harmed by the agent's tortious conduct. Unless an applicable statute provides otherwise, an actor remains subject to liability although the actor acts as an agent or an employee, with actual or apparent authority, or within the scope of employment.

Section 7.02—Duty to Principal; Duty to Third Party

An agent's breach of a duty owed to the principal is not an independent basis for the agent's tort liability to a third party. An agent is subject to tort liability to a third party harmed by the agent's conduct only when the agent's conduct breaches a duty that the agent owes to the third party.

Section 7.03—Principal's Liability—In General

(1) A principal is subject to direct liability to a third party harmed by an agent's conduct when

(a) as stated in § 7.04, the agent acts with actual authority or the principal ratifies the agent's conduct and

(i)   the agent's conduct is tortious, or

(ii) the agent's conduct, if that of the principal, would subject the principal to tort liability; or

(b) as stated in § 7.05, the principal is negligent in selecting, supervising, or otherwise controlling the agent; or

(c) as stated in § 7.06, the principal delegates performance of a duty to use care to protect other persons or their property to an agent who fails to perform the duty.

(2) A principal is subject to vicarious liability to a third party harmed by an agent's conduct when

(a) as stated in § 7.07, the agent is an employee who commits a tort while acting within the scope of employment; or

(b) as stated in § 7.08, the agent commits a tort when acting with apparent authority in dealing with a third party on or purportedly on behalf of the principal.

Section 7.04—Agent Acts with Actual Authority

A principal is subject to liability to a third party harmed by an agent's conduct when the agent's conduct is within the scope of the agent's actual authority or ratified by the principal; and

(1) the agent's conduct is tortious, or

(2) the agent's conduct, if that of the principal, would subject the principal to tort liability.

Section 7.08—Agent Acts with Apparent Authority

A principal is subject to vicarious liability for a tort committed by an agent in dealing or communicating with a third party on or purportedly on behalf of the principal when actions taken by the agent with apparent authority constitute the tort or enable the agent to conceal its commission.

1. EMPLOYEE VERSUS INDEPENDENT CONTRACTOR

Narayanasamy v. Issa

435 F. Supp. 3d 388 (D.R.I. 2020)

Needing a ride from T.F. Green Airport to his hotel, Mr. Lokeshwaran Narayanasamy used the Uber Application on his cell phone to summon a driver. Defendant Claudette Issa, a registered Uber driver, responded and picked him up. During the trip, Ms. Issa's car collided with a vehicle abandoned by the roadside after breaking down. Both Mr. Narayanasamy and Ms. Issa suffered injuries.

Claiming Ms. Issa was negligent, Mr. Narayanasamy, along with his wife Savitry Krishnamurthy and their minor child (collectively "the Narayanasamys"), seeks compensation from Uber under a theory of *respondeat superior*.

Uber moves for summary judgment, claiming that Ms. Issa is not an agent, servant, or employee of Uber as a matter of law, and thus it cannot be held liable under any *respondeat superior* theory.

The question here is whether Ms. Issa is an Uber employee rendering Uber liable for the injuries resulting from the car accident. In its motion, Uber argues that it cannot be held liable as a matter of law for Ms. Issa's negligence because she is an independent contractor not an Uber employee. Mr. Narayanasamy counters that the Court should look into the reality of the relationship between Ms. Issa and Uber—one that he believes bears many hallmarks of an employer-employee relationship— and should deny summary judgment because there is a dispute over that relationship.

The parties do not appear to dispute, however, that whether a relationship between parties constitutes an employer-employee relationship is a mixed question of fact and law and "depends in each case upon its particular facts taken as a whole." Therefore, a person's status in the work world—whether an employee or an independent contractor— should be decided by a jury when enough facts could support either finding.

At the motion for summary judgment stage, the Court's only determination is whether the Narayanasamy's have set forth enough evidence that if believed, a jury could determine that the driver, Ms. Issa was an employee of Uber.

Under Rhode Island law, the test to determine whether a person is an employee or an independent contractor is " 'based on the employer's right or power to exercise control over the method and means of performing the work and not merely the exercise of actual control.' "

Uber asserts that the evidence shows that it is merely a software provider with no actual or apparent control or authority over drivers like Ms. Issa. As evidence that Ms. Issa is not an employee, Uber cites to the

Technology Services Agreement (TSA) executed between Ms. Issa and [a wholly owned subsidiary of Uber—Raiser, LLC—] which states she is an independent contractor. Uber also points to the General Assembly's determination that Uber drivers are independent contractors. [EDS.— Rhode Island classifies a licensed entity that "uses a digital network to connect transportation network company riders to transportation network operators who provide prearranged rides" as a transportation network company (TNC). R.I. Gen. Laws § 39–14.2–16.] Finally, Uber relies on Ms. Issa's deposition testimony where she agrees that she is an independent contractor.

In addition to the TNC statute and the TSA that all drivers sign, Uber points to the fact that the driver controls the method and means of how they provide their services to riders, whether they chose to work or not work on any given day or any given time, whether to accept rides, what route to take, how to drive their car, whether also to work for a competitor (such as Lyft), and drivers provide their own equipment. Also, Uber does not pay the driver, the riders do.

On the other side of the road, Mr. Narayanasamy assert[s] that Uber is a service provider and employer of driver/partners. Their view of the evidence is that Uber "controls" their drivers, so it assumes liability for their actions. For example, they argue that:

1. *Uber controls the finances:* Uber unilaterally sets and controls fares; Uber pays its drivers and can alter payment if the driver receives a complaint; a rider's terms and financial relationship is with Uber directly not the driver; Uber collects the fares through a rider's credit card and the drivers have no option to collect fares directly from riders; fares set by Uber vary based on demand and peak times; Uber solely decides when and if prices surge to higher levels.

2. *Uber controls the branding and marketing:* Uber provides drivers with Uber logos for their vehicles; drivers are prohibited from having business cards or soliciting rides outside the Uber App; Uber sends riders using the Uber App a message that they can rely on Uber to provide "safe, reliable" rides, and that Uber has "peace of mind designed into every ride;" Uber expressly assures its riders that it actively screens drivers, and acts on ratings so that the riders may have "peace of mind."

3. *Uber imposes requirements on the drivers:* Uber has guidelines for quality, cleanliness, and behavior standards; Uber exercises substantial regulation and control over driver performance by reserving the right "at any time in Company's sole discretion to deactivate or otherwise restrict" access to the Uber App; Uber has threatened drivers with "deactivation" for issues such as having a poor attitude or not taking the most efficient/direct route on a trip, a rider complaining about a bad smelling car, trying to settle disputes directly with riders, asking riders to be paid for damage done to the

driver's vehicle, low customer ratings, cancelling too many rides, or for failing to accept enough rides while "on-duty."

4. *Uber handles disputes and adjudications:* Uber handles and adjudicates any rider disputes; in resolving disputes, Uber may reduce a rider's fare in its sole discretion and thereby, a driver's income.

5. *Relationship directly between Uber and the rider:* Uber maintains an ongoing relationship with riders through in-App advertisements and solicitations; Uber often offers riders reduced fares, special fare packages, free hotel stays, and other promotions, such as "Uber cash" that are credits that can be used to pay for rides, scooters, or bicycles, or food delivery through Uber's "UberEats" App; Uber periodically runs contest giveaways for riders including concert tickets and vacations as a marketing strategy; riders may also join special membership levels such as "Uber Gold" and "Uber VIP" to enjoy special privileges; Uber offers a "24/7" support team to address any rider concerns.

6. *Uber provides benefits to drivers:* Uber offers paid liability and comprehensive collision insurance, and rights to participate in health insurance offerings for which Uber has negotiated group rates; for applicants who do not have their own car, Uber offers "the Uber rental car program" so that drivers can get a ready-to-go car at a low commitment; if a driver does not have their own smartphone, Uber will provide one for business use.

7. *Employer-like activities:* Uber requires driver applicants to upload their driver's license information, vehicle's registration, and insurance; applicants must pass a background check; Uber encourages drivers to work as much time for Uber and not look for other employment; Uber drivers must agree to Uber's rules and oversight.

These facts raise disputes here such that "reasonable people could differ on whether a worker is an employee or an independent contractor based on the evidence in the case." The Court therefore finds that "the question is not for a court to decide; it must go to the jury," and declines to dismiss Uber on summary judgment.

[EDS.—On March 9, 2020, the parties filed a joint Stipulation of Dismissal and the case was dismissed with prejudice. Also in 2022, California voters voted in support of Proposition 22, allowing companies like Uber, Lyft, and DoorDash to treat ride-hail and food-delivery app-based drivers as independent contractors instead of employees. However, in 2021, the Alameda Superior Court of California ruled that Proposition 22 is unconstitutional and unenforceable.]

2. SCOPE OF EMPLOYMENT

In considering whether a tortious act occurred within the scope of employment, there is a circuit split. Some courts, such as Second Circuit in *Bushey*, use the foreseeability test. Others, such as the Utah Supreme Court in *Clover*, use the purpose test.

Restatement (Third) of Agency

Section 7.07—Employee Acting Within Scope of Employment

(1) An employer is subject to vicarious liability for a tort committed by its employee acting within the scope of employment.

(2) An employee acts within the scope of employment when performing work assigned by the employer or engaging in a course of conduct subject to the employer's control. An employee's act is not within the scope of employment when it occurs within an independent course of conduct not intended by the employee to serve any purpose of the employer.

(3) For purposes of this section,

(a) an employee is an agent whose principal controls or has the right to control the manner and means of the agent's performance of work, and

(b) the fact that work is performed gratuitously does not relieve a principal of liability.

Ira S. Bushey & Sons, Inc. v. United States

398 F.2d 167 (2d Cir. 1968)

■ FRIENDLY, CIRCUIT JUDGE.

While the United States Coast Guard vessel Tamaroa was being overhauled in a floating drydock located in Brooklyn's Gowanus Canal, a seaman returning from shore leave late at night, in the condition for which seamen are famed, turned some wheels on the drydock wall. He thus opened valves that controlled the flooding of the tanks on one side of the drydock. Soon the ship listed, slid off the blocks and fell against the wall. Parts of the drydock sank, and the ship partially did—fortunately without loss of life or personal injury. The drydock owner sought and was granted compensation by the District Court for the Eastern District of New York in an amount to be determined; the United States appeals.

The Tamaroa had gone into drydock on February 28, 1963; her keel rested on blocks permitting her drive shaft to be removed and repairs to be made to her hull. The contract between the Government and Bushey provided in part:

(o) The work shall, whenever practical, be performed in such manner as not to interfere with the berthing and messing of

> personnel attached to the vessel undergoing repair, and
> provision shall be made so that personnel assigned shall have
> access to the vessel at all times, it being understood that such
> personnel will not interfere with the work or the contractor's
> workmen.

Access from shore to ship was provided by a route past the security guard at the gate, through the yard, up a ladder to the top of one drydock wall and along the wall to a gangway leading to the fantail deck, where men returning from leave reported at a quartermaster's shack.

Seaman Lane, whose prior record was unblemished, returned from shore leave a little after midnight on March 14. He had been drinking heavily; the quartermaster made mental note that he was "loose." For reasons not apparent to us or very likely to Lane, he took it into his head, while progressing along the gangway wall, to turn each of three large wheels some twenty times; unhappily, as previously stated, these wheels controlled the water intake valves. After boarding ship at 12:11 A.M., Lane mumbled to an off-duty seaman that he had "turned some valves" and also muttered something about "valves" to another who was standing the engineering watch. Neither did anything; apparently Lane's condition was not such as to encourage proximity. At 12:20 A.M. a crew member discovered water coming into the drydock. By 12:30 A.M. the ship began to list, the alarm was sounded and the crew were ordered ashore. Ten minutes later the vessel and dock were listing over 20 degrees; in another ten minutes the ship slid off the blocks and fell against the drydock wall.

The Government attacks imposition of liability on the ground that Lane's acts were not within the scope of his employment. It relies heavily on § 228(1) of the Restatement of Agency 2d which says that "conduct of a servant is within the scope of employment if, but only if: [. . .] (c) it is actuated, at least in part by a purpose to serve the master." [EDS.—This is similar to § 7.07 of the Restatement of Agency 2d.] Courts have gone to considerable lengths to find such a purpose, as witness a well-known opinion in which Judge Learned Hand concluded that a drunken boatswain who routed the plaintiff out of his bunk with a blow, saying "Get up, you big [SOB], and turn to," and then continued to fight, might have thought he was acting in the interest of the ship. It would be going too far to find such a purpose here; while Lane's return to the Tamaroa was to serve his employer, no one has suggested how he could have thought turning the wheels to be, even if—which is by no means clear— he was unaware of the consequences.

In light of the highly artificial way in which the motive test has been applied, the district judge believed himself obliged to test the doctrine's continuing vitality by referring to the larger purposes *respondeat superior* is supposed to serve. He concluded that the old formulation failed this test. We do not find his analysis so compelling, however, as to constitute a sufficient basis in itself for discarding the old doctrine. It is not at all clear, as the court below suggested, that expansion of liability in the manner here suggested will lead to a more efficient allocation of resources. As the most astute exponent of this theory has emphasized, a more efficient allocation can only be expected if there is some reason to believe that imposing a particular cost on the enterprise will lead it to consider whether steps should be taken to prevent a recurrence of the accident. And the suggestion that imposition of liability here will lead to more intensive screening of employees rests on highly questionable premises. The unsatisfactory quality of the allocation of resource rationale is especially striking on the facts of this case. It could well be that application of the traditional rule might induce drydock owners, prodded by their insurance companies, to install locks on their valves to avoid similar incidents in the future, while placing the burden on shipowners is much less likely to lead to accident prevention. It is true, of course, that in many cases the plaintiff will not be in a position to insure, and so expansion of liability will, at the very least, serve *respondeat superior*'s loss spreading function. But the fact that the defendant is better able to afford damages is not alone sufficient to justify legal responsibility, and this overarching principle must be taken into account in deciding whether to expand the reach of *respondeat superior*.

A policy analysis thus is not sufficient to justify this proposed expansion of vicarious liability. This is not surprising since *respondeat superior*, even within its traditional limits, rests not so much on policy grounds consistent with the governing principles of tort law as in a deeply rooted sentiment that a business enterprise cannot justly disclaim responsibility for accidents which may fairly be said to be characteristic of its activities. It is in this light that the inadequacy of the motive test becomes apparent. Whatever may have been the case in the past, a doctrine that would create such drastically different consequences for the actions of the drunken boatswain in Nelson and those of the drunken seaman here reflects a wholly unrealistic attitude toward the risks characteristically attendant upon the operation of a ship. We concur in the statement of Mr. Justice Rutledge in a case involving violence injuring a fellow-worker, in this instance in the context of workmen's compensation:

> Men do not discard their personal qualities when they go to work. Into the job they carry their intelligence, skill, habits of care and rectitude. Just as inevitably they take along also their tendencies to carelessness and camaraderie, as well as emotional make-up. In bringing men together, work brings these qualities together, causes frictions between them, creates occasions for lapses into carelessness, and for fun-making and emotional flare-up. . . . These expressions of human nature are incidents inseparable from working together. They involve risks of injury and these risks are inherent in the working environment.

Put another way, Lane's conduct was not so "unforeseeable" as to make it unfair to charge the Government with responsibility. We agree with a leading treatise that "what is reasonably foreseeable in this context (of *respondeat superior*) [. . .] is quite a different thing from the foreseeably unreasonable risk of harm that spells negligence [. . .] The foresight that should impel the prudent man to take precautions is not the same measure as that by which he should perceive the harm likely to flow from his long-run activity in spite of all reasonable precautions on his own part. . . . The employer should be held to expect risks, to the public also, which arise 'out of and in the course of' his employment of labor." Here it was foreseeable that crew members crossing the drydock might do damage, negligently or even intentionally, such as pushing a Bushey employee or kicking property into the water.

Moreover, the proclivity of seamen to find solace for solitude by copious resort to the bottle while ashore has been noted in opinions too numerous to warrant citation. Once all this is granted, it is immaterial that Lane's precise action was not to be foreseen. [. . .]

One can readily think of cases that fall on the other side of the line. If Lane had set fire to the bar where he had been imbibing or had caused an accident on the street while returning to the drydock, the Government would not be liable; the activities of the "enterprise" do not reach into areas where the servant does not create risks different from those attendant on the activities of the community in general. We agree with the district judge that if the seaman "upon returning to the drydock, recognized the Bushey security guard as his wife's lover and shot him," vicarious liability would not follow; the incident would have related to the seaman's domestic life, not to his seafaring activity, and it would have been the most unlikely happenstance that the confrontation with the paramour occurred on a drydock rather than at the traditional spot. Here Lane had come within the closed-off area where his ship lay, to occupy a berth to which the Government insisted he have access, and while his act is not readily explicable, at least it was not shown to be due entirely to facets of his personal life. The risk that seamen going and coming from the Tamaroa might cause damage to the drydock is enough to make it fair that the enterprise bear the loss. It is not a fatal objection that the rule we lay down lacks sharp contours; in the end, as Judge Andrews said in a related context, "it is all a question (of expediency,) [. . .] of fair judgment, always keeping in mind the fact that we endeavor to make a rule in each case that will be practical and in keeping with the general understanding of Mankind." [. . .]

Affirmed.

Clover v. Snowbird Ski Resort

808 P.2d 1037 (Utah 1991)

Plaintiff Margaret Clover sought to recover damages for injuries sustained as the result of a ski accident in which Chris Zulliger, an employee of defendant Snowbird Corporation ("Snowbird"), collided with her. From the entry of summary judgment in favor of defendants, Clover appeals.

[. . .] At the time of the accident, Chris Zulliger was employed by Snowbird as a chef at the Plaza Restaurant. [. . .] He [. . .] had several conversations with Peter Mandler, the manager of the Plaza and Mid-Gad Restaurants, during which Mandler directed him to make periodic stops at the Mid-Gad to monitor operations.

On December 5, 1985, the date of the accident, Zulliger was scheduled to begin work at the Plaza Restaurant at 3 p.m. Prior to beginning work, he had planned to go skiing with Barney Norman, who was also employed as a chef at the Plaza. [. . .] On the morning of the accident, Mandler asked Zulliger to inspect the operation of the Mid-Gad prior to beginning work at the Plaza.

Zulliger and Norman stopped at the Mid-Gad in the middle of their first run. At the restaurant, they had a snack, inspected the kitchen, and talked to the personnel for approximately fifteen to twenty minutes. Zulliger and Norman then skied four runs before heading down the mountain to begin work. On their final run, Zulliger and Norman took a route that was often taken by Snowbird employees to travel from the top of the mountain to the Plaza. About mid-way down the mountain, at a point above the Mid-Gad, Zulliger decided to take a jump off a crest on the side of an intermediate run. He had taken this jump many times before. A skier moving relatively quickly is able to become airborne at that point because of the steep drop off on the downhill side of the crest. Due to this drop off, it is impossible for skiers above the crest to see skiers below the crest. The jump was well known to Snowbird. In fact, the Snowbird ski patrol often instructed people not to jump off the crest. There was also a sign instructing skiers to ski slowly at this point in the run. Zulliger, however, ignored the sign and skied over the crest at a significant speed. Clover, who had just entered the same ski run from a point below the crest, either had stopped or was traveling slowly below the crest. When Zulliger went over the jump, he collided with Clover, who was hit in the head and severely injured.

Clover brought claims against [. . .] Snowbird, alleging that [. . .] Snowbird is liable for Zulliger's negligence because at the time of the collision, he was acting within the scope of his employment. [. . .]

Under the doctrine of *respondeat superior*, employers are held vicariously liable for the torts their employees commit when the employees are acting within the scope of their employment. [. . .] In *Birkner [v. Salt Lake County]*, we observed that the Utah cases that have addressed the issue of whether an employee's actions, as a matter of law, are within or without the scope of employment have focused on three criteria. "First, an employee's conduct must be of the general kind the employee is employed to perform. [. . .] In other words, the employee must be about the employer's business and the duties assigned by the employer, as opposed to being wholly involved in a personal endeavor." Second, the employee's conduct must occur substantially within the hours and ordinary spatial boundaries of the employment. "Third, the employee's conduct must be motivated at least in part, by the purpose of serving the employer's interest." Under specific factual situations, such as when the employee's conduct serves a dual purpose or when the employee takes a personal detour in the course of carrying out his employer's directions, this court has occasionally used variations of this approach. These variations, however, are not departures from the criteria advanced in *Birkner*. Rather, they are methods of applying the criteria in specific factual situations.

[. . .] The difficulty, of course, arises from the fact that Zulliger did not return to the Plaza after he finished inspecting the facilities at the Mid-Gad. Rather, he skied four more runs and rode the lift to the top of the mountain before he began his return to the base. Snowbird claims that this fact shows that Zulliger's primary purpose for skiing on the day of the accident was for his own pleasure and that therefore, as a matter of law, he was not acting within the scope of his employment. In support of this proposition, Snowbird cites *Whitehead v. Variable Annuity Life Insurance. Whitehead* concerned the dual purpose doctrine. Under this doctrine, if an employee's actions are motivated by the dual purpose of benefiting the employer and serving some personal interest, the actions will usually be considered within the scope of employment. However, if the primary motivation for the activity is personal, "even though there may be some transaction of business or performance of duty merely incidental or adjunctive thereto, the [person] should not be deemed to be in the scope of his employment." In situations where the scope of employment issue concerns an employee's trip, a useful test in determining if the transaction of business is purely incidental to a personal motive is "whether the trip is one which would have required the employer to send another employee over the same route or to perform the same function if the trip had not been made."

In *Whitehead,* we held that an employee's commute home was not within the scope of employment, notwithstanding the plaintiff's contention that because the employee planned to make business calls from his house, there was a dual purpose for the commute. In so holding, we noted that the business calls could have been made as easily from any other place as from the employee's home. The instant case is distinguishable from *Whitehead* in that the activity of inspecting the Mid-Gad necessitates travel to the restaurant. Furthermore, there is evidence that the manager of both the Mid-Gad and the Plaza wanted an employee to inspect the restaurant and report back by 3 p.m. If Zulliger had not inspected the restaurant, it would have been necessary to send a second employee to accomplish the same purpose. Furthermore, the second employee would have most likely used the ski lifts and ski runs in traveling to and from the restaurant.

There is ample evidence that there was a predominant business purpose for Zulliger's trip to the Mid-Gad. Therefore, this case is better analyzed under our decisions dealing with situations where an employee has taken a personal detour in the process of carrying out his duties. This court has decided several cases in which employees deviated from their duties for wholly personal reasons and then, after resuming their duties, were involved in accidents. In situations where the detour was such a substantial diversion from the employee's duties that it constituted an abandonment of employment, we held that the employee, as a matter of law, was acting outside the scope of employment. However, in situations where reasonable minds could differ on whether the detour constituted a slight deviation from the employee's duties or an abandonment of employment, we have left the question for the jury.

Under the circumstances of the instant case, it is entirely possible for a jury to reasonably believe that at the time of the accident, Zulliger had resumed his employment and that Zulliger's deviation was not substantial enough to constitute a total abandonment of employment. First, a jury could reasonably believe that by beginning his return to the base of the mountain to begin his duties as a chef and to report to Mandler concerning his observations at the Mid-Gad, Zulliger had resumed his employment. In past cases, in holding that the actions of an employee were within the scope of employment, we have relied on the fact that the employee had resumed the duties of employment prior to the time of the accident. This is an important factor because if the employee has resumed the duties of employment, the employee is then "about the employer's business" and the employee's actions will be "motivated, at least in part, by the purpose of serving the employer's interest." The fact that due to Zulliger's deviation, the accident occurred at a spot above the Mid-Gad does not disturb this analysis. In situations where accidents have occurred substantially within the normal spatial boundaries of employment, we have held that employees may be within the scope of employment if, after a personal detour, they return to their duties and an accident occurs.

Second, a jury could reasonably believe that Zulliger's actions in taking four ski runs and returning to the top of the mountain do not constitute a complete abandonment of employment. It is important to note that by taking these ski runs, Zulliger was not disregarding his employer's directions. [. . .] [F]ar from directing its employees not to ski at the resort, Snowbird issued its employees season ski passes as part of their compensation.

These two factors, along with other circumstances—such as, throughout the day Zulliger was on Snowbird's property, there was no specific time set for inspecting the restaurant, and the act of skiing was the method used by Snowbird employees to travel among the different locations of the resort—constitute sufficient evidence for a jury to conclude that Zulliger, at the time of the accident, was acting within the scope of his employment.

In light of the genuine issues of material fact in regard to each of Clover's claims, summary judgment was inappropriate.

Reversed and remanded for further proceedings.

Norwood v. Simon Property Group, Inc.
200 A.D.3d 891 (N.Y. App. Div. 2021)

[. . .] On the evening of April 23, 2011, the plaintiff, along with several friends, went to the AMC Lowes Roosevelt Field 8 movie theater at the Roosevelt Field Mall located in Garden City. According to the defendant Eric C. Adams, one of the theater managers who was working that evening, the group was "causing a ruckus" near the theater entrance before they came inside. Some group members were "hitting" the glass entrance doors. Roosevelt Field Mall security guards were notified; they instructed the group to buy tickets to a movie or leave.

The group members purchased their tickets and were waiting in line at the concession stand in the theater lobby when a verbal dispute began between the plaintiff and Adams regarding something the plaintiff said about a concession stand worker. Adams asked the plaintiff to leave the theater. [. . .]

As the incident escalated, one of the plaintiff's friends began to "get aggressive" with Adams; he told Adams to "get out of here" and "mind [his] business." Adams then removed a collapsible baton from one of his pants pockets and extended it. He kept the baton by his side; he did not swing it or otherwise use it to make contact with the plaintiff or any of his friends. The plaintiff, upon noticing the baton, laughed at Adams. According to Adams, the plaintiff also said that he "[had] something for [Adams] in the car." Adams walked away. [. . .]

The plaintiff and his friends asked for, and were given, refunds for their tickets. They left the theater, stopping on the sidewalk just outside the entrance.

When the plaintiff and his friends left the theater, Adams walked out of the theater and went to his vehicle. Adams retrieved an airsoft pistol (a pellet gun), [. . .] and then returned to the sidewalk area in front of the theater where the plaintiff and his friends had congregated. When asked during his deposition why he returned to the front of the theater, Adams stated, "I'm the manager, and I can't leave." He also indicated that he believed that the plaintiff might have gone to his own vehicle to retrieve a weapon.

There, the altercation between the plaintiff and Adams resumed. The accounts of what happened next differ. The plaintiff testified that Adams pointed the pellet gun at him. Adams denied doing so. In either case, the plaintiff and his friends scattered, running in different directions. A security guard told Adams to go back inside the theater. Adams complied and was subsequently arrested.

The plaintiff commenced this action against Simon Property Group, Inc. (hereinafter Simon), AMC Entertainment, Inc., and AMC Lowes Roosevelt Field 8 (hereinafter together the AMC defendants, and collectively with Simon, the defendants), and Adams alleging causes of action sounding in intentional infliction of emotional distress, assault and battery, vicarious liability, negligent hiring, training, and supervision, and negligence, among other things. [. . .] [T]he Supreme Court, among other things, granted [defendants' motion for summary judgment]. The plaintiff appeals.

"[T]he doctrine of *respondeat superior* renders a master vicariously liable for a tort committed by his servant while acting within the scope of his employment." *Riviello v. Waldron*. The applicability of this theory of liability turns on a determination of "whether the act was done while the servant was doing his master's work, no matter how irregularly, or with what disregard of instructions" *Id*. Put another way, an employer is not "necessarily excused [from vicarious liability] merely because his employees, acting in furtherance of his interests, exhibit human failings and perform negligently or otherwise than in an authorized manner" *Id*. On the other hand, an employer "cannot be held vicariously liable for its employee's alleged tortious conduct if the employee was acting solely for personal motives unrelated to the furtherance of the employer's business." *Zwibel v. Midway Auto. Group*. [. . .]

As an initial matter, the defendants established, prima facie, that Adams was not employed by Simon, and was employed, instead, by the AMC defendants. [T]he Supreme Court properly granted that branch of the defendants' motion which was for summary judgment dismissing the vicarious liability cause of action insofar as asserted against Simon.

We reach the opposite conclusion, however, with respect to the AMC defendants. In support of their motion, the defendants submitted, among other things, a copy of the "AMC Theatres Manager Handbook," which, in relevant part, prohibits managers from "[p]ossessing, brandishing, or using a weapon while on AMC premises or while engaged in AMC business." The Handbook, however, also includes a "Guest Service Protocol" section, which states that, if guests are "disruptive or potentially violent," managers "may need to have them escorted off of the property," as part of their "obligation to protect . . . guests, associates [and themselves]." Consistent with this expectation, the general manager of the theater, Adams's supervisor, stated, during his deposition, that managers, like Adams, have security-related responsibilities, including ensuring that the theater is safe for customers and dealing with unruly patrons. And the plaintiff, during his deposition, stated that he believed Adams was a security guard.

When a business employs security guards or bouncers to maintain order, the use of physical force may be within the scope of their employment. Adams did not hold either of these job titles, but his responsibilities included maintaining order at the theater, ensuring the safety of customers and staff, and, if necessary, facilitating the removal from the theater of "disruptive or potentially violent" customers. The accomplishment of these ends by means prohibited by the AMC defendants' policy was not necessarily unforeseeable. After all, an employee's "disregard of instructions" is an almost inevitable feature of vicarious liability claims involving intentional torts. *Riviello v. Waldron.* Moreover, "specifically instruct[ing]" employees "to refrain from [certain kinds of behavior when dealing] with customers does not compel [the] conclusion that, as a matter of law," the prohibited conduct is outside the scope of employment. *Jaccarino v. Supermarkets Gen. Corp.* Unquestionably, Adams's response to the plaintiff and his friends was "in poor judgment" and contrary to the AMC defendants' policy, but "this in itself does not absolve [the AMC] defendants of liability for his acts." *Ramos v. Jake Realty Co.*

Contrary to the defendants' contention, they failed to establish, as a matter of law, that Adams's conduct was motivated solely by the desire to respond to a perceived slight from the plaintiff and his friends. A jury could perhaps conclude that Adams's actions towards the plaintiff were so motivated, but it could also find that he acted primarily with his employer's interests in mind, by ensuring that a group of individuals that he perceived as unruly, and perhaps even violent, left the theater before they engaged in more serious misconduct. [. . .]

Accordingly, the defendants failed to demonstrate their prima facie entitlement to judgment as a matter of law dismissing the vicarious liability cause of action insofar as asserted against the AMC defendants. [. . .]

3. FRANCHISE TORTS

Unique issues arise when the tortfeasor is a franchise of a larger corporate entity. Who should be liable for the tort—the franchise owner only, or the larger corporate entity (as a principal)?

Bartholomew v. Burger King Corp.
15 F. Supp. 3d 1043 (D. Haw. 2014)

I. INTRODUCTION

This is a tort action arising from an incident in which Plaintiff Clark Bartholomew ("Bartholomew") allegedly sustained injuries from eating a Triple Whopper sandwich imbedded with two needle-shaped metal objects at a Burger King Restaurant franchised to Defendant Army and Air Force Exchange Service ("AAFES").

On October 12, 2011, Bartholomew, his wife, and his son ("Plaintiffs") filed this action alleging tortious conduct by Defendants Burger King Corporation ("Burger King"), AAFES, and CTI Foods Holding Company ("CTI"), the hamburger patty supplier.

Currently before the court is Burger King's February 3, 2014 Motion for Summary Judgment arguing that Burger King cannot be liable for Bartholomew's injuries as a mere franchisor with insufficient control over the AAFES restaurant. Based on the following, the Court DENIES the Motion for Summary Judgment.

II. BACKGROUND

On December 1, 2010, Bartholomew's wife ordered a Triple Whopper meal at the AAFES restaurant and took it home for Bartholomew. While eating the sandwich, Bartholomew bit into a needle-like object, which pierced his tongue. Two days later, Bartholomew experienced stomach pain and sought medical attention. Apparently, another needle-like object was lodged in his small intestine requiring hospitalization.

He was placed on bed rest until December 9, 2010.

On May 15, 2009, Burger King and AAFES entered into a Franchise Agreement and Development Agreement ("Franchise Agreement"). Under the Franchise Agreement, AAFES is a franchisee of a Burger King Restaurant located at Schofield Barracks, Hawaii, but AAFES "is not an agent, partner, joint venture or employee of [Burger King]." According to the Franchise Agreement, Burger King has "no control over the terms and conditions of employment of AAFES' employees," and AAFES "must indicate the Independent ownership of the Restaurant and . . . that the Restaurant is operated by an Independent operator." At all relevant times, Burger King had no employees or management personnel at the AAFES restaurant. The Franchise Agreement also provides that AAFES must "comply strictly at all times with all elements of the Burger King System" and it reserves an "unrestricted right to enter the Restaurant" for inspection to the franchisor. Thus, the Franchise Agreement disclaims any agency relationship between Burger King and AAFES but requires AAFES to strictly adhere to the Burger King brand standards.

The Franchise Agreement incorporates the Burger King Mod Manual, an extensive manual that details food assembly procedures, crisis management procedures (including food tampering and food-related injuries), and quality assurance standards. The manual describes a precise method by which employees are to assemble the Triple Whopper Sandwich from spreading "3/4 [ounces] of mayonnaise evenly from edge to edge" of the bun crown to placing "three meat patties on the bun heel." The manual also has extensive "required" instructions for storage and broiling of beef patties. Finally, the manual mandates that "[o]nly products, supplies, and equipment on the Approved Brands List (ABL) or Approved Equipment List (AEL) are authorized for use in your restaurant." [. . .]

III. DISCUSSION

Burger King's Motion seeks summary judgment as to all claims, and ultimately turns on whether it, as a mere franchisor, may be held liable for injuries arising from the consumption of a sandwich produced by a franchisee. Because the cause of the alleged negligence remains in dispute, this court cannot conclude, at this summary judgment stage, that Burger King has no possible liability.

A. General Principles of Franchisor Liability

Hawaii has very little case law specifically addressing franchisor tort liability. *Ottensmeyer v. Baskin*, however, recognized that liability for a franchisor could arise from the actual or apparent agency of the franchisee. *Ottensmeyer*, thus, makes clear that Hawaii recognizes tort liability for franchisors although it does not describe exact parameters for such liability.

Many cases from other jurisdictions, however, describe the well-accepted general principles of franchisor liability—franchisors may be liable where they control or have the right to control day-to-day operations of the franchisee sufficient to establish an agency relationship.

In addition to this actual agency based liability, courts may find the franchisor liable where the franchisor has control of or the right to control the specific instrumentality of the harm. In fact, "there is an emerging judicial consensus to apply a franchisor liability test that considers the franchisor's control or right of control over the instrumentality that is alleged to have caused the harm." *Papa John's Int'l, Inc. v. McCoy.*

And this rule makes sense—an instrumentality-focused franchisor liability test allows courts to assess liability against those who were in the best position to prevent the harm. For example, a franchisor who exerts considerable control over the temperatures of food products may be held liable for injuries resulting from temperatures that were too high or too low. In contrast, that same franchisor would not be liable for a slip and fall where the franchisee had exclusive control over upkeep of the premises. Given the "emerging judicial consensus" and the soundness of this approach to franchisor liability, the court concludes that Hawaii would also embrace a test that focuses on the nexus between the franchisor's control and the instrumentality of the harm.

In addition to liability under the control test, a franchisor may also be liable for the tortious acts of the franchisee if an apparent agency relationship exists. Under the doctrine of apparent agency, vicarious liability arises where a franchisor represents to consumers that a franchisee is the agent of the franchisor causing a consumer to justifiably rely upon the apparent agency.

B. Application of Principles of Franchisor Liability

1. Negligence Liability-Based Counts: Negligence; Negligent Infliction of Emotional Distress; Negligent Training, Retention, Supervision, and/or Hiring; and Statutory Tort Liability

Burger King first argues that it cannot be liable for the counts of negligence because it had no control over the AAFES restaurant. In this regard, [*Miller v. McDonald's Corp.*] is especially instructive—the facts are directly on point. In *Miller*, a fast-food patron was injured when she bit into a sapphire imbedded in her Big Mac, the signature sandwich of the fast-food franchisor. Miller reversed summary judgment in favor of the franchisor because there were sufficient facts for a jury to find that the franchisor had "the right to control the way in which [the franchisee] performed at least food handling and preparation." The court held that if a franchisor details specific procedures that employees must follow with respect to "food handling and preparation," there may be sufficient control on the part of the franchisor to establish *respondeat superior* liability for injuries resulting from that food.

Plaintiffs contend that Burger King maintains a "tight grip on the daily worldwide, burger-by-burger operations" and has strict specifications regarding preparation of the Triple Whopper as well as ingredient supply. In support of these contentions, Plaintiffs point to various provisions in the franchise agreement including detailed Whopper assembly instructions and a requirement that "only products, supplies and equipment on the Approved Brands List [. . .] are authorized for use in your restaurant." These provisions create a genuine issue of fact—one that severely undermines Burger King's assertion that "the Restaurant was under the exclusive control of AAFES."

Burger King points out that the franchise agreement states that "the franchisee is responsible for the day-to-day operation of his/her business," and that AAFES "is not an agent, partner, joint venture or employee of [Burger King]." But a disclaimer of agency in a franchise agreement will not, by itself, defeat liability where the circumstances indicate that the requisite control exists. There is clearly an issue of material fact as to whether Burger King retained the requisite control over the Triple Whopper consumed by Bartholomew. [. . .]

3. Liability Based on Apparent Agency

Questions of fact also preclude summary judgment on an apparent agency theory. As stated, vicarious liability arises where a franchisor represents to consumers that a franchisee is the agent of the franchisor causing a consumer to justifiably rely upon the apparent agency. Thus, if AAFES was the apparent agent of Burger King, Burger King is liable for the torts of AAFES.

The fast-food franchise model relies upon a public perception of a "national system of restaurants with common products and common standards of quality." In this case, although the franchise agreement required AAFES to post a sign notifying the public of its ownership and operation of the establishment, it is unclear whether AAFES actually posted such a sign. Further, a single sign indicating that a franchisee owns the particular restaurant at issue may not necessarily overcome the public perception of agency.

Ottensmeyer examined the franchise relationship and apparent agency. The court reversed summary judgment in favor of the franchisor, Miss Universe, Inc., and the franchisee, holding that there were jury issues as to whether "the manifestations of control apparent to the [pageant] contestants" were "sufficient indications of actual or apparent authority on the part of [the franchisee]." Although the franchisor/franchisee agreement had a provision "expressly disclaim[ing] any agency on the part of the franchisee," *Ottensmeyer* emphasized that such contract language was not dispositive. Instead, "consideration of the whole record" controls the determination of apparent agency.

Similarly, the Burger King/AAFES Franchise Agreement disavows any agency relationship between Burger King and AAFES. However, other "manifestations of control," such as the branding efforts of Burger King and the potential lack of AAFES signage at the AAFES restaurant, might create a relationship of apparent agency, and is, therefore, a genuine issue of material fact. Indeed, there is a "Burger King" sign outside of the AAFES restaurant, the architectural and color scheme of the restaurant matches that of other Burger King restaurants, and numerous materials inside the restaurant bear the "Burger King" logo. These factors could lead a fact finder to conclude that the Plaintiffs justifiably relied upon an apparent agency relationship between AAFES and Burger King. [. . .]

V. CONCLUSION

For the reasons discussed above, the court DENIES Defendant Burger King Corporation's Motion for Summary Judgment.

[EDS.—Bartholomew and Burger King ultimately settled for $50,000.]

4. INHERENTLY DANGEROUS ACTIVITIES

Hatch v. V.P. Fair Foundation, Inc.
990 S.W.2d 126 (Mo. App. 2d. 1999)

V.P. Fair organizes an annual multi-day fair in downtown St. Louis to celebrate the Fourth of July. [. . .] In 1993, V.P. Fair contracted with

Northstar for the provision of a bungee jumping attraction. [. . .] [On July 5, Hatch] was to be the first jumper of the day. A Northstar employee placed a harness around Hatch's waist and ankles, and fastened the bungee cord to the harness. Hatch walked to the bungee cage where he joined Paul Murray, Northstar's jumpmaster, and a reporter and cameraman from a local television station. A crane lifted the bungee cage 170 feet above the ground, and Murray opened the cage door and straightened out the bungee cord inside the cage. Murray then directed Hatch to the front of the cage and told him that he was locked in and safe to jump. Unfortunately, no one had attached the bungee cord to the crane, and when Hatch leaped off the platform, he plunged 170 feet to the ground. [. . .] As a result of the fall, Hatch sustained serious injuries to his back, legs, and shoulders. A tape depicting the premises, the preparation for the jump, and the jump itself was shown to the jury. [. . .]

After his fall, Hatch instituted this lawsuit against Northstar and V.P. Fair. [. . .] [T]he court found that V.P. Fair could be liable under a premises liability theory only if bungee jumping was an inherently dangerous activity.

The [question] of [. . .] whether bungee jumping constituted an inherently dangerous activity [was] submitted to the jury. The jury [. . .] found that bungee jumping was an inherently dangerous activity and returned a verdict in favor of Hatch and against V.P. Fair on the premises liability claim. The jury awarded Hatch $5,000,000 in damages, and the trial court entered a judgment against defendants in that amount. Defendants filed post-trial motions for judgment notwithstanding the verdict, new trial, and remittitur. The trial court granted V.P. Fair's motion for judgment notwithstanding the verdict. [. . .] This appeal followed.

On appeal, [. . .] Hatch argues that the trial court erred in granting V.P. Fair's motion for judgment notwithstanding the verdict on the basis of its finding that as a matter of law bungee jumping is not an inherently dangerous activity.

In general, a landowner owes a duty of ordinary and reasonable care to invitees to prevent injury to the invitee. A well-recognized exception to this general rule exists when a landowner hires an independent contractor. A landowner is not vicariously liable for injuries to third parties caused by the negligence of the independent contractor or his employees. Thus, by hiring an independent contractor, the landowner may shift the duty to use reasonable and ordinary care to prevent injury to the independent contractor.

Nevertheless, there are at least two exceptions under which a non-negligent landowner may be held vicariously liable for the negligence of an independent contractor: the landowner control exception and the inherently dangerous activity exception. As previously stated, in this opinion we reach only the application of the inherently dangerous activity exception.

[. . .] Under this exception, a landowner who hires an independent contractor to perform an inherently dangerous activity has a nondelegable duty to take special precautions to prevent injury from the activity. The landowner "remains liable for the torts of the contractor, simply for commissioning the activity. The liability attaches without any need for showing that the employer is in any respect negligent. It is purely vicarious." *Ballinger v. Gascosage Elec. Coop.*

A landowner who hires an independent contractor to perform an inherently dangerous activity, however, is not vicariously liable for every act of an independent contractor that causes injury to a third party. According to the Restatement (Second) of Torts, the inherently dangerous activity exception applies only where "the harm results from the negligence of the contractor in failing to take precautions against the danger involved in the work itself, which the employer should contemplate at the time of the contract." Restatement (Second) of Torts sec. 427 cmt. d (1965). On the other hand, if the contractor's negligence is "collateral," the general rule of landowner non-liability applies.

The Restatement defines collateral negligence as "negligence which is unusual or abnormal, or foreign to the normal or contemplated risks of doing the work, as distinguished from negligence which creates only the normal or contemplated risk." Restatement (Second) of Torts sec. 426 cmt. a (1965). Under this rule,

> a landowner is not required to contemplate or anticipate abnormal or unusual kinds of negligence on the part of the contractor, or negligence in the performance of the operative details of the work which ordinarily may be expected to be carried out with proper care, *unless the circumstances under which the work is done give him warning of some special reason to take precautions, or some special risk of harm to others inherent in the work.*

Restatement (Second) of Torts sec. 426 cmt. b (1965).

[. . .] In its judgment notwithstanding the verdict, the trial court first concluded that bungee jumping was not inherently dangerous as a matter of law because the evidence indicated that bungee jumping could be done safely. In so holding, the trial court relied on *dicta* found in *Reed v. Ocello*, in which this Court stated "if there is a safe way to perform the activity, it is not inherently dangerous, and the general rule of landowner non-liability applies."

In our view the *dicta* in *Reed* [. . .] directly contradicts *Ballinger v. Gascosage Electric Cooperative,* in which the court stated that "[t]he essence of inherent danger . . . is the need for special precaution. It is not sufficient for the defendant to show that the work can be done safely." [. . .] Accordingly, the trial court erred in entering judgment notwithstanding the verdict in favor of V.P. Fair.

To initially determine whether an activity is inherently dangerous, the trial judge should begin by ascertaining the nature of the activity and the manner in which the activity is ordinarily performed. If after considering these factors the trial court concludes the activity does not involve some peculiar risk of harm, then the activity is not inherently dangerous as a matter of law. If the trial court does not so find, then the question should be submitted to the jury pursuant to [state law].

In this case, while there was evidence that the activity could be done safely, there was also evidence, including Northstar's release form, which would support a conclusion that by its very nature the activity involves some peculiar risk of physical harm. Thus, the trial court erred in determining as a matter of law that bungee jumping is not inherently dangerous.

Having found sufficient evidence to support a finding that the bungee jump in this case was inherently dangerous, we must next determine if Northstar's failure to attach the bungee cord is an act of collateral negligence. In its judgment notwithstanding the verdict, the trial court found that Northstar's failure to attach the bungee cord was an act of collateral negligence. Collateral negligence would preclude a finding that the V.P. Fair is vicariously liable. We conclude that the trial court misinterpreted the collateral negligence rule.

Collateral negligence occurs when the negligence is unusual or foreign to the normal contemplated risks of performing the activity. A landowner is not immune from liability simply because the independent contractor's negligence contributed to the third party's injury. Instead, the proper focus for the factfinder is whether the landowner contemplated or should have contemplated the type of negligence committed by the independent contractor. As to what an employer is and is not expected to contemplate, the Restatement provides the following example:

> [A]n employer may hire a contractor to make an excavation, reasonably expecting that the contractor will proceed in the normal and usual manner with bulldozer or with pick and shovel. When the contractor, for his own reasons, decides to use blasting instead, and the blasting is done in a negligent manner, so that it injures the plaintiff, such negligence is "collateral" to the contemplated risk, and the employer is not liable. If, on the other hand, the blasting is provided for or contemplated by the contract, the negligence in the course of the operation is within the risk contemplated, and the employer is responsible for it.

The test is whether or not the independent contractor's acts were or should have been within the contemplation of the landowner. The Restatement provides that a landowner may be required to contemplate abnormal or unusual kinds of negligence if the circumstances under which the activity is performed give the landowner warning of special reasons to take precautions or some special risk of harm to others inherent in the activity. Here, because of the extreme height involved,

V.P. Fair should have been aware of a special risk of injury to bungee jumping participants if Northstar failed to properly attach the bungee cord. V.P. Fair had the opportunity to argue to the jury that Northstar's actions were not and should not have been within its contemplation. The participant's safety in making a bungee jump depends in large part on the security of the bungee cord. The risk that a participant could be injured as a result of any failure of the cord, its attachment, or the persons operating the jump is a peculiar risk that V.P. Fair should have contemplated. Accordingly, Hatch made a submissible case under the inherently dangerous activity exception.

The trial court properly instructed the jury under MAI 16.08 to determine whether bungee jumping was inherently dangerous. We are satisfied that in considering whether the activity of bungee jumping was inherently dangerous, the jury reasonably could have found that unless adequate precautions were taken, bungee jumping necessarily presents a substantial risk of harm. In addition, the jury reasonably could have found that the risk of injury from a fall is a risk that inheres in bungee jumping itself in the absence of adequate precautions and that the risk was not negligently created solely as the result of the improper manner in which Northstar performed the work. Because Hatch made a submissible case under the inherently dangerous activity exception, the trial court erred in entering judgment notwithstanding the verdict.

The case is remanded with directions to reinstate the verdict against V.P. Fair and to enter judgment thereon.

G. TERMINATION OF THE AGENCY RELATIONSHIP

As a general rule, once an agent's authority is terminated, the agent no longer has the right to act on the principal's behalf. This section reviews the events that terminate an agent's authority.

Restatement (Third) of Agency
Section 3.06—Termination of Actual Authority—In General

An agent's actual authority may be terminated by:

(1) the agent's death, cessation of existence, or suspension of powers as stated in § 3.07(1) and (3); or

(2) the principal's death, cessation of existence, or suspension of powers as stated in § 3.07(2) and (4); or

(3) the principal's loss of capacity, as stated in § 3.08(1) and (3); or

(4) an agreement between the agent and the principal or the occurrence of circumstances on the basis of which the agent should reasonably conclude that the principal no longer would assent to the agent's taking action on the principal's behalf, as stated in § 3.09; or

(5) a manifestation of revocation by the principal to the agent, or of renunciation by the agent to the principal, as stated in § 3.10(1); or

(6) the occurrence of circumstances specified by statute.

Section 3.07—Death, Cessation of Existence, and Suspension of Powers

(1) The death of an individual agent terminates the agent's actual authority.

(2) The death of an individual principal terminates the agent's actual authority. The termination is effective only when the agent has notice of the principal's death. The termination is also effective as against a third party with whom the agent deals when the third party has notice of the principal's death. [. . .]

Section 3.08—Loss of Capacity

(1) An individual principal's loss of capacity to do an act terminates the agent's actual authority to do the act. The termination is effective only when the agent has notice that the principal's loss of capacity is permanent or that the principal has been adjudicated to lack capacity. The termination is also effective as against a third party with whom the agent deals when the third party has notice that the principal's loss of capacity is permanent or that the principal has been adjudicated to lack capacity.

(2) A written instrument may make an agent's actual authority effective upon a principal's loss of capacity, or confer it irrevocably regardless of such loss.

(3) If a principal that is not an individual loses capacity to do an act, its agent's actual authority to do the act is terminated.

Section 3.09—Termination by Agreement or by Occurrence of Changed Circumstances

An agent's actual authority terminates (1) as agreed by the agent and the principal, subject to the provisions of § 3.10; or (2) upon the occurrence of circumstances on the basis of which the agent should reasonably conclude that the principal no longer would assent to the agent's taking action on the principal's behalf.

Section 3.10—Manifestation Terminating Actual Authority

(1) Notwithstanding any agreement between principal and agent, an agent's actual authority terminates if the agent renounces it by a manifestation to the principal or if the principal revokes the agent's actual authority by a manifestation to the agent. A revocation or a renunciation is effective when the other party has notice of it. [. . .]

Section 3.11—Termination of Apparent Authority

(1) The termination of actual authority does not by itself end any apparent authority held by an agent.

(2) Apparent authority ends when it is no longer reasonable for the third party with whom an agent deals to believe that the agent continues to act with actual authority.

Olander v. State Farm Mutual Auto Insurance Company
317 F.3d 807 (8th Cir. 2003)

Brian Olander became a State Farm insurance agent in Mandan, North Dakota in 1981. In August 1996, Olander was charged with murder after a violent altercation with a neighboring landowner. When Olander refused to take a leave of absence until the criminal charges were resolved, State Farm terminated his agency agreement and assigned other agents to serve the State Farm policyholders previously served by Olander's agency. In 1999, Olander commenced this diversity action against State Farm, alleging wrongful termination of the agency agreement and related claims. The district court granted State Farm's motion for summary judgment, concluding that Section III.A. of the written State Farm Agent's Agreement unambiguously made the parties' contractual relationship terminable at will. Section III.A. provides:

> This Agreement will terminate upon your death. You or State Farm have the right to terminate this Agreement by written notice delivered to the other or mailed to the other's last known address. The date of termination shall be the date specified in the notice, but in the event no date is specified, the date of termination shall be the date of delivery if the notice is delivered, or the date of the postmark, if the notice is mailed. Either party can accelerate the date of termination specified by the other by giving written notice of termination in accordance with this paragraph.

On appeal, a divided panel of this court reversed. The panel concluded that two other provisions of the Agreement create an ambiguity as to whether it was terminable only for cause; therefore, summary judgment was inappropriate because extrinsic evidence is admissible to construe this essential contract term. [. . .] [W]e granted State Farm's petition for rehearing en banc and now affirm.

The issue on appeal may be quickly summarized. If the Agreement was terminable at will by either party, then Olander has no wrongful termination claim, and his related claims were properly dismissed as well. Under North Dakota law, the construction of a written contract is initially a question of law. Olander argues that extrinsic evidence—most of it pre-dating his State Farm Agent's Agreement—establishes State Farm's intent that its agents be terminated only for cause. Under North Dakota law, such evidence is not admissible to vary the terms of an unambiguous written contract. "However, if a written contract is ambiguous, extrinsic evidence may be considered to show the parties' intent." *Des Lacs Valley Land Corp.* "A contract is ambiguous when rational arguments can be made for different positions about its meaning. . . . When a contract is ambiguous, the terms of the contract and the parties' intent become questions of fact." *Kaler v. Kraemer.* Here, the district court concluded the contract is unambiguous and refused to consider Olander's extrinsic evidence. Our panel disagreed. Whether a written contract is ambiguous must be determined from the four corners of the document, construing the contract as a whole. Ambiguity is a question of law that we review de novo, just as we review the grant of summary judgment de novo.

Section III of the State Farm Agent's Agreement is entitled "Termination of Agreement." Other than providing that the Agreement terminates upon the death of the agent (which confirms this is a personal services contract), Section III does not specify the *grounds* for termination. It simply provides, "You [the agent] or State Farm have the right to terminate this Agreement by written notice delivered to the other." In many cases, a contract's silence on an issue creates an ambiguity. But in this case, the contract's silence is itself unambiguous. The general rule in this country has long been that a personal services contract of indefinite duration may be terminated at will by either party. [. . .]

North Dakota has codified this general rule for contracts of employment. The Supreme Court of North Dakota has also applied the rule to personal services contracts, under which agents and professionals who are not employees provide on-going services of indefinite duration. That the Supreme Court of North Dakota would apply the general rule to Section III.A. of the State Farm Agent's Agreement is confirmed by *Wadeson v. Am. Family Mut. Ins. Co.* In *Wadeson,* a contract between an insurer and its district manager provided, like Section III.A., that it "may be terminated by any party as to its interest by giving written notice to the other," without specifying the grounds for termination. The court held that the contract was terminable at will, not only for good cause.

Thus, the North Dakota general rule establishes that the Agreement's silence as to its duration is, without more, an unambiguous declaration that it is terminable at will by either party. Seeking to avoid the general rule, Olander argues, and the panel majority agreed, that two other provisions of the Agreement create an ambiguity that requires the consideration of extrinsic evidence.

First, Section III.B. of the Agreement provides: "In the event [State Farm] terminate[s] this Agreement, you are entitled upon request to a review in accordance with the termination review procedures approved by the Board of Directors of [State Farm], as amended from time to time." The panel majority surmised that "one rational explanation for the existence of the review procedure is to ensure that any termination was made for good cause, and not capriciously." However, two courts have squarely rejected the contention that this provision renders the State Farm Agent's Agreement ambiguous. Another court construed a Farmers

Insurance Exchange agency contract as unambiguously terminable at will despite a similar review provision[.] [. . .]

Similarly, many other cases have held that an employer's contract termination procedures did not render an employment relationship terminable only for cause.

Second, the panel majority relied upon the statement in the Agreement's preamble that the parties "expect that by entering into this Agreement, and by the full and faithful observance and performance of the obligations and responsibilities herein set forth, a mutually satisfactory relationship will be established and maintained." However, this hortatory language may not properly serve to create an ambiguity in an otherwise unambiguous termination provision. When one operative term in a contract is unambiguous, as the termination provision is here, other provisions must be read so that they are consistent with the plain meaning of the unambiguous term.

To our knowledge, every court but one has interpreted the State Farm Agent's Agreement as being unambiguously terminable at will. The one exception is the Ninth Circuit's unpublished opinion in *Sandberg v. State Farm Mut. Auto. Ins. Co.*. However, in holding that summary judgment was inappropriate on the terminable-at-will issue, the court in *Sandberg* applied California law, which, unlike North Dakota law, permits the consideration of extrinsic evidence on the question of whether a contract is ambiguous.

Moreover, the court in *Sandberg* affirmed the grant of summary judgment in State Farm's favor. Applying the definition of good cause under California law—"a fair and honest reason, regulated by good faith, that is not trivial, arbitrary or capricious, unrelated to business needs or goals, or pretextual"—the court concluded that State Farm had good cause to terminate an agent who had sued State Farm seeking punitive damages for fraud. Here, Olander was terminated after he was indicted for murder and refused to take a leave of absence until the criminal proceedings were resolved. Thereafter, a jury convicted him of manslaughter, and he spent many months in prison before the Supreme Court of North Dakota reversed his conviction. Though he was ultimately acquitted after a second trial, State Farm's summary judgment motion was supported by an affidavit from the Director of Agent Licensing and Investigations for the North Dakota Insurance Department averring that, had Olander not lost his agent's license when he was terminated by State Farm, "at the time of his conviction of a felony, the Department would have taken action in some form to suspend and/or possibly revoke his license." These events make it clear that, if the definition of good cause under California law applied in this case (which of course it does not), State Farm would be entitled to summary judgment on the ground that it had good cause to protect its business interests by terminating Olander in August 1996.

Because the State Farm Agent's Agreement was unambiguously terminable at will as a matter of law, the district court properly declined to consider the extrinsic evidence submitted by Olander in granting State Farm's motion for summary judgment. Accordingly, the judgment of the district court is affirmed. [. . .]

H. REVIEW PROBLEMS

1.   Vinny wants to buy a used car, but he knows his negotiating skills are not as good as his friend Lisa's. Vinny gives Lisa the cash he is willing to spend on the car, and Lisa heads to the local used car lot. Although Lisa does not work as a mechanic, she has an inordinate amount of experience working on used cars. At the used car lot, Lisa selects the perfect car for Vinny. She does not, however, inspect the car. Instead, she trusts the word of the salesman. Unfortunately for Vinny, the car was recently in an accident that rendered it both unsafe to drive and almost valueless. An inspection would have revealed this information, whether Lisa conducted it herself or asked a mechanic to do it. Frustrated, Vinny consults you as his attorney to see if he might be able to recover the money he paid for the car from Lisa. What is your advice?[5]

2.   While serving as the mayor of the City of Colton, CA and as a member of the Colton City Council, Gaytan accepted bribes that influenced his vote on several city land use issues. Gaytan pleaded guilty to bribery after federal charges were brought against him and was ordered to pay restitution to the City in the total amount of the bribes received, which he appeals. Gaytan argues that the City (his principal) did not suffer any actual loss when he accepted the bribe money. In this case, has Gaytan breached his duties as an agent and is he accountable for the bribe money he has received?[6]

3.   Taylor is a salesperson who sells solar panels over the phone. They are employed by Universal Builders, who pays them minimum wage plus a commission for any sales that result from their phone sales. The company also employs door-to-door salespeople who earn a higher wage and commission. One day, while off-duty and at a block party, Taylor learns that a neighbor is thinking about installing solar panels. Taylor visits the neighbor's home and provides a ballpark estimate. Then, Taylor tells their supervisor that they have identified a prospect, and that they would give the name of the prospect to the supervisor if the supervision would give Taylor the same pay and commission as door-to-door salespeople. When the supervisor refused to pay Taylor more, Taylor refused to give the supervisor the name of the prospect. Did Taylor violate their duty of loyalty?[7]

4.   In December 2015, HotWheels, a car manufacturer, entered into a loan agreement with the IronBank. HotWheels guaranteed the repayment of

---

[5]   *See* RESTATEMENT (THIRD) OF AGENCY § 8.08, cmt. e, illus. 5.

[6]   *See* United States v. Gaytan, 342 F.3d 1010 (9th Cir. 2003).

[7]   *See* Smith v. Unemployment Comp. Bd. of Review, 28 Pa. Cmwlth. 98 (Pa. Commw. Ct. 1977).

the loan granting the IronBank a lien (*i.e.*, a form of secured interest) on its inventory. Three years later, needing to raise capital to convert its production to electric vehicles, HotWheels entered a larger loan with the IronBank. For this second loan, the lender required security interests in HotWheels' real estate properties. In 2020, HotWheels decided to repay the first loan and instructed LittleGreen LLP, its counsel, to prepare the documents necessary to repay the IronBank and to release the security interest the lender held in HotWheels' inventory. A LittleGreen partner assigned the work to an associate and instructed him to prepare a closing checklist and all the necessary documents to repay the loan and terminate the security interest. The associate prepared the documents and shared the documents with the partner, who approved the work and circulated them with HotWheels' internal counsels, the IronBank, and its own counsel, Polished Shoes LLP. All parties agreed on the terms of the transaction. In early 2021, HotWheels filed for bankruptcy. In the process, IronBank realized that, when processing the repayment of the 2015 loan, it had inadvertently terminated all security interests on both the original loan and the 2020 loan, making it a *de facto* unsecured creditor. After investigation, the parties realized that the LittleGreen associate made a clerical mistake in reporting the correct information of the security interests, including in the final repayment documents reference to all security interests granted by HotWheels to IronBank, and not only the interest to the lien of the 2015 loan. Can IronBank be on the hook for the termination of all security interests?[8]

5.   Betty Simpson worked for Bradford White. White had previously granted Simpson power of attorney to close a real estate deal. In a separate transaction, White asked Simpson to attend an auction and bid up to $250,000 on another property White wished to acquire. Simpson won the auction, but for $327,500. To cover the overage, Simpson offered to sell a portion of the property to the Thomases, claiming she had the authority to sell the property. The Thomases accepted Simpson's offer. While White was upset when he learned what Simpson had done, he ratified Simpson's winning bid. But then, White contacted the Thomases informing them Simpson did not have the authority to sell the land and he would not sell them the land. The Thomases sued White seeking to bind him to Simpson's representations. Is White bound by Simpson's representations?[9]

6.   Barth, Inc., hired Florence to manage its principal asset: an apartment complex. Florence listed the apartment complex for sale. The listing agreement disclosed "Barth, Inc." as the owner. Florence helped the listing agent show Newberry the property. Newberry subsequently purchased the apartment complex. Barth, Inc., however, refused to deliver the property to Newberry on the theory that Florence had no authority to sell the property. Newberry sued Barth, Inc. and Florence

---

[8]   *See* Off. Comm. of Unsecured Creditors of Motors Liquidation Co. v. JPMorgan Chase Bank, N.A., No. 13–2187, 2015 WL 252318 (2d Cir. Jan. 21, 2015).

[9]   *See* White v. Thomas, No. CA 90–157, 1991 WL 31212 (Mar. 6, 1991).

for specific performance. At trial, Florence testified she thought she had authority to list the property on behalf of the corporation. How should the trial court rule?[10]

7. Todd and C.A. Taylor hired Ramsay-Gerding Construction Co. as their general contractor to build a hotel. Ramsay-Gerding hired a subcontractor to install a stucco plaster exterior and accompanying accessories. During construction, the Taylors became concerned the stucco may rust. Ramsay-Gerding organized a meeting with the subcontractor and Mike McDonald, the territory manager for the stucco manufacturer. During the meeting, McDonald asserted the stucco system was "bullet-proof" against rust but suggested that a corrosion inhibitor would provide additional protection. Mr. Taylor seemed unconvinced, so McDonald said, "Mr. Taylor, you know you're getting a five-year warranty?" By the end of their meeting, Mr. Taylor agreed to move forward with installing the stucco and corrosion inhibitor. After construction was completed, McDonald sent a letter to the stucco installer on corporate letterhead confirming the manufacturer's warranty. The letter was signed, "Mike McDonald, Territory Manager OR." The stucco installer forwarded the letter to Ramsay-Gerding, who forwarded it to the Taylors. Later that year, the Taylors noticed discoloration on the exterior walls of the hotel. The Taylors sued Ramsay-Gerding for breach of contract and the stucco manufacturer for breach of warranty. Ramsay-Gerding also sued the stucco manufacturer for breach of warranty and contribution. At trial, the stucco manufacturer moved for a directed verdict on the breach of warrant claim, arguing that McDonald did not have authority to bind the corporation. How should the judge rule?[11]

8. BitCo., which buys computer hardware for lease to end-users, sued CryptoMine for breach of contract to purchase computer core memories. After a meeting between BitCo.'s sole employee Joyce, CryptoMine salesman Kays, and Kays' boss Ava, the parties commenced negotiations which resulted in Kays giving Joyce a written document containing the terms of sale of memory units from CryptoMine to BitCo. The document had signature blocks for a representative of each party to sign. Joyce signed on behalf of BitCo., but no one from CryptoMine signed the document. Shortly after Joyce signed the document, Ava circulated an intra-office memorandum stating that CryptoMine had an agreement with BitCo. for the purchase of computer core memories, and that at Joyce's request all communications with BitCo. concerning the sale would be handled through Kays. A few days later, Kays sent a letter to Joyce confirming the delivery dates and installation instructions for the core memories. As it turns out, neither Kays nor Ava had actual authority to issue this kind of delivery letter. Delivery letters at CryptoMine are only supposed to be entered into by higher-ups. Later on, CryptoMine fails to deliver the items promised to BitCo., and BitCo. sues for damages. CryptoMine argues that the people who issued their

---

[10] *See* Newberry v. Barth, Inc., 252 N.W.2d 711 (Iowa 1977).
[11] *See* Taylor v. Ramsay-Gerding Constr. Co., 196 P.3d 532 (Or. 2008).

delivery letter had no authority to do so, and thus CryptoMine is off the hook for the failed delivery. Did Kays have authority to issue the delivery letter? If so, what kind?[12]

9. Luca owns and operates a dry cleaner doing business under the name "Luca's Dry Cleaners." Luca purchases all his dry-cleaning supplies from Sudsy Solutions each week. Luca sells the business to a local dry-cleaning chain but remains on as the manager. The company continues to operate as Luca's Dry Cleaners. The new owner directs Luca to buy two specific cleaning solutions from its discount supplier. Luca, however, continues purchasing all his supplies from Sudsy. The new owner then instructs Luca not to pay Sudsy for the order. When Sudsy's local salesperson follows up with Luca, Luca blames the new owner for the issue. Sudsy sues the local dry-cleaning chain in small claims court. Will Sudsy prevail?[13]

10. William was a janitor at a Filene's Basement in Boston. To do his job, he wheeled a 4' by 4' cart around the store, collecting trash. On particularly busy days, William would sometimes need to "sideswipe" a few customers, but not with enough force to harm them, in order to squeeze his way around the aisles. On one particularly busy day, he sideswiped a customer, Bertha. Bertha was a regular at Filene's. In the past, she had blocked his cart, accused him of stealing her purse, and otherwise stood in the way of his work. On this occasion, Bertha, upset, followed William and said, "If you would say 'excuse me,' people would get out of your way." She claimed that she said this in a "ladylike" manner, without hostility—but that William punched her in the face. Is Filene's liable to Bertha for William's actions?[14]

---

[12] *See* Three-Seventy Leasing Corp. v. Ampex Corp., 528 F.2d 993 (5th Cir. 1976).

[13] *See id.* § 2.06, cmt. c, illus. 3.

[14] *See* Miller v. Federated Department Stores, Inc., 364 Mass. 340 (1973).

CHAPTER II

PARTNERSHIP LAW

A partnership is the association of two or more persons to carry on a business for profit as co-owners.*

State partnership law sets the rights and obligations of partners and establishes the default rules that govern a partnership's formation, its dissolution, and every aspect in between these two major events. Most partnership laws, however, are defaults. They generally recognize parties' freedom to contract through a partnership agreement that defines the obligations and duties of partners and the organization of the partnership.

Most jurisdictions have adopted versions of one of two uniform partnership statutes: the Uniform Partnership Act of 1914 (the "UPA") and the Revised Uniform Partnership Act of 1999 (the "RUPA"). Most states have adopted RUPA, although several states still have UPA-based statutes.

A. PARTNERSHIP DEFINED

Revised Uniform Partnership Act
Section 102—Definitions.

(1) "Business" includes every trade, occupation, and profession.

(2) "Contribution" [. . .] means property or a benefit described in Section 403 which is provided by a person to a partnership to become a partner or in the person's capacity as a partner. [. . .]

(4) "Distribution" means a transfer of money or other property from a partnership to a person on account of a transferable interest or in a person's capacity as a partner. The term:

    (A) includes:

        (i) a redemption or other purchase by a partnership of a transferable interest; and

        (ii) a transfer to a partner in return for the partner's relinquishment of any right to participate as a partner in the management or conduct of the partnership's business or have access to records or other information concerning the partnership's business; and

    (B) does not include amounts constituting reasonable compensation for present or past service or payments made in the ordinary course

---

*   REVISED UNIF. P'SHIP ACT § 102(11) (Unif. L. Comm'n 2014).

of business under a bona fide retirement plan or other bona fide benefits program. [. . .]

(10) "Partner" means a person that:

(A) has become a partner in a partnership under Section 402 or was a partner in a partnership when the partnership became subject to this [act] under Section 110; and

(B) has not dissociated as a partner under Section 601.

(11) "Partnership", except in [Article] 11, means an association of two or more persons to carry on as co-owners a business for profit formed under this [act] or that becomes subject to this [act] under [Article] 11 or Section 110. The term includes a limited liability partnership.

(12) "Partnership agreement" means the agreement, whether or not referred to as a partnership agreement and whether oral, implied, in a record, or in any combination thereof, of all the partners of a partnership concerning the matters described in Section 105(a). The term includes the agreement as amended or restated.

(13) "Partnership at will" means a partnership in which the partners have not agreed to remain partners until the expiration of a definite term or the completion of a particular undertaking.

(14) "Person" means an individual, business corporation, nonprofit corporation, partnership, limited partnership, limited liability company, [general cooperative association,] limited cooperative association, unincorporated nonprofit association, statutory trust, business trust, common-law business trust, estate, trust, association, joint venture, public corporation, government or governmental subdivision, agency, or instrumentality, or any other legal or commercial entity. [. . .]

Section 104—Governing Law.

The internal affairs of a partnership and the liability of a partner as a partner for a debt, obligation, or other liability of the partnership are governed by:

(1) in the case of a limited liability partnership, the law of this state; and

(2) in the case of a partnership that is not a limited liability partnership, the law of the jurisdiction in which the partnership has its principal office. Section 201—Partnership as Entity.

A partnership is an entity distinct from its partners. [. . .]

Section 203—Partnership Property.

Property acquired by a partnership is property of the partnership and not of the partners individually.

Section 204—When Property is Partnership Property.

(a) Property is partnership property if acquired in the name of:

(1) the partnership; or

(2) one or more partners with an indication in the instrument transferring title to the property of the person's capacity as a partner or of the existence of a partnership but without an indication of the name of the partnership.

(b) Property is acquired in the name of the partnership by a transfer to:

(1) the partnership in its name; or

(2) one or more partners in their capacity as partners in the partnership, if the name of the partnership is indicated in the instrument transferring title to the property.

(c) Property is presumed to be partnership property if purchased with partnership assets, even if not acquired in the name of the partnership or of one or more partners with an indication in the instrument transferring title to the property of the person's capacity as a partner or of the existence of a partnership.

(d) Property acquired in the name of one or more of the partners, without an indication in the instrument transferring title to the property of the person's capacity as a partner or of the existence of a partnership and without use of partnership assets, is presumed to be separate property, even if used for partnership purposes.

B. PARTNERSHIP FORMATION

Revised Uniform Partnership Act
Section 202—Formation of Partnership.

(a) Except as otherwise provided in subsection (b), the association of two or more persons to carry on as co-owners a business for profit forms a partnership, whether or not the persons intend to form a partnership. [. . .]

(c) In determining whether a partnership is formed, the following rules apply:

(1) Joint tenancy, tenancy in common, tenancy by the entireties, joint property, common property, or part ownership does not by itself establish a partnership, even if the co-owners share profits made by the use of the property.

(2) The sharing of gross returns does not by itself establish a partnership, even if the persons sharing them have a joint or common right or interest in property from which the returns are derived.

(3) A person who receives a share of the profits of a business is presumed to be a partner in the business, unless the profits were received in payment:

(A) of a debt by installments or otherwise;

(B) for services as an independent contractor or of wages or other compensation to an employee;

(C) of rent;

(D) of an annuity or other retirement or health benefit to a beneficiary, representative, or designee of a deceased or retired partner;

(E) of interest or other charge on a loan, even if the amount of payment varies with the profits of the business, including a direct or indirect present or future ownership of the collateral, or rights to income, proceeds, or increase in value derived from the collateral; or

(F) for the sale of the goodwill of a business or other property by installments or otherwise.

Section 105—Partnership Agreement; Scope, Function, and Limitations.

(a) Except as otherwise provided in subsections (c) and (d), the partnership agreement governs:

(1) relations among the partners as partners and between the partners and the partnership;

(2) the business of the partnership and the conduct of that business; and

(3) the means and conditions for amending the partnership agreement.

(b) To the extent the partnership agreement does not provide for a matter described in subsection (a), this [act] governs the matter.

(c) A partnership agreement may not:

(1) vary the law applicable under Section 104(1); [. . .]

(3) vary the provisions of Section 307 [Transfer of Partnership Property];

(4) unreasonably restrict the duties and rights under Section 408, but the partnership agreement may impose reasonable restrictions on the availability and use of information obtained under that section and may define appropriate remedies, including liquidated damages, for a breach of any reasonable restriction on use;

(5) alter or eliminate the duty of loyalty or the duty of care, except as otherwise provided in subsection (d);

(6) eliminate the contractual obligation of good faith and fair dealing under Section 409(d), but the partnership agreement may prescribe the standards, if not manifestly unreasonable, by which the performance of the obligation is to be measured; [. . .]

(8) relieve or exonerate a person from liability for conduct involving bad faith, willful or intentional misconduct, or knowing violation of law;

(9) vary the power of a person to dissociate as a partner under Section 602(a), except to require that the notice under Section 601(1) to be in a record;

(10) vary the grounds for expulsion specified in Section 601(5);

(11) vary the causes of dissolution specified in Section 801(4) or (5);

(12) vary the requirement to wind up the partnership's business as specified in Section 802(a), (b)(1), and (d); [. . .]

(d) Subject to subsection (c)(8), [. . .]

   (1) The partnership agreement may:

      (A) specify the method by which a specific act or transaction that would otherwise violate the duty of loyalty may be authorized or ratified by one or more disinterested and independent persons after full disclosure of all material facts; [. . .]

   (3) If not manifestly unreasonable, the partnership agreement may:

      (A) alter or eliminate the aspects of the duty of loyalty stated in Section 409(b);

      (B) identify specific types or categories of activities that do not violate the duty of loyalty;

      (C) alter the duty of care, but may not authorize conduct involving bad faith, willful or intentional misconduct, or knowing violation of law; and

      (D) alter or eliminate any other fiduciary duty. [. . .]

In re Marriage of Hassiepen

646 N.E.2d 1348 (Ill. 1995)

[EDS.—The partnership question in this case arises out of a child support dispute between Cynthia Hassiepen and her ex-husband, Kevin Von Behren. After the couple's divorce, Kevin began living with, and eventually married, a woman named Brenda. To determine how much of their businesses' profits was attributable to Kevin as income for the purposes of calculating child support, the court first had to decide whether the Von Behren businesses were sole proprietorships owned by Kevin or partnerships owned by both Kevin and Brenda.]

In 1985, Kevin began living with Brenda. [. . .] [H]e and Brenda decided to start an electrical contracting business, called Von Behren Electric. Kevin started this business with only an old pickup truck and a drill which his father had given him. Brenda's credit cards were used to purchase other business supplies and materials. Brenda handled the general office work, including taking phone calls, picking up mail, preparing bills, banking, and preparing bids. Kevin performed the electrical contracting work. When they began the business, Brenda was also a court reporter, and she continued to receive income from this job for about two years thereafter.

After Kevin and Brenda began living together, they opened a joint checking account, which they used for all personal and business transactions. They did not pay themselves wages or a salary, but instead withdrew money from the account for both personal or business reasons. They put any money received into this joint account. At the time of the 1993 hearings, they continued this practice for handling money.

Von Behren Electric proved to be quite prosperous. In November 1991, Kevin and Brenda incorporated Von Behren Electric upon the advice of their accountant, Carol Nelson. Nelson kept track of their expenses, separating all their transactions into personal and business categories. She also prepared a yearly profit and loss statement for the business. After incorporating, Kevin and Brenda paid themselves an annual salary of $12,000 each. However, if they needed any additional money for personal expenses, they would merely withdraw this from the joint checking account. [. . .]

[EDS.—Kevin's ex-wife Cynthia sued for an adjustment to child support, prompting this action.] In October 1993, the trial court made the following findings regarding child support: [. . .]

(2) Kevin began his electrical business in 1987 and his income and net worth have increased substantially since then;

(3) Kevin's ability to pay increased child support has increased;

(4) the children's needs have substantially increased; [. . .]

(6) Brenda became involved in the electrical business with Kevin in 1987;

(7) Kevin and Brenda commingled their liquid assets for a substantial portion of their relationship together;

(8) Brenda was substantially and integrally involved in the Von Behren Electric, Inc., business and other enterprises and shared in the economic results of the businesses;

(9) their business relationship is an equal partnership;

(10) throughout Kevin's business career, he commingled his business and personal expenses and accounts;

(11) Kevin did not incorporate to avoid child support; nonetheless, the corporate veil of Von Behren Electric, Inc., should be broken and the corporation shall be considered Kevin's and Brenda's alter ego;

(12) no significant difference exists in how Kevin operates Von Behren Electric, Inc., compared to his prior habits of

> commingling of accounts and expenses, lack of corporate
> structure, and his management style; [. . .]

Based upon these findings, the trial court (1) denied Kevin's petition to decrease or suspend child support; (2) increased child support to $1,500 per month beginning November 1993 and retroactive to September 1993 [. . .]. After a hearing on the parties' post-trial motions, the court supplemented its October 1993 order by a docket entry which stated that Kevin's "net income for purposes of child support was determined by considering approximately 50% of [Kevin's] net income from his 1992 corporate and individual Federal and State income tax returns." [. . .]

Cynthia appeals [. . .] the trial court's decision[ ] regarding the increase in child support [. . .].

II. Analysis

Were Kevin and Brenda Business Partners?

Cynthia first argues that the trial court erred in finding that Kevin and Brenda were partners in Von Behren Electric and Von Behren Properties. Essentially, Cynthia claims that Kevin is sole owner of the two businesses and that Brenda is one of his employees. As a result, Cynthia contends that all of the net income from Von Behren Electric and Von Behren Properties should be accorded to Kevin, not just half of this income as determined by the trial court based upon its finding that a partnership existed. Kevin responds that the court did not abuse its discretion by finding a partnership.

The existence of a partnership is a question of the parties' intent and is based upon all the facts and circumstances surrounding the formation of the relationship at issue. As a result, the formalities of a written partnership agreement are unnecessary to prove the existence of a partnership. A partnership arises when (1) parties join together to carry on a venture for their common benefit, (2) each party contributes property or services to the venture, and (3) each party has a community of interest in the profits of the venture. [. . .]

[T]he Uniform Partnership Act defines a partnership as "an association of two or more persons to carry on as . . . a business for profit . . . ." Further, the receipt of a share of the business profits is *prima facie* evidence that a person is a partner in the business. The party asserting the existence of the partnership carries the burden of proving its existence. [. . .] [T]he existence of a partnership is a question of fact.

Cynthia points to the following facts which she claims support a conclusion that Kevin and Brenda were not partners in the Von Behren businesses: [. . .]

(3) Kevin put "sole proprietorship" on the top (in bold letters) of his tax return schedules for 1988 through 1991;

(4) no written partnership agreement exists;

(5) they never filed a partnership tax return;

(6) they never informed Nelson, their accountant, that they were a partnership;

(7) Brenda's name is not on any of the legal documents or deeds for the real estate known as Von Behren Properties;

(8) all business vehicles are titled in Kevin's name;

(9) no business signs indicated that either business was a partnership;

(10) business cards for Von Behren Electric, Inc., state "Kevin Von Behren/Owner"; and

(11) when Kevin answered interrogatories for this case, he stated that he was sole owner and that Brenda worked for him.

Kevin asserts that the following facts support his claim that he and Brenda were partners in the Von Behren businesses:

(1) in 1987, he and Brenda verbally agreed to "start an electrical contracting business to see if they could make some money out of it";

(2) Brenda's credit cards were used to obtain credit when they began the electrical business because he had no credit available after going through bankruptcy;

(3) all money earned by the electrical business was put into their joint checking account;

(4) neither he nor Brenda received wages from the electrical business;

(5) Brenda gave up her court reporting career to work full-time for the business;

(6) Brenda was not paid separately for her work for the business; and

(7) Brenda performed integral duties for the business, including paying all bills, managing the business, coordinating employees and equipment, handling the payroll, taking phone calls, and dealing with other important matters.

Kevin further claims that the lack of proper written formalities for their electrical business does not negate their original agreement to "start a business and make some money together." Also, Kevin asserts that Von Behren Properties was handled in the same manner as the electrical business, and thus should be treated as a similar entity.

After reviewing the evidence, the trial court found that Brenda was involved with Kevin in the electrical contracting business when it began in 1987. Also, the court noted that "Brenda was substantially and integrally involved in the Von Behren electrical business and other enterprises and shared in the economic results of the business[es]," and concluded that their business relationship was a partnership. Based upon our review of the record, we cannot say that this conclusion was against the manifest weight of the evidence.

Obviously, Kevin and Brenda are not sophisticated business people. While the trial court should consider the absence of written formalities, that is only one factor to consider when determining if a partnership exists. The trial court must review all facts and circumstances surrounding the formation of the business. In this case, both Kevin and Brenda provided services for the businesses, Brenda provided credit for the initial operations of the business, and Kevin contributed assets to the business. Also, all the money earned by the business was put into their joint account and used for reinvestment in the businesses or for their personal needs. Accordingly, we conclude that the trial court did not err by finding that Kevin sustained his burden of proving that his businesses were partnerships with Brenda. Consequently, the trial court did not err in according Kevin only half of the income from the two businesses.

Energy Transfer Partners, L.P. v. Enterprise Products Partners, L.P.

593 S.W.3d 732 (Tex. 2020)

The issue in this case is whether Texas law permits parties to conclusively agree that, as between themselves, no partnership will exist unless certain conditions are satisfied. We hold that it does and that the parties here made such an agreement. [. . .]

I

Cushing, Oklahoma is a major trading hub for crude oil. For decades, the United States imported most of its crude oil from abroad to its Gulf Coast refineries, where the oil was processed and shipped north through Cushing. In 2008, new technology enabled oil production in the Dakotas and Canada, resulting in oil being transported to Cushing from the north. But no pipeline existed to move oil stored at Cushing south. An excess supply accumulated, driving down the price of oil sold there. Sensing economic opportunity, major pipeline companies began exploring ways to move oil south from Cushing.

Among them were [Energy Transfer Partners, L.P., "ETP"] and [Enterprise Products Partners, L.P., "Enterprise"], competitors that are among the ten largest energy companies in the United States. Enterprise co-owned with ConocoPhillips a pipeline called Seaway that sent oil north to Cushing from the Texas Gulf Coast. Enterprise lobbied ConocoPhillips for years to reverse the pipeline's direction, but ConocoPhillips refused. Enterprise also talked to Canadian pipeline company Enbridge about a joint project but to no result.

In March 2011, Enterprise approached ETP about converting a pipeline called Old Ocean into one that could move oil south from Cushing. Old

Ocean transports natural gas from Sweeny, Texas, near the Coast, up to
Maypearl, near Dallas. ETP owns the pipeline, but Enterprise holds a
long-term lease on it. Converting the pipeline to one for transporting oil
and extending it the rest of the way to Cushing would require a massive
investment from the parties and committed customers willing to pay a
sufficient tariff to justify the investment.

The parties agreed to explore the viability of the project, which they
dubbed "Double E." In three written agreements, they reiterated their
intent that neither party be bound to proceed until each company's board
of directors had approved the execution of a formal contract. The
Confidentiality Agreement, signed in March 2011, recited that
Enterprise and ETP had "entered into discussions with each other in
connection with a possible transaction involving a joint venture to
provide crude oil transportation [from Cushing to Houston] utilizing [the]
Old Ocean Pipeline." The agreement laid out the parties' rights and
responsibilities with respect to confidential information exchanged
during the discussions and then stated:

> The Parties agree that unless and until a definitive agreement
> between the Parties with respect to the Potential Transaction
> has been executed and delivered, and then only to the extent of
> the specific terms of such definitive agreement, no Party hereto
> will be under any legal obligation of any kind whatsoever with
> respect to any transaction by virtue of this Agreement or any
> written or oral expression with respect to such a transaction by
> any Party or their respective Representatives, except, in the
> case of this Agreement, for the matters specifically agreed to
> herein . . . .

In April, the parties also signed a Letter Agreement with an attached
"Non-Binding Term Sheet." The Letter Agreement again recited that the
parties were "entering discussions regarding a proposed joint venture
transaction involving the construction (or conversion, as applicable) and
operation of a pipeline to move crude oil" from Cushing to Houston, and
that the "letter [was] intended only to set forth the general terms of the
Transaction between the Parties, . . . contained in the term sheet
attached." The letter then stated:

> Neither this letter nor the JV Term Sheet create any binding or
> enforceable obligations between the Parties and, except for the
> Confidentiality Agreement . . . , no binding or enforceable
> obligations shall exist between the Parties with respect to the
> Transaction unless and until the Parties have received their
> respective board approvals and definitive agreements
> memorializing the terms and conditions of the Transaction have
> been negotiated, executed and delivered by both of the Parties.
> Unless and until such definitive agreements are executed and
> delivered by both of the Parties, either [Enterprise] or ETP, for
> any reason, may depart from or terminate the negotiations with

respect to the Transaction at any time without any liability or obligation to the other, whether arising in contract, tort, strict liability or otherwise.

The Non-Binding Term Sheet sketched out the basic features of the potential transaction and envisioned that a "mutually agreeable Limited Liability Company Agreement would be entered into" to govern the joint venture.

Finally, in April the parties also signed a Reimbursement Agreement that provided the terms under which ETP would reimburse Enterprise for half the cost of the project's engineering work. That agreement, like the other two, recognized that the parties were "in the process of negotiating mutually agreeable definitive agreements" for the project and stated that nothing in it would "be deemed to create or constitute a joint venture, a partnership, a corporation, or any entity taxable as a corporation, partnership or otherwise." ETP's pleadings acknowledge that "as of the date of [these agreements] . . . the parties had not yet formed a partnership."

By May, the parties had formed an integrated team to pursue Double E. The biggest piece of the puzzle was obtaining sufficient shipping commitments. To do so, the parties needed to convince shippers that their pipeline would be the first to market. During the spring and summer of 2011, they marketed Double E to potential customers as a "50/50 JV" and prepared engineering plans for the project. The parties also explored the possibility of building a new pipeline from scratch rather than retrofitting Old Ocean, but they continued to market the Old Ocean conversion to potential customers.

[The Double E project struggled to attract shippers, who found the pipeline shipping costs too high. Only] [. . .] Chesapeake Energy Corp. committed to ship 100,000 barrels daily. ETP was hopeful that Chesapeake's commitment would draw in other shippers who had been holding out. [. . .] [Given the poor results,] Enterprise had begun preparing its exit by resuming negotiations with Enbridge. Enterprise ended its relationship with ETP orally on August 15 and then in writing a few days later.

The next month, ConocoPhillips announced that it would sell its interest in the Seaway pipeline. Enbridge bought it, making Enbridge co-owner of the pipeline with Enterprise. Enterprise and Enbridge obtained an anchor shipper commitment from Chesapeake, which resulted in their securing many additional commitments during the open season. Enterprise and Enbridge invested billions to reverse the direction of the pipeline and make other modifications needed to move oil from Cushing to the Gulf. The new pipeline, called Wrangler, opened in June 2012, and it has been a financial success.

ETP sued. Its theory at trial was that despite the disclaimers in the parties' written agreements, they had formed a partnership to "market and pursue" a pipeline through their conduct, and Enterprise breached its statutory duty of loyalty by pursuing the Wrangler project with Enbridge. [EDS.—The jury found that ETP and Enterprise created a partnership to market and pursue a pipeline project to transport crude oil from Cushing, Oklahoma to the Gulf Coast and that Enterprise breached its duty of loyalty to ETP; and the trial court rendered judgment on the verdict for ETP for a total of $535,794,777.40.]

The court of appeals reversed and rendered judgment for Enterprise. The court concluded that the Texas Business Organizations Code (TBOC) allows parties to contract for conditions precedent to partnership formation; that the Letter Agreement in particular created two here that were not met—(1) execution of "definitive agreements memorializing the terms and conditions of the Transaction" that (2) have "received [each party's] respective board approvals"; and that ETP had the burden either to obtain a jury finding that the conditions were waived or to prove waiver conclusively, which it failed to do. We granted ETP's petition for review.

II

Section 152.051(b) [EDS.—see RUPA Section 102(11)] of the TBOC states that "an association of two or more persons to carry on a business for profit as owners creates a partnership, regardless of whether: (1) the persons intend to create a partnership; or (2) the association is called a 'partnership,' 'joint venture,' or other name." Under § 152.052(a),

Factors indicating that persons have created a partnership include the persons':

    (1) receipt or right to receive a share of profits of the business;

    (2) expression of an intent to be partners in the business;

    (3) participation or right to participate in control of the business;

    (4) agreement to share or sharing:

        (A) losses of the business; or

        (B) liability for claims by third parties against the business; and

    (5) agreement to contribute or contributing money or property to the business.

Section 152.003 provides that "[t]he principles of law and equity and the other partnership provisions supplement this chapter unless otherwise provided by this chapter or the other partnership provisions."

[. . .] TBOC Chapter 152 [. . .] sets out a nonexclusive list of factors to be considered in a totality-of-the-circumstances test. Under § 152.052(a)(2), "expression of an intent to be partners in the business" is just one factor of the totality-of-the-circumstances test. *Ingram v. Degree*. We acknowledged in *Ingram* that the statute "does not by its terms give the parties' intent or expression of intent any greater weight than the other factors." *Id.* Moreover, under § 152.051(b), persons can create a partnership regardless of whether they intend to. This provision derives from Section 202(a) of the Revised Uniform Partnership Act. A comment to that section drafted by the Uniform Law Commission warns that parties "may inadvertently create a partnership despite their expressed subjective intention not to do so." But in *Ingram* we expressed skepticism that the Legislature "intended to spring surprise or accidental partnerships on independent business persons." *Ingram.* Can persons override the default test for partnership formation in Chapter 152 by agreeing not to be partners until conditions precedent are satisfied? *Ingram* did not involve such an agreement, and our discussion there of the role of intent in the partnership-formation analysis did not contemplate one.

Section 152.003 imports other "principles of law and equity" into the partnership-formation analysis, and the use of the word "include" in § 152.052(a) makes the factors enumerated there nonexclusive. [. . .] Texas courts regularly enforce conditions precedent to contract formation and reject legal claims that are artfully pleaded to skirt unambiguous contract language, especially when that language is the result of arm's-length negotiations between sophisticated business entities. *JPMorgan Chase Bank, N.A. v. Orca Assets G.P., L.L.C.*

[. . .] ETP argues that the TBOC's totality-of-the-circumstances test controls partnership formation to the exclusion of the common law and that the parties' intent with respect to the creation of a partnership is just one factor to be weighed with the others in § 152.052(a). The submission of the case to the jury reflects this theory. Question 1 instructed the jury on the rule of § 152.051(b) that parties can form a partnership even if they do not intend to and on the multi-factor test in § 152.052(a). Question 1 also told the jury that "[n]o single fact may be stated as a complete and final test of partnership." It then asked the jury whether a partnership was created. Under ETP's view, submitted to the jury, parties cannot through contract language preclude the creation of a partnership until a specific condition has occurred or been performed. ETP argues that the key to avoiding an accidental partnership is to "avoid the conduct that establishes a partnership under the statute."

Enterprise urges the primacy of freedom of contract and argues that if parties cannot by contract protect themselves from the creation of an unwanted partnership, detrimental economic consequences to the State and constant litigation will ensue. [. . .]

We maintain our view expressed a decade ago in *Ingram* that the Legislature did not "intend[ ] to spring surprise or accidental partnerships" on parties. *Ingram.* Section 152.003 expressly authorizes supplementation of the partnership-formation rules of Chapter 152 with "principles of law and equity", and perhaps no principle of law is as deeply engrained in Texas jurisprudence as freedom of contract. We hold that parties can contract for conditions precedent to preclude the unintentional formation of a partnership under Chapter 152 and that, as a matter of law, they did so here.

III

An agreement not to be partners unless certain conditions are met will ordinarily be conclusive on the issue of partnership formation as between the parties.[34] [. . .]

In *Ingram*, we explained that when analyzing the second factor of § 152.052(a)'s totality-of-the-circumstances test, "expression of an intent to be partners in the business":

> Courts should only consider evidence not specifically probative of the other factors. In other words, evidence of profit or loss sharing, control, or contribution of money or property should not be considered evidence of an expression of intent to be partners. Otherwise, all evidence could be an "expression" of the parties' intent, making the intent factor a catch-all for evidence of any of the factors, and the separate "expression of intent" inquiry would be eviscerated.

Similarly, where waiver of a condition precedent to partnership formation is at issue, only evidence directly tied to the condition precedent is relevant. Evidence that would be probative of expression of intent under § 152.051(a)—such as "the parties' statements that they are partners, one party holding the other party out as a partner on the business's letterhead or name plate, or in a signed partnership agreement"—is not relevant. Nor is evidence that would be probative of any of the other § 152.052(a) factors. Otherwise, a party in ETP's position could claim waiver in virtually every case.

ETP has not pointed to any evidence that Enterprise specifically disavowed the Letter Agreement's requirement of definitive, board-of-directors-approved agreements or that Enterprise intentionally acted inconsistently with that requirement. ETP's challenge to the court of appeals' holding is premised on the argument we have already rejected that the effect of the conditions precedent in the Letter Agreement was subsumed in Question 1. The only record evidence that ETP points to— the parties held themselves out as partners and worked closely together on the Double E project—is not relevant to the issue of waiver of definitive, board-approved agreements.

* * * * *

We hold that parties can conclusively negate the formation of a partnership under Chapter 152 of the TBOC through contractual conditions precedent. ETP and Enterprise did so as a matter of law here,

---

[34] Such an agreement would not, of course, bind third parties, and we do not consider its effect on them.

and there is no evidence that Enterprise waived the conditions. The judgment of the court of appeals is affirmed.

1. DISTINGUISHING PARTNERSHIPS FROM OTHER BUSINESS RELATIONSHIPS

a. PARTNERS OR EMPLOYER AND EMPLOYEE

Brodsky v. Stadlen
138 A.D.2d 662 (N.Y. 1988)

[. . .] In 1979 the parties were involved in the production of the show "Lewis J. Stadlen as Groucho!" The defendants were the coauthors of the play. The defendant Stadlen was its producer and star, and the defendant Flinn was its director and choreographer. The plaintiff, an attorney who teaches entertainment law, performed legal work, conducted negotiations and acted as general manager for the production. The plaintiff claims that the production company which produced the play was a partnership between the three men. The defendants deny this allegation.

There is no written partnership agreement as such between the parties. Therefore, we must determine whether a partnership in fact existed from the conduct, intention, and relationship between the parties. The Supreme Court found that there was not a partnership, but rather an employer-employee relationship between the defendant Stadlen and the plaintiff. We agree.

No one characteristic of a business relationship is determinative in finding the existence of a partnership in fact. Case law reveals a series of factors to be considered in determining whether or not there is a partnership: (1) sharing of profits, (2) sharing of losses, (3) ownership of partnership assets, (4) joint management and control, (5) joint liability to creditors, (6) intention of the parties, (7) compensation, (8) contribution of capital, and (9) loans to the organization.

The credible evidence in this case shows that the plaintiff was an employee who was entitled to 2% of gross profits as well as a fixed salary every week the show was performed during his employment. He performed legal services, ran the office, and acted as general manager. There is no indication he was liable for the losses of the enterprise. He did, however, advance money which was repaid by the defendant Stadlen. It has been noted that such loans of cash by one person to another for the purposes of business during the existence of the claimed relationship usually negates the notion of partnership. *Smith v. Maine.* So too, the failure of a party to contribute capital is strongly indicative that no partnership exists. *Id.*

The plaintiff relies heavily on certain documents which refer to the production company, known as Diana Enterprises, as a partnership. It should be noted that calling an organization a partnership does not make it one. Indeed, the defendants indicated no intention to enter into a partnership arrangement with its concomitant joint management and control with the plaintiff. In fact the defendant Flinn made no management decisions and little or no contribution beyond directing the play prior to its first performance. We do not find that these documents establish a partnership. [. . .]

disc'l holding

b.   PARTNERS OR LENDER AND BORROWER

Martin v. Peyton
246 N.Y. 213 (N.Y. 1927)

[. . .] Partnership results from contract, express or implied. If denied it may be proved by the production of some written instrument; by testimony as to some conversation; by circumstantial evidence. If nothing else appears the receipt by the defendant of a share of the profits of the business is enough.

Assuming some written contract between the parties the question may arise whether it creates a partnership. If it be complete; if it expresses in good faith the full understanding and obligation of the parties, then it is for the court to say whether a partnership exists. It may, however, be a mere sham intended to hide the real relationship. [. . .] Mere words will not blind us to realities. Statements that no partnership is intended are not conclusive. If as a whole a contract contemplates an association of two or more persons to carry on as co-owners a business for profit a partnership there is. [. . .] On the other hand, if it be less than this no partnership exists. Passing on the contract as a whole, an arrangement for sharing profits is to be considered. [. . .] But it is to be weighed in connection with all the rest. It is not decisive. It may be merely the method adopted to pay a debt or wages, as interest on a loan or for other reasons. [. . .]

In the case before us the claim that the defendants became partners in the firm of Knauth, Nachod Kuhne, doing business as bankers and brokers, depends upon the interpretation of certain instruments. There is nothing in their subsequent acts determinative of or indeed material upon this question. [. . .] "The plaintiff's claim," he stipulates, "is a claim of actual partnership [. . .]."

Remitted then, as we are, to the documents themselves, we refer to circumstances surrounding their execution only so far as is necessary to make them intelligible. And we are to remember that although the intention of the parties to avoid liability as partners is clear, although in language precise and definite they deny any design to then join the firm of K. N. & K.; although they say their interests in profits should be construed merely as a measure of compensation for loans, not an interest in profits as such; although they provide that they shall not be liable for any losses or treated as partners, the question still remains whether in fact they agree to so associate themselves with the firm as to 'carry on as co-owners a business for profit.

In the spring of 1921 the firm of K. N. & K. found itself in financial difficulties. John R. Hall was one of the partners. He was a friend of Mr. Peyton. From him he obtained the loan of almost $500,000 of Liberty bonds, which K. N. & K. might use as collateral to secure bank advances. This, however, was not sufficient. The firm and its members had engaged in unwise speculations, and it was deeply involved. Mr. Hall was also intimately acquainted with George W. Perkins, Jr., and with Edward W. Freeman. He also knew Mrs. Peyton and Mrs. Perkins and Mrs. Freeman. All were anxious to help him. He therefore, representing K. N. & K., entered into negotiations with them. While they were pending a proposition was made that Mr. Peyton, Mr. Perkins, and Mr. Freeman, or some of them, should become partners. It met a decided refusal. Finally an agreement was reached. It is expressed in three documents, executed on the same day, all a part of the one transaction. They were drawn with care and are unambiguous. We shall refer to them as "the agreement," "the indenture," and "the option."

We have no doubt as to their general purpose. The respondents [Peyton, Perkins and Freeman] were to loan K. N. & K. $2,500,000 worth of liquid securities, which were to be returned to them on or before April 15, 1923. The firm might hypothecate them to secure loans totaling $2,000,000, using the proceeds as its business necessities required. To insure respondents against loss K. N. & K. were to turn over to them a large number of their own securities which may have been valuable, but which were of so speculative a nature that they could not be used as collateral for bank loans. In compensation for the loan the respondents were to receive 40 per cent. of the profits of the firm until the return was made, not exceeding, however, $500,000, and not less than $100,000. Merely because the transaction involved the transfer of securities and not of cash does not prevent its being a loan, within the meaning of section 11. The respondents also were given an option to join the firm if they, or any of them, expressed a desire to do so before June 4, 1923. [. . .]

As representing the lenders, Mr. Peyton and Mr. Freeman are called "trustees." The loaned securities when used as collateral are not to be mingled with other securities of K. N. & K., and the trustees at all times are to be kept informed of all transactions affecting them. To them shall be paid all dividends and income accruing therefrom. They may also substitute for any of the securities loaned securities of equal value. With their consent the firm may sell any of its securities held by the respondents, the proceeds to go, however, to the trustees. In other similar ways the trustees may deal with these same securities, but the securities loaned shall always be sufficient in value to permit of their hypothecation for $2,000,000. If they rise in price, the excess may be withdrawn by the defendants. If they fall, they shall make good the deficiency.

So far, there is no hint that the transaction is not a loan of securities with a provision for compensation. Later a somewhat closer connection with the firm appears. Until the securities are returned, the directing management of the firm is to be in the hands of John R. Hall, and his life is to be insured for $1,000,000, and the policies are to be assigned as further collateral security to the trustees. These requirements are not unnatural. Hall was the one known and trusted by the defendants. Their acquaintance with the other members of the firm was of the slightest. These others had brought an old and established business to the verge of bankruptcy. As the respondents knew, they also had engaged in unsafe speculation. The respondents were about to loan $2,500,000 of good securities. As collateral they were to receive others of problematical value. What they required seems but ordinary caution. Nor does it imply an association in the business.

The trustees are to be kept advised as to the conduct of the business and consulted as to important matters. They may inspect the firm books and are entitled to any information they think important. Finally, they may veto any business they think highly speculative or injurious. Again we hold this but a proper precaution to safeguard the loan. The trustees may not initiate any transaction as a partner may do. They may not bind the firm by any action of their own. Under the circumstances the safety of the loan depended upon the business success of K. N. & K. This success was likely to be compromised by the inclination of its members to engage in speculation. No longer, if the respondents were to be protected, should it be allowed. The trustees therefore might prohibit it, and that their prohibition might be effective, information was to be furnished them. Not dissimilar agreements have been held proper to guard the interests of the lender.

As further security each member of K. N. & K. is to assign to the trustees their interest in the firm. No loan by the firm to any member is permitted and the amount each may draw is fixed. No other distribution of profits is to be made. So that realized profits may be calculated the existing capital is stated to be $700,000, and profits are to be realized as promptly as good business practice will permit. In case the trustees think this is not done, the question is left to them and to Mr. Hall, and if they differ then to an arbitrator. There is no obligation that the firm shall continue the business. It may dissolve at any time. Again we conclude there is nothing here not properly adapted to secure the interest of the respondents as lenders. If their compensation is dependent on a percentage of the profits, still provision must be made to define what these profits shall be.

The "indenture" is substantially a mortgage of the collateral delivered by K. N. & K. to the trustees to secure the performance of the "agreement." It certainly does not strengthen the claim that the respondents were partners.

Finally we have the "option." It permits the respondents, or any of them, or their assignees or nominees to enter the firm at a later date if they desire to do so by buying 50 per cent or less of the interests therein of all or any of the members at a stated price. Or a corporation may, if the respondents and the members agree, be formed in place of the firm. Meanwhile, apparently with the design of protecting the firm business against improper or ill-judged action which might render the option valueless, each member of the firm is to place his resignation in hands of Mr. Hall. If at any time he and the trustees agree that such resignation should be accepted, that member shall then retire, receiving the value of his interest calculated as of the date of such retirement.

This last provision is somewhat unusual, yet it is not enough in itself to show that on June 4, 1921, a present partnership was created, nor taking these various papers as a whole do we reach such a result. It is quite true that even if one or two or three like provisions contained in such a contract do not require this conclusion, yet it is also true that when taken together a point may come where stipulations immaterial separately cover so wide a field that we should hold a partnership exists. As in other branches of the law, a question of degree is often the determining factor. Here that point has not been reached. The judgment appealed should be affirmed.

2. PARTNERSHIP BY ESTOPPEL

Revised Uniform Partnership Act
Section 308—Liability of Purported Partner.

(a) If a person, by words or conduct, purports to be a partner, or consents to being represented by another as a partner, in a partnership or with one or more persons not partners, the purported partner is liable to a person to whom the representation is made, if that person, relying on the representation, enters into a transaction with the actual or purported partnership. If the representation, either by the purported partner or by a person with the purported partner's consent, is made in a public manner, the purported partner is liable to a person who relies upon the purported partnership even if the purported partner is not aware of being held out as a partner to the claimant. If partnership liability results, the purported partner is liable with respect to that liability as if the purported partner were a partner. If no partnership liability results, the purported partner is liable with respect to that liability jointly and severally with any other person consenting to the representation.

(b) If a person is thus represented to be a partner in an existing partnership, or with one or more persons not partners, the purported partner is an agent of persons consenting to the representation to bind them to the same extent and in the same manner as if the purported partner were a partner, with respect to persons who enter into transactions in reliance upon the representation. If all of the partners of the existing partnership consent to the representation, a partnership act or obligation results. If fewer than all of the partners of the existing partnership consent to the representation, the person acting and the partners consenting to the representation are jointly and severally liable. [. . .]

First American Corp. v. Price Waterhouse LLP
988 F.Supp. 353 (S.D.N.Y. 1997)

[EDS.—First American Corporation ("FAC"), a privately-held bank holding company wholly owned by Credit and Commerce American Holdings Co. N.V. ("CCAH"), petitioned to compel disclosure of information regarding an audit of Bank of Credit and Commerce International ("BCCI"). FAC alleges that BCCI committed fraud. FAC seeks disclosure from an entity that FAC calls "Price Waterhouse-World Wide" as well as other Price Waterhouse entities: Price Waterhouse-United Kingdom ("PW-UK"), Price Waterhouse North Caribbean Firm ("PW-Cayman"), Price Waterhouse Luxembourg Firm ("PW-Lux"), and Price Waterhouse Arab Emirates Firm ("PW-Emirates").]

[. . .] [BCCI perpetrated one of the] largest bank fraud[s] in world history [. . .]. During BCCI's growth to an organization of international proportions, it created fictitious loans, stole deposits, incurred hundreds of millions of dollars in losses from reckless trading operations, accepted illicit funds from drug launderers and corrupt dictators, and blatantly violated banking and criminal laws in virtually every jurisdiction in which it operated. The result was a $10.5 billion bank failure, and the loss of billions of dollars of depositors' savings.

[. . .] FAC [sued] to recover for alleged fraud perpetrated by the BCCI, which allegedly obtained ownership and control of FAC in contravention of U.S. banking laws, by acquiring FAC through a series of fictitious loans to nominee shareholders of CCAH, the ultimate holding company for First American, with CCAH shares pledged as security for those loans. In so doing, BCCI evaded requirements of U.S. banking law that a bank receive approval from U.S. bank regulators, such as the Federal Reserve Board, before acquiring a U.S. bank. The DC Action includes claims for civil RICO violations, common law fraud, breach of fiduciary duty, reckless and negligent misconduct, and civil conspiracy.

Activities of Various Price Waterhouse Firms in Relation to BCCI

The Price Waterhouse firms were the auditors of BCCI (Overseas) Limited ("BCCI-Overseas"), a Cayman Islands bank, from its inception in 1975, and were the worldwide auditors for the entire BCCI group from 1987 until the bank was closed in June 1991. Specifically, Price Waterhouse-Cayman acted as auditor of BCCI-Overseas from its incorporation until closure. Price Waterhouse-Luxembourg was the auditor of BCCI International S.A. ("BCCI-International") and BCCI

Holdings (Luxembourg) S.A. ("BCCI-Holdings") from 1987 onwards. PW-US was appointed by BCCI to issue an audit opinion of BCCI's operations in this country.

The efforts of these separate PW firms were coordinated by PW-UK. PW-UK assisted PW-Cayman with its audits of BCCI-Overseas from 1985 onwards, and was responsible for the worldwide audit of BCCI-Holdings from 1987 onwards. [. . .] As part of its coordination of worldwide audits, PW-UK would instruct and direct the efforts of accounting firms in those territories where BCCI-Holdings' subsidiaries carried on material business. In the United States, the appointed accounting firm was PW-US.

In October 1990, PW-UK became members of a Committee of Investigation set up by the Abu Dhabi Government to investigate problem lending within BCCI. This investigation was conducted in conditions of strict secrecy. In early 1991, PW-UK was also appointed by the Bank of England to report on irregularities in BCCI's business. On July 5, 1991, based in part on PW-UK's reports, banking regulators around the world took steps to close BCCI.

After BCCI's closure, the liquidators of BCCI-Overseas, BCCI-Holdings, and BCCI-International commenced proceedings in England (the "Liquidators' Action") against PW-UK, PW-Cayman, and PW-Lux for breach of contract and/or negligence. [. . .]

The Subpoenas

The instant motion to compel discovery arises from two subpoenas served by FAC on PW-US and on Newton, a partner of PW-UK now residing in New York (the "Subpoenas"). The first subpoena was addressed to "Price Waterhouse" and was served in August 1997, at PW-US' main office at 1251 Avenue of the Americas. [EDS.—The second subpoena relates to a separate issue and has been edited out of this case.] [. . .]

"Schedule A" attached to the Subpoenas defined "Price Waterhouse" as:

> the worldwide accounting firm of Price Waterhouse that operates or has operated as a partnership by estoppel in the United States, United Kingdom, Cayman Islands and Luxembourg, including, but not limited to any other affiliated divisions, entities or Price Waterhouse firms, and any affiliated parents, subsidiaries, partnerships, divisions, affiliates, successors and predecessors, and each of their partners, employees, agents, representatives or any other persons acting or purporting to act for or on their behalf.

The Subpoenas separately define "Price Waterhouse-US", "Price Waterhouse-UK", "Price Waterhouse-Cayman", and "Price Waterhouse-Emirates" each as an "entity or division of [the purported worldwide firm of] Price Waterhouse" operating in the designated location.

The Subpoenas requested documents from "Price Waterhouse (including Price Waterhouse-UK, Price Waterhouse-Luxembourg, Price Waterhouse-Cayman and Price Waterhouse-Emirates)" related to CCAH and BCCI, and any services performed by "Price Waterhouse" for those companies.

On September 3, 1997, PW-US served its objections to the Subpoena on the following grounds: (1) there is no single legal entity "Price Waterhouse" that includes the various Price Waterhouse partnerships or entities operating in the United States, the United Kingdom, the Cayman Islands, the United Arab Emirates and Luxembourg, nor is there any "partnership by estoppel" between these entities; (2) the documents listed in the Subpoenas which are in the possession of the other Price Waterhouse partnerships were not in the control of PW-US; (3) PW-US is not the appropriate vehicle for serving, obtaining jurisdiction over and/or taking discovery from any of the individual Price Waterhouse firms operating outside the U.S., therefore no proper service had been made on these firms, and no jurisdiction established by serving PW-US [. . .].

Discussion

Jurisdiction over All Price Waterhouse Firms via Partnership By Estoppel

FAC asserts jurisdiction over PW-UK, PW-Cayman, PW-Luxembourg and PW-Emirates via service on PW-US on the grounds that Price Waterhouse must be treated as a world-wide partnership, according to the doctrine of partnership by estoppel. The doctrine of partnership by estoppel, which is part of the Uniform Partnership Act, has been codified in New York law and states that:

> When a person, by words spoken or written or by conduct, represents himself, or consents to another representing him to anyone, as a partner in an existing partnership or with one or more persons not actual partners, he is liable to any such person to whom such representation has been made, who has, on the faith of such representation, given credit to the actual or apparent partnership, and if he has made such representation or consented to its being made in a public manner he is liable to such person, whether the representation has or has not been made or communicated to such person so giving credit by or with the knowledge of the apparent partner making the representation or consenting to its being made.

[. . .] Partnership by estoppel should not be lightly invoked and generally presents issues of fact. *Royal Bank and Trust Company v. Weintraub, Gold & Alper.*

Partnership by estoppel thus contains two elements. First, that sufficient indicia of partnership be presented to the injured party to constitute a representation that the partnership exists. [. . .]

Second, the injured party must have relied on this representation to his or her detriment. *Milano v. Freed.* [. . .]

As evidence of representations of partnership, FAC asserts that Price Waterhouse represented itself to BCCI as a worldwide partnership, and characterized its numerous geographic locations as offices, rather than separate partnerships or entities. The former CEO and the former CFO of BCCI each testified that PW-Cayman and PW-UK represented themselves to BCCI as one integrated firm, and that Price Waterhouse brochures were submitted to BCCI emphasizing Price Waterhouse's global integration as a critical strength of the firm. Communications from Price Waterhouse to BCCI referred to Price Waterhouse as the "sole auditor" of BCCI. A partner in PW-UK signed financial statements for 1987 for BCCI Overseas, BCCI Holdings and BCCI International on behalf of "Price Waterhouse" without any geographic limitation. This practice of certifying BCCI's financial statements simply by "Price Waterhouse" continued until BCCI collapsed in June 1991.

FAC cites the 1985 audit of BCCI Overseas as a particular example of the manner in which Price Waterhouse's separate offices function as a single partnership. During the 1985 audit, PW-UK discovered that BCCI Overseas had experienced losses of nearly $1 billion from 1981 through 1985, and took control of the audit from PW-Cayman. This shift in control was portrayed to BCCI as simply a shift from one portion of the world-wide entity to another.

FCA also cites the relationship between PW-US and PW-UK as one of partnership rather than separate entities. FCA asserts that PW-UK controlled and managed the worldwide audit of BCCI from 1987 onwards, working with PW-US as its partner and using PW-US as its agent. A partner in PW-UK, Christopher Cowan, testified that PW-UK used its sister PW offices as agents:

> At the end of the day I think it comes down to effectively an agency relationship . . . if the ultimate responsibility [for the audit] is of, shall we say, the Grand Cayman firm and they seek to use services of the U.K. firm then they are effectively contracting to use those services, so they are acting as their agent.

Finally, FAC also asserts that Price Waterhouse markets itself as a worldwide entity in its brochures and advertisements.

While the facts set forth above may establish representations of partnership and reliance as to BCCI, they do not demonstrate such representations and reliance by FAC. FAC contends that it relied upon the above representations "as part of the BCCI group". However, it is not clear that such indirect reliance satisfies the requirements of New York law. Courts have required a stronger showing of reliance before imposing liability based on partnership by estoppel. In *Milano*, a medical malpractice action, the Second Circuit held that although one of the defendant doctors had represented herself as a partner in the doctors' group, nothing in the record indicated that the plaintiffs had selected the group on the strength of her representations. [. . .] Without a direct influence to act, liability could not be imposed.

In *Young v. Federal Deposit Insurance Corporation*, the Fourth Circuit applied South Carolina law, which has adopted the identical provision regarding partnership by estoppel from the Uniform Partnership Act as that codified in New York law. The Circuit held that the plaintiff investor could not establish personal jurisdiction over Price Waterhouse-Bahamas ("PW-Bahamas") in South Carolina under the doctrine of partnership by estoppel, because he had not contended that he relied upon PW-Bahamas brochures in making his decision to invest. *Id.* In the instant case, without the requisite showing of direct reliance to its detriment on Price Waterhouse's representations of partnership, FAC cannot establish that worldwide partnership and its corollary, personal jurisdiction. [. . .]

[EDS.—The Court, while rejecting FAC's claim that jurisdiction over PW-UK could be established via partnership by estoppel, granted the motion to compel discovery as to PW-UK on the ground of personal jurisdiction arising from its employment of New York-based PW-US.]

C. PARTNERS' FIDUCIARY DUTIES

Revised Uniform Partnership Act
Section 409—Standards of Conduct for Partners.

(a)　A partner owes to the partnership and the other partners the duties of loyalty and care stated in subsections (b) and (c).

(b)　The fiduciary duty of loyalty of a partner includes the duties:

(1)　to account to the partnership and hold as trustee for it any property, profit, or benefit derived by the partner:

(A)　in the conduct or winding up of the partnership's business;

(B)　from a use by the partner of the partnership's property; or

(C)　from the appropriation of a partnership opportunity;

(2)　to refrain from dealing with the partnership in the conduct or winding up of the partnership business as or on behalf of a person having an interest adverse to the partnership; and

(3)　to refrain from competing with the partnership in the conduct of the partnership's business before the dissolution of the partnership.

(c)　The duty of care of a partner in the conduct or winding up of the partnership business is to refrain from engaging in grossly negligent or reckless conduct, willful or intentional misconduct, or a knowing violation of law.

(d) A partner shall discharge the duties and obligations under this [act] or under the partnership agreement and exercise any rights consistently with the contractual obligation of good faith and fair dealing.

(e) A partner does not violate a duty or obligation under this [act] or under the partnership agreement solely because the partner's conduct furthers the partner's own interest.

(f) All the partners may authorize or ratify, after full disclosure of all material facts, a specific act or transaction by a partner that otherwise would violate the duty of loyalty.

(g) It is a defense to a claim under subsection (b)(2) and any comparable claim in equity or at common law that the transaction was fair to the partnership.

(h) If, as permitted by subsection (f) or the partnership agreement, a partner enters into a transaction with the partnership which otherwise would be prohibited by subsection (b)(2), the partner's rights and obligations arising from the transaction are the same as those of a person that is not a partner.

1. DUTY OF LOYALTY AND BUSINESS OPPORTUNITIES

Meinhard v. Salmon
249 N.Y. 458 (N.Y. 1928)

■ CARDOZO, C.J.

On April 10, 1902, Louisa M. Gerry leased to the defendant Walter J. Salmon the premises known as the Hotel Bristol at the northwest corner of Forty-Second Street and Fifth Avenue in the City of New York. The lease was for a term of 20 years, commencing May 1, 1902, and ending April 30, 1922. The lessee undertook to change the hotel building for use as shops and offices at a cost of $200,000. Alterations and additions were to be accretions to the land.

Salmon, while in course of treaty with the lessor as to the execution of the lease, was in course of treaty with Meinhard, the plaintiff, for the necessary funds. The result was a joint venture with terms embodied in a writing. Meinhard was to pay to Salmon half of the moneys requisite to reconstruct, alter, manage, and operate the property. Salmon was to pay to Meinhard 40 per cent of the net profits for the first five years of the lease and 50 per cent for the years thereafter. If there were losses, each party was to bear them equally. Salmon, however, was to have sole power to "manage, lease, underlet and operate" the building. There were to be certain pre-emptive rights for each in the contingency of death.

The two were coadventurers, subject to fiduciary duties akin to those of partners. As to this we are all agreed. The heavier weight of duty rested, however, upon Salmon. He was a coadventurer with Meinhard, but he was manager as well. During the early years of the enterprise, the building, reconstructed, was operated at a loss. If the relation had then ended, Meinhard as well as Salmon would have carried a heavy burden. Later the profits became large with the result that for each of the investors there came a rich return. For each the venture had its phases of fair weather and of foul. The two were in it jointly, for better or for worse.

When the lease was near its end, Elbridge T. Gerry had become the owner of the reversion. He owned much other property in the neighborhood, one lot adjoining the Bristol building on Fifth Avenue and four lots on Forty-Second Street. He had a plan to lease the entire tract for a long term to some one who would destroy the buildings then existing and put up another in their place. In the latter part of 1921, he submitted such a project to several capitalists and dealers. He was unable to carry it through with any of them. Then, in January, 1922, with less than four months of the lease to run, he approached the defendant Salmon. The result was a new lease to the Midpoint Realty Company, which is owned and controlled by Salmon, a lease covering the whole tract, and involving a huge outlay. The term is to be twenty years, but successive covenants for renewal will extend it to a maximum of eighty years at the will of either party. The existing buildings may remain unchanged for seven years. They are then to be torn down, and a new building to cost $ 3,000,000 is to be placed upon the site. The rental, which under the Bristol lease was only $ 55,000, is to be from $ 350,000 to $ 475,000 for the properties so combined. Salmon personally guaranteed the performance by the lessee of the covenants of the new lease until such time as the new building had been completed and fully paid for.

The lease between Gerry and the Midpoint Realty Company was signed and delivered on January 25, 1922. Salmon had not told Meinhard anything about it. Whatever his motive may have been, he had kept the negotiations to himself. Meinhard was not informed even of the bare existence of a project. The first that he knew of it was in February, when the lease was an accomplished fact. He then made demand on the defendants that the lease be held in trust as an asset of the venture, making offer upon the trial to share the personal obligations incidental to the guaranty. The demand was followed by refusal, and later by this suit. A referee gave judgment for the plaintiff, limiting the plaintiff's interest in the lease, however, to 25 per cent. The limitation was on the theory that the plaintiff's equity was to be restricted to one-half of so much of the value of the lease as was contributed or represented by the occupation of the Bristol site. Upon cross-appeals to the Appellate Division, the judgment was modified so as to enlarge the equitable interest to one-half of the whole lease. With this enlargement of plaintiff's interest, there went, of course, a corresponding enlargement of his attendant obligations. The case is now here on an appeal by the defendants.

Joint adventurers, like copartners, owe to one another, while the enterprise continues, the duty of the finest loyalty. Many forms of conduct permissible in a workaday world for those acting at arm's length, are forbidden to those bound by fiduciary ties. A trustee is held to something stricter than the morals of the market place. Not honesty alone, but the punctilio of an honor the most sensitive, is then the standard of behavior. [. . .] Uncompromising rigidity has been the attitude of courts of equity when petitioned to undermine the rule of undivided loyalty by the "disintegrating erosion" of particular exceptions. [. . .]

The owner of the reversion, Mr. Gerry, had vainly striven to find a tenant who would favor his ambitious scheme of demolition and construction. Baffled in the search, he turned to the defendant Salmon in possession of the Bristol, the keystone of the project. He figured to himself beyond a doubt that the man in possession would prove a likely customer. To the eye of an observer, Salmon held the lease as owner in his own right, for himself and no one else. In fact he held it as a fiduciary, for himself and another, sharers in a common venture. If this fact had been proclaimed, if the lease by its terms had run in favor of a partnership, Mr. Gerry, we may fairly assume, would have laid before the partners, and not merely before one of them, his plan of reconstruction. The pre-emptive privilege, or, better, the pre-emptive opportunity, that was thus an incident of the enterprise, Salmon appropriate to himself in secrecy and silence. He might have warned Meinhard that the plan had been submitted, and that either would be free to compete for the award. [. . .] The trouble about his conduct is that he excluded his coadventurer from any chance to compete, from any chance to enjoy the opportunity for benefit that had come to him alone by virtue of his agency. This chance, if nothing more, he was under a duty to concede. The price of its denial is an extension of the trust at the option and for the benefit of the one whom he excluded.

No answer is it to say that the chance would have been of little value even if seasonably offered. Such a calculus of probabilities is beyond the science of the chancery. Salmon, the real estate operator, might have been preferred to Meinhard, the woolen merchant. On the other hand, Meinhard might have offered better terms, or reinforced his offer by alliance with the wealth of others. Perhaps he might even have persuaded the lessor to renew the Bristol lease alone [. . .] All these opportunities were cut away from him through another's intervention. He knew that Salmon was the manager. As the time drew near for the expiration of the lease, he would naturally assume from silence, if from nothing else, that the lessor was willing to extend it for a term of years, or at least to let it stand as a lease from year to year. Not impossibly the lessor would have done so, whatever his protestations of unwillingness, if Salmon had not given assent to a project more attractive. [. . .] At least, there was nothing in the situation to give warning to any one that while the lease was still in being, there had come to the manager an offer of extension which he had locked within his breast to be utilized by himself alone. The very fact that Salmon was in control with exclusive powers of direction charged him the more obviously with the duty of disclosure, since only through disclosure could opportunity be equalized. If he might cut off renewal by a purchase for his own benefit when four months were to pass before the lease would have an end, he might do so with equal right while there remained as many years. He might steal a march on his comrade under cover of the darkness, and then hold the captured ground. Loyalty and comradeship are not so easily abjured.

Little profit will come from a dissection of the precedents. [. . .] Authority is, of course, abundant that one partner may not appropriate to his own use a renewal of a lease, though its term is to begin at the expiration of the partnership. The lease at hand with its many changes is not strictly a renewal. Even so, the standard of loyalty for those in trust relations is without the fixed divisions of a graduated scale. [. . .] Equity refuses to confine within the bounds of classified transactions its precept of a loyalty that is undivided and unselfish. Certain at least it is that a "man obtaining his locus standi, and his opportunity for making such arrangements, by the position he occupies as a partner, is bound by his obligation to his co-partners in such dealings not to separate his interest from theirs, but, if he acquires any benefit, to communicate it to them" *Cassels v. Stewart* [. . .]. If conflicting inferences are possible as to abuse or opportunity, the trier of the facts must make the choice between them. [. . .] A constructive trust is then the remedial device through which preference of self is made subordinate to loyalty to others [. . .].

We have no thought to hold that Salmon was guilty of a conscious purpose to defraud. Very likely he assumed in all good faith that with the approaching end of the venture he might ignore his coadventurer and take the extension for himself. He had given to the enterprise time and labor as well as money. He had made it a success. Meinhard, who had given money, but neither time nor labor, had already been richly paid. There might seem to be something grasping in his insistence upon more. Such recriminations are not unusual when coadventurers fall out. They are not without their force if conduct is to be judged by the common standards of competitors. That is not to say that they have pertinency here. Salmon had put himself in a position in which thought of self was to be renounced, however hard the abnegation. He was much more than a coadventurer. He was a managing coadventurer. For him and for those like him the rule of undivided loyalty is relentless and supreme. A different question would be here if there were lacking any nexus of relation between the business conducted by the manager and the opportunity brought to him as an incident of management. For this problem, as for most, there are distinctions of degree. If Salmon had received from Gerry a proposition to lease a building at a location far removed, he might have held for himself the privilege thus acquired, or so we shall assume. Here the subject-matter of the new lease was an extension and enlargement of the subject-matter of the old one. A managing coadventurer appropriating the benefit of such a lease without warning to his partner might fairly expect to be reproached with conduct that was underhand, or lacking, to say the least, in reasonable candor, if the partner were to surprise him in the act of signing the new instrument. Conduct subject to that reproach does not receive from equity a healing benediction.

A question remains as to the form and extent of the equitable interest to be allotted to the plaintiff. The trust as declared has been held to attach to the lease which was in the name of the defendant corporation. We think it ought to attach at the option of the defendant Salmon to the shares of stock which were owned by him or were under his control. The difference may be important if the lessee shall wish to execute an assignment of the lease, as it ought to be free to do with the consent of the lessor. On the other hand, an equal division of the shares might lead to other hardships. It might take away from Salmon the power of control and management which under the plan of the joint venture he was to have from first to last. The number of shares to be allotted to the plaintiff should, therefore, be reduced to such an extent as may be necessary to preserve to the defendant Salmon the expected measure of dominion. To that end an extra share should be added to his half.

Subject to this adjustment, we agree with the Appellate Division that the plaintiff's equitable interest is to be measured by the value of half of the entire lease, and not merely by half of some undivided part. A single building covers the whole area. Physical division is impracticable along the lines of the Bristol site, the keystone of the whole. Division of interests and burdens is equally impracticable. [. . .] The lease as it has been executed is single and entire. If confusion has resulted from the union of adjoining parcels, the trustee who consented to the union must bear the inconvenience. [. . .]

The judgment should be modified by providing that at the option of the defendant Salmon there may be substituted for a trust attaching to the lease a trust attaching to the shares of stock, with the result that one-half of such shares together with one additional share will in that event be allotted to the defendant Salmon and the other shares to the plaintiff, and as so modified the judgment should be affirmed with costs.

■ ANDREWS, J. (dissenting).

[. . .] Was the transaction in view of all the circumstances surrounding it unfair and inequitable? [. . .] There was no general partnership, merely a joint venture for a limited object, to end at a fixed time. The new lease, covering additional property, containing many new and unusual terms and conditions, with a possible duration of eighty years, was more nearly the purchase of the reversion than the ordinary renewal with which the authorities are concerned. [. . .]

[. . .] Were this a general partnership between Mr. Salmon and Mr. Meinhard, I should have little doubt as to the correctness of this result, assuming the new lease to be an offshoot of the old. Such a situation involves questions of trust and confidence to a high degree; it involves questions of good will; many other considerations. As has been said, rarely if ever may one partner without the knowledge of the other acquire for himself the renewal of a lease held by the firm, even if the new lease is to begin after the firm is dissolved. Warning of such an intent, if he is managing partner, may not be sufficient to prevent the application of this rule.

We have here a different situation governed by less drastic principles. I assume that where parties engage in a joint enterprise each owes to the other the duty of the utmost good faith in all that relates to their common venture. Within its scope they stand in a fiduciary relationship. I assume prima facie that even as between joint adventurers one may not secretly obtain a renewal of the lease of property actually used in the joint adventure where the possibility of renewal is expressly or impliedly involved in the enterprise. I assume also that Mr. Meinhard had an equitable interest in the Bristol Hotel lease. Further, that an expectancy of renewal inhered in that lease. Two questions then arise. Under his contract did he share in that expectancy? And if so, did that expectancy mature into a graft of the original lease? To both questions my answer is "no." [. . .]

What then was the scope of the adventure into which the two men entered? It is to be remembered that before their contract was signed Mr. Salmon had obtained the lease of the Bristol property. Very likely the matter had been earlier discussed between them. The $5,000 advance by Mr. Meinhard indicates that fact. But it has been held that the written contract defines their rights and duties. Having the lease, Mr. Salmon assigns no interest in it to Mr. Meinhard. He is to manage the property. It is for him to decide what alterations shall be made and to fix the rents. But for 20 years from May 1, 1902, Salmon is to make all advances from his own funds and Meinhard is to pay him personally on demand one-half of all expenses incurred and all losses sustained "during the full term of said lease," and during the same period Salmon is to pay him a part of the net profits. There was no joint capital provided.

It seems to me that the venture so inaugurated had in view a limited object and was to end at a limited time. There was no intent to expand it into a far greater undertaking lasting for many years. The design was to exploit a particular lease. Doubtless in it Mr. Meinhard had an equitable interest, but in it alone. This interest terminated when the joint adventure terminated. There was no intent that for the benefit of both any advantage should be taken of the chance of renewal—that the adventure should be continued beyond that date. Mr. Salmon has done all he promised to do in return for Mr. Meinhard's undertaking when he distributed profits up to May 1, 1922. Suppose this lease, nonassignable without the consent of the lessor, had contained a renewal option. Could Mr. Meinhard have exercised it? Could he have insisted that Mr. Salmon do so? Had Mr. Salmon done so could he insist that the agreement to share losses still existed, or could Mr. Meinhard have claimed that the joint adventure was still to continue for 20 or 80 years? I do not think so. The adventure by its express terms ended on May 1, 1922. The contract by its language and by its whole import excluded the idea that the tenant's expectancy was to subsist for the benefit of the plaintiff. On that date whatever there was left of value in the lease reverted to Mr. Salmon, as it would had the lease been for thirty years instead of twenty. Any equity which Mr. Meinhard possessed was in the particular lease itself, not in any possibility of renewal. There was nothing unfair in Mr. Salmon's conduct. [. . .]

So far I have treated the new lease as if it were a renewal of the old. As already indicated, I do not take that view. Such a renewal could not be obtained. Any expectancy that it might be had vanished. What Mr. Salmon obtained was not a graft springing from the Bristol lease, but something distinct and different—as distinct as if for a building across Fifth avenue. I think also that in the absence of some fraudulent or unfair act the secret purchase of the reversion even by one partner is rightful. Substantially this is such a purchase. Because of the mere label of a transaction we do not place it on one side of the line or the other. Here is involved the possession of a large and most valuable unit of property for eighty years, the destruction of all existing structures and the erection of a new and expensive building covering the whole. No fraud, no deceit, no calculated secrecy is found. Simply that the arrangement was made without the knowledge of Mr. Meinhard. I think this not enough.

The judgment of the courts below should be reversed and a new trial ordered, with costs in all courts to abide the event.

2. GRABBING AND LEAVING

Gibbs v. Breed, Abbott & Morgan
710 N.Y.S.2d 578 (2000)

Plaintiffs Charles Gibbs and Robert Sheehan are former partners of Breed, Abbott & Morgan (BAM) who specialize in trust and estate law. They withdrew from BAM in July 1991 to join Chadbourne & Parke (Chadbourne), and brought this action for monies due to them under their BAM partnership agreement. Defendants asserted various counterclaims alleging that plaintiffs breached their fiduciary duty to BAM. [. . .] The counterclaims were severed and tried without a jury. Plaintiffs appeal from the trial court's determination that, in the course of both partners' planning and eventually implementing their withdrawal from BAM, they breached their fiduciary duty to the partnership. Plaintiffs also appeal from the trial court's determination that $1,861,045 in damages resulted from these transgressions.

From January 1991 until July 1991, plaintiffs were the only partners in the trusts and estates department (T/E) at BAM; plaintiff Gibbs was the head of the department. A third partner, Paul Lambert, had been the former head of the department, and he had obtained many, if not most, of the department's clients. In 1989 he had left the firm to become the United States Ambassador to Ecuador and was still on leave in 1991. Lambert intended to return to the firm upon completion of his term as ambassador. The BAM trusts and estates department also employed three associate attorneys, Warren Whitaker (fifteenth year), Austin Wilkie (fourth year), and Joseph Scorese (first year); two accountants, Lois Wetzel and Ellen Furst; and two paralegals, Lee Ann Riley and Ruth Kramer.

Gibbs had become dissatisfied with BAM, and in January 1991 he began interviews to locate a new affiliation. He also approached Sheehan to persuade him to move with him. Sheehan and Gibbs subsequently conducted a number of joint interviews with prospective employers. In May 1991, Ambassador Lambert visited BAM, and Gibbs told him that he had been interviewing. Lambert relayed this information to the other partners. In early June, plaintiffs informed the executive committee that they had received an offer from two firms: McDermott, Will & Emery and Bryan Cave.

On June 19, 1991, both plaintiffs informed Stephen Lang, BAM's presiding partner, that they had accepted offers to join Chadbourne. Lang asked Gibbs not to discuss his departure with any of the T/E associates, and Gibbs agreed not to do so. On June 20, 1991, Lawrence Warble, a BAM partner who was named temporary head of the T/E department, met with its associates and nonlegal personnel to inform them that plaintiffs were leaving the firm.

On June 24, 1991, Gibbs and Sheehan sent Chadbourne a memo listing the names of the personnel in the T/E department at BAM, their respective salaries, their annual billable hours, and the rate at which BAM billed out these employees to clients. The memo included other information about the attorneys, including the colleges and law schools they attended and their Bar admissions. This list had been prepared by Sheehan on April 26, 1991, months before the partners announced they were leaving. Sheehan specifically testified that the memo was prepared in anticipation of discussions with prospective firms, and both Gibbs and Sheehan testified at trial that the recruitment of certain associates and support personnel was discussed with different firms between March and May, as the partners were considering various affiliations. While Gibbs and Sheehan were still partners at BAM, Chadbourne interviewed four BAM employees that Gibbs had indicated he was interested in bringing to Chadbourne with him. On June 27, 1991, plaintiffs submitted their written resignations. Before Gibbs and Sheehan left BAM, they wrote letters to clients served by them, advising that they were leaving BAM and that other attorneys at BAM could serve them. These letters did not mention the fact that the two partners were moving to Chadbourne. Although the partnership agreement required 45 days' notice of an intention to withdraw, BAM waived this provision upon plaintiffs' production of their final billings for work previously performed. Gibbs left BAM on July 9, 1991, and Sheehan left on July 11, 1991, both taking various documents, including their respective "chronology" or desk files. With the assistance of his chronology file, Gibbs began to contact his former clients on July 11, 1991. On July 11th, Chadbourne made employment offers to Whitaker, Wilkie, Wetzel, and Riley. Wilkie, Wetzel, and Riley accepted that same day; Whitaker accepted on July 15, 1991. In the following weeks, 92 of the 201 BAM T/E clients moved their business to Chadbourne.

After hearing all the testimony and the parties' arguments, the trial court determined that Gibbs' actions in persuading his partner Sheehan to leave BAM, "and the way in which the leave was orchestrated, were done, at least partially, with the intention of crippling BAM's trusts and estates (T/E) department," and constituted a breach of loyalty to BAM. The court also found that Gibbs and Sheehan had breached their fiduciary duties to BAM by sending Chadbourne the April 26, 1991 memo detailing personal information about the individuals in the T/E department at BAM, because this gave Chadbourne a competitive advantage in offering employment to other members of the department. Finally, the court found that Gibbs and Sheehan breached their fiduciary duties to BAM by taking their chronology files with them to Chadbourne. Specifically, the court concluded that by taking their respective chronology files, the partners "to a large degree hobbled their former partners in their effort to rebuild the Trusts and Estates department, in order to maintain a viable department, and in their ability to serve clients without undue disruption." [. . .]

The members of a partnership owe each other a duty of loyalty and good faith, and "[a]s a fiduciary, a partner must consider his or her partners' welfare, and refrain from acting for purely private gain" *Meehan v. Shaughnessy*. Partners are constrained by such duties throughout the life of the partnership and "[t]he manner in which partners plan for and implement withdrawals . . . is [still] subject to the constraints imposed on them by virtue of their status as fiduciaries" [. . .]. According the trial court's findings on issues of fact and credibility appropriate deference, we uphold that portion of the court's liability determination which found that plaintiffs breached their fiduciary duty as partners of the firm they were about to leave by supplying confidential employee information to Chadbourne while still partners at BAM [. . .]. However, we find no breach with respect to Gibbs' interactions with Sheehan, or with respect to either partner's removal of his desk files from BAM.

Defendants did not establish that Gibbs breached any duty to BAM by discussing with Sheehan a joint move to another firm, or that Sheehan's decision was based upon anything other than his own personal interests. In addition, while in certain situations "[A] lawyer's removal or copying, without the firm's consent, of materials from a law firm that do not belong to the lawyer, that are the property of the law firm, and that are intended by the lawyer to be used in his new affiliation, could constitute dishonesty, which is professional misconduct under [Model] Rule 8.4 (c)" (DC Bar Legal Ethics Comm Opn 273, at 192), here, the partners took their desk copies of recent correspondence with the good faith belief that they were entitled to do so.

Contrary to the finding of the trial court [. . .], we find no breach of duty in plaintiffs taking their desk files. These were comprised of duplicates of material maintained in individual client files, the partnership agreement was silent as to these documents, and removal was apparently common practice for departing attorneys [. . .].

However, the record supports the court's finding that both partners committed a breach of their fiduciary duty to the BAM partners by supplying Chadbourne, and presumably the other partnerships they considered joining, with the April 26, 1991 memorandum describing the members of BAM's T/E department, their salaries, and other confidential information, such as billing rates and average billable hours, taken from personnel files. Moreover, a closer examination of the record does not support the dissent's conclusion that these partners did not engage in surreptitious recruiting. The partners may not have discussed with firm employees the possibility of moving with them prior to June 20, 1991, but they indicated to Chadbourne the employees they were interested in prior to this date, and Gibbs specifically testified that he refrained from telling one of his partners, to whom he had a duty of loyalty, about his future plans to recruit specific associates and support staff from the partnership.

There is no evidence of improper client solicitation in this case, nor is it an issue on this appeal. Although the analogy could be useful in concluding that Gibbs did not breach his fiduciary duty to the partnership by working with Sheehan to find a new affiliation, the fiduciary restraints upon a partner with respect to client solicitation are not analogous to those applicable to employee recruitment. By contrast to the lawyer-client relationship, a partner does not have a fiduciary duty to the employees of a firm which would limit his duty of loyalty to the partnership. Thus, recruitment of firm employees has been viewed as distinct and "permissible on a more limited basis than . . . solicitation of clients" [. . .]. Prewithdrawal recruitment is generally allowed "only after the firm has been given notice of the lawyer's intention to withdraw" [. . .]. Robert W. Hillman, *Loyalty in the Law Firm*.

However, here Sheehan prepared a memo in April of 1991, well in advance of even deciding, much less informing his partners of his intention to withdraw. There is ample support in the record for the trial court's finding that the preparation and sending of the April 26, 1991 memo, combined with the subsequent hiring of certain trusts and estates personnel, constituted an egregious breach of plaintiff's fiduciary duty to BAM. [. . .] Sheehan's disclosure of confidential BAM data to even one firm was a direct breach of his duty of loyalty to his partners. Because the memo gave Chadbourne confidential BAM employment data as well as other information reflecting BAM's valuation of each employee, Chadbourne was made privy to information calculated to give it an unfair advantage in recruiting certain employees [. . .].

While partners may not be restrained from inviting qualified personnel to change firms with them [. . .], here Gibbs and Sheehan began their recruiting while still members of the firm and prior to serving notice of their intent to withdraw. They did so without informing their partners that they were disseminating confidential firm data to competitors. Their actions, while still members of the firm, were intended to and did place BAM in the position of not knowing which of their employees were targets and what steps would be appropriate for them to take in order to retain these critical employees. The dissent's analysis, that once the firm was notified of the partners' departure, there was no breach of fiduciary duty, is flawed. The breach occurred in April of 1991 and could not be cured by any after-the-fact notification by the fiduciary who committed the breach that he was withdrawing from the firm. Chadbourne still had the unfair advantage of the confidential information from the April 1991 memo, and still had the upper hand, which was manifested by its ability to tailor its offers and incentives to the BAM recruits.

Contrary to the dissent, I would characterize the memo distributed to prospective competitors as confidential. The data was obtained from BAM personnel files which Sheehan had unique access to as a BAM partner. The dissent's statement that such financial information is generally known to "headhunters" is without foundation. [. . .]

For example, the BAM partnership agreement, which is included in the record, reveals that the approximately 40 partners in the firm earn substantially different percentages of the firm's earnings. No professional publication would be privy to these financials. With respect to the specific associates and support staff whose compensation was disseminated in the April 1991 memo, the information disclosed to Chadbourne incorporated these individuals' bonuses. Bonus payments are confidential [. . .]. Sheehan abused his fiduciary duty to the partnership by accessing personnel files to obtain the actual gross compensation of the associates and support staff he and Gibbs wished to bring with them, including bonuses, and disclosing this information to Chadbourne.

Moreover, the memo contained more than a list of salaries. It itemized each of the employee's annual billable hours, and the rates at which BAM billed these employees out to their clients, information which was not otherwise publicly available. These facts go directly to a potential employee's value and were accessible only to members of the BAM partnership. Selected partners providing BAM's confidential information, which they were able to obtain by virtue of their position as fiduciaries, to Chadbourne was an act of disloyalty to their partnership. The confidential information placed Chadbourne, as a competing prospective employer, in the advantageous position of conducting interviews of the associates and support staff with more knowledge than any firm could obtain through independent research, as well as providing it with information BAM partners did not know it had, thereby prejudicing their own efforts to retain their associates and support staff. [. . .]

Accordingly, the order, Supreme Court, New York County (Herman Cahn, J.), entered October 1, 1998, which [. . .] determined that plaintiffs had breached their fiduciary duty to defendants, should be modified, on the law, to limit such conclusion to the act of disseminating confidential employee information, and otherwise affirmed [. . .].

■ SAXE, J. (concurring in part and dissenting in part)

The trial court concluded that plaintiffs breached their fiduciary duty to their former partners in several ways. First, that plaintiff Charles Gibbs improperly "solicited" his partner Robert Sheehan to leave Breed, Abbott with him; second, that it was improper for the two attorneys to take their chronological correspondence files with them; lastly, that the plaintiffs furnished to their new law firm, prior to their departure from Breed, Abbott, confidential information regarding their support staff, whom Chadbourne then hired. The trial court also explicitly found that plaintiffs' move to Chadbourne & Parke was "orchestrated to cripple" Breed, Abbott.

The evidence before the trial court fails to support its findings that plaintiffs violated their fiduciary duty to their partners at Breed, Abbott. I agree with the majority's holding that Gibbs's predeparture discussions with Sheehan cannot constitute a breach of Gibbs's fiduciary duty to Breed, Abbott, and that plaintiffs' removal of their desk chronology files breached no obligation to their former partners. However, I disagree with the conclusion that defendants are entitled to damages based upon plaintiffs having provided Chadbourne with information about other employees of the firm's trusts and estates department, which information was provided in the interests of bringing these employees along with them in their move to Chadbourne.

Persuading a Partner to Leave the Firm as a Team

Turning first to the trial court's finding that Gibbs "actively encouraged" or "persuaded" Sheehan to leave the firm with him, and "orchestrated" their move to cripple Breed, Abbott's trusts and estates department, there is no established fiduciary duty that can be stretched to cover Gibbs's conduct. The standard employed by the trial court, if applied generally, would too severely restrict attorneys' rights to change affiliations, compete with former partners, and offer clients full freedom of choice with respect to retaining counsel.

Initially, the "solicitation" of one's own partners to make a joint move simply does not qualify as a breach of fiduciary duty. [. . .]

[. . .] The Court recognized that an attorney's fiduciary duty is not violated by "taking steps to locate alternative space and affiliations." *Graubard Mollen Dannett & Horowitz v. Moskovitz*. The Court also noted that "departing partners have been permitted to inform firm clients with whom they have a prior professional relationship about their impending withdrawal and new practice, and to remind the client of its freedom to retain counsel of its choice [citations omitted]," although it added that "[i]deally, such approaches would take place only after notice to the firm of the partner's plans to leave [citations omitted]" *Id.* [. . .]

The "solicitation" of one's own partners to make a joint move is fundamentally different than the solicitation of firm clients [. . .].

Although clients are not, technically, an "asset" or "property" of the firm, subject to possession, the rules regarding their solicitation treat them as something of an equivalent [. . .]. The wrongfulness in preresignation solicitation of clients lies in directly and unfairly competing with the firm for *business,* while still a partner of it, taking unfair advantage of knowledge the firm lacks. [. . .]

Law partners "are bound by a fiduciary duty requiring 'the punctilio of an honor the most sensitive' " *Meinhard v. Salmon.* Yet, neither this duty nor any rules of ethics prohibit partners in a law firm from leaving the firm, or from competing with their former firm immediately upon their departure, or even from making plans while still a member of the firm to compete with it following their departure [. . .]. What is prohibited is *actual* competition with the firm while still a member of it.

[. . .] The prohibition against secretly soliciting clients, or removing client files, prior to one's resignation, is founded upon the prohibition against taking unfair advantage of the knowledge of his impending departure, while his partners are still unaware of it. It constitutes not a mere plan to compete in the future with his former law partners, but a present act of direct competition with those to whom he still owes a duty of loyalty.

An equally important principle in these circumstances, providing something of a counterweight to the duty of loyalty partners owe one another, is "the important value of client freedom of choice in legal representation" *Graubard Mollen Dannett & Horowitz v. Moskovitz.* Imposition of a limitation which restricts the ability of a departing partner to offer the client the ability to continue to serve as counsel may violate the ethical prohibition against restricting an attorney's practice of law. [. . .]

A partner planning a move necessarily makes numerous arrangements in anticipation of withdrawal, to ensure a smooth transition, including ensuring the capability of continuing to serve those former clients who choose to retain the departing partner. *Meehan v. Shaughnessy.* The same considerations apply equally when two partners plan a joint move. *Id.* The fact that one partner conceived of the move first and approached the other with the idea, or even convinced an initially content colleague to embark upon a joint departure, cannot change the attorneys' right to leave their firm. [. . .]

The observation of the trial court that plaintiffs' joint departure "denuded" Breed, Abbott's trusts and estates department is irrelevant to the issue of breach of fiduciary duty. Where a department of a law firm contains two active partners, a few associates and support staff, a decision by the two partners to withdraw from the firm will of necessity "denude" the department, and may indeed even "cripple" it, at least temporarily. However, it does not follow that the departure violates the duty owed by the departing partners to the firm. Partners' freedom to withdraw from a firm simply cannot be reconciled with a requirement that their departure be arranged in such a way as to protect the integrity of the department, and ensure its continued profit levels.

[. . .] We can [ ] assume that as a result of the withdrawal, the old firm may well be economically damaged. Yet, the mere fact of such damage does not make it compensable.

Associates and Other Staff

Once it is recognized that partners in law firms do not breach their duty to the other members of their firm by speaking to colleagues about leaving the firm, there is no logic to prohibiting partners from inviting selected employees to apply for a position at the new firm as well, absent contractual obligations not at issue here. Support staff, like clients, are not the exclusive property of a firm with which they are affiliated. [. . .]

The April 26, 1991 Memo

Under the circumstances, plaintiffs' preliminary compilation of information regarding the salaries, billable hours and standard billing rates of the employees they sought to bring with them, and their providing it to Chadbourne after giving notice to Breed, Abbott, provides no support for a liability determination against them.

[. . .] [W]hile plaintiffs obtained the salary information regarding the associates and staff in question through their position as partners at Breed, Abbott, it was information that could as easily have been obtained elsewhere. The concept that this information is some sort of trade secret does not comport with the realities of the practice of law.

It is only the partners' fiduciary duty, rather than the label "confidential information," that limits their right to disclose information about their present firm to members of a contemplated new affiliation, and this limitation applies only where disclosure of the information would constitute an act of direct competition with their present firm. [. . .]

Desk Chronology Files

As to the finding of the trial court that plaintiffs breached their fiduciary duty to their former partners by taking their desk chronology files, in this respect, too, the trial court imposed a non-existent duty. [. . .]

Individual attorneys may be answerable subsequently for actions taken while still a member of their former firm. In such circumstances, these documents could be necessary to defend against, for example, claims of ethical violations or malpractice. As long as the removal of duplicate documents properly in their possession does not hinder or interfere with the former firm's ability to continue serving as counsel for the clients, there is no reason why retaining the duplicates would constitute a breach of fiduciary duty. It does not give plaintiffs an unfair advantage in the competition for clients.

I perceive nothing in plaintiffs' conduct constituting any violation of fiduciary duty, and accordingly, I would reverse and dismiss the counterclaims in their entirety.

3.   OBLIGATION OF GOOD FAITH TO FELLOW PARTNERS

Bohatch v. Butler & Binion
977 S.W.2d 543 (Tex. 1998)

[. . .] [Colette] Bohatch became an associate in the Washington, D.C., office of Butler & Binion in 1986 after working for several years as Deputy Assistant General Counsel at the Federal Energy Regulatory Commission. John McDonald, the managing partner of the office, and Richard Powers, a partner, were the only other attorneys in the Washington office. The office did work for Pennzoil almost exclusively.

Bohatch was made partner in February 1990. She then began receiving internal firm reports showing the number of hours each attorney worked, billed, and collected. From her review of these reports, Bohatch became concerned that McDonald was overbilling Pennzoil and discussed the matter with Powers. Together they reviewed and copied portions of McDonald's time diary. Bohatch's review of McDonald's time entries increased her concern.

On July 15, 1990, Bohatch met with Louis Paine, the firm's managing partner, to report her concern that McDonald was overbilling Pennzoil. Paine said he would investigate. Later that day, Bohatch told Powers about her conversation with Paine.

The following day, McDonald met with Bohatch and informed her that Pennzoil was not satisfied with her work and wanted her work to be supervised. Bohatch testified that this was the first time she had ever heard criticism of her work for Pennzoil.

The next day, Bohatch repeated her concerns to Paine and to R. Hayden Burns and Marion E. McDaniel, two other members of the firm's management committee, in a telephone conversation. Over the next month, Paine and Burns investigated Bohatch's complaint. They reviewed the Pennzoil bills and supporting computer print-outs for those bills. They then discussed the allegations with Pennzoil in-house counsel John Chapman, the firm's primary contact with Pennzoil. Chapman, who had a long-standing relationship with McDonald, responded that Pennzoil was satisfied that the bills were reasonable.

In August, Paine met with Bohatch and told her that the firm's investigation revealed no basis for her contentions. He added that she should begin looking for other employment, but that the firm would continue to provide her a monthly draw, insurance coverage, office space, and a secretary. After this meeting, Bohatch received no further work assignments from the firm.

In January 1991, the firm denied Bohatch a year-end partnership distribution for 1990 and reduced her tentative distribution share for 1991 to zero. In June, the firm paid Bohatch her monthly draw and told her that this draw would be her last. Finally, in August, the firm gave Bohatch until November to vacate her office.

By September, Bohatch had found new employment. She filed this suit on October 18, 1991, and the firm voted formally to expel her from the partnership three days later, October 21, 1991. [. . .]

The court of appeals held that the firm's only duty to Bohatch was not to expel her in bad faith. The court of appeals stated that " '[b]ad faith' in this context means only that partners cannot expel another partner for self-gain." Finding no evidence that the firm expelled Bohatch for self-gain, the court concluded that Bohatch could not recover for breach of fiduciary duty. However, the court concluded that the firm breached the partnership agreement when it reduced Bohatch's tentative partnership distribution for 1991 to zero without notice, and when it terminated her draw three months before she left. The court concluded that Bohatch was entitled to recover $35,000 in lost earnings for 1991 but none for 1990, and no mental anguish damages. Accordingly, the court rendered judgment for Bohatch for $35,000 plus $225,000 in attorney's fees.

We have long recognized as a matter of common law that "[t]he relationship between . . . partners . . . is fiduciary in character, and imposes upon all the participants the obligation of loyalty to the joint concern and of the utmost good faith, fairness, and honesty in their dealings with each other with respect to matters pertaining to the enterprise." *Fitz-Gerald v. Hull.* Yet, partners have no obligation to remain partners; "at the heart of the partnership concept is the principle that partners may choose with whom they wish to be associated." *Gelder Med. Group v. Webber.* The issue presented, one of first impression, is whether the fiduciary relationship between and among partners creates an exception to the at-will nature of partnerships; that is, in this case, whether it gives rise to a duty not to expel a partner who reports suspected overbilling by another partner.

[. . .] [N]either statutory nor contract law principles answer the question of whether the firm owed Bohatch a duty not to expel her. The Texas Uniform Partnership Act addresses expulsion of a partner only in the context of dissolution of the partnership. In this case, as provided by the partnership agreement, Bohatch's expulsion did not dissolve the partnership. [. . .] [T]he partnership agreement contemplates expulsion of a partner and prescribes procedures to be followed, but it does not specify or limit the grounds for expulsion. Thus, while Bohatch's claim that she was expelled in an *improper way* is governed by the partnership agreement, her claim that she was expelled for an *improper reason* is not. Therefore, we look to the common law to find the principles governing Bohatch's claim that the firm breached a duty when it expelled her.

Courts in other states have held that a partnership may expel a partner for purely business reasons. [. . .] Further, courts recognize that a law firm can expel a partner to protect relationships both within the firm and with clients. Finally, many courts have held that a partnership can expel a partner without breaching any duty in order to resolve a "fundamental schism." *Waite v. Sylvester*.

The fiduciary duty that partners owe one another does not encompass a duty to remain partners or else answer in tort damages. Nonetheless, Bohatch and several distinguished legal scholars urge this Court to recognize that public policy requires a limited duty to remain partners— i.e., a partnership must retain a whistleblower partner. They argue that such an extension of a partner's fiduciary duty is necessary because permitting a law firm to retaliate against a partner who in good faith reports suspected overbilling would discourage compliance with rules of professional conduct and thereby hurt clients.

While this argument is not without some force, we must reject it. A partnership exists solely because the partners choose to place personal confidence and trust in one another. [. . .] Just as a partner can be expelled, without a breach of any common law duty, over disagreements about firm policy or to resolve some other "fundamental schism," a partner can be expelled for accusing another partner of overbilling without subjecting the partnership to tort damages. Such charges, whether true or not, may have a profound effect on the personal confidence and trust essential to the partner relationship. Once such charges are made, partners may find it impossible to continue to work together to their mutual benefit and the benefit of their clients.

We are sensitive to the concern expressed by the dissenting Justices that "retaliation against a partner who tries in good faith to correct or report perceived misconduct virtually assures that others will not take these appropriate steps in the future." However, the dissenting Justices do not explain how the trust relationship necessary both for the firm's existence and for representing clients can survive such serious accusations by one partner against another. The threat of tort liability for expulsion would tend to force partners to remain in untenable circumstance—suspicious of and angry with each other—to their own detriment and that of their clients whose matters are neglected by lawyers distracted with intra-firm frictions.

Although concurring in the Court's judgment, Justice Hecht criticizes the Court for failing to "address amici's concerns that failing to impose liability will discourage attorneys from reporting unethical conduct." To address the scholars' concerns, he proposes that a whistleblower be protected from expulsion, but only if the report, irrespective of being made in good faith, is proved to be correct. We fail to see how such an approach encourages compliance with ethical rules more than the approach we adopt today. Furthermore, the amici's position is that a reporting attorney must be in good faith, not that the attorney must be right. In short, Justice Hecht's approach ignores the question Bohatch presents, the amici write about, and the firm challenges—whether a partnership violates a fiduciary duty when it expels a partner who in good faith reports suspected ethical violations. The concerns of the amici are best addressed by a rule that clearly demarcates an attorney's ethical duties and the parameters of tort liability, rather than redefining "whistleblower."

We emphasize that our refusal to create an exception to the at-will nature of partnerships in no way obviates the ethical duties of lawyers. Such duties sometimes necessitate difficult decisions, as when a lawyer suspects overbilling by a colleague. The fact that the ethical duty to report may create an irreparable schism between partners neither excuses failure to report nor transforms expulsion as a means of resolving that schism into a tort.

We hold that the firm did not owe Bohatch a duty not to expel her for reporting suspected overbilling by another partner.

Breach of the Partnership Agreement

The court of appeals concluded that the firm breached the partnership agreement by reducing Bohatch's tentative distribution for 1991 to zero without the requisite notice. The firm contests this finding on the ground that the management committee had the right to set tentative and year-end bonuses. However, the partnership agreement guarantees a monthly draw of $7,500 per month regardless of the tentative distribution. Moreover, the firm's right to reduce the bonus was contingent upon providing proper notice to Bohatch. The firm does not dispute that it did not give Bohatch notice that the firm was reducing her tentative distribution. Accordingly, the court of appeals did not err in finding the firm liable for breach of the partnership agreement. Moreover, because Bohatch's damages sound in contract, and because she sought attorney's fees at trial [. . .], we affirm the court of appeals' award of Bohatch's attorney's fees.

We affirm the court of appeals' judgment.

■ SPECTOR, joined by PHILLIPS, CHIEF JUSTICE, dissenting.

> [W]hat's the use you learning to do right when it's troublesome
> to do right and ain't no trouble to do wrong, and the wages is
> just the same?
>
> —*The Adventures of Huckleberry Finn*

The issue in this appeal is whether law partners violate a fiduciary duty
by retaliating against one partner for questioning the billing practices of
another partner. I would hold that partners violate their fiduciary duty
to one another by punishing compliance with the Disciplinary Rules of
Professional Conduct. Accordingly, I dissent.

[. . .] The majority views the partnership relationship among lawyers as
strictly business. I disagree. The practice of law is a profession first, then
a business. Moreover, it is a self-regulated profession subject to the Rules
promulgated by this Court.

As attorneys, we take an oath to "honestly demean [ourselves] in the
practice of law; and . . . discharge [our] duty to [our] *client[s]* to the best
of [our] ability." Tex. Gov't Code § 82.037 (emphasis added). This oath of
honesty and duty is not mere "self-adulatory bombast" but mandated by
the Legislature. *See Schware v. Board of Bar Exam'rs* (Frankfurter, J.
concurring) (noting that the rhetoric used to describe the esteemed role
of the legal profession has real meaning). As attorneys, we bear
responsibilities to our clients and the bar itself that transcend ordinary
business relationships.

Certain requirements imposed by the Rules have particular relevance in
this case. Lawyers may not charge unconscionable fees. Partners and
supervisory attorneys have a duty to take reasonable remedial action to
avoid or mitigate the consequences of known violations by other lawyers
in their firm. Lawyers who know that another lawyer has violated a rule
of professional conduct in a way that raises a substantial question as to
that lawyer's honesty or fitness as a lawyer must report that violation.
[. . .]

In sum, attorneys organizing together to practice law are subject to a
higher duty toward their clients and the public interest than those in
other occupations. As a natural consequence, this duty affects the special
relationship among lawyers who practice law together.

It is true that no high court has considered the issue of whether expulsion
of a partner for complying with ethical rules violates law partners'
fiduciary duty. The dearth of authority in this area does not, however,
diminish the significance of this case. Instead, the scarcity of guiding case
law only heightens the importance of this Court's decision.

[. . .] In *Wieder v. Skala,* the New York Court of Appeals held in an at-
will employment context that an associate terminated for reporting
another associate's misconduct had a valid claim for breach of contract
against his law firm based on an implied-in-law obligation to comply with

the rules of the profession. The court recognized that "[i]ntrinsic to [the hiring of an attorney to practice law] . . . was the unstated but essential compact that in conducting the firm's legal practice both plaintiff and the firm would do so in compliance with the prevailing rules of conduct and ethical standards of the profession." To find otherwise would amount to "nothing less than a frustration of the only legitimate purpose of the employment relationship," that is, "the lawful and ethical practice of law." The plaintiff was not just an employee, but also an "independent officer[ ] of the court responsible in a broader public sense for [his] professional obligations."

Only one reported case involves an attorney who was punished solely for failing to report another lawyer's misconduct. The case is more notable for its rarity and effect than for the holding itself. The Illinois Supreme Court suspended an attorney for one year for failing to report misconduct pursuant to a settlement agreement forbidding reporting of unprivileged information about the conversion of client funds by another attorney. Aware of the possible practical effect of its holding in setting an ethical standard for attorneys, the court found that "public discipline is necessary in this case to carry out the purposes of attorney discipline." *In re Himmel.* Together these cases illustrate that lawyers, by their agreements, may not sidestep their ethical obligations.

I believe that the fiduciary relationship among law partners should incorporate the rules of the profession promulgated by this Court. Although the evidence put on by Bohatch is by no means conclusive, applying the proper presumptions of a no-evidence review, this trial testimony amounts to some evidence that Bohatch made a good-faith report of suspected overbilling in an effort to comply with her professional duty. Further, it provides some evidence that the partners of Butler & Binion began a retaliatory course of action *before* any investigation of the allegation had begun.

In light of this Court's role in setting standards to govern attorneys' conduct, it is particularly inappropriate for the Court to deny recourse to attorneys wronged for adhering to the Disciplinary Rules. I would hold that in this case the law partners violated their fiduciary duty by retaliating against a fellow partner who made a good-faith effort to alert her partners to the possible overbilling of a client.

[. . .] The Court's writing in this case sends an inappropriate signal to lawyers and to the public that the rules of professional responsibility are subordinate to a law firm's other interests. Under the majority opinion's vision for the legal profession, the wages would not even be the same for "doing right"; they diminish considerably and leave an attorney who acts ethically and in good faith without recourse. Accordingly, I respectfully dissent.

D. RIGHTS AND LIABILITIES OF PARTNERS

1. PARTNER'S RIGHTS

Revised Uniform Partnership Act
Section 301—Partner Agent of Partnership.

Subject to the effect of a statement of partnership authority under Section 303:

(1) Each partner is an agent of the partnership for the purpose of its business. An act of a partner, including the signing of an instrument in the partnership name, for apparently carrying on in the ordinary course the partnership business or business of the kind carried on by the partnership binds the partnership, unless the partner did not have authority to act for the partnership in the particular matter and the person with which the partner was dealing knew or had notice that the partner lacked authority.

(2) An act of a partner which is not apparently for carrying on in the ordinary course the partnership's business or business of the kind carried on by the partnership binds the partnership only if the act was actually authorized by all the other partners.

Section 307—Actions by and Against Partnership and Partners.

(a) A partnership may sue and be sued in the name of the partnership.

(b) To the extent not inconsistent with Section 306, a partner may be joined in an action against the partnership or named in a separate action.

(c) A judgment against a partnership is not by itself a judgment against a partner. A judgment against a partnership may not be satisfied from a partner's assets unless there is also a judgment against the partner.

(d) A judgment creditor of a partner may not levy execution against the assets of the partner to satisfy a judgment based on a claim against the partnership unless the partner is personally liable for the claim under Section 306 and:

> (1) a judgment based on the same claim has been obtained against the partnership and a writ of execution on the judgment has been returned unsatisfied in whole or in part;

> (2) the partnership is a debtor in bankruptcy;

> (3) the partner has agreed that the creditor need not exhaust partnership assets;

> (4) a court grants permission to the judgment creditor to levy execution against the assets of a partner based on a finding that partnership assets subject to execution are clearly insufficient to satisfy the judgment, that exhaustion of partnership assets is excessively burdensome, or that the grant of permission is an appropriate exercise of the court's equitable powers; or

(5) liability is imposed on the partner by law or contract independent of the existence of the partnership. [. . .]

Section 401—Partner's Rights and Duties.

(a) Each partner is entitled to an equal share of the partnership distributions and, except in the case of a limited liability partnership, is chargeable with a share of the partnership losses in proportion to the partner's share of the distributions.

(b) A partnership shall reimburse a partner for any payment made by the partner in the course of the partner's activities on behalf of the partnership, if the partner complied with this section and Section 409 in making the payment.

(c) A partnership shall indemnify and hold harmless a person with respect to any claim or demand against the person and any debt, obligation, or other liability incurred by the person by reason of the person's former or present capacity as a partner, if the claim, demand, debt, obligation, or other liability does not arise from the person's breach of this section or Section 407 or 409.

(d) In the ordinary course of its business, a partnership may advance reasonable expenses, including attorney's fees and costs, incurred by a person in connection with a claim or demand against the person by reason of the person's former or present capacity as a partner, if the person promises to repay the partnership if the person ultimately is determined not to be entitled to be indemnified under subsection (c).

(e) A partnership may purchase and maintain insurance on behalf of a partner against liability asserted against or incurred by the partner in that capacity or arising from that status even if, under Section 105(c)(7), the partnership agreement could not eliminate or limit the person's liability to the partnership for the conduct giving rise to the liability.

(f) A partnership shall reimburse a partner for an advance to the partnership beyond the amount of capital the partner agreed to contribute.

(g) A payment or advance made by a partner which gives rise to a partnership obligation under subsection (b) or (f) constitutes a loan to the partnership which accrues interest from the date of the payment or advance.

(h) Each partner has equal rights in the management and conduct of the partnership's business.

(i) A partner may use or possess partnership property only on behalf of the partnership.

(j) A partner is not entitled to remuneration for services performed for the partnership, except for reasonable compensation for services rendered in winding up the business of the partnership.

(k)   A difference arising as to a matter in the ordinary course of business of a partnership may be decided by a majority of the partners. An act outside the ordinary course of business of a partnership and an amendment to the partnership agreement may be undertaken only with the affirmative vote or consent of all the partners.

Section 408—Rights of Information of Partners and Persons Dissociated as Partners.

(a)   A partnership shall keep its books and records, if any, at its principal office.

(b)   On reasonable notice, a partner may inspect and copy during regular business hours [. . .] any record maintained by the partnership regarding the partnership's business, financial condition, and other circumstances, to the extent the information is material to the partner's rights and duties under the partnership agreement or this [act].

(c)   The partnership shall furnish to each partner:

(1)   without demand, any information concerning the partnership's business, financial condition, and other circumstances which the partnership knows and is material to the proper exercise of the partner's rights and duties under the partnership agreement or this [act], except to the extent the partnership can establish that it reasonably believes the partner already knows the information; and

(2) on demand, any other information concerning the partnership's business, financial condition, and other circumstances, except to the extent the demand or the information demanded is unreasonable or otherwise improper under the circumstances. [. . .]

(j) In addition to any restriction or condition stated in its partnership agreement, a partnership, as a matter within the ordinary course of its business, may impose reasonable restrictions and conditions on access to and use of information to be furnished under this section, including designating information confidential and imposing nondisclosure and safeguarding obligations on the recipient. [. . .]

Section 501—Partner Not Co-Owner of Partnership Property.

A partner is not a co-owner of partnership property and has no interest in partnership property which can be transferred, either voluntarily or involuntarily.

Section 502—Nature of Transferable Interest.

A transferable interest is personal property.

Section 503—Transfer of Transferable Interest.

(a)   A transfer, in whole or in part, of a transferable interest:

(1)   is permissible;

(2)   does not by itself cause a person's dissociation as a partner or a dissolution and winding up of the partnership business; and

(3) [. . .] does not entitle the transferee to:

(A) participate in the management or conduct of the partnership's business; or

(B) except as otherwise provided in subsection (c), have access to records or other information concerning the partnership's business.

(b) A transferee has the right to:

(1) receive, in accordance with the transfer, distributions to which the transferor would otherwise be entitled; and

(2) seek under Section 801(5) a judicial determination that it is equitable to wind up the partnership business.

(c) In a dissolution and winding up of a partnership, a transferee is entitled to an account of the partnership's transactions only from the date of dissolution. [. . .]

(e) A transfer of a transferable interest in violation of a restriction on transfer contained in the partnership agreement is ineffective if the intended transferee has knowledge or notice of the restriction at the time of transfer.

(f) Except as otherwise provided in Section 601(4)(B), if a partner transfers a transferable interest, the transferor retains the rights of a partner other than the transferable interest transferred and retains all the duties and obligations of a partner. [. . .]

Section 305—Partnership Liable for Partner's Actionable Conduct.

(a) A partnership is liable for loss or injury caused to a person, or for a penalty incurred, as a result of a wrongful act or omission, or other actionable conduct, of a partner acting in the ordinary course of business of the partnership or with authority of the partnership.

(b) If, in the course of the partnership's business or while acting with authority of the partnership, a partner receives or causes the partnership to receive money or property of a person not a partner, and the money or property is misapplied by a partner, the partnership is liable for the loss.

Section 306—Partner's Liability.

(a) Except as otherwise provided in subsections (b) and (c), all partners are liable jointly and severally for all debts, obligations, and other liabilities of the partnership unless otherwise agreed by the claimant or provided by law.

(b) A person that becomes a partner is not personally liable for a debt, obligation, or other liability of the partnership incurred before the person became a partner.

(c) A debt, obligation, or other liability of a partnership incurred while the partnership is a limited liability partnership is solely the debt, obligation, or other liability of the limited liability partnership. A partner is not personally liable, directly or indirectly, by way of contribution or otherwise, for a debt, obligation, or other liability of the limited liability partnership solely by reason of being or acting as a partner. This subsection applies:

> (1) despite anything inconsistent in the partnership agreement that existed immediately before the vote or consent required to become a limited liability partnership under Section 901(b); and

> (2) regardless of the dissolution of the limited liability partnership. [. . .]

National Biscuit Co. v. Stroud
106 S.E.2d 692 (N.C. 1959)

C. N. Stroud and Earl Freeman entered into a general partnership to sell groceries under the firm name of Stroud's Food Center. There is nothing in the agreed statement of facts to indicate or suggest that Freeman's power and authority as a general partner were in any way restricted or limited by the articles of partnership in respect to the ordinary and legitimate business of the partnership. Certainly, the purchase and sale of bread were ordinary and legitimate business of Stroud's Food Center during its continuance as a going concern.

Several months prior to February 1956 Stroud advised plaintiff that he personally would not be responsible for any additional bread sold by plaintiff to Stroud's Food Center. After such notice, [plaintiff] from 6 February 1956 to 25 February 1956, at the request of Freeman, sold and delivered bread in the amount of $171.04 to Stroud's Food Center.

[T]his Court said [that a] partnership is, by operation of law, a power to each to bind the partnership in any manner legitimate to the business. [. . .] What either partner does with a third person is binding on the partnership. [. . .]

Section 59–39 [of North Carolina's Uniform Partnership Act] is entitled "Partner Agent of Partnership as to Partnership Business," and subsection (1) reads: "Every partner is an agent of the partnership for the purpose of its business, and the act of every partner, including the execution in the partnership name of any instrument, for apparently carrying on in the usual way the business of the partnership of which he is a member binds the partnership, unless the partner so acting has in fact no authority to act for the partnership in the particular matter, and the person with whom he is dealing has knowledge of the fact that he has no such authority." Section 59–39(4) states: "No act of a partner in contravention of a restriction on authority shall bind the partnership to persons having knowledge of the restriction."

Section 59–45 provides that "all partners are jointly and severally liable for the acts and obligations of the partnership."

Section 59–48 is captioned "Rules Determining Rights and Duties of Partners." Subsection (e) thereof reads: "All partners have equal rights in the management and conduct of the partnership business." Subsection (h) hereof is as follows: "Any difference arising as to ordinary matters connected with the partnership business may be decided by a majority of the partners; but no act in contravention of any agreement between the partners may be done rightfully without the consent of all the partners."

Freeman as a general partner with Stroud, with no restrictions on his authority to act within the scope of the partnership business so far as the agreed statement of facts shows, had under the Uniform Partnership Act "equal rights in the management and conduct of the partnership business." Under Section 59–48(h) Stroud, his co-partner, could not restrict the power and authority of Freeman to buy bread for the partnership as a going concern, for such a purchase was an "ordinary matter connected with the partnership business," for the purpose of its business and within its scope, because in the very nature of things Stroud was not, and could not be, a majority of the partners. Therefore, Freeman's purchases of bread from plaintiff for Stroud's Food Center as a going concern bound the partnership and his co-partner Stroud. [. . .]

In Crane on Partnership, it is said: "In cases of an even division of the partners as to whether or not an act within the scope of the business should be done, of which disagreement a third person has knowledge, it seems that logically no restriction can be placed upon the power to act. The partnership being a going concern, activities within the scope of the business should not be limited, save by the expressed will of the majority deciding a disputed question; half of the members are not a majority."

At the close of business on 25 February 1956 Stroud and Freeman by agreement dissolved the partnership. By their dissolution agreement all of the partnership assets, including cash on hand, bank deposits and all accounts receivable, with a few exceptions, were assigned to Stroud, who bound himself by such written dissolution agreement to liquidate the firm's assets and discharge its liabilities. It would seem a fair inference from the agreed statement of facts that the partnership got the benefit of the bread sold and delivered by plaintiff to Stroud's Food Center, at Freeman's request, from 6 February 1956 to 25 February 1956. But whether it did or not, Freeman's acts, as stated above, bound the partnership and Stroud. [. . .]

Covalt v. High
100 N.M. 700 (N.M. Ct. Appeals 1983)

Can a partner recover damages against his co-partner for the co-partner's failure or refusal to negotiate and obtain an increase in the amount of rental of partnership property? Under the circumstances herein, we hold no right of recovery exists.

The plaintiff, Louis E. Covalt, filed suit against defendant, William L. High [. . .]. Covalt alleged High had breached his fiduciary duty as a partner resulting in a loss of increased rentals. [. . .] [At trial,] Covalt was awarded judgment against William L. High, individually, in the sum of $9,500, plus prejudgment interest in the sum of $2,269.

High appeals [. . .]. The single issue presented on appeal is whether the trial court erred by ruling that High breached a fiduciary duty of fairness to his former partner Covalt by failing to negotiate and obtain an increase in the amount of rental for the partnership realty.

FACTS

Covalt and High were corporate officers and shareholders in CSI [Concrete Systems, Inc.]. Covalt owned 25% of the stock and High owned the remaining 75% of the stock. Both men received remuneration from the corporation in the form of salaries and bonuses. In late 1971, after both High and Covalt had become corporate officers, they orally agreed to the formation of a partnership. The partnership bought real estate and constructed an office and warehouse building on the land. In February, 1973, CSI leased the building from the partnership for a five-year term. Following the expiration of the initial term of the lease, CSI remained a tenant of the building; the corporation and the partnership orally agreed to certain rental increases. The corporation made substantial improvements to the leasehold. Under the original lease any improvements to the premises were to accrue to the partnership upon termination of the lease.

In December, 1978, Covalt resigned his corporate position and was employed by a competitor of CSI. Covalt, however, remained a partner with High in the ownership of the land and the building rented to CSI. On January 9, 1979, Covalt wrote to High demanding that the monthly rent for the partnership real estate leased to CSI be increased from $1,850 to $2,850 per month. Upon receipt of the letter, High informed Covalt he would determine if the rent could be increased. Thereafter, however, High did not agree to the increased rent and took no action to renegotiate the amount of the monthly rent payable.

At the trial, High testified that he felt CSI could not afford a higher rent and that the corporation had a poor financial status. The trial court, however, adopted findings that CSI could afford the requested rental increase and that High's failure to assent to his partner's demand was a breach of his fiduciary duty. The trial court also found that at the time of Covalt's demand, a reasonable monthly rental would have been $2,850 per month or more.

The trial court adopted findings of fact, that:

> 18. At all material times, William High was the managing partner of the partnership and had a duty of utmost fairness to his partner, Mr. Covalt, which required him to obtain a reasonable rental on the property.

55. William High refused to see that the rental on the Richmond property was raised to $2,850 a month, and said refusal was a breach of his fiduciary duty of utmost fairness to his partner, Louis Covalt.

The court also found that the partnership between High and Covalt was dissolved by written agreement dated August 27, 1980. Under the terms of the dissolution, High paid Covalt $170,000, in cash, plus installment payments for his one-half interest as a partner, and for other property in which the two parties held joint interests.

The court further found that the rental rate in effect when the written lease expired on January 31, 1978, was $1,850 per month, no other written lease was ever executed by the partnership and CSI, and that the partners never had any specific agreement as to how the partnership would set the rent to be charged CSI. As between the partners, that calculation was left up to High. The court adopted a finding that High, as Covalt's partner, did not agree with Covalt's demand to raise the monthly rental payable by CSI.

The trial court also found:

34. On January 9, 1979, when Covalt made his demand on [CSI] for a rental increase, High, as President of [CSI] owed a duty to the Corporation and all shareholders, including Covalt, to exercise his best judgment to operate the Corporation as profitably as possible.

35. That High, in failing or refusing to accede to the demand by Covalt to raise the rent, was fulfilling this duty owed to the Corporation and its shareholders, including Covalt.

Based on the foregoing findings, the trial court concluded that High breached his fiduciary duty to Covalt, resulting in damage to Covalt in the sum of $9,500 as lost rentals, plus prejudgment interest through April 30, 1982, in the amount of $2,269.66.

FIDUCIARY DUTY AS A PARTNER

Did High breach a fiduciary partnership duty to Covalt warranting an award of damages?

The status resulting from the formation of a partnership creates a fiduciary relationship between partners. The status of partnership requires of each member an obligation of good faith and fairness in their dealings with one another, and a duty to act in furtherance of the common benefit of all partners in transactions conducted within the ambit of partnership affairs. NMSA 1978, § 54–1–21. As a fiduciary, each partner has a duty to fully disclose to the other, all material facts which may affect the business of the partnership. NMSA 1978, § 54–1–20. As stated in the text, J. Crane & A. Bromberg, *Crane & Bromberg on Partnership*, "[a] partner must account for any profit acquired in a manner injurious to the interests of the partnership * * *."

The problems which have arisen between the parties herein, emphasize the importance of formulating written partnership agreements detailing the rights and obligations of the partners. Here, at the time of Covalt's demand for an increase in rents, both he and High simultaneously occupied the positions of corporate shareholders in CSI and as partners engaged in the ownership and rental of real property to the same corporation. Prior to Covalt's resignation as a corporate officer, he also served as vice president of CSI. The trial court found that High occupied the position of managing partner of the partnership.

Except where the partners expressly agree to the contrary, it is a fundamental principle of the law of partnership that all partners have equal rights in the management and conduct of the business of the partnership. NMSA 1978, § 54–1–18(E); *see also Rogers v. McDonald*. As specified in the Uniform Partnership Act adopted by New Mexico, where there is a difference of opinion between the partners as to the management or conduct of the partnership business, the decision of the majority must govern. NMSA 1978, § 54–1–18(H).

Under Section 54–1–18(E), Covalt was legally invested with an equal voice in the management of the partnership affairs. Assuming, but not deciding, that High's status as a managing partner is not to be considered, neither partner had the right to impose his will or decision concerning the operation of the partnership business upon the other. The fact that a proposal may in fact benefit the partnership does not mandate acceptance by all the partners. As specified in Section 54–1–18(H), "any difference arising as to ordinary matters connected with the partnership business may be decided by a majority of the partners; but no act in contravention of any agreement between the partners may be done rightfully without the consent of all the partners."

As stated in *Lindley on the Law of Partnership*, as to differences arising in the ordinary scope of the partnership business:

> [I]f the partners are equally divided, those who forbid a change must have their way * * *. [O]ne partner cannot either engage a new or dismiss an old servant against the will of his co-partner; nor, if the lease of the partnership place of business expires, insist on renewing the lease and continuing the business at the old place.

In *Summers v. Dooley*, the Supreme Court of Idaho was confronted with a similar problem arising out of a partnership of two individuals. There, the partners were engaged in a trash collection business and each contributed to the necessary labor. Over the objection of one partner, the other hired an additional employee. The disagreement over the hiring and compensation of the new employee resulted in a suit between the partners. The one partner sought to compel his co-partner to contribute to the expenses for hiring the additional man. The court held that, based upon the Idaho statute, mirroring the Uniform Partnership Act and identical to that adopted by New Mexico, the statutory language that any differences between partners as to the ordinary course of partnership business " 'may be decided by a majority of the partners,' " is mandatory rather than permissive in nature.

In keeping with *Lindley* and *Summers,* as between the partners themselves, in the absence of an agreement of a majority of the partners—an act involving the partnership business may not be compelled by the co-partner. If the parties are evenly divided as to a business decision affecting the partnership, and in the absence of a written provision in the partnership agreement providing for such contingency, then, as between the partners, the power to exercise discretion on behalf of the partners is suspended so long as the division continues. The rule is different, however, as to transactions between partners and third parties. *See Dotson v. Grice* (holding that in dealing with third parties a partner has the authority to act on behalf of the partnership in the usual way, even without the consent of the other partner).

Similarly, it is observed in 1 J. Barrett & E. Seago, *Partners and Partnerships Law and Taxation*:

> Where the partnership consists of only two partners there is ordinarily no question of one partner controlling the other and there is no majority. The rights of each of the two partners are equal. If the partners are unable to agree and if the partnership agreement does not provide an acceptable means for settlement of this disagreement, the only course of action is to dissolve the partnership.

At the time of the formation of the partnership, both Covalt and High were officers and shareholders of CSI. Each was aware of the potential for conflict between their duties as corporate officers to further the business of the corporation, and that of their role as partners in leasing realty to the corporation for the benefit of the partnership business. In the posture of being both a landlord and representatives of the tenant they had conflicting loyalties and fiduciary duties. After Covalt's resignation as an officer of the corporation he continued to remain a shareholder of the corporation. Each party's conflict of interest was known to the other and was acquiesced in when the partnership was formed.

Under the facts herein, in the absence of a mutual agreement between the partners to increase the rent of the partnership realty, we hold that one partner may not recover damages for the failure of the co-partner to acquiesce in a demand by the plaintiff that High negotiate and execute an increase in the monthly rentals of partnership property with CSI. Thus, there was no breach of a fiduciary duty. In the absence of a mutual agreement, or a written instrument detailing the rights of the parties, the remedy for such an impasse is a dissolution of the partnership.

Costs on appeal including costs to appellant in Court of Appeals Cause No. 5881 wherein we remanded this appeal for proper findings and conclusions, are awarded to appellant; the judgment awarding damages is reversed.

IT IS SO ORDERED.

RNR Investments Limited Partnership v. Peoples First Community Bank

812 So.2d 561 (Fla. Dist. Ct. App. 2002)

Factual and Procedural History

[. . .] RNR is a Florida limited partnership formed pursuant to chapter 620, Florida Statutes, to purchase vacant land in Destin, Florida, and to construct a house on the land for resale. Bernard Roeger was RNR's general partner and Heinz Rapp, Claus North, and S.E. Waltz, Inc., were limited partners. The agreement of limited partnership provides for various restrictions on the authority of the general partner. [. . .]

[T]he agreement required th[at] [. . .]

> The General Partner shall not incur debts, liabilities or obligations of the Partnership [for more than $650,000] unless the General Partner shall receive the prior written consent of the Limited Partner.

In June 1998, RNR, through its general partner, entered into a construction loan agreement, note and mortgage in the principal amount of $990,000 [with Peoples First Community Bank]. [. . .] From June 25, 1998 through Mar. 13, 2000, the bank disbursed the aggregate sum of $952,699, by transfers into RNR's bank account. [. . .] No representative of RNR objected to any draw of funds or asserted that the amounts disbursed were not associated with the construction of the house.

RNR defaulted under the terms of the note and mortgage by failing to make payments due in July 2000 and all monthly payments due thereafter. The Bank filed a complaint seeking foreclosure. RNR filed an answer and affirmative defenses. In its first affirmative defense, RNR alleged that the Bank had failed to review the limitations on the general partner's authority in RNR's limited partnership agreement. RNR asserted that the Bank had negligently failed to investigate and to realize that the general partner had no authority to execute notes, a mortgage and a construction loan agreement and was estopped from foreclosing. The Bank filed a motion for summary judgment with supporting affidavits attesting to the amounts due and owing and the amount of disbursements under the loan.

In opposition to the summary judgment motion, [. . .] [RNR President] stated that the partners anticipated that RNR would need to finance the construction of the residence, but that [. . .] the partnership agreement limited the amount of any loan the general partner could obtain on behalf of RNR [. . .] unless the general partner received the prior written consent of the limited partners [and] that the limited partners understood and orally agreed that the general partner would seek financing in the approximate amount of $650,000. Further, [RNR President] stated:

> Even though the limited partners had orally agreed to this amount, a written consent was never memorialized, and to my surprise, the [Bank], either through its employees or attorney, TTT never requested the same from any of the limited partners at any time prior to [or] after the closing on the loan from the [Bank] to RNR.

[RNR President] alleged that the partners learned in the spring of 2000 that, instead of obtaining a loan for $650,000, Roeger had obtained a loan for $990,000, which was secured by RNR's property. He stated that the limited partners did not consent to Roeger obtaining a loan from the Bank [. . .] either orally or in writing and that the limited partners were never contacted by the Bank as to whether they had consented to a loan amount of $990,000.

RNR asserts that a copy of the limited partnership agreement was maintained at its offices. Nevertheless, the record contains no copy of an Approved Budget of the partnership or any evidence that would show that a copy of RNR's partnership agreement or any partnership budget was given to the Bank or that any notice of the general partner's restricted authority was provided to the Bank. [. . .]

Apparent Authority of the General Partner

[. . .] Florida Revised Uniform Partnership Act (FRUPA), provides:

> Each partner is an agent of the partnership for the purpose of its business. An act of a partner, including the execution of an instrument in the partnership name, for apparently carrying on in the ordinary scope of partnership business or business of the kind carried on by the partnership, in the geographic area in which the partnership operates, binds the partnership unless the partner had no authority to act for the partnership in the particular manner and the person with whom the partner was dealing knew or had received notification that the partner lacked authority.

Thus, even if a general partner's actual authority is restricted by the terms of the partnership agreement, the general partner possesses the apparent authority to bind the partnership in the ordinary course of partnership business or in the business of the kind carried on by the partnership, unless the third party "knew or had received a notification that the partner lacked authority [. . .]." *Id.* "Knowledge" and "notice" under FRUPA are defined [in the statute]. [U]nder FRUPA [. . .] "[a] person knows a fact if the person has actual knowledge of the fact [. . .]." Further, a third party has notice of a fact if that party "(a) [k]nows of the fact; (b) [h]as received notification of the fact; or (c) [h]as reason to know the fact exists from all other facts known to the person at the time in question." [. . .]

[. . .] "Absent actual knowledge, third parties have no duty to inspect the partnership agreement or inquire otherwise to ascertain the extent of a partner's actual authority in the ordinary course of business, . . . even if they have some reason to question it [. . .]." The apparent authority provisions reflect a policy by the drafters that "the risk of loss from partner misconduct more appropriately belongs on the partnership than on third parties who do not knowingly participate in or take advantage of the misconduct [. . .]." J. Dennis Hayes, *Notice and Notification Under the Revised Uniform Partnership Act* [. . .]

Analysis

Under [FRUPA], the determination of whether a partner is acting with authority to bind the partnership involves a two-step analysis. The first step is to determine whether the partner purporting to bind the partnership apparently is carrying on the partnership business in the usual way or a business of the kind carried on by the partnership. An affirmative answer on this step ends the inquiry, unless it is shown that the person with whom the partner is dealing actually knew or had received a notification that the partner lacked authority. Here, it is undisputed that, in entering into the loan, the general partner was carrying on the business of RNR in the usual way. The dispositive question in this appeal is whether there are issues of material fact as to whether the Bank had actual knowledge or notice of restrictions on the general partner's authority.

RNR argues that, as a result of the restrictions on the general partner's authority in the partnership agreement, the Bank had constructive knowledge of the restrictions and was obligated to inquire as to the general partner's specific authority to bind RNR in the construction loan. We cannot agree. Under [FRUPA], the Bank could rely on the general partner's apparent authority, unless it had *actual knowledge* or *notice* of restrictions on that authority. While the RNR partners may have agreed upon restrictions that would limit the general partner to borrowing no more than $650,000 on behalf of the partnership, RNR does not contend and nothing before us would show that the Bank had actual knowledge or notice of any restrictions on the general partner's authority. Here, the partnership could have protected itself by [. . .] providing notice to the Bank of the specific restrictions on the authority of the general partner.

RNR relies on *Green River Assocs. v. Mark Twain Kansas City Bank* [. . .], as authority for its argument that the Bank was negligent in providing financing in reliance upon the apparent authority of the general partner. RNR's reliance is misplaced. In *Green River*, the express language of the partnership agreement, known to the bank, required that the proceeds of the loan be deposited in the partnership bank account. The court found that, when the bank wired partnership money to an account of an entity other than the partnership, the bank knew that its actions were contrary to the partnership agreement. Therefore, the court reasoned, the bank could not argue that the general partner had apparent authority to direct the bank to disburse the funds to a non-partnership account. *Id.* As a result, because the bank paid the loan proceeds to an entity other than the borrower, the court concluded that the partnership's note was void for lack of consideration. *Id.* Interestingly, Green River rejected the partnership's claim based upon the bank's alleged negligence. *Id.* Here, unlike *Green River,* all funds advanced by the Bank were paid into RNR's account. There is no basis for arguing a failure of consideration. Further, there is no fact in the record that would show that the Bank had actual knowledge or notice of restrictions on the general partner's authority.

Because there is no disputed issue of fact concerning whether the Bank had actual knowledge or notice of restrictions on the general partner's authority to borrow, summary judgment [for the Bank] was proper.

2.   DISTRIBUTING PROFITS AND LOSSES

Revised Uniform Partnership Act
Section 405—Sharing of and Right to Distributions Before Dissolution.

(a)   Any distribution made by a partnership before its dissolution and winding up must be in equal shares among partners, except to the extent necessary to comply with a transfer effective under Section 503 or charging order in effect under Section 504.

(b)   Subject to Section 701, a person has a right to a distribution before the dissolution and winding up of a partnership only if the partnership decides to make an interim distribution.

(c)   A person does not have a right to demand or receive a distribution from a partnership in any form other than money. Except as otherwise provided in Section 806, a partnership may distribute an asset in kind only if each part of the asset is fungible with each other part and each person receives a percentage of the asset equal in value to the person's share of distributions.

(d)   If a partner or transferee becomes entitled to receive a distribution, the partner or transferee has the status of, and is entitled to all remedies available to, a creditor of the partnership with respect to the distribution. However, the partnership's obligation to make a distribution is subject to offset for any amount owed to the partnership by the partner or a person dissociated as partner on whose account the distribution is made.

Kessler v. Antinora

653 A.2d 579 (N.J. Super. Ct. 1995)

I

Plaintiff Robert H. Kessler and defendant Richard Antinora entered into a written agreement for the purpose of building and selling a single-family residence on a lot in Wayne in Passaic County. The concept of the agreement seemed simple: Kessler was to provide the money and Antinora was to act as general contractor. Profits would be divided—60% to Kessler, 40% to Antinora—after Kessler was repaid. No thought was given to losses. The venture lost money. Kessler sued Antinora to recover 40% of his financial losses or $65,742. The Law Division judge ruled in Kessler's favor on summary judgment. We disagree, reverse the judgment in Kessler's favor, and order judgment in Antinora's favor.

II

On April 15, 1987 Kessler and Antinora executed a seven-page written agreement titled "JOINT VENTURE PARTNERSHIP AGREEMENT." The agreement contemplated a single venture: buying a lot in Wayne and building and selling a residence on it. Under the agreement Kessler agreed to "provide all necessary funds to purchase land and construct a one-family dwelling and disburse all funds to pay bills." Antinora agreed to "actually construct the dwelling and be the general contractor of the job."

The agreement provided for distribution of the proceeds of the venture:

> 9. Distribution. Upon or about completion of the dwelling it shall be placed for sale. Upon sale of same, and after deducting all monies expended by Robert Kessler plus interest at prime plus one point and/or including interest or any funds borrowed for the project, not to exceed prime plus one point, engineering fees, architectural fees, legal fees, broker fees, if any, and any other costs connected with the project, the parties, Robert Kessler and Richard Antinora, shall divide the net profits as follows:
>
> Robert Kessler—sixty (60%) percent
>
> Richard Antinora—forty (40%) percent

The agreement was silent about losses. There was no provision to compensate Antinora for any services other than the 40% profit clause.

Both parties complied with the agreement. Kessler provided the funds; Antinora supervised and delivered the finished house. This took over three years. Meanwhile, the real estate market soured. The house sold on September 1, 1991 for $420,000. The cost incurred in building and selling the house was $498,917.

Kessler was repaid all but $78,917 of the money he advanced pursuant to the contract. He also claimed unreimbursed interest of $85,440 for his self-characterized "loan" to the partnership. Kessler thus claimed a total loss of $164,357. He sought and obtained his summary judgment in the Law Division for 40% of this amount, or $65,742.80. No amount was presented on the value of Antinora's services over the three-year period as general contractor.

Antinora contended that the agreement was basically for a joint venture, silent as to losses, and that both parties risked and lost their unrecovered contributions—Kessler's money and Antinora's labor. The Law Division judge disagreed. [Applying New Jersey's Uniform Partnership Law, the] judge ruled that Antinora was liable for 40% of Kessler's monetary losses and inferentially rejected any recognition of Antinora's "in kind" loss.

III

We conclude that New Jersey's allegedly applicable section of the Uniform Partnership Law does not control here because of the specific terms of the agreement between the parties. The pertinent statutory section states:

> [. . .] The rights and duties of the partners in relation to the partnership shall be determined, subject to any agreement between them, by the following rules:
>
> a.   Each partner shall be repaid his contributions, whether by way of capital or advances to the partnership property and share equally in the profits and surplus remaining after all liabilities, including those to partners, are satisfied; and must contribute towards the losses, whether of capital or otherwise, sustained by the partnership according to his share in the profits. [. . .]

We find the agreement controlling over the statute. The agreement said that upon sale of the house "and after deducting all monies expended by Robert Kessler plus interest," fees, and other costs the "parties [Kessler and Antinora] shall divide net profits" 60% and 40%. We conclude that the agreement evinced a clear intent that Kessler would be repaid his investment from the sale of the house only, not by Antinora. There is no suggestion in the agreement that any of Kessler's risked and lost money would be repaid in part by Antinora. Nor is there any suggestion that Antinora's risked labor would be repaid in part by Kessler.

We find particularly persuasive the reasoning of the California Supreme Court in *Kovacik v. Reed*, 315 P.2d 314 (Cal. 1957). There the parties orally agreed to participate in a kitchen remodeling venture for Sears Roebuck & Company. Kovacik agreed to invest $10,000 in the venture and Reed agreed to become the job estimator and supervisor. They agreed to share the profits on a 50–50 basis. Possible losses were not discussed. Despite their efforts, the venture was unsuccessful and [Kovacik lost $8,680 of his investment.] Kovacik sued Reed to recover one-half the money losses he endured. [. . .]

The California Supreme Court acknowledged the general rule of partnership law that in the absence of an agreement, "the law presumes that partners and joint adventurers intended to participate equally in the profits and losses of the common enterprise, irrespective of any inequality in the amounts each contributed to the capital employed in the venture, with the losses being shared by them in the same proportions as they share the profits." [. . .]

The California court then observed that this "general rule" did not [apply] where one party contributed the money and the other the labor, stating:

> However, it appears that in the cases in which the above stated general rule has been applied, each of the parties had contributed capital consisting of either money or land or other tangible property, or else was to receive compensation for services rendered to the common undertaking which was to be paid before computation of the profits or losses. Where, however, as in the present case, one partner or joint adventurer contributes the money capital as against the other's skill and labor, all the cases cited, and which our research has discovered, hold that neither party is liable to the other for contribution for any loss sustained. Thus, upon loss of the money the party who contributed it is not entitled to recover any part of it from the party who contributed only services. [. . .]

The rationale which the California decision and the earlier cited cases adopted was where one party contributes money and the other services, in the event of a loss, each loses his own capital—one in the form of money, the other in labor. *Ibid.* A corollary view was that the parties have implicitly agreed, by their conduct and contract, to share profits and that their contributions of money and sweat equity have been valued in an equal ratio. Thus, upon the loss of both some money and labor, the loss falls upon each proportionately without any legal recourse. Thus, Kovacik lost $8,680 of his $10,000 while Reed lost all of his labor.

Likewise, in the case before us, Kessler lost some of his money—$65,472, plus disputed interest, but Antinora lost all of the value of his labor on the three-year project. The Arizona Court of Appeals in *Ellingson v. Sloan,* has also recognized that in a joint venture "[t]he term 'losses' is not limited to monetary losses, but includes time expenditures and out-of-pocket expenses, especially where one party in a joint venture furnishes property and the other only services." id, citing *Kovacik v. Reed.* The point of the Arizona case is that rendering services to an ultimately losing venture represents a valuable contribution, even though the laboring venturer risked no money capital. [. . .]

We conclude that the "JOINT VENTURE PARTNERSHIP AGREEMENT" here did contemplate repayment to Kessler of his investment but only from the proceeds of the sale of the house, not from his coventurer Antinora. This is what the parties said, the only truly reliable evidence of what they intended. Our interpretation of the agreement between the parties accords with the result reached under the common-law cases discussed, and with our overall sense of fairness. Each party shoulders a loss, one in determinative dollars; the other in labor, difficult, if not impossible, to quantify. The parties did not think about losses in casting their agreement and any attempt by the law now to reconstruct their then non-existent intent on the subject would be speculative.

Reversed for entry of summary judgment for the defendant Antinora.

E. PARTNERSHIP DISSOCIATION AND DISSOLUTION

1. DISSOCIATION

a. PARTNERS' DISSOCIATION GENERALLY

Revised Uniform Partnership Act
Section 601—Events Causing Dissociation.

A person is dissociated as a partner when:

(1) the partnership knows or has notice of the person's express will to withdraw as a partner, but, if the person has specified a withdrawal date later than the date the partnership knew or had notice, on that later date;

(2) an event stated in the partnership agreement as causing the person's dissociation occurs;

(3) the person is expelled as a partner pursuant to the partnership agreement;

(4) the person is expelled as a partner by the affirmative vote or consent of all the other partners if:

    (A) it is unlawful to carry on the partnership business with the person as a partner;

    (B) there has been a transfer of all of the person's transferable interest in the partnership, other than:

        (i)   a transfer for security purposes; or

        (ii) a charging order in effect under Section 504 which has not been foreclosed;

    (C) the person is an entity and:

        (i)   the partnership notifies the person that it will be expelled as a partner because the person has filed a statement of dissolution or the equivalent, the person has been administratively dissolved, the person's charter or the equivalent has been revoked, or the person's right to conduct business has been suspended by the person's jurisdiction of formation; and

        (ii) not later than 90 days after the notification, the statement of dissolution or the equivalent has not been withdrawn, rescinded, or revoked, or the person's charter or the equivalent or right to conduct business has not been reinstated; or

(D) the person is an unincorporated entity that has been dissolved and whose activities and affairs are being wound up;

(5) on application by the partnership or another partner, the person is expelled as a partner by judicial order because the person:

(A) has engaged or is engaging in wrongful conduct that has affected adversely and materially, or will affect adversely and materially, the partnership's business;

(B) has committed willfully or persistently, or is committing willfully or persistently, a material breach of the partnership agreement or a duty or obligation under Section 409; or

(C) has engaged or is engaging in conduct relating to the partnership's business which makes it not reasonably practicable to carry on the business with the person as a partner;

(6) the person:

(A) becomes a debtor in bankruptcy;

(B) signs an assignment for the benefit of creditors; or

(C) seeks, consents to, or acquiesces in the appointment of a trustee, receiver, or liquidator of the person or of all or substantially all the person's property;

(7) in the case of an individual:

(A) the individual dies;

(B) a guardian or general conservator for the individual is appointed; or

(C) a court orders that the individual has otherwise become incapable of performing the individual's duties as a partner under this [act] or the partnership agreement; [. . .]

(15) the partnership dissolves and completes winding up.

Section 602—Power to Dissociate as Partners; Wrongful Dissociation.

(a) A person has the power to dissociate as a partner at any time, rightfully or wrongfully, by withdrawing as a partner by express will under Section 601(1).

(b) A person's dissociation as a partner is wrongful only if the dissociation:

(1) is in breach of an express provision of the partnership agreement; or

(2) in the case of a partnership for a definite term or particular undertaking, occurs before the expiration of the term or the completion of the undertaking and:

(A) the person withdraws as a partner by express will, unless the withdrawal follows not later than 90 days after another person's dissociation by death or otherwise under Section 601(6) through (10) or wrongful dissociation under this subsection;

(B) the person is expelled as a partner by judicial order under Section 601(5);

(C) the person is dissociated under Section 601(6); or

(D) in the case of a person that is not a trust other than a business trust, an estate, or an individual, the person is expelled or otherwise dissociated because it willfully dissolved or terminated.

(c) A person that wrongfully dissociates as a partner is liable to the partnership and to the other partners for damages caused by the dissociation. The liability is in addition to any debt, obligation, or other liability of the partner to the partnership or the other partners.

Section 603—Effect of Dissociation.

(a) If a person's dissociation results in a dissolution and winding up of the partnership business, [Article] 8 applies; otherwise, [Article] 7 applies.

(b) If a person is dissociated as a partner:

(1) the person's right to participate in the management and conduct of the partnership's business terminates, except as otherwise provided in Section 802(c); and

(2) the person's duties and obligations under Section 409 end with regard to matters arising and events occurring after the person's dissociation, except to the extent the partner participates in winding up the partnership's business pursuant to Section 802.

(c) A person's dissociation does not of itself discharge the person from any debt, obligation, or other liability to the partnership or the other partners which the person incurred while a partner.

Corrales v. Corrales
198 Cal.App.4th 221 (2011)

[. . .]

FACTS

The brothers Corrales, Rudy and Richard, formed RC Electronics (RCE) in 1989, according to a written partnership agreement with an indefinite term. RCE repaired, refurbished, and sold computer tape drives. The brothers agreed that Rudy would be responsible for running the business, while Richard would supply financing and business know-how. [. . .]

Rudy's wife, Pamela, came on board shortly after RCE started up; she became the office manager and was responsible for preparing the company's business records. Their two daughters also worked for RCE.

The business was quite successful for several years, and Rudy and Richard realized substantial sums from it. In 2004, however, Richard discovered that Rudy, Pamela, and their daughters had formed a competing business, PK Electronics (PKE), to perform the same services performed by RCE, but without Richard. When Richard inquired about PKE, Rudy refused to tell him anything and cut off all communication with him.

Richard sent Rudy a "Notice of Dissociation," dated April 12, 2005, in which he stated that he was withdrawing from the partnership. Richard and Rudy sued each other in 2006 in separate lawsuits. Richard sued Rudy, Pamela, the two daughters, PKE, and RCE for breach of contract, breach of fiduciary duty, fraud, conspiracy, misappropriation of trade secrets, and accounting. Rudy sued Richard for breach of contract, common counts, fraud, negligent misrepresentation, breach of fiduciary duty, and "Cal. Corp.Code, § 16703."

[. . .] The court adopted Rudy's expert's valuation [of the business for buyout purposes]. The court also found that Rudy had concealed the existence of PKE from Richard, but held that Richard had not proved any damages arising from the concealment.

Richard has appealed on two issues. First, he asserts that there was no evidence to support Rudy's expert's valuation of the business and that the court should have picked one of his expert's valuations. Second, he asserts that he did prove damages arising from Rudy's breach of his fiduciary duty to RCE by forming and doing business through PKE.

DISCUSSION

[. . .]

I.   Dissociation vs. Dissolution

[. . .] The California Revised Uniform Partnership Act (RUPA) applies to the dispute between Rudy and Richard. The RUPA defines a partnership as "an association of two or more persons to carry on as coowners a business for profit . . . ." (§ 16101, subd. (9).) A " '[p]artnership at will' " is one "in which the partners have not agreed to remain partners until the expiration of a definite term or the completion of a particular undertaking." (§ 16101, subd. (11).)

A.   Dissociation

The RUPA, adopted in 1996, applies to all partnerships as of 1999. Section 16601, subdivision (1) allows dissociation upon "[t]he partnership's having notice of the partner's express will to withdraw as a partner or on a later date specified by the partner." Under Section

16701, subdivision (a), the partnership must buy out the dissociated partner's interest in the partnership. Section 16701, subdivision (b) sets out the process by which the interest is to be valued.

Dissociation was a new feature of the RUPA, one not present in former law. Under former law, a partnership was simply a group of people; when a partner died, withdrew, or was expelled, the partnership automatically dissolved and had to be reconstituted, unless the partnership agreement specifically provided otherwise. Dissociation permits the remaining partners to carry on partnership business without the withdrawing partner and without having to start from scratch.

B. Dissolution

Partnership dissolution occurs "[i]n a partnership at will, by the express will to dissolve and wind up the partnership business of at least half of the partners, including partners ... who have dissociated within the preceding 90 days, and for which purpose a dissociation under paragraph (1) of Section 16601 constitutes an expression of that partner's will to dissolve and wind up the partnership business." (§ 16801, subd. (1).) The procedure to be followed upon dissolution, however, differs from the buyout procedure of section 16701. There is no buyout. Instead, the partnership's creditors are paid, and then the partners settle accounts between or among themselves, pursuant to section 16807.

When Richard withdrew from RCE, the partnership dissolved by operation of law; by definition, a partnership must consist of at least two persons. (§ 16101, subd. (9).) A person cannot dissociate from a dissolved partnership, and the buyout rule of section 16701 does not apply to a two-person partnership when one partner leaves. When that happens, the dissolution procedures take over. The partnership is wound up, its business is completed, and the partners make whatever adjustments are necessary to their own accounts after paying the creditors. (§ 16807.)

Section 16701 is found in a chapter of the RUPA that applies to a "partner's dissociation when business [is] not wound up." The purpose of dissociation is to allow the partnership to continue with the remaining partners. When a partner withdraws from a two-person partnership, however, the business cannot continue as before. One person cannot carry on a business as a partnership. (§ 16101, subd. (9).

The use of the buyout remedy of section 16701 was error, and we must reverse the judgment and remand it to the trial court with instructions to enter a judicial dissolution of the partnership under sections 16801 and 16807. The parties could peruse these code sections themselves and stipulate to a distribution of assets after the creditors are paid to minimize the time they spend before the trial judge. Or they can retry the case using the correct procedure.

II. Damages for Breach of Fiduciary Duty

Substantial evidence supports the trial court's conclusion Rudy formed PKE to compete with RCE, but without Richard. Section 16404 identifies "refrain[ing] from competing with the partnership in the conduct of the partnership business before the dissolution of the partnership" as one aspect of a partner's duty of loyalty toward the partnership and the other partners. (§ 16404, subd. (b)(3).) The court found, however, that Richard had not proved any damages arising from the breach; Richard appeals from this ruling.

A more fundamental issue is whether Richard was entitled to damages at all. Ordinarily partners cannot sue each other for damages based on partnership business, at least not until there has been an action for dissolution and accounting. [. . .]

In this case, there was no evidence showing that Rudy converted to his own use all the partnership assets or destroyed the business. [. . .] Richard was the one who withdrew from the partnership, thereby terminating it. Accordingly it does not appear the exception to the general rule applies here.

The parties must do an accounting, in order to comply with section 16807. If, as seems likely, the court finds that PKE [. . .] improperly competed with RCE, then any funds earned by these entities that could have been earned by RCE can be folded into the accounting and distributed according to section 16807.

DISPOSITION

The matter is reversed and remanded to the trial court for entry of an order of dissolution of the RCE partnership under sections 16801 and 16807. Any funds the court determines were improperly obtained by Rudy's competing business entities are to be included in the assets of the partnership for winding up purposes. The parties shall bear their own costs on appeal.

b.   PARTNER'S DISSOCIATION WITHOUT WINDING UP THE
     PARTNERSHIP BUSINESS

Revised Uniform Partnership Act

Section 701—Purchase of Interest of Person Dissociated as Partners.

(a) If a person is dissociated as a partner without the dissociation resulting in a dissolution and winding up of the partnership business under Section 801, the partnership shall cause the person's interest in the partnership to be purchased for a buyout price determined pursuant to subsection (b).

(b) The buyout price of the interest of a person dissociated as a partner is the amount that would have been distributable to the person under Section 806(b) if, on the date of dissociation, the assets of the partnership were sold and the partnership were wound up, with the sale price equal to the greater of:

(1) the liquidation value; or

(2) the value based on a sale of the entire business as a going concern without the person.

(c) Interest accrues on the buyout price from the date of dissociation to the date of payment, but damages for wrongful dissociation under Section 602(b), and all other amounts owing, whether or not presently due, from the person dissociated as a partner to the partnership, must be offset against the buyout price.

(d) A partnership shall defend, indemnify, and hold harmless a person dissociated as a partner whose interest is being purchased against all partnership liabilities, whether incurred before or after the dissociation, except liabilities incurred by an act of the person under Section 702.

(e) If no agreement for the purchase of the interest of a person dissociated as a partner is reached not later than 120 days after a written demand for payment, the partnership shall pay, or cause to be paid, in money to the person the amount the partnership estimates to be the buyout price and accrued interest, reduced by any offsets and accrued interest under subsection (c). [. . .]

(h) A person that wrongfully dissociates as a partner before the expiration of a definite term or the completion of a particular undertaking is not entitled to payment of any part of the buyout price until the expiration of the term or completion of the undertaking, unless the person establishes to the satisfaction of the court that earlier payment will not cause undue hardship to the business of the partnership. A deferred payment must be adequately secured and bear interest. [. . .]

Section 702—Power to Bind and Liability of Person Dissociated as Partner.

(a) After a person is dissociated as a partner without the dissociation resulting in a dissolution and winding up of the partnership business and before the partnership is merged out of existence, converted, or domesticated under [Article] 11, or dissolved, the partnership is bound by an act of the person only if:

(1) the act would have bound the partnership under Section 301 before dissociation; and

(2) at the time the other party enters into the transaction:

(A) less than two years has passed since the dissociation; and

(B) the other party does not know or have notice of the dissociation and reasonably believes that the person is a partner.

(b) If a partnership is bound under subsection (a), the person dissociated as a partner which caused the partnership to be bound is liable:

(1) to the partnership for any damage caused to the partnership arising from the obligation incurred under subsection (a); and

(2) if a partner or another person dissociated as a partner is liable for the obligation, to the partner or other person for any damage caused to the partner or other person arising from the liability.

Section 703—Liability of Person Dissociated as Partner to Other Persons.

(a) Except as otherwise provided in subsection (b), a person dissociated as a partner is not liable for a partnership obligation incurred after dissociation.

(b) A person that is dissociated as a partner is liable on a transaction entered into by the partnership after the dissociation only if:

(1) a partner would be liable on the transaction; and

(2) at the time the other party enters into the transaction:

(A) less than two years has passed since the dissociation; and

(B) the other party does not have knowledge or notice of the dissociation and reasonably believes that the person is a partner.

(c) By agreement with a creditor of a partnership and the partnership, a person dissociated as a partner may be released from liability for a debt, obligation, or other liability of the partnership.

(d) A person dissociated as a partner is released from liability for a debt, obligation, or other liability of the partnership if the partnership's creditor, with knowledge or notice of the person's dissociation but without the person's consent, agrees to a material alteration in the nature or time of payment of the debt, obligation, or other liability.

Section 704—Statement of Dissociation.

(a) A person dissociated as a partner or the partnership may deliver to the [Secretary of State] for filing a statement of dissociation stating the name of the partnership and that the person has dissociated from the partnership.

(b) A statement of dissociation is a limitation on the authority of a person dissociated as a partner for the purposes of Section 303.

Section 705—Continued Use of Partnership Name.

Continued use of a partnership name, or the name of a person dissociated as a partner as part of the partnership name, by partners continuing the business does not of itself make the person dissociated as a partner liable for an obligation of the partners or the partnership continuing the business.

Section 801—Events Causing Dissolution.

A partnership is dissolved, and its business must be wound up, upon the occurrence of any of the following:

(1) in a partnership at will, the partnership knows or has notice of a person's express will to withdraw as a partner, other than a partner that has dissociated under Section 601(2) through (10), but, if the person has specified a withdrawal date later than the date the partnership knew or had notice, on the later date;

(2) in a partnership for a definite term or particular undertaking:

(A) within 90 days after a person's dissociation by death or otherwise under Section 601(6) through (10) or wrongful dissociation under Section 602(b), the affirmative vote or consent of at least half of the remaining partners to wind up the partnership business, for which purpose a person's rightful dissociation pursuant to Section 602(b)(2)(A) constitutes that partner's consent to wind up the partnership business;

(B) the affirmative vote or consent of all the partners to wind up the partnership business; or

(C) the expiration of the term or the completion of the undertaking;

(3) an event or circumstance that the partnership agreement states causes dissolution;

(4) on application by a partner, the entry by [the appropriate court] of an order dissolving the partnership on the grounds that:

(A) the conduct of all or substantially all the partnership's business is unlawful;

(B) the economic purpose of the partnership is likely to be unreasonably frustrated;

(C) another partner has engaged in conduct relating to the partnership business which makes it not reasonably practicable to carry on the business in partnership with that partner; or

(D) it is otherwise not reasonably practicable to carry on the partnership business in conformity with the partnership agreement;

(5) on application by a transferee, the entry by [the appropriate court] of an order dissolving the partnership on the ground that it is equitable to wind up the partnership business:

(A) after the expiration of the term or completion of the undertaking, if the partnership was for a definite term or particular undertaking at the time of the transfer or entry of the charging order that gave rise to the transfer; or

(B) at any time, if the partnership was a partnership at will at the time of the transfer or entry of the charging order that gave rise to the transfer; or

(6) the passage of 90 consecutive days during which the partnership does not have at least two partners.

Robertson v. Jacobs Cattle Co.

285 Neb. 859 (2013)

[. . .]

I.   FACTS

Jacobs Cattle Company is a family partnership that was formally organized on January 1, 1979. The original partners were Leonard Jacobs and his wife, Ardith Jacobs; their children Dennis Jacobs, Duane Jacobs, and Patricia Robertson; and the respective spouses of those children, Debbie Jacobs, Carolyn Sue Jacobs, and James E. Robertson. At some point, Debbie withdrew from the partnership and Dennis acquired her interest.

Leonard died in March 1997. Probate proceedings determined that his capital interest in the partnership at the time of his death was 34 percent.

1.   PARTNERSHIP AGREEMENT

The operative partnership agreement became effective on June 19, 1997. The partners were identified as Ardith, in her capacity as trustee of the Leonard Jacobs Family Trust and in her capacity as trustee of the Ardith Jacobs Living Revocable Trust; Duane; Carolyn; Patricia; James; and Dennis.

Pertinent provisions of the agreement include the following:

4.   *TERM*

. . . This Partnership shall continue until terminated by mutual agreement, operation of law or as hereinafter provided. . . . .

7.   *MANAGEMENT*

Ardith Jacobs, Trustee of the Ardith Jacobs Living Revocable Trust shall have general management authority to conduct day to day business on behalf of the Partnership, and Ardith Jacobs shall have the authority to bind the Partnership; provided however, a vote of 6 Partners shall have authority to override a decision made by Ardith Jacobs. Votes can be cast by Partners as follows: [Ardith and Dennis each have two votes; Patricia, James, Duane, and Carolyn each have one vote.]

Matters that cannot be agreed upon shall be submitted to Arbitration as established hereinbelow. . . . .

11.   *PROFITS AND LOSSES*

The net profits and net losses of the Partnership shall be distributable or chargeable, as the case may be, to each of the Partners in proportion to the votes they have herein as set forth in paragraph 7. The term "net profits" and "net losses" shall mean the net profits and net losses of the Partnership as determined by generally accepted accounting principles. . . .

17. *QUARTERLY MEETING*

A quarterly meeting of all Partners shall be held on the first Monday following the close of the preceding quarter. The purpose of the meeting is to discuss business operations, profits, losses, capital accounts, income accounts, and all other Partnership business. . . . [. . .]

2. PARTNERSHIP BUSINESS

The partnership owns approximately 1,525 acres of land in Valley County. The land is mostly farmland and pasture and is unencumbered. A real estate appraiser valued the land as of January 1, 2011, at $4,545,000, and as of September 20, 2011, at $5,135,000. [. . .]

The partnership rented its land to others. Patricia and James, Dennis, and Duane and Carolyn all rented land from the partnership, although James did not sign a lease. At least some of the land was rented for less than its fair rental value.

Since June 19, 1997, the partnership has not returned a profit and there have been no distributions of net profits to the partners. Since Leonard's death, no partner has contributed new land or capital to the partnership.

3. PARTNERSHIP ISSUES

In July 2004, the attorney for the partnership sent a letter to the partners informing them that none of the tenants had paid their rent for 2004. There were no partnership meetings after January 2005. In late 2004 or early 2005, Ardith terminated the services of Robert D. Stowell as the attorney for the partnership. In April 2005, Ardith retained a new attorney for the partnership. In 2005, Ardith terminated the services of Mick Puckett as the accountant for the partnership and hired a new accountant. Puckett was the last certified public accountant agreeable to all of the partners, and Stowell was the last attorney agreeable to all partners.

In March 2005, Dennis and Patricia were involved in a physical altercation. As a result, Dennis pled no contest to criminal assault charges. On April 28, Patricia and James were served with a notice to quit the leased premises for nonpayment of rent. Around the same time, Duane was also notified that he needed to quit the premises he was leasing due to nonpayment of rent. Duane eventually paid his rent, but on May 4, the partnership sued Patricia and James for rents due for the years 2003 and 2004. Ardith alone made the decision to file the lawsuit. On August 11, a court entered judgment against Patricia for unpaid rent. The court did not enter judgment against James because his name was not on the lease. The land which the partnership had leased to Patricia was later rented to Dennis.

II. PROCEDURAL HISTORY

1.   PLEADINGS

In July 2007, appellants filed [. . .] for dissolution of the partnership against the partnership, Ardith, and Dennis (collectively appellees). The complaint sought a dissolution and winding up of the partnership under the Uniform Partnership Act of 1998 (1998 UPA). [. . .]

2.   SEPTEMBER 20, 2011, INTERLOCUTORY ORDER

After conducting a bench trial, the district court entered an order on September 20, 2011. The court concluded that appellants did not prove the occurrence of events authorizing dissolution [. . .] because (1) nothing had occurred to interfere with the partnership's ability to buy, own, and rent land; (2) no partners took steps to override decisions made by Ardith and "[j]ust because a partner does not like the decision of the managing partner does not make it impracticable to continue the partnership with that partner"; and (3) Ardith had not acted beyond the partner restrictions specified in the partnership agreement. The court reasoned that nothing had occurred to make the partnership agreement difficult or impossible with which to comply, and it dismissed appellants' dissolution claims.

However, the court found that appellants' failure to pay rent in a timely manner supported appellees' request that appellants be dissociated from the partnership [. . .]. The court reasoned that because the primary purpose of the partnership was to rent land, appellants' delinquency in paying rent materially and adversely affected the partnership business and made it not practicable for the partnership to carry on with appellants as partners. The court thus ordered dissociation of appellants by judicial expulsion [. . .] and ordered the partnership to purchase appellants' interests in the partnership [. . .]. The court specifically ordered the parties to prepare buyout proposals and found that the value of partnership assets was "to be determined as of the date of the dissociation, which is the date this judgment is filed."

3.   FINAL JUDGMENT

On November 4, 2011, the partnership filed a buyout proposal with the district court. The proposal set out the value of the partnership based on its assets and liabilities [. . .], and then proposed that each appellant be paid $275,941.96. Although the proposal did not contain mathematical calculations, it stated that this sum represented each appellant's "equal partnership fractional interest." [. . .]

Appellants filed written objections to the proposed buyout [. . .]. [. . .] Appellants submitted an alternative buyout proposal which [. . .] generally calculated the buyout price based on the provision in paragraph 11 of the partnership agreement allocating profit percentages to the partners' income accounts. The alternative buyout proposal generally requested that each appellant receive 12.5 percent of the partnership's liquidation value. [. . .]

[After much back and forth, t]he district court ultimately approved the partnership's proposed buyout, with minor alterations not related to appellants' stated objections. In computing the amount appellants were entitled to as a result of the required buyout, the district court arrived at a liquidation value for the partnership by subtracting the partnership's liabilities from its assets. The assets included the appreciated value of the partnership's land. The court then distributed the liquidation value to each partner based on his or her capital account, so appellants each received 5.33 percent of the total liquidation value. [. . .]

III. ASSIGNMENTS OF ERROR

Appellants assign, restated and summarized, that the district court erred in (1) failing to dissolve the partnership under § 67–439(5); (2) determining that James, Duane, and Carolyn failed to pay rent to the partnership and that all appellants engaged in wrongful conduct and should be dissociated from the partnership under § 67–431(5); (3) determining the amount of the buyouts of appellants and failing to include in the buyout amount of each appellant one-eighth of the net profits which would have resulted from capital gains arising from the liquidation of the partnership's assets. [. . .]

On cross-appeal, appellees assign that the district court erred in [ ] holding the date of dissociation was September 20, 2011, rather than May 2005, when appellants failed to pay their rents [. . .].

V.   ANALYSIS

The legal framework for our analysis is the 1998 UPA, which is Nebraska's counterpart to the model act known as the Revised Uniform Partnership Act (RUPA). [. . .]

The 1998 UPA replaced the original Uniform Partnership Act and brought about significant changes in partnership law. Prior law required an at-will partnership to dissolve upon any partner's expressed will to dissolve the partnership. RUPA, on which the 1998 UPA is based, sought to avoid mandatory dissolution of partnerships by making a partnership a distinct entity from its partners. As we noted in *Shoemaker v. Shoemaker,*

> "RUPA's underlying philosophy differs radically from [the original Uniform Partnership Act], thus laying the foundation for many of its innovative measures. RUPA adopts the "entity" theory of partnership as opposed to the "aggregate" theory that the [original Uniform Partnership Act] espouses. Under the aggregate theory, a partnership is characterized by the collection of its individual members, with the result being that if one of the partners dies or withdraws, the partnership ceases to exist. On the other hand, RUPA's entity theory allows for the partnership to continue even with the departure of a member because it views the partnership as 'an entity distinct from its partners.' "

RUPA, as embodied by our 1998 UPA, provides gap-filling rules that control only when a question is not resolved by the parties' express provisions in an agreement. The parties agree that this case must be resolved by application of the statutory principles of the 1998 UPA.

1. DISSOCIATION OR DISSOLUTION?

The parties are in general agreement that they cannot continue in partnership with each other. They differ as to the appropriate remedy to be employed in ending their relationship. Appellants contend that the partnership should have been dissolved. Appellees argue that the district court correctly dissociated appellants from the partnership because this allows the partnership itself to continue with Ardith and Dennis as its remaining partners.

The statutory provisions governing dissociation and dissolution are similar but not identical. Dissolution of a partnership is governed by § 67–439 [EDS.—see RUPA Section 801(4)], which provides that "[a] partnership is dissolved, and its business must be wound up, only upon the occurrence of any of the following events," which include

> (5)   On application by a partner, a judicial determination that:
>
> (a)   The economic purpose of the partnership is likely to be unreasonably frustrated;
>
> (b)   Another partner has engaged in conduct relating to the partnership business which makes it not reasonably practicable to carry on the business in partnership with that partner; or
>
> (c)   It is not otherwise reasonably practicable to carry on the partnership business in conformity with the partnership agreement[.]

The district court concluded that none of these circumstances existed because (1) nothing had occurred which would frustrate the partnership's ability to buy, sell, or own land, and (2) Ardith, as managing partner, had authority on behalf of the partnership to take the actions with which appellants disagreed.

Dissociation is a new concept introduced by RUPA "to denote the change in the relationship caused by a partner's ceasing to be associated in the carrying on of the business." Under RUPA, "the dissociation of a partner does not necessarily cause a dissolution and winding up of the business of the partnership." Section 67–431 [EDS.—see RUPA Section 601(4)], lists events which may trigger a partner's dissociation, including

> (5)   On application by the partnership or another partner, the partner's expulsion by judicial determination because:
>
> (a)   The partner engaged in wrongful conduct that adversely and materially affected the partnership business;

(b) The partner willfully or persistently committed a material breach of the partnership agreement or of a duty owed to the partnership or the other partners under section 67–424; or

(c) The partner engaged in conduct relating to the partnership business which makes it not reasonably practicable to carry on the business in partnership with the partner.

In this case, the district court concluded that the grounds for dissociation stated in § 67–431(5)(a) and (c) were met by the failure of appellants to pay timely rent for the land leased from the partnership.

With these principles in mind, we first consider appellants' argument that the district court erred in determining that there were grounds to dissociate them from the partnership. Given that the sole business of the partnership was to own farmland which it leased to others, we have no difficulty concluding that the failure of appellants who executed leases to pay timely rents constituted wrongful conduct that adversely and materially affected the partnership business and made it not reasonably practical to carry on the partnership business with the existing partners. And we are not persuaded by the argument that James bore no responsibility for the nonpayment of rent because he had not signed a lease. [. . .] James testified that he owed money to the partnership prior to 2010. There is a reasonable inference that James knew that rent had not been paid to the partnership of which he and Patricia were both partners. Thus, regardless of whether he was legally obligated on the lease, James engaged in conduct which satisfied the grounds for dissociation stated in § 67–431(5)(a) and (c) to the same extent as the other appellants.

Next, we consider whether the district court erred in concluding that appellants failed to establish grounds for dissolution of the partnership. Appellees argue the district court correctly decided this issue because no wrongdoing on the part of Ardith or Dennis has been proved. But even appellees acknowledge that "much acrimony exists between and among the parties." At oral argument, appellees' counsel conceded that there were unspecified grounds for dissolution of the partnership, but argued that dissociation was nevertheless the appropriate remedy. We perceive this concession as agreement that the somewhat autocratic manner in which Ardith conducted the affairs of the partnership in recent years, even if not in violation of the partnership agreement, would constitute grounds for dissolution under § 67–439(5)(b), i.e., "conduct relating to the partnership business which makes it not reasonably practicable to carry on the business in partnership with that partner." We find no other possible grounds for dissolution. As we have noted, such conduct is also grounds for dissociation under § 67–431(5)(c), and the record supports the district court's determination that appellants engaged in such conduct. Thus, we conclude that there are grounds for dissolution of the partnership under § 67–439(5)(b) and dissociation of appellants under § 67–431(5)(a) and (c).

Under the RUPA model upon which our statutes are based, the dissociation of a partner does not necessarily cause a dissolution and winding up of the partnership's business. Generally, the partnership must be dissolved and its business wound up only upon the occurrence of one of the events listed in § 801 of RUPA, upon which Nebraska's § 67–439 is based. The question we must resolve is whether dissolution is mandatory where the conduct of multiple partners constitutes grounds for dissolution under § 67–439(5)(b) and also constitutes grounds for dissociation pursuant to § 67–431(5)(c).

We have found no authority on this precise point. But the decision of the Supreme Court of Connecticut in *Brennan v. Brennan Associates* provides helpful guidance. In that case, the court concluded that a single partner's conduct fell within Connecticut's statutory equivalents of our §§ 67–431(5)(c) and 67–439(5)(b) such that it was not practicable for the remaining partners to carry on the business of the partnership with that partner. The court rejected an argument that the conduct would justify judicial dissolution of the partnership but not dissociation of the offending partner, concluding that "an irreparable deterioration of a relationship between partners is a valid basis to order dissolution, and, therefore, is a valid basis for the alternative remedy of dissociation." A Kansas appellate court in *Giles v. Giles Land Co., L.P.* followed the reasoning of Brennan in concluding that a court did not err in dissociating a partner where the evidence established that his conduct would justify either dissociation or dissolution under that state's counterparts to our §§ 67–431(5)(c) and 67–439(5)(b).

We perceive no good reason to apply a different rule where the conduct of multiple partners makes it "not reasonably practicable to carry on the business in partnership" with each other. Construing the dissolution remedy as mandatory in this circumstance would be contrary to the entity theory of partnership embodied in RUPA. As we noted in *Shoemaker,* a main purpose of RUPA is "to prevent mandatory dissolution" of a partnership. Accordingly, we hold that where a court determines that the conduct of one or more partners constitutes grounds for dissociation by judicial expulsion under § 67–431(5)(c) and dissolution under § 67–439(5)(b), and there are no other grounds for dissolution, the court may in its discretion order either dissociation by expulsion of one or more partners or dissolution of the partnership.

We conclude that dissociation by judicial expulsion of appellants is an appropriate remedy under the facts of this case. Individually and in trust, Ardith and Dennis have a capital interest in the partnership of approximately 78 percent. Pursuant to the partnership agreement, Ardith has general management authority to conduct the day-to-day business on behalf of the partnership. We agree with the finding of the district court that there is no apparent reason why the partnership cannot continue to exist and function in accordance with the partnership agreement with Ardith and Dennis as its sole partners. Accordingly, we conclude that the first and second assignments of error as restated above are without merit.

2. ISSUES PERTAINING TO BUYOUT PRICE

The remaining issues pertain to the district court's calculation of the buyout price which the dissociated partners are to receive for their interests in the partnership. This price is governed by § 67–434(2) [EDS.—see RUPA Section 701(b)], which provides:

> The buyout price of a dissociated partner's interest is the amount that would have been distributable to the dissociating partner under subsection (2) of section 67–445 if, on the date of dissociation, the assets of the partnership were sold at a price equal to the greater of the liquidation value or the value based on a sale of the entire business as a going concern without the dissociated partner and the partnership were wound up as of that date. Interest must be paid from the date of dissociation to the date of payment.

Section 67–445(2) [EDS.—see RUPA Section 806], provides in pertinent part:

> Each partner is entitled to a settlement of all partnership accounts upon winding up the partnership business. In settling accounts among the partners, profits and losses that result from the liquidation of the partnership assets must be credited and charged to the partners' accounts. The partnership shall make a distribution to a partner in an amount equal to any excess of the credits over the charges in the partner's account. A partner shall contribute to the partnership an amount equal to any excess of the charges over the credits in the partner's account but excluding from the calculation charges attributable to an obligation for which the partner is not personally liable under section 67–418.

(a)   Date of Dissociation

The district court determined the date of dissociation was September 20, 2011 the date it entered its order that appellants were dissociated by judicial expulsion [. . .]. [. . .] [A]ppellees contend that the court should have found the date of dissociation to be in May 2005, when the nonpayment of rent which the district court determined to be grounds for dissociation occurred. [. . .]

[. . .] The events which may result in dissociation are listed in § 67–431 [EDS.—see RUPA Section 601]. Some of these, such as a partner's withdrawal or expulsion pursuant to the partnership agreement, occur without any judicial intervention. But in this case, the dissociation occurred as a result of expulsion by judicial determination pursuant to

§ 67–431(5). Appellants were not dissociated from the partnership until the district court determined that they had engaged in conduct described in § 67–431(5)(a) and (c). [. . .]

(b) Appellants' Share of Appreciated Value of Land

The land owned by the partnership is a capital asset. Under the operative partnership agreement, the partners each had a capital account. The value of the capital account was "directly proportionate to [each partner's] original Capital contributions as later adjusted for draws taken from the Partnership." At the time of dissociation, the capital account of each appellant was approximately 5.33 percent of the total capital in the partnership.

Each partner also had an income account under the partnership agreement. Net profits and net losses of the partnership were to be "credited or debited to the individual income accounts [of each partner] as soon as practicable after the close of each fiscal year." The agreement provided that the "term[s] 'net profits' and 'net losses' shall mean the net profits and net losses of the Partnership as determined by generally accepted accounting principles." It further noted that "[t]he net profits and net losses of the Partnership" were distributable or chargeable "to each of the Partners in proportion to the votes they have." Under the agreement, Ardith had two votes (one as trustee for each trust), Dennis had two votes, and appellants each had one vote, for a total of eight votes. Thus, appellants each had a 12.5 percent share of net profits and losses in their income account.

The district court expressly found that appellants' "interests in the partnership shall be purchased by the partnership as required by Neb.Rev.Stat.Sec. 67–434." In its ruling, the district court considered the value of the partnership's assets, including the appreciated value of the land, less the partnership's liabilities, and arrived at a liquidation value for the partnership. It then accepted appellees' argument that the proper buyout price was calculated by applying each partner's capital account percentage to the partnership's total liquidation value. [. . .]

It is clear from the plain language of § 67–434(2) that the proper calculation must be based upon the assumption that the partnership assets, here the land, were sold on the date of dissociation, even though no actual sale occurs. Here, the initial question is whether selling the partnership land on the date of dissociation would result in a capital gain and "profits" in the context of § 67–445(2). We consider this to be a question of statutory interpretation.

The term "capital gain" means "profit realized when a capital asset is sold or exchanged." The term "profit" is generally defined as the "excess of revenues over expenditures in a business transaction." *Pittman v. Western Engineering Co.* We are required to give the language of a statute its plain and ordinary meaning. Accordingly, we conclude that the capital gain which would be realized upon a hypothetical liquidation of the partnership's land on the date of dissociation (as required by § 67–434(2)) would constitute "profits" within the meaning of the phrase in § 67–445(2).

VI. CONCLUSION

Based upon our de novo review and for the reasons discussed, we conclude that the district court did not err in dissociating appellants from the partnership by judicial expulsion as of September 20, 2011. We also conclude that the district court did not err in declining to dissolve the partnership. [. . .]

2. DISSOLUTION, WINDING UP, AND TERMINATION

Revised Uniform Partnership Act
Section 802—Winding Up.

(a) A dissolved partnership shall wind up its business and, except as otherwise provided in Section 803, the partnership continues after dissolution only for the purpose of winding up.

(b) In winding up its business, the partnership:

(1) shall discharge the partnership's debts, obligations, and other liabilities, settle and close the partnership's business, and marshal and distribute the assets of the partnership; and

(2) may:

(A) deliver to the [Secretary of State] for filing a statement of dissolution stating the name of the partnership and that the partnership is dissolved;

(B) preserve the partnership business and property as a going concern for a reasonable time;

(C) prosecute and defend actions and proceedings, whether civil, criminal, or administrative;

(D) transfer the partnership's property;

(E) settle disputes by mediation or arbitration;

(F) deliver to the [Secretary of State] for filing a statement of termination stating the name of the partnership and that the partnership is terminated; and

(G) perform other acts necessary or appropriate to the winding up.

(c) A person whose dissociation as a partner resulted in dissolution may participate in winding up as if still a partner, unless the dissociation was wrongful. [. . .]

Section 804—Power to Bind Partnership After Dissolution.

(a) A partnership is bound by a partner's act after dissolution which:

(1) is appropriate for winding up the partnership business; or

(2) would have bound the partnership under Section 301 before dissolution if, at the time the other party enters into the transaction, the other party does not know or have notice of the dissolution.

(b) A person dissociated as a partner binds a partnership through an act occurring after dissolution if:

(1) at the time the other party enters into the transaction:

(A) less than two years has passed since the dissociation; and

(B) the other party does not know or have notice of the dissociation and reasonably believes that the person is a partner; and

(2) the act:

(A) is appropriate for winding up the partnership's business; or

(B) would have bound the partnership under Section 301 before dissolution and at the time the other party enters into the transaction the other party does not know or have notice of the dissolution.

Section 805—Liability After Dissolution of Partner and Person Dissociated as Partner.

(a) If a partner having knowledge of the dissolution causes a partnership to incur an obligation under Section 804(a) by an act that is not appropriate for winding up the partnership business, the partner is liable:

(1) to the partnership for any damage caused to the partnership arising from the obligation; and

(2) if another partner or person dissociated as a partner is liable for the obligation, to that other partner or person for any damage caused to that other partner or person arising from the liability.

(b) Except as otherwise provided in subsection (c), if a person dissociated as a partner causes a partnership to incur an obligation under Section 804(b), the person is liable:

(1) to the partnership for any damage caused to the partnership arising from the obligation; and

(2) if a partner or another person dissociated as a partner is liable for the obligation, to the partner or other person for any damage caused to the partner or other person arising from the obligation.

(c) A person dissociated as a partner is not liable under subsection (b) if:

(1) Section 802(c) permits the person to participate in winding up; and

(2) the act that causes the partnership to be bound under Section 804(b) is appropriate for winding up the partnership's business.

Section 806—Disposition of Assets in Winding Up; When Contributions Required.

(a) In winding up its business, a partnership shall apply its assets, including the contributions required by this section, to discharge the partnership's obligations to creditors, including partners that are creditors.

(b) After a partnership complies with subsection (a), any surplus must be distributed in the following order, subject to any charging order in effect under Section 504:

(1) to each person owning a transferable interest that reflects contributions made and not previously returned, an amount equal to the value of the unreturned contributions; and

(2) among persons owning transferable interests in proportion to their respective rights to share in distributions immediately before the dissolution of the partnership.

(c) If a partnership's assets are insufficient to satisfy all its obligations under subsection (a), [. . .], the following rules apply:

(1) Each person that was a partner when the obligation was incurred and that has not been released from the obligation under Section 703(c) and (d) shall contribute to the partnership for the purpose of enabling the partnership to satisfy the obligation. The contribution due from each of those persons is in proportion to the right to receive distributions in the capacity of a partner in effect for each of those persons when the obligation was incurred.

(2) If a person does not contribute the full amount required under paragraph (1) with respect to an unsatisfied obligation of the partnership, the other persons required to contribute by paragraph (1) on account of the obligation shall contribute the additional amount necessary to discharge the obligation. The additional contribution due from each of those other persons is in proportion to the right to receive distributions in the capacity of a partner in effect for each of those other persons when the obligation was incurred.

(3) If a person does not make the additional contribution required by paragraph (2), further additional contributions are determined and due in the same manner as provided in that paragraph.

(d) A person that makes an additional contribution under subsection (c)(2) or (3) may recover from any person whose failure to contribute under subsection (c)(1) or (2) necessitated the additional contribution. A person may not recover under this subsection more than the amount additionally contributed. A person's liability under this subsection may not exceed the amount the person failed to contribute.

(e) If a partnership does not have sufficient surplus to comply with subsection (b)(1), any surplus must be distributed among the owners of transferable interests in proportion to the value of the respective unreturned contributions.

(f) All distributions made under subsections (b) and (c) must be paid in money.

Bertolla v. Bill
774 So.2d 497 (Alabama 1999)

This case involves a family farming partnership, A. Bertolla & Sons ("ABS"), which was formed in Baldwin County, in the early 1900's. [. . .] Alessandro Bertolla immigrated to Baldwin County, and began a farming operation in the early 1900's. [. . .]

Alessandro died in 1935 and his five sons continued to operate ABS. [. . .]

In October, 1954, the four surviving brothers, Angelo, Rudolph, John P. and Alexander entered into the first written partnership agreement. [. . .]

In 1979, a new partnership agreement was drafted. The four new partners added in 1979 were Viola Bertolla and Mary Bertolla Bill, sisters of the original partners; John Eddie Bertolla, the son of John P. Bertolla; and Andy Bertolla, the son of Alexander Bertolla, each acquiring 10% of the partnership. They joined Rudolph F. Bertolla and John P. Bertolla who each owned 30%. The new partners paid the then book value of a 10 percent partnership interest; approximately $115,000 each. A formal partnership agreement was drawn up and signed by all of the partners. It read in pertinent part, as follows:

> 5. The term during which the partnership shall continue is for an indefinite period and until terminated as herein provided or by operation of law. [. . .]
>
> 6. The parties shall each draw from the partnership such sums and at such times as may be mutually agreed upon and in the proportions hereinafter set forth shall share in all profits and losses of the business as follows: [Rudolph F. Bertolla 30%; John P. Bertolla 30%; Viola Bertolla 10%; Mary Bill 10%; John Edward Bertolla 10%; Alexander A. Bertolla 10%.]
>
> 7. Each of the partners is to devote such time and attention to the affairs of the business as may be deemed necessary by the partnership and is not to engage in any other competing business without the consent of the other partners.
>
> 8. Proper books of account shall be kept [. . .].
>
> 9. No partner shall, without the consent of the other partners, use the firm's name, credit or property for other than partnership purposes, or sign or endorse negotiable paper or become surety for third persons, or engage in any speculation or knowingly do any act by which the interests of the partnership

shall be imperiled or prejudiced, except with the written consent of the other partners.

10. Any partner may withdraw from the partnership upon giving six (6) months written notice to the other partner or partners of his intention so to do. In the event of the withdrawal of a partner, or in the event of the death of a partner, the partnership shall terminate. Immediately upon such death or withdrawal, the surviving or remaining partners shall determine if the partnership shall continue and shall cause to be made by an independent accountant an audit of the books of the business to determine the net worth of said business as shown by the books as of the date of said death or withdrawal. The surviving or remaining partners shall thereupon have an option for a period of sixty (60) days, exercisable by written notice to such withdrawing partner or to the personal representatives or heirs of such deceased partner, to purchase the interest of the withdrawing or deceased partner at 100 (100%) of the book value thereof, as shown by such audit, making payment therefor as follows: Within one hundred twenty (120) days of the exercise of said option, the withdrawing partner or the heirs, executor or administrators of the deceased partner shall be paid then percent (10%) of the purchase price, and the balance thereof shall be payable over a period of eight (8) years, commencing eighteen (18) months from the date of death or withdrawal, in equal annual installments, together with interest at the rate of seven percent (7%) per annum on the reducing principal balance outstanding from time to time. It is understood however, that the remaining partner or partners may prepay such payments in whole or in part in any amounts and at any time or times he or they may deem advisable. If all of the surviving or remaining partners elect to purchase the interest of the withdrawing or deceased partner, such purchase shall be in the proportions held by each such partner. If any partner elects not to participate in such purchase, such partner may continue to hold his or her original share and the remaining partners may purchase such withdrawing or deceased partner's share proportionately.

12. Notwithstanding any other provision of this agreement, it is understood and agreed by the parties hereto that the management and control of the affairs of the partnership shall remain with Rudolph F. Bertolla, John P. Bertolla, and Viola A. Bertolla, and the remaining partners will not undertake any act or enter into any commitment on behalf of or in the name of the corporation without the prior consent and authorization of Rudolph F. Bertolla, John P. Bertolla and Viola A. Bertolla . . . .
[. . .]

[Several deaths, disputes, and buyouts] resulted in Andy (son of Alexander) and Mary each with a 50% interest in the partnership. In 1989, Andy and Mary assigned 3% each of their respective interest to Mike Bill, Mary's son.

The testimony reflects that almost as soon as the management of the partnership was vested in Andy and Mary by the elderly partners in 1986, Andy began active management of the partnership with a complete disregard for Mary, contrary to the written agreement. For example, Andy spent $21,000 fixing up an old farm house on the property, without partnership approval. Andy paid bonuses during losing years to their nephew Adam Bertolla (son of John Eddie and who runs the operation of the Loxley farm) and their nephew Ray Bertolla (son of John Eddie and who runs the operation of the Belforest farm) without partnership consent. Andy put the partnership into a new business venture without consulting Mary. Rebecca Carr, a former bookkeeper at Bertolla Farm Supply testified that Andy closed the doors to his office to purposefully exclude Mary when he met with representatives from McFarland Cattle, one of the partnership's most significant accounts. Ms. Carr testified that Andy was very rude to Mary and that the relationship between them was very tense. Andy executed a $26,500 promissory note to a feed lot in Texas without consulting Mary or Mike, again in violation of the provisions of the partnership agreement.

In 1992, Mary's concerns increased when the regular financial reports detailed the partnership's losses. These losses totaled $1,170,200. Andy ignored Mary's concerns and began to attack her verbally. She broke out in hives as a result of his verbal abuse. Mary testified that Andy just would not quit spending. [. . .]

In the fall of 1994, Andy told Mary that the partnership was losing money because their bookkeeper was stealing. Mary responded that Andy was spending too much—that was the reason the partnership was losing money. Andy did not tell Mary that he had already hired Buddy Russell, another accountant to check out the books. Mary did not learn about a special audit Andy had Buddy Russell make, until this litigation began. The report confirmed that the bookkeeper was not stealing, and that Andy was spending too much. Russell's report suggested that Andy eliminate pecan farming, but Andy refused. He stated that it didn't make any difference what anybody else thought, he was going to continue to farm. Andy then ordered that the bookkeeper keep a time card on Mary at Bertolla Farm Supply.

In 1995 Andy began secretly tape recording his 85 year old Aunt Mary in hopes that she would say that she would withdraw from the partnership. Mary refused to withdraw and insisted that the partnership be dissolved. Mary asked Kenny Hanak, an accountant and family friend, to hold a partnership meeting in his office. On February 23, 1995, Mary and Mike, through Hanak, told Andy that they wanted to dissolve the partnership. Andy taped this meeting also. Ultimately a vote was taken and Mary and

Mike voted their 53% to dissolve the partnership. Andy would not accept the vote and vowed to continue farming.

After Andy refused to accept the vote to dissolve the partnership, Mary and Mike signed, as representatives of the partnership, quitclaim deeds that removed their combined 53% interest from the partnership. Mary and Mike had their attorney write Andy's lawyer to notify Andy that he should make no further purchases in the partnership's name. Despite this notification, Andy signed a note to purchase a cotton picker for $154,977. Mary and Mike sent notifications to McMillan and Harrison that Andy was no longer authorized to buy supplies from Bertolla Farm Supply. Despite these measures, Andy continued to farm and make charges on these accounts.

In 1996, plaintiff Mary Bertolla Bill and her son, Mike Charles Bill, filed this suit against Andy and the partnership, for dissolution, breach of partnership agreement, breach of fiduciary duty and an accounting. Andy answered, admitting that ABS was dissolved, but asserting that the Bills could only get book value for their interests under the partnership agreement. [. . .]

[. . .] The trial court's order of January 26, 1998, found [. . .]:

[. . .]1.   [. . .][I]t is not reasonably practicable for the partners to carry on the business in partnership together and the circumstances render a dissolution equitable. Therefore, A. Bertolla & Sons, an Alabama general partnership, is dissolved as of the date of this order.

2.   The partners, Mary Bertolla Bill, Michael Charles Bill, and Andrew A. Bertolla shall wind up the partnership affairs in accordance with the provisions of this order.

3.   As of the date of this order no partner is due to account to the partnership or the other partners; all assets of the partnership are in the possession of the partnership and no marshalling is required; partnership property consists of all real and personal property in the partnership name; the assets and liabilities of the partnership are as shown by the evidence and no contributions of the partners are necessary.

4.   The partnership assets shall be sold by the partnership at private sale as follows: the stocks, bonds, and other securities shall be sold within thirty (30) days of the date of this order; all other property shall be immediately placed on the market and sold as soon as practicable thereafter subject to the approval of the Court.

5.   All partnership liabilities shall be paid as soon as possible in the following order: those owing to creditors other than partners within thirty (30) days after the sale of stocks, bonds and other securities; those owing to partners other than for capital and profits immediately thereafter; those owing to

partners in respect of capital immediately thereafter; and those owing to partners in respect of profits immediately thereafter.

6. Any liability of the partnership to partners with respect to capital and profits, all proceeds of sales paid to partners, and all other payments paid to partners shall be made according to their respective partnership interest in the following proportions: Mary Bertolla Bill 47%; Michael Charles Bill 6%; and Alexander A. Bertolla 47%. [. . .]

The defendant filed a motion to alter amend or vacate which was granted in part and denied in part. On May 4, 1998, the trial court issued an amended order which called for an accounting and the in-kind distribution of the securities to the partners according to their interests. The partnership's real property was to be placed on the market, sold and the proceeds distributed in accordance with the original order.

As previously stated, the question before us is whether the trial court is plainly and palpably in error or manifestly unjust in ordering this partnership to be dissolved and the assets distributed according to each partner's interest. ABS is an Alabama general partnership, governed by the Alabama Partnership Act [. . .]. The plaintiffs sought a judicial dissolution of the ABS partnership. Section 10–8–92(a), Ala.Code 1975, provides for judicial dissolution of a partnership:

(a) On application by or for a partner, the court shall order a dissolution whenever:

(1) A partner has been declared in any judicial proceeding or is otherwise shown to be a person of unsound mind;

(2) A partner becomes in any other way incapable of performing his part of the partnership contract;

(3) A partner has been guilty of such conduct as tends to affect prejudicially the carrying on of the business;

(4) A partner willfully or persistently commits a breach of the partnership agreement, or otherwise so conducts himself in matters relating to the partnership business that it is not reasonably practicable to carry on the business in partnership with him;

(5) The business of the partnership can only be carried on at a loss; or

(6) Other circumstances render a dissolution equitable.

The trial judge based his ruling that the partnership must be dissolved upon four days of trial testimony. While Andy contends that there is no evidence in the record to support any of the grounds the trial court relied upon to dissolve the partnership, the evidence supports the trial court's order of dissolution on the ground of the impracticability of the partners carrying on the business. The evidence clearly shows that it was "not reasonably practicable" for them to remain in partnership. § 10–8–

92(a)(4). Every witness who was asked whether Andy and Mary could
continue in partnership with each other answered that they could not. It
is well settled that partners who cannot interact with each other should
not have to remain bound together in partnership. *Owen v. Cohen.*

The evidence also supports judicial dissolution on the ground of Andy's
misconduct. Section § 10–8–92(a)(3) allows judicial dissolution when "a
partner has been guilty of such conduct as tends to affect prejudicially
the carrying on of the business." This statute codifies Alabama caselaw
that authorizes dissolution of a partnership on the ground of the
misconduct of a partner. *Brooke v. Tucker.* 59A Am.Jur.2d *Partnership*
§ 857 (1987) lists certain acts as conducted by a partner that are
sufficient to warrant judicial dissolution: 1) Unilateral decisions as to the
management of the partnership; 2) Exclusion of partner from
partnership affairs; 3) Willful and persistent breach of partnership
agreement; 4) Refusal to discuss partnership affairs; 5) Misappropriation
of partnership funds; 6) Negligent and incompetent handling of
partnership affairs. The record supports judicial dissolution in this case
because there was evidence that Andy some 16 times breached the
partnership agreement's prohibition against signing negotiable
instruments without authority. Accountant Carl Johnson testified that
Mary's concerns related to the farm losses were legitimate. Without the
"nest egg" of securities from the profits run by the shipping business
which were put away by Mary's brothers, Andy would have bankrupted
the partnership. The testimony in the record demonstrating Andy's
misconduct as a partner is sufficient to support the trial court's order.

While Andy contends that Mary withdrew from the partnership, the facts
do not support this conclusion. Andy's attempt to trick Mary into saying
she would withdraw while secretly tape recording his conversations with
her failed. Courts interpreting the Uniform Partnership Act have held
that a request for judicial dissolution is not tantamount to withdrawal by
the requesting partner. *Cooper v. Isaacs.*

Mary denies that she withdrew from the partnership and notes that,
although Andy alleges she withdrew, he completely failed to perform any
of the conditions precedent to exercise the option available to remaining
partners when a partner withdraws, all contained in paragraph 10 of the
partnership agreement. Andy did not act immediately, did not have an
audit performed, did not exercise the option to buy at book value within
60 days, and has not paid any of the money that would be due to Mary or
Mike because of the alleged "withdrawal."

When the ABS partnership agreement was written, the provisions for
buyouts of deceased partners' shares were structured to qualify for
special estate tax treatment. Andy argues that the provisions of the
partnership agreement which were written to take advantage of the tax
laws restrict lifetime transfers of partnership interests to book values
and also restrict a partner's right to dissolve.

However, these provisions, which at the time took advantage of favorable tax laws, do not control the rights of partners to dissolve an at-will partnership. Alabama partnership law controls. The ABS partnership agreement does not expressly provide for the distribution of partnership assets upon dissolution. The distribution of the partnership assets is governed by the provisions of the Uniform Partnership Act, under which each partner is entitled to receive the fair market value of his or her interest in the partnership. § 10–8–97, Ala.Code 1975. Andy argues that the assets of the partnership should be distributed according to their book value, drawing upon the "unless otherwise agreed" language of § 10–8–97. However, a plain reading of the partnership agreement does not support this conclusion. Furthermore, it would be inherently unfair. The book value of the partnership assets at the time of the trial was approximately $1.5 million; the fair market value of the assets at the time of trial was $24.5 million. The trial judge correctly ordered the sale for distribution of the assets to the partners according to their interests. This is required by the Alabama Partnership Act. It is also the fair and equitable resolution to this case. *See Mahan v. Mahan.*

The Alabama Uniform Partnership Act expressly authorizes the dissolution of the partnership as ordered by the trial court. The distribution of the assets of the partnership is based upon facts provided by the accountants for both the Bills and Andy Bertolla. Findings of fact based on *More tenus* evidence are presumed correct even though there may have been conflicting evidence. *Deloney v. Chappell.* In light of the evidence from the record set out above, our review of the record, and the attendant presumptions of correctness accompanying that evidence, the judgment of the trial court is affirmed. *Arzonico v. Wells.*

AFFIRMED.

Pav-Saver Corp. v. Vasso Corp.

493 N.E.2d 423 (Ill. App. Ct. 1986)

The matter before us arises out of the dissolution of the parties' partnership, the Pav-Saver Manufacturing Company. The facts are not in dispute, and only those needed to explain our disposition on the issues on appeal will be stated.

Plaintiff, Pav-Saver Corporation ("PSC") is the owner of the Pav-Saver trademark and certain patents for the design and marketing of concrete paving machines. Harry Dale is the inventor of the Pav-Saver "slip-form" paver and the majority shareholder of PSC, located in Moline, Illinois. H. Moss Meersman is an attorney who is also the owner and sole shareholder of Vasso Corporation. In 1974 Dale, individually, together with PSC and Meersman formed Pav-Saver Manufacturing Company for the manufacture and sale of Pav-Saver machines. Dale agreed to contribute his services, PSC contributed the patents and trademark necessary to the proposed operation, and Meersman agreed to obtain financing for it. The partnership agreement was drafted by Meersman and approved by Attorney Charles Peart, president of PSC. The agreement contained two paragraphs which lie at the heart of the appeal and cross-appeal before us:

"3.   The duties, obligations and functions of the respective partners shall be:

A.   Meersman shall provide whatever financing is necessary for the joint venture, as required.

B.   (1) PAV-SAVER shall grant to the partnership without charge the exclusive right to use on all machines manufactured and sold, its trademark 'PAV-SAVER' during the term of this Agreement. In order to preserve and maintain the good will and other values of the trademark PAV-SAVER, it is agreed between the parties that PAV-SAVER Corporation shall have the right to inspect from time to time the quality of machines upon which the licensed trademark PAV-SAVER is used or applied on machines for laying concrete pavement where such machines are manufactured and/or sold. Any significant changes in structure, materials or components shall be disclosed in writing or by drawings to PAV-SAVER Corporation.

(2) PAV-SAVER grants to the partnership exclusive license without charge for its patent rights in and to its Patent # 3,377,933 for the term of this agreement and exclusive license to use its specifications and drawings for the Slip-form paving machine known as Model MX 6-33, plus any specifications and drawings for any extensions, additions and attachments for said machine for said term. It being understood and agreed that same shall remain the property of PAV-SAVER and all copies shall be returned to PAV-SAVER at the expiration of this partnership. Further, PAV-SAVER, so long as this agreement is honored and is in force, grants a license under any patents of PAV-SAVER granted in the United States and/or other countries applicable to the Slip-Form paving machine."

[. . .]

"11. It is contemplated that this joint venture partnership shall be permanent, and same shall not be terminated or dissolved by either party except upon mutual approval of both parties. If, however, either party shall terminate or dissolve said relationship, the terminating party shall pay to the other party, as liquidated damages, a sum equal to four (4) times the gross royalties received by PAV-SAVER

Corporation in the fiscal year ending July 31, 1973, as shown by their corporate financial statement. Said liquidated damages to be paid over a ten (10) year period next immediately following the termination, payable in equal installments."

In 1976, upon mutual consent, the PSC/Dale/Meersman partnership was dissolved and replaced with an identical one between PSC and Vasso, so as to eliminate the individual partners.

It appears that the Pav-Saver Manufacturing Company operated and thrived according to the parties' expectations until around 1981, when the economy slumped, sales of the heavy machines dropped off significantly, and the principals could not agree on the direction that the partnership should take to survive. On March 17, 1983, Attorney Charles Peart, on behalf of PSC, wrote a letter to Meersman terminating the partnership and invoking the provisions of paragraph 11 of the parties' agreement.

In response, Meersman moved into an office on the business premises of the Pav-Saver Manufacturing Company, physically ousted Dale, and assumed a position as the day-to-day manager of the business. PSC then sued in the circuit court of Rock Island County for a court-ordered dissolution of the partnership, return of its patents and trademark, and an accounting. Vasso counterclaimed for declaratory judgment that PSC had wrongfully terminated the partnership and that Vasso was entitled to continue the partnership business, and other relief pursuant to the Illinois Uniform Partnership Act. [. . .] After protracted litigation, the trial court ruled that PSC had wrongfully terminated the partnership; that Vasso was entitled to continue the partnership business and to possess the partnership assets, including PSC's trademark and patents; that PSC's interest in the partnership was $165,000, based on a $330,000 valuation for the business; and that Vasso was entitled to liquidated damages in the amount of $384,612, payable pursuant to paragraph 11 of the partnership agreement. Judgment was entered accordingly.

Both parties appealed. PSC takes issue with the trial court's failure to order the return of its patents and trademark or, in the alternative, to assign a value to them in determining the value of the partnership assets. Further, neither party agrees with the trial court's enforcement of their agreement for liquidated damages. In its cross-appeal, PSC argues that the amount determined by the formula in paragraph 11 is a penalty. Vasso, on the other hand, contends in its appeal that the amount is unobjectionable, but the installment method of pay-out should not be enforced.

In addition to the afore-cited paragraphs of the parties' partnership agreement, the resolution of this case is controlled by the dissolution provision of the Uniform Partnership Act (Ill. Rev. Stat. 1983, ch. 106½, pars. 29–43). The Act provides:

"(2) When dissolution is caused in contravention of the partnership agreement the rights of the partners shall be as follows:

(a) Each partner who has not caused dissolution wrongfully shall have:

[. . .]

II. The right, as against each partner who has caused the dissolution wrongfully, to damage for breach of the agreement.

(b) The partners who have not caused the dissolution wrongfully, if they all desire to continue the business in the same name, either by themselves or jointly with others, may do so, during the agreed term for the partnership and for that purpose may possess the partnership property, provided they secure the payment by bond approved by the court, or pay to any partner who has caused the dissolution wrongfully, the value of his interest in the partnership at the dissolution, less any damages recoverable under clause (2a II) of this section, and in like manner indemnify him against all present or future partnership liabilities.

(c) A partner who has caused the dissolution wrongfully shall have: [. . .]

II. If the business is continued under paragraph (2b) of this section the right as against his co-partners and all claiming through them in respect of their interests in the partnership, to have the value of his interest in the partnership, less any damages caused to his co-partners by the dissolution, ascertained and paid to him in cash, or the payment secured by bond approved by the court and to be released from all existing liabilities of the partnership; but in ascertaining the value of the partner's interest the value of the good will of the business shall not be considered.

Initially we must reject PSC's argument that the trial court erred in refusing to return Pav-Saver's patents and trademark pursuant to paragraph 3 of the partnership agreement, or in the alternative that the court erred in refusing to assign a value to PSC's property in valuing the partnership assets. The partnership agreement on its face contemplated a "permanent" partnership, terminable only upon mutual approval of the parties. It is undisputed that PSC's unilateral termination was in contravention of the agreement. The wrongful termination necessarily invokes the provisions of the Uniform Partnership Act so far as they concern the rights of the partners. Upon PSC's notice terminating the partnership, Vasso elected to continue the business pursuant to section 38(2)(b) of the Uniform Partnership Act. As correctly noted by Vasso, the statute was enacted "to cover comprehensively the problem of dissolution [. . .] [and] to stabilize business." [citation omitted] Ergo, despite the parties' contractual direction that PSC's patents would be returned to it upon the mutually approved expiration of the partnership (paragraph 3), the right to possess the partnership property and continue in business upon a wrongful termination must be derived from and is controlled by the statute. Evidence at trial clearly established that the Pav-Saver machines being manufactured by the partnership could not be produced or marketed without PSC's patents and trademark. Thus, to continue in business pursuant to the statutorily-granted right of the party not causing the wrongful dissolution, it is essential that paragraph 3 of the parties' agreement—the return to PSC of its patents—not be honored.

Similarly, we find no merit in PSC's argument that the trial court erred in not assigning a value to the patents and trademark. The only evidence adduced at trial to show value of this property was testimony relating to good will. It was unrefuted that the name Pav-Saver enjoys a good reputation for a good product and reliable service. However, inasmuch as the Uniform Partnership Act specifically states that "the value of the good will of the business shall not be considered" (Ill.Rev.Stat.1983, ch. 106½, par. 38(2)(c)(II)), we find that the trial court properly rejected PSC's good will evidence of the value of its patents and trademark in valuing its interest in the partnership business.

[EDS.—The court then rejects the argument that the amount of liquidated damages awarded to Vasso pursuant to the formula is a "penalty" and unreasonable.]

Affirmed.

■ JUSTICE STOUDER concurring in part-dissenting in part.

I generally agree with the result of the majority. I cannot, however, accept the majority's conclusion the defendant is entitled to retention of the patents.

The [provisions in the] Uniform Partnership Act [. . .] are best viewed as "default" standards because they apply in the absence of contrary agreements. [. . .] When the partnership contract contains provisions, imposing on one or more of the partners obligations differing from those which the law ordinarily infers from the partnership relation, the courts should strive to construe these provisions so as to give effect to the honest intentions of the partners as shown by the language of the contract and their conduct under it.

The plaintiff (PSC) brought this action at law seeking dissolution of the partnership before expiration of the agreed term of its existence. Under the Uniform Partnership Act where dissolution is caused by an act in violation of the partnership agreement, the other partner(s) are accorded certain rights. The partnership agreement is a contract, and even though a partner may have the power to dissolve, he does not necessarily have the right to do so. Therefore, if the dissolution he causes is a violation of the agreement, he is liable for any damages sustained by the innocent partner(s) as a result thereof. The innocent partner(s) also have the option to continue the business in the firm name provided they pay the partner causing the dissolution the value of his interest in the partnership. [. . .]

The duties and obligations of partners arising from a partnership relation are regulated by the express contract as far as they are covered thereby. A written agreement is not necessary but where it does exist it constitutes the measure of the partners' rights and obligations. While the rights and duties of the partners in relation to the partnership are governed by the Uniform Partnership Act, the uniform act also provides that such rules are subject to any agreement between the parties. [. . .] It is where the express contract does not cover the situation or question which arises that they are determined under the applicable law, The Uniform Partnership Act.

The partnership agreement entered into by PSC and Vasso in pertinent part provides:

> 3.B.(2) [PSC] grants to the partnership exclusive license without charge for its patent rights [. . .] for the term of this agreement. [. . .] [I]t being understood and agreed that same shall remain the property of [PSC] [. . .] and shall be returned to [PSC] at the expiration of this partnership.

The majority holds this provision in the contract is unenforceable. The only apparent reason for such holding is that its enforcement would affect defendant's option to continue the business. No authority is cited to support such a rule.

The partnership agreement further provides:

> 11. [. . .] If either party shall terminate or dissolve said [partnership], the terminating party shall pay to the other party as liquidated damages [. . .] [$384,612].

This provision becomes operative at the same time as the provision relating to the return of the patents. [. . .]

Here, express terms of the partnership agreement deal with the status of the patents and measure of damages, the question is settled thereby. I think it clear the parties agreed the partnership only be allowed the use of the patents during the term of the agreement. The agreement having been terminated, the right to use the patents is terminated. The provisions in the contract do not conflict with the statutory option to continue the business and even if there were a conflict the provisions of the contract should prevail. The option to continue the business does not carry with it any guarantee or assurance of success and it may often well be that liquidation rather than continuation would be the better option for a partner not at fault.

As additional support for my conclusion, it appears the liquidated damages clause was insisted upon by the defendant because of earlier conduct of the plaintiff withdrawing from a former partnership. Thus, the existence of the liquidated damages clause recognizes the right of plaintiff to withdraw the use of his patents in accordance with the specific terms of the partnership agreement. Since liquidated damages depends on return of the patents, I would vacate that part of the judgment providing defendant is entitled to continue use of the patents and provide that use shall remain with plaintiff.

Congel v. Malfitano
31 N.Y.3d 272 (2018)

[. . .]

I.

In 1985, defendant and seven others entered into a written agreement (the agreement) to form a general partnership known as "Poughkeepsie Galleria Company" (the Partnership), for the ownership, operation, and management of a shopping mall. The mall opened in 1987 and continues to operate today. Defendant initially had a 2.25% ownership interest in the Partnership, which increased to 3.08% by the mid-2000s. In addition to the minority partners, the Partnership had a majority owner, Moselle Associates, which controlled a little over 56% of the Partnership.

The agreement provided that the Partnership "shall continue until it is terminated as hereinafter provided." In a subsequent provision, the agreement stated that the Partnership would dissolve upon "[t]he election by the Partners to dissolve the Partnership" or "[t]he happening of any event which makes it unlawful for the business of the Partnership to be carried on or for the Partners to carry it on in Partnership."

The agreement further stated that "[a]ll decisions to be made by the Partners shall be made by the casting of votes at a meeting of such Partners" and that "[t]he affirmative vote of no less than fifty-one percent (51%)" of the partners "shall be required to approve any matter presented for decision." Day-to-day control of the Partnership was vested in a three-member Executive Committee, comprised of Robert J. Congel, Bruce A. Kenan, and James A. Tuozzolo, the plaintiffs in this case. The Executive Committee had "the exclusive right to manage the business of the Partnership," although a majority of partners had the authority to "overrule or modify" the Committee's decisions, "withdraw or modify" any power granted to the Committee, or remove its members.

In the mid-2000s, defendant decided to withdraw from the Partnership. [. . .] He explored the option of a buyout of his interest, but negotiations failed.

On November 24, 2006, defendant wrote to his partners: "[I]n accordance with Section 62 (1) (b) of the Partnership Law, and as a general partner of the Partnership I hereby elect to dissolve the Partnership and by this notice the Partnership is hereby dissolved."

Partnership Law § 62(1)(b) states that a partner may unilaterally dissolve a partnership, without violating the partnership agreement, if "no definite term or particular undertaking is specified" in the agreement and the partnership is therefore "at will." Defendant insisted that his partners were compelled to liquidate. The Partnership was in the process of negotiating a mortgage refinancing, and defendant recorded a notice of pendency on the Poughkeepsie Galleria property.

The partners took the position that defendant had wrongfully dissolved the Partnership, and they continued the business, in the same name as before, pursuant to Partnership Law § 69(2)(b). That provision states, with certain conditions, that when dissolution is caused in violation of a partnership agreement, "[t]he partners who have not caused the dissolution wrongfully, if they all desire to continue the business in the same name. . . may do so, during the agreed term for the partnership and for that purpose may possess the partnership property."

In January 2007, plaintiffs, as the Partnership's Executive Committee and on behalf of the Partnership, commenced this breach of contract action, seeking a declaratory ruling that defendant had wrongfully dissolved the Partnership, as well as damages. [. . .]

Defendant answered and interposed several counterclaims, including the allegation that the dissolution precluded the Partnership from refinancing or taking any business actions other than winding up, and a claim for judicial dissolution under Partnership Law § 63(1) [. . .] [and] insisting that the Partnership qualified as an "at-will" partnership, which can be dissolved without violation of the partnership agreement, under Partnership Law § 62(1)(b).

[. . .] Supreme Court granted summary judgment to plaintiffs, holding that the Partnership was not an "at-will" partnership, because it specified a "particular undertaking" within the meaning of Partnership Law § 62(1)(b), and that defendant's dissolution of the Partnership breached the agreement. [. . .]

In April 2009, the Appellate Division upheld Supreme Court's ruling on the wrongfulness of the dissolution, albeit on different grounds, finding that the agreement specified a "definite term" or temporal limit under Partnership Law § 62(1)(b). [. . .]

Partnership Law § 69(2)(c)(II) states that when a partner dissolves a partnership in contravention of the partnership agreement, and the remaining partners continue the business in the same name, the dissolving partner has

"the right as against his copartners . . . to have the value of his interest in the partnership, less any damages caused to his copartners by the dissolution, ascertained and paid to him in cash, or the payment secured by bond approved by the court, and to be released from all existing liabilities of the partnership; but in ascertaining the value of the partner's interest the value of the good-will of the business shall not be considered."

Consequently, in November 2011, Supreme Court conducted a bench trial to establish the value of defendant's interest in the Partnership, taking into account the value of goodwill, and the amount of damages, if any, that defendant owed to plaintiffs. At the outset of trial, the parties stipulated that the value of defendant's interest in the Partnership as of November 24, 2006 was $4,850,000. [. . .]

Supreme Court ruled that the stipulated value of $4,850,000 would be reduced by 15% or $727,500 to represent the value of the Partnership's goodwill. [. . .] The trial court explained that "[a] potential purchaser of the Poughkeepsie Galleria would more than likely pay more for an established going concern that already has tenant retail stores that attract a loyal customer base," and in this manner "would pay extra for the acquisition of goodwill." [. . .]

Next, Supreme Court applied a 35% or $1,442,875 marketability discount, to the stipulated value as reduced by goodwill, to account for the limited marketability of defendant's interest, generating a discounted value of $2,679,625. [. . .]

Defendant appealed, and plaintiffs cross-appealed.

Defendant contended, among other things, that the Appellate Division should overturn its 2009 rulings holding that he had wrongfully dissolved the Partnership [. . .].

Upon remand, Supreme Court issued an amended judgment applying the minority discount and further reducing defendant's interest in the Partnership to $911,072.50; ruling that the plaintiffs were entitled to $1,822,460.25 in fees and statutory interest; and concluding that defendant owed plaintiffs $911,387.75.

We granted defendant leave to appeal. [. . .] The appeal brings up for review the Appellate Division's 2009 and 2016 orders.

II.

The first issue, as framed by the parties, is whether defendant's unilateral dissolution of the Partnership violated the agreement. The trial court and the Appellate Division both ruled that the dissolution was wrongful, but focused on whether the agreement specified a "definite term" or "particular undertaking" under Partnership Law § 62(1)(b). Defendant contends that the Partnership was "at will" because the agreement did not contain a "definite term" or "particular undertaking" under the statute. Plaintiffs urge us to affirm on an alternative ground, namely that because the agreement sets out the methods of dissolving the Partnership in accordance with the agreement, the wrongfulness of defendant's dissolution can be decided without recourse to the statute. We agree with plaintiffs on this issue.

The governing law of partnerships in New York is the Partnership Law of 1919, which enacted into law the original Uniform Partnership Act (UPA). It is well established, however, that "[t]he Partnership Law's provisions are, for the most part, default requirements that come into play in the absence of an agreement" *Ederer v. Gursky*. The statutory scheme

> "applies only when there is either no partnership agreement governing the partnership's affairs, the agreement is silent on a particular point, or the agreement contains provisions contrary to law. Where an agreement addresses a particular issue, the terms of the agreement control, and the rights and obligations of the parties are determined by reference to principles of contract law. Thus, an agreement specifying the circumstances under which a partnership may be dissolved is not at will." *BPR Group Ltd. Partnership v. Bendetson*.

Indeed, partners may, "absent prohibitory provisions of the statutes or of rules of the common law relating to partnerships, or considerations of public policy, . . . include in the partnership articles any agreement" the partners desire to include. *Cohen v. Lord, Day & Lord*. "[T]he partners of either a general or limited partnership, as between themselves, may include in the partnership articles any agreement they wish concerning the sharing of profits and losses, priorities of distribution on winding up of the partnership affairs and other matters. If complete, as between the partners, the agreement so made controls." *Lanier v. Bowdoin*.

[. . .] The Partnership Law provides that dissolution does not violate a partnership agreement if it occurs "[b]y the termination of the definite term or particular undertaking specified in the agreement." Partnership Law § 62(1)(a). [. . .] [I]f "no definite term or particular undertaking is specified" in the partnership agreement, then the partnership is said to be an "at-will" partnership, and a unilateral dissolution "[b]y the express will of any partner" does not violate the partnership agreement. Partnership Law § 62(1)(b). [. . .]

By contrast, [. . .], "[w]hen the agreement specifies a durational term, or a defined project, an attempt unilaterally to dissolve the partnership would violate the partnership agreement." *Scholastic, Inc. v. Harris*. While "partners are statutorily empowered to dissolve the partnership at any time, wrongfully dissolving partners may be liable to the expelled partner for breach of the partnership agreement" *Dawson v. White & Case*.

[. . .] Here, the agreement stated that the Partnership "shall continue until it is terminated as hereinafter provided," and, in a subsequent provision, stated that the Partnership would dissolve upon "[t]he election by the Partners to dissolve the Partnership" or "[t]he happening of any event which makes it unlawful for the business of the Partnership to be carried on or for the Partners to carry it on in Partnership." The partners clearly intended that the methods provided in the agreement for dissolution were the only methods whereby the partnership would dissolve <u>in accordance with the agreement</u>, and by implication that unilateral dissolution would breach the agreement.

[. . .] Accordingly, this was plainly not intended to be an "at-will" partnership. [. . .]

IV.

With respect to the reduction for goodwill, Partnership Law § 69(2)(c)(II) gives a partner who dissolves a partnership in contravention of the partnership agreement the right "to have the value of his interest in the partnership, less any damages caused to his copartners by the dissolution, ascertained and paid to him in cash, . . . but in ascertaining the value of the partner's interest the value of the good-will of the business shall not be considered." [. . .] Defendant argues that he should not have been assessed a goodwill deduction.

Goodwill is an intangible asset of a business, corresponding in this context to what a buyer would pay for the business, over and above its value as a mere sum of tangible assets, because of the patronage and support of regular customers. [. . .] [T]he goodwill question is a factual one. [. . .] Here, the trial court found, based on the expert testimony and other evidence, that the shopping mall and the mall's tenants attract regular, loyal shoppers, and there is record support for the affirmed finding that the value of the Partnership included, in addition to its real property and cash, a goodwill component. [. . .]

VI.

The final question we must resolve is whether a minority discount may be applied in the calculation of the value of a wrongfully dissolving partner's interest in a partnership, pursuant to Partnership Law § 69(2)(c)(II), when the remaining partners continue the business under Partnership Law § 69(2)(b). A minority discount is a standard tool in valuation of a financial interest, designed to reflect the fact that the price an investor is willing to pay for a minority ownership interest in a business, whether a corporation or a partnership, is less because the owner of a minority interest lacks control of the business.

Defendant contends that, as a matter of law, minority discounts are not applicable in the valuation of a minority partner's interest after the partner exits a business that remains a going concern. This issue is properly preserved, but we cannot agree with defendant on the merits.

[. . .] Partnership Law § 69 (2) (c) (II) contemplates a valuation of a wrongfully dissolving partner's interest based on treating the partnership as a going concern, rather than an asset to be liquidated. [. . .] Given that the focus is on one partner's interest in a persisting concern, we agree with the Massachusetts high court that a minority discount is applicable, because a minority interest is worth less to anyone buying that interest alone.

Notably, New York, like Massachusetts, has not adopted the 1997 Uniform Partnership Act commonly known as RUPA. The dissent's discussion of RUPA and of cases from states that have adopted RUPA does not illuminate the law in New York. In particular, while RUPA, "[b]y focusing on a top-down valuation keyed to a sale of all of the assets of the partnership, ... directs the analysis away from a valuation of the interests of a particular partner," so that "a minority discount is inappropriate" (dissenting op. at 302), we conclude that the same cannot be said of the UPA.

[. . .] [W]rongful dissolution of a partnership may happen at any time, and valuation of a partner's interest occurs only if the remaining partners have agreed to continue their business as if nothing changed. Unlike shareholder dissent and appraisal, wrongful dissolution is not necessarily preceded by upheaval "inimical to the position of the minority" (*Friedman*, so trial courts need not substitute a "fair value" for the actual value a third party would pay. Indeed, here the upheaval took the form of an action by a minority partner inimical to the majority's interests.

[. . .] In sum, defendant provides no basis for concluding that a minority discount is inapplicable as a matter of law to the valuation of the interest of a wrongfully dissolving partner when the remaining partners continue the partnership. We note, finally, that the parties to a partnership agreement may contract out of application of a minority discount to the valuation of their interests, just as they may contract around statutory provisions. Defendant does not assert that the agreement precluded use of a minority discount in this manner.

VII.

For these reasons, Supreme Court properly determined the value of defendant's interest in the Partnership [. . .].

Accordingly, the judgment appealed from and the orders of the Appellate Division brought up for review should be modified, without costs, by remitting the case to Supreme Court, for further proceedings in accordance with this opinion, and, as so modified, affirmed.

■ FEINMAN, J. (dissenting in part).

[. . .] I do not join Part VI, the majority's holding that the trial court was required to apply a minority discount to the value of a partner's interests under Partnership Law § 69 (2)(c)(II). [. . .]

Section 69 distinguishes between wrongful and non-wrongful dissolutions. If the partnership's dissolution was not wrongful, then "each partner . . . may have the partnership property applied to discharge its liabilities, and the surplus applied to pay in cash the net amount owing to the respective partners." Partnership Law § 69[1]. In effect, "the withdrawing partner, unless otherwise agreed, has the right, upon dissolution, to compel the 'winding up' or liquidation of the company, and receive the value of [its] interest in the partnership" *Estate of Watts v. C.I.R.* Where dissolution is wrongful and the partners do not elect to continue the existence of the partnership under § 69(2)(b), the result is the same, except that the wrongful dissolver's right to payment must be set off against "damages for breach of the agreement." Partnership Law § 69[2][a][I]-[II], [c][I]. If the partnership is continued, however, the Partnership Law states only that the wrongful dissolver is entitled to "the value of [the partner's] interest in the partnership," excluding goodwill and set off against contractual damages. *Id.* § 69[2][c][II]. Although this procedure results in a technical dissolution, its economic effect in most cases is that a partner is allowed to cash out of the partnership and withdraw at any time, subject to its obligation to compensate the remaining partners for any losses they incur as a result of the breach of the partnership agreement. In this context, whether the "value of [the partner's] interest in the partnership" is subject to a discount for that partner's lack of control is the issue now before us.

Here, the majority insists that the "value of [the partner's] interest in the partnership" could only mean "the price at which [the interest] would change hands between a willing buyer and a willing seller" "as if that interest were being sold piecemeal and the rest of the business continuing as a going concern". But the majority does not explain why this is so. [. . .]

[. . .] The UPA left it unclear how a wrongful dissolver's buyout price should be calculated or whether any discounts should be applied. [. . .]

The RUPA resolved this ambiguity by explicitly defining the "buyout price" of a withdrawing partner as "the amount that would have been distributable to the dissociating partner . . . if, on the date of dissociation, the assets of the partnership were sold at a price equal to the greater of the liquidation value or the value based on a sale of the entire business as a going concern." RUPA § 701[b]. In other words, a dissociating partner would be entitled to its proportionate share in the value of the business as a going concern, set off against contractual damages, but without an individualized inquiry into the marketability of its particular slice of the partnership.

[. . .] The only departures from the UPA specifically noted in the Official Comment are the exclusion of the goodwill discount and the elimination of a partner's right to elect profits in lieu of interest under UPA § 42 (see RUPA § 701[b] cmt). [. . .]

In the context of corporate appraisals and judicial dissolutions, minority discounts have been soundly rejected in New York and in the vast majority of jurisdictions across the country. *In re Dissolution of Penepent Corp., Inc.* [. . .] In most states, including New York, minority stockholders must receive their "proportionate interest in the going concern value of the corporation as a whole, that is, what a willing purchaser, in an arm's length transaction, would offer for the *corporation* as an operating business" [. . .].

Two primary rationales have emerged from the case law. First, many courts, including this one, have explained that the exclusion is partially motivated by a desire to deter unfair squeeze-outs and safeguard minority shareholders from oppression [. . .].

The second rationale transposes much more easily to the partnership context. As many courts have observed, there is an analytical flaw in applying a minority discount where the actual purchasers of the minority interest are the remaining shareholders, rather than a hypothetical "willing buyer." The purchasers are not entering into a noncontrolling position, but merely consolidating and increasing whatever degree of control they already have over the business.

Minority discounts would essentially randomize the partnership's liability in many wrongful dissolution cases, hindering the dissolving partner's ability to settle the dispute out of court based on a reliable and predictable computation of the "value of [its] interest."

Finally, if the purpose of the minority discount is to deter or punish "wrongful" conduct, [. . .] then it is certainly a peculiar way to do so. The brunt of this penalty will fall disproportionately on minority partners, the class of partners whose withdrawal is *least* likely to cause a disturbance, but whose exit rights are *most* important, due precisely to their lack of control over the business. This would "inflict a double penalty" upon the minority partner; the partner not only lacks control over operational decision making, but would then receive less than a proportionate value *because* of that lack of control. Indeed, by the majority's own logic, if a wrongful dissolver is a majority or controlling partner—precisely the kind of partner whose dissociation will most damage the business—that partner may now be entitled to a *control premium* under Partnership Law § 69(2)(c)(II), since this would reflect the amount that a willing third-party buyer would pay for a majority stake. The structure of Partnership Law § 69(2)(c)(II) already deters wrongful dissolution in two ways: by requiring the dissolving partner to pay damages, and by discounting the value of its partnership interests attributable to goodwill. A further discount for a lack of control is cumulative and unnecessary in light of these other provisions.

In defining the "value of [the partner's] interest in the partnership," the question does not turn on whether a particular method of valuation is 'accurate,' but whether that valuation will lead to an allocation of wealth as between these partners that best advances the legislative scheme. "Value" can mean many different things, and the definition we embrace should be guided by the ends that the legislature sought to implement when it enacted the Partnership Law. Here, the court applied a minority discount of $1,768,552.50 to appellant's partnership interests, which were stipulated to be worth $4,850,000 without adjustments (see majority op. at 284, 76 N.Y.S.3d at 879, 101 N.E.3d at 347). The question is, in an action for wrongful dissolution, where the partnership is continued as a going concern, which party has the greater right to that $1,768,552.50 portion of appellant's interests—the controlling partners, or appellant himself? For the reasons discussed above, I believe this question should resolve in appellant's favor, and the order of the Appellate Division should be modified accordingly. [. . .]

Karrick v. Hannaman

168 U.S. 328 (1897)

Synopsis

Appeal from the Supreme Court of the Territory of Utah.

This was a suit brought April 17, 1890, in the Third judicial district court of the territory of Utah, by Hannaman against Karrick, for the dissolution of a partnership formed February 3, 1886, by an agreement in writing, by which they agreed to become partners in a mercantile and laundry business for the term of five years from that date, with a capital stock of $25,000, of which the plaintiff was to furnish $5,000, and the defendant $20,000. The defendant lent the plaintiff the sum of $5,000 for five years, for which the plaintiff gave a promissory note, payable at the end of that time, and secured by mortgage upon his interest in the partnership property. The plaintiff was to give his entire time and attention to the partnership business, and the defendant was to devote to it only such time as he should see fit; the plaintiff to have the control and management of the business generally and entirely, except as the defendant might designate, and such matters to be subject to mutual agreement; one half of the net profits of the business to go to the defendant in repayment of $15,000 of the capital stock furnished by him, and the other half to be allowed to remain in the business, except that each partner might draw out not exceeding $125 a month for personal expenses; the profits and losses to be shared equally, and neither party to have any other salary or compensation for services; and the title and interest of the partners in the partnership property to be proportionate to their respective contributions to the capital.

The complaint alleged the following facts: The parties carried on business in conformity with the agreement until February 1, 1888, when the defendant took exclusive possession of all the partnership business [. . .] and ever afterwards prevented the plaintiff from participating in any manner in the business or deriving any benefits therefrom. The plaintiff, until that date, performed his part of the agreement, and was ever after ready and willing to perform it, and so informed the defendant. From that date, the defendant wrongfully, and in fraud of the plaintiff's rights, carried on and controlled the partnership business for his own exclusive benefit, and applied to his own use, from the proceeds and profits of the same, large sums of money, exceeding the proportion to which he was entitled. On January 1, 1890, the defendant, without the plaintiff's knowledge or assent, sold and delivered to the Bast-Marshall Mercantile Company all the assets and property of the partnership. The complaint prayed for a dissolution of the partnership, the appointment of a receiver, an injunction against interfering with the property, its application to the payment of the partnership debts, and a division of the remainder between the partners, the setting aside and cancellation of any transfer or assignment to the Bast-Marshall Mercantile Company, and an account.

The defendant, Karrick, in his answer, admitted the partnership, and his own taking possession on February 1, 1888, but denied the other allegations of the complaint, and alleged that the plaintiff mismanaged the business in various particulars specified, and that, when the defendant took possession, the partnership was insolvent, and heavily in debt, and the plaintiff was owing to it a large sum of money, and was insolvent, and the partnership was then dissolved by mutual consent.

The Bast-Marshall Mercantile Company was originally made a defendant, and filed a separate answer; but the plaintiff afterwards dismissed his suit as against that company. The case was referred, by consent of the remaining parties, to a referee, to report his findings of fact and conclusions of law to the court. [. . .]

From the findings of fact, the referee concluded, as matter of law, that the partnership was not dissolved, but that it expired February 3, 1891, according to the terms of the agreement; that the profits and losses of the partnership business should be divided equally between the parties, after crediting each with his advances to and investments in the partnership; and that the sum of $12,040.53 was therefore owing to the plaintiff. The court adopted the referee's findings of fact and conclusions of law, and entered a decree accordingly.

The defendant appealed to the supreme court of the territory, which held that [. . .] the defendant could not dissolve the partnership, without reasonable cause, and without the plaintiff's consent, before the expiration of the term stipulated in the partnership articles; and, therefore, that the partnership had not been dissolved by the acts of the defendant; but that, as each partner was permitted by those articles to draw out of the partnership $125 a month for personal expenses, the defendant should have been allowed the sum of $3,000 as personal expenses for the two years during which he conducted the business of the firm; and that the judgment should be modified by deducting one-half of this sum, and, so modified, be affirmed for the sum of $10,540.53. 9 Utah, 236, 33 Pac. 1039. The defendant appealed to this court.

Opinion

■ MR. JUSTICE GRAY, after stating the facts in the foregoing language, delivered the opinion of the court.

[. . .] The principal question of law discussed in the opinion of the supreme court of the territory, and at the argument in this court, was whether a partnership which, by the co-partnership articles, is to continue for a specified time, can be dissolved by one partner at his own will, without the assent of the other, before the expiration of that time.

It is universally conceded that a contract of partnership, containing no stipulation as to the time during which it shall continue in force, does not endure for the life of the partners, or of either of them, nor for any longer time than their mutual consent, but may be dissolved by either partner at his own will, at any time. *Peacock v. Peacock.*

Upon the question how far the status or relation of a partnership, which by the partnership agreement is to continue for a certain number of years, can be determined by one partner without the consent of the other before the expiration of that time, there has been some difference of opinion.

The principal reasons and authorities in favor of the position that a contract of partnership for a definite time cannot be dissolved at the mere will of one partner are stated or referred to in the opinion of the supreme court of the territory in this case, reported in 9 Utah, 236, 33 Pac. 1039.

Those which support the opposite view may be summed up as follows: A contract of partnership is one by which two or more persons agree to carry on a business for their common benefit, each contributing property or services, and having a community of interest in the profits. It is, in effect, a contract of mutual agency, each partner acting as a principal in his own behalf and as agent for his co-partner. *Meehan v. Valentine.* Every partnership creates a personal relation between the partners, rests upon their mutual consent, and exists between them only. [. . .] No partnership can efficiently or beneficially carry on its business without the mutual confidence and co-operation of all the partners. Even when, by the partnership articles, they have covenanted with each other that the partnership shall continue for a certain period, the partnership may be dissolved at any time, at the will of any partner, so far as to put an end to the partnership relation and to the authority of each partner to act for all, but rendering the partner who breaks his covenant liable to an action at law for damages, as in other cases of breaches of contract. *Skinner v. Dayton.* According to the authorities just cited, the only difference, so far as concerns the right of dissolution by one partner, between a partnership for an indefinite period and one for a specified term, is this: In the former case, the dissolution is no breach of the partnership agreement, and affords the other partner no ground of complaint. In the latter case, such a dissolution before the expiration of the time stipulated is a breach of the agreement, and, as such, to be compensated in damages; but in either case the action of one partner does actually dissolve the partnership.

A court of equity, doubtless, will not assist the partner breaking his contract to procure a dissolution of the partnership, because, upon familiar principles, a partner who has not fully and fairly performed the partnership agreement on his part has no standing in a court of equity to enforce any rights under the agreement. *Marble Co. v. Ripley.* But, generally speaking, neither will it interfere at the suit of the other partner to prevent the dissolution, because, while it may compel the execution of articles of partnership so as to put the parties in the same position as if the articles had been executed as agreed, it will seldom, if ever, specifically compel subsequent performance of the contract by either party, the contract of partnership being of an essentially personal character. Batten, Spec. Perf. 165–167. Especially where, by the partnership agreement, as in the case at bar, the defendant is to supply all or most of the capital, and the plaintiff is to furnish his personal services, the agreement cannot be specifically enforced against the plaintiff, and will not be enforced against the defendant. *Stocker v. Wedderburn*. [. . .]

We are not prepared, therefore, to assent to the opinion of the court below that a partnership for a definite time cannot be dissolved by one partner at his own will, and without the consent of his co-partner, within that time; and, consequently, that the partnership between these parties was not dissolved on February 1, 1888, when the defendant assumed exclusive possession and control of the business and property of the partnership, and excluded the plaintiff from any participation therein. But it is unnecessary to express an opinion upon this point, because, however it might be decided, it would not affect the conclusion in favor of the plaintiff in the present case.

Even if the partnership should be considered as having been actually dissolved at that date, yet the dissolution did not put an end to the plaintiff's right to his share in the property and the profits of the partnership. In a case in which both parties, in their pleadings, assumed the partnership to have been dissolved, this court, speaking by Mr. Justice Miller, held that drunkenness and dishonesty on the part of one partner, and his consequent exclusion from the business, did not authorize his co-partner, "of his own motion, to treat the partnership as ended, and to take himself all the benefits of their joint labors and joint property," or exempt him from responsibility to account to the excluded partner. *Ambler v. Whipple*. [. . .]

A partner who assumes to dissolve the partnership before the end of the term agreed on in the partnership articles is liable, in an action at law against him by his co-partner for the breach of the agreement, to respond in damages for the value of the profits which the plaintiff would otherwise have received. *Bagley v. Smith*. In a court of equity, a partner who, after a dissolution of the partnership carries on the business with the partnership property, is liable, at the election of the other partner or his representative, to account for the profits thereof, subject to proper allowances. *Ambler v. Whipple*.

In the case at bar, by the terms of the agreement in writing, dated February 3, 1886, under which the partnership was formed, it was to continue for five years,—that is to say, until February 3, 1891. The plaintiff was to contribute $5,000, and the defendant $20,000, to the capital. The defendant lent the plaintiff the sum of $5,000, for which the plaintiff gave his promissory note, payable at the end of the five years. The plaintiff was to have the general management of the business. Each partner might draw out not exceeding $125 a month for personal expenses. The profits and losses were to be shared equally, and neither partner was to have any other compensation for services; and their title in the partnership property was to be in proportion to their contributions to the capital.

By the facts found by the courts of the territory, it appears that the business was carried on according to the agreement for two years, or until February 1, 1888; that the defendant then took exclusive possession of the property and the business of the partnership, and thenceforth carried on the business profitably and for his own benefit, and excluded the plaintiff from any participation in the business or the profits, although the plaintiff was, as he informed the defendant, ready and willing to perform his part of the partnership agreement; and the defendant, on January 1, 1890, a year before the expiration of the term agreed on, and without the plaintiff's knowledge or assent, sold out and delivered to a stranger all the property of the partnership.

The judgment of the court of first instance charged the defendant with the amount of capital paid by the plaintiff into the partnership, deducting, however, the whole amount of the plaintiff's promissory note payable to the defendant at the end of the term of five years, and further charged the defendant with half of the net profits of the business during the two years that he carried it on, after ousting the plaintiff, and before selling out to a stranger, and with half of the wrongful disbursements of the defendant afterwards. The supreme court of the territory, affirming the judgment in other respects, held that, as by the agreement of partnership each partner was permitted to draw out a certain sum monthly for personal expenses, the defendant was entitled to such an allowance monthly for the two years during which he conducted the business, and the same should be deducted from the profits to be accounted for, and the judgment in favor of the plaintiff reduced accordingly. The court made no such allowance to the plaintiff; and, in accordance with the partnership articles, neither partner was allowed any compensation for his services other than his half of the profits.

It does not appear to have been suggested by the defendant in either of the courts of the territory, and could not successfully be contended, that, in estimating the damages or the profits which the plaintiff was entitled to recover, any deduction should be made by reason of his not having performed during those two years the services, as manager of the business, which he had agreed by the partnership articles to perform. No finding as to the value of such services was made or requested; and the defendant himself, not only refused to let the plaintiff, as he offered to do, perform them during those two years, but, in his answer and at the hearing before the referee, insisted that the plaintiff's services as manager were of no benefit to the partnership.

The result is that, whether the partnership should or should not be considered to have been dissolved when the defendant ousted the plaintiff and assumed the exclusive possession and control of the property and business of the partnership, the defendant has shown no ground for reversing or modifying the final decree of the supreme court of the territory.

Decree affirmed.

3.   BUYOUT AGREEMENTS

G & S Investments v. Belman

700 P.2d 1358 (Ariz. Ct. App. 1984)

This case involves a partnership dispute arising out of the misconduct and subsequent death of Thomas N. Nordale. [. . .] [The] principal issue[] in this case: whether the surviving general partner, G & S Investments, is entitled to continue the partnership after the death of Nordale, and how the value of Nordale's interest in partnership property is to be computed. The trial court, after making findings of fact and conclusions of law, entered judgment in favor of G & S Investments, finding that it had the right to continue the partnership and that the estate was owed $4,867.57. [. . .]

[. . .] Century Park, Ltd., is a limited partnership which was formed to receive ownership of a 62-unit apartment complex in Tucson. In 1982 the general partners were G & S Investments (51 per cent) and Nordale (25.5 per cent). The remaining partnership interest was owned by the limited partners, Jones and Chapin.

In 1979 Nordale began using cocaine, which caused a personality change. He became suspicious of his partners and other people, and he could not communicate with other people. He stopped going to work and stopped keeping normal business hours. He stopped returning phone calls and became hyperactive, agitated and angry toward people for no reason. Commencing in 1980 he made threats to some of the other partners, stating that he was going to get them and fix them.

Nordale lived in the apartment complex. This led to several problems [, including solicitation of tenants for sex]. Despite repeated demands, he refused to give up possession or pay rent on an apartment that the partnership had allowed him to use temporarily during his divorce. His lifestyle in the apartment complex created a great deal of tension and disturbance and frightened the tenants. At least one tenant was lost because of the disturbances.

Fundamental business and management disputes also arose. Nordale irrationally insisted upon converting the apartment complex into condominiums despite adverse tax consequences and mortgage interest rates that were at an all-time high. He also insisted on raising the rents despite the fact that recent attempts to do so had resulted in mass vacancies which had a devastating economic effect on the partnership enterprise.

By 1981 Gary Gibson and Steven Smith (G & S Investments) had come to the conclusion that Nordale was incapable of making rational business decisions and that they should seek a dissolution of the partnership which would allow them to carry on the business and buy out Nordale's interest.

The original complaint, filed on September 11, 1981, sought a judicial dissolution and the right to carry on the business and buy out Nordale's interest. [. . .] The key allegations of the complaint were as follows:

> "5. Defendant has become incapable of performing his part of Century Park's Articles of Limited Partnership ('the articles'), has been guilty of such conduct as tends to affect prejudicially the carrying on of Century Park's business, has willfully or persistently committed breaches of Century Park's articles and breaches of his fiduciary duties to Century Park and its partners, and otherwise has so conducted himself in matters relating to Century Park's business that it is not reasonably practicable to carry on the business in partnership with him.
>
> 6. Defendant wrongfully has caused a dissolution of Century Park in contravention of Century Park's articles and has acted with wreckless [sic] disregard of the rights of Century Park and its partners. [. . .]

8. [. . .] [P]laintiffs cannot agree with defendant on the management of Century Park's business and the disposition of Century Park's assets." [. . .]

After the filing of the complaint, on February 16, 1982, Nordale died. On June 28, 1982, appellees filed a supplemental complaint invoking their right to continue the partnership and acquire Nordale's interest under article 19 of the partnership's Articles of Limited Partnership. The key provisions of article 19 are as follows:

> "(a) In the interest of a continuity of the partnership it is agreed that upon the death, retirement, insanity or resignation of one of the general partners . . . that the surviving or remaining general partners may continue the partnership business. [. . .]
>
> (e) Rules as to resignation or retirement [which under Article 19(d) includes death]. [. . .]
>
>> (2) In the event the surviving or remaining general partner shall desire to continue the partnership

business, *he shall purchase the interest of the retiring or resigning general partner."* [. . .]

The Filing of the Original Complaint

Appellant contends that the mere filing of the complaint acted as a dissolution of the partnership, requiring the liquidation of the assets and distribution of the net proceeds to the partners. He takes this position because he believes the estate will receive more money under this theory than if the other partners are allowed to carry on the business upon payment of the amount which was due to Nordale under the partnership agreement. Appellees contend that the filing of the complaint did not cause a dissolution but that the wrongful conduct of Nordale, in contravention of the partnership agreement, gave the court the power to dissolve the partnership and allow them to carry on the business by themselves. We agree with appellees.

Contrary to appellant's contention, Nordale's conduct was in contravention of the partnership agreement. Nordale's conduct affected the carrying on of the business and made it impracticable to continue in partnership with him. His conduct was wrongful and was in contravention of the partnership agreement, thus allowing the court to permit appellees to carry on the business. [UPA (1914) § 32] authorizes the court to dissolve a partnership when:

(2) A partner becomes in any other way incapable of performing his part of the partnership contract.

(3) A partner has been guilty of such conduct as tends to affect prejudicially the carrying on of the business.

(4) A partner willfully or persistently commits a breach of the partnership agreement, or otherwise so conducts himself in matters relating to the partnership business that it is not reasonably practicable to carry on the business in partnership with him.

In the case of *Cooper v. Isaacs*, the court was met with the same contention made here, to-wit, that the mere filing of the complaint acted as a dissolution. The court rejected this contention. To paraphrase the reasoning of the court in *Cooper v. Isaacs*, because the Uniform Partnership Act provides for dissolution for cause by decree of court and appellees have alleged facts which would entitle them to a dissolution on this ground if proven, their filing of the complaint cannot be said to effect a dissolution, wrongful or otherwise, under the act; dissolution would occur only when decreed by the court or when brought about by other acts.

Article 19 of the Articles of Partnership

Article 19 of the Articles of Partnership provides that upon the death, retirement, insanity or resignation of one of the general partners the surviving or remaining general partners may continue the partnership business. It further provides that should the surviving or remaining general partners desire to continue the partnership business, they must purchase the interest of the retiring or resigning general partner. Appellant contends that by filing the complaint in this case the appellees caused Mr. Nordale to act in reliance on the complaint, to his detriment, and that appellees are therefore estopped from asserting the right to proceed under article 19. [. . .]

The Buy-Out Formula

Article 19(e)(2)(i) contains the following buy-out provision:

The amount shall be calculated as follows:

> By the addition of the sums of the amount of the resigning or retiring general partner's capital account plus an amount equal to the average of the prior three years' profits and gains actually paid to the general partner, or as agreed upon by the general partners, provided said agreed sum does not exceed the calculated sum in dollars.

Appellant claims that the term "capital account" in article 19(e)(2)(i) is ambiguous. The estate relies on the testimony of an accountant, Jon Young, that the term "capital account" is ambiguous merely because there is no definition of the term in the articles. He claimed that it was not clear whether the cost basis or the fair market value of the partnership's assets should be used in determining the capital account. Even on direct examination, however, Young admitted that [. . .] the buy-out formula takes the capital account of the deceased partner and adds to that amount the average of the prior three years' earnings. On cross-examination he admitted that generally accepted accounting principles require the partnership capital accounts be maintained on a cost basis and that he has never seen a partnership in which the capital accounts in the books and records were based on the fair market value. He also admitted that his interpretation was contrary to the literal import of the words used in the agreement and that the words used were not ambiguous and that he had no knowledge of the actual intent of the parties. The sole reason given by Young for his opinion that "capital account" should not be interpreted in accordance with its literal meaning and with generally accepted accounting principles was that he himself had never seen a buy-out provision for real property based on a cost basis of the assets.

In contrast, Gibson and Smith testified that the parties actually intended and understood "capital account" to mean exactly what it literally says, the account which shows a partner's capital contribution to the partnership plus profits minus losses. Smith, an accountant, further testified that while there is a relationship between the capital accounts and valuation of the partnership assets, the valuation of the assets does not affect the actual entries made on the capital account.

There was no dispute that Nordale's capital account showed a negative balance of $44,510.09, which the court found to be a fact and concluded that the purchase price of Nordale's interest should be calculated in accordance with article 19(e)(2), the capital account, and that his interest in the partnership was zero, instead of the fair market value of his interest in the partnership which would have amounted to the sum of $76,714.24.

Appellant contends that the conclusions of the trial court were erroneous, that fair market value should have been used instead of the balance in the capital account and that, even then, the fair market value which the court found was far in excess of the $76,714.24. We disagree with appellant and agree with the trial court's conclusions.

The words "capital account" are not ambiguous and clearly mean the partner's capital account as it appears on the books of the partnership. Our conclusion is further buttressed by the entire language of article 19(e)(2)(i) which requires, for a buy-out, the payment of the amount of the partner's capital account plus other sums. This is "capital account" language and not "fair market value" language. [. . .]

In this case, assuming that the terms "book value" and "capital account" are functional equivalents, Nordale's capital account had not been manipulated in any way. There is no reason why the general rule and the agreement of the parties should not apply. [. . .]

Because partnerships result from contract, the rights and liabilities of the partners among themselves are subject to such agreements as they may make. [. . .]

Partnership buy-out agreements are valid and binding although the purchase price agreed upon is less or more than the actual value of the interest at the time of death. [. . .]

We do not have the power to rewrite article 19 based upon subjective notions of fairness arising long after the agreement was made or because the agreement did not turn out to be an advantageous one. Modern business practice mandates that the parties be bound by the contract they enter into, absent fraud or duress. [. . .] It is not the province of this court to act as a post-transaction guardian for either party.

Judgment affirmed.

F. REVIEW PROBLEMS

1. Rhode Island Builder's Association, Inc. ("RIBA") contracted with Sherman Exposition Management, Inc. ("SEM") to produce home shows for RIBA in Rhode Island. The agreement included the following provisions: RIBA agreed to (1) sponsor and endorse only shows produced by SEM and (2) permit SEM to use RIBA's name for promotional purposes. In return, SEM agreed to (1) obtain all necessary leases, licenses, permits and insurance, (2) indemnify RIBA for show-related losses "of whatever sort," (3) accord RIBA the right to accept or reject

any exhibitor, (4) audit show income, and (5) advance all the capital required to finance the shows. In addition, the parties agreed to share net show profits: 55% to SEM; 45% to RIBA. Southex Exhibitions, Inc. ("Southex"), which acquired SEM, sued RIBA to enjoin a home show, alleging that the agreement between RIBA and Southern's predecessor, SEM established a partnership and that RIBA breached its fiduciary duties by dissolving the parentship. Did the agreement between RIBA and SEM established a partnership?[1]

2.   Katherine Andrews brought an action for attorney malpractice against defendants Barry Elwell (who represented Andrews in Lawrence Juvenile Court), as well as against Paul Pappas, John Carlson, and Neil Colicchio. Pappas, Carlson, and Colicchio moved for summary judgment in their favor on the grounds that they cannot be held vicariously liable for Elwell's alleged negligence. Elwell shared an office with Pappas and Carlson during his representation of Andrews; Colicchio also shared the office beginning "some time" in 2002. During the representation, whenever Andrews called Elwell's office, someone answered the telephone by stating "Pappas, Carlson, and Elwell," and Andrews would ask for Elwell. Elwell made several representations to the court and others that he was affiliated, in some way, with Pappas, Carlson, and later Colicchio. On January 8, 2003, Elwell sent a letter to Andrews's new attorney, which used letterhead bearing the title "PAPPAS, CARLSON, ELWELL & COLICCHIO: ATTORNEYS AT LAW." In addition, the attorney liability insurance policy for the years 2002–03 that names "Pappas, Carlson, Elwell & Colicchio" as the insured. On what grounds can Ms Andrews succeed in her claims against Elwell, Pappas, Carlson, and Colicchio?[2]

3.   Padgett Carroll and Walter Charles Fulton debtor operated a trucking business under the name of C & F Trucking. Mr. Carroll contributed a semi-truck which Fulton drove for the business. The profits earned from the business were to be divided between the parties. In July 1982, Mr. Carroll purchased 1972 Great Dane 42 foot van from Fruehauf Corporation for C & F Trucking. The seller's invoice for the trailer listed C & F Trucking as the purchaser of the trailer. The Arkansas certificate of title for the trailer was signed by the Mr Fulton and listed C & F Trucking as the owner. In December 1982, Fulton filed a voluntary Chapter 7 bankruptcy petition. On January 24, 1983, Fulton amended his petition to reflect that he had been engaged in business as a partner in C & F Trucking. Fulton's schedules listed the 42 foot trailer s one of his assets. Who owns the van?[3]

4.   Senior Living Properties (SLP) operates nursing homes. ZC Specialty Insurance Company (Zurich) guaranteed SLP's mortgage for new nursing homes with a $146 million surety bond. Zurich and SLP entered into agreements that gave Zurich influence over SLP's contracts and

---

[1]   See 279 F.3d 94 (1st Cir. 2002).

[2]   See Andrews v. Elwell, 367 F.Supp.2d 35 (2005), United States District Court, D. Massachusetts.

[3]   See In re Fulton—43 B.R. 273 (Bankr. M.D. Tenn. 1984).

business decisions. One agreement gave Zurich "sole discretion" to protect its interest by amending debt agreements between SLP and another creditor. Zurich had the right to inspect SLP's books and records, and SLP provided Zurich with financial statements and information. Zurich regularly attended SLP's quarterly board meetings and member meetings, and SLP agreed to give Zurich at least ten business days' notice so that Zurich could attend. On SLP's behalf, Zurich negotiated a twenty-year management contract with a nursing home management company, Complete Care Services (CCS). Zurich retained "sole and absolute discretion" to execute a new management agreement and choose a replacement management company. SLP's agreements also gave Zurich "ultimate control" over the nursing homes' day-to-day operations. Zurich monitored SLP's performance, then called CCS to address problems and concerns about individual nursing homes. CCS also issued monthly reports to Zurich, SPL's board, and another creditor.

Ultimately, SLP defaulted on the mortgage. SLP's trustee argues that Zurich operated nursing homes as SLP's partner, and, as a result, Zurich is liable for SLP's debts. In response, Zurich claims that it formed a creditor-debtor relationship with SLP rather than a partnership because a lender may include management review provisions in contracts to protect its position, and formal indications of a partnership, such as a partnership agreement, are absent. Is Zurich only a creditor, or does a partnership exist?[4]

5.   Tobias, Lindsay, and Lucille associated to acquire a property to "flip" it for a profit. Tobias and Lindsay formed Flipping LLC to purchase the property and obtain development funding. Flipping LLC then purchased a property using a loan from Dime Bank, which holds a lien on the property. Lucille formed SparklingReno LLC to facilitate the development of the property. On August 30, 2019, Flipping LLC and SparklingReno LLC entered into a Development Agreement with the purpose of attracting additional funding to develop the property and complete the project. These are some of the main provisions of the Development Agreement:

1.   Flipping LLC will source and provide equity and debt financing to fund the project.

2.   SparklingReno LLC will act as the general contractor to develop the property and will invoice Flipping LLC at cost for all land development expenditures.

3.   SparklingReno LLC will oversee sales to end buyers, build homes on the lots, and deposit the proceeds in an escrow fund.

4.   Flipping LLC must approve the critical path at its sole discretion and must agree to all expenditures in advance.

---

[4]   See Lain v. ZC Specialty Ins. Co. (In re Senior Living Props., L.L.C.), 309 B.R. 223 (Bankr. N.D. Tex., 2004).

5. Flipping LLC and SparklingReno LLC have joint authority to approve disbursements from the escrow fund. Disbursements were to be split between Flipping LLC and SparklingReno LLC.

6. The Development Agreement contains a provision that "[N]othing in this Agreement shall be construed, deemed or interpreted by the parties or by any third person to create the relationship of principal and agent or of partnership, joint venture or any other association other than that of debtor-creditor between the parties."

Did the parties form a partnership when they entered the Development Agreement? Why?[5]

6. Rachel was an experienced M&A attorney who opened her own boutique firm. Louis began working for Rachel as an associate in 2010. For the first years of their relationship, Rachel paid Louis a salary from which the applicable taxes were deducted. Rachel also gave Louis a one-third referral fee for any case he brought into the office. On August 30, 2014, the parties entered into a written agreement. The Agreement did not characterize the relationship between Rachel and Louis as employer and employee or as a partnership, although prior drafts had variously called the document an "Associate Arrangement" and a "Partnership Arrangement." Instead, the final document signed by the parties was simply titled an "Agreement" and referred to an "arrangement" based on Rachel and Louis's prior "excellent relationship in the law practice *heretofore* owned solely by Rachel."

The Agreement provided for Louis to share in the firm's net income on a percentage basis, which would have increased over time, and discontinued the previous agreement on salary and fee-sharing provisions. Nevertheless, Louis was "guaranteed" a specified minimum annual payment "regardless of the amount of net practice income." From 2020 forward, however, Louis's annual share of the net profits was fixed at 25% with no guaranteed minimum payment. The Agreement provided for Louis's vacation and benefits.

The Agreement further required each party to purchase term life insurance on the other's life, with the premiums to be paid out of the purchasing attorney's share of the profits. The apparent purpose of the life insurance policies was to fund a buyout of the deceased attorney's interest in the firm. The Agreement also specifically provided that Rachel would make all decisions with respect to management of the practice. It also characterized Louis as "an independent contractor" who would be "solely responsible for all taxes payable upon his remuneration."

The Agreement provided that the agreement could "be terminated for any reason by either party with the giving of 60 days written notice by one party to the other."

---

[5] *See* In re Cavu/Rock Properties Project I, LLC, 516 B.R. 414, 416 (Bankr. W.D. Tex. 2014), *aff'd*, 530 B.R. 349 (W.D. Tex. 2015), *aff'd*, 637 Fed. Appx. 123 (5th Cir. 2016).

Did Rachel and Louis form a partnership?[6]

7.   CookieDough Corporation and Brick LLC formed a limited partnership for the construction of a 10-floor building known as "Sweet Paradise." The partners intended to erect the building in downtown Washington, D.C. Brick was the sole limited partner with a 20% interest. CookieDough was the sole general partner with an 80% interest. CookieDough and Brick agreed on a variety of things to complete the "Sweet Paradise" project. CookieDough agreed to raise the large sums of money needed to construct what was intended to be a fancy building and guaranteed (1) full payment by the partnership of the principal and interest on the amount borrowed to complete the project, and (2) the completion on time of the construction of the building. Regarding this latter aspect, Brick LLC agreed to indemnify up to 1/3 of CookieDough's liability for its guarantees.

In their capacities as partners, CookieDough and Brick understood there might be a need for additional partnership capital in the future. Thus, they agreed that under certain circumstances, the general partner, CookieDough, could "call" for the partners to contribute more money. If Brick LLC failed to contribute its share of additional capital, CookieDough could "cram down" (i.e., CookieDough could pay the capital Brick failed to pay, and take over Brick's interest in the partnership).

In the partnership agreement, the partners agreed on a contractual definition of "business judgment" that required parties to perform their duties "with ordinary prudence and in a manner characteristic of businesspersons in similar circumstances." They also agreed that liability would not arise out of a mistake in judgment and that no exculpation from liability shall apply in situations of bad faith.

Sometime after the agreement was signed, the real estate market in Washington collapsed, CookieDough made a capital call, Brick refused to meet the call, and CookieDough "crammed down" on Brick.

Brick sued CookieDough for breach of fiduciary duties. On what ground? What party is more likely to succeed and why?[7]

8.   Meehan and Boyle were partners of the law firm Parker Coulter. After Meehan and Boyle terminated their relationship with Parker Coulter to start their own firm, they commenced this action both to recover amounts they claim the defendants, their former partners, owed them under the partnership agreement, and to obtain a declaration as to amounts they owed the defendants for work done at Parker Coulter on cases they removed to their new firm. The defendants counterclaimed that Meehan and Boyle violated their fiduciary duties and breached the partnership agreement when they departed Parker Coutler. Parker Coulter asserted that Meehan and Boyle breached their fiduciary duties

---

  [6] *See* Nadel v. Starkman, No. A–4204–08T1, 2010 WL 4103626 (N.J. Super. Ct. App. Div. Oct. 20, 2010).

  [7] *See* Opus Corp. v. International Business Machines Corp., 141 F.3d 1261 (8th Cir. 1998).

to the partnership through various improper actions. Which of the following actions may justify a breach of fiduciary duty?

a. Meehan and Boyle made some logistical arrangement to set up their new firm, such as leasing office space and preparing a list of clients expected to leave Parker Coulter;

b. Meehan and Boyle obtained clients' consent to move to the new law firm and the correspondence to clients was sent on Parker Coulter's letterhead;

c. Prior to their departure, Meehan and Boyle were asked on three occasions by their partners whether they were leaving the firm. They denied that they were leaving;

d. Meehan and Boyle worked slowly on cases and clients, including on cases and clients that were paid on a contingency basis, on the theory that those payments could then be earned by the new firm;

e. Meehan and Boyle asked employees to join their new firm.[8]

9. John Summers and E.A. Dooley run a trash-collecting business. They agree that if either is unable to work, the non-working partner would provide a replacement worker at his own expense. In 1962, Dooley became unable to work and, at his own expense, hired an employee to take his place. In July 1966, Summers approached his partner Dooley regarding the hiring of an additional employee, but Dooley refused. If Summers proceeds in hiring the employee and personally pays him, does the partnership need to reimburse half of the costs?[9]

10. Kelly Giles is a general partner in a family farming limited partnership, Giles Land Company, L.P.. Kelly filed suit against the partnership and his partners, arguing that he had not been provided access to partnership books and records. The remaining members of the partnership—his parents and sibling—then filed a counterclaim requesting that Kelly be dissociated from the partnership under RUPA 601.

The other partners of Giles Land Company, L.P. provide evidence that:

• Kelly did not trust the other general partners and that he did not trust some of his sisters who are limited partners in the partnership;

• The relationship between Kelly and the other family members was irreparably broken. At a partnership meeting, Kelly turned to each of the general partners and said that they would each die and that when he was the last man standing, he would then control the partnership.

---

[8] *See* Meehan v. Shaughnessy, 535 N.E.2d 1255 (Mass. 1989).
[9] *See* Summers v. Dooley, 481 P.2d 318 (Idaho 1971).

On what ground can the partnership dissociate Kelly? If the partners decide to seek a judicial dissociation of Kelly, what do would be the best reasons to advance in court?[10]

11. Cohen and Owen entered into an oral agreement to run a bowling alley. Owen lends $7000 to the partnership, with the understanding that the amount so contributed was to be considered a loan to the partnership and was to be repaid to Owen out of the prospective profits of the business as soon as it could reasonably do so. After a few months, differences arose between the partner with regard to the management of the partnership affairs, and their respective rights and duties under their agreement. What kind of partnership was formed by Cohen and Owen? What do parties need to show to seek judicial dissolution? Owen v. Cohen, 119 P.2d 713 (1941).[11]

G. STANDARD GENERAL PARTNERSHIP AGREEMENT

This standard general partnership agreement is adapted from Alan S. Gutterman's Standard General Partnership Agreement (2020).

Article 1—Parties

The parties to this agreement, Antonin Scalia of 3301 Fairfax Drive, Arlington, Virginia, and Ruth Bader Ginsburg of 3302 Fairfax Drive, Arlington, Virginia, agree to form a partnership pursuant to the Virginia partnership law on the terms and conditions set forth.

Article 2—Purpose

The partnership shall be for the purpose of engaging in the business of legal publication and in such other related business as may be agreed on by the partners.

Article 3—Name of Partnership

The name of the partnership shall be FYRE Dissents.

Article 4—Place of Business

The principal place of business of the partnership shall be 3300 Fairfax Drive, Arlington, Virginia, and such other place or places as may be agreed on by the partners.

Article 5—Duration

The partnership shall commence on January 1, 202X, and continue until December 31, 203X, or until dissolved pursuant to this agreement.

Article 6—Capital Contributions

6.1 Partnership Capital. The initial capital of the partnership shall consist of the sum of $100,000.

---

10   *See* Giles v. Giles Land Co., L.P., 279 P.3d 139 (Kan. App. 2012).
11   *See* Owen v. Coehn, 119 P.2d 713 (Cal. 1941).

6.2 Initial Contributions. The initial contribution of each partner shall be as follows:

(a) Antonin Scalia: $50,000

(b) Ruth Bader Ginsburg: 3300 Fairfax Drive, Arlington, Virginia, with tax assessed value of $50,000 (the "storefront")

6.3 Subsequent Capital Contributions

(a) Subsequent capital contributions, as such are needed by the partnership, shall be made by each partner in proportion to his or her respective distributive share (as defined in this agreement).

(b) In the event any partner fails to make such subsequent capital contribution, the partners who have contributed their shares may consider the sums so advanced as loans to the partnership.

6.4 When Initial Contribution to be Made. Each partner shall make an initial contribution of capital to the capital of the partnership on or before January 15, 202X (the "contribution date").

6.5 Effect of Failure to Make Initial Contribution

(a) If any partner fails to make an entire initial contribution to the capital of the partnership on or before the *contribution date*, this agreement shall be of no further effect.

(b) On the happening of this contingency all contributions which have been made shall be returned to the partners who have made these contributions.

6.6 Interest on Capital Contributions. No partner shall receive, or be entitled to receive, interest on contributions to capital.

Article 7—Partnership Property

7.1 Partnership Property. Subject to the provisions of this Article, all property originally paid or brought into, or transferred to, the partnership as contributions to capital by the partners, or subsequently acquired by purchase or otherwise, on account of the partnership, is partnership property.

7.2 Title to Property. It is agreed that the *storefront* is being made available to the partnership by Ruth Bader Ginsburg solely for the use of the partnership and is to remain the property of Justice Ginsburg and is to be returned to her on December 31, 203X, or when the partnership is dissolved, if prior to that date.

7.3 Property to be in Partnership Name. The title to all partnership property shall be held in the name of the partnership.

Article 8—Rights, Duties, and Liabilities of Partners

8.1 Other Business Activities Prohibited. No partner, during the continuance of the partnership, shall pursue, or become directly or indirectly interested in, any business or occupation which is in conflict either with the business of the partnership or with the duties and responsibilities of the partner to the partnership.

8.2 Time Partners to Devote to Business. Each partner shall devote to the business of the partnership the following amount of time:

Name	Time Devoted to Business
Antonin Scalia	2,400 hours per year
Ruth Bader Ginsburg	2,400 hours per year

8.3 Salaries. Each partner, for time devoted to the business of the partnership, shall receive, in addition to his or her share in any profits, the following salary:

Name	Salary
Antonin Scalia	$100,000 per year
Ruth Bader Ginsburg	$100,000 per year

8.4 Vacations and Leaves of Absence. Each partner shall be entitled to 10 days of vacation and 10 days of leave of absence for illness or disability per annum, commencing from January 1, 202X, with no impairment of rights to the partner's share of the profits or of any other rights under this agreement.

8.5 Suretyship Obligations. The parties covenant that they presently are not, and agree that they shall not during the existence of the partnership, without the written consent of all the partners, become obligated under any bond, suretyship or security agreement, bail contract, or as co-signer for any individual, partnership, or corporation, and shall not knowingly cause or allow anything to be done in which partnership property may be attached or taken in execution.

Article 9—Management of Business

9.1 Participation in Management.

(a) Except as otherwise provided in this agreement, all partners shall have equal rights in the management and conduct of the partnership.

(b) Decisions shall be by majority vote (each partner having one vote) except as provided in this Article.

9.2 Matters Requiring Unanimity. During the continuance of the partnership, no partner shall, without the consent of all the partners, do any of the following:

(a) Assign the partnership property in trust for creditors or on the assignee's promise to pay the debts of the partnership;

(b) Dispose of the good will of the business;

(c) Submit a partnership claim or liability to arbitration or reference;

(d) Confess a judgment against the partnership;

(e) Do any act which would make it impossible to carry on the ordinary business of the partnership;

(f) Make, execute, or deliver in the name of the partnership any bond, trust deed, mortgage, indemnity bond, guarantee, surety bond, or accommodation paper or accommodation indorsement;

(g) Borrow money in the name of the partnership or use as collateral any partnership property;

(h) Assign, pledge, transfer, release, or compromise any debt owing to, or claim of, the partnership except for full payment;

(i) Convey any real property of the partnership;

(j) Pledge or transfer in any manner, except to another partner, his or her individual interest in the partnership; or

(k) Undertake or complete any act for which unanimity is required under any other provision of this agreement.

9.3 Contracts. For purposes of the partnership business, but subject to any limitations and restrictions imposed by this agreement, each partner shall have equal power and authority in using the partnership name and in binding the partnership, in making contracts and purchasing goods, and in otherwise trading, buying, selling, and managing on behalf of the partnership.

9.4 Employment and Dismissal of Personnel. No partner shall hire any person for employment by the partnership or dismiss, except in case of gross misconduct, any person in the employment of the partnership without the consent of all the partners.

9.5 Indemnity by Partnership. The partnership will indemnify each partner in respect of payments made and personal liabilities reasonably incurred by each partner in the ordinary and proper conduct of the partnership business, or for the preservation of its business or property.

9.6 Bank Deposits and Accounts. All partnership funds shall be deposited in the name of the partnership in accounts in the Real Good Bank at 3211 Washington Boulevard, Arlington, Virginia. All checks, drafts, or other withdrawal slips drawn on partnership accounts must be signed by two partners.

Article 10—Profits and Losses

10.1   Sharing of Profits

(a) The partners shall be entitled to the net profits arising from the operation of the partnership business that remain after the payment of the expenses of conducting the business of the partnership.

(b) Each partner shall be entitled to the distributive share of the profits specified below:

Name	Percentage
Antonin Scalia	50%
Ruth Bader Ginsburg	50%

(c) The distributive share of the profits shall be determined and paid to the partners on the 31st day of December of each year.

10.2   Losses. All losses that occur in the operation of the partnership business shall be paid out of the capital of the partnership and the profits of the business, or, if such sources are deficient in funds to cover such losses, by the partners in the following shares:

Name	Percentage
Antonin Scalia	50%
Ruth Bader Ginsburg	50%

Article 11—Books, Records, and Accounts

11.1   Books of Account. Books of account shall be kept by the partners, and proper entries made of all the sales, purchases, receipts, payments, engagements, transactions, and property of the partnership.

11.2   Method of Accounting. All accounts of the partnership shall be kept on the accrual basis. All matters of accounting for which there is no provision in this agreement are to be governed by generally accepted methods of accounting.

11.3   Place Where Books and Records to be Kept

(a) The partnership books of account, and all securities, papers, and writings of the partnership shall be kept at the principal place of business at 3300 Fairfax Drive, Arlington, Virginia, or in an alternative place where the business shall be carried on.

(b) Each partner shall have free access at all times to examine and copy the partnership books.

11.4   Capital Accounts

(a) A capital account shall be maintained on the partnership books on behalf of each partner.

(b) This account shall be credited with that partner's contributions to the capital of the partnership and shall be debited and credited in the manner prescribed in this Article.

11.5   Income Accounts

(a) An income account shall be maintained on the partnership books on behalf of each partner.

(b) This account shall be closed to the capital account of the partner at the close of each fiscal year.

(c) As soon as practicable after the close of each fiscal year, and at such other times as the partners may decide, the income account of each partner shall be credited with that partner's distributive share of profits and debited with his or her share of the losses.

(d) Any losses to be debited to a partner's income account that exceed the credit balance of the account shall be debited to that partner's individual capital account.

(e) If, as a result of debiting a partner's individual capital account with the excess losses, his or her capital account is depleted, future profits of that partner shall be credited to his or her capital account until the depletion has been eliminated.

11.6 Drawing Accounts

(a) A drawing account, to which withdrawals shall be debited, shall be maintained on the partnership books on behalf of each partner.

(b) Withdrawals may be made subject to such limitations as the partners may from time to time adopt.

(c) The drawing account shall be closed to the income account at the close of each fiscal year.

11.7 Tax Year. The taxable year of the partnership shall commence on June 1st and end on May 31st.

Article 12—Accounting Between Partners

Each partner shall, on every reasonable request, give to the other partners a true accounting of all transactions relating to the business of the partnership, and full information of all letters, accounts, writings, and other things which shall come into his or her possession or to his or her knowledge concerning the business of the partnership.

Article 13—Admission of Partners

Additional partners may be admitted to this partnership on terms as may be agreed on in writing between the partners and the new partners. The terms so agreed on shall constitute an amendment to this partnership agreement.

Article 14—Withdrawal or Retirement of Partners

14.1 Notice. In the event any partner shall desire to withdraw or retire from the partnership, or becomes disabled so that he or she is unable to fulfill obligations to the partnership as specified in this agreement, the partner shall give 45 days' notice in writing by registered or certified mail to the other partners at each other partner's last known address.

14.2   **Special Circumstances.** If any partner is adjudged incompetent or insane, then his or her guardian shall give notice to each of the other partners in the manner provided above.

Article 15—Expulsion of Partners

If any partner is adjudged insane or incompetent, or becomes disabled to the extent that he or she will be unable for a period of one year to fulfill obligations to the partnership as specified in this agreement, or fails for any other reason to fulfill such obligations, the partner may be expelled from membership in the partnership by a majority vote of the other partners, the expulsion to become effective after 10 days' notice of expulsion to the partner. The notice shall briefly state the grounds for the expulsion.

Article 16—Competitive Activities

Any partner who is no longer associated with the partnership shall not, without the consent in writing of the active partners in the partnership, conduct or otherwise engage in the legal publication business within Arlington, Virginia, for a period of two years after dissociation.

Article 17—Dissolution, Winding Up; Liquidation

17.1   **Causes of Dissolution.** The partnership shall be dissolved on the happening of any of the following events:

(a) Termination of the term as specified in this agreement;

(b) Withdrawal, retirement, or expulsion of any partner;

(c) Death, disability, or bankruptcy of any partner;

(d) Unanimous agreement of the parties;

(e) An event that makes it unlawful for all or substantially all of the business of the partnership to be continued; or

(f) Judicial dissolution on application of a partner.

17.2   **Right to Continue Business After Dissolution**

(a) On dissolution of the partnership, the remaining partners shall have the right to elect to continue the business of the partnership under the same name, by themselves, or with any additional persons they may choose.

(b) If the partners remaining desire to continue the business, but not together, the partnership shall be liquidated pursuant to this Article.

17.3   **Payment if Partnership Continued After Dissolution**

(a) If, on dissolution, the remaining partners elect to continue the partnership business under this Article, they shall pay to any dissociating partner, the value of that partner's interest, as determined by this Article, as of the date of dissolution.

(b) This payment shall be made within three months of dissolution.

17.4   Value of Partner's Interest. The value of a partner's interest in the partnership shall be computed by:

(a) adding the totals of

    (1)   the partner's capital account,

    (2)   the partner's income account, and

    (3)   any other amounts owed to the partner by the partnership, and

(b) subtracting from the sum of the above totals the sum of the totals of

    (1)   the partner's drawing account, and

    (2)   any amount owed by the partner to the partnership.

17.5   Winding Up and Liquidation.

(a) On dissolution of the partnership, if the partnership business is not continued pursuant to this Article, it shall be wound up and liquidated as quickly as circumstances will allow.

(b) The assets of the partnership shall be applied to partnership liabilities in the following order:

    (1)   Amounts owing to creditors other than partners;

    (2)   Amounts owing to partners other than for capital and profits;

    (3)   Amounts owing to partners in respect to capital; and

    (4)   Amounts owing to partners in respect to profits.

Article 18—Arbitration

It is agreed that disputes arising under this agreement, or under any instrument made to carry out the terms of this agreement, shall be submitted to arbitration in accordance with the arbitration laws of the State of Virginia.

Article 19—Notices to Partners

All notices to the partners pursuant to this agreement shall be in writing and shall be deemed effective when given by personal delivery or by certified or registered mail or similar delivery service, postage prepaid, to the partners at their addresses as shown from time to time on the records of the Partnership, and shall be deemed given when mailed or delivered.

Article 20—Amendments

This agreement, except with respect to vested rights of the partners, may be amended at any time by a majority vote of the partners.

/s/ Antonin Scalia
Antonin Scalia

/s/ Ruth Bader Ginsburg
Ruth Bader Ginsburg

Dated: December 31, 202X

CHAPTER III

CORPORATE ORGANIZATION AND PURPOSE

Corporations are business entities that play a central role in the economy and society. They allow entrepreneurs to raise, pool, and partition assets for economic purposes. They are separate legal entities from their founders and investors, and are the centers of legal rights, obligations, and duties.

Each state has adopted its own corporate law. State corporate law sets allowable corporate structures and the rights and obligations of shareholders, directors, and officers of the firm. Case law is layered on top of that and is particularly important in defining the scope of fiduciary obligations.

This book focuses on Delaware law. More than 1,000,000 business entities and more than 66% of the Fortune 500 corporations are incorporated in Delaware. As a result, the Delaware judiciary and corporate law have become the most authoritative source of corporate law.

A. CORPORATION DEFINED

Burwell v. Hobby Lobby Stores, Inc.
573 U.S. 682 (2014)

■ JUSTICE ALITO delivered the opinion of the Court.

We must decide in these cases whether the Religious Freedom Restoration Act of 1993 (RFRA) [. . .] permits the United States Department of Health and Human Services (HHS) to demand that three closely held corporations provide health insurance coverage for methods of contraception that violate the sincerely held religious beliefs of the companies' owners. We hold that the regulations that impose this obligation violate RFRA, which prohibits the Federal Government from taking any action that substantially burdens the exercise of religion unless that action constitutes the least restrictive means of serving a compelling government interest.

In holding that the HHS mandate is unlawful, we reject HHS's argument that the owners of the companies forfeited all RFRA protection when they decided to organize their businesses as corporations rather than sole proprietorships or general partnerships. The plain terms of RFRA make it perfectly clear that Congress did not discriminate in this way against men and women who wish to run their businesses as for-profit corporations in the manner required by their religious beliefs. [. . .]

David and Barbara Green and their three children are Christians who own and operate two family businesses. Forty-five years ago, David Green started an arts-and-crafts store that has grown into a nationwide chain called Hobby Lobby. There are now 500 Hobby Lobby stores, and the company has more than 13,000 employees. Hobby Lobby is organized as a for-profit corporation under Oklahoma law. One of David's sons started an affiliated business, Mardel, which operates Christian bookstores and employs close to 400 people. Mardel is also organized as a for-profit corporation under Oklahoma law. Though these two businesses have expanded over the years, they remain closely held, and David, Barbara, and their children retain exclusive control of both companies. David serves as the CEO of Hobby Lobby, and his three children serve as the president, vice president, and vice CEO.

Hobby Lobby's statement of purpose commits the Greens to "[h]onoring the Lord in all [they] do by operating the company in a manner consistent with Biblical principles." Each family member has signed a pledge to run the businesses in accordance with the family's religious beliefs and to use the family assets to support Christian ministries. In accordance with those commitments, Hobby Lobby and Mardel stores close on Sundays, even though the Greens calculate that they lose millions in sales annually by doing so. The businesses refuse to engage in profitable transactions that facilitate or promote alcohol use; they contribute profits to Christian missionaries and ministries; and they buy hundreds of full-page newspaper ads inviting people to "know Jesus as Lord and Savior."

[. . .] The first question that we must address is whether th[e RFRA] provision applies to regulations that govern the activities of for-profit corporations like Hobby Lobby [. . .]. HHS contends that neither th[is] company nor [its] owners can even be heard under RFRA. According to HHS, the compan[y] cannot sue because [it] seek[s] to make a profit for [its] owners, and the owners cannot be heard because the regulations, at least as a formal matter, apply only to the compan[y] and not to the owners as individuals. HHS's argument would have dramatic consequences.

Consider this Court's decision in *Braunfeld v. Brown*. In that case, five Orthodox Jewish merchants who ran small retail businesses in Philadelphia challenged a Pennsylvania Sunday closing law as a violation of the Free Exercise Clause. Because of their faith, these merchants closed their shops on Saturday, and they argued that requiring them to remain shut on Sunday threatened them with financial ruin. The Court entertained their claim (although it ruled against them on the merits), and if a similar claim were raised today under RFRA against a jurisdiction still subject to the Act [. . .], the merchants would be entitled to be heard. According to HHS, however, if these merchants chose to incorporate their businesses—without in any way changing the size or nature of their businesses—they would forfeit all RFRA (and free exercise) rights. HHS would put these merchants to a difficult choice: either give up the right to seek judicial protection of their religious liberty or forgo the benefits, available to their competitors, of operating as corporations. [. . .]

A corporation is simply a form of organization used by human beings to achieve desired ends. [. . .] When rights, whether constitutional or statutory, are extended to corporations, the purpose is to protect the rights of these people. [. . .]

As we noted above, RFRA applies to "a person's" exercise of religion [. . .] and RFRA itself does not define the term "person." We therefore look to the Dictionary Act, which we must consult "[i]n determining the meaning of any Act of Congress, unless the context indicates otherwise." 1 U.S.C. § 1.

Under the Dictionary Act, "the wor[d] 'person' . . . include[s] corporations, companies, associations, firms, partnerships, societies, and joint stock companies, as well as individuals." [. . .] Thus, unless there is something about the RFRA context that "indicates otherwise," the Dictionary Act provides a quick, clear, and affirmative answer to the question whether the companies involved in these cases may be heard.

We see nothing in RFRA that suggests a congressional intent to depart from the Dictionary Act definition, and HHS makes little effort to argue otherwise. [. . .]

This concession effectively dispatches any argument that the term "person" as used in RFRA does not reach the closely held corporations involved in these cases. No known understanding of the term "person" includes *some* but not all corporations. The term "person" sometimes encompasses artificial persons (as the Dictionary Act instructs), and it sometimes is limited to natural persons. But no conceivable definition of the term includes natural persons and nonprofit corporations, but not for-profit corporations. [. . .]

The principal argument advanced by HHS and the principal dissent regarding RFRA protection for Hobby Lobby [. . .] focuses not on the statutory term "person," but on the phrase "exercise of religion." According to HHS and the dissent, these corporations are not protected by RFRA because they cannot exercise religion. [. . .]

Is it because of the corporate form? The corporate form alone cannot provide the explanation because [. . .] HHS concedes that nonprofit corporations can be protected by RFRA. The dissent suggests that nonprofit corporations are special because furthering their religious "autonomy . . . often furthers individual religious freedom as well." [. . .] But this principle applies equally to for-profit corporations: Furthering their religious freedom also "furthers individual religious freedom." In these cases, for example, allowing Hobby Lobby [. . .] to assert RFRA claims protects the religious liberty of the Greens [*i.e.*, the controlling shareholders of Hobby Lobby].

If the corporate form is not enough, what about the profit-making objective? [. . .] [T]he Court explained [. . .] the "exercise of religion" involves "not only belief and profession but the performance of (or abstention from) physical acts" that are "engaged in for religious reasons." [. . .] Business practices that are compelled or limited by the tenets of a religious doctrine fall comfortably within that definition. Thus, a law that "operates so as to make the practice of . . . religious beliefs more expensive" in the context of business activities imposes a burden on the exercise of religion. [. . .]

Some lower court judges have suggested that RFRA does not protect for-profit corporations because the purpose of such corporations is simply to make money. This argument flies in the face of modern corporate law. "Each American jurisdiction today either expressly or by implication authorizes corporations to be formed under its general corporation act for *any lawful purpose* or business." [. . .] While it is certainly true that a central objective of for-profit corporations is to make money, modern corporate law does not require for-profit corporations to pursue profit at the expense of everything else, and many do not do so. For-profit corporations, with ownership approval, support a wide variety of charitable causes, and it is not at all uncommon for such corporations to further humanitarian and other altruistic objectives. Many examples come readily to mind. So long as its owners agree, a for-profit corporation may take costly pollution-control and energy-conservation measures that go beyond what the law requires. A for-profit corporation that operates facilities in other countries may exceed the requirements of local law regarding working conditions and benefits. If for-profit corporations may pursue such worthy objectives, there is no apparent reason why they may not further religious objectives as well.

HHS would draw a sharp line between nonprofit corporations (which, HHS concedes, are protected by RFRA) and for-profit corporations (which HHS would leave unprotected), but the actual picture is less clear-cut. Not all corporations that decline to organize as nonprofits do so in order to maximize profit. For example, organizations with religious and charitable aims might organize as for-profit corporations because of the potential advantages of that corporate form, such as the freedom to participate in lobbying for legislation or campaigning for political candidates who promote their religious or charitable goals. In fact, recognizing the inherent compatibility between establishing a for-profit corporation and pursuing nonprofit goals, States have increasingly adopted laws formally recognizing hybrid corporate forms. Over half of the States, for instance, now recognize the "benefit corporation," a dual-purpose entity that seeks to achieve both a benefit for the public and a profit for its owners.*

In any event, the objectives that may properly be pursued by the compan[y] in th[is] case[ ] [are] governed by the laws of the State[ ] in which [it was] incorporated—[. . .] Oklahoma—and the laws of th[is] State[ ] permit[s] for-profit corporations to pursue "any lawful purpose" or "act," including the pursuit of profit in conformity with the owners' religious principles. Okla. Stat., Tit. 18, §§ 1002, 1005 (West 2012) ("[E]very corporation, whether profit or not for profit" may "be incorporated or organized . . . to conduct or promote any lawful business or purposes"); *see also* § 1006(A)(3); Brief for State of Oklahoma as *Amicus Curiae* in No. 13–354.

Finally, HHS contends that Congress could not have wanted RFRA to apply to for-profit corporations because it is difficult as a practical matter to ascertain the sincere "beliefs" of a corporation. HHS goes so far as to raise the specter of "divisive, polarizing proxy battles over the religious identity of large, publicly traded corporations such as IBM or General Electric." [. . .]

[This case], however, do[es] not involve publicly traded corporations, and it seems unlikely that the sort of corporate giants to which HHS refers will often assert RFRA claims. HHS has not pointed to any example of a publicly traded corporation asserting RFRA rights, and numerous practical restraints would likely prevent that from occurring. For example, the idea that unrelated shareholders—including institutional investors with their own set of stakeholders—would agree to run a corporation under the same religious beliefs seems improbable. In any event, we have no occasion in these cases to consider RFRA's applicability to such companies. The compan[y] in the case[ ] before us [is a] closely held corporation[ ], [. . .] owned and controlled by members of a single family, and no one has disputed the sincerity of their religious beliefs.

HHS has also provided no evidence that the purported problem of determining the sincerity of an asserted religious belief moved Congress to exclude for-profit corporations from RFRA's protection. [. . .]

HHS and the principal dissent express concern about the possibility of disputes among the owners of corporations, but that is not a problem that arises because of RFRA or that is unique to this context. The owners of

---

* EDS.—Delaware's statute on public benefit corporation, DGCL § 362, states:

(a) A "public benefit corporation" is a for-profit corporation [. . .] that is intended to produce a public benefit or public benefits and to operate in a responsible and sustainable manner. To that end, a public benefit corporation shall be managed in a manner that balances the stockholders' pecuniary interests, the best interests of those materially affected by the corporation's conduct, and the public benefit or public benefits identified in its certificate of incorporation. [. . .]

(b) "Public benefit" means a positive effect (or reduction of negative effects) on 1 or more categories of persons, entities, communities or interests (other than stockholders in their capacities as stockholders) including, but not limited to, effects of an artistic, charitable, cultural, economic, educational, environmental, literary, medical, religious, scientific or technological nature. [. . .]"

closely held corporations may—and sometimes do—disagree about the conduct of business. [. . .] And even if RFRA did not exist, the owners of a company might well have a dispute relating to religion. For example, some might want a company's stores to remain open on the Sabbath in order to make more money, and others might want the stores to close for religious reasons. State corporate law provides a ready means for resolving any conflicts by, for example, dictating how a corporation can establish its governing structure. *See, e.g., ibid; id.*, § 3:2; Del. Code Ann., Tit. 8, § 351 (2011) (providing that certificate of incorporation may provide how "the business of the corporation shall be managed"). Courts will turn to that structure and the underlying state law in resolving disputes.

For all these reasons, we hold that a federal regulation's restriction on the activities of a for-profit closely held corporation must comply with RFRA.

■ JUSTICE GINSBURG, with whom JUSTICE SOTOMAYOR joins, and with whom JUSTICE BREYER and JUSTICE KAGAN join as to all but Part III–C–1, dissenting.

In a decision of startling breadth, the Court holds that commercial enterprises, including corporations, along with partnerships and sole proprietorships, can opt out of any law (saving only tax laws) they judge incompatible with their sincerely held religious beliefs. [. . .] In the Court's view, RFRA demands accommodation of a for-profit corporation's religious beliefs no matter the impact that accommodation may have on third parties who do not share the corporation owners' religious faith—in these cases, thousands of women employed by Hobby Lobby [. . .] or dependents of persons th[is] corporation[] employ[s]. Persuaded that Congress enacted RFRA to serve a far less radical purpose, and mindful of the havoc the Court's judgment can introduce, I dissent. [. . .]

RFRA's compelling interest test [. . .] applies to government actions that "substantially burden *a person's exercise of religion*." [. . .] This reference, the Court submits, incorporates the definition of "person" found in the Dictionary Act, 1 U. S. C. § 1, which extends to "corporations, companies, associations, firms, partnerships, societies, and joint stock companies, as well as individuals." [. . .] The Dictionary Act's definition, however, controls only where "context" does not "indicat[e] otherwise". Here, context does so indicate. RFRA speaks of "a person's *exercise of religion*." [. . .]

Until this litigation, no decision of this Court recognized a for-profit corporation's qualification for a religious exemption from a generally applicable law, whether under the Free Exercise Clause or RFRA. The absence of such precedent is just what one would expect, for the exercise of religion is characteristic of natural persons, not artificial legal entities. As Chief Justice Marshall observed nearly two centuries ago, a corporation is "an artificial being, invisible, intangible, and existing only in contemplation of law." *Trustees of Dartmouth College v. Woodward.*

Corporations, Justice Stevens more recently reminded, "have no consciences, no beliefs, no feelings, no thoughts, no desires." *Citizens United v. Federal Election Comm'n.* [. . .]

The First Amendment's free exercise protections, the Court has indeed recognized, shelter churches and other nonprofit religion-based organizations. "For many individuals, religious activity derives meaning in large measure from participation in a larger religious community," and "furtherance of the autonomy of religious organizations often furthers individual religious freedom as well." [. . .] The Court's "special solicitude to the rights of religious organizations," [. . .] however, is just that. No such solicitude is traditional for commercial organizations. Indeed, until today, religious exemptions had never been extended to any entity operating in "the commercial, profit-making world." [. . .]

The reason why is hardly obscure. Religious organizations exist to foster the interests of persons subscribing to the same religious faith. Not so of for-profit corporations. Workers who sustain the operations of those corporations commonly are not drawn from one religious community. Indeed, by law, no religion-based criterion can restrict the work force of for-profit corporations. [. . .]

The Court notes that for-profit corporations may support charitable causes and use their funds for religious ends, and therefore questions the distinction between such corporations and religious nonprofit organizations. [. . .] Again, the Court forgets that religious organizations exist to serve a community of believers. For-profit corporations do not fit that bill. [. . .] To reiterate, "for-profit corporations are different from religious non-profits in that they use labor to make a profit, rather than to perpetuate [the] religious value[s] [shared by a community of believers]." *Gilardi v. United States Dept. of Health and Human Servs.*

Citing *Braunfeld v. Brown*, the Court questions why, if "a sole proprietorship that seeks to make a profit may assert a free-exercise claim, [Hobby Lobby [. . .]] can't . . . do the same?" [. . .] But even accepting, *arguendo*, the premise that unincorporated business enterprises may gain religious accommodations under the Free Exercise Clause, the Court's conclusion is unsound. In a sole proprietorship, the business and its owner are one and the same. By incorporating a business, however, an individual separates herself from the entity and escapes personal responsibility for the entity's obligations. One might ask why the separation should hold only when it serves the interest of those who control the corporation. In any event, *Braunfeld* is hardly impressive authority for the entitlement Hobby Lobby [. . .] seek[s]. [. . .]

The Court's determination that RFRA extends to for-profit corporations is bound to have untoward effects. Although the Court attempts to cabin its language to closely held corporations, its logic extends to corporations of any size, public or private. Little doubt that RFRA claims will proliferate, for the Court's expansive notion of corporate personhood—combined with its other errors in construing RFRA—invites for-profit entities to seek religion-based exemptions from regulations they deem offensive to their faith. [. . .]

[. . .] Working for Hobby Lobby [. . .] should not deprive employees of the preventive care available to workers at the shop next door, at least in the absence of directions from the Legislature or Administration to do so.

Why should decisions of this order be made by Congress or the regulatory authority, and not this Court? Hobby Lobby [. . .] surely do[es] not stand alone as commercial enterprises seeking exemptions from generally applicable laws on the basis of their religious beliefs. *See, e.g., Newman* v. *Piggie Park Enterprises, Inc.* (owner of restaurant chain refused to serve black patrons based on his religious beliefs opposing racial integration); *In re Minnesota ex rel. McClure* (born-again Christians who owned closely held, for-profit health clubs believed that the Bible proscribed hiring or retaining an "individua[l] living with but not married to a person of the opposite sex," "a young, single woman working without her father's consent or a married woman working without her husband's consent," and any person "antagonistic to the Bible," including "fornicators and homosexuals"; *Elane Photography, LLC* v. *Willock*, (for-profit photography business owned by a husband and wife refused to photograph a lesbian couple's commitment ceremony based on the religious beliefs of the company's owners). Would RFRA require exemptions in cases of this ilk? And if not, how does the Court divine which religious beliefs are worthy of accommodation, and which are not? Isn't the Court disarmed from making such a judgment given its recognition that "courts must not presume to determine . . . the plausibility of a religious claim"? *Ante,* at 37.

Would the exemption the Court holds RFRA demands for employers with religiously grounded objections to the use of certain contraceptives extend to employers with religiously grounded objections to blood transfusions (Jehovah's Witnesses); antidepressants (Scientologists); medications derived from pigs, including anesthesia, intravenous fluids, and pills coated with gelatin (certain Muslims, Jews, and Hindus); and vaccinations (Christian Scientists, among others)? According to counsel for Hobby Lobby, "each one of these cases . . . would have to be evaluated on its own . . . apply[ing] the compelling interest-least restrictive alternative test." [. . .]

For the reasons stated, I would reverse the judgment of the Court of Appeals for the Tenth Circuit and affirm the judgment of the Court of Appeals for the Third Circuit.

■ JUSTICE BREYER and JUSTICE KAGAN, dissenting.

We agree with Justice Ginsburg that the plaintiffs' challenge to the contraceptive coverage requirement fails on the merits. We need not and do not decide whether either for-profit corporations or their owners may bring claims under the Religious Freedom Restoration Act of 1993.

Accordingly, we join all but Part III–C–1 of Justice Ginsburg's dissenting opinion.

Delaware General Corporation Law

Section 101. Incorporators; how corporation formed; purposes.

(a) Any person, partnership, association or corporation, singly or jointly with others, and without regard to such person's or entity's residence, domicile or state of incorporation, may incorporate or organize a corporation under this chapter by filing with the Division of Corporations in the Department of State a certificate of incorporation which shall be executed, acknowledged and filed in accordance with § 103 of this title.

(b) A corporation may be incorporated or organized under this chapter to conduct or promote any lawful business or purposes [. . .]

Section 106. Commencement of corporate existence.

Upon the filing with the Secretary of State of the certificate of incorporation, executed and acknowledged in accordance with § 103 of this title, the incorporator or incorporators who signed the certificate, [. . .] shall, from the date of such filing, be and constitute a body corporate [. . .].

Section 102. Contents of certificate of incorporation.

(a) The certificate of incorporation shall set forth:

(1) The name of the corporation, which (i) shall contain 1 of the words "association," "company," "corporation," "club," "foundation," "fund," "incorporated," "institute," "society," "union," "syndicate," or "limited," (or abbreviations thereof, with or without punctuation) [. . .]

(3) The nature of the business or purposes to be conducted or promoted. It shall be sufficient to state, either alone or with other businesses or purposes, that the purpose of the corporation is to engage in any lawful act or activity for which corporations may be organized under the General Corporation Law of Delaware [. . .];

(4) If the corporation is to be authorized to issue only 1 class of stock, the total number of shares of stock which the corporation shall have authority to issue and the par value of each of such shares, or a statement that all such shares are to be without par value. If the corporation is to be authorized to issue more than 1 class of stock, the certificate of incorporation shall set forth the total number of shares of all classes of stock which the corporation shall have authority to issue and the number of shares of each class and shall specify each class the shares of which are to be without par value and each class the shares of which are to have par value and the par value of the shares of each such class. The certificate of incorporation shall also set forth a statement of the designations and the powers,

preferences and rights, and the qualifications, limitations or restrictions thereof, which are permitted by § 151 of this title in respect of any class or classes of stock or any series of any class of stock of the corporation and the fixing of which by the certificate of incorporation is desired, and an express grant of such authority as it may then be desired to grant to the board of directors to fix by resolution or resolutions any thereof that may be desired but which shall not be fixed by the certificate of incorporation. [. . .]

(b) In addition to the matters required to be set forth in the certificate of incorporation by subsection (a) of this section, the certificate of incorporation may also contain any or all of the following matters:

(1) Any provision for the management of the business and for the conduct of the affairs of the corporation, and any provision creating, defining, limiting and regulating the powers of the corporation, the directors, and the stockholders, or any class of the stockholders, or the governing body, members [. . .]; if such provisions are not contrary to the laws of this State. Any provision which is required or permitted by any section of this chapter to be stated in the bylaws may instead be stated in the certificate of incorporation; [. . .]

(3) Such provisions as may be desired granting to the holders of the stock of the corporation, or the holders of any class or series of a class thereof, the preemptive right to subscribe to any or all additional issues of stock of the corporation of any or all classes or series thereof, or to any securities of the corporation convertible into such stock. No stockholder shall have any preemptive right to subscribe to an additional issue of stock or to any security convertible into such stock unless, and except to the extent that, such right is expressly granted to such stockholder in the certificate of incorporation. [. . .]

(4) Provisions requiring for any corporate action, the vote of a larger portion of the stock or of any class or series thereof, or of any other securities having voting power, or a larger number of the directors, than is required by this chapter;

(5) A provision limiting the duration of the corporation's existence to a specified date; otherwise, the corporation shall have perpetual existence;

(6) A provision imposing personal liability for the debts of the corporation on its stockholders to a specified extent and upon specified conditions; otherwise, the stockholders of a corporation shall not be personally liable for the payment of the corporation's debts except as they may be liable by reason of their own conduct or acts;

(7) A provision eliminating or limiting the personal liability of a director or officer to the corporation or its stockholders for monetary damages for breach of fiduciary duty as a director or officer, provided that such provision shall not eliminate or limit the liability of:

(i)   A director or officer for any breach of the director's or officer's duty of loyalty to the corporation or its stockholders;

(ii) A director or officer for acts or omissions not in good faith or which involve intentional misconduct or a knowing violation of law;

(iii) A director under § 174 of this title;

(iv) A director or officer for any transaction from which the director or officer derived an improper personal benefit; or

(v)   An officer in any action by or in the right of the corporation.

No such provision shall eliminate or limit the liability of a director or officer for any act or omission occurring prior to the date when such provision becomes effective.

An amendment, repeal or elimination of such a provision shall not affect its application with respect to an act or omission by a director or officer occurring before such amendment, repeal or elimination unless the provision provides otherwise at the time of such act or omission. [. . .]

Section 109. Bylaws.

(a) The original or other bylaws of a corporation may be adopted, amended or repealed by the incorporators, by the initial directors of a corporation [. . .] if they were named in the certificate of incorporation, or, before a corporation [. . .] has received any payment for any of its stock, by its board of directors. After a corporation [. . .] has received any payment for any of its stock, the power to adopt, amend or repeal bylaws shall be in the stockholders entitled to vote. [. . .]Notwithstanding the foregoing, any corporation may, in its certificate of incorporation, confer the power to adopt, amend or repeal bylaws upon the directors [. . .]. The fact that such power has been so conferred upon the directors or governing body, as the case may be, shall not divest the stockholders or members of the power, nor limit their power to adopt, amend or repeal bylaws.

(b) The bylaws may contain any provision, not inconsistent with law or with the certificate of incorporation, relating to the business of the corporation, the conduct of its affairs, and its rights or powers or the rights or powers of its stockholders, directors, officers or employees. The bylaws may not contain any provision that would impose liability on a stockholder for the attorneys' fees or expenses of the corporation or any other party in connection with an internal corporate claim, as defined in § 115 of this title.

Section 121. General powers.

(a) In addition to the powers enumerated in § 122 of this title, every corporation, its officers, directors and stockholders shall possess and may exercise all the powers and privileges granted by this chapter or by any other law or by its certificate of incorporation, together with any powers incidental thereto, so far as such powers and privileges are necessary or convenient to the conduct, promotion or attainment of the business or purposes set forth in its certificate of incorporation. [. . .]

Section 122. Specific powers.

Every corporation created under this chapter shall have power to:

(1) Have perpetual succession by its corporate name, unless a limited period of duration is stated in its certificate of incorporation;

(2) Sue and be sued in all courts and participate, as a party or otherwise, in any judicial, administrative, arbitrative or other proceeding, in its corporate name; [. . .]

(4) Purchase, receive, take by grant, gift, devise, bequest or otherwise, lease, or otherwise acquire, own, hold, improve, employ, use and otherwise deal in and with real or personal property, or any interest therein, wherever situated, and to sell, convey, lease, exchange, transfer or otherwise dispose of, or mortgage or pledge, all or any of its property and assets, or any interest therein, wherever situated;

(5) Appoint such officers and agents as the business of the corporation requires and to pay or otherwise provide for them suitable compensation;

(6) Adopt, amend and repeal bylaws;

(7) Wind up and dissolve itself in the manner provided in this chapter;

(8) Conduct its business, carry on its operations and have offices and exercise its powers within or without this State;

(9) Make donations for the public welfare or for charitable, scientific or educational purposes, and in time of war or other national emergency in aid thereof;

(10) Be an incorporator, promoter or manager of other corporations of any type or kind;

(11) Participate with others in any corporation, partnership, limited partnership, joint venture or other association of any kind [. . .];

(12) Transact any lawful business which the corporation's board of directors shall find to be in aid of governmental authority;

(13) Make contracts [. . .];

(14) Lend money for its corporate purposes, invest and reinvest its funds, and take, hold and deal with real and personal property as security for the payment of funds so loaned or invested;

(15) Pay pensions and establish and carry out pension, profit sharing, stock option, stock purchase, stock bonus, retirement, benefit, incentive and compensation plans, trusts and provisions for any or all of its directors, officers and employees [. . .];

(16) Provide insurance for its benefit on the life of any of its directors, officers or employees [. . .].

(17) Renounce, in its certificate of incorporation or by action of its board of directors, any interest or expectancy of the corporation in, or in being offered an opportunity to participate in, specified business opportunities or specified classes or categories of business opportunities that are presented to the corporation or 1 or more of its officers, directors or stockholders.

Section 151. Classes and series of stock; redemption; rights.

(a) Every corporation may issue 1 or more classes of stock or 1 or more series of stock within any class thereof, any or all of which classes may be of stock with par value or stock without par value and which classes or series may have such voting powers, full or limited, or no voting powers, and such designations, preferences and relative, participating, optional or other special rights, and qualifications, limitations or restrictions thereof, as shall be stated and expressed in the certificate of incorporation or of any amendment thereto, or in the resolution or resolutions providing for the issue of such stock adopted by the board of directors pursuant to authority expressly vested in it by the provisions of its certificate of incorporation. Any of the voting powers, designations, preferences, rights and qualifications, limitations or restrictions of any such class or series of stock may be made dependent upon facts ascertainable outside the certificate of incorporation or of any amendment thereto, or outside the resolution or resolutions providing for the issue of such stock adopted by the board of directors pursuant to authority expressly vested in it by its certificate of incorporation, provided that the manner in which such facts shall operate upon the voting powers, designations, preferences, rights and qualifications, limitations or restrictions of such class or series of stock is clearly and expressly set forth in the certificate of incorporation or in the resolution or resolutions providing for the issue of such stock adopted by the board of directors. [. . .]

(b) Any stock of any class or series may be made subject to redemption by the corporation at its option or at the option of the holders of such stock or upon the happening of a specified event; [. . .]

(c) The holders of preferred or special stock of any class or of any series thereof shall be entitled to receive dividends at such rates, on such conditions and at such times as shall be stated in the certificate of incorporation or in the resolution or resolutions providing for the issue of such stock adopted by the board of directors as hereinabove provided, payable in preference to, or in such relation to, the dividends payable on any other class or classes or of any other series of stock, and cumulative or noncumulative as shall be so stated and expressed. When dividends upon the preferred and special stocks, if any, to the extent of the preference to which such stocks are entitled, shall have been paid or declared and set apart for payment, a dividend on the remaining class or classes or series of stock may then be paid out of the remaining assets of the corporation available for dividends as elsewhere in this chapter provided.

(d) The holders of the preferred or special stock of any class or of any series thereof shall be entitled to such rights upon the dissolution of, or upon any distribution of the assets of, the corporation as shall be stated in the certificate of incorporation or in the resolution or resolutions providing for the issue of such stock adopted by the board of directors as hereinabove provided.

(e) Any stock of any class or of any series thereof may be made convertible into, or exchangeable for, at the option of either the holder or the corporation or upon the happening of a specified event, shares of any other class or classes or any other series of the same or any other class or classes of stock of the corporation, at such price or prices or at such rate or rates of exchange and with such adjustments as shall be stated in the certificate of incorporation or in the resolution or resolutions providing for the issue of such stock adopted by the board of directors as hereinabove provided.

(f) If any corporation shall be authorized to issue more than 1 class of stock or more than 1 series of any class, the powers, designations, preferences and relative, participating, optional, or other special rights of each class of stock or series thereof and the qualifications, limitations or restrictions of such preferences and/or rights shall be set forth in full or summarized on the face or back of the certificate which the corporation shall issue to represent such class or series of stock[. . .]

Section 152. Issuance of stock; lawful consideration; fully paid stock.

(a) The consideration, as determined pursuant to § 153(a) and (b) of this title, for subscriptions to, or the purchase of, the capital stock to be issued by a corporation shall be paid in the form and in the manner that the board of directors shall determine. The board of directors may authorize capital stock to be issued for consideration consisting of cash, any tangible or intangible property or any benefit to the corporation, or any combination thereof. Stock may be issued in 1 or more transactions, in the numbers, at the times and for the consideration as set forth in a resolution of the board of directors.

B. PIERCING THE CORPORATE VEIL

Walkovszky v. Carlton
18 N.Y.2d 414 (N.Y. Ct. App. 1966)

■ FULD, JUDGE.

This case involves what appears to be a rather common practice in the taxicab industry of vesting the ownership of a taxi fleet in many corporations, each owning only one or two cabs.

The complaint alleges that the plaintiff was severely injured four years ago in New York City when he was run down by a taxicab owned by the defendant Seon Cab Corporation and negligently operated at the time by the defendant Marchese. The individual defendant, Carlton, is claimed to be a stockholder of 10 corporations, including Seon, each of which has but two cabs registered in its name, and it is implied that only the minimum automobile liability insurance required by law (in the amount of $10,000) is carried on any one cab. Although seemingly independent of one another, these corporations are alleged to be "operated . . . as a single entity, unit and enterprise" with regard to financing, supplies, repairs, employees and garaging, and all are named as defendants. The plaintiff asserts that he is also entitled to hold their stockholders personally liable for the damages sought because the multiple corporate structure constitutes an unlawful attempt "to defraud members of the general public" who might be injured by the cabs. [. . .]

The law permits the incorporation of a business for the very purpose of enabling its proprietors to escape personal liability but, manifestly, the privilege is not without its limits. Broadly speaking, the courts will disregard the corporate form, or, to use accepted terminology, "pierce the corporate veil," whenever necessary "to prevent fraud or to achieve equity." In determining whether liability should be extended to reach assets beyond those belonging to the corporation, we are guided, as Judge Cardozo noted, by "general rules of agency." *Berkey v. Third Ave. Ry. Co.* In other words, whenever anyone uses control of the corporation to further his own rather than the corporation's business, he will be liable for the corporation's acts "upon the principle of *respondeat superior* applicable even where the agent is a natural person." *Rapid Tr. Subway Constr. Co. v. City of New York.* Such liability, moreover, extends not only to the corporation's commercial dealings but to its negligent acts as well.

In *Mangan v. Terminal Transp. System*, the plaintiff was injured as a result of the negligent operation of a cab owned and operated by one of four corporations affiliated with the defendant Terminal. Although the defendant was not a stockholder of any of the operating companies, both the defendant and the operating companies were owned, for the most part, by the same parties. The defendant's name (Terminal) was conspicuously displayed on the sides of all of the taxis used in the enterprise and, in point of fact, the defendant actually serviced, inspected, repaired and dispatched them. These facts were deemed to provide sufficient cause for piercing the corporate veil of the operating company—the nominal owner of the cab which injured the plaintiff—and holding the defendant liable. The operating companies were simply instrumentalities for carrying on the business of the defendant without imposing upon it financial and other liabilities incident to the actual ownership and operation of the cabs.

In the case before us, the plaintiff has explicitly alleged that none of the corporations "had a separate existence of their own" and, as indicated above, all are named as defendants. However, it is one thing to assert that a corporation is a fragment of a larger corporate combine which actually conducts the business. It is quite another to claim that the corporation is a "dummy" for its individual stockholders who are in reality carrying on the business in their personal capacities for purely personal rather than corporate ends. Either circumstance would justify treating the corporation as an agent and piercing the corporate veil to reach the principal but a different result would follow in each case. In the first, only a larger *corporate* entity would be held financially responsible while, in the other, the stockholder would be personally liable. Either the stockholder is conducting the business in his individual capacity or he is not. If he is, he will be liable; if he is not, then it does not matter—insofar as his personal liability is concerned—that the enterprise is actually being carried on by a larger "enterprise entity." *See* Berle, *The Theory of Enterprise Entity.* [. . .]

The individual defendant is charged with having "organized, managed, dominated and controlled" a fragmented corporate entity but there are no allegations that he was conducting business in his individual capacity. Had the taxicab fleet been owned by a single corporation, it would be readily apparent that the plaintiff would face formidable barriers in attempting to establish personal liability on the part of the corporation's stockholders. The fact that the fleet ownership has been deliberately split up among many corporations does not ease the plaintiff's burden in that respect. The corporate form may not be disregarded merely because the assets of the corporation, together with the mandatory insurance coverage of the vehicle which struck the plaintiff, are insufficient to assure him the recovery sought. If Carlton were to be held individually liable on those facts alone, the decision would apply equally to the thousands of cabs which are owned by their individual drivers who conduct their businesses through corporations organized pursuant to [. . .] the Business Corporation Law [. . .] and carry the minimum insurance required [. . .]. These taxi owner-operators are entitled to form such corporations and we agree with the court at Special Term that, if the insurance coverage required by statute "is inadequate for the protection of the public, the remedy lies not with the courts but with the Legislature." *Elenkrieg v. Siebrecht.* It may very well be sound policy to require that certain corporations must take out liability insurance which will afford adequate compensation to their potential tort victims. However, the responsibility for imposing conditions on the privilege of incorporation has been committed by the Constitution to the Legislature and it may not be fairly implied, from any statute, that the Legislature intended, without the slightest discussion or debate, to require of taxi corporations that they carry automobile liability insurance over and above that mandated by the Vehicle and Traffic Law.

This is not to say that it is impossible for the plaintiff to state a valid cause of action against the defendant Carlton. However, the simple fact is that the plaintiff has just not done so here. While the complaint alleges that the separate corporations were undercapitalized and that their assets have been intermingled, it is barren of any "sufficiently particular(ized) statements" (CPLR 3013) that the defendant Carlton and his associates are actually doing business in their individual capacities, shuttling their personal funds in and out of the corporations "without regard to formality and to suit their immediate convenience." *Weisser v. Mursam Shoe Corp.* Such a "perversion of the privilege to do business in a corporate form" would justify imposing personal liability on the individual stockholders. *Berkey v. Third Ave. Ry. Co.* Nothing of the sort has in fact been charged, and it cannot reasonably or logically be inferred from the happenstance that the business of Seon Cab Corporation may actually be carried on by a larger corporate entity composed of many corporations which, under general principles of agency, would be liable to each other's creditors in contract and in tort.

In point of fact, the principle relied upon in the complaint to sustain the imposition of personal liability is not agency but fraud. Such a cause of action cannot withstand analysis. If it is not fraudulent for the owner-operator of a single cab corporation to take out only the minimum required liability insurance, the enterprise does not become either illicit or fraudulent merely because it consists of many such corporations. The plaintiff's injuries are the same regardless of whether the cab which strikes him is owned by a single corporation or part of a fleet with ownership fragmented among many corporations. Whatever rights he may be able to assert against parties other than the registered owner of the vehicle come into being not because he has been defrauded but because, under the principle of *respondeat superior*, he is entitled to hold the whole enterprise responsible for the acts of its agents.

In sum, then, the complaint falls short of adequately stating a cause of action against the defendant Carlton in his individual capacity.

The order of the Appellate Division should be reversed, with costs in this court and in the Appellate Division, the certified question answered in the negative and the order of the Supreme Court, Richmond County, reinstated, with leave to serve an amended complaint.

■ KEATING, JUDGE (dissenting).

The defendant Carlton [. . .] was a principal shareholder and organizer of the defendant corporation which owned the taxicab. The corporation was one of 10 organized by the defendant, each containing two cabs and each cab having the "minimum liability" insurance coverage mandated by the Vehicle and Traffic Law. The sole assets of these operating corporations are the vehicles themselves and they are apparently subject to mortgages.

From their inception these corporations were intentionally undercapitalized for the purpose of avoiding responsibility for acts which were bound to arise as a result of the operation of a large taxi fleet having cars out on the street 24 hours a day and engaged in public transportation. And during the course of the corporations' existence all income was continually drained out of the corporations for the same purpose.

The issue presented by this action is whether the policy of this State, which affords those desiring to engage in a business enterprise the privilege of limited liability through the use of the corporate device, is so strong that it will permit that privilege to continue no matter how much it is abused, no matter how irresponsibly the corporation is operated, no matter what the cost to the public. I do not believe that it is.

Under the circumstances of this case the shareholders should all be held individually liable to this plaintiff for the injuries he suffered. At least, the matter should not be disposed of on the pleadings by a dismissal of the complaint. [. . .]

In *Anderson v. Abbott*, the defendant shareholders had organized a holding company and transferred to that company shares which they held in various national banks in return for shares in the holding company. The holding company did not have sufficient assets to meet the double liability requirements of the governing Federal statutes which provided that the owners of shares in national banks were personally liable for corporate obligations "to the extent of the amount of their stock therein, at the par value thereof, in addition to the amount invested in such shares" 12 U.S.C.A. § 63 (repealed 1959).

The court had found that these transfers were made in good faith, that other defendant shareholders who had purchased shares in the holding company had done so in good faith and that the organization of such a holding company was entirely legal. Despite this finding, the Supreme Court, speaking through Mr. Justice DOUGLAS, pierced the corporate veil of the holding company and held all the shareholders, even those who had no part in the organization of the corporation, individually responsible for the corporate obligations as mandated by the statute. [. . .]

The policy of this State has always been to provide and facilitate recovery for those injured through the negligence of others. The automobile, by its very nature, is capable of causing severe and costly injuries when not operated in a proper manner. The great increase in the number of automobile accidents combined with the frequent financial irresponsibility of the individual driving the car led to the adoption of section 388 of the Vehicle and Traffic Law which had the effect of imposing upon the owner of the vehicle the responsibility for its negligent operation. It is upon this very statute that the cause of action against both the corporation and the individual defendant is predicated. [. . .]

In addition the Legislature, still concerned with the financial irresponsibility of those who owned and operated motor vehicles, enacted a statute requiring minimum liability coverage for all owners of automobiles. [. . .]

The defendant Carlton claims that, because the minimum amount of insurance required by the statute was obtained, the corporate veil cannot and should not be pierced despite the fact that the assets of the corporation which owned the cab were "trifling compared with the business to be done and the risks of loss" which were certain to be encountered. I do not agree.

The Legislature in requiring minimum liability insurance of $10,000, no doubt, intended to provide at least some small fund for recovery against those individuals and corporations who just did not have and were not able to raise or accumulate assets sufficient to satisfy the claims of those who were injured as a result of their negligence. It certainly could not have intended to shield those individuals who organized corporations, with the specific intent of avoiding responsibility to the public, where the operation of the corporate enterprise yielded profits sufficient to purchase additional insurance. Moreover, it is reasonable to assume that the Legislature believed that those individuals and corporations having substantial assets would take out insurance far in excess of the minimum in order to protect those assets from depletion. Given the costs of hospital care and treatment and the nature of injuries sustained in auto collisions, it would be unreasonable to assume that the Legislature believed that the minimum provided in the statute would in and of itself be sufficient to recompense "innocent victims of motor vehicle accidents [. . .] for the injury and financial loss inflicted upon them."

The defendant, however, argues that the failure of the Legislature to increase the minimum insurance requirements indicates legislative acquiescence in this scheme to avoid liability and responsibility to the public. In the absence of a clear legislative statement, approval of a scheme having such serious consequences is not to be so lightly inferred.

The defendant contends that the court will be encroaching upon the legislative domain by ignoring the corporate veil and holding the individual shareholder. [. . .] This argument was answered by Mr. Justice DOUGLAS in *Anderson* v. *Abbott* where he wrote that: "In the field in which we are presently concerned, judicial power hardly oversteps the bounds when it refuses to lend its aid to a promotional project which would circumvent or undermine a legislative policy. [. . .] Judicial interference to cripple or defeat a legislative policy is one thing; judicial interference with the plans of those *whose corporate or other devices would circumvent that policy is quite another*. Once the purpose or effect of the scheme is clear, once the legislative policy is plain, we would indeed forsake a great tradition to say we were helpless to fashion the instruments for appropriate relief."

The defendant contends that a decision holding him personally liable would discourage people from engaging in corporate enterprise.

What I would merely hold is that a participating shareholder of a corporation vested with a public interest, organized with capital insufficient to meet liabilities which are certain to arise in the ordinary course of the corporation's business, may be held personally responsible for such liabilities. Where corporate income is not sufficient to cover the cost of insurance premiums above the statutory minimum or where initially adequate finances dwindle under the pressure of competition, bad times or extraordinary and unexpected liability, obviously the shareholder will not be held liable [. . .].

The only types of corporate enterprises that will be discouraged as a result of a decision allowing the individual shareholder to be sued will be those such as the one in question, designed solely to abuse the corporate privilege at the expense of the public interest.

For these reasons I would vote to affirm the order of the Appellate Division.

Sea-Land Services, Inc. v. Pepper Source

941 F.2d 519 (7th Cir. 1991)

This spicy case finds its origin in several shipments of Jamaican sweet peppers. Appellee Sea-Land Services, Inc. ("Sea-Land"), an ocean carrier, shipped the peppers on behalf of The Pepper Source ("PS"), one of the appellants here. PS then stiffed Sea-Land on the freight bill, which was rather substantial. Sea-Land filed a federal diversity action for the money it was owed. On December 2, 1987, the district court entered a default judgment in favor of Sea-Land and against PS in the amount of $86,767.70. But PS was nowhere to be found; it had been "dissolved" in mid-1987 for failure to pay the annual state franchise tax. Worse yet for Sea-Land, even had it not been dissolved, PS apparently had no assets. With the well empty, Sea-Land could not recover its judgment against PS. Hence the instant lawsuit.

In June 1988, Sea-Land brought this action against Gerald J. Marchese and five business entities he owns: PS, Caribe Crown, Inc., Jamar Corp., Salescaster Distributors, Inc., and Marchese Fegan Associates. Marchese also was named individually. Sea-Land sought by this suit to pierce PS's corporate veil and render Marchese personally liable for the judgment owed to Sea-Land, and then "reverse pierce" Marchese's other corporations so that they, too, would be on the hook for the $87,000. Thus, Sea-Land alleged in its complaint that all of these corporations "are alter egos of each other and hide behind the veils of alleged separate corporate existence for the purpose of defrauding plaintiff and other creditors." Not only are the corporations alter egos of each other, alleged Sea-Land, but also they are alter egos of Marchese, who should be held individually liable for the judgment because he created and manipulated these corporations and their assets for his own personal uses. (Hot on the heels of the filing of Sea-Land's complaint, PS took the necessary steps to be reinstated as a corporation in Illinois.)[. . .]

In December 1989, Sea-Land moved for summary judgment.

In an order dated June 22, 1990, the court granted Sea-Land's motion. The court discussed and applied the test for corporate veil-piercing explicated in *Van Dorn Co. v. Future Chemical and Oil Corp.* Analyzing Illinois law, we held in *Van Dorn* that a corporate entity will be disregarded and the veil of limited liability pierced when two requirements are met:

> [F]irst, there must be such unity of interest and ownership that the separate personalities of the corporation and the individual [or other corporation] no longer exist; and second, circumstances must be such that adherence to the fiction of separate corporate existence would sanction a fraud or promote injustice.

As for determining whether a corporation is so controlled by another to justify disregarding their separate identities, the Illinois cases, as we summarized them in *Van Dorn,* focus on four factors: "(1) the failure to maintain adequate corporate records or to comply with corporate formalities, (2) the commingling of funds or assets, (3) undercapitalization, and (4) one corporation treating the assets of another corporation as its own."

[. . .] [The] district court in the instant case laid the template of *Van Dorn* over the facts of this case [and] entered judgment in favor of Sea-Land and against PS, Caribe Crown, Jamar, Salescaster, Tie-Net, and Marchese individually. These defendants were held jointly liable for Sea-Land's $87,000 judgment, as well as for post-judgment interest under Illinois law. From that judgment Marchese and the other defendants brought a timely appeal.

Because this is an appeal from a grant of summary judgment, our review is *de novo.* Thus, our task is to examine the evidence for ourselves, apply the same standard as the district court (namely, the *Van Dorn* test), and determine whether there is no genuine issue of material fact and whether Sea-Land is entitled to judgment as a matter of law.

The first and most striking feature that emerges from our examination of the record is that these corporate defendants are, indeed, little but Marchese's playthings. Marchese is the sole shareholder of PS, Caribe Crown, Jamar, and Salescaster. He is one of the two shareholders of Tie-

Net. Except for Tie-Net, none of the corporations ever held a single corporate meeting. (At the handful of Tie-Net meetings held by Marchese and Andre [EDS.—George Andre owned the other half of Tie-Net], no minutes were taken.) During his deposition, Marchese did not remember any of these corporations ever passing articles of incorporation, bylaws, or other agreements. As for physical facilities, Marchese runs all of these corporations (including Tie-Net) out of the same, single office, with the same phone line, the same expense accounts, and the like. And how he does "run" the expense accounts! When he fancies to, Marchese "borrows" substantial sums of money from these corporations—interest free, of course. The corporations also "borrow" money from each other when need be, which left at least PS completely out of capital when the Sea-Land bills came due. What's more, Marchese has used the bank accounts of these corporations to pay all kinds of personal expenses, including alimony and child support payments to his ex-wife, education expenses for his children, maintenance of his personal automobiles, health care for his pet—the list goes on and on. Marchese did not even have a personal bank account! (With "corporate" accounts like these, who needs one?)

And Tie-Net is just as much a part of this as the other corporations. On appeal, Marchese makes much of the fact that he shares ownership of Tie-Net, and that Sea-Land has not been able to find an example of funds flowing from PS to Tie-Net to the detriment of Sea-Land and PS's other creditors. So what? The record reveals that, in all material senses, Marchese treated Tie-Net like his other corporations: he "borrowed" over $30,000 from Tie-Net; money and "loans" flowed freely between Tie-Net and the other corporations; and Marchese charged up various personal expenses (including $460 for a picture of himself with President Bush) on Tie-Net's credit card. Marchese was not deterred by the fact that he did not hold all of the stock of Tie-Net; why should his creditors be?[2]

In sum, we agree with the district court that there can be no doubt that the "shared control/unity of interest and ownership" part of the *Van Dorn* test is met in this case: corporate records and formalities have not been maintained; funds and assets have been commingled with abandon; PS, the offending corporation, and perhaps others have been undercapitalized; and corporate assets have been moved and tapped and "borrowed" without regard to their source. Indeed, Marchese basically punted this part of the inquiry before the district court by coming forward with little or no evidence in response to Sea-Land's extensively supported argument on these points. That fact alone was enough to do him in; opponents to summary judgment motions cannot simply rest on their

---

[2] We note that the record evidence in this case, if true, establishes that for years Marchese flagrantly has disregarded the tax code concerning the treatment of corporate funds. Yet, when we inquired at oral argument whether Marchese currently is under investigation by the IRS, his counsel informed us that to his knowledge he is not. Marchese also stated in his deposition that he never has been audited by the IRS. If these statements are true, and the IRS has so far shown absolutely no interest in Marchese's financial shenanigans with his "corporations," how and why that has occurred may be the biggest puzzles in this litigation.

laurels, but must come forward with specific facts showing that there is a genuine issue for trial. Regarding the elements that make up the first half of the *Van Dorn* test, Marchese and the other defendants have not done so. Thus, Sea-Land is entitled to judgment on these points.

The second part of the *Van Dorn* test is more problematic, however. "Unity of interest and ownership" is not enough; Sea-Land also must show that honoring the separate corporate existences of the defendants "would sanction a fraud or promote injustice." This last phrase truly is disjunctive:

> Although an intent to defraud creditors would surely play a part if established, the Illinois test does not require proof of such intent. Once the first element of the test is established, *either* the sanctioning of a fraud (intentional wrongdoing) or the promotion of injustice, will satisfy the second element.

Seizing on this, Sea-Land has abandoned the language in its two complaints that make repeated references to "fraud" by Marchese, and has chosen not to attempt to *prove* that PS and Marchese intended to defraud it [. . .]. Instead, Sea-Land has argued that honoring the defendants' separate identities would "promote injustice."

But what, exactly, does "promote injustice" mean, and how does one establish it [. . .]? [. . .] To start with, as the above passage from *Van Dorn* makes clear, "promote injustice" means something less than an affirmative showing of fraud—but how much less? In its one-sentence treatment of this point, the district court held that it was enough that "Sea-Land would be denied a judicially-imposed recovery." Sea-Land defends this reasoning on appeal, arguing that "permitting the appellants to hide behind the shield of limited liability would clearly serve as an injustice against appellee" because it would "impermissibly deny appellee satisfaction." But that cannot be what is meant by "promote injustice." [. . .] [I]f an unsatisfied judgment is enough for the "promote injustice" feature of the test, then *every* plaintiff will pass on that score, and *Van Dorn* collapses into a one-step "unity of interest and ownership" test.

Because we cannot abide such a result, we will undertake our own review of Illinois cases to determine how the "promote injustice" feature of the veil-piercing inquiry has been interpreted. [. . .]

[W]e see that the courts that properly have pierced corporate veils to avoid "promoting injustice" have found that, unless it did so, some "wrong" beyond a creditor's inability to collect would result: the common sense rules of adverse possession would be undermined; former partners would be permitted to skirt the legal rules concerning monetary obligations; a party would be unjustly enriched; a parent corporation that caused a sub's liabilities and its inability to pay for them would escape those liabilities; or an intentional scheme to squirrel assets into a liability-free corporation while heaping liabilities upon an asset-free corporation would be successful. Sea-Land, although it alleged in its complaint the kind of intentional asset- and liability-shifting found in *Van Dorn*, has yet to come forward with evidence akin to the "wrongs" found in these cases. Apparently, it believed, as did the district court, that its unsatisfied judgment was enough. That belief was in error, and the entry of summary judgment premature. We, therefore, reverse the judgment and remand the case to the district court.

C. ORGANIZATIONAL DOCUMENTS

Boilermakers Local 154 Retirement Fund v. Chevron Corporation

73 A.3d 934 (Del. Ch. 2013)

■ STRINE, CHANCELLOR.

I. Introduction

The board of Chevron, the oil and gas major, has adopted a bylaw providing that litigation relating to Chevron's internal affairs should be conducted in Delaware, the state where Chevron is incorporated and whose substantive law Chevron's stockholders know governs the corporation's internal affairs. The board of the logistics company FedEx, which is also incorporated in Delaware and whose internal affairs are also therefore governed by Delaware law, has adopted a similar bylaw providing that the forum for litigation related to FedEx's internal affairs should be the Delaware Court of Chancery. The boards of both companies have been empowered in their certificates of incorporation to adopt bylaws under 8 Del. C. § 109(a).

The plaintiffs, stockholders in Chevron and FedEx, have sued the boards for adopting these "forum selection bylaws." The plaintiffs' complaints are nearly identical and were filed only a few days apart by clients of the same law firm. In Count I, the plaintiffs claim that the bylaws are statutorily invalid because they are beyond the board's authority under the Delaware General Corporation Law ("DGCL"). [. . .] In Count IV, the plaintiffs allege that the bylaws are contractually invalid, and therefore cannot be enforced like other contractual forum selection clauses under the test adopted by the Supreme Court of the United States in *The Bremen v. Zapata Off-Shore Co.* [. . .] because they were unilaterally adopted by the Chevron and FedEx boards using their power to make bylaws. Because the two bylaws are similar, present common legal issues, and are the target of near-identical complaints, [this] court decided to address them together. [. . .]

II. Background And Procedural Posture

A. The Chevron And FedEx Forum Selection Bylaws

Critical to the resolution of this motion is an understanding of who has the power to adopt, amend, and repeal the bylaws, and what subjects the bylaws may address under the DGCL. 8 Del. C. § 109(a) identifies who has the power to adopt, amend, and repeal the bylaws:

> [T]he power to adopt, amend or repeal bylaws shall be in the stockholders entitled to vote .... Notwithstanding the foregoing, any corporation may, in its certificate of incorporation, confer the power to adopt, amend or repeal bylaws upon the directors .... The fact that such power has been so conferred upon the directors ... shall not divest the stockholders ... of the power, nor limit their power to adopt, amend or repeal bylaws.

8 Del. C. § 109(b) states the subject matter the bylaws may address:

> The bylaws may contain any provision, not inconsistent with law or with the certificate of incorporation, relating to the business of the corporation, the conduct of its affairs, and its rights or powers or the rights or powers of its stockholders, directors, officers or employees.

Both Chevron's and FedEx's certificates of incorporation conferred on the boards the power to adopt bylaws under 8 Del. C. § 109(a). Thus, all investors who bought stock in the corporations whose forum selection bylaws are at stake knew that (i) the DGCL allows for bylaws to address the subjects identified in 8 Del. C. § 109(b), (ii) the DGCL permits the certificate of incorporation to contain a provision allowing directors to adopt bylaws unilaterally, and (iii) the certificates of incorporation of Chevron and FedEx contained a provision conferring this power on the boards.

Acting consistent with the power conferred to the board in Chevron's certificate of incorporation, the board amended the bylaws and adopted a forum selection bylaw. Generally speaking, a forum selection bylaw is a provision in a corporation's bylaws that designates a forum as the exclusive venue for certain stockholder suits against the corporation, either as an actual or nominal defendant, and its directors and employees. On September 29, 2010, the board of Chevron, a Delaware corporation headquartered in California, adopted a forum selection bylaw that provided:

> Unless the Corporation consents in writing to the selection of an alternative forum, the Court of Chancery of the State of Delaware shall be the sole and exclusive forum for (i) any derivative action or proceeding brought on behalf of the Corporation, (ii) any action asserting a claim of breach of a fiduciary duty owed by any director, officer or other employee of the Corporation to the Corporation or the Corporation's stockholders, (iii) any action asserting a claim arising pursuant to any provision of the Delaware General Corporation Law, or (iv) any action asserting a claim governed by the internal affairs doctrine. Any person or entity purchasing or otherwise

acquiring any interest in shares of capital stock of the Corporation shall be deemed to have notice of and consented to the provisions of this [bylaw].

Several months later, on March 14, 2011, the board of FedEx, a Delaware corporation headquartered in Tennessee, adopted a forum selection bylaw identical to Chevron's. Like Chevron, FedEx's board had been authorized by the certificate of incorporation to adopt bylaws without a stockholder vote, and the FedEx board adopted the bylaw unilaterally. [. . .]

In their briefing, the boards of Chevron and FedEx state that the forum selection bylaws are intended to cover four types of suit, all relating to internal corporate governance:

- *Derivative suits.* The issue of whether a derivative plaintiff is qualified to sue on behalf of the corporation and whether that derivative plaintiff has or is excused from making demand on the board is a matter of corporate governance, because it goes to the very nature of who may speak for the corporation.

- *Fiduciary duty suits.* The law of fiduciary duties regulates the relationships between directors, officers, the corporation, and its stockholders.

- *D.G.C.L. suits.* The Delaware General Corporation Law provides the underpinning framework for all Delaware corporations. That statute goes to the core of how such corporations are governed.

- *Internal affairs suits.* As the U.S. Supreme Court has explained, "internal affairs," in the context of corporate law, are those "matters peculiar to the relationships among or between the corporation and its current officers, directors, and shareholders." *Edgar v. MITE Corp.*

That is, the description of the forum selection bylaws by the Chevron and FedEx boards is consistent with what the plain language of the bylaws suggests: that these bylaws are not intended to regulate *what* suits may be brought against the corporations, only *where* internal governance suits may be brought.

B. The Defendant Boards Have Identified Multiforum Litigation Over Single Corporate Transactions Or Decisions As The Reason Why They Adopted The Bylaws

The Chevron and FedEx boards say that they have adopted forum selection bylaws in response to corporations being subject to litigation over a single transaction or a board decision in more than one forum simultaneously, so-called "multiforum litigation." The defendants' opening brief argues that the boards adopted the forum selection bylaws to address what they perceive to be the inefficient costs of defending against the same claim in multiple courts at one time. The brief describes how, for jurisdictional purposes, a corporation is a citizen both of the state where it is incorporated and of the state where it has its principal place of business. Because a corporation need not be, and frequently is not, headquartered in the state where it is incorporated, a corporation may be subject to personal jurisdiction as a defendant in a suit involving corporate governance matters in two states. Therefore, any act that the corporation or its directors undertake is potentially subject to litigation in at least two states. Furthermore, both state and federal courts may have jurisdiction over the claims against the corporation. The result is that any act that the corporation or its directors undertake may be challenged in various forums within those states simultaneously. The boards of Chevron and FedEx argue that multiforum litigation, when it is brought by dispersed stockholders in different forums, directly or derivatively, to challenge a single corporate action, imposes high costs on the corporations and hurts investors by causing needless costs that are ultimately born by stockholders, and that these costs are not justified by rational benefits for stockholders from multiforum filings.

Thus, the boards of Chevron and FedEx claim to have tried to minimize or eliminate the risk of what they view as wasteful duplicative litigation by adopting the forum selection bylaws. Chevron and FedEx are not the only boards to have recently unilaterally adopted these clauses: in the last three years, over 250 publicly traded corporations have adopted such provisions. [. . .]

C.   The Plaintiffs Challenge The Forum Selection Bylaws

Within the course of three weeks in February 2012, a dozen complaints were filed in this court against Delaware corporations, including Chevron and FedEx, whose boards had adopted forum selection bylaws without stockholder votes. As a threshold issue, these complaints, which were all substantively identical and filed by clients of the same accomplished law firm, alleged that the boards of the defendant corporations had no authority to adopt the bylaws, and sought a declaration that the bylaws were invalid and a breach of fiduciary duty. [. . .]

IV. Legal Analysis

A.   The Board-Adopted Forum Selection Bylaws Are Statutorily Valid

[. . .] [T]he court structures its analysis to mirror the two facial claims of invalidity as they have been presented in the complaints. First, the court looks at Count I's challenge that the "bylaw[s are] invalid because [they are] beyond the authority granted in 8 Del. C. § 109(b)." As to that claim, the court must determine whether the adoption of the forum selection bylaws was beyond the board's authority in the sense that they do not address a proper subject matter under 8 Del. C. § 109(b). [. . .]

Thus, the court must decide if the bylaws are facially invalid under the DGCL because they do not relate to the business of the corporations, the conduct of their affairs, or the rights of the stockholders.

After first making that determination, the court then addresses Count IV's challenge that "the bylaw[s are] not a valid and enforceable forum selection provision." That is, even if forum selection bylaws regulate proper subject matter under 8 Del. C. § 109(b), the plaintiffs allege that forum selection bylaws are contractually invalid because they have been unilaterally adopted by the board.

1. The Forum Selection Bylaws Regulate A Proper Subject Matter Under 8 Del. C. § 109(b)

Having challenged whether the bylaws are authorized by 8 Del. C. § 109(b), the plaintiffs have to confront the broad subjects that § 109(b) permits bylaws to address. The DGCL provides that bylaws may address any subject, "not inconsistent with law or with the certificate of incorporation, relating to the business of the corporation, the conduct of its affairs, and its rights or powers or the rights or powers of its stockholders, directors, officers or employees." [. . .] As a matter of easy linguistics, the forum selection bylaws address the "rights" of the stockholders, because they regulate where stockholders can exercise their right to bring certain internal affairs claims against the corporation and its directors and officers. They also plainly relate to the conduct of the corporation by channeling internal affairs cases into the courts of the state of incorporation, providing for the opportunity to have internal affairs cases resolved authoritatively by our Supreme Court if any party wishes to take an appeal. That is, because the forum selection bylaws address internal affairs claims, the subject matter of the actions the bylaws govern relates quintessentially to "the corporation's business, the conduct of its affairs, and the rights of its stockholders [*qua* stockholders]."

Perhaps recognizing the weakness of any argument that the forum selection bylaws fall outside the plain language of 8 Del. C. § 109(b), the plaintiffs try to argue that judicial gloss put on the language of the statute renders the bylaws facially invalid. The plaintiffs contend that the bylaws do not regulate permissible subject matters under 8 Del. C. § 109(b), because they attempt to regulate an "external" matter, as opposed to, an "internal" matter of corporate governance. The plaintiffs attempt to support this argument with a claim that traditionally there have only been three appropriate subject matters of bylaws: stockholder meetings, the board of directors and its committees, and officerships.

But even if one assumes that judicial statements could limit the plain statutory words in the way the plaintiffs claim (which is dubious), the judicial decisions do not aid the plaintiffs. The plaintiffs take a cramped view of the proper subject matter of bylaws. The bylaws of Delaware corporations have a "procedural, process-oriented nature." It is doubtless true that our courts have said that bylaws typically do not contain substantive mandates, but direct how the corporation, the board, and its stockholders may take certain actions. 8 Del. C. § 109(b) has long been understood to allow the corporation to set "self-imposed rules and regulations [that are] deemed expedient for its convenient functioning." The forum selection bylaws here fit this description. They are process-oriented, because they regulate *where* stockholders may file suit, not *whether* the stockholder may file suit or the kind of remedy that the stockholder may obtain on behalf of herself or the corporation. The bylaws also clearly address cases of the kind that address "the business of the corporation, the conduct of its affairs, and . . . the rights or powers of its stockholders, directors, officers or employees," because they govern where internal affairs cases governed by state corporate law may be heard. These are the kind of claims most central to the relationship between those who manage the corporation and the corporation's stockholders.

By contrast, the bylaws would be regulating external matters if the board adopted a bylaw that purported to bind a plaintiff, even a stockholder plaintiff, who sought to bring a tort claim against the company based on a personal injury she suffered that occurred on the company's premises or a contract claim based on a commercial contract with the corporation. The reason why those kinds of bylaws would be beyond the statutory language of 8 Del. C. § 109(b) is obvious: the bylaws would not deal with the rights and powers of the plaintiff-stockholder *as a stockholder*. As noted earlier, the defendants themselves read the forum selection bylaws in a natural way to cover only internal affairs claims brought by stockholders *qua* stockholders. [. . .]

The plaintiffs' argument, then, reduces to the claim that the bylaws do not speak to a "traditional" subject matter, and should be ruled invalid for that reason alone. [. . .]

[T]he court concludes that forum selection bylaws are statutorily valid under Delaware law, and Count I of the plaintiffs' complaints is dismissed. [. . .]

2. The Board-Adopted Bylaws Are Not Contractually Invalid As Forum Selection Clauses Because They Were Adopted Unilaterally By The Board

Despite the contractual nature of the stockholders' relationship with the corporation under our law, the plaintiffs argue, in Count IV of their complaints, that the forum selection bylaws by their nature are different and cannot be adopted by the board unilaterally. The plaintiffs' argument is grounded in the contention that a board-adopted forum selection bylaw cannot be a *contractual* forum selection clause because the stockholders do not vote in advance of its adoption to approve it. The plaintiffs acknowledge that contractual forum selection clauses are "prima facie valid" under *The Bremen v. Zapata Off-Shore Co.* and *Ingres Corp. v. CA, Inc.,* and that they are presumptively enforceable. But, the plaintiffs say, the forum selection bylaws are contractually invalid in this case, because they were adopted by a board, rather than by Chevron's and FedEx's dispersed stockholders. The plaintiffs argue that this method of adopting a forum selection clause is invalid as a matter of contract law, because it does not require the assent of the stockholders who will be affected by it. Thus, in the plaintiffs' view, there are two types of bylaws: (i) contractually binding bylaws that are adopted by stockholders; (ii) non-contractually binding bylaws that are adopted by boards using their statutory authority conferred by the certificate of incorporation.

By this artificial bifurcation, the plaintiffs misapprehend fundamental principles of Delaware corporate law. Our corporate law has long rejected the so-called "vested rights" doctrine. That vested rights view, which the plaintiffs have adopted as their own, "asserts that boards cannot modify bylaws in a manner that arguably diminishes or divests pre-existing shareholder rights absent stockholder consent." As then-Vice Chancellor, now Justice, Jacobs explained in the *Kidsco* case, under Delaware law, where a corporation's articles or bylaws "put all on notice that the by-laws may be amended at any time, *no vested rights can arise that would contractually prohibit an amendment.*"

In an unbroken line of decisions dating back several generations, our Supreme Court has made clear that the bylaws constitute a binding part of the contract between a Delaware corporation and its stockholders. Stockholders are on notice that, as to those subjects that are subject of regulation by bylaw under 8 Del. C. § 109(b), the board itself may act unilaterally to adopt bylaws addressing those subjects. Such a change by the board is not extra-contractual simply because the board acts unilaterally; rather it is the kind of change that the overarching statutory and contractual regime the stockholders buy into explicitly allows the board to make on its own. In other words, the Chevron and FedEx stockholders have assented to a contractual framework established by the DGCL and the certificates of incorporation that explicitly recognizes that stockholders will be bound by bylaws adopted unilaterally by their boards. Under that clear contractual framework, the stockholders assent to not having to assent to board-adopted bylaws. The plaintiffs' argument that stockholders must approve a forum selection bylaw for it to be contractually binding is an interpretation that contradicts the plain terms of the contractual framework chosen by stockholders who buy stock in Chevron and FedEx. Therefore, when stockholders have authorized a board to unilaterally adopt bylaws, it follows that the bylaws are not contractually invalid simply because the board-adopted bylaw lacks the contemporaneous assent of the stockholders. [. . .]

Even so, the statutory regime provides protections for the stockholders, through the indefeasible right of the stockholders to adopt and amend bylaws themselves. "[B]y its terms Section 109(a) vests in the shareholders a power to adopt, amend or repeal bylaws that is legally sacrosanct, *i.e.,* the power cannot be non-consensually eliminated or limited by anyone other than the legislature itself." *CA, Inc. v. AFSCME*

Emps. Pension Plan. Thus, even though a board may, as is the case here, be granted authority to adopt bylaws, stockholders can check that authority by repealing board-adopted bylaws. And, of course, because the DGCL gives stockholders an annual opportunity to elect directors, stockholders have a potent tool to discipline boards who refuse to accede to a stockholder vote repealing a forum selection clause. Thus, a corporation's bylaws are part of an inherently flexible contract between the stockholders and the corporation under which the stockholders have powerful rights they can use to protect themselves if they do not want board-adopted forum selection bylaws to be part of the contract between themselves and the corporation.

[. . .] Unlike cruise ship passengers, who have no mechanism by which to change their tickets' terms and conditions, stockholders retain the right to modify the corporation's bylaws. [. . .]

In sum, stockholders contractually assent to be bound by bylaws that are valid under the DGCL—that is an essential part of the contract agreed to when an investor buys stock in a Delaware corporation. Where, as here, the certificate of incorporation has conferred on the board the power to adopt bylaws, and the board has adopted a bylaw consistent with 8 Del. C. § 109(b), the stockholders have assented to that new bylaw being contractually binding. Thus, Count IV of the complaints cannot survive and the bylaws are contractually valid as a facial matter. [. . .]

V. Conclusion

For these reasons, the court finds that the challenged bylaws are statutorily valid under 8 Del. C. § 109(b), and are contractually valid and enforceable as forum selection clauses. Judgment is entered for the defendants dismissing Counts I and IV of the plaintiffs' complaints against Chevron and FedEx, with prejudice. IT IS SO ORDERED.*

Delaware General Corporation Law
Section 115. Forum selection provisions.

The certificate of incorporation or the bylaws may require, consistent with applicable jurisdictional requirements, that any or all internal corporate claims shall be brought solely and exclusively in any or all of the courts in this State, and no provision of the certificate of incorporation or the bylaws may prohibit bringing such claims in the courts of this State. "Internal corporate claims" means claims, including claims in the right of the corporation, (i) that are based upon a violation of a duty by a current or former director or officer or stockholder in such capacity, or (ii) as to which this title confers jurisdiction upon the Court of Chancery.

---

* EDS.—In 2015, Delaware adopted a statutory provision on forum selection clauses.

D. AUTHORITY OF OFFICERS

Sarissa Capital Domestic Fund LP v. Innoviva, Inc.
2017 WL 6209597 (Del. Ch. 2017)

■ SLIGHTS, VICE CHANCELLOR.

[EDS.—Sarissa is a dissident shareholder of Innoviva. In early 2017, Sarissa mounted a proxy contest to replace members of Innoviva's board of directors. This action concerns the *de jure* composition of the board.]

Sarissa's proxy contest commenced in February 2017. In its proxy materials, Sarissa charged that Innoviva's incumbent directors were "grossly overpaid . . . in the face of poor stock performance" and were "failing to fulfill [their] duty of oversight." Thus, Sarissa reckoned, Innoviva was "not be[ing] run for the benefit of shareholders[.]" [. . .]

In early April 2017, three leading proxy advisory firms recommended that Innoviva stockholders vote for Sarissa's director nominees. Following the issuance of those recommendations, the parties began exploring a potential settlement of the proxy contest. The chief negotiators during these discussions were Sarissa's founder and Chief Investment Officer, Alexander Denner and the then-Vice Chairman of Innoviva's Board, James Tyree.

Two days out from the annual meeting, the proxy solicitors in both camps reported that the vote was too close to call. This uncertainty drove the parties to intensify their settlement discussions. Denner and Tyree reconnected and spoke on the phone several times that day. During those calls, Denner offered that Sarissa would end its proxy campaign if Innoviva would (1) expand its Board from seven members to nine members; (2) appoint two of Sarissa's nominees to the Board as directors; *and* (3) forgo a "standstill."[3] In response, Tyree indicated that Innoviva would be willing to expand its Board from seven to nine members, and to appoint two of Sarissa's nominees to the Board as directors, but insisted that Sarissa agree to a standstill and the issuance of a conciliatory joint press release announcing the settlement.

Later that day, Tyree provided an update to the Board regarding the settlement discussions. The key area of disagreement at that point was the standstill—from both parties' perspectives, that term was a "deal breaker."

The Board reconvened the next morning [. . .] regarding the status of the proxy contest and settlement discussions with Sarissa. With less than twenty-four hours to go before the vote, the outcome of the proxy contest

---

[3] In a proxy contest settlement agreement, a "standstill" provision typically provides that, for a fixed period of time, the dissident stockholder may not (1) acquire more than a certain percentage of the corporation's outstanding voting stock; (2) engage in the solicitation of voting proxies; or (3) make any tender offer or merger proposal in respect of the corporation or its shareholders. [. . .]

still [. . .] remained in doubt, as several of Innoviva's largest shareholders—including [. . .] Vanguard and BlackRock [. . .]—had not yet indicated how they would vote at the annual meeting. [. . .]

After discussing Innoviva's options, the Board remained adamant that an Innoviva-Sarissa settlement would require a standstill. Innoviva's position changed, however, once it learned—shortly after noon that day—that Vanguard planned to vote for Sarissa's nominees. Having lost Vanguard's vote, Innoviva's Board expected that it would lose BlackRock's vote as well, thereby ensuring that "at least two of Sarissa's three [nominees] would be elected to the Board . . . ." [. . .] [T]he "clock was ticking down" for Innoviva to reach a settlement with Sarissa and thereby avert an (expected) electoral defeat.

The Board reconvened later that afternoon for another telephonic meeting. During that meeting, the Board determined that: (1) Innoviva would settle with Sarissa without a standstill; (2) as part of that settlement, Innoviva would expand its Board from seven to nine members and appoint any two of Sarissa's three nominees to the expanded Innoviva Board; *and* (3) the settlement would require Sarissa to include a conciliatory quote about Innoviva in a joint press announcing the settlement. At the meeting's close, the Board authorized Tyree to convey to Denner that Innoviva would settle with Sarissa on those terms.

Tyree phoned Denner shortly thereafter to convey Innoviva's revised settlement proposal. Denner promptly accepted, and so confirmed Sarissa's assent to the essential terms of a Sarissa-Innoviva settlement. At the end of their call, Tyree and Denner confirmed they "had a deal" and that they would leave it to others on their respective teams to prepare the "paperwork . . . to get it done." Neither Tyree nor Denner indicated, however, that the settlement was contingent upon the execution of the "paperwork."

Following Tyree and Denner's call, the parties' attorneys worked to memorialize the agreed-upon deal in writing and finalize the language of the parties' joint press release. With the confirmatory writing finalized, and the press release nearly finalized, Innoviva learned that BlackRock had voted in favor of the Board's slate of directors, effectively ensuring that the Board's nominees would win election. Having snatched victory from the jaws of defeat, Innoviva's Board changed course. It resolved to cease discussions with Sarissa and proceed with the stockholder vote at Innoviva's annual meeting the following day. Tyree made contact with Denner that evening to advise him, in essence, that the "deal" that had been struck during their phone conversation hours before was now "no deal."

Sarissa filed this action under 8 Del. C. § 225 on the day of the annual meeting. It seeks a declaration that the parties entered into a binding settlement agreement the afternoon of April 19, 2017—during the Denner/Tyree telephone call. According to Sarissa, during that call,

Tyree orally bound Innoviva to a settlement agreement with the following terms:

1. Innoviva would expand its Board from seven members to nine, and two of Sarissa's nominees would be added as directors, without requiring a standstill;

2. Sarissa would terminate its proxy contest, withdraw its nomination notice and dismiss its then-pending books-and-records action against Innoviva;

3. Sarissa and Innoviva would announce the settlement in a mutually conciliatory joint press release; *and*

4. Innoviva would issue new proxy materials with the two Sarissa nominees included on the Board's slate, and Innoviva's 2017 annual meeting would be adjourned (for no more than thirty days) so that those new materials could be prepared and issued.

Sarissa also asks the Court to "specifically enforce the terms of the parties' agreement and order Innoviva and its directors and management to expand the size of the [Board] to nine and appoint [two of its nominees] to the Board."

Innoviva, for its part, argues that the parties never entered into a binding settlement agreement. In this regard, Innoviva contends that—

1. The parties never reached a meeting of the minds on all material terms of a settlement;

2. The parties did not intend to enter into a binding oral contract, but instead understood that any contract would have to be memorialized in an executed written agreement; and

3. Tyree lacked authority to bind Innoviva to the alleged oral contract. [. . .]

II. ANALYSIS

[. . .]

A. Tyree Had Authority to Enter Into an Oral Settlement Agreement With Sarissa on Behalf on Innoviva

An individual corporate director may negotiate a settlement on behalf of the corporation—and bind the corporation to an agreed-upon settlement—provided the director has actual or apparent authority to do so. For the reasons set forth below, I conclude that Tyree had both actual and apparent authority to bind Innoviva to an oral settlement agreement with Sarissa.

1. Tyree Had Actual Authority

Actual authority requires an extant agency relationship. An agency relationship "arises when one person [or entity] (a 'principal') manifests assent to another person [or entity] (an 'agent') that the agent shall act on the principal's behalf and subject to the principal's control, and the agent manifests assent or otherwise consents so to act." *Estate of Eller v. Bartron*. Actual authority, then, "is created by a principal's manifestation to an agent that, as reasonably understood by the agent, expresses the principal's assent that the agent take action on the principal's behalf." Restatement of Agency § 3.01.

Where the principal is a corporation, such assent may be manifested in provisions of the corporation's certificate of incorporation or bylaws, or otherwise through board action. Thus, a corporation's governance documents may grant actual authority to certain of its directors and officers to bind the corporation in contract—whether to a particular contract or type of contract, or more generally. Alternatively, a corporation's board of directors, as such, may cause the corporation to manifest assent that a particular director or officer shall have the power to bind the corporation in contract, provided the corporation's certificate and bylaws do not prohibit such action by the board.

The scope of an agent's actual authority is determined by the agent's reasonable understanding of the principal's manifestations and objectives. Accordingly, "[a]n agent has actual authority to take action designated or implied in the principal's manifestations to the agent and [to take] acts necessary or incidental to achieving the principal's objectives, as the agent reasonably understands the principal's manifestations and objectives when the agent determines how to act." Restatement of Agency § 2.02(1).

In this case, Tyree had actual authority to bind Innoviva to an oral settlement agreement with Sarissa within certain parameters. This authority can be traced to the express manifestations of Innoviva's Board (and thus, Innoviva) prior to and during the Board's April 19 afternoon meeting [. . .], and Tyree's reasonable understanding of those manifestations. Before that meeting, Innoviva's Board had appointed Tyree to act as Innoviva's "lead negotiator" in settlement discussions with Sarissa, and Tyree had accepted that appointment, thus creating a specific agency relationship between Tyree and Innoviva. And during that meeting, Innoviva's Board manifested assent that Tyree contact Denner "to negotiate to see if a settlement agreement including a press release between Sarissa and [Innoviva] could be reached." In that regard, the Board also manifested assent that Tyree convey to Denner the following:

- that Innoviva was willing to settle with Sarissa without a standstill;

- that, as part of that settlement, Innoviva would expand its Board from seven to nine members and appoint any two of Sarissa's nominees to the Board to fill the resulting vacancies; *and*

- that Sarissa would be required to include a conciliatory quote about Innoviva in the joint press release announcing the settlement.

The Board's authorization of Tyree to offer these terms on the afternoon of April 19, came in the midst of the Board's expectation that BlackRock would vote for "at least two" of Sarissa's director nominees, meaning (1) that "at least two" of Sarissa's three nominees would be elected to the seven-member Board; *and* (2) that "at least two" of Innoviva's existing directors would be replaced. [. . .] And with the revelation of BlackRock's (expected) vote for Sarissa's nominees, Sarissa would no longer have an incentive to settle its proxy contest. Thus, for Innoviva's Board, the "clock was ticking down" for Innoviva to reach a binding settlement with Sarissa—and thereby avert an (expected) electoral rout.

Under these circumstances, Tyree reasonably understood the Board's (and thus Innoviva's) manifestations to him during the Board's April 19 afternoon meeting to express Innoviva's assent that (1) within the Settlement Agreement Parameters, Tyree was authorized to make an oral settlement offer on Innoviva's behalf; *and* (2) Denner's oral acceptance of that offer (on Sarissa's behalf) would bind Innoviva to the settlement. And the record reflects that this was, in fact, Tyree's understanding. Accordingly, Tyree had actual authority to convey to Denner an oral settlement offer on behalf of Innoviva (on the terms approved by the Board) *and* to bind Innoviva to a settlement with Sarissa on those terms.

2. Tyree Had Apparent Authority

Unlike actual authority, apparent authority does not depend on the existence of an underlying agency relationship, and may arise even where no such relationship exists. Apparent authority "is the power held by an agent or other actor to affect a principal's legal relations with third parties when a third party reasonably believes the actor has authority to act on behalf of the principal and that belief is traceable to the principal's manifestations." *Vichi v. Koninklijke Philips Elecs., N.V.* Thus, even if a person lacks actual authority to bind an entity to a contract with a third party, the person still may have *apparent* authority to do so. For instance, a non-agent director has apparent authority to bind the corporation to a contract with a third party if (1) the third party reasonably believes that the director has such authority; and (2) that belief is traceable to the corporation's manifestations.

A corporate principal may make a manifestation to a third party concerning an agent's authority "by placing [the] agent in charge of a transaction or situation." In particular, where a corporate principal has designated an agent as its "exclusive channel of communication" with a third party, that designation can "constitute a manifestation of [the corporation's] assent to be bound in accordance with ... communication[s]" made through that channel. Restatement of Agency § 3.03.

Here, the evidence clearly reveals that Tyree had apparent authority to bind Innoviva to a settlement agreement with Sarissa. *First*, Denner, Sarissa's principal, believed that Tyree spoke on behalf of Innoviva's Board (and so Innoviva), and thus was authorized to enter into a settlement agreement on Innoviva's behalf. *Second*, it was reasonable for Denner to believe this. Tyree was Innoviva's "lead negotiator" in settlement discussions with Sarissa and the only Innoviva Board member with whom Denner negotiated during the critical April 18–19 time period. In addition, there is no evidence that Innoviva then communicated (or otherwise indicated) to Denner that Tyree was not authorized to enter into a settlement agreement on Innoviva's behalf. *Finally*, Denner's reasonable belief that Tyree was authorized to take such action on Innoviva's behalf is traceable to Innoviva's manifestations, namely, (1) Innoviva's having appointed Tyree as Innoviva's "lead negotiator" in settlement discussions with Sarissa; *and* (2) Innoviva's having permitted Tyree to serve as Innoviva's exclusive channel of settlement-related communications with Denner during the critical April 18–19 time period. For these reasons, I find that Tyree had apparent authority to bind Innoviva to a settlement agreement with Sarissa.

3. There Was No Improper Delegation of the Board's Duties

Innoviva contends that Tyree "did not have authority . . . to enter into the alleged oral agreement because this would involve an improper delegation of the Board's fiduciary and statutory duties." Specifically, Innoviva argues that, under 8 Del. C. §§ 141(b),* 223(a)(1) and Section 3.9 of Innoviva's Bylaws, "decisions regarding who should fill Board vacancies cannot be delegated to an individual director or a third person, but must be decided by the entire Board acting by majority vote." Innoviva's argument, however, misapprehends the facts proven at trial and the statutory and bylaw provisions upon which it relies. [. . .]

During the Board's April 19 afternoon meeting, the Board conditionally resolved to expand the size of the Board from seven to nine members [. . .]. This was done in anticipation of Innoviva's entry into a settlement with Sarissa. The Board also authorized Tyree to represent (or offer) to Denner that the Board would appoint (presumably by later vote) any two of Sarissa's three nominees to the Board if the proxy contest was settled. That is to say, if Sarissa accepted Innoviva's settlement proposal, then Innoviva's Board would be expanded from seven to nine members, and "a majority . . . of [the seven] directors then in office" would vote to appoint any two of Sarissa's three nominees to fill the resulting Board vacancies—consistent with Section 3.9 of Innoviva's Bylaws.

---

* EDS.—This section of the statute notes:

(b) The board of directors of a corporation shall consist of 1 or more members, each of whom shall be a natural person. The number of directors shall be fixed by, or in the manner provided in, the bylaws, unless the certificate of incorporation fixes the number of directors, in which case a change in the number of directors shall be made only by amendment of the certificate.

Here, it was Innoviva's Board that made the foregoing determinations, not Tyree. Indeed, the settlement terms that Tyree was authorized to convey to Denner were *Innoviva's* settlement terms, *i.e.*, the settlement terms approved by Innoviva's Board. Under these circumstances, as proven by Sarissa at trial, I am satisfied that Tyree's authority to bind Innoviva to an oral settlement agreement with Sarissa on terms approved by Innoviva's Board was entirely consistent with Section 141(b)'s and 223(a)(1)'s requirements that the creation and filling of new directorships be properly authorized by the board of directors in accordance with the corporation's governing documents. [. . .]

III. CONCLUSION

In an article for the *Financial Times*, investment banker and commentator, Frank Partnoy, writes that, in the spirit of deliberative decision-making:

> [W]e should generally delay the moment of decision until the last possible instant. If we have an hour, we should wait 59 minutes before responding. If we have a year, we should wait 364 days. Even if we have just half a second, we should wait as long as we can.

Here, with the clock ticking, Innoviva waited to solve its impending electoral drubbing until the last possible moment, just before the votes were to be counted. When it sensed that a loss would be announced at any moment, it did what it thought it had to do to manage the risk and keep its incumbents on the Board—it deliberately struck a deal with Sarissa at the 59th minute. Its efforts to walk away from that deal, after discovering that the risk it thought it perceived was not real, will not be countenanced.

For the foregoing reasons, judgment will be entered in favor of Sarissa on its claim for breach of contract as follows: (1) a decree of specific performance ordering Innoviva to perform its obligations under the Sarissa-Innoviva Settlement Agreement; and (2) a declaratory judgment that Bickerstaff and Kostas are rightful members of the Innoviva Board pursuant to 8 Del. C. § 225. [. . .]

E. SEPARATION OF OWNERSHIP AND CONTROL

In 2012, Charlie Craig and David Mullins, two men from Colorado, tried to order a wedding cake from Masterpiece Cakeshop in Lakewood, Colorado. Craig and Mullins had already been legally married in Massachusetts, although same-sex marriage was still banned in Colorado in 2012. Masterpiece Cakeshop's owner, Jack Phillips, told the couple that he would not create the cake due to his Christian beliefs. The couple complained to the Colorado Civil Rights Commission under the Colorado Anti-Discrimination Act, which prohibits businesses open to the public from discriminating against their customers on the basis of sexual orientation. The case eventually wound its way to the U.S. Supreme

Court. The question was whether applying Colorado's public accommodations law to compel Phillips to create expression that violates his sincerely held religious beliefs about marriage violates the Free Speech or Free Exercise Clauses of the First Amendment. Although this case was not a corporate law issue, 34 business law professors filed the following amicus brief in the Supreme Court case.

Brief of Amici Curiae Corporate Law Professors in Support of Respondents Masterpiece Cakeshop, Ltd. v. Colorado Civ. Rights Comm'n

INTEREST OF AMICI CURIAE

Amici are 34 law professors whose research and teaching focus on corporate governance law, securities law, or constitutional law as applied to corporations and other business entities. [. . .]

ARGUMENT

I. **Because of the Separate Legal Personality of Corporations and Shareholders, the Constitutional Interests of Shareholders Should Not Be Projected onto the Corporation.**

The viability of the constitutional claims of petitioner Masterpiece Cakeshop, Ltd., a corporation chartered under Colorado law, depends on the Court's willingness to assume the corporation holds sincere beliefs that operate to exempt it from otherwise applicable law. It is not the corporation that holds any such beliefs, however, but rather one of its shareholders, Jack Phillips. It is shareholder Phillips who "is a cake artist," who refused to sell a wedding cake to a same-sex couple because of "his" religious beliefs. Phillips characterizes the question to be decided as whether Colorado can compel "him" to violate "his" sincere religious beliefs, not the beliefs of the corporation in which he owns shares.

Thus, it is not the company but rather Phillips who asserts a "deep religious faith," and who "meticulously crafts each wedding cake." [. . .] He does not assert a compelled speech claim on behalf of the company but states it is "his artistic expression" at issue. *Id.* [. . .]

Masterpiece Cakeshop, Ltd., meanwhile, is a "Colorado corporation" whose shareholders are Phillips and his wife. While Phillips repeatedly equates his interests with those of the corporation, in the company's most recent incarnation, Phillips does not even appear in its chartering documents. [. . .] While Phillips represents that he and his spouse are the only shareholders, he does not specify his percentage of share ownership, nor does he state that he is the majority owner. [. . .]

Under Colorado law, a public accommodation must be a "place of business," and the Colorado Civil Rights Division determined that Masterpiece Cakeshop was a public accommodation and subject to CADA [the Colorado Anti Discrimination Act]. [. . .]

As for the constitutional claims of the corporation, they can succeed only if the company can claim Phillips's religious beliefs as its own. But Phillips and Masterpiece Cake shop are not the same. They are not identical for purposes of corporate law, and they should not be deemed identical for purposes of First Amendment law.

A.   Corporate separateness—i.e., legal personhood—is the core principle of corporate governance.

The first principle of corporate law is that for-profit corporations are entities that possess legal interests of their own and a legal identity separate and distinct from their shareholders. This legal "personhood" holds true whether the for-profit corporation has two, two hundred, or two million shareholders. In each scenario, the corporate entity is distinct in its legal interests and existence from those who contribute capital to it.

This Court has repeatedly recognized this principle of strict separation [. . .]. This separation is [. . .] the sine qua non of the wealth-creating legal innovation of the corporate form. The rationale behind corporate separateness is to encourage entrepreneurial activity by founders, investment by passive investors, and risk-taking by corporate managers. The corporate veil is a profound but simple device helping to achieve all three of these goals. Indeed, it is impossible to imagine a workable legal framework for corporate governance without such separation.

"After all," the Court has emphasized, "incorporation's basic purpose is to create a distinct legal entity, with legal rights, obligations, powers, and privileges different from those of the natural individuals who created it, who own it, or whom it employs." *Cedric Kushner Promotions, Ltd. v. King.*

The centrality of corporate separateness is well established and longstanding. *See Burnet v. Clark* (a "corporation and its stockholders are generally to be treated as separate entities"); *New Colonial Ice Co. v. Helvering* ("As a general rule, a corporation and its stockholders are deemed separate entities . . . ."); *William Blackstone, Commentaries on the Laws of England* ("[I]t has been found necessary . . . to constitute artificial persons, who may maintain a perpetual succession, and enjoy a kind of legal immortality. These artificial persons are called bodies politic, bodies corporate, . . .or corporations . . . .").

Because the corporation is a separate entity, its shareholders are not responsible for its debts. This "privilege of limited liability," as protected by the corporate veil, is "the corporation's most precious characteristic." William W. Cook, *The Principles of Corporation Law*. Although the term "corporation" sometimes calls to mind large, publicly traded enterprises, incorporation provides equally critical benefits to smaller businesses even when their shares are not publicly traded. One of the most compelling reasons for a small business to incorporate is so that its shareholders can acquire the protection of the corporate veil. By incorporating a business, the founders and investors insulate their personal assets from risk. Absent significant misconduct and fraud, shareholders in a corporation cannot lose any more than their original investment. If the corporation cannot pay its bills, the creditors—not the shareholders—bear the loss, with only very narrow exceptions.

Even where a single shareholder owns all the corporation's shares (which is presumably not the case with Masterpiece Cakeshop), the corporate veil cannot be pierced absent significant misconduct or fraud on the part of the shareholder. [. . .]

Because of these benefits, founders of even small businesses routinely choose the corporate form or another limited liability business form for the organization of a company. If entrepreneurs want to remain legally identified with their businesses, they can organize them as sole proprietorships or partnerships. But the cost of doing so is the exposure to much greater financial and legal risks. The corporate form insulates entrepreneurs from those risks and acts as a subsidy to entrepreneurs and shareholders by offering a way to shift those risks to creditors, tort victims, and the public at large. [. . .]

In the present case, Masterpiece Cakeshop argues it should be exempt from CADA because of the religious values of a (presumably) controlling shareholder, while seeking to maintain the benefits of corporate separateness for all other purposes. The company has benefited from its separateness in countless ways, and Phillips has been insulated from actual and potential corporate liabilities since inception. Yet now the company and the shareholder ask this Court to disregard that separateness in connection with a government regulation they would rather not obey. Petitioners want to argue, in effect, that the corporate veil is only a one-way ratchet: its shareholders can get protection from tort or contract liability by standing behind the veil, but the corporation can ask a court to disregard the corporate veil whenever the company is required by law to act in a way that offends a shareholder's beliefs. Petitioners cannot have their cake and eat it too. As this Court has said, "One who has created a corporate arrangement, chosen as a means of carrying out his business purposes, does not have the choice of disregarding the corporate entity in order to avoid the obligations which the statute lays upon it for the protection of the public." *Schenley Distillers Corp. v. United States* [. . .].

The Court should not assume it can disregard this principle of separateness with closely held companies such as Masterpiece Cakeshop and not cause significant uncertainty, infighting, and litigation with regard to other companies. If the Court sought to limit its holding to private or even family companies with a dominant shareholder, courts will be forced to resolve questions about what degree and type of ownership constitutes "control"—a question to which corporate law provides no ready answer [. . .]—and what degree of unanimity among shareholders would allow them to project their views onto the corporate entity. [. . .] Moreover, the Court should not presume all privately held corporations are tiny. " "Closely held" is not synonymous with "small." " *Burwell v. Hobby Lobby Stores, Inc. (Ginsburg, J., dissenting).* Some of the nation's most prominent corporations—Mars ($35 billion in revenues, 80,000 employees), Cargill ($110 billion in revenues, 150,000 employees), Bechtel ($33 billion in revenues, 58,000 employees), Uber ($6.5 billion in revenues, 12,000 employees), and Koch Industries ($100 billion in revenues, 100,000 employees), for example—are privately held.

Nor should the Court assume that "family owned" companies are small or even closely held. Walmart and Ford are both examples of large publicly traded corporations with major share ownership retained in one family. If this Court were to relax the rule of separateness in this case, it is hardly clear how lower courts would delineate which corporations could claim the beliefs of their shareholders and which could not.

Thus, Petitioners not only ask this Court to constitutionalize a view of corporations that displaces the fundamental principle of separateness, but to do so in a way that invites years of litigation to define the contours of that displacement.[7]

B. Corporate separateness should not be ignored in constitutional law.

[. . .] Petitioners do not seem to recognize the necessity of persuasion here, failing to make any argument at all as to why Phillips's constitutional interests should be projected onto the corporation. Petitioners either ignore the issue or hope this Court will. This Court has left no doubt that for-profit corporations and their trade associations may raise free speech claims. But the Court does not equate the interests of corporations with their shareholders for the purpose of free speech analysis. On the contrary—corporations are holders of their own rights. The Court has recognized corporate speech rights in order to preserve the " "open marketplace" of ideas protected by the First Amendment," *Citizens United* (quoting *N.Y. State Bd. of Elections v. López Torres*), and to protect the company's, consumers', and society's interest in "the free flow of commercial information," *Va. State Bd. of Pharmacy v. Va. Citizens Consumer Council, Inc.* The asserted interests are those of the company itself, not the company's shareholders. In this respect, for-profit corporations are distinct from membership associations, in that the latter represent and embody the legal interests of their members, are deemed to share the values of their members, and have standing to sue on their members' behalf. Corporations, in contrast, are legally distinct entities whose shareholders may have idiosyncratic investment objectives, distinctive and variable economic needs, and a diversity of political and religious beliefs. ExxonMobil and Masterpiece Cakeshop are not the Boy Scouts or the NAACP. Though this Court may have once theorized

---

7   [. . .] In companies where a dominant shareholder sincerely holds certain political or religious views, would non-religious directors and officers violate their fiduciary duties if they failed to assert the shareholder's views as a basis for an accommodation for the company?

corporations as akin to membership associations in some cases, this characterization no longer fits modern corporations, modern shareholding, or modern corporate law.

Corporations stand in their own shoes as a matter of free speech law. Corporations, to be sure, can and should have a role to play in public discourse, but courts should not merely presume that corporations act as conduits for the shareholders' points of view or have standing to assert their shareholders' constitutional interests.

This Court has long recognized this distinction between shareholders and corporations in other constitutional contexts. This Court has recognized the distinction even between a sole shareholder and the corporation for purposes of the Fifth Amendment.

Jack Phillips is both a shareholder of Masterpiece Cakeshop and its employee. No one is challenging the sincerity of Phillips's beliefs. But CADA does not require him to do, say, or create anything as a shareholder that even arguably violates his beliefs. To the extent CADA requires him to act contrary to his beliefs, it is doing so in his role of an employee of a company determined to be a public accommodation under Colorado law. The rights of employees to assert a religious objection to a work requirement of an employer or to a requirement of state or federal anti-discrimination law is a separate question, one on which amici take no position. But there is no doubt that if Masterpiece has a corporate speech interest at issue here, it is not because it has an employee who disagrees with Colorado law. For the company to have a claim, it would have to allege that the company *qua* company has been coerced into saying or doing something contrary to "those properties which the charter of its creation confers upon it, either expressly, or as incidental to its very existence." *Trs. of Dartmouth Coll. v. Woodward.* There is nothing inherent in the operation of Masterpiece Cakeshop or in its chartering documents that would make obedience to state anti-discrimination law inconsistent with "its very existence."

This is not to say that corporations cannot assert First Amendment interests, but merely that courts should take care that the rights asserted belong to the corporation and not to someone else. If Phillips has an individual First Amendment interest here, it cannot be used as the basis for a regulatory waiver for the company. Even if the individual employee could assert a constitutional right to be exempted from CADA's obligations for employees of a public accommodation (a question on which amici take no position), the company cannot leverage a solitary employee's or shareholder's objections to a regulation as the basis for a company-wide exemption. [. . .]

CONCLUSION

This Court should affirm the judgment of the court of appeals.

F. CORPORATE PURPOSE

A.P. Smith Mfg. Co. v. Barlow
98 A.2d 581 (N.J. 1953)

The [A.P. Smith Manufacturing C]ompany [. . .] was incorporated in 1896 and is engaged in the manufacture and sale of valves, fire hydrants and special equipment, mainly for water and gas industries. [. . .] On July 24, 1951 the board of directors adopted a resolution which set forth that it was in the corporation's best interests to join with others in the 1951 Annual Giving to Princeton University, and appropriated the sum of $1,500 to be transferred by the corporation's treasurer to the university as a contribution towards its maintenance. When this action was questioned by stockholders the corporation instituted a declaratory judgment action in the Chancery Division and trial was had in due course.

Mr. Hubert F. O'Brien, the president of the company, testified that he considered the contribution to be a sound investment, that the public expects corporations to aid philanthropic and benevolent institutions, that they obtain good will in the community by so doing, and that their charitable donations create favorable environment for their business operations. In addition, he expressed the thought that in contributing to liberal arts institutions, corporations were furthering their self-interest in assuring the free flow of properly trained personnel for administrative and other corporate employment. Mr. Frank W. Abrams, chairman of the board of the Standard Oil Company of New Jersey, testified that corporations are expected to acknowledge their public responsibilities in support of the essential elements of our free enterprise system. He indicated that it was not "good business" to disappoint "this reasonable and justified public expectation," nor was it of good business for corporations "to take substantial benefits from their membership in the economic community while avoiding the normally accepted obligations of citizenship in the social community." Mr. Irving S. Olds, former chairman of the board of the United States Steel Corporation, pointed out that corporations have a self-interest in the maintenance of liberal education as the bulwark of good government. He stated that "Capitalism and free enterprise owe their survival in no small degree to the existence of our private, independent universities" and that if American business does not aid in their maintenance, it is not "properly protecting the long-range interest of its stockholders, its employees and its customers." Similarly, Dr. Harold W. Dodds, President of Princeton University, suggested that if private institutions of higher learning were replaced by governmental institutions, our society would be vastly different and private enterprise in other fields would fade out rather promptly. Further on he stated that "democratic society will not long endure if it does not nourish within itself strong centers of non-governmental fountains of knowledge, opinions of all sorts not governmentally or politically originated. If the time comes when all these centers are absorbed into government, then freedom as we know it, I submit, is at an end."

The objecting stockholders have not disputed any of the foregoing testimony nor the showing of great need by Princeton and other private institutions of higher learning and the important public service being rendered by them for democratic government and industry alike. Similarly, they have acknowledged that for over two decades there has been state legislation on our books which expresses a strong public policy in favor of corporate contributions such as that being questioned by them. Nevertheless, they have taken the position that [. . .] the plaintiff's certificate of incorporation does not expressly authorize the contribution and under common-law principles the company does not possess any implied or incidental power to make it. [. . .]

In his discussion of the early history of business corporations, Professor Williston refers to a 1702 publication where the author stated flatly that "The general intent and end of all civil incorporations is for better government." [. . .] As a concomitant, the common-law rule developed that those who managed the corporation could not disburse any corporate funds for philanthropic or other worthy public cause unless the expenditure would benefit the corporation. *Hutton v. West Cork* [. . .] During the 19th Century when corporations were relatively few and small and did not dominate the country's wealth, the common-law rule did not significantly interfere with the public interest. But the 20th Century has presented a different climate. Control of economic wealth has passed largely from individual entrepreneurs to dominating corporations and calls upon the corporations for reasonable philanthropic donations have come to be made with increased public support. In many instances such contributions have been sustained by the courts within the common-law doctrine upon liberal findings that the donations tended reasonably to promote the corporate objectives. [. . .]

When the wealth of the nation was primarily in the hands of individuals they discharged their responsibilities as citizens by donating freely for charitable purposes. With the transfer of most of the wealth to corporate hands and the imposition of heavy burdens of individual taxation, they have been unable to keep pace with increased philanthropic needs. They have therefore, with justification, turned to corporations to assume the modern obligations of good citizenship in the same manner as humans do. Congress and state legislatures have enacted laws which encourage corporate contributions, and much has recently been written to indicate the crying need and adequate legal basis therefor . . . . In actual practice corporate giving has correspondingly increased. [. . .] It seems to us that just as the conditions prevailing when corporations were originally created required that they serve public as well as private interests, modern conditions require that corporations acknowledge and discharge social as well as private responsibilities as members of the communities within which they operate. Within this broad concept there is no difficulty in sustaining, as incidental to their proper objects and in aid of the public welfare, the power of corporations to contribute corporate funds within reasonable limits in support of academic institutions. But even if we confine ourselves to the terms of the common-law rule in its application to current conditions, such expenditures may likewise readily be justified as being for the benefit of the corporation; indeed, if need be the matter may be viewed strictly in terms of actual survival of the corporation in a free enterprise system. [. . .]

In 1930 a statute was enacted in our State which expressly provided that any corporation could cooperate with other corporations and natural persons in the creation and maintenance of community funds and charitable, philanthropic or benevolent instrumentalities conducive to public welfare, and could for such purposes expend such corporate sums as the directors "deem expedient and as in their judgment will contribute to the protection of the corporate interests." L.1930, c. 105; L.1931, c. 290; R.S. 14:3–13, N.J.S.A. See 53 N.J.L.J. 335 (1930). [. . .]

In 1950 a more comprehensive statute was enacted. [. . .] In this enactment the Legislature declared that it shall be the public policy of our State and in furtherance of the public interest and welfare that encouragement be given to the creation and maintenance of institutions engaged in community fund, hospital, charitable, philanthropic, educational, scientific or benevolent activities or patriotic or civic activities conducive to the betterment of social and economic conditions; and it expressly empowered corporations acting singly or with others to contribute reasonable sums to such institutions. [. . .]

In the light of all of the foregoing we have no hesitancy in sustaining the validity of the donation by the plaintiff. There is no suggestion that it was made indiscriminately or to a pet charity of the corporate directors in furtherance of personal rather than corporate ends. On the contrary, it was made to a preeminent institution of higher learning, was modest in amount and well within the limitations imposed by the statutory enactments, and was voluntarily made in the reasonable belief that it would aid the public welfare and advance the interests of the plaintiff as a private corporation and as part of the community in which it operates. We find that it was a lawful exercise of the corporation's implied and incidental powers under common-law principles and that it came within the express authority of the pertinent state legislation. As has been indicated, there is now widespread belief throughout the nation that free and vigorous non-governmental institutions of learning are vital to our democracy and the system of free enterprise and that withdrawal of corporate authority to make such contributions within reasonable limits would seriously threaten their continuance. Corporations have come to recognize this and with their enlightenment have sought in varying measures, as has the plaintiff by its contribution, to insure and strengthen the society which gives them existence and the means of aiding themselves and their fellow citizens. Clearly then, the appellants, as individual stockholders whose private interests rest entirely upon the well-being of the plaintiff corporation, ought not be permitted to close their eyes to present-day realities and thwart the long-visioned corporate action in recognizing and voluntarily discharging its high obligations as a constituent of our modern social structure.

The judgment entered in the Chancery Division is in all respects Affirmed.

Dodge v. Ford Motor Co.
170 N.W. 668 (Mich. 1919)

The Ford Motor Company is a corporation, organized and existing under Act No. 232 of the Public Acts of 1903 [. . .].

The articles of association were executed June 16, 1903 [. . .]. Article II of the articles of association reads:

> "The purpose or purposes of this corporation are as follows: To purchase, manufacture and placing on the market for sale of automobiles or the purchase, manufacture and placing on the market for sale of motors and of devices and appliances incident to their construction and operation."

The parties in the first instance associating, who signed the articles, included Henry Ford, whose subscription was for 255 shares, John F. Dodge, Horace E. Dodge, the plaintiffs, Horace H. Rackham and James Couzens, who each subscribed for 50 shares, and several other persons. The company began business in the month of June, 1903. [. . .]

[. . .] The business of the company continued to expand. The cars it manufactured met a public demand, and were profitably marketed, so that, in addition to regular quarterly dividends equal to 5 per cent. monthly on the capital stock of $2,000,000, its board of directors declared and the company paid special dividends [. . .].

No special dividend having been paid after October, 1915 (a special dividend of $2,000,000 was declared in November, 1916, before the filing of the answers), the plaintiffs, who together own 2,000 shares, or one-tenth of the entire capital stock of the Ford Motor Company, on the 2d of November, 1916, filed in the circuit court for the county of Wayne, in chancery, their bill of complaint [. . .] in which bill they charge that since 1914 they have not been represented on the board of directors of the Ford Motor Company, and that since that time the policy of the board of directors has been dominated and controlled absolutely by Henry Ford, the president of the company, who owns and for several years has owned 58 per cent. of the entire capital stock of the company; [. . .] Setting up that on the 31st of July, 1916, the end of its last fiscal year, [. . .] Henry Ford gave out for publication a statement of the financial condition of the company [. . .] that for a number of years a regular dividend, payable quarterly, equal to 5 per cent. monthly upon the authorized capital stock, and the special dividends hereinbefore referred to, had been paid, it is charged that notwithstanding the earnings for the fiscal year ending July 31, 1916, the Ford Motor Company has not since that date declared any special dividends:

"And the said Henry Ford, president of the company, has declared it to be the settled policy of the company not to pay in the future any special dividends, but to put back into the business for the future all of the earnings of the company, other than the regular dividend of five per cent. (5%) monthly upon the authorized capital stock of the company—two million dollars ($2,000,000)."

This declaration of the future policy [. . .] was published in the public press in the city of Detroit and throughout the United States in substantially the following language:

" 'My ambition,' declared Mr. Ford, 'is to employ still more men; to spread the benefits of this industrial system to the greatest possible number, to help them build up their lives and their homes. To do this, we are putting the greatest share of our profits back into the business.' "

It is charged further that the said Henry Ford stated to plaintiffs personally, in substance, that as all the stockholders had received back in dividends more than they had invested they were not entitled to receive anything additional to the regular dividend of 5 per cent. a month, and that it was not his policy to have larger dividends declared in the future, and that the profits and earnings of the company would be put back into the business for the purpose of extending its operations and increasing the number of its employees, and that [. . .] the stockholders would have no right to complain. It is charged [. . .] that the said Henry Ford,—

"dominating and controlling the policy of said company, has declared it to be his purpose—and he has actually engaged in negotiations looking to carrying such purposes into effect—to invest millions of dollars of the company's money in the purchase of iron ore mines in the Northern Peninsula of Michigan or State of Minnesota; to acquire by purchase or have built ships for the purpose of transporting such ore to smelters to be erected on the River Rouge adjacent to Detroit in the county of Wayne and State of Michigan; and to construct and install steel manufacturing plants to produce steel products to be used in the manufacture of cars at the factory of said company; and by this means to deprive the stockholders of the company of the fair and reasonable returns upon their investment by way of dividends to be declared upon their stockholding interest in said company."

[. . .] Plaintiffs ask for an injunction to restrain the carrying out of the alleged declared policy of Mr. Ford and the company, for a decree requiring the distribution to stockholders of at least 75 per cent. of the accumulated cash surplus, and for the future that they be required to distribute all of the earnings of the company except such as may be reasonably required for emergency purposes in the conduct of the business. [. . .]

[T]he case for plaintiffs must rest upon the claim, and the proof in support of it, that the proposed expansion of the business of the corporation, involving the further use of profits as capital, ought to be enjoined because inimical to the best interests of the company and its shareholders, and upon the further claim that in any event the withholding of the special dividend asked for by plaintiffs is arbitrary action of the directors requiring judicial interference. [. . .]

The rule which will govern courts in deciding these questions is not in dispute. It is, of course, differently phrased by judges and by authors, and [. . .] the facts before the court [. . .] must be considered. This court, in *Hunter v. Roberts, Throp & Co.*, recognized the rule in the following language:

> "It is a well-recognized principle of law that the directors of a corporation, and they alone, have the power to declare a dividend of the earnings of the corporation, and to determine its amount. Courts of equity will not interfere in the management of the directors unless it is clearly made to appear that they are guilty of fraud or misappropriation of the corporate funds, or refuse to declare a dividend when the corporation has a surplus of net profits which it can, without detriment to its business, divide among its stockholders, and when a refusal to do so would amount to such an abuse of discretion as would constitute a fraud, or breach of that good faith which they are bound to exercise towards the stockholders."

[. . .] When plaintiffs made their complaint and demand for further dividends, the Ford Motor Company had concluded its most prosperous year of business. The demand for its cars at the price of the preceding year continued. It could make and could market in the year beginning August 1, 1916, more than 500,000 cars. [. . .] [I]t reasonably might have expected a profit for the year of upwards of $60,000,000. It had assets of more than $132,000,000, a surplus of almost $112,000,000, and its cash on hand and municipal bonds were nearly $54,000,000. Its total liabilities, including capital stock, was a little over $20,000,000. It had declared no special dividend during the business year except the October, 1915, dividend. It had been the practice, under similar circumstances, to declare larger dividends. Considering only these facts, a refusal to declare and pay further dividends appears to be not an exercise of discretion on the part of the directors, but an arbitrary refusal to do what the circumstances required to be done. [. . .] In justification, the defendants have offered testimony tending to prove, and which does prove, the following facts: It had been the policy of the corporation for a considerable time to annually reduce the selling price of cars, while keeping up, or improving, their quality. As early as in June, 1915, a general plan for the expansion of the productive capacity of the concern by a practical duplication of its plant had been talked over by the executive officers and directors and agreed upon; not all of the details having been settled, and no formal action of directors having been taken. The erection of a smelter was considered, and engineering and other data in connection therewith secured. In consequence, it was determined not to reduce the selling price of cars for the year beginning August 1, 1915, but to maintain the price and to accumulate a large surplus to pay for the proposed expansion of plant and equipment, and perhaps to build a plant for smelting ore. It is hoped, by Mr. Ford, that eventually 1,000,000 cars will be annually produced. The contemplated changes will permit the increased output.

The plan, as affecting the profits of the business for the year beginning August 1, 1916, and thereafter, calls for a reduction in the selling price of the cars. It is true that this price might be at any time increased, but the plan called for the reduction in price of $80 a car. The capacity of the plant, without the additions thereto voted to be made [. . .] would produce more than 600,000 cars annually. This number, and more, could have been sold for $440 instead of $360, a difference [. . .] of at least $48,000,000. In short, the plan [. . .] is not intended to produce immediately a more profitable business, but a less profitable one; not only less profitable than formerly, but less profitable than it is admitted it might be made. The apparent immediate effect will be to diminish the value of shares and the returns to shareholders.

It is the contention of plaintiffs that the apparent effect of the plan is intended to be the continued and continuing effect of it, and that it is deliberately proposed [. . .] to continue the corporation henceforth as a semi-eleemosynary institution and not as a business institution. In support of this contention, they point to the attitude and to the expressions of Mr. Henry Ford.

Mr. Henry Ford is the dominant force in the business of the Ford Motor Company. No plan of operations could be adopted unless he consented, and no board of directors can be elected whom he does not favor. One of the directors of the company has no stock. One share was assigned to him to qualify him for the position, but it is not claimed that he owns it. A business, one of the largest in the world, and one of the most profitable, has been built up. It employs many men, at good pay.

"My ambition," said Mr. Ford, "is to employ still more men, to spread the benefits of this industrial system to the greatest possible number, to help them build up their lives and their homes. To do this we are putting the greatest share of our profits back in the business."

"With regard to dividends, the company paid sixty per cent. on its capitalization of two million dollars, or $1,200,000, leaving $58,000,000 to reinvest for the growth of the company. This is Mr. Ford's policy at present, and it is understood that the other stockholders cheerfully accede to this plan."

He had made up his mind in the summer of 1916 that no dividends other than the regular dividends should be paid, "for the present."

> **Q.** For how long? Had you fixed in your mind any time in the future, when you were going to pay—
>
> **A.** No.
>
> **Q.** That was indefinite in the future?
>
> **A.** That was indefinite; yes, sir.

The record, and especially the testimony of Mr. Ford, convinces that he has to some extent the attitude towards shareholders of one who has dispensed and distributed to them large gains and that they should be content to take what he chooses to give. His testimony creates the impression, also, that he thinks the Ford Motor Company has made too much money, has had too large profits, and that, although large profits might be still earned, a sharing of them with the public, by reducing the price of the output of the company, ought to be undertaken. We have no doubt that certain sentiments, philanthropic and altruistic, creditable to Mr. Ford, had large influence in determining the policy to be pursued by the Ford Motor Company [. . .].

It is said by his counsel that—

> "Although a manufacturing corporation cannot engage in humanitarian works as its principal business, the fact that it is organized for profit does not prevent the existence of implied powers to carry on with humanitarian motives such charitable works as are incidental to the main business of the corporation."

And again:

> "As the expenditures complained of are being made in an expansion of the business which the company is organized to carry on, and for purposes within the powers of the corporation as hereinbefore shown, the question is as to whether such expenditures are rendered illegal because influenced to some extent by humanitarian motives and purposes on the part of the members of the board of directors."

In discussing this proposition, counsel have referred to [. . .] cases [. . .] which [. . .] turn finally upon the point, the question, whether it appears that the directors were not acting for the best interests of the corporation. We do not draw in question, nor do counsel for the plaintiffs do so, the validity of the general proposition stated by counsel nor the soundness of the opinions delivered in the cases cited. The case presented here is not like any of them. The difference between an incidental humanitarian expenditure of corporate funds for the benefit of the employees, like the building of a hospital for their use and the employment of agencies for the betterment of their condition, and a general purpose and plan to benefit mankind at the expense of others, is obvious. There should be no confusion (of which there is evidence) of the duties which Mr. Ford conceives that he and the stockholders owe to the general public and the duties which in law he and his codirectors owe to protesting, minority stockholders. A business corporation is organized and carried on primarily for the profit of the stockholders. The powers of the directors are to be employed for that end. The discretion of directors is to be exercised in the choice of means to attain that end, and does not extend to a change in the end itself, to the reduction of profits, or to the nondistribution of profits among stockholders in order to devote them to other purposes.

There is committed to the discretion of directors, a discretion to be exercised in good faith, the infinite details of business, including the wages which shall be paid to employees, the number of hours they shall work, the conditions under which labor shall be carried on, and the price for which products shall be offered to the public. It is said by appellants that the motives of the board members are not material and will not be inquired into by the court so long as their acts are within their lawful powers. As we have pointed out [. . .] it is not within the lawful powers of a board of directors to shape and conduct the affairs of a corporation for the merely incidental benefit of shareholders and for the primary purpose of benefiting others, and no one will contend that, if the avowed purpose of the defendant directors was to sacrifice the interests of shareholders, it would not be the duty of the courts to interfere.

We are not, however, persuaded that we should interfere with the proposed expansion of the business of the Ford Motor Company. In view of the fact that the selling price of products may be increased at any time, the ultimate results of the larger business cannot be certainly estimated. The judges are not business experts. It is recognized that plans must often be made for a long future, for expected competition, for a continuing as well as an immediately profitable venture. The experience of the Ford Motor Company is evidence of capable management of its affairs. [. . .] We are not satisfied that the alleged motives of the directors, in so far as they are reflected in the conduct of the business, menace the interests of shareholders. [. . .]

Assuming the general plan and policy of expansion and the details of it to have been sufficiently, formally, approved at the October and November, 1917, meetings of directors, and assuming further that the plan and policy and the details agreed upon were for the best ultimate interest of the company and therefore of its shareholders, what does it amount to in justification of a refusal to declare and pay a special dividend or dividends? The Ford Motor Company was able to estimate with nicety its income and profit. It could sell more cars than it could make. Having ascertained what it would cost to produce a car and to sell it, the profit upon each car depended upon the selling price. That being fixed, the yearly income and profit was determinable, and, within slight variations, was certain.

There was appropriated—voted—for the smelter $11,325,000. As to the remainder voted, there is no available way for determining how much had been paid before the action of directors was taken and how much was paid thereafter; but assuming that the plans required an expenditure sooner or later of $9,895,000 for duplication of the plant, and for land and other expenditures $3,000,000, the total is $24,220,000. The company was continuing business, at a profit—a cash business. If the total cost of proposed expenditures had been immediately withdrawn in cash from the cash surplus (money and bonds) on hand August 1, 1916, there would have remained nearly $30,000,000.

Defendants say, and it is true, that a considerable cash balance must be at all times carried by such a concern. But, as has been stated, there was a large daily, weekly, monthly, receipt of cash. The output was practically continuous and was continuously, and within a few days, turned into cash. Moreover, the contemplated expenditures were not to be immediately made. The large sum appropriated for the smelter plant was payable over a considerable period of time. So that, without going further, it would appear that, accepting and approving the plan of the directors, it was their duty to distribute on or near the 1st of August, 1916, a very large sum of money to stockholders.

In reaching this conclusion, we do not ignore, but recognize, the validity of the proposition that plaintiffs have from the beginning profited by, if they have not lately, officially, participated in, the general policy of expansion pursued by this corporation. We do not lose sight of the fact that it had been, upon an occasion, agreeable to the plaintiffs to increase the capital stock to $100,000,000 by a stock dividend of $98,000,000. These things go only to answer other contentions now made by plaintiffs, and do not and cannot operate to estop them to demand proper dividends upon the stock they own. It is obvious that an annual dividend of 60 per cent. upon $2,000,000, or $1,200,000, is the equivalent of a very small dividend upon $100,000,000, or more.

The decree of the court below fixing and determining the specific amount to be distributed to stockholders is affirmed. [. . .] Plaintiffs will recover interest at 5 per cent. per annum upon their proportional share of said dividend from the date of the decree of the lower court. [. . .]

Shlensky v. Wrigley
95 Ill.App.2d 173 (1968)

Plaintiff is a minority stockholder of defendant corporation, Chicago National League Ball Club. Defendant corporation owns and operates the major league professional baseball team known as the Chicago Cubs. The corporation also engages in the operation of Wrigley Field, the Cubs' home park [. . .]. The individual defendants are directors of the Cubs and have served for varying periods of years. Defendant Philip K. Wrigley is also president of the corporation and owner of approximately 80% of the stock therein.

Plaintiff alleges that since night baseball was first played in 1935 nineteen of the twenty major league teams have scheduled night games. In 1966, out of a total of 1620 games in the major leagues, 932 were played at night. Plaintiff alleges that every member of the major leagues, other than the Cubs, scheduled substantially all of its home games in 1966 at night, exclusive of opening days, Saturdays, Sundays, holidays and days prohibited by league rules. Allegedly this has been done for the specific purpose of maximizing attendance and thereby maximizing revenue and income.

The Cubs, in the years 1961–65, sustained operating losses from its direct baseball operations. Plaintiff attributes those losses to inadequate attendance at Cubs' home games. He concludes that if the directors continue to refuse to install lights at Wrigley Field and schedule night baseball games, the Cubs will continue to sustain comparable losses and its financial condition will continue to deteriorate. [. . .]

Plaintiff compares attendance at Cubs' games with that of the Chicago White Sox, an American League club, whose weekday games were generally played at night. The weekend attendance figures for the two teams was similar; however, the White Sox week-night games drew many more patrons than did the Cubs' weekday games.

Plaintiff alleges that the funds for the installation of lights can be readily obtained through financing and the cost of installation would be far more than offset and recaptured by increased revenues and incomes resulting from the increased attendance.

Plaintiff further alleges that defendant Wrigley has refused to install lights, not because of interest in the welfare of the corporation but because of his personal opinions "that baseball is a 'daytime sport' and that the installation of lights and night baseball games will have a deteriorating effect upon the surrounding neighborhood." It is alleged that he has admitted that he is not interested in whether the Cubs would benefit financially from such action because of his concern for the neighborhood, and that he would be willing for the team to play night games if a new stadium were built in Chicago.

Plaintiff alleges that the other defendant directors, with full knowledge of the foregoing matters, have [. . .] permitted [Wrigley] to dominate the board of directors in matters involving the installation of lights and scheduling of night games, even though they knew he was not motivated by a good faith concern as to the best interests of defendant corporation, but solely by his personal views set forth above. It is charged that the directors are acting for a reason or reasons contrary and wholly unrelated to the business interests of the corporation; that such arbitrary and capricious acts constitute mismanagement and waste of corporate assets, and that the directors have been negligent in failing to exercise reasonable care and prudence in the management of the corporate affairs.

The question on appeal is whether plaintiff's amended complaint states a cause of action. It is plaintiff's position that fraud, illegality and conflict of interest are not the only bases for a stockholder's derivative action against the directors. [D]efendants argue that the courts will not step in and interfere with honest business judgment of the directors unless there is a showing of fraud, illegality or conflict of interest.

The cases in this area are numerous and each differs from the others on a factual basis. However, the courts have pronounced certain ground rules which appear in all cases and which are then applied to the given factual situation. The court in *Wheeler v. Pullman Iron and Steel Company*, said:

> [. . .] The majority of shares of its stock, or the agents by the holders thereof lawfully chosen, must be permitted to control the business of the corporation in their discretion, when not in violation of its charter or some public law, or corruptly and fraudulently subversive of the rights and interests of the corporation or of a shareholder.

[. . .] In *Davis v. Louisville Gas & Electric Co.*, a minority shareholder sought to have the directors enjoined from amending the certificate of incorporation. The court said [. . .]:

> We have then a conflict in view between the responsible managers of a corporation and an overwhelming majority of its stockholders on the one hand and a dissenting minority on the other—a conflict touching matters of business policy [. . .]. The response which courts make to such applications is that it is not their function to resolve for corporations questions of policy and business management. The judgment of the directors of corporations enjoys the benefit of a presumption that it was formed in good faith and was designed to promote the best interests of the corporation they serve. [. . .]

[Citing *Helfman v. American Light & Traction Company*], the court in *Toebelman v. Missouri-Kansas Pipe Line Co.*, said [. . .] "In a purely business corporation . . . the authority of the directors in the conduct of the business of the corporation must be regarded as absolute when they act within the law, and the court is without authority to substitute its judgment for that of the directors."

Plaintiff in the instant case argues that the directors are acting for reasons unrelated to the financial interest and welfare of the Cubs. However, we are not satisfied that the motives assigned to Philip K. Wrigley, and through him to the other directors, are contrary to the best interests of the corporation and the stockholders. For example, it appears to us that the effect on the surrounding neighborhood might well be considered by a director who was considering the patrons who would or would not attend the games if the park were in a poor neighborhood. Furthermore, the long run interest of the corporation in its property value at Wrigley Field might demand all efforts to keep the neighborhood from deteriorating. By these thoughts we do not mean to say that we have decided that the decision of the directors was a correct one. That is beyond our jurisdiction and ability. [T]he decision is one properly before directors and the motives alleged in the amended complaint showed no fraud, illegality or conflict of interest in their making of that decision.

[. . .] [W]e feel that unless the conduct of the defendants at least borders on one of the elements, the courts should not interfere. The trial court in the instant case acted properly in dismissing plaintiff's amended complaint.

We feel that plaintiff's amended complaint was also defective in failing to allege damage to the corporation. [. . .] There is no allegation that the night games played by the other nineteen teams enhanced their financial position or that the profits, if any, of those teams were directly related to the number of night games scheduled. There is an allegation that the installation of lights and scheduling of night games in Wrigley Field would have resulted in large amounts of additional revenues and incomes from increased attendance and related sources of income. Further, the cost of installation of lights, funds for which are allegedly readily available by financing, would be more than offset and recaptured by increased revenues. However, no allegation is made that there will be a net benefit to the corporation from such action, considering all increased costs.

Plaintiff claims that the losses of defendant corporation are due to poor attendance at home games. However, it appears from the amended complaint [. . .] that factors other than attendance affect the net earnings or losses. For example, in 1962, attendance at home and road games decreased appreciably as compared with 1961, and yet the loss from direct baseball operation and of the whole corporation was considerably less.

The record shows that plaintiff did not feel he could allege that the increased revenues would be sufficient to cure the corporate deficit. The only cost plaintiff was at all concerned with was that of installation of lights. No mention was made of operation and maintenance of the lights or other possible increases in operating costs of night games and we cannot speculate as to what other factors might influence the increase or decrease of profits if the Cubs were to play night home games. [. . .]

[P]laintiff's allegation that the minority stockholders and the corporation have been seriously and irreparably damaged by the wrongful conduct of the defendant directors is a mere conclusion and not based on well pleaded facts in the amended complaint.

Finally, we do not agree with plaintiff's contention that failure to follow the example of the other major league clubs in scheduling night games constituted negligence. [. . .] Directors are elected for their business capabilities and judgment and the courts cannot require them to forego their judgment because of the decisions of directors of other companies. Courts may not decide these questions in the absence of a clear showing of dereliction of duty on the part of the specific directors and mere failure to "follow the crowd" is not such a dereliction.

Affirmed.

Business Roundtable Statement on the Purpose of a Corporation

[EDS.—The Business Roundtable is an association of more than 200 chief executive officers of major U.S. companies. In 2019, the Business Roundtable issued the following statement.]

Americans deserve an economy that allows each person to succeed through hard work and creativity and to lead a life of meaning and dignity. We believe the free-market system is the best means of generating good jobs, a strong and sustainable economy, innovation, a healthy environment and economic opportunity for all. Businesses play a vital role in the economy by creating jobs, fostering innovation, and providing essential goods and services. Businesses make and sell consumer products; manufacture equipment and vehicles; support the national defense; grow and produce food; provide health care; generate and deliver energy; and offer financial, communications and other services that underpin economic growth. While each of our individual companies serves its own corporate purpose, we share a fundamental commitment to all of our stakeholders. We commit to:

- Delivering value to our customers. We will further the tradition of American companies leading the way in meeting or exceeding customer expectations.

- Investing in our employees. This starts with compensating them fairly and providing important benefits. It also includes supporting them through training and education that help develop new skills for a rapidly changing world. We foster diversity and inclusion, dignity and respect.

- Dealing fairly and ethically with our suppliers. We are dedicated to serving as good partners to the other companies, large and small, that help us meet our missions.

- Supporting the communities in which we work. We respect the people in our communities and protect the environment by embracing sustainable practices across our businesses.

- Generating long-term value for shareholders, who provide the capital that allows companies to invest, grow and innovate. We are committed to transparency and effective engagement with shareholders.

Each of our stakeholders is essential. We commit to deliver value to all of them, for the future success of our companies, our communities and our country.

G. THE NATURE OF THE CORPORATION: A FINAL VIEW

United States Constitution
First Amendment

Congress shall make no law respecting an establishment of religion, or prohibiting the free exercise thereof; or abridging the freedom of speech, or of the press; or the right of the people peaceably to assemble, and to petition the Government for a redress of grievances.

Citizens United v. Federal Election Commission
558 U.S. 310 (2010)

■ JUSTICE KENNEDY delivered the opinion of the Court.

Federal law prohibits corporations and unions from using their general treasury funds to make independent expenditures for speech defined as an "electioneering communication" or for speech expressly advocating the election or defeat of a candidate. 2 U.S.C. § 441b.* * * * [. . .] *Austin* [*v. Mich. Chamber of Com.*] had held that political speech may be banned based on the speaker's corporate identity.

In this case we are asked to reconsider *Austin* [. . .]. It has been noted that "*Austin* was a significant departure from ancient First Amendment principles," *Federal Election Comm'n v. Wisconsin Right to Life, Inc.,* [. . .] (2007) *(WRTL)* [. . .]. We agree with that conclusion and hold that *stare decisis* does not compel the continued acceptance of *Austin.* The Government may regulate corporate political speech through disclaimer and disclosure requirements, but it may not suppress that speech altogether. We turn to the case now before us.

I

A

Citizens United is a nonprofit corporation. It brought this action in the United States District Court for the District of Columbia. A three-judge court later convened to hear the cause. The resulting judgment gives rise to this appeal.

Citizens United has an annual budget of about $12 million. Most of its funds are from donations by individuals; but, in addition, it accepts a small portion of its funds from for-profit corporations.

In January 2008, Citizens United released a film entitled *Hillary: The Movie.* [. . .] *Hillary* mentions Senator [Hillary] Clinton by name and depicts interviews with political commentators and other persons, most of them quite critical of Senator Clinton. *Hillary* was released in theaters and on DVD, but Citizens United wanted to increase distribution by making it available through video-on-demand.

[T]o promote the film, [Citizens United] produced two 10-second ads and one 30-second ad for *Hillary*. Each [television] ad includes a short (and, in our view, pejorative) statement about Senator Clinton, followed by the name of the movie and the movie's Web site address. Citizens United desired to promote the video-on-demand offering by running advertisements on broadcast and cable television.

B

Before the Bipartisan Campaign Reform Act of 2002 (BCRA), federal law prohibited—and still does prohibit—corporations and unions from using general treasury funds to make direct contributions to candidates or independent expenditures that expressly advocate the election or defeat of a candidate, through any form of media, in connection with certain qualified federal elections. [. . .] Corporations and unions are barred from using their general treasury funds for express advocacy or electioneering communications. They may establish, however, a "separate segregated fund" (known as a political action committee, or PAC) for these purposes. 2 U.S.C. § 441b(b)(2). The moneys received by the segregated fund are limited to donations from stockholders and employees of the corporation or, in the case of unions, members of the union. [. . .].

C

Citizens United wanted to make *Hillary* available through video-on-demand within 30 days of the 2008 primary elections. It feared, however, that both the film and the ads would be covered by § 441b's ban on corporate-funded independent expenditures, thus subjecting the corporation to civil and criminal penalties under § 437g. In December 2007, Citizens United sought declaratory and injunctive relief against the FEC. It argued that (1) § 441b is unconstitutional as applied to *Hillary;* and (2) BCRA's disclaimer and disclosure requirements, BCRA §§ 201 and 311, are unconstitutional as applied to *Hillary* and to the three ads for the movie.

The District Court denied Citizens United's motion for a preliminary injunction [. . .] [and] held that § 441b was facially constitutional under *McConnell,* and that § 441b was constitutional as applied to *Hillary* because it was "susceptible of no other interpretation than to inform the electorate that Senator Clinton is unfit for office, that the United States would be a dangerous place in a President Hillary Clinton world, and that viewers should vote against her." [. . .]

III

The First Amendment provides that "Congress shall make no law . . . abridging the freedom of speech." [. . .]

The law before us is an outright ban, backed by criminal sanctions. Section 441b makes it a felony for all corporations—including nonprofit advocacy corporations—either to expressly advocate the election or defeat of candidates or to broadcast electioneering communications within 30 days of a primary election and 60 days of a general election. [. . .]

Section 441b is a ban on corporate speech notwithstanding the fact that a PAC created by a corporation can still speak. A PAC is a separate association from the corporation. So the PAC exemption from § 441b's expenditure ban does not allow corporations to speak. Even if a PAC could somehow allow a corporation to speak—and it does not—the option to form PACs does not alleviate the First Amendment problems with § 441b. PACs are burdensome alternatives; they are expensive to administer and subject to extensive regulations. For example, every PAC must appoint a treasurer, forward donations to the treasurer promptly, keep detailed records of the identities of the persons making donations, preserve receipts for three years, and file an organization statement and report changes to this information within 10 days. [. . .]

PACS have to comply with [. . .] regulations just to speak. This might explain why fewer than 2,000 of the millions of corporations in this country have PACs. [. . .] PACs, furthermore, must exist before they can speak. Given the onerous restrictions, a corporation may not be able to establish a PAC in time to make its views known regarding candidates and issues in a current campaign.

Section 441b's prohibition on corporate independent expenditures is thus a ban on speech. As a "restriction on the amount of money a person or group can spend on political communication during a campaign," that statute "necessarily reduces the quantity of expression by restricting the number of issues discussed, the depth of their exploration, and the size of the audience reached." *Buckley v. Valeo*. Were the Court to uphold these restrictions, the Government could repress speech by silencing certain voices at any of the various points in the speech process. [. . .] If § 441b applied to individuals, no one would believe that it is merely a time, place, or manner restriction on speech. Its purpose and effect are to silence entities whose voices the Government deems to be suspect.

[. . .] Laws that burden political speech are "subject to strict scrutiny," which requires the Government to prove that the restriction "furthers a compelling interest and is narrowly tailored to achieve that interest." *WRTL*. While it might be maintained that political speech simply cannot be banned or restricted as a categorical matter, the quoted language from *WRTL* provides a sufficient framework for protecting the relevant First Amendment interests in this case. We shall employ it here. [. . .]

Quite apart from the purpose or effect of regulating content [. . .] the Government may commit a constitutional wrong when by law it identifies certain preferred speakers. By taking the right to speak from some and giving it to others, the Government deprives the disadvantaged person or class of the right to use speech to strive to establish worth, standing, and respect for the speaker's voice. The Government may not by these means deprive the public of the right and privilege to determine for itself what speech and speakers are worthy of consideration. [. . .]

The Court has upheld a narrow class of speech restrictions that operate to the disadvantage of certain persons [. . .] based on an interest in allowing governmental entities to perform their functions. [. . .] The corporate independent expenditures at issue in this case, however, would not interfere with governmental functions, so these cases are inapposite. [. . .]

We find no basis for the proposition that, in the context of political speech, the Government may impose restrictions on certain disfavored speakers. Both history and logic lead us to this conclusion.

A

1

The Court has recognized that First Amendment protection extends to corporations. [. . .]

This protection has been extended by explicit holdings to the context of political speech. [. . .] Under the rationale of these precedents, political speech does not lose First Amendment protection "simply because its source is a corporation." [. . .] ("The identity of the speaker is not decisive in determining whether speech is protected. Corporations and other associations, like individuals, contribute to the 'discussion, debate, and the dissemination of information and ideas' that the First Amendment seeks to foster" (quoting *Bellotti* [. . .]). The Court has thus rejected the argument that political speech of corporations or other associations should be treated differently under the First Amendment simply because such associations are not "natural persons." [. . .]

At least since the latter part of the 19th century, the laws of some States and of the United States imposed a ban on corporate direct contributions to candidates. [. . .] Yet not until 1947 did Congress first prohibit independent expenditures by corporations and labor unions in § 304 of the Labor Management Relations Act, 1947, 61 Stat. 159 (codified at 2 U.S.C. § 251 (1946 ed., Supp. I)). In passing this Act Congress overrode the veto of President Truman, who warned that the expenditure ban was a "dangerous intrusion on free speech." Message from the President of the United States, H.R. Doc. No. 334, 80th Cong., 1st Sess., 9 (1947). [. . .]

2

[. . .] [*First Nat. Bank of Boston v.] Bellotti* reaffirmed the First Amendment principle that the Government cannot restrict political speech based on the speaker's corporate identity. *Bellotti* could not have been clearer when it struck down a state-law prohibition on corporate independent expenditures related to referenda issues:

> "We thus find no support in the First . . . Amendment, or in the decisions of this Court, for the proposition that speech that otherwise would be within the protection of the First Amendment loses that protection simply because its source is a corporation that cannot prove, to the satisfaction of a court, a material effect on its business or property. . . [That proposition] amounts to an impermissible legislative prohibition of speech based on the identity of the interests that spokesmen may represent in public debate over controversial issues and a requirement that the speaker have a sufficiently great interest in the subject to justify communication. [. . .]

3

Thus the law stood until *Austin*. *Austin* "uph[eld] a direct restriction on the independent expenditure of funds for political speech for the first time in [this Court's] history." [. . .]. There, the Michigan Chamber of Commerce sought to use general treasury funds to run a newspaper ad supporting a specific candidate. Michigan law, however, prohibited corporate independent expenditures that supported or opposed any candidate for state office. A violation of the law was punishable as a felony. The Court sustained the speech prohibition.

To bypass [. . .] *Bellotti*, the *Austin* Court identified a new governmental interest in limiting political speech: an antidistortion interest. *Austin* found a compelling governmental interest in preventing "the corrosive and distorting effects of immense aggregations of wealth that are accumulated with the help of the corporate form and that have little or no correlation to the public's support for the corporation's political ideas." [. . .]

B

The Court is thus confronted with conflicting lines of precedent: a pre-*Austin* line that forbids restrictions on political speech based on the speaker's corporate identity and a post-*Austin* line that permits them. [. . .]

In its defense of the corporate-speech restrictions in § 441b, the Government notes the antidistortion rationale on which *Austin* and its progeny rest in part, yet it all but abandons reliance upon it. It argues instead that two other compelling interests support *Austin*'s holding that corporate expenditure restrictions are constitutional: an anticorruption interest [. . .], and a shareholder-protection interest [. . .]. We consider the three points in turn.

1

As for *Austin*'s antidistortion rationale, the Government does little to defend it. [. . .]

If the First Amendment has any force, it prohibits Congress from fining or jailing citizens, or associations of citizens, for simply engaging in political speech. If the antidistortion rationale were to be accepted, however, it would permit Government to ban political speech simply because the speaker is an association that has taken on the corporate form. The Government contends that *Austin* permits it to ban corporate expenditures for almost all forms of communication stemming from a corporation. [. . .]

Political speech is "indispensable to decisionmaking in a democracy, and this is no less true because the speech comes from a corporation rather than an individual." *Bellotti*. [. . .] This protection for speech is inconsistent with *Austin*'s antidistortion rationale. *Austin* sought to defend the antidistortion rationale as a means to prevent corporations from obtaining "an unfair advantage in the political marketplace" by using "resources amassed in the economic marketplace." [. . .] But *Buckley* rejected the premise that the Government has an interest "in equalizing the relative ability of individuals and groups to influence the outcome of elections." [. . .] *Buckley* was specific in stating that "the skyrocketing cost of political campaigns" could not sustain the governmental prohibition. The First Amendment's protections do not depend on the speaker's "financial ability to engage in public discussion." [. . .]

Either as support for its antidistortion rationale or as a further argument, the *Austin* majority undertook to distinguish wealthy individuals from corporations on the ground that "[s]tate law grants corporations special advantages—such as limited liability, perpetual life, and favorable treatment of the accumulation and distribution of assets." This does not suffice, however, to allow laws prohibiting speech. "It is rudimentary that the State cannot exact as the price of those special advantages the forfeiture of First Amendment rights." [. . .]

It is irrelevant for purposes of the First Amendment that corporate funds may "have little or no correlation to the public's support for the corporation's political ideas." *Austin*. All speakers, including individuals and the media, use money amassed from the economic marketplace to fund their speech. The First Amendment protects the resulting speech, even if it was enabled by economic transactions with persons or entities who disagree with the speaker's ideas. [. . .]

Austin's antidistortion rationale would produce the dangerous, and unacceptable, consequence that Congress could ban political speech of media corporations. [. . .] Media corporations are now exempt from § 441b's ban on corporate expenditures. [. . .] Yet media corporations accumulate wealth with the help of the corporate form, the largest media corporations have "immense aggregations of wealth," and the views expressed by media corporations often "have little or no correlation to the public's support" for those views. [. . .] Thus, under the Government's reasoning, wealthy media corporations could have their voices diminished to put them on par with other media entities. There is no precedent for permitting this under the First Amendment. [. . .]

The law's exception for media corporations is, on its own terms, all but an admission of the invalidity of the antidistortion rationale. [. . .]

There is simply no support for the view that the First Amendment, as originally understood, would permit the suppression of political speech by media corporations. The Framers may not have anticipated modern business and media corporations. [. . .] Yet television networks and major newspapers owned by media corporations have become the most important means of mass communication in modern times. The First Amendment was certainly not understood to condone the suppression of political speech in society's most salient media. It was understood as a response to the repression of speech and the press that had existed in England and the heavy taxes on the press that were imposed in the Colonies. [. . .] At the founding, speech was open, comprehensive, and vital to society's definition of itself; there were no limits on the sources of speech and knowledge. [. . .] The Framers may have been unaware of certain types of speakers or forms of communication, but that does not mean that those speakers and media are entitled to less First Amendment protection than those types of speakers and media that provided the means of communicating political ideas when the Bill of Rights was adopted.

Austin interferes with the "open marketplace" of ideas protected by the First Amendment [ ] It permits the Government to ban the political speech of millions of associations of citizens. [. . .] Most of these are small corporations without large amounts of wealth. [. . .]

By suppressing the speech of manifold corporations, both for-profit and nonprofit, the Government prevents their voices and viewpoints from reaching the public and advising voters on which persons or entities are hostile to their interests. [. . .]

The purpose and effect of this law is to prevent corporations, including small and nonprofit corporations, from presenting both facts and opinions to the public. This makes *Austin*'s antidistortion rationale all the more an aberration. "[T]he First Amendment protects the right of corporations to petition legislative and administrative bodies." *Bellotti* [. . .]

Even if § 441b's expenditure ban were constitutional, wealthy corporations could still lobby elected officials, although smaller corporations may not have the resources to do so. And wealthy individuals and unincorporated associations can spend unlimited amounts on independent expenditures. [. . .] Yet certain disfavored associations of citizens—those that have taken on the corporate form—are penalized for engaging in the same political speech. [. . .]

2

What we have said also shows the invalidity of other arguments made by the Government. For the most part relinquishing the antidistortion rationale, the Government falls back on the argument that corporate political speech can be banned in order to prevent corruption or its appearance. In *Buckley,* the Court found this interest "sufficiently important" to allow limits on contributions but did not extend that reasoning to expenditure limits. [. . .] When *Buckley* examined an expenditure ban, it found "that the governmental interest in preventing corruption and the appearance of corruption [was] inadequate to justify [the ban] on independent expenditures." [. . .]

[. . .] The *Buckley* Court [. . .] sustained limits on direct contributions in order to ensure against the reality or appearance of corruption. [. . .]

[. . .] The anticorruption interest is not sufficient to displace the speech here in question. [. . .]

3

The Government contends further that corporate independent expenditures can be limited because of its interest in protecting dissenting shareholders from being compelled to fund corporate political speech. This asserted interest, like *Austin*'s antidistortion rationale, would allow the Government to ban the political speech even of media corporations. [. . .] Assume, for example, that a shareholder of a corporation that owns a newspaper disagrees with the political views the newspaper expresses. *Austin* [. . .]. Under the Government's view, that potential disagreement could give the Government the authority to restrict the media corporation's political speech. The First Amendment does not allow that power. There is, furthermore, little evidence of abuse that cannot be corrected by shareholders "through the procedures of corporate democracy." *Bellotti* [. . .]

Those reasons are sufficient to reject this shareholder-protection interest; and, moreover, the statute is both underinclusive and overinclusive. As to the first, if Congress had been seeking to protect dissenting shareholders, it would not have banned corporate speech in only certain media within 30 or 60 days before an election. A dissenting shareholder's interests would be implicated by speech in any media at any time. As to the second, the statute is overinclusive because it covers all corporations, including nonprofit corporations and for-profit corporations with only single shareholders. As to other corporations, the remedy is not to restrict speech but to consider and explore other regulatory mechanisms. The regulatory mechanism here, based on speech, contravenes the First Amendment. [. . .]

C

Our precedent is to be respected unless the most convincing of reasons demonstrates that adherence to it puts us on a course that is sure error. "Beyond workability, the relevant factors in deciding whether to adhere to the principle of *stare decisis* include the antiquity of the precedent, the reliance interests at stake, and of course whether the decision was well reasoned." [. . .]

These considerations counsel in favor of rejecting *Austin,* which itself contravened this Court's earlier precedents in *Buckley* and *Bellotti.* [. . .]

For the reasons above, it must be concluded that *Austin* was not well reasoned.

[. . .]

Austin is overruled, so it provides no basis for allowing the Government to limit corporate independent expenditures. As the Government appears to concede, overruling Austin "effectively invalidate[s] not only BCRA Section 203, but also [. . .] 441b's prohibition on the use of corporate treasury funds for express advocacy." [. . .] Section 441b's restrictions on corporate independent expenditures are therefore invalid and cannot be applied to *Hillary.*

■ CHIEF JUSTICE ROBERTS, with whom JUSTICE ALITO joins, concurring.

The Government urges us in this case to uphold a direct prohibition on political speech. It asks us to embrace a theory of the First Amendment that would allow censorship not only of television and radio broadcasts, but of pamphlets, posters, the Internet, and virtually any other medium that corporations and unions might find useful in expressing their views on matters of public concern. Its theory, if accepted, would empower the Government to prohibit newspapers from running editorials or opinion pieces supporting or opposing candidates for office, so long as the newspapers were owned by corporations—as the major ones are. First Amendment rights could be confined to individuals, subverting the vibrant public discourse that is at the foundation of our democracy. The Court properly rejects that theory, and I join its opinion in full. The First Amendment protects more than just the individual on a soapbox and the lonely pamphleteer. [. . .]

■ JUSTICE SCALIA, with whom JUSTICE ALITO joins, and with whom JUSTICE THOMAS joins in part, concurring.

I join the opinion of the Court.

I write separately to address Justice STEVENS' discussion of *"Original Understandings,"* [. . .] This section of the dissent purports to show that today's decision is not supported by the original understanding of the First Amendment. The dissent attempts this demonstration, however, in splendid isolation from the text of the First Amendment. It never shows why "the freedom of speech" that was the right of Englishmen did not include the freedom to speak in association with other individuals, including association in the corporate form. To be sure, in 1791 (as now) corporations could pursue only the objectives set forth in their charters; but the dissent provides no evidence that their speech in the pursuit of those objectives could be censored.

Instead of taking this straightforward approach to determining the Amendment's meaning, the dissent embarks on a detailed exploration of the Framers' views about the "role of corporations in society." [. . .] The Framers did not like corporations, the dissent concludes, and therefore it follows (as night the day) that corporations had no rights of free speech. Of course the Framers' personal affection or disaffection for corporations is relevant only insofar as it can be thought to be reflected in the understood meaning of the text they enacted—not, as the dissent suggests, as a freestanding substitute for that text. But the dissent's distortion of proper analysis is even worse than that. Though faced with a constitutional text that makes no distinction between types of speakers, the dissent feels no necessity to provide even an isolated statement from the founding era to the effect that corporations are *not* covered, but places the burden on appellant to bring forward statements showing that they *are. Ibid.* ("[T]here is not a scintilla of evidence to support the notion that anyone believed [the First Amendment] would preclude regulatory distinctions based on the corporate form").

Despite the corporation-hating quotations the dissent has dredged up, it is far from clear that by the end of the 18th century corporations were despised. If so, how came there to be so many of them? The dissent's statement that there were few business corporations during the 18th century—"only a few hundred during all of the 18th century"—is misleading. [. . .]. There were approximately 335 charters issued to business corporations in the United States by the end of the 18th century. [. . .] This was a "considerable extension of corporate enterprise in the field of business," *Davis, Essays in the Earlier History of American Corporations* [. . .] and represented "unprecedented growth" *Id.* [. . .]. Moreover, what seems like a small number by today's standards surely does not indicate the relative importance of corporations when the Nation was considerably smaller. As I have previously noted, "[b]y the end of the eighteenth century the corporation was a familiar figure in American economic life." *McConnell* v. *Federal Election Comm'n* [. . .]

Even if we thought it proper to apply the dissent's approach of excluding from First Amendment coverage what the Founders disliked, and even if we agreed that the Founders disliked founding-era corporations, modern corporations might not qualify for exclusion. Most of the Founders' resentment toward corporations was directed at the state-granted monopoly privileges that individually chartered corporations enjoyed. Modern corporations do not have such privileges, and would probably have been favored by most of our enterprising Founders—excluding, perhaps, Thomas Jefferson and others favoring perpetuation of an agrarian society. Moreover, if the Founders' specific intent with respect to corporations is what matters, why does the dissent ignore the Founders' views about other legal entities that have more in common with modern business corporations than the founding-era corporations? At the time of the founding, religious, educational, and literary corporations were incorporated under general incorporation statutes, much as business corporations are today. [. . .] There were also small unincorporated business associations, which some have argued were the " 'true progenitors' " of today's business corporations. [. . .] Were all of these silently excluded from the protections of the First Amendment?

The lack of a textual exception for speech by corporations cannot be explained on the ground that such organizations did not exist or did not speak. To the contrary, colleges, towns and cities, religious institutions, and guilds had long been organized as corporations at common law and under the King's charter, [. . .], and as I have discussed, the practice of incorporation only expanded in the United States. Both corporations and voluntary associations actively petitioned the Government and expressed their views in newspapers and pamphlets. [. . .] The dissent offers no evidence—none whatever—that the First Amendment's unqualified text was originally understood to exclude such associational speech from its protection.

Historical evidence relating to the textually similar clause "the freedom of . . . the press" also provides no support for the proposition that the First Amendment excludes conduct of artificial legal entities from the scope of its protection. The freedom of "the press" was widely understood to protect the publishing activities of individual editors and printers. [. . .] But these individuals often acted through newspapers, which (much like corporations) had their own names, outlived the individuals who had founded them, could be bought and sold, were sometimes owned by more than one person, and were operated for profit. [. . .] Their activities were not stripped of First Amendment protection simply because they were carried out under the banner of an artificial legal entity. And the notion which follows from the dissent's view, that modern newspapers, since they are incorporated, have free-speech rights only at the sufferance of Congress, boggles the mind. [. . .]

The dissent says that when the Framers "constitutionalized the right to free speech in the First Amendment, it was the free speech of individual Americans that they had in mind." [. . .] That is no doubt true. All the provisions of the Bill of Rights set forth the rights of individual men and women—not, for example, of trees or polar bears. But the individual person's right to speak includes the right to speak *in association with other individual persons.* Surely the dissent does not believe that speech by the Republican Party or the Democratic Party can be censored because it is not the speech of "an individual American." It is the speech of many individual Americans, who have associated in a common cause, giving the leadership of the party the right to speak on their behalf. The association of individuals in a business corporation is no different—or at least it cannot be denied the right to speak on the simplistic ground that it is not "an individual American."

But to return to, and summarize, my principal point, which is the conformity of today's opinion with the original meaning of the First Amendment. The Amendment is written in terms of "speech," not speakers. Its text offers no foothold for excluding any category of speaker, from single individuals to partnerships of individuals, to unincorporated associations of individuals, to incorporated associations of individuals— and the dissent offers no evidence about the original meaning of the text to support any such exclusion. We are therefore simply left with the question whether the speech at issue in this case is "speech" covered by the First Amendment. No one says otherwise. A documentary film critical of a potential Presidential candidate is core political speech, and its nature as such does not change simply because it was funded by a corporation. Nor does the character of that funding produce any reduction whatever in the "inherent worth of the speech" and "its capacity for informing the public," *First Nat. Bank of Boston v. Bellotti* [. . .] Indeed, to exclude or impede corporate speech is to muzzle the principal agents of the modern free economy. We should celebrate rather than condemn the addition of this speech to the public debate.

■ JUSTICE STEVENS, with whom JUSTICE GINSBURG, JUSTICE BREYER and JUSTICE SOTOMAYOR join, concurring in part and dissenting in part.

The real issue in this case concerns how, not if, the appellant may finance its electioneering. Citizens United is a wealthy nonprofit corporation that runs a political action committee (PAC) with millions of dollars in assets. Under the Bipartisan Campaign Reform Act of 2002 (BCRA), it could have used those assets to televise and promote *Hillary: The Movie* wherever and whenever it wanted to. It also could have spent unrestricted sums to broadcast *Hillary* at any time other than the 30 days before the last primary election. Neither Citizens United's nor any other corporation's speech has been "banned". All that the parties dispute is whether Citizens United had a right to use the funds in its general treasury to pay for broadcasts during the 30-day period. The notion that the First Amendment dictates an affirmative answer to that question is, in my judgment, profoundly misguided. Even more misguided is the notion that the Court must rewrite the law relating to campaign expenditures by *for-profit* corporations and unions to decide this case.

The basic premise underlying the Court's ruling is its iteration, and constant reiteration, of the proposition that the First Amendment bars regulatory distinctions based on a speaker's identity, including its "identity" as a corporation. While that glittering generality has rhetorical appeal, it is not a correct statement of the law. Nor does it tell us when a corporation may engage in electioneering that some of its shareholders oppose. It does not even resolve the specific question whether Citizens United may be required to finance some of its messages with the money in its PAC. The conceit that corporations must be treated identically to natural persons in the political sphere is not only inaccurate but also inadequate to justify the Court's disposition of this case.

In the context of election to public office, the distinction between corporate and human speakers is significant. Although they make enormous contributions to our society, corporations are not actually members of it. They cannot vote or run for office. Because they may be managed and controlled by nonresidents, their interests may conflict in fundamental respects with the interests of eligible voters. The financial resources, legal structure, and instrumental orientation of corporations raise legitimate concerns about their role in the electoral process. Our lawmakers have a compelling constitutional basis, if not also a democratic duty, to take measures designed to guard against the potentially deleterious effects of corporate spending in local and national races.

The majority's approach to corporate electioneering marks a dramatic break from our past. Congress has placed special limitations on campaign spending by corporations [. . .]. We have unanimously concluded that this "reflects a permissible assessment of the dangers posed by those entities to the electoral process," [. . .] and have accepted the "legislative judgment that the special characteristics of the corporate structure require particularly careful regulation" [. . .]. The Court today rejects a century of history when it treats the distinction between corporate and individual campaign spending as an invidious novelty born of *Austin* [. . .]. I emphatically dissent from its principal holding.

III

The novelty of the Court's procedural dereliction and its approach to *stare decisis* is matched by the novelty of its ruling on the merits. The ruling rests on several premises. First, the Court claims that *Austin* and *McConnell* have "banned" corporate speech. Second, it claims that the First Amendment precludes regulatory distinctions based on speaker identity, including the speaker's identity as a corporation. Third, it claims that *Austin* and *McConnell* were radical outliers in our First Amendment tradition and our campaign finance jurisprudence. Each of these claims is wrong. [. . .]

Identity-Based Distinctions

The second pillar of the Court's opinion is its assertion that "the Government cannot restrict political speech based on the speaker's . . . identity." [. . .] The case on which it relies for this proposition is *First Nat. Bank of Boston v. Bellotti* [. . .].

[. . .] "Our jurisprudence over the past 216 years has rejected an absolutist interpretation" of the First Amendment. [. . .] Yet in a variety of contexts, we have held that speech can be regulated differentially on account of the speaker's identity, when identity is understood in categorical or institutional terms. The Government routinely places special restrictions on the speech rights of students, prisoners, members of the Armed Forces, foreigners, and its own employees. When such restrictions are justified by a legitimate governmental interest, they do not necessarily raise constitutional problems. [. . .]

The same logic applies to this case with additional force because it is the identity of corporations, rather than individuals, that the Legislature has taken into account. As we have unanimously observed, legislatures are entitled to decide "that the special characteristics of the corporate structure require particularly careful regulation" in an electoral context. [. . .] Not only has the distinctive potential of corporations to corrupt the electoral process long been recognized, but within the area of campaign finance, corporate spending is also "furthest from the core of political expression, since corporations' First Amendment speech and association interests are derived largely from those of their members and of the public in receiving information [. . .]. Campaign finance distinctions based on corporate identity tend to be less worrisome, in other words, because the "speakers" are not natural persons, much less members of our political community, and the governmental interests are of the highest order. Furthermore, when corporations, as a class, are distinguished from noncorporations, as a class, there is a lesser risk that regulatory distinctions will reflect invidious discrimination or political favoritism.

If taken seriously, our colleagues' assumption that the identity of a speaker has *no* relevance to the Government's ability to regulate political speech would lead to some remarkable conclusions. Such an assumption would have accorded the propaganda broadcasts to our troops by "Tokyo Rose" during World War II the same protection as speech by Allied commanders. More pertinently, it would appear to afford the same protection to multinational corporations controlled by foreigners as to individual Americans: To do otherwise, after all, could " 'enhance the relative voice' " of some (*i.e.,* humans) over others (*i.e.,* nonhumans). [. . .] Under the majority's view, I suppose it may be a First Amendment problem that corporations are not permitted to vote, given that voting is, among other things, a form of speech.

In short, the Court dramatically overstates its critique of identity-based distinctions, without ever explaining why corporate identity demands the same treatment as individual identity. Only the most wooden approach to the First Amendment could justify the unprecedented line it seeks to draw.

Our First Amendment Tradition

[. . .]

1.   *Original Understandings*

Let us start from the beginning. The Court invokes "ancient First Amendment principles," [. . .] and original understandings, [. . .] to defend today's ruling, yet it makes only a perfunctory attempt to ground its analysis in the principles or understandings of those who drafted and ratified the Amendment. [. . .]

This is not only because the Framers and their contemporaries conceived of speech more narrowly than we now think of it, [. . .] but also because they held very different views about the nature of the First Amendment right and the role of corporations in society. Those few corporations that existed at the founding were authorized by grant of a special legislative charter. Corporate sponsors would petition the legislature, and the legislature, if amenable, would issue a charter that specified the corporation's powers and purposes and "authoritatively fixed the scope and content of corporate organization," including "the internal structure of the corporation." [. . .] Corporations were created, supervised, and conceptualized as quasi-public entities, "designed to serve a social function for the state." [. . .] It was "assumed that [they] were legally privileged organizations that had to be closely scrutinized by the legislature because their purposes had to be made consistent with public welfare." [. . .]

The individualized charter mode of incorporation reflected the "cloud of disfavor under which corporations labored" in the early years of this Nation. [. . .] Thomas Jefferson famously fretted that corporations would subvert the Republic. General incorporation statutes, and widespread acceptance of business corporations as socially useful actors, did not emerge until the 1800's. [. . .]

The Framers thus took it as a given that corporations could be comprehensively regulated in the service of the public welfare. Unlike our colleagues, they had little trouble distinguishing corporations from human beings, and when they constitutionalized the right to free speech in the First Amendment, it was the free speech of individual Americans that they had in mind. While individuals might join together to exercise their speech rights, business corporations, at least, were plainly not seen as facilitating such associational or expressive ends. Even "the notion that business corporations could invoke the First Amendment would probably have been quite a novelty," given that "at the time, the legitimacy of every corporate activity was thought to rest entirely in a concession of the sovereign." [. . .] In light of these background practices and understandings, it seems to me implausible that the Framers believed "the freedom of speech" would extend equally to all corporate speakers, much less that it would preclude legislatures from taking limited measures to guard against corporate capture of elections.

[. . .] This case sheds a revelatory light on the assumption of some that an impartial judge's application of an originalist methodology is likely to yield more determinate answers, or to play a more decisive role in the decisional process, than his or her views about sound policy. [. . .]

1. Legislative and Judicial Interpretation

A century of more recent history puts to rest any notion that today's ruling is faithful to our First Amendment tradition. At the federal level, the express distinction between corporate and individual political spending on elections stretches back to 1907, when Congress passed the Tillman Act [. . .] banning all corporate contributions to candidates. [. . .]

By the time Congress passed FECA in 1971, the bar on corporate contributions and expenditures had become such an accepted part of federal campaign finance regulation that when a large number of plaintiffs, including several nonprofit corporations, challenged virtually every aspect of FECA in *Buckley,* [. . .] no one even bothered to argue that the bar as such was unconstitutional. *Buckley* famously (or infamously) distinguished direct contributions from independent expenditures [. . .], but its silence on corporations only reinforced the understanding that corporate expenditures could be treated differently from individual expenditures. [. . .]

Thus, it was unremarkable, in a 1982 case holding that Congress could bar nonprofit corporations from soliciting nonmembers for PAC funds, that then-Justice Rehnquist wrote for a unanimous Court that [. . .] "The governmental interest in preventing both actual corruption and the appearance of corruption of elected representatives has long been recognized," the unanimous Court observed, "and there is no reason why it may not . . . be accomplished by treating . . . corporations . . . differently from individuals."

The corporate/individual distinction was not questioned by the Court's disposition, in 1986, of a challenge to the expenditure restriction as applied to a distinctive type of nonprofit corporation. [. . .] In *MCFL,* [. . .] we stated again "that 'the special characteristics of the corporate structure require particularly careful regulation,'" [. . .] and again we acknowledged that the Government has a legitimate interest in "regulat[ing] the substantial aggregations of wealth amassed by the special advantages which go with the corporate form" [. . .]. What the Court held by a 5-to-4 vote was that a limited class of corporations must be allowed to use their general treasury funds for independent expenditures, because Congress' interests in protecting shareholders and "restrict[ing] 'the influence of political war chests funneled through the corporate form,'" [. . .] did not apply to corporations that were structurally insulated from those concerns. [. . .]

Four years later, in *Austin,* [. . .] we considered whether corporations falling outside the *MCFL* exception could be barred from using general treasury funds to make independent expenditures in support of, or in opposition to, candidates. We held they could be. Once again recognizing the importance of "the integrity of the marketplace of political ideas" in candidate elections, [. . .] we noted that corporations have "special advantages—such as limited liability, perpetual life, and favorable treatment of the accumulation and distribution of assets," [. . .]—that allow them to spend prodigious general treasury sums on campaign messages that have "little or no correlation" with the beliefs held by actual persons [. . .]. In light of the corrupting effects such spending might have on the political process, we permitted the State of Michigan to limit corporate expenditures on candidate elections to corporations' PACs, which rely on voluntary contributions and thus "reflect actual public support for the political ideas espoused by corporations" [. . .]. Notwithstanding our colleagues' insinuations that *Austin* deprived the public of general "ideas," "facts," and " 'knowledge,' " the decision addressed only candidate-focused expenditures and gave the State no license to regulate corporate spending on other matters.

In the 20 years since *Austin,* we have reaffirmed its holding and rationale a number of times [. . .].

2.   Buckley and Bellotti

Against this extensive background of congressional regulation of corporate campaign spending, and our repeated affirmation of this regulation as constitutionally sound, the majority dismisses *Austin* as "a significant departure from ancient First Amendment principles." How does the majority attempt to justify this claim? Selected passages from two cases, *Buckley* [. . .] and *Bellotti,* [. . .] do all of the work. In the Court's view, *Buckley* and *Bellotti* decisively rejected the possibility of distinguishing corporations from natural persons in the 1970's [. . .].

* * *

In sum, over the course of the past century Congress has demonstrated a recurrent need to regulate corporate participation in candidate elections to " '[p]reserv[e] the integrity of the electoral process, preven[t] corruption, . . . sustai[n] the active, alert responsibility of the individual citizen,' " protect the expressive interests of shareholders, and " '[p]reserv [e] . . . the individual citizen's confidence in government.' " [. . .] These understandings provided the combined impetus behind the Tillman Act in 1907, [. . .] the Taft-Hartley Act in 1947, [. . .] FECA in 1971, [. . .] and BCRA in 2002 [. . .]. Continuously for over 100 years, this line of "[c]ampaign finance reform has been a series of reactions to documented threats to electoral integrity obvious to any voter, posed by large sums of money from corporate or union treasuries." Time and again, we have recognized these realities in approving measures that Congress and the States have taken. None of the cases the majority cites is to the contrary. The only thing new about *Austin* was the dissent, with its stunning failure to appreciate the legitimacy of interests recognized in the name of democratic integrity since the days of the Progressives.

IV

Having explained why this is not an appropriate case in which to revisit *Austin* and *McConnell* and why these decisions sit perfectly well with "First Amendment principles," [. . .] I come at last to the interests that are at stake. The majority recognizes that *Austin* and *McConnell* may be defended on anticorruption, antidistortion, and shareholder protection rationales. [. . .] It badly errs both in explaining the nature of these rationales, which overlap and complement each other, and in applying them to the case at hand.

The Anticorruption Interest

[. . .] On numerous occasions we have recognized Congress' legitimate interest in preventing the money that is spent on elections from exerting an " 'undue influence on an officeholder's judgment' " and from creating " 'the appearance of such influence,' " beyond the sphere of *quid pro quo* relationships. [. . .] Corruption can take many forms. Bribery may be the paradigm case. But the difference between selling a vote and selling access is a matter of degree, not kind. And selling access is not qualitatively different from giving special preference to those who spent money on one's behalf. Corruption operates along a spectrum, and the majority's apparent belief that *quid pro quo* arrangements can be neatly demarcated from other improper influences does not accord with the theory or reality of politics [. . .].

[. . .] When private interests are seen to exert outsized control over officeholders solely on account of the money spent on (or withheld from) their campaigns, the result can depart so thoroughly "from what is pure or correct" in the conduct of Government, [. . .] that it amounts to a "subversion. . . of the . . . electoral process" [. . .]. At stake in the legislative efforts to address this threat is therefore not only the legitimacy and quality of Government but also the public's faith therein, not only "the capacity of this democracy to represent its constituents [but also] the confidence of its citizens in their capacity to govern themselves," *WRTL* [. . .]. "Take away Congress' authority to regulate the appearance of undue influence and 'the cynical assumption that large donors call the tune could jeopardize the willingness of voters to take part in democratic governance.' " [. . .]

The cluster of interrelated interests threatened by such undue influence and its appearance has been well captured under the rubric of "democratic integrity." *WRTL* (Souter, J., dissenting). This value has underlined a century of state and federal efforts to regulate the role of corporations in the electoral process.

Unlike the majority's myopic focus on *quid pro quo* scenarios and the free-floating "First Amendment principles" on which it rests so much weight, this broader understanding of corruption has deep roots in the Nation's history. "During debates on the earliest [campaign finance] reform acts, the terms 'corruption' and 'undue influence' were used nearly interchangeably." [. . .]. Long before *Buckley,* we appreciated that "[t]o say that Congress is without power to pass appropriate legislation to safeguard . . . an election from the improper use of money to influence the result is to deny to the nation in a vital particular the power of self protection." [. . .] And whereas we have no evidence to support the notion that the Framers would have wanted corporations to have the same rights as natural persons in the electoral context, we have ample evidence to suggest that they would have been appalled by the evidence of corruption that [. . .] that the Court today discounts to irrelevance. It is fair to say that "[t]he Framers were obsessed with corruption" [. . .]. They discussed corruption "more often in the Constitutional Convention than factions, violence, or instability." Teachout 352. When they brought our constitutional order into being, the Framers had their minds trained on a threat to republican self-government that this Court has lost sight of.

Quid Pro Quo Corruption

[. . .] Corporations, as a class, tend to be more attuned to the complexities of the legislative process and more directly affected by tax and appropriations measures that receive little public scrutiny; they also have vastly more money with which to try to buy access and votes. *See* Supp. Brief for Appellee 17 (stating that the Fortune 100 companies earned revenues of $13.1 trillion during the last election cycle). Business corporations must engage the political process in instrumental terms if they are to maximize shareholder value. The unparalleled resources, professional lobbyists, and single-minded focus they bring to this effort, I believed, make *quid pro quo* corruption and its appearance inherently more likely when they (or their conduits or trade groups) spend unrestricted sums on elections. [. . .]

Austin and Corporate Expenditures

Just as the majority gives short shrift to the general societal interests at stake in campaign finance regulation, it also overlooks the distinctive considerations raised by the regulation of *corporate* expenditures. The majority fails to appreciate that *Austin*'s antidistortion rationale is itself an anticorruption rationale, [. . .] tied to the special concerns raised by corporations. Understood properly, "antidistortion" is simply a variant on the classic governmental interest in protecting against improper influences on officeholders that debilitate the democratic process. It is manifestly not just an " 'equalizing' " ideal in disguise. [. . .]

1.   *Antidistortion*

The fact that corporations are different from human beings might seem to need no elaboration, except that the majority opinion almost completely elides it. *Austin* set forth some of the basic differences. Unlike natural persons, corporations have "limited liability" for their owners and managers, "perpetual life," separation of ownership and control, "and favorable treatment of the accumulation and distribution of assets . . . that enhance their ability to attract capital and to deploy their resources in ways that maximize the return on their shareholders' investments." [. . .] Unlike voters in U.S. elections, corporations may be foreign controlled. Unlike other interest groups, business corporations have been "effectively delegated responsibility for ensuring society's economic welfare"; they inescapably structure the life of every citizen. " '[T]he resources in the treasury of a business corporation,' " furthermore, " 'are not an indication of popular support for the corporation's political ideas.' " [. . .] " 'They reflect instead the economically motivated decisions of investors and customers. The availability of these resources may make a corporation a formidable political presence, even though the power of the corporation may be no reflection of the power of its ideas.' " [. . .]

It might also be added that corporations have no consciences, no beliefs, no feelings, no thoughts, no desires. Corporations help structure and facilitate the activities of human beings, to be sure, and their "personhood" often serves as a useful legal fiction. But they are not themselves members of "We the People" by whom and for whom our Constitution was established.

These basic points help explain why corporate electioneering is not only more likely to impair compelling governmental interests, but also why restrictions on that electioneering are less likely to encroach upon First Amendment freedoms. One fundamental concern of the First Amendment is to "protec[t] the individual's interest in self-expression." [. . .] Freedom of speech helps "make men free to develop their faculties," [. . .] it respects their "dignity and choice," [. . .] and it facilitates the value of "individual self-realization." [. . .] Corporate speech, however, is derivative speech, speech by proxy.

It is an interesting question "who" is even speaking when a business corporation places an advertisement that endorses or attacks a particular candidate. Presumably it is not the customers or employees, who typically have no say in such matters. It cannot realistically be said to be the shareholders, who tend to be far removed from the day-to-day decisions of the firm and whose political preferences may be opaque to management. Perhaps the officers or directors of the corporation have the best claim to be the ones speaking, except their fiduciary duties generally prohibit them from using corporate funds for personal ends. Some individuals associated with the corporation must make the decision to place the ad, but the idea that these individuals are thereby fostering their self-expression or cultivating their critical faculties is fanciful. It is entirely possible that the corporation's electoral message will *conflict* with their personal convictions. Take away the ability to use general treasury funds for some of those ads, and no one's autonomy, dignity, or political equality has been impinged upon in the least.

Corporate expenditures are distinguishable from individual expenditures in this respect. I have taken the view that a legislature may place reasonable restrictions on individuals' electioneering expenditures in the service of the governmental interests explained above, and in recognition of the fact that such restrictions are not direct restraints on speech but rather on its financing. [. . .] But those restrictions concededly present a tougher case, because the primary conduct of actual, flesh-and-blood persons is involved. Some of those individuals might feel that they need to spend large sums of money on behalf of a particular candidate to vindicate the intensity of their electoral preferences. This is obviously not the situation with business corporations, as their routine practice of giving "substantial sums to *both* major national parties" makes pellucidly clear. [. . .] "[C]orporate participation" in elections, any business executive will tell you, "is more transactional than ideological." [. . .]

[. . .] [S]ome corporations have affirmatively urged Congress to place limits on their electioneering communications. These corporations fear that officeholders will shake them down for supportive ads, that they will have to spend increasing sums on elections in an ever-escalating arms race with their competitors, and that public trust in business will be eroded. [. . .] A system that effectively forces corporations to use their shareholders' money both to maintain access to, and to avoid retribution from, elected officials may ultimately prove more harmful than beneficial to many corporations. It can impose a kind of implicit tax. [. . .]

[. . .] Corporate "domination" of electioneering, [. . .] can generate the impression that corporations dominate our democracy. When citizens turn on their televisions and radios before an election and hear only corporate electioneering, they may lose faith in their capacity, as citizens, to influence public policy. A Government captured by corporate interests, they may come to believe, will be neither responsive to their needs nor willing to give their views a fair hearing. The predictable result is cynicism and disenchantment: an increased perception that large spenders " 'call the tune' " and a reduced " 'willingness of voters to take part in democratic governance.' " [. . .] To the extent that corporations are allowed to exert undue influence in electoral races, the speech of the eventual winners of those races may also be chilled. Politicians who fear that a certain corporation can make or break their reelection chances may be cowed into silence about that corporation. On a variety of levels, unregulated corporate electioneering might diminish the ability of citizens to "hold officials accountable to the people," [. . .] and disserve the goal of a public debate that is "uninhibited, robust, and wide-open." [. . .]

The majority's unwillingness to distinguish between corporations and humans similarly blinds it to the possibility that corporations' "war chests" and their special "advantages" in the legal realm, [. . .] may translate into special advantages in the market for legislation. When large numbers of citizens have a common stake in a measure that is under consideration, it may be very difficult for them to coordinate resources on behalf of their position. The corporate form, by contrast, "provides a simple way to channel rents to only those who have paid their dues, as it were. If you do not own stock, you do not benefit from the larger dividends or appreciation in the stock price caused by the passage of private interest legislation." [. . .] Corporations, that is, are uniquely equipped to seek laws that favor their owners, not simply because they have a lot of money but because of their legal and organizational structure. Remove all restrictions on their electioneering, and the door may be opened to a type of rent seeking that is "far more destructive" than what noncorporations are capable of. [. . .]. It is for reasons such as these that our campaign finance jurisprudence has long appreciated that "the 'differing structures and purposes' of different entities 'may require different forms of regulation in order to protect the integrity of the electoral process.' " [. . .]

In critiquing *Austin*'s antidistortion rationale and campaign finance regulation more generally, our colleagues place tremendous weight on the example of media corporations. [. . .] The press plays a unique role not only in the text, history, and structure of the First Amendment but also in facilitating public discourse; as the *Austin* Court explained, "media corporations differ significantly from other corporations in that their resources are devoted to the collection of information and its dissemination to the public" [. . .]. Our colleagues have raised some interesting and difficult questions about Congress' authority to regulate electioneering by the press, and about how to define what constitutes the press. *But that is not the case before us.* Section 203 does not apply to media corporations, and even if it did, Citizens United is not a media corporation. [. . .]

2. *Shareholder Protection*

[. . .] Interwoven with *Austin*'s concern to protect the integrity of the electoral process is a concern to protect the rights of shareholders from a kind of coerced speech: electioneering expenditures that do not "reflec[t] [their] support." [. . .] When corporations use general treasury funds to praise or attack a particular candidate for office, it is the shareholders, as the residual claimants, who are effectively footing the bill. Those shareholders who disagree with the corporation's electoral message may find their financial investments being used to undermine their political convictions.

The PAC mechanism, by contrast, helps ensure that those who pay for an electioneering communication actually support its content and that managers do not use general treasuries to advance personal agendas. *Ibid.* It " 'allows corporate political participation without the temptation to use corporate funds for political influence, quite possibly at odds with the sentiments of some shareholders or members.' " [. . .] A rule that privileges the use of PACs thus does more than facilitate the political speech of like-minded shareholders; it also curbs the rent seeking behavior of executives and respects the views of dissenters. *Austin*'s acceptance of restrictions on general treasury spending "simply allows people who have invested in the business corporation for purely economic reasons"—the vast majority of investors, one assumes—"to avoid being taken advantage of, without sacrificing their economic objectives." [. . .]

The Court dismisses this interest on the ground that abuses of shareholder money can be corrected "through the procedures of corporate democracy," [. . .] and, it seems, through Internet-based disclosures. [. . .] I fail to understand how this addresses the concerns of dissenting union members, who will also be affected by today's ruling, and I fail to understand why the Court is so confident in these mechanisms. By "corporate democracy," presumably the Court means the rights of shareholders to vote and to bring derivative suits for breach of fiduciary duty. In practice, however, many corporate lawyers will tell you that "these rights are so limited as to be almost nonexistent," given the internal authority wielded by boards and managers and the expansive protections afforded by the business judgment rule. [. . .] Modern technology may help make it easier to track corporate activity, including electoral advocacy, but it is utopian to believe that it solves the problem. Most American households that own stock do so through intermediaries such as mutual funds and pension plans, [. . .] which makes it more difficult both to monitor and to alter particular holdings. [. . .] Moreover, if the corporation in question operates a PAC, an investor who sees the company's ads may not know whether they are being funded through the PAC or through the general treasury.

If and when shareholders learn that a corporation has been spending general treasury money on objectionable electioneering, they can divest. Even assuming that they reliably learn as much, however, this solution is only partial. The injury to the shareholders' expressive rights has already occurred; they might have preferred to keep that corporation's stock in their portfolio for any number of economic reasons; and they may incur a capital gains tax or other penalty from selling their shares, changing their pension plan, or the like. The shareholder protection rationale has been criticized as underinclusive, in that corporations also spend money on lobbying and charitable contributions in ways that any particular shareholder might disapprove. But those expenditures do not implicate the selection of public officials, an area in which "the interests of unwilling . . . corporate shareholders [in not being] forced to subsidize that speech" "are at their zenith." [. . .]

H. REVIEW PROBLEMS

1. In the mid-2010s, there was a notable uptick in the number of class action securities cases filed against public companies. Blue Apron Holdings, Inc., Roku, Inc., and Stitch Fix, Inc. are Delaware corporations. Before their 2017 initial public offerings, all three adopted provisions in their charters that required shareholders who brought class action claims under Section 11 of the Securities Act of 1933 to bring those suits in federal court. These companies noted that their goal was to consolidate securities actions into one forum for efficiency purposes. Plaintiff Matthew Sciabacucchi purchased shares of each company and sought declaratory action in the Delaware Court of Chancery seeking to invalidate the provisions. Sciabacucchi argued that organizational documents such as charters cannot bind a plaintiff to a particular forum. Are these "federal forum provisions" valid under Delaware law? (Hint: *See* DGCL § 102(b)(1))[1]

---

[1]   *See* Salzberg v. Sciabacucchi, 227 A.3d 102 (Del. 2020).

2. In merger transactions, stockholders of Delaware corporations have a statutory right to an appraisal under DGCL § 262. An appraisal is a judicial determination of the fair price for the transaction. Authentix Acquisition Co. has a stockholder agreement that provides certain rights to its stockholders in a merger. The agreement also requires stockholders to refrain from exercising their appraisal rights in a merger. Authentix has engaged in a merger and stockholders who signed the stockholder agreement now seek appraisal. The question before the court is whether stockholders can waive their right to appraisal. How is a court likely to decide?[2]

---

[2] *See* Manti Holdings LLC v. Authentix Acquisition Co., 251 A.3d. 1199 (Del. 2021).

CHAPTER IV

SHAREHOLDERS, MANAGEMENT AND CONTROL

A. SHAREHOLDER FRANCHISE

Blasius Industries, Inc. v. Atlas Corp.

564 A.2d 651 (Del. Ch. 1988)

■ ALLEN, CHANCELLOR.

[. . .]

Blasius Acquires a 9% Stake in Atlas.

Blasius is a new stockholder of Atlas. It began to accumulate Atlas shares for the first time in July 1987. On October 29, it filed a Schedule 13D with the Securities Exchange Commission disclosing that, with affiliates, it then owed 9.1% of Atlas' common stock. It stated in that filing that it intended to encourage management of Atlas to consider a restructuring of the Company or other transaction to enhance shareholder values. It also disclosed that Blasius was exploring the feasibility of obtaining control of Atlas, including instituting a tender offer or seeking "appropriate" representation on the Atlas board of directors.

Blasius has recently come under the control of two individuals, Michael Lubin and Warren Delano, who after experience in the commercial banking industry, had, for a short time, run a venture capital operation for a small investment banking firm. [. . .]

The prospect of Messrs. Lubin and Delano involving themselves in Atlas' affairs was not a development welcomed by Atlas' management. Atlas had a new CEO, defendant Weaver, who had, over the course of the past year or so, overseen a business restructuring of a sort . . ., [and who] wrote in his diary on October 30, 1987:

> 13D by Delano & Lubin came in today. Had long conversation
> w/ MAH & Mark Golden [of Goldman, Sachs] on issue. All agree
> we must dilute these people down by the acquisition of another
> Co. w/stock, or merger or something else.

The Blasius Proposal of A Leverage Recapitalization Or Sale.

Immediately after filing its 13D on October 29, Blasius' representatives sought a meeting with the Atlas management. Atlas dragged its feet. A meeting was arranged for December 2, 1987 following the regular meeting of the Atlas board. [. . .]

At that meeting, Messrs. Lubin and Delano suggested that Atlas engage in a leveraged restructuring and distribute cash to shareholders. In such a transaction, which is by this date a commonplace form of transaction, a corporation typically raises cash by sale of assets and significant borrowings and makes a large one-time cash distribution to shareholders. The shareholders are typically left with cash and an equity interest in a smaller, more highly leveraged enterprise. Lubin and Delano gave the outline of a leveraged recapitalization for Atlas as they saw it.

Immediately following the meeting, the Atlas representatives expressed among themselves an initial reaction that the proposal was infeasible. On December 7, Mr. Lubin sent a letter detailing the proposal. [. . .]

Atlas Asks Its Investment Banker to Study the Proposal.

This written proposal was distributed to the Atlas board on December 9 and Goldman Sachs was directed to review and analyze it.

The proposal met with a cool reception from management. On December 9, Mr. Weaver issued a press release expressing surprise that Blasius would suggest using debt to accomplish what he characterized as a substantial liquidation of Atlas at a time when Atlas' future prospects were promising. [. . .]

Blasius attempted on December 14 and December 22 to arrange a further meeting with the Atlas management without success. During this period, Atlas provided Goldman Sachs with projections for the Company. Lubin was told that a further meeting would await completion of Goldman's analysis. A meeting after the first of the year was proposed.

The Delivery of Blasius' Consent Statement.

On December 30, 1987, Blasius caused Cede & Co. (the registered owner of its Atlas stock) to deliver to Atlas a signed written consent (1) adopting a precatory resolution recommending that the board develop and implement a restructuring proposal, (2) amending the Atlas bylaws to, among other things, expand the size of the board from seven to fifteen members—the maximum number under Atlas' charter, and (3) electing eight named persons to fill the new directorships. [. . .]

The reaction was immediate. Mr. Weaver conferred with Mr. Masinter, the Company's outside counsel and a director, who viewed the consent as an attempt to take control of the Company. They decided to call an emergency meeting of the board, even though a regularly scheduled meeting was to occur only one week hence, on January 6, 1988. The point of the emergency meeting was to act on their conclusion (or to seek to have the board act on their conclusion) "that we should add at least one and probably two directors to the board . . ." (Tr. 85, Vol. II). A quorum of directors, however, could not be arranged for a telephone meeting that day. A telephone meeting was held the next day. At that meeting, the board voted to amend the bylaws to increase the size of the board from seven to nine and appointed John M. Devaney and Harry J. Winters, Jr. to fill those newly created positions. Atlas' Certificate of Incorporation creates staggered terms for directors; the terms to which Messrs.

Devaney and Winters were appointed would expire in 1988 and 1990, respectively.

The Motivation of the Incumbent Board In Expanding the Board and Appointing New Members.

In increasing the size of Atlas' board by two and filling the newly created positions, the members of the board realized that they were thereby precluding the holders of a majority of the Company's shares from placing a majority of new directors on the board through Blasius' consent solicitation, should they want to do so. Indeed the evidence establishes that that was the principal motivation in so acting.

The conclusion that, in creating two new board positions on December 31 and electing Messrs. Devaney and Winters to fill those positions the board was principally motivated to prevent or delay the shareholders from possibly placing a majority of new members on the board, is critical to my analysis of the central issue posed by the first filed of the two pending cases. If the board in fact was not so motivated, but rather had taken action completely independently of the consent solicitation, which merely had an incidental impact upon the possible effectuation of any action authorized by the shareholders, it is very unlikely that such action would be subject to judicial nullification. [. . . .] The board, as a general matter, is under no fiduciary obligation to suspend its active management of the firm while the consent solicitation process goes forward. [. . .]

In this setting, I conclude that, while the addition of these qualified men would, under other circumstances, be clearly appropriate as an independent step, such a step was in fact taken in order to impede or preclude a majority of the shareholders from effectively adopting the course proposed by Blasius. Indeed, while defendants never forsake the factual argument that that action was simply a continuation of business as usual, they, in effect, admit from time to time this overriding purpose. For example, everyone concedes that the directors understood on December 31 that the effect of adding two directors would be to preclude stockholders from effectively implementing the Blasius proposal. Mr. Weaver, for example, testifies as follows:

> Q: Was it your view that by electing these two directors, Atlas was preventing Blasius from electing a majority of the board?
>
> A: I think that is a component of my total overview. I think in the short term, yes, it did.

Directors Farley and Bongiovanni admit that the board acted to slow the Blasius proposal down. [. . .]

This candor is praiseworthy, but any other statement would be frankly incredible. The timing of these events is, in my opinion, consistent only with the conclusion that Mr. Weaver and Mr. Masinter originated, and the board immediately endorsed, the notion of adding these competent, friendly individuals to the board, not because the board felt an urgent need to get them on the board immediately for reasons relating to the operations of Atlas' business, but because to do so would, for the moment, preclude a majority of shareholders from electing eight new board members selected by Blasius. As explained below, I conclude that, in so acting, the board was not selfishly motivated simply to retain power. [. . .]

The January 6 Rejection of the Blasius Proposal.

On January 6, the board convened for its scheduled meeting. At that time, it heard a full report from its financial advisor concerning the feasibility of the Blasius restructuring proposal. [. . .]

The board then voted to reject the Blasius proposal. Blasius was informed of that action. [. . .]

II.

Plaintiff attacks the December 31 board action as a selfishly motivated effort to protect the incumbent board from a perceived threat to its control of Atlas. Their conduct is said to constitute a violation of the principle, applied in such cases as *Schnell v. Chris Craft Industries,* Del.Supr., 285 A.2d 437 (1971), that directors hold legal powers subjected to a supervening duty to exercise such powers in good faith pursuit of what they reasonably believe to be in the corporation's interest.* [. . .]

III.

One of the principal thrusts of plaintiffs' argument is that, in acting to appoint two additional persons of their own selection, including an officer of the Company, to the board, defendants were motivated not by any view that Atlas' interest (or those of its shareholders) required that action, but rather they were motivated improperly, by selfish concern to maintain their collective control over the Company. That is, plaintiffs say that the evidence shows there was no policy dispute or issue that really motivated this action, but that asserted policy differences were pretexts for entrenchment for selfish reasons. If this were found to be factually true, one would not need to inquire further. The action taken would constitute a breach of duty. [. . .]

While I am satisfied that the evidence is powerful, indeed compelling, that the board was chiefly motivated on December 31 to forestall or preclude the possibility that a majority of shareholders might place on the Atlas board eight new members sympathetic to the Blasius proposal, it is less clear with respect to the more subtle motivational question:

---

   * EDS.—"[M]anagement has attempted to utilize the corporate machinery and the Delaware Law for the purpose of perpetuating itself in office; and, to that end, for the purpose of obstructing the legitimate efforts of dissident stockholders in the exercise of their rights to undertake a proxy contest against management. These are inequitable purposes, contrary to established principles of corporate democracy. The advancement by directors of the by-law date of a stockholders' meeting, for such purposes, may not be permitted to stand. When the by-laws of a corporation designate the date of the annual meeting of stockholders, it is to be expected that those who intend to contest the reelection of incumbent management will gear their campaign to the by-law date. It is not to be expected that management will attempt to advance that date in order to obtain an inequitable advantage in the contest." *Schnell.*

whether the existing members of the board did so because they held a good faith belief that such shareholder action would be self-injurious and shareholders needed to be protected from their own judgment.

On balance, I cannot conclude that the board was acting out of a self-interested motive in any important respect on December 31. I conclude rather that the board saw the "threat" of the Blasius recapitalization proposal as posing vital policy differences between itself and Blasius. It acted, I conclude, in a good faith effort to protect its incumbency, not selfishly, but in order to thwart implementation of the recapitalization that it feared, reasonably, would cause great injury to the Company.

The real question the case presents, to my mind, is whether, in these circumstances, the board, even if it *is* acting with subjective good faith (which will typically, if not always, be a contestable or debatable judicial conclusion), may validly act for the principal purpose of preventing the shareholders from electing a majority of new directors. The question thus posed is not one of intentional wrong (or even negligence), but one of authority *as between the fiduciary and the beneficiary* (not simply legal authority, *i.e.,* as between the fiduciary and the world at large).

IV.

It is established in our law that a board may take certain steps-such as the purchase by the corporation of its own stock-that have the effect of defeating a threatened change in corporate control, when those steps are taken advisedly, in good faith pursuit of a corporate interest, and are reasonable in relation to a threat to legitimate corporate interests posed by the proposed change in control. [. . .]. Does this rule—that the reasonable exercise of good faith and due care generally validates, in equity, the exercise of legal authority even if the act has an entrenchment effect—apply to action designed for the primary purpose of interfering with the effectiveness of a stockholder vote? Our authorities, as well as sound principles, suggest that the central importance of the franchise to the scheme of corporate governance, requires that, in this setting, that rule not be applied and that closer scrutiny be accorded to such transaction.

1.   *Why the deferential business judgment rule does not apply to board acts taken for the primary purpose of interfering with a stockholder's vote, even if taken advisedly and in good faith.*

A.   *The question of legitimacy.*

The shareholder franchise is the ideological underpinning upon which the legitimacy of directorial power rests. Generally, shareholders have only two protections against perceived inadequate business performance. They may sell their stock (which, if done in sufficient numbers, may so affect security prices as to create an incentive for altered managerial performance), or they may vote to replace incumbent board members.

It has, for a long time, been conventional to dismiss the stockholder vote as a vestige or ritual of little practical importance. It may be that we are now witnessing the emergence of new institutional voices and arrangements that will make the stockholder vote a less predictable affair than it has been. Be that as it may, however, whether the vote is seen functionally as an unimportant formalism, or as an important tool of discipline, it is clear that it is critical to the theory that legitimates the exercise of power by some (directors and officers) over vast aggregations of property that they do not own. Thus, when viewed from a broad, institutional perspective, it can be seen that matters involving the integrity of the shareholder voting process involve consideration not present in any other context in which directors exercise delegated power.

B.   Questions of this type raise issues of the allocation of authority as between the board and the shareholders.

The distinctive nature of the shareholder franchise context also appears when the matter is viewed from a less generalized, doctrinal point of view. From this point of view, as well, it appears that the ordinary considerations to which the business judgment rule originally responded are simply not present in the shareholder voting context. That is, a decision by the board to act for the primary purpose of preventing the effectiveness of a shareholder vote inevitably involves the question who, as between the principal and the agent, has authority with respect to a matter of internal corporate governance. That, of course, is true in a very specific way in this case which deals with the question who should constitute the board of directors of the corporation, but it will be true in every instance in which an incumbent board seeks to thwart a shareholder majority. A board's decision to act to prevent the shareholders from creating a majority of new board positions and filling them does not involve the exercise of *the corporation's power* over its property, or with respect to *its* rights or obligations; rather, it involves allocation, between shareholders as a class and the board, of effective power with respect to governance of the corporation. This need not be the case with respect to other forms of corporate action that may have an entrenchment effect [. . .]. Action designed principally to interfere with the effectiveness of a vote inevitably involves a conflict between the board and a shareholder majority. Judicial review of such action involves a determination of the legal and equitable obligations of an agent towards his principal. This is not, in my opinion, a question that a court may leave to the agent finally to decide so long as he does so honestly and competently; that is, it may not be left to the agent's business judgment.

2.   What rule does apply: per se invalidity of corporate acts intended primarily to thwart effective exercise of the franchise or is there an intermediate standard?

Plaintiff argues for a rule of *per se* invalidity once a plaintiff has established that a board has acted for the primary purpose of thwarting the exercise of a shareholder vote. [. . .]

A *per se* rule that would strike down, in equity, any board action taken for the primary purpose of interfering with the effectiveness of a corporate vote would have the advantage of relative clarity and predictability. It also has the advantage of most vigorously enforcing the concept of corporate democracy. The disadvantage it brings along is, of course, the disadvantage a *per se* rule always has: it may sweep too broadly.

In two recent cases dealing with shareholder votes, this court struck down board acts done for the primary purpose of impeding the exercise of stockholder voting power. In doing so, a *per se* rule was not applied. Rather, it was said that, in such a case, the board bears the heavy burden of demonstrating a compelling justification for such action.[. . .]

In my view, our inability to foresee now all of the future settings in which a board might, in good faith, paternalistically seek to thwart a shareholder vote, counsels against the adoption of a *per se* rule invalidating, in equity, every board action taken for the sole or primary purpose of thwarting a shareholder vote, even though I recognize the transcending significance of the franchise to the claims to legitimacy of our scheme of corporate governance. It may be that some set of facts would justify such extreme action. This, however, is not such a case.

3. *Defendants have demonstrated no sufficient justification for the action of December 31 which was intended to prevent an unaffiliated majority of shareholders from effectively exercising their right to elect eight new directors.*

The board was not faced with a coercive action taken by a powerful shareholder against the interests of a distinct shareholder constituency (such as a public minority). It was presented with a consent solicitation by a 9% shareholder. Moreover, here it had time (and understood that it had time) to inform the shareholders of its views on the merits of the proposal subject to stockholder vote. The only justification that can, in such a situation, be offered for the action taken is that the board knows better than do the shareholders what is in the corporation's best interest. While that premise is no doubt true for any number of matters, it is irrelevant (except insofar as the shareholders wish to be guided by the board's recommendation) when the question is who should comprise the board of directors. The theory of our corporation law confers power upon directors as the agents of the shareholders; it does not create Platonic masters. It may be that the Blasius restructuring proposal was or is unrealistic and would lead to injury to the corporation and its shareholders if pursued. Having heard the evidence, I am inclined to think it was not a sound proposal. The board certainly viewed it that way, and that view, held in good faith, entitled the board to take certain steps to evade the risk it perceived. It could, for example, expend corporate funds to inform shareholders and seek to bring them to a similar point of view. [. . .]. But there is a vast difference between expending corporate funds to inform the electorate and exercising power for the primary purpose of foreclosing effective shareholder action. A majority of the shareholders, who were not dominated in any respect, could view the matter differently than did the board. If they do, or did, they are entitled to employ the mechanisms provided by the corporation law and the Atlas certificate of incorporation to advance that view. They are also entitled, in my opinion, to restrain their agents, the board, from acting for the principal purpose of thwarting that action.

I therefore conclude that, even finding the action taken was taken in good faith, it constituted an unintended violation of the duty of loyalty that the board owed to the shareholders. I note parenthetically that the concept of an unintended breach of the duty of loyalty is unusual but not novel. [. . .] That action will, therefore, be set aside by order of this court.

Coster v. UIP Companies, Inc.

2023 WL 4239581 (Del. 2023)

■ SEITZ, CHIEF JUSTICE:

[. . .]

I.

[. . .] UIP Companies, Inc. is a real estate services company [. . .] [that] [. . .] operates through various subsidiaries that provide a range of services to investment properties in the Washington, D.C. area. [. . .] [UIP has two equal stockholders: Wout Coster and Steven Schwat, each with a one-half interest in UIP.]

In 2013, Wout notified Schwat and Peter Bonnell, a senior UIP executive, that he had been diagnosed with leukemia. Shortly after, the group began negotiations for a buyout in which Bonnell and Heath Wilkinson, another UIP executive, would purchase Wout's shares in the company. [. . .]

Unfortunately, negotiations were unsuccessful. While the parties agreed on a non-binding term sheet in April 2014 in which Wout would receive $2,125,000 for his half of UIP shares, the parties continued to go back and forth over the deal terms. Wout did not feel comfortable with the terms so "[n]o deal was ever finalized." Wout passed away on April 8, 2015, and his widow, Marion Coster ("Coster"), inherited his UIP interests.*

Immediately after Wout's death, Schwat and Bonnell continued exploring buyout options with Coster. Discussions continued throughout 2015 with no resolution. During this time, Coster became "very distressed about her financial situation" as she had not received income distributions or the benefits she had expected. By May 2016, "Coster appeared primarily interested in a lump sum buyout or arrangement that would provide her with a consistent stream of income."

[. . .] Negotiations between the parties continued throughout 2016 and into 2017 as Coster sought an independent valuation of UIP.

---

* EDS.—This decision refers to Mr. Coster as "Wout" and Marion Coster as "Coster" to avoid name confusion.

A.

In August 2017, Coster provided UIP with a $7.3 million valuation and demanded to inspect UIP books and records. Coster followed up with a second inspection demand in October 2017. Then, "[a]fter much back and forth about the adequacy of the documents provided, on April 4, 2018, Coster called for a UIP stockholders special meeting to elect new board members." At this time, UIP had a five-member board composed of Schwat, Bonnell, and Stephen Cox, UIP's Chief Financial Officer. Two seats were vacant due to Wout's passing and Cornelius Bruggen's departure in 2011.

The stockholder meeting took place on May 22, 2018. Coster, represented by counsel, raised multiple motions affecting the size and composition of the board. Predictably, each of Coster's motions failed due to Schwat's opposition. Later that day, the UIP board reduced the number of board seats to three through unanimous written consent.

A second stockholder meeting followed on June 4, 2018. The meeting also ended in deadlock as Schwat and Coster each opposed the other's respective motions. With the deadlock, Schwat, Bonnell, and Cox remained UIP's directors.

B.

Coster filed a complaint in the Court of Chancery seeking appointment of a custodian under 8 *Del. C.* § 226(a)(1) (the "Custodian Action").[16] Coster's "complaint mainly sought to impose a neutral tie-breaker to facilitate director election["] [. . .]. Coster "sought the appointment of a custodian with broad oversight and managerial powers."

Coster's request for a "broadly empowered" custodian rather than one specifically tailored to target the stockholder deadlock "posed new risks to the Company." [. . .] "Facing this threat to the Company," the UIP board decided to "issue the equity that they had long promised to Bonnell." Having conducted its own valuation that "valued a 100-percent, noncontrolling equity interest in UIP at $123,869," the UIP board offered, and Bonnell purchased, a one-third interest in the company for $41,289.67 (the "Stock Sale").

The Stock Sale diluted Coster's ownership interest from one half to one third and negated her ability to block stockholder action as a half owner of the company. The Stock Sale also mooted the Custodian Action. Coster responded by filing suit and sought to cancel the Stock Sale.

C.

In its opinion following trial, the Court of Chancery upheld the Stock Sale under the entire fairness standard of review. According to the court, once

---

[16] 8 *Del. C.* § 226 allows for the Court of Chancery to appoint a custodian "upon application of any stockholder ... when ... [a]t any meeting held for the election of directors the stockholders are so divided that they have failed to elect successors to directors whose terms have expired or would have expired upon qualification of their successors."

the Stock Sale "satisfie[d] Delaware's most onerous standard of review," no further review was required. The deadlock broken, the court did not need to consider appointing a custodian and dismissed the action.

D.

In the first appeal, this Court did not disturb the Court of Chancery's entire fairness decision but remanded with instructions to review the Stock Sale under *Schnell* and *Blasius*. As explained in our first decision, while entire fairness is "Delaware's most onerous standard of review," it is "not [a] substitute for further equitable review" under *Schnell* or *Blasius* when the board interferes with director elections:

> In a vacuum, it might be that the price at which the board agreed to sell the one-third UIP equity interest to Bonnell was entirely fair, as was the process to set the price for the stock. But "inequitable action does not become permissible simply because it is legally possible." If the board approved the Stock Sale for inequitable reasons, the Court of Chancery should have cancelled the Stock Sale. And if the board, acting in good faith, approved the Stock Sale for the "primary purpose of thwarting" Coster's vote to elect directors or reduce her leverage as an equal stockholder, it must "demonstrat[e] a compelling justification for such action" to withstand judicial scrutiny.

> After remand, if the court decides that the board acted for inequitable purposes or in good faith but for the primary purpose of disenfranchisement without a compelling justification, it should cancel the Stock Sale and decide whether a custodian should be appointed for UIP. *Coster I*

In the first appellate decision, we recounted the "undisputed facts or facts found by the court" that could "support the conclusion, under *Schnell*, that the UIP board approved the Stock Sale for inequitable reasons." Those facts included that "[t]he Stock Sale occurred while buyout negotiations stalled between UIP's two equal stockholders," that "[t]he Stock Sale entrenched the existing board in control of UIP," and the Court of Chancery's finding that "Defendants obviously desired to eliminate Plaintiff's ability to block stockholder action, including the election of directors, and the leverage that accompanied those rights." We recognized, however, "that the [Court of Chancery] made other findings inconsistent with this conclusion," and therefore gave the Court of Chancery the "opportunity to review all of its factual findings in any manner it sees fit in light of its new focus on *Schnell/Blasius* review."

E.

On remand, the Court of Chancery found that the UIP board had not acted for inequitable purposes under *Schnell* and had compelling justifications for the Stock Sale under *Blasius*. For Coster's *Schnell* claim, the court held that "the UIP board had multiple reasons for approving the Stock Sale" and that "the UIP board's decision did not totally lack a good faith basis." The court also found that the UIP board was primarily motivated by "retaining and rewarding Bonnell, mooting the Custodian Action, and undermining [Coster's] leverage."

Turning to *Blasius* review, the court concluded that "[i]n the exceptionally unique circumstances of this case, Defendants have met the onerous burden of demonstrating a compelling justification." The court's compelling justification analysis largely borrowed from *Unocal's* reasonableness and proportionality test for defensive measures adopted by a board in response to a takeover threat. As the court explained:

> To satisfy the compelling justification standard, "the directors must show that their actions were reasonable in relation to their legitimate objective, and did not preclude the stockholders from exercising their right to vote or coerce them into voting a particular way." "In this context, the shift from 'reasonable' to 'compelling' requires that the directors establish a closer fit between means and ends."

The court found that the threat posed by the Custodian Action was "an existential crisis" that justified the UIP board's actions and "that the Stock Sale was appropriately tailored to achieve the goal of mooting the Custodian Action while also achieving other important goals, such as implementing the succession plan that Wout favored and rewarding Bonnell."

II.

In her second appeal, Coster has challenged the Court of Chancery's ruling on both remand questions. This Court reviews the Court of Chancery's legal conclusions *de novo* but defers to the Court of Chancery's factual findings supported by the record. [. . .]

A.

In her lead argument on appeal, Coster argues that the Court of Chancery erred when it limited its *Schnell* review to board action totally lacking a good faith basis. To frame our analysis, it is helpful to review again the circumstances of *Schnell* and *Blasius*. Both cases involved board action that interfered with director elections in contests for control—*Schnell*, a proxy solicitation, and *Blasius*, a consent solicitation.

In *Schnell*, the incumbent Chris-Craft board faced the prospect of a difficult proxy fight to retain their seats. In response to the threat to their tenure as board members, the board accelerated the annual meeting date and moved the meeting to a more remote location. The director defendants mounted no real defense to the Court of Chancery suit except to argue that their actions did not violate the Delaware General Corporation Law ("DGCL") or Chris-Craft's bylaws and were therefore legal.

The Court of Chancery was persuaded by the board's legal authorization defense and dismissed the case. On appeal, the Supreme Court took a dim view of the board's intentional efforts to obstruct the insurgent's proxy contest. As the Court held, even though the board's actions met all legal requirements, the Chris-Craft board was "attempt[ing] to utilize the corporate machinery and the Delaware Law for the purpose of perpetuating itself in office; and, to that [sic] end, for the purpose of obstructing legitimate efforts of dissident stockholders in the exercise of their rights to undertake a proxy contest against management." In Justice Herrmann's oft-quoted words, "inequitable action does not become permissible simply because it is legally possible." The Supreme Court ordered the Chris-Craft board to reinstate the original meeting date.

In *Blasius*, the Court of Chancery explored how *Schnell* operates in contested election cases, and specifically how *Schnell* was not the end of the road for judicial review of good faith board actions that interfered with director elections. Like *Schnell*, *Blasius* involved an incumbent board facing a consent solicitation aimed at replacing a majority of the board. Atlas Industries had a staggered board. Only seven of the authorized fifteen board seats were occupied. With a majority of stockholders behind the effort, an insurgent could in one action amend the company's bylaws, increase the board size to fifteen, and elect a new board majority of eight members.

If the Atlas board had acted on a clear day to establish new seats and to fill the vacancies, the circumstances would have been different. But for the Atlas board, the skies were cloudy, and it was raining. It faced a serious consent solicitation. In response, the board added two seats and filled the newly created positions with directors friendly to management. Now, Blasius had to win not one, but two elections to control the board.

Two other points were important to the court's decision. First, Blasius enticed stockholders to vote for its nominees with a business plan that would give stockholders upfront cash and a later debenture redemption, all premised on a highly leveraged and speculative business strategy. And second, the Atlas board had its own turn-around strategy that it believed in good faith was a better choice for Atlas stockholders than Blasius' risky plan that could lead to Atlas' bankruptcy.

Blasius argued that the board's corporate maneuvers were "a selfishly motivated effort to protect the incumbent board from a perceived threat to its control of Atlas." The Chancellor turned to *Schnell* to evaluate this claim. According to the court, if the board was not "principally motivated" to interfere with the consent solicitation and instead "had taken action completely independently of the consent solicitation [. . .], it is very unlikely that such action would be subject to judicial nullification." On the other hand, if "there was no policy dispute or issue that really motivated this action" or "policy differences were pretexts for entrenchment for selfish reasons," then the court "would not need to inquire further." The Atlas board's actions "would constitute a breach of duty." The Chancellor found that the Atlas board did not act out of a desire to entrench the existing board but out of a good faith belief that Blasius was an existential threat to Atlas and its stockholders. Thus, under *Schnell*, the Atlas board was not principally motivated to interfere with the election of directors for selfish reasons. But the court was still left with the fact that the Atlas board, even if well-intentioned, had nonetheless acted to thwart Blasius's consent solicitation. Thus, the "real question the case present[ed]" was whether a board, even if acting in good faith, "may validly act for the principal purpose of preventing the shareholders from electing a majority of new directors."

To answer the ultimate question, the court had to answer another question—whether there should be a "*per se* rule that would strike down, in equity, any board action taken for the primary purpose of interfering with the effectiveness of a corporate vote." A rigid rule had the advantage of "clarity and predictability." [. . .]

Ultimately, Chancellor Allen concluded that, even if the board acted in good faith, it did not justify its interference with the stockholder franchise. The court did not propose to "invalidat[e], in equity, every board action taken for the sole or primary purpose of thwarting a shareholder vote." But the board could not rely on the justification that it "knows better than do the shareholders what is in the corporation's best interest."

B.

[. . .] "[A]lmost all of the post-*Schnell* decisions involved situations where boards of directors deliberately employed various legal strategies either to frustrate or completely disenfranchise a shareholder vote." While the Supreme Court was a bit hyperbolic to say that only claims that tear the fabric of our law come within *Schnell*, the Chancellor was correct in this case to cabin *Schnell* and its equitable review to those cases where the board acts within its legal power, but is motivated for selfish reasons to interfere with the stockholder franchise.

C.

The Court of Chancery in this case also interpreted *Blasius* with a sensitivity to how, in practice, the Supreme Court and the Court of Chancery have effectively folded *Blasius* into *Unocal* review. As discussed earlier, Chancellor Allen in *Blasius* was skeptical of the board's authority, even if acting in good faith, to protect the stockholders from themselves when it came to corporate elections. As Chancellor Allen noted, "[t]he shareholder franchise is the ideological underpinning upon which the legitimacy of directorial power rests. Generally, shareholders have only two protections against perceived inadequate business performance. They may sell their stock . . . or they may vote to replace incumbent board members." Given the stakes involved, the court decided that the board's justifications must be subject to enhanced scrutiny.

Blasius first applied that enhanced review by requiring a board, even if acting in good faith, to demonstrate a "compelling justification" for interfering with the stockholder franchise. But another standard of review could also apply when the board interferes with the stockholder vote during a contest for control. In *Unocal Corporation v. Mesa Petroleum Company*, this Court noted the "omnipresent specter" that incumbent directors might take action to further their own interests or those of incumbent management "rather than those of the corporation and its shareholders." When stockholders challenge a board's use of anti-takeover measures, the board must show (i) that "they had reasonable grounds for believing that a danger to corporate policy and effectiveness existed," and (ii) that the response was "reasonable in relation to the threat posed." A defensive measure is an unreasonable response in relation to the threat if it is either draconian—coercive or preclusive—or falls outside a range of reasonable responses.

In *Stroud v. Grace*, our Court first recognized how both *Blasius* and *Unocal* review were called for in a proxy fight involving a tender offer:

> Board action interfering with the exercise of the franchise often arose during a hostile contest for control where an acquiror launched both a proxy fight and a tender offer. Such action necessarily invoked both *Unocal* and *Blasius*. We note that the two "tests" are not mutually exclusive because both recognize the inherent conflicts of interest that arise when shareholders are not permitted free exercise of their franchise.
>
> . . . In certain circumstances, a court must recognize the special import of protecting the shareholders' franchise within *Unocal*'s requirement that any defensive measure be proportionate and "reasonable in relation to the threat posed." A board's unilateral decision to adopt a defensive measure touching "upon issues of control" that purposefully disenfranchises its shareholders is strongly suspect under *Unocal*, and cannot be sustained without a "compelling justification."

After *Stroud*, the Court of Chancery in *Chesapeake Corporation v. Shore* went a step further and suggested merging the two standards of review in contested election cases. A single standard of review was possible, according to the court, by "infus[ing] . . . *Unocal* analyses with the spirit animating *Blasius*." [. . .]

In *MM Companies v. Liquid Audio, Inc.*, the Supreme Court took the formal step to incorporate *Blasius* "within *Unocal*." In *Liquid Audio*, MM had tried for some time to take control of Liquid Audio. When it looked likely that MM's nominees would gain board seats at the annual meeting, the Liquid Audio board responded by expanding the board from five to seven members and filling the new seats. With a staggered board, the board expansion defeated MM's ability to control the board following the annual meeting.

MM filed suit to enjoin the incumbent board's action. To invalidate the board's expansion, the Supreme Court applied *Blasius* "within *Unocal*" as the standard of review:

> When the *primary purpose* of a board of directors' defensive measure is to interfere with or impede the effective exercise of the shareholder franchise in a contested election for directors, the board must first demonstrate a compelling justification for such action as a condition precedent to any judicial consideration of reasonableness and proportionately.... To invoke the *Blasius* compelling justification standard of review within an application of the *Unocal* standard of review, the defensive actions of the board only need to be taken for the primary purpose of interfering with or impeding the effectiveness of the stockholder vote in a contested election for directors.

Even though the Supreme Court in *Liquid Audio* combined *Blasius* and *Unocal* review, it did not solve the practical problem of how to turn *Unocal*'s reasonableness review and *Blasius*' "primary purpose" and "compelling justification" elements into a useful standard of review. [. . .]

In *Mercier v. Inter-Tel (Del.)*, [. . .] [t]he minority stockholders [. . .] claimed that a special committee of independent directors breached its fiduciary duties by rescheduling stockholder special meeting to consider a proposed merger. The committee also set a new record date. Instead of applying *Schnell* and *Blasius* "within *Unocal*," the Court of Chancery turned to *Unocal* and its "reasonableness" review but applied it with greater sensitivity to the interests at stake because the "director action . . . could have the effect of influencing the outcome of corporate director elections or other stockholder votes having consequences for corporate control."

According to the court, the committee bore the burden of proof under a modified *Unocal* review (1) to identify "a legitimate corporate objective" supporting its decision to move the special stockholders' meeting date and to change the record date; (2) "to show that their motivations were proper and not selfish;" and (3) to demonstrate that, even if not disloyal, "their actions were reasonable in relation to their legitimate objective and did not preclude the stockholders from exercising their right to vote or coerce them into voting a particular way." [. . .] The court decided that the board's action satisfied *Unocal* review because the board's meeting and record date changes (1) allowed additional time for stockholders to consider the proposed merger; (2) protected the financial best interests of the stockholders; and (3) was neither preclusive nor coercive as the stockholders would ultimately be free to vote as they desired. The court refused to enjoin the board from rescheduling the special meeting date.

As Chancellor Allen did in *Blasius*, the court in *Mercier* also rejected "[t]he notion that directors know better than the stockholders" who should run the company. The court explained that the "know better" defense, standing alone, "is no justification at all" for the board to interfere with a contest for corporate control. [. . .]

D.

In *Unocal*, the Supreme Court remarked that "our corporate law is not static." Experience has shown that *Schnell* and *Blasius* review, as a matter of precedent and practice, have been and can be folded into *Unocal* review to accomplish the same ends—enhanced judicial scrutiny of board action that interferes with a corporate election or a stockholder's voting rights in contests for control. When *Unocal* is applied in this context, it can "subsume[] the question of loyalty that pervades all fiduciary duty cases, which is whether the directors have acted for proper reasons" and "thus address[] issues of good faith such as were at stake in *Schnell*." *Unocal* can also be applied with the sensitivity *Blasius* review brings to protect the fundamental interests at stake—the free exercise of the stockholder vote as an essential element of corporate democracy.

As we explained in our earlier decision in this case, the court's review is situationally specific and is independent of other standards of review. When a stockholder challenges board action that interferes with the election of directors or a stockholder vote in a contest for corporate control, the board bears the burden of proof. First, the court should review whether the board faced a threat "to an important corporate interest or to the achievement of a significant corporate benefit." The threat must be real and not pretextual, and the board's motivations must be proper and not selfish or disloyal. As Chancellor Allen stated long ago, the threat cannot be justified on the grounds that the board knows what is in the best interests of the stockholders.

Second, the court should review whether the board's response to the threat was reasonable in relation to the threat posed and was not preclusive or coercive to the stockholder franchise. To guard against unwarranted interference with corporate elections or stockholder votes in contests for corporate control, a board that is properly motivated and has identified a legitimate threat must tailor its response to only what is necessary to counter the threat. The board's response to the threat cannot deprive the stockholders of a vote or coerce the stockholders to vote a particular way.

Applying *Unocal* review in this case with sensitivity to the stockholder franchise is no stretch for our law. Here, the UIP board issued stock to break a director election deadlock and moot a custodian action. [. . .]

E.

[. . .] [After the Supreme Court remanded the case, the Chancery Court reviewed all of its factual findings and] supplemented the earlier factual findings with the following:*

---

   *   EDS.—These were the original factual findings identified by the Chancery Court in *Coster I:*

- "Without making any meaningful effort to negotiate board composition, Plaintiff filed a complaint in this Court seeking the appointment of a custodian;"

- "Plaintiff's request for custodial relief was extremely broad. Plaintiff did not present a tailored request for relief that targeted the stockholder deadlock. Rather, she asked the court to empower a custodian to 'exercise full authority and control over the Company, its operations, and management;' "

- "The threat of a court-appointed custodian so broadly empowered posed new risks to the Company. The appointment of a custodian with these powers would have given rise to broad termination rights in SPE contracts and threatened UIP's revenue stream, as UIP's business model is dependent on the continued viability of those contracts;"

- "Facing this threat to the Company," the UIP board "identified a solution" to issue equity "long promised to Bonnell" that "implent[ed] a succession plan" proposed "on a clear day;"

- The Stock Sale would "moot the Custodian Action and eliminate the risks the appointment of a custodian posed to UIP" and would "eliminate the stockholder leverage that Plaintiff was using to try to force a buyout at a price detrimental to the Company;"

- "The Stock Sale occurred while buyout negotiations stalled between UIP's two equal stockholders;

- The stockholders could not elect a new board because of the deadlock, which led to the Custodian Action;

- A majority of the board members approving the sale were interested in the Stock Sale;

- Schwat and Bonnell were friends and "from the inception of Wout's transition planning negotiation, Schwat and Bonnell appeared to be aligned in negotiations against Wout;"

- Schwat and Bonnell "worked together to develop the plan to moot the Custodian Action and neutralize the threat of [Coster] controlling the Company;"

- The defendants were "in a rush for the [McLean] [V]aluation" until the defendants "determined to answer the [plaintiff's] complaint and then subsequently amend the answer after the sale of stock to Bonnell was completed[,]" which permitted them to "file[ ] an amended answer, which stated an intention to move for judgment on the pleadings because the Custodian Action had been mooted by the Stock Sale;"

- The Stock Sale put UIP stock in the hands of fellow board member Bonnell, who was aligned with the holdover board;

- The Stock Sale entrenched the existing board in control of UIP; and

- "Defendants obviously desired to eliminate Plaintiff's ability to block stockholder action, including the election of directors, and the leverage that accompanied those rights." "

- The UIP board's motives were not "pretexts for entrenchment for selfish reasons" or "post-hoc justifications;" and

- "[T]hese were genuine motivations for their actions that stood alongside the more problematic purposes that [Coster I] identified and the Appellate Decision collected."

After its additional fact findings, the Court of Chancery [. . .] found that the UIP board faced a threat—which the court described as an "existential crisis"—to UIP's existence through a deadlocked stockholder vote and the risk of a custodian appointment. Although the court thought that some of the board's reasons for approving the Stock Sale were problematic, on balance the court held that the board was properly motivated in responding to the threat. According to the court, the UIP board acted in good faith "to advance the best interests of UIP" by "reward[ing] and retain[ing] an essential employee," "implement[ing] a succession plan that Wout had favored," and "moot[ing] the Custodian Action to avoid risk of default under key contracts." The court also relied on its earlier finding that the UIP board issued UIP stock to Bonnell at an entirely fair price.

The Court of Chancery also found that the UIP board responded reasonably and proportionately to the threat posed when it approved the Stock Sale and mooted the Custodian Action. As it held, "in the exceptionally unique circumstances of this case," without the Stock Sale, the possibility that a custodian appointed with broad powers would jeopardize key contracts caused an existential crisis at UIP. The Stock Sale, the court held, "was appropriately tailored to achieve the goal of mooting the Custodian Action" while implementing the succession plan and retaining Bonnell. And the court noted that there were more aggressive options that could have been, but were not, pursued to break the deadlock.

Finally, the board's response to the existential threat posed by the stockholder deadlock and custodian action was not preclusive or coercive. Although the Stock Sale effectively foreclosed Coster from perpetuating the deadlock facing UIP, the new three-way ownership of the company presented a potentially more effective way for her to exercise actual control. As the Court of Chancery noted, Schwat and Bonnell are not bound to vote together, meaning Coster could cast a swing vote at stockholder meetings. As an equal one third owner with the two other stockholders, Coster can join forces with either one of UIP's other owners "at some point in the future. A realistic path to control of UIP negates the preclusive impact of the Stock Sale.

III.

The judgment of the Court of Chancery is affirmed.

B. Shareholder Voting

Delaware General Corporation Law
Section 211. Meetings of stockholders.

(a) (1) Meetings of stockholders may be held at such place, either within or without this State as may be designated by or in the manner provided in the certificate of incorporation or bylaws, or if not so designated, as determined by the board of directors. [. . .][T]he board of directors may, in its sole discretion, determine that the meeting shall not be held at any place, but may instead be held solely by means of remote communication as authorized by paragraph (a)(2) of this section.

(2) If authorized by the board of directors in its sole discretion, [. . .] stockholders and proxyholders not physically present at a meeting of stockholders may, by means of remote communication:

a. Participate in a meeting of stockholders; and

b. Be deemed present in person and vote at a meeting of stockholders[.] [. . .]

(b) Unless directors are elected by written consent in lieu of an annual meeting as permitted by this subsection, an annual meeting of stockholders shall be held for the election of directors on a date and at a time designated by or in the manner provided in the bylaws. Stockholders may, unless the certificate of incorporation otherwise provides, act by written consent to elect directors; provided, however, that, if such consent is less than unanimous, such action by written consent may be in lieu of holding an annual meeting only if all of the directorships to which directors could be elected at an annual meeting held at the effective time of such action are vacant and are filled by such action. Any other proper business may be transacted at the annual meeting.

(c) A failure to hold the annual meeting at the designated time or to elect a sufficient number of directors to conduct the business of the corporation shall not affect otherwise valid corporate acts or work a forfeiture or dissolution of the corporation except as may be otherwise specifically provided in this chapter[. . .][T]he Court of Chancery may summarily order a meeting to be held upon the application of any stockholder or director. The shares of stock represented at such meeting, either in person or by proxy, and entitled to vote thereat, shall constitute a quorum for the purpose of such meeting, notwithstanding any provision of the certificate of incorporation or bylaws to the contrary. [. . .]

(d) Special meetings of the stockholders may be called by the board of directors or by such person or persons as may be authorized by the certificate of incorporation or by the bylaws. [. . .]

Section 212. Voting rights of stockholders; proxies; limitations.

(a) Unless otherwise provided in the certificate of incorporation and subject to § 213 of this title, each stockholder shall be entitled to 1 vote for each share of capital stock held by such stockholder. If the certificate of incorporation provides for more or less than 1 vote for any share, on any matter, every reference in this chapter to a majority or other proportion of stock, voting stock or shares shall refer to such majority or other proportion of the votes of such stock, voting stock or shares.

(b) Each stockholder entitled to vote at a meeting of stockholders or to express consent or dissent to corporate action in writing without a meeting may authorize another person or persons to act for such stockholder by proxy, but no such proxy shall be voted or acted upon after 3 years from its date, unless the proxy provides for a longer period. [. . .]

Section 213. Fixing date for determination of stockholders of record.

(a) In order that the corporation may determine the stockholders entitled to notice of any meeting of stockholders or any adjournment thereof, the board of directors may fix a record date, which record date shall not precede the date upon which the resolution fixing the record date is adopted by the board of directors, and which record date shall not be more than 60 nor less than 10 days before the date of such meeting. If the board of directors so fixes a date, such date shall also be the record date for determining the stockholders entitled to vote at such meeting unless the board of directors determines, at the time it fixes such record date, that a later date on or before the date of the meeting shall be the date for making such determination. If no record date is fixed by the board of directors, the record date for determining stockholders entitled to notice of and to vote at a meeting of stockholders shall be at the close of business on the day next preceding the day on which notice is given, or, if notice is waived, at the close of business on the day next preceding the day on which the meeting is held. [. . .]

Section 214. Cumulative voting.

The certificate of incorporation of any corporation may provide that at all elections of directors of the corporation, or at elections held under specified circumstances, each holder of stock or of any class or classes or of a series or series thereof shall be entitled to as many votes as shall equal the number of votes which (except for such provision as to cumulative voting) such holder would be entitled to cast for the election of directors with respect to such holder's shares of stock multiplied by the number of directors to be elected by such holder, and that such holder may cast all of such votes for a single director or may distribute them among the number to be voted for, or for any 2 or more of them as such holder may see fit.

Section 216. Quorum and required vote for stock corporations.

Subject to this chapter in respect of the vote that shall be required for a specified action, the certificate of incorporation or bylaws of any corporation authorized to issue stock may specify the number of shares and/or the amount of other securities having voting power the holders of which shall be present or represented by proxy at any meeting in order to constitute a quorum for, and the votes that shall be necessary for, the transaction of any business, but in no event shall a quorum consist of less than ⅓ of the shares entitled to vote at the meeting, except that, where a separate vote by a class or series or classes or series is required, a quorum shall consist of no less than ⅓ of the shares of such class or series or classes or series. In the absence of such specification in the certificate of incorporation or bylaws of the corporation:

(1) A majority of the shares entitled to vote, present in person or represented by proxy, shall constitute a quorum at a meeting of stockholders;

(2) In all matters other than the election of directors, the affirmative vote of the majority of shares present in person or represented by proxy at the meeting and entitled to vote on the subject matter shall be the act of the stockholders;

(3) Directors shall be elected by a plurality of the votes of the shares present in person or represented by proxy at the meeting and entitled to vote on the election of directors; and

(4) Where a separate vote by a class or series or classes or series is required, a majority of the outstanding shares of such class or series or classes or series, present in person or represented by proxy, shall constitute a quorum entitled to take action with respect to that vote on that matter and, in all matters other than the election of directors, the affirmative vote of the majority of shares of such class or series or classes or series present in person or represented by proxy at the meeting shall be the act of such class or series or classes or series.

A bylaw amendment adopted by stockholders which specifies the votes that shall be necessary for the election of directors shall not be further amended or repealed by the board of directors.

Section 218. Voting trusts and other voting agreements.

(a) One stockholder or 2 or more stockholders may by agreement in writing deposit capital stock of an original issue with or transfer capital stock to any person or persons, or entity or entities authorized to act as trustee, for the purpose of vesting in such person or persons, entity or entities, who may be designated voting trustee, or voting trustees, the right to vote thereon for any period of time determined by such agreement, upon the terms and conditions stated in such agreement. The agreement may contain any other lawful provisions not inconsistent with such purpose. After delivery of a copy of the agreement to the registered office of the corporation in this State or the principal place of business of the corporation, which copy shall be open to the inspection of any stockholder of the corporation or any beneficiary of the trust under the agreement [. . .], certificates of stock or uncertificated stock shall be issued to the voting trustee or trustees to represent any stock of an original issue so deposited with such voting trustee or trustees. [. . .] The voting trustee or trustees may vote the stock so issued or transferred during the period specified in the agreement. [. . .]

(b) Any amendment to a voting trust agreement shall be made by a written agreement [. . .].

(c) An agreement between 2 or more stockholders, if in writing and signed by the parties thereto, may provide that in exercising any voting rights, the shares held by them shall be voted as provided by the agreement, or as the parties may agree, or as determined in accordance with a procedure agreed upon by them.

(d) This section shall not be deemed to invalidate any voting or other agreement among stockholders or any irrevocable proxy which is not otherwise illegal.

Section 222. Notice of meetings and adjourned meetings.

(a) Whenever stockholders are required or permitted to take any action at a meeting, a notice of the meeting shall be given in accordance with § 232 of this title, and such notice shall state the place, if any, date and hour of the meeting, the means of remote communications, if any, by which stockholders and proxy holders may be deemed to be present in person and vote at such meeting, the record date for determining the stockholders entitled to vote at the meeting, if such date is different from the record date for determining stockholders entitled to notice of the meeting, and, in the case of a special meeting, the purpose or purposes for which the meeting is called.

(b) Unless otherwise provided in this chapter, the notice of any meeting shall be given not less than 10 nor more than 60 days before the date of the meeting to each stockholder entitled to vote at such meeting as of the record date for determining the stockholders entitled to notice of the meeting. [. . .]

Section 228. Consent of stockholders or members in lieu of meeting.

(a) Unless otherwise provided in the certificate of incorporation, any action required by this chapter to be taken at any annual or special meeting of stockholders of a corporation, or any action which may be taken at any annual or special meeting of such stockholders, may be taken without a meeting, without prior notice and without a vote, if a consent or consents, setting forth the action so taken, shall be signed by the holders of outstanding stock having not less than the minimum number of votes that would be necessary to authorize or take such action at a meeting at which all shares entitled to vote thereon were present and voted and shall be delivered to the corporation in the manner required by this section. [. . .]

(c) A consent must be set forth in writing or in an electronic transmission. [. . .]

(d) (1) A consent permitted by this section shall be delivered: (i) to the principal place of business of the corporation; (ii) to an officer or agent of the corporation having custody of the book in which proceedings of meetings of stockholders or members are recorded; (iii) to the registered office of the corporation in this State by hand or by certified or registered mail, return receipt requested[.][. . .]

(e) Prompt notice of the taking of the corporate action without a meeting by less than unanimous consent shall be given to those stockholders or members who have not consented and who, if the action had been taken at a meeting, would have been entitled to notice of the meeting if the record date for notice of such meeting had been the date that consents signed by a sufficient number of holders or members to take the action were delivered to the corporation as provided in this section. In the event that the action which is consented to is such as would have required the filing of a certificate under any other section of this title, if such action had been voted on by stockholders or by members at a meeting thereof, the certificate filed under such other section shall state, in lieu of any statement required by such section concerning any vote of stockholders or members, that consent has been given in accordance with this section.

Section 112. Access to proxy solicitation materials.

The bylaws may provide that if the corporation solicits proxies with respect to an election of directors, it may be required, to the extent and subject to such procedures or conditions as may be provided in the bylaws, to include in its proxy solicitation materials (including any form of proxy it distributes), in addition to individuals nominated by the board of directors, 1 or more individuals nominated by a stockholder. Such procedures or conditions may include any of the following:

> (1) A provision requiring a minimum record or beneficial ownership, or duration of ownership, of shares of the corporation's capital stock, by the nominating stockholder, and defining beneficial ownership to take into account options or other rights in respect of or related to such stock;

> (2) A provision requiring the nominating stockholder to submit specified information concerning the stockholder and the stockholder's nominees, including information concerning ownership by such persons of shares of the corporation's capital stock, or options or other rights in respect of or related to such stock;

> (3) A provision conditioning eligibility to require inclusion in the corporation's proxy solicitation materials upon the number or

proportion of directors nominated by stockholders or whether the stockholder previously sought to require such inclusion;

(4) A provision precluding nominations by any person if such person, any nominee of such person, or any affiliate or associate of such person or nominee, has acquired or publicly proposed to acquire shares constituting a specified percentage of the voting power of the corporation's outstanding voting stock within a specified period before the election of directors;

(5) A provision requiring that the nominating stockholder undertake to indemnify the corporation in respect of any loss arising as a result of any false or misleading information or statement submitted by the nominating stockholder in connection with a nomination; and

(6) Any other lawful condition.

Section 113. Proxy expense reimbursement.

(a) The bylaws may provide for the reimbursement by the corporation of expenses incurred by a stockholder in soliciting proxies in connection with an election of directors, subject to such procedures or conditions as the bylaws may prescribe, including:

(1) Conditioning eligibility for reimbursement upon the number or proportion of persons nominated by the stockholder seeking reimbursement or whether such stockholder previously sought reimbursement for similar expenses;

(2) Limitations on the amount of reimbursement based upon the proportion of votes cast in favor of 1 or more of the persons nominated by the stockholder seeking reimbursement, or upon the amount spent by the corporation in soliciting proxies in connection with the election;

(3) Limitations concerning elections of directors by cumulative voting pursuant to § 214 of this title; or

(4) Any other lawful condition. [. . .]

Ringling Bros.-Barnum & Bailey Combined Shows v. Ringling
29 Del. Ch. 610 (1947)

■ PEARSON, JUDGE.

The Court of Chancery was called upon to review an attempted election of directors at the 1946 annual stockholders meeting of the corporate defendant. The pivotal questions concern an agreement between two of the three present stockholders, and particularly the effect of this agreement with relation to the exercise of voting rights by these two stockholders. At the time of the meeting, the corporation had outstanding 1000 shares of capital stock held as follows: 315 by petitioner Edith

Conway Ringling; 315 by defendant Aubrey B. Ringling Haley [. . .]; and 370 by defendant John Ringling North. The purpose of the meeting was to elect the entire board of seven directors. The shares could be voted cumulatively. Mrs. Ringling asserts that by virtue of the operation of an agreement between her and Mrs. Haley, the latter was bound to vote her shares for an adjournment of the meeting, or in the alternative, for a certain slate of directors. Mrs. Haley contends that she was not so bound for reason that the agreement was invalid, or at least revocable.

The two ladies entered into the agreement in 1941. [. . .] The agreement recites that each party was the owner [. . .] of 300 shares of the capital stock of the defendant corporation; that in 1938 these shares had been deposited under a voting trust agreement which would terminate in 1947, or earlier, upon the elimination of certain liability of the corporation; that each party also owned 15 shares individually; that the parties had 'entered into an agreement in April 1934 providing for joint action by them in matters affecting their ownership of stock and interest in' the corporate defendant; that the parties desired 'to continue to act jointly in all matters relating to their stock ownership or interest in' the corporate defendant (and the other corporation). The agreement then provides as follows:

'Now, Therefore, in consideration of the mutual covenants and agreements hereinafter contained the parties hereto agree as follows:

'1.   Neither party will sell any shares of stock or any voting trust certificates in either of said corporations to any other person whosoever, without first making a written offer to the other party hereto of all of the shares or voting trust certificates proposed to be sold, for the same price and upon the same terms and conditions as in such proposed sale, and allowing such other party a time of not less than 180 days from the date of such written offer within which to accept same.

'2.   In exercising any voting rights to which either party may be entitled by virtue of ownership of stock or voting trust certificates held by them in either of said corporation, each party will consult and confer with the other and the parties will act jointly in exercising such voting rights in accordance with such agreement as they may reach with respect to any matter calling for the exercise of such voting rights.

'3.   In the event the parties fail to agree with respect to any matter covered by paragraph 2 above, the question in disagreement shall be submitted for arbitration to Karl D. Loos, of Washington, D. C. as arbitrator and his decision thereon shall be binding upon the parties hereto. Such arbitration shall be exercised to the end of assuring for the respective corporations good management and such participation therein by the members of the Ringling family as the experience, capacity and ability of each may warrant. The parties may at any time by written agreement designate any other individual to act as arbitrator in lieu of said Loos.

'4.   Each of the parties hereto will enter into and execute such voting trust agreement or agreements and such other instruments as, from time to time they may deem advisable and as they may be advised by counsel are appropriate to effectuate the purposes and objects of this agreement.

'5.   This agreement shall be in effect from the date hereof and shall continue in effect for a period of ten years unless sooner terminated by mutual agreement in writing by the parties hereto.

'6.   The agreement of April 1934 is hereby terminated.

'7.   This agreement shall be binding upon and inure to the benefit of the heirs, executors, administrators and assigns of the parties hereto respectively.'

The Mr. Loos mentioned in the agreement is an attorney and has represented both parties since 1937, and, before and after the voting trust was terminated in late 1942, advised them with respect to the exercise of their voting rights. At the annual meetings in 1943 and the two following years, the parties voted their shares in accordance with mutual understandings arrived at as a result of discussions. In each of these years, they elected five of the seven directors. Mrs. Ringling and Mrs. Haley each had sufficient votes, independently of the other, to elect two of the seven directors. By both voting for an additional candidate, they could be sure of his election regardless of how Mr. North, the remaining stockholder, might vote.[1]

Some weeks before the 1946 meeting, they discussed with Mr. Loos the matter of voting for directors. They were in accord that Mrs. Ringling should cast sufficient votes to elect herself and her son; and that Mrs. Haley should elect herself and her husband; but they did not agree upon a fifth director. The day before the meeting, the discussions were continued, Mrs. Haley being represented by her husband since she could not be present because of illness. In a conversation with Mr. Loos, Mr. Haley indicated that he would make a motion for an adjournment of the meeting for sixty days, in order to give the ladies additional time to come to an agreement about their voting. On the morning of the meeting, however, he stated that because of something Mrs. Ringling had done, he

---

[1]   Each lady was entitled to cast 2205 votes (since each had the cumulative voting rights of 315 shares, and there were 7 vacancies in the directorate). The sum of the votes of both is 4410, which is sufficient to allow 882 votes for each of 5 persons. Mr. North, holding 370 shares, was entitled to cast 2590 votes, which obviously cannot be divided so as to give to more than two candidates as many as 882 votes each. It will be observed that in order for Mrs. Ringling and Mrs. Haley to be sure to elect five directors (regardless of how Mr. North might vote) they must act together in the sense that their combined votes must be divided among five different candidates and at least one of the five must be voted for by both Mrs. Ringling and Mrs. Haley.

would not consent to a postponement. Mrs. Ringling then made a demand upon Mr. Loos to act under the third paragraph of the agreement 'to arbitrate the disagreement' between her and Mrs. Haley in connection with the manner in which the stock of the two ladies should be voted. At the opening of the meeting, Mr. Loos read the written demand and stated that he determined and directed that the stock of both ladies be voted for an adjournment of sixty days. Mrs. Ringling then made a motion for adjournment and voted for it. Mr. Haley, as proxy for his wife, and Mr. North voted against the motion. Mrs. Ringling (herself or through her attorney, it is immaterial which,) objected to the voting of Mrs. Haley's stock in any manner other than in accordance with Mr. Loos' direction. The chairman ruled that the stock could not be voted contrary to such direction, and declared the motion for adjournment had carried. Nevertheless, the meeting proceeded to the election of directors. Mrs. Ringling stated that she would continue in the meeting 'but without prejudice to her position with respect to the voting of the stock and the fact that adjournment had not been taken.' Mr. Loos directed Mrs. Ringling to cast her votes

> 882 for Mrs. Ringling,
>
> 882 for her son, Robert, and
>
> 441 for a Mr. Dunn, who had been a member of the board for several years.

She complied. Mr. Loos directed that Mrs. Haley's votes be cast

> 882 for Mrs. Haley,
>
> 882 for Mr. Haley, and
>
> 441 for Mr. Dunn.

Instead of complying, Mr. Haley attempted to vote his wife's shares

> 1103 for Mrs. Haley, and
>
> 1102 for Mr. Haley.

Mr. North voted his shares

> 864 for a Mr. Woods,
>
> 863 for a Mr. Griffin, and
>
> 863 for Mr. North.

The chairman ruled that the five candidates proposed by Mr. Loos, together with Messrs. Woods and North, were elected. The Haley-North group disputed this ruling insofar as it declared the election of Mr. Dunn; and insisted that Mr. Griffin, instead, had been elected. A director's meeting followed in which Mrs. Ringling participated after stating that she would do so 'without prejudice to her position that the stockholders' meeting had been adjourned and that the directors' meeting was not properly held.' Mr. Dunn and Mr. Griffin, although each was challenged by an opposing faction, attempted to join in voting as directors for different slates of officers. Soon after the meeting, Mrs. Ringling instituted this proceeding.

The Vice Chancellor determined that the agreement to vote in accordance with the direction of Mr. Loos was valid as a 'stock pooling agreement' with lawful objects and purposes, and that it was not in violation of any public policy of this state. He held that where the arbitrator acts under the agreement and one party refuses to comply with his direction, 'the Agreement constitutes the willing party . . . an implied agent possessing the irrevocable proxy of the recalcitrant party for the purpose of casting the particular vote'. It was ordered that a new election be held before a master, with the direction that the master should recognize and give effect to the agreement if its terms were properly invoked.

Before taking up defendants' objections to the agreement, let us analyze particularly what it attempts to provide with respect to voting, including what functions and powers it attempts to repose in Mr. Loos, the 'arbitrator'. The agreement recites that the parties desired 'to continue to act jointly in all matters relating to their stock ownership or interest in' the corporation. The parties agreed to consult and confer with each other in exercising their voting rights and to act jointly—that is, concertedly; unitedly; towards unified courses of action—in accordance with such agreement as they might reach. Thus, so long as the parties agree for whom or for what their shares shall be voted, the agreement provides no function for the arbitrator. His role is limited to situations where the parties fail to agree upon a course of action. In such cases, the agreement directs that 'the question in disagreement shall be submitted for arbitration' to Mr. Loos 'as arbitrator and his decision thereon shall be binding upon the parties'. These provisions are designed to operate in aid of what appears to be a primary purpose of the parties, 'to act jointly' in exercising their voting rights, by providing a means for fixing a course of action whenever they themselves might reach a stalemate.

Should the agreement be interpreted as attempting to empower the arbitrator to carry his directions into effect? Certainly there is no express delegation or grant of power to do so, either by authorizing him to vote the shares or to compel either party to vote them in accordance with his directions. The agreement expresses no other function of the arbitrator than that of deciding questions in disagreement which prevent the effectuation of the purpose 'to act jointly'. The power to enforce a decision does not seem a necessary or usual incident of such a function. Mr. Loos is not a party to the agreement. It does not contemplate the transfer of any shares or interest in shares to him, or that he should undertake any duties which the parties might compel him to perform. They provided that they might designate any other individual to act instead of Mr. Loos. The agreement does not attempt to make the arbitrator a trustee of an express trust. What the arbitrator is to do is for the benefit of the parties, not for his own benefit. Whether the parties accept or reject his decision is no concern of his, so far as the agreement or the surrounding circumstances reveal. We think the parties sought to bind each other, but to be bound only to each other, and not to empower the arbitrator to enforce decisions he might make.

From this conclusion, it follows necessarily that no decision of the arbitrator could ever be enforced if both parties to the agreement were unwilling that it be enforced, for the obvious reason that there would be no one to enforce it. Under the agreement, something more is required after the arbitrator has given his decision in order that it should become compulsory: at least one of the parties must determine that such decision shall be carried into effect. Thus, any 'control' of the voting of the shares, which is reposed in the arbitrator, is substantially limited in action under the agreement in that it is subject to the overriding power of the parties themselves.

The agreement does not describe the undertaking of each party with respect to a decision of the arbitrator other than to provide that it 'shall be binding upon the parties'. It seems to us that this language, considered with relation to its context and the situations to which it is applicable, means that each party promised the other to exercise her own voting rights in accordance with the arbitrator's decision. The agreement is silent about any exercise of the voting rights of one party by the other. The language with reference to situations where the parties arrive at an understanding as to voting plainly suggests 'action' by each, and 'exercising' voting rights by each, rather than by one for the other. There is no intimation that this method should be different where the arbitrator's decision is to be carried into effect. Assuming that a power in each party to exercise the voting rights of the other might be a relatively more effective or convenient means of enforcing a decision of the arbitrator than would be available without the power, this would not justify implying a delegation of the power in the absence of some indication that the parties bargained for that means. The method of voting actually employed by the parties tends to show that they did not construe the agreement as creating powers to vote each other's shares; for at meetings prior to 1946 each party apparently exercised her own voting rights, and at the 1946 meeting, Mrs. Ringling, who wished to enforce the agreement, did not attempt to cast a ballot in exercise of any voting rights of Mrs. Haley. We do not find enough in the agreement or in the circumstances to justify a construction that either party was empowered to exercise voting rights of the other.

Having examined what the parties sought to provide by the agreement, we come now to defendants' contention that the voting provisions are illegal and revocable. They say that the courts of this state have definitely established the doctrine 'that there can be no agreement, or any device whatsoever, by which the voting power of stock of a Delaware corporation may be irrevocably separated from the ownership of the stock, except by an agreement which complies with Section 18' of the Corporation Law,

Rev. Code 1935, § 2050, and except by a proxy coupled with an interest. [. . .] The statute reads, in part, as follows:

'Sec. 18. Fiduciary Stockholders; Voting Power of; Voting Trusts:-Persons holding stock in a fiduciary capacity shall be entitled to vote the shares so held, and persons whose stock is pledged shall be entitled to vote, unless in the transfer by the pledgor on the books of the corporation he shall have expressly empowered the pledgee to vote thereon, in which case only the pledgee, or his proxy may represent said stock and vote thereon.

'One or more stockholders may by agreement in writing deposit capital stock of an original issue with or transfer capital stock to any person or persons, or corporation or corporations authorized to act as trustee, for the purpose of vesting in said person or persons, corporation or corporations, who may be designated Voting Trustee or Voting Trustees, the right to vote thereon for any period of time determined by such agreement, not exceeding ten years, upon the terms and conditions stated in such agreement. Such agreement may contain any other lawful provisions not inconsistent with said purpose. * * * Said Voting Trustees may vote upon the stock so issued or transferred during the period in such agreement specified; stock standing in the names of such Voting Trustees may be voted either in person or by proxy, and in voting said stock, such Voting Trustees shall incur no responsibility as stockholder, trustee or otherwise, except for their own individual malfeasance.'

[. . .] The statute authorizes, among other things, the deposit or transfer of stock in trust for a specified purpose, namely, 'vesting' in the transferee 'the right to vote thereon' for a limited period; and prescribes numerous requirements in this connection. Accordingly, it seems reasonable to infer that to establish the relationship and accomplish the purpose which the statute authorizes, its requirements must be complied with. But the statute does not purport to deal with agreements whereby shareholders attempt to bind each other as to how they shall vote their shares. Various forms of such pooling agreements, as they are sometimes called, have been held valid and have been distinguished from voting trusts [. . .] We think the particular agreement before us does not violate Section 18 or constitute an attempted evasion of its requirements, and is not illegal for any other reason. Generally speaking, a shareholder may exercise wide liberality of judgment in the matter of voting, and it is not objectionable that his motives may be for personal profit, or determined by whims or caprice, so long as he violates no duty owed his fellow shareholders. [. . .] The ownership of voting stock imposes no legal duty to vote at all. A group of shareholders may, without impropriety, vote their respective shares so as to obtain advantages of concerted action. They may lawfully contract with each other to vote in the future in such way as they, or a majority of their group, from time to time determine. [. . .] Reasonable provisions for cases of failure of the group to reach a determination because of an even division in their ranks seem unobjectionable. The provision here for submission to the arbitrator is plainly designed as a deadlock-breaking measure, and the arbitrator's decision cannot be enforced unless at least one of the parties (entitled to cast one-half of their combined votes) is willing that it be enforced. We find the provision reasonable. It does not appear that the agreement enables the parties to take any unlawful advantage of the outside shareholder, or of any other person. It offends no rule of law or public policy of this state of which we are aware.

Legal consideration for the promises of each party is supplied by the mutual promises of the other party. The undertaking to vote in accordance with the arbitrator's decision is a valid contract. The good faith of the arbitrator's action has not been challenged and, indeed, the record indicates that no such challenge could be supported. Accordingly, the failure of Mrs. Haley to exercise her voting rights in accordance with his decision was a breach of her contract. It is no extenuation of the breach that her votes were cast for two of the three candidates directed by the arbitrator. His directions to her were part of a single plan or course of action for the voting of the shares of both parties to the agreement, calculated to utilize an advantage of joint action by them which would bring about the election of an additional director. The actual voting of Mrs. Haley's shares frustrates that plan to such an extent that it should not be treated as a partial performance of her contract.

Throughout their argument, defendants make much of the fact that all votes cast at the meeting were by the registered shareholders. The Court of Chancery may, in a review of an election, reject votes of a registered shareholder where his voting of them is found to be in violation of rights of another person. [. . .] It seems to us that upon the application of Mrs. Ringling, the injured party, the votes representing Mrs. Haley's shares should not be counted. Since no infirmity in Mr. North's voting has been demonstrated, his right to recognition of what he did at the meeting should be considered in granting any relief to Mrs. Ringling; for her rights arose under a contract to which Mr. North was not a party. With this in mind, we have concluded that the election should not be declared invalid, but that effect should be given to a rejection of the votes representing Mrs. Haley's shares. No other relief seems appropriate in this proceeding. Mr. North's vote against the motion for adjournment was sufficient to defeat it. With respect to the election of directors, the return of the inspectors should be corrected to show a rejection of Mrs. Haley's votes, and to declare the election of the six persons for whom Mr. North and Mrs. Ringling voted.

This leaves one vacancy in the directorate[; t]he question of what to do about such a vacancy was not considered by the court below and has not been argued here. For this reason, and because an election of directors at the 1947 annual meeting (which presumably will be held in the near future) may make a determination of the question unimportant, we shall not decide it on this appeal. If a decision of the point appears important to the parties, any of them may apply to raise it in the Court of Chancery, after the mandate of this court is received there.

An order should be entered directing a modification of the order of the Court of Chancery in accordance with this opinion.

Espinoza v. Zuckerberg

124 A.3d 47 (Del. Ch. 2015)

■ BOUCHARD, C.

[. . .]

I. BACKGROUND

A. The Parties

Nominal Defendant Facebook, Inc. is a Delaware corporation with headquarters in California. Hundreds of millions of people use Facebook's social networking website and mobile applications. [. . .]

Defendant Mark Zuckerberg is the founder of Facebook. Zuckerberg has served as Facebook's Chief Executive Officer since July 2004 and as the Chairman of Facebook's board of directors since January 2012. Zuckerberg, principally due to his ownership of the super-voting Class B shares, controlled approximately 61.6% of the total voting power of Facebook's common stock as of February 28, 2014. Defendant Sheryl K. Sandberg has served as Facebook's Chief Operating Officer since March 2008 and as a Facebook director since June 2012.

Defendants Donald E. Graham, Peter A. Thiel, Marc. L. Andreessen, Reed Hastings, Erskine B. Bowles, and Susan D. Desmond-Hellmann were members of Facebook's board of directors when the Verified Complaint was filed on June 6, 2014, and at all times relevant to this opinion. All of the defendant directors other than Zuckerberg and Sandberg were non-employee directors.

Plaintiff Ernesto Espinoza alleges he has been a Facebook stockholder at all relevant times. [. . .]

C. The Board Approves Compensation for Non-Employee Directors

On August 21, 2013, the Compensation Committee, consisting of Graham and Thiel, discussed the compensation of Facebook's non-management directors. The following day, Facebook's board considered the topic at a regular meeting and unanimously approved a proposal to increase the annual cash retainer paid to Audit Committee members from $50,000 to $70,000, to raise the annual cash retainer paid to the Audit Committee Chair from $70,000 to $100,000, and to provide non-employee directors with annual [Restricted Stock Unit] grants at a value of $300,000 per year, subject to the board's approval of an implementation plan.

Zuckerberg attended this meeting. A few weeks later, the Facebook board formally approved a plan implementing the proposal by unanimous written consent.

As a result of the board's approval of the compensation plan, Facebook's six non-employee directors received RSU grants in 2013 (the "2013 Compensation"). [. . .]

D. Procedural Posture

On June 6, 2014, plaintiff filed a derivative complaint on behalf of Facebook against the eight members of its board of directors concerning the 2013 Compensation. The complaint asserts three causes of action: breach of fiduciary duty "for awarding and/or receiving excessive compensation at the expense of the Company" (Count I), waste of corporate assets (Count II), and unjust enrichment (Count III). [. . .]

On August 18, 2014, defendants moved for summary judgment [. . .]. On the same day, Zuckerberg filed an affidavit in support of the summary judgment motion declaring as follows:

> [. . .] Although I was never presented with an opportunity to approve formally the 2013 equity awards to Facebook's Non-Executive Directors or the Annual Compensation Program in my capacity as a Facebook stockholder, had an opportunity presented itself, I would have done so. If put to a vote, I would vote in favor of the 2013 equity awards to Facebook's Non-Executive Directors, as well as the Annual Compensation Program, and if presented with a stockholder written consent approving them, I would sign it. [. . .]

Zuckerberg never executed a written consent under 8 Del C. § 228, which would have triggered an obligation to notify non-consenting stockholders of the action taken. [. . .]

II. LEGAL ANALYSIS

[. . .]

B. Count I: Breach of Fiduciary Duty

Plaintiff asserts in Count I that defendants violated their fiduciary duty of loyalty "by awarding and/or receiving" the 2013 Compensation, thereby causing injury to Facebook. Plaintiff argues that the entire fairness standard must apply to this transaction because six of the eight board members received the 2013 Compensation, and thus a majority of the board was interested in the transaction. [. . .]

Directors are necessarily interested in their compensation, which is a benefit they receive that does not accrue to stockholders generally. Thus, where, as here, directors make decisions about their own compensation, those decisions presumptively will be reviewed as self-dealing transactions under the entire fairness standard rather than under the business judgment rule. A decision dominated by interested directors can gain the protection of the business judgment rule, however, if a fully-informed disinterested majority of stockholders ratifies the transaction. [. . .]

Here, defendants contend that the business judgment rule should apply to their approval of the 2013 Compensation on the theory that Zuckerberg [. . .] ratified the 2013 Compensation in his capacity as a Facebook stockholder by virtue of statements he made in his affidavit and his deposition after this action was filed. Plaintiff responds that these acts do not constitute a valid form of stockholder ratification (and thus do not permit invocation of the business judgment rule) because Zuckerberg did not express assent as a stockholder in a manner permitted by the Delaware General Corporation Law ("DGCL"). [. . .]

1.   The Methods for Taking Stockholder Action Under the DGCL

The DGCL provides two methods for stockholders to express assent on a matter concerning the affairs of the corporation: (1) by voting in person or by proxy at a meeting of stockholders, or (2) by written consent. In both cases, the statute contains a number of formal requirements that [. . .] ensure precision in stockholder voting and transparency to all stockholders. [. . .]

Today, under Section 228 of the DGCL, unless the certificate of incorporation restricts the use of written consents, any action that may be taken at any annual or special meeting of stockholders may be taken by majority stockholder consent (or whatever other voting threshold applies for a particular act) "without a meeting, without prior notice and without a vote."

Significantly, although Section 228 permits stockholders to take action by written consent without prior notice, "[p]rompt notice of the taking of the corporate action" by written consent must be provided to the non-consenting stockholders. Thus, Section 228 ensures some level of transparency for non-consenting stockholders. [. . .]

This Court has recognized more broadly that, "[b]ecause Section 228 permits immediate action without prior notice to minority stockholders, the statute involves great potential for mischief and its requirements must be strictly complied with if any semblance of corporate order is to be maintained." [. . .] Thus, even if a controlling stockholder manifests a clear intent to ratify a decision outside of a stockholder meeting, the ratification will not be effective unless it complies with the technical requirements of Section 228.

In sum, the provisions of the DGCL governing the ability of stockholders to take action, whether by voting at a meeting or by written consent, demonstrate the importance of ensuring precision, both in defining the exact nature of the corporate action to be authorized, and in verifying that the requirements for taking such an action are met, including that the transaction received enough votes to be effective. They also demonstrate the importance of providing transparency to stockholders, whose rights are affected by the actions of the majority. In particular, stockholders have the right to participate in a meeting at which a vote is to be taken after receiving notice and all material information or, in the case of action taken by written consent, to receive prompt notice after the fact of the action taken.

2. Defendants' Authorities Are Inapposite and Do Not Warrant Deviation from the Corporate Formalities of the DGCL

Defendants argue that Zuckerberg, as Facebook's controlling stockholder, should be permitted to ratify the decision of an interested board of directors without complying with the formalities of the provisions of the DGCL for taking stockholder action. [. . .]

Defendants advance several arguments in an attempt to make this case, beginning with reliance on general principles of ratification under the law of agency. In particular, defendants assert that Chancellor Allen's decision in *Lewis v. Vogelstein* affirms the applicability of common law ratification in the corporate context.

In *Vogelstein,* stockholders challenged certain option grants [. . .] for the directors of Mattel, Inc., which plan had been approved by the stockholders of the company at an annual meeting. Because the challenged transaction had been approved at a formal meeting of stockholders, the Court had no occasion to consider the question presented here [. . .]. The Court's inquiry focused instead on the legal effect of a concededly valid form of stockholder ratification on judicial review of the option grants in question. In analyzing this question, Chancellor Allen explained how "[r]atification is a concept deriving from the law of agency," but went on to elaborate that "[a]pplication of these general ratification principles to shareholder ratification is complicated by three other factors," namely (1) the lack of a single individual acting as principal—a factor not present here, (2) a purpose to demonstrate compliance with fiduciary duties rather than to validate unauthorized conduct, and (3) the existence of the DGCL as a statutory overlay. The Chancellor commented that these "differences between shareholder ratification of director action and classic ratification by a single principal . . . lead to a difference in the effect of a valid ratification in the shareholder context."

I do not read *Vogelstein* as a wholesale endorsement of importing general principles of common law ratification into the corporate context, as defendants suggest. To the contrary, the decision demonstrates the need to be sensitive to the peculiarities of the corporate context when applying general principles of ratification. [. . .]

3. Existing Authority and the Policies Underlying the Stockholder Approval Provisions of the DGCL Suggest that Formalities Must Be Followed to Effectuate Ratification in the Corporate Context

Defendants observe that there "is no case or statute that requires a stockholder vote or written consent for ratification purposes if the approval of a stockholder majority can be expressed another way." [. . .] [R]eferences in existing case law to ratification in the context of a stockholder "vote," as well as policy considerations underlying the provisions of the DGCL for taking stockholder action, support the conclusion that adherence to formalities should be required in this context.

One foundational case is *Gantler v. Stephens*. As the Supreme Court recently noted, *Gantler* is a narrow decision focused on defining a specific legal term, "ratification." (internal quotes omitted) In *Gantler*, the Supreme Court held that the scope of "the shareholder ratification doctrine must be limited . . . to circumstances where a fully informed shareholder vote approves director action that does *not* legally require shareholder approval in order to become legally effective." In my view, *Gantler*'s use of the phrase "fully informed shareholder ***vote***" in defining the concept of ratification was deliberate and was not intended to mean something less formal than an actual stockholder vote (or an action by written consent in lieu thereof).

Recently, in *Corwin v. KKR*, which confirmed that stockholder approval from a statutorily required vote can be used to invoke the business judgment rule the same way an approval from a voluntary vote can, the Supreme Court again used specific voting language to explain the doctrine of ratification in the corporate context. Specifically, the Supreme Court stated that "the doctrine applies only to fully informed, uncoerced stockholder votes," thereby implicitly excluding less formal methods of stockholder approval.

Another example is 8 Del. C. § 144(a)(2), which prevents the voiding of a director's interested transaction if the "transaction is specifically approved in good faith by vote of the stockholders." [. . .]

In my opinion, the policies underlying the DGCL provisions governing the taking of stockholder action further support the conclusion that stockholders—including controlling stockholders like Zuckerberg—must observe statutory formalities when seeking to ratify director action. Doing so will avoid ambiguity and misinterpretation by ensuring that actions taken by stockholders are defined with precision and—where a single controlling stockholder is not present—that the requisite level of approval was obtained, and will promote transparency for the benefit of all stockholders. [. . .]

Defendants contend that formal processes such as a stockholder vote or a written consent can be convenient methods of ratification for groups of stockholders [. . .] but that they are not necessary for a controlling stockholder whose will can be clearly expressed without formalities. They argue that permitting many sorts of acts to constitute ratification poses no problem of imprecision, because "[b]y virtue of his voting control, Mr. Zuckerberg can be the singular voice of Facebook's stockholders . . . ." I disagree. Although an affidavit is a relatively formal expression, once the statutory framework is removed, the possibilities for ambiguity in expressing approval are seemingly limitless—if affidavits are sufficient, what about meeting minutes, press releases, conversations with directors, or even "Liking" a Facebook post of a proposed corporate action? Such an approach would require directors, stockholders, and courts to engage in the inefficient exercise of divining the intentions of a controlling stockholder, and would cut away at the certainty and precision that make the formalities of stockholder meetings or statutorily compliant written consents beneficial.

Zuckerberg's deposition testimony illustrates the problem. Discussing Facebook's board of directors, Zuckerberg testified that "[t]hese are the people who I want . . . and who I think will serve the company best, and I think that the compensation plan that we have is doing its job of attracting and retaining them over the long term." It is far from clear that Zuckerberg intended that statement to be a definitive ratification of a specific corporate act. The year of the compensation in question is not mentioned, and Zuckerberg provides no language indicating final approval of a past compensation act. [. . .]

Failing to adhere to corporate formalities to effect stockholder ratification also impinges on the rights of minority stockholders. [. . .] Although minority stockholders have no power to alter a controlling stockholder's binding decisions absent a fiduciary breach, they are entitled to the benefits of the formalities imposed by the DGCL, including prompt notification under Section 228(e). This requirement promotes transparency and enables minority stockholders to stay abreast of corporate decision-making and maintain the accountability of boards of directors and controlling stockholders. In this vein, this Court has commented that the written consent procedure keeps minority stockholders' voting rights intact, even if those rights are rendered moot when a majority stockholder executes a decision.

It is therefore of no moment that Zuckerberg undisputedly controls Facebook. Although he can outvote all other stockholders, [. . .] he still must adhere to corporate formalities (and his fiduciary obligations) when doing so, because his rights as a stockholder are no greater than the rights of any other stockholder—he simply holds more voting power.

[. . .] If Zuckerberg does not need to provide written consents to ratify the 2013 Compensation, why require written consents for any other action he takes? Such a regime would essentially negate most requirements under Delaware law to notify stockholders of meaningful events.

Balanced against the informational costs of a less formal system of stockholder approval are the financial costs of formalities. Defendants argue that Facebook chose to avoid "the added expense of a stockholder vote or action by written consent" since it was not obliged to follow those legal requirements when securing Zuckerberg's ratification. But Section 228 already serves as a convenient method of avoiding the expense of a stockholder vote. [. . .] Indeed, the burden and expense of this litigation undoubtedly dwarf the burden of Zuckerberg signing an appropriate form of consent in this case. [. . .]

For the reasons stated above, I hold that stockholder ratification of an interested transaction, so as to shift the standard of review from entire fairness to the business judgment presumption, cannot be achieved without complying with the statutory formalities in the DGCL for taking stockholder action. Consequently, neither Zuckerberg's affidavit nor his deposition testimony ratified the Facebook board's decision to approve the 2013 Compensation [. . .].

The entire fairness standard of review requires defendants to establish that the "transaction was the product of both fair dealing and fair price." Because defendants relied solely on a ratification defense, they did not attempt to produce evidence of entire fairness sufficient to show an entitlement to judgment as a matter of law, nor have they demonstrated that there is no genuine issue of material fact as to the entire fairness of the 2013 Compensation. [. . .]

III. CONCLUSION

For the foregoing reasons, defendants' motion for summary judgment as to Count [. . .] I (breach of fiduciary duty) [. . .] is denied [. . .].

C. PROXY FIGHTS

Rosenfeld v. Fairchild Engine & Airplane Corporation

309 N.Y. 168 (N.Y. 1955)

In a stockholder's derivative action brought by plaintiff, an attorney, who owns 25 out of the company's over 2,300,000 shares, he seeks to compel the return of $261,522, paid out of the corporate treasury to reimburse both sides in a proxy contest for their expenses. The Appellate Division has unanimously affirmed a judgment [. . .] dismissing plaintiff's complaint on the merits, and we agree. Exhaustive opinions were written by both courts below, and it will serve no useful purpose to review the facts again.

Of the amount in controversy $106,000 were spent out of corporate funds by the old board of directors while still in office in defense of their position in said contest; $28,000 were paid to the old board by the new board after the change of management following the proxy contest, to compensate the former directors for such of the remaining expenses of their unsuccessful defense as the new board found was fair and reasonable; payment of $127,000, representing reimbursement of expenses to members of the prevailing group, was expressly ratified by a 16 to 1 majority vote of the stockholders.

The essential facts are not in dispute, and, since the determinations below are amply supported by the evidence, we are bound by the findings affirmed by the Appellate Division. The Appellate Division found that the difference between plaintiff's group and the old board "went deep into the policies of the company", and that among these Ward's contract was one of the "main points of contention". The Official Referee found that the controversy "was based on an understandable difference in policy between the two groups, at the very bottom of which was the Ward employment contract".

By way of contrast with the findings here, in *Lawyers' Advertising Co. v. Consolidated Ry., Lighting & Refrigerating Co.*, which was an action to recover for the cost of publishing newspaper notices not authorized by the board of directors, it was expressly found that the proxy contest there involved was "by one faction in its contest with another for the control of the corporation ... a contest for the perpetuation of their offices and control." We there said by way of dicta that under such circumstances the publication of certain notices on behalf of the management faction was not a corporate expenditure which the directors had the power to authorize.

Other jurisdictions and our own lower courts have held that management may look to the corporate treasury for the reasonable expenses of soliciting proxies to defend its position in a bona fide policy contest.

It should be noted that plaintiff does not argue that the aforementioned sums were fraudulently extracted from the corporation; indeed, his counsel conceded that "the charges were fair and reasonable," but denied "they were legal charges which may be reimbursed for." This is therefore not a case where a stockholder challenges specific items, which, on examination, the trial court may find unwarranted, excessive or otherwise improper. Had plaintiff made such objections here, the trial court would have been required to examine the items challenged.

If directors of a corporation may not in good faith incur reasonable and proper expenses in soliciting proxies in these days of giant corporations with vast numbers of stockholders, the corporate business might be seriously interfered with because of stockholder indifference and the difficulty of procuring a quorum, where there is no contest. In the event of a proxy contest, if the directors may not freely answer the challenges of outside groups and in good faith defend their actions with respect to corporate policy for the information of the stockholders, they and the corporation may be at the mercy of persons seeking to wrest control for their own purposes, so long as such persons have ample funds to conduct a proxy contest. The test is clear. When the directors act in good faith in a contest over policy, they have the right to incur reasonable and proper expenses for solicitation of proxies and in defense of their corporate policies, and are not obliged to sit idly by. The courts are entirely competent to pass upon their bona fides in any given case, as well as the nature of their expenditures when duly challenged.

It is also our view that the members of the so-called new group could be reimbursed by the corporation for their expenditures in this contest by affirmative vote of the stockholders. With regard to these ultimately successful contestants, as the Appellate Division below has noted, there was, of course, "no duty . . . to set forth the facts, with corresponding obligation of the corporation to pay for such expense." However, where a majority of the stockholders chose in this case by a vote of 16 to 1 to reimburse the successful contestants for achieving the very end sought and voted for by them as owners of the corporation, we see no reason to deny the effect of their ratification nor to hold the corporate body powerless to determine how its own moneys shall be spent.

The rule then which we adopt is simply this: In a contest over policy, as compared to a purely personal power contest, corporate directors have the right to make reasonable and proper expenditures, subject to the scrutiny of the courts when duly challenged, from the corporate treasury for the purpose of persuading the stockholders of the correctness of their position and soliciting their support for policies which the directors believe, in all good faith, are in the best interests of the corporation. The stockholders, moreover, have the right to reimburse successful contestants for the reasonable and bona fide expenses incurred by them in any such policy contest, subject to like court scrutiny. That is not to say, however, that corporate directors can, under any circumstances, disport themselves in a proxy contest with the corporation's moneys to an unlimited extent. Where it is established that such moneys have been spent for personal power, individual gain or private advantage, and not in the belief that such expenditures are in the best interests of the stockholders and the corporation, or where the fairness and reasonableness of the amounts allegedly expended are duly and successfully challenged, the courts will not hesitate to disallow them.

The judgment of the Appellate Division should be affirmed, without costs.
[. . .]

Levin v. Metro-Goldwyn-Mayer Inc.

264 F. Supp. 797 (S.D.N.Y. 1967)

This action was filed by six stockholders of Metro-Goldwyn-Mayer, Inc. (MGM), a Delaware corporation with its principal place of business in New York. The defendants named are MGM and five of the thirteen members of its Board of Directors. They are part of present MGM corporate management; all of them serve as officers or as members of the Executive Committee.

Plaintiff, Philip Levin, is and has been a director of MGM since February, 1965 and all of the plaintiffs hold substantial blocks of MGM common stock.

The present action flows from a conflict for corporate control between present management—called "the O'Brien group" and "the Levin group." Each group intends to nominate a slate of directors at the MGM stockholder annual meeting which is to be held on February 23, 1967; each has been actively soliciting proxies for this meeting. [. . .]

Plaintiffs complain of the manner, method and means employed by defendants in the solicitation of proxies for the coming annual meeting of MGM stockholders. Specifically, plaintiffs charged that the defendants, in connection with the proxy solicitation contest, have wrongfully committed MGM to pay for the services of specially retained attorneys, a public relations firm and proxy soliciting organizations, and, in addition, have improperly used the offices and employees of MGM in proxy solicitation and the good-will and business contacts of MGM to secure support for the present management. Plaintiffs, in their complaint, pray for temporary and permanent injunctive relief against defendants' continuing this method of solicitation of proxies and against defendants' voting the proxies so obtained at the annual meeting. They also seek money damages of $2,500,000 on behalf of MGM from the individual defendants. [. . .]

Although disapproving of the proxy solicitation methods of "the O'Brien group", and of certain financial and business policies applied in the conduct of corporate activities of MGM, Levin heretofore has described Robert H. O'Brien, the President and the Chief Executive Officer of MGM, as "able and dedicated." In a letter to MGM stockholders sent out in May, 1966, Levin wrote of the Directors—"I have never impugned the integrity of any of my fellow board members."

Plaintiffs' counsel during the presentation of their arguments have stated that no charge is made by plaintiffs that defendants or any of them or any one acting for them or on their behalf have made any false or fraudulent statements in their solicitation of proxies. Plaintiffs make no charge of corruption in the conduct of the corporate affairs for direct personal gain or profit by any of the defendants.

Plaintiffs maintain the injunctive relief sought is required to prevent (1) the unlawful use of the corporate organization—its employees, good-will and offices and of corporate funds in the solicitation of proxies, (2) the retention of "the four top proxy-soliciting concerns and the passing of their bill for their services to the corporation rather than to the individuals" and (3) the employment at corporate expense of special counsel "for the sole and exclusive and no other purpose than the waging of a proxy contest on behalf of the individual defendants who have every right to pay for his valuable services" with their own private funds, particularly in view of the fact that regularly employed attorneys are available to represent the corporate interests of MGM.

Because of the nature of plaintiffs' allegations, we weigh the merits of this application for injunctive relief against the financial and business background of MGM. As of August 31, 1966, MGM had total assets of $251,132,000 and a gross income for its 1966 fiscal year of approximately $185,000,000. It is one of the major producers and distributors of motion pictures in the world and markets to exhibitors films produced by others as well as its own films. MGM has 31 branch distribution offices in the United States. It operates 49 theatres in foreign countries, and it licenses its feature productions and its "shorts" to local as well as network affiliated television stations. It operates a record manufacturing plant, pressing records for its own labels and for others and it produces and distributes records for itself and others. It also has a majority stockholding in one of the leading music publishing companies. MGM's gross revenue in the past fiscal year from music publishing and record distribution are stated to have been over $30,000,000. MGM owns and operates a motion picture producing studio in California and another in England, where feature films are produced by it, often involving expenditure of eight to ten million dollars on a single production. MGM is one of the "giants" in the entertainment industry.

Much has been said by the defendants of the need for expert knowledge in the entertainment field, in the specialized demands for financing, and in the management of an enterprise of the magnitude and diversity of MGM. This is undoubtedly required. Defendants point with unabashed pride to the results they have achieved in their direction of the affairs of MGM. We do not question that the successful operation of MGM has been accomplished in no small measure by diligent and intelligent application to corporate affairs and by the exercise of sound and informed business judgment. The decision as to the continuance of the present management, however, rests entirely with the stockholders. A court may not override or dictate on a matter of this nature to stockholders.

It is quite plain that the differences between "the O'Brien group" and "the Levin group" are much more than mere personality conflicts. These might readily be resolved by reasoning and hard-headed, profit-minded business men. There are definite business policies advocated by each group, so divergent that reconciliation does not seem possible. They appear so evident from the papers before us that detailed analysis would be a waste of time. However, in such a situation the right of an independent stockholder to be fully informed is of supreme importance. The controlling question presented on this application is whether illegal or unfair means of communication, such as demand judicial intervention, are being employed by the present management. We find that they are not and conclude that the injunctive relief now sought should be denied.

The proxy statement filed by MGM under date of January 6, 1967, opens with the statement that "MGM will bear all cost in connection with the management solicitation of proxies." It discloses the purpose of the management to solicit proxies and "to request brokerage houses, custodians, nominees and others who hold stock in their names to solicit proxies from the persons who own such stock, pursuant to the rules of the New York Stock Exchange." It sets forth that MGM will reimburse them "for their out-of-pocket expenses and reasonable clerical expenses." It discloses the employment of Georgeson & Co. at $15,000 and Kissel-Blake Organization, Inc. at $5,000 for services and estimated out-of-pocket expenses. It informs the reader that "officers and regular employees of MGM and its subsidiaries" may request the return of proxies for which no additional compensation will be paid them. It advises that "Proxies may also be solicited in newspapers or other publications" and that the total amount which it is estimated will be spent in the management solicitation is $125,000 "exclusive of amounts normally expended for a solicitation for an election of directors and costs represented by salaries and wages of regular employees and officers."

We do not find the amounts recited to be paid excessive, or the method of operation disclosed by MGM management to be unfair or illegal. It contravenes no federal statute or S.E.C rule or regulation. It provides for orderly dissemination of information to the public investors and the methods and procedures outlined in the management proxy statement follow those set forth in "the Levin group" proxy statement issued under the auspices of "MGM Stockholder's Committee for Better Management." This "Levin group" statement discloses that R. A. Drennan & Co., Inc. has been hired at a fee (and reimbursement of expenses) not to exceed $17,000; that as of January 19, 1967 approximately $35,000 had been expended by the "Committee" and that it is estimated that the total expenditures for solicitation will amount to approximately $175,000; "all expenses will be paid by Philip J. Levin, his wife and corporations wholly owned by them." It is however noted that "no decision has yet been made as to whether reimbursement will be requested from the Company. However, if reimbursement from the Company is sought, it will be submitted to a vote of the stockholders." [. . .]

D. SHAREHOLDER PROPOSALS

Rules and Regulations Under the Securities Exchange Act of 1934
Rule 14a–8: Shareholder Proposals

This section addresses when a company must include a shareholder's proposal in its proxy statement and identify the proposal in its form of proxy when the company holds an annual or special meeting of shareholders. [. . .]

(a) *Question 1:* What is a proposal?

A shareholder proposal is your recommendation or requirement that the company and/or its board of directors take action, which you intend to present at a meeting of the company's shareholders. Your proposal should state as clearly as possible the course of action that you believe the company should follow. If your proposal is placed on the company's proxy card, the company must also provide in the form of proxy means for shareholders to specify by boxes a choice between approval or disapproval, or abstention. Unless otherwise indicated, the word "proposal" as used in this section refers both to your proposal, and to your corresponding statement in support of your proposal (if any).

(b) **Question 2:** Who is eligible to submit a proposal, and how do I demonstrate to the company that I am eligible?

    (1) To be eligible to submit a proposal, you must satisfy the following requirements:

        (i) You must have continuously held:

            (A) At least $2,000 in market value of the company's securities entitled to vote on the proposal for at least three years; or

            (B) At least $15,000 in market value of the company's securities entitled to vote on the proposal for at least two years; or

            (C) At least $25,000 in market value of the company's securities entitled to vote on the proposal for at least one year; or

            (D) The amounts specified in paragraph (b)(3) of this section. This paragraph (b)(1)(i)(D) will expire on the same date that § 240.14a–8(b)(3) expires; and

        (ii) You must provide the company with a written statement that you intend to continue to hold the requisite amount of securities, determined in accordance with paragraph (b)(1)(i)(A) through (C) of this section, through the date of the shareholders' meeting for which the proposal is submitted; and

        (iii) You must provide the company with a written statement that you are able to meet with the company in person or via teleconference no less than 10 calendar days, nor more than 30 calendar days, after submission of the shareholder proposal. You must include your contact information as well as business days and specific times that you are available to discuss the proposal with the company. [. . .]

        (iv) If you use a representative to submit a shareholder proposal on your behalf, you must provide the company with written documentation that:

            (A) Identifies the company to which the proposal is directed;

            (B) Identifies the annual or special meeting for which the proposal is submitted;

            (C) Identifies you as the proponent and identifies the person acting on your behalf as your representative;

            (D) Includes your statement authorizing the designated representative to submit the proposal and otherwise act on your behalf;

(E) Identifies the specific topic of the proposal to be submitted;

(F) Includes your statement supporting the proposal; and

(G) Is signed and dated by you. [. . .]

(2) One of the following methods must be used to demonstrate your eligibility to submit a proposal:

(i) If you are the registered holder of your securities, which means that your name appears in the company's records as a shareholder, the company can verify your eligibility on its own, although you will still have to provide the company with a written statement that you intend to continue to hold the requisite amount of securities[. . .].

(ii) If, like many shareholders, you are not a registered holder, the company likely does not know that you are a shareholder, or how many shares you own. In this case, at the time you submit your proposal, you must prove your eligibility to the company in one of two ways:

(A) The first way is to submit to the company a written statement from the "record" holder of your securities (usually a broker or bank) verifying that, at the time you submitted your proposal, you continuously held at least $2,000, $15,000, or $25,000 in market value of the company's securities entitled to vote on the proposal for at least three years, two years, or one year, respectively. You must also include your own written statement that you intend to continue to hold the requisite amount of securities [. . .] through the date of the shareholders' meeting for which the proposal is submitted; or

(B) The second way to prove ownership applies only if you were required to file, and filed, a Schedule 13D (§ 240.13d–101), Schedule 13G (§ 240.13d–102), Form 3 (§ 249.103 of this chapter), Form 4 (§ 249.104 of this chapter), and/or Form 5 (§ 249.105 of this chapter), or amendments to those documents or updated forms, demonstrating that you meet at least one of the share ownership requirements under paragraph (b)(1)(i)(A) through (C) of this section. [. . .]

(c) *Question 3:* How many proposals may I submit?

Each person may submit no more than one proposal, directly or indirectly, to a company for a particular shareholders' meeting. A person may not rely on the securities holdings of another person for the purpose of meeting the eligibility requirements and submitting multiple proposals for a particular shareholders' meeting.

(d) *Question 4:* How long can my proposal be?

The proposal, including any accompanying supporting statement, may not exceed 500 words.

(e) **Question 5:** What is the deadline for submitting a proposal?

(1) If you are submitting your proposal for the company's annual meeting, you can in most cases find the deadline in last year's proxy statement. However, if the company did not hold an annual meeting last year, or has changed the date of its meeting for this year more than 30 days from last year's meeting, you can usually find the deadline in one of the company's quarterly reports on Form 10-Q (§ 249.308a of this chapter), or in shareholder reports of investment companies under § 270.30d–1 of this chapter of the Investment Company Act of 1940. [. . .]

(f) **Question 6:** What if I fail to follow one of the eligibility or procedural requirements explained in answers to Questions 1 through 4 of this section?

(1) The company may exclude your proposal, but only after it has notified you of the problem, and you have failed adequately to correct it. Within 14 calendar days of receiving your proposal, the company must notify you in writing of any procedural or eligibility deficiencies, as well as of the time frame for your response. Your response must be postmarked, or transmitted electronically, no later than 14 days from the date you received the company's notification. [. . .] If the company intends to exclude the proposal, it will later have to make a submission under § 240.14a–8 and provide you with a copy under Question 10 below, § 240.14a–8(j).

(2) If you fail in your promise to hold the required number of securities through the date of the meeting of shareholders, then the company will be permitted to exclude all of your proposals from its proxy materials for any meeting held in the following two calendar years.

(g) **Question 7:** Who has the burden of persuading the Commission or its staff that my proposal can be excluded?

Except as otherwise noted, the burden is on the company to demonstrate that it is entitled to exclude a proposal.

(h) **Question 8:** Must I appear personally at the shareholders' meeting to present the proposal?

(1) Either you, or your representative who is qualified under state law to present the proposal on your behalf, must attend the meeting to present the proposal. [. . .]

(2) If the company holds its shareholder meeting in whole or in part via electronic media, and the company permits you or your representative to present your proposal via such media, then you may appear through electronic media rather than traveling to the meeting to appear in person.

(3) If you or your qualified representative fail to appear and present the proposal, without good cause, the company will be permitted to exclude all of your proposals from its proxy materials for any meetings held in the following two calendar years.

(i) *Question 9:* If I have complied with the procedural requirements, on what other bases may a company rely to exclude my proposal?

(1) *Improper under state law*: If the proposal is not a proper subject for action by shareholders under the laws of the jurisdiction of the company's organization;

> **Note to paragraph (i)(1):** Depending on the subject matter, some proposals are not considered proper under state law if they would be binding on the company if approved by shareholders. In our experience, most proposals that are cast as recommendations or requests that the board of directors take specified action are proper under state law. [. . .] **(2)** *Violation of law:* If the proposal would, if implemented, cause the company to violate any state, federal, or foreign law to which it is subject; [. . .]

(3) *Violation of proxy rules:* If the proposal or supporting statement is contrary to any of the Commission's proxy rules, including § 240.14a–9, which prohibits materially false or misleading statements in proxy soliciting materials;

(4) *Personal grievance; special interest:* If the proposal relates to the redress of a personal claim or grievance against the company or any other person, or if it is designed to result in a benefit to you, or to further a personal interest, which is not shared by the other shareholders at large;

(5) *Relevance:* If the proposal relates to operations which account for less than 5 percent of the company's total assets at the end of its most recent fiscal year, and for less than 5 percent of its net earnings and gross sales for its most recent fiscal year, and is not otherwise significantly related to the company's business;

(6) *Absence of power/authority:* If the company would lack the power or authority to implement the proposal;

(7) *Management functions:* If the proposal deals with a matter relating to the company's ordinary business operations;

(8) *Director elections:* If the proposal:

(i) Would disqualify a nominee who is standing for election;

(ii) Would remove a director from office before his or her term expired;

(iii) Questions the competence, business judgment, or character of one or more nominees or directors;

(iv) Seeks to include a specific individual in the company's proxy materials for election to the board of directors; or

(v) Otherwise could affect the outcome of the upcoming election of directors.

(9) *Conflicts with company's proposal:* If the proposal directly conflicts with one of the company's own proposals to be submitted to shareholders at the same meeting; [. . .]

(10) *Substantially implemented:* If the company has already substantially implemented the proposal; [. . .]

(11) *Duplication:* If the proposal substantially duplicates another proposal previously submitted to the company by another proponent that will be included in the company's proxy materials for the same meeting;

(12) *Resubmissions:* If the proposal addresses substantially the same subject matter as a proposal, or proposals, previously included in the company's proxy materials within the preceding five calendar years if the most recent vote occurred within the preceding three calendar years and the most recent vote was:

(i) Less than 5 percent of the votes cast if previously voted on once;

(ii) Less than 15 percent of the votes cast if previously voted on twice; or

(iii) Less than 25 percent of the votes cast if previously voted on three or more times.

(13) *Specific amount of dividends:* If the proposal relates to specific amounts of cash or stock dividends.

(j) *Question 10:* What procedures must the company follow if it intends to exclude my proposal?

(1) If the company intends to exclude a proposal from its proxy materials, it must file its reasons with the Commission no later than 80 calendar days before it files its definitive proxy statement and form of proxy with the Commission. The company must simultaneously provide you with a copy of its submission. The Commission staff may permit the company to make its submission later than 80 days before the company files its definitive proxy statement and form of proxy, if the company demonstrates good cause for missing the deadline.

[. . .]

(m) *Question 13:* What can I do if the company includes in its proxy statement reasons why it believes shareholders should not vote in favor of my proposal, and I disagree with some of its statements?

(1) The company may elect to include in its proxy statement reasons why it believes shareholders should vote against your proposal. [. . .]

(2) However, if you believe that the company's opposition to your proposal contains materially false or misleading statements that may violate our anti-fraud rule, § 240.14a–9, you should promptly send to the Commission staff and the company a letter explaining the reasons for your view, along with a copy of the company's statements opposing your proposal. To the extent possible, your letter should include specific factual information demonstrating the inaccuracy of the company's claims. Time permitting, you may wish to try to work out your differences with the company by yourself before contacting the Commission staff.

(3) We require the company to send you a copy of its statements opposing your proposal before it sends its proxy materials, so that you may bring to our attention any materially false or misleading statements, under the following timeframes:

> **(i)** If our no-action response requires that you make revisions to your proposal or supporting statement as a condition to requiring the company to include it in its proxy materials, then the company must provide you with a copy of its opposition statements no later than 5 calendar days after the company receives a copy of your revised proposal; or

> **(ii)** In all other cases, the company must provide you with a copy of its opposition statements no later than 30 calendar days before its files definitive copies of its proxy statement and form of proxy under § 240.14a–6.

Trinity Wall Street v. Wal-Mart Stores, Inc.
792 F.3d 323 (3d Cir. 2015)

■ AMBRO, CIRCUIT JUDGE.

I.   Introduction

"[T]he secret of successful retailing is to give your customers what they want." Sam Walton. This case involves one shareholder's attempt to affect how Wal-Mart goes about doing that.

Appellant Wal-Mart Stores, Inc., the world's largest retailer, and one of its shareholders, Appellee Trinity Wall Street—an Episcopal parish headquartered in New York City that owns Wal-Mart stock—are locked in a heated dispute. It stems from Wal-Mart's rejection of Trinity's request to include its shareholder proposal in Wal-Mart's proxy materials for shareholder consideration.

Trinity's proposal, while linked to Wal-Mart's sale of high-capacity firearms (guns that can accept more than ten rounds of ammunition) at about one-third of its 3,000 stores, is nonetheless broad. It asks Wal-Mart's Board of Directors to develop and implement standards for management to use in deciding whether to sell a product that (1) "especially endangers public safety"; (2) "has the substantial potential to impair the reputation of Wal-Mart"; and/or (3) "would reasonably be considered by many offensive to the family and community values integral to the Company's promotion of its brand." Standing in Trinity's way, among other things, is a rule of the Securities and Exchange Commission, known as the "ordinary business" exclusion. ("Rule 14a–8(i)(7)"). As its name suggests, the rule lets a company omit a shareholder proposal from its proxy materials if the proposal relates to its ordinary business operations.

Wal-Mart obtained what is known as a "no-action letter" from the staff of the SEC's Division of Corporate Finance, thus signaling that there would be no recommendation of an enforcement action against the company if it omitted the proposal from its proxy materials. Trinity thereafter filed suit in federal court, seeking to enjoin Wal-Mart's exclusion of the proposal. The core of the dispute is whether the proposal was excludable under the ordinary business exclusion. Although the District Court initially denied Trinity's request, it handed the church a victory on the merits some seven months later by holding that, because the proposal concerned the company's Board (rather than its management) and focused principally on governance (rather than how Wal-Mart decides what to sell), it was outside Wal-Mart's ordinary business operations. Wal-Mart appeals, seeking a ruling that it could exclude Trinity's proposal from its 2015 proxy materials and did not err in excluding the proposal from its 2014 proxy materials.

II. Facts and Procedural History

Public companies publish and circulate a proxy statement in advance of their annual shareholders' meeting. The statement "includes information about items or initiatives on which the shareholders are asked to vote[.]" *Apache Corp. v. Chevedden*. It can also include shareholder proposals—a device that allows shareholders to ask for a vote on company matters. Predictably, companies don't easily surrender control of their proxy statement and often lean on an SEC rule to justify excluding a given shareholder proposal. But doing so can trigger a protracted legal battle that escalates from an exchange of views before the SEC to a federal lawsuit. This is one such case.

A. Trinity Objects to Wal-Mart's Sale of Assault Rifles.

Trinity [is] one of the wealthiest religious institutions in the United States, with a balance sheet of over $800 million in assets and real estate valued at approximately $3 billion. Its strong financial footing, according to Trinity, empowers it to "pursue a mission of good works beyond the reach of other religious institutions." Part of that mission is to reduce violence in society.

Alarmed by the spate of mass murders in America, in particular the shooting at Sandy Hook Elementary School in December 2012, Trinity resolved to use its investment portfolio to address the ease of access to rifles equipped with high-capacity magazines (the weapon of choice of the

Sandy Hook shooter and other mass murderers). Its principal focus was Wal-Mart.

During its review of Wal-Mart's merchandising practices, Trinity discovered what it perceived as a major inconsistency. Despite the retailer's stated mission to "make a difference on the big issues that matter to us all," it continued in some states to sell the Bushmaster AR-15 (a model of assault rifle). [. . .] [A]pparently due to safety concerns, it has stopped selling (1) handguns in the United States; (2) high-capacity magazines separate from a gun; and (3) guns through its website. Trinity attributes these perceived inconsistencies to the "lack of written policies and Board oversight concerning its approach to products that could have momentous consequences for both society and corporate reputation and brand value[.]"

B. Trinity's Shareholder Proposal.

Trinity pressed Wal-Mart to explain its continued sale of the Bushmaster AR-15. Wal-Mart's response was as follows:

> There are many viewpoints on this topic and many in our country remain engaged in the conversations about the sale and regulation of certain firearms. In areas of the country where we sell firearms, we have a long standing commitment to do so safely and responsibly. [. . .]

Unmoved, Trinity drafted a shareholder proposal aimed at filling the governance gap it perceived. The proposal, which is the subject of this appeal, provides:

> Resolved:
>
> Stockholders request that the Board amend the Compensation, Nominating and Governance Committee charter . . . as follows:
>
> "Providing oversight concerning [and the public reporting of] the formulation and implementation of . . . policies and standards that determine whether or not the Company should sell a product that:
>
> 1)   especially endangers public safety and well-being;
>
> 2)   has the substantial potential to impair the reputation of the Company; and/or
>
> 3)   would reasonably be considered by many offensive to the family and community values integral to the Company's promotion of its brand."

The narrative part of the proposal makes clear it is intended to cover Wal-Mart's sale of certain firearms. [. . .]

The proposal also included a supporting statement asserting in relevant part that

> [t]he company respects family and community interests by choosing not to sell certain products such as music that depicts

violence or sex and high capacity magazines separately from a gun, but lacks policies and standards to ensure transparent and consistent merchandizing decisions across product categories. This results in the company's sale of products, such as guns equipped with high capacity magazines, that facilitate mass killings, even as it prohibits sales of passive products such as music that merely depict such violent rampages. [. . .]

While guns equipped with high capacity magazines are just one example of a product whose sale poses significant risks to the public and to the company's reputation and brand, their sale illustrates a lack of reasonable consistency that this proposal seeks to address through Board level oversight.

The purpose of the proposal [. . .] is to

allow[ ] the company to make a transparent choice considering both the business and ethical (community impact) aspects of the matter. Anti-violence concerns can be broadly considered, including for example the sale of video games glorifying violence, as well as other merchandising decisions that are inconsistent with the well-being of the community and/or Wal-Mart's brand value and desired reputation.

C. Wal-Mart Seeks a No-Action Letter from the SEC.

On January 30, 2014, Wal-Mart notified Trinity and the [SEC] of its belief that it could exclude the proposal from its 2014 proxy materials under Rule 14a–8(i)(7). Trinity predictably disagreed, stating that its proposal didn't "meddl[e] in ordinary course decision-making" but focused on "big picture oversight and supervision that is the responsibility of the Board." In support of that assertion, Trinity offered three reasons why its proposal was not excludable:

1. [It] addresses corporate governance through Board oversight of important merchandising policies and is substantially removed from particularized decision-making in the ordinary course of business;

2. [It] concerns the Company's standards for avoiding community harm while fostering public safety and corporate ethics and does not relate exclusively to any individual product; and

3. [It] raises substantial issues of public policy, namely a concern for the safety and welfare of the communities served by the Company's stores.

Trinity also touted the proposal as not dictating "the specifics of how that Board oversight will operate or how best to report publicly on the policies being followed by the Company and their implementation," not seeking to "determine what products should or should not be sold by the Company," allowing policy development "not by shareholders, but by management, using its knowledge and discretion," and addressing "the ethical responsibility of the Company to take account of public safety and well-being, and the related risks of damage to the Company's reputation and brand."

On March 20, 2014, the Commission's Corp. Fin. staff issued a "no-action" letter siding with Wal-Mart. It noted [. . .] "[p]roposals concerning the sale of particular products and services are generally excludable under [the rule]."* [. . .]

Because no-action letters are not binding—they reflect only informal views of the [SEC's] staff and are not decisions on the merits—Trinity's proposal still had life.

D.   Trinity Takes Its Fight to Federal Court: Round One

On April 1, 2014, and just 17 days before Wal-Mart's proxy materials were due at the printer, Trinity filed a declaratory judgment action against Wal-Mart in the District of Delaware. It sought a declaration that "Wal-Mart's decision to omit the proposal from [its] 2014 Proxy Materials violates Section 14(a) of the 1934 Act and Rule 14a–8." [. . .]

Viewing the proposal as one dealing "with guns on the shelves and not guns in society," the Court, in a ruling from the bench, held that the proposal related to an "ordinary business matter" and was thus excludable under Rule 14a–8(i)(7). *Id.* It explained that

> [. . .] While the specific proposal is crafted as one directed solely to policy and oversight and therefore arguably arises in the difficult and seemingly novel perhaps intersection between ordinary business . . . on the [one] hand [and corporate governance] on the other hand, ultimately I'm not persuaded that I'm likely to conclude at the end of the day on the merits that it therefore does not fall within the exception given the rule for ordinary business.

Id. (emphases omitted). [. . .]

E.   Round Two

Wal-Mart thereafter moved to dismiss both counts of Trinity's amended complaint. The District Court granted Wal-Mart's motion only in part. Most notably, [. . .] and in direct tension with its earlier decision, the

---

* EDS.—This is an excerpt from the SEC "No action letter": "There are two elements to consider with respect to this exclusion. First, the degree to which certain decisions are "fundamental to management's ability to run a company on a day-to-day basis." Second, the degree to which a proposal seeks to "micro-manage the company." The Proposal seeks neither to supplant management's day-to-day decision-making nor to micro-manage the Company. Instead, the Proposal focuses on corporate governance by requesting that the charter of a Board committee include a mandate to supervise the formulation and implementation, and public reporting of the formulation and implementation, of the interplay between the Company's general policies and standards that determine whether or not the Company should sell a product and the strategic considerations of endangering public safety and well-being, and the related risks of significant harm to the Company's reputation and brand. Implementation of the Proposal would not constitute meddling in ordinary course decision-making. It requests engagement on broad strategic considerations at the Board level." [. . .]

Court on summary judgment held that the proposal was *not* excludable under Rule 14a–8(i)(7).

With more time to deliberate, the Court concluded that, although the proposal "could (and almost certainly would) shape what products are sold by Wal-Mart," it is "best viewed as dealing with matters that are *not* related to Wal-Mart's ordinary business operations." Thus Rule 14(a)–8 could not block its inclusion in Wal-Mart's proxy materials. The Court fastened its holding to the view that the proposal wasn't a directive to management but to the Board to "oversee the development and effectuation of a Wal-Mart policy." In this way, "[a]ny direct impact of adoption of Trinity's proposal would be felt at the Board level; it would then be for [it] to determine what, if any, policy should be formulated and implemented." Stated differently, the day-to-day responsibility for implementing whatever policies the Board develops was outside the scope of the proposal.

In the alternative, the Court held that even if the proposal does tread on the core of Wal-Mart's business—the products it sells—it "nonetheless 'focuses on sufficiently significant social policy issues' " that "transcend[ ] the day-to-day business matters" of the company, making the proposal "appropriate for a shareholder vote." Among the policy issues the District Court noted are "the social and community effects of sales of high capacity firearms at the world's largest retailer and the impact this could have on Wal-Mart's reputation, particularly if such a product sold at Wal-Mart is misused and people are injured or killed as a result."

The Court also found helpful how "Trinity [. . .] carefully drafted its proposal . . . to not dictate what products should be sold or how the policies regarding sales of certain types of products should be formulated or implemented." It stressed the difference between Trinity's proposal and the generally excludable proposals that ask a company to report on its "policies and reporting obligations regarding possible toxic and hazardous products offered for sale."

Finally, the District Court addressed Wal-Mart's secondary argument that Trinity's proposal is excludable under Rule 14a–8(i)(3) for being "so inherently vague or indefinite that neither the stockholders voting on the proposal, nor the company in implementing the proposal (if adopted), would be able to determine with any reasonable certainty exactly what actions or measures the proposal requires." It acknowledged that "Wal-Mart is undoubtedly correct that the 'broad variety of products offered by [it] and the numerous customers, employees and communities around the world with whom [it] works' mean that 'there is no *single* set of 'family and community values' that would be readily identifiable as being 'integral to the company's promotion of its brand.' " But it doesn't "follow from this that shareholders voting on the proposal, or the Committee in implementing it (if approved), would be unable to determine with reasonable certainty what the Committee needs to do." "Instead, it merely illustrates . . . that the [p]roposal properly leaves the details of any policy formulation and implementation to the discretion of the Committee, showing once more that [it] does not dictate any particular outcome or micro-manage Wal-Mart's day-to-day business." Wal-Mart appeals from both of the Court's holdings on the merits.

III. Regulatory Background

[. . .]

C. Shareholder Proposals

[. . .] A shareholder can garner support [for their proposal] in one of two ways. It can "pay to issue a separate proxy statement, which must satisfy all the disclosure requirements applicable to management's proxy statement." *Apache Corp.* Or the shareholder can go the Rule 14a–8 route and have the company include its proposal (and a supporting statement) in the proxy materials at the company's expense.

D. Exclusion of Shareholder Proposals

[. . .] Rule 14a–8 restricts the company-subsidy to "shareholders who offer 'proper' proposals." Palmiter at 879. A "proper" proposal is one that doesn't fit within one of Rule 14a–8's exclusionary grounds—which are both substantive and procedural.

[. . .] If a company wants to invoke one of these grounds to exclude a proposal, the process is as follows. First, it must notify the shareholder in writing of the problem with the proposal within 14 days of receiving it and inform the shareholder that it has 14 days to respond. If the company finds the shareholder's response unpersuasive and still wants to exclude the proposal, it then must file with the SEC's Corp. Fin. staff the reasons why it believes the proposal is excludable no later than 80 days before the company files its proxy materials with the SEC. In this letter, the company may also ask the staff for a no-action letter to support the exclusion of a proposal. If the shareholder wants to respond, it can file a submission noting why exclusion would be improper.

The staff will respond in one of two ways: (1) with a no-action letter, specifying that the company may omit the shareholder proposal under the exclusion(s) it relied on; or (2) that it is "unable to concur" with the company. A shareholder dissatisfied with the staff's response can, as Trinity did here, pursue its rights against the company in federal court.

E. SEC Interpretive Releases on the "Ordinary Business" Exclusion

The ordinary business exclusion has been called the "most perplexing" of all the 14a–8 bars. This stems from the opaque term "ordinary business," which is neither self-defining nor consistent in its meaning across different corporate contexts. Neither the courts nor Congress have offered a corrective. Rather, and "[f]rom the beginning, Rule 14a–8 jurisprudence—both in quality and quantity—has rested almost exclusively with the [SEC] . . . ." Palmiter at 880. [. . .]

IV. Analysis

The principal issue we address is whether Trinity's proposal was excludable because it related to Wal-Mart's ordinary business operations. In doing so, we evaluate the District Court's primary and alternative holdings. To repeat, it held that Trinity's proposal doesn't meddle in the nuts-and-bolts of Wal-Mart's business because it was a directive to the Board (rather than management) to set standards to guide certain merchandising decisions. And in the alternative the proposal is not excludable because it implicates a significant social policy—the sale of high-capacity firearms by the world's largest retailer—that transcends Wal-Mart's ordinary business. In this case (and we agree with the Commission that our determination counsels a case-by-case inquiry) we conclude that the proposal is excludable under the ordinary business proviso and that the significant social policy intended by the proposal is here no exception to that exclusion.

A. Trinity's Proposal Relates to Wal-Mart's Ordinary Business Operations

We employ a two-part analysis to determine whether Trinity's proposal "deals with a matter relating to the company's ordinary business operations [.]" 17 C.F.R. § 240.14a–8(i)(7). Under the first step, we discern the "subject matter" of the proposal. Under the second, we ask whether that subject matter relates to Wal-Mart's ordinary business operations. If the answer to the second question is yes, Wal-Mart must still convince us that Trinity's proposal does not raise a significant policy issue that transcends the nuts and bolts of the retailer's business.

1. What is the subject matter of Trinity's proposal?

Beginning with the first step, we are mindful of the Commission's consistent nod to substance over form and its distaste for clever drafting. [. . .] Thus, even though Trinity's proposal asks for the development of a specific merchandising policy—and not a review, report or examination— we still ask whether the *subject matter* of the action it calls for is a matter of ordinary business.

Applying that principle, we part ways with the District Court. We perceive it put undue weight on the distinction between a directive to management and a request for Board action. In the District Court's view, if the proposal had directed management to arrange its product assortment in a certain way, it would have been excludable. But because it merely asked the *"Board* [to] oversee the development and effectuation of a Wal-Mart policy," it was not. The concern with this line of reasoning is that the SEC [has] rejected the proposed bright line whereby shareholder proposals involving "matters that would be handled by management personnel without referral to the board . . . generally would be excludable," but those involving "matters that would require action by the board would not be." Thus, though the District Court's rationale and holding are not implausible, we do not adopt them.

Distancing itself from the District Court's formal approach, Trinity argues that the subject matter of its proposal is the improvement of "corporate governance over strategic matters of community responsibility, reputation for good corporate citizenship, and brand reputation, none of which can be considered ordinary business," and the focus is on the "shortcomings in Wal-Mart's corporate governance and oversight over policy matters." We cannot agree. [. . .] Trinity's contention, like the District Court's analysis, relies "on how [the proposal] is framed and to whom, rather than [its] substance." Contrary to what Trinity would have us believe, the immediate consequence of the adoption of a proposal—here the improvement of corporate governance through the formulation and implementation of a merchandising policy— is not its subject matter. [. . .] For example, under Trinity's position, the subject matter of a proposal that calls for a report on how a restaurant chain's menu promotes sound dietary habits would be corporate governance as opposed to important matters involving the promotion of public health. [. . .] The subject matter of the proposal is instead its *ultimate* consequence—here a potential change in the way Wal-Mart decides which products to sell. Indeed, as even the District Court acknowledged, if the company were to adopt Trinity's proposal, then, whatever the nature of the forthcoming policy, it "could (and almost certainly would) shape what products are sold by Wal-Mart[.]"

[. . .] For us, the subject matter of Trinity's proposal is how Wal-Mart approaches merchandising decisions involving products that (1) especially endanger public-safety and well-being, (2) have the potential to impair the reputation of the Company, and/or (3) would reasonably be considered by many offensive to the family and community values integral to the company's promotion of the brand. A contrary holding— that the proposal's subject matter is "improved corporate governance"— would allow drafters to evade Rule 14a–8(i)(7)'s reach by styling their proposals as requesting board oversight or review. We decline to go in that direction.

2. Does Wal-Mart's approach to whether it sells particular products relate to its ordinary business operations?

Reaching the second step of the analysis, we ask whether the subject matter of Trinity's proposal relates to day-to-day matters of Wal-Mart's business. Wal-Mart says the answer is yes because, even though the proposal doesn't demand any specific changes to the make-up of its product offerings—a point on which Trinity hangs its hat [. . .]—it "seeks to have a [B]oard committee address policies that could (and almost certainly would) shape what products are sold by Wal-Mart." That is, Trinity's proposal is just a sidestep from "a shareholder referendum on how [Wal-Mart] selects its inventory." And thus its subject matter strikes at the core of Wal-Mart's business.

We agree. A retailer's approach to its product offerings is the bread and butter of its business. As *amicus* the National Association of

Manufacturers notes, "Product selection is a complicated task influenced by economic trends, data analytics, demographics, customer preferences, supply chain flexibility, shipping costs and lead-times, and a host of other factors best left to companies' management and boards of directors." Though a retailer's merchandising approach is not beyond shareholder comprehension, the particulars of that approach involve operational judgments that are ordinary-course matters.

Moreover, that the proposal doesn't direct management to stop selling a particular product or prescribe a matrix to follow is, we think, a straw man. A proposal need only *relate* to a company's ordinary business to be excludable. *Cf.* 17 C.F.R. § 240.14a–8(i)(7) (exclusion is proper where a proposal deals with a matter "*relating* to the company's ordinary business operations") (emphasis added). It need not dictate any particular outcome. To make the point even clearer, suppose that Trinity's proposal had merely asked Wal-Mart's Board to *reconsider* whether to continue selling a given product. Though the request doesn't dictate a particular outcome, we have no doubt it would be excludable [. . .] as the action sought relates to Wal-Mart's ordinary business operations. This is so even though it doesn't suggest any changes. The same is true here. In short, so long as the subject matter of the proposal *relates*—that is, bears on—a company's ordinary business operations, the proposal is excludable unless some other exception to the exclusion applies.

Failing all of this, Trinity retreats to friendlier territory. It contends that, even if the subject matter of its proposal concerns Wal-Mart's ordinary business operations, it focuses on a significant and transcendent social policy issue: Wal-Mart's approach to the risk that the sale of a product can cause "harm to [its] customers or its brand and reputation." We address that issue next.

B. Trinity's Proposal Does Not Focus on a Significant Policy Issue that Transcends Wal-Mart's Day-to-Day Business Operations.

As discussed above, there is a significant social policy exception to the default rule of excludability for proposals that relate to a company's ordinary business operations. For the SEC staff this means that when "a proposal's underlying subject matter transcends the day-to-day business matters of the company and raises policy issues so significant that it would be appropriate for a shareholder vote, the proposal generally will not be excludable under Rule 14a–8(i)(7)." SEC Staff Legal Bulletin No. 14E.

The difficulty in this case is divining the line between proposals that focus on sufficiently significant social policy issues that transcend a company's ordinary business (not excludable) from those that don't (excludable). Even the Commission admits that the social-policy exception "raise[s] difficult interpretive questions." No doubt that is because the calculus is complex. Yet we cannot sidestep what some may deem an unreckonable area. Thus we wade in.

We think the inquiry is again best split into two steps. The first is whether the proposal focuses on a significant policy (be it social or, as noted below, corporate). If it doesn't, the proposal fails to fit within the social-policy exception to Rule 14a–8(i)(7)'s exclusion. If it does, we reach the second step and ask whether the significant policy issue transcends the company's ordinary business operations.

1. Does Trinity's proposal raise a significant social policy issue?

We first turn to whether Trinity's proposal focuses on a "sufficiently significant" policy issue [. . .]. The District Court said yes because the proposal at its core dealt with "the social and community effects of sales of high capacity firearms at the world's largest retailer." However, even Trinity concedes its proposal "is not directed solely to Wal-Mart's sale of guns." Rather it asks Wal-Mart's Board to oversee merchandising decisions for *all* "products especially dangerous to reputation, brand value, or the community that a family retailer such as Wal-Mart should carefully consider whether or not to sell."

Wal-Mart, on the other hand, contends that neither the Commission nor its staff has ever countenanced "such a broad and nebulous concept of significant policy issue." We disagree. True enough, the Commission has adopted what can only be described as a "we-know-it-when-we-see-it" approach. Yet it is hard to counter that Trinity's proposal doesn't touch the bases of what are significant concerns in our society and corporations in that society. Thus we deem that its proposal raises a matter of sufficiently significant policy. [. . .]

2. Even if Trinity's proposal raises a significant policy issue, does that issue transcend Wal-Mart's ordinary business operations?

To repeat, where "a proposal's underlying subject matter transcends the day-to-day business matters of the company *and* raises policy issues so significant that it would be appropriate for a shareholder vote, the proposal generally will not be excludable under Rule 14a–8(i)(7)." What this means is that, to shield its proposal from the ordinary business exclusion, a shareholder must do more than focus its proposal on a significant policy issue; the subject matter of its proposal must "transcend" the company's ordinary business. The Commission used the latter term, we believe, to refer to a policy issue that is divorced from how a company approaches the nitty-gritty of its core business. Thus [. . .], we think the transcendence requirement plays a pivotal role in the social-policy exception calculus. Without it shareholders would be free to submit "proposals dealing with ordinary business matters yet cabined in social policy concern." *Apache Corp. v. New York City Emps.' Ret. Sys.*

For major retailers of myriad products, a policy issue is rarely transcendent if it treads on the meat of management's responsibility: crafting a product mix that satisfies consumer demand. This explains why the Commission's staff, almost as a matter of course, allows retailers to exclude proposals that "concern[] the sale of particular products and services." On the other hand, if a significant policy issue disengages from the core of a retailer's business (deciding whether to sell certain goods that customers want), it is more likely to transcend its daily business dealings.

To illustrate the distinction, a proposal that asks a supermarket chain to evaluate its sale of sugary sodas because of the effect on childhood obesity should be excludable because, although the proposal raises a significant social policy issue, the request is too entwined with the fundamentals of the daily activities of a supermarket running its business: deciding which food products will occupy its shelves. So too would a proposal that, out of concern for animal welfare, aims to limit which food items a grocer sells.

By contrast, a proposal raising the impropriety of a supermarket's discriminatory hiring or compensation practices generally is not excludable because, even though human resources management is a core business function, it is disengaged from the essence of a supermarket's business. The same goes for proposals asking for information on the environmental effect of constructing stores near environmentally sensitive sites.

With those principles in mind, we turn to Trinity's proposal. Trinity says it focuses on "*both* corporate policy and social policy"—specifically, the "transcendent policy issue of under what policies and standards and with what Board oversight Wal-Mart handles [] merchandising decisions" for products that are "especially dangerous to [the company's] reputation, brand value, or the community." "In an age of mass shootings, increased violence, and concerns about product safety," Trinity argues, "the [p]roposal goes to the heart of Wal-Mart's impact on and approach to social welfare as well as the risks such impact and approach may have to Wal-Mart's reputation and brand image and its community."

But is how a retailer weighs safety in deciding which products to sell too enmeshed with its day-to-day business? We think it is in this instance. As we noted before, the essence of a retailer's business is deciding what products to put on its shelves—decisions made daily that involve a careful balancing of financial, marketing, reputational, competitive and other factors. The emphasis management places on safety to the consumer or the community is fundamental to its role in managing the company in the best interests of its shareholders and cannot, "as a practical matter, be subject to direct shareholder oversight."

It is thus not surprising that the SEC's Corp. Fin. staff consistently allows retailers to omit proposals that address their product menu. For example, it has indicated that a proposal trying to stop a retailer from selling or promoting products that connote negative stereotypes is excludable. It has done the same for proposals aiming to restrict a retailer's promotion of products that pose a threat to public health, [. . .] as well as those proposals targeting a retailer's approach to product safety.

For further support of the view that a policy issue does not transcend a company's ordinary business operations where it targets day-to-day decision-making, we look to the difference in treatment of stop-selling proposals sent to retailers and those sent to pure-play manufacturers. A policy matter relating to a product is far more likely to transcend a company's ordinary business operations when the product is that of a manufacturer with a narrow line.

But the outcome changes where those same policy proposals are directed at retailers who sell thousands of products.

The reason for the difference, in our view, is that a manufacturer with a very narrow product focus—like a tobacco or gun manufacturer—exists principally to sell the product it manufactures. Its daily business deliberations do not involve whether to continue to sell the product to which it owes its reason for being. As such, a stop-selling proposal generally isn't excludable because it relates to the seller's very existence. Quite the contrary for retailers. They typically deal with thousands of products amid many options for each, precisely the sort of business decisions a retailer makes many times daily. Thus, and in contrast to the manufacturing context, a stop-selling proposal implicates a retailer's ordinary business operations and is in turn excludable. Although Trinity's proposal is not strictly a stop-selling proposal, it still targets the same basic business decision: how to weigh safety risks in the merchandising calculus.

Trinity's claim that its proposal raises a "significant" and "transcendent" *corporate* policy is likewise insufficient to fit that proposal within the social-policy exception to exclusion. The relevant question to us is whether Wal-Mart's consideration of the risk that certain products pose to its "economic success" and "reputation for good corporate citizenship" is enmeshed with the way it runs its business and the retailer-consumer interaction. We think the answer is yes. Decisions relating to what products Wal-Mart sells in its rural locations versus its urban sites will vary considerably, and these are quintessentially calls made by management. Wal-Mart serves different Americas with different values. Its customers in rural America want different products than its customers in cities, and that management decides how to deal with these differing desires is not an issue typical for its Board of Directors. Indeed, catering to "small-town America" is how Wal-Mart built its business. And whether to put emphasis on brand integrity and brand protection, or none at all, is naturally a decision shareholders as well as directors entrust management to make in the exercise of their experience and business judgment.

We also agree with Wal-Mart's contention (and seemingly the position of the SEC's Corp. Fin. staff) that a company can omit a shareholder proposal concerning its reputation or brand when what the proposal seeks is woven with the way the company conducts its business.

We thus hold that, even if Trinity's proposal raises sufficiently significant social and corporate policy issues, those policies do not transcend the ordinary business operations of Wal-Mart. For a policy issue here to transcend Wal-Mart's business operations, it must target something more than the choosing of one among tens of thousands of products it sells. Trinity's proposal fails that test and is properly excludable under Rule 14a–8(i)(7).

■ SHWARTZ, CIRCUIT JUDGE, with whom JUDGE VANASKIE joins as to Part III, concurring in the judgment.

[W]hile I agree with my colleagues that the proposal is excludable based on the ordinary business exclusion, I believe that the test that it has fashioned for determining when an exception to this exclusion applies may remove many company actions over which shareholders should have a say from shareholder oversight.

SEC Rule 14a–8 requires a public company to include a shareholder proposal "in its proxy statement . . . when [the company] holds an annual or special meeting of shareholders." The rule thus "affords shareholders access to management proxy solicitations," both "to sound out management views and to communicate with other shareholders on matters of major import." *Amalgamated Clothing & Textile Workers Union v. Wal-Mart Stores, Inc.* Such access, however, is not unfettered. In addition to eligibility and procedural requirements, SEC Rule 14a–8 is "limited by thirteen content-based exceptions," two of which Wal-Mart argues apply here: Rule 14a–8(i)(7) and Rule 14a–8(i)(3).

Rule 14a–8(i)(7) allows a company to exclude proposals that "deal [ ] with a matter relating to the company's ordinary business operations." The SEC has explained that the determination of whether a particular shareholder proposal implicates a company's ordinary business operations "rests on two central considerations": (1) whether the "subject matter" of the proposal involves "tasks . . . fundamental to management's ability to run a company on a day-to-day basis"; and (2) "the degree to which the proposal seeks to 'micro-manage' the company by probing too deeply into matters of a complex nature upon which shareholders . . . would not be in a position to make an informed judgment."

There is an exception to this exclusion. Specifically, proposals "relating to" ordinary business operations "but focusing on sufficiently significant social policy issues . . . generally would not be considered excludable," notwithstanding their relationship to ordinary business, "because the proposals would transcend the day-to-day business matters and raise policy issues so significant that it would be appropriate for a shareholder vote." The Majority would limit proposals invoking the "significant social policy exception" to only those concerning matters that are "disengaged from the essence of" a company's business. [. . .]

[. . .] [T]he Majority's test for the "significant social policy exception" to the ordinary business exclusion is inconsistent with the purpose of § 14 of the Securities Exchange Act of 1934 and Rule 14a–8. [. . .]

The Majority's test, insofar as it practically gives companies carte blanche to exclude any proposal raising social policy issues that are directly related to core business operations, undermines the principle of fair corporate suffrage animating Rule 14a–8: shareholders' "ability to exercise their right—some would say their duty—to control the important decisions which affect them in their capacity as . . . owners of [a] corporation." *Med. Comm. for Human Rights v. SEC*. Section 14(a) of the Exchange Act ensures that "[a] corporation is run for the benefit of its stockholders and not for that of its managers," *SEC v. Transamerica Corp.* and "Congress intended by its enactment of [§] 14 . . . to give true vitality to the concept of corporate democracy," *Med. Comm. for Human Rights*. Permitting shareholders to vote on important social issues, including those that may be closely related to a company's ordinary business, is consistent with these principles, and I would not interpret the ordinary business exclusion to prohibit it.

Lovenheim v. Iroquois Brands, Ltd.

618 F. Supp. 554 (D.D.C. 1985)

[. . .] Plaintiff Peter C. Lovenheim, [a shareholder of] [. . .] Iroquois Brands, Ltd. [. . .], seeks to bar Iroquois [. . .] from excluding from the proxy materials being sent to all shareholders [. . .] information concerning a proposed resolution [that he presented about] [. . .] the procedure used to force-feed geese for production of pate de foie gras in France,[2] [and] [. . .] imported by Iroquois. [. . .] [He] calls upon the Directors of Iroquois [. . .] to:

> form a committee to study the methods by which its French supplier produces pate de foie gras, and report to the shareholders its findings and opinions, based on expert consultation, on whether this production method causes undue distress, pain or suffering to the animals involved and, if so, whether further distribution of this product should be

---

[2] Pate de foie gras is made from the liver of geese. According to Mr. Lovenheim's affidavit, force-feeding is frequently used in order to expand the liver and thereby produce a larger quantity of pate. Mr. Lovenheim's affidavit also contains a description of the force-feeding process:

> Force-feeding usually begins when the geese are four months old. On some farms where feeding is mechanized, the bird's body and wings are placed in a metal brace and its neck is stretched. Through a funnel inserted 10–12 inches down the throat of the goose, a machine pumps up to 400 grams of corn-based mash into its stomach. An elastic band around the goose's throat prevents regurgitation. When feeding is manual, a handler uses a funnel and stick to force the mash down.

[. . .] Plaintiff contends that such force-feeding is a form of cruelty to animals. [. . .]. Plaintiff has offered no evidence that force-feeding is used by Iroquois[. . .]'s supplier in producing the pate imported by Iroquois[. . .]. However his proposal calls upon the committee he seeks to create to investigate this question.

discontinued until a more humane production method is developed. [. . .]

Mr. Lovenheim's right to compel Iroquois [. . .] to insert information concerning his proposal in the proxy materials turns on the applicability of section 14(a) of the Securities Exchange Act of 1934, [. . .], and the shareholder proposal rule promulgated by the Securities and Exchange Commission ("SEC"), Rule 14a–8. That rule states in pertinent part:

> If any security holder of an issuer notifies the issuer of his intention to present a proposal for action at a forthcoming meeting of the issuer's security holders, the issuer shall set forth the proposal in its proxy statement and identify it in its form of proxy and provide means by which security holders [presenting a proposal may present in the proxy statement a statement of not more than 200 words in support of the proposal].

Iroquois [. . .] has refused to allow information concerning Mr. Lovenheim's proposal to be included in proxy materials [. . .] rel[ying] on [. . .] exception [. . .] Rule 14a–8(c)(5), [which] [. . .] provides that an issuer of securities "may omit a proposal and any statement in support thereof" from its proxy statement and form of proxy:

> if the proposal relates to operations which account for less than 5 percent of the issuer's total assets at the end of its most recent fiscal year, and for less than 5 percent of its net earnings and gross sales for its most recent fiscal year, and is not otherwise significantly related to the issuer's business. [. . .]

Applicability of Rule 14a–8(c)(5) Exception

[. . .] [T]he likelihood of plaintiff's prevailing in this litigation turns primarily on the applicability to plaintiff's proposal of the exception to the shareholder proposal rule contained in Rule 14a–8(c)(5).

Iroquois['s] reliance on the argument that this exception applies is based on the following information contained in the affidavit of its president: Iroquois[. . .] has annual revenues of $141 million with $6 million in annual profits and $78 million in assets. In contrast, its pate de foie gras sales were just $79,000 last year, representing a net loss on pate sales of $3,121. Iroquois [. . .] has only $34,000 in assets related to pate. Thus none of the company's net earnings and less than .05 percent of its assets are implicated by plaintiff's proposal. [. . .] These levels are obviously far below the five percent threshold set forth in the first portion of the exception claimed by Iroquois [. . .].

Plaintiff does not contest that his proposed resolution relates to a matter of little economic significance to Iroquois [. . .]. Nevertheless he contends that the Rule 14a–8(c)(5) exception is not applicable as it cannot be said that his proposal "is not otherwise significantly related to the issuer's business" as is required by the final portion of that exception. In other words, plaintiff's argument that Rule 14a–8 does not permit omission of his proposal rests on the assertion that the rule and statute on which it is based do not permit omission merely because a proposal is not economically significant where a proposal has "ethical or social significance."[8]

Iroquois[. . .] challenges plaintiff's view that ethical and social proposals cannot be excluded even if they do not meet the economic or five percent test. Instead, Iroquois [. . .] views the exception solely in economic terms as permitting omission of any proposals relating to a de minimis share of assets and profits. Iroquois [. . .] asserts that since corporations are economic entities, only an economic test is appropriate.

The Court would note that the applicability of the Rule 14a–8(c)(5) exception to Mr. Lovenheim's proposal represents a close question given the lack of clarity in the exception itself. In effect, plaintiff relies on the word "otherwise," suggesting that it indicates the drafters of the rule intended that other noneconomic tests of significance be used. Iroquois[. . .] relies on the fact that the rule examines other significance in relation to the issuer's business. Because of the apparent ambiguity of the rule, the Court considers the history of the shareholder proposal rule in determining the proper interpretation of the most recent version of that rule.

Prior to 1983, paragraph 14a–8(c)(5) excluded proposals "not significantly related to the issuer's business" but did not contain an objective economic significance test such as the five percent of sales, assets, and earnings specified in the first part of the current version. Although a series of SEC decisions through 1976 allowing issuers to exclude proposals challenging compliance with the Arab economic boycott of Israel allowed exclusion if the issuer did less than one percent of their business with Arab countries or Israel, the Commission stated later in 1976 that it did "not believe that subparagraph (c)(5) should be hinged solely on the economic relativity of a proposal." [. . .] Thus the Commission required inclusion "in many situations in which the related business comprised less than one percent" of the company's revenues, profits or assets "where the proposal has raised *policy questions* important enough to be considered 'significantly related' to the issuer's business."

As indicated above, the 1983 revision adopted the five percent test of economic significance in an effort to create a more objective standard. Nevertheless, in adopting this standard, the Commission stated that

---

[8]   The assertion that the proposal is significant in an ethical and social sense relies on plaintiff's argument that "the very availability of a market for products that may be obtained through the inhumane force-feeding of geese cannot help but contribute to the continuation of such treatment." Plaintiff's brief characterizes the humane treatment of animals as among the foundations of western culture and cites in support of this view the Seven Laws of Noah, an animal protection statute enacted by the Massachusetts Bay Colony in 1641, numerous federal statutes enacted since 1877, and animal protection laws existing in all fifty states and the District of Columbia. An additional indication of the significance of plaintiff's proposal is the support of such leading organizations in the field of animal care as the American Society for the Prevention of Cruelty to Animals and The Humane Society of the United States for measures aimed at discontinuing use of force-feeding. [. . .]

proposals will be includable notwithstanding their "failure to reach the specified economic thresholds if a significant relationship to the issuer's business is demonstrated on the face of the resolution or supporting statement." [. . .] Thus it seems clear based on the history of the rule that "the meaning of 'significantly related' is not *limited* to economic significance." [. . .]

The only decision in this Circuit cited by the parties relating to the scope of section 14 and the shareholder proposal rule is *Medical Committee for Human Rights v. SEC*. That case concerned an effort by shareholders of Dow Chemical Company to advise other shareholders of their proposal directed at prohibiting Dow's production of napalm. Dow had relied on the counterpart of the 14a–8(c) (5) exemption then in effect to exclude the proposal from proxy materials and the SEC accepted Dow's position without elaborating on its basis for doing so. In remanding the matter back to the SEC [. . .], the Court noted what it termed "substantial questions" as to whether an interpretation of the shareholder proposal rule "which permitted omission of [a] proposal as one motivated primarily by *general* political or social concerns would conflict with the congressional intent underlying section 14(a) of the [Exchange] Act."

Iroquois [. . .] attempts to distinguish *Medical Committee for Human Rights* as a case where a company sought to exclude a proposal that, unlike Mr. Lovenheim's proposal, was economically significant merely because the motivation of the proponents was political. The argument is not without appeal given the fact that the *Medical Committee* Court was confronted with a regulation that contained no reference to economic significance. [. . .] Yet the *Medical Committee* decision contains language suggesting that the Court assumed napalm was not economically significant to Dow:

> The management of Dow Chemical Company is repeatedly quoted in sources which include the company's own publications as proclaiming that the decision to continue manufacturing and marketing napalm was made not *because* of business considerations, but *in spite* of them; that management in essence decided to pursue a course of activity which generated little profit for the shareholders . . . . [. . .]

[T]he Court therefore holds that in light of the ethical and social significance of plaintiff's proposal and the fact that it implicates significant levels of sales, plaintiff has shown a likelihood of prevailing on the merits with regard to the issue of whether his proposal is "otherwise significantly related" to Iroquois/Delaware's business. [. . .]

IV. CONCLUSION

For the reasons discussed above, the Court concludes that plaintiff's motion for preliminary injunction should be granted.

E. SHAREHOLDER INSPECTION RIGHTS

Delaware General Corporation Law
Section 220. Inspection of books and records.

[. . .] (b) Any stockholder, in person or by attorney or other agent, shall, upon written demand under oath stating the purpose thereof, have the right during the usual hours for business to inspect for any proper purpose, and to make copies and extracts from:

(1) The corporation's stock ledger, a list of its stockholders, and its other books and records; and

(2) A subsidiary's books and records, to the extent that:

a. The corporation has actual possession and control of such records of such subsidiary; or

b. The corporation could obtain such records through the exercise of control over such subsidiary, provided that as of the date of the making of the demand:

1. The stockholder inspection of such books and records of the subsidiary would not constitute a breach of an agreement between the corporation or the subsidiary and a person or persons not affiliated with the corporation; and

2. The subsidiary would not have the right under the law applicable to it to deny the corporation access to such books and records upon demand by the corporation.

In every instance where the stockholder is other than a record holder of stock in a stock corporation, or a member of a nonstock corporation, the demand under oath shall state the person's status as a stockholder, be accompanied by documentary evidence of beneficial ownership of the stock, and state that such documentary evidence is a true and correct copy of what it purports to be. A proper purpose shall mean a purpose reasonably related to such person's interest as a stockholder. [. . .]

(c) If the corporation, or an officer or agent thereof, refuses to permit an inspection sought by a stockholder or attorney or other agent acting for the stockholder pursuant to subsection (b) of this section or does not reply to the demand within 5 business days after the demand has been made, the stockholder may apply to the Court of Chancery for an order to compel such inspection. The Court of Chancery is hereby vested with exclusive jurisdiction to determine whether or not the person seeking inspection is entitled to the inspection sought. The Court may summarily order the corporation to permit the stockholder to inspect the corporation's stock ledger, an existing list of stockholders, and its other books and records, and to make copies or extracts therefrom; or the Court may order the corporation to furnish to the stockholder a list of its stockholders as of a specific date on condition that the stockholder first pay to the corporation the reasonable cost of obtaining and furnishing such list and on such other conditions as the Court deems appropriate. Where the stockholder seeks to inspect the corporation's books and records, other than its stock ledger or list of stockholders, such stockholder shall first establish that:

(1) Such stockholder is a stockholder;

(2) Such stockholder has complied with this section respecting the form and manner of making demand for inspection of such documents; and

(3) The inspection such stockholder seeks is for a proper purpose.

Where the stockholder seeks to inspect the corporation's stock ledger or list of stockholders and establishes that such stockholder is a stockholder and has complied with this section respecting the form and manner of making demand for inspection of such documents, the burden of proof shall be upon the corporation to establish that the inspection such stockholder seeks is for an improper purpose. The Court may, in its discretion, prescribe any limitations or conditions with reference to the inspection, or award such other or further relief as the Court may deem just and proper. The Court may order books, documents and records, pertinent extracts therefrom, or duly authenticated copies thereof, to be brought within this State and kept in this State upon such terms and conditions as the order may prescribe.

(d) Any director shall have the right to examine the corporation's stock ledger, a list of its stockholders and its other books and records for a purpose reasonably related to the director's position as a director. The Court of Chancery is hereby vested with the exclusive jurisdiction to determine whether a director is entitled to the inspection sought. The Court may summarily order the corporation to permit the director to inspect any and all books and records, the stock ledger and the list of stockholders and to make copies or extracts therefrom. The burden of proof shall be upon the corporation to establish that the inspection such director seeks is for an improper purpose. The Court may, in its discretion, prescribe any limitations or conditions with reference to the inspection, or award such other and further relief as the Court may deem just and proper.

AmerisourceBergen Corporation v. Lebanon County Employees' Retirement Fund

243 A.3d 417 (Del. 2020)

■ TRAYNOR, JUSTICE:

I. BACKGROUND

During the ongoing opioid epidemic, AmerisourceBergen, one of the country's largest opioid distributors, has been investigated by numerous law-enforcement and government agencies. [. . .]

A. Factual Background

Federal regulations require opioid distributors to maintain effective controls and reporting systems to ensure that drug shipments stay within "legitimate medical, scientific, and industrial channels." In 2007, the federal Drug Enforcement Administration (the "DEA") suspended AmerisourceBergen's license at its Orlando, Florida distribution center, concluding that AmerisourceBergen had not maintained effective controls there in part because it failed to flag rogue pharmacies [. . .].

AmerisourceBergen settled with the DEA and agreed to implement and maintain at all its facilities a "compliance program designed to detect and prevent diversion of controlled substances." Following the settlement, AmerisourceBergen continued to work with the DEA to implement an anti-diversion program and to develop an industry standard for opioid-distribution compliance.

Despite these efforts, since 2012 AmerisourceBergen has been the subject of several governmental reports, investigations, and state and federal lawsuits. Federal prosecutors in ten states and the attorneys general of forty-one states have either subpoenaed the company's documents or named it as a defendant in litigation. Two congressional investigations found that AmerisourceBergen failed to address suspicious order monitoring in violation of federal law.

In 2019, the New York Attorney General filed a complaint, naming AmerisourceBergen, among other opioid distributors and manufacturers, as a defendant [alleging] that the AmerisourceBergen's policies failed to properly identify suspicious orders and that the Company " 'ha[d] consistently stood out as compared to its major competitors [because of] its unwillingness to identify suspicious orders, even among customers that regularly exceeded their thresholds and presented multiple red flags of diversion.' "

AmerisourceBergen is also a defendant in multi-district litigation in the United States District Court for the Northern District of Ohio [where plaintiffs] allege that AmerisourceBergen has failed to implement and maintain effective systems to flag suspicious orders [. . .]. In an effort to settle the ongoing Multidistrict Litigation, the Company and two other opioid distributors, offered to pay $10 billion. The regulators rejected the offer and demanded $45 billion.

To date, AmerisourceBergen "has spent more than $1 billion in connection with opioid-related lawsuits and investigations." Analysts estimate that AmerisourceBergen could spend up to $100 billion to reach a global settlement.

C. Procedural History

In May 2019, amidst this "flood of government investigations and lawsuits relating to AmerisourceBergen's opioid practices," the Plaintiffs served a Section 220 demand on AmerisourceBergen, requesting inspection of thirteen categories of books and records (the "Demand"). The Plaintiffs requested Board Materials from May 1, 2010 to date concerning certain settlements, acquisitions, investigations, and other events related to AmerisourceBergen's operations and its potential involvement in the opioid crisis.

The Demand listed four investigatory purposes:

> (i) to investigate possible breaches of fiduciary duty, mismanagement, and other violations of law by members of the Company's Board of Directors and management ... in connection with [the Company]'s distribution of prescription opioid medications;

> (ii) to consider any remedies to be sought in respect of the aforementioned conduct;

> (iii) to evaluate the independence and disinterestedness of the members of the Board; and

> (iv) to use information obtained through inspection of the Company's books and records to evaluate possible litigation or other corrective measures with respect to some or all of these matters.

AmerisourceBergen rejected the Demand in its entirety, claiming that the Demand did not state a proper purpose and that, even if the Plaintiffs' purpose were proper, the scope of the inspection was overbroad. In July 2019, the Plaintiffs filed this action in the Court of Chancery, seeking to compel production of the requested documents. [. . .]

In its memorandum opinion following trial on a paper record, the Court of Chancery found that the Plaintiffs had demonstrated a proper purpose sufficient to warrant the inspection of Formal Board Materials. In reaching this conclusion, the Court of Chancery made several subsidiary findings. The court found that the Plaintiffs had established a credible basis, through "strong circumstantial evidence," to suspect that "AmerisourceBergen's situation did not result from any ordinary business decision that, in hindsight, simply turned out poorly," but instead may have been the product of the Company's violation of positive law. The Plaintiffs had not, according to the court, "approached AmerisourceBergen as part of an indiscriminate fishing expedition or out of mere curiosity." The court also rejected AmerisourceBergen's contention that the Plaintiffs' sole purpose in seeking the inspection was to investigate a potential *Caremark*[18] claim, noting that the Plaintiffs' demand "reserved the ability to consider all courses of action that their investigation might warrant pursuing." And finally, the court rejected AmerisourceBergen's contention that the Plaintiffs were required to show the wrongdoing they sought to investigate was "actionable" wrongdoing, but that, even if they were, it would be premature to consider the merits-based defenses advanced by AmerisourceBergen.

Next, because the Plaintiffs had satisfied their burden of proof under Section 220, the court concluded that the Plaintiffs were entitled to Formal Board Materials relating to most of the events listed in the Demand. [. . .]

On appeal, AmerisourceBergen challenges the Court of Chancery's opinion on [two] grounds. First, AmerisourceBergen argues that the Court of Chancery erroneously found that the Plaintiffs had stated a proper purpose and need not "identify the objectives of the investigation." Second, the Company asserts that the court erroneously determined that the Plaintiffs had established a credible basis from which the court could suspect wrongdoing and that such wrongdoing need not be *actionable*. [. . .]

II. STANDARD OF REVIEW

We review *de novo* whether a stockholder's stated purpose for demanding inspection under Section 220 is a "proper purpose." When a stockholder seeks to investigate corporate wrongdoing, the Court of Chancery's determination that a credible basis to infer wrongdoing exists is a mixed finding of fact and law, to which we afford considerable deference. This Court reviews the scope of relief ordered in a books and records action for abuse of discretion.

III. ANALYSIS

A stockholder's right to inspect a corporation's books and records was "recognized at common law because '[a]s a matter of self-protection, the stockholder was entitled to know how his agents were conducting the affairs of the corporation of which he or she was a part owner.' " Section 220(c) provides that stockholders who seek to inspect a corporation's books and records must establish that "(1) [s]uch stockholder is a stockholder; (2) [s]uch stockholder has complied with [Section 220] respecting the form and manner of making demand for inspection of such documents; and (3) [t]he inspection such stockholder seeks is for a proper purpose." A proper purpose is a "purpose reasonably related to such person's interest as a stockholder."

---

[18] *In re Caremark Int'l Inc. Derivative Litig.*, 698 A.2d 959 (Del. Ch. 1996); *see Stone ex rel. AmSouth Bancorporation v. Ritter*, 911 A.2d 362, 370 (Del. 2006) (holding that Caremark imposes director oversight liability where: "(a) the directors utterly failed to implement any reporting or information system or controls; *or* (b) having implemented such a system or controls, consciously failed to monitor or oversee its operations thus disabling themselves from being informed of risks or problems requiring their attention") (emphasis in original).

Myriad proper purposes have been accepted under Delaware law including: "the determination of the value of one's equity holdings, evaluating an offer to purchase shares, inquiring into the independence of directors, investigation of a director's suitability for office, testing the propriety of the company's public disclosures, investigation of corporate waste, and investigation of possible mismanagement or self-dealing." "[M]ere disagreement with a business decision" will fail to establish a proper purpose. Once a stockholder shows that its primary purpose is reasonably related to its interest as a stockholder, the fact that it may also have "a further or secondary purpose . . . is irrelevant."

For over a quarter-century, this Court has repeatedly encouraged stockholders suspicious of a corporation's management or operations to exercise this right to obtain the information necessary to meet the particularization requirements that are applicable in derivative litigation. Section 220 has thus become a widely used tool for stockholders seeking information about corporate wrongdoing, mismanagement, or waste. This development, in turn, sparked "[t]he evolution of [our] jurisprudence in section 220 actions[,] reflect[ing] judicial efforts to maintain a proper balance between the rights of shareholders to obtain information based upon credible allegations of corporation mismanagement and the rights of directors to manage the business of the corporation without undue interference from stockholders."

To avoid "indiscriminate fishing expedition[s]," a bare allegation of possible waste, mismanagement, or breach of fiduciary duty, without more, will not entitle a stockholder to a Section 220 inspection. Rather, a stockholder seeking to investigate wrongdoing must show, by a preponderance of the evidence, a credible basis from which the court can infer there is "possible mismanagement as would warrant further investigation." Although not an insubstantial threshold, the credible basis standard is the "lowest possible burden of proof." A stockholder need not show that corporate wrongdoing or mismanagement has occurred in fact, but rather the "threshold may be satisfied by a credible showing, through documents, logic, testimony or otherwise, that there are legitimate issues of wrongdoing." Once a stockholder has established a proper purpose, the stockholder will be entitled only to the "books and records that are necessary and essential to accomplish the stated, proper purpose."

A. The Plaintiffs' Proper Purpose

In the Court of Chancery, AmerisourceBergen argued that the Plaintiffs failed to demonstrate a credible basis to investigate a *Caremark* claim, which, according to the Company, was "the only purported purpose of the Demand." The court disagreed with AmerisourceBergen's characterization of the Demand, noting that the Demand "signaled that [the Plaintiffs] are not solely interested in filing a derivative lawsuit . . . [and] are open to considering other possible remedies, corrective measures, and methods of addressing the wrongdoing that they believe has occurred." The court further understood AmerisourceBergen to "maintain[ ] that if a stockholder wants to investigate wrongdoing and use the resulting documents to achieve an end other than filing litigation, the stockholder must say so in the demand."

After a thoughtful analysis of Section 220's proper-purpose requirement, which included a review of a line of authority in the Court of Chancery requiring stockholders who want to investigate corporate wrongdoing "to state up-front what they plan[ ] to do with the fruits of the inspection," the court concluded that, although "the Demand did not recite ends to which the [P]laintiff[s] might put the books and records[,] . . . they were not required to do so. Instead the [P]laintiffs reserved the ability to consider all possible courses of action that their investigation might warrant pursuing." We, too, reject AmerisourceBergen's characterization of the Plaintiffs' Demand as solely limited to pursuing derivative litigation. And we agree with the Court of Chancery's observation that a stockholder is not required to state the objectives of his investigation.

AmerisourceBergen acknowledges that investigating corporate wrongdoing is a widely recognized proper purpose under Section 220. Yet it claims that "whether that purpose in a specific case is reasonably related to the stockholder's interest as a stockholder cannot be ascertained in a vacuum." According to AmerisourceBergen, "[t]he objectives of the investigation will dictate whether the purpose is in fact a proper purpose." And AmerisourceBergen contends that, unless those objectives are explicitly disclosed in the stockholder's demand, "the corporation [will be] impaired, if not entirely thwarted in its efforts to evaluate the propriety of the demand's purpose" without resorting to litigation.

AmerisourceBergen concedes that this Court has not considered whether a stockholder must state in its demand the objectives of an investigation of corporate wrongdoing. Therefore, the Company relies heavily on *Northwest Industries, Inc. v. B.F. Goodrich Co.* ("*Northwest Industries*"), a case involving a stockholder's request to inspect the company's list of stockholders. The majority in *Northwest Industries* held that, in that context, a demand that contained "a mere statement" that the purpose of the inspection was "to communicate with other stockholders" was inadequate. In the majority's view:

> [Section] 220 required Goodrich to state in its demand the substance of its intended communication sufficiently to enable Northwest, and the courts if necessary, to determine whether there was a reasonable relationship between its purpose, i.e., the intended communication, and Goodrich's interest as a stockholder of Northwest.

But a request to inspect a list of stockholders is fundamentally different than a request to inspect books and records in furtherance of an investigation of corporate wrongdoing. A corporation cannot discern whether the inspection of its list of stockholders for the purpose of communicating with other stockholders is related to the stockholder's interest as a stockholder without a disclosure of the substance of the intended communication. By contrast, corporate wrongdoing is, as the Court of Chancery noted, in and of itself "a legitimate matter of concern that is reasonably related to [a stockholder's] interest[ ] as [a] stockholder[ ]."

We have recognized that, when a stockholder investigates meritorious allegations of possible mismanagement, waste, or wrongdoing, it serves the interests of all stockholders "and should increase stockholder return." It follows that, under such circumstances, the stockholder's purpose is proper. Of course, a mere statement of suspicion is inadequate. If the stockholder cannot present a credible basis from which the court can infer wrongdoing or mismanagement, it is likely that the stockholder's demand is an "indiscriminate fishing expedition." But where a stockholder meets this low burden of proof from which possible wrongdoing or mismanagement can be inferred, a stockholder's purpose will be deemed proper under Delaware law. [. . .]

D. The Relevance of Actionability

The previous argument—that the Plaintiffs' sole purpose in seeking to inspect AmerisourceBergen's books and records is to pursue a *Caremark* claim and the court should not consider other potential uses of the documents—would not, standing alone, suffice to defeat the Plaintiffs' inspection rights. After all, AmerisourceBergen concedes that the evaluation of litigation options is an appropriate objective of an investigative Section 220 demand. As the Court of Chancery recognized, however, AmerisourceBergen's attempt to cabin the Plaintiffs' use of its books and records to their pursuit of a *Caremark* claim, merely set the stage for AmerisourceBergen's "launching [of] merits-based strikes on the lawsuit that AmerisourceBergen expects the Plaintiffs to file someday." Such strikes are justified, AmerisourceBergen contends, because the Plaintiffs must establish that the wrongdoing they seek to investigate is *actionable* wrongdoing. And, according to AmerisourceBergen, the Plaintiffs' claims are not actionable because they are legally barred by a Section 102(b)(7) exculpatory provision in its certificate of incorporation and by laches.

The Court of Chancery rejected AmerisourceBergen's argument on three grounds. First, the court found that the argument failed for the "threshold reason . . . [that] [t]he [P]laintiffs are not seeking the books and records for the sole purpose of investigating a potential *Caremark* claim . . . [and thus] can use the fruits of their investigation for other purposes." Second, the court held that "to obtain books and records, a stockholder does not have to introduce evidence from which a court could infer the existence of an actionable claim." Third, the court found that, in any event, AmerisourceBergen's Section 102(b)(7) and laches defenses were unavailing. As to the Section 102(b)(7) defense, the court found that "[t]he issues that the [P]laintiffs wish to investigate could well lead to non-exculpated claims." And as to the laches defense, it was not clear to the court that the Plaintiffs' potential derivative claims were time-barred, given the possibility that the doctrines of fraudulent concealment and equitable tolling could apply. Our agreement with the Court of Chancery on any one of these three grounds would be sufficient to lay AmerisourceBergen's argument to rest; we happen to agree on all three.

As mentioned, the *sine qua non* of AmerisourceBergen's contention that the Plaintiffs must establish a credible basis from which actionable wrongdoing can be inferred is that the Plaintiffs "are only seeking to investigate a *Caremark* claim." To support this claim, AmerisourceBergen contends that the Demand, as well as the Plaintiffs' complaint and pre-trial briefing, is "littered with assertions" that the company's board of directors "ignored red flags"—language that suggests an investigation of a *Caremark* failed-oversight claim. AmerisourceBergen asserts that the Plaintiffs' engagement letters with counsel "unquestionably establish" that the Plaintiffs are only seeking books and records in contemplation of litigation.

AmerisourceBergen's assertions go too far. A stockholder may state more than one purpose for inspection and use the information obtained for more than one purpose. As already mentioned, a stockholder may use the information supporting a claim of mismanagement obtained through an inspection for purposes other than bringing litigation. Although AmerisourceBergen correctly identifies several references to potential litigation in the Demand, the Demand also states that the information sought will be used "to evaluate ... other corrective measures with respect to all or some of these matters." The Demand also contemplates a "[p]ossible course[ ] of conduct [to] include making a demand on the Company's Board of Directors to take action." In our view, the Court of Chancery's determination that the Plaintiffs contemplated purposes *other than* litigation is supported by a fair reading of the Demand. We need go no further than that to dispose of AmerisourceBergen's "actionability" argument. We nevertheless take this opportunity to dispel the notion that a stockholder who demonstrates a credible basis from which the court can infer wrongdoing or mismanagement must demonstrate that the wrongdoing or mismanagement is actionable.

As noted above, under Section 220, a stockholder who wishes to investigate corporate wrongdoing must present a credible basis from which the court can infer that wrongdoing may have occurred. It bears repeating that this test "reflects judicial efforts to maintain a proper balance between the rights of shareholders to obtain information based upon credible allegations of corporation mismanagement and the rights of directors to manage the business of the corporation without undue interference from stockholders." Having struck that balance, this Court has not required stockholders to prove that the wrongdoing they seek to investigate is actionable. To the contrary, we have stated that a stockholder is not required to prove that wrongdoing occurred, only that there is "possible mismanagement that would warrant further investigation."

It is true that the Court of Chancery has disallowed inspections for the purpose of investigating mismanagement and wrongdoing when the stockholder's sole objective is to pursue litigation that faces an insurmountable procedural obstacle. [. . .] For example, in *Polygon Global Opportunities Master Fund v. West Corp.* ("*Polygon*"), where the stockholder lacked standing to bring the anticipated claim, the Court of Chancery denied inspection even in the face of a credible showing of wrongdoing. Likewise, the court has denied inspection by stockholders whose sole purpose is to evaluate litigation options when the claims under consideration are time barred, as was the case in *Graulich v. Dell, Inc.* ("*Graulich*"), or otherwise precluded, as in *West Coast Management.* It should be stressed that, in each of these instances, the sole reason for the stockholder's demand was to pursue litigation and the obstacle that blocked the stockholder's path was the product of a determinate procedural history and based on undisputed facts. [. . .] Given the obvious futility of the litigation the stockholder claims to have in mind, the investigation can only be seen as assuaging the stockholder's idle curiosity or a fishing expedition.

Yet AmerisourceBergen points us to two more recent Court of Chancery opinions, one of which we summarily affirmed, that considered merits-based defenses, not to the Section 220 action before the court but, to the anticipated plenary action that might follow. In *Southeastern Pennsylvania Transportation Authority v. AbbVie, Inc.* ("*AbbVie*"), the Section 220 plaintiffs sought to inspect the company's books and records to investigate possible breaches of fiduciary duties and mismanagement

[. . .] AbbVie challenged the propriety of this purpose on the grounds that AbbVie's certificate of incorporation exculpated its directors from liability for a breach of duty of care in accordance with Section 102(b)(7) of the DGCL. Therefore, according to AbbVie, the stockholders were without a remedy in a derivative action against the directors for a breach of the duty of care, hence, "investigating any such breach [was] futile and not a proper purpose for a Section 220 demand."

In addressing AbbVie's defense, the Court of Chancery acknowledged that it had "not squarely addressed the issue of whether, when a stockholder seeks to investigate corporate wrongdoing *solely* for the purpose of evaluating whether to bring a derivative action, the 'proper purpose' requirement under Section 220 is limited to investigating non-exculpated corporate wrongdoing."

[. . .] [T]he court concluded that:

> [. . .] the proper purpose requirement under that statute requires that, if a stockholder seeks inspection solely to evaluate whether to bring derivative litigation, the corporate wrongdoing

which he seeks to investigate must necessarily be justiciable. Because a Section 102(b)(7) exculpatory provision serves as a bar to stockholders recovering for certain director liability in litigation, a stockholder seeking to use Section 220 to investigate corporate wrongdoing solely to evaluate whether to bring derivative litigation has stated a proper purpose only insofar as the investigation targets non-exculpated corporate wrongdoing. Here, that means that [the stockholders'] stated purpose to investigate whether wrongdoing is proper only to investigate whether AbbVie's directors breached their fiduciary duty of loyalty.

To skirt the exculpatory provision, the stockholders alleged that the AbbVie directors breached the duty of loyalty by acting in bad faith or by committing waste. The court found that the stockholders could not clear either of these hurdles and therefore denied the stockholders' demand for inspection, and the stockholders appealed to this Court. [. . .]

Soon after we affirmed *AbbVie*, the Court of Chancery decided *Beatrice Corwin Living Irrevocable Trust v. Pfizer, Inc.* ("*Pfizer*"). Here, in the Court of Chancery, AmerisourceBergen relied on *Pfizer* in support of its argument that, "[w]here a stockholder seeks to investigate mismanagement or wrongdoing solely for potential litigation, the evidence the stockholder presents to establish a credible basis must be evidence of 'actionable corporate wrongdoing.'"

In *Pfizer* [. . .] the court noted that the stockholder had failed to address the Pfizer board's reliance on an unqualified opinion from the company's auditors that Pfizer's financial statements were prepared in accordance with generally accepted accounting principles. The court observed that "[u]nder 8 *Del. C.* § 141(e), directors are 'fully protected' in relying in good faith on the expert's opinions as to matters the director reasonably believes are within the expert's competence, provided the expert was selected with reasonable care." And because the stockholder failed to present any evidence to overcome § 141(e)'s presumptions, the court found the stockholder's "credible basis argument" wanting. [. . .]

This trend, if it can be called that, has met with resistance in other Court of Chancery decisions, as evidenced by the case under consideration here. For instance, in *Amalgamated Bank v. Yahoo! Inc.* ("*Yahoo!*") a case that bears a resemblance to the one before us now, the court found that, even where the plaintiff's likelihood of prevailing on a non-exculpated claim appeared slim but where the plaintiff had established a credible basis from which the Court of Chancery could infer mismanagement, the potential for exculpation would not warrant defeat the stockholder's inspection rights. [. . .]

And as recently as last month in *Pettry v. Gilead Sciences, Inc.* ("*Gilead*"), the Court of Chancery granted a stockholder's inspection request over the corporation's objections that the stockholder lacked standing to pursue follow-on derivative claims, which, in any event, would be time-barred and barred by the corporation's exculpatory charter provision.

It could be said that the Court of Chancery opinions on both sides of this apparent divide can be harmonized; on one side stand *Polygon*, *West Coast Management*, *Graulich*, *AbbVie*, and *Pfizer*, where the stockholder's sole purpose for seeking inspection is to pursue litigation, and on the other stand this case, *Yahoo!* and *Gilead*, where the stockholders have not limited themselves to pursuing litigation. Under the first set of circumstances, one might contend that defenses to the anticipated litigation, including merits-based defenses, should be considered in the Section 220 proceeding, but not in the second.

We think, however, that the apparent tension that has developed between these two approaches should be relieved in a manner that better serves the purpose and nature of Section 220 proceedings, which, after all, are intended to be "summary," and thus "managed expeditiously." It has become evident that the interjection of merits-based defenses—defenses that turn on the quality of the wrongdoing to be investigated—interferes with that process. As the Court of Chancery has noted, a Section 220 proceeding "is not the time for a merits assessment of Plaintiffs' potential claims against [the corporation's] fiduciaries." We therefore reaffirm the "credible basis" test as the standard by which investigative inspections under Section 220 are to be judged. To obtain books and records, a stockholder must show, by a preponderance of the evidence, a credible basis from which the Court of Chancery can infer there is possible mismanagement or wrongdoing warranting further investigation. The stockholder need not demonstrate that the alleged mismanagement or wrongdoing is actionable. To the extent that our summary affirmance in *AbbVie* suggests otherwise, we hereby overrule it.

In the rare case in which the stockholder's sole reason for investigating mismanagement or wrongdoing is to pursue litigation and a purely procedural obstacle, such as standing or the statute of limitations, stands in the stockholder's way such that the court can determine, without adjudicating merits-based defenses, that the anticipated litigation will be dead on arrival, the court may be justified in denying inspection. But in all other cases, the court should—as the Court of Chancery did here—defer the consideration of defenses that do not directly bear on the stockholder's inspection rights, but only on the likelihood that the stockholder might prevail in another action.

[. . .]

F. SHAREHOLDER DERIVATIVE ACTIONS

1. DIRECT V. DERIVATIVE SUITS

Rules of the Court of Chancery of the State of Delaware

Rule 23.1. Derivative actions by shareholders.

(a) In a derivative action brought by one or more shareholders or members to enforce a right of a corporation or of an unincorporated association, the corporation or association having failed to enforce a right which may properly be asserted by it, the complaint shall allege that the plaintiff was a shareholder or member at the time of the transaction of which the plaintiff complains or that the plaintiff's share or membership thereafter devolved on the plaintiff by operation of law. The complaint shall also allege with particularity the efforts, if any, made by the plaintiff to obtain the action the plaintiff desires from the directors or comparable authority and the reasons for the plaintiff's failure to obtain the action or for not making the effort.

(b) Each person seeking to serve as a representative plaintiff on behalf of a corporation or unincorporated association pursuant to this Rule shall file with the Register in Chancery an affidavit stating that the person has not received, been promised or offered and will not accept any form of compensation, directly or indirectly, for prosecuting or serving as a representative party in the derivative action in which the person or entity is a named party except (i) such fees, costs or other payments as the Court expressly approves to be paid to or on behalf of such person, or (ii) reimbursement, paid by such person's attorneys, of actual and reasonable out-of-pocket expenditures incurred directly in connection with the prosecution of the action. The affidavit required by this subpart shall be filed within 10 days after the earliest of the affiant filing the complaint, filing a motion to intervene in the action or filing a motion seeking appointment as a representative party in the action. An affidavit provided pursuant to this subpart shall not be construed to be a waiver of the attorney-client privilege. [. . .]

Tooley v. Donaldson, Lufkin, & Jenrette, Inc.

845 A.2d 1031 (Del. 2004)

■ VEASEY, CHIEF JUSTICE:

Facts

Patrick Tooley and Kevin Lewis are former minority stockholders of Donaldson, Lufkin & Jenrette, Inc. (DLJ), a Delaware corporation engaged in investment banking. DLJ was acquired by Credit Suisse Group in the Fall of 2000. Before that acquisition, AXA Financial, Inc., which owned 71% of DLJ stock, controlled DLJ. Pursuant to a stockholder agreement between AXA and Credit Suisse, AXA agreed to exchange with Credit Suisse its DLJ stockholdings for a mix of stock and cash. The consideration received by AXA consisted primarily of stock. Cash made up one-third of the purchase price. Credit Suisse intended to acquire the remaining minority interests of publicly-held DLJ stock through a cash tender offer, followed by a merger of DLJ into a Credit Suisse subsidiary.

The tender offer price was set at $90 per share in cash. The tender offer was to expire 20 days after its commencement. The merger agreement, however, authorized two types of extensions. First, Credit Suisse could unilaterally extend the tender offer if certain conditions were not met, such as SEC regulatory approvals or certain payment obligations. Alternatively, DLJ and Credit Suisse could agree to postpone acceptance by Credit Suisse of DLJ stock tendered by the minority stockholders.

Credit Suisse availed itself of both types of extensions to postpone the closing of the tender offer. The tender offer was initially set to expire on October 5, 2000, but Credit Suisse invoked the five-day unilateral extension provided in the agreement. Later, by agreement between DLJ and Credit Suisse, it postponed the merger a second time so that it was then set to close on November 2, 2000.

Plaintiffs challenge the second extension that resulted in a 22-day delay. They contend that this delay was not properly authorized and harmed minority stockholders while improperly benefitting AXA. They claim damages representing the time-value of money lost through the delay.

The Decision of the Court of Chancery

The order of the Court of Chancery dismissing the complaint, and the Memorandum Opinion upon which it is based, state that the dismissal is based on the plaintiffs' lack of standing to bring the claims asserted therein. Thus, when plaintiffs tendered their shares, they lost standing under Court of Chancery Rule 23.1, the contemporaneous holding rule. The ruling before us on appeal is that the plaintiffs' claim is derivative, purportedly brought on behalf of DLJ. The Court of Chancery, relying upon our confusing jurisprudence on the direct/derivative dichotomy, based its dismissal on the following ground: "Because this delay affected all DLJ shareholders equally, plaintiffs' injury was not a special injury, and this action is, thus, a derivative action, at most."

[. . .] The Court of Chancery correctly noted that "[t]he Court will independently examine the nature of the wrong alleged and any potential relief to make its own determination of the suit's classification . . . . Plaintiffs' classification of the suit is not binding." The trial court's analysis was hindered, however, because it focused on the confusing concept of "special injury" as the test for determining whether a claim is derivative or direct. The trial court's premise was as follows:

> In order to bring a *direct* claim, a plaintiff must have experienced some "special injury." A special injury is a wrong

that "is separate and distinct from that suffered by other shareholders, . . . or a wrong involving a contractual right of a shareholder, such as the right to vote, or to assert majority control, which exists independently of any right of the corporation." *Moran v. Household Int'l Inc.*

In our view, the concept of "special injury" that appears in some Supreme Court and Court of Chancery cases is not helpful to a proper analytical distinction between direct and derivative actions. We now disapprove the use of the concept of "special injury" as a tool in that analysis.

The Proper Analysis to Distinguish Between Direct and Derivative Actions

The analysis must be based solely on the following questions: Who suffered the alleged harm—the corporation or the suing stockholder individually—and who would receive the benefit of the recovery or other remedy? This simple analysis is well imbedded in our jurisprudence, but some cases have complicated it by injection of the amorphous and confusing concept of "special injury."

The Chancellor, in the very recent *Agostino* case, correctly points this out and strongly suggests that we should disavow the concept of "special injury." In a scholarly analysis of this area of the law, he also suggests that the inquiry should be whether the stockholder has demonstrated that he or she has suffered an injury that is not dependent on an injury to the corporation. In the context of a claim for breach of fiduciary duty, the Chancellor articulated the inquiry as follows: "Looking at the body of the complaint and considering the nature of the wrong alleged and the relief requested, has the plaintiff demonstrated that he or she can prevail without showing an injury to the corporation?" We believe that this approach is helpful in analyzing the first prong of the analysis: what person or entity has suffered the alleged harm? The second prong of the analysis should logically follow.

A Brief History of Our Jurisprudence

The derivative suit has been generally described as "one of the most interesting and ingenious of accountability mechanisms for large formal organizations." *Kramer v. Western Pacific Industries, Inc.* It enables a stockholder to bring suit on behalf of the corporation for harm done to the corporation. Because a derivative suit is being brought on behalf of the corporation, the recovery, if any, must go to the corporation. A stockholder who is directly injured, however, does retain the right to bring an individual action for injuries affecting his or her legal rights as a stockholder. Such a claim is distinct from an injury caused to the corporation alone. In such individual suits, the recovery or other relief flows directly to the stockholders, not to the corporation.

Determining whether an action is derivative or direct is sometimes difficult and has many legal consequences, some of which may have an expensive impact on the parties to the action. For example, if an action is derivative, the plaintiffs are then required to comply with the requirements of Court of Chancery Rule 23.1, that the stockholder: (a) retain ownership of the shares throughout the litigation; (b) make presuit demand on the board; and (c) obtain court approval of any settlement. Further, the recovery, if any, flows only to the corporation. The decision whether a suit is direct or derivative may be outcome-determinative. Therefore, it is necessary that a standard to distinguish such actions be clear, simple and consistently articulated and applied by our courts.

In *Elster v. American Airlines, Inc.*, the stockholder sought to enjoin the grant and exercise of stock options because they would result in a dilution of her stock personally. In *Elster,* the alleged injury was found to be derivative, not direct, because it was essentially a claim of mismanagement of corporate assets. Then came the complication in the analysis: The Court held that where the alleged injury is to both the corporation *and* to the stockholder, the stockholder must allege a "special injury" to maintain a direct action. The Court did not define "special injury," however. By implication, decisions in later cases have interpreted *Elster* to mean that a "special injury" is alleged where the wrong is inflicted upon the stockholder alone or where the stockholder complains of a wrong affecting a particular right. Examples would be a preemptive right as a stockholder, rights involving control of the corporation or a wrong affecting the stockholder, *qua* individual holder, and not the corporation.

In *Bokat v. Getty Oil Co.,* a stockholder of a subsidiary brought suit against the director of the parent corporation for causing the subsidiary to invest its resources wastefully, resulting in a loss to the subsidiary. The claim in *Bokat* was essentially for mismanagement of corporate assets. Therefore, the Court held that any recovery must be sought on behalf of the corporation, and the claim was, thus, found to be derivative.

In describing how a court may distinguish direct and derivative actions, the *Bokat* Court stated that a suit must be maintained derivatively if the injury falls equally upon all stockholders. Experience has shown this concept to be confusing and inaccurate. It is confusing because it appears to have been intended to address the fact that an injury to the corporation tends to diminish each share of stock equally because corporate assets or their value are diminished. In that sense, the *indirect* injury to the stockholders arising out of the harm to the corporation comes about solely by virtue of their stockholdings. It does not arise out of any independent or direct harm to the stockholders, individually. That concept is also inaccurate because a direct, individual claim of stockholders that does not depend on harm to the corporation can also fall on all stockholders equally, without the claim thereby becoming a derivative claim.

In *Lipton v. News International, Plc.,* this Court applied the "special injury" test. There, a stockholder began acquiring shares in the defendant corporation presumably to gain control of the corporation. In response, the defendant corporation agreed to an exchange of its shares with a friendly buyer. Due to the exchange and a supermajority voting requirement on certain stockholder actions, the management of the defendant corporation acquired a veto power over any change in management.

The *Lipton* Court concluded that the critical analytical issue in distinguishing direct and derivative actions is whether a "special injury" has been alleged. There, the Court found a "special injury" because the board's manipulation worked an injury upon the plaintiff-stockholder unlike the injury suffered by other stockholders. That was because the plaintiff-stockholder was actively seeking to gain control of the defendant corporation. Therefore, the Court found that the claim was direct. Ironically, the Court could have reached the same correct result by simply concluding that the manipulation directly and individually harmed the stockholders, without injuring the corporation.

In *Kramer v. Western Pacific Industries, Inc.*, this Court found to be derivative a stockholder's challenge to corporate transactions that occurred six months immediately preceding a buy-out merger. The stockholders challenged the decision by the board of directors to grant stock options and golden parachutes to management. The stockholders argued that the claim was direct because their share of the proceeds from the buy-out sale was reduced by the resources used to pay for the options and golden parachutes. Once again, our analysis was that to bring a direct action, the stockholder must allege something other than an injury resulting from a wrong to the corporation. We interpreted *Elster* to require the court to determine the nature of the action based on the "nature of the wrong alleged" and the relief that could result. That was, and is, the correct test. The claim in *Kramer* was essentially for mismanagement of corporate assets. Therefore, we found the claims to be derivative. That was the correct outcome.

In *Grimes v. Donald,* we sought to distinguish between direct and derivative actions in the context of employment agreements granted to certain officers that allegedly caused the board to abdicate its authority. Relying on the *Elster* and *Kramer* precedents that the court must look to the nature of the wrong and to whom the relief will go, we concluded that the plaintiff was not seeking to recover any damages for injury to the corporation. Rather, the plaintiff was seeking a declaration of the invalidity of the agreements on the ground that the board had abdicated its responsibility to the stockholders. Thus, based on the relief requested, we affirmed the judgment of the Court of Chancery that the plaintiff was entitled to pursue a direct action.

Grimes was followed by *Parnes v. Bally Entertainment Corp.*, which held, among other things, that the injury to the stockholders must be "independent of any injury to the corporation." As the Chancellor correctly noted in *Agostino,* neither *Grimes* nor *Parnes* applies the purported "special injury" test.

Thus, two confusing propositions have encumbered our caselaw governing the direct/derivative distinction. The "special injury" concept, applied in cases such as *Lipton,* can be confusing in identifying the nature of the action. The same is true of the proposition that stems from *Bokat*—that an action cannot be direct if all stockholders are equally affected or unless the stockholder's injury is separate and distinct from that suffered by other stockholders. The proper analysis has been and should remain that stated in *Grimes*; *Kramer* and *Parnes*. That is, a court should look to the nature of the wrong and to whom the relief should go. The stockholder's claimed direct injury must be independent of any alleged injury to the corporation. The stockholder must demonstrate that the duty breached was owed to the stockholder and that he or she can prevail without showing an injury to the corporation.

Standard to Be Applied in This Case

In this case it cannot be concluded that the complaint alleges a derivative claim. There is no derivative claim asserting injury to the corporate entity. There is no relief that would go the corporation. Accordingly, there is no basis to hold that the complaint states a derivative claim.

But, it does not necessarily follow that the complaint states a direct, individual claim. While the complaint purports to set forth a direct claim, in reality, it states no claim at all. The trial court analyzed the complaint and correctly concluded that it does not claim that the plaintiffs have any rights that have been injured. Their rights have not yet ripened. The contractual claim is nonexistent until it is ripe, and that claim will not be ripe until the terms of the merger are fulfilled, including the extensions of the closing at issue here. Therefore, there is no direct claim stated in the complaint before us.

Accordingly, the complaint was properly dismissed. But, due to the reliance on the concept of "special injury" by the Court of Chancery, the ground set forth for the dismissal is erroneous, there being no derivative claim. That error is harmless, however, because, in our view, there is no direct claim either. [. . .]

Brookfield Asset Management, Inc. v. Rosson

261 A.3d 1251 (Del. 2021)

■ VALIHURA, JUSTICE:

[. . .]

I.   Relevant Facts and Procedural Background

[EDS.—This case involves TerraForm Power, Inc., a publicly traded Delaware corporation that owns and operates wind and solar farms. Plaintiffs are Martin Rosson and the City of Dearborn Police and Fire Revised Retirement Fund (*i.e.* the appellees), who owned TerraForm stock and sued the Board of TerraForm for breach of fiduciary duties.

Brookfield Asset Management (*i.e.* the appellant) beneficially owned 61.5% of TerraForm at the time of the Complaint.

As matter of background, Brookfield was the controlling stockholder of Terraform and (i) had the power to appoint Terraform's CEO, CFO, and General Counsel pursuant to a Master Services Agreement and governance agreement; and (ii) pursuant to TerraForm's Charter and its majority holdings, Brookfield had the right to designate four of Terraform's seven directors and used that power to designate four members of Brookfield's senior management. The Charter required that the TerraForm Board have a Conflicts Committee composed of the three non-Brookfield directors, responsible for reviewing and approving material transactions and matters in which a conflict may exist between TerraForm and Brookfield.

Brookfield approached TerraForm regarding the opportunity to acquire a foreign company, Saeta Yields. To finance the acquisition of Saeta Yields, Brookfield steered TerraForm towards a backstopped equity offering. Brookfield and TerraForm informed the Conflicts Committee that, in addition to funding the Saeta Acquisition with debt, TerraForm would raise approximately $600–$700 million of equity in the public markets. The Conflicts Committee approved a $400 million public equity offering at $10.66 per share as part of the funding for the takeover of Saeta Yields. And Brookfield indicated that in addition to participating up to its *pro rata* portion of the equity offering (*i.e.*, 51 percent), it was willing to backstop all the equity offering. However, a few month after the agreement was reached, Brookfield, TerraForm management, and the Conflicts Committee restructured the offering as a private placement of TerraForm's stock worth $650 million to Brookfield at $10.66 per share, which represented a discount on the $11.77 trading piece at which TerraForm traded the time it completed the acquisition of Saeta Yields, or the $17.30 a share, at the time the Complaint was filed.

Plaintiffs filed a verified derivative and purported class action complaint against Brookfield and alleged that Brookfield caused TerraForm to issue its stock in a Private Placement for inadequate value, diluting both the financial and voting interest of the minority stockholders. The Complaint also alleges that the Company was damaged as a result. The trial court consolidated the two actions. Defendants moved to dismiss Plaintiffs' direct claims on the basis that they are entirely derivative.

In a merger completed after the Complaint's filing, affiliates of Brookfield acquired all of TerraForm's stock. As a result, Defendants argue that Plaintiffs lost standing to pursue their derivative claims, as they were no longer stockholders of TerraForm.

The Court of Chancery rejected Plaintiffs' arguments that they have standing to pursue direct claims against the Defendants under *Tooley* explaining that dilution claims are classically derivative, *i.e.*, "the quintessence of a claim belonging to an entity: that fiduciaries, acting in a way that breaches their duties, have caused the entity to exchange assets at a loss." *Tooley v. Donaldson, Lufkin & Jennette, Inc.*]

"Notwithstanding its conclusion that the Plaintiffs had failed to state direct claims under *Tooley*, the court nevertheless found that Plaintiffs had stated direct claims because the claims were predicated on facts similar to those presented in *Gentile v. Rossette*. In Gentile, this Court determined that "the plaintiffs pled two independent harms arising from the transaction: (1) that the corporation was caused to overpay (in stock) for the debt forgiveness, and (2), the minority stockholders lost a significant portion of the cash value and voting power of the minority interest." Regarding Gentile, the Court of Chancery observed that the current law is, as a matter of doctrine, unsatisfying. But it concluded that it was "not free to decide cases in a way that deviates from binding Supreme Court precedent." Accordingly, it held that

> [C]onsistent with *Gentile*, the Plaintiffs have made a sufficient pleading that Brookfield is TerraForm's controller, that Brookfield caused TerraForm to issue excessive shares of its stock in exchange for insufficient consideration, and that the exchange caused an increase in the percentage of the outstanding shares owned by Brookfield, and a corresponding decrease in the share percentage owned by the public (minority) stockholders. [. . .]"

Bound by this Court's decision in *Gentile*, the Court of Chancery determined that Plaintiffs had standing to assert direct claims and denied the Defendants' Motion to Dismiss. [. . .]

Defendants submitted an application to the trial court for certification of an interlocutory appeal of the Court of Chancery's decision denying their motion to dismiss. [. . .] This Court accepted the interlocutory appeal on December 14, 2020.

Appellees contend on cross-appeal that the Court of Chancery erred in holding that they had failed to plead reasonably conceivable direct claims for voting power dilution. [. . .]

III. Analysis

A. Standing is a Threshold Question

In [*El Paso Pipeline GP Co. v. Brinckerhoff*], we explained that " '[t]he concept of standing, in its procedural sense, refers to the right of a party to invoke the jurisdiction of a court to enforce a claim or redress a grievance.' " [. . .]

We explained further in *El Paso* that "[d]erivative standing is a 'creature of equity' that was created to enable a court of equity to exercise jurisdiction over corporate claims asserted by stockholders 'to prevent a complete failure of justice on behalf of the corporation.' " A plaintiff may lose standing in a variety of ways during the progress of litigation. In corporate derivative litigation, for example, a plaintiff's standing is extinguished as a result of loss of plaintiff's status as a stockholder. Once standing is lost, "the court lacks the power to adjudicate the matter, and the action will be dismissed as moot unless an exception applies." Thus, the question of derivative standing is "'properly a threshold question that the [c]ourt may not avoid.'"

B. The Test for Derivative Standing: *Tooley* and *Gentile*'s Carve-Out

1. First, the *Tooley* Test for Direct Versus Derivative Standing

A derivative suit enables a stockholder to bring a suit on behalf of the corporation for harm done to the corporation. Because a derivative suit is brought on behalf of the corporation, any recovery must go to the corporation. However, a stockholder who is directly injured retains the right to bring an individual action for injuries affecting his or her legal rights as a stockholder. "Such a claim is distinct from an injury caused to the corporation alone." *In re J.P. Morgan Chase & Co. S'holder Litig.* In such individual suits, "the recovery or other relief flows directly to the stockholders, not to the corporation." *Id.* Classification of a particular claim as derivative or direct can be difficult. Further, "[t]he decision whether a suit is direct or derivative may be outcome-determinative." *Tooley v. Donaldson.* Such is the case here as the central question is whether Plaintiffs have direct standing to pursue their claims or whether their claims are entirely derivative. If the latter, then their claims were extinguished in the Merger, and they lack standing to pursue them.

In *Tooley*, this Court undertook to create a simple test of straightforward application to distinguish direct claims from derivative claims. Under the *Tooley* test, the determination of whether a stockholder's claim is direct or derivative "must turn *solely* on the following questions: (1) who suffered the alleged harm (the corporation or the stockholders, individually); and (2) who would receive the benefit of any recovery or other remedy (the corporation or the stockholders, individually)?" [. . .]

2. The *Gentile* Carve-Out from the *Tooley* Test

Two years after deciding *Tooley*, this Court decided *Gentile*. *Gentile* involved a controlling stockholder and transactions that resulted in an improper transfer of both economic value and voting power from the minority stockholders to the controlling stockholder. There, a corporation's CEO and controlling stockholder forgave a portion of the company's $3 million debt to him in exchange for additional equity. [. . .] Without disclosing the underlying transaction, the board secured a stockholder vote authorizing the shares needed to issue the additional equity.

The share issuance increased the CEO's equity position from 61.19 percent to 93.49 percent. The minority stockholders suffered a corresponding decrease in their interest from 38.81 percent to 6.51 percent. When the CEO later negotiated a merger between the corporation and its only competitor, the CEO received a generous put agreement that was not disclosed to the other stockholders. The trial court dismissed the ensuing stockholders litigation after concluding that the claims were exclusively derivative and that the plaintiff stockholders' standing had been extinguished following the merger.

This Court reversed and allowed the plaintiffs to proceed with direct claims. The Court reasoned that there were two independent aspects of the plaintiffs' claims, namely, the overpayment claim and the minority's significant loss of cash value and voting power. These claims constituted "a species of corporate overpayment claim" that was "both derivative and direct in character." Accordingly, this Court held that "[u]nlike the typical overpayment transaction, a dual-natured claim arises where:

> (1) a stockholder having a majority or effective control causes the corporation to issue "excessive" shares of its stock in exchange for assets of the controlling stockholder that have a lesser value; and (2) the exchange causes an increase in the percentage of the outstanding shares owned by the controlling shareholder, and a corresponding decrease in the share percentage owned by the public (minority) shareholders.

The Court in *Gentile* clearly recognized that allowing direct standing to assert a corporate dilution/overpayment claim was a deviation from the norm:

> Normally, claims of corporate overpayment are treated as causing harm solely to the corporation and, thus, are regarded as derivative. The reason (expressed in *Tooley* terms) is that the corporation is both the party that suffers the injury (a reduction in its assets or their value) as well as the party to whom the remedy (a restoration of the improperly reduced value) would flow. In the typical corporate overpayment case, a claim against the corporation's fiduciaries for redress is regarded as exclusively derivative, irrespective of whether the currency or form of overpayment is cash or the corporation's stock. Such claims are not normally regarded as direct, because any dilution in value of the corporation's stock is merely the unavoidable result (from an accounting standpoint) of the reduction in the value of the entire corporate entity, of which each share of equity represents an equal fraction. In the eyes of the law, such equal "injury" to the shares resulting from a corporate overpayment is not viewed as, or equated with, harm to specific shareholders individually.

The *Gentile* panel addressed the tension with *Tooley* by acknowledging that "[a]lthough the corporation suffered harm (in the form of a diminution of its net worth), the minority shareholders also suffered a harm that was unique to them and independent of any injury to the corporation." Focusing on the identity of the alleged wrongdoer, the Court stated that, the harm to the minority plaintiffs "resulted from a breach of a fiduciary duty owed to them by the controlling shareholder, namely, not to cause the corporation to effect a transaction that would benefit the fiduciary at the expense of the minority shareholders." Thus, in Gentile the Court held that the value represented by the corporate overpayment is "an entitlement that may be claimed by the public shareholders directly and without regard to any claim the corporation may have."

3. Plaintiffs Have Standing Under *Gentile* but Not *Tooley*

In this case, the Vice Chancellor determined that [. . .] the Complaint does not state direct claims under "a classic *Tooley* analysis," but that it does under *Gentile*. We agree.

[. . .] [T]o plead a direct claim under *Tooley*, a "stockholder must demonstrate that the duty breached was owed to the stockholder and that he or she can prevail without showing an injury to the corporation." [. . .] The claim is derivative because they allege an overpayment (or over-issuance) of shares to the controlling stockholder constituting harm to the corporation for which it has a claim to compel the restoration of the value of the overpayment. Clearly, the gravamen of the Complaint is that the Private Placement was unfair and that TerraForm suffered harm. Further, they seek rescissory damages on behalf of TerraForm. If the Private Placement was for inadequate consideration, the worth of the stockholder's interest is reduced to the extent TerraForm was harmed—as the Vice Chancellor put it, "a classic derivative claim." The alleged economic dilution in the value of the corporation's stock is the unavoidable result of the reduction in the value of the entire corporate entity, of which each share of equity represents an equal fraction. Dilution is a typical result of a corporation's raising funds through the issuance of additional new shares. As the Court in *Gentile* recognized, normally such equal "injury" to the shares resulting from a corporate overpayment is not equated to specific, individual harm to stockholders. Here, the economic and voting power dilution that allegedly harmed the stockholders flowed indirectly to them in proportion to, and via, their shares in TerraForm, and thus any remedy should flow to them the same way, derivatively via the corporation.

[. . .] Because we agree with the Vice Chancellor that Plaintiffs' claims do fit precisely into the *Gentile* paradigm, we now explain why *Gentile* should be overruled.

C. *Gentile* Should be Overruled

1. *Gentile*'s Tension with *Tooley*

Appellants persuasively argue that, "[g]iven the clear conflict between *Gentile* and *Tooley*, the confusion *Gentile* imposes on *Tooley's* straightforward and easy-to-apply analysis, and the policy reasons for removing the exception . . ., this Court should exercise its discretion to overrule *Gentile*. After careful consideration of the relevant doctrinal, practical, and policy considerations, we agree. [. . .]

[. . .] [W]e agree with Appellants that certain aspects of *Gentile* are in tension with *Tooley*. [. . .] One aspect is Gentile's conclusion that the economic and voting dilution was an injury to stockholders *independent* of any injury to the corporation. [. . .]

[. . .] [I]n *Tooley*, this Court stated that "[t]he stockholder's claimed direct injury must be independent of any alleged injury to the corporation." In *Gentile*, this Court acknowledged that the corporation was injured also, but nevertheless, found the plaintiffs' claims to be both derivative and direct:

> Because the means used to achieve that result is an overpayment (or "over-issuance") of shares to the controlling stockholder, the corporation is harmed and has a claim to compel the restoration of the value of the overpayment. That claim, by definition, is derivative.

It went on to find a "separate, and direct, claim arising out of that same transaction." The direct claim was "an improper transfer—or expropriation—of economic value and voting power from the public shareholders to the majority or controlling stockholder."

The gravamen of Plaintiffs' Complaint is that the Private Placement allegedly harmed the Company by issuing shares to Brookfield for an unfairly low price and harmed the stockholders indirectly through economic and voting power dilution proportional to their shareholdings. Thus, the harm to the stockholders was not independent of the harm to the Company, but rather flowed indirectly to them in proportion to, and via their shares in, TerraForm. We agree with the Vice Chancellor that under *Tooley*, this alleged corporate overpayment in stock and consequent dilution of minority interest falls "neatly" into *Tooley*'s derivative category. [. . .]

2.   *The Gentile "Carve-Out" is Superfluous*

[. . .] [W]e see no practical need for the "*Gentile* carve-out." [. . .]

D.   Appellees Cross-Appeal Contention that They Have Direct Standing Regardless of *Gentile* is Meritless

Appellees also separately argue on cross-appeal that they have direct standing to proceed without *Gentile* because the transaction consolidated Brookfield's control of the corporate levers of power, and so the Board violated its fiduciary duties by approving the transaction without compensating the minority shareholders for the further diminution of their voting power. Appellees argue that because entrenchment works a disenfranchisement felt by the minority stockholders as voters, they have direct standing apart from *Gentile*. [. . .]

Appellees' direct disenfranchisement argument is twofold. First, Plaintiffs contend that the Private Placement allowed Brookfield to expand their majority voting control enough that a subsequent sale would not eliminate their majority status (the "Entrenchment Claim"). Second, the Private Placement brought Brookfield near to *super*majority voting control, a threshold that, if they crossed it, would permit them to unilaterally alter certain provisions of the corporate charter without Appellees' consent (the "Supermajority Claim"). Appellees emphasize that theirs was a *substantial* loss of voting power.

The Entrenchment Claim fails because Plaintiffs fail to allege any facts supporting a reasonably conceivable inference that Brookfield, absent the Private Placement, would have permitted a dilution of their equity stake sufficient to relinquish their majority control. Brookfield's stake in TerraForm declined slightly in the 2019 equity issuance because, concurrently with the $250 million October 2019 public offering of close to fifteen million shares at $16.77 per share, Brookfield made a further investment in a private placement (of close to three million shares) at the same price. [. . .]

[. . .] Plaintiffs fail to allege that anyone knew in June 2018 that TerraForm would conduct an offering in October 2019. Moreover, it would have to be reasonably conceivable that even had the Private Placement not occurred, Brookfield would not have participated on a *pro rata* basis in the 2019 offering, thereby choosing to forego its majority stake. Because a control premium has value, we agree it is not reasonably conceivable that Brookfield would have declined to participate in the 2019 offering if that would translate into Brookfield forfeiting majority control for no premium.

Nor does the Supermajority Claim hit the mark [. . .]. To overcome the supermajority threshold, Brookfield needed to expand its equity stake to exceed two-thirds of the Company's voting shares. [. . .] Brookfield never achieved the level of control necessary to unilaterally remove the supermajority voting rights, and Brookfield never attempted to abrogate the rights through the 2019 offering. [. . .] [W]e agree that Plaintiffs' entrenchment claims fail.

IV. Conclusion

For the foregoing reasons, this Court overrules *Gentile* and REVERSES the Court of Chancery's denial of Defendant's Motion to Dismiss for lack of standing.

2. DEMAND FUTILITY

United Food and Commercial Workers Union v. Zuckerberg
262 A.3d 1034 (Del. 2021)

■ MONTGOMERY-REEVES, JUSTICE:

[. . .]

I.   RELEVANT FACTS AND PROCEDURAL BACKGROUND

A.   The Parties and Relevant Non-Parties

Appellee Facebook is a Delaware corporation with its principal place of business in California. [. . .]

Appellant Tri-State has continuously owned stock in Facebook since September 2013.

Appellee Mark Zuckerberg founded Facebook and has served as its chief executive officer since July 2014. Zuckerberg controls a majority of Facebook's voting power and has been the chairman of Facebook's board of directors since January 2012.

Appellee Marc Andreessen has served as a Facebook director since June 2008 [. . .].

Appellee Peter Thiel has served as a Facebook director since April 2005. [. . .]

Appellee Reed Hastings began serving as a Facebook director in June 2011 and was still a director when Tri-State filed its complaint. [. . .] In addition to his work as a Facebook director, Hastings founded and serves as the chief executive officer and chairman of Netflix, Inc. ("Netflix").

Appellee Erskine B. Bowles began serving as a Facebook director in September 2011 and was still a director when Tri-State filed its complaint [. . .].

Appellee Susan D. Desmond-Hellman began serving as a Facebook director in March 2013 and was still a director when Tri-State filed its complaint [. . .].

[EDS.—Three other directors, Sheryl Sandberg, Kenneth I. Chenault, and Jeffery Zients, are of limited relevance to this suit.]

B.   Zuckerberg Takes the Giving Pledge

According to the allegations in the complaint, in December 2010, Zuckerberg took the Giving Pledge, a movement championed by Bill Gates and Warren Buffet that challenged wealthy business leaders to donate a majority of their wealth to philanthropic causes. [. . .]

In March 2015, Zuckerberg began working on an accelerated plan to complete the Giving Pledge by making annual donations of $2 to $3 billion worth of Facebook stock. Zuckerberg asked Facebook's general counsel to look into the plan. Facebook's legal team cautioned Zuckerberg that he could only sell a small portion of his stock—$3 to $4 billion based on the market price—without dipping below majority voting control. To avoid this problem, the general counsel suggested that Facebook could follow the "Google playbook" and issue a new class of non-voting stock that Zuckerberg could sell without significantly diminishing his voting power. The legal team recommended that the board form a special committee of independent directors to review and approve the plan and noted that litigation involving Google's reclassification resulted in a $522 million settlement. Zuckerberg instructed Facebook's legal team to "start figuring out how to make this happen."

C. The Special Committee Approves the Reclassification

At an August 20, 2015 meeting of Facebook's board, Zuckerberg formally proposed that Facebook issue a new class of non-voting shares, which would allow him to sell a substantial amount of stock without losing control of the company. Zuckerberg also disclosed that he had hired Simpson Thacher & Bartlett LLP to give him personal legal advice about "what creating a new class of stock might look like."

A couple of days later, Facebook established a special committee, which was composed of three purportedly independent directors: Andreessen, Bowles, and Desmond-Hellman (the "Special Committee"). The board charged the Special Committee with evaluating the Reclassification, considering alternatives, and making a recommendation to the full board. The board also authorized the Special Committee to retain legal counsel, financial advisors, and other experts.

Facebook management recommended and the Special Committee hired Wachtell, Lipton, Rosen & Katz ("Wachtell") as the committee's legal advisor. [. . .]

Following the recommendation of Bowles, the Special Committee hired Evercore Group L.L.C. ("Evercore") as its financial advisor. Evercore was founded by Roger Altman, a personal friend of Bowles who had helped him with various political efforts. Evercore's team leader observed that it had been hired "in the second inning" and that negotiations were well underway before it began to advise the Special Committee on the Reclassification.

As the negotiations progressed, the Special Committee largely agreed to give Zuckerberg the terms that he wanted and did not consider alternatives or demand meaningful concessions. [. . .] [T]he Special Committee asked for only small concessions from Zuckerberg, such as a sunset provision that was designed to discourage Zuckerberg from leaving the company despite the absence of any demonstrable reason to believe that Zuckerberg would step away from his existing Facebook duties.

On November 9, 2015, Zuckerberg publicly reaffirmed the Giving Pledge. The next day, Zuckerberg circulated a draft announcement within Facebook that would disclose his intent to begin making large annual donations to complete the pledge. [. . .]

A few weeks later, Zuckerberg published a post on his Facebook page announcing that he planned to begin making large donations of his Facebook stock. The post noted that Zuckerberg intended to "remain Facebook's CEO for many, many years to come" and did not mention that his plan hinged on the Special Committee's approval of the Reclassification. The Special Committee did not try to use the public announcement as leverage to extract more concessions from Zuckerberg.

Throughout the negotiations about the Reclassification, Andreessen engaged in facially dubious back-channel communications with Zuckerberg about the Special Committee's deliberations. [. . .]

On April 13, 2016, the Special Committee recommend that the full board approve the Reclassification. The next day, Facebook's full board accepted the Special Committee's recommendation and voted to approve the Reclassification. Zuckerberg and Sandberg abstained from voting on the Reclassification.

D. Facebook Settles a Class Action Challenging the Reclassification

On April 27, 2016, Facebook revealed the Reclassification to the public. The announcement was timed to coincide with the company's best-ever quarterly earnings report. Evercore's project leader, Altman, sent Desmond-Hellmann an email remarking, "Anytime [Facebook] announces earnings like that, no one will care about an equity recapitalization."

On April 29, 2016, the first class action was filed in the Court of Chancery challenging the Reclassification. [. . .] [I]n May 2016 the Court of Chancery consolidated thirteen cases into a single class action (the "Reclassification Class Action").

On June 20, 2016, Facebook held its annual stockholders meeting. Among other things, the stockholders were asked to vote on the Reclassification. Zuckerberg voted all of his stock in favor of the plan. Including Zuckerberg's votes, a majority of Facebook's stockholders approved the Reclassification. More than three-quarters of the minority stockholders voted against the Reclassification.

On June 24, 2016, Facebook agreed that it would not go forward with the Reclassification while the Reclassification Class Action was pending. The Court of Chancery certified the Reclassification Class Action in April 2017 and tentatively scheduled the trial for September 26, 2017. About a week before the trial was scheduled to begin, Zuckerberg asked the board to abandon the Reclassification. [. . .]

By January 3, 2019, Zuckerberg had sold about $5.6 billion worth of Facebook stock without the Reclassification.

E. Tri-State Files a Class Action Seeking to Recoup the Money that Facebook Spent Defending and Settling the Reclassification Class Action

Facebook spent about $21.8 million defending the Reclassification Class Action, including more than $17 million on attorneys' fees. Additionally, Facebook paid $68.7 million to the plaintiffs attorneys in the Reclassification Class Action to settle a claim under the corporate benefit doctrine.

On September 12, 2018, Tri-State filed a derivative action in the Court of Chancery seeking to recoup the money that Facebook spent defending and settling the Reclassification Class Action. The complaint asserted a single count alleging that Zuckerberg, Andreessen, Thiel, Hastings, Bowles, and Desmond-Hellmann (collectively, the "Director Defendants") breached their fiduciary duties of care and loyalty by improperly negotiating and approving the Reclassification. When Tri-State filed its complaint, Facebook's board was composed of nine directors: Zuckerberg, Andreessen, Bowles, Desmond-Hellman, Hastings, Thiel, Sandberg, Chenault, and Zients (collectively, the "Demand Board").

The complaint alleged that demand was excused as futile under Court of Chancery Rule 23.1 because "the Reclassification was not the product of a valid exercise of business judgment" and because "a majority of the Board face[d] a substantial likelihood of liability[ ] and/or lack[ed] independence." Facebook and the Director Defendants moved to dismiss the complaint under Court of Chancery Rule 23.1 for failing to comply with the demand requirement.

On October 26, 2020, the Court of Chancery issued a memorandum opinion dismissing the complaint for failing to comply with Rule 23.1. The court held that demand was required because the complaint did not contain particularized allegations raising a reasonable doubt that a majority of the Demand Board received a material personal benefit from the Reclassification, faced a substantial likelihood of liability for approving the Reclassification, or lacked independence from another interested party.

Tri-State appeals the Court of Chancery's judgment dismissing the derivative complaint under Rule 23.1 for failing to make a demand on the board or plead with particularity facts establishing that demand would be futile.

II. STANDARD OF REVIEW

"[O]ur review of decisions of the Court of Chancery applying Rule 23.1 is *de novo* and plenary." *Brehm v. Eisner.*

III. ANALYSIS

"A cardinal precept" of Delaware law is "that directors, rather than shareholders, manage the business and affairs of the corporation." *Aronson v. Lewis.* This precept is reflected in Section 141(a) of the Delaware General Corporation Law ("DGCL"), which provides that "[t]he business and affairs of every corporation organized under this chapter *shall be managed by or under the direction of a board of directors* except as may be otherwise provided in this chapter or in [a corporation's] certificate of incorporation." The board's authority to govern corporate affairs extends to decisions about what remedial actions a corporation should take after being harmed, including whether the corporation should file a lawsuit against its directors, its officers, its controller, or an outsider.

"In a derivative suit, a stockholder seeks to displace the board's [decision-making] authority over a litigation asset and assert the corporation's claim." Op. at 16. Thus, "[b]y its very nature[,] the derivative action" encroaches "on the managerial freedom of directors" by seeking to deprive the board of control over a corporation's litigation asset. *Aronson*. "In order for a stockholder to divest the directors of their authority to control the litigation asset and bring a derivative action on behalf of the corporation, the stockholder must" (1) make a demand on the company's board of directors or (2) show that demand would be futile. *Lenois v. Lawal*. The demand requirement is a substantive requirement that " '[e]nsure[s] that a stockholder exhausts his intracorporate remedies,' 'provide[s] a safeguard against strike suits,' and 'assure[s] that the stockholder affords the corporation the opportunity to address an alleged wrong without litigation and to control any litigation which does occur.' "

Court of Chancery Rule 23.1 implements the substantive demand requirement at the pleading stage by mandating that derivative complaints "allege with particularity the efforts, if any, made by the plaintiff to obtain the action the plaintiff desires from the directors or comparable authority and the reasons for the plaintiff's failure to obtain the action or for not making the effort." To comply with Rule 23.1, the plaintiff must meet "stringent requirements of factual particularity that differ substantially from . . . permissive notice pleadings." *Brehm v. Eisner* When considering a motion to dismiss a complaint for failing to comply with Rule 23.1, the Court does not weigh the evidence, must accept as true all of the complaint's particularized and well-pleaded allegations, and must draw all reasonable inferences in the plaintiff's favor.

The plaintiff in this action did not make a pre-suit demand. Thus, the question before the Court is whether demand is excused as futile. This Court has articulated two tests to determine whether the demand requirement should be excused as futile: the *Aronson* test and the *Rales* test. The *Aronson* test applies where the complaint challenges a decision made by the same board that would consider a litigation demand. Under *Aronson*, demand is excused as futile if the complaint alleges particularized facts that raise a reasonable doubt that "(1) the directors are disinterested and independent[,] [or] (2) the challenged transaction was otherwise the product of a valid business judgment." This reflects the "rule . . . that where officers and directors are under an influence which sterilizes their discretion, they cannot be considered proper persons to conduct litigation on behalf of the corporation. Thus, demand would be futile."

The *Rales* test applies in all other circumstances. Under *Rales*, demand is excused as futile if the complaint alleges particularized facts creating a "reasonable doubt that, as of the time the complaint is filed," a majority of the demand board "could have properly exercised its independent and disinterested business judgment in responding to a demand." "Fundamentally, *Aronson* and *Rales* both 'address the same question of whether the board can exercise its business judgment on the corporat[ion]'s behalf" in considering demand." For this reason, the Court of Chancery has recognized that the broader reasoning of *Rales* encompasses *Aronson*, and therefore the *Aronson* test is best understood as a special application of the *Rales* test.

While Delaware law recognizes that there are circumstances where making a demand would be futile because a majority of the directors "are under an influence which sterilizes their discretion" and "cannot be considered proper persons to conduct litigation on behalf of the corporation," *Aronson v. Lewis* the demand requirement is not excused lightly because derivative litigation upsets the balance of power that the DGCL establishes between a corporation's directors and its stockholders. Thus, the demand-futility analysis provides an important doctrinal check that ensures the board is not improperly deprived of its decision-making authority, while at the same time leaving a path for stockholders to file a derivative action where there is reason to doubt that the board could bring its impartial business judgment to bear on a litigation demand.

In this case, Tri-State alleged that demand was excused as futile for several reasons, including that the board's negotiation and approval of the Reclassification would not be "protected by the business judgment rule" because "[t]heir approval was not fully informed" or "duly considered," and that a majority of the directors on the Demand Board lacked independence from Zuckerberg. The Court of Chancery held that Tri-State failed to plead with particularity facts establishing that demand was futile and dismissed the complaint because it did not comply with Court of Chancery Rule 23.1.

On appeal, Tri-State raises two issues with the Court of Chancery's demand-futility analysis. First, Tri-State argues that the Court of Chancery erred by holding that exculpated care violations do not satisfy the second prong of the *Aronson* test. Second, Tri-State argues that its complaint contained particularized allegations establishing that a majority of the directors on the Demand Board were beholden to Zuckerberg. [. . .]

A. Exculpated Care Violations Do Not Satisfy *Aronson's* Second Prong

The directors and officers of a Delaware corporation owe two overarching fiduciary duties—the duty of care and the duty of loyalty. "[P]redicated upon concepts of gross negligence," the duty of care requires that fiduciaries inform themselves of material information before making a business decision and act prudently in carrying out their duties. *Aronson v. Lewis* The duty of loyalty " 'requires an undivided and unselfish loyalty to the corporation' and 'demands that there shall be no conflict between duty and self-interest.' " *City of Fort Myers Gen. Emps.' Pension Fund v. Haley*

Tri-State alleges that the Director Defendants breached their duty of care in negotiating and approving the Reclassification. Section 102(b)(7) of the DGCL authorizes corporations to adopt a charter provision insulating directors from liability for breaching their duty of care [. . .].

Facebook's charter contains a Section 102(b)(7) clause; as such, the Director Defendants face no risk of personal liability from the allegations asserted in this action. Thus, Tri-State's demand-futility allegations raise the question whether a derivative plaintiff can rely on exculpated care violations to establish that demand is futile under the second prong of the Aronson test. The Court of Chancery held that exculpated care claims do not excuse demand because the second prong of the *Aronson* test focuses on whether a director faces a substantial likelihood of liability. Tri-State argues that this analysis was wrong because *Aronson's* second prong focuses on whether the challenged transaction "satisfies the applicable standard of review," not on whether directors face a substantial likelihood of liability. [. . .]

1. The second prong of *Aronson* focuses on whether the directors face a substantial likelihood of liability

The main question on appeal is whether allegations of exculpated care violations can establish that demand is excused under *Aronson's* second prong. According to Tri-State, the second prong excuses demand whenever the complaint raises a reasonable doubt that the challenged transaction was a valid exercise of business judgment, regardless of whether the directors face a substantial likelihood of liability for approving the challenged transaction. Thus, exculpated care violations can establish that demand is futile.

Tri-State's argument hinges on the plain language of *Aronson's* second prong, which focuses on whether "the challenged transaction was . . . the product of a valid business judgment":

> [I]n determining demand futility, the Court of Chancery . . . must decide whether, under the particularized facts alleged, a reasonable doubt is created that: (1) the directors are disinterested and independent and (2) *the challenged transaction was otherwise the product of a valid business judgment.* Hence, the Court of Chancery must make two inquiries, one into the independence and disinterestedness of the directors and *the other into the substantive nature of the challenged transaction and the board's approval thereof. Aronson v. Lewis*

Later opinions issued by this Court contain similar language that can be read to suggest that *Aronson's* second prong focuses on the propriety of the challenged transaction. These passages do not address, however, why *Aronson* used the standard of review as a proxy for whether the board could impartially consider a litigation demand. The likely answer is that, before the General Assembly adopted Section 102(b)(7) in 1995, rebutting the business judgment rule through allegations of care violations exposed directors to a substantial likelihood of liability. Thus, even if the demand board was independent and disinterested with respect to the challenged transaction, the litigation presented a threat that would "sterilize [the board's] discretion" with respect to a demand.

Aronson supports this conclusion. [. . .] At that time, if the business judgment rule did not apply, allowing the derivative litigation to go forward would expose the directors to a substantial likelihood of liability for breach-of-care claims supported by well-pleaded factual allegations. It is reasonable to doubt that a director would be willing to take that personal risk. Thus, demand is excused.

On the other hand, if the business judgment rule would apply, allowing the derivative litigation to go forward would expose the directors to a minimal threat of liability. A remote threat of liability is not a good enough reason to deprive the board of control over the corporation's litigation assets. Thus, demand is required.

Although not unanimous, the weight of Delaware authority since the enactment of Section 102(b)(7) supports holding that exculpated care violations do not excuse demand under *Aronson's* second prong. [. . .]

Accordingly, this Court affirms the Court of Chancery's holding that exculpated care claims do not satisfy *Aronson's* second prong. This Court's decisions construing *Aronson* have consistently focused on whether the demand board has a connection to the challenged transaction that would render it incapable of impartially considering a litigation demand. When *Aronson* was decided, raising a reasonable doubt that directors breached their duty of care exposed them to a substantial likelihood of liability and protracted litigation, raising doubt as to their ability to impartially consider demand. The ground has since shifted, and exculpated breach of care claims no longer pose a threat that neutralizes director discretion. These developments must be factored into demand-futility analysis, and Tri-State has failed to provide a reasoned explanation of why rebutting the business judgment rule should automatically render directors incapable of impartially considering a litigation demand given the current landscape. For these reasons, the Court of Chancery's judgment is affirmed.

2. Tri-State's other arguments do not change the analysis

Tri-State raises a few more counterarguments that do not change the Court's analysis.

First, Tri-State argues that construing the second prong of *Aronson* to focus on whether directors face a substantial likelihood of liability erases any distinction between the two prongs of the *Aronson* test. The argument goes like this. If directors face a substantial likelihood of liability for approving the challenged transaction, then they are interested with respect to the challenged transaction. This argument misconstrues *Aronson*. The first prong of *Aronson* focuses on whether the directors had a personal interest in the challenged transaction (i.e., a personal financial benefit from the challenged transaction that is not equally shared by the stockholders). This is a different consideration than whether the directors face a substantial likelihood of liability for approving the challenged transaction, even if they received nothing personal from the challenged transaction. The second prong excuses demand in that circumstance. Thus, the first and second prongs of *Aronson* perform separate functions, even if those functions are complementary.

Second, Tri-State argues that this holding places an unfair burden on plaintiffs and will fail to deter controllers from pressuring boards to approve unfair transactions. Although not entirely clear, Tri-State appears to argue that because the entire fairness standard of review applies *ab initio* to a conflicted-controller transaction, demand is automatically excused under Aronson's second prong. As the Court of Chancery has explained, the theory that demand should be excused simply because an alleged controlling stockholder stood on both sides of the transaction is "inconsistent with Delaware Supreme Court authority that focuses the test for demand futility exclusively on the ability of a corporation's board of directors to impartially consider a demand to institute litigation on behalf of the corporation—including litigation implicating the interests of a controlling stockholder."

Further, Tri-State's argument presumes that a stockholder has a general right to control corporate claims. Not so. The directors are tasked with managing the affairs of the corporation, including whether to file action on behalf of the corporation. A stockholder can only displace the directors if the stockholder alleges with particularity that "the directors are under an influence which sterilizes their discretion" such that "they cannot be considered proper persons to conduct litigation on behalf of the corporation." *Aronson v. Lewis* As such, enforcing the demand requirement where a stockholder has only alleged exculpated conduct does not "undermine shareholder rights;" instead, it recognizes the delegation of powers outlined in the DGCL.

Finally, Tri-State's argument collapses the distinction between the board's capacity to consider a litigation demand and the propriety of the challenged transaction. It is entirely possible that an independent and disinterested board, exercising its impartial business judgment, could decide that it is not in the corporation's best interest to spend the time and money to pursue a claim that is likely to succeed. Yet, Tri-State asks the Court to deprive directors and officers of the power to make such a decision, at least where the derivative action would challenge a conflicted-controller transaction. This rule may have its benefits, but it runs counter to the "cardinal precept" of Delaware law that independent and disinterested directors are generally in the best position to manage a corporation's affairs, including whether the corporation should exercise its legal rights.

For these reasons, Tri-State cannot satisfy the demand requirement by pleading—for reasons unrelated to the conduct or interests of a majority of the directors on the demand board—that the entire fairness standard of review would apply to the Reclassification. Rather, to satisfy Rule 23.1, Tri-State must plead with particularity facts establishing that a majority of the directors on the demand board are subject to an influence that would sterilize their discretion with respect to the litigation demand.

[. . .]

3. This Court adopts the Court of Chancery's three-part test for demand futility

This issue raises one more question—whether the three-part test for demand futility the Court of Chancery applied below is consistent with *Aronson, Rales,* and their progeny. The Court of Chancery noted [. . .]:

> The composition of the Board in this case exemplifies the difficulties that the *Aronson* test struggles to overcome. The Board has nine members, six of whom served on the Board when it approved the Reclassification. Under a strict reading of *Rales,* because the Board does not have a new majority of directors, *Aronson* provides the governing test. But one of those six directors abstained from the vote on the Reclassification, meaning that the *Aronson* analysis only has traction for five of the nine. Aronson does not provide guidance about what to do with either the director who abstained or the two directors who joined the Board later. The director who abstained from voting on the Reclassification suffers from other conflicts that renders her incapable of considering a demand, yet a strict reading of Aronson only focuses on the challenged decision and therefore would not account for those conflicts. Similarly, the plaintiff alleges that one of the directors who subsequently joined the Board has conflicts that render him incapable of considering a demand, but a strict reading of Aronson would not account for that either. Precedent thus calls for applying *Aronson,* but its analytical framework is not up to the task. The *Rales* test, by contrast, can accommodate all of these considerations.

The court also suggested that in light of the developments discussed above, "*Aronson* is broken in its own right [. . .] [p]erhaps the time has come to move on from *Aronson* entirely."

To address these concerns, the Court of Chancery applied the following three-part test on a director-by-director basis to determine whether demand should be excused as futile:

(i) whether the director received a material personal benefit from the alleged misconduct that is the subject of the litigation demand;

(ii) whether the director would face a substantial likelihood of liability on any of the claims that are the subject of the litigation demand; and

(iii) whether the director lacks independence from someone who received a material personal benefit from the alleged misconduct that is the subject of the litigation demand or who would face a substantial likelihood of liability on any of the claims that are the subject of the litigation demand.

This approach treated "*Rales* as the general demand futility test," while "draw[ing]" upon *Aronson*-like principles when evaluating whether particular directors face a substantial likelihood of liability as a result of having participated in the decision to approve the Reclassification."

This Court adopts the Court of Chancery's three-part test as the universal test for assessing whether demand should be excused as futile. [. . .] Blending the Aronson test with the Rales test is appropriate because "both appropriate and necessary that the common law evolve in an orderly fashion to incorporate [. . .] developments. The Court of Chancery's three-part test achieves that important goal. [. . .]

Accordingly, from this point forward, courts should ask the following three questions on a director-by-director basis when evaluating allegations of demand futility:

(i) whether the director received a material personal benefit from the alleged misconduct that is the subject of the litigation demand;

(ii) whether the director faces a substantial likelihood of liability on any of the claims that would be the subject of the litigation demand; and

(iii) whether the director lacks independence from someone who received a material personal benefit from the alleged misconduct that would be the subject of the litigation demand or who would face a substantial likelihood of liability on any of the claims that are the subject of the litigation demand.

If the answer to any of the questions is "yes" for at least half of the members of the demand board, then demand is excused as futile. It is no longer necessary to determine whether the Aronson test or the Rales test governs a complaint's demand-futility allegations.

B. The Complaint Does Not Plead with Particularity Facts Establishing that Demand Would Be Futile

The second issue on appeal is whether Tri-State's complaint pleaded with particularity facts establishing that a litigation demand on Facebook's board would be futile. The Court resolves this issue by applying the three-part test adopted above on a director-by-director basis.

The Demand Board was composed of nine directors. Tri-State concedes on appeal that two of those directors, Chenault and Zients, could have impartially considered a litigation demand. And Facebook does not argue on appeal that Zuckerberg, Sandberg, or Andreessen could have impartially considered a litigation demand. Thus, in order to show that demand is futile, Tri-State must sufficiently allege that two of the following directors could not impartially consider demand: Thiel, Hastings, Bowles, and Desmond-Hellmann.[. . .]

[W]e hold that Tri-State failed to raise a reasonable doubt that either Thiel, Hastings, or Bowles was beholden to Zuckerberg.

1. Hastings

The complaint does not raise a reasonable doubt that Hastings lacked independence from Zuckerberg. According to the complaint, Hastings was not independent because:

- "Netflix purchased advertisements from Facebook at relevant times," and maintains "ongoing and potential future business relationships with" Facebook. [. . .]

- "Hastings has . . . publicly supported large philanthropic donations by founders during their lifetimes. Indeed, both Hastings and Zuckerberg have been significant contributors . . . [to] a well-known foundation known for soliciting and obtaining large contributions from company founders and which manages donor funds for both Hastings . . . and Zuckerberg . . . ."

These allegations do not raise a reasonable doubt that Hastings was beholden to Zuckerberg. Even if Netflix purchased advertisements from Facebook, the complaint does not allege that those purchases were material to Netflix or that Netflix received anything other than arm's length terms under those agreements. [. . .]

[. . .] Nor is it apparent how donating to the same charitable fund would result in Hastings feeling obligated to serve Zuckerberg's interests." Accordingly, the Court affirms the Court of Chancery's holding that the complaint does not raise a reasonable doubt about Hastings's independence.

2. Thiel

The complaint does not raise a reasonable doubt that Thiel lacked independence from Zuckerberg. According to the complaint, Thiel was not independent because:

- "Thiel was one of the early investors in Facebook," is "its longest-tenured board member besides Zuckerberg," and "has . . . been instrumental to Facebook's business strategy and direction over the years."

- "Thiel has a personal bias in favor of keeping founders in control of the companies they created . . . ."

- The venture capital firm at which Thiel is a partner, Founders Fund, "gets 'good deal flow' " from its "high-profile association with Facebook."

- "According to Facebook's 2018 Proxy Statement, the Facebook shares owned by the Founders Fund (i.e., by Thiel and Andreessen) will be released from escrow in connection with" an acquisition.
- "Thiel is Zuckerberg's close friend and mentor."
- In October 2016, Thiel made a $1 million donation to an "organization that paid [a substantial sum to] Cambridge Analytica" and "cofounded the Cambridge [. . .] Analytica-linked data firm Palantir." Even though "[t]he Cambridge Analytica scandal has exposed Facebook to regulatory investigations" and litigation, Zuckerberg did not try to remove Thiel from the board.
- Similarly, Thiel's "acknowledge[ment] that he secretly funded various lawsuits aimed at bankrupting [the] news website Gawker Media" lead to "widespread calls for Zuckerberg to remove Thiel from Facebook's Board given Thiel's apparent antagonism toward a free press." Zuckerberg ignored those calls and did not seek to remove Thiel from Facebook's board.

These allegations do not raise a reasonable doubt that Thiel is beholden to Zuckerberg. The complaint does not explain why Thiel's status as a long-serving board member, early investor, or his contributions to Facebook's business strategy make him beholden to Zuckerberg. And for the same reasons provided above, a director's good faith belief that founder controller maximizes value does not raise a reasonable doubt that the director lacks independence from a corporation's founder.

While the complaint alleges that Founders Fund "gets 'good deal flow'" from Thiel's "high-profile association with Facebook, the complaint does not identify a single deal that flowed to—or is expected to flow to—Founders Fund through this association, let alone any deals that would be material to Thiel's interests. The complaint also fails to draw any connection between Thiel's continued status as a director and the vesting of Facebook stock related to the acquisition. And alleging that Thiel is a personal friend of Zuckerberg is insufficient to establish a lack of independence. The final pair of allegations suggest that because "Zuckerberg stood by Thiel" in the face of public scandals, "Thiel feels a sense of obligation to Zuckerberg." These allegations can only raise a reasonable doubt about Thiel's independence if remaining a Facebook director was financially or personally material to Thiel. As the Court of Chancery noted below, given Thiel's wealth and stature, "[t]he complaint does not support an inference that Thiel's service on the Board is financially material to him. Nor does the complaint sufficiently allege that serving as a Facebook director confers such cachet that Thiel's independence is compromised." Accordingly, this Court affirms the Court of Chancery's holding that the complaint does not raise a reasonable doubt about Thiel's independence.

3. Bowles

The complaint does not raise a reasonable doubt that Bowles lacked independence from Zuckerberg. According to the complaint, [Bowles] was not independent because:

- "Bowles is beholden to the entire board" because it granted "a waiver of the mandatory retirement age for directors set forth in Facebook's Corporate Governance Guidelines," allowing "Bowles to stand for reelection despite having reached 70 years old before" the May 2018 annual meeting.

- "Morgan Stanley—a company for which [Bowles] . . . served as a longstanding board member at the time (2005–2017)—directly benefited by receiving over $2 million in fees for its work . . . in connection with the Reclassification . . . ."

- Bowles "ensured that Evercore and his close friend Altman financially benefitted from the Special Committee's engagement" without properly vetting Evercore's competency or considering alternatives.

These allegations do not raise a reasonable doubt that Bowles is beholden to Zuckerberg or the other members of the Demand Board. The complaint does not make any particularized allegation explaining why the board's decision to grant Bowles a waiver from the mandatory retirement age would compromise his ability to impartially consider a litigation demand or engender a sense of debt to the other directors. For example, the complaint does not allege that Bowles was expected to do anything in exchange for the waiver, or that remaining a director was financially or personally material to Bowles.

The complaint's allegations regarding Bowles's links to financial advisors are similarly ill-supported. None of these allegations suggest that Bowles received a personal benefit from the Reclassification, or that Bowles's ties to these advisors made him beholden to Zuckerberg as a condition of sending business to Morgan Stanley, Evercore, or his "close friend Altman." Accordingly, this Court affirms the Court of Chancery's holding that the complaint does not raise a reasonable doubt about Bowles's independence.

IV. CONCLUSION

For the reasons provided above, the Court of Chancery's judgment is affirmed.

G. SPECIAL COMMITTEES

Zapata Corp. v. Maldonado
430 A.2d 779 (Del. 1981)

■ QUILLEN, JUSTICE:

[. . .] In June, 1975, William Maldonado, a stockholder of Zapata, instituted a derivative action in the Court of Chancery on behalf of Zapata against ten officers and/or directors of Zapata, alleging, essentially, breaches of fiduciary duty. Maldonado did not first demand that the board bring this action, stating instead such demand's futility because all directors were named as defendants and allegedly participated in the acts specified.

By June, 1979, four of the defendant-directors were no longer on the board, and the remaining directors appointed two new outside directors to the board. The board then created an "Independent Investigation Committee" (Committee), composed solely of the two new directors, to investigate Maldonado's actions, as well as a similar derivative action then pending in Texas, and to determine whether the corporation should continue any or all of the litigation. The Committee's determination was stated to be "final, . . . not . . . subject to review by the Board of Directors and . . . in all respects . . . binding upon the Corporation."

Following an investigation, the Committee concluded, in September, 1979, that each action should "be dismissed forthwith as their continued maintenance is inimical to the Company's best interests . . . ." Consequently, Zapata moved for dismissal or summary judgment in the three derivative actions.

On March 18, 1980, the Court of Chancery, in a reported opinion, the basis for the order of April 9, 1980, denied Zapata's motions, holding that Delaware law does not sanction this means of dismissal. More specifically, it held that the "business judgment" rule is not a grant of authority to dismiss derivative actions and that a stockholder has an individual right to maintain derivative actions in certain instances. [. . .]

[. . .] We limit our review in this interlocutory appeal to whether the Committee has the power to cause the present action to be dismissed.

We begin with an examination of the carefully considered opinion of the Vice Chancellor which states, in part, that the "business judgment" rule does not confer power "to a corporate board of directors to terminate a derivative suit." His conclusion is particularly pertinent because several federal courts, applying Delaware law, have held that the business judgment rule enables boards (or their committees) to terminate derivative suits, decisions now in conflict with the holding below.

As the term is most commonly used, and given the disposition below, we can understand the Vice Chancellor's comment that "the business judgment rule is irrelevant to the question of whether the Committee has the authority to compel the dismissal of this suit." Corporations, existing because of legislative grace, possess authority as granted by the legislature. Directors of Delaware corporations derive their managerial decision making power, which encompasses decisions whether to initiate, or refrain from entering, litigation, from 8 *Del.C.* § 141 (a). This statute is the fount of directorial powers. The "business judgment" rule is a judicial creation that presumes propriety, under certain circumstances, in a board's decision. Viewed defensively, it does not create authority. In this sense the "business judgment" rule is not relevant in corporate decision making until after a decision is made. It is generally used as a defense to an attack on the decision's soundness. The board's managerial decision making power, however, comes from § 141(a). The judicial creation and legislative grant are related because the "business judgment" rule evolved to give recognition and deference to directors' business expertise when exercising their managerial power under § 141(a).

In the case before us, although the corporation's decision to move to dismiss or for summary judgment was, literally, a decision resulting from an exercise of the directors' (as delegated to the Committee) business judgment, the question of "business judgment", in a defensive sense, would not become relevant until and unless the decision to seek termination of the derivative lawsuit was attacked as improper. [. . .]

Thus, the focus in this case is on the power to speak for the corporation as to whether the lawsuit should be continued or terminated. [. . .]

Accordingly, we turn first to the Court of Chancery's conclusions concerning the right of a plaintiff stockholder in a derivative action. We find that its determination that a stockholder, once demand is made and refused, possesses an independent, individual right to continue a derivative suit for breaches of fiduciary duty over objection by the corporation, [. . .] as an absolute rule, is erroneous. [. . .]

McKee v. Rogers [. . .] stated "as a general rule" that "a stockholder cannot be permitted. . . to invade the discretionary field committed to the judgment of the directors and sue in the corporation's behalf when the managing body refuses. This rule is a well settled one." [. . .]

The *McKee* rule, of course, should not be read so broadly that the board's refusal will be determinative in every instance. Board members, owing a well-established fiduciary duty to the corporation, will not be allowed to cause a derivative suit to be dismissed when it would be a breach of their fiduciary duty. Generally disputes pertaining to control of the suit arise in two contexts.

Consistent with the purpose of requiring a demand, a board decision to cause a derivative suit to be dismissed as detrimental to the company, after demand has been made and refused, will be respected unless it was wrongful. A claim of a wrongful decision not to sue is thus the first exception and the first context of dispute. Absent a wrongful refusal, the stockholder in such a situation simply lacks legal managerial power. [. . .]

But it cannot be implied that, absent a wrongful board refusal, a stockholder can never have an individual right to initiate an action. [. . .]

A demand, when required and refused (if not wrongful), terminates a stockholder's legal ability to initiate a derivative action. But where demand is properly excused, the stockholder does possess the ability to initiate the action on his corporation's behalf.

These conclusions, however, do not determine the question before us. Rather, they merely bring us to the question to be decided. It is here that we part company with the Court below. Derivative suits enforce corporate rights and any recovery obtained goes to the corporation. [. . .] We see no inherent reason why the "two phases" of a derivative suit, the stockholder's suit to compel the corporation to sue and the corporation's suit, should automatically result in the placement in the hands of the litigating stockholder sole control of the corporate right throughout the litigation. To the contrary, it seems to us that such an inflexible rule would recognize the interest of one person or group to the exclusion of all others within the corporate entity. Thus, we reject the view of the Vice Chancellor as to the first aspect of the issue on appeal.

The question to be decided becomes: When, if at all, should an authorized board committee be permitted to cause litigation, properly initiated by a derivative stockholder in his own right, to be dismissed? As noted above, a board has the power to choose not to pursue litigation when demand is made upon it, so long as the decision is not wrongful. If the board determines that a suit would be detrimental to the company, the board's determination prevails. Even when demand is excusable, circumstances may arise when continuation of the litigation would not be in the corporation's best interests. Our inquiry is whether, under such circumstances, there is a permissible procedure under § 141(a) by which a corporation can rid itself of detrimental litigation. If there is not, a single stockholder in an extreme case might control the destiny of the entire corporation [. . .]: "To allow one shareholder to incapacitate an entire board of directors merely by leveling charges against them gives too much leverage to dissident shareholders." But, when examining the means, including the committee mechanism examined in this case, potentials for abuse must be recognized. This takes us to the second and third aspects of the issue on appeal.

Before we pass to equitable considerations as to the mechanism at issue here, it must be clear that an independent committee possesses the corporate power to seek the termination of a derivative suit. Section 141(c) allows a board to delegate all of its authority to a committee. Accordingly, a committee with properly delegated authority would have the power to move for dismissal or summary judgment if the entire board did.

Even though demand was not made in this case and the initial decision of whether to litigate was not placed before the board, Zapata's board, it seems to us, retained all of its corporate power concerning litigation decisions. If Maldonado had made demand on the board in this case, it could have refused to bring suit. Maldonado could then have asserted that the decision not to sue was wrongful and, if correct, would have been allowed to maintain the suit. The board, however, never would have lost its statutory managerial authority. The demand requirement itself evidences that the managerial power is retained by the board. When a derivative plaintiff is allowed to bring suit after a wrongful refusal, the board's authority to choose whether to pursue the litigation is not challenged although its conclusion—reached through the exercise of that authority—is not respected since it is wrongful. Similarly, Rule 23.1, by excusing demand in certain instances, does not strip the board of its corporate power. It merely saves the plaintiff the expense and delay of making a futile demand resulting in a probable tainted exercise of that authority in a refusal by the board or in giving control of litigation to the opposing side. But the board entity remains empowered under § 141(a) to make decisions regarding corporate litigation. The problem is one of member disqualification, not the absence of power in the board.

The corporate power inquiry then focuses on whether the board, tainted by the self-interest of a majority of its members, can legally delegate its authority to a committee of two disinterested directors. We find our statute clearly requires an affirmative answer to this question. [. . .]

We do not think that the interest taint of the board majority is per se a legal bar to the delegation of the board's power to an independent committee composed of disinterested board members. The committee can properly act for the corporation to move to dismiss derivative litigation that is believed to be detrimental to the corporation's best interest.

Our focus now switches to the Court of Chancery which is faced with a stockholder assertion that a derivative suit, properly instituted, should continue for the benefit of the corporation and a corporate assertion, properly made by a board committee acting with board authority, that the same derivative suit should be dismissed as inimical to the best interests of the corporation.

At the risk of stating the obvious, the problem is relatively simple. If, on the one hand, corporations can consistently wrest bona fide derivative actions away from well-meaning derivative plaintiffs through the use of the committee mechanism, the derivative suit will lose much, if not all, of its generally-recognized effectiveness as an intra-corporate means of policing boards of directors. [. . .] If, on the other hand, corporations are unable to rid themselves of meritless or harmful litigation and strike suits, the derivative action, created to benefit the corporation, will produce the opposite, unintended result. [. . .] It thus appears desirable to us to find a balancing point where bona fide stockholder power to bring corporate causes of action cannot be unfairly trampled on by the board of directors, but the corporation can rid itself of detrimental litigation.

As we noted, the question has been treated by other courts as one of the "business judgment" of the board committee. If a "committee, composed of independent and disinterested directors, conducted a proper review of the matters before it, considered a variety of factors and reached, in good faith, a business judgment that [the] action was not in the best interest of [the corporation]", the action must be dismissed. [. . .] The issues become solely independence, good faith, and reasonable investigation. The ultimate conclusion of the committee, under that view, is not subject to judicial review.

[. . .]

The context here is a suit against directors where demand on the board is excused. We think some tribute must be paid to the fact that the lawsuit was properly initiated. It is not a board refusal case. Moreover, this complaint was filed in June of 1975 and, while the parties undoubtedly would take differing views on the degree of litigation activity, we have to be concerned about the creation of an "Independent Investigation Committee" four years later, after the election of two new outside directors. Situations could develop where such motions could be filed after years of vigorous litigation for reasons unconnected with the merits of the lawsuit.

Moreover, notwithstanding our conviction that Delaware law entrusts the corporate power to a properly authorized committee, we must be mindful that directors are passing judgment on fellow directors in the same corporation and fellow directors, in this instance, who designated them to serve both as directors and committee members. The question naturally arises whether a "there but for the grace of God go I" empathy might not play a role. And the further question arises whether inquiry as to independence, good faith and reasonable investigation is sufficient safeguard against abuse, perhaps subconscious abuse.

[. . .]

Whether the Court of Chancery will be persuaded by the exercise of a committee power resulting in a summary motion for dismissal of a derivative action, where a demand has not been initially made, should rest, in our judgment, in the independent discretion of the Court of Chancery. We thus steer a middle course between those cases which yield to the independent business judgment of a board committee and this case as determined below which would yield to unbridled plaintiff stockholder control. [. . .]

After an objective and thorough investigation of a derivative suit, an independent committee may cause its corporation to file a pretrial motion to dismiss in the Court of Chancery. The basis of the motion is the best interests of the corporation, as determined by the committee. The motion should include a thorough written record of the investigation and its findings and recommendations. Under appropriate Court supervision, akin to proceedings on summary judgment, each side should have an opportunity to make a record on the motion. As to the limited issues presented by the motion noted below, the moving party should be prepared to meet the normal burden under Rule 56 that there is no genuine issue as to any material fact and that the moving party is entitled to dismiss as a matter of law. The Court should apply a two-step test to the motion.

First, the Court should inquire into the independence and good faith of the committee and the bases supporting its conclusions. Limited discovery may be ordered to facilitate such inquiries. The corporation should have the burden of proving independence, good faith and a reasonable investigation, rather than presuming independence, good faith and reasonableness. If the Court determines either that the committee is not independent or has not shown reasonable bases for its conclusions, or, if the Court is not satisfied for other reasons relating to the process, including but not limited to the good faith of the committee, the Court shall deny the corporation's motion. If, however, the Court is satisfied under Rule 56 standards that the committee was independent and showed reasonable bases for good faith findings and recommendations, the Court may proceed, in its discretion, to the next step.

The second step provides, we believe, the essential key in striking the balance between legitimate corporate claims as expressed in a derivative stockholder suit and a corporation's best interests as expressed by an independent investigating committee. The Court should determine, applying its own independent business judgment, whether the motion should be granted. This means, of course, that instances could arise where a committee can establish its independence and sound bases for its good faith decisions and still have the corporation's motion denied. The second step is intended to thwart instances where corporate actions meet the criteria of step one, but the result does not appear to satisfy its spirit, or where corporate actions would simply prematurely terminate a stockholder grievance deserving of further consideration in the corporation's interest. The Court of Chancery of course must carefully consider and weigh how compelling the corporate interest in dismissal is when faced with a non-frivolous lawsuit. The Court of Chancery should, when appropriate, give special consideration to matters of law and public policy in addition to the corporation's best interests.

If the Court's independent business judgment is satisfied, the Court may proceed to grant the motion, subject, of course, to any equitable terms or conditions the Court finds necessary or desirable.

The interlocutory order of the Court of Chancery is reversed and the cause is remanded for further proceedings consistent with this opinion.

In re Oracle Corp. Derivative Litigation
824 A.2d 917 (Del. Ch. 2003)

■ STRINE, VICE CHANCELLOR.

[. . .]

I.   *Factual Background*

A.   *Summary of the Plaintiffs' Allegations*

The Delaware Derivative Complaint centers on alleged insider trading by four members of Oracle's board of directors—Lawrence Ellison, Jeffrey Henley, Donald Lucas, and Michael Boskin (collectively, the "Trading Defendants"). Each of the Trading Defendants had a very different role at Oracle.

Ellison is Oracle's Chairman, Chief Executive Officer, and its largest stockholder, owning nearly twenty-five percent of Oracle's voting shares. By virtue of his ownership position, Ellison is one of the wealthiest men in America. By virtue of his managerial position, Ellison has regular access to a great deal of information about how Oracle is performing on a week-to-week basis.

Henley is Oracle's Chief Financial Officer, Executive Vice President, and a director of the corporation. Like Ellison, Henley has his finger on the pulse of Oracle's performance constantly.

Lucas is a director who chairs Oracle's Executive Committee and its Finance and Audit Committee. [. . .]

Boskin is a director, Chairman of the Compensation Committee, and a member of the Finance and Audit Committee. [. . .]

According to the plaintiffs, each of these Trading Defendants possessed material, non-public information demonstrating that Oracle would fail to meet the earnings and revenue guidance it had provided to the market in December 2000. [. . .]

[EDS.—The guidance projected that Oracle would earn 12 cents per share and generate revenues of over $2.9 billion in the third quarter of its fiscal year 2001 (December1, 2000 to February 28, 2001). Plaintiffs also allege that the Trading Defendants, on the base of these information, which made the attainment of the earnings and revenue guidance extremely difficult, engaged in substantial trading activities, selling million of dollars' worth of Oracle shares] [. . .]:

- On January 3, 2001, Lucas sold 150,000 shares of Oracle common stock at $30 per share, reaping proceeds of over $4.6 million. These sales constituted 17% of Lucas's Oracle holdings.

- On January 4, 2001, Henley sold one million shares of Oracle stock at approximately $32 per share, yielding over $32.3 million. These sales represented 7% of Henley's Oracle holdings.

- On January 17, 2001, Boskin sold 150,000 shares of Oracle stock at over $33 per share, generating in excess of $5 million. These sales were 16% of Boskin's Oracle holdings.

- From January 22 to January 31, 2001, Ellison sold over 29 million shares at prices above $30 per share, producing over $894 million. Despite the huge proceeds generated by these sales, they constituted the sale of only 2% of Ellison's Oracle holdings.

Into early to mid-February, Oracle allegedly continued to assure the market that it would meet its December guidance. Then, on March 1, 2001, the company announced that rather than posting 12 cents per share in quarterly earnings and 25% license revenue growth as projected, the company's earnings for the quarter would be 10 cents per share and license revenue growth only 6%. The stock market reacted swiftly and negatively to this news, with Oracle's share price dropping as low as $15.75 before closing at $16.88—a 21% decline in one day. These prices were well below the above $30 per share prices at which the Trading Defendants sold in January 2001. [. . .]

B. *The Plaintiffs' Claims in the Delaware Derivative Action*

The plaintiffs make two central claims in their amended complaint in the Delaware Derivative Action. First, the plaintiffs allege that the Trading Defendants breached their duty of loyalty by misappropriating inside information and using it as the basis for trading decisions. [. . .]

Second, as to the other defendants—who are the members of the Oracle board who did not trade—the plaintiffs allege a *Caremark* violation, in the sense that the board's indifference to the deviation between the company's December guidance and reality was so extreme as to constitute subjective bad faith. [. . .]

D. *The Formation of the Special Litigation Committee*

On February 1, 2002, Oracle formed the SLC in order to investigate the Delaware Derivative Action and to determine whether Oracle should press the claims raised by the plaintiffs, settle the case, or terminate it. Soon after its formation, the SLC's charge was broadened to give it the same mandate as to all the pending derivative actions, wherever they were filed.

The SLC was granted full authority to decide these matters without the need for approval by the other members of the Oracle board.

E. *The Members of the Special Litigation Committee*

Two Oracle board members were named to the SLC. Both of them joined the Oracle board on October 15, 2001, more than a half a year after Oracle's 3Q FY 2001 closed. The SLC members also share something else: both are tenured professors at Stanford University.

Professor Hector Garcia-Molina is Chairman of the Computer Science Department at Stanford and holds the Leonard Bosack and Sandra Lerner Professorship in the Computer Science and Electrical Engineering Departments at Stanford. [. . .]

The other SLC member, Professor Joseph Grundfest, is the W.A. Franke Professor of Law and Business at Stanford University. He directs the University's well-known Directors' College and the Roberts Program in Law, Business, and Corporate Governance at the Stanford Law School. Grundfest is also the principal investigator for the Law School's Securities Litigation Clearinghouse. Immediately before coming to Stanford, Grundfest served for five years as a Commissioner of the Securities and Exchange Commission. [. . .]

As will be discussed more specifically later, Grundfest also serves as a steering committee member and a senior fellow of the Stanford Institute for Economic Policy Research, and releases working papers under the "SIEPR" banner.

For their services, the SLC members were paid $250 an hour, a rate below that which they could command for other activities, such as consulting or expert witness testimony. Nonetheless, during the course of their work, the SLC members became concerned that (arguably scandal-driven) developments in the evolving area of corporate governance as well as the decision in *Telxon v. Meyerson,* might render the amount of their compensation so high as to be an argument against their independence. Therefore, Garcia-Molina and Grundfest agreed to give up any SLC-related compensation if their compensation was deemed by this court to impair their impartiality.

F.   *The SLC Members Are Recruited to the Board*

The SLC members were recruited to the board primarily by defendant Lucas, with help from defendant Boskin. The wooing of them began in the summer of 2001. Before deciding to join the Oracle board, Grundfest, in particular, did a good deal of due diligence. [. . .]

Grundfest then met with defendants Ellison and Henley [. . .]. Grundfest received answers that were consistent enough with what he called the "exogenous" information about the case to form sufficient confidence to at least join the Oracle board. Grundfest testified that [. . .] Ellison's and Henley's explanations of their conduct were plausible [and] these were reputable businessmen with whom he felt comfortable serving as a fellow director, and that Henley had given very impressive answers to difficult questions regarding the way Oracle conducted its financial reporting operations.

G.   *The SLC's Advisors*

The most important advisors retained by the SLC were its counsel from Simpson Thacher & Bartlett LLP. [. . .] [P]laintiffs have not challenged its independence. [. . .]

H. *The SLC's Investigation and Report*

The SLC's investigation was, by any objective measure, extensive. The SLC reviewed an enormous amount of paper and electronic records. SLC counsel interviewed seventy witnesses, some of them twice. SLC members participated in several key interviews, including the interviews of the Trading Defendants. [. . .]

In the end, the SLC produced an extremely lengthy Report totaling 1,110 pages (excluding appendices and exhibits) that concluded that Oracle should not pursue the plaintiffs' claims against the Trading Defendants or any of the other Oracle directors serving during the 3Q FY 2001. [. . .]

Thus, taking into account all the relevant information sources, the SLC concluded that [the defendants] did not possess material, nonpublic information. [. . .]

In this same regard, the Report also noted that Oracle insiders felt especially confident about meeting 3Q FY 2001 guidance because the company closed a large transaction involving Covisint in December—a transaction that produced revenue giving the company a boost in meeting its guidance. [. . .]

Moreover, as the SLC Report points out, the idea that the Trading Defendants acted with *scienter* in trading in January 2001 was problematic in light of several factors. Implicitly the first and foremost is the reality that Oracle is a functioning business with real products of value. Although it is plausible to imagine a scenario where someone of Ellison's wealth would cash out, fearing the imminent collapse of a house of cards he had sold to an unsuspecting market, this is not the situation that Ellison faced in January 2001.

As of that time, Oracle faced no collapse, even if it, like other companies, had to deal with a slowing economy. And, as the SLC points out, Ellison sold only two percent of his holdings. [. . .] In view of Oracle's basic health, Ellison's huge wealth, and his retention of ninety-eight percent of his shares, the SLC concluded that any inference that Ellison acted with *scienter* and attempted to reap improper trading profits was untenable.

The same reasoning also motivated the SLC's conclusions as to Henley, who sold only seven percent of his stake in Oracle. Both Ellison and Henley stood to expose a great deal of their personal wealth to substantial risk by undertaking a scheme to cash out a small portion of their holdings and risking a greater injury to Oracle, a company in which they retained a far greater stake than they had sold. [. . .]

Of course, the amount of the proceeds each of the Trading Defendants generated was extremely large. By selling only two percent of his holdings, Ellison generated nearly a billion dollars, enough to flee to a small island nation with no extradition laws and to live like a Saudi prince. But given Oracle's fundamental health as a company and his retention of ninety-eight percent of his shares, Ellison (the SLC found) had no need to take desperate—or, for that matter, even slightly risky—measures. The same goes for the other Trading Defendants; there was simply nothing special or urgent about their financial circumstances in January 2001 that would have motivated (or did motivate, in the SLC's view) the Trading Defendants to cash out because they believed that Oracle would miss its earnings guidance. [. . .]

For these and other reasons, the SLC concluded that the plaintiffs' allegations that the Trading Defendants had breached their fiduciary duty of loyalty by using inside information about Oracle to reap illicit trading gains were without merit. [. . .] Therefore, the SLC determined to seek dismissal of the Delaware Derivative Action and the other derivative actions.

II. *The SLC Moves to Terminate*

Consistent with its Report, the SLC moved to terminate this litigation. [. . .]

III. *The Applicable Procedural Standard*

In order to prevail on its motion to terminate the Delaware Derivative Action, the SLC must persuade me that: (1) its members were independent; (2) that they acted in good faith; and (3) that they had reasonable bases for their recommendations. If the SLC meets that burden, I am free to grant its motion or may, in my discretion, undertake my own examination of whether Oracle should terminate and permit the suit to proceed if I, in my oxymoronic judicial "business judgment," conclude that procession is in the best interests of the company. This two-step analysis comes, of course, from *Zapata*. [. . .]

As I understand it, this standard requires me to determine whether, on the basis of the undisputed factual record, I am convinced that the SLC was independent, acted in good faith, and had a reasonable basis for its recommendation. If there is a material factual question about these issues causing doubt about any of these grounds, I read *Zapata* and its progeny as requiring a denial of the SLC's motion to terminate.

In this case, the plaintiffs principally challenge the SLC's independence and the reasonableness of its recommendation. For reasons I next explain, I need examine only the more difficult question, which relates to the SLC's independence.

IV. *Is the SLC Independent?*

A. *The Facts Disclosed in the Report*

In its Report, the SLC took the position that its members were independent. In support of that position, the Report noted several factors including:

- the fact that neither Grundfest nor Garcia-Molina received compensation from Oracle other than as directors;

- the fact that neither Grundfest nor Garcia-Molina were on the Oracle board at the time of the alleged wrongdoing;

- the fact that both Grundfest and Garcia-Molina were willing to return their compensation as SLC members if necessary to preserve their status as independent;

- the absence of any other material ties between Oracle, the Trading Defendants, and any of the other defendants, on the one hand, and Grundfest and Garcia-Molina, on the other; and

- the absence of any material ties between Oracle, the Trading Defendants, and any of the other defendants, on the one hand, and the SLC's advisors, on the other.

Noticeably absent from the SLC Report was any disclosure of several significant ties between Oracle or the Trading Defendants and Stanford University, the university that employs both members of the SLC. In the Report, it was only disclosed that:

- defendant Boskin was a Stanford professor;

- the SLC members were aware that Lucas had made certain donations to Stanford; and

- among the contributions was a donation of $50,000 worth of stock that Lucas donated to Stanford Law School after Grundfest delivered a speech to a venture capital fund meeting in response to Lucas's request. It happens that Lucas's son is a partner in the fund and that approximately half the donation was allocated for use by Grundfest in his personal research.

B. *The "Stanford" Facts that Emerged During Discovery*

In view of the modesty of these disclosed ties, it was with some shock that a series of other ties among Stanford, Oracle, and the Trading Defendants emerged during discovery. [. . .]Before discussing these facts, I begin with certain features of the record [. . .] that are favorable to the SLC. Initially, I am satisfied that neither of the SLC members is compromised by a fear that support for the procession of this suit would endanger his ability to make a nice living. Both of the SLC members are distinguished in their fields and highly respected. Both have tenure, which could not have been stripped from them for making a determination that this lawsuit should proceed.

Nor have the plaintiffs developed evidence that either Grundfest or Garcia-Molina have fundraising responsibilities at Stanford. Although Garcia-Molina is a department chairman, the record is devoid of any indication that he is required to generate contributions. And even though Grundfest heads up Stanford's Directors' College, the plaintiffs have not argued that he has a fundraising role in that regard. For this reason, it is important to acknowledge up front that the SLC members occupy positions within the Stanford community different from that of the University's President, deans, and development professionals, all of whom, it can be reasonably assumed, are required to engage heavily in the pursuit of contributions to the University.

This is an important point of departure for discussing the multitude of ties that have emerged among the Trading Defendants, Oracle, and Stanford during discovery in this case. In evaluating these ties, the court is not faced with the relatively easier call of considering whether these ties would call into question the impartiality of an SLC member who was a key fundraiser at Stanford or who was an untenured faculty member subject to removal without cause. Instead, one must acknowledge that the question is whether the ties I am about to identify would be of a material concern to two distinguished, tenured faculty members whose current jobs would not be threatened by whatever good faith decision they made as SLC members.

With this question in mind, I begin to discuss the specific ties that allegedly compromise the SLC's independence, beginning with those involving Professor Boskin.

1. *Boskin*

Defendant Michael J. Boskin is the T.M. Friedman Professor of Economics at Stanford University. During the Administration of President George H.W. Bush, Boskin occupied the coveted and important position of Chairman of the President's Council of Economic Advisors. He returned to Stanford after this government service, continuing a teaching career there that had begun many years earlier.

During the 1970s, Boskin taught Grundfest when Grundfest was a Ph.D. candidate. [. . .][T]he two have remained in contact over the years, speaking occasionally about matters of public policy.

Furthermore, both Boskin and Grundfest are senior fellows and steering committee members at the Stanford Institute for Economic Policy Research, which was previously defined as "SIEPR." According to the SLC, the title of senior fellow is largely an honorary one. According to SIEPR's own web site, however, "[s]enior fellows actively participate in SIEPR research and participate in its governance."

Likewise, the SLC contends that Grundfest went MIA as a steering committee member, having failed to attend a meeting since 1997. The SIEPR web site, however, identifies its steering committee as having the role of "advising the director [of SIEPR] and guiding [SIEPR] on matters pertaining to research and academics." Because Grundfest allegedly did not attend to these duties, his service alongside Boskin in that capacity is, the SLC contends, not relevant to his independence.

That said, the SLC does not deny that both Boskin and Grundfest publish working papers under the SIEPR rubric and that SIEPR helps to publicize their respective works. Indeed, as I will note later in this opinion, Grundfest, in the same month the SLC was formed, addressed a meeting of some of SIEPR's largest benefactors [. . .]. The SLC just claims that the SIEPR affiliation is one in which SIEPR basks in the glow of Boskin and Grundfest, not the other way around, and that the mutual service of the two as senior fellows and steering committee members is not a collegial tie of any significance. [. . .]

2. *Lucas*

As noted in the SLC Report, the SLC members admitted knowing that Lucas was a contributor to Stanford. They also acknowledged that he had donated $50,000 to Stanford Law School in appreciation for Grundfest having given a speech at his request. About half of the proceeds were allocated for use by Grundfest in his research.

[. . .] Lucas is a Stanford alumnus, [. . .] a very loyal alumnus.

[. . .] The Richard M. Lucas Foundation has given $11.7 million to Stanford since its 1981 founding. [. . .]

The SLC Report did not mention the Richard M. Lucas Foundation or its grants to Stanford. [. . .]

From his own personal funds, Lucas has contributed $4.1 million to Stanford [. . .].

3. *Ellison*

There can be little doubt that Ellison is a major figure in the community in which Stanford is located. [. . .] One of the wealthiest men in America, Ellison is a major figure in the nation's increasingly important information technology industry. Given his wealth, Ellison is also in a position to make—and, in fact, he has made—major charitable contributions.

Some of the largest of these contributions have been made through the Ellison Medical Foundation, which makes grants to universities and laboratories to support biomedical research relating to aging and infectious diseases. [. . .]

During the time Ellison has been CEO of Oracle, the company itself has also made over $300,000 in donations to Stanford. Not only that, when Oracle established a generously endowed educational foundation—the Oracle Help Us Help Foundation—to help further the deployment of educational technology in schools serving disadvantaged populations, it named Stanford as the "appointing authority," which gave Stanford the right to name four of the Foundation's seven directors. [. . .]

Taken together, these facts suggest that Ellison (when considered as an individual and as the key executive and major stockholder of Oracle) had, at the very least, been involved in several endeavors of value to Stanford.

Beginning in the year 2000 and continuing well into 2001—the same year that Ellison made the trades the plaintiffs contend were suspicious and the same year the SLC members were asked to join the Oracle board— Ellison and Stanford discussed a much more lucrative donation. The idea

Stanford proposed for discussion was the creation of an Ellison Scholars Program modeled on the Rhodes Scholarship at Oxford. The proposed budget for Stanford's answer to Oxford: $170 million. [. . .]

As part of his proposal for the Ellison Scholars Program, Shoven [EDS.— the Director of SIEPR] suggested that three of the four Trading Defendants—Ellison, Lucas, and Boskin—be on the Program board. In the hypothetical curriculum that Shoven presented to Ellison, he included a course entitled "Legal Institutions and the Modern Economy" to be taught by Grundfest. [. . .]

In order to buttress the argument that Stanford did not feel beholden to him, Ellison shared with the court the (otherwise private) fact that one of his children had applied to Stanford in October 2000 and was not admitted. If Stanford felt comfortable rejecting Ellison's child, the SLC contends, why should the SLC members hesitate before recommending that Oracle press insider trading-based fiduciary duty claims against Ellison?

But the fact remains that Ellison was still talking very publicly and seriously about the possibility of endowing a graduate interdisciplinary studies program at Stanford during the summer *after* his child was rejected from Stanford's undergraduate program.

C. *The SLC's Argument*

The SLC contends that even together, these facts regarding the ties among Oracle, the Trading Defendants, Stanford, and the SLC members do not impair the SLC's independence. In so arguing, the SLC places great weight on the fact that none of the Trading Defendants have the practical ability to deprive either Grundfest or Garcia-Molina of their current positions at Stanford. Nor, given their tenure, does Stanford itself have any practical ability to punish them for taking action adverse to Boskin, Lucas, or Ellison—each of whom, as we have seen, has contributed (in one way or another) great value to Stanford as an institution. As important, neither Garcia-Molina nor Grundfest are part of the official fundraising apparatus at Stanford; thus, it is not their on-the-job duty to be solicitous of contributors [. . .].

In so arguing, the SLC focuses on the language of previous opinions of this court and the Delaware Supreme Court that indicates that a director is not independent only if he is dominated and controlled by an interested party, such as a Trading Defendant. The SLC also emphasizes that much of our jurisprudence on independence focuses on economically consequential relationships between the allegedly interested party and the directors who allegedly cannot act independently of that director. [. . .] Putting a point on this, the SLC cites certain decisions of Delaware courts concluding that directors who are personal friends of an interested party were not, by virtue of those personal ties, to be labeled non-independent.

More subtly, the SLC argues that university professors simply are not inhibited types, unwilling to make tough decisions even as to fellow professors and large contributors. What is tenure about if not to provide professors with intellectual freedom, even in non-traditional roles such as special litigation committee members? No less ardently [. . .], the SLC contends that Garcia-Molina and Grundfest [. . .] were not, in fact, influenced by the facts identified heretofore. Indeed, the SLC argues, how could they have been influenced by many of these facts when they did not learn them until the post-Report discovery process? If it boils down to the simple fact that both share with Boskin the status of a Stanford professor, how material can this be when there are 1,700 others who also occupy the same position?

D. *The Plaintiffs' Arguments*

[. . .] Taken in their totality, the plaintiffs contend, these connections simply constitute too great a bias-producing factor for the SLC to meet its burden to prove its independence.

Even more, the plaintiffs argue that the SLC's failure to identify many of these connections in its Report is not an asset proving its independence, but instead a fundamental flaw in the Report itself, which is the document in which the SLC is supposed to demonstrate its own independence and the reasonableness of its investigation. By failing to focus on these connections when they were obviously discoverable [. . .] the SLC calls into doubt not only its independence, but its competence. If it could not ferret out these things, by what right should the court trust its investigative acumen?

In support of its argument, the plaintiffs note that the Delaware courts have adopted a flexible, fact-based approach to the determination of directorial independence. This test focuses on whether the directors, for any substantial reason, cannot act with only the best interests of the corporation in mind, and not just on whether the directors face pecuniary damage for acting in a particular way.

E. *The Court's Analysis of the SLC's Independence*

[. . .] I begin with an important reminder: the SLC bears the burden of proving its independence. It must convince me.

But of what? According to the SLC, its members are independent unless they are essentially subservient to the Trading Defendants—*i.e.*, they are under the "domination and control" of the interested parties. If the SLC is correct and this is the central inquiry in the independence determination, they would win. Nothing in the record suggests to me that either Garcia-Molina or Grundfest are dominated and controlled by any of the Trading Defendants, by Oracle, or even by Stanford.

But, in my view, an emphasis on "domination and control" would serve only to fetishize much-parroted language, at the cost of denuding the independence inquiry of its intellectual integrity. Take an easy example. Imagine if two brothers were on a corporate board, each successful in different businesses and not dependent in any way on the other's beneficence in order to be wealthy. The brothers are brothers, they stay in touch and consider each other family, but each is opinionated and strong-willed. A derivative action is filed targeting a transaction involving one of the brothers. The other brother is put on a special litigation committee to investigate the case. If the test is domination and control, then one brother could investigate the other. Does any sensible person think that is our law? I do not think it is.

And it should not be our law. Delaware law should not be based on a reductionist view of human nature that simplifies human motivations on the lines of the least sophisticated notions of the law and economics movement. *Homo sapiens* is not merely *homo economicus.* We may be thankful that an array of other motivations exist that influence human behavior; not all are any better than greed or avarice, think of envy, to name just one. But also think of motives like love, friendship, and collegiality, think of those among us who direct their behavior as best they can on a guiding creed or set of moral values.

Nor should our law ignore the social nature of humans. To be direct, corporate directors are generally the sort of people deeply enmeshed in social institutions. Such institutions have norms, expectations that, explicitly and implicitly, influence and channel the behavior of those who participate in their operation. [. . .] In being appropriately sensitive to this factor, our law also cannot assume—absent some proof of the point— that corporate directors are, as a general matter, persons of unusual social bravery, who operate heedless to the inhibitions that social norms generate for ordinary folk.

For all these reasons, this court has previously held that the Delaware Supreme Court's teachings on independence can be summarized thusly:

At bottom, the question of independence turns on whether a director is, *for any substantial reason,* incapable of making a decision with only the best interests of the corporation in mind. That is, the Supreme Court cases ultimately focus on impartiality and objectivity. [. . .]

1.   *The Contextual Nature of the Independence Inquiry Under Delaware Law*

In examining whether the SLC has met its burden to demonstrate that there is no material dispute of fact regarding its independence, the court must bear in mind the function of special litigation committees under our jurisprudence. Under Delaware law, the primary means by which corporate defendants may obtain a dismissal of a derivative suit is by showing that the plaintiffs have not met their pleading burden under the [*Brookfield Asset Management, Inc. v. Rosson* test] In simple terms, these tests permit a corporation to terminate a derivative suit if its board is comprised of directors who can impartially consider a demand.

Special litigation committees are permitted as a last chance for a corporation to control a derivative claim in circumstances when a majority of its directors cannot impartially consider a demand. By vesting the power of the board to determine what to do with the suit in a committee of independent directors, a corporation may retain control over whether the suit will proceed, so long as the committee meets the standard set forth in *Zapata*.

In evaluating the independence of a special litigation committee, this court must take into account the extraordinary importance and difficulty of such a committee's responsibility. [. . .] Denying a fellow director the ability to proceed on a matter important to him may not be easy, but it must, as a general matter, be less difficult than finding that there is reason to believe that the fellow director has committed serious wrongdoing and that a derivative suit should proceed against him.

The difficulty of making this decision is compounded in the special litigation committee context because the weight of making the moral judgment necessarily falls on less than the full board. A small number of directors feels the moral gravity—and social pressures—of this duty alone.

For all these reasons, the independence inquiry is critically important if the special litigation committee process is to retain its integrity, a quality that is, in turn, essential to the utility of that process.

[. . .] Thus, in assessing the independence of the Oracle SLC, I necessarily examine the question of whether the SLC can independently make the difficult decision entrusted to it: to determine whether the Trading Defendants should face suit for insider trading-based allegations of breach of fiduciary duty. An affirmative answer by the SLC to that question would have potentially huge negative consequences for the Trading Defendants, not only by exposing them to the possibility of a large damage award but also by subjecting them to great reputational harm. To have Professors Grundfest and Garcia-Molina declare that Oracle should press insider trading claims against the Trading Defendants would have been, to put it mildly, "news." Relatedly, it is reasonable to think that an SLC determination that the Trading Defendants had likely engaged in insider trading would have been accompanied by a recommendation that they step down as fiduciaries until their ultimate culpability was decided. [. . .]

2. *The SLC Has Not Met Its Burden to Demonstrate the Absence of a Material Dispute of Fact About Its Independence*

Using the contextual approach I have described, I conclude that the SLC has not met its burden to show the absence of a material factual question about its independence. I find this to be the case because the ties among the SLC, the Trading Defendants, and Stanford are so substantial that they cause reasonable doubt about the SLC's ability to impartially consider whether the Trading Defendants should face suit. [. . .]

As SLC members, Grundfest and Garcia-Molina were already being asked to consider whether the company should level extremely serious accusations of wrongdoing against fellow board members. As to Boskin, both SLC members faced another layer of complexity: the determination of whether to have Oracle press insider trading claims against a fellow professor at their university. Even though Boskin was in a different academic department from either SLC member, it is reasonable to assume that the fact that Boskin was also on faculty would—to persons possessing typical sensibilities and institutional loyalty—be a matter of more than trivial concern. Universities are obviously places of at-times intense debate, but they also see themselves as communities. In fact, Stanford refers to itself as a "community of scholars." To accuse a fellow professor—whom one might see at the faculty club or at inter-disciplinary presentations of academic papers—of insider trading cannot be a small thing—even for the most callous of academics.

As to Boskin, Grundfest faced an even more complex challenge than Garcia-Molina. Boskin was a professor who had taught him and with whom he had maintained contact over the years. Their areas of academic interest intersected, putting Grundfest in contact if not directly with Boskin, then regularly with Boskin's colleagues. [. . .] Having these ties, Grundfest (I infer) would have more difficulty objectively determining whether Boskin engaged in improper insider trading than would a person who was not a fellow professor, had not been a student of Boskin, had not kept in touch with Boskin over the years, and who was not a senior fellow and steering committee member at SIEPR.

In so concluding, I necessarily draw on a general sense of human nature. It may be that Grundfest is a very special person who is capable of putting these kinds of things totally aside. But the SLC has not provided evidence that that is the case. [. . .] Human nature being what it is, it is entirely possible that Grundfest would in fact be tougher on Boskin than he would on someone with whom he did not have such connections. The inference I draw is subtly, but importantly, different. What I infer is that a person in Grundfest's position would find it difficult to assess Boskin's conduct without pondering his own association with Boskin and their mutual affiliations. Although these connections might produce bias in either a tougher or laxer direction, the key inference is that these connections would be on the mind of a person in Grundfest's position, putting him in the position of either causing serious legal action to be brought against a person with whom he shares several connections (an awkward thing) or not doing so (and risking being seen as having engaged in favoritism toward his old professor and SIEPR colleague).

The same concerns also exist as to Lucas. For Grundfest to vote to accuse Lucas of insider trading would require him to accuse SIEPR's Advisory Board Chair and major benefactor of serious wrongdoing—of conduct that violates federal securities laws. Such action would also require

Grundfest to make charges against a man who recently donated $50,000 to Stanford Law School after Grundfest made a speech at his request.

And, for both Grundfest and Garcia-Molina, service on the SLC demanded that they consider whether an extremely generous and influential Stanford alumnus should be sued by Oracle for insider trading. Although they were not responsible for fundraising, as sophisticated professors they undoubtedly are aware of how important large contributors are to Stanford, and they share in the benefits that come from serving at a university with a rich endowment. A reasonable professor giving any thought to the matter would obviously consider the effect his decision might have on the University's relationship with Lucas, it being (one hopes) sensible to infer that a professor of reasonable collegiality and loyalty cares about the well-being of the institution he serves.

In so concluding, I give little weight to the SLC's argument that it was unaware of just how substantial Lucas's beneficence to Stanford has been. I do so for two key reasons. Initially, it undermines, rather than inspires, confidence that the SLC did not examine the Trading Defendant's ties to Stanford more closely in preparing its Report. The Report's failure to identify these ties is important because it is the SLC's burden to show independence. In forming the SLC, the Oracle board should have undertaken a thorough consideration of the facts bearing on the independence of the proposed SLC members from the key objects of the investigation.

The purported ignorance of the SLC members about all of Lucas's donations to Stanford is not helpful to them. [. . .] It is improbable that Grundfest was not aware that Lucas was the Chair of SIEPR's Advisory Board [. . .] Grundfest would have had to be extremely insensitive to his own working environment not to have considered Lucas an extremely generous alumni benefactor of Stanford, and at SIEPR and the Law School in particular. [. . .]

In concluding that the facts regarding Lucas's relationship with Stanford are materially important, I must address a rather odd argument of the SLC's. The argument goes as follows. Stanford has an extremely large endowment. Lucas's contributions, while seemingly large, constitute a very small proportion of Stanford's endowment and annual donations. Therefore, Lucas could not be a materially important contributor to Stanford and the SLC's independence could not be compromised by that factor. [. . .]

But missing from that syllogism is any acknowledgement of the role that Stanford's solicitude to benefactors like Lucas might play in the overall size of its endowment and campus facilities. Endowments and buildings grow one contribution at a time, and they do not grow by callous indifference to alumni who (personally and through family foundations) have participated in directing contributions of the size Lucas has. Buildings and conference centers are named as they are as a recognition of the high regard universities have for donors (or at least, must feign convincingly). The SLC asks me to believe that what universities like Stanford say in thank you letters and public ceremonies is not in reality true; that, in actuality, their contributors are not materially important to the health of those academic institutions. This is a proposition that the SLC has not convinced me is true, and that seems to contradict common experience.

Nor has the SLC convinced me that tenured faculty are indifferent to large contributors to their institutions [. . .]. The idea that faculty members would not be concerned that action of that kind might offend a large contributor who a university administrator or fellow faculty colleague (e.g., Shoven at SIEPR) had taken the time to cultivate strikes me as implausible and as resting on a narrow-minded understanding of the way that collegiality works in institutional settings.

In view of the ties involving Boskin and Lucas alone, I would conclude that the SLC has failed to meet its burden on the independence question.

[. . .] The notion that anyone in Palo Alto can accuse Ellison of insider trading without harboring some fear of social awkwardness seems a stretch. That being said, I do not mean to imply that the mere fact that Ellison is worth tens of billions of dollars and is the key force behind a very important social institution in Silicon Valley disqualifies all persons who live there from being independent of him. Rather, it is merely an acknowledgement of the simple fact that accusing such a significant person in that community of such serious wrongdoing is no small thing.

Given that general context, Ellison's relationship to Stanford itself contributes to my overall doubt, when heaped on top of the ties involving Boskin and Lucas. During the period when Grundfest and Garcia-Molina were being added to the Oracle board, Ellison was publicly considering making extremely large contributions to Stanford. Although the SLC denies knowledge of these public statements, Grundfest claims to have done a fair amount of research before joining the board, giving me doubt that he was not somewhat aware of the possibility that Ellison might bestow large blessings on Stanford. This is especially so when I cannot rule out the possibility that Grundfest had been told by Lucas about, but has now honestly forgotten, the negotiations over the Ellison Scholars Program.

Of course, the SLC says these facts are meaningless because Stanford rejected Ellison's child for admission. I am not sure what to make of this fact, but it surely cannot bear the heavy weight the SLC gives it. [. . .] Suffice to say that after the rejection took place, it did not keep Ellison from making public statements in *Fortune* magazine on August 13, 2001 about his consideration of making a huge donation to Stanford, at the same time when the two SLC members were being courted to join the Oracle board. [. . .]

Taken in isolation, the facts about Ellison might well not be enough to compromise the SLC's independence. But that is not the relevant inquiry. The pertinent question is whether, given *all* the facts, the SLC has met its independence burden.

When viewed in that manner, the facts about Ellison buttress the conclusion that the SLC has not met its burden. Whether the SLC members had precise knowledge of all the facts that have emerged is not essential, what is important is that by any measure this was a social atmosphere painted in too much vivid Stanford Cardinal red for the SLC members to have reasonably ignored it. Summarized fairly, two Stanford professors were recruited to the Oracle board in summer 2001 and soon asked to investigate a fellow professor and two benefactors of the University. On Grundfest's part, the facts are more substantial, because his connections—through his personal experiences, SIEPR, and the Law School—to Boskin and to Lucas run deeper.

It seems to me that the connections outlined in this opinion would weigh on the mind of a reasonable special litigation committee member deciding whether to level the serious charge of insider trading against the Trading Defendants. As indicated before, this does not mean that the SLC would be less inclined to find such charges meritorious, only that the connections identified would be on the mind of the SLC members in a way that generates an unacceptable risk of bias. That is, these connections generate a reasonable doubt about the SLC's impartiality because they suggest that material considerations other than the best interests of Oracle could have influenced the SLC's inquiry and judgments.

[. . .] To conclude that the Oracle SLC was not independent is not a conclusion that the two accomplished professors who comprise it are not persons of good faith and moral probity, it is solely to conclude that they were not situated to act with the required degree of impartiality. *Zapata* requires independence to ensure that stockholders do not have to rely upon special litigation committee members who must put aside personal considerations that are ordinarily influential in daily behavior in making the already difficult decision to accuse fellow directors of serious wrongdoing.

Finally, the SLC has made the argument that a ruling against it will chill the ability of corporations to locate qualified independent directors in the academy. This is overwrought. If there are 1,700 professors at Stanford alone, as the SLC says, how many must there be on the west coast of the United States, at institutions without ties to Oracle and the Trading Defendants as substantial as Stanford's? [. . .]

Rather than form an SLC whose membership was free from bias-creating relationships, Oracle formed a committee fraught with them. As a result, the SLC has failed to meet its *Zapata* burden, and its motion to terminate must be denied. [. . .] In the absence of a finding that the SLC was independent, its subjective good faith and the reasonableness of its conclusions would not be sufficient to justify termination. Without confidence that the SLC was impartial, its findings do not provide the assurance our law requires for the dismissal of a derivative suit without a merits inquiry.

V. *Conclusion*

The SLC's motion to terminate is DENIED. IT IS SO ORDERED.

H. DIRECTOR INDEPENDENCE

Beam ex rel. Martha Stewart Living Omnimedia, Inc. v. Stewart

845 A.2d 1040 (Del. 2004)

■ VEASEY, CHIEF JUSTICE:

[. . .]

Facts

The plaintiff, Monica A. Beam, owns shares of Martha Stewart Living Omnimedia, Inc. ("MSO"). Beam filed a derivative action in the Court of Chancery against Martha Stewart [and] the five other members of MSO's board of directors [. . .].

In the single claim at issue on appeal [. . .], Beam alleged that Stewart breached her fiduciary duties of loyalty and care by illegally selling ImClone stock in December of 2001 and by mishandling the media attention that followed, thereby jeopardizing the financial future of MSO. The Court of Chancery dismissed [this claim] under Court of Chancery Rule 23.1 because Beam failed to plead particularized facts demonstrating pre-suit demand futility.

When Beam filed the complaint in the Court of Chancery, the MSO board of directors consisted of six members: [Chairman, Chief Executive Officer, and majority shareholder] Stewart, [President and Chief Operating Officer] Sharon L. Patrick, Arthur C. Martinez, Darla D. Moore, Naomi O. Seligman, and Jeffrey W. Ubben. The Chancellor concluded that the complaint alleged sufficient facts to support the conclusion that two of the directors, Stewart and Patrick, were not disinterested or independent for purposes of considering a pre-suit demand.

The Court of Chancery found that [. . .] Stewart [was] an interested party and therefore unable to consider demand. The Court also found that Patrick's position [. . .] raised a reasonable doubt as to her ability objectively to consider demand. The defendants do not challenge the Court's conclusions with respect to Patrick and Stewart.

We now address the plaintiff's allegations concerning the independence of the other board members. [EDS.—If three directors on the six-director board are deemed non-independent, there is not a majority of independent directors, and demand would be futile.] We must determine if the following allegations of the complaint, and the reasonable inferences that may flow from them, create a reasonable doubt of the independence of [. . .] Moore or Seligman: [. . .]

> 5.   Defendant Darla D. Moore is a director of the Company, a position she has held since September 2001. [. . .] Moore is a longstanding friend of defendant Stewart. In November 1995, she attended a wedding reception hosted by Stewart's personal lawyer, Allen Grubman, for his daughter. Also in attendance [was] Stewart. In August 1996, *Fortune* carried an article highlighting Moore's close personal relationship with [. . .] defendant Stewart. When [Charlotte] Beers, a longtime friend and confidante to Stewart, resigned from the Company's board in September 2001, Moore was nominated to replace her.

> 6.   Defendant Naomi O. Seligman ("Seligman") is a director of the Company, a position that she has held since September 1999. [. . .] According to a story appearing on July 2, 2002 in *The Wall Street Journal*, Seligman contacted the Chief Executive Officer of John Wiley & Sons (a publishing house) at defendant Stewart's behest last year to express concern over its planned publication of a biography that was critical of Stewart. [. . .]

> 8.   [. . .] Moore [and] [Seligman] are hereinafter referred to collectively as the Director Defendants. By reason of Stewart's overwhelming voting control over the Company, each of the Director Defendants serves at her sufferance. Each of the Director Defendants receive [sic] valuable perquisites and benefits by reason of their service on the Company's Board. [. . .]

Director Independence

[. . .] A director will be considered unable to act objectively with respect to a pre-suit demand if he or she is interested in the outcome of the litigation or is otherwise not independent. A director's interest may be shown by demonstrating a potential personal benefit or detriment to the director as a result of the decision. "In such circumstances, a director cannot be expected to exercise his or her independent business judgment without being influenced by the . . . personal consequences resulting from the decision." *Rales v. Blasband.* The primary basis upon which a director's independence must be measured is whether the director's decision is based on the corporate merits of the subject before the board, rather than extraneous considerations or influences. This broad statement of the law requires an analysis of whether the director is disinterested in the underlying transaction and, even if disinterested, whether the director is otherwise independent. More precisely in the context of the present case, the independence inquiry requires us to determine whether there is a reasonable doubt that any one of these three directors is capable of objectively making a business decision to assert or not assert a corporate claim against Stewart.

Independence Is a Contextual Inquiry

Independence is a fact-specific determination made in the context of a particular case. The court must make that determination by answering the inquiries: independent from whom and independent for what purpose? To excuse presuit demand in this case, the plaintiff has the burden to plead particularized facts that create a reasonable doubt sufficient to rebut the presumption that either Moore [or] Seligman [. . .] was independent of defendant Stewart.

In order to show lack of independence, the complaint of a stockholder-plaintiff must create a reasonable doubt that a director is not so "beholden" to an interested director (in this case Stewart) that his or her "discretion would be sterilized." [. . .] The "reasonable doubt" standard "is sufficiently flexible and workable to provide the stockholder with 'the keys to the courthouse' in an appropriate case where the claim is not based on mere suspicions or stated solely in conclusory terms." *Grimes v. Donald.*

Personal Friendship

A variety of motivations, including friendship, may influence the demand futility inquiry. But, to render a director unable to consider demand, a relationship must be of a bias-producing nature. Allegations of mere personal friendship or a mere outside business relationship, standing alone, are insufficient to raise a reasonable doubt about a director's independence. In this connection, we adopt as our own the Chancellor's analysis in this case:

> [S]ome professional or personal friendships, which may border on or even exceed familial loyalty and closeness, may raise a reasonable doubt whether a director can appropriately consider demand. This is particularly true when the allegations raise serious questions of either civil or criminal liability of such a close friend. Not all friendships, or even most of them, rise to this level and the Court cannot make a *reasonable* inference that a particular friendship does so without specific factual allegations to support such a conclusion. *Litt v. Wycoff.*

The facts alleged by Beam regarding the relationships between Stewart and these other members of MSO's board of directors largely boil down to a "structural bias" argument, which presupposes that the professional and social relationships that naturally develop among members of a board impede independent decisionmaking.[29] This Court addressed the structural bias argument in *Aronson v. Lewis:*

---

[29] *See* DENNIS J. BLOCK ET AL., THE BUSINESS JUDGMENT RULE 1765 (5th ed. 1998) (describing the "'structural bias' viewpoint . . . [as holding] that the judgment of seemingly disinterested directors—who are not defendants in a litigation or participants in wrongdoing alleged in a litigation—is inherently corrupted by the 'common cultural bond' and 'natural empathy and collegiality' shared by most directors") [. . .] [.]

> Critics will charge that [by requiring the independence of only a majority of the board] we are ignoring the structural bias common to corporate boards throughout America, as well as the other unseen socialization processes cutting against independent discussion and decisionmaking in the boardroom. The difficulty with structural bias in a demand futile case is simply one of establishing it in the complaint for purposes of Rule 23.1. We are satisfied that discretionary review by the Court of Chancery of complaints alleging specific facts pointing to bias on a particular board will be sufficient for determining demand futility.

In the present case, the plaintiff attempted to plead affinity beyond mere friendship between Stewart and the other directors, but her attempt is not sufficient to demonstrate demand futility. Even if the alleged friendships may have preceded the directors' membership on MSO's board and did not necessarily arise out of that membership, these relationships are of the same nature as those giving rise to the structural bias argument.

Allegations that Stewart and the other directors moved in the same social circles, attended the same weddings, developed business relationships before joining the board, and described each other as "friends," even when coupled with Stewart's 94% voting power, are insufficient, without more, to rebut the presumption of independence. They do not provide a sufficient basis from which reasonably to infer that [. . .] Moore and Seligman may have been beholden to Stewart. Whether they arise before board membership or later as a result of collegial relationships among the board of directors, such affinities—standing alone—will not render pre-suit demand futile.

The Court of Chancery in the first instance, and this Court on appeal, must review the complaint on a case-by-case basis to determine whether it states with particularity facts indicating that a relationship—whether it preceded or followed board membership—is so close that the director's independence may *reasonably* be doubted. This doubt might arise either because of financial ties, familial affinity, a particularly close or intimate personal or business affinity or because of evidence that in the past the relationship caused the director to act non-independently vis à vis an interested director. No such allegations are made here. Mere allegations that they move in the same business and social circles, or a characterization that they are close friends, is not enough to negate independence for demand excusal purposes.

That is not to say that personal friendship is always irrelevant to the independence calculus. But, for presuit demand purposes, friendship must be accompanied by substantially more in the nature of serious allegations that would lead to a reasonable doubt as to a director's independence. That a much stronger relationship is necessary to overcome the presumption of independence at the demand futility stage

becomes especially compelling when one considers the risks that
directors would take by protecting their social acquaintances in the face
of allegations that those friends engaged in misconduct. To create a
reasonable doubt about an outside director's independence, a plaintiff
must plead facts that would support the inference that because of the
nature of a relationship or additional circumstances other than the
interested director's stock ownership or voting power, the non-interested
director would be more willing to risk his or her reputation than risk the
relationship with the interested director.

Specific Allegations Concerning Seligman and Moore

1.   Seligman

Beam's allegations concerning Seligman's lack of independence raise an
additional issue not present in the Moore [relationship]. Those
allegations are not necessarily based on a purported friendship between
Seligman and Stewart. Rather, they are based on a specific past act by
Seligman that, Beam claims, indicates Seligman's lack of independence
from Stewart. Beam alleges that Seligman called John Wiley & Sons at
Stewart's request in order to prevent an unfavorable publication
reference to Stewart. The Chancellor concluded, properly in our view,
that this allegation does not provide particularized facts from which one
may reasonably infer improper influence.

The bare fact that Seligman contacted Wiley, on whose board Seligman
also served, to dissuade Wiley from publishing unfavorable references to
Stewart, even if done at Stewart's request, is insufficient to create a
reasonable doubt that Seligman is capable of considering presuit demand
free of Stewart's influence. Although the court should draw all *reasonable*
inferences in Beam's favor, neither improper influence by Stewart over
Seligman nor that Seligman was beholden to Stewart is a reasonable
inference from these allegations.

Indeed, the reasonable inference is that Seligman's purported
intervention on Stewart's behalf was of benefit to MSO and *its*
reputation, which is allegedly tied to *Stewart's* reputation, as the
Chancellor noted. A motivation by Seligman to benefit the company every
bit as much as Stewart herself is the only reasonable inference supported
by the complaint, when all of its allegations are read in context.

2.   Moore

The Court of Chancery concluded that the plaintiff's allegations with
respect to Moore's social relationship with Stewart presented "quite a
close call" and suggested ways that the "balance could have been tipped."
Although we agree that there are ways that the balance could be tipped
so that mere allegations of social relationships would become allegations
casting reasonable doubt on independence, we do not agree that the facts
as alleged present a "close call" with respect to Moore's independence.
These allegations center on: (a) Moore's attendance at a wedding
reception for the daughter of Stewart's lawyer where Stewart [was] also

present; (b) a *Fortune* magazine article focusing on the close personal relationships among Moore, Stewart and [Charlotte] Beers; and (c) the fact that Moore replaced Beers on the MSO board. In our view, these bare social relationships clearly do not create a reasonable doubt of independence.

3. Stewart's 94% Stock Ownership

Beam attempts to bolster her allegations regarding the relationships between Stewart and Seligman and Moore by emphasizing Stewart's overwhelming voting control of MSO. That attempt also fails to create a reasonable doubt of independence. A stockholder's control of a corporation does not excuse presuit demand on the board without particularized allegations of relationships between the directors and the controlling stockholder demonstrating that the directors are beholden to the stockholder. As noted earlier, the relationships alleged by Beam do not lead to the inference that the directors were beholden to Stewart and, thus, unable independently to consider demand. Coupling those relationships with Stewart's overwhelming voting control of MSO does not close that gap. [. . .]

Conclusion

Because Beam did not plead facts sufficient to support a reasonable inference that at least one MSO director in addition to Stewart and Patrick was incapable of considering demand, Beam was required to make demand on the board before pursuing a derivative suit. Hence, presuit demand was not excused. [. . .]

I. REVIEW PROBLEMS

1. On October 28, 2021, the stockholders of Defendant, CytoDyn Inc. will hold their annual meeting. At that meeting, among other things, the stockholders will elect the latest iteration of CytoDyn's board of directors. CytoDyn's bylaws require stockholders to provide advance notice of matters they wish to place on the agenda for the annual meeting (*i.e.*, the so-called advance notice bylaw), including their intent to nominate candidates for election to the board. A group of dissident CytoDyn stockholders submitted a nomination notice on the eve of the notice deadline. CytoDyn's incumbent board disagreed with the nomination and rejected the nomination notice arguing that the nomination notice had structural deficiencies. How do you think the Chancery Court should decide on the plaintiff dissident stockholders' request for injunction requiring the board to place the plaintiffs' nominees on the ballot for the CytoDyn annual meeting scheduled for October 2021? Do you think the Court should apply the *Blasius* standard or simply engage in a contractual analysis of the bylaws?[1]

2. Amalgamated Bank served as trustee of two funds that held Yahoo! Inc. stock. After the hiring and subsequently firing of Yahoo! Inc. stock Chief

---

[1] *See* Rosenbaum v. CytoDyn Inc., C.A. No. 2021-0728-JRS (Del. Ch. Oct. 13, 2021).

Operating Officer, Henrique de Castro, Amalgamated demanded to inspect the books and records of respondent Yahoo! Inc. pursuant to Section 220 of the DGCL. Amalgamated's stated purpose to inspect Yahoo!'s books and record was "investigating the potential mismanagement, including mismanagement in connection with the payment of compensation to a corporation's officers and directors." De Castro was a former executive of Google Inc., and his termination without cause cost a severance payment of approximately $60 million to Yahoo!. On what ground(s) can Yahoo! reject the demand? Do you think Amalgamated Bank has a proper purpose to inspect the respondent's books and records?[2]

3. Zynga Inc. is a Delaware corporation that develops mobile games. Zynga insiders may not sell stock until three days after an earnings announcement. A Zynga shareholder sued, alleging that several of Zynga's top managers and directors and its controlling shareholder were given an exemption to the company's usual rule, allowing them to sell shares before a Zynga announcement that caused a large drop in stock prices. The plaintiff alleges that the insiders who participated in the sale breached their fiduciary duties. The shareholder did not make a pre-suit demand on Zynga's board before filing suit, claiming that a majority of the company's board lacked independence, so demand would have been futile. Among other things, the plaintiff notes that:

- There are nine directors on Zynga's board, and three of them participated in the transaction.

- The plaintiff has identified three additional directors whom he does not believe are independent: Directors A, B, and C. None of these directors were involved with the transaction. In his complaint, the plaintiff states that:

  o Director A co-owns a private plane with one of the directors who participated in the transaction and has described him as a "close family friend."

  o Director B is a partner at a venture capital firm that owns 9.2% of Zynga's equity. The firm has also invested heavily in a company that was founded by one of the directors who sold stock.

  o In its public disclosures, Zynga states that Director C cannot be considered independent under the NASDAQ Listing Rules, which provide that a director is not independent if she has a "relationship which, in the opinion of the Company's board of directors, would interfere with the exercise of independent judgment in carrying out the responsibilities of a director." NASDAQ Marketplace Rule 5605(a)(2). The plaintiff highlights this disclosure in his complaint but does not explain why

---

[2] *See* Amalgamated Bank v. Yahoo! Inc., 132 A.3d 752 (Del. Del. Ch. 2016).

Zynga considers Director C to lack independence under the Listing Rules.

Zynga motions to dismiss the complaint on the theory that the plaintiff failed to make a pre-suit demand on the board. You are a trial court judge. Would you permit the suit to proceed, or would you dismiss it?[3]

---

[3]   *See Sandys v. Pincus*, 152 A.3d 124 (Del. 2016).

CHAPTER V

FIDUCIARY DUTIES OF DIRECTORS AND OFFICERS

A. THE ROLES OF DIRECTORS AND OFFICERS

Delaware General Corporation Law
Section 141. Board of directors; powers; number, qualifications, terms and quorum; committees; classes of directors; nonstock corporations; reliance upon books; action without meeting; removal.

(a) The business and affairs of every corporation organized under this chapter shall be managed by or under the direction of a board of directors, except as may be otherwise provided in this chapter or in its certificate of incorporation. [. . .]

(b) The board of directors of a corporation shall consist of 1 or more members, each of whom shall be a natural person. The number of directors shall be fixed by, or in the manner provided in, the bylaws, unless the certificate of incorporation fixes the number of directors, in which case a change in the number of directors shall be made only by amendment of the certificate. Directors need not be stockholders unless so required by the certificate of incorporation or the bylaws. The certificate of incorporation or bylaws may prescribe other qualifications for directors. Each director shall hold office until such director's successor is elected and qualified or until such director's earlier resignation or removal. Any director may resign at any time upon notice given in writing or by electronic transmission to the corporation. [. . .] A majority of the total number of directors shall constitute a quorum for the transaction of business unless the certificate of incorporation or the bylaws require a greater number. Unless the certificate of incorporation provides otherwise, the bylaws may provide that a number less than a majority shall constitute a quorum which in no case shall be less than ½ of the total number of directors. The vote of the majority of the directors present at a meeting at which a quorum is present shall be the act of the board of directors unless the certificate of incorporation or the bylaws shall require a vote of a greater number. [. . .]

(c) [. . .] (2)   The board of directors may designate 1 or more committees, each committee to consist of 1 or more of the directors of the corporation. [. . .] Any such committee, to the extent provided in the resolution of the board of directors, or in the bylaws of the corporation, shall have and may exercise all the powers and authority of the board of directors in the management of the business and affairs of the corporation, and may authorize the seal of the corporation to be affixed to all papers which may require it; but no such committee shall have the power or authority in reference to the following matter: (i) approving or adopting, or recommending to the stockholders, any action or matter (other than the election or removal of directors) expressly required by this chapter to be submitted to stockholders for approval or (ii) adopting, amending or repealing any bylaw of the corporation. [. . .]

(d) The directors of any corporation organized under this chapter may, by the certificate of incorporation or by an initial bylaw, or by a bylaw adopted by a vote of the stockholders, be divided into 1, 2 or 3 classes; the term of office of those of the first class to expire at the first annual meeting held after such classification becomes effective; of the second class 1 year thereafter; of the third class 2 years thereafter; and at each annual election held after such classification becomes effective, directors shall be chosen for a full term, as the case may be, to succeed those whose terms expire. [. . .]

(e) A member of the board of directors, or a member of any committee designated by the board of directors, shall, in the performance of such member's duties, be fully protected in relying in good faith upon the records of the corporation and upon such information, opinions, reports or statements presented to the corporation by any of the corporation's officers or employees, or committees of the board of directors, or by any other person as to matters the member reasonably believes are within such other person's professional or expert competence and who has been selected with reasonable care by or on behalf of the corporation.

(f) Unless otherwise restricted by the certificate of incorporation or bylaws, (1) any action required or permitted to be taken at any meeting of the board of directors or of any committee thereof may be taken without a meeting if all members of the board or committee, as the case may be, consent thereto in writing, or by electronic transmission, and (2) a consent may be documented, signed and delivered in any manner permitted by § 116 of this title. [. . .]

(g) Unless otherwise restricted by the certificate of incorporation or bylaws, the board of directors of any corporation organized under this chapter may hold its meetings, and have an office or offices, outside of this State.

(h) Unless otherwise restricted by the certificate of incorporation or bylaws, the board of directors shall have the authority to fix the compensation of directors.

(i) Unless otherwise restricted by the certificate of incorporation or bylaws, members of the board of directors of any corporation, or any committee designated by the board, may participate in a meeting of such board, or committee by means of conference telephone or other communications equipment by means of which all persons participating in the meeting can hear each other, and participation in a meeting pursuant to this subsection shall constitute presence in person at the meeting. [. . .]

(k) Any director or the entire board of directors may be removed, with or without cause, by the holders of a majority of the shares then entitled to vote at an election of directors, except as follows:

(1) Unless the certificate of incorporation otherwise provides, in the case of a corporation whose board is classified as provided in subsection (d) of this section, stockholders may effect such removal only for cause; or

(2) In the case of a corporation having cumulative voting, if less than the entire board is to be removed, no director may be removed without cause if the votes cast against such director's removal would be sufficient to elect such director if then cumulatively voted at an election of the entire board of directors, or, if there be classes of directors, at an election of the class of directors of which such director is a part. [. . .]

Section 142. Officers; titles, duties, selection, term; failure to elect; vacancies.

(a) Every corporation organized under this chapter shall have such officers with such titles and duties as shall be stated in the bylaws or in a resolution of the board of directors [. . .]. One of the officers shall have the duty to record the proceedings of the meetings of the stockholders and directors in a book to be kept for that purpose. Any number of offices may be held by the same person unless the certificate of incorporation or bylaws otherwise provide.

(b) Officers shall be chosen in such manner and shall hold their offices for such terms as are prescribed by the bylaws or determined by the board of directors or other governing body. Each officer shall hold office until such officer's successor is elected and qualified or until such officer's earlier resignation or removal. Any officer may resign at any time upon written notice to the corporation. [. . .]

(e) Any vacancy occurring in any office of the corporation by death, resignation, removal or otherwise, shall be filled as the bylaws provide. In the absence of such provision, the vacancy shall be filled by the board of directors or other governing body.

Section 145. Indemnification of officers, directors, employees and agents; insurance.

(a) A corporation shall have power to indemnify any person who was or is a party or is threatened to be made a party to any threatened, pending or completed action, suit or proceeding, whether civil, criminal, administrative or investigative (other than an action by or in the right of the corporation) by reason of the fact that the person is or was a director, officer, employee or agent of the corporation, or is or was serving at the request of the corporation as a director, officer, employee or agent of another corporation, partnership, joint venture, trust or other enterprise, against expenses (including attorneys' fees), judgments, fines and amounts paid in settlement actually and reasonably incurred by the person in connection with such action, suit or proceeding if the person acted in good faith and in a manner the person reasonably believed to be in or not opposed to the best interests of the corporation, and, with respect to any criminal action or proceeding, had no reasonable cause to believe the person's conduct was unlawful. [. . .]

(b) A corporation shall have power to indemnify any person who was or is a party or is threatened to be made a party to any threatened, pending or completed action or suit by or in the right of the corporation to procure a judgment in its favor by reason of the fact that the person is or was a director, officer, employee or agent of the corporation, or is or was serving at the request of the corporation as a director, officer, employee or agent of another corporation, partnership, joint venture, trust or other enterprise against expenses (including attorneys' fees) actually and reasonably incurred by the person in connection with the defense or settlement of such action or suit if the person acted in good faith and in a manner the person reasonably believed to be in or not opposed to the best interests of the corporation and except that no indemnification shall be made in respect of any claim, issue or matter as to which such person shall have been adjudged to be liable to the corporation unless and only to the extent that the Court of Chancery or the court in which such action or suit was brought shall determine upon application that, despite the adjudication of liability but in view of all the circumstances of the case, such person is fairly and reasonably entitled to indemnity for such expenses which the Court of Chancery or such other court shall deem proper.

(c) (1)   To the extent that a present or former director or officer of a corporation has been successful on the merits or otherwise in defense of any action, suit or proceeding referred to in subsections (a) and (b) of this section, or in defense of any claim, issue or matter therein, such person shall be indemnified against expenses (including attorneys' fees) actually and reasonably incurred by such person in connection therewith. [. . .]

(d) Any indemnification under subsections (a) and (b) of this section (unless ordered by a court) shall be made by the corporation only as authorized in the specific case upon a determination that indemnification of the present or former director, officer, employee or agent is proper in the circumstances because the person has met the applicable standard of conduct set forth in subsections (a) and (b) of this section. Such determination shall be made, with respect to a person who is a director or officer of the corporation at the time of such determination:

(1) By a majority vote of the directors who are not parties to such action, suit or proceeding, even though less than a quorum; or

(2) By a committee of such directors designated by majority vote of such directors, even though less than a quorum; or

(3) If there are no such directors, or if such directors so direct, by independent legal counsel in a written opinion; or

(4) By the stockholders.

(e) Expenses (including attorneys' fees) incurred by an officer or director of the corporation in defending any civil, criminal, administrative or investigative action, suit or proceeding may be paid by the corporation in advance of the final disposition of such action, suit or proceeding upon receipt of an undertaking by or on behalf of such director or officer to repay such amount if it shall ultimately be determined that such person is not entitled to be indemnified by the corporation as authorized in this section. Such expenses (including attorneys' fees) incurred by former directors and officers or other employees and agents of the corporation or by persons serving at the request of the corporation as directors, officers, employees or agents of another corporation, partnership, joint venture, trust or other enterprise may be so paid upon such terms and conditions, if any, as the corporation deems appropriate. [. . .]

(g) A corporation shall have power to purchase and maintain insurance on behalf of any person who is or was a director, officer, employee or agent of the corporation, or is or was serving at the request of the corporation as a director, officer, employee or agent of another corporation, partnership, joint venture, trust or other enterprise against any liability asserted against such person and incurred by such person in any such capacity, or arising out of such person's status as such, whether or not the corporation would have the power to indemnify such person against such liability under this section. [. . .]

B. DUTY OF CARE

Kamin v. American Express Company
383 N.Y.S.2d 807 (N.Y. Sup. Ct. 1976)

In this stockholders' derivative action, the individual defendants, who are the directors of the American Express Company, move for an order dismissing the complaint for failure to state a cause of action [. . .], and alternatively, for summary judgment [. . .].

The complaint is brought derivatively by two minority stockholders of the American Express Company, asking for a declaration that a certain dividend in kind is a waste of corporate assets, directing the defendants not to proceed with the distribution, or, in the alternative, for monetary damages. [. . .]

[T]he complaint alleges that in 1972 American Express acquired for investment 1,954,418 shares of common stock of Donaldson, Lufken and Jenrette, Inc. (hereafter DLJ), a publicly traded corporation, at a cost of $29.9 million. It is further alleged that the current market value of those shares is approximately $4.0 million. On July 28, 1975, it is alleged, the

Board of Directors of American Express declared a special dividend to all stockholders of record pursuant to which the shares of DLJ would be distributed in kind. Plaintiffs contend further that if American Express were to sell the DLJ shares on the market, it would sustain a capital loss of $25 million, which could be offset against taxable capital gains on other investments. Such a sale, they allege, would result in tax savings to the company of approximately $8 million, which would not be available in the case of the distribution of DLJ shares to stockholders. It is alleged that on October 8, 1975 and October 16, 1975, plaintiffs demanded that the directors rescind the previously declared dividend in DLJ shares and take steps to preserve the capital loss which would result from selling the shares. This demand was rejected by the Board of Directors on October 17, 1975.

It is apparent that all the previously-mentioned allegations of the complaint go to the question of the exercise by the Board of Directors of business judgment in deciding how to deal with the DLJ shares. The crucial allegation [is]:

> [. . .] All of the defendant Directors engaged in or acquiesced in or negligently permitted the declaration and payment of the Dividend in violation of the fiduciary duty owed by them to Amex to care for and preserve Amex's assets in the same manner as a man of average prudence would care for his own property.

Plaintiffs never moved for temporary injunctive relief, and did nothing to bar the actual distribution of the DLJ shares. The dividend was in fact paid on October 31, 1975. [. . .]

Examination of the complaint reveals that there is no claim of fraud or self-dealing, and no contention that there was any bad faith or oppressive conduct. The law is quite clear as to what is necessary to ground a claim for actionable wrongdoing[:]

> In actions by stockholders, which assail the acts of their directors or trustees, courts will not interfere unless the powers have been illegally or unconscientiously executed; or unless it be made to appear that the acts were fraudulent or collusive, and destructive of the rights of the stockholders. Mere errors of judgment are not sufficient as grounds for equity interference, for the powers of those entrusted with corporate management are largely discretionary. *Leslie v. Lorillard.*

More specifically, the question of whether or not a dividend is to be declared or a distribution of some kind should be made is exclusively a matter of business judgment for the Board of Directors[:]

> ... Courts will not interfere with such discretion unless it be first made to appear that the directors have acted or are about to act in bad faith and for a dishonest purpose. It is for the directors to say, acting in good faith of course, when and to what

extent dividends shall be declared ... [...] *Liebman v. Auto Strop Co.*

Thus, a complaint must be dismissed if all that is presented is a decision to pay dividends rather than pursuing some other course of conduct. A complaint which alleges merely that some course of action other than that pursued by the Board of Directors would have been more advantageous gives rise to no cognizable cause of action. Courts have more than enough to do in adjudicating legal rights and devising remedies for wrongs. The directors' room rather than the courtroom is the appropriate forum for thrashing out purely business questions which will have an impact on profits, market prices, competitive situations, or tax advantages. As stated by Cardozo, J., [...] the substitution of someone else's business judgment for that of the directors "is no business for any court to follow." *Holmes v. St. Joseph Lead Co.*, quoting from *Gamble v. Queens County Water Co.*

It is not enough to allege, as plaintiffs do here, that the directors made an imprudent decision, which did not capitalize on the possibility of using a potential capital loss to offset capital gains. More than imprudence or mistaken judgment must be shown[:]

> Questions of policy of management, expediency of contracts or action, adequacy of consideration, lawful appropriation of corporate funds to advance corporate interests, are left solely to their honest and unselfish decision, for their powers therein are without limitation and free from restraint, and the exercise of them for the common and general interests of the corporation may not be questioned, although the results show that what they did was unwise or inexpedient. *Pollitz v. Wabash Railroad Co.*

Section 720(a)(1)(A) of the Business Corporation Law permits an action against directors for "the neglect of, or failure to perform, or other violation of his duties in the management and disposition of corporate assets committed to his charge." This does not mean that a director is chargeable with ordinary negligence for having made an improper decision, or having acted imprudently. The "neglect" referred to in the statute is neglect of duties (i.e., malfeasance or nonfeasance) and not misjudgment. To allege that a director "negligently permitted the declaration and payment" of a dividend without alleging fraud, dishonesty or nonfeasance, is to state merely that a decision was taken with which one disagrees.

Nor does this appear to a be a case in which a potentially valid cause of action is inartly stated. The defendants have moved alternatively for summary judgment and have submitted affidavits [...], and plaintiffs likewise have submitted papers enlarging upon the allegations of the complaint. The affidavits of the defendants and the exhibits annexed thereto demonstrate that the objections raised by the plaintiffs to the proposed dividend action were carefully considered and unanimously rejected by the Board at a special meeting called precisely for that purpose at the plaintiffs' request. The minutes of the special meeting indicate that the defendants were fully aware that a sale rather than a distribution of the DLJ shares might result in the realization of a substantial income tax saving. Nevertheless, they concluded that there were countervailing considerations primarily with respect to the adverse effect such a sale, realizing a loss of $25 million, would have on the net income figures in the American Express financial statement. Such a reduction of net income would have a serious effect on the market value of the publicly traded American Express stock. This was not a situation in which the defendant directors totally overlooked facts called to their attention. They gave them consideration, and attempted to view the total picture in arriving at their decision. While plaintiffs contend that according to their accounting consultants the loss on the DLJ stock would still have to be charged against current earnings even if the stock were distributed, the defendants' accounting experts assert that the loss would be a charge against earnings only in the event of a sale, whereas in the event of distribution of the stock as a dividend, the proper accounting treatment would be to charge the loss only against surplus. [. . .]

The only hint of self-interest which is raised, not in the complaint but in the papers on the motion, is that four of the twenty directors were officers and employees of American Express and members of its Executive Incentive Compensation Plan. Hence, it is suggested, by virtue of the action taken earnings may have been overstated and their compensation affected thereby. Such a claim is highly speculative and standing alone can hardly be regarded as sufficient to support an inference of self-dealing. There is no claim or showing that the four company directors dominated and controlled the sixteen outside members of the Board. Certainly, every action taken by the Board has some impact on earnings and may therefore affect the compensation of those whose earnings are keyed to profits. That does not disqualify the inside directors, nor does it put every policy adopted by the Board in question. All directors have an obligation, using sound business judgment, to maximize income for the benefit of all persons having a stake in the welfare of the corporate entity. What we have here as revealed both by the complaint and by the affidavits and exhibits, is that a disagreement exists between two minority stockholders and a unanimous Board of Directors as to the best way to handle a loss already incurred on an investment. The directors are entitled to exercise their honest business judgment on the information before them, and to act within their corporate powers. That they may be mistaken, that other courses of action might have differing consequences, or that their action might benefit some shareholders more than others presents no basis for the superimposition of judicial judgment, so long as it appears that the directors have been acting in good faith. The question of to what extent a dividend shall be declared and the manner in which it shall be paid is ordinarily subject only to the qualification that the dividend be paid out of surplus. The Court will not interfere unless a clear case is made out of fraud, oppression, arbitrary action, or breach of trust.

In this case it clearly appears that the plaintiffs have failed as a matter of law to make out an actionable claim. Accordingly, the motion by the defendants for summary judgment and dismissal of the complaint is granted.

Smith v. Van Gorkom

488 A.2d 858 (Del. 1985)

■ HORSEY, JUSTICE, for the majority.

I.

[. . .]

-A-

Trans Union was a publicly-traded, diversified holding company, the principal earnings of which were generated by its railcar leasing business. During the period here involved, the Company had a cash flow of hundreds of millions of dollars annually. However, the Company had difficulty in generating sufficient taxable income to offset increasingly large investment tax credits (ITCs). Accelerated depreciation deductions had decreased available taxable income against which to offset accumulating ITCs. [. . .]

In the late 1970's, together with other capital-intensive firms, Trans Union lobbied in Congress to have ITCs refundable in cash to firms which could not fully utilize the credit. [. . .] By the end of August, Van Gorkom was convinced that Congress would neither accept the refundability concept nor curtail further accelerated depreciation.

[. . .] In July 1980, Trans Union Management prepared the annual revision of the Company's Five Year Forecast. [. . .] The report referred to the ITC situation as a "nagging problem" and, given that problem, the leasing company "would still appear to be constrained to a tax breakeven." The report then listed four alternative uses of the projected 1982–1985 equity surplus: (1) stock repurchase; (2) dividend increases; (3) a major acquisition program; and (4) combinations of the above. The sale of Trans Union was not among the alternatives. [. . .]

-B-

On August 27, 1980, [Trans Union's Chairman and Chief Executive Officer] Van Gorkom met with Senior Management of Trans Union. Van Gorkom reported [. . .] his desire to find a solution to the tax credit problem more permanent than a continued program of acquisitions. Various alternatives were suggested and discussed preliminarily, including the sale of Trans Union to a company with a large amount of taxable income.

Donald Romans, Chief Financial Officer of Trans Union, stated that his department had done a "very brief bit of work on the possibility of a leveraged buy-out," [. . .] [which] consisted of a "preliminary study" of the cash which could be generated by the Company if it participated in a leveraged buy-out. [. . .]

On September 5, at another Senior Management meeting which Van Gorkom attended, Romans again brought up the idea of a leveraged buy-out as a "possible strategic alternative" to the Company's acquisition program. Romans and Bruce S. Chelberg, President and Chief Operating Officer of Trans Union, had been working on the matter in preparation for the meeting. According to Romans: They did not "come up" with a price for the Company. They merely "ran the numbers" at $50 a share and at $60 a share with the "rough form" of their cash figures at the time. [. . .] It was intended to determine the cash flow needed to service the debt that would "probably" be incurred in a leveraged buy-out, based on "rough calculations" without "any benefit of experts to identify what the limits were to that, and so forth." [. . .]

At this meeting, Van Gorkom stated that he would be willing to take $55 per share for his own 75,000 shares. He vetoed the suggestion of a leveraged buy-out by Management, however, as involving a potential conflict of interest for Management. Van Gorkom, a certified public accountant and lawyer, had been an officer of Trans Union for 24 years, its Chief Executive Officer for more than 17 years, and Chairman of its Board for 2 years. It is noteworthy in this connection that he was then approaching 65 years of age and mandatory retirement.

For several days following the September 5 meeting, Van Gorkom pondered the idea of a sale. He had participated in many acquisitions as a manager and director of Trans Union and as a director of other companies. He was familiar with acquisition procedures, valuation methods, and negotiations; and he privately considered the pros and cons of whether Trans Union should seek a privately or publicly-held purchaser.

Van Gorkom decided to meet with Jay A. Pritzker, a well-known corporate takeover specialist and a social acquaintance [. . .] [and] assembled a proposed per share price for sale of the Company and a financing structure by which to accomplish the sale [. . .] without consulting either his Board or any members of Senior Management except one: Carl Peterson, Trans Union's Controller. Telling Peterson that he wanted no other person on his staff to know what he was doing, but without telling him why, Van Gorkom directed Peterson to calculate the feasibility of a leveraged buy-out at an assumed price per share of $55. Apart from the Company's historic stock market price, and Van Gorkom's long association with Trans Union, the record is devoid of any competent evidence that $55 represented the per share intrinsic value of the Company.

Having thus chosen the $55 figure, based solely on the availability of a leveraged buy-out, Van Gorkom multiplied the price per share by the number of shares outstanding to reach a total value of the Company of $690 million. Van Gorkom told Peterson to use this $690 million figure and to assume a $200 million equity contribution by the buyer. [. . .]

Van Gorkom arranged a meeting with Pritzker at the latter's home on Saturday, September 13, 1980. [. . .]

Van Gorkom then reviewed with Pritzker his calculations based upon his proposed price of $55 per share. Although Pritzker mentioned $50 as a more attractive figure, no other price was mentioned. However, Van Gorkom stated that to be sure that $55 was the best price obtainable, Trans Union should be free to accept any better offer. Pritzker demurred, stating that his organization would serve as a "stalking horse" for an "auction contest" only if Trans Union would permit Pritzker to buy 1,750,000 shares of Trans Union stock at market price which Pritzker could then sell to any higher bidder. [. . .]

On Monday, September 15, Pritzker advised Van Gorkom that he was interested in the $55 cash-out merger proposal and requested more information on Trans Union. Van Gorkom agreed to meet privately with Pritzker, accompanied by Peterson, Chelberg, and Michael Carpenter, Trans Union's consultant from the Boston Consulting Group. The meetings took place on September 16 and 17. Van Gorkom was "astounded that events were moving with such amazing rapidity."

On Thursday, September 18, Van Gorkom met again with Pritzker. At that time, Van Gorkom knew that Pritzker intended to make a cash-out merger offer at Van Gorkom's proposed $55 per share. [. . .] At this point, Pritzker insisted that the Trans Union Board act on his merger proposal within the next three days, stating to Van Gorkom: "We have to have a decision by no later than Sunday [evening, September 21] before the opening of the English stock exchange on Monday morning." Pritzker's lawyer was then instructed to draft the merger documents, to be reviewed by Van Gorkom's lawyer, "sometimes with discussion and sometimes not, in the haste to get it finished."

On Friday, September 19, Van Gorkom, Chelberg, and Pritzker consulted with Trans Union's lead bank regarding the financing of Pritzker's purchase of Trans Union [and retained outside legal counsel for Trans Union]. [. . .] Van Gorkom did not consult with [anyone].

On Friday, September 19, Van Gorkom called a special meeting of the Trans Union Board for noon the following day. He also called a meeting of the Company's Senior Management to convene at 11:00 a.m., prior to the meeting of the Board. No one, except Chelberg and Peterson, was told the purpose of the meetings. Van Gorkom did not invite Trans Union's investment banker, Salomon Brothers or its Chicago-based partner, to attend.

Of those present at the Senior Management meeting on September 20, only Chelberg and Peterson had prior knowledge of Pritzker's offer. Van Gorkom disclosed the offer and described its terms, but he furnished no copies of the proposed Merger Agreement. Romans announced that his department had done a second study which showed that, for a leveraged buy-out, the price range for Trans Union stock was between $55 and $65 per share. Van Gorkom neither saw the study nor asked Romans to make it available for the Board meeting.

Senior Management's reaction to the Pritzker proposal was completely negative. No member of Management, except Chelberg and Peterson, supported the proposal. Romans objected to the price as being too low; he was critical of the timing [. . .]; and he took the position that the agreement to sell Pritzker one million newly-issued shares at market price would inhibit other offers, as would the prohibitions against soliciting bids and furnishing inside information to other bidders. Romans argued that the Pritzker proposal was a "lock up" and amounted to "an agreed merger as opposed to an offer." Nevertheless, Van Gorkom proceeded to the Board meeting as scheduled without further delay.

Ten directors served on the Trans Union Board, five inside (defendants Bonser, O'Boyle, Browder, Chelberg, and Van Gorkom) and five outside (defendants Wallis, Johnson, Lanterman, Morgan and Reneker). [. . .] Of the outside directors, four were corporate chief executive officers and one was the former Dean of the University of Chicago Business School. None was an investment banker or trained financial analyst. All members of the Board were well informed about the Company and its operations as a going concern. They were familiar with the current financial condition of the Company, as well as operating and earnings projections reported in the recent Five Year Forecast. The Board generally received regular and detailed reports and was kept abreast of the accumulated investment tax credit and accelerated depreciation problem.

Van Gorkom began the Special Meeting of the Board with a twenty-minute oral presentation. Copies of the proposed Merger Agreement were delivered too late for study before or during the meeting. [. . .] He discussed his initial meeting with Pritzker and his motivation in arranging that meeting. Van Gorkom did not disclose to the Board, however, the methodology by which he alone had arrived at the $55 figure, or the fact that he first proposed the $55 price in his negotiations with Pritzker.

Van Gorkom outlined the terms of the Pritzker offer as follows: Pritzker would pay $55 in cash for all outstanding shares of Trans Union stock upon completion of which Trans Union would be merged into New T Company, a subsidiary wholly-owned by Pritzker and formed to implement the merger; for a period of 90 days, Trans Union could receive, but could not actively solicit, competing offers; the offer had to be acted on by the next evening, Sunday, September 21; Trans Union could only furnish to competing bidders published information, and not proprietary information; the offer was subject to Pritzker obtaining the necessary financing by October 10, 1980; if the financing contingency were met or waived by Pritzker, Trans Union was required to sell to Pritzker one million newly-issued shares of Trans Union at $38 per share.

Van Gorkom took the position that putting Trans Union "up for auction" through a 90-day market test would validate a decision by the Board that $55 was a fair price. He told the Board that the "free market will have an opportunity to judge whether $55 is a fair price." Van Gorkom framed the decision before the Board not as whether $55 per share was the highest price that could be obtained, but as whether the $55 price was a fair price that the stockholders should be given the opportunity to accept or reject.

Attorney Brennan advised the members of the Board that they might be sued if they failed to accept the offer and that a fairness opinion was not required as a matter of law.

Romans attended the meeting as chief financial officer of the Company. He told the Board that he had not been involved in the negotiations with Pritzker and knew nothing about the merger proposal until the morning of the meeting [. . .]. Romans told the Board that, in his opinion, $55 was "in the range of a fair price," but "at the beginning of the range."

Chelberg, Trans Union's President, supported Van Gorkom's presentation and representations. [. . .]

The Board meeting of September 20 lasted about two hours. Based solely upon Van Gorkom's oral presentation, Chelberg's supporting representations, Romans' oral statement, Brennan's legal advice, and their knowledge of the market history of the Company's stock, the directors approved the proposed Merger Agreement. However, the Board later claimed to have attached two conditions to its acceptance: (1) that Trans Union reserved the right to accept any better offer that was made during the market test period; and (2) that Trans Union could share its proprietary information with any other potential bidders. While the Board now claims to have reserved the right to accept any better offer received after the announcement of the Pritzker agreement (even though the minutes of the meeting do not reflect this), it is undisputed that the Board did not reserve the right to actively solicit alternate offers.

The Merger Agreement was executed by Van Gorkom during the evening of September 20 at a formal social event that he hosted for the opening of the Chicago Lyric Opera. Neither he nor any other director read the agreement prior to its signing and delivery to Pritzker.

On Monday, September 22, the Company issued a press release announcing that Trans Union had entered into a "definitive" Merger Agreement with an affiliate of the Marmon Group, Inc., a Pritzker holding company. Within 10 days of the public announcement, dissent among Senior Management over the merger had become widespread. Faced with threatened resignations of key officers, Van Gorkom met with Pritzker who agreed to several modifications of the Agreement. [. . .]

Van Gorkom reconvened the Board on October 8 and secured the directors' approval of the proposed amendments—sight unseen. The Board also authorized the employment of Salomon Brothers, its investment banker, to solicit other offers for Trans Union during the proposed "market test" period.

The next day, October 9, Trans Union issued a press release announcing: (1) that Pritzker had obtained "the financing commitments necessary to consummate" the merger with Trans Union; (2) that Pritzker had acquired one million shares of Trans Union common stock at $38 per share; (3) that Trans Union was now permitted to actively seek other offers and had retained Salomon Brothers for that purpose; and (4) that if a more favorable offer were not received before February 1, 1981, Trans Union's shareholders would thereafter meet to vote on the Pritzker proposal.

[. . .] The amendments were considerably at variance with Van Gorkom's representations of the amendments to the Board on October 8 [. . .] and [. . .] placed serious constraints on Trans Union's ability to negotiate a better deal and withdraw from the Pritzker agreement. Nevertheless, Van Gorkom proceeded to execute what became the October 10 amendments to the Merger Agreement without conferring further with the Board members and apparently without comprehending the actual implications of the amendments.

Salomon Brothers' efforts over a three-month period from October 21 to January 21 produced only one serious suitor for Trans Union—General Electric Credit Corporation. However, GE Credit was unwilling to make an offer for Trans Union unless Trans Union first rescinded its Merger Agreement with Pritzker. When Pritzker refused, GE Credit terminated further discussions with Trans Union in early January.

In the meantime, in early December, the investment firm of Kohlberg, Kravis, Roberts & Co. ("KKR"), the only other concern to make a firm offer for Trans Union, withdrew its offer under circumstances hereinafter detailed.

On December 19, this litigation was commenced. [. . .]

On February 10, the stockholders of Trans Union approved the Pritzker merger proposal. Of the outstanding shares, 69.9% were voted in favor of the merger; 7.25% were voted against the merger; and 22.85% were not voted.

II.

We turn to the issue of the application of the business judgment rule to the September 20 meeting of the Board.

Under Delaware law, the business judgment rule is the offspring of the fundamental principle, codified in 8 Del.C.§ 141(a), that the business and affairs of a Delaware corporation are managed by or under its board of directors. [. . .] Aronson v. Lewis; Zapata Corp. v. Maldonado. In carrying out their managerial roles, directors are charged with an unyielding fiduciary duty to the corporation and its shareholders. *Loft, Inc. v. Guth.* The business judgment rule exists to protect and promote the full and free exercise of the managerial power granted to Delaware directors. *Zapata Corp. v. Maldonado* [. . .]. The rule itself "is a presumption that in making a business decision, the directors of a corporation acted on an informed basis, in good faith and in the honest belief that the action taken was in the best interests of the company." *Aronson v. Lewis* [. . .]. Thus, the party attacking a board decision as uninformed must rebut the presumption that its business judgment was an informed one. *Id.*

The determination of whether a business judgment is an informed one turns on whether the directors have informed themselves "prior to making a business decision, of all material information reasonably available to them." *Id.*

Under the business judgment rule there is no protection for directors who have made "an unintelligent or unadvised judgment." *Mitchell v. Highland-Western Glass.* A director's duty to inform himself in preparation for a decision derives from the fiduciary capacity in which he serves the corporation and its stockholders. *Lutz v. Boas. See Weinberger v. UOP, Inc.; Guth v. Loft.* Since a director is vested with the responsibility for the management of the affairs of the corporation, he must execute that duty with the recognition that he acts on behalf of others. Such obligation does not tolerate faithlessness or self-dealing. But fulfillment of the fiduciary function requires more than the mere absence of bad faith or fraud. Representation of the financial interests of others imposes on a director an affirmative duty to protect those interests and to proceed with a critical eye in assessing information of the type and under the circumstances present here. *See Lutz; Guth.* [. . .]

Thus, a director's duty to exercise an informed business judgment is in the nature of a duty of care, as distinguished from a duty of loyalty. Here, there were no allegations of fraud, bad faith, or self-dealing, or proof thereof. Hence, it is presumed that the directors reached their business judgment in good faith, *Allaun v. Consolidated Oil Co.,* and considerations of motive are irrelevant to the issue before us. [. . .]

We think the concept of gross negligence is also the proper standard for determining whether a business judgment reached by a board of directors was an informed one.

In the specific context of a proposed merger of domestic corporations, a director has a duty under 8 Del.C. § 251(b), along with his fellow directors, to act in an informed and deliberate manner in determining whether to approve an agreement of merger before submitting the proposal to the stockholders.

It is against those standards that the conduct of the directors of Trans Union must be tested, as a matter of law and as a matter of fact, regarding their exercise of an informed business judgment in voting to approve the Pritzker merger proposal.

III.

[. . .] The issue of whether the directors reached an informed decision to "sell" the Company on September 20, 1980 must be determined only upon the basis of the information then reasonably available to the directors and relevant to their decision to accept the Pritzker merger proposal. [. . .] [T]he question of whether the directors reached an informed business judgment in agreeing to sell the Company, pursuant to the terms of the September 20 Agreement presents, in reality, two questions: (A) whether the directors reached an informed business judgment on September 20, 1980; and (B) if they did not, whether the directors' actions taken subsequent to September 20 were adequate to cure any infirmity in their action taken on September 20. We first consider the directors' September 20 action in terms of their reaching an informed business judgment.

-A-

On the record before us, we must conclude that the Board of Directors did not reach an informed business judgment on September 20, 1980 in voting to "sell" the Company for $55 per share pursuant to the Pritzker cash-out merger proposal. Our reasons, in summary, are as follows:

The directors (1) did not adequately inform themselves as to Van Gorkom's role in forcing the "sale" of the Company and in establishing the per share purchase price; (2) were uninformed as to the intrinsic value of the Company; and (3) given these circumstances, at a minimum, were grossly negligent in approving the "sale" of the Company upon two hours' consideration, without prior notice, and without the exigency of a crisis or emergency.

As has been noted, the Board based its September 20 decision to approve the cash-out merger primarily on Van Gorkom's representations. None of the directors, other than Van Gorkom and Chelberg, had any prior knowledge that the purpose of the meeting was to propose a cash-out merger of Trans Union. No members of Senior Management were present, other than Chelberg, Romans and Peterson; and the latter two had only learned of the proposed sale an hour earlier. Both general counsel Moore and former general counsel Browder attended the meeting, but were equally uninformed as to the purpose of the meeting and the documents to be acted upon.

Without any documents before them concerning the proposed transaction, the members of the Board were required to rely entirely upon Van Gorkom's 20-minute oral presentation of the proposal. No written summary of the terms of the merger was presented; the directors were given no documentation to support the adequacy of $55 price per share for sale of the Company; and the Board had before it nothing more than Van Gorkom's statement of his understanding of the substance of an agreement which he admittedly had never read, nor which any member of the Board had ever seen.

[. . .] Under 8 Del.C. § 141(e), "directors are fully protected in relying in good faith on reports made by officers." The term "report" has been liberally construed to include reports of informal personal investigations by corporate officers. *Cheff v. Mathes.* However, there is no evidence that any "report," as defined under § 141(e), concerning the Pritzker proposal, was presented to the Board on September 20. Van Gorkom's oral presentation of his understanding of the terms of the proposed Merger Agreement, which he had not seen, and Romans' brief oral statement of his preliminary study regarding the feasibility of a leveraged buy-out of Trans Union do not qualify as § 141(e) "reports" for these reasons: The former lacked substance because Van Gorkom was basically uninformed as to the essential provisions of the very document about which he was talking. Romans' statement was irrelevant to the issues before the Board since it did not purport to be a valuation study. At a minimum for a report to enjoy the status conferred by § 141(e), it must be pertinent to the subject matter upon which a board is called to act, and otherwise be entitled to good faith, not blind, reliance. Considering all of the surrounding circumstances—hastily calling the meeting without prior notice of its subject matter, the proposed sale of the Company without any prior consideration of the issue or necessity therefor, the urgent time constraints imposed by Pritzker, and the total absence of any documentation whatsoever—the directors were duty bound to make reasonable inquiry of Van Gorkom and Romans, and if they had done so, the inadequacy of that upon which they now claim to have relied would have been apparent. [. . .]

(1)

A substantial premium may provide one reason to recommend a merger, but in the absence of other sound valuation information, the fact of a premium alone does not provide an adequate basis upon which to assess the fairness of an offering price. Here, the judgment reached as to the adequacy of the premium was based on a comparison between the historically depressed Trans Union market price and the amount of the Pritzker offer. Using market price as a basis for concluding that the premium adequately reflected the true value of the Company was a clearly faulty, indeed fallacious, premise, as the defendants' own evidence demonstrates.

The record is clear that before September 20, Van Gorkom and other members of Trans Union's Board knew that the market had consistently undervalued the worth of Trans Union's stock, despite steady increases in the Company's operating income in the seven years preceding the merger. The Board related this occurrence in large part to Trans Union's inability to use its ITCs as previously noted. Van Gorkom testified that he did not believe the market price accurately reflected Trans Union's true worth; and several of the directors testified that, as a general rule, most chief executives think that the market undervalues their companies' stock. Yet, on September 20, Trans Union's Board apparently believed that the market stock price accurately reflected the value of the Company for the purpose of determining the adequacy of the premium for its sale.

In the Proxy Statement, however, the directors reversed their position. There, they stated that, although the earnings prospects for Trans Union were "excellent," they found no basis for believing that this would be reflected in future stock prices. With regard to past trading, the Board stated that the prices at which the Company's common stock had traded in recent years did not reflect the "inherent" value of the Company. But having referred to the "inherent" value of Trans Union, the directors ascribed no number to it. Moreover, nowhere did they disclose that they had no basis on which to fix "inherent" worth beyond an impressionistic reaction to the premium over market and an unsubstantiated belief that the value of the assets was "significantly greater" than book value. By their own admission they could not rely on the stock price as an accurate measure of value. Yet, also by their own admission, the Board members assumed that Trans Union's market price was adequate to serve as a basis upon which to assess the adequacy of the premium for purposes of the September 20 meeting.

The parties do not dispute that a publicly-traded stock price is solely a measure of the value of a minority position and, thus, market price represents only the value of a single share. Nevertheless, on September 20, the Board assessed the adequacy of the premium over market, offered by Pritzker, solely by comparing it with Trans Union's current and historical stock price. [. . .]

Indeed, as of September 20, the Board had no other information on which to base a determination of the intrinsic value of Trans Union as a going concern. As of September 20, the Board had made no evaluation of the Company designed to value the entire enterprise, nor had the Board ever previously considered selling the Company or consenting to a buy-out merger. Thus, the adequacy of a premium is indeterminate unless it is assessed in terms of other competent and sound valuation information that reflects the value of the particular business.

Despite the foregoing facts and circumstances, there was no call by the Board, either on September 20 or thereafter, for any valuation study or documentation of the $55 price per share as a measure of the fair value of the Company in a cash-out context. It is undisputed that the major asset of Trans Union was its cash flow. Yet, at no time did the Board call for a valuation study taking into account that highly significant element of the Company's assets.

We do not imply that an outside valuation study is essential to support an informed business judgment; nor do we state that fairness opinions by independent investment bankers are required as a matter of law. Often insiders familiar with the business of a going concern are in a better position than are outsiders to gather relevant information; and under appropriate circumstances, such directors may be fully protected in relying in good faith upon the valuation reports of their management. *See* 8 Del.C. § 141(e). *See also Cheff* [. . .].

Here, the record establishes that the Board did not request its Chief Financial Officer, Romans, to make any valuation study or review of the proposal to determine the adequacy of $55 per share for sale of the Company. [. . .]

Had the Board, or any member, made an inquiry of Romans, [. . .] [he] would have presumably also informed the Board of his view, and the widespread view of Senior Management, that the timing of the offer was wrong and the offer inadequate.

The record also establishes that the Board accepted without scrutiny Van Gorkom's representation as to the fairness of the $55 price per share for sale of the Company—a subject that the Board had never previously considered. The Board thereby failed to discover that [. . .] Van Gorkom had arrived at the $55 figure based on calculations designed solely to determine the feasibility of a leveraged buy-out.

[. . .] Thus, the record compels the conclusion that on September 20 the Board lacked valuation information adequate to reach an informed business judgment as to the fairness of $55 per share for sale of the Company.

(2)

This brings us to the post-September 20 "market test" upon which the defendants ultimately rely to confirm the reasonableness of their September 20 decision to accept the Pritzker proposal. In this connection, the directors present a two-part argument: (a) that by making a "market test" of Pritzker's $55 per share offer a condition of their September 20 decision to accept his offer, they cannot be found to have acted impulsively or in an uninformed manner on September 20; and (b) that the adequacy of the $17 premium for sale of the Company was conclusively established over the following 90 to 120 days by the most reliable evidence available—the marketplace. Thus, the defendants impliedly contend that the "market test" eliminated the need for the Board to perform any other form of fairness test either on September 20, or thereafter.

[. . .] [But, t]here is no evidence: (a) that the Merger Agreement was effectively amended to give the Board freedom to put Trans Union up for auction sale to the highest bidder; or (b) that a public auction was in fact permitted to occur. The minutes of the Board meeting make no reference to any of this. Indeed, the record compels the conclusion that the directors had no rational basis for expecting that a market test was attainable, given the terms of the Agreement as executed during the evening of September 20.

[. . .] [T]he press release issued on September 22, with the authorization of the Board, stated that Trans Union had entered into "definitive agreements" with the Pritzkers; and the press release did not even disclose Trans Union's limited right to receive and accept higher offers. Accompanying this press release was a further public announcement that Pritzker had been granted an option to purchase at any time one million shares of Trans Union's capital stock at 75 cents above the then-current price per share.

Thus, notwithstanding what several of the outside directors later claimed to have "thought" occurred at the meeting, the record compels the conclusion that Trans Union's Board had no rational basis to conclude on September 20 or in the days immediately following, that the Board's acceptance of Pritzker's offer was conditioned on (1) a "market test" of the offer; and (2) the Board's right to withdraw from the Pritzker Agreement and accept any higher offer received before the shareholder meeting.

(3)

The directors' unfounded reliance on both the premium and the market test as the basis for accepting the Pritzker proposal undermines the defendants' remaining contention that the Board's collective experience and sophistication was a sufficient basis for finding that it reached its September 20 decision with informed, reasonable deliberation. [. . .]

(4)

Part of the defense is based on a claim that the directors relied on legal advice rendered at the September 20 meeting by James Brennan, Esquire, who was present at Van Gorkom's request. Unfortunately, Brennan did not appear and testify at trial even though his firm participated in the defense of this action. There is no contemporaneous evidence of the advice given by Brennan on September 20 [. . .].

[. . .] We conclude that Trans Union's Board was grossly negligent in that it failed to act with informed reasonable deliberation in agreeing to the Pritzker merger proposal on September 20; and we further conclude that the Trial Court erred as a matter of law in failing to address that question before determining whether the directors' later conduct was sufficient to cure its initial error. [. . .]

-B-

We now examine the Board's post-September 20 conduct for the purpose of determining first, whether it was informed and not grossly negligent; and second, if informed, whether it was sufficient to legally rectify and cure the Board's derelictions of September 20.

(1)

[. . .] The public announcement of the Pritzker merger resulted in an "en masse" revolt of Trans Union's Senior Management. [. . .]

Instead of reconvening the Board, Van Gorkom again privately met with Pritzker, informed him of the developments, and sought his advice. Pritzker then made the following suggestions for overcoming Management's dissatisfaction: (1) that the Agreement be amended to permit Trans Union to solicit, as well as receive, higher offers; and (2) that the shareholder meeting be postponed from early January to February 10, 1981. In return, Pritzker asked Van Gorkom to obtain a commitment from Senior Management to remain at Trans Union for at least six months after the merger was consummated.

Van Gorkom then advised Senior Management that the Agreement would be amended to give Trans Union the right to solicit competing offers through January, 1981, if they would agree to remain with Trans Union. Senior Management was temporarily mollified; and Van Gorkom then called a special meeting of Trans Union's Board for October 8.

Thus, the primary purpose of the October 8 Board meeting was to amend the Merger Agreement, in a manner agreeable to Pritzker, to permit Trans Union to conduct a "market test." [. . .] In a brief session, the directors approved Van Gorkom's oral presentation of the substance of the proposed amendments, the terms of which were not reduced to writing until October 10. But rather than waiting to review the amendments, the Board again approved them sight unseen and adjourned, giving Van Gorkom authority to execute the papers when he received them.

[. . .] The next day, October 9, and before the Agreement was amended, Pritzker moved swiftly to off-set the proposed market test amendment. First, Pritzker informed Trans Union that he had completed arrangements for financing its acquisition and that the parties were thereby mutually bound to a firm purchase and sale arrangement. Second, Pritzker announced the exercise of his option to purchase one million shares of Trans Union's treasury stock at $38 per share—75 cents above the current market price. Trans Union's Management responded the same day by issuing a press release announcing: (1) that all financing arrangements for Pritzker's acquisition of Trans Union had been completed; and (2) Pritzker's purchase of one million shares of Trans Union's treasury stock at $38 per share.

The next day, October 10, Pritzker delivered to Trans Union the proposed amendments to the September 20 Merger Agreement. [. . .] The record does not affirmatively establish that Trans Union's directors ever read the October 10 amendments.

The October 10 amendments to the Merger Agreement did authorize Trans Union to solicit competing offers, but the amendments had more far-reaching effects. The most significant change was in the definition of the third-party "offer" available to Trans Union as a possible basis for withdrawal from its Merger Agreement with Pritzker. Under the October 10 amendments, a better *offer* was no longer sufficient to permit Trans Union's withdrawal. Trans Union was now permitted to terminate the

Pritzker Agreement and abandon the merger only if, prior to February 10, 1981, Trans Union had either consummated a merger (or sale of assets) with a third party or had entered into a "definitive" merger agreement more favorable than Pritzker's and for a greater consideration—subject only to stockholder approval. Further, the "extension" of the market test period to February 10, 1981 was circumscribed by other amendments which required Trans Union to file its preliminary proxy statement on the Pritzker merger proposal by December 5, 1980 and use its best efforts to mail the statement to its shareholders by January 5, 1981. Thus, the market test period was effectively reduced, not extended. [. . .]

In our view, the record compels the conclusion that the directors' conduct on October 8 exhibited the same deficiencies as did their conduct on September 20. The Board permitted its Merger Agreement with Pritzker to be amended in a manner it had neither authorized nor intended. [. . .]

We conclude that the Board acted in a grossly negligent manner on October 8; and that Van Gorkom's representations on which the Board based its actions do not constitute "reports" under § 141(e) on which the directors could reasonably have relied. [. . .]

V.

The defendants ultimately rely on the stockholder vote of February 10 for exoneration. The defendants contend that the stockholders' "overwhelming" vote approving the Pritzker Merger Agreement had the legal effect of curing any failure of the Board to reach an informed business judgment in its approval of the merger.

[. . .] The settled rule in Delaware is that "where a majority of fully informed stockholders ratify action of even interested directors, an attack on the ratified transaction normally must fail." *Gerlach v. Gillam.* The question of whether shareholders have been fully informed such that their vote can be said to ratify director action, "turns on the fairness and completeness of the proxy materials submitted by the management to the . . . shareholders." *Michelson v. Duncan.* [. . .]

In *Lynch v. Vickers Energy Corp.*, [. . .] this Court held that corporate directors owe to their stockholders a fiduciary duty to disclose all facts germane to the transaction at issue in an atmosphere of complete candor. We defined "germane" in the tender offer context as all "information such as a reasonable stockholder would consider important in deciding whether to sell or retain stock." *Id.* [. . .] In reality, "germane" means material facts.

Applying this standard to the record before us, we find that Trans Union's stockholders were not fully informed of all facts material to their vote on the Pritzker Merger. [. . .]

VI.

To summarize: we hold that the directors of Trans Union breached their fiduciary duty to their stockholders (1) by their failure to inform themselves of all information reasonably available to them and relevant to their decision to recommend the Pritzker merger; and (2) by their failure to disclose all material information such as a reasonable stockholder would consider important in deciding whether to approve the Pritzker offer.

We hold, therefore, that the Trial Court committed reversible error in applying the business judgment rule in favor of the director defendants in this case.

On remand, the Court of Chancery shall conduct an evidentiary hearing to determine the fair value of the shares represented by the plaintiffs' class, based on the intrinsic value of Trans Union on September 20, 1980. Such valuation shall be made in accordance with *Weinberger* [. . .] Thereafter, an award of damages may be entered to the extent that the fair value of Trans Union exceeds $55 per share. [. . .]

■ MCNEILLY, JUSTICE, dissenting.

The majority opinion reads like an advocate's closing address to a hostile jury. And I say that not lightly. Throughout the opinion great emphasis is directed only to the negative, with nothing more than lip service granted the positive aspects of this case. [. . .]

Trans Union's Board of Directors consisted of ten men, five of whom were "inside" directors and five of whom were "outside" directors. [. . .] At the time the merger was proposed the inside five directors had collectively been employed by the Company for 116 years and had 68 years of combined experience as directors. [. . .] The five "outside" directors had 78 years of combined experience as chief executive officers, and 53 years cumulative service as Trans Union directors.

The inside directors wear their badge of expertise in the corporate affairs of Trans Union on their sleeves. But what about the outsiders? Dr. Wallis is or was an economist and math statistician, a professor of economics at Yale University, dean of the graduate school of business at the University of Chicago, and Chancellor of the University of Rochester. Dr. Wallis had been on the Board of Trans Union since 1962. He also was on the Board of Bausch & Lomb, Kodak, Metropolitan Life Insurance Company, Standard Oil and others.

William B. Johnson is a University of Pennsylvania law graduate, President of Railway Express until 1966, Chairman and Chief Executive of I.C. Industries Holding Company, and member of Trans Union's Board since 1968.

Joseph Lanterman, a Certified Public Accountant, is or was President and Chief Executive of American Steel, on the Board of International Harvester, Peoples Energy, Illinois Bell Telephone, Harris Bank and

Trust Company, Kemper Insurance Company and a director of Trans Union for four years.

Graham Morgan is a chemist, was Chairman and Chief Executive Officer of U.S. Gypsum, and in the 17 and 18 years prior to the Trans Union transaction had been involved in 31 or 32 corporate takeovers.

Robert Reneker attended University of Chicago and Harvard Business Schools. He was President and Chief Executive of Swift and Company, director of Trans Union since 1971, and member of the Boards of seven other corporations including U.S. Gypsum and the *Chicago Tribune*.

Directors of this caliber are not ordinarily taken in by a "fast shuffle." I submit they were not taken into this multi-million dollar corporate transaction without being fully informed and aware of the state of the art as it pertained to the entire corporate panoroma of Trans Union. True, even directors such as these, with their business acumen, interest and expertise, can go astray. I do not believe that to be the case here. These men knew Trans Union like the back of their hands and were more than well qualified to make on the spot informed business judgments concerning the affairs of Trans Union including a 100% sale of the corporation. Lest we forget, the corporate world of then and now operates on what is so aptly referred to as "the fast track." These men were at the time an integral part of that world, all professional business men, not intellectual figureheads. [. . .]

City of Coral Springs Police Officers' Pension Plan v. Jack Dorsey et al.

2023 WL 3316246 (Del. Ch. 2023)

■ McCORMICK, C.

The plaintiff, a stockholder of Block, Inc., filed this derivative suit challenging Block's acquisition of TIDAL—a music streaming company associated with rapper, producer, and entrepreneur Shawn Carter. [. . .]

I. FACTUAL BACKGROUND

[. . .]

A. Block And Its Board

Block, a California-based company, offers products and services that help businesses facilitate payment processing and help individuals transfer money electronically. [. . .]

Dorsey founded Block and took the Company public in 2015. He is Block's President and CEO, and he serves as Chairman of Block's Board of Directors (the "Board"). According to Block's public filings, Dorsey held between 48.08% and 51.32% of the Company's total stockholder voting power at relevant times.

At the time of the acquisition, the Board comprised eleven members: Dorsey and Defendants Roelof Botha, Amy Brooks, Paul Deighton,

Randy Garutti, Jim McKelvey, Mary Meeker, Anna Patterson, Lawrence Summers, David Viniar, and Darren Walker (collectively, "Defendants").

B. Carter's Acquisition And Attempted Revamp Of TIDAL

Carter, known professionally as "Jay-Z," is a rapper, record producer, and entrepreneur. In 2015, a group of recording artists led by Carter acquired a Norwegian music streaming company, formerly called Aspiro, for $56 million and rebranded it as TIDAL. Carter spearheaded these efforts and served as the public face of TIDAL. He also held a 27% stake in the company. Along with his partners, Carter launched a campaign for TIDAL to break into the music streaming industry as an artist-friendly platform.

The campaign was unsuccessful. By mid-2020, TIDAL had amassed only 2.1 million paying subscribers, which compared poorly to competitors like Spotify (138 million paying subscribers), Apple Music (60 million), and Amazon Music (55 million). TIDAL had logged multimillion-dollar losses for each of the preceding ten quarters. Carter personally extended a $50 million loan to TIDAL in 2020.

TIDAL's operations also showed signs of distress. Between 2015 and 2020, TIDAL had churned through five different CEOs. The Company's contracts with music labels were semi-formal at best; some had expired. TIDAL had incurred substantial unpaid liabilities to music labels for streaming fees. In a public fallout, TIDAL lost its exclusive streaming arrangement with recording artist Kanye West. To top it all off, the Company was facing an ongoing criminal investigation in Norway for artificially inflating its streaming numbers.

C. Dorsey Proposes That Block Acquire TIDAL.

Dorsey and Carter are friends. They share interests in cryptocurrency and philanthropy. Dorsey publicly supported Carter's acquisition of TIDAL in 2015 [. . .].

While their families were summering together in the Hamptons, Dorsey and Carter began discussing a potential acquisition of TIDAL by Block. On August 25, 2020, Dorsey joined the Board's regularly scheduled meeting by videoconference from the Hamptons. During the meeting, Dorsey raised the idea that Block acquire TIDAL. The meeting minutes reflect the Board's discussion of strategic rationales, proposed valuations, and the Company's potential integration strategies. The Board then "instructed management to continue to evaluate such transactions including through additional due diligence and negotiation of a letter of intent." The Board resolved to establish a transaction committee to review any potential acquisition of TIDAL by unanimous written consent (the "Transaction Committee").

The proposed Transaction Committee members were four independent directors: Botha, Brooks, Meeker, and Walker (the "Committee Defendants"). The resolution authorized the Transaction Committee to retain advisers to evaluate a potential acquisition and granted it the authority to approve a purchase. All directors excluding Dorsey signed their written consents on August 26, 2020. Two days later, on August 28, Dorsey executed his written consent, and the Transaction Committee was officially formed.

Meanwhile, Dorsey drafted and submitted a non-binding letter of intent for Block to purchase TIDAL for $554.8 million.

D.   The Transaction Committee's First Meeting

The Transaction Committee convened by videoconference for its first meeting on September 29, 2020. The meeting lasted 35 minutes. Dorsey and members of Block's legal team attended the meeting and were present for its duration. The Transaction Committee discussed TIDAL's competitive landscape and Block's proposed product development strategies. Dorsey then "provided his perspective on the transaction as well as the interim management strategy should the transaction move forward."

In advance of its first meeting, the Transaction Committee received three reports from Block management analyzing a potential acquisition of TIDAL. The reports included general background on the music industry, an outline of Block's strategic goals in entering the industry, and a preliminary analysis of the investments Block would need to make into TIDAL to make it successful. None of the three reports contained management's valuation of the proposed acquisition. The third report, delivered the day before the Transaction Committee's first meeting, was the first time that management informed the Transaction Committee that Dorsey and his team had submitted a letter of intent a month earlier.

E.   The Transaction Committee's Second Meeting

Block management provided the Transaction Committee with its fourth written report on October 14, 2020. Management reported that TIDAL had only amassed 2.1 million paying subscribers and that growing this number would prove difficult. Management reasoned that "Spotify is synonymous with music streaming," and Apple Music and Amazon Music had largely captured the remaining market share. The report also apprised the board that TIDAL had generated negative EBITDA of $39 million in 2019 and of Carter's $50 million loan to the company.

Management further revealed that TIDAL operated under semi-formal or expired arrangements with these labels, capitalizing on the influence of the prominent artists who were partial owners of TIDAL. The report warned that TIDAL's relationships with these labels could sour following an acquisition by Block.

The report highlighted other potential risks in an acquisition, such as the ongoing criminal probe by the Norwegian government and a federal lawsuit brought by artists alleging that TIDAL had withheld their owed royalties. TIDAL's relationships with its artists were also faltering, and rapper Kanye West had withdrawn from his exclusive streaming arrangement with TIDAL for one of his albums due to piracy issues.

Management set an "[e]xpected purchase price" of $550–750 million. They reached this conclusion based on: comparables analyses with Spotify, Apple Music, and Amazon Music; comparables analyses with private precedent transactions; discounted cash flows analysis derived from TIDAL's management forecasts; and TIDAL's representations that it was in discussions with an undisclosed third party for a loan that valued TIDAL at $500–600 million.

The Transaction Committee convened for its second meeting on October 20, 2020. Dorsey and his management team presented on the October 14 report and additional financial information from TIDAL. Among other things, management informed the Transaction Committee that TIDAL had recorded multimillion-dollar losses in each of its previous ten quarters. These losses, management reported, would dilute Block's earnings for at least three years and potentially create volatility in its stock price. Management's presentation acknowledged that TIDAL's existing contracts with its artists had expired, yet management valued TIDAL's "intangible" artist relationships at $231 million. Management also presented on TIDAL's accrued liabilities of $127 million, primarily from amounts owed to record labels for streaming fees.

In a section called "Committee Q&A," the presentation addressed 18 multi-part, complex questions from Transaction Committee members [. . .]. One member asked, "Who are internal advocates for transactions? Is there sufficient buy in?" The slide reported that Dorsey was still "the primary sponsor of the deal" and that he was "the only one who is strongly advocating to move forward." The slide also stated that there was "substantial push back from Core members," i.e., Block's senior executives, and that neither of Block's two business unit leaders, Alyssa Henry and Brian Grassadonia, were advocating for the transaction.

Another Transaction Committee member asked whether TIDAL artists had any legal commitment to maintain their relationship with the platform following a merger. The presentation stated that "existing artists will have no legal obligation to [Block]; we are counting on their economic incentives as owners to drive future contributions to the growth and success of [TIDAL]." In response to a follow-up question requesting a "Drilldown" on the specifics of artists' commitment, the presentation again acknowledged that the agreements "may be difficult to enforce legally, we will largely be relying on Jay-Z's influence with them" to secure performance. When asked about the value of these artist relationships, management responded that "we do not have a concrete view on the value of the artist shareholders."

One Transaction Committee member asked for the one-month, six-month, and one-to-three-year plans for assimilating and building the business. The response admitted that "[w]e do not have this level of detail at this stage" and acknowledged that "the lack of a clear operational/strategic lead here remains one of the greatest risks." In the "Investor Relations Plan" section, the presentation described the framing to investors as follows: "While it is a big opportunity, the bet we are taking today is small relative to the size of Square."

Despite these concerns, management informed the Transaction Committee that they intended to enter a deal term sheet in which Block would acquire approximately 90% of TIDAL at an enterprise valuation of $490 million. Certain member artists would retain the remaining 10% stake.

The October 20 meeting lasted an hour, and Dorsey was present for the entirety of the meeting. In closing, the Transaction Committee "instructed management to continue pursuing the transaction and update the Committee as negotiations progress."

The Transaction Committee updated the full Board at its regularly scheduled meeting the next day, October 21. According to the Board minutes, Transaction Committee member Brooks provided an update on "the work that the deal team has undertaken and the discussions that the Transaction Committee of the Board have had in connection with the review of the target and the negotiation of a potential term sheet." The Transaction Committee's update was one of 14 items of business discussed at the October 21 Board meeting.

F. Block And TIDAL Agree On A Term Sheet.

On November 10, 2020, Block entered a term sheet to purchase a majority interest in TIDAL. A few days later, Dorsey and Carter were spotted vacationing together in Hawaii.

The Transaction Committee did not convene again until January 22, 2021. The meeting lasted an hour, according to the minutes. Dorsey and his team presented to the Transaction Committee members on the proposed transaction. Based on TIDAL's failure to meet its management's forecasts for 2020, and the likely scenario that T-Mobile would soon pull out of a significant partnership with TIDAL, Block's management reduced its valuation of TIDAL to $350 million.

Block's management estimated that TIDAL would generate its own negative EBITDA of $15.8 million in 2021, $24.5 million in 2022, and $32.4 million in 2023. Based on management's projected capital infusions that Block would need to make into its TIDAL investment, they predicted the acquisition would generate negative EBITDA for Block of $35.6 million in 2021, $55 million in 2022, and $68.3 million in 2023.

Management downplayed the bad news as minor within the greater scheme of Block's financial success. [. . .] Management also responded to questions about the acquisition's scale, noting that a $350 million purchase price would only constitute 0.35% of Block's $100 billion market capitalization.

Like in the October 20 meeting, the Transaction Committee pressed management for more details on artists' legal obligations to continue working with TIDAL postacquisition. Management responded that "whether an artist contributes to the platform or not, there would be no recourse for [Block] to take." When pressed on the basis for "how we will win" in the market, the presentation stated plainly that the "[m]ost important driver here will be Jack's and Jay's vision."

Ultimately, Dorsey proposed a purchase price of $309 million to acquire an 88% stake in TIDAL, implying a $350 million total enterprise valuation. Carter would retain an 8% stake, and other artist partners would hold the remaining 4% interest. The presentation set forth the acquisition as more of an assumption than an open question: "We will update the Committee once we have finalized terms we are comfortable with, and unless there are additional remaining questions, we can circulate a UWC to the Committee to approve the transaction."

The Transaction Committee concluded that management should continue pursuing the transaction and update it as negotiations progressed. The Transaction Committee provided the full Board with an update on the proposed transaction at its regularly scheduled meeting on February 11.

G. The Transaction Committee Approves The Acquisition.

Without any further meetings, the Transaction Committee approved the acquisition by unanimous written consent on February 25, 2021. The Company announced the deal on March 4, after which its stock price decreased by 7%. [. . .]

Block closed the deal on April 30, 2021[and] it ultimately paid $237.3 million for an ownership interest of 86.23%. [. . .]

H. This Litigation

Plaintiff City of Coral Springs Police Officers' Pension Plan ("Plaintiff") is a beneficial owner of Block common stock. Before filing this action, Plaintiff made a demand for books and records pursuant to 8 Del. C. § 220, and Block produced documents in response.

Plaintiff filed this derivative action on January 27, 2022. The Complaint asserts two causes of action challenging the TIDAL acquisition as a breach of fiduciary duty—Count I against Dorsey as a controller and Count II against the directors on the Board at the time the transaction was approved. Defendants moved to dismiss the Complaint. [. . .]

II. LEGAL ANALYSIS

Defendants moved to dismiss the Amended Complaint pursuant to Court of Chancery Rules 23.1 and 12(b)(6). Because the Rule 23.1 motion results in dismissal, the court does not reach the Rule 12(b)(6) motion.

"A cardinal precept of [Delaware law] is that directors, rather than shareholders, manage the business and affairs of the corporation." *Aronson v. Lewis; Brehm v. Eisner* "In a derivative suit, a stockholder seeks to displace the board's authority over a litigation asset and assert the corporation's claim." *United Food & Com. Workers Union & Participating Food Indus. Empls. Tri-State Pension Fund v. Zuckerberg.* Because derivative litigation impinges on the managerial freedom of directors in this way, "a stockholder only can pursue a cause of action belonging to the corporation if (i) the stockholder demanded that the directors pursue the corporate claim and they wrongfully refused to do so or (ii) demand is excused because the directors are incapable of making an impartial decision regarding the litigation." *Id.* The demand requirement is a substantive principle under Delaware law. *Id.* Rule 23.1 is the "procedural embodiment of this substantive principle." *Rales v. Blasband.*

Under Rule 23.1, stockholder plaintiffs must "allege with particularity the efforts, if any, made by the plaintiff to obtain the action the plaintiff desires from the directors or comparable authority and the reasons for the plaintiff's failure to obtain the action or for not making the effort." *Ct. Ch. R. 23.1(a).* Stockholders choosing to allege demand futility must meet the "heightened pleading requirements," *Zuckerberg* alleging "particularized factual statements that are essential to the claim." *Brehm.* [. . .]

In *Zuckerberg*, the Delaware Supreme Court affirmed and thereby adopted Vice Chancellor Laster's "universal test" for demand futility that blends elements of the two precursor tests: *Aronson* and *Rales*. When conducting a demand futility analysis under Zuckerberg, Delaware courts ask, on a director-by-director basis:

(i) whether the director received a material personal benefit from the alleged misconduct that is the subject of the litigation demand;

(ii) whether the director faces a substantial likelihood of liability on any of the claims that would be the subject of the litigation demand; and

(iii) whether the director lacks independence from someone who received a material personal benefit from the alleged misconduct that would be the subject of the litigation demand or who would face a substantial likelihood of liability on any of the claims that are the subject of the litigation demand. *United Food & Com. Workers Union & Participating Food Indus. Empls. Tri-State Pension Fund v. Zuckerberg, 262 A.3d 1034, 1059 (Del. 2021)*

"If the answer to any of the questions is 'yes' for at least half of the members of the demand board, then demand is excused as futile." *Id.* While the Zuckerberg test displaced the prior tests from Aronson and Rales, cases properly applying Aronson and Rales remain good law. *Id.*

As of the date when Plaintiff filed their complaint, the Board comprised twelve directors: Dorsey, Carter, the Committee Defendants, and the remaining six Defendants (Deighton, Garutti, McKelvey, Patterson, Summers, and Viniar). To defeat Defendants' Rule 23.1 motion, Plaintiff must impugn the impartiality of at least six directors under *Zuckerberg*. [. . .]

Plaintiff focuses its arguments on Carter, Dorsey, and the four Committee Defendants. Plaintiff argues that: Carter is disqualified because he received a material personal benefit from the TIDAL acquisition; Dorsey's relationship with Carter made him incapable of impartially considering a demand concerning the TIDAL acquisition; and the Committee Defendants face a substantial likelihood of liability from claims challenging the TIDAL acquisition.

The analysis as to Carter and Dorsey goes Plaintiff's way. Defendants concede that Carter is interested in the transaction. And there are good arguments that Dorsey lacks independence from Carter for the purpose of the TIDAL acquisition. When supported by specific factual allegations, "professional or personal friendships, which may border on or even exceed familial loyalty and closeness, may raise a reasonable doubt whether a director can appropriately consider demand." *Beam* [. . .]. Two recent Delaware Supreme Court decisions addressing the independence analysis under Rule 23.1 urge the court to evaluate personal relationships in a commonsense manner.[43] Applying this commonsense approach to Dorsey and Carter's relationship, Plaintiff has the better side of the argument. It is reasonably conceivable that Dorsey used corporate coffers to bolster his relationship with Carter. But the court need not delve too deeply into this issue, because Plaintiff has failed to meet its burden as to the remaining ten directors.

Plaintiff argues that demand is futile as to the Committee Defendants because they face a substantial likelihood of liability from the subject matter of the litigation demand. Where, as here, the corporation's certificate of incorporation exculpates its directors from liability to the fullest extent permitted by law, the substantial-likelihood standard requires that a plaintiff "plead particularized facts providing a reason to believe that the individual director was self-interested, beholden to an interested party, or acted in bad faith." *Zuckerberg Del. Ch. 2020*. A

---

[43] *See* Sandys v. Pincus, 152 A.3d 124 (Del. 2016) (reversing the trial court's determination that plaintiff had failed to adequately allege that a director lacked independence from a CEO with whom the director co-owned a private jet, holding that the co-ownership is "suggestive of the type of very close personal relationship that, like family ties, one would expect to heavily influence a human's ability to exercise impartial judgment"); Marchand v. Barnhill, 212 A.3d 805, 818–20 (Del. 2019) (reversing the trial court's determination that the plaintiff had failed to adequately allege that a director lacked independence from the controller and Kruse family where the director started as the Kruse patriarch's administrative assistant and, over the course of a 28-year career with the company, rose to the high managerial position of CFO, became a director due to the support of the Kruse family, and was the honorary beneficiary of the Kruse family's charitable efforts that led to a $450,000 donation to a key local college, observing that "our law has recognized that deep and longstanding friendships are meaningful to human beings and that any realistic consideration of the question of independence must give weight to these important relationships and their natural effect on the ability of the parties to act impartially toward each other").

stockholder need not show a probability of success to meet the substantial-likelihood standard; the standard requires only a showing that "the claims have some merit." *Id.*

Plaintiff does not argue that the Committee Defendants acted in a self-interested manner or that they were beholden to an interested party. Rather, Plaintiff argues that the Committee Defendants failed to act in good faith when approving the TIDAL acquisition. [. . .]

[. . .] The Delaware Supreme Court has described a non-exhaustive set of circumstances forming a failure to act in good faith:

> A failure to act in good faith may be shown, for instance, where the fiduciary intentionally acts with a purpose other than that of advancing the best interests of the corporation, where the fiduciary acts with the intent to violate applicable positive law, or where the fiduciary intentionally fails to act in the face of a known duty to act, demonstrating a conscious disregard for his duties. There may be other examples of bad faith yet to be proven or alleged, but these three are the most salient. *Stone v. Ritter.*

Pleading a failure to act in good faith requires the plaintiff to "plead particularized facts that demonstrate that the directors acted with scienter, i.e., that they had 'actual or constructive knowledge' that their conduct was legally improper." *In re Citigroup Inc. S'holder Deriv. Litig.*

That is, to allege a lack of good faith, a plaintiff must allege that the actor knew that he was acting "inconsistent with his fiduciary duties." *McElrath v. Kalanick* "Gross negligence, without more, is insufficient to get out from under an exculpated breach of the duty of care." *Id.*

Generally, this court is not in the business of second-guessing board decisions made by disinterested and independent directors. Of course, there are some business decisions that are so suspect that it is reasonably conceivable that the decision makers were not acting to advance the best interest of the corporation. Two cases relied on by the parties in briefing help delineate the boundaries of this principle—*Disney*, denying a motion to dismiss where the plaintiff adequately alleged that the board acted in bad faith, and *McElrath*, granting a motion to dismiss where the plaintiff failed to adequately allege that the board acted in bad faith.

In *Disney*, a stockholder sued Disney's departing CEO, Eisner, and its board for breach of fiduciary duty in connection with the hiring and firing of Eisner's longtime friend Ovitz as President. The narrative set out in the Disney complaint was quite stark. As alleged, Eisner "unilaterally" made the hiring decision. The board did not receive any presentations on the terms of the employment contract, did not ask questions about the proposed agreement, received only a summary of the employment agreement's terms, approved the hire while the employment agreement was still a "work in progress," did not engage in further review once it had authorized the hire, and did not retain any outside experts to consult on the agreement. Negotiation of the unresolved employment terms took place solely between Eisner, Ovitz, and their attorneys. The compensation committee followed up with meetings to receive updates on the negotiations but did not otherwise engage in the process. The final agreement differed vastly from the initial summary that the board had approved. And when Eisner terminated Ovitz a year later, the employment agreement allowed Ovitz to reap substantial exit benefits, which the board permitted without further investigation.

On these facts, then-Chancellor Chandler denied the defendants' motion to dismiss for failure to plead demand futility, holding that the plaintiff had adequately pled that the directors failed to act in good faith. The well-pled allegations portrayed more than mere negligent or grossly negligent conduct, and instead suggested "that the defendant directors consciously and intentionally disregarded their responsibilities, adopting a 'we don't care about the risks' attitude concerning a material corporate decision." *Disney* Put differently, the facts as alleged gave rise to the inference that the directors "knew that they were making material decisions without adequate information and without adequate deliberation, and that they simply did not care if the decisions caused the corporation and its stockholders to suffer injury or loss." *Id.* The Chancellor weighed the board's "ostrich-like" approach and concluded that the plaintiff had adequately alleged that "the defendant directors' conduct fell outside the protection of the business judgment rule," *id.* and that conclusion was sufficient to render demand futile under the second prong of *Aronson*.

Distinguishable allegations resulted in a different outcome in *McElrath*. There, a stockholder challenged Uber's acquisition of a self-driving car project from Google. Uber's CEO, Travis Kalanick, negotiated the acquisition. Uber's diligence materials included a report from a computer forensic investigation firm finding that some of the target's employees had retained confidential information from Google following their departure. When the misuse of confidential information was later revealed, Uber suffered financially and reputationally. The plaintiff brought derivative claims against Kalanick and the directors who approved the transaction. To plead bad faith as to a majority of the board, the plaintiff constructed a narrative that the board was on notice that Kalanick might ignore intellectual property issues because Kalanick's prior business had been sued for copyright violations, Uber had a practice of hiring employees from competitors to steal trade secrets, and the merger agreement contained an abnormal indemnification clause that prevented Uber from seeking indemnification from the target's employees for non-compete and infringement claims.

The defendants moved to dismiss the complaint for failure to plead demand futility, and Vice Chancellor Glasscock granted the motion. The Delaware Supreme Court affirmed on appeal, identifying a number of factors that made it unreasonable to infer that Uber's board acted in bad faith. The high court observed that "[b]y any reasonable measure, the Uber board of directors approved a flawed transaction," but that did not give rise to a "real threat of personal liability" sufficient to disqualify a majority of the board for Rule 23.1 purposes. In reaching this conclusion, the court observed that the board did more than just rubberstamp the deal: they heard a presentation summarizing the transaction, reviewed the risk of litigation with Google, discussed due diligence, and asked questions. When the board asked questions about diligence and litigation risk, they received answers indicating that the risk was present, but not necessarily prevalent enough to kill the deal, and the board concluded that the diligence was "okay." The high court rejected the appellant's appeal to Disney by noting important distinctions—unlike the board in Disney, the Uber directors heard a presentation from the CEO on the transaction, met to consider the acquisition, and enlisted the assistance of outside counsel and an investigative firm to help with due diligence. The high court affirmed this court's dismissal based on the plaintiff's failure to show that the directors faced a substantial likelihood of liability.

Here, as in McErath, it is clear that the TIDAL acquisition was a "flawed" business decision "[b]y any reasonable measure." The question is whether, as in Disney, Plaintiff adequately alleged that the majority of the board acted in bad faith when approving it.

Plaintiff's counsel took an admirable stab at packaging the facts of this case into the mold of Disney. As Plaintiff tells it, Dorsey pulled some Eisner-level moves by pushing the deal forward singlehandedly, with the Transaction Committee playing an "ostrich-like" role. Plaintiff alleges that Dorsey caused Block to submit a letter of intent to purchase TIDAL before the Transaction Committee was even formed. The Transaction Committee then allowed Dorsey to handle negotiations. After discussing the opportunity for only thirty-five minutes during their first meeting in September, the Transaction Committee encouraged Dorsey to move forward. In advance of its second meeting in October, management provided a report that showed just how dire TIDAL's market position looked.

To be sure, the Transaction Committee asked many questions throughout the process, and Plaintiff concedes this much. Plaintiff argues, however, that the court should not credit the Transaction Committee for asking questions given the answers it received. As Plaintiff sees it, the problem was not that the Transaction Committee failed to ask questions—it is that the answers did not seem to matter.

Before its October meeting, the Transaction Committee asked whether any other members of senior management supported the acquisition; in response, the committee learned that there were none, aside from Dorsey. The Transaction Committee asked whether the artist commitments, which formed the basis for at least half of management's valuation of TIDAL, were legally enforceable; in response, the committee learned that Block would have "no recourse" if the artists decided to walk away. The Transaction Committee asked for near- and long-term plans for integrating TIDAL into Block's business; in response, the committee learned that management had not created these plans and that this remained "one of the biggest risks."

After the October meeting, the Transaction Committee went dark for three months while Dorsey negotiated the purchase price. Ultimately, without any further meetings, the Transaction Committee approved the acquisition by unanimous written consent.

Although the facts emphasized by Plaintiff do not generate tremendous confidence in the Transaction Committee's process, they fall short of supporting an inference of bad faith. Effectively, Plaintiff asks the court to presume bad faith based on the merits of the deal alone. Plaintiff does not allege that the Transaction Committee lacked a business reason for wanting to acquire TIDAL—the presentation materials show management's strategic goals for expanding Block into the music industry. Plaintiff does not attempt allege that any of the Committee Defendants were in any way beholden to Dorsey. Plaintiff acknowledge that the Committee Defendants did not sit idly by while Dorsey presented. They asked many appropriate questions before the October 20 meeting, and they asked many appropriate follow-up questions in advance of the next meeting on January 22. The Transaction Committee were presented with over twenty single-spaced slides providing management's detailed answers to each of these questions. Over the course of negotiations, and even inexplicably after the deal was publicly announced, the purchase price dropped considerably. On these facts, the Transaction Committee's actions more closely resemble those in McElrath than Disney. Plaintiff has alleged sufficient facts to make a reasonable person question the business wisdom of the TIDAL acquisition, but Plaintiff has failed to plead that the Committee Defendants acted in bad faith and thus faced a substantial likelihood of liability for that decision.

Plaintiff's allegations as to the remaining six non-Committee Defendant directors are even more attenuated. Plaintiff's only allegations as to those defendants are that they failed to meaningfully supervise the Transaction Committee's process. According to Plaintiff, the rest of the Board should have intervened to stop the TIDAL acquisition. Because Plaintiff has not adequately alleged that the Transaction Committee's approval of the TIDAL acquisition rose to the level of bad faith, it is difficult to imagine how the Board's lack of "supervision" of that process did so. Plaintiff's allegations as to the remaining directors fail.

III. CONCLUSION

Ultimately, the demand requirement is a manifestation of the business judgment rule, which exists in part to "free fiduciaries making risky business decisions in good faith from the worry that if those decisions do not pan out in the manner they had hoped, they will put their personal net worths at risk." *In re Massey Energy Co.* In this case, the demand requirement operates as intended. Because Plaintiff failed to adequately allege with particularity facts giving rise to a reasonable doubt that a majority of the Board was disinterested or lacked independence with respect to the TIDAL acquisition, Plaintiff failed to plead that demand was futile. Defendants' motion to dismiss pursuant to Rule 23.1 is granted.

C. DUTY OF LOYALTY

Delaware General Corporation Law
Section 144. Interested directors; quorum.

(a) No contract or transaction between a corporation and 1 or more of its directors or officers, or between a corporation and any other corporation, partnership, association, or other organization in which 1 or more of its directors or officers, are directors or officers, or have a financial interest, shall be void or voidable solely for this reason, or solely because the director or officer is present at or participates in the meeting of the board or committee which authorizes the contract or transaction, or solely because any such director's or officer's votes are counted for such purpose, if:

(1) The material facts as to the director's or officer's relationship or interest and as to the contract or transaction are disclosed or are known to the board of directors or the committee, and the board or committee in good faith authorizes the contract or transaction by the affirmative votes of a majority of the disinterested directors, even though the disinterested directors be less than a quorum; or

(2) The material facts as to the director's or officer's relationship or interest and as to the contract or transaction are disclosed or are known to the stockholders entitled to vote thereon, and the contract or transaction is specifically approved in good faith by vote of the stockholders; or

(3) The contract or transaction is fair as to the corporation as of the time it is authorized, approved or ratified, by the board of directors, a committee or the stockholders.

(b) Common or interested directors may be counted in determining the presence of a quorum at a meeting of the board of directors or of a committee which authorizes the contract or transaction.

1. CONFLICTS OF INTEREST

Benihana of Tokyo, Inc. v. Benihana, Inc.
906 A.2d 114 (Del. 2006)

[. . .]

■ BERGER, JUSTICE:

[. . .]

Factual and Procedural Background

Rocky Aoki founded Benihana of Tokyo, Inc. (BOT), and its subsidiary, Benihana, which own and operate Benihana restaurants in the United States and other countries. Aoki owned 100% of BOT until 1998, when he pled guilty to insider trading charges. In order to avoid licensing problems created by his status as a convicted felon, Aoki transferred his stock to the Benihana Protective Trust. The trustees of the Trust were Aoki's three children (Kana Aoki Nootenboom, Kyle Aoki and Kevin Aoki) and Darwin Dornbush (who was then the family's attorney, a Benihana director, and, effectively, the company's general counsel).

Benihana, a Delaware corporation, has two classes of common stock. There are approximately 6 million shares of Class A common stock outstanding. Each share has 1/10 vote and the holders of Class A common are entitled to elect 25% of the directors. There are approximately 3 million shares of Common stock outstanding. Each share of Common has one vote and the holders of Common stock are entitled to elect the remaining 75% of Benihana's directors. Before the transaction at issue, BOT owned 50.9% of the Common stock and 2% of the Class A stock. The nine member board of directors is classified and the directors serve three-year terms.

In 2003, shortly after Aoki married Keiko Aoki, conflicts arose between Aoki and his children. In August, the children were upset to learn that Aoki had changed his will to give Keiko control over BOT. Joel Schwartz, Benihana's president and chief executive officer, also was concerned about this change in control. He discussed the situation with Dornbush, and they briefly considered various options, including the issuance of sufficient Class A stock to trigger a provision in the certificate of incorporation that would allow the Common and Class A to vote together for 75% of the directors.

The Aoki family's turmoil came at a time when Benihana also was facing challenges. Many of its restaurants were old and outmoded. Benihana hired WD Partners to evaluate its facilities and to plan and design appropriate renovations. The resulting Construction and Renovation Plan anticipated that the project would take at least five years and cost $56 million or more. Wachovia offered to provide Benihana a $60 million line of credit for the Construction and Renovation Plan, but the restrictions Wachovia imposed made it unlikely that Benihana would be able to borrow the full amount. Because the Wachovia line of credit did not assure that Benihana would have the capital it needed, the company retained Morgan Joseph & Co. to develop other financing options.

On January 9, 2004, after evaluating Benihana's financial situation and needs, Fred Joseph, of Morgan Joseph, met with Schwartz, Dornbush and John E. Abdo, the board's executive committee. Joseph expressed concern that Benihana would not have sufficient available capital to complete the Construction and Renovation Plan and pursue appropriate acquisitions. Benihana was conservatively leveraged, and Joseph discussed various financing alternatives, including bank debt, high yield debt, convertible debt or preferred stock, equity and sale/leaseback options.

The full board met with Joseph on January 29, 2004. He reviewed all the financing alternatives that he had discussed with the executive committee, and recommended that Benihana issue convertible preferred stock. Joseph explained that the preferred stock would provide the funds needed for the Construction and Renovation Plan and also put the company in a better negotiating position if it sought additional financing from Wachovia.

Joseph gave the directors a board book, marked "Confidential," containing an analysis of the proposed stock issuance (the Transaction). The book included, among others, the following anticipated terms: (i) issuance of $20,000,000 of preferred stock, convertible into Common stock; (ii) dividend of 6% +/− 0.5%; (iii) conversion premium of 20% +/− 2.5%; (iv) buyer's approval required for material corporate transactions; and (v) one to two board seats to the buyer. At trial, Joseph testified that the terms had been chosen by looking at comparable stock issuances and analyzing the Morgan Joseph proposal under a theoretical model.

The board met again on February 17, 2004, to review the terms of the Transaction. The directors discussed Benihana's preferences and Joseph predicted what a buyer likely would expect or require. [. . .] As the Court of Chancery found, the board understood that the preferred terms were akin to a "wish list."

Shortly after the February meeting, Abdo contacted Joseph and told him that BFC Financial Corporation was interested in buying the new convertible stock. In April 2005, Joseph sent BFC a private placement memorandum. Abdo negotiated with Joseph for several weeks. They agreed to the Transaction on the following basic terms: (i) $20 million issuance in two tranches of $10 million each, with the second tranche to be issued one to three years after the first; (ii) BFC obtained one seat on the board, and one additional seat if Benihana failed to pay dividends for two consecutive quarters; (iii) BFC obtained preemptive rights on any new voting securities; (iv) 5% dividend; (v) 15% conversion premium; (vi) BFC had the right to force Benihana to redeem the preferred stock in full after ten years; and (vii) the stock would have immediate "as if converted" voting rights. Joseph testified that he was satisfied with the negotiations, as he had obtained what he wanted with respect to the most important points.

On April 22, 2004, Abdo sent a memorandum to Dornbush, Schwartz and Joseph, listing the agreed terms of the Transaction. He did not send the memorandum to any other members of the Benihana board. Schwartz did tell Becker, Sturges, Sano, and possibly Pine that BFC was the potential buyer. At its next meeting, held on May 6, 2004, the entire board was officially informed of BFC's involvement in the Transaction. Abdo made a presentation on behalf of BFC and then left the meeting. Joseph distributed an updated board book, which explained that Abdo had approached Morgan Joseph on behalf of BFC, and included the negotiated terms. The trial court found that the board was not informed that Abdo had negotiated the deal on behalf of BFC. But the board did know that Abdo was a principal of BFC. After discussion, the board reviewed and approved the Transaction, subject to the receipt of a fairness opinion.

On May 18, 2004, after he learned that Morgan Joseph was providing a fairness opinion, Schwartz publicly announced the stock issuance. Two days later, Aoki's counsel sent a letter asking the board to abandon the Transaction and pursue other, more favorable, financing alternatives. The letter expressed concern about the directors' conflicts, the dilutive effect of the stock issuance, and its "questionable legality." Schwartz gave copies of the letter to the directors at the May 20 board meeting, and Dornbush advised that he did not believe that Aoki's concerns had merit. Joseph and another Morgan Joseph representative then joined the meeting by telephone and opined that the Transaction was fair from a financial point of view. The board then approved the Transaction.

During the following two weeks, Benihana received three alternative financing proposals. Schwartz asked Becker, Pine and Sturges to act as an independent committee and review the first offer. The committee decided that the offer was inferior and not worth pursuing. Morgan Joseph agreed with that assessment. Schwartz referred the next two proposals to Morgan Joseph, with the same result.

On June 8, 2004, Benihana and BFC executed the Stock Purchase Agreement. On June 11, 2004, the board met and approved resolutions ratifying the execution of the Stock Purchase Agreement and authorizing the stock issuance. Schwartz then reported on the three alternative proposals that had been rejected by the ad hoc committee and Morgan Joseph. On July 2, 2004, BOT filed this action against all of Benihana's directors, except Kevin Aoki, alleging breaches of fiduciary duties; and against BFC, alleging that it aided and abetted the fiduciary violations. Three months later, as the parties were filing their pre-trial briefs, the board again reviewed the Transaction. After considering the allegations in the amended complaint, the board voted once more to approve it. [. . .]

Discussion

Before addressing the directors' conduct and motivation, we must decide whether Benihana's certificate of incorporation authorized the board to issue preferred stock with preemptive rights. Article 4, ¶ 2 of the certificate provides that, "[n]o stockholder shall have any preemptive right to subscribe to or purchase any issue of stock . . . of the corporation. . . ." Article 4(b) authorizes the board to issue:

> Preferred Stock of any series and to state in the resolution or resolutions providing for the issuance of shares of any series the voting powers, if any, designations, preferences and relative, participating, optional or other special rights, and the qualifications, limitations or restrictions of such series to the full extent now or hereafter permitted by the law of the State of Delaware. . . .

BOT contends that Article 4, ¶ 2 clearly and unambiguously prohibits preemptive rights. BOT acknowledges that Article 4(b) gives the board so-called "blank check" authority to designate the rights and preferences of Benihana's preferred stock. Reading the two provisions together, BOT argues that they give the board blank check authority to designate rights and preferences as to all enumerated matters *except* preemptive rights.

The trial court reviewed the history of 8 *Del. C.* § 102, and decided that the boilerplate language in Article 4, ¶ 2 merely confirms that no stockholder has preemptive rights under common law. As a result, the seemingly absolute language in ¶ 2 has no bearing on the availability of contractually created preemptive rights. The trial court explained:

> Before the 1967 amendments, § 102(b)(3) provided that a certificate of incorporation may contain provisions "limiting or denying to the stockholders the preemptive rights to subscribe to any or all additional issues of stock of the corporation." As a result, a common law rule developed that shareholders possess preemptive rights unless the certificate of incorporation provided otherwise. In 1967 the Delaware Legislature reversed this presumption. Section 102(b)(3) was amended to provide in relevant part: "No stockholder shall have any preemptive right . . . unless, and except to the extent that, such right is expressly granted to him in the certificate of incorporation."
>
> Thereafter, companies began including boilerplate language in their charters to clarify that no shareholder possessed preemptive rights under common law.
>
> The blank check provision in Benihana's Certificate of Incorporation suggests that the certificate was never intended to limit Benihana's ability to issue preemptive rights by contract to purchasers of preferred stock. Therefore, I do not read Article 4 of the charter as doing anything more than confirming that the common law presumption does not apply and that the

Certificate of Incorporation itself does not grant any preemptive rights. *Benihana of Tokyo, Inc. v. Benihana, Inc.*

It is settled law that certificates of incorporation are contracts, subject to the general rules of contract and statutory construction. *Staar Surgical Co. v. Waggoner; Lawson v. Household Finance Corporation.* Thus, if the charter language is clear and unambiguous, it must be given its plain meaning. *Northwestern National Ins. Co. v. Esmark, Inc.* If there is ambiguity, however, the language must be construed in a manner that will harmonize the apparent conflicts and give effect to the intent of the drafters. *Anchor Motor Freight v. Ciabattoni.* The Court of Chancery properly applied these principles, and we agree with its conclusion that the Benihana certificate does not prohibit the issuance of preferred stock with preemptive rights.

Even if the Benihana board had the power to issue the disputed stock, BOT maintains that the trial court erred in finding that it acted properly in approving the Transaction. Specifically, BOT argues that the Court of Chancery erred: (1) by applying 8 *Del. C.* § 144(a)(1), because the board did not know all material facts before it approved the Transaction; (2) by applying the business judgment rule, because Abdo breached his fiduciary duties; and (3) by finding that the board's primary purpose in approving the Transaction was not to dilute BOT's voting power.

A.   Section 144(a)(1) Approval

Section 144 of the Delaware General Corporation Law provides a safe harbor for interested transactions, like this one, if "[t]he material facts as to the director's . . . relationship or interest and as to the contract or transaction are disclosed or are known to the board of directors . . . and the board . . . in good faith authorizes the contract or transaction by the affirmative votes of a majority of the disinterested directors. . . ." After approval by disinterested directors, courts review the interested transaction under the business judgment rule, *Cede & Co. v. Technicolor, Inc.*, which "is a presumption that in making a business decision, the directors of a corporation acted on an informed basis, in good faith and in the honest belief that the action taken was in the best interest of the company." *Aronson v. Lewis.*

BOT argues that § 144(a)(1) is inapplicable because, when they approved the Transaction, the disinterested directors did not know that Abdo had negotiated the terms for BFC. Abdo's role as negotiator is material, according to BOT, because Abdo had been given the confidential term sheet prepared by Joseph and knew which of those terms Benihana was prepared to give up during negotiations. We agree that the board needed to know about Abdo's involvement in order to make an informed decision. The record clearly establishes, however, that the board possessed that material information when it approved the Transaction on May 6, 2004 and May 20, 2004.

Shortly before the May 6 meeting, Schwartz told Becker, Sturges and Sano that BFC was the proposed buyer. Then, at the meeting, Abdo made the presentation on behalf of BFC. Joseph's board book also explained that Abdo had made the initial contact that precipitated the negotiations. The board members knew that Abdo is a director, vice-chairman, and one of two people who control BFC. Thus, although no one ever said, "Abdo negotiated this deal for BFC," the directors understood that he was BFC's representative in the Transaction. As Pine testified, "whoever actually did the negotiating, [Abdo] as a principal would have to agree to it. So whether he sat in the room and negotiated it or he sat somewhere else and was brought the results of someone else's negotiation, he was the ultimate decision-maker." Accordingly, we conclude that the disinterested directors possessed all the material information on Abdo's interest in the Transaction, and their approval at the May 6 and May 20 board meetings satisfies § 144(a)(1).*

B. Abdo's alleged fiduciary violation

BOT next argues that the Court of Chancery should have reviewed the Transaction under an entire fairness standard because Abdo breached his duty of loyalty when he used Benihana's confidential information to negotiate on behalf of BFC. This argument starts with a flawed premise. The record does not support BOT's contention that Abdo used any confidential information against Benihana. Even without Joseph's comments at the February 17 board meeting, Abdo knew the terms a buyer could expect to obtain in a deal like this. Moreover, as the trial court found, "the negotiations involved give and take on a number of points" and Benihana "ended up where [it] wanted to be" for the most important terms. Abdo did not set the terms of the deal; he did not deceive the board; and he did not dominate or control the other directors' approval of the Transaction. In short, the record does not support the claim that Abdo breached his duty of loyalty. *Cinerama, Inc. v. Technicolor, Inc.*

C. Dilution of BOT's voting power

Finally, BOT argues that the board's primary purpose in approving the Transaction was to dilute BOT's voting control. BOT points out that Schwartz was concerned about BOT's control in 2003 and even discussed with Dornbush the possibility of issuing a huge number of Class A shares. Then, despite the availability of other financing options, the board decided on a stock issuance, and agreed to give BFC "as if converted"

---

*   EDS.—The Chancery Court embraced a different view on the effects of 8 Del. C. § 144(a)(1). According to the Chancery Court, § 144 "merely protects against invalidation of a transaction 'solely' because it is an interested one." It further notes that "[n]othing in the statute sanctions unfairness to [the Company] or removes the transaction from judicial scrutiny" and that "satisfying the requirements of § 144 only means that the BFC Transaction is not void or voidable solely because of the conflict of interest." Moreover, "the satisfaction of §§ 144(a)(1) or (a)(2) alone does not always have the opposite effect of invoking business judgment rule review . . . ."

voting rights. According to BOT, the trial court overlooked this powerful evidence of the board's improper purpose.

It is settled law that, "corporate action . . . may not be taken for the sole or primary purpose of entrenchment." *Williams v. Geier*. Here, however, the trial court found that "the primary purpose of the . . . Transaction was to provide what the directors subjectively believed to be the best financing vehicle available for securing the necessary funds to pursue the agreed upon Construction and Renovation Plan for the Benihana restaurants." That factual determination has ample record support, especially in light of the trial court's credibility determinations. Accordingly, we defer to the Court of Chancery's conclusion that the board's approval of the Transaction was a valid exercise of its business judgment, for a proper corporate purpose.

Conclusion

Based on the foregoing, the judgment of the Court of Chancery is affirmed.

2. CORPORATE OPPORTUNITY DOCTRINE

Personal Touch Holding Corp. v. Glaubach
No. 11199–CB, 2019 WL 937180 (Del. Ch. Feb. 25, 2019)

■ BOUCHARD, C.

I. BACKGROUND

In 1974, Felix Glaubach, an orthodontist, and non-party Robert Marx, a lawyer, co-founded [. . .] Personal Touch Holding Corp. [. . .] They later became equal partners in the business.

Personal Touch is a Delaware corporation with its principal place of business in Lake Success, New York. The Company provides home healthcare services, including nursing, physical therapy, and long-term care. It currently operates through various subsidiaries with locations in seven different states.

Glaubach served as President of the Company from December 13, 2010 until June 24, 2015, when he was terminated from that position. Glaubach, together with his wife and family trusts, currently holds approximately 27% of the Company's outstanding common stock. At the time of trial, Glaubach was about eighty-eight years old, and had been married to his wife for over fifty-eight years.

Glaubach and Marx currently serve as special directors of the Company's board of directors (the "Board"), entitling them to three votes each. The Board has four other members, each of whom is entitled to one vote. [. . .]

Two other individuals prominent in this action are David Slifkin and his wife, Dr. Trudy Balk. Slifkin joined the Company in 1990 and served as its CEO from January 31, 2011 until December 7, 2015. Slifkin resigned as CEO on the heels of an internal investigation that uncovered his central role in a tax evasion scheme involving many Company employees. Balk joined the Company in 1980 and was its Vice President of Operations when she left the Company in July 2014. [. . .]

On or about February 28, 2013, Jim Clifford, the Director of Management Services at AAA New York, informed Mike Macagnone, the Director of Employee Services at the Company, that the building located next door to one of the Company's subsidiaries in Jamaica, New York (the "AAA Building") was for sale. The Company had been seeking additional office space in Jamaica, New York for several years and was especially interested in the AAA Building due to its location. Management believed that the AAA Building could be used to relocate the Company's corporate offices, to expand the Company's operations in the area, as additional office space for one of the Company's subsidiaries, or as storage.

On March 4, 2013, Slifkin emailed Marx and Glaubach stating that the AAA Building "is up for sale and the asking price seems reasonable." Two days later, Marx, Glaubach, and Macagnone met with Clifford to see the building and discuss a price. Marx told Clifford that the Company was "very interested" in the property but that the asking price of $ 1,200,000 was "a little high." Marx then offered Clifford $ 1 million in cash for the building. [. . .]

Less than one month later, Clifford informed Marx that AAA could not proceed with a sale at that time because its relocation plans had fallen through. Marx continued to inquire with Clifford about the AAA Building for several months. During one of those inquiries, Clifford told Marx that AAA wants "to move and we'll call you as soon as we have anything."

On November 1, 2013, one of the Company's subsidiaries entered into a five-year lease with Personal Touch Realty LLC to rent a property in Jamaica, New York (the "Jamaica Property"). Marx and Glaubach each owned fifty percent of Personal Touch Realty LLC at all relevant times. Only Marx and Glaubach signed the lease—Marx for Personal Touch Realty LLC and Glaubach for the Company. Marx set the rental rate for the Jamaica Property.

On or around January 1, 2014, Glaubach hired David Reich as "Assistant to the President" with a salary of $ 100,000 per year. Glaubach asserts he hired Reich primarily to assist him in exposing fraud that he suspected was occurring within the Company. Reich was an employee of the Company from January 8, 2014 until April 15, 2015, during which time he was paid a total of approximately $ 209,440. Also during this time period, Reich assisted Glaubach in acquiring the AAA Building for himself.

In 2014, Glaubach instructed Reich to contact Clifford to see whether AAA was ready to sell the AAA Building. Reich and Clifford discussed the sale of the building during the summer of 2014. Both were under the impression at the time that they were negotiating the sale of the building to the Company. Clifford continued to have this impression until September 24, 2014.

At some point before September 24, Glaubach told Reich that he wanted to buy the AAA Building himself in order to develop it or sell it for a profit. Glaubach did not want anyone at the Company to know about his negotiations regarding the AAA Building and made efforts to keep them secret. Reich thus stopped using his Company email account and began using a personal one in his communications about the AAA Building. Reich also suggested meeting with Clifford in a conference room in Reich's temple rather than on Company grounds because there were "a lot of blabbermouths" in the Company's offices. [. . .]

In May 2016, after the Audit Committee identified the Jamaica Property lease as a related-party transaction, the Company obtained an appraisal, which indicated that the Company was paying above-market rent to Personal Touch Realty LLC, the entity owned fifty-fifty by Glaubach and Marx. The appraisal indicated that the amount of above-market rent due on the lease was approximately $ 1,270,000.

Marx obtained his own appraisal suggesting that the lease was below-market. Nonetheless, in May 2017, Marx entered into a settlement agreement with the Company in which he agreed to provide $ 400,000 of consideration to the Company, consisting of $ 100,000 in cash and a $ 300,000 reduction in his share of rent that otherwise would be owed under the lease in the future. [. . .]

III. ANALYSIS

[. . .]

A. Glaubach Usurped a Corporate Opportunity by Secretly Acquiring the AAA Building for Himself

The Company contends that Glaubach breached his fiduciary duty of loyalty by usurping the corporate opportunity of acquiring the AAA Building for himself. I agree for the reasons explained below.

Eighty years ago, in its seminal decision of *Guth v. Loft, Inc.*, our Supreme Court described the corporate opportunity doctrine as follows:

> [I]f there is presented to a corporate officer or director a business opportunity which the corporation is financially able to undertake, is, from its nature, in the line of the corporation's business and is of practical advantage to it, is one in which the corporation has an interest or a reasonable expectancy, and, by embracing the opportunity, the self-interest of the officer or director will be brought into conflict with that of his corporation, the law will not permit him to seize the opportunity for himself.

In *Broz v. Cellular Information Systems, Inc.*, our Supreme Court more recently explained that:

> The corporate opportunity doctrine, as delineated by *Guth* and its progeny, holds that a corporate officer or director may not

take a business opportunity for his own if: (1) the corporation is financially able to exploit the opportunity; (2) the opportunity is within the corporation's line of business; (3) the corporation has an interest or expectancy in the opportunity; and (4) by taking the opportunity for his own, the corporate fiduciary will thereby be placed in a position inimicable to his duties to the corporation.

Although these four factors are articulated in the conjunctive, the Supreme Court in *Broz* emphasized "that the tests enunciated in *Guth* and subsequent cases provide guidelines to be considered by a reviewing court in balancing the equities of an individual case" and that "[n]o one factor is dispositive and all factors must be taken into account insofar as they are applicable." Consistent with this approach, the Supreme Court previously referred to the "line of business" and "interest or expectancy" factors in the disjunctive, suggesting that proof of either factor could sustain a corporate opportunity claim (*Equity Corp. v. Millton*)[.] [. . .]

1. The Company Was Financially Able to Acquire the AAA Building

Although Delaware courts have not delineated a clear standard for determining whether a corporation is financially able to avail itself of a corporate opportunity, our Supreme Court has opined (albeit in dictum) that this court may consider "a number of options and standards for determining financial inability, including but not limited to, a balancing standard, temporary insolvency standard, or practical insolvency standard." *Yiannatsis v. Stephanis by Sterianou*. [. . .]

Glaubach purchased the AAA Building for $ 1.8 million in February 2015 and gave AAA six months of free rent as part of the transaction. This equates, at most, to an acquisition price of approximately $ 2.4 million, as discussed below. Applying any reasonable standard of financial ability, I am convinced that the Company was financially able to acquire the AAA Building in this price range during the time period when purchase discussions were occurring with AAA.

Marx and Goff (an Outside Director) both testified that they believed the Company could afford to purchase the AAA Building, with Goff explaining that Slifkin, the Company's CEO at the time, reported at a February 2015 Board meeting that the Company "could easily finance the acquisition of the AAA Building." Their views are substantiated by evidence that the Company generated well over $ 300 million in revenues and earned approximately $ 15 million in EBITDAE in 2014, had cash on hand of approximately $ 30.4 million as of December 31, 2014, and that its annualized EBITDAE for "2015 and beyond" was expected as of April 2015 to increase from approximately $ 15 million to approximately $ 20 million after a planned acquisition. On the other side of the ledger, the record is devoid of any evidence indicating that the Company's financial position was precarious when the AAA Building was purchased, and Glaubach offered no evidence suggesting that the Company was not financially able to purchase it for what he paid.

2. The Company Had a Clear Interest and Expectancy in Acquiring the AAA Building

With respect to the third *Broz* factor, I find that the Company clearly had an interest and expectancy in acquiring the AAA Building. It is stipulated that the Company "had been seeking additional office space in the Jamaica, New York area for years and was particularly interested in the AAA Building because it was located next door to the offices of one of the Company's key operating subsidiaries" and "could be used to relocate the Company's corporate offices, for expansion of the Company's Jamaica operations, as offices for the Company's other subsidiaries and for storage."

The Company's general interest in acquiring the AAA Building became an actual opportunity in March 2013, when Slifkin learned that the AAA Building was for sale. On March 4, 2013, Slifkin reported this news to Marx and Glaubach in an email, explaining that the "asking price seems reasonable" and discussing several ways the Company could use the property. Two days later, Marx and Glaubach met with Clifford of AAA to inspect the building and negotiate a price for the Company to purchase it. Glaubach understood at the time that it was the Company that was the intended purchaser of the building. Marx's negotiations with Clifford stalled not because the Company lost interest in the property, but because AAA's plans to move to a different location fell through for a time. Clifford reassured Marx, however, that "we want to move and we'll call you as soon as we have anything."

While the Company was waiting to hear back from AAA, Glaubach stepped in to take the opportunity for himself by instructing his assistant (Reich) to contact Clifford to see whether AAA was ready to sell the building. Tellingly, when Reich and Clifford were engaged in discussions during the summer of 2014, they were both under the impression that the Company was to be the purchaser of the building. And when Reich learned later that Glaubach wanted the building for himself, he took steps at Glaubach's direction to conceal his negotiations with AAA from others at the Company. [. . .]

Glaubach's assertion that the Company lost interest in acquiring the AAA Building is not supported by the record. To the contrary, after Marx initiated a dialogue with AAA to acquire the building, AAA's representative expressly told him that he would contact Marx when AAA was ready to move forward. [. . .] In sum, the record clearly supports the conclusion that the Company was keenly interested in, and had a reasonable expectation of, acquiring the AAA Building at all relevant times.

3.   The Line of Business Inquiry

The second *Broz* factor asks whether the opportunity to acquire the AAA Building was within Personal Touch's line of business. Noting that the Company historically had leased office space and that it had owned a piece of real estate only once before, Glaubach argues that owning real estate is not in the Company's line of business. Quoting the Company's own brief, Glaubach contends that the Company's "two main *lines of business*" consist of "(i) a managed long-term healthcare program that provides home-based services to patients who would otherwise be in nursing homes; and (ii) a more traditional home care operation, which is in seven states and provides home healthcare aides, nurses, physical therapy and other home-based healthcare services." [. . .]

Consistent with its doctrinal moorings in the duty of loyalty, the "line of business" concept was intended to be applied flexibly. [. . .] Delaware courts accordingly have "broadly interpreted" the "nature of the corporation's business" when "determining whether a corporation has an interest in a line of business." *Dweck v. Nasser*; *In re Riverstone Nat'l, Inc. S'holder Litig.*

In my opinion, Glaubach takes a crabbed view of the line of business inquiry that misses the central point of the corporate opportunity doctrine. Although the record bears out that the Company historically did not purchase real estate to house its operations, the Company has never been engaged in the business of purchasing and leasing real estate. Personal Touch is a healthcare provider, not a commercial real estate venture. Applying the line of business concept flexibly, the sensible way to consider the issue in the context of this case is that, irrespective of its past practice of leasing office space, the Company was presented with a rare opportunity to acquire a building with a highly desirable location that it could use to relocate or expand its healthcare operations. In that sense, the opportunity to acquire the AAA Building fit within the Company's existing line of business. [. . .]

[. . .] Even if the opportunity to acquire the AAA Building could be said not to fall within the Company's existing line of business under a strict interpretation of that concept, that is not fatal to the Company's claim. To the contrary, it is sufficient that the Company had a clear interest and expectancy in the property at the time the opportunity to acquire it arose.

4.   Glaubach Acted Inimicably to His Fiduciary Duties

The fourth *Broz* factor prohibits a corporate officer or director from taking an opportunity for his own if "the corporate fiduciary will thereby be placed in a position inimicable to his duties to the corporation." Elaborating on this factor, the Supreme Court explained that "the corporate opportunity doctrine is implicated only in cases where the fiduciary's seizure of an opportunity results in a conflict between the fiduciary's duties to the corporation and the self-interest of the director as actualized by the exploitation of the opportunity." *Broz*. That is what occurred here.

After learning about the opportunity to purchase the AAA Building from Slifkin, Glaubach attended the initial meeting with Marx and Clifford in March 2013 and knew full well that the Company was interested in purchasing it. Putting his self-interest above his duty of loyalty to Personal Touch, Glaubach chose to compete directly with the Company to acquire for himself an admittedly "vital property" while making concerted efforts to conceal his activities from the Company until after he had closed on the deal. Indeed, Glaubach did not disclose to his fellow directors his efforts to buy the building for himself even when Marx was updating the Board about his efforts to purchase the property for the Company in Glaubach's presence.

Removing any doubt about the importance of the building to the Company and the conflicted nature of what Glaubach did, Glaubach sought to lease the building to the Company almost immediately after he purchased it. In short, Glaubach was acutely aware of the value the opportunity to acquire the AAA Building presented to the Company because of the building's unique location and, instead of looking out for the interests of Personal Touch, he secretly thwarted its ability to take advantage of that opportunity so that he could profit personally by acquiring the building for himself.

Finally, I reject Glaubach's contention that he "did not place himself in a position 'inimical' to his corporate duties by purchasing the building" based on Section 2.2 of his Employment Agreement. That provision states simply that "[t]he Company acknowledges that [Glaubach] has business interests outside of the Company and will continue to devote a material portion of his business time, attention and affairs to such other business interests." Nothing in this provision allows Glaubach to compete with the Company for opportunities in which it has an interest or expectancy. Indeed, the preceding sentence in Section 2.2 states that Glaubach "shall not engage, directly or indirectly, in any other business, employment or occupation which is competitive with the business of the Company."

* * *

For the reasons explained above, balancing each of the *Broz* factors and considering them in a holistic fashion, the court concludes that Glaubach breached his fiduciary duty of loyalty by usurping the opportunity to purchase the AAA Building. [. . .]

The Company contends an appropriate measure of damages is the increase in value of the building from February 2015, when Glaubach acquired it, to the date of trial. In response, Glaubach appears to suggest that no damages may be awarded until such time, if ever, that Glaubach actually sells the AAA Building and realizes a profit on it. I reject Glaubach's argument, for which no legal support is provided and which would lead to the inequitable result of affording the Company no remedy for Glaubach's breach of duty. In my view, the Company has advanced a logical theory for quantifying damages that can be reasonably estimated based on record evidence. [. . .]

IV. CONCLUSION

For the reasons explained above, judgment will be entered in the Company's favor on Count I of the Amended Complaint, in part, entitling the Company to an award of damages in the amount of $ 2,735,000 and declaratory relief. [. . .]

3.   DUTY OF CANDOR

City of Fort Myers Gen. Employees' Pension Fund v. Haley
235 A.3d 702 (Del. 2020)

■ VALIHURA, JUSTICE, for the Majority.

I.   Factual and Procedural Background

[EDS.—In late 2014, after a few years of unsatisfactory results, Willis Group Holdings Public Limited Company began a review of strategic alternatives, and started to study a possible business combination with its peer, Towers Watson & Co.]

[. . .] On June 29, 2015, the Towers Board once again convened and was advised by [its advisor] Merrill Lynch that the transaction was financially fair to the Towers' stockholders, even though the merger consideration valued each share of Towers stock at $125.13, a nine percent discount to Towers' unaffected trading price [. . .]. [EDS.—The transaction was unanimously approved by the board.] The finalized merger agreement was conditioned on stockholder approval, and called for mutual termination fees not to exceed $45 million in the event a majority of the stockholders of either entity failed to approve the transaction. Haley [, the Chairman and CEO of Towers] would serve as the CEO and a director on the Board of the post-merger entity, and each company was to designate six directors to the twelve-member Board. Concurrent with the parties' execution of the merger agreement, ValueAct [the second largest shareholders of Willis with approximately 103 percent of Willis's outstanding stock] executed a voting agreement with Towers, agreeing to vote its Willis shares in favor of the merger.

[. . .] [After the merger] was announced on June 30, 2015, [. . .] Towers stock price dropped. [. . .]

On September 2015, ValueAct reached out to Haley and presented him with a three-page document entitled, "Towers Watson Compensation Review September 2015." The document, referred to by ValueAct personnel as an "executive compensation proposal," illustrated the value of Haley's long-term equity incentive compensation over a three-year period under three different scenarios: Haley's then-current plan over his last three years at Towers, worth approximately $24 million; Haley's then-current plan approximately doubled at the post-merger company to account for increased market capitalization (i.e., double that of Towers); and ValueAct's proposed plan (the "Proposal"), which provided Haley an opportunity allegedly worth more than $140 million. Haley testified in the related appraisal action that he understood that under the Proposal, he could earn upwards of $165 million. The document also showed that ValueAct's Proposal would provide Haley with a long-term equity incentive compensation amount greater than that of the CEOs at two peer companies, both of which had greater market capitalizations than the post-merger entity. [. . .]

At the same time, Driehaus Capital Management LLC ("Driehaus"), a Towers stockholder, commenced a public campaign against the merger. [. . .]

Driehaus then filed an opposition letter with the SEC on October 8, 2015, stressing that "[o]ver the last few weeks, other shareholders have reached out with a number of their own concerns regarding the value destructive deal . . . we believe that the transaction will be voted down by Towers' shareholders." [. . .]

On October 13, 2015, Towers and Willis issued the proxy statement soliciting votes in favor of the merger, and setting the stockholder meetings for November 18, 2015. Notably, the proxy statement did not mention the Proposal, any discussions about the management's post-merger compensation, or the extent of ValueAct's role in the merger process.

On October 22, 2015, Driehaus filed another opposition letter with the SEC, noting that the price of Towers stock had dropped 12.2 percent since the merger announcement.

On October 26, 2015, after preparing with the help of ValueAct, Haley met with Institutional Shareholder Services ("ISS") to discuss the merger. [. . .]

On November 5, 2015, ISS issued a recommendation to stockholders to vote against the merger. During his deposition in the appraisal action, Ryan Birtwell, a partner at ValueAct, explained his surprise: "[I]t is challenging to get a 'yes' vote in a situation where ISS has recommended a vote against a deal." [. . .] The same day, Glass Lewis recommended that Towers stockholders vote against the merger and seek a better price.

With stockholder approval in a precarious place, [. . .] ValueAct developed a series of strategies designed to generate positive market sentiment for the deal. First, ValueAct had Willis issue a press release highlighting the benefits of the merger to the Towers stockholders. ValueAct then instructed Willis to talk to its legal team to look into whether Towers could change its bylaws so that non-votes would not count as "no" votes. Next, ValueAct and Haley worked together to solicit

Towers' largest stockholders, including The Vanguard Group and BlackRock, Inc., to vote to approve the merger. [. . .]

On November 3, 2015, Towers publicly responded to Driehaus, filing an investor presentation with the SEC, touting Towers' existing compensation practices, and seeking to "set the record straight." It accused Driehaus of making demonstrably false statements regarding compensation to support its allegations of a conflict of interest. It further asserted that Towers' executive compensation growth had been modest, and was far outpaced by total shareholder return. It did not refer to ValueAct's compensation proposal. [. . .]

In light of the uncertainty of stockholder approval, Haley and Ubben [ValueAct's Chief Investment Officer] agreed to increase the special dividend to $10.00 per share. According to Plaintiffs, "Haley viewed the $10.00 special dividend not as the best deal he could get for Towers stockholders (to whom he owed fiduciary duties) but, rather, as the minimum amount necessary to secure the Stockholder Approval he needed to push the Merger through so he could secure the massive compensation Proposal Ubben had promised him." [. . .]

The Towers Board convened on November 17 to discuss the transaction. [. . .] [I]n the meeting, Haley did not disclose his post-closing compensation discussions with ValueAct or ValueAct's Proposal. [. . .]

The next morning, Towers and Willis adjourned their respective stockholder meetings. That day, only 43.45 percent of the then-submitted votes of Towers stockholders were "for" the merger.

Later that day, the Willis Board agreed to the special dividend, conditioned on eliminating the termination fee for Willis, and increasing the termination fee for Towers to $60 million. The Towers Board met that afternoon and unanimously approved the new terms, subject to a final fairness opinion from Merrill Lynch. The opinion was given the next day. Based on the revised terms, the merger consideration was now valued at $128.30 per Towers share, a seven percent discount to the unaffected trading price. [. . .]

On November 27, 2015, Towers filed the proxy update, disclosing that Towers executed an amendment to the voting agreement with ValueAct and confirming that the voting agreement was still in effect. But according to Plaintiffs, the proxy update failed to disclose Haley's proposed compensation package or ValueAct's role in the merger negotiations.

Towers convened a special stockholders meeting on December 11, 2015 to vote on the merger, and 62 percent of the Towers stockholders voted in favor of it. Willis also held a special meeting that day and received 95.5 percent votes in favor. [. . .]

E. Haley's Executive Compensation Negotiations

[. . .] On December 20, 2015, [Wendy] Lane [Chairman of the Compensation Committee] contacted Ubben "to catch up on the conversations" between Haley and him regarding compensation. Alex Baum, a partner and Vice President of ValueAct, [. . .] explained that, although Haley liked the Proposal, he wanted "even more leverage."

About a month after the merger closed, SBCG circulated a proposal for Haley's equity incentive plan to Wickes (formerly Towers' Managing Director of Benefits). SBCG's proposal would have provided Haley with significantly less long-term equity incentive compensation than ValueAct's original Proposal. [. . .] The Compensation Committee finalized Haley's compensation plan on March 1, 2016. Haley's employment agreement differed in some ways from the ValueAct Proposal, but notably, the employment agreement provided more potential upside than the Proposal. The Court of Chancery noted that the Proposal offered a 300 percent payout of long-term equity, while the Willis Towers definitive proxy statement refers to a 350 percent maximum opportunity under Haley's employment agreement. [. . .]

G. The Court of Chancery Proceedings in This Matter

In the proceedings below, Plaintiffs relied on *Cinerama, Inc. v. Technicolor, Inc.*, and argued that Haley suffered a material conflict, which he failed to disclose to the Towers Board, and which a reasonable Board member would have regarded as significant in evaluating the proposed transaction. [. . .]

Defendants moved to dismiss, [. . .] argu[ing] that the business judgment rule presumptively applies given the nature of the merger and that the Plaintiffs failed to plead facts sufficient to rebut the business judgment rule. [. . .]

Plaintiffs did not dispute that the business judgment rule presumptively applied. Instead, they attempted to rebut the business judgment rule and invoke the entire fairness standard based solely on Haley's alleged conflict of interest.

The Court of Chancery granted the Defendants' motion to dismiss. The court focused on Plaintiffs' claim that Haley's failure to inform the Towers Board of the Proposal constituted deceptive silence and fraud upon the Board[.] [. . .]

The Plaintiffs filed a timely notice of appeal on August 22, 2019. Plaintiffs appeal the dismissal only as to Haley. [. . .]

III. Analysis

A. The Court of Chancery Erred in Dismissing Plaintiffs' Claim Against Haley.

Plaintiffs' theory on appeal is that Haley breached his fiduciary duty of loyalty by selling out Towers' public stockholders in exchange for a massive compensation package, promised by Ubben and ValueAct. [. . .]

We hold that Plaintiffs' theory is reasonably conceivable as pleaded and the claim should survive a motion to dismiss.

The business judgment rule presumptively applies because Towers' stockholders exchanged their shares in one widely-held public company for shares in another widely-held public company. *In re Santa Fe Pac. Corp. S'holder Litig.* Thus, to state a claim, Plaintiffs must rebut the presumption that Towers' directors "acted on an informed basis [i.e., with due care], in good faith and in the honest belief that the action taken was in the best interest of the company." *Cede & Co. v. Technicolor, Inc.*

As the claims asserted against Haley focus on the conduct of a single director, both sides agree that in order to rebut the presumption of the business judgment rule, Plaintiffs must adequately allege that (i) the director was "materially self-interested" in the transaction, (ii) the director failed to disclose his "interest in the transaction to the board," and (iii) "a reasonable board member would have regarded the existence of [the director's] material interest as a significant fact in the evaluation of the proposed transaction." *Cinerama, Inc.; see also Mills Acq. Co. v. Macmillan, Inc.; Weinberger v. UOP, Inc.* "Absent such a showing, the mere presence of a conflicted director or an act of disloyalty by a director, does not deprive the board of the business judgment rule's presumption of loyalty." *Goodwin v. Live Entm't, Inc.*

In dismissing Plaintiffs' claims, the Court of Chancery held that, given what the Towers Board knew, the alleged self-interest was immaterial, and that a reasonable director would not have considered the Proposal to be significant when evaluating the merger. [. . .]

[. . .] We consider first whether Plaintiffs have adequately alleged that Haley was materially self-interested in the merger. [. . .]

The issue here is whether the alleged omissions meet the legal definition of materiality. We hold that the Plaintiffs have adequately alleged that the Proposal altered the nature of the potential conflict that the Towers Board knew of in a material way. "Material," in this context, means that the information is "relevant and of a magnitude to be important to directors in carrying out their fiduciary duty of care in decisionmaking." *Brehm v. Eisner.* It is elementary that under Delaware law the duty of candor imposes an unremitting duty on fiduciaries, including directors and officers, to "not use superior information or knowledge to mislead others in the performance of their own fiduciary obligations." *Mills Acquisition Co. v. Macmillan, Inc.* Further, "[c]orporate officers and directors are not permitted to use their position of trust and confidence to further their private interests." *Guth v. Loft.* [. . .]

[. . .] [I]t is "uncontroversial" that "material information about a potential director conflict should be disclosed to the board." [. . .] Plaintiffs have adequately alleged that the Board would have found it material that its lead negotiator had been presented with a compensation proposal having a potential upside of nearly five times his compensation at Towers, and that he was presented with this Proposal during an atmosphere of deal uncertainty and before they authorized him to renegotiate the merger consideration.

[. . .] [I]n *Morrison v. Berry*, [. . .] we reiterated the basic principle that "directors have an 'unremitting obligation' to deal candidly with their fellow directors." There, we considered allegations that a CEO had concealed from the Board that he and a bidder had an agreement that contemplated his "rolling over" his equity interest. In considering whether the alleged omissions were material to the stockholders, we held that, "[a] reasonable stockholder would want to know the facts showing that [the CEO] had not been forthcoming with the board about his agreement with [the bidder] . . . ." [. . .]

In this case, [. . .] [a] reasonable stockholder likely would consider important [. . .] information about Haley discussing and receiving the Proposal amidst deal completion uncertainty, and information concerning Haley's relationship with ValueAct, and whether that relationship impaired his "ability to negotiate in good faith on behalf of Towers Watson shareholders." This is evident from the inquiries Towers received from certain significant stockholders regarding Haley's discussions with ValueAct.

[. . .] The fact that the Proposal was a not concrete agreement and had milestones requiring "Herculean" efforts did not relieve Haley of his duty to disclose to the Towers Board the deepening of the potential conflict, particularly in an atmosphere of considerable deal uncertainty. As this Court said in the seminal case, *Guth v. Loft*, a director's duty of loyalty "requires an undivided and unselfish loyalty to the corporation" and "demands that there shall be no conflict between duty and self-interest." [. . .] We emphasize that we make no finding that he did, in fact, subordinate the Towers stockholders' interests to his own, but at this point [. . .] we accept the well-pleaded allegations as true.

Nor does the fact that Haley's compensation agreement ultimately differed from the Proposal negate its materiality [. . .]. Ubben's influence over Haley's compensation was allegedly enough to convince Haley to agree to unfavorable terms in the merger renegotiations in order to benefit himself by obtaining a lucrative compensation deal. ValueAct was a significant Willis stockholder and proponent of the transaction. Ubben was involved in the negotiations, participated in driving Willis's negotiating strategy, and was likely to be a Board and compensation committee member of the post-merger entity. Thus, Plaintiffs have adequately pleaded that Haley subjectively believed that the compensation increase set forth in the Proposal was attainable, and that the Proposal carried weight, even if it were of a non-binding nature.

Next, we conclude that Plaintiffs adequately allege that Haley failed to inform the Towers Board of his deepened interest in the transaction. That Haley kept the Towers Board generally apprised of negotiations, as the Court of Chancery found, does not rebut Plaintiffs' contention that

Haley failed to adequately disclose his self-interest to the Board. Even assuming that Haley kept the Towers Board generally apprised of the negotiations, he allegedly did not disclose that he had received the Proposal and had discussed executive compensation with ValueAct and Ubben. [. . .] Even more, Plaintiffs allege [. . .] that Board member and Compensation Committee Chair Ray testified that "he would have wanted to know that Haley was discussing his compensation at the future company with Ubben and ValueAct, but did not receive such information, let alone information as to the magnitude of the raise that Haley stood to receive." Thus, Plaintiffs have adequately pleaded that Haley failed to disclose the Proposal to the Towers Board.

Finally, Plaintiffs have adequately pleaded that a reasonable Board member would have regarded Haley's material interest in the Proposal as a significant fact in evaluating the merger. This conclusion is also supported by Ray's testimony that he would have wanted to know that Haley was discussing his compensation at the future company with Ubben and ValueAct. [. . .]

Thus, we conclude that Plaintiffs have alleged sufficiently that Haley was materially interested in the merger, that he failed to disclose his interest in the Proposal to the Towers Board, and that a reasonable Board member would have regarded the existence of Haley's material interest as a significant fact in the evaluation of the merger. Accordingly, we hold that Plaintiffs have adequately pleaded their claim for breach of fiduciary duty against Haley and, thus, the claim will survive a motion to dismiss. [. . .]

IV. Conclusion

For the reasons set forth above, we REVERSE the Court of Chancery's opinion, and REMAND for proceedings consistent with this opinion.

D. OBLIGATION OF GOOD FAITH

1. IN GENERAL

In re Walt Disney Co. Derivative Litigation
906 A.2d 27 (Del. 2006)

■ JACOBS, JUSTICE.

I. The Facts

[. . .] The critical events flow from what turned out to be an unfortunate hiring decision at Disney, a company that for over half a century has been one of America's leading film and entertainment enterprises.

In 1994 Disney lost in a tragic helicopter crash its President and Chief Operating Officer, Frank Wells, who together with Michael Eisner, Disney's Chairman and Chief Executive Officer, had enjoyed remarkable success at the Company's helm. Eisner temporarily assumed Disney's presidency, but only three months later, heart disease required Eisner to undergo quadruple bypass surgery. Those two events persuaded Eisner and Disney's board of directors that the time had come to identify a successor to Eisner.

Eisner's prime candidate for the position was Michael Ovitz, who was the leading partner and one of the founders of Creative Artists Agency ("CAA"), the premier talent agency whose business model had reshaped the entire industry. By 1995, CAA had 550 employees and a roster of about 1400 of Hollywood's top actors, directors, writers, and musicians. That roster generated about $150 million in annual revenues and an annual income of over $20 million for Ovitz, who was regarded as one of the most powerful figures in Hollywood.

Eisner and Ovitz had enjoyed a social and professional relationship that spanned nearly 25 years. Although in the past the two men had casually discussed possibly working together, in 1995, when Ovitz began negotiations to leave CAA and join Music Corporation of America ("MCA"), Eisner became seriously interested in recruiting Ovitz to join Disney. [. . .]

A. Negotiation Of The Ovitz Employment Agreement

Eisner and Irwin Russell, who was a Disney director and chairman of the compensation committee, first approached Ovitz about joining Disney. [. . .] Both Russell and Eisner negotiated with Ovitz, over separate issues and concerns. From his talks with Eisner, Ovitz gathered that Disney needed his skills and experience to remedy Disney's current weaknesses, which Ovitz identified as poor talent relationships and stagnant foreign growth. Seeking assurances from Eisner that Ovitz's vision for Disney was shared, at some point during the negotiations Ovitz came to believe that he and Eisner would run Disney, and would work together in a relation akin to that of junior and senior partner. Unfortunately, Ovitz's belief was mistaken, as Eisner had a radically different view of what their respective roles at Disney should be.

Russell assumed the lead in negotiating the financial terms of the Ovitz employment contract. In the course of negotiations, Russell learned from Ovitz's attorney, Bob Goldman, that Ovitz owned 55% of CAA and earned approximately $20 to $25 million a year from that company. From the beginning Ovitz made it clear that he would not give up his 55% interest in CAA without "downside protection." Considerable negotiation then ensued over downside protection issues. During the summer of 1995, the parties agreed to a draft version of Ovitz's employment agreement (the "OEA"). [. . .] [T]he draft agreement included the following terms:

> Under the proposed OEA, Ovitz would receive a five-year contract with two tranches of options. The first tranche consisted of three million options vesting in equal parts in the third, fourth, and fifth years, and if the value of those options at the end of the five years had not appreciated to $50 million,

Disney would make up the difference. The second tranche consisted of two million options that would vest immediately if Disney and Ovitz opted to renew the contract.

The proposed OEA sought to protect both parties in the event that Ovitz's employment ended prematurely, and provided that absent defined causes, neither party could terminate the agreement without penalty. If Ovitz, for example, walked away, for any reason other than those permitted under the OEA, he would forfeit any benefits remaining under the OEA and could be enjoined from working for a competitor. Likewise, if Disney fired Ovitz for any reason other than gross negligence or malfeasance, Ovitz would be entitled to a non-fault payment (Non-Fault Termination or "NFT"), which consisted of his remaining salary, $7.5 million a year for unaccrued bonuses, the immediate vesting of his first tranche of options and a $10 million cash out payment for the second tranche of options. [. . .]

As the basic terms of the OEA were crystallizing, Russell prepared and gave Ovitz and Eisner a "case study" to explain those terms. In that study, Russell also expressed his concern that the negotiated terms represented an extraordinary level of executive compensation. Russell acknowledged, however, that Ovitz was an "exceptional corporate executive" and "highly successful and unique entrepreneur" who merited "downside protection and upside opportunity. Both would be required to enable Ovitz to adjust to the reduced cash compensation he would receive from a public company, in contrast to the greater cash distributions and other perquisites more typically available from a privately held business. But, Russell did caution that Ovitz's salary would be at the top level for any corporate officer and significantly above that of the Disney CEO. Moreover, the stock options granted under the OEA would exceed the standards applied within Disney and corporate America and would "raise very strong criticism." Russell shared this original case study only with Eisner and Ovitz. He also recommended another, additional study of this issue.

To assist in evaluating the financial terms of the OEA, Russell recruited Graef Crystal, an executive compensation consultant, and Raymond Watson, a member of Disney's compensation committee and a past Disney board chairman who had helped structure Wells' and Eisner's compensation packages. [. . .]

Crystal was philosophically opposed to a pay package that would give Ovitz the best of both worlds—low risk and high return.

[. . .] Addressing Crystal's concerns, Russell made clear that the guarantee would not function as Crystal believed it might. Crystal then revised his original letter, adjusting the value of the OEA (assuming a two year renewal) to $24.1 million per year. Up to that point, only three Disney directors—Eisner, Russell and Watson—knew the status of the negotiations with Ovitz and the terms of the draft OEA.

While Russell, Watson and Crystal were finalizing their analysis of the OEA, Eisner and Ovitz reached a separate agreement. [. . .] After deliberating, Ovitz accepted those terms, and that evening Ovitz, Eisner, Sid Bass and their families celebrated Ovitz's decision to join Disney.

[. . .] The next day, August 13, Eisner met with Ovitz, Russell, Sanford Litvack (an Executive Vice President and Disney's General Counsel), and Stephen Bollenbach (Disney's Chief Financial Officer) to discuss the decision to hire Ovitz. [. . .] Litvack and Bollenbach were emphatic that they would not report to Ovitz, but would continue to report to Eisner. Despite Ovitz's concern about his "shrinking authority" as Disney's future President, Eisner was able to provide sufficient reassurance so that ultimately Ovitz acceded to Litvack's and Bollenbach's terms.

On August 14, Eisner and Ovitz signed a letter agreement (the "OLA"), which outlined the basic terms of Ovitz's employment, and stated that the agreement (which would ultimately be embodied in a formal contract) was subject to approval by Disney's compensation committee and board of directors. Russell called Sidney Poitier, a Disney director and compensation committee member, to inform Poitier of the OLA and its terms. Poitier believed that hiring Ovitz was a good idea because of Ovitz's reputation and experience. Watson called Ignacio Lozano, another Disney director and compensation committee member, who felt that Ovitz would successfully adapt from a private company environment to Disney's public company culture. [. . .]

That same day, a press release made the news of Ovitz's hiring public. The reaction was extremely positive: Disney was applauded for the decision, and Disney's stock price rose 4.4% in a single day, thereby increasing Disney's market capitalization by over $1 billion. [. . .]

On September 26, 1995, the Disney compensation committee (which consisted of Messrs. Russell, Watson, Poitier and Lozano) met for one hour to consider, among other agenda items, the proposed terms of the OEA. A term sheet was distributed at the meeting, although a draft of the OEA was not. [. . .] The committee voted unanimously to approve the OEA terms, subject to "reasonable further negotiations within the framework of the terms and conditions" described in the OEA.

Immediately after the compensation committee meeting, the Disney board met in executive session. The board was told about the reporting structure to which Ovitz had agreed, but the initial negative reaction of Litvack and Bollenbach to the hiring was not recounted. Eisner led the discussion relating to Ovitz, and Watson then explained his analysis, and both Watson and Russell responded to questions from the board. After further deliberation, the board voted unanimously to elect Ovitz as President. [. . .]

B. Ovitz's Performance As President of Disney

Ovitz's tenure as President of the Walt Disney Company officially began on October 1, 1995, the date that the OEA was executed. When Ovitz took office, the initial reaction was optimistic, and Ovitz did make some positive contributions while serving as President of the Company. By the fall of 1996, however, it had become clear that Ovitz was "a poor fit with his fellow executives." [. . .]

[. . .] On September 30, 1996, the Disney board met. During an executive session of that meeting, and in small group discussions where Ovitz was not present, Eisner told the other board members of the continuing problems with Ovitz's performance. [. . .]

Those interchanges set the stage for Ovitz's eventual termination as Disney's President.

C. Ovitz's Termination At Disney

[. . .] During this period Eisner was also working with Litvack to explore whether they could terminate Ovitz under the OEA for cause. If so, Disney would not owe Ovitz the NFT payment. From the very beginning, Litvack advised Eisner that he did not believe there was cause to terminate Ovitz under the OEA. Litvack's advice never changed.

At the end of November 1996, Eisner again asked Litvack if Disney had cause to fire Ovitz and thereby avoid the costly NFT payment. Litvack proceeded to examine that issue more carefully. He studied the OEA, refreshed himself on the meaning of "gross negligence" and "malfeasance," and reviewed all the facts concerning Ovitz's performance of which he was aware. [. . .] Although the Chancellor was critical of Litvack and Eisner for lacking sufficient documentation to support his conclusion and the work they did to arrive at that conclusion, the Court found that Eisner and Litvack "did in fact make a concerted effort to determine if Ovitz could be terminated for cause, and that despite these efforts, they were unable to manufacture the desired result."

Litvack also believed that it would be inappropriate, unethical and a bad idea to attempt to coerce Ovitz (by threatening a for-cause termination) into negotiating for a smaller NFT package than the OEA provided. [. . .] Litvack believed that attempting to avoid legitimate contractual obligations would harm Disney's reputation as an honest business partner and would affect its future business dealings.

The Disney board next met on November 25. [. . .] An executive session took place after the board meeting, from which Ovitz was excluded. At that session, Eisner informed the directors who were present that he intended to fire Ovitz by year's end, and that he had asked Gary Wilson, a board member and friend of Ovitz, to speak with Ovitz while Wilson and Ovitz were together on vacation during the upcoming Thanksgiving holiday.

Shortly after the November 25 board meeting and executive session, the Ovitz and Wilson families left on their yacht for a Thanksgiving trip to the British Virgin Islands. [. . .]

After returning from the Thanksgiving trip, Ovitz met with Eisner on December 3, to discuss his termination. Ovitz asked for several concessions, all of which Eisner ultimately rejected. [. . .]

On December 11, Eisner met with Ovitz to agree on the wording of a press release to announce the termination, and to inform Ovitz that he would not receive any of the additional items that he requested. [. . .] After his December 11 meeting with Eisner, Ovitz never returned to Disney.

Ovitz's termination was memorialized in a letter, dated December 12, 1996, that Litvack signed on Eisner's instruction. The board was not shown the letter, nor did it meet to approve its terms. A press release announcing Ovitz's termination was issued that same day. [. . .] None of the board members at that time, or at any other time, objected to Ovitz's termination, and most, if not all, of them thought it was the appropriate step for Eisner to take. [. . .]

A December 27, 1996 letter from Litvack to Ovitz, which Ovitz signed, memorialized the termination, accelerated Ovitz's departure date from January 31, 1997 to December 31, 1996, and informed Ovitz that he would receive roughly $38 million in cash and that the first tranche of three million options would vest immediately. By the terms of that letter agreement, Ovitz's tenure as an executive and a director of Disney officially ended on December 27, 1996. Shortly thereafter, Disney paid Ovitz what was owed under the OEA for an NFT, minus a holdback of $1 million pending final settlement of Ovitz's accounts. One month after Disney paid Ovitz, the plaintiffs filed this action.

II. Summary of Appellants' Claims of Error

The appellants' [. . .] claims against the Disney defendants [. . .] encompass [. . .] the claims that the Disney defendants breached their fiduciary duties to act with due care and in good faith by (1) approving the OEA, and specifically, its NFT provisions; and (2) approving the NFT severance payment to Ovitz upon his termination—a payment that is also claimed to constitute corporate waste. [. . .] [EDS.—The appellants advance claims against Ovitz asserting that Ovitz "breached his fiduciary duties of care and loyalty to Disney by (i) negotiating for and accepting the NFT severance provisions of the OEA, and (ii) negotiating a full NFT payout in connection with his termination.]

III. The Claims Against Ovitz

A. Claims Based Upon Ovitz's Conduct Before Assuming Office At Disney

First, appellants contend that the Court of Chancery erred by dismissing their claim, as a summary judgment matter, that Ovitz had breached his fiduciary duties to Disney by negotiating and entering into the OEA. On summary judgment the Chancellor determined that Ovitz had breached no fiduciary duty to Disney, because Ovitz did not become a fiduciary until he formally assumed office on October 1, 1995, by which time the essential terms of the NFT provision had been negotiated. Therefore, the

Court of Chancery held, Ovitz's pre-October 1 conduct was not constrained by any fiduciary duty standard. [EDS.—The Supreme Court affirms the findings of the Chancellor.]

B. Claims Based Upon Ovitz's Conduct During His Termination As President

The appellants' second claim is that the Court of Chancery erroneously concluded that Ovitz breached no fiduciary duty, including his duty of loyalty, by receiving the NFT payment upon his termination as President of Disney. The Chancellor found:

> Ovitz did not breach his fiduciary duty of loyalty by receiving the NFT payment because he played no part in the decisions: (1) to be terminated and (2) that the termination would not be for cause under the OEA. Ovitz did possess fiduciary duties as a director and officer while these decisions were made, but by not improperly interjecting himself into the corporation's decisionmaking process nor manipulating that process, he did not breach the fiduciary duties he possessed in that unique circumstance. Furthermore, Ovitz did not "engage" in a transaction with the corporation—rather, the corporation imposed an unwanted transaction upon him.
>
> Once Ovitz was terminated without cause (as a result of decisions made entirely without input or influence from Ovitz), he was contractually entitled, without any negotiation or action on his part, to receive the benefits provided by the OEA for a termination without cause, benefits for which he negotiated at arm's length *before* becoming a fiduciary.

[EDS.—The Supreme Court affirmed that the Court of Chancery made no error in determining that Ovitz did not breach any fiduciary duty that he owed to Disney when negotiating for, or when receiving severance payments under, the non-fault termination clause of the OEA.]

IV. The Claims Against the Disney Defendants

[. . .]

A. Claims Arising From The Approval Of The OEA And Ovitz's Election As President

[. . .] For clarity of presentation we address the claimed errors relating to the fiduciary duty of care rulings separately from those that relate to the directors' fiduciary duty to act in good faith.

1. *The Due Care Determinations*

The plaintiff-appellants advance [. . .] contentions to support their claim that the Chancellor reversibly erred by concluding that the plaintiffs had failed to establish a violation of the Disney defendants' duty of care. The appellants claim that the Chancellor erred by: (1) treating as distinct questions whether the plaintiffs had established by a preponderance of the evidence either gross negligence or a lack of good faith; (2) ruling that the old board was not required to approve the OEA; [. . .] (4) concluding that the compensation committee members did not breach their duty of care in approving the NFT provisions of the OEA; and (5) holding that the remaining members of the old board (*i.e.,* the directors who were not members of the compensation committee) had not breached their duty of care in electing Ovitz as Disney's President.

(a) Treating Due Care and Bad Faith as Separate Grounds for Denying the Business Judgement Rule Review

This argument is best understood against the backdrop of the presumptions that cloak director action being reviewed under the business judgment standard. Our law presumes that "in making a business decision the directors of a corporation acted on an informed basis, in good faith, and in the honest belief that the action taken was in the best interests of the company." *Aronson v. Lewis.* Those presumptions can be rebutted if the plaintiff shows that the directors breached their fiduciary duty of care or of loyalty or acted in bad faith. If that is shown, the burden then shifts to the director defendants to demonstrate that the challenged act or transaction was entirely fair to the corporation and its shareholders.

Because no duty of loyalty claim was asserted against the Disney defendants, the only way to rebut the business judgment rule presumptions would be to show that the Disney defendants had either breached their duty of care or had not acted in good faith. At trial, the plaintiff-appellants attempted to establish both grounds, but the Chancellor determined that the plaintiffs had failed to prove either. [. . .]

(b) Ruling that the Full Disney Board Was Not Required to Consider and Approve the OEA

The appellants next challenge the Court of Chancery's determination that the full Disney board was not required to consider and approve the OEA, because the Company's governing instruments allocated that decision to the compensation committee. This challenge also cannot survive scrutiny. [. . .]

The Delaware General Corporation Law (DGCL) expressly empowers a board of directors to appoint committees and to delegate to them a broad range of responsibilities, which may include setting executive compensation. Nothing in the DGCL mandates that the entire board must make those decisions. At Disney, the responsibility to consider and approve executive compensation was allocated to the compensation committee, as distinguished from the full board. The Chancellor's ruling—that executive compensation was to be fixed by the compensation committee—is legally correct. [. . .]

(d) Holding That the Compensation Committee Members Did Not Fail To Exercise Due Care in Approving the OEA

The appellants next challenge the Chancellor's determination that although the compensation committee's decision-making process fell far short of corporate governance "best practices," the committee members breached no duty of care in considering and approving the NFT terms of the OEA. That conclusion is reversible error, the appellants claim, because the record establishes that the compensation committee members did not properly inform themselves of the material facts and, hence, were grossly negligent in approving the NFT provisions of the OEA.

The appellants advance five reasons why a reversal is compelled: (i) not all committee members reviewed a draft of the OEA; (ii) the minutes of the September 26, 1995 compensation committee meeting do not recite any discussion of the grounds for which Ovitz could receive a non-fault termination; (iii) the committee members did not consider any comparable employment agreements or the economic impact of extending the exercisability of the options being granted to Ovitz; (iv) Crystal did not attend the September 26, 1995 committee meeting, nor was his letter distributed to or discussed with Poitier and Lozano; and (v) Poitier and Lozano did not review the spreadsheets generated by Watson. These contentions amount essentially to an attack upon underlying factual findings that will be upheld where they result from the Chancellor's assessment of live testimony. Levitt v. Bouvier.

Although the appellants have balkanized their due care claim into several fragmented parts, the overall thrust of that claim is that the compensation committee approved the OEA with NFT provisions that could potentially result in an enormous payout, without informing themselves of what the full magnitude of that payout could be. Rejecting that claim, the Court of Chancery found that the compensation committee members were adequately informed. The issue thus becomes whether that finding is supported by the evidence of record. We conclude that it is.

In our view, a helpful approach is to compare what actually happened here to what would have occurred had the committee followed a "best practices" (or "best case") scenario, from a process standpoint. In a "best case" scenario, all committee members would have received, before or at the committee's first meeting on September 26, 1995, a spreadsheet or similar document prepared by (or with the assistance of) a compensation expert (in this case, Graef Crystal). Making different, alternative assumptions, the spreadsheet would disclose the amounts that Ovitz could receive under the OEA in each circumstance that might foreseeably arise. [. . .] That spreadsheet, which ultimately would become an exhibit to the minutes of the compensation committee meeting, would form the basis of the committee's deliberations and decision.

[. . .] Regrettably, the committee's informational and decision making process used here was not so tidy. That is one reason why the Chancellor found that although the committee's process did not fall below the level required for a proper exercise of due care, it did fall short of what best practices would have counseled. [. . .]

If measured in terms of the documentation that would have been generated if "best practices" had been followed, that record leaves much to be desired. [. . .] But, the Chancellor also found that despite its imperfections, the evidentiary record was sufficient to support the conclusion that the compensation committee had adequately informed itself of the potential magnitude of the entire severance package, including the options, that Ovitz would receive in the event of an early NFT.

The OEA was specifically structured to compensate Ovitz for walking away from $150 million to $200 million of anticipated commissions from CAA over the five-year OEA contract term. [. . .] Accordingly, the Court of Chancery had a sufficient evidentiary basis in the record from which to find that, at the time they approved the OEA, the compensation committee members were adequately informed of the potential magnitude of an early NFT severance payout. [. . .]

For these reasons, we uphold the Chancellor's determination that the compensation committee members did not breach their fiduciary duty of care in approving the OEA.

(e) Holding that the Remaining Disney Directors Did Not Fail to Exercise Due Care In Approving the Hiring of Ovitz as the President of Disney

[. . .] The appellants argue that the Disney directors breached their duty of care by failing to inform themselves of all material information reasonably available with respect to Ovitz's employment agreement. [. . .] The only properly reviewable action of the entire board was its decision to elect Ovitz as Disney's President. In that context the sole issue, as the Chancellor properly held, is "whether [the remaining members of the old board] properly exercised their business judgment and acted in accordance with their fiduciary duties when they elected Ovitz to the Company's presidency." [. . .]

The Chancellor found and the record shows the following: well in advance of the September 26, 1995 board meeting the directors were fully aware that the Company needed—especially in light of Wells' death and Eisner's medical problems—to hire a "number two" executive and potential successor to Eisner. [. . .] The directors thus knew of Ovitz's skills, reputation and experience, all of which they believed would be highly valuable to the Company. The directors also knew that to accept a position at Disney, Ovitz would have to walk away from a very successful business—a reality that would lead a reasonable person to believe that Ovitz would likely succeed in similar pursuits elsewhere in the industry. [. . .]

The board was also informed of the key terms of the OEA (including Ovitz's salary, bonus and options) [. . .]. Relying upon the compensation committee's approval of the OEA and the other information furnished to them, the Disney directors, after further deliberating, unanimously elected Ovitz as President.

Based upon this record, we uphold the Chancellor's conclusion that, when electing Ovitz to the Disney presidency the remaining Disney directors were fully informed of all material facts, and that the appellants failed to establish any lack of due care on the directors' part.

(f) The Good Faith Determinations

The Court of Chancery held that the business judgment rule presumptions protected the decisions of the compensation committee and the remaining Disney directors, not only because they had acted with due care but also because they had not acted in bad faith. That latter ruling, the appellants claim, was reversible error because the Chancellor formulated and then applied an incorrect definition of bad faith.

In its Opinion the Court of Chancery defined bad faith as follows:

> Upon long and careful consideration, I am of the opinion that the concept of intentional dereliction of duty, a conscious disregard for one's responsibilities, is an appropriate (although not the only) standard for determining whether fiduciaries have acted in good faith. Deliberate indifference and inaction in the face of a duty to act is, in my mind, conduct that is clearly disloyal to the corporation. It is the epitome of faithless conduct.

The precise question is whether the Chancellor's articulated standard for bad faith corporate fiduciary conduct—intentional dereliction of duty, a conscious disregard for one's responsibilities—is legally correct. In approaching that question, we note that the Chancellor characterized that definition as "an appropriate (although not the only) standard for determining whether fiduciaries have acted in good faith." That observation is accurate and helpful, because as a matter of simple logic, at least three different categories of fiduciary behavior are candidates for the "bad faith" pejorative label.

The first category involves so-called "subjective bad faith," that is, fiduciary conduct motivated by an actual intent to do harm. That such conduct constitutes classic, quintessential bad faith is a proposition so well accepted in the liturgy of fiduciary law that it borders on axiomatic. [. . .] [N]o such conduct is claimed to have occurred, or did occur, in this case.

The second category of conduct, which is at the opposite end of the spectrum, involves lack of due care—that is, fiduciary action taken solely by reason of gross negligence and without any malevolent intent. In this case, appellants assert claims of gross negligence to establish breaches not only of director due care but also of the directors' duty to act in good faith. Although the Chancellor found, and we agree, that the appellants failed to establish gross negligence, to afford guidance we address the issue of whether gross negligence (including a failure to inform one's self of available material facts), without more, can also constitute bad faith. The answer is clearly no.

From a broad philosophical standpoint, that question is more complex than would appear, if only because (as the Chancellor and others have observed) "issues of good faith are (to a certain degree) inseparably and necessarily intertwined with the duties of care and loyalty . . . ." But, in the pragmatic, conduct-regulating legal realm which calls for more precise conceptual line drawing, the answer is that grossly negligent conduct, without more, does not and cannot constitute a breach of the fiduciary duty to act in good faith. The conduct that is the subject of due care may overlap with the conduct that comes within the rubric of good faith in a psychological sense, but from a legal standpoint those duties are and must remain quite distinct. Both our legislative history and our common law jurisprudence distinguish sharply between the duties to exercise due care and to act in good faith, and highly significant consequences flow from that distinction.

The Delaware General Assembly has addressed the distinction between bad faith and a failure to exercise due care (i.e., gross negligence) in two separate contexts. The first is Section 102(b)(7) of the DGCL, which authorizes Delaware corporations, by a provision in the certificate of incorporation, to exculpate their directors from monetary damage liability for a breach of the duty of care. That exculpatory provision affords significant protection to directors of Delaware corporations. The statute carves out several exceptions, however, including most relevantly, "for acts or omissions not in good faith. . . ." Thus, a corporation can exculpate its directors from monetary liability for a breach of the duty of care, but not for conduct that is not in good faith. To adopt a definition of bad faith that would cause a violation of the duty of care automatically to become an act or omission "not in good faith," would eviscerate the protections accorded to directors by the General Assembly's adoption of Section 102(b)(7).

A second legislative recognition of the distinction between fiduciary conduct that is grossly negligent and conduct that is not in good faith, is Delaware's indemnification statute, found at 8 Del C. § 145. To oversimplify, subsections (a) and (b) of that statute permit a corporation to indemnify (inter alia) any person who is or was a director, officer, employee or agent of the corporation against expenses (including attorneys' fees), judgments, fines and amounts paid in settlement of specified actions, suits or proceedings, where (among other things): (i) that person is, was, or is threatened to be made a party to that action, suit or proceeding, and (ii) that person "acted in good faith and in a manner the person reasonably believed to be in or not opposed to the best interests of the corporation. . . ." Thus, under Delaware statutory law a director or officer of a corporation can be indemnified for liability (and litigation expenses) incurred by reason of a violation of the duty of care, but not for a violation of the duty to act in good faith.

Section 145, like Section 102(b)(7), evidences the intent of the Delaware General Assembly to afford significant protections to directors (and, in the case of Section 145, other fiduciaries) of Delaware corporations. To adopt a definition that conflates the duty of care with the duty to act in good faith by making a violation of the former an automatic violation of the latter, would nullify those legislative protections and defeat the General Assembly's intent. There is no basis in policy, precedent or common sense that would justify dismantling the distinction between gross negligence and bad faith.

That leaves the third category of fiduciary conduct, which falls in between the first two categories of (1) conduct motivated by subjective bad intent and (2) conduct resulting from gross negligence. This third category is what the Chancellor's definition of bad faith—intentional dereliction of duty, a conscious disregard for one's responsibilities—is intended to capture. The question is whether such misconduct is properly treated as a non-exculpable, nonindemnifiable violation of the fiduciary duty to act in good faith. In our view it must be, for at least two reasons.

First, the universe of fiduciary misconduct is not limited to either disloyalty in the classic sense (i.e., preferring the adverse self-interest of the fiduciary or of a related person to the interest of the corporation) or gross negligence. Cases have arisen where corporate directors have no conflicting self-interest in a decision, yet engage in misconduct that is more culpable than simple inattention or failure to be informed of all facts material to the decision. To protect the interests of the corporation and its shareholders, fiduciary conduct of this kind, which does not involve disloyalty (as traditionally defined) but is qualitatively more culpable than gross negligence, should be proscribed. A vehicle is needed to address such violations doctrinally, and that doctrinal vehicle is the duty to act in good faith. [. . .]

Second, the legislature has also recognized this intermediate category of fiduciary misconduct, which ranks between conduct involving subjective bad faith and gross negligence. [. . .] Because the statute exculpates directors only for conduct amounting to gross negligence, the statutory denial of exculpation for "acts . . . not in good faith" must encompass the intermediate category of misconduct captured by the Chancellor's definition of bad faith.

For these reasons, we uphold the Court of Chancery's definition as a legally appropriate, although not the exclusive, definition of fiduciary bad faith. [. . .]

B. Claims Arising From The Payment Of The NFT Severance Payout To Ovitz

The appellants advance three alternative claims (each accompanied by assorted subsidiary arguments) whose overall thrust is that even if the OEA approval was legally valid, the NFT severance payout to Ovitz pursuant to the OEA was not. [. . .] The appellants argued [. . .] by permitting Ovitz to be terminated without cause, Litvack and Eisner acted in bad faith and without exercising due care. Rejecting that claim, the Chancellor determined independently, as a matter of fact and law, that (1) Ovitz had not engaged in any conduct as President that constituted gross negligence or malfeasance—the standard for an NFT under the OEA; and (2) in arriving at that same conclusion in 1996, Litvack and Eisner did not breach their fiduciary duty of care or their duty to act in good faith. [. . .]

At the trial level, the appellants attempted to show, as a factual matter, that Ovitz's conduct as President met the standard for a termination for cause, because (i) Ovitz intentionally failed to follow Eisner's directives and was insubordinate, (ii) Ovitz was a habitual liar, and (iii) Ovitz violated Company policies relating to expenses and to reporting gifts he gave while President of Disney. The Court found the facts contrary to appellants' position. As to the first accusation, the Court found that many of Ovitz's efforts failed to produce results "often because his efforts reflected an opposite philosophy than that held by Eisner, Iger, and Roth. This does not mean that Ovitz intentionally failed to follow Eisner's directives or that he was insubordinate." As to the second, the Court found that:

> [. . .] As a neutral fact-finder, I find that the evidence simply does not support either of those assertions.

And, as to the third accusation, the Court found "that Ovitz was not in violation of The Walt Disney Company's policies relating to expenses or giving and receiving gifts." Accordingly, the appellants' claim that the Chancellor incorrectly determined that Ovitz could not legally be terminated for cause lacks any factual foundation.

In conclusion, Litvack gave the proper advice and came to the proper conclusions when it was necessary. He was adequately informed in his decisions, and he acted in good faith for what he believed were the best interests of the Company.

With respect to Eisner, the Chancellor found that faced with a situation where he was unable to work well with Ovitz, who required close and constant supervision, Eisner had three options: 1) keep Ovitz as President and continue trying to make things work; 2) keep Ovitz at Disney, but in a role other than as President; or 3) terminate Ovitz. The first option was unacceptable, and the second would have entitled Ovitz to the NFT, or at the very least would have resulted in a costly lawsuit to determine whether Ovitz was so entitled. After an unsuccessful effort to "trade" Ovitz to Sony, that left only the third option, which was to terminate Ovitz and pay the NFT. The Chancellor found that in choosing this alternative, Eisner had breached no duty and had exercised his business judgment [. . .]

Even though the Chancellor found much to criticize in Eisner's "imperial CEO" style of governance, nothing has been shown to overturn the factual basis for the Court's conclusion that, in the end, Eisner's conduct satisfied the standards required of him as a fiduciary.

To summarize, the Court of Chancery correctly determined that the decisions of the Disney defendants to approve the OEA, to hire Ovitz as President, and then to terminate him on an NFT basis, were protected business judgments, made without any violations of fiduciary duty. Having so concluded, it is unnecessary for the Court to reach the appellants' contention that the Disney defendants were required to prove that the payment of the NFT severance to Ovitz was entirely fair. [. . .]

V.   The Waste Claim

The appellants' final claim is that even if the approval of the OEA was protected by the business judgment rule presumptions, the payment of the severance amount to Ovitz constituted waste. This claim is rooted in the doctrine that a plaintiff who fails to rebut the business judgment rule presumptions is not entitled to any remedy unless the transaction constitutes waste. *In re J.P. Stevens & Co., Inc. S'holders Litig.* The Court of Chancery rejected the appellants' waste claim, and the appellants claim that in so doing the Court committed error.

To recover on a claim of corporate waste, the plaintiffs must shoulder the burden of proving that the exchange was "so one sided that no business person of ordinary, sound judgment could conclude that the corporation has received adequate consideration." *Brehm*. A claim of waste will arise only in the rare, "unconscionable case where directors irrationally squander or give away corporate assets." *Id.* This onerous standard for waste is a corollary of the proposition that where business judgment presumptions are applicable, the board's decision will be upheld unless it cannot be "attributed to any rational business purpose." *Sinclair Oil Corp. v. Levien.*

The claim that the payment of the NFT amount to Ovitz, without more, constituted waste is meritless on its face, because at the time the NFT amounts were paid, Disney was contractually obligated to pay them. The payment of a contractually obligated amount cannot constitute waste, unless the contractual obligation is itself wasteful. Accordingly, the proper focus of a waste analysis must be whether the amounts required to be paid in the event of an NFT were wasteful *ex ante*.

[. . .] The approval of the NFT provisions in the OEA had a rational business purpose: to induce Ovitz to leave CAA, at what would otherwise be a considerable cost to him, in order to join Disney. The Chancellor found that the evidence does not support any notion that the OEA irrationally incentivized Ovitz to get himself fired. Ovitz had no control over whether or not he would be fired, either with or without cause. To suggest that at the time he entered into the OEA Ovitz would engineer an early departure at the cost of his extraordinary reputation in the entertainment industry and his historical friendship with Eisner, is not only fanciful but also without proof in the record. Indeed, the Chancellor found that it was "patently unreasonable to assume that Ovitz intended to perform just poorly enough to be fired quickly, but not so poorly that he could be terminated for cause."

We agree. Because the appellants have failed to show that the approval of the NFT terms of the OEA was not a rational business decision, their waste claim must fail.

VI. Conclusion

For the reasons stated above, the judgment of the Court of Chancery is affirmed.

2. *CAREMARK* DUTIES

Marchand v. Barnhill
212 A.3d 805 (Del. 2019)

■ STRINE, CHIEF JUSTICE.

I. Background

Founded in 1907 in Brenham, Texas, Blue Bell Creameries USA, Inc. ("Blue Bell"), a Delaware corporation, produces and distributes ice cream under the Blue Bell banner. [. . .]

As a U.S. food manufacturer, Blue Bell operates in a heavily regulated industry. [. . .]

Specifically, FDA regulations require food manufacturers to conduct operations "with adequate sanitation principles" and, in line with that obligation, "must prepare . . . and implement a written food safety plan." [. . .] Appropriate corporate officials must monitor these preventative controls.

Not only is Blue Bell subject to federal regulations, but it must also adhere to various state regulations. At the time of the *listeria* outbreak, Blue Bell operated in three states, and each had issued rules and regulations regarding the proper handling and production of food to ensure food safety.

[. . .] The complaint starts by observing that, as a single-product food company, food safety is of obvious importance to Blue Bell. But despite the critical nature of food safety for Blue Bell's continued success, the complaint alleges that management turned a blind eye to red and yellow flags that were waved in front of it by regulators and its own tests, and the board—by failing to implement any system to monitor the company's food safety compliance programs—was unaware of any problems until it was too late.

According to the complaint, Blue Bell's issues began to emerge in 2009. At that time, Paul Kruse, Blue Bell's President and CEO, and his cousin, Paul Bridges, were responsible for the three plants Blue Bell operated in Texas, Oklahoma, and Alabama. The complaint alleges that, despite being responsible for overseeing plant operations, Paul Kruse and Bridges failed to respond to signs of trouble in the run up to the *listeria* outbreak. From 2009 to 2013 several regulators found troubling compliance failures at Blue Bell's facilities

[. . .] In 2013, "the Company had five positive tests" for *listeria*, and in January 2014, "the Company received a presumptive positive *[l]isteria* result reports from the third party laboratory for the [Oklahoma] facility on January 20, 2014 and the samples reported positive for a second time on January 24, 2014."

Although management had received reports about *listeria*'s growing presence in Blue Bell's plants, the complaint alleges that the board never received any information about *listeria* or more generally about food safety issues. [. . .]

During the rest of 2014, Blue Bell's problems accelerated, but the board remained uninformed about Blue Bell's problems. [. . .]

Over the course of 2014, Blue Bell received ten positive tests for *listeria*. [. . .]

Despite management's knowledge of the growing problem, the complaint alleges that this information never made its way to the board, and the board continued to be uninformed about (and thus unaware of) the problem. Minutes from the board's 2014 meetings are bereft of reports on the *listeria* issues. Only during the September meeting is sanitation discussed, when Bridges informed the board that "[t]he recent Silliker audit [Blue Bell's third-party auditor for sanitation issues in 2014] went well." This lone reference to a third-party audit is the only instance, until the *listeria* outbreak forced the recall of Blue Bell's products, of *any* board-level discussion regarding food safety.

[. . .] Based on this chronology of events, the plaintiffs have fairly pled that:

- Blue Bell had no board committee charged with monitoring food safety;

- Blue Bell's full board did not have a process where a portion of the board's meetings each year, for example either quarterly or biannually, were specifically devoted to food safety compliance; and

- The Blue Bell board did not have a protocol requiring or have any expectation that management would deliver key food safety compliance reports or summaries of these reports to the board on a consistent and mandatory basis. In fact, it is inferable that there was no expectation of reporting to the board of any kind.

In short, the complaint pleads that the Blue Bell board had made no effort at all to implement a board-level system of mandatory reporting of any kind. [. . .]

Blue Bell's *listeria* problem spread in 2015. Starting in January 2015, one of Blue Bell's product tests had positive coliform levels above legal limits. The same result appeared in February 2015. And by this point, the problem spread to Blue Bell's products and spiraled out of control.

On February 13, 2015, "Blue Bell received notification that the Texas Department of State Health Services also had positive tests for *[l]isteria* in Blue Bell samples." [. . .] The board met on February 19, 2015, following Blue Bell's annual stockholders meeting, but there was no *listeria* discussion.

Four days later, Blue Bell initiated a limited recall. Two days after that, Blue Bell's board met, and Bridges reported that "[t]he FDA is working with Texas health inspectors regarding the Company's recent recall of products. More information is developing and should be known within the next days or weeks." Despite two years of evidence that *listeria* was a growing problem for Blue Bell, this is the first time the board discussed the issue, according to the complaint and the incorporated board minutes. Instead of holding more frequent emergency board meetings to receive constant updates on the troubling fact that life-threatening bacteria was found in its products, Blue Bell's board left the company's response to management.

And the problem got worse, with awful effects. [. . .] And by March 23, 2015, Blue Bell was forced to recall more products. Two days later, Blue Bell's board met and adopted a resolution "express[ing] support for Blue Bell's CEO, management, and employees and encourag[ing] them to ensure that everything Blue Bell manufacture[s] and distributes is a wholesome and good testing [sic] product that our consumers deserve and expect."

Blue Bell expanded the recall two weeks later, and less than a month later, on April 20, 2015, Blue Bell "instituted a recall of all products." By this point, the Center for Disease Controls and Prevention ("CDC") had begun an investigation and discovered that the source of the *listeria* outbreak in Kansas was caused by Blue Bell's Texas and Oklahoma plants. Ultimately, five adults in Kansas and three adults in Texas were sickened by Blue Bell's products; three of the five Kansas adults died because of complications due to *listeria* infection. The CDC issued a recall to grocers and retailers, alerting them to the contamination and warning them against selling the products.

After Blue Bell's full product recall, the FDA inspected each of the company's three plants. Each was found to have major deficiencies. [. . .]

Most of these findings, the complaint alleges, are unsurprising because similar deficiencies were found by the FDA and state regulators in the run up to the *listeria* outbreak, yet according to the FDA's inspection after the fact, it appeared that neither management nor the board made progress on remedying these deficiencies.

After the fact, various news outlets interviewed former Blue Bell employees who "claimed that Company management ignored complaints about factory conditions in [the Texas facility]." One former employee "reported [that] spilled ice cream was left to pool on the floor, 'creating an environment where bacteria could flourish.'" Another former employee described being "instructed to pour ice cream and fruit that dripped off his machine into mix to be used later." [. . .]

C. The Court of Chancery Dismisses the Case

[. . .] [T]he plaintiff, a Blue Bell stockholder, sued Blue Bell's management and board derivatively, asserting [. . .] the board's violation of its duty of loyalty, under *Caremark*, by failing to implement any reporting system and therefore failing to inform itself about Blue Bell's food safety compliance. The Court of Chancery dismissed both claims[.] [. . .]

The plaintiff timely appealed from that dismissal.

B. The *Caremark* Claim

[. . .] Although *Caremark* claims are difficult to plead and ultimately to prove out, we nonetheless disagree with the Court of Chancery's decision to dismiss the plaintiff's claim against the Blue Bell board.

Under *Caremark* and *Stone v. Ritter*, a director must make a good faith effort to oversee the company's operations. Failing to make that good faith effort breaches the duty of loyalty and can expose a director to liability. In other words, for a plaintiff to prevail on a *Caremark* claim, the plaintiff must show that a fiduciary acted in bad faith—"the state of mind traditionally used to define the mindset of a disloyal director."

Bad faith is established, under *Caremark*, when "the directors [completely] fail[ ] to implement any reporting or information system or controls[,] or . . . having implemented such a system or controls, consciously fail[ ] to monitor or oversee its operations thus disabling themselves from being informed of risks or problems requiring their attention." In short, to satisfy their duty of loyalty, directors must make a good faith effort to implement an oversight system and then monitor it.

[. . .] But *Caremark* does have a bottom-line requirement that is important: the board must make a good faith effort—*i.e.*, try—to put in place a reasonable board-level system of monitoring and reporting. Thus, our case law gives deference to boards and has dismissed *Caremark* cases even when illegal or harmful company activities escaped detection, when the plaintiffs have been unable to plead that the board failed to make the required good faith effort to put a reasonable compliance and reporting system in place.

[. . .] [W]e are not examining the effectiveness of a board-level compliance and reporting system after the fact. Rather, we are focusing on whether the complaint pleads facts supporting a reasonable inference that the board did not undertake good faith efforts to put a board-level system of monitoring and reporting in place.

Under *Caremark*, a director may be held liable if she acts in bad faith in the sense that she made no good faith effort to ensure that the company had in place any "system of controls." Here, the plaintiff did as our law encourages and sought out books and records about the extent of board-level compliance efforts at Blue Bell regarding what has to be one of the most central issues at the company: whether it is ensuring that the only product it makes—ice cream—is safe to eat. Using these books and records, the complaint fairly alleges that before the *listeria* outbreak engulfed the company:

- no board committee that addressed food safety existed;

- no regular process or protocols that required management to keep the board apprised of food safety compliance practices, risks, or reports existed;

- no schedule for the board to consider on a regular basis, such as quarterly or biannually, any key food safety risks existed;

- during a key period leading up to the deaths of three customers, management received reports that contained what could be considered red, or at least yellow, flags, and the board minutes of the relevant period revealed no evidence that these were disclosed to the board;

- the board was given certain favorable information about food safety by management, but was not given important reports that presented a much different picture; and

- the board meetings are devoid of any suggestion that there was any regular discussion of food safety issues.

And the complaint goes on to allege that after the *listeria* outbreak, the FDA discovered a number of systematic deficiencies in all of Blue Bell's plants—such as plants being constructed "in such a manner as to [not] prevent drip and condensate from contaminating food, food-contact surfaces, and food-packing material"—that might have been rectified had any reasonable reporting system that required management to relay food safety information to the board on an ongoing basis been in place.

In sum, the complaint supports an inference that no system of board-level compliance monitoring and reporting existed at Blue Bell. Although *Caremark* is a tough standard for plaintiffs to meet, the plaintiff has met it here. When a plaintiff can plead an inference that a board has undertaken no efforts to make sure it is informed of a compliance issue intrinsically critical to the company's business operation, then that supports an inference that the board has not made the good faith effort that *Caremark* requires.

[. . .] [T]he fact that Blue Bell nominally complied with FDA regulations does not imply that the *board* implemented a system to monitor food safety *at the board level*. [. . .] At best, Blue Bell's compliance with these requirements shows only that management was following, in a nominal way, certain standard requirements of state and federal law. It does not rationally suggest that the board implemented a reporting system to monitor food safety or Blue Bell's operational performance. The mundane reality that Blue Bell is in a highly regulated industry and complied with some of the applicable regulations does not foreclose any pleading-stage inference that the directors' lack of attentiveness rose to the level of bad faith indifference required to state a *Caremark* claim.

In answering the plaintiff's argument, the Blue Bell directors also stress that management regularly reported to them on "operational issues." This response is telling. In decisions dismissing *Caremark* claims, the plaintiffs usually lose because they must concede the existence of board-level systems of monitoring and oversight such as a relevant committee, a regular protocol requiring board-level reports about the relevant risks, or the board's use of third-party monitors, auditors, or consultants. For example, in *Stone v. Ritter*, although the company paid $50 million in fines related "to the failure by bank employees" to comply with "the federal Bank Secrecy Act," the "[b]oard dedicated considerable resources to the [Bank Secrecy Act] compliance program and put into place numerous procedures and systems to attempt to ensure compliance." Accordingly, this Court affirmed the Court of Chancery's dismissal of a *Caremark* claim. [. . .] Here, the Blue Bell directors just argue that because Blue Bell management, in its discretion, discussed general operations with the board, a *Caremark* claim is not stated.

But if that were the case, then *Caremark* would be a chimera. At every board meeting of any company, it is likely that management will touch on some operational issue. Although *Caremark* may not require as much as some commentators wish, it does require that a board make a good faith effort to put in place a reasonable system of monitoring and reporting about the corporation's central compliance risks. In Blue Bell's case, food safety was essential and mission critical. [. . .]

If *Caremark* means anything, it is that a corporate board must make a good faith effort to exercise its duty of care. A failure to make that effort constitutes a breach of the duty of loyalty. Where, as here, a plaintiff has followed our admonishment to seek out relevant books and records and then uses those books and records to plead facts supporting a fair inference that no reasonable compliance system and protocols were established as to the obviously most central consumer safety and legal compliance issue facing the company, that the board's lack of efforts resulted in it not receiving official notices of food safety deficiencies for several years, and that, as a failure to take remedial action, the company exposed consumers to *listeria*-infected ice cream, resulting in the death and injury of company customers, the plaintiff has met his onerous pleading burden and is entitled to discovery to prove out his claim.

III. Conclusion

We therefore reverse the Court of Chancery's decision and remand for proceedings consistent with this opinion.

E. THE INTERSECTION OF DEMAND AND DUTIES

In re Citigroup Shareholders Derivative Litigation
964 A.2d 106 (Del. Ch. 2009)

■ CHANDLER, CHANCELLOR.

I. BACKGROUND

A. The Parties

Citigroup is a global financial services company whose businesses provide a broad range of financial services to consumers and businesses. Citigroup was incorporated in Delaware in 1988 and maintains its principal executive offices in New York, New York.

Defendants in this action are current and former directors and officers of Citigroup. The complaint names thirteen members of the Citigroup board of directors on November 9, 2007 [. . .]. Plaintiffs allege that a majority of the director defendants were members of the Audit and Risk Management Committee ("ARM Committee") in 2007 and were considered audit committee financial experts [. . .].

Plaintiffs [. . .] are all owners of shares of Citigroup stock.

B. Citigroup's Exposure to the Subprime Crisis

Plaintiffs allege that since as early as 2006, defendants have caused and allowed Citigroup to engage in subprime lending[2] that ultimately left the Company exposed to massive losses by late 2007. [. . .]

Much of Citigroup's exposure to the subprime lending market arose from its involvement with collateralized debt obligations ("CDOs")—repackaged pools of lower rated securities that Citigroup created by acquiring asset-backed securities, including residential mortgage backed securities ("RMBSs"), and then selling rights to the cash flows from the securities in classes, or tranches, with different levels of risk and return. Included with at least some of the CDOs created by Citigroup was a "liquidity put"—an option that allowed the purchasers of the CDOs to sell them back to Citigroup at original value.

According to plaintiffs, Citigroup's alleged $55 billion subprime exposure was in two areas of the Company's Securities & Banking Unit. [. . .]

By late 2007, it was apparent that Citigroup faced significant losses on its subprime-related assets [. . .].

---

[2] "Subprime" generally refers to borrowers who do not qualify for prime interest rates, typically due to weak credit histories, low credit scores, high debt-burden ratios, or high loan-to-value ratios.

C. Plaintiffs' Claims

Plaintiffs allege that defendants are liable to the Company for breach of fiduciary duty for (1) failing to adequately oversee and manage Citigroup's exposure to the problems in the subprime mortgage market, even in the face of alleged "red flags" and (2) failing to ensure that the Company's financial reporting and other disclosures were thorough and accurate. [. . .] [T]he "red flags" alleged in the eighty-six page Complaint are generally statements from public documents that reflect worsening conditions in the financial markets, including the subprime and credit markets, and the effects those worsening conditions had on market participants, including Citigroup's peers. By way of example only, plaintiffs' "red flags" include the following:

- *May 27, 2005:* Economist Paul Krugman of the *New York Times* said he saw "signs that America's housing market, like the stock market at the end of the last decade, is approaching the final, feverish stages of a speculative bubble."

- *May 2006:* Ameriquest Mortgage, one of the United States' leading wholesale subprime lenders, announced the closing of each of its 229 retail offices and reduction of 3,800 employees. [. . .]

- *April 18, 2007:* Freddie Mac announced plans to refinance up to $20 billion of loans held by subprime borrowers who would be unable to afford their adjustable-rate mortgages at the reset rate.

- *July 10, 2007:* Standard and Poor's and Moody's downgraded bonds backed by subprime mortgages.

- *August 1, 2007:* Two hedge funds managed by Bear Stearns that invested heavily in subprime mortgages declared bankruptcy.

- *August 9, 2007:* American International Group, one of the largest United States mortgage lenders, warned that mortgage defaults were spreading beyond the subprime sector, with delinquencies becoming more common among borrowers in the category just above subprime.

- *October 18, 2007:* Standard & Poor's cut the credit ratings on $23.35 billion of securities backed by pools of home loans that were offered to borrowers during the first half of the year. The downgrades even hit securities rated AAA, which was the highest of the ten investment-grade ratings and the rating of government debt. [. . .]

III. THE MOTION TO DISMISS UNDER RULE 23.1

A. The Legal Standard for Demand Excused

[. . .] [T]o show demand futility where the subject of the derivative suit is not a business decision of the board, a plaintiff must allege particularized facts that "create a reasonable doubt that, as of the time the complaint is filed, the board of directors could have properly exercised its independent and disinterested business judgment in responding to a demand." *Rales v. Blasband.*

[. . .] To establish that demand is excused under Rule 23.1, the pleadings must comply with "stringent requirements of factual particularity" and set forth "particularized factual statements that are essential to the claim." "A prolix complaint larded with conclusory language . . . does not comply with these fundamental pleading mandates." *Brehm.*

[. . .] Demand is not excused solely because the directors would be deciding to sue themselves. Rather, demand will be excused based on a possibility of personal director liability only in the rare case when a plaintiff is able to show director conduct that is "so egregious on its face that board approval cannot meet the test of business judgment, and a substantial likelihood of director liability therefore exists." *Aronson.*

B. Demand Futility Regarding Plaintiffs' Fiduciary Duty Claims

Plaintiffs' argument is based on a theory of director liability famously articulated by former-Chancellor Allen in *In re Caremark*. [. . .] In *Caremark,* the plaintiffs alleged that the directors were liable because they should have known that certain officers and employees were violating the federal Anti-Referral Payments Law. In analyzing these claims, the Court began, appropriately, by reviewing the duty of care and the protections of the business judgment rule.

With regard to director liability standards, the Court distinguished between (1) "*a board decision* that results in a loss because that decision was ill advised or 'negligent'" and (2) "an *unconsidered failure of the board to act* in circumstances in which due attention would, arguably, have prevented the loss." *Caremark.* In the former class of cases, director action is analyzed under the business judgment rule, which prevents judicial second guessing of the decision if the directors employed a rational process and considered all material information reasonably available—a standard measured by concepts of gross negligence. As former-Chancellor Allen explained:

> [. . .] [W]hether a judge or jury considering the matter after the fact, believes a decision substantively wrong, or degrees of wrong extending through "stupid" to "egregious" or "irrational," provides no ground for director liability, so long as the court determines that the process employed was either rational or employed in *a good faith* effort to advance corporate interests. To employ a different rule—one that permitted an "objective"

evaluation of the decision—would expose directors to substantive second guessing by ill-equipped judges or juries, which would, in the long-run, be injurious to investor interests.

[. . .]

[W]here directors are alleged to be liable for a failure to monitor liability creating activities, the *Caremark* Court stated that while directors could be liable for a failure to monitor, "only a sustained or systematic failure of the board to exercise oversight—such as an utter failure to attempt to assure a reasonable information and reporting system exists—will establish the lack of good faith that is a necessary condition to liability."

In *Stone v. Ritter,* the Delaware Supreme Court approved the *Caremark* standard for director oversight liability and made clear that liability was based on the concept of good faith, which the *Stone* Court held was embedded in the fiduciary duty of loyalty and did not constitute a freestanding fiduciary duty that could independently give rise to liability. As the *Stone* Court explained:

Caremark articulates the necessary conditions predicate for director oversight liability: (a) the directors utterly failed to implement any reporting or information system or controls; *or* (b) having implemented such a system or controls, consciously failed to monitor or oversee its operations thus disabling themselves from being informed of risks or problems requiring their attention. In either case, imposition of liability requires a showing that the directors knew that they were not discharging their fiduciary obligations. [. . .]

Thus, to establish oversight liability a plaintiff must show that the directors *knew* they were not discharging their fiduciary obligations or that the directors demonstrated a *conscious* disregard for their responsibilities such as by failing to act in the face of a known duty to act. The test is rooted in concepts of bad faith; indeed, a showing of bad faith is a *necessary condition* to director oversight liability.

1. Plaintiffs' Caremark Allegations

Plaintiffs' theory of how the director defendants will face personal liability is a bit of a twist on the traditional *Caremark* claim. In a typical *Caremark* case, plaintiffs argue that the defendants are liable for damages that arise from a failure to properly monitor or oversee employee misconduct or violations of law. [. . .]

In contrast, plaintiffs' *Caremark* claims are based on defendants' alleged failure to properly monitor Citigroup's *business risk,* specifically its exposure to the subprime mortgage market. [. . .] [P]laintiffs allege that the director defendants are personally liable under *Caremark* for failing to "make a good faith attempt to follow the procedures put in place or fail[ing] to assure that adequate and proper corporate information and reporting systems existed that would enable them to be fully informed regarding Citigroup's risk to the subprime mortgage market." Plaintiffs point to so-called "red flags" that should have put defendants on notice of the problems in the subprime mortgage market and further allege that the board should have been especially conscious of these red flags because a majority of the directors (1) served on the Citigroup board during its previous Enron related conduct and (2) were members of the ARM Committee and considered financial experts.

Although these claims are framed by plaintiffs as *Caremark* claims, plaintiffs' theory essentially amounts to a claim that the director defendants should be personally liable to the Company because they failed to fully recognize the risk posed by subprime securities. [. . .] Delaware Courts have faced these types of claims many times and have developed doctrines to deal with them—the fiduciary duty of care and the business judgment rule. [. . .]

The business judgment rule "is a presumption that in making a business decision the directors of a corporation acted on an informed basis, in good faith and in the honest belief that the action taken was in the best interests of the company." *Aronson.* The burden is on plaintiffs, the party challenging the directors' decision, to rebut this presumption. Thus, absent an allegation of interestedness or disloyalty to the corporation, the business judgment rule prevents a judge or jury from second guessing director decisions if they were the product of a rational process and the directors availed themselves of all material and reasonably available information. The standard of director liability under the business judgment rule "is predicated upon concepts of gross negligence." *Id.*

Additionally, Citigroup has adopted a provision in its certificate of incorporation pursuant to 8 Del. C. § 102(b)(7) that exculpates directors from personal liability for violations of fiduciary duty, except for, among other things, breaches of the duty of loyalty or actions or omissions not in good faith or that involve intentional misconduct or a knowing violation of law. [. . .] Here, plaintiffs have not alleged that the directors were interested in the transaction and instead root their theory of director personal liability in bad faith.

[. . .] A plaintiff can [. . .] plead bad faith by alleging with particularity that a director *knowingly* violated a fiduciary duty or failed to act in violation of a *known* duty to act, demonstrating a *conscious* disregard for her duties.

Turning now specifically to plaintiffs' *Caremark* claims, [. . .] a plaintiff can show that the director defendants will be liable if their acts or omissions constitute bad faith. A plaintiff can show bad faith conduct by, for example, properly alleging particularized facts that show that a director *consciously* disregarded an obligation to be reasonably informed about the business and its risks or *consciously* disregarded the duty to monitor and oversee the business.

The Delaware Supreme Court made clear in *Stone* that directors of Delaware corporations have certain responsibilities to implement and monitor a system of oversight; however, this obligation does not eviscerate the core protections of the business judgment rule—protections designed to allow corporate managers and directors to pursue risky transactions without the specter of being held personally liable if those decisions turn out poorly. Accordingly, the burden required for a plaintiff to rebut the presumption of the business judgment rule by showing gross negligence is a difficult one, and the burden to show bad faith is even higher. [. . .] The presumption of the business judgment rule, the protection of an exculpatory § 102(b)(7) provision, and the difficulty of proving a *Caremark* claim together function to place an extremely high burden on a plaintiff to state a claim for personal director liability for a failure to see the extent of a company's business risk.

[. . .] The essence of the business judgment of managers and directors is deciding how the company will evaluate the trade-off between risk and return. Businesses—and particularly financial institutions—make returns by taking on risk; a company or investor that is willing to take on more risk can earn a higher return. Thus, in almost any business transaction, the parties go into the deal with the knowledge that, even if they have evaluated the situation correctly, the return could be different than they expected.

It is almost impossible for a court, in hindsight, to determine whether the directors of a company properly evaluated risk and thus made the "right" business decision. In any investment there is a chance that returns will turn out lower than expected, and generally a smaller chance that they will be far lower than expected. When investments turn out poorly, it is possible that the decision-maker evaluated the deal correctly but got "unlucky" in that a huge loss—the probability of which was very small—actually happened. It is also possible that the decision-maker improperly evaluated the risk posed by an investment and that the company suffered large losses as a result.

Business decision-makers must operate in the real world, with imperfect information, limited resources, and an uncertain future. To impose liability on directors for making a "wrong" business decision would cripple their ability to earn returns for investors by taking business risks. Indeed, this kind of judicial second guessing is what the business judgment rule was designed to prevent, and even if a complaint is framed under a *Caremark* theory, this Court will not abandon such bedrock principles of Delaware fiduciary duty law. [. . .]

a.   The Complaint Does Not Properly Allege Demand Futility for Plaintiffs' Fiduciary Duty Claims

In this case, plaintiffs allege that the defendants are liable for failing to properly monitor the risk that Citigroup faced from subprime securities. While it may be possible for a plaintiff to meet the burden under some set of facts, plaintiffs in this case have failed to state a *Caremark* claim sufficient to excuse demand based on a theory that the directors did not fulfill their oversight obligations by failing to monitor the business risk of the company.

The allegations in the Complaint amount essentially to a claim that Citigroup suffered large losses and that there were certain warning signs that could or should have put defendants on notice of the business risks related to Citigroup's investments in subprime assets. Plaintiffs then conclude that because defendants failed to prevent the Company's losses associated with certain business risks, they must have consciously ignored these warning signs or knowingly failed to monitor the Company's risk in accordance with their fiduciary duties. Such conclusory allegations, however, are not sufficient to state a claim for failure of oversight that would give rise to a substantial likelihood of personal liability, which would require particularized factual allegations demonstrating bad faith by the director defendants.

[. . .] Citigroup had procedures and controls in place that were designed to monitor risk. [. . .] Citigroup established the ARM Committee and in 2004 amended the ARM Committee charter to include the fact that one of the purposes of the ARM Committee was to assist the board in fulfilling its oversight responsibility relating to policy standards and guidelines for risk assessment and risk management. The ARM Committee was also charged with [. . .] (1) discussing with management and independent auditors the annual audited financial statements, (2) reviewing with management an evaluation of Citigroup's internal control structure, and (3) discussing with management Citigroup's major credit, market, liquidity, and operational risk exposures and the steps taken by management to monitor and control such exposures, including Citigroup's risk assessment and risk management policies. According to plaintiffs' own allegations, the ARM Committee met eleven times in 2006 and twelve times in 2007.

Plaintiffs nevertheless argue that the director defendants breached their duty of oversight either because the oversight mechanisms were not adequate or because the director defendants did not make a good faith effort to comply with the established oversight procedures. To support this claim, the Complaint alleges numerous facts that plaintiffs argue should have put the director defendants on notice of the impending problems in the subprime mortgage market and Citigroup's exposure thereto. [. . .]

Plaintiffs argue that demand is excused because a majority of the director defendants face a substantial likelihood of personal liability because they were charged with management of Citigroup's risk as members of the ARM Committee and as audit committee financial experts and failed to properly oversee and monitor such risk. [. . .] Plaintiffs fail to plead any particularized factual allegations that raise a reasonable doubt that the director defendants acted in good faith.

The warning signs alleged by plaintiffs are not evidence that the directors consciously disregarded their duties or otherwise acted in bad faith; at most they evidence that the directors made bad business decisions. The "red flags" in the Complaint amount to little more than portions of public documents that reflected the worsening conditions in the subprime mortgage market and in the economy generally. Plaintiffs fail to plead "particularized facts suggesting that the Board was presented with 'red flags' alerting it to potential misconduct" at the Company. [. . .] Nothing about plaintiffs' "red flags" supports plaintiffs' conclusory allegation that "defendants have not made a good faith attempt to assure that adequate and proper corporate information and reporting systems existed that would enable them to be fully informed regarding Citigroup's risk to the subprime mortgage market." Indeed, plaintiffs' allegations do not even specify how the board's oversight mechanisms were inadequate or how the director defendants knew of these inadequacies and consciously ignored them. Rather, plaintiffs seem to hope the Court will accept the conclusion that since the Company suffered large losses, and since a properly functioning risk management system would have avoided such losses, the directors must have breached their fiduciary duties in allowing such losses. [. . .]

These types of conclusory allegations are exactly the kinds of allegations that do not state a claim for relief under *Caremark*.

To recognize such claims under a theory of director oversight liability would undermine the long established protections of the business judgment rule. [. . .][T]he mere fact that a company takes on business risk and suffers losses—even catastrophic losses—does not evidence misconduct, and without more, is not a basis for personal director liability. That there were signs in the market that reflected worsening conditions and suggested that conditions may deteriorate even further is not an invitation for this Court to disregard the presumptions of the business judgment rule and conclude that the directors are liable because they did not properly evaluate business risk. [. . .]

Director oversight duties are designed to ensure reasonable reporting and information systems exist that would allow directors to know about and prevent wrongdoing that could cause losses for the Company. There are significant differences between failing to oversee employee fraudulent or criminal conduct and failing to recognize the extent of a Company's business risk. [. . .] While it may be tempting to say that directors have the same duties to monitor and oversee business risk, imposing *Caremark*-type duties on directors to monitor business risk is fundamentally different. Citigroup was in the business of taking on and managing investment and other business risks. To impose oversight liability on directors for failure to monitor "excessive" risk would involve courts in conducting hindsight evaluations of decisions at the heart of the business judgment of directors. Oversight duties under Delaware law are not designed to subject directors, even expert directors, to *personal liability* for failure to predict the future and to properly evaluate business risk. [. . .]

IV. CONCLUSION

[. . .] Ultimately, the discretion granted directors and managers allows them to maximize shareholder value in the long term by taking risks without the debilitating fear that they will be held personally liable if the company experiences losses. This doctrine also means, however, that when the company suffers losses, shareholders may not be able to hold the directors personally liable. [. . .]

F. CONTROLLING SHAREHOLDERS' DUTY OF LOYALTY

Sinclair Oil Corp. v. Levien
280 A.2d 717 (Del. 1971)

■ WOLCOTT, CHIEF JUSTICE.

This is an appeal by the defendant, Sinclair Oil Corporation (hereafter Sinclair), from an order of the Court of Chancery, in a derivative action requiring Sinclair to account for damages sustained by its subsidiary, Sinclair Venezuelan Oil Company (hereafter Sinven), organized by Sinclair for the purpose of operating in Venezuela, as a result of dividends paid by Sinven, the denial to Sinven of industrial development, and a breach of contract between Sinclair's wholly-owned subsidiary, Sinclair International Oil Company, and Sinven.

Sinclair, operating primarily as a holding company, is in the business of exploring for oil and of producing and marketing crude oil and oil products. At all times relevant to this litigation, it owned about 97% Of Sinven's stock. The plaintiff owns about 3000 of 120,000 publicly held shares of Sinven. Sinven, incorporated in 1922, has been engaged in petroleum operations primarily in Venezuela and since 1959 has operated exclusively in Venezuela.

Sinclair nominates all members of Sinven's board of directors. The Chancellor found as a fact that the directors were not independent of Sinclair. Almost without exception, they were officers, directors, or employees of corporations in the Sinclair complex. By reason of Sinclair's domination, it is clear that Sinclair owed Sinven a fiduciary duty. Sinclair concedes this.

The Chancellor held that because of Sinclair's fiduciary duty and its control over Sinven, its relationship with Sinven must meet the test of intrinsic fairness. The standard of intrinsic fairness involves both a high degree of fairness and a shift in the burden of proof. Under this standard the burden is on Sinclair to prove, subject to careful judicial scrutiny, that its transactions with Sinven were objectively fair.

Sinclair argues that the transactions between it and Sinven should be tested, not by the test of intrinsic fairness with the accompanying shift of the burden of proof, but by the business judgment rule. [. . .]

We think, however, that Sinclair's argument in this respect is misconceived. When the situation involves a parent and a subsidiary, with the parent controlling the transaction and fixing the terms, the test of intrinsic fairness, with its resulting shifting of the burden of proof, is applied. *Sterling v. Mayflower Hotel Corp.* The basic situation for the application of the rule is the one in which the parent has received a benefit to the exclusion and at the expense of the subsidiary. [. . .]

A parent does indeed owe a fiduciary duty to its subsidiary when there are parent-subsidiary dealings. However, this alone will not evoke the intrinsic fairness standard. This standard will be applied only when the fiduciary duty is accompanied by self-dealing—the situation when a parent is on both sides of a transaction with its subsidiary. Self-dealing occurs when the parent, by virtue of its domination of the subsidiary, causes the subsidiary to act in such a way that the parent receives something from the subsidiary to the exclusion of, and detriment to, the minority stockholders of the subsidiary.

We turn now to the facts. The plaintiff argues that, from 1960 through 1966, Sinclair caused Sinven to pay out such excessive dividends that the industrial development of Sinven was effectively prevented, and it became in reality a corporation in dissolution.

From 1960 through 1966, Sinven paid out $108,000,000 in dividends ($38,000,000 in excess of Sinven's earnings during the same period). The Chancellor held that Sinclair caused these dividends to be paid during a period when it had a need for large amounts of cash. Although the dividends paid exceeded earnings, the plaintiff concedes that the payments were made in compliance with 8 Del.C. § 170, authorizing payment of dividends out of surplus or net profits. However, the plaintiff attacks these dividends on the ground that they resulted from an improper motive—Sinclair's need for cash. The Chancellor, applying the intrinsic fairness standard, held that Sinclair did not sustain its burden of proving that these dividends were intrinsically fair to the minority stockholders of Sinven. [. . .]

We do not accept the argument that the intrinsic fairness test can never be applied to a dividend declaration by a dominated board, although a dividend declaration by a dominated board will not inevitably demand the application of the intrinsic fairness standard. If such a dividend is in essence self-dealing by the parent, then the intrinsic fairness standard is the proper standard. For example, suppose a parent dominates a subsidiary and its board of directors. The subsidiary has outstanding two classes of stock, X and Y. Class X is owned by the parent and Class Y is owned by minority stockholders of the subsidiary. If the subsidiary, at the direction of the parent, declares a dividend on its Class X stock only, this might well be self-dealing by the parent. It would be receiving something from the subsidiary to the exclusion of and detrimental to its minority stockholders. This self-dealing, coupled with the parent's fiduciary duty, would make intrinsic fairness the proper standard by which to evaluate the dividend payments.

Consequently it must be determined whether the dividend payments by Sinven were, in essence, self-dealing by Sinclair. The dividends resulted in great sums of money being transferred from Sinven to Sinclair. However, a proportionate share of this money was received by the minority shareholders of Sinven. Sinclair received nothing from Sinven to the exclusion of its minority stockholders. As such, these dividends were not self-dealing. We hold therefore that the Chancellor erred in applying the intrinsic fairness test as to these dividend payments. The business judgment standard should have been applied.

We conclude that the facts demonstrate that the dividend payments complied with the business judgment standard and with 8 Del.C. § 170. The motives for causing the declaration of dividends are immaterial unless the plaintiff can show that the dividend payments resulted from improper motives and amounted to waste. The plaintiff contends only that the dividend payments drained Sinven of cash to such an extent that it was prevented from expanding.

The plaintiff proved no business opportunities which came to Sinven independently and which Sinclair either took to itself or denied to Sinven. As a matter of fact, with two minor exceptions which resulted in losses, all of Sinven's operations have been conducted in Venezuela, and Sinclair had a policy of exploiting its oil properties located in different countries by subsidiaries located in the particular countries.

From 1960 to 1966 Sinclair purchased or developed oil fields in Alaska, Canada, Paraguay, and other places around the world. The plaintiff contends that these were all opportunities which could have been taken by Sinven. The Chancellor concluded that Sinclair had not proved that its denial of expansion opportunities to Sinven was intrinsically fair. He based this conclusion on the following findings of fact. Sinclair made no real effort to expand Sinven. The excessive dividends paid by Sinven resulted in so great a cash drain as to effectively deny to Sinven any ability to expand. During this same period Sinclair actively pursued a company-wide policy of developing through its subsidiaries new sources of revenue, but Sinven was not permitted to participate and was confined in its activities to Venezuela.

However, the plaintiff could point to no opportunities which came to Sinven. Therefore, Sinclair usurped no business opportunity belonging to Sinven. Since Sinclair received nothing from Sinven to the exclusion of and detriment to Sinven's minority stockholders, there was no self-dealing. Therefore, business judgment is the proper standard by which to evaluate Sinclair's expansion policies.

Since there is no proof of self-dealing on the part of Sinclair, it follows that the expansion policy of Sinclair and the methods used to achieve the desired result must, as far as Sinclair's treatment of Sinven is concerned, be tested by the standards of the business judgment rule. Accordingly, Sinclair's decision, absent fraud or gross overreaching, to achieve expansion through the medium of its subsidiaries, other than Sinven, must be upheld.

Even if Sinclair was wrong in developing these opportunities as it did, the question arises, with which subsidiaries should these opportunities have been shared? No evidence indicates a unique need or ability of Sinven to develop these opportunities. The decision of which subsidiaries would be used to implement Sinclair's expansion policy was one of business judgment with which a court will not interfere absent a showing of gross and palpable overreaching. No such showing has been made here.

Next, Sinclair argues that the Chancellor committed error when he held it liable to Sinven for breach of contract.

In 1961 Sinclair created Sinclair International Oil Company (hereafter International), a wholly owned subsidiary used for the purpose of coordinating all of Sinclair's foreign operations. All crude purchases by Sinclair were made thereafter through International.

On September 28, 1961, Sinclair caused Sinven to contract with International whereby Sinven agreed to sell all of its crude oil and refined products to International at specified prices. The contract provided for minimum and maximum quantities and prices. The plaintiff contends that Sinclair caused this contract to be breached in two respects. Although the contract called for payment on receipt, International's payments lagged as much as 30 days after receipt. Also, the contract required International to purchase at least a fixed minimum amount of crude and refined products from Sinven. International did not comply with this requirement.

Clearly, Sinclair's act of contracting with its dominated subsidiary was self-dealing. Under the contract Sinclair received the products produced by Sinven, and of course the minority shareholders of Sinven were not able to share in the receipt of these products. If the contract was breached, then Sinclair received these products to the detriment of Sinven's minority shareholders. We agree with the Chancellor's finding that the contract was breached by Sinclair, both as to the time of payments and the amounts purchased.

Although a parent need not bind itself by a contract with its dominated subsidiary, Sinclair chose to operate in this manner. As Sinclair has received the benefits of this contract, so must it comply with the contractual duties.

Under the intrinsic fairness standard, Sinclair must prove that its causing Sinven not to enforce the contract was intrinsically fair to the minority shareholders of Sinven. Sinclair has failed to meet this burden. Late payments were clearly breaches for which Sinven should have sought and received adequate damages. As to the quantities purchased,

Sinclair argues that it purchased all the products produced by Sinven. This, however, does not satisfy the standard of intrinsic fairness. Sinclair has failed to prove that Sinven could not possibly have produced or someway have obtained the contract minimums. As such, Sinclair must account on this claim. [. . .]

We will therefore reverse that part of the Chancellor's order that requires Sinclair to account to Sinven for damages sustained as a result of dividends paid between 1960 and 1966, and by reason of the denial to Sinven of expansion during that period. We will affirm the remaining portion of that order and remand the cause for further proceedings.

In Re Tesla Motors, Inc. Stockholder Litigation
2018 WL 1560293 (Del. Ch. 2018)

■ SLIGHTS, VICE CHANCELLOR.

The question addressed in this Memorandum Opinion is whether Plaintiffs have adequately pled that Elon Musk is a controlling stockholder of Tesla, Inc. ("Tesla" or the "Company"). [. . .]

I. FACTUAL BACKGROUND

[. . .]

A. The Parties and Relevant Non-Parties

Plaintiffs are Tesla stockholders[.] [. . .]

Nominal Defendant Tesla is a public Delaware corporation headquartered in Palo Alto, California that designs, develops, manufactures and sells electric vehicles and energy storage products. Tesla's Board comprises seven members: Elon Musk ("Musk"), Brad W. Buss, Robyn M. Denholm, Ira Ehrenpreis, Antonio J. Gracias, Stephen T. Jurvetson and Kimbal Musk ("Kimbal").

Non-party SolarCity was a public Delaware corporation headquartered in San Mateo, California that was founded by Musk and his cousins, Peter and Lyndon Rive ("Peter" and "Lyndon"). It principally operated as a solar energy system installer. Its board of directors (the "SolarCity Board") included Musk, Gracias, Lyndon, Peter, Nancy Pfund, and John H.N. Fisher. Lyndon served as SolarCity's CEO and Peter as its Chief Technology Officer ("CTO").

Defendant Musk is Tesla's largest stockholder. At the time of the Acquisition, Musk owned approximately 22.1% of Tesla's common stock. He serves as Chairman of the Tesla Board (since April 2004) and as Tesla's CEO (since October 2008) and Chief Product Architect. He also led Tesla's pre-initial public offering ("IPO") funding rounds. Tesla has acknowledged in its Securities and Exchange Commission filings that Musk is not an independent director.

As Tesla's Chief Product Architect, Musk plays a key role in the design of all Tesla products. He also contributes "significantly and actively" to

Tesla by "recruiting executives and engineers, [. . .] raising capital for [the Company] and bringing investors to and raising public awareness of the Company." In its SEC filings, Tesla states that it is "highly dependent on the services of Elon Musk," and acknowledges that if it were to lose Musk's services, the loss would "disrupt [Tesla's] operations, delay the development and introduction of [its] vehicles and services, and negatively impact [its] business, prospects and operating results as well as cause [its] stock price to decline." [. . .] On an August 1, 2016 conference call (the same day Tesla announced the Acquisition), Musk repeatedly referred to Tesla as "my company."

Musk also served as the Chairman of the SolarCity Board since its formation in 2006. He was SolarCity's largest stockholder, holding approximately 21.9% of the common stock prior to the Acquisition. As a result of the Acquisition, Musk's SolarCity holdings were converted to over $500 million of Tesla shares. It is alleged that Musk has publicly maintained that Tesla, SolarCity and SpaceX form a "pyramid" on top of which he sits, and that it is "important that there not be some sort of house of cards that crumbles if one element of the pyramid . . . falters."

Defendant Buss has been a Tesla Board member since 2009. [. . .] From August 2014 until February 2016, Buss served as SolarCity's Chief Financial Officer ("CFO"), for which he received total compensation of $32 million. After his departure from SolarCity's management, Buss remained at SolarCity as either an employee or consultant through at least December 31, 2016. [. . .]

Defendant Denholm has been a Tesla Board member since August 2014. [. . .]

Defendant Ehrenpreis has been a Tesla Board member since May 2007. [. . .] Ehrenpreis is an investor in, and serves on the board of directors of, Mapbox, Inc., which provides custom online maps. Tesla and Mapbox entered into an agreement in December 2015 pursuant to which Tesla pays Mapbox ongoing fees, including $5 million over the first twelve months of the agreement.

Ehrenpreis is also a managing partner and co-owner of a venture capital firm, DBL Partners, which he co-founded with fellow managing partner and co-owner Nancy Pfund. Pfund was an observer on the Tesla Board from 2006 to 2010. She was also a member of the SolarCity Board and one of two members of the SolarCity Board's special committee that negotiated and approved the Acquisition. Pfund is the managing director and founder of DBL Investors, LLC ("DBL Investors"), which contributed at least $3.6 million over three of SolarCity's funding rounds. [. . .] She is a close friend of Musk's and has said that "[h]e's always been a master of the universe in my mind."

Defendant Gracias has served on the Tesla Board since May 2007. Gracias has been Tesla's Lead Independent Director since September 2010. [. . .] Musk and Gracias are close friends; indeed, Musk gave

Gracias the second Tesla Roadster ever made. Gracias also served on SolarCity's Board at the time of the Acquisition and beneficially owned 211,854 shares of SolarCity common stock.

In addition, Gracias is founder, managing partner, CEO, Chief Investment Officer, director and sole owner of private equity firm Valor Management Corp., which does business as Valor Equity Partners ("Valor"). Valor and Gracias have participated in several pre-IPO funding rounds for Tesla and SolarCity. [. . .] Prior to Tesla's IPO, Valor owned nearly five million Tesla shares. Gracias and his Valor funds also contributed nearly $25 million to SolarCity's pre-IPO preferred stock financing round. Musk has invested $2 million in each of two Valor funds.

Defendant Jurvetson has served as a Tesla Board member since June 2009. [. . .] Musk and Jurvetson are also close friends, evidenced in part by the fact that Musk gave Jurvetson the first Tesla Model S and the second Tesla Model X ever made.

Jurvetson is a managing director of venture capital firm Draper Fisher Jurvetson ("DFJ"). [. . .] Musk invests in DFJ and one of Musk's trusts is a limited partner in a DFJ fund.

Defendant Kimbal has served on the Tesla Board since April 2004. He is Musk's brother and cousin of Lyndon and Peter, SolarCity's co-founders. [. . .] He owns an unspecified amount of Tesla shares. At the time of the Acquisition, Kimbal also beneficially owned 147,541 shares of SolarCity common stock. Additionally, Kimbal is a limited partner in two Valor funds, and Musk has invested in one of those funds.

The Company's SEC filings acknowledge that the "concentration of ownership among [Tesla's] existing executive officers, directors and their affiliates may prevent new investors from influencing significant corporate decisions," and that "these stockholders will be able to exercise a significant level of control over all matters requiring stockholder approval, including the election of directors, amendment of our certificate of incorporation and approval of significant corporate transactions."

B. The Tesla-SolarCity Connections

[. . .] Musk became involved with Tesla soon after it was formed. In 2004, Musk led Tesla's Series A round of financing and became Chairman of the Board pursuant to a Series A voting agreement. Over the next few years, Musk participated in Tesla's Series B, C, D and E venture funding rounds. Musk led the Series B round of funding and co-led the Series C round. Prior to Tesla's IPO, Musk had invested approximately $70 million in the Company.

"In November 2007, Musk forced founder and then-CEO [Martin] Eberhard out of the Company." He appointed himself CEO in October 2008. Around that time, Tesla encountered financial trouble. Musk personally borrowed $20 million from SpaceX in early 2009 to help "keep Tesla afloat."

Since Tesla's IPO in 2010, Musk has been the Company's largest stockholder, owning between 26.5% and 29% of its outstanding common stock. [. . .] By September 2016, Musk owned 22.1% of Tesla's outstanding common stock.

Musk, Lyndon and Peter founded SolarCity in 2006. [. . .] It completed an IPO in December 2012 and since then has suffered losses in every quarter except three. Musk owned 21.9%, Lyndon owned 3.9% and Peter owned 3.8% of SolarCity's outstanding common stock at the time of the Acquisition.

C.   SolarCity's Liquidity Challenges

During the three years immediately preceding Tesla's June 2016 offer to acquire SolarCity, SolarCity's debt increased thirteen-fold, totaling $3.56 billion as of June 2016. By any measure, SolarCity was in the midst of a liquidity crisis. [. . .]

In February 2016, a SolarCity Board presentation (the "February 2016 SolarCity Board Presentation") acknowledged that the company faced "significant liquidity concerns" [. . .]. To make matters worse, $1.23 billion of SolarCity's debt was scheduled to become due by the end of 2017. Musk, Gracias and Buss attended the February 2016 meeting and were well aware of SolarCity's "significant liquidity concerns" at the time Musk brought the proposed acquisition of SolarCity to the Tesla Board.

The debt and equity markets were effectively closed to SolarCity. [. . .] The credit markets were no more forgiving. SolarCity already held substantial debt and had recently attempted to raise capital via bond offerings ("Solar Bonds"). [. . .]

D.   Musk Persistently Presents the SolarCity Transaction to the Board

The Tesla Board held a special meeting on February 29, 2016. At the meeting, Musk and Tesla CFO, Jason Wheeler, presented a preliminary plan for Tesla to acquire SolarCity. Musk led the presentation. The stated purpose of the proposed transaction was "to complement the Company's Energy business, grow the Sales operations of the Company and to create other product, service and operational synergies through the combination of the companies." Musk's focus was on a potential acquisition of SolarCity; he did not mention and the Board did not consider other companies in the solar industry or other strategic transactions. The Board "decided not to proceed with an offer to SolarCity at [that] time [. . .]."

Two weeks passed, and Musk was before the Tesla Board again to propose a possible acquisition of SolarCity (and only SolarCity) during the Board's March 15, 2016 meeting. And, again, the Board deferred the discussion.

Less than three months later, on May 31, 2016, at a regularly scheduled meeting of the Board, Musk was back to propose (again) a possible acquisition of SolarCity. [. . .] The minutes of the meeting reflect that "the Board discussed the possibility of evaluating an acquisition of SolarCity Corporation . . . as a potential target of opportunity in the solar energy space." Once again, SolarCity was the only target on which the Board trained its sight.

[. . .] "Despite the Tesla Board members' obvious conflicts in considering an acquisition of SolarCity, the Tesla Board did not form a special committee" to consider the potential acquisition.

The Tesla Board called a special meeting for June 20, 2016 (the "June 2016 Special Meeting") "to further explore a potential strategic transaction between the Company and a participant in the solar energy industry." Musk opened the meeting by "remind[ing] the board that the issue [of acquiring SolarCity] had been raised and discussed but ultimately deferred at previous meetings and review[ing] some of the strategic considerations that the board had evaluated at those previous meetings." It is alleged that, as if on cue, the Board heeded Musk's "tacit order" and promptly authorized its advisors to make an offer for SolarCity.

The Board's first meeting with Evercore occurred during the June 2016 Special Meeting, the same meeting where the Board approved the offer to acquire SolarCity. The meeting minutes reflect that although Evercore's presentation included a brief analysis of "various potential targets," the Board did not discuss potential acquisitions of any target other than SolarCity. This is surprising, to say the least, given that "Goldman Sachs & Co., which was a co-underwriter in Tesla's $2 billion secondary stock offering that was issued just weeks earlier, publicly stated that SolarCity was the 'worst positioned' company in the solar energy sector for capitalizing on future growth in the industry."

Musk and Gracias, both directors of Tesla and SolarCity, recused themselves from the June 2016 Special Meeting while the remaining members of the Board voted to approve the offer for SolarCity. But both remained for the entirety of the meeting while the potential acquisition of SolarCity was discussed, and Musk led most of those discussions. When the time came for the vote, the Board approved and adopted the offer on the same terms discussed when Musk and Gracias were present.

E. The Offer for SolarCity

On June 21, 2016, Tesla announced its offer to acquire SolarCity in a stock-for-stock transaction [. . .].

Musk was active in his sponsorship and backing of the Offer and the eventual Acquisition both before and after the announcement of the deal. First, during a June 22, 2016, call with investors and analysts [. . .] Musk stated:

> Like the opinion is unanimous for both companies. So, I mean, unless there's something discovered that like that I have no idea about or just that nobody on the board has any idea about, which

is extremely unlikely, then the board would—the independent board members would recommend in favor of completing a transaction somewhere in the price range that was mentioned, most likely.

Then, during the due diligence period, Musk reached out to "certain institutional investors" to garner support for the Acquisition. It is alleged that [. . .] "[. . .] Elon Musk forced the Tesla Board into a position in which they had no choice but to follow through with the Acquisition."

And finally [. . .] on July 20, 2016, Musk published his "Master Plan, Part Deux" to Tesla's website. This "manifesto" of sorts updated the original Master Plan that Musk published in 2006 [. . .]. The Master Plan, Part Deux, states, in relevant part:

> [. . .] The point of all this was, and remains, accelerating the advent of sustainable energy, so that we can imagine far into the future and life is still good.

> [. . .] We can't do this well if Tesla and SolarCity are different companies, which is why we need to combine and break down the barriers inherent to being separate companies. [. . .]

F. Due Diligence Reveals SolarCity's Liquidity Crisis and Other Issues

In a July 5, 2016 presentation to the Tesla Board, Evercore warned the Board that SolarCity had $3.164 billion in outstanding debt as of March 31, 2016, and that significant debt would mature in a three-to-five year window. [. . .]

In more bad news, due diligence revealed issues with SolarCity's new manufacturing facility planned for Buffalo, New York (the "Buffalo Factory"). [. . .] As discovered in Tesla's due diligence, SolarCity's Buffalo Factory was behind schedule, its costs were projected to be higher than those carried in the industry [. . .].

H. Tesla and SolarCity Announce the Merger Agreement

On August 1, 2016, Tesla and SolarCity announced they had executed an Agreement and Plan of Merger dated July 31, 2016 (the "Merger Agreement"), pursuant to which Tesla would acquire SolarCity in an all-stock deal. [. . .] The Acquisition price valued SolarCity at approximately $2.6 billion. [. . .]

The Complaint alleges the Acquisition was a bailout of SolarCity that benefited six of the seven members of the Tesla Board and/or their family members, businesses and business partners. Specifically, the Acquisition benefited: (a) Musk, Kimbal and their cousins, Peter and Lyndon; (b) Gracias and the investment fund he manages; (c) Jurvetson, his venture capital firm and his firm's managing director; (d) Ehrenpreis' venture capital partner; and (e) Buss.

I. The Tesla Stockholders Approve the Acquisition

On November 17, 2016, Tesla stockholders voted to approve the Acquisition. The Merger Agreement excluded from the vote certain Tesla stockholders (and their affiliates) who were also directors or executive officers of SolarCity [. . .].

The Acquisition closed on November 21, 2016. Musk, Lyndon and Peter became executive officers of the surviving SolarCity subsidiary of Tesla. And with the stroke of a pen, Tesla's debt load nearly doubled.

J. Procedural Posture

[EDS.—The Complaint asserted several claims, including a derivative claim for breach of fiduciary duty against Musk as Tesla's controlling stockholder for using his control to orchestrate Board approval of the Acquisition.]

[. . .] This is the Court's decision on Defendants' motion to dismiss the Complaint.

II. ANALYSIS

[. . .] Defendants' showcase defense rests on *Corwin*. Although Tesla stockholder approval of the Acquisition was not required by the Delaware General Corporation Law, the Tesla Board submitted the Acquisition for stockholder approval anyway. Defendants maintain that the fully informed, uncoerced vote of the disinterested stockholders mandates business judgment review of Plaintiffs' breach of fiduciary duty claims and dismissal of the Complaint. Plaintiffs disagree on several grounds; first among them, Plaintiffs maintain that, as a matter of law, *Corwin* does not apply because the Acquisition benefited Tesla's controlling stockholder, Musk. Because I agree the Complaint pleads facts that allow reasonable inferences that Musk was a controlling stockholder and that Plaintiffs' claims against all Defendants are subject to entire fairness review, I begin and end my analysis of the motion to dismiss there. [. . .]

A. The Controlling Stockholder Inquiry

In the seminal *Kahn v. Lynch Communications Systems, Inc.*, the Supreme Court observed that Delaware courts will deem a stockholder a controlling stockholder when the stockholder: (1) owns more than 50% of the voting power of a corporation or (2) owns less than 50% of the voting power of the corporation but "*exercises control* over the business affairs of the corporation." Plaintiffs do not dispute that Musk holds only 22.1% of the voting power in Tesla. Thus, the operative question is whether Musk, as a minority blockholder, "*exercises control* over the business affairs of [Tesla]." Further refined, the inquiry is whether Musk "exercised actual domination and control over . . . [the] directors." In this regard, his power must have been "so potent that independent directors . . . [could not] freely exercise their judgment."

"The requisite degree of control can be shown to exist generally or 'with regard to the particular transaction that is being challenged.'" *Carsanaro v. Bloodhound Techs., Inc.*

B. It Is Reasonably Conceivable That Musk Is Tesla's Controlling Stockholder

The parties proffer several factors to inform the Court's determination of whether the Complaint adequately pleads Musk's controller status. They include: (1) Musk's ability to influence the stockholder vote to effect significant change at Tesla, including the removal of Board members; (2) Musk's influence over the Board as Tesla's visionary, CEO and Chairman of the Board; (3) Musk's strong connections with members of the Tesla Board and the fact that a majority of the Tesla Board was "interested," as that term is defined in our law, in the Acquisition; and (4) Tesla's and Musk's acknowledgement of Musk's control in its public filings. [. . .]

1. Musk's Control of the Vote

Musk is a 22.1% stockholder. In the controlling stockholder context, this ownership stake is "relatively low" reflecting a "small block." Even so, "there is no absolute percentage of voting power that is required in order for there to be a finding that a controlling stockholder exists." *In re PNB Holding Co. Shareholder Litigation.* Indeed, "[a]ctual control over business affairs may stem from sources extraneous to stock ownership." *In re Zhongpin Inc. Stockholder Litigation.* [. . .]

Defendants view the controlling stockholder question as turning on the minority blockholder's ability to control the outcome of a contested election and the resulting perception of members of the board of directors that their future on the board rests in the alleged controller's hands. According to Defendants, since Musk's 22.1% voting power is inadequate to dominate a contested election, he cannot be deemed a controlling stockholder. [. . .] I disagree.

The ability of an alleged controller to influence a contested election is a significant consideration. [. . .] But alleged control of the ballot box is not always dispositive of the controlling stockholder inquiry in the minority stockholder context. [. . .] "[T]he focus of the [controller] inquiry [is] on the *de facto* power of a significant (but less than majority) shareholder, which, when *coupled with other factors*, gives that shareholder the ability to dominate the corporate decision-making process." *Superior Vision Services, Inc. v. ReliaStar Life Ins. Co.* [. . .]

All tallied, the facts pled regarding Musk's ability to exercise the equivalent of majority voting control extend beyond mere conclusory statements that he could control the vote. [. . .]

2. Musk's Control Over Tesla's Board

That Musk is the "face of Tesla" [. . .] is not dispositive of the controller question. [. . .] [I]n *Dell*, our Supreme Court relied on this Court's post-trial fact findings to conclude that a management buyout of Dell, Inc. led by Dell's founder and CEO, Michael Dell, was not a controlling stockholder transaction. In reaching that conclusion, however, this Court emphasized that after Mr. Dell announced his intent to pursue the MBO: (1) he immediately advised Dell's board he "did not want to proceed further without approval of the Board, and that he would not engage a financial advisor without first informing the Board"; (2) the board formed an independent committee to negotiate with Mr. Dell and Mr. Dell did not participate in any of the board level discussions regarding a sale of the company; (3) the committee actively explored alternatives to Mr. Dell's MBO proposal and Mr. Dell committed to work with any competing bidders; (4) Mr. Dell agreed to "to join up with whoever" in the event a superior proposal emerged; (5) when the negotiations reached an impasse over price, Mr. Dell agreed to roll over his shares at a lower price than the deal price to resolve the stalemate; and (6) importantly, Mr. Dell entered into a voting agreement that required him and his affiliates to vote their shares "in the same proportion as the number of [s]hares voted by the [u]naffiliated [s]tockholders ... that are voted in favor of the adoption" of either (i) the MBO merger agreement or (ii) a superior proposal. These facts, and perhaps others, allowed the trial court to determine that [. . .] Mr. Dell did not "dominate the corporate decision-making process." They also provided a basis for the court to resist the instinctive appeal of the "face of the company" argument when engaging in the controlling stockholder analysis.

[. . .] [T]here were practically no steps taken to separate Musk from the Board's consideration of the Acquisition. He brought the proposal to the Board not once, not twice, but three times. He then led the Board's discussions regarding the Acquisition throughout its laser focus on SolarCity and was responsible for engaging the Board's advisors. [. . .] [T]he Board never considered forming a committee of disinterested, independent directors to consider the *bona fides* of the Acquisition. It took that role upon itself, notwithstanding the obvious conflicts of its members [. . .].

3. The Board Level Conflicts

The question of whether a board is comprised of independent or disinterested directors is relevant to the controlling stockholder inquiry because the answer, in turn, will inform the court's determination of whether the board was free of the controller's influence such that it could exercise independent judgment in its decision-making. Even an independent, disinterested director can be dominated in his decision-making by a controlling stockholder. [. . .]

In this case, the Board did not form a special committee to consider the transaction, and it is reasonably conceivable that a majority of the five Board members who voted to approve the Offer and Acquisition [. . .] were interested in the Acquisition or not independent of Musk. Tesla's SEC filings concede Buss and Kimbal are not independent directors. [. . .] DFJ, Jurvetson's venture capital firm, has invested in Tesla three times between 2006 and 2008, and held Tesla stock as recently as late 2014. [. . .] And Jurvetson himself owned 417,450 shares of SolarCity common stock as of the Acquisition.

In addition to the Board level conflicts [. . .] the Company paid approximately $2.6 billion in Tesla stock to acquire SolarCity, a severely distressed company on the brink of bankruptcy but for the Acquisition. [. . .]

4.   Musk and Tesla Acknowledge Musk's Influence

[. . .] Plaintiffs argue that Tesla and Musk himself have made similar concessions of Musk's powerful influence over the Company and its Board. [. . .]

[N]either Tesla nor Musk have expressly conceded that Musk is a controlling stockholder. [. . .] The public acknowledgements of Musk's substantially outsized influence, however, do bear on the controlling stockholder inquiry when coupled with the other well-pled allegations of Musk's control over the Company and its Board.

[. . .] Specifically, the combination of well-pled facts relating to Musk's voting influence, his domination of the Board during the process leading up to the Acquisition against the backdrop of his extraordinary influence within the Company generally, the Board level conflicts that diminished the Board's resistance to Musk's influence, and the Company's and Musk's own acknowledgements of his outsized influence, all told, satisfy Plaintiffs' burden to plead that Musk's status as a Tesla controlling stockholder is reasonably conceivable. [. . .]

III. CONCLUSION

For the foregoing reasons, Defendants' motion to dismiss is DENIED. [. . .]

Tornetta v. Musk

250 A.3d 793 (Del. Ch. 2019)

■ SLIGHTS, VICE CHANCELLOR.

In January 2018, Tesla, Inc.'s board of directors (the "Board") approved an incentive-based compensation plan for its chief executive officer, Elon Musk, called the 2018 Performance Award (the "Award"). The Board then submitted the Award to Tesla's stockholders for approval. The stockholders who voted at the specially called meeting overwhelmingly approved the Award and Tesla implemented it thereafter. A Tesla stockholder has brought direct and derivative claims against Musk and members of the Board alleging the Award is excessive and the product of breaches of fiduciary duty. Defendants move to dismiss under Court of Chancery Rule 12(b)(6).

A board of directors' decision to fix the compensation of the company's executive officers is about as work-a-day as board decisions get. It is a decision entitled to great judicial deference. When the board submits its decision to grant executive incentive compensation to stockholders for approval, and secures that approval, the decision typically is entitled to even greater deference. But this is not a typical case. Plaintiff has well pled that Musk, the beneficiary of the Award, is also Tesla's controlling stockholder. And the size of the Award is extraordinary; it allows Musk the potential to earn stock options with a value upwards of $55.8 billion.

Defendants' motion to dismiss presents the gating question that frequently dictates the pleadings stage disposition of a breach of fiduciary duty claim: under what standard of review will the court adjudicate the claim? If the court reviews the fiduciary conduct under the deferential business judgment rule, the claim is unlikely to proceed beyond the proverbial starting line. If, on the other hand, the court reviews the conduct under the entire fairness standard, the claim is likely to proceed at least through discovery, if not trial. Given the high stakes and costs of corporate fiduciary duty litigation, defendants understandably are prone to call the "standard of review" question at the earliest opportunity, usually at the pleadings stage.

In this case, the standard of review question presents issues of first impression in Delaware. On the one hand, as noted, board decisions to award executive compensation are given great deference under our law, particularly when approved by unaffiliated stockholders. On the other hand, as pled, the Award is a transaction with a conflicted controlling stockholder and, as such, it ought to provoke heightened judicial suspicion.

Defendants maintain the stockholder vote approving the Award ratified the Board's decision to adopt it and thereby ratcheted any heightened scrutiny of the Award that might be justified down to business judgment review. By Defendants' lights, Plaintiff's only legally viable claim is waste, which he has not adequately pled. In response, Plaintiff argues stockholder ratification cannot alter the standard of review with respect to conflicted controller transactions. The only possible exception to this proposition Plaintiff will acknowledge is that Defendants might have avoided entire fairness review had they implemented the dual protections outlined in the seminal *In re MFW Shareholders Litigation*. Defendants admittedly did not follow the *MFW* roadmap. And they reject any suggestion they were required to do so in order to earn business judgment deference. According to Defendants, any such requirement would extend *MFW* beyond its intended bounds and ignore the Delaware law of stockholder ratification.

This court's earnest deference to board determinations relating to executive compensation does not jibe with our reflexive suspicion when a board transacts with a controlling stockholder. Delaware courts have long recognized the risks to sound corporate governance posed by conflicted controllers and generally review these transactions for entire fairness. This doctrinal suspicion has its costs, however. A rule holding corporate fiduciaries personally accountable for *all* transactions with conflicted controllers *unless* the fiduciaries demonstrate the transaction is entirely fair will necessarily suppress at least some beneficial transactions.

This tension was front and center in *MFW*, albeit in the context of a transformational transaction, and the court resolved it by approving a process whereby consummation of the transaction is conditioned from the beginning on the informed and impartial approval of decision makers at both the board and stockholder levels. As the court explained, preserving the integrity of the decisions at both levels in the conflicted controller context is key to allaying the court's suspicions such that our preference for presumptive deference can be restored. . .

MFW addressed a post-closing stockholder challenge to a freeze-out merger, and neither the Court of Chancery nor the Supreme Court provided any indication their holdings were intended to apply outside of that context. Subsequent decisions of this court, however, have applied the *MFW* framework to controller transactions involving the sale of a company to a third party and a stock reclassification. In both cases, however, as Defendants observe, the transactions at issue "fundamentally alter[ed] the corporate contract" and, therefore, were subject by statute to approval by both the board of directors and a majority of outstanding shares entitled to vote. Indeed, this is the line Defendants would have the Court draw in delineating *MFW*'s reach; the dual protections endorsed by *MFW* should be required to earn business judgment deference only with respect to transformational conflicted controller transactions where the Delaware General Corporation Law requires the approval of both the corporation's managers and owners.

There is symmetry in Defendants' view of *MFW*. If a controlling stockholder seeks to draw the corporation into a transaction that, by statute, cannot be consummated without the approval of both the board and the stockholders, then it makes sense to require the controller to condition consummation on the informed approval of both independent board members and unaffiliated stockholders if he wishes to secure our law's most deferential standard of review at the threshold. But does it make sense to impose those same dual protections on the controller and the board as a predicate to application of the business judgment rule in instances where the DGCL does not require both board and stockholder approval? Or, should the fiduciaries in that context be able to trigger business judgment review through traditional stockholder ratification?

To answer this question, I have returned to first principles. In instances where the beneficiary of a transaction is a controlling stockholder, [as Chief Justice Strine wrote in a case and in a law review article,] "there is an obvious fear that even putatively independent directors may owe or feel a more-than-wholesome allegiance to the interests of the controller, rather than to the corporation and its public stockholders." Because the conflicted controller, as the "800-pound gorilla," is able to exert coercive influence over the board and unaffiliated stockholders, "our law has required that [ ] transaction[s] [with conflicted controllers] be reviewed for substantive fairness even if the transaction was negotiated by independent directors or approved by the minority stockholders." In these circumstances, stockholder approval of the conflicted controller transaction, alone, will not justify business judgment deference.

The controlling stockholder's potentially coercive influence is no less present, and no less consequential, in instances where the board is negotiating the controlling stockholder's compensation than it is when the board is negotiating with the controller to effect a "transformational" transaction. In my view, stockholder ratification, without more, does not counterpoise the risk of coercion in either context.

Having determined entire fairness is the standard by which the Award must be reviewed, it is appropriate to consider whether, in circumstances like this, the Board could have structured the approval process leading to the Award in a way that provides a "feasible way for defendants to get [cases] dismissed on the pleadings." As I see it, *MFW* provides the answer. In this regard, I share Defendants' view that neither the Chancery nor Supreme Court opinions in *MFW* can be read to endorse an application of *MFW* beyond the squeeze-out merger. But that does not mean *MFW*'s dual protections cannot be potent neutralizers in other applications. In this case, had the Board conditioned the consummation of the Award upon the approval of an independent, fully-functioning committee of the Board and a statutorily compliant vote of a majority of the unaffiliated stockholders, the Court's suspicions regarding the controller's influence would have been assuaged and deference to the Board and stock- holder decisions would have been justified. As that did not happen here, Defendants' motion to dismiss the breach of fiduciary duty claims must be denied.

I.   BACKGROUND

A.   The Parties

Nominal Defendant, Tesla, is a public Delaware corporation headquartered in Palo Alto, California. It designs, manufactures and sells electric vehicles and energy storage systems.

At the time the Complaint was filed, Tesla's Board comprised nine members: Musk, Kimbal Musk, Antonio J. Gracias, Stephen T. Jurvetson, Ira Ehrenpreis, Brad W. Buss, Robyn M. Denholm, James Murdoch and Linda Johnson Rice. The members of the Board's Compensation Committee at the time of the Award were Ehrenpreis (Chair), Gracias, Denholm and Buss.

Defendant, Musk, is Tesla's largest stockholder. At the time the Award was approved, Musk owned approximately 21.9% of Tesla's common stock and served as Tesla's Chairman (from April 2004 until September 2018), CEO (since October 2008) and Chief Product Architect. For purposes of this motion to dismiss only, it is not disputed Plaintiff has well pled that Musk is Tesla's controlling stockholder.

In addition to his roles at Tesla, Musk is the majority shareholder, Chairman, CEO and Chief Technology Officer of Space Exploration Technologies Corporation ("SpaceX"), a private company that develops and launches rockets to deliver commercial satellites into space. SpaceX plans, eventually, to deliver humans to space as well. It is alleged SpaceX is one of the world's most valuable private companies.

B. Musk's Historical Compensation as CEO

Musk assumed his role as Tesla's CEO in 2008 and, at that time, was paid $1 per year annual salary with no equity compensation. In December 2009, Musk was awarded options that vested on a three-year schedule contingent on his continued service with Tesla. He also received options contingent on achieving certain operating milestones. After Tesla's initial public offering in 2010, Musk continued to receive $1 in annual salary with no equity awards in that year or in 2011.

In 2012, Musk had nearly reached all the operational milestones set for him in the 2009 option grant. With this in mind, the Compensation Committee retained an outside consultant to review Musk's compensation. Following its review, the Compensation Committee recommended, and the Board adopted, an entirely performance-based option award for Musk (the "2012 Award").

The 2012 Award consisted of ten tranches of stock options, each tranche representing 0.5% of Tesla's shares outstanding on the date of the grant. The vesting of each tranche was entirely contingent on Tesla achieving both a market capitalization milestone and an operational milestone. If the milestones were missed, Musk received nothing. The 2012 Award had a ten year term; if a tranche did not vest within the term, it would expire.

Each of the ten market capitalization milestones in the 2012 Award required an increase of $4 billion in Tesla's market capitalization, compared to Tesla's market capitalization of $3.2 billion when the award was granted. The operational milestones included producing and designing new vehicle models, increasing production of an existing vehicle (Tesla's Model S) and increasing gross margin. Within five years of the Board approving the 2012 Award, Tesla had achieved all of the market capitalization milestones and was on the verge of reaching all but one of the operational milestones.

C. The 2018 Performance Award

As 2018 approached, the Compensation Committee realized a new compensation package for Musk would soon be necessary. Accordingly, it retained outside counsel and Compensia, the same executive compensation firm that assisted in the design of the 2012 Award, to review Musk's compensation. In considering a new package, the Compensation Committee also solicited the advice of Tesla's other directors (excluding Kimbal Musk).

The Compensation Committee was faced with a difficult question: how to keep Musk focused on Tesla given his other business interests. By 2017, SpaceX was among the largest private companies in the world and Musk played an active role in SpaceX's management. The Compensation Committee viewed Musk as instrumental to Tesla's success and keeping him locked in on Tesla was a top priority.

Using the 2012 Award as a model, the Compensation Committee began crafting a new compensation package in mid-2017. The Compensation Committee proposed a 10-year grant of stock options that would vest in twelve tranches, again contingent upon reaching market capitalization and operational milestones. After conferring with Tesla's largest institutional investors, the company tied the operational milestones to increases in total revenue and adjusted EBITDA.

Over a series of meetings in 2017, the Compensation Committee and Musk negotiated the milestones at which the options would vest, the overall size of the grant and how share dilution would affect the Award. The full Board approved the Award at its January 2018 meeting.

Each of the Award's market capitalization milestones requires a $50 billion increase in Tesla's market capitalization. Reaching the first market capitalization milestone would roughly double Tesla's market capitalization as of the date the Award was approved, and reaching all 12 would likely make Tesla one of the most valuable public companies in the world. The Award's annual revenue milestones range from $20 billion to $175 billion, and the adjusted EBITDA milestones range from $1.5 billion to $14 billion.

Upon reaching the twin milestones corresponding to each tranche of the Award, options held by Musk representing 1% of Tesla's current total outstanding shares will vest. By tying the shares Musk receives to outstanding shares at the time of the grant, as opposed to 1% of the fully diluted shares at the time of vesting, the cost of dilution is born by Musk. The Award restricts Musk's ability to sell vested shares for five years, tying him more closely to Tesla. Any options that do not vest within ten years are forfeited, and no options will vest if, at the time the relevant milestone is met, Musk is not serving as either CEO or both Executive Chairman and Chief Product Officer with the CEO reporting directly to him. The Award also provides that milestones will be adjusted if Tesla makes acquisitions having a material impact on reaching any milestone, ensuring the milestones will be met through organic growth, not acquisitions.

If none of the tranches of options vest, Musk will earn nothing under the Award. Alternatively, if every market capitalization and operational milestone is reached, options will vest with a maximum potential value of $55.8 billion. Tesla estimated the Award's preliminary aggregate fair value at $2.615 billion on its proxy statement.

D. The 2018 Stockholder Vote

The Board conditioned implementation of the Award on the approval of a majority of the disinterested shares voting at a March 21, 2018, special meeting of Tesla stockholders. On February 8, 2018, Tesla submitted its proxy statement describing the Award and recommending that shareholders vote to approve it. The proxy statement described the Award in detail and expressly conditioned its approval on receiving a majority vote of the shares not owned by Musk or Kimbal Musk. It explained that a failure to vote (assuming a quorum was present at the meeting) would not be counted as a no vote (as it would for a vote on a merger), but instead would have no effect on the vote.

The Award was approved by the shareholders, with 81% of voting shares and 80% of shares present and entitled to vote cast in favor. At the final tally, 73% of disinterested shares at the meeting (those not affiliated with either Musk or Kimbal Musk) voted in favor of the Award. This equated to approximately 47% of the total disinterested shares outstanding.

E. Procedural History

[. . .] Plaintiff filed his Complaint in which he asserts [. . .]: a direct and derivative claim for breach of fiduciary duty against Musk in his capacity as Tesla's controlling shareholder for causing Tesla to adopt the Award; a direct and derivative claim for breach of fiduciary duty against the Director Defendants for approving the Award; [. . .and] a derivative claim for waste against the Director Defendants.

On August 30, 2018, Defendants filed a motion to dismiss the Complaint under Court of Chancery Rule 12(b)(6). The Court heard argument on May 9, 2019.

II. ANALYSIS

A. The Fiduciary Duty Claims

I resolve Defendants' motion to dismiss the breach of fiduciary duty claims in two parts. First, I address the proper standard of review. As explained below, I conclude entire fairness is the applicable standard at this pleadings stage given Plaintiff's well-pled allegations. Next, I address whether Plaintiff has stated viable breach of fiduciary duty claims as viewed through the lens of entire fairness, and conclude he has.

1. The Standard of Review

As in nearly all pleadings stage challenges to the viability of a breach of fiduciary duty claim in the corporate context, deciding the proper standard of review in this case will be outcome determinative. In this regard, Defendants urge the Court to keep its sights trained on the nature of the decision at issue here, and for good reason. A board's decision to grant executive compensation is usually entitled to "great deference." But Defendants acknowledge (for purposes of this motion only) that Musk is a controlling shareholder and that he dominated the Board and the Compensation Committee during the time the Award was negotiated and approved. Thus, in the absence of stockholder ratification, Defendants acknowledge (for purposes of this motion only) that the Court must review the Award for entire fairness.

Citing seminal Delaware authority, however, Defendants maintain the Court must review the Award under the business judgment rule because Tesla's stockholders have overwhelmingly approved all aspects of Musk's compensation. Plaintiff disagrees on two grounds. First, he argues the stockholder vote was structurally inadequate to ratify breaches of fiduciary duty because a majority of all outstanding disinterested shares did not vote to approve the Award. Second, he argues even if the vote might otherwise be adequate to ratify the Award, it cannot, as a matter of equity, ratify an incentive compensation plan where the company's controlling stockholder is the beneficiary. I address the arguments in turn.

a.   The Structure of the Vote

According to Plaintiff, the 2018 stockholder vote approving the Award did not produce ratifying effects because "Delaware law is clear that the 'cleansing effect of ratification' requires the *affirmative* approval of a majority of *all* disinterested shares, not a mere majority of whatever subset of disinterested shares actually votes." Defendants make two points in response, both persuasive.

First, Plaintiff's principal supporting authority, *PNB*, involved a cash-out merger where, by statute, the stockholder vote required to approve the transaction was an affirmative vote of the majority of all outstanding shares. No such statutory requirement existed with respect to the Award.

Defendants' second point expands on their first. Tesla submitted the Award for stockholder approval in accordance with the statute that governs stockholder votes on non-extraordinary stockholder action, like approval of executive compensation plans. Section 216 of the Delaware General Corporation Law (titled "Quorum and required vote for stock corporations") prescribes the default requirements a stockholder vote must meet to approve a corporate action when the DGCL does not otherwise dictate a different voting structure for a "specified action." Section 216(1) sets the default minimum for a quorum:

(1)   A majority of the shares entitled to vote, present in person or represented by proxy, shall constitute a quorum at a meeting of stockholders. And Section 216(2) sets the default minimum for the affirmative voting threshold:

(2)   In all matters other than the election of directors, the affirmative vote of the majority of shares present in person or represented by proxy at the meeting and entitled to vote on the subject matter shall be the act of the stockholders.

When a stockholder vote governed by Section 216 meets the prescribed quorum and voting requirements, the outcome "shall be the act of the stockholders," even though the number of shares voted in favor of the corporate action at issue may have been less than a majority of the outstanding shares entitled to vote.

The stockholder vote approving the Award fell under the default quorum and voting threshold requirements of Section 216 because no other provision of the DGCL dictates "the vote that shall be required for" the issuance of options or other compensation to directors or officers, and Tesla's charter and bylaws did not specify different requirements. And the vote clearly satisfied the statutory requirements: (1) a majority of Tesla's outstanding shares entitled to vote were present at the meeting, and (2) a majority of the shares present at the meeting and entitled to vote did, in fact, vote to approve the Award.

Given these undisputed facts, there is no basis to say the stockholder vote approving the Award did not produce a ratifying effect. The vote met the quorum and voting threshold requirements of Section 216 even when considering only the disinterested shares: (1) a majority (64%) of Tesla's outstanding disinterested shares entitled to vote were present at the meeting, and (2) a majority (73%) of those disinterested shares were voted in favor of the Award. In the ordinary course, therefore, the stockholder vote would justify business judgment deference.

b. Stockholder Ratification Does Not Justify Business Judgment Deference Because the Award Benefits a Conflicted Controller

In the realm of criminal jurisprudence, it is accepted that "death (capital punishment) is different." I suppose the same could be said of conflicted controller transactions in our corporate fiduciary jurisprudence; they are, in a word, "different." Our courts are steadfast in requiring corporate fiduciaries to prove entire fairness when a controller stands on both sides of a transaction. These cases range from squeeze-out mergers, to asset purchases, to consulting agreements. And when conflicted controllers are involved, our courts will not allow the controller to rely upon stockholder approval of the transaction at the pleadings stage to "cleanse" otherwise well-pled breaches of fiduciary duty.

Disparate treatment of controlling shareholder transactions makes good sense. It is settled in Delaware that stockholder votes will not ratify director action if there is "a showing that the structure or circumstances of the vote were impermissibly coercive." "The determination of whether coercion was in-equitable in a particular circumstance is a relationship-driven inquiry." And, without doubt, our law recognizes the relationship between a controlling stockholder and minority stockholders is fertile ground for potent coercion. Indeed, as our Supreme Court has observed:

> Even where no coercion is intended, shareholders voting on a parent subsidiary merger might perceive that their disapproval could risk retaliation of some kind by the controlling stockholder. . . . At the very least, the potential for that perception, and its possible impact upon a shareholder vote,

could never be fully eliminated. . . . Given that uncertainty, a court might well conclude that even minority shareholders who have ratified a . . . merger need procedural protections beyond . . . full disclosure of all material facts. *Kahn v. Lynch.*

In *Pure Resources*, then-Vice Chancellor Strine aptly described the controlling stockholder as an "800-pound gorilla whose urgent hunger for the rest of the bananas is likely to frighten . . . minority stockholders [who] would fear retribution from the gorilla if they defeated the merger and he did not get his way." Chancellor Allen called controlling shareholder transactions "the context in which the greatest risk of undetectable bias may be present. . . ."

Defendants acknowledge the threat of coercion inherent in conflicted controller transactions but argue the concern is less pressing, and less worthy of protection, in transactions, like the Award, that do not "alter the corporate contract." I disagree. While stockholders generally would have no reason to feel coerced when casting a non-binding, statutory Say on Pay vote, or when asked to approve a board-endorsed executive compensation plan, I discern no reason to think minority stockholders would feel any less coerced when voting against the controlling CEO's compensation plan than they would when voting to oppose a transformational transaction involving the controller. In both instances, minority stockholders would have reason to fear controller retribution, e.g., the controller "force[ing] a squeeze-out or cut[ting] dividends . . . ."

Indeed, in the CEO compensation context, the minority knows full well the CEO is staying with the company whether *vel non* his compensation plan is approved. As our Supreme Court observed in *Tremont II*:

> [I]n a transaction such as the one considered . . . the controlling shareholder will continue to dominate the company regardless of the outcome of the transaction. The risk is thus created that those who pass upon the propriety of the transaction might perceive that disapproval may result in retaliation by the controlling shareholder.

These words apply with equal force to the compensation setting.

Having found no principled basis to distinguish the coercive implications of controller compensation transactions from other (even transformational) conflicted controller transactions, I can find no basis to conclude, on the pleadings, that the stockholder vote approving the Award would not be subject to the coercive forces inherent in controlling stockholder transactions. Since Plaintiff has well pled the Compensation Committee and Board processes with respect to the Award were also subject to the controller's coercive influence, at this stage, I must conclude the Award was not duly approved by either of Tesla's qualified decision makers. Entire fairness, therefore, is the appropriate standard of review at this pleadings stage.

c. What is a Controlling Stockholder/CEO to Do?

Our law recognizes the costs and downstream implications of fiduciary litigation in the corporate context and has provided road maps to avoid such consequences. [. . .] *MFW* provides a roadmap that allows fiduciaries to engage in conflicted controller transactions worthy of pleadings stage business judgment deference. In the conflicted controller context, in particular, *MFW*'s "dual protections" are meant to "neutralize" the conflicted controller's "presumptively coercive influence" so that judicial second-guessing is no longer required.

Defendants see no place for *MFW* here. They rely heavily on a "statutory rubric" argument, claiming *MFW*'s dual protections, devised in the context of a squeeze-out merger, mimic the approvals required by 8 *Del C.* § 251 but have no practical application to transactions where our law does not mandate approval at both the board and stockholder levels. [. . .]

[. . .] I do agree with Defendants that nothing in *MFW* or its progeny would suggest the Supreme Court intended to extend the holding to other transactions involving controlling stockholders. That does not mean, however, that *MFW*'s dual protections cannot provide useful safeguards here. Just as in the squeeze-out context, preconditioning a controller's compensation package on both the approval of a fully functioning, independent committee *and* an informed, uncoerced vote of the majority of the minority stockholders will dilute the looming coercive influence of the controller. With *MFW*'s dual protections in place, the minority stockholders can cast their votes knowing the controller has agreed at the outset to negotiate his compensation award with an independent, fully functioning committee of the board, to condition consummation of the award on that committee's endorsement, and to allow the unaffiliated stockholders to have the final say. Under these circumstances, the minority stockholders have far less reason to fear that the controller will retaliate if the committee or minority stockholder votes do not go his way.

Had the Board ensured from the outset of "substantive economic negotiations" that both of Tesla's qualified decision makers—an independent, fully functioning Compensation Committee *and* the minority stockholders—were able to engage in an informed review of the Award, followed by meaningful (i.e., otherwise uncoerced) approval, the Court's reflexive suspicion of Musk's coercive influence over the outcome would be abated. Business judgment deference at the pleadings stage would then be justified. Plaintiff has well pled, however, that the Board level review was not divorced from Musk's influence. Entire fairness, therefore, must abide.

2. Plaintiff Has Adequately Pled the Award Was Not Entirely Fair

[. . .] As things stand, Plaintiff is obliged to plead and prove the Award was not the "product of both fair dealing and fair price." "Often, whether the price paid in a transaction was fair is the 'paramount concern.'"

Because this inquiry is fact intensive, it is rare the court will dismiss a fiduciary duty claim on a Rule 12(b)(6) motion when entire fairness is the governing standard of review.

While Plaintiff alleges both unfair process and unfair price, his focus, not surprisingly, is on the Award's unfair price. Specifically, Plaintiff alleges the Award has a potential value that is orders of magnitude higher than what other highly paid CEOs earn. According to Plaintiff, the "fair value estimate of the Plan" is either $2.6 billion or $3.7 billion, dwarfing the compensation of "the world's most successful technology executives." While Defendants dispute Plaintiff's calculation of the Award's present value, it is reasonably conceivable the present fair value of the Award is, as Plaintiff alleges, well in excess of that paid to Musk's peers.

Defendants urge me to consider that the Award is entirely performance based and aligns Musk's incentives with those of the other stockholders. This is particularly important, say Defendants, since Musk has several other business interests, including SpaceX, that might distract him from his work at Tesla. Moreover, given the extraordinary market capitalization and performance milestones built into the Award, Defendants observe it is quite possible Musk will never see the full value of the Award. On the other hand, if Musk leads Tesla to achieve the milestones, then Tesla will be one of the most valuable companies in the world and all stakeholders will have reaped the benefits of Musk's incentivized focus. These are all factors I would consider, if uncontested, on summary judgment or, if contested, at trial. Indeed, they may well carry the day in those contexts. But, on the pled facts, albeit lodged on the "very outer margins of adequacy," it is reasonably conceivable the Award is unfair. Accordingly, Defendant's motion to dismiss Counts I & II must be denied. [. . .]

D. The Waste Claim

Plaintiff also alleges the Award is "so one-sided that no person acting in good faith pursuant to Tesla's interests could have approved its terms." Not coincidentally, Plaintiff's waste allegations, summarily pled, mirror the standard for waste, where the plaintiff "must allege facts showing that no person of ordinary sound business judgment could view the benefits received in the transaction as a fair exchange for the consideration paid by the corporation."

While Plaintiff has adequately pled the Award is unfair, "[t]he pleading burden on a plaintiff attacking a corporate transaction as wasteful is necessarily higher than that of a plaintiff challenging a transaction as 'unfair.'" This is especially so with respect to the Award given that the majority of disinterested stockholders voting at the special meeting approved the Award, and our law recognizes as axiomatic, even on the pleadings, "that stockholders would be unlikely to approve a transaction that is wasteful." The well-pled facts fail to support a reasonable inference that no person of "ordinary sound business judgment" would have granted the Award, a fact made even more clear in the light of the informed stockholder vote that approved it. Defendant's motion to dismiss Count IV is granted.

III. CONCLUSION

For the foregoing reasons, the motion to dismiss is DENIED as to Counts I, II and III, and GRANTED as to Count IV.

G. REVIEW PROBLEMS

1. In *In re Columbia Pipeline Grp., Inc.*, an exculpatory provision in the corporation's charter limited directors' liability under § 102(b)(7). The court considered the personal liability of defendants Skaggs and Smith, the CEO and CFO of NiSource (Columbia's parent company), for allegedly breaching their fiduciary duties in merger-related dealings with TransCanada. The defendants filed a motion to dismiss for failure to state a claim. The success of the defendants' motion to dismiss depended on whether the plaintiffs pleaded claims that were exculpated under § 102(b)(7), including claims against directors or claims of duty of care breaches, or non-exculpated claims, which cannot be dismissed at the pleading stage regardless of any exculpatory provisions in the charter.[1]

   The court considered the following facts to determine whether to grant the defendants' motion to dismiss:

   - The CEO and CFO had potentially conflicting interests, namely their plans to sell NiSource before their anticipated retirement so that they could retire with "materially greater" change-of-control benefits.

   - A January 7 meeting with TransCanada's representative, during which Smith (NiSource's CFO) invited a bid and told TransCanada's rep that it did not face competition. The court explained that Smith's statements and TransCanada's bid in response breached the standstill provision, which prohibited TransCanada from making an offer to purchase the company without a written invitation from the board.

   - The defendants' "material misstatements" to the board about their dealings with TransCanada that, according to the plaintiffs, undermined the Company's ability to extract a higher price from TransCanada.

   - The plaintiffs claimed that the defendants favored TransCanada with exclusivity after periods of exclusivity had expired, which was disadvantageous to other bidders during merger negotiations.

     (a) Considering each of these facts, which fiduciary duty did the CEO or CFO breach (duty of care, duty of loyalty,

---

[1] *See* In re Columbia Pipeline Grp., Inc., No. CV 2018–0484–JTL, 2021 WL 772562 (Del. Ch. Mar. 1, 2021).

obligation of good faith)? Consider their potential breaches separately.

(b) Does the corporation's exculpatory provision shield Skaggs from liability for his actions in his capacity as NiSource's CEO? *Hint*: do directors and officers have the same liability under § 102(b)(7)?

(c) If Skaggs and Smith had acted as directors rather than as officers, which facts might support personal liability (non-exculpation) or limited liability (exculpation) for money damages owed to shareholders or to the corporation? *Hint*: which facts support or weigh against a finding that Skaggs or Smith breached his duty of loyalty?

2. Pritchard and Baird had three directors: Lillian Pritchard and her sons Charles and William. The corporate minutes reflect perfunctory activities by the directors. Contrary to the industry custom of segregating funds, P&B comingled funds extensively and engaged in a variety of non-standard financial practices. In particular, Charles and William caused P&B to loan money to each of them in amounts far exceeding their salaries, totaling about $12 million (in 1970s dollars). When P&B went bankrupt, Lillian was sued for breach of the duty of care. She did not engage at all in her work as a director: she knew virtually nothing of the corporation or its affairs, visited its office only once, and never sought or read its annual financial filings. Lillian, in her defense, argued that she was elderly and infirm, especially after the recent death of her husband. Further, she argued that she could not be found liable for breach of the duty of care because she did not fail in the performance of her duties—instead, she did not perform her duties at all. What is a court likely to find?[28]

3. Celanese Corporation decided to produce a series of radio advertisements featuring refined music. The directors had an informal discussion about the new advertisements, after which one director decided to consult his wife, Jean, who is "a singer of wide experience." With the management's approval, Jean then spoke to Celanese's advertising agency, suggesting several singers while also offering her own services. The ad agency hired all of the suggested singers, including Jean herself, paying them each market rates. A stockholder sued the directors, alleging that the hiring of Jean is a conflict of interest. The stockholder also argued that the conflict was exacerbated by the fact that the directors did not have a formal meeting about the matter. What is the likely result? And what actions should have been taken to conform with best practices?[29]

4. Plaintiffs—a group of stockholders—wish to sue Boeing's board in a derivative suit. They allege that Boeing rushed its development of the 737 MAX airplane, including resolving a serious mechanical issue by installing questionable software that ended up causing two fatal

---

[28] *See* Francis v. United Jersey Bank, 432 A.2d 814 (1981).
[29] *See* Bayer v. Beran, 39 N.Y.S.2d 2 (N.Y. Sup. Ct. 1944).

airplane crashes. During development of the plane and software, there were many red flags raised, including by the Federal Aviation Authority, Boeing's own analyses, and Boeing's employees. Some complaints made it to senior management, but none to the board. After the first crash, both the full board and a safety committee of the board met to review information from management. The Department of Justice opened a criminal investigation to determine whether the company had defrauded the FAA in obtaining certifications for the 737 MAX. Management assured the board that the plane and its software were safe, so the board decided not to conduct additional internal investigations. What duties, if any, did the board most likely breach?[30]

5.   McDonald's is one of the world's largest employers. Plaintiffs—a group of stockholders—have sued Fairhurst, the Company's Executive Vice President and Global Chief People Officer, for breach of fiduciary duties. Fairhurst, who served from 2015 until his termination with cause in 2019, was the executive officer with day-to-day responsibility for ensuring that the company provided its employees with a safe and respectful workplace. The plaintiffs allege that during his tenure, Fairhurst allowed a corporate culture to develop that condoned sexual harassment and misconduct. The complaint alleges that starting in late 2016, McDonald's faced public scrutiny over sexual harassment and misconduct. Subsequently, Fairhurst himself engaged in several acts of sexual harassment. Fairhurst was disciplined for a November 2018 incident, then terminated in November 2019 after he committed another act of sexual harassment. The complaint cites statements from employees who asserted that under Fairhurst's watch, the human resources department turned a blind eye to complaints about sexual harassment. In 2018, the Company faced a series of public issues relating to sexual harassment, including coordinated complaints filed by restaurant workers and a ten-city strike. Should the plaintiffs bring a direct or derivative suit? Does the *Caremark/Marchand* duty of oversight apply also to corporate officers? On what ground can Fairhurst be held accountable for a breach of fiduciary duty to McDonald's?[31]

6.   A group of McDonald's stockholders file a derivative suit against the corporate directors alleging that the company suffered harm in the form of employee lawsuits, lost employee trust, and a damaged reputation because directors knew about the sexual harassment problems that McDonalds's was facing and consciously ignored them. In particular, plaintiffs allege that the following events alerted the board to the threats to the company: (a) a wave of complaints filed with the Equal Employment Opportunity Commission alleging acts of sexual harassment and retaliation, (b) a ten-city employee strike, and (c) an inquiry from a U.S. Senator seeking to investigate the company's harassment and misconduct issues. Further, the directors knew that the company's head human resources officer was terminated for sexual

---

[30]   *See* In Re The Boeing Company Derivative Litigation, 2021 WL 4059934 (Del. Ch. 2021).

[31]   *See* In re McDonald's Corporation Stockholder Derivative Litigation, C.A. No. 2021-0324-JTL (Jan. 25, 2023).

harassment. They also worked with the company management on a response that included (a) hiring outside consultants, (b) revising the Company's policies, (c) implementing new training programs, (d) providing new levels of support to franchisees, and (e) taking other steps to establish a renewed commitment to a safe and respectful workplace. What are the directors' best arguments to successfully defend against the breach of duty of oversight?[32]

7. AmSouth Bancorporation is a Delaware corporation operating a banking business. AmSouth Bancorporation and its subsidiary AmSouth Bank were required to paid more than $50 millions in fines to resolve government and regulatory investigations relating to failures to comply with the Bank Secrecy Act and various anti-money laundering regulations. Two employees orchestrated a Ponzi scheme to defraud investors using on AmSouth Bank accounts. Stockholders of AmSouth Bancorporation filed a derivative suit against the directors of AmSouth Bancorporation, alleging a *Caremark* claim. If the defendant directors can show through expert reports that longstanding Bank Secrecy Act/anti-money laundering compliance programs were in place and that those programs were properly operated, how is a Delaware Court likely to decide the case?[33]

---

[32] *See* In re McDonald's Corporation Stockholder Derivative Litigation, C.A. No. 2021-0324-JTL (Mar. 1, 2023).

[33] *See* Stone v. Ritter, 911 A.2d 362 (Del. 2006).

CHAPTER VI

MERGERS AND ACQUISITIONS

A. MERGERS AND ACQUISITIONS DEFINED

Delaware General Corporation Law
Section 251. Merger or consolidation of domestic corporations.

(a) Any 2 or more corporations of this State may merge into a single surviving corporation, which may be any 1 of the constituent corporations or may consolidate into a new resulting corporation formed by the consolidation, pursuant to an agreement of merger or consolidation, as the case may be, complying and approved in accordance with this section.

(b) The board of directors of each corporation which desires to merge or consolidate shall adopt a resolution approving an agreement of merger or consolidation and declaring its advisability. [. . .]

(c) The agreement [. . .] shall be submitted to the stockholders of each constituent corporation at an annual or special meeting for the purpose of acting on the agreement. [. . .] If a majority of the outstanding stock of the corporation entitled to vote thereon shall be voted for the adoption of the agreement, that fact shall be certified on the agreement by the secretary or assistant secretary of the corporation, provided that such certification on the agreement shall not be required if a certificate of merger or consolidation is filed in lieu of filing the agreement. If the agreement shall be so adopted and certified by each constituent corporation, it shall then be filed and shall become effective, in accordance with § 103 of this title. [. . .]

(f) Notwithstanding the requirements of subsection (c) of this section, unless required by its certificate of incorporation, no vote of stockholders of a constituent corporation surviving a merger shall be necessary to authorize a merger if (1) the agreement of merger does not amend in any respect the certificate of incorporation of such constituent corporation, (2) each share of stock of such constituent corporation outstanding immediately prior to the effective date of the merger is to be an identical outstanding or treasury share of the surviving corporation after the effective date of the merger, and (3) either no shares of common stock of the surviving corporation and no shares, securities or obligations convertible into such stock are to be issued or delivered under the plan of merger, or the authorized unissued shares or the treasury shares of common stock of the surviving corporation to be issued or delivered under the plan of merger plus those initially issuable upon conversion of any other shares, securities or obligations to be issued or delivered under such plan do not exceed 20% of the shares of common stock of such constituent corporation outstanding immediately prior to the effective date of the merger. No vote of stockholders of a constituent corporation shall be necessary to authorize a merger or consolidation if no shares of the stock of such corporation shall have been issued prior to the adoption by the board of directors of the resolution approving the agreement of merger or consolidation. [. . .]

(h) Notwithstanding the requirements of subsection (c) of this section, unless expressly required by its certificate of incorporation, no vote of stockholders of a constituent corporation that has a class or series of stock that is listed on a national securities exchange or held of record by more than 2,000 holders immediately prior to the execution of the agreement of merger by such constituent corporation shall be necessary to authorize a merger if:

 (1) The agreement of merger expressly:

  a. Permits or requires such merger to be effected under this subsection; and

  b. Provides that such merger shall be effected as soon as practicable following the consummation of the offer referred to in paragraph (h)(2) of this section if such merger is effected under this subsection;

 (2) A corporation consummates an offer for all of the outstanding stock of such constituent corporation on the terms provided in such agreement of merger that, absent this subsection, would be entitled to vote on the adoption or rejection of the agreement of merger; provided, however, that such offer may be conditioned on the tender of a minimum number or percentage of shares of the stock of such constituent corporation, or of any class or series thereof, and such offer may exclude any excluded stock and provided further that the corporation may consummate separate offers for separate classes or series of the stock of such constituent corporation; [. . .]

 (3) Immediately following the consummation of the offer referred to in paragraph (h)(2) of this section, the stock irrevocably accepted for purchase or exchange pursuant to such offer and received by the depository prior to expiration of such offer, together with the stock otherwise owned by the consummating corporation or its affiliates and any rollover stock, equals at least such percentage of the shares of stock of such constituent corporation, and of each class or series thereof, that, absent this subsection, would be required to adopt the agreement of merger by this chapter and by the certificate of incorporation of such constituent corporation;

 (4) The corporation consummating the offer referred to in paragraph (h)(2) of this section merges with or into such constituent corporation pursuant to such agreement; and

 (5) Each outstanding share (other than shares of excluded stock) of each class or series of stock of such constituent corporation that is

the subject of and is not irrevocably accepted for purchase or exchange in the offer referred to in paragraph (h)(2) of this section is to be converted in such merger into, or into the right to receive, the same amount and kind of cash, property, rights or securities to be paid for shares of such class or series of stock of such constituent corporation irrevocably accepted for purchase or exchange in such offer.

(6)   As used in this section only, the term:

    a.   "Affiliate" means, in respect of the corporation making the offer referred to in paragraph (h)(2) of this section, any person that (i) owns, directly or indirectly, all of the outstanding stock of such corporation or (ii) is a direct or indirect wholly-owned subsidiary of such corporation or of any person referred to in clause (i) of this definition;

If an agreement of merger is adopted without the vote of stockholders of a corporation pursuant to this subsection, the secretary or assistant secretary of the surviving corporation shall certify on the agreement that the agreement has been adopted pursuant to this subsection and that the conditions specified in this subsection (other than the condition listed in paragraph (h)(4) of this section) have been satisfied; provided that such certification on the agreement shall not be required if a certificate of merger is filed in lieu of filing the agreement. The agreement so adopted and certified shall then be filed and shall become effective, in accordance with § 103 of this title. Such filing shall constitute a representation by the person who executes the agreement that the facts stated in the certificate remain true immediately prior to such filing.

Section 259. Status, rights, liabilities, of constituent and surviving or resulting corporations following merger or consolidation.

(a)   When any merger or consolidation shall have become effective under this chapter, for all purposes of the laws of this State the separate existence of all the constituent corporations, or of all such constituent corporations except the one into which the other or others of such constituent corporations have been merged, as the case may be, shall cease and the constituent corporations shall become a new corporation, or be merged into 1 of such corporations, as the case may be, possessing all the rights, privileges, powers and franchises as well of a public as of a private nature, and being subject to all the restrictions, disabilities and duties of each of such corporations so merged or consolidated [. . .]

Section 262. Appraisal rights.

(a) Any stockholder of a corporation of this State who holds shares of stock on the date of the making of a demand pursuant to subsection (d) of this section with respect to such shares, who continuously holds such shares through the effective date of the merger, consolidation, or conversion, who has otherwise complied with subsection (d) of this section and who has neither voted in favor of the merger, consolidation or conversion nor consented thereto in writing pursuant to § 228 of this title shall be entitled to an appraisal by the Court of Chancery of the fair value of the stockholder's shares of stock under the circumstances described in subsections (b) and (c) of this section. [. . .]

Section 271. Sale, lease or exchange of assets; consideration; procedure.

(a) Every corporation may at any meeting of its board of directors or governing body sell, lease or exchange all or substantially all of its property and assets, including its goodwill and its corporate franchises, [. . .] as its board of directors or governing body deems expedient and for the best interests of the corporation when and as authorized by a resolution adopted by the holders of a majority of the outstanding stock of the corporation entitled to vote thereon [. . .].

B. DEAL STRUCTURES

Hariton v. Arco Electronics, Inc.

188 A.2d 123 (Del. Ch. 1963)

■ SOUTHERLAND, CHIEF JUSTICE.

This case involves a sale of assets under § 271 of the corporation law, 8 Del. C. It presents for decision the question presented, but not decided, in *Heilbrunn v. Sun Chemical Corporation*. It may be stated as follows:

> A sale of assets is effected under § 271 in consideration of shares of stock of the purchasing corporation. The agreement of sale embodies also a plan to dissolve the selling corporation and distribute the shares so received to the stockholders of the seller, so as to accomplish the same result as would be accomplished by a merger of the seller into the purchaser. Is the sale legal?

The facts are these:

The defendant Arco and Loral Electronics Corporation, a New York corporation, are both engaged, in somewhat different forms, in the electronic equipment business. In the summer of 1961 they negotiated for an amalgamation of the companies. As of October 27, 1961, they entered into a 'Reorganization Agreement and Plan.' The provisions of this Plan pertinent here are in substance as follows:

> 1.   Arco agrees to sell all its assets to Loral in consideration (inter alia) of the issuance to it of 283,000 shares of Loral.
>
> 2.   Arco agrees to call a stockholders meeting for the purpose of approving the Plan and the voluntary dissolution.

> 3.   Arco agrees to distribute to its stockholders all the Loral shares received by it as a part of the complete liquidation of Arco.

At the Arco meeting all the stockholders voting (about 80%) approved the Plan. It was thereafter consummated.

Plaintiff, a stockholder who did not vote at the meeting, sued to enjoin the consummation of the Plan on the grounds (1) that it was illegal, and (2) that it was unfair. The second ground was abandoned. Affidavits and documentary evidence were filed, and defendant moved for summary judgment and dismissal of the complaint. The Vice Chancellor granted the motion and plaintiff appeals.

The question before us we have stated above. Plaintiff's argument that the sale is illegal runs as follows:

> The several steps taken here accomplish the same result as a merger of Arco into Loral. In a "true" sale of assets, the stockholder of the seller retains the right to elect whether the selling company shall continue as a holding company. Moreover, the stockholder of the selling company is forced to accept an investment in a new enterprise without the right of appraisal granted under the merger statute. § 271 cannot therefore be legally combined with a dissolution proceeding under § 275 and a consequent distribution of the purchaser's stock. Such a proceeding is a misuse of the power granted under § 271, and a *de facto* merger results.

The foregoing is a brief summary of plaintiff's contention.

Plaintiff's contention that this sale has achieved the same result as a merger is plainly correct. The same contention was made to us in *Heilbrunn*. Accepting it as correct, we noted that this result is made possible by the overlapping scope of the merger statute and section 271, mentioned in *Sterling v. Mayflower Hotel Corp*. We also adverted to the increased use, in connection with corporate reorganization plans, of § 271 instead of the merger statute. Further, we observed that no Delaware case has held such procedure to be improper, and that two cases appear to assume its legality. *Finch v. Warrior Cement Corporation*, and *Argenbright v. Phoenix Finance Co*. But we were not required in the Heilbrunn case to decide the point.

We now hold that the reorganization here accomplished through § 271 and a mandatory plan of dissolution and distribution is legal. This is so because the sale-of-assets statute and the merger statute are independent of each other. They are, so to speak, of equal dignity, and the framers of a reorganization plan may resort to either type of corporate mechanics to achieve the desired end. This is not an anomalous result in our corporation law. As the Vice Chancellor pointed out, the elimination of accrued dividends, though forbidden under a charter amendment

(*Keller v. Wilson & Co.*) may be accomplished by a merger. *Federal United Corporation v. Havender.* [. . .]

Plaintiff concedes, as we read his brief, that if the several steps taken in this case had been taken separately they would have been legal. That is, he concedes that a sale of assets, followed by a separate proceeding to dissolve and distribute, would be legal, even though the same result would follow. This concession exposes the weakness of his contention. To attempt to make any such distinction between sales under § 271 would be to create uncertainty in the law and invite litigation.

We are in accord with the Vice Chancellor's ruling, and the judgment below is affirmed.

Gimbel v. Signal Companies, Inc.

316 A.2d 619 (Del. Ch. 1974)

■ QUILLEN, CHANCELLOR:

Facts

This action was commenced on December 24, 1973 by plaintiff, a stockholder of the Signal Companies, Inc. ("Signal"). The complaint seeks, among other things, injunctive relief to prevent the consummation of the pending sale by Signal to Burmah Oil Incorporated ("Burmah") of all of the outstanding capital stock of Signal Oil and Gas Company ("Signal Oil"), a wholly-owned subsidiary of Signal. The effective sale price exceeds 480 million dollars. The sale was approved at a special meeting of the Board of Directors of Signal held on December 21, 1973.

The agreement provides that the transaction will be consummated on January 15, 1974 or upon the obtaining of the necessary governmental consents, whichever occurs later, but, in no event, after February 15, 1974 unless mutually agreed. The consents evidently have been obtained. On Monday, December 24, 1973, on the occasion of the plaintiff's application for a temporary restraining order, counsel for Signal and Signal Oil reported to this Court that the parties would not consummate this transaction prior to this Court's decision on the plaintiff's application for a preliminary injunction or January 15, 1974, whichever should occur first.

In light of that representation, no temporary restraining order was entered and the matter was set down for a hearing on plaintiff's application for a preliminary injunction [. . .]. This is the Court's decision on plaintiff's application for a preliminary injunction to prevent the sale of Signal Oil to Burmah pending trial on the merits of plaintiff's contentions.

Standard

In applying the law to the transaction in question, the Court believes it is first desirable to review the standards for a preliminary injunction . . . . In exercising its discretion, the Court must ask itself two familiar questions, which have long constituted the backdrop for evaluating the merits of any plaintiff's plea for a preliminary injunction. Stated briefly, the first question is: 'Has the plaintiff satisfied the Court that there is a reasonable probability of his ultimate success on final hearing?' ... The second question can be stated as follows: 'Has the plaintiff satisfied the Court that he will suffer irreparable injury if the Court fails to issue the requested preliminary injunction?' [. . .] Moreover, this second question of irreparable injury to the plaintiff should injunctive relief be denied has a corollary which requires the Court to consider potential hardship to the defendant [. . .].

Partly because of the enormous amount of money involved in this case, it is easy to discuss the irreparable injury aspect. From the plaintiff's point of view, the imminent threat of the closing of the sale does present a situation where it may be impossible to 'unscramble the eggs.' [. . .] While the remedy of rescission is available, it is not difficult to imagine the various obstacles to such a remedy including, tax consequences, accounting practices, business reorganizations, management decisions concerning capital investments, dividends, etc. and a host of other problems which as a practical matter will make rescission very difficult indeed [. . .]. On the other hand, the harm to Signal of entering an injunction is also massive. Under the contract, if the transaction is delayed by litigation, Burmah has a right to withdraw and the Court has no legal power to prevent such withdrawal. The loss of Signal's legal right to enforce the contract is itself irreparable harm.

In summary on the question of irreparable harm, it appears to me that there is irreparable harm to the losing side on this preliminary injunction application in the event the loser should ultimately prevail on the merits. Thus, in this case, the Court feels that the emphasis in analysis on this application for a preliminary injunction should focus on whether the plaintiff has a reasonable probability of success in this lawsuit.

Shareholder Vote

Turning specifically to the pleadings in this case, the complaint contains three separate counts [. . .]. In Count 3, the plaintiff alleges a class action on behalf of all Signal stockholders who, according to the complaint, were entitled to vote upon the proposed sale [. . .] [D]oes the sale require authorization by a majority of the outstanding stock of Signal pursuant to 8 Del. C. § 271(a)? [. . .]

I turn first to the question of 8 Del. C. § 271(a) which requires majority stockholder approval for the sale of 'all or substantially all' of the assets of a Delaware corporation. A sale of less than all or substantially all assets is not covered by negative implication from the statute. Folk, The Delaware General Corporation Law, Section 271, p. 400, ftnt. 3; 8 Del. C. § 141(a).

It is important to note in the first instance that the statute does not speak of a requirement of shareholder approval simply because an independent, important branch of a corporate business is being sold. The plaintiff cites several non-Delaware cases for the proposition that shareholder approval of such a sale is required. But that is not the language of our statute. Similarly, it is not our law that shareholder approval is required upon every 'major' restructuring of the corporation. Again, it is not necessary to go beyond the statute. The statute requires shareholder approval upon the sale of 'all or substantially all' of the corporation's assets. That is the sole test to be applied. While it is true that test does not lend itself to a strict mathematical standard to be applied in every case, the qualitative factor can be defined to some degree notwithstanding the limited Delaware authority. But the definition must begin with and ultimately necessarily relate to our statutory language.

[. . .] The key language in the Court of Chancery opinion in [a precedent case] is the suggestion that 'the critical factor in determining the character of a sale of assets is generally considered not the amount of property sold but whether the sale is in fact an unusual transaction or one made in the regular course of business of the seller.' [. . .] Professor Folk suggests from the opinion that 'the statute would be inapplicable if the assets sale is 'one made in furtherance of express corporate objects in the ordinary and regular course of the business.' *Folk, supra*, Section 271, p. 401.

But any 'ordinary and regular course of the business' test in this context obviously is not intended to limit the directors to customary daily business activities. Indeed, a question concerning the statute would not arise unless the transaction was somewhat out of the ordinary. While it is true that a transaction in the ordinary course of business does not require shareholder approval, the converse is not true. Every transaction out of normal routine does not necessarily require shareholder approval. The unusual nature of the transaction must strike at the heart of the corporate existence and purpose [. . .] It is in this sense that the 'unusual transaction' judgment is to be made and the statute's applicability determined. If the sale is of assets quantitatively vital to the operation of the corporation and is out of the ordinary and substantially affects the existence and purpose of the corporation, then it is beyond the power of the Board of Directors. With these guidelines, I turn to Signal and the transaction in this case.

Signal or its predecessor was incorporated in the oil business in 1922. But, beginning in 1952, Signal diversified its interests. In 1952, Signal acquired a substantial stock interest in American President lines. From 1957 to 1962 Signal was the sole owner of Laura Scudders, a nation-wide snack food business. In 1964, Signal acquired Garrett Corporation which is engaged in the aircraft, aerospace, and uranium enrichment business. In 1967, Signal acquired Mack Trucks, Inc., which is engaged in the manufacture and sale of trucks and related equipment. Also in 1968, the oil and gas business was transferred to a separate division and later in 1970 to the Signal Oil subsidiary. Since 1967, Signal has made acquisition of or formed substantial companies none of which are involved or related with the oil and gas industry. *See* Walkup affidavit, docket number 34. As indicated previously, the oil and gas production development of Signal's business is now carried on by Signal Oil, the sale of the stock of which is an issue in this lawsuit [. . .].

Based on the company's figures, Signal Oil represents only about 26% of the total assets of Signal. While Signal Oil represents 41% of Signal's total net worth, it produces only about 15% of Signal's revenues and earnings. Moreover, the additional tables shown in Signal's brief from the Chitiea affidavit are also interesting in demonstrating the low rate of return which has been realized recently from the oil and gas operation [. . .] While it is true, based on the experience of the Signal-Burmah transaction and the record in this lawsuit, that Signal Oil is more valuable than shown by the company's books, even if, as plaintiff suggests in his brief, the $761,000,000 value attached to Signal Oil's properties by the plaintiff's expert Paul V. Keyser, Jr., were substituted as the asset figure, the oil and gas properties would still constitute less than half the value of Signal's total assets. Thus, from a straight quantitative approach, I agree with Signal's position that the sale to Burmah does not constitute a sale of 'all or substantially all' of Signal's assets.

In addition, if the character of the transaction is examined, the plaintiff's position is also weak. While it is true that Signal's original purpose was oil and gas and while oil and gas is still listed first in the certificate of incorporation, the simple fact is that Signal is now a conglomerate engaged in the aircraft and aerospace business, the manufacture and sale of trucks and related equipment, and other businesses besides oil and gas. The very nature of its business, as it now in fact exists, contemplates the acquisition and disposal of independent branches of its corporate business. Indeed, given the operations since 1952, it can be said that such acquisitions and dispositions have become part of the ordinary course of business. The facts that the oil and gas business was historically first and that authorization for such operations are listed first in the certificate do not prohibit disposal of such interest. As Director Harold M. Williams testified, business history is not 'compelling' and 'many companies go down the drain because they try to be historic.'

It is perhaps true, as plaintiff has argued, that the advent of multi-business corporations has in one sense emasculated § 271 since one business may be sold without shareholder approval when other substantial businesses are retained. But it is one thing for a corporation to evolve over a period of years into a multi-business corporation, the operations of which include the purchase and sale of whole businesses, and another for a single business corporation by a one transaction revolution to sell the entire means of operating its business in exchange for money or a separate business. In the former situation, the processes of corporate democracy customarily have had the opportunity to restrain or otherwise control over a period of years. Thus, there is a chance for some shareholder participation. The Signal development illustrates the difference. For example, when Signal, itself formerly called Signal Oil and Gas Company, changed its name in 1968, it was for the announced 'need for a new name appropriate to the broadly diversified activities of Signal's multi-industry complex.'

The situation is also dramatically illustrated financially in this very case. Independent of the contract with Burmah, the affidavit of Signal's Board Chairman shows that over $200,000,000 of Signal Oil's refining and marketing assets have been sold in the past five years. This activity, prior to the sale at issue here, in itself constitutes a major restructuring of the corporate structure.

I conclude that measured quantitively and qualitatively, the sale of the stock of Signal Oil by Signal to Burmah does not constitute a sale of 'all or substantially all' of Signal's assets. This conclusion is supported by the closest case involving Delaware law which was been cited to the Court. Accordingly, insofar as the complaint rests on 8 Del. C. § 271(a), in my judgment, it has no reasonable probability of ultimate success.

City of North Miami Beach General Employees' Retirement Plan v. Dr Pepper Snapple Group, Inc.

189 A.3d 188 (Del. Ch. 2018)

■ QUILLEN, CHANCELLOR:

Earlier this year, Dr Pepper Snapple Group, Inc. and Keurig Green Mountain, Inc. announced an agreement to combine their businesses to create a more diversified beverage company. The transaction is structured so that Keurig will become an indirect wholly-owned subsidiary of Dr Pepper through a reverse triangular merger. Dr Pepper stockholders will receive $103.75 per share in a special cash dividend and will retain their shares of Dr Pepper, which will account for 13% of the shares of the combined company. The indirect owners of Keurig will receive shares of Dr Pepper and will hold the remaining 87% of the equity of the combined company.

The Merger is depicted in the diagram below:

The Merger

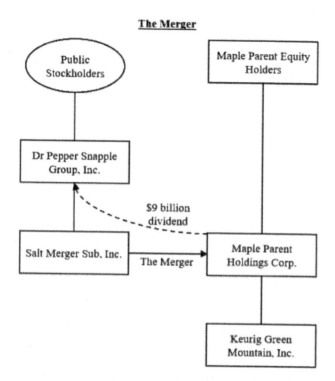

Dr Pepper's stockholders are not being asked to vote to approve the Merger. Rather, as described in a preliminary proxy statement [. . .] Dr Pepper's stockholders will vote on two proposals necessary to effectuate the transactions contemplated by the Merger Agreement [. . .] First, Dr Pepper's stockholders will "vote on a proposal to approve the issuance of [Dr Pepper] common stock as merger consideration pursuant to the [Merger Agreement]" (the "Share Issuance Proposal"). Second, Dr Pepper's stockholders will "vote on a proposal to approve an amendment to the certificate of incorporation of [Dr Pepper] to provide for [ ] an increase in authorized shares to permit issuance of a sufficient number of shares as merger consideration" (the "Charter Amendment Proposal") [. . .] The Preliminary Proxy informs Dr Pepper's stockholders that they do not have appraisal rights in connection with the Merger. Specifically, it states that "Section 262 of the DGCL does not provide for appraisal rights in connection with the transactions contemplated by the merger agreement for holders of shares of [Dr Pepper] common stock."

This action boils down to the purely legal question of whether Dr Pepper's stockholders have appraisal rights in connection with the Merger under 8 Del. C. § 262. For the reasons explained below, I find that they do not. Thus, the motions for summary judgment of Dr Pepper and Maple Parent will be granted, and plaintiffs' motion will be denied . . . .

Section 262(b) imposes a threshold requirement for determining when appraisal rights are available in connection with a merger or consolidation effected under the Delaware General Corporation Law:

> Appraisal rights shall be available for *the shares of any class or series of stock of a constituent corporation in a merger or consolidation* to be effected pursuant to § 251 . . ., § 252, § 254, § 255, § 256, § 257, § 258, § 263 or § 264 of this title [. . .]

Thus, as a statutory matter, appraisal is available in a merger or consolidation governed by Section 262(b) only for the stock of a "constituent corporation."

The Delaware General Corporation Law does not explicitly define the term "constituent corporation," but a number of its provisions give insight into the meaning of the term. Together, they clearly imply that "constituent corporations" are entities that actually were merged or combined in the transaction and *not* a parent of such entities.

For example, Section 251(a) provides: "Any 2 or more corporations of this State may merge into a single surviving corporation, which may be any 1 of the constituent corporations or may consolidate into a new resulting corporation formed by the consolidation." Because this statute provides that the entity surviving a merger may be either (i) a "new resulting" entity of a consolidation *or* (ii) one of two or more "constituent corporations" to a merger, the term "constituent corporations" must mean the corporations actually being merged or consolidated [. . .]

In the same vein, this court has interpreted the term "constituent corporations" to mean only those legal entities actually being combined in a transaction. Specifically, in *In re Inergy L.P. Unitholder Litig.*, the court considered whether the unitholders of a limited partnership (Inergy) were entitled to vote on a proposed merger under Inergy's partnership agreement. The court explained that the answer "turns on whether Inergy is actively 'merging' or 'consolidating' with another entity so that it is a constituent party to such merger or consolidation." Although Inergy was a contractual party to the merger agreement, the court concluded that it was "clear" that Inergy was "not a constituent of the merger between Holdings and MergerCo." Accordingly, the court found that Inergy's unitholders were unlikely to succeed on their claim that they were entitled to vote on the merger.

In analyzing the issue, the *Inergy* court analogized to the use of triangular mergers in the corporate context, *i.e.*, where "a parent corporation can acquire a target corporation by setting up a subsidiary to merge with the target." The court explained that the "effect of this arrangement is that the parent does not become a constituent to the merger between the target and the subsidiary" and thus the stockholders of the parent "generally are not entitled to vote on the merger." This conclusion is consistent with this court's observation in *Lewis v. Ward* that the stockholders of a parent corporation of a merging subsidiary in a triangular merger "generally do not have the right to vote on the merger, nor are they entitled to appraisal."

The authorities discussed above support interpreting the term "constituent corporation" in Section 262 to mean only an entity that actually is being merged or combined with another entity in a merger or consolidation and thus does not include a parent of such entities [. . .]

The authorities discussed above uniformly support, and I so hold, that the term "constituent corporation" in Section 262 plainly means only an entity that actually is being merged or combined with another entity in a merger or consolidation and thus does *not* include a parent of such entities. Applying this definition, it is clear that the "constituent corporations" in the Merger are Maple Parent and Merger Sub and that Dr Pepper is not a constituent corporation in the Merger.

The transaction here is structured as a reverse triangular merger, where parent Dr Pepper causes its subsidiary Merger Sub to merge with and into Maple Parent, resulting in Maple Parent becoming a wholly-owned subsidiary of Dr Pepper. The fact that Merger Sub merely functions as an intermediary entity, solely formed to facilitate the Merger, does not confer Merger Sub's status as a constituent corporation on its parent Dr Pepper. Accordingly, because Dr Pepper is not a constituent corporation in the Merger, its stockholders are not entitled to appraisal rights under 8 Del. C. § 262.

C. THE ACQUISITION AGREEMENT

Akorn, Inc. v. Fresenius Kabi AG

2018 WL 4719347 (Del. Ch. 2018)

■ LASTER, VICE CHANCELLOR:

Pursuant to an agreement and plan of merger dated April 24, 2017 (the "Merger Agreement"), Fresenius Kabi AG agreed to acquire Akorn, Inc. [. . .]

[. . .] Closing, however, was not a foregone conclusion. First, Fresenius's obligation to close was conditioned on Akorn's representations having been true and correct both at signing and at closing, except where the failure to be true and correct would not reasonably be expected to have a contractually defined "Material Adverse Effect." If this condition was not met and could not be cured by the Outside Date, then Fresenius could terminate the Merger Agreement. Fresenius could not exercise this termination right, however, if Fresenius was in material breach of its own obligations under the Merger Agreement.

Second, Fresenius's obligation to close was conditioned on Akorn having complied in all material respects with its obligations under the Merger Agreement. Once again, if this condition was not met and could not be cured by the Outside Date, then Fresenius could terminate the Merger

Agreement. Here too, Fresenius could not exercise the termination right if Fresenius was in material breach of its own obligations under the Merger Agreement.

Third, Fresenius's obligation to close was conditioned on Akorn not having suffered a Material Adverse Effect. The failure of this condition did not give Fresenius a right to terminate. Once the Outside Date passed, however, either Fresenius or Akorn could terminate, as long as the terminating party's own breach of the Merger Agreement had not been a principal cause of or resulted in the parties' failure to close before the Outside Date.

Akorn and Fresenius entered into the Merger Agreement shortly after announcing their results for the first quarter of 2017. During the second quarter of 2017, Akorn's business performance fell off a cliff, delivering results that fell materially below Akorn's prior-year performance on a year-over-year basis. The dismal results shocked Fresenius, because on the same date that the parties signed the Merger Agreement, Akorn had reaffirmed its full-year guidance for 2018 at Fresenius's request. Akorn's performance fell well below the guidance, forcing management to adjust Akorn's full-year guidance downward. Fresenius consulted with Akorn about the reasons for the sudden decline, which Akorn attributed to unexpected competition and the loss of a key contract.

Akorn's CEO reassured Fresenius that the downturn was temporary, but Akorn's performance continued to slide in July and again in August 2018. By September, Fresenius's management team had become concerned that Akorn had suffered a Material Adverse Effect, although its legal counsel was not certain at that point that Fresenius could satisfy the high burden imposed by Delaware law.

In October 2017, Fresenius received a letter from an anonymous whistleblower who made disturbing allegations about Akorn's product development process failing to comply with regulatory requirements. In November 2017, Fresenius received a longer version of the letter that provided additional details and made equally disturbing allegations about Akorn's quality compliance programs. The letters called into question whether Akorn's representations regarding regulatory compliance were accurate and whether Akorn had been operating in the ordinary course of business.

Fresenius provided the letters to Akorn. Although Fresenius understood that Akorn would have to investigate the allegations in the ordinary course of business, Fresenius informed Akorn that Fresenius also needed to conduct its own investigation into the allegations. Under the Merger Agreement, Fresenius had bargained for a right of reasonable access to Akorn's officers, employees, and information so that Fresenius could evaluate Akorn's contractual compliance and determine whether the conditions to closing were met. Invoking this right, Fresenius had expert attorneys and advisors investigate the issues raised by the whistleblower letters.

Fresenius's investigation uncovered serious and pervasive data integrity problems that rendered Akorn's representations about its regulatory compliance sufficiently inaccurate that the deviation between Akorn's actual condition and its as-represented condition would reasonably be expected to result in a Material Adverse Effect. During the course of the investigation, tensions escalated between the parties. Matters came to a head after Akorn downplayed its problems and oversold its remedial efforts in a presentation to its primary regulator, the United States Food and Drug Administration ("FDA"). As one of Akorn's own experts recognized at trial, Akorn was not fully transparent with the FDA. Put more bluntly, the presentation was misleading. From Fresenius's standpoint, Akorn was not conducting its operations in the ordinary course of business, providing an additional basis for termination.

During this same period, Akorn's business performance continued to deteriorate. In mid-April 2018, Fresenius sent Akorn a letter explaining why conditions to closing could not be met and identifying contractual bases for terminating the Merger Agreement. Fresenius nevertheless offered to extend the Outside Date if Akorn believed that further investigation would enable Akorn to resolve its difficulties. Akorn declined.

On April 22, 2018, Fresenius gave notice that it was terminating the Merger Agreement. Fresenius asserted that Akorn's representations regarding regulatory compliance were so incorrect that the deviation would reasonably be expected to result in a Material Adverse Effect. Fresenius also cited Akorn's failure to comply in all material respects with its contractual obligations under the Merger Agreement, including Akorn's obligation to use commercially reasonable efforts to operate in the ordinary course of business in all material respects. Fresenius also cited the section in the Merger Agreement that conditioned Fresenius's obligation to close on Akorn not having suffered a Material Adverse Effect.

Akorn responded by filing this action, which seeks a declaration that Fresenius's attempt to terminate the Merger Agreement was invalid and a decree of specific performance compelling Fresenius to close. Fresenius answered and filed counterclaims, contending it validly terminated the Merger Agreement and is not required to close. [. . .]

II. LEGAL ANALYSIS

The disputes in this case are primarily contractual. Fresenius contends that it terminated the Merger Agreement in accordance with its terms. Akorn contends that Fresenius did not validly terminate the Merger Agreement and seeks an order of specific performance to compel Fresenius to close the Merger. Both parties are highly sophisticated and crafted the Merger Agreement with the assistance of expert counsel. The pertinent provisions are dense and complex.

The analysis turns on three conditions that Akorn must meet before Fresenius is obligated to close the Merger:

- [other conditions omitted]
- Under Section 6.02(c), Akorn must not have suffered a Material Adverse Effect (the "General MAE Condition").

The failure of the General MAE Condition does not give Fresenius an independent right to terminate the Merger Agreement, but it does give Fresenius the right to refuse to close. [. . .]The General MAE Condition is not tied to a particular representation about a particular issue, leading this decision to describe the resulting event as a "General MAE." [. . .]The sudden and sustained drop in Akorn's business performance constituted a General MAE. [. . .]

A. The Failure Of The General MAE Condition

From the standpoint of contract interpretation, the most straightforward issue is whether Akorn suffered a General MAE. Starting with this issue is also helpful because much of the commentary on MAE clauses has focused on General MAEs. Because Fresenius seeks to establish a General MAE to excuse its performance under the Merger Agreement, Fresenius bore the burden of proving that a General MAE had occurred. This decision concludes that Akorn suffered a General MAE.

In any M&A transaction, a significant deterioration in the selling company's business between signing and closing may threaten the fundamentals of the deal. "Merger agreements typically address this problem through complex and highly-negotiated 'material adverse change' or 'MAC' clauses, which provide that, if a party has suffered a MAC within the meaning of the agreement, the counterparty can costlessly cancel the deal."

Despite the attention that contracting parties give to these provisions, MAE clauses typically do not define what is "material." Commentators have argued that parties find it efficient to leave the term undefined because the resulting uncertainty generates productive opportunities for renegotiation. Parties also risk creating more problems when they attempt to include specific quantitative thresholds, both during the negotiations and for purposes of subsequent litigation. "What constitutes an MAE, then, is a question that arises only when the clause is invoked and must be answered by the presiding court."

Rather than devoting resources to defining more specific tests for materiality, the current practice is for parties to negotiate exceptions and exclusions from exceptions that allocate categories of MAE risk. "The typical MAE clause allocates general market or industry risk to the buyer, and company-specific risks to the seller." From a drafting perspective, the MAE provision accomplishes this by placing the general risk of an MAE on the seller, then using exceptions to reallocate specific categories of risk to the buyer. Exclusions from the exceptions therefore return risks to the seller. A standard exclusion from the buyer's acceptance of general market or industry risk returns the risk to the seller when the seller's business is uniquely affected. To accomplish the reallocation, the relevant exceptions are "qualified by a concept of disproportionate effect." "For example, a buyer might revise the carve-out relating to industry conditions to exclude changes that disproportionately affect the target as compared to other companies in the industries in which such target operates."

A more nuanced analysis of the types of issues addressed by MAE provisions reveals four categories of risk: systematic risks, indicator risks, agreement risks, and business risks.

- Systematic risks are "beyond the control of all parties (even though one or both parties may be able to take steps to cushion the effects of such risks) and . . . will generally affect firms beyond the parties to the transaction."

- Indicator risks signal that an MAE may have occurred. For example, a drop in the seller's stock price, a credit rating downgrade, or a failure to meet a financial projection is not itself an adverse change, but rather evidence of such a change.

- "Agreement risks include all risks arising from the public announcement of the merger agreement and the taking of actions contemplated thereunder by the parties." Agreement risks include endogenous risks related to the cost of getting from signing to closing, e.g., potential employee flight.

- Business risks are those "arising from the ordinary operations of the party's business (other than systematic risks), and over such risks the party itself usually has significant control." "The most obvious" business risks are those "associated with the ordinary business operations of the party—the kinds of negative events that, in the ordinary course of operating the business, can be expected to occur from time to time, including those that, although known, are remote."

Generally speaking, the seller retains the business risk. The buyer assumes the other risks.

In this case, as a condition to Fresenius's obligation to close, Akorn must not have suffered a General MAE. Section 6.02 of the Merger Agreement, titled "Conditions to the Obligations of [Fresenius Kabi] and Merger Sub," states:

> The obligations of [Fresenius Kabi] and Merger Sub to effect the Merger shall be subject to the satisfaction (or written waiver by [Fresenius Kabi], if permissible under applicable law) on or prior to the Closing Date of the following conditions:
>
> * * *

(c) <u>No Material Adverse Effect</u>. Since the date of this Agreement there shall not have occurred and be continuing any effect, change, event or occurrence that, individually or in the aggregate, has had or would reasonably be expected to have a Material Adverse Effect.

The effect of this condition is to place the general risk of an MAE on Akorn.

The Merger Agreement defines the concept of a "Material Adverse Effect" in customary albeit complex and convoluted prose. The following reproduction of the definition adds formatting to enhance legibility:

"Material Adverse Effect" means any effect, change, event or occurrence that, individually or in the aggregate

(i)   would prevent or materially delay, interfere with, impair or hinder the consummation of the [Merger] or the compliance by the Company with its obligations under this Agreement or

(ii) has a material adverse effect on the business, results of operations or financial condition of the Company and its Subsidiaries, taken as a whole;

<u>provided</u>, <u>however</u>, that none of the following, and no effect, change, event or occurrence arising out of, or resulting from, the following, shall constitute or be taken into account in determining whether a Material Adverse Effect has occurred, is continuing or would reasonably be expected to occur: any effect, change, event or occurrence

(A) generally affecting (1) the industry in which the Company and its Subsidiaries operate or (2) the economy, credit or financial or capital markets, in the United States or elsewhere in the world, including changes in interest or exchange rates, monetary policy or inflation, or

(B) to the extent arising out of, resulting from or attributable to

(1) changes or prospective changes in Law or in GAAP or in accounting standards, or any changes or prospective changes in the interpretation or enforcement of any of the foregoing, or any changes or prospective changes in general legal, regulatory, political or social conditions,

(2) the negotiation, execution, announcement or performance of this Agreement or the consummation of the [Merger] (other than for purposes of any representation or warranty contained in Sections 3.03(c) and 3.04), including the impact thereof on relationships, contractual or otherwise, with customers, suppliers, distributors, partners, employees or regulators, or any litigation arising from allegations of breach of fiduciary

duty or violation of Law relating to this Agreement or the [Merger],

(3) acts of war (whether or not declared), military activity, sabotage, civil disobedience or terrorism, or any escalation or worsening of any such acts of war (whether or not declared), military activity, sabotage, civil disobedience or terrorism,

(4) pandemics, earthquakes, floods, hurricanes, tornados or other natural disasters, weather-related events, force majeure events or other comparable events,

(5) any action taken by the Company or its Subsidiaries that is required by this Agreement or at [Fresenius Kabi's] written request,

(6) any change or prospective change in the Company's credit ratings,

(7) any decline in the market price, or change in trading volume, of the shares of the Company or

(8) any failure to meet any internal or public projections, forecasts, guidance, estimates, milestones, budgets or internal or published financial or operating predictions of revenue, earnings, cash flow or cash position (it being understood that the exceptions in clauses (6), (7) and (8) shall not prevent or otherwise affect a determination that the underlying cause of any such change, decline or failure referred to therein (if not otherwise falling within any of the exceptions provided by clause (A) and clauses (B)(1) through (8) hereof) is a Material Adverse Effect); provided further, however, that any effect, change, event or occurrence referred to in clause (A) or clauses (B)(3) or (4) may be taken into account in determining whether there has been, or would reasonably be expected to be, a Material Adverse Effect to the extent such effect, change, event or occurrence has a disproportionate adverse affect [sic] on the Company and its Subsidiaries, taken as a whole, as compared to other participants in the industry in which the Company and its Subsidiaries operate (in which case the incremental disproportionate impact or impacts may be taken into account in determining whether there has been, or would reasonably be expected to be, a Material Adverse Effect).

As is common, the definition starts with a general statement of what constitutes an MAE. It next carves out certain types of events that otherwise could give rise to an MAE. It then creates two broad exceptions to the carve-outs. One is that while the carve-outs confirm that certain evidentiary indicators of an MAE will not themselves constitute an MAE, such as a decline in the seller's market price or an adverse change in its credit rating, those carve-outs do not foreclose the underlying cause of the negative events from being used to establish an MAE, unless it otherwise falls within a different carve-out. The other is that four of the identified carve-outs will give rise to an MAE if the effect, change, event or occurrence has had a disproportionately adverse effect on the Company.

Fresenius relies on subpart (ii) of the MAE definition, which establishes (subject to the carve-outs and their exceptions) that an MAE means "any effect, change, event or occurrence that, individually or in the aggregate that . . . (ii) has a material adverse effect on the business, results of operations or financial condition of the Company and its Subsidiaries, taken as a whole." This aspect of the MAE definition adheres to the general practice and defines "Material Adverse Effect" self-referentially as something that "has a material adverse effect."

The subsequent exceptions to the definition and exclusions from the exceptions implement a standard risk allocation between buyer and seller. Through the exceptions in subparts (A)(1) and (A)(2), Fresenius accepted the systematic risks related to Akorn's industry and "the economy, credit or financial or capital markets, in the United States or elsewhere in the world, including changes in interest or exchange rates, monetary policy or inflation." Through the exceptions in subparts (B)(3) and (B)(4), Fresenius also accepted the systematic risks related to acts of war, violence, pandemics, disasters, and other *force majeure* events. Each of these allocations is subject to a disproportionate-effect exclusion that returns the risk to Akorn to the extent that an event falling into one of these categories disproportionately affects Akorn "as compared to other participants in the industry." Under subpart (B)(1), Fresenius also assumes the systematic risk relating to changes in GAAP or applicable law. This exception is not subject to a disproportionate-effect exclusion and therefore would remain with Fresenius in any event.

The exceptions in subparts (B)(2) and (B)(5) identify agreement risks. Through these exceptions, Fresenius assumes these risks.

The exceptions in subparts (B)(6), (B)(7), and (B)(8) identify indicator risks. The MAE definition explicitly treats these risks as indicators, first by excluding them through the exceptions, then by confirming that although these indicators would not independently give rise to an MAE, the underlying cause of a change in the indicators could give rise to an MAE.

What remains is business risk, which Akorn retains. Scholars view this outcome as economically efficient because the seller "is better placed to prevent such risks (i.e., is the cheaper cost avoider) and has superior knowledge about the likelihood of the materializations of such risks that cannot be prevented (i.e., is the superior risk bearer)."

1. Whether The Magnitude Of The Effect Was Material

The first step in analyzing whether a General MAE has occurred is to determine whether the magnitude of the downward deviation in the affected company's performance is material: "[U]nless the court concludes that the company has suffered an MAE as defined in the language coming before the proviso, the court need not consider the application of the [. . .] carve-outs." Whether the party asserting the existence of an MAE has adduced sufficient evidence to carry its burden of proof is a question of fact.

"A buyer faces a heavy burden when it attempts to invoke a material adverse effect clause in order to avoid its obligation to close." "A short-term hiccup in earnings should not suffice; rather the Material Adverse Effect should be material when viewed from the longer-term perspective of a reasonable acquiror." "In the absence of evidence to the contrary, a corporate acquirer may be assumed to be purchasing the target as part of a long-term strategy." "The important consideration therefore is whether there has been an adverse change in the target's business that is consequential to the company's long-term earnings power over a commercially reasonable period, which one would expect to be measured in years rather than months."

> This, of course, is not to say that evidence of a significant decline in earnings by the target corporation during the period after signing but prior to the time appointed for closing is irrelevant. Rather, it means that for such a decline to constitute a material adverse effect, poor earnings results must be expected to persist significantly into the future.

Put differently, the effect should "substantially threaten the overall earnings potential of the target in a durationally-significant manner."

The *Hexion* decision teaches that when evaluating the magnitude of a decline, a company's performance generally should be evaluated against its results during the same quarter of the prior year, which minimizes the effect of seasonal fluctuations. The *Hexion* court declined to find an MAE where the seller's 2007 EBITDA was only 3% below its 2006 EBITDA, and where according to its management forecasts, its 2008 EBITDA would be only 7% below its 2007 EBITDA. Even using the buyer's more conservative forecasts, the seller's 2008 EBTIDA would still be only 11% below its 2007 EBITDA. The average of analyst estimates for the seller's 2009 EBITDA was only 3.6% below the seller's average results during the prior three years. The court noted that the buyer had contemplated scenarios consistent with these results.

In their influential treatise, Lou R. Kling and Eileen T. Nugent observe that most courts which have considered decreases in profits in the 40% or higher range found a material adverse effect to have occurred. Chancellor Allen posited that a decline in earnings of 50% over two consecutive quarters would likely be an MAE. Courts in other jurisdictions have reached similar conclusions. These precedents do not foreclose the possibility that a buyer could show that percentage changes of a lesser magnitude constituted an MAE. Nor does it exclude the possibility that a buyer might fail to prove that percentage changes of a greater magnitude constituted an MAE.

An example of the latter scenario is *IBP*, where Chief Justice Strine held while serving as a Vice Chancellor that a 64% drop in quarterly earnings did not constitute a material adverse effect. There, a major producer of beef suffered a large quarterly decline in performance primarily due to widely known cycles in the meat industry, exacerbated by a harsh winter that also affected the buyer. After the bad quarter and the onset of spring, "IBP began to perform more in line with its recent year results." The Chief Justice concluded that "IBP remain[ed] what the baseline evidence suggests it was—a consistently but erratically profitable company struggling to implement a strategy that will reduce the cyclicality of its earnings." The Chief Justice nevertheless noted that "the question of whether IBP has suffered a Material Adverse Effect remains a close one" and that he was "confessedly torn about the correct outcome." He further posited that

> [i]f IBP had continued to perform on a straight-line basis using its first quarter 2001 performance, it would generate earnings from operations of around $200 million. This sort of annual performance would be consequential to a reasonable acquiror and would deviate materially from the range in which IBP had performed during the recent past [thus giving rise to an MAE].

[. . .] In this case, Fresenius made the showing necessary to establish a General MAE. At trial, Professor Daniel Fischel testified credibly and persuasively that Akorn's financial performance has declined materially since the signing of the Merger Agreement and that the underlying causes of the decline were durationally significant. The factual record supports Fischel's opinions.

[. . .] Notably, Akorn's performance during the first quarter of 2017—before the Merger Agreement was signed—did not exhibit the downturn that the ensuing three quarters did. But immediately after the signing of the Merger Agreement, Akorn's performance dropped off a cliff.

Akorn's dramatic downturn in performance is durationally significant. It has already persisted for a full year and shows no sign of abating. More importantly, Akorn's management team has provided reasons for the decline that can reasonably be expected to have durationally significant effects. When reporting on Akorn's bad results during the second quarter of FY 2017, [Akorn CEO] Rai attributed Akorn's poor performance to unexpected new market entrants who competed with Akorn's three top products—ephedrine, clobetasol, and lidocaine. He noted that Akorn also faced a new competitor for Nembutal, another important product, which Akorn management had not foreseen. As Rai testified, "There were way more [competitors] than what [Akorn] had potentially projected in [its] forecast for 2017," and the new competition resulted in unexpected price erosion. Akorn also unexpectedly lost a key contract to sell progesterone, resulting in a loss of revenue where Akorn had been forecasting growth. When explaining its third quarter results, Akorn described its poor performance as "[d]riven mostly by unanticipated supply interruptions and unfavorable impact from competition across [the] portfolio." Akorn also noted that its "[a]verage product pricing [was] lower than expected due to [an] unfavorable customer/contract mix and price erosion [that was] not considered in our forecast." There is every reason to think that the additional competition will persist and no reason to believe that Akorn will recapture its lost contract. [. . .]

To contest this powerful evidence of a Material Adverse Effect, Akorn contends that any assessment of the decline in Akorn's value should be measured not against its performance as a standalone entity, but rather against its value to Fresenius as a synergistic buyer. In my view, the plain language of the definition of an MAE makes clear that any MAE must be evaluated on a standalone basis. First, the broad definition of an MAE refers to any "material adverse effect on the business, results of operations or financial condition *of the Company and its Subsidiaries,* taken as a whole." If the parties had contemplated a synergistic approach, the definition would have referred to the surviving corporation or the combined company. Second, subpart (B)(2) of the definition carves out any effects resulting from "the negotiation, execution, announcement or performance of this Agreement or the consummation of the [Merger,]" and the generation of synergies is an effect that results from the consummation of the Merger. A review of precedent does not reveal any support for Akorn's argument; every prior decision has looked at changes in value relative to the seller as a standalone company. Akorn's desire to include synergies is understandable—it increases the denominator for purposes of any percentage-based comparison—but it is not supported by the Merger Agreement or the law.

Akorn also argues that as long as Fresenius can make a profit from the acquisition, an MAE cannot have occurred. The MAE definition does not include any language about the profitability of the deal to the buyer; it focuses solely on the value of the seller. Assessing whether Fresenius can make a profit would introduce a different, non-contractual standard. It would effectively require that Fresenius show a goodwill impairment before it could prove the existence of an MAE. The parties could have bargained for that standard, but they did not. Requiring a loss before a buyer could show an MAE also would ignore the fact that acquirers evaluate rates of return when choosing among competing projects, including acquisitions. A buyer might make money on an absolute basis, but the opportunity cost on a relative basis would be quite high.

More broadly, the black-letter doctrine of frustration of purpose already operates to discharge a contracting party's obligations when his "principal purpose is substantially frustrated without his fault by the occurrence of an event the non-occurrence of which was a basic assumption on which the contract was made." This common law doctrine "provides an escape for an acquirer if the target experiences a catastrophe during the executory period." "It is not reasonable to conclude that sophisticated parties to merger agreements, who expend considerable resources drafting and negotiating MAC clauses, intend them to do nothing more than restate the default rule." In lieu of the default rule that performance may be excused only where a contract's principal purpose is completely or nearly completely frustrated, a contract could "lower this bar to an achievable level by providing for excuse when the value of counterperformance has 'materially' (or 'considerably' or 'significantly') diminished." That is what the parties did in this case. It should not be necessary for Fresenius to show a loss on the deal before it can rely on the contractual exit right it negotiated.

The record in this case established the existence of a sustained decline in business performance that is durationally significant and which would be material to a reasonable buyer. Akorn suffered a General MAE . [. . .]

III. CONCLUSION

Akorn brought this action seeking a decree of specific performance that would compel Fresenius to close. Akorn cannot obtain specific performance because three conditions to closing failed: the General MAE Condition [and others].

D. CONTROLLING SHAREHOLDERS AND SQUEEZE OUT MERGERS

Weinberger v. UOP, Inc.
457 A.2d 701 (Del. 1983)

■ MOORE, JUSTICE:

This post-trial appeal was reheard en banc from a decision of the Court of Chancery. It was brought by the class action plaintiff below, a former shareholder of UOP, Inc., who challenged the elimination of UOP's minority shareholders by a cash-out merger between UOP and its majority owner, The Signal Companies, Inc. Originally, the defendants in this action were Signal, UOP, certain officers and directors of those companies, and UOP's investment banker, Lehman Brothers Kuhn Loeb, Inc. The present Chancellor held that the terms of the merger were fair to the plaintiff and the other minority shareholders of UOP. Accordingly, he entered judgment in favor of the defendants.

Numerous points were raised by the parties, but we address only [. . .] [t]he fairness of the merger in terms of adequacy of the price paid for the minority shares and the remedy appropriate to that issue [. . .].

In considering the nature of the remedy available under our law to minority shareholders in a cash-out merger, we believe that it is, and hereafter should be, an appraisal under 8 Del.C. § 262 as hereinafter construed. We therefore overrule *Lynch v. Vickers Energy Corp.* (*Lynch II*) to the extent that it purports to limit a stockholder's monetary relief to a specific damage formula. But to give full effect to section 262 within the framework of the General Corporation Law we adopt a more liberal, less rigid and stylized, approach to the valuation process than has heretofore been permitted by our courts. While the present state of these proceedings does not admit the plaintiff to the appraisal remedy per se, the practical effect of the remedy we do grant him will be co-extensive with the liberalized valuation and appraisal methods we herein approve for cases coming after this decision. [. . .]

I.

[. . .] Signal is a diversified, technically based company operating through various subsidiaries. Its stock is publicly traded on the New York, Philadelphia and Pacific Stock Exchanges. UOP, formerly known as Universal Oil Products Company, was a diversified industrial company engaged in various lines of business, including petroleum and petrochemical services and related products, construction, fabricated metal products, transportation equipment products, chemicals and plastics, and other products and services including land development, lumber products and waste disposal. Its stock was publicly held and listed on the New York Stock Exchange.

In 1974 Signal sold one of its wholly-owned subsidiaries for $420,000,000 in cash. While looking to invest this cash surplus, Signal became interested in UOP as a possible acquisition. Friendly negotiations ensued, and Signal proposed to acquire a controlling interest in UOP at a price of $19 per share. UOP's representatives sought $25 per share. In the arm's length bargaining that followed, an understanding was reached whereby Signal agreed to purchase from UOP 1,500,000 shares of UOP's authorized but unissued stock at $21 per share.

This purchase was contingent upon Signal making a successful cash tender offer for 4,300,000 publicly held shares of UOP, also at a price of $21 per share. This combined method of acquisition permitted Signal to acquire 5,800,000 shares of stock, representing 50.5% of UOP's outstanding shares. The UOP board of directors advised the company's shareholders that it had no objection to Signal's tender offer at that price. Immediately before the announcement of the tender offer, UOP's common stock had been trading on the New York Stock Exchange at a fraction under $14 per share.

The negotiations between Signal and UOP occurred during April 1975, and the resulting tender offer was greatly oversubscribed. However, Signal limited its total purchase of the tendered shares so that, when coupled with the stock bought from UOP, it had achieved its goal of becoming a 50.5% shareholder of UOP.

Although UOP's board consisted of thirteen directors, Signal nominated and elected only six. Of these, five were either directors or employees of Signal. The sixth, a partner in the banking firm of Lazard Freres & Co., had been one of Signal's representatives in the negotiations and bargaining with UOP concerning the tender offer and purchase price of the UOP shares.

However, the president and chief executive officer of UOP retired during 1975, and Signal caused him to be replaced by James V. Crawford, a long-time employee and senior executive vice president of one of Signal's wholly-owned subsidiaries. Crawford succeeded his predecessor on UOP's board of directors and also was made a director of Signal.

By the end of 1977 Signal basically was unsuccessful in finding other suitable investment candidates for its excess cash, and by February 1978 considered that it had no other realistic acquisitions available to it on a friendly basis. Once again its attention turned to UOP.

The trial court found that at the instigation of certain Signal management personnel, including William W. Walkup, its board chairman, and Forrest N. Shumway, its president, a feasibility study was made concerning the possible acquisition of the balance of UOP's outstanding shares. This study was performed by two Signal officers, Charles S. Arledge, vice president (director of planning), and Andrew J. Chitiea, senior vice president (chief financial officer). Messrs. Walkup, Shumway, Arledge and Chitiea were all directors of UOP in addition to their membership on the Signal board.

Arledge and Chitiea concluded that it would be a good investment for Signal to acquire the remaining 49.5% of UOP shares at any price up to $24 each. Their report was discussed between Walkup and Shumway who, along with Arledge, Chitiea and Brewster L. Arms, internal counsel for Signal, constituted Signal's senior management. [. . .] It was ultimately agreed that a meeting of Signal's executive committee would be called to propose that Signal acquire the remaining outstanding stock of UOP through a cash-out merger in the range of $20 to $21 per share.

The executive committee meeting was set for February 28, 1978. As a courtesy, UOP's president, Crawford, was invited to attend, although he was not a member of Signal's executive committee. On his arrival, and prior to the meeting, Crawford was asked to meet privately with Walkup and Shumway. He was then told of Signal's plan to acquire full ownership of UOP and was asked for his reaction to the proposed price range of $20 to $21 per share. Crawford said he thought such a price would be "generous," and that it was certainly one which should be submitted to UOP's minority shareholders for their ultimate consideration. He stated, however, that Signal's 100% ownership could cause internal problems at UOP. He believed that employees would have to be given some assurance of their future place in a fully-owned Signal subsidiary. Otherwise, he feared the departure of essential personnel. Also, many of UOP's key employees had stock option incentive programs which would be wiped out by a merger. Crawford therefore urged that some adjustment would have to be made, such as providing a comparable incentive in Signal's shares, if after the merger he was to maintain his quality of personnel and efficiency at UOP.

[. . .] Crawford voiced no objection to the $20 to $21 price range, nor did he suggest that Signal should consider paying more than $21 per share for the minority interests.

[. . .] [I]t was the consensus that a price of $20 to $21 per share would be fair to both Signal and the minority shareholders of UOP. Signal's executive committee authorized its management "to negotiate" with UOP "for a cash acquisition of the minority ownership in UOP, Inc., with the intention of presenting a proposal to [Signal's] board of directors [. . .] on March 6, 1978." Immediately after this February 28, 1978 meeting, Signal issued a press release stating [that Signal and UOP were] conducting negotiations for the acquisition by Signal of 49.5 percent of UOP [. . .].

The announcement also referred to the fact that the closing price of UOP's common stock on that day was $14.50 per share.

Two days later, on March 2, 1978, Signal issued a second press release stating that its management would recommend a price in the range of $20 to $21 per share for UOP's 49.5% minority interest. This announcement referred to Signal's earlier statement that "negotiations" were being conducted for the acquisition of the minority shares.

Between Tuesday, February 28, 1978 and Monday, March 6, 1978, a total of four business days, Crawford spoke by telephone with all of UOP's non-Signal, i.e., outside, directors. Also during that period, Crawford retained Lehman Brothers to render a fairness opinion as to the price offered the minority for its stock. [. . .]

Crawford telephoned [James W.] Glanville, [a long-time director of UOP and a partner in Lehman Brothers who had acted as a financial advisor to UOP for many years], [. . .] gave his assurance that Lehman Brothers had no conflicts that would prevent it from accepting the task. Glanville's immediate personal reaction was that a price of $20 to $21 would certainly be fair, since it represented almost a 50% premium over UOP's market price. [. . .]

During this period Crawford also had several telephone contacts with Signal officials. In only one of them, however, was the price of the shares discussed. In a conversation with Walkup, Crawford advised that as a result of his communications with UOP's non-Signal directors, it was his feeling that the price would have to be the top of the proposed range, or $21 per share, if the approval of UOP's outside directors was to be obtained. But again, he did not seek any price higher than $21.

Glanville assembled a three-man Lehman Brothers team to do the work on the fairness opinion. These persons examined relevant documents and information concerning UOP, including its annual reports and its Securities and Exchange Commission filings from 1973 through 1976, as well as its audited financial statements for 1977, its interim reports to shareholders, and its recent and historical market prices and trading volumes. In addition, on Friday, March 3, 1978, two members of the

Lehman Brothers team flew to UOP's headquarters in Des Plaines, Illinois, to perform a "due diligence" visit, during the course of which they interviewed Crawford as well as UOP's general counsel, its chief financial officer, and other key executives and personnel.

As a result, the Lehman Brothers team concluded that "the price of either $20 or $21 would be a fair price for the remaining shares of UOP." They telephoned this impression to Glanville, who was spending the weekend in Vermont.

On Monday morning, March 6, 1978, Glanville and the senior member of the Lehman Brothers team flew to Des Plaines to attend the scheduled UOP directors meeting. Glanville looked over the assembled information during the flight. The two had with them the draft of a "fairness opinion letter" in which the price had been left blank. Either during or immediately prior to the directors' meeting, the two-page "fairness opinion letter" was typed in final form and the price of $21 per share was inserted.

On March 6, 1978, both the Signal and UOP boards were convened to consider the proposed merger. Telephone communications were maintained between the two meetings. Walkup, Signal's board chairman, and also a UOP director, attended UOP's meeting with Crawford in order to present Signal's position and answer any questions that UOP's non-Signal directors might have. Arledge and Chitiea, along with Signal's other designees on UOP's board, participated by conference telephone. All of UOP's outside directors attended the meeting either in person or by conference telephone.

First, Signal's board unanimously adopted a resolution authorizing Signal to propose to UOP a cash merger of $21 per share as outlined in a certain merger agreement and other supporting documents. This proposal required that the merger be approved by a majority of UOP's outstanding minority shares voting at the stockholders meeting at which the merger would be considered, and that the minority shares voting in favor of the merger, when coupled with Signal's 50.5% interest would have to comprise at least two-thirds of all UOP shares. Otherwise the proposed merger would be deemed disapproved.

UOP's board then considered the proposal. Copies of the agreement were delivered to the directors in attendance, and other copies had been forwarded earlier to the directors participating by telephone. They also had before them UOP financial data for 1974–1977, UOP's most recent financial statements, market price information, and budget projections for 1978. In addition they had Lehman Brothers' hurriedly prepared fairness opinion letter finding the price of $21 to be fair. Glanville, the Lehman Brothers partner, and UOP director, commented on the information that had gone into preparation of the letter.

Signal also suggests that the Arledge-Chitiea feasibility study, indicating that a price of up to $24 per share would be a "good investment" for

Signal, was discussed at the UOP directors' meeting. The Chancellor made no such finding, and our independent review of the record, detailed *infra,* satisfies us by a preponderance of the evidence that there was no discussion of this document at UOP's board meeting. Furthermore, it is clear beyond peradventure that nothing in that report was ever disclosed to UOP's minority shareholders prior to their approval of the merger.

After consideration of Signal's proposal, Walkup and Crawford left the meeting to permit a free and uninhibited exchange between UOP's non-Signal directors. Upon their return a resolution to accept Signal's offer was then proposed and adopted. While Signal's men on UOP's board participated in various aspects of the meeting, they abstained from voting. However, the minutes show that each of them "if voting would have voted yes."

On March 7, 1978, UOP sent a letter to its shareholders advising them of the action taken by UOP's board with respect to Signal's offer. This document pointed out, among other things, that on February 28, 1978 "both companies had announced negotiations were being conducted."

Despite the swift board action of the two companies, the merger was not submitted to UOP's shareholders until their annual meeting on May 26, 1978. In the notice of that meeting and proxy statement sent to shareholders in May, UOP's management and board urged that the merger be approved. [. . .]

When Signal's stock was added to the minority shares voting in favor, a total of 76.2% of UOP's outstanding shares approved the merger while only 2.2% opposed it.

By its terms the merger became effective on May 26, 1978, and each share of UOP's stock held by the minority was automatically converted into a right to receive $21 cash.

II.

A.

A primary issue mandating reversal is the preparation by two UOP directors, Arledge and Chitiea, of their feasibility study for the exclusive use and benefit of Signal. This document was of obvious significance to both Signal and UOP. Using UOP data, it described the advantages to Signal of ousting the minority at a price range of $21–$24 per share. [. . .]

Having written those words, solely for the use of Signal, it is clear from the record that neither Arledge nor Chitiea shared this report with their fellow directors of UOP. We are satisfied that no one else did either. This conduct hardly meets the fiduciary standards applicable to such a transaction. While Mr. Walkup, Signal's chairman of the board and a UOP director, attended the March 6, 1978 UOP board meeting and testified at trial that he had discussed the Arledge-Chitiea report with the UOP directors at this meeting, the record does not support this assertion. Perhaps it is the result of some confusion on Mr. Walkup's part. In any event Mr. Shumway, Signal's president, testified that he made sure the Signal outside directors had this report prior to the March 6, 1978 Signal board meeting, but he did not testify that the Arledge-Chitiea report was also sent to UOP's outside directors.

Mr. Crawford, UOP's president, could not recall that any documents, other than a draft of the merger agreement, were sent to UOP's directors before the March 6, 1978 UOP meeting. Mr. Chitiea, an author of the report, testified that it was made available to Signal's directors, but to his knowledge it was not circulated to the outside directors of UOP. He specifically testified that he "didn't share" that information with the outside directors of UOP with whom he served.

None of UOP's outside directors who testified stated that they had seen this document. The minutes of the UOP board meeting do not identify the Arledge-Chitiea report as having been delivered to UOP's outside directors. This is particularly significant since the minutes describe in considerable detail the materials that actually were distributed. While these minutes recite Mr. Walkup's presentation of the Signal offer, they do not mention the Arledge-Chitiea report or any disclosure that Signal considered a price of up to $24 to be a good investment. If Mr. Walkup had in fact provided such important information to UOP's outside directors, it is logical to assume that these carefully drafted minutes would disclose it. The post-trial briefs of Signal and UOP contain a thorough description of the documents purportedly available to their boards at the March 6, 1978, meetings. Although the Arledge-Chitiea report is specifically identified as being available to the Signal directors, there is no mention of it being among the documents submitted to the UOP board. [. . .]

Actually, it appears that a three-page summary of figures was given to all UOP directors. Its first page is identical to one page of the Arledge-Chitiea report, but this dealt with nothing more than a justification of the $21 price. Significantly, the contents of this three-page summary are what the minutes reflect Mr. Walkup told the UOP board. However, nothing contained in either the minutes or this three-page summary reflects Signal's study regarding the $24 price.

The Arledge-Chitiea report speaks for itself in supporting the Chancellor's finding that a price of up to $24 was a "good investment" for Signal. It shows that a return on the investment at $21 would be 15.7% versus 15.5% at $24 per share. This was a difference of only two-tenths of one percent, while it meant over $17,000,000 to the minority. Under such circumstances, paying UOP's minority shareholders $24 would have had relatively little long-term effect on Signal, and the Chancellor's findings concerning the benefit to Signal, even at a price of $24, were obviously correct. *Levitt v. Bouvier.*

Certainly, this was a matter of material significance to UOP and its shareholders. Since the study was prepared by two UOP directors, using UOP information for the exclusive benefit of Signal, and nothing whatever was done to disclose it to the outside UOP directors or the minority shareholders, a question of breach of fiduciary duty arises. This problem occurs because there were common Signal-UOP directors participating, at least to some extent, in the UOP board's decision-making processes without full disclosure of the conflicts they faced.

B.

In assessing this situation, the Court of Chancery was required to:

> examine what information defendants had and to measure it against what they gave to the minority stockholders, in a context in which 'complete candor' is required. In other words, the limited function of the Court was to determine whether defendants had disclosed all information in their possession germane to the transaction in issue. And by 'germane' we mean, for present purposes, information such as a reasonable shareholder would consider important in deciding whether to sell or retain stock.

> ... Completeness, not adequacy, is both the norm and the mandate under present circumstances.

Lynch v. Vickers Energy Corp. (*Lynch I*). This is merely stating in another way the long-existing principle of Delaware law that these Signal designated directors on UOP's board still owed UOP and its shareholders an uncompromising duty of loyalty.

Given the absence of any attempt to structure this transaction on an arm's length basis, Signal cannot escape the effects of the conflicts it faced, particularly when its designees on UOP's board did not totally abstain from participation in the matter. There is no "safe harbor" for such divided loyalties in Delaware. When directors of a Delaware corporation are on both sides of a transaction, they are required to demonstrate their utmost good faith and the most scrupulous inherent fairness of the bargain. *Gottlieb v. Heyden Chemical Corp.* The requirement of fairness is unflinching in its demand that where one stands on both sides of a transaction, he has the burden of establishing its entire fairness, sufficient to pass the test of careful scrutiny by the courts. *Sterling v. Mayflower Hotel Corp.*; *Bastian v. Bourns, Inc.*; *David J. Greene & Co. v. Dunhill International Inc.*

There is no dilution of this obligation where one holds dual or multiple directorships, as in a parent-subsidiary context. *Levien v. Sinclair Oil Corp.* Thus, individuals who act in a dual capacity as directors of two corporations, one of whom is parent and the other subsidiary, owe the same duty of good management to both corporations, and in the absence of an independent negotiating structure (*see* note 7, *supra*), or the directors' total abstention from any participation in the matter, this duty is to be exercised in light of what is best for both companies. *Warshaw v. Calhoun.* The record demonstrates that Signal has not met this obligation.

C.

The concept of fairness has two basic aspects: fair dealing and fair price. The former embraces questions of when the transaction was timed, how it was initiated, structured, negotiated, disclosed to the directors, and how the approvals of the directors and the stockholders were obtained. The latter aspect of fairness relates to the economic and financial considerations of the proposed merger, including all relevant factors: assets, market value, earnings, future prospects, and any other elements that affect the intrinsic or inherent value of a company's stock. Moore, *The "Interested" Director or Officer Transaction*; Nathan & Shapiro, *Legal Standard of Fairness of Merger Terms Under Delaware Law. See Tri-Continental Corp. v. Battye*; 8 Del.C. § 262(h). However, the test for fairness is not a bifurcated one as between fair dealing and price. All aspects of the issue must be examined as a whole since the question is one of entire fairness. However, in a non-fraudulent transaction we recognize that price may be the preponderant consideration outweighing other features of the merger. Here, we address the two basic aspects of fairness separately because we find reversible error as to both.

D.

Part of fair dealing is the obvious duty of candor required by *Lynch I, supra.* Moreover, one possessing superior knowledge may not mislead any stockholder by use of corporate information to which the latter is not privy. *Lank v. Steiner.* Delaware has long imposed this duty even upon persons who are not corporate officers or directors, but who nonetheless are privy to matters of interest or significance to their company. *Brophy v. Cities Service Co.* With the well-established Delaware law on the subject, and the Court of Chancery's findings of fact here, it is inevitable that the obvious conflicts posed by Arledge and Chitiea's preparation of their "feasibility study," derived from UOP information, for the sole use and benefit of Signal, cannot pass muster.

The Arledge-Chitiea report is but one aspect of the element of fair dealing. How did this merger evolve? It is clear that it was entirely initiated by Signal. The serious time constraints under which the principals acted were all set by Signal. It had not found a suitable outlet for its excess cash and considered UOP a desirable investment, particularly since it was now in a position to acquire the whole company for itself. For whatever reasons, and they were only Signal's, the entire transaction was presented to and approved by UOP's board within four business days. Standing alone, this is not necessarily indicative of any lack of fairness by a majority shareholder. It was what occurred, or more properly, what did not occur, during this brief period that makes the time constraints imposed by Signal relevant to the issue of fairness.

The structure of the transaction, again, was Signal's doing. So far as negotiations were concerned, it is clear that they were modest at best. Crawford, Signal's man at UOP, never really talked price with Signal, except to accede to its management's statements on the subject, and to convey to Signal the UOP outside directors' view that as between the $20–$21 range under consideration, it would have to be $21. The latter is not a surprising outcome, but hardly arm's length negotiations. Only the protection of benefits for UOP's key employees and the issue of Lehman Brothers' fee approached any concept of bargaining.

As we have noted, the matter of disclosure to the UOP directors was wholly flawed by the conflicts of interest raised by the Arledge-Chitiea report. All of those conflicts were resolved by Signal in its own favor without divulging any aspect of them to UOP.

This cannot but undermine a conclusion that this merger meets any reasonable test of fairness. The outside UOP directors lacked one material piece of information generated by two of their colleagues, but shared only with Signal. True, the UOP board had the Lehman Brothers' fairness opinion, but that firm has been blamed by the plaintiff for the hurried task it performed, when more properly the responsibility for this lies with Signal. There was no disclosure of the circumstances surrounding the rather cursory preparation of the Lehman Brothers' fairness opinion. Instead, the impression was given UOP's minority that a careful study had been made, when in fact speed was the hallmark, and Mr. Glanville, Lehman's partner in charge of the matter, and also a UOP director, having spent the weekend in Vermont, brought a draft of the "fairness opinion letter" to the UOP directors' meeting on March 6, 1978 with the price left blank. We can only conclude from the record that the rush imposed on Lehman Brothers by Signal's timetable contributed to the difficulties under which this investment banking firm attempted to perform its responsibilities. Yet, none of this was disclosed to UOP's minority.

Finally, the minority stockholders were denied the critical information that Signal considered a price of $24 to be a good investment. Since this would have meant over $17,000,000 more to the minority, we cannot conclude that the shareholder vote was an informed one. Under the circumstances, an approval by a majority of the minority was meaningless. *Lynch I*; *Cahall v. Lofland.*

Given these particulars and the Delaware law on the subject, the record does not establish that this transaction satisfies any reasonable concept of fair dealing, and the Chancellor's findings in that regard must be reversed.

E.

Turning to the matter of price, plaintiff also challenges its fairness. His evidence was that on the date the merger was approved the stock was worth at least $26 per share. In support, he offered the testimony of a chartered investment analyst who used two basic approaches to valuation: a comparative analysis of the premium paid over market in ten other tender offer-merger combinations, and a discounted cash flow analysis.

In this breach of fiduciary duty case, the Chancellor perceived that the approach to valuation was the same as that in an appraisal proceeding. Consistent with precedent, he rejected plaintiff's method of proof and accepted defendants' evidence of value as being in accord with practice under prior case law. This means that the so-called "Delaware block" or weighted average method was employed wherein the elements of value, i.e., assets, market price, earnings, etc., were assigned a particular weight and the resulting amounts added to determine the value per share. This procedure has been in use for decades. *See In re General Realty & Utilities Corp.* However, to the extent it excludes other generally accepted techniques used in the financial community and the courts, it is now clearly outmoded. It is time we recognize this in appraisal and other stock valuation proceedings and bring our law current on the subject.

While the Chancellor rejected plaintiff's discounted cash flow method of valuing UOP's stock, as not corresponding with "either logic or the existing law," it is significant that this was essentially the focus, i.e., earnings potential of UOP, of Messrs. Arledge and Chitiea in their evaluation of the merger. Accordingly, the standard "Delaware block" or weighted average method of valuation, formerly employed in appraisal and other stock valuation cases, shall no longer exclusively control such proceedings. We believe that a more liberal approach must include proof of value by any techniques or methods which are generally considered acceptable in the financial community and otherwise admissible in court, subject only to our interpretation of 8 Del.C. § 262(h), *infra. See also* D.R.E. 702–05. This will obviate the very structured and mechanistic procedure that has heretofore governed such matters. *See Jacques Coe & Co. v. Minneapolis-Moline Co.; Tri-Continental Corp. v. Battye; In re General Realty and Utilities Corp., supra.*

Fair price obviously requires consideration of all relevant factors involving the value of a company. This has long been the law of Delaware as stated in *Tri-Continental Corp.*:

> The basic concept of value under the appraisal statute is that the stockholder is entitled to be paid for that which has been taken from him, viz., his proportionate interest in a going concern. By value of the stockholder's proportionate interest in the corporate enterprise is meant the true or intrinsic value of his stock which has been taken by the merger. In determining what figure represents this true or intrinsic value, the appraiser and the courts must take into consideration all factors and elements which reasonably might enter into the fixing of value. Thus, market value, asset value, dividends, earning prospects, the nature of the enterprise and any other facts which were known or which could be ascertained as of the date of merger and which throw any light on *future prospects* of the merged corporation are not only pertinent to an inquiry as to the value

of the dissenting stockholders' interest, but *must be considered* by the agency fixing the value. (Emphasis added.)

This is not only in accord with the realities of present day affairs, but it is thoroughly consonant with the purpose and intent of our statutory law. Under 8 Del.C. § 262(h), the Court of Chancery:

> shall appraise the shares, determining their *fair* value exclusive of any element of value arising from the accomplishment or expectation of the merger, together with a fair rate of interest, if any, to be paid upon the amount determined to be the *fair* value. In determining such *fair* value, the Court shall take into account *all relevant factors* . . . (Emphasis added) [. . .]

It is significant that section 262 now mandates the determination of "fair" value based upon "all relevant factors." Only the speculative elements of value that may arise from the "accomplishment or expectation" of the merger are excluded. We take this to be a very narrow exception to the appraisal process, designed to eliminate use of *pro forma* data and projections of a speculative variety relating to the completion of a merger. But elements of future value, including the nature of the enterprise, which are known or susceptible of proof as of the date of the merger and not the product of speculation, may be considered. When the trial court deems it appropriate, fair value also includes any damages, resulting from the taking, which the stockholders sustain as a class. If that was not the case, then the obligation to consider "all relevant factors" in the valuation process would be eroded. We are supported in this view not only by *Tri-Continental Corp.*, but also by the evolutionary amendments to section 262.

Prior to an amendment in 1976, the earlier relevant provision of section 262 stated:

> (f) The appraiser shall determine the value of the stock of the stockholders [. . .] The Court shall by its decree determine the value of the stock of the stockholders entitled to payment therefor [. . .]

The first references to "fair" value occurred in a 1976 amendment to section 262(f), which provided:

> (f) [. . .] the Court shall appraise the shares, determining their fair value exclusively of any element of value arising from the accomplishment or expectation of the merger [. . .].

It was not until the 1981 amendment to section 262 that the reference to "fair value" was repeatedly emphasized and the statutory mandate that the Court "take into account all relevant factors" appeared [section 262(h)]. Clearly, there is a legislative intent to fully compensate shareholders for whatever their loss may be, subject only to the narrow limitation that one cannot take speculative effects of the merger into account.

Although the Chancellor received the plaintiff's evidence, his opinion indicates that the use of it was precluded because of past Delaware practice. While we do not suggest a monetary result one way or the other, we do think the plaintiff's evidence should be part of the factual mix and weighed as such. Until the $21 price is measured on remand by the valuation standards mandated by Delaware law, there can be no finding at the present stage of these proceedings that the price is fair. Given the lack of any candid disclosure of the material facts surrounding establishment of the $21 price, the majority of the minority vote, approving the merger, is meaningless.

The plaintiff has not sought an appraisal, but rescissory damages of the type contemplated by *Lynch v. Vickers Energy Corp.* (*Lynch II*). In view of the approach to valuation that we announce today, we see no basis in our law for *Lynch II*'s exclusive monetary formula for relief. On remand the plaintiff will be permitted to test the fairness of the $21 price by the standards we herein establish, in conformity with the principle applicable to an appraisal—that fair value be determined by taking "into account all relevant factors" [*see* 8 Del.C. § 262(h), *supra*]. In our view this includes the elements of rescissory damages if the Chancellor considers them susceptible of proof and a remedy appropriate to all the issues of fairness before him. To the extent that *Lynch II* purports to limit the Chancellor's discretion to a single remedial formula for monetary damages in a cash-out merger, it is overruled.

While a plaintiff's monetary remedy ordinarily should be confined to the more liberalized appraisal proceeding herein established, we do not intend any limitation on the historic powers of the Chancellor to grant such other relief as the facts of a particular case may dictate. The appraisal remedy we approve may not be adequate in certain cases, particularly where fraud, misrepresentation, self-dealing, deliberate waste of corporate assets, or gross and palpable overreaching are involved. *Cole v. National Cash Credit Association.* Under such circumstances, the Chancellor's powers are complete to fashion any form of equitable and monetary relief as may be appropriate, including rescissory damages. Since it is apparent that this long completed transaction is too involved to undo, and in view of the Chancellor's discretion, the award, if any, should be in the form of monetary damages based upon entire fairness standards, i.e., fair dealing and fair price.

Obviously, there are other litigants, like the plaintiff, who abjured an appraisal and whose rights to challenge the element of fair value must be preserved. *See* 8 Del.C. § 262(a), (d) & (e). Accordingly, the quasi-appraisal remedy we grant the plaintiff here will apply only to: (1) this case; (2) any case now pending on appeal to this Court; (3) any case now pending in the Court of Chancery which has not yet been appealed but which may be eligible for direct appeal to this Court; (4) any case challenging a cash-out merger, the effective date of which is on or before February 1, 1983; and (5) any proposed merger to be presented at a shareholders' meeting, the notification of which is mailed to the stockholders on or before February 23, 1983. Thereafter, the provisions of 8 Del.C. § 262, as herein construed, respecting the scope of an appraisal and the means for perfecting the same, shall govern the financial remedy available to minority shareholders in a cash-out merger. Thus, we return to the well established principles of *Stauffer v. Standard Brands, Inc.* and *David J. Greene & Co. v. Schenley Industries, Inc.*, mandating a stockholder's recourse to the basic remedy of an appraisal. [. . .]

The judgment of the Court of Chancery, finding both the circumstances of the merger and the price paid the minority shareholders to be fair, is reversed. The matter is remanded for further proceedings consistent herewith. Upon remand the plaintiff's post-trial motion to enlarge the class should be granted.

REVERSED AND REMANDED.

Kahn v. M & F Worldwide Corp.

88 A.3d 635 (Del. 2014)

■ HOLLAND, JUSTICE:

This is an appeal from a final judgment entered by the Court of Chancery in a proceeding that arises from a 2011 acquisition by MacAndrews & Forbes Holdings, Inc. ("M & F" or "MacAndrews & Forbes")—a 43% stockholder in M & F Worldwide Corp. ("MFW")—of the remaining common stock of MFW (the "Merger"). From the outset, M & F's proposal to take MFW private was made contingent upon two stockholder-protective procedural conditions. First, M & F required the Merger to be negotiated and approved by a special committee of independent MFW directors (the "Special Committee"). Second, M & F required that the Merger be approved by a majority of stockholders unaffiliated with M & F. The Merger closed in December 2011, after it was approved by a vote of 65.4% of MFW's minority stockholders.

[. . .] The Appellants [. . .] sought post-closing relief against M & F, Ronald O. Perelman, and MFW's directors (including the members of the Special Committee) for breach of fiduciary duty. Again, the Appellants were provided with extensive discovery. The Defendants then moved for summary judgment, which the Court of Chancery granted.

Court of Chancery Decision

The Court of Chancery found that the case presented a "novel question of law," specifically, "what standard of review should apply to a going private merger conditioned upfront by the controlling stockholder on approval by both a properly empowered, independent committee and an informed, uncoerced majority-of-the-minority vote." The Court of Chancery held that business judgment review, rather than entire fairness, should be applied to a very limited category of controller mergers. That category consisted of mergers where the controller voluntarily relinquishes its control—such that the negotiation and approval process replicate those that characterize a third-party merger.

The Court of Chancery held that, rather than entire fairness, the business judgment standard of review should apply "if, *but only if:* (i) the controller conditions the transaction on the approval of both a Special Committee and a majority of the minority stockholders; (ii) the Special Committee is independent; (iii) the Special Committee is empowered to freely select its own advisors and to say no definitively; (iv) the Special Committee acts with care; (v) the minority vote is informed; and (vi) there is no coercion of the minority."

The Court of Chancery found that those prerequisites were satisfied and that the Appellants had failed to raise any genuine issue of material fact indicating the contrary. The court then reviewed the Merger under the business judgment standard and granted summary judgment for the Defendants.

[EDS.—The Appellants argued that the standard of review should have been entire fairness because the Special Litigation Committee was not disinterested and independent, not fully empowered, and was not effective; in addition, they claimed that in freeze out mergers by a controlling shareholder the applicable standard of review should be entire fairness notwithstanding the conditioning of the deal on both Special Committee approval and a favorable majority of the minority vote. The Defendants contended that the judicial standard of review should be the business judgment rule, because the merger was conditioned *ab initio* on two procedural protections that together operated to replicate an arm's-length merger: the employment of an active, unconflicted negotiating agent free to turn down the transaction; and a requirement that any transaction negotiated by that agent be approved by a majority of the disinterested stockholders.]

FACTS

MFW and M & F

MFW is a holding company incorporated in Delaware. Before the Merger that is the subject of this dispute, MFW was 43.4% owned by MacAndrews & Forbes, which in turn is entirely owned by Ronald O. Perelman. [. . .]

The MFW board had thirteen members. They were: Ronald Perelman, Barry Schwartz, William Bevins, Bruce Slovin, Charles Dawson, Stephen Taub, John Keane, Theo Folz, Philip Beekman, Martha Byorum, Viet Dinh, Paul Meister, and Carl Webb. Perelman, Schwartz, and Bevins were officers of both MFW and MacAndrews & Forbes. Perelman was the Chairman of MFW and the Chairman and CEO of MacAndrews & Forbes; Schwartz was the President and CEO of MFW and the Vice Chairman and Chief Administrative Officer of MacAndrews & Forbes; and Bevins was a Vice President at MacAndrews & Forbes.

The Taking MFW Private Proposal

In May 2011, Perelman began to explore the possibility of taking MFW private. At that time, MFW's stock price traded in the $20 to $24 per share range. MacAndrews & Forbes engaged a bank, Moelis & Company, to advise it. After preparing valuations based on projections that had been supplied to lenders by MFW in April and May 2011, Moelis valued MFW at between $10 and $32 a share.

On June 10, 2011, MFW's shares closed on the New York Stock Exchange at $16.96. The next business day, June 13, 2011, Schwartz sent a letter proposal ("Proposal") to the MFW board to buy the remaining MFW shares for $24 in cash. The Proposal stated, in relevant part:

> The proposed transaction would be subject to the approval of the Board of Directors of the Company [*i.e.,* MFW] and the negotiation and execution of mutually acceptable definitive transaction documents. It is our expectation that the Board of Directors will appoint a special committee of independent directors to consider our proposal and make a recommendation to the Board of Directors. *We will not move forward with the transaction unless it is approved by such a special committee. In addition, the transaction will be subject to a non-waivable condition requiring the approval of a majority of the shares of the Company not owned by M & F or its affiliates* [. . .]

In connection with this proposal, [. . .] we encourage the special committee to retain its own legal and financial advisors to assist it in its review.

MacAndrews & Forbes filed this letter with the U.S. Securities and Exchange Commission ("SEC") and issued a press release disclosing substantially the same information.

The Special Committee Is Formed

The MFW board met the following day to consider the Proposal. At the meeting, Schwartz presented the offer on behalf of MacAndrews & Forbes. Subsequently, Schwartz and Bevins, as the two directors present who were also directors of MacAndrews & Forbes, recused themselves from the meeting, as did Dawson, the CEO of HCHC, who had previously expressed support for the proposed offer.

The independent directors then invited counsel from Willkie Farr & Gallagher—a law firm that had recently represented a Special Committee of MFW's independent directors in a potential acquisition of a subsidiary of MacAndrews & Forbes—to join the meeting. The independent directors decided to form the Special Committee, and resolved further that:

> [T]he Special Committee is empowered to: (i) make such investigation of the Proposal as the Special Committee deems appropriate; (ii) evaluate the terms of the Proposal; (iii)

negotiate with Holdings [*i.e.,* MacAndrews & Forbes] and its representatives any element of the Proposal; (iv) negotiate the terms of any definitive agreement with respect to the Proposal (it being understood that the execution thereof shall be subject to the approval of the Board); (v) report to the Board its recommendations and conclusions with respect to the Proposal, including a determination and *recommendation as to whether the Proposal is fair and in the best interests of the stockholders of the Company other than Holdings* and its affiliates and should be approved by the Board; and (vi) determine to elect not to pursue the Proposal [. . .]

[. . .] [T]he Board shall not approve the Proposal without a prior favorable recommendation of the Special Committee [. . .]

[T]he Special Committee [is] empowered to retain and employ legal counsel, a financial advisor, and such other agents as the Special Committee shall deem necessary or desirable in connection with these matters [. . .].

The Special Committee consisted of Byorum, Dinh, Meister (the chair), Slovin, and Webb. The following day, Slovin recused himself because, although the MFW board had determined that he qualified as an independent director under the rules of the New York Stock Exchange, he had "some current relationships that could raise questions about his independence for purposes of serving on the Special Committee."

ANALYSIS

What Should Be The Review Standard?

Where a transaction involving self-dealing by a controlling stockholder is challenged, the applicable standard of judicial review is "entire fairness," with the defendants having the burden of persuasion. *Kahn v. Tremont Corp.*; *Weinberger v. UOP, Inc.*; *Rosenblatt v. Getty Oil Co.* In other words, the defendants bear the ultimate burden of proving that the transaction with the controlling stockholder was entirely fair to the minority stockholders. In *Kahn v. Lynch Communication Systems, Inc.*, however, this Court held that in "entire fairness" cases, the defendants may shift the burden of persuasion to the plaintiff if either (1) they show that the transaction was approved by a well-functioning committee of independent directors; or (2) they show that the transaction was approved by an informed vote of a majority of the minority stockholders.

This appeal presents a question of first impression: what should be the standard of review for a merger between a controlling stockholder and its subsidiary, where the merger is conditioned *ab initio* upon the approval of both an independent, adequately-empowered Special Committee that fulfills its duty of care, and the uncoerced, informed vote of a majority of the minority stockholders. The question has never been put directly to this Court.

Almost two decades ago, in *Kahn v. Lynch,* we held that the approval by *either* a Special Committee *or* the majority of the noncontrolling stockholders of a merger with a buying controlling stockholder would shift the burden of proof under the entire fairness standard from the defendant to the plaintiff. *Lynch* did not involve a merger conditioned by the controlling stockholder on both procedural protections. The Appellants submit, nonetheless, that statements in *Lynch* and its progeny could be (and were) read to suggest that even if both procedural protections were used, the standard of review would remain entire fairness. However, in *Lynch* and the other cases that Appellants cited, *Southern Peru* and *Kahn v. Tremont,* the controller did not give up its voting power by agreeing to a non-waivable majority-of-the-minority condition. That is the vital distinction between those cases and this one. The question is what the legal consequence of that distinction should be in these circumstances.

The Court of Chancery held that the consequence should be that the business judgment standard of review will govern going private mergers with a controlling stockholder that are conditioned *ab initio* upon (1) the approval of an independent and fully-empowered Special Committee that fulfills its duty of care and (2) the uncoerced, informed vote of the majority of the minority stockholders.

The Court of Chancery rested its holding upon the premise that the common law equitable rule that best protects minority investors is one that encourages controlling stockholders to accord the minority both procedural protections. A transactional structure subject to both conditions differs fundamentally from a merger having only one of those protections, in that:

> By giving controlling stockholders the opportunity to have a going private transaction reviewed under the business judgment rule, a strong incentive is created to give minority stockholders much broader access to the transactional structure that is most likely to effectively protect their interests. . . . That structure, it is important to note, is critically different than a structure that uses only *one* of the procedural protections. The "or" structure does not replicate the protections of a third-party merger under the DGCL approval process, because it only requires that one, and not both, of the statutory requirements of director and stockholder approval be accomplished by impartial decisionmakers. The "both" structure, by contrast, replicates the arm's-length merger steps of the DGCL by "requir[ing] two independent approvals, which it is fair to say serve independent integrity-enforcing functions." *In re MFW S'holders Litig.*

Before the Court of Chancery, the Appellants acknowledged that "this transactional structure is the optimal one for minority shareholders." Before us, however, they argue that neither procedural protection is adequate to protect minority stockholders, because "possible ineptitude and timidity of directors" may undermine the special committee protection, and because majority-of-the-minority votes may be unduly influenced by arbitrageurs that have an institutional bias to approve virtually any transaction that offers a market premium, however insubstantial it may be. Therefore, the Appellants claim, these protections, even when combined, are not sufficient to justify "abandon[ing]" the entire fairness standard of review.

With regard to the Special Committee procedural protection, the Appellants' assertions regarding the MFW directors' inability to discharge their duties are not supported either by the record or by well-established principles of Delaware law. As the Court of Chancery correctly observed:

> Although it is possible that there are independent directors who have little regard for their duties or for being perceived by their company's stockholders (and the larger network of institutional investors) as being effective at protecting public stockholders, the court thinks they are likely to be exceptional, and certainly our Supreme Court's jurisprudence does not embrace such a skeptical view.

Regarding the majority-of-the-minority vote procedural protection, as the Court of Chancery noted, "plaintiffs themselves do not argue that minority stockholders will vote against a going private transaction because of fear of retribution." Instead, as the Court of Chancery summarized, the Appellants argued as follows:

> [Plaintiffs] just believe that most investors like a premium and will tend to vote for a deal that delivers one and that many long-term investors will sell out when they can obtain most of the premium without waiting for the ultimate vote. But that argument is not one that suggests that the voting decision is not voluntary, it is simply an editorial about the motives of investors and does not contradict the premise that a majority-of-the-minority condition gives minority investors a free and voluntary opportunity to decide what is fair for themselves.

Business Judgment Review Standard Adopted

We hold that business judgment is the standard of review that should govern mergers between a controlling stockholder and its corporate subsidiary, where the merger is conditioned *ab initio* upon both the approval of an independent, adequately-empowered Special Committee that fulfills its duty of care; and the uncoerced, informed vote of a majority of the minority stockholders. We so conclude for several reasons.

First, entire fairness is the highest standard of review in corporate law. It is applied in the controller merger context as a substitute for the dual statutory protections of disinterested board and stockholder approval, because both protections are potentially undermined by the influence of the controller. However, as this case establishes, that undermining influence does not exist in every controlled merger setting, regardless of the circumstances. The simultaneous deployment of the procedural protections employed here create a countervailing, offsetting influence of equal—if not greater—force. That is, where the controller irrevocably and publicly disables itself from using its control to dictate the outcome of the negotiations and the shareholder vote, the controlled merger then acquires the shareholder-protective characteristics of third-party, arm's-length mergers, which are reviewed under the business judgment standard.

Second, the dual procedural protection merger structure optimally protects the minority stockholders in controller buyouts. As the Court of Chancery explained:

> [W]hen these two protections are established up-front, a potent tool to extract good value for the minority is established. From inception, the controlling stockholder knows that it cannot bypass the special committee's ability to say no. And, the controlling stockholder knows it cannot dangle a majority-of-the-minority vote before the special committee late in the process as a deal-closer rather than having to make a price move.

Third, and as the Court of Chancery reasoned, applying the business judgment standard to the dual protection merger structure:

> [. . .] is consistent with the central tradition of Delaware law, which defers to the informed decisions of impartial directors, especially when those decisions have been approved by the disinterested stockholders on full information and without coercion. Not only that, the adoption of this rule will be of benefit to minority stockholders because it will provide a strong incentive for controlling stockholders to accord minority investors the transactional structure that respected scholars believe will provide them the best protection, a structure where stockholders get the benefits of independent, empowered negotiating agents to bargain for the best price and say no if the agents believe the deal is not advisable for any proper reason, plus the critical ability to determine for themselves whether to accept any deal that their negotiating agents recommend to them. A transactional structure with both these protections is fundamentally different from one with only one protection.

Fourth, the underlying purposes of the dual protection merger structure utilized here and the entire fairness standard of review both converge and are fulfilled at the same critical point: price. Following *Weinberger v. UOP, Inc.,* this Court has consistently held that, although entire fairness review comprises the dual components of fair dealing and fair price, in a non-fraudulent transaction "price may be the preponderant consideration outweighing other features of the merger." The dual protection merger structure requires two price-related pretrial determinations: first, that a fair price was achieved by an empowered, independent committee that acted with care; and, second, that a fully-informed, uncoerced majority of the minority stockholders voted in favor of the price that was recommended by the independent committee.

The New Standard Summarized

To summarize our holding, in controller buyouts, the business judgment standard of review will be applied *if and only if:* (i) the controller conditions the procession of the transaction on the approval of both a Special Committee and a majority of the minority stockholders; (ii) the Special Committee is independent; (iii) the Special Committee is empowered to freely select its own advisors and to say no definitively; (iv) the Special Committee meets its duty of care in negotiating a fair price; (v) the vote of the minority is informed; and (vi) there is no coercion of the minority.

If a plaintiff that can plead a reasonably conceivable set of facts showing that any or all of those enumerated conditions did not exist, that complaint would state a claim for relief that would entitle the plaintiff to proceed and conduct discovery. *Cent. Mortg. Co. v. Morgan Stanley Mortg. Capital Holdings LLC.* If, after discovery, triable issues of fact remain about whether either or both of the dual procedural protections were established, or if established were effective, the case will proceed to a trial in which the court will conduct an entire fairness review. *Ams. Mining Corp. v. Theriault.*

This approach is consistent with *Weinberger, Lynch* and their progeny. A controller that employs and/or establishes only one of these dual procedural protections would continue to receive burden-shifting within the entire fairness standard of review framework. Stated differently, unless *both* procedural protections for the minority stockholders are established *prior to trial,* the ultimate judicial scrutiny of controller buyouts will continue to be the entire fairness standard of review. *Theriault.* [. . .]

Dual Protection Inquiry

To reiterate, in this case, the controlling stockholder conditioned its offer upon the MFW Board agreeing, *ab initio,* to both procedural protections, *i.e.,* approval by a Special Committee and by a majority of the minority stockholders. For the combination of an effective committee process and majority-of-the-minority vote to qualify (jointly) for business judgment review, each of these protections must be effective singly to warrant a burden shift.

In *Kahn v. Tremont Corp.,* this Court held that "[t]o obtain the benefit of burden shifting, the controlling stockholder must do more than establish a perfunctory special committee of outside directors."

Rather, the special committee must "function in a manner which indicates that the controlling stockholder did not dictate the terms of the transaction and that the committee exercised real bargaining power 'at an arms-length.' " *Kahn*. As we have previously noted, deciding whether an independent committee was effective in negotiating a price is a process so fact-intensive and inextricably intertwined with the merits of an entire fairness review (fair dealing and fair price) that a pretrial determination of burden shifting is often impossible. *Theriault*. Here, however, the Defendants have successfully established a record of independent committee effectiveness and process that warranted a grant of summary judgment entitling them to a burden shift prior to trial. [. . .]

The Special Committee Was Independent

The Appellants do not challenge the independence of the Special Committee's Chairman, Meister. They claim, however, that the three other Special Committee members—Webb, Dinh, and Byorum—were beholden to Perelman because of their prior business and/or social dealings with Perelman or Perelman-related entities.

The Appellants first challenge the independence of Webb. They urged that Webb and Perelman shared a "longstanding and lucrative business partnership" between 1983 and 2002 which included acquisitions of thrifts and financial institutions, and which led to a 2002 asset sale to Citibank in which Webb made "a significant amount of money." The Court of Chancery concluded, however, that the fact of Webb having engaged in business dealings with Perelman nine years earlier did not raise a triable fact issue regarding his ability to evaluate the Merger impartially. *Beam ex rel. Martha Stewart Living Omnimedia, Inc. v. Stewart*. We agree.

Second, the Appellants argued that there were triable issues of fact regarding Dinh's independence. The Appellants demonstrated that between 2009 and 2011, Dinh's law firm, Bancroft PLLC, advised M & F and Scientific Games (in which M & F owned a 37.6% stake), during which time the Bancroft firm earned $200,000 in fees. The record reflects that Bancroft's limited prior engagements, which were inactive by the time the Merger proposal was announced, were fully disclosed to the Special Committee soon after it was formed. The Court of Chancery found that the Appellants failed to proffer any evidence to show that compensation received by Dinh's law firm was material to Dinh, in the sense that it would have influenced his decisionmaking with respect to the M & F proposal. The only evidence of record, the Court of Chancery concluded, was that these fees were "*de minimis*" and that the Appellants had offered no contrary evidence that would create a genuine issue of material fact. *See* Ct. Ch. R. 56(e).

The Court of Chancery also found that the relationship between Dinh, a Georgetown University Law Center professor, and M & F's Barry Schwartz, who sits on the Georgetown Board of Visitors, did not create a triable issue of fact as to Dinh's independence. No record evidence suggested that Schwartz could exert influence on Dinh's position at Georgetown based on his recommendation regarding the Merger. Indeed,

Dinh had earned tenure as a professor at Georgetown before he ever knew Schwartz.

The Appellants also argue that Schwartz's later invitation to Dinh to join the board of directors of Revlon, Inc. "illustrates the ongoing personal relationship between Schwartz and Dinh." There is no record evidence that Dinh expected to be asked to join Revlon's board at the time he served on the Special Committee. Moreover, the Court of Chancery noted, Schwartz's invitation for Dinh to join the Revlon board of directors occurred months after the Merger was approved and did not raise a triable fact issue concerning Dinh's independence from Perelman. We uphold the Court of Chancery's findings relating to Dinh.

Third, the Appellants urge that issues of material fact permeate Byorum's independence and, specifically, that Byorum "had a business relationship with Perelman from 1991 to 1996 through her executive position at Citibank." The Court of Chancery concluded, however, the Appellants presented no evidence of the nature of Byorum's interactions with Perelman while she was at Citibank. Nor was there evidence that after 1996 Byorum had an ongoing economic relationship with Perelman that was material to her in any way. Byorum testified that any interactions she had with Perelman while she was at Citibank resulted from her role as a senior executive, because Perelman was a client of the bank at the time. Byorum also testified that she had no business relationship with Perelman between 1996 and 2007, when she joined the MFW Board.

The Appellants also contend that Byorum performed advisory work for Scientific Games in 2007 and 2008 as a senior managing director of Stephens Cori Capital Advisors ("Stephens Cori"). The Court of Chancery found, however, that the Appellants had adduced no evidence tending to establish that the $100,000 fee Stephens Cori received for that work was material to either Stephens Cori or to Byorum personally. Stephens Cori's engagement for Scientific Games, which occurred years before the Merger was announced and the Special Committee was convened, was fully disclosed to the Special Committee, which concluded that "it was not material, and it would not represent a conflict." We uphold the Court of Chancery's findings relating to Byorum as well.

[. . .] To show that a director is not independent, a plaintiff must demonstrate that the director is "beholden" to the controlling party "or so under [the controller's] influence that [the director's] discretion would be sterilized." *Rales v. Blasband*. Bare allegations that directors are friendly with, travel in the same social circles as, or have past business relationships with the proponent of a transaction or the person they are investigating are not enough to rebut the presumption of independence. *Martha Stewart*.

A plaintiff seeking to show that a director was not independent must satisfy a materiality standard. The court must conclude that the director in question had ties to the person whose proposal or actions he or she is evaluating that are sufficiently substantial that he or she could not objectively discharge his or her fiduciary duties. *Cinerama, Inc. v. Technicolor.* Consistent with that predicate materiality requirement, the existence of some financial ties between the interested party and the director, without more, is not disqualifying. The inquiry must be whether, applying a subjective standard, those ties were *material,* in the sense that the alleged ties could have affected the impartiality of the individual director. *Cinerama.* [. . .]

The Court of Chancery found that to the extent the Appellants claimed the Special Committee members, Webb, Dinh, and Byorum, were beholden to Perelman based on prior economic relationships with him, the Appellants never developed or proffered evidence showing the materiality of those relationships [. . .].

The record supports the Court of Chancery's holding that none of the Appellants' claims relating to Webb, Dinh or Byorum raised a triable issue of material fact concerning their individual independence or the Special Committee's collective independence.

The Special Committee Was Empowered

It is undisputed that the Special Committee was empowered to hire its own legal and financial advisors, and it retained Willkie Farr & Gallagher LLP as its legal advisor. After interviewing four potential financial advisors, the Special Committee engaged Evercore Partners ("Evercore"). The qualifications and independence of Evercore and Willkie Farr & Gallagher LLP are not contested.

Among the powers given the Special Committee in the board resolution was the authority to "report to the Board its recommendations and conclusions with respect to the [Merger], including a determination and recommendation as to whether the Proposal is fair and in the best interests of the stockholders. . . ." The Court of Chancery also found that it was "undisputed that the [S]pecial [C]ommittee was empowered not simply to 'evaluate' the offer, like some special committees with weak mandates, but to negotiate with [M & F] over the terms of its offer to buy out the noncontrolling stockholders. This negotiating power was accompanied by the clear authority to say no definitively to [M & F]" and to "make that decision stick." MacAndrews & Forbes promised that it would not proceed with any going private proposal that did not have the support of the Special Committee. Therefore, the Court of Chancery concluded, "the MFW committee did not have to fear that if it bargained too hard, MacAndrews & Forbes could bypass the committee and make a tender offer directly to the minority stockholders." [. . .]

The Special Committee Exercised Due Care

The Special Committee insisted from the outset that MacAndrews (including any "dual" employees who worked for both MFW and MacAndrews) be screened off from the Special Committee's process, to ensure that the process replicated arm's-length negotiations with a third party. In order to carefully evaluate M & F's offer, the Special Committee held a total of eight meetings during the summer of 2011.

From the outset of their work, the Special Committee and Evercore had projections that had been prepared by MFW's business segments in April and May 2011. Early in the process, Evercore and the Special Committee asked MFW management to produce new projections that reflected management's most up-to-date, and presumably most accurate, thinking. Consistent with the Special Committee's determination to conduct its analysis free of any MacAndrews influence, MacAndrews—including "dual" MFW/MacAndrews executives who normally vetted MFW projections—were excluded from the process of preparing the updated financial projections. Mafco, the licorice business, advised Evercore that all of its projections would remain the same. Harland Clarke updated its projections. On July 22, 2011, Evercore received new projections from HCHC, which incorporated the updated projections from Harland Clarke. Evercore then constructed a valuation model based upon all of these updated projections. [. . .]

In scrutinizing the Special Committee's execution of its broad mandate, the Court of Chancery determined there was no "evidence indicating that the independent members of the special committee did not meet their duty of care. . . ." To the contrary, the Court of Chancery found, the Special Committee "met frequently and was presented with a rich body of financial information relevant to whether and at what *price* a going private transaction was advisable." The Court of Chancery ruled that "the plaintiffs d[id] not make any attempt to show that the MFW Special Committee failed to meet its duty of care. . . ." Based on the undisputed record, the Court of Chancery held that, "there is no triable issue of fact regarding whether the [S]pecial [C]ommittee fulfilled its duty of care." In the context of a controlling stockholder merger, a pretrial determination that the *price* was negotiated by an empowered independent committee that acted with care would shift the burden of persuasion to the plaintiffs under the entire fairness standard of review. *Kahn v. Lynch Commc'n Sys.*

Majority of Minority Stockholder Vote

We now consider the second procedural protection invoked by M & F— the majority-of-the-minority stockholder vote. Consistent with the second condition imposed by M & F at the outset, the Merger was then put before MFW's stockholders for a vote. On November 18, 2011, the stockholders were provided with a proxy statement, which contained the history of the Special Committee's work and recommended that they vote in favor of the transaction at a price of $25 per share.

The proxy statement disclosed, among other things, that the Special Committee had countered M & F's initial $24 per share offer at $30 per share, but only was able to achieve a final offer of $25 per share. The proxy statement disclosed that the MFW business divisions had discussed with Evercore whether the initial projections Evercore received reflected management's latest thinking. It also disclosed that the updated projections were lower. The proxy statement also included the five separate price ranges for the value of MFW's stock that Evercore had generated with its different valuation analyses.

Knowing the proxy statement's disclosures of the background of the Special Committee's work, of Evercore's valuation ranges, and of the analyses supporting Evercore's *fairness opinion,* MFW's stockholders— representing more than 65% of the minority shares—approved the Merger. In the controlling stockholder merger context, it is settled Delaware law that an uncoerced, informed majority-of-the-minority vote, without any other procedural protection, is itself sufficient to shift the burden of persuasion to the plaintiff under the entire fairness standard of review. *Rosenblatt v. Getty Oil Co.* The Court of Chancery found that "the plaintiffs themselves do not dispute that the majority-of-the-minority vote was fully informed and uncoerced, because they fail to allege any failure of disclosure or any act of coercion."

Both Procedural Protections Established

Based on a highly extensive record, the Court of Chancery concluded that the procedural protections upon which the Merger was conditioned— approval by an independent and empowered Special Committee and by a uncoerced informed majority of MFW's minority stockholders—had *both* been undisputedly established *prior to trial.* We agree and conclude the Defendants' motion for summary judgment was properly granted on all of those issues.

Business Judgment Review Properly Applied

We have determined that the business judgment rule standard of review applies to this controlling stockholder buyout. Under that standard, the claims against the Defendants must be dismissed unless no rational person could have believed that the merger was favorable to MFW's minority stockholders. In this case, it cannot be credibly argued (let alone concluded) that no rational person would find the Merger favorable to MFW's minority stockholders.

Conclusion

For the above-stated reasons, the judgment of the Court of Chancery is affirmed.

E. TAKEOVER DEFENSES AND FIDUCIARY DUTIES

Cheff v. Mathes
199 A.2d 548 (Del.Ch. 1964)

■ CAREY, JUSTICE.

This is an appeal from the decision of the Vice-Chancellor in a derivative suit holding certain directors of Holland Furnace Company liable for loss allegedly resulting from improper use of corporate funds to purchase shares of the company. Because a meaningful decision upon review turns upon a complete understanding of the factual background, a somewhat detailed summary of the evidence is required.

Holland Furnace Company, a corporation of the State of Delaware, manufactures warm air furnaces, air conditioning equipment, and other home heating equipment. At the time of the relevant transactions, the board of directors was composed of the seven individual defendants. Mr. Cheff had been Holland's Chief Executive Officer since 1933, received an annual salary of $77,400, and personally owned 6,000 shares of the company. He was also a director. Mrs. Cheff, the wife of Mr. Cheff, was a daughter of the founder of Holland and had served as a director since 1922. She personally owned 5,804 shares of Holland and owned 47.9 percent of Hazelbank United Interest, Inc. Hazelbank is an investment vehicle for Mrs. Cheff and members of the Cheff-Landwehr family group, which owned 164,950 shares of the 883,585 outstanding shares of Holland. As a director, Mrs. Cheff received a compensation of $200.00 for each monthly board meeting, whether or not she attended the meeting.

The third director, Edgar P. Landwehr, is the nephew of Mrs. Cheff and personally owned 24,010 shares of Holland and 8.6 percent of the outstanding shares of Hazelbank. He received no compensation from Holland other than the monthly director's fee.

Robert H. Trenkamp is an attorney who first represented Holland in 1946. In May 1953, he became a director of Holland and acted as general counsel for the company. During the period in question, he received no retainer from the company, but did receive substantial sums for legal services rendered the company. Apart from the above-described payments, he received no compensation from Holland other than the monthly director's fee. He owned 200 shares of Holland Furnace stock. Although he owned no shares of Hazelbank, at the time relevant to this controversy, he was serving as a director and counsel of Hazelbank.

[EDS.—The other directors were John D. Ames, a partner in an investment firm, who was considered by the other members of the Holland board to be the financial advisor to the board; Ralph G. Boalt, a manufacturer and distributor of cosmetics; and George Spatta, the President of a large manufacturer of earth moving equipment.]

The board of directors of Hazelbank included the five principal shareholders: Mrs. Cheff; Leona Kolb, who was Mrs. Cheff's daughter; Mr. Landwehr; Mrs. Bowles, who was Mr. Landwehr's sister; Mrs. Putnam, who was also Mr. Landwehr's sister; Mr. Trenkamp; and Mr. William DeLong, an accountant.

Prior to the events in question, Holland employed approximately 8500 persons and maintained 400 branch sales offices located in 43 states. The volume of sales had declined from over $41,000,000 in 1948 to less than $32,000,000 in 1956. Defendants contend that the decline in earnings is attributable to the artificial post-war demand generated in the 1946–1948 period. In order to stabilize the condition of the company, the sales department apparently was reorganized and certain unprofitable branch offices were closed. By 1957 this reorganization had been completed and the management was convinced that the changes were manifesting beneficial results. The practice of the company was to directly employ the retail salesman, and the management considered that practice—unique in the furnace business—to be a vital factor in the company's success.

During the first five months of 1957, the monthly trading volume of Holland's stock on the New York Stock Exchange ranged between 10,300 shares to 24,200 shares. In the last week of June 1957, however, the trading increased to 37,800 shares, with a corresponding increase in the market price. In June of 1957, Mr. Cheff met with Mr. Arnold H. Maremont, who was President of Maremont Automotive Products, Inc. and Chairman of the boards of Motor Products Corporation and Allied Paper Corporation. Mr. Cheff testified, on deposition, that Maremont generally inquired about the feasibility of merger between Motor Products and Holland. Mr. Cheff testified that, in view of the difference in sales practices between the two companies, he informed Mr. Maremont that a merger did not seem feasible. In reply, Mr. Maremont stated that, in the light of Mr. Cheff's decision, he had no further interest in Holland nor did he wish to buy any of the stock of Holland.

None of the members of the board apparently connected the interest of Mr. Maremont with the increased activity of Holland stock. However, Mr. Trenkamp and Mr. Staal, the Treasurer of Holland, unsuccessfully made an informal investigation in order to ascertain the identity of the purchaser or purchasers. The mystery was resolved, however, when Maremont called Ames in July of 1957 to inform the latter that Maremont then owned 55,000 shares of Holland stock. At this juncture, no requests for change in corporate policy were made, and Maremont made no demand to be made a member of the board of Holland.

Ames reported the above information to the board at its July 30, 1957 meeting. Because of the position now occupied by Maremont, the board elected to investigate the financial and business history of Maremont and corporations controlled by him. Apart from the documentary evidence produced by this investigation, which will be considered infra, Staal testified, on deposition, that 'leading bank officials' had indicated that Maremont 'had been a participant, or had attempted to be, in the liquidation of a number of companies.' Staal specifically mentioned only one individual giving such advice, the Vice President of the First National Bank of Chicago. Mr. Cheff testified, at trial, of Maremont's alleged participation in liquidation activities. Mr. Cheff testified that: 'Throughout the whole of the Kalamazoo-Battle Creek area, and Detroit too, where I spent considerable time, he is well known and not highly regarded by any stretch.' This information was communicated to the board.

On August 23, 1957, at the request of Maremont, a meeting was held between Mr. Maremont and Cheff. At this meeting, Cheff was informed that Motor Products then owned approximately 100,000 shares of Holland stock. Maremont then made a demand that he be named to the board of directors, but Cheff refused to consider it. Since considerable controversy has been generated by Maremont's alleged threat to liquidate the company or substantially alter the sales force of Holland, we believe it desirable to set forth the testimony of Cheff on this point: 'Now we have 8500 men, direct employees, so the problem is entirely different. He indicated immediately that he had no interest in that type of distribution, that he didn't think it was modern, that he felt furnaces could be sold as he sold mufflers, through half a dozen salesmen in a wholesale way.'

Testimony was introduced by the defendants tending to show that substantial unrest was present among the employees of Holland as a result of the threat of Maremont to seek control of Holland. Thus, Mr. Cheff testified that the field organization was considering leaving in large numbers because of a fear of the consequences of a Maremont acquisition; he further testified that approximately '25 of our key men' were lost as the result of the unrest engendered by the Maremont proposal. Staal, corroborating Cheff's version, stated that a number of branch managers approached him for reassurances that Maremont was not going to be allowed to successfully gain control. Moreover, at approximately this time, the company was furnished with a Dun and Bradstreet report, which indicated the practice of Maremont to achieve quick profits by sales or liquidations of companies acquired by him. The defendants were also supplied with an income statement of Motor Products, Inc., showing a loss of $336,121.00 for the period in 1957.

On August 30, 1957, the board was informed by Cheff of Maremont's demand to be placed upon the board and of Maremont's belief that the retail sales organization of Holland was obsolete. The board was also informed of the results of the investigation by Cheff and Staal. Predicated upon this information, the board authorized the purchase of company stock on the market with corporate funds, ostensibly for use in a stock option plan.

Subsequent to this meeting, substantial numbers of shares were purchased and, in addition, Mrs. Cheff made alternate personal purchases of Holland stock. As a result of purchases by Maremont, Holland and Mrs. Cheff, the market price rose. On September 13, 1957, Maremont wrote to each of the directors of Holland and requested a broad engineering survey to be made for the benefit of all stockholders. During September, Motor Products released its annual report, which indicated that the investment in Holland was a 'special situation' as opposed to the normal policy of placing the funds of Motor Products into 'an active company'. On September 4th, Maremont proposed to sell his current holdings of Holland to the corporation for $14.00 a share. However, because of delay in responding to this offer, Maremont withdrew the offer. At this time, Mrs. Cheff was obviously quite concerned over the prospect of a Maremont acquisition, and had stated her willingness to expend her personal resources to prevent it.

On September 30, 1957, Motor Products Corporation, by letter to Mrs. Bowles, made a buy-sell offer to Hazelbank. At the Hazelbank meeting of October 3, 1957, Mrs. Bowles presented the letter to the board. The board took no action, but referred the proposal to its finance committee. Although Mrs. Bowles and Mrs. Putnam were opposed to any acquisition of Holland stock by Hazelbank, Mr. Landwehr conceded that a majority of the board were in favor of the purchase. Despite this fact, the finance committee elected to refer the offer to the Holland board on the grounds that it was the primary concern of Holland.

Thereafter, Mr. Trenkamp arranged for a meeting with Maremont, which occurred on October 14–15, 1957, in Chicago. Prior to this meeting, Trenkamp was aware of the intentions of Hazelbank and Mrs. Cheff to purchase all or portions of the stock then owned by Motor Products if Holland did not so act. As a result of the meeting, there was a tentative agreement on the part of Motor Products to sell its 155,000 shares at $14.40 per share. On October 23, 1957, at a special meeting of the Holland board, the purchase was considered. All directors, except Spatta, were present. The dangers allegedly posed by Maremont were again reviewed by the board. Trenkamp and Mrs. Cheff agree that the latter informed the board that either she or Hazelbank would purchase part or all of the block of Holland stock owned by Motor Products if the Holland board did not so act. The board was also informed that in order for the corporation to finance the purchase, substantial sums would have to be borrowed from commercial lending institutions. A resolution authorizing the purchase of 155,000 shares from Motor Products was adopted by the board. The price paid was in excess of the market price prevailing at the time, and the book value of the stock was approximately $20.00 as compared to approximately $14.00 for the net quick asset value. The transaction was subsequently consummated. The stock option plan mentioned in the minutes has never been implemented. In 1959, Holland stock reached a high of $15.25 a share.

On February 6, 1958, plaintiffs, owners of 60 shares of Holland stock, filed a derivative suit in the court below naming all of the individual directors of Holland, Holland itself and Motor Products Corporation as defendants. The complaint alleged that all of the purchases of stock by Holland in 1957 were for the purpose of insuring the perpetuation of control by the incumbent directors. The complaint requested that the transaction between Motor Products and Holland be rescinded and, secondly, that the individual defendants account to Holland for the alleged damages. Since Motor Products was never served with process, the initial remedy became inapplicable. Ames was never served nor did he enter an appearance.

After trial, the Vice Chancellor found the following facts: (a) Holland directly sells to retail consumers by means of numerous branch offices. There were no intermediate dealers. (b) Immediately prior to the complained-of transactions, the sales and earnings of Holland had declined and its marketing practices were under investigation by the Federal Trade Commission. (c) Mr. Cheff and Trenkamp had received substantial sums as Chief Executive and attorney of the company, respectively. (d) Maremont, on August 23rd, 1957, demanded a place on the board. (e) At the October 14th meeting between Trenkamp, Staal and Maremont, Trenkamp and Staal were authorized to speak for Hazelbank and Mrs. Cheff as well as Holland. Only Mr. Cheff, Mrs. Cheff, Mr. Landwehr, and Mr. Trenkamp clearly understood, prior to the October 23rd meeting, that either Hazelbank or Mrs. Cheff would have utilized their funds to purchase the Holland stock if Holland had not acted. (g) There was no real threat posed by Maremont and no substantial evidence of intention by Maremont to liquidate Holland. (h) Any employee unrest could have been caused by factors other than Maremont's intrusion and 'only one important employee was shown to have left, and his motive for leaving is not clear.' (1) The Court rejected the stock option plan as a meaningful rationale for the purchase from Maremont or the prior open market purchases.

The Court then found that the actual purpose behind the purchase was the desire to perpetuate control, but because of its finding that only the four above-named directors knew of the 'alternative', the remaining directors were exonerated. No appeal was taken by plaintiffs from that decision. [. . .]

Under the provisions of 8 Del.C. § 160, a corporation is granted statutory power to purchase and sell shares of its own stock. Such a right, as embodied in the statute, has long been recognized in this State. [. . .] The charge here is not one of violation of statute, but the allegation is that the true motives behind such purchases were improperly centered upon perpetuation of control. In an analogous field, courts have sustained the use of proxy funds to inform stockholders of management's views upon the policy questions inherent in an election to a board of directors, but have not sanctioned the use of corporate funds to advance the selfish desires of directors to perpetuate themselves in office. [. . .] Similarly, if the actions of the board were motivated by a sincere belief that the buying out of the dissident stockholder was necessary to maintain what the board believed to be proper business practices, the board will not be held liable for such decision, even though hindsight indicates the decision was not the wisest course. [. . .] On the other hand, if the board has acted solely or primarily because of the desire to perpetuate themselves in office, the use of corporate funds for such purposes is improper. [. . .]

Our first problem is the allocation of the burden of proof to show the presence or lack of good faith on the part of the board in authorizing the purchase of shares. Initially, the decision of the board of directors in authorizing a purchase was presumed to be in good faith and could be overturned only by a conclusive showing by plaintiffs of fraud or other misconduct. [. . .] However [. . .]

> 'We must bear in mind the inherent danger in the purchase of shares with corporate funds to remove a threat to corporate policy when a threat to control is involved. The directors are of necessity confronted with a conflict of interest, and an objective decision is difficult. * * * Hence, in our opinion, the burden should be on the directors to justify such a purchase as one primarily in the corporate interest.'

[. . .] To say that the burden of proof is upon the defendants is not to indicate, however, that the directors have the same 'self-dealing interest' as is present, for example, when a director sells property to the corporation. The only clear pecuniary interest shown on the record was held by Mr. Cheff, as an executive of the corporation, and Trenkamp, as its attorney. The mere fact that some of the other directors were substantial shareholders does not create a personal pecuniary interest in the decisions made by the board of directors, since all shareholders would presumably share the benefit flowing to the substantial shareholder. [. . .] Accordingly, these directors other than Trenkamp and Cheff, while called upon to justify their actions, will not be held to the same standard of proof required of those directors having personal and pecuniary interest in the transaction.

As noted above, the Vice Chancellor found that the stock option plan, mentioned in the minutes as a justification for the purchases, was not a motivating reason for the purchases. This finding we accept, since there is evidence to support it; in fact, Trenkamp admitted that the stock option plan was not the motivating reason. The minutes of October 23, 1957 dealing with the purchase from Maremont do not, in fact, mention the option plan as a reason for the purchase. While the minutes of the October 1, 1957 meeting only indicated the stock option plan as the motivating reason, the defendants are not bound by such statements and may supplement the minutes by oral testimony to show that the motivating reason was genuine fear of an acquisition by Maremont. [. . .]

Plaintiffs urge that the sale price was unfair in view of the fact that the price was in excess of that prevailing on the open market. However, as conceded by all parties, a substantial block of stock will normally sell at a higher price than that prevailing on the open market, the increment being attributable to a 'control premium'. Plaintiffs argue that it is inappropriate to require the defendant corporation to pay a control premium, since control is meaningless to an acquisition by a corporation of its own shares. However, it is elementary that a holder of a substantial number of shares would expect to receive the control premium as part of his selling price, and if the corporation desired to obtain the stock, it is unreasonable to expect that the corporation could avoid paying what any other purchaser would be required to pay for the stock. In any event, the financial expert produced by defendant at trial indicated that the price paid was fair and there was no rebuttal. Ames, the financial man on the board, was strongly of the opinion that the purchase was a good deal for the corporation. The Vice Chancellor made no finding as to the fairness of the price other than to indicate the obvious fact that the market price was increasing as a result of open market purchases by Maremont, Mrs. Cheff and Holland.

The question then presented is whether or not defendants satisfied the burden of proof of showing reasonable grounds to believe a danger to corporate policy and effectiveness existed by the presence of the Maremont stock ownership. It is important to remember that the directors satisfy their burden by showing good faith and reasonable investigation; the directors will not be penalized for an honest mistake of judgment, if the judgment appeared reasonable at the time the decision was made. [. . .]

In holding that employee unrest could as well be attributed to a condition of Holland's business affairs as to the possibility of Maremont's intrustion, the Vice Chancellor must have had in mind one or both of two matters: (1) the pending proceedings before the Federal Trade Commission concerning certain sales practices of Holland; (2) the decrease in sales and profits during the preceding several years. Any other possible reason would be pure speculation. In the first place, the adverse decision of the F.T.C. was not announced until *after* the complained-of transaction. Secondly, the evidence clearly shows that the downward trend of sales and profits had reversed itself, presumably because of the reorganization which had then been completed. Thirdly, everyone who testified on the point said that the unrest was due to the possible threat presented by Maremont's purchases of stock. There was, in fact, no *testimony* whatever of any connection between the unrest and either the F.T.C. proceedings or the business picture.

The Vice Chancellor found that there was no substantial evidence of a liquidation posed by Maremont. This holding overlooks an important contention. The fear of the defendants, according to their testimony, was not limited to the possibility of liquidation; it included the alternate possibility of a material change in Holland's sales policies, which the board considered vital to its future success. The *unrebutted* testimony before the court indicated: (1) Maremont had deceived Cheff as to his original intentions, since his open market purchases were contemporaneous with his disclaimer of interest in Holland; (2) Maremont had given Cheff some reason to believe that he intended to eliminate the retail sales force of Holland; (3) Maremont demanded a place on the board; (4) Maremont substantially increased his purchases after having been refused a place on the board; (5) the directors had good reason to believe that unrest among key employees had been engendered by the Maremont threat; (6) the board had received advice from Dun and Bradstreet indicating the past liquidation or quick sale activities of

Motor Products; (7) the board had received professional advice from the firm of Merril Lynch, Fenner & Beane, who recommended that the purchase from Motor Products be carried out; (8) the board had received competent advice that the corporation was over-capitalized; (9) Staal and Cheff had made informal personal investigations from contacts in the business and financial community and had reported to the board of the alleged poor reputation of Maremont. The board was within its rights in relying upon that investigation, since 8 Del.C. § 141(f) allows the directors to reasonably rely upon a report provided by corporate officers. [. . .]

Accordingly, we are of the opinion that the evidence presented in the court below leads inevitably to the conclusion that the board of directors, based upon direct investigation, receipt of professional advice, and personal observations of the contradictory action of Maremont and his explanation of corporate purpose, believed, with justification, that there was a reasonable threat to the continued existence of Holland, or at least existence in its present form, by the plan of Maremont to continue building up his stock holdings. We find no evidence in the record sufficient to justify a contrary conclusion. The opinion of the Vice Chancellor that employee unrest may have been engendered by other factors or that the board had no grounds to suspect Maremont is not supported in any manner by the evidence.

As noted above, the Vice-Chancellor found that the purpose of the acquisition was the improper desire to maintain control, but, at the same time, he exonerated those individual directors whom he believed to be unaware of the possibility of using non-corporate funds to accomplish this purpose. Such a decision is inconsistent with his finding that the motive was improper, within the rule enunciated in Bennett. If the actions were in fact improper because of a desire to maintain control, then the presence or absence of a non-corporate alternative is irrelevant, as corporate funds may not be used to advance an improper purpose even if there is no non-corporate alternative available. Conversely, if the actions were proper because of a decision by the board made in good faith that the corporate interest was served thereby, they are not rendered improper by the fact that some individual directors were willing to advance personal funds if the corporation did not. It is conceivable that the Vice Chancellor considered this feature of the case to be of significance because of his apparent belief that any excess corporate funds should have been used to finance a subsidiary corporation. That action would not have solved the problem of Holland's over-capitalization. In any event, this question was a matter of business judgment, which furnishes no justification for holding the directors personally responsible in this case.

Accordingly, the judgment of the court below is reversed and remanded with instruction to enter judgment for the defendants.

Unocal Corp. v. Mesa Petroleum Co.

493 A.2d 946 (Del. Ch. 1985)

■ MOORE, JUSTICE.

We confront an issue of first impression in Delaware—the validity of a corporation's self-tender for its own shares which excludes from participation a stockholder making a hostile tender offer for the company's stock. The Court of Chancery granted a preliminary injunction to the plaintiffs, Mesa Petroleum Co., Mesa Asset Co., Mesa Partners II, and Mesa Eastern, Inc. (collectively "Mesa")[1], enjoining an exchange offer of the defendant, Unocal Corporation (Unocal) for its own stock. [. . .]

I.

[. . .] On April 8, 1985, Mesa, the owner of approximately 13% of Unocal's stock, commenced a two-tier "front loaded" cash tender offer for 64 million shares, or approximately 37%, of Unocal's outstanding stock at a price of $54 per share. The "back-end" was designed to eliminate the remaining publicly held shares by an exchange of securities purportedly worth $54 per share. However [. . .] Mesa issued a supplemental proxy statement to Unocal's stockholders disclosing that the securities offered in the second-step merger would be highly subordinated [. . .]. Unocal has rather aptly termed such securities "junk bonds".

Unocal's board consists of eight independent outside directors and six insiders. It met on April 13, 1985, to consider the Mesa tender offer. Thirteen directors were present, and the meeting lasted nine and one-half hours. The directors were given no agenda or written materials prior to the session. However, detailed presentations were made by legal counsel regarding the board's obligations under both Delaware corporate law and the federal securities laws. The board then received a presentation from Peter Sachs on behalf of Goldman Sachs & Co. [. . .] and Dillon, Read & Co. [. . .] discussing the bases for their opinions that the Mesa proposal was wholly inadequate. [. . .] The Court of Chancery found that the Sachs presentation was designed to apprise the directors of the scope of the analyses performed rather than the facts and numbers used in reaching the conclusion that Mesa's tender offer price was inadequate.

Mr. Sachs also presented various defensive strategies available to the board if it concluded that Mesa's two-step tender offer was inadequate and should be opposed. One of the devices outlined was a self-tender by Unocal for its own stock with a reasonable price range of $70 to $75 per share. The cost of such a proposal would cause the company to incur $6.1–6.5 billion of additional debt, and a presentation was made informing the board of Unocal's ability to handle it. The directors were told that the

---

[1]   T. Boone Pickens, Jr., is President and Chairman of the Board of Mesa Petroleum and President of Mesa Asset and controls the related Mesa entities.

primary effect of this obligation would be to reduce exploratory drilling, but that the company would nonetheless remain a viable entity.

The eight outside directors, comprising a clear majority of the thirteen members present, then met separately with Unocal's financial advisors and attorneys. Thereafter, they unanimously agreed to advise the board that it should reject Mesa's tender offer as inadequate, and that Unocal should pursue a self-tender to provide the stockholders with a fairly priced alternative to the Mesa proposal. The board then reconvened and unanimously adopted a resolution rejecting as grossly inadequate Mesa's tender offer. Despite the nine and one-half hour length of the meeting, no formal decision was made on the proposed defensive self-tender.

On April 15, the board met again with four of the directors present by telephone and one member still absent. This session lasted two hours. Unocal's Vice President of Finance and its Assistant General Counsel made a detailed presentation of the proposed terms of the exchange offer. A price range between $70 and $80 per share was considered, and ultimately the directors agreed upon $72. The board was also advised about the debt securities that would be issued, and the necessity of placing restrictive covenants upon certain corporate activities until the obligations were paid. The board's decisions were made in reliance on the advice of its investment bankers [. . .]. Based upon this advice, and the board's own deliberations, the directors unanimously approved the exchange offer. Their resolution provided that if Mesa acquired 64 million shares of Unocal stock through its own offer (the Mesa Purchase Condition), Unocal would buy the remaining 49% outstanding for an exchange of debt securities having an aggregate par value of $72 per share. The board resolution also stated that the offer would be subject to other conditions that had been described to the board at the meeting, [. . .] including the exclusion of Mesa from the proposal (the Mesa exclusion). [. . .]

Unocal's exchange offer was commenced on April 17, 1985, and Mesa promptly challenged it by filing this suit in the Court of Chancery. On April 22, the Unocal board met again and was advised by Goldman Sachs and Dillon Read to waive the Mesa Purchase Condition as to 50 million shares [. . .] in response to a perceived concern of the shareholders that, if shares were tendered to Unocal, no shares would be purchased by either offeror. The directors were also advised that they should tender their own Unocal stock into the exchange offer as a mark of their confidence in it.

[. . .] Legal counsel advised that under Delaware law Mesa could only be excluded for what the directors reasonably believed to be a valid corporate purpose. The directors' discussion centered on the objective of adequately compensating shareholders at the "back-end" of Mesa's proposal, which the latter would finance with "junk bonds". To include Mesa would defeat that goal, because under the proration aspect of the exchange offer (49%) every Mesa share accepted by Unocal would displace one held by another stockholder. Further, if Mesa were permitted to tender to Unocal, the latter would in effect be financing Mesa's own inadequate proposal.

On April 24, 1985 Unocal issued a supplement to the exchange offer describing the partial waiver of the Mesa Purchase Condition. On May 1, 1985, in another supplement, Unocal extended the withdrawal, proration and expiration dates of its exchange offer to May 17, 1985.

Meanwhile, on April 22, 1985, Mesa amended its complaint in this action to challenge the Mesa exclusion. A preliminary injunction hearing was scheduled for May 8, 1985. However, on April 23, 1985, Mesa moved for a temporary restraining order in response to Unocal's announcement that it was partially waiving the Mesa Purchase Condition. After expedited briefing, the Court of Chancery heard Mesa's motion on April 26.

On April 29, 1985, the Vice Chancellor temporarily restrained Unocal from proceeding with the exchange offer unless it included Mesa. The trial court recognized that directors could oppose, and attempt to defeat, a hostile takeover which they considered adverse to the best interests of the corporation. However, the Vice Chancellor decided that in a selective purchase of the company's stock, the corporation bears the burden of showing: (1) a valid corporate purpose, and (2) that the transaction was fair to all of the stockholders, including those excluded.

Unocal immediately sought certification of an interlocutory appeal to this Court pursuant to Supreme Court Rule 42(b). [. . .]

II.

The issues we address involve these fundamental questions: Did the Unocal board have the power and duty to oppose a takeover threat it reasonably perceived to be harmful to the corporate enterprise, and if so, is its action here entitled to the protection of the business judgment rule?

Mesa contends that the discriminatory exchange offer violates the fiduciary duties Unocal owes it. Mesa argues that because of the Mesa exclusion the business judgment rule is inapplicable, because the directors by tendering their own shares will derive a financial benefit that is not available to all Unocal stockholders. Thus, it is Mesa's ultimate contention that Unocal cannot establish that the exchange offer is fair to all shareholders, and argues that the Court of Chancery was correct in concluding that Unocal was unable to meet this burden.

Unocal answers that it does not owe a duty of "fairness" to Mesa [. . .]. Specifically, Unocal contends that its board of directors reasonably and in good faith concluded that Mesa's $54 two-tier tender offer was coercive and inadequate, and that Mesa sought selective treatment for itself. Furthermore, Unocal argues that the board's approval of the exchange offer was made in good faith, on an informed basis, and in the exercise of due care. Under these circumstances, Unocal contends that its directors properly employed this device to protect the company and its stockholders from Mesa's harmful tactics.

III.

We begin with the basic issue of the power of a board of directors of a Delaware corporation to adopt a defensive measure of this type. Absent such authority, all other questions are moot. Neither issues of fairness nor business judgment are pertinent without the basic underpinning of a board's legal power to act.

The board has a large reservoir of authority upon which to draw. Its duties and responsibilities proceed from the inherent powers conferred by 8 Del.C. § 141(a), respecting management of the corporation's "business and affairs". Additionally, the powers here being exercised derive from 8 Del.C. § 160(a), conferring broad authority upon a corporation to deal in its own stock. From this it is now well established that in the acquisition of its shares a Delaware corporation may deal selectively with its stockholders, provided the directors have not acted out of a sole or primary purpose to entrench themselves in office.

Finally, the board's power to act derives from its fundamental duty and obligation to protect the corporate enterprise, which includes stockholders, from harm reasonably perceived, irrespective of its source. Thus, we are satisfied that in the broad context of corporate governance, including issues of fundamental corporate change, a board of directors is not a passive instrumentality.

Given the foregoing principles, we turn to the standards by which director action is to be measured. In *Pogostin v. Rice*, we held that the business judgment rule [. . .] is applicable in the context of a takeover. The business judgment rule is a "presumption that in making a business decision the directors of a corporation acted on an informed basis, in good faith and in the honest belief that the action taken was in the best interests of the company." *Aronson v. Lewis*. A hallmark of the business judgment rule is that a court will not substitute its judgment for that of the board if the latter's decision can be "attributed to any rational business purpose." *Sinclair Oil Corp. v. Levien*.

When a board addresses a pending takeover bid it has an obligation to determine whether the offer is in the best interests of the corporation and its shareholders. [. . .] Because of the omnipresent specter that a board may be acting primarily in its own interests, [. . .] there is an enhanced duty which calls for judicial examination at the threshold before the protections of the business judgment rule may be conferred. [. . .]

In the face of this inherent conflict directors must show that they had reasonable grounds for believing that a danger to corporate policy and effectiveness existed because of another person's stock ownership. However, they satisfy that burden "by showing good faith and reasonable investigation. . . ." *Cheff v. Mathes*. Furthermore, such proof is materially enhanced, as here, by the approval of a board comprised of a majority of outside independent directors who have acted in accordance with the foregoing standards.

IV.

A.

In the board's exercise of corporate power to forestall a takeover bid our analysis begins with the basic principle that corporate directors have a fiduciary duty to act in the best interests of the corporation's stockholders. [. . .] [T]heir duty of care extends to protecting the corporation and its owners from perceived harm whether a threat originates from third parties or other shareholders. But such powers are not absolute. A corporation does not have unbridled discretion to defeat any perceived threat by any Draconian means available.

The restriction placed upon a selective stock repurchase is that the directors may not have acted solely or primarily out of a desire to perpetuate themselves in office. Of course, to this is added the further caveat that inequitable action may not be taken under the guise of law. The standard of proof [. . .] is designed to ensure that a defensive measure to thwart or impede a takeover is indeed motivated by a good faith concern for the welfare of the corporation and its stockholders, which in all circumstances must be free of any fraud or other misconduct. However, this does not end the inquiry.

B.

[. . .] If a defensive measure is to come within the ambit of the business judgment rule, it must be reasonable in relation to the threat posed. This entails an analysis by the directors of the nature of the takeover bid and its effect on the corporate enterprise. Examples of such concerns may include: inadequacy of the price offered, nature and timing of the offer, questions of illegality, the impact on "constituencies" other than shareholders (i.e., creditors, customers, employees, and perhaps even the community generally), the risk of nonconsummation, and the quality of securities being offered in the exchange. [. . .] While not a controlling factor, it also seems to us that a board may reasonably consider the basic stockholder interests at stake, including those of short term speculators, whose actions may have fueled the coercive aspect of the offer at the expense of the long term investor. Here, the threat posed was viewed by the Unocal board as a grossly inadequate two-tier coercive tender offer coupled with the threat of greenmail.

Specifically, the Unocal directors had concluded that the value of Unocal was substantially above the $54 per share offered in cash at the front end. Furthermore, they determined that the subordinated securities to be exchanged in Mesa's announced squeeze out of the remaining shareholders in the "back-end" merger were "junk bonds" worth far less than $54. It is now well recognized that such offers are a classic coercive measure designed to stampede shareholders into tendering at the first tier, even if the price is inadequate, out of fear of what they will receive at the back end of the transaction. Wholly beyond the coercive aspect of an inadequate two-tier tender offer, the threat was posed by a corporate raider with a national reputation as a "greenmailer".

In adopting the selective exchange offer, the board stated that its objective was either to defeat the inadequate Mesa offer or, should the offer still succeed, provide the 49% of its stockholders, who would otherwise be forced to accept "junk bonds", with $72 worth of senior debt. We find that both purposes are valid.

However, such efforts would have been thwarted by Mesa's participation in the exchange offer. First, if Mesa could tender its shares, Unocal would effectively be subsidizing the former's continuing effort to buy Unocal stock at $54 per share. Second, Mesa could not, by definition, fit within the class of shareholders being protected from its own coercive and inadequate tender offer.

Thus, we are satisfied that the selective exchange offer is reasonably related to the threats posed. [. . .] [T]he board's decision to offer what it determined to be the fair value of the corporation to the 49% of its shareholders, who would otherwise be forced to accept highly subordinated "junk bonds", is reasonable and consistent with the directors' duty to ensure that the minority stockholders receive equal value for their shares.

V.

Mesa contends that it is unlawful, and the trial court agreed, for a corporation to discriminate in this fashion against one shareholder. It argues correctly that no case has ever sanctioned a device that precludes a raider from sharing in a benefit available to all other stockholders. [. . .]

However, our corporate law is not static. It must grow and develop in response to, indeed in anticipation of, evolving concepts and needs. [. . .] Various defensive tactics, which provided no benefit whatever to the raider, evolved. [. . .] Litigation, supported by corporate funds, aimed at the raider has long been a popular device.

More recently, as the sophistication of both raiders and targets has developed, a host of other defensive measures to counter such ever mounting threats has evolved and received judicial sanction. These include defensive charter amendments and other devices bearing some rather exotic, but apt, names: Crown Jewel, White Knight, Pac Man, and Golden Parachute. Each has highly selective features, the object of which is to deter or defeat the raider.

Thus, while the exchange offer is a form of selective treatment, given the nature of the threat posed here the response is neither unlawful nor unreasonable. If the board of directors is disinterested, has acted in good faith and with due care, its decision in the absence of an abuse of discretion will be upheld as a proper exercise of business judgment.

To this Mesa responds that the board is not disinterested, because the directors are receiving a benefit from the tender of their own shares, which because of the Mesa exclusion, does not devolve upon all stockholders equally. However, Mesa concedes that if the exclusion is valid, then the directors and all other stockholders share the same benefit. The answer of course is that the exclusion is valid, and the directors' participation in the exchange offer does not rise to the level of a disqualifying interest. [. . .]

Nor does this become an "interested" director transaction merely because certain board members are large stockholders. [. . .] [T]hat fact alone does not create a disqualifying "personal pecuniary interest" to defeat the operation of the business judgment rule. *Cheff v. Mathes.*

Mesa also argues that the exclusion permits the directors to abdicate the fiduciary duties they owe it. However, that is not so. The board continues to owe Mesa the duties of due care and loyalty. But in the face of the destructive threat Mesa's tender offer was perceived to pose, the board had a supervening duty to protect the corporate enterprise, which includes the other shareholders, from threatened harm.

Mesa contends that the basis of this action is punitive, and solely in response to the exercise of its rights of corporate democracy. Nothing precludes Mesa, as a stockholder, from acting in its own self-interest. However, Mesa, while pursuing its own interests, has acted in a manner which a board consisting of a majority of independent directors has reasonably determined to be contrary to the best interests of Unocal and its other shareholders. In this situation, there is no support in Delaware law for the proposition that, when responding to a perceived harm, a corporation must guarantee a benefit to a stockholder who is deliberately provoking the danger being addressed. There is no obligation of self-sacrifice by a corporation and its shareholders in the face of such a challenge.

Here, the Court of Chancery specifically found that the "directors' decision [to oppose the Mesa tender offer] was made in the good faith belief that the Mesa tender offer is inadequate." [. . .] [W]e are satisfied that Unocal's board has met its burden of proof.

VI.

In conclusion, there was directorial power to oppose the Mesa tender offer, and to undertake a selective stock exchange made in good faith and upon a reasonable investigation pursuant to a clear duty to protect the corporate enterprise. Further, the selective stock repurchase plan chosen by Unocal is reasonable in relation to the threat that the board rationally and reasonably believed was posed by Mesa's inadequate and coercive two-tier tender offer. Under those circumstances the board's action is entitled to be measured by the standards of the business judgment rule. Thus, unless it is shown by a preponderance of the evidence that the directors' decisions were primarily based on perpetuating themselves in office, or some other breach of fiduciary duty such as fraud, overreaching, lack of good faith, or being uninformed, a Court will not substitute its judgment for that of the board.

In this case that protection is not lost merely because Unocal's directors have tendered their shares in the exchange offer. Given the validity of the Mesa exclusion, they are receiving a benefit shared generally by all other stockholders except Mesa. In this circumstance the test of *Aronson v. Lewis* is satisfied. If the stockholders are displeased with the action of their elected representatives, the powers of corporate democracy are at their disposal to turn the board out.

With the Court of Chancery's findings that the exchange offer was based on the board's good faith belief that the Mesa offer was inadequate, that the board's action was informed and taken with due care, that Mesa's prior activities justify a reasonable inference that its principle objective was greenmail, and implicitly, that the substance of the offer itself was reasonable and fair to the corporation and its stockholders if Mesa were included, we cannot say that the Unocal directors have acted in such a manner as to have passed an "unintelligent and unadvised judgment". *Mitchell v. Highland-Western Glass Co.* The decision of the Court of Chancery is therefore REVERSED, and the preliminary injunction is VACATED.

Moran v. Household International, Inc.

500 A.2d 1346 (Del 1985)

■ MCNEILLY, JUSTICE:

This case presents to this Court for review the most recent defensive mechanism in the arsenal of corporate takeover weaponry—the Preferred Share Purchase Rights Plan ("Rights Plan" or "Plan"). The validity of this mechanism has attracted national attention.

I.

[. . .] On August 14, 1984, the Board of Directors of Household International, Inc. adopted the Rights Plan by a fourteen to two vote. The intricacies of the Rights Plan are contained in a 48-page document entitled "Rights Agreement". Basically, the Plan provides that Household common stockholders are entitled to the issuance of one Right per common share under certain triggering conditions. There are two triggering events that can activate the Rights. The first is the announcement of a tender offer for 30 percent of Household's shares ("30% trigger") and the second is the acquisition of 20 percent of Household's shares by any single entity or group ("20% trigger").

If an announcement of a tender offer for 30 percent of Household's shares is made, the Rights are issued and are immediately exercisable to purchase 1/100 share of new preferred stock for $100 and are redeemable by the Board for $.50 per Right. If 20 percent of Household's shares are acquired by anyone, the Rights are issued and become non-redeemable and are exercisable to purchase 1/100 of a share of preferred. If a Right is not exercised for preferred, and thereafter, a merger or consolidation occurs, the Rights holder can exercise each Right to purchase $200 of the common stock of the tender offeror for $100. This "flip-over" provision of the Rights Plan is at the heart of this controversy.[. . .]

Household did not adopt its Rights Plan during a battle with a corporate raider, but as a preventive mechanism to ward off future advances. The Vice-Chancellor found that as early as February 1984, Household's management became concerned about the company's vulnerability as a takeover target and began considering amending its charter to render a takeover more difficult. [. . .] Against this factual background, the Plan was approved.

II.

The primary issue here is the applicability of the business judgment rule as the standard by which the adoption of the Rights Plan should be reviewed. Much of this issue has been decided by our recent decision in *Unocal Corp. v. Mesa Petroleum Co.* [. . .]

This case is distinguishable from the ones cited, since here we have a defensive mechanism adopted to ward off possible future advances and not a mechanism adopted in reaction to a specific threat. This distinguishing factor does not result in the Directors losing the protection of the business judgment rule. To the contrary, pre-planning for the contingency of a hostile takeover might reduce the risk that, under the pressure of a takeover bid, management will fail to exercise reasonable judgment. Therefore, in reviewing a pre-planned defensive mechanism it seems even more appropriate to apply the business judgment rule.

Of course, the business judgment rule can only sustain corporate decision making or transactions that are within the power or authority of the Board. Therefore, before the business judgment rule can be applied it must be determined whether the Directors were authorized to adopt the Rights Plan.

III.

Appellants vehemently contend that the Board of Directors was unauthorized to adopt the Rights Plan. First, appellants contend that no provision of the Delaware General Corporation Law authorizes the issuance of such Rights. Secondly, appellants, along with the SEC, contend that the Board is unauthorized to usurp stockholders' rights to receive hostile tender offers. Third, appellants and the SEC also contend that the Board is unauthorized to fundamentally restrict stockholders' rights to conduct a proxy contest. We address each of these contentions in turn.

A.

[. . .] Household contends that the Rights Plan was issued pursuant to 8 *Del.C.* §§ 151(g) and 157. It explains that the Rights are authorized by § 157 and the issue of preferred stock underlying the Rights is authorized by § 151. [. . .]

Having concluded that sufficient authority for the Rights Plan exists in 8 *Del.C.* § 157, we note the inherent powers of the Board conferred by 8 *Del.C.* § 141(a), concerning the management of the corporation's "business and *affairs*" (emphasis added), also provides the Board additional authority upon which to enact the Rights Plan.

B.

[. . .] In addition, the Rights Plan is not absolute. When the Household Board of Directors is faced with a tender offer and a request to redeem the Rights, they will not be able to arbitrarily reject the offer. They will be held to the same fiduciary standards any other board of directors would be held to in deciding to adopt a defensive mechanism, the same standard as they were held to in originally approving the Rights Plan.

In addition, appellants contend that the deterrence of tender offers will be accomplished by what they label "a fundamental transfer of power from the stockholders to the directors." They contend that this transfer of power, in itself, is unauthorized.

The Rights Plan will result in no more of a structural change than any other defensive mechanism adopted by a board of directors. The Rights Plan does not destroy the assets of the corporation. The implementation of the Plan neither results in any outflow of money from the corporation nor impairs its financial flexibility. It does not dilute earnings per share and does not have any adverse tax consequences for the corporation or its stockholders. The Plan has not adversely affected the market price of Household's stock.

Comparing the Rights Plan with other defensive mechanisms, it does less harm to the value structure of the corporation than do the other mechanisms. Other mechanisms result in increased debt of the corporation. *See Whittaker Corp. v. Edgar, supra* (sale of "prize asset"), *Cheff v. Mathes, supra,* (paying greenmail to eliminate a threat), *Unocal Corp. v. Mesa Petroleum Co., supra,* (discriminatory self-tender).

There is little change in the governance structure as a result of the adoption of the Rights Plan. The Board does not now have unfettered discretion in refusing to redeem the Rights. The Board has no more discretion in refusing to redeem the Rights than it does in enacting any defensive mechanism.

The contention that the Rights Plan alters the structure more than do other defensive mechanisms because it is so effective as to make the corporation completely safe from hostile tender offers is likewise without merit. . . . [T]here are numerous methods to successfully launch a hostile tender offer.

V.

In conclusion, the Household Directors receive the benefit of the business judgment rule in their adoption of the Rights Plan.

The Directors adopted the Plan pursuant to statutory authority in 8 *Del.C.* §§ 141, 151, 157. We reject appellants' contentions that the Rights Plan strips stockholders of their rights to receive tender offers, and that the Rights Plan fundamentally restricts proxy contests.

The Directors adopted the Plan in the good faith belief that it was necessary to protect Household from coercive acquisition techniques. The Board was informed as to the details of the Plan. In addition, Household has demonstrated that the Plan is reasonable in relation to the threat posed. Appellants, on the other hand, have failed to convince us that the Directors breached any fiduciary duty in their adoption of the Rights Plan.

While we conclude for present purposes that the Household Directors are protected by the business judgment rule, that does not end the matter. The ultimate response to an actual takeover bid must be judged by the Directors' actions at that time, and nothing we say here relieves them of their basic fundamental duties to the corporation and its stockholders use of the Plan will be evaluated when and if the issue arises.

AFFIRMED.

Revlon, Inc. v. MacAndrews and Forbes Holdings, Inc.

506 A.2d 173 (Del. 1986)

■ MOORE, JUSTICE:

[. . .][1]

I.

[. . .] The prelude to this controversy began in June 1985, when Ronald O. Perelman, chairman of the board and chief executive officer of Pantry Pride, met with his counterpart at Revlon, Michel C. Bergerac, to discuss a friendly acquisition of Revlon by Pantry Pride. Perelman suggested a price in the range of $40–50 per share, but the meeting ended with Bergerac dismissing those figures as considerably below Revlon's intrinsic value. All subsequent Pantry Pride overtures were rebuffed, perhaps in part based on Mr. Bergerac's strong personal antipathy to Mr. Perelman.

---

[1] The nominal plaintiff, MacAndrews & Forbes Holdings, Inc., is the controlling stockholder of Pantry Pride. For all practical purposes their interests in this litigation are virtually identical, and we hereafter will refer to Pantry Pride as the plaintiff.

Thus, on August 14, Pantry Pride's board authorized Perelman to acquire Revlon, either through negotiation in the $42–$43 per share range, or by making a hostile tender offer at $45. Perelman then met with Bergerac and outlined Pantry Pride's alternate approaches. Bergerac remained adamantly opposed to such schemes and conditioned any further discussions of the matter on Pantry Pride executing a standstill agreement prohibiting it from acquiring Revlon without the latter's prior approval.

On August 19, the Revlon board met specially to consider the impending threat of a hostile bid by Pantry Pride. At the meeting, Lazard Freres, Revlon's investment banker, advised the directors that $45 per share was a grossly inadequate price for the company. [. . .] Lazard Freres explained to the board that Pantry Pride's financial strategy for acquiring Revlon would be through "junk bond" financing followed by a break-up of Revlon and the disposition of its assets. With proper timing, according to the experts, such transactions could produce a return to Pantry Pride of $60 to $70 per share, while a sale of the company as a whole would be in the "mid 50" dollar range. Martin Lipton, special counsel for Revlon, recommended two defensive measures: first, that the company repurchase up to 5 million of its nearly 30 million outstanding shares; and second, that it adopt a Note Purchase Rights Plan. Under this plan, each Revlon shareholder would receive as a dividend one Note Purchase Right (the Rights) for each share of common stock, with the Rights entitling the holder to exchange one common share for a $65 principal Revlon note at 12% interest with a one-year maturity. The Rights would become effective whenever anyone acquired beneficial ownership of 20% or more of Revlon's shares, unless the purchaser acquired all the company's stock for cash at $65 or more per share. In addition, the Rights would not be available to the acquiror, and prior to the 20% triggering event the Revlon board could redeem the rights for 10 cents each. Both proposals were unanimously adopted.

Pantry Pride made its first hostile move on August 23 with a cash tender offer for any and all shares of Revlon at $47.50 per common share and $26.67 per preferred share, subject to (1) Pantry Pride's obtaining financing for the purchase, and (2) the Rights being redeemed, rescinded or voided.

The Revlon board met again on August 26. The directors advised the stockholders to reject the offer. Further defensive measures also were planned. On August 29, Revlon commenced its own offer for up to 10 million shares, exchanging for each share of common stock tendered one Senior Subordinated Note (the Notes) of $47.50 principal at 11.75% interest, due 1995, and one-tenth of a share of $9.00 Cumulative Convertible Exchangeable Preferred Stock valued at $100 per share. [. . .] Revlon stockholders tendered 87 percent of the outstanding shares (approximately 33 million), and the company accepted the full 10 million shares on a pro rata basis. The new Notes contained covenants which limited Revlon's ability to incur additional debt, sell assets, or pay dividends unless otherwise approved by the "independent" (non-management) members of the board.

At this point, both the Rights and the Note covenants stymied Pantry Pride's attempted takeover. The next move came on September 16, when Pantry Pride announced a new tender offer at $42 per share, conditioned upon receiving at least 90% of the outstanding stock. Pantry Pride also indicated that it would consider buying less than 90%, and at an increased price, if Revlon removed the impeding Rights. While this offer was lower on its face than the earlier $47.50 proposal, Revlon's investment banker, Lazard Freres, described the two bids as essentially equal in view of the completed exchange offer.

The Revlon board held a regularly scheduled meeting on September 24 [where] [t]he directors rejected the latest Pantry Pride offer and authorized management to negotiate with other parties interested in acquiring Revlon. Pantry Pride remained determined in its efforts and continued to make cash bids for the company, offering $50 per share on September 27, [. . .] $53 on October 1, and [. . .] $56.25 on October 7.

In the meantime, Revlon's negotiations with Forstmann* and the investment group Adler & Shaykin had produced results. The Revlon directors met on October 3 to consider Pantry Pride's $53 bid and to examine possible alternatives to the offer. Both Forstmann and Adler & Shaykin made certain proposals to the board. As a result, the directors unanimously agreed to a leveraged buyout by Forstmann. The terms of this accord were as follows: each stockholder would get $56 cash per share; management would purchase stock in the new company by the exercise of their Revlon "golden parachutes";** Forstmann would assume Revlon's $475 million debt incurred by the issuance of the Notes; and Revlon would redeem the Rights and waive the Notes covenants for Forstmann or in connection with any other offer superior to Forstmann's. The board [. . .] indicated that the outside directors would waive the covenants in due course. Part of Forstmann's plan was to sell Revlon's Norcliff Thayer and Reheis divisions to American Home Products for $335 million. Before the merger, Revlon was to sell its cosmetics and fragrance division to Adler & Shaykin for $905 million. These transactions would facilitate the purchase by Forstmann or any other acquiror of Revlon.

When the merger, and thus the waiver of the Notes covenants, was announced, the market value of these securities began to fall. The Notes, which originally traded near par, around $100, dropped to $87.50 by October 8. One director later reported (at the October 12 meeting) a

---

* EDS.—"Forstmann" refers to Forstmann Little & Co. and an affiliated limited partnership.

** EDS.—In the Court's words, "golden parachutes" refer to "termination agreements providing substantial bonuses and other benefits for managers and certain directors upon a change in control of a company."

"deluge" of telephone calls from irate noteholders, and on October 10 the Wall Street Journal reported threats of litigation by these creditors.

Pantry Pride countered with a new proposal on October 7, raising its $53 offer to $56.25, subject to nullification of the Rights, a waiver of the Notes covenants, and the election of three Pantry Pride directors to the Revlon board. On October 9, representatives of Pantry Pride, Forstmann and Revlon conferred in an attempt to negotiate the fate of Revlon, but could not reach agreement. At this meeting Pantry Pride announced that it would engage in fractional bidding and top any Forstmann offer by a slightly higher one. It is also significant that Forstmann, to Pantry Pride's exclusion, had been made privy to certain Revlon financial data. Thus, the parties were not negotiating on equal terms.

Again privately armed with Revlon data, Forstmann met on October 11 with Revlon's special counsel and investment banker. On October 12, Forstmann made a new $57.25 per share offer, based on several conditions.[6] The principal demand was a lock-up option to purchase Revlon's Vision Care and National Health Laboratories divisions for $525 million, some $100–$175 million below the value ascribed to them by Lazard Freres, if another acquiror got 40% of Revlon's shares. Revlon also was required to accept a no-shop provision. The Rights and Notes covenants had to be removed as in the October 3 agreement. There would be a $25 million cancellation fee to be placed in escrow, and released to Forstmann if the new agreement terminated or if another acquiror got more than 19.9% of Revlon's stock. Finally, there would be no participation by Revlon management in the merger. In return, Forstmann agreed to support the par value of the Notes, which had faltered in the market, by an exchange of new notes. Forstmann also demanded immediate acceptance of its offer, or it would be withdrawn. The board unanimously approved Forstmann's proposal because: (1) it was for a higher price than the Pantry Pride bid, (2) it protected the noteholders, and (3) Forstmann's financing was firmly in place.[7] The board further agreed to redeem the rights and waive the covenants on the preferred stock in response to any offer above $57 cash per share. The covenants were waived, contingent upon receipt of an investment banking opinion that the Notes would trade near par value once the offer was consummated.

---

[6] Forstmann's $57.25 offer ostensibly is worth $1 more than Pantry Pride's $56.25 bid. However, the Pantry Pride offer was immediate, while the Forstmann proposal must be discounted for the time value of money because of the delay in approving the merger and consummating the transaction. The exact difference between the two bids was an unsettled point of contention even at oral argument.

[7] Actually, at this time about $400 million of Forstmann's funding was still subject to two investment banks using their "best efforts" to organize a syndicate to provide the balance. Pantry Pride's entire financing was not firmly committed at this point either, although Pantry Pride represented in an October 11 letter to Lazard Freres that its investment banker, Drexel Burnham Lambert, was highly confident of its ability to raise the balance of $350 million. Drexel Burnham had a firm commitment for this sum by October 18.

Pantry Pride, which had initially sought injunctive relief from the Rights plan on August 22, filed an amended complaint on October 14 challenging the lock-up, the cancellation fee, and the exercise of the Rights and the Notes covenants. Pantry Pride also sought a temporary restraining order to prevent Revlon from placing any assets in escrow or transferring them to Forstmann. Moreover, on October 22, Pantry Pride again raised its bid, with a cash offer of $58 per share conditioned upon nullification of the Rights, waiver of the covenants, and an injunction of the Forstmann lock-up.

On October 15, the Court of Chancery prohibited the further transfer of assets, and eight days later enjoined the lock-up, no-shop, and cancellation fee provisions of the agreement. The trial court concluded that the Revlon directors had breached their duty of loyalty by making concessions to Forstmann, out of concern for their liability to the noteholders, rather than maximizing the sale price of the company for the stockholders' benefit.

II.

To obtain a preliminary injunction, a plaintiff must demonstrate both a reasonable probability of success on the merits and some irreparable harm which will occur absent the injunction. [. . .]

A.

[. . .] The ultimate responsibility for managing the business and affairs of a corporation falls on its board of directors. 8 *Del.C.* § 141(a). [. . .] [T]he directors owe fiduciary duties of care and loyalty to the corporation and its shareholders. These principles apply with equal force when a board approves a corporate merger pursuant to 8 *Del.C.* § 251(b); and of course they are the bedrock of our law regarding corporate takeover issues. While the business judgment rule may be applicable to the actions of corporate directors responding to takeover threats, the principles upon which it is founded—care, loyalty and independence—must first be satisfied.

If the business judgment rule applies, there is a "presumption that in making a business decision the directors of a corporation acted on an informed basis, in good faith and in the honest belief that the action taken was in the best interests of the company." *Aronson v. Lewis.* However, when a board implements anti-takeover measures there arises "the omnipresent specter that a board may be acting primarily in its own interests, rather than those of the corporation and its shareholders [. . .]" *Unocal Corp. v. Mesa Petroleum Co.* This potential for conflict places upon the directors the burden of proving that they had reasonable grounds for believing there was a danger to corporate policy and effectiveness, a burden satisfied by a showing of good faith and reasonable investigation. In addition, the directors must analyze the nature of the takeover and its effect on the corporation in order to ensure balance—that the responsive action taken is reasonable in relation to the threat posed.

B.

The first relevant defensive measure adopted by the Revlon board was the Rights Plan, which would be considered a "poison pill" in the current language of corporate takeovers—a plan by which shareholders receive the right to be bought out by the corporation at a substantial premium on the occurrence of a stated triggering event. By 8 *Del.C.* §§ 141 and 122(13), the board clearly had the power to adopt the measure. Thus, the focus becomes one of reasonableness and purpose.

The Revlon board approved the Rights Plan in the face of an impending hostile takeover bid by Pantry Pride at $45 per share, a price which Revlon reasonably concluded was grossly inadequate. Lazard Freres had so advised the directors, and had also informed them that Pantry Pride was a small, highly leveraged company bent on a "bust-up" takeover by using "junk bond" financing to buy Revlon cheaply, sell the acquired assets to pay the debts incurred, and retain the profit for itself.[12] In adopting the Plan, the board protected the shareholders from a hostile takeover at a price below the company's intrinsic value, while retaining sufficient flexibility to address any proposal deemed to be in the stockholders' best interests.

To that extent the board acted in good faith and upon reasonable investigation. Under the circumstances it cannot be said that the Rights Plan as employed was unreasonable, considering the threat posed. Indeed, the Plan was a factor in causing Pantry Pride to raise its bids from a low of $42 to an eventual high of $58. At the time of its adoption the Rights Plan afforded a measure of protection consistent with the directors' fiduciary duty in facing a takeover threat perceived as detrimental to corporate interests. Far from being a "show-stopper," as the plaintiffs had contended in [*Moran v. Household International, Inc.*], the measure spurred the bidding to new heights, a proper result of its implementation.

Although we consider adoption of the Plan to have been valid under the circumstances, its continued usefulness was rendered moot by the directors' actions on October 3 and October 12. At the October 3 meeting the board redeemed the Rights conditioned upon consummation of a merger with Forstmann, but further acknowledged that they would also be redeemed to facilitate any more favorable offer. On October 12, the board unanimously passed a resolution redeeming the Rights in connection with any cash proposal of $57.25 or more per share. Because all the pertinent offers eventually equalled [*sic*] or surpassed that amount, the Rights clearly were no longer any impediment in the contest

---

[12] As we noted in *Moran*, a "bust-up" takeover generally refers to a situation in which one seeks to finance an acquisition by selling off pieces of the acquired company, presumably at a substantial profit.

for Revlon. This mooted any question of their propriety under *Moran* or *Unocal*.

C.

The second defensive measure adopted by Revlon to thwart a Pantry Pride takeover was the company's own exchange offer for 10 million of its shares. The directors' general broad powers to manage the business and affairs of the corporation are augmented by the specific authority conferred under 8 *Del.C.* § 160(a), permitting the company to deal in its own stock. However, when exercising that power in an effort to forestall a hostile takeover, the board's actions are strictly held to the fiduciary standards outlined in *Unocal*. These standards require the directors to determine the best interests of the corporation and its stockholders, and impose an enhanced duty to abjure any action that is motivated by considerations other than a good faith concern for such interests.

The Revlon directors concluded that Pantry Pride's $47.50 offer was grossly inadequate. In that regard the board acted in good faith, and on an informed basis, with reasonable grounds to believe that there existed a harmful threat to the corporate enterprise. The adoption of a defensive measure, reasonable in relation to the threat posed, was proper and fully accorded with the powers, duties, and responsibilities conferred upon directors under our law.

D.

However, when Pantry Pride increased its offer to $50 per share, and then to $53, it became apparent to all that the break-up of the company was inevitable. The Revlon board's authorization permitting management to negotiate a merger or buyout with a third party was a recognition that the company was for sale. The duty of the board had thus changed from the preservation of Revlon as a corporate entity to the maximization of the company's value at a sale for the stockholders' benefit. This significantly altered the board's responsibilities under the *Unocal* standards. It no longer faced threats to corporate policy and effectiveness, or to the stockholders' interests, from a grossly inadequate bid. The whole question of defensive measures became moot. The directors' role changed from defenders of the corporate bastion to auctioneers charged with getting the best price for the stockholders at a sale of the company.

III.

This brings us to the lock-up with Forstmann and its emphasis on shoring up the sagging market value of the Notes in the face of threatened litigation by their holders. Such a focus was inconsistent with the changed concept of the directors' responsibilities at this stage of the developments. The impending waiver of the Notes covenants had caused the value of the Notes to fall, and the board was aware of the noteholders' ire as well as their subsequent threats of suit. The directors thus made support of the Notes an integral part of the company's dealings with

Forstmann, even though their primary responsibility at this stage was to the equity owners.

The original threat posed by Pantry Pride—the break-up of the company—had become a reality which even the directors embraced. Selective dealing to fend off a hostile but determined bidder was no longer a proper objective. Instead, obtaining the highest price for the benefit of the stockholders should have been the central theme guiding director action. Thus, the Revlon board could not make the requisite showing of good faith by preferring the noteholders and ignoring its duty of loyalty to the shareholders. The rights of the former already were fixed by contract. The noteholders required no further protection, and when the Revlon board entered into an auction-ending lock-up agreement with Forstmann on the basis of impermissible considerations at the expense of the shareholders, the directors breached their primary duty of loyalty.

The Revlon board argued that it acted in good faith in protecting the noteholders because *Unocal* permits consideration of other corporate constituencies. Although such considerations may be permissible, there are fundamental limitations upon that prerogative. A board may have regard for various constituencies in discharging its responsibilities, provided there are rationally related benefits accruing to the stockholders. However, such concern for non-stockholder interests is inappropriate when an auction among active bidders is in progress, and the object no longer is to protect or maintain the corporate enterprise but to sell it to the highest bidder. [. . .]

A lock-up is not *per se* illegal under Delaware law. [. . .] Such options can entice other bidders to enter a contest for control of the corporation, creating an auction for the company and maximizing shareholder profit. Current economic conditions in the takeover market are such that a "white knight" like Forstmann might only enter the bidding for the target company if it receives some form of compensation to cover the risks and costs involved. However, while those lock-ups which draw bidders into the battle benefit shareholders, similar measures which end an active auction and foreclose further bidding operate to the shareholders' detriment. [. . .]

In [*Hanson Trust PLC, et al. v. ML SCM Acquisition Inc.*], the bidder, Hanson, sought control of SCM by a hostile cash tender offer. SCM management joined with Merrill Lynch to propose a leveraged buy-out of the company at a higher price, and Hanson in turn increased its offer. Then, despite very little improvement in its subsequent bid, the management group sought a lock-up option to purchase SCM's two main assets at a substantial discount. The SCM directors granted the lock-up without adequate information as to the size of the discount or the effect the transaction would have on the company. Their action effectively ended a competitive bidding situation. The Hanson Court invalidated the lock-up because the directors failed to fully inform themselves about the value of a transaction in which management had a strong self-interest.

"In short, the Board appears to have failed to ensure that negotiations for alternative bids were conducted by those whose only loyalty was to the shareholders." *Hanson Trust*.

The Forstmann option had a similar destructive effect on the auction process. Forstmann had already been drawn into the contest on a preferred basis, so the result of the lock-up was not to foster bidding, but to destroy it. The board's stated reasons for approving the transactions were: (1) better financing, (2) noteholder protection, and (3) higher price. [. . .] [A]ny distinctions between the rival bidders' methods of financing the proposal were nominal at best, and such a consideration has little or no significance in a cash offer for any and all shares. The principal object, contrary to the board's duty of care, appears to have been protection of the noteholders over the shareholders' interests.

While Forstmann's $57.25 offer was objectively higher than Pantry Pride's $56.25 bid, the margin of superiority is less when the Forstmann price is adjusted for the time value of money. In reality, the Revlon board ended the auction in return for very little actual improvement in the final bid. The principal benefit went to the directors, who avoided personal liability to a class of creditors to whom the board owed no further duty under the circumstances. Thus, when a board ends an intense bidding contest on an insubstantial basis, and where a significant by-product of that action is to protect the directors against a perceived threat of personal liability for consequences stemming from the adoption of previous defensive measures, the action cannot withstand the enhanced scrutiny which *Unocal* requires of director conduct.

In addition to the lock-up option, the Court of Chancery enjoined the no-shop provision as part of the attempt to foreclose further bidding by Pantry Pride. The no-shop provision, like the lock-up option, while not *per se* illegal, is impermissible under the *Unocal* standards when a board's primary duty becomes that of an auctioneer responsible for selling the company to the highest bidder. The agreement to negotiate only with Forstmann ended rather than intensified the board's involvement in the bidding contest.

It is ironic that the parties even considered a no-shop agreement when Revlon had dealt preferentially, and almost exclusively, with Forstmann throughout the contest. After the directors authorized management to negotiate with other parties, Forstmann was given every negotiating advantage that Pantry Pride had been denied: cooperation from management, access to financial data, and the exclusive opportunity to present merger proposals directly to the board of directors. Favoritism for a white knight to the total exclusion of a hostile bidder might be justifiable when the latter's offer adversely affects shareholder interests, but when bidders make relatively similar offers, or dissolution of the company becomes inevitable, the directors cannot fulfill their enhanced *Unocal* duties by playing favorites with the contending factions. Market forces must be allowed to operate freely to bring the target's shareholders the best price available for their equity. Thus, as the trial court ruled, the shareholders' interests necessitated that the board remain free to negotiate in the fulfillment of that duty.

The court below similarly enjoined the payment of the cancellation fee, pending a resolution of the merits, because the fee was part of the overall plan to thwart Pantry Pride's efforts. We find no abuse of discretion in that ruling.

IV.

Having concluded that Pantry Pride has shown a reasonable probability of success on the merits, we address the issue of irreparable harm. The Court of Chancery ruled that unless the lock-up and other aspects of the agreement were enjoined, Pantry Pride's opportunity to bid for Revlon was lost. The court also held that the need for both bidders to compete in the marketplace outweighed any injury to Forstmann. Given the complexity of the proposed transaction between Revlon and Forstmann, the obstacles to Pantry Pride obtaining a meaningful legal remedy are immense. We are satisfied that the plaintiff has shown the need for an injunction to protect it from irreparable harm, which need outweighs any harm to the defendants.

V.

In conclusion, the Revlon board was confronted with a situation not uncommon in the current wave of corporate takeovers. A hostile and determined bidder sought the company at a price the board was convinced was inadequate. The initial defensive tactics worked to the benefit of the shareholders, and thus the board was able to sustain its *Unocal* burdens in justifying those measures. However, in granting an asset option lock-up to Forstmann, [. . .] the directors allowed considerations other than the maximization of shareholder profit to affect their judgment, and followed a course that ended the auction for Revlon [. . .] to the ultimate detriment of its shareholders. No such defensive measure can be sustained when it represents a breach of the directors' fundamental duty of care. In that context the board's action is not entitled to the deference accorded it by the business judgment rule. The measures were properly enjoined. The decision of the Court of Chancery, therefore, is AFFIRMED.

Paramount Communications, Inc. v. Time Inc.

571 A.2d 1140 (Del. 1989)

■ HORSEY, JUSTICE:

Paramount Communications, Inc. ("Paramount") and two other groups of plaintiffs ("Shareholder Plaintiffs"), shareholders of Time Incorporated ("Time"), a Delaware corporation, separately filed suits in the Delaware Court of Chancery seeking a preliminary injunction to halt Time's tender offer for 51% of Warner Communication, Inc.'s ("Warner") outstanding shares at $70 cash per share. The court below consolidated the cases and, following the development of an extensive record, after discovery and an evidentiary hearing, denied plaintiffs' motion. In a 50-page unreported opinion and order entered July 14, 1989, the Chancellor refused to enjoin Time's consummation of its tender offer, concluding that the plaintiffs were unlikely to prevail on the merits. [. . .]

Shareholder Plaintiffs [. . .] assert a claim based on *Revlon v. MacAndrews & Forbes Holdings, Inc.* They argue that the original Time-Warner merger agreement of March 4, 1989 resulted in a change of control which effectively put Time up for sale, thereby triggering *Revlon* duties. Those plaintiffs argue that Time's board breached its *Revlon* duties by failing, in the face of the change of control, to maximize shareholder value in the immediate term. [. . .]

I.

Time is a Delaware corporation with its principal offices in New York City. Time's traditional business is publication of magazines and books; however, Time also provides pay television programming through its Home Box Office, Inc. and Cinemax subsidiaries. In addition, Time owns and operates cable television franchises through its subsidiary, American Television and Communication Corporation. During the relevant time period, Time's board consisted of sixteen directors. Twelve of the directors were "outside," nonemployee directors. Four of the directors were also officers of the company. [. . .]

As early as 1983 and 1984, Time's executive board began considering expanding Time's operations into the entertainment industry. In 1987, Time established a special committee of executives to consider and propose corporate strategies for the 1990s. The consensus of the committee was that Time should move ahead in the area of ownership and creation of video programming. This expansion, as the Chancellor noted, was predicated upon two considerations: first, Time's desire to have greater control, in terms of quality and price, over the film products delivered by way of its cable network and franchises; and second, Time's concern over the increasing globalization of the world economy. Some of Time's outside directors [. . .] had opposed this move as a threat to the editorial integrity and journalistic focus of Time. Despite this concern, the board recognized that a vertically integrated video enterprise to complement Time's existing HBO and cable networks would better enable it to compete on a global basis.

In late spring of 1987, a meeting took place between Steve Ross, CEO of Warner Brothers, and [N.J.] Nicholas [the president and COO] of Time. Ross and Nicholas discussed the possibility of a joint venture between the two companies through the creation of a jointly-owned cable company. Time would contribute its cable system and HBO. Warner would contribute its cable system and provide access to Warner Brothers Studio. The resulting venture would be a larger, more efficient cable network, able to produce and distribute its own movies on a worldwide basis. Ultimately the parties abandoned this plan, determining that it was impractical for several reasons, chief among them being tax considerations.

On August 11, 1987, Gerald M. Levin, Time's vice chairman and chief strategist, wrote J. Richard Munro [Time's CEO] a confidential memorandum in which he strongly recommended a strategic consolidation with Warner. In June 1988, Nicholas and Munro sent to each outside director a copy of the "comprehensive long-term planning document" prepared by the committee of Time executives that had been examining strategies for the 1990s. The memo included reference to and a description of Warner as a potential acquisition candidate.

Thereafter, Munro and Nicholas held meetings with Time's outside directors to discuss, generally, long-term strategies for Time and, specifically, a combination with Warner. Nearly a year later, Time's board reached the point of serious discussion of the "nuts and bolts" of a consolidation with an entertainment company. On July 21, 1988, Time's board met, with all outside directors present. The meeting's purpose was to consider Time's expansion into the entertainment industry on a global scale. Management presented the board with a profile of various entertainment companies in addition to Warner, including Disney, 20th Century Fox, Universal, and Paramount.

Without any definitive decision on choice of a company, the board approved in principle a strategic plan for Time's expansion. The board gave management the "go-ahead" to continue discussions with Warner concerning the possibility of a merger. [. . .] [M]ost of the outside directors agreed that a merger involving expansion into the entertainment field promised great growth opportunity for Time. [. . .]

The board's consensus was that a merger of Time and Warner was feasible, but only if Time controlled the board of the resulting corporation and thereby preserved a management committed to Time's journalistic integrity. To accomplish this goal, the board stressed the importance of carefully defining in advance the corporate governance provisions that would control the resulting entity. Some board members expressed concern over whether such a business combination would place Time "*in play.*" The board discussed the wisdom of adopting further defensive measures to lessen such a possibility.

Of a wide range of companies considered by Time's board as possible merger candidates, Warner Brothers, Paramount, Columbia, M.C.A., Fox, MGM, Disney, and Orion, the board, in July 1988, concluded that Warner was the superior candidate for a consolidation. Warner stood out on a number of counts. Warner had just acquired Lorimar and its film studios. Time-Warner could make movies and television shows for use on HBO. Warner had an international distribution system, which Time could use to sell films, videos, books and magazines. Warner was a giant in the music and recording business, an area into which Time wanted to expand. None of the other companies considered had the musical clout of

Warner. Time and Warner's cable systems were compatible and could be easily integrated; none of the other companies considered presented such a compatible cable partner. Together, Time and Warner would control half of New York City's cable system; Warner had cable systems in Brooklyn and Queens; and Time controlled cable systems in Manhattan and Queens. Warner's publishing company would integrate well with Time's established publishing company. Time sells hardcover books and magazines, and Warner sells softcover books and comics. Time-Warner could sell all of these publications and Warner's videos by using Time's direct mailing network and Warner's international distribution system. Time's network could be used to promote and merchandise Warner's movies.

In August 1988, Levin, Nicholas, and Munro, acting on instructions from Time's board, continued to explore a business combination with Warner. By letter dated August 4, 1988, management informed the outside directors of proposed corporate governance provisions to be discussed with Warner. The provisions incorporated the recommendations of several of Time's outside directors.

From the outset, Time's board favored an all-cash or cash and securities acquisition of Warner as the basis for consolidation. Bruce Wasserstein, Time's financial advisor, also favored an outright purchase of Warner. However, Steve Ross, Warner's CEO, was adamant that a business combination was only practicable on a stock-for-stock basis. [. . .]

Eventually Time acquiesced in Warner's insistence on a stock-for-stock deal, but talks broke down over corporate governance issues. [. . .] Negotiations ended when the parties reached an impasse. Time's board refused to compromise on its position on corporate governance. Time, and particularly its outside directors, viewed the corporate governance provisions as critical for preserving the "Time Culture" through a pro-Time management at the top.[. . .]

Throughout the fall of 1988 Time pursued its plan of expansion into the entertainment field; Time held informal discussions with several companies, including Paramount. Capital Cities/ABC approached Time to propose a merger. Talks terminated, however, when Capital Cities/ABC suggested that it was interested in purchasing Time or in controlling the resulting board. Time steadfastly maintained it was not placing itself up for sale.

Warner and Time resumed negotiations in January 1989. [. . .] [M]any of the details of the original stock-for-stock exchange agreement remained intact. In addition, Time's senior management agreed to long-term contracts.

Time insider directors [. . .] met with Warner's financial advisors to decide upon a stock exchange ratio. Time's board had recognized the potential need to pay a premium in the stock ratio in exchange for dictating the governing arrangement of the new Time-Warner. [. . .] The board discussed premium rates of 10%, 15% and 20%. Wasserstein also suggested paying a premium for Warner due to Warner's rapid growth rate. The market exchange ratio of Time stock for Warner stock was .38 in favor of Warner. Warner's financial advisors informed its board that any exchange rate over .400 was a fair deal and any exchange rate over .450 was "one hell of a deal." The parties ultimately agreed upon an exchange rate favoring Warner of .465. On that basis, Warner stockholders would have owned approximately 62% of the common stock of Time-Warner.

On March 3, 1989, Time's board, with all but one director in attendance, met and unanimously approved the stock-for-stock merger with Warner. Warner's board likewise approved the merger. The agreement called for Warner to be merged into a wholly-owned Time subsidiary with Warner becoming the surviving corporation. The common stock of Warner would then be converted into common stock of Time at the agreed upon ratio. Thereafter, the name of Time would be changed to Time-Warner, Inc.

The rules of the New York Stock Exchange required that Time's issuance of shares to effectuate the merger be approved by a vote of Time's stockholders. The Delaware General Corporation Law required approval of the merger by a majority of the Warner stockholders. Delaware law did not require any vote by Time stockholders. The Chancellor concluded that the agreement was the product of "an arms-length negotiation between two parties seeking individual advantage through mutual action."

The resulting company would have a 24-member board, with 12 members representing each corporation. The company would have co-CEO's, at first Ross and Munro, then Ross and Nicholas, and finally, after Ross' retirement, by Nicholas alone. The board would create an editorial committee with a majority of members representing Time. A similar entertainment committee would be controlled by Warner board members. A two-thirds supermajority vote was required to alter CEO successions but an earlier proposal to have supermajority protection for the editorial committee was abandoned. Warner's board suggested raising the compensation levels for Time's senior management under the new corporation. Warner's management, as with most entertainment executives, received higher salaries than comparable executives in news journalism. Time's board, however, rejected Warner's proposal to equalize the salaries of the two management teams.

At its March 3, 1989 meeting, Time's board adopted several defensive tactics. Time entered an automatic share exchange agreement with Warner. Time would receive 17,292,747 shares of Warner's outstanding common stock (9.4%) and Warner would receive 7,080,016 shares of Time's outstanding common stock (11.1%). Either party could trigger the exchange. Time sought out and paid for "confidence" letters from various banks with which it did business. In these letters, the banks promised not to finance any third-party attempt to acquire Time. Time argues these agreements served only to preserve the confidential relationship between itself and the banks. The Chancellor found these agreements to be inconsequential and futile attempts to "dry up" money for a hostile takeover. Time also agreed to a "no-shop" clause, preventing Time from considering any other consolidation proposal, thus relinquishing its power to consider other proposals, regardless of their merits. Time did so at Warner's insistence. Warner did not want to be left "on the auction block" for an unfriendly suitor, if Time were to withdraw from the deal.

Time's board simultaneously established a special committee of outside directors [. . .] to oversee the merger. The committee's assignment was to resolve any impediments that might arise in the course of working out the details of the merger and its consummation.

Time representatives lauded the lack of debt to the United States Senate and to the President of the United States. Public reaction to the announcement of the merger was positive. Time-Warner would be a media colossus with international scope. The board scheduled the stockholder vote for June 23; and a May 1 record date was set. On May 24, 1989, Time sent out extensive proxy statements to the stockholders regarding the approval vote on the merger. In the meantime, with the merger proceeding without impediment, the special committee had concluded, shortly after its creation, that it was not necessary either to retain independent consultants, legal or financial, or even to meet. Time's board was unanimously in favor of the proposed merger with Warner; and, by the end of May, the Time-Warner merger appeared to be an accomplished fact.

On June 7, 1989, these wishful assumptions were shattered by Paramount's surprising announcement of its all-cash offer to purchase all outstanding shares of Time for $175 per share. The following day, June 8, the trading price of Time's stock rose from $126 to $170 per share. Paramount's offer was said to be "fully negotiable."

Time found Paramount's "fully negotiable" offer to be in fact subject to at least three conditions. First, Time had to terminate its merger agreement and stock exchange agreement with Warner, and remove certain other of its defensive devices, including the redemption of Time's shareholder rights. Second, Paramount had to obtain the required cable franchise transfers from Time in a fashion acceptable to Paramount in its sole discretion. Finally, the offer depended upon a judicial determination that section 203 of the General Corporate Law of Delaware (The Delaware Anti-Takeover Statute) was inapplicable to any Time-Paramount merger. While Paramount's board had been privately advised that it could take months, perhaps over a year, to forge and consummate the deal, Paramount's board publicly proclaimed its ability to close the offer by July 5, 1989. Paramount executives later conceded that none of its directors believed that July 5th was a realistic date to close the transaction.

On June 8, 1989, Time formally responded to Paramount's offer. Time's chairman and CEO, J. Richard Munro, sent an aggressively worded letter to Paramount's CEO, Martin Davis. Munro's letter attacked Davis' personal integrity and called Paramount's offer "smoke and mirrors." Time's nonmanagement directors were not shown the letter before it was sent. However, at a board meeting that same day, all members endorsed management's response as well as the letter's content.

Over the following eight days, Time's board met three times to discuss Paramount's $175 offer. The board viewed Paramount's offer as inadequate and concluded that its proposed merger with Warner was the better course of action. Therefore, the board declined to open any negotiations with Paramount and held steady its course toward a merger with Warner.

In June, Time's board of directors met several times. During the course of their June meetings, Time's outside directors met frequently without management, officers or directors being present. At the request of the outside directors, corporate counsel was present during the board meetings and, from time to time, the management directors were asked to leave the board sessions. During the course of these meetings, Time's financial advisors informed the board that, on an auction basis, Time's per share value was materially higher than Warner's $175 per share offer. After this advice, the board concluded that Paramount's $175 offer was inadequate.

At these June meetings, certain Time directors expressed their concern that Time stockholders would not comprehend the long-term benefits of the Warner merger. Large quantities of Time shares were held by institutional investors. The board feared that even though there appeared to be wide support for the Warner transaction, Paramount's cash premium would be a tempting prospect to these investors. In mid-June, Time sought permission from the New York Stock Exchange to alter its rules and allow the Time-Warner merger to proceed without stockholder approval. Time did so at Warner's insistence. The New York Stock Exchange rejected Time's request on June 15; and on that day, the value of Time stock reached $182 per share.

The following day, June 16, Time's board met to take up Paramount's offer. The board's prevailing belief was that Paramount's bid posed a threat to Time's control of its own destiny and retention of the "Time Culture." Even after Time's financial advisors made another presentation of Paramount and its business attributes, Time's board maintained its position that a combination with Warner offered greater potential for Time. Warner provided Time a much desired production capability and an established international marketing chain. Time's advisors suggested various options, including defensive measures. The board considered and rejected the idea of purchasing Paramount in a "Pac Man" defense. The board considered other defenses, including a recapitalization, the acquisition of another company, and a material change in the present capitalization structure or dividend policy. The board determined to retain its same advisors even in light of the changed circumstances. The board rescinded its agreement to pay its advisors a bonus based on the consummation of the Time-Warner merger and agreed to pay a flat fee for any advice rendered. Finally, Time's board formally rejected Paramount's offer.

At the same meeting, Time's board decided to recast its consolidation with Warner into an outright cash and securities acquisition of Warner by Time; and Time so informed Warner. Time accordingly restructured its proposal to acquire Warner as follows: Time would make an immediate all-cash offer for 51% of Warner's outstanding stock at $70 per share. The remaining 49% would be purchased at some later date for a mixture of cash and securities worth $70 per share. To provide the funds required for its outright acquisition of Warner, Time would assume 7–10 billion dollars worth of debt, thus eliminating one of the principal transaction-related benefits of the original merger agreement. Nine billion dollars of the total purchase price would be allocated to the purchase of Warner's goodwill.

Warner agreed but insisted on certain terms. Warner sought a control premium and guarantees that the governance provisions found in the original merger agreement would remain intact. Warner further sought agreements that Time would not employ its poison pill against Warner and that, unless enjoined, Time would be legally bound to complete the transaction. Time's board agreed to these last measures only at the insistence of Warner. For its part, Time was assured of its ability to extend its efforts into production areas and international markets, all the while maintaining the Time identity and culture. The Chancellor found the initial Time-Warner transaction to have been negotiated at arms length and the restructured Time-Warner transaction to have resulted from Paramount's offer and its expected effect on a Time shareholder vote.

On June 23, 1989, Paramount raised its all-cash offer to buy Time's outstanding stock to $200 per share. Paramount still professed that all aspects of the offer were negotiable. Time's board met on June 26, 1989 and formally rejected Paramount's $200 per share second offer. The board reiterated its belief that, despite the $25 increase, the offer was still inadequate. The Time board maintained that the Warner transaction offered a greater long-term value for the stockholders and, unlike Paramount's offer, did not pose a threat to Time's survival and its "culture." Paramount then filed this action in the Court of Chancery.

II.

The Shareholder Plaintiffs first assert a *Revlon* claim. They contend that the March 4 Time-Warner agreement effectively put Time up for sale, triggering *Revlon* duties, requiring Time's board to enhance short-term shareholder value and to treat all other interested acquirors on an equal basis. The Shareholder Plaintiffs base this argument on two facts: (i) the ultimate Time-Warner exchange ratio of .465 favoring Warner, resulting in Warner shareholders' receipt of 62% of the combined company; and (ii) the subjective intent of Time's directors as evidenced in their statements that the market might perceive the Time-Warner merger as putting Time up "for sale" and their adoption of various defensive measures.

The Shareholder Plaintiffs further contend that Time's directors, in structuring the original merger transaction to be "takeover-proof," triggered *Revlon* duties by foreclosing their shareholders from any prospect of obtaining a control premium. In short, plaintiffs argue that Time's board's decision to merge with Warner imposed a fiduciary duty to maximize immediate share value and not erect unreasonable barriers to further bids. Therefore, they argue, the Chancellor erred in finding: that Paramount's bid for Time did not place Time "for sale"; that Time's transaction with Warner did not result in any transfer of control; and that the combined Time-Warner was not so large as to preclude the possibility of the stockholders of Time-Warner receiving a future control premium. [. . .]

The Court of Chancery posed the pivotal question presented by this case to be: Under what circumstances must a board of directors abandon an in-place plan of corporate development in order to provide its shareholders with the option to elect and realize an immediate control premium? As applied to this case, the question becomes: Did Time's board, having developed a strategic plan of global expansion to be launched through a business combination with Warner, come under a fiduciary duty to jettison its plan and put the corporation's future in the hands of its shareholders?

While we affirm the result reached by the Chancellor, we think it unwise to place undue emphasis upon long-term versus short-term corporate strategy. Two key predicates underpin our analysis. First, Delaware law imposes on a board of directors the duty to manage the business and affairs of the corporation. 8 *Del.C.* § 141(a). This broad mandate includes a conferred authority to set a corporate course of action, including time frame, designed to enhance corporate profitability. Thus, the question of "long-term" versus "short-term" values is largely irrelevant because directors, generally, are obliged to chart a course for a corporation which is in its best interests without regard to a fixed investment horizon. Second, absent a limited set of circumstances as defined under *Revlon,* a board of directors, while always required to act in an informed manner, is not under any *per se* duty to maximize shareholder value in the short term, even in the context of a takeover. In our view, the pivotal question presented by this case is: "Did Time, by entering into the proposed merger with Warner, put itself up for sale?" [. . .]

A.

We first take up plaintiffs' principal *Revlon* argument, summarized above. In rejecting this argument, the Chancellor found the original Time-Warner merger agreement not to constitute a "change of control" and concluded that the transaction did not trigger *Revlon* duties. [. . .] The Chancellor's findings of fact are supported by the record and his conclusion is correct as a matter of law. However, we premise our rejection of plaintiffs' *Revlon* claim on different grounds, namely, the absence of any substantial evidence to conclude that Time's board, in negotiating with Warner, made the dissolution or break-up of the corporate entity inevitable, as was the case in *Revlon*.

Under Delaware law there are, generally speaking and without excluding other possibilities, two circumstances which may implicate *Revlon* duties. The first, and clearer one, is when a corporation initiates an active bidding process seeking to sell itself or to effect a business reorganization involving a clear break-up of the company. *See, e.g., Mills Acquisition Co. v. Macmillan, Inc.* However, *Revlon* duties may also be triggered where, in response to a bidder's offer, a target abandons its long-term strategy and seeks an alternative transaction involving the breakup of the company. Thus, in *Revlon*, when the board responded to Pantry Pride's offer by contemplating a "bust-up" sale of assets in a leveraged acquisition, we imposed upon the board a duty to maximize immediate shareholder value and an obligation to auction the company fairly. If, however, the board's reaction to a hostile tender offer is found to constitute only a defensive response and not an abandonment of the corporation's continued existence, *Revlon* duties are not triggered, though *Unocal* duties attach. *See, e.g., Ivanhoe Partners v. Newmont Mining Corp.*

The plaintiffs insist that even though the original Time-Warner agreement may not have worked "an objective change of control," the transaction made a "sale" of Time inevitable. Plaintiffs rely on the subjective intent of Time's board of directors and principally upon certain board members' expressions of concern that the Warner transaction *might* be viewed as effectively putting Time up for sale. Plaintiffs argue that the use of a lock-up agreement, a no-shop clause, and so-called "dry-up" agreements prevented shareholders from obtaining a control premium in the immediate future and thus violated *Revlon*.

We agree with the Chancellor that such evidence is entirely insufficient to invoke *Revlon* duties; and we decline to extend *Revlon*'s application to corporate transactions simply because they might be construed as putting a corporation either "in play" or "up for sale." *See Citron v. Fairchild Camera; Macmillan.* The adoption of structural safety devices alone does not trigger *Revlon*. Rather, as the Chancellor stated, such devices are properly subject to a *Unocal* analysis. [. . .]

B.

We turn now to plaintiffs' *Unocal* claim. We begin by noting, as did the Chancellor, that our decision does not require us to pass on the wisdom of the board's decision to enter into the original Time-Warner agreement. That is not a court's task. Our task is simply to review the record to determine whether there is sufficient evidence to support the

Chancellor's conclusion that the initial Time-Warner agreement was the product of a proper exercise of business judgment. [. . .]

We have purposely detailed the evidence of the Time board's deliberative approach, beginning in 1983–84, to expand itself. Time's decision in 1988 to combine with Warner was made only after what could be fairly characterized as an exhaustive appraisal of Time's future as a corporation. After concluding in 1983–84 that the corporation must expand to survive, and beyond journalism into entertainment, the board combed the field of available entertainment companies. By 1987 Time had focused upon Warner; by late July 1988 Time's board was convinced that Warner would provide the best "fit" for Time to achieve its strategic objectives. The record attests to the zealousness of Time's executives, fully supported by their directors, in seeing to the preservation of Time's "culture," i.e., its perceived editorial integrity in journalism. We find ample evidence in the record to support the Chancellor's conclusion that the Time board's decision to expand the business of the company through its March 3 merger with Warner was entitled to the protection of the business judgment rule. [. . .]

The Chancellor reached a different conclusion in addressing the Time-Warner transaction as revised three months later. He found that the revised agreement was defense-motivated and designed to avoid the potentially disruptive effect that Paramount's offer would have had on consummation of the proposed merger were it put to a shareholder vote. Thus, the court declined to apply the traditional business judgment rule to the revised transaction and instead analyzed the Time board's June 16 decision under *Unocal*. The court ruled that *Unocal* applied to all director actions taken, following receipt of Paramount's hostile tender offer, that were reasonably determined to be defensive. Clearly that was a correct ruling and no party disputes that ruling.

In *Unocal*, we held that before the business judgment rule is applied to a board's adoption of a defensive measure, the burden will lie with the board to prove (a) reasonable grounds for believing that a danger to corporate policy and effectiveness existed; and (b) that the defensive measure adopted was reasonable in relation to the threat posed. [. . .] Directors satisfy the first part of the *Unocal* test by demonstrating good faith and reasonable investigation. We have repeatedly stated that the refusal to entertain an offer may comport with a valid exercise of a board's business judgment. [. . .]

Unocal involved a two-tier, highly coercive tender offer. In such a case, the threat is obvious: shareholders may be compelled to tender to avoid being treated adversely in the second stage of the transaction. [. . .] In subsequent cases, the Court of Chancery has suggested that an all-cash, all-shares offer, falling within a range of values that a shareholder might reasonably prefer, cannot constitute a legally recognized "threat" to shareholder interests sufficient to withstand a *Unocal* analysis. [. . .] In those cases, the Court of Chancery determined that whatever threat existed related only to the shareholders and only to price and not to the corporation.

From those decisions by our Court of Chancery, Paramount and the individual plaintiffs extrapolate a rule of law that an all-cash, all-shares offer with values reasonably in the range of acceptable price cannot pose any objective threat to a corporation or its shareholders. Thus, Paramount would have us hold that only if the value of Paramount's offer were determined to be clearly inferior to the value created by management's plan to merge with Warner could the offer be viewed—objectively—as a threat.

Implicit in the plaintiffs' argument is the view that a hostile tender offer can pose only two types of threats: the threat of coercion that results from a two-tier offer promising unequal treatment for nontendering shareholders; and the threat of inadequate value from an all-shares, all-cash offer at a price below what a target board in good faith deems to be the present value of its shares. [. . .] Since Paramount's offer was all-cash, the only conceivable "threat," plaintiffs argue, was inadequate value. We disapprove of such a narrow and rigid construction of *Unocal,* for the reasons which follow.

Plaintiffs' position represents a fundamental misconception of our standard of review under *Unocal* principally because it would involve the court in substituting its judgment as to what is a "better" deal for that of a corporation's board of directors. To the extent that the Court of Chancery has recently done so in certain of its opinions, we hereby reject such approach as not in keeping with a proper *Unocal* analysis. [. . .]

The usefulness of *Unocal* as an analytical tool is precisely its flexibility in the face of a variety of fact scenarios. *Unocal* is not intended as an abstract standard; neither is it a structured and mechanistic procedure of appraisal. Thus, we have said that directors may consider, when evaluating the threat posed by a takeover bid, the "inadequacy of the price offered, nature and timing of the offer, questions of illegality, the impact on 'constituencies' other than shareholders . . . the risk of nonconsummation, and the quality of securities being offered in the exchange." [. . .] The open-ended analysis mandated by *Unocal* is not intended to lead to a simple mathematical exercise: that is, of comparing the discounted value of Time-Warner's expected trading price at some future date with Paramount's offer and determining which is the higher. Indeed, in our view, precepts underlying the business judgment rule militate against a court's engaging in the process of attempting to appraise and evaluate the relative merits of a long-term versus a short-term investment goal for shareholders. To engage in such an exercise is a distortion of the *Unocal* process and, in particular, the application of the second part of *Unocal's* test, discussed below.

In this case, the Time board reasonably determined that inadequate value was not the only legally cognizable threat that Paramount's all-cash, all-shares offer could present. Time's board concluded that

Paramount's eleventh hour offer posed other threats. One concern was that Time shareholders might elect to tender into Paramount's cash offer in ignorance or a mistaken belief of the strategic benefit which a business combination with Warner might produce. Moreover, Time viewed the conditions attached to Paramount's offer as introducing a degree of uncertainty that skewed a comparative analysis. Further, the timing of Paramount's offer to follow issuance of Time's proxy notice was viewed as arguably designed to upset, if not confuse, the Time stockholders' vote. Given this record evidence, we cannot conclude that the Time board's decision of June 6 that Paramount's offer posed a threat to corporate policy and effectiveness was lacking in good faith or dominated by motives of either entrenchment or self-interest.

Paramount also contends that the Time board had not duly investigated Paramount's offer. Therefore, Paramount argues, Time was unable to make an informed decision that the offer posed a threat to Time's corporate policy. Although the Chancellor did not address this issue directly, his findings of fact do detail Time's exploration of the available entertainment companies, including Paramount, before determining that Warner provided the best strategic "fit." In addition, the court found that Time's board rejected Paramount's offer because Paramount did not serve Time's objectives or meet Time's needs. Thus, the record does, in our judgment, demonstrate that Time's board was adequately informed of the potential benefits of a transaction with Paramount. We agree with the Chancellor that the Time board's lengthy pre-June investigation of potential merger candidates, including Paramount, mooted any obligation on Time's part to halt its merger process with Warner to reconsider Paramount. Time's board was under no obligation to negotiate with Paramount. [. . .] Time's failure to negotiate cannot be fairly found to have been uninformed. The evidence supporting this finding is materially enhanced by the fact that twelve of Time's sixteen board members were outside independent directors. [. . .]

We turn to the second part of the *Unocal* analysis. The obvious requisite to determining the reasonableness of a defensive action is a clear identification of the nature of the threat. As the Chancellor correctly noted, this "requires an evaluation of the importance of the corporate objective threatened; alternative methods of protecting that objective; impacts of the 'defensive' action, and other relevant factors." [. . .] It is not until both parts of the *Unocal* inquiry have been satisfied that the business judgment rule attaches to defensive actions of a board of directors. [. . .] As applied to the facts of this case, the question is whether the record evidence supports the Court of Chancery's conclusion that the restructuring of the Time-Warner transaction, including the adoption of several preclusive defensive measures, was a *reasonable response* in relation to a perceived threat.

Paramount argues that, assuming its tender offer posed a threat, Time's response was unreasonable in precluding Time's shareholders from accepting the tender offer or receiving a control premium in the immediately foreseeable future. Once again, the contention stems, we believe, from a fundamental misunderstanding of where the power of corporate governance lies. Delaware law confers the management of the corporate enterprise to the stockholders' duly elected board representatives. 8 *Del.C.* § 141(a). The fiduciary duty to manage a corporate enterprise includes the selection of a time frame for achievement of corporate goals. That duty may not be delegated to the stockholders. *Van Gorkom.* Directors are not obliged to abandon a deliberately conceived corporate plan for a short-term shareholder profit unless there is clearly no basis to sustain the corporate strategy. *See, e.g., Revlon.*

Although the Chancellor blurred somewhat the discrete analyses required under *Unocal,* he did conclude that Time's board reasonably perceived Paramount's offer to be a significant threat to the planned Time-Warner merger and that Time's response was not "overly broad." We have found that even in light of a valid threat, management actions that are coercive in nature or force upon shareholders a management-sponsored alternative to a hostile offer may be struck down as unreasonable and non-proportionate responses. [. . .]

Here, on the record facts, the Chancellor found that Time's responsive action to Paramount's tender offer was not aimed at "cramming down" on its shareholders a management-sponsored alternative, but rather had as its goal the carrying forward of a pre-existing transaction in an altered form. Thus, the response was reasonably related to the threat. The Chancellor noted that the revised agreement and its accompanying safety devices did not preclude Paramount from making an offer for the combined Time-Warner company or from changing the conditions of its offer so as not to make the offer dependent upon the nullification of the Time-Warner agreement. Thus, the response was proportionate. We affirm the Chancellor's rulings as clearly supported by the record. Finally, we note that although Time was required, as a result of Paramount's hostile offer, to incur a heavy debt to finance its acquisition of Warner, that fact alone does not render the board's decision unreasonable so long as the directors could reasonably perceive the debt load not to be so injurious to the corporation as to jeopardize its well being.

C.

Conclusion

Applying the test for grant or denial of preliminary injunctive relief, we find plaintiffs failed to establish a reasonable likelihood of ultimate success on the merits. Therefore, we affirm.

Paramount Communications, Inc. v.
QVC Network, Inc.

637 A.2d 34 (Del. 1994)

■ VEASEY, CHIEF JUSTICE.

In this appeal we review an order of the Court of Chancery dated November 24, 1993 (the "November 24 Order"), preliminarily enjoining certain defensive measures designed to facilitate a so-called strategic alliance between Viacom Inc. ("Viacom") and Paramount Communications Inc. ("Paramount") approved by the board of directors of Paramount (the "Paramount Board" or the "Paramount directors") and to thwart an unsolicited, more valuable, tender offer by QVC Network Inc. ("QVC"). [. . .]

This action arises out of a proposed acquisition of Paramount by Viacom through a tender offer followed by a second-step merger (the "Paramount-Viacom transaction"), and a competing unsolicited tender offer by QVC. The Court of Chancery granted a preliminary injunction. [. . .]

I. FACTS

[. . .] Paramount is a Delaware corporation with its principal offices in New York City. Approximately 118 million shares of Paramount's common stock are outstanding and traded on the New York Stock Exchange. The majority of Paramount's stock is publicly held by numerous unaffiliated investors. Paramount owns and operates a diverse group of entertainment businesses, including motion picture and television studios, book publishers, professional sports teams, and amusement parks.

There are 15 persons serving on the Paramount Board. Four directors are officer-employees of Paramount: Martin S. Davis ("Davis"), Paramount's Chairman and Chief Executive Officer since 1983; Donald Oresman ("Oresman"), Executive Vice-President, Chief Administrative Officer, and General Counsel; Stanley R. Jaffe, President and Chief Operating Officer; and Ronald L. Nelson, Executive Vice President and Chief Financial Officer. Paramount's 11 outside directors are distinguished and experienced business persons who are present or former senior executives of public corporations or financial institutions.

Viacom is a Delaware corporation with its headquarters in Massachusetts. Viacom is controlled by Sumner M. Redstone ("Redstone"), its Chairman and Chief Executive Officer, who owns indirectly approximately 85.2 percent of Viacom's voting Class A stock and approximately 69.2 percent of Viacom's nonvoting Class B stock through National Amusements, Inc. ("NAI"), an entity 91.7 percent owned by Redstone. Viacom has a wide range of entertainment operations, including a number of well-known cable television channels such as MTV, Nickelodeon, Showtime, and The Movie Channel. Viacom's equity co-investors in the Paramount-Viacom transaction include NYNEX Corporation and Blockbuster Entertainment Corporation.

QVC is a Delaware corporation with its headquarters in West Chester, Pennsylvania. QVC has several large stockholders, including Liberty Media Corporation, Comcast Corporation, Advance Publications, Inc., and Cox Enterprises Inc. Barry Diller ("Diller"), the Chairman and Chief Executive Officer of QVC, is also a substantial stockholder. QVC sells a variety of merchandise through a televised shopping channel. QVC has several equity co-investors in its proposed combination with Paramount including BellSouth Corporation and Comcast Corporation.

Beginning in the late 1980s, Paramount investigated the possibility of acquiring or merging with other companies in the entertainment, media, or communications industry. Paramount considered such transactions to be desirable, and perhaps necessary, in order to keep pace with competitors in the rapidly evolving field of entertainment and communications. Consistent with its goal of strategic expansion, Paramount made a tender offer for Time Inc. in 1989, but was ultimately unsuccessful. *See Paramount Communications, Inc. v. Time Inc. ("Time-Warner").*

Although Paramount had considered a possible combination of Paramount and Viacom as early as 1990, recent efforts to explore such a transaction began at a dinner meeting between Redstone and Davis on April 20, 1993. Robert Greenhill ("Greenhill"), Chairman of Smith Barney Shearson Inc. ("Smith Barney"), attended and helped facilitate this meeting. After several more meetings between Redstone and Davis, serious negotiations began taking place in early July.

It was tentatively agreed that Davis would be the chief executive officer and Redstone would be the controlling stockholder of the combined company, but the parties could not reach agreement on the merger price and the terms of a stock option to be granted to Viacom. With respect to price, Viacom offered a package of cash and stock (primarily Viacom Class B nonvoting stock) with a market value of approximately $61 per share, but Paramount wanted at least $70 per share.

Shortly after negotiations broke down in July 1993, two notable events occurred. First, Davis apparently learned of QVC's potential interest in Paramount, and told Diller over lunch on July 21, 1993, that Paramount was not for sale. Second, the market value of Viacom's Class B nonvoting stock increased from $46.875 on July 6 to $57.25 on August 20. QVC claims (and Viacom disputes) that this price increase was caused by open market purchases of such stock by Redstone or entities controlled by him.

On August 20, 1993, discussions between Paramount and Viacom resumed when Greenhill arranged another meeting between Davis and Redstone. After a short hiatus, the parties negotiated in earnest in early September, and performed due diligence with the assistance of their financial advisors, Lazard Freres & Co. ("Lazard") for Paramount and

Smith Barney for Viacom. On September 9, 1993, the Paramount Board was informed about the status of the negotiations and was provided information by Lazard, including an analysis of the proposed transaction.

On September 12, 1993, the Paramount Board met again and unanimously approved the Original Merger Agreement whereby Paramount would merge with and into Viacom. The terms of the merger provided that each share of Paramount common stock would be converted into 0.10 shares of Viacom Class A voting stock, 0.90 shares of Viacom Class B nonvoting stock, and $9.10 in cash. In addition, the Paramount Board agreed to amend its "poison pill" Rights Agreement to exempt the proposed merger with Viacom. The Original Merger Agreement also contained several provisions designed to make it more difficult for a potential competing bid to succeed. We focus, as did the Court of Chancery, on three of these defensive provisions: a "no-shop" provision (the "No-Shop Provision"), the Termination Fee, and the Stock Option Agreement.

First, under the No-Shop Provision, the Paramount Board agreed that Paramount would not solicit, encourage, discuss, negotiate, or endorse any competing transaction unless: (a) a third party "makes an unsolicited written, bona fide proposal, which is not subject to any material contingencies relating to financing"; and (b) the Paramount Board determines that discussions or negotiations with the third party are necessary for the Paramount Board to comply with its fiduciary duties.

Second, under the Termination Fee provision, Viacom would receive a $100 million termination fee if: (a) Paramount terminated the Original Merger Agreement because of a competing transaction; (b) Paramount's stockholders did not approve the merger; or (c) the Paramount Board recommended a competing transaction.

The third and most significant deterrent device was the Stock Option Agreement, which granted to Viacom an option to purchase approximately 19.9 percent (23,699,000 shares) of Paramount's outstanding common stock at $69.14 per share if any of the triggering events for the Termination Fee occurred. In addition to the customary terms that are normally associated with a stock option, the Stock Option Agreement contained two provisions that were both unusual and highly beneficial to Viacom: (a) Viacom was permitted to pay for the shares with a senior subordinated note of questionable marketability instead of cash, thereby avoiding the need to raise the $1.6 billion purchase price (the "Note Feature"); and (b) Viacom could elect to require Paramount to pay Viacom in cash a sum equal to the difference between the purchase price and the market price of Paramount's stock (the "Put Feature"). Because the Stock Option Agreement was not "capped" to limit its maximum dollar value, it had the potential to reach (and in this case did reach) unreasonable levels.

After the execution of the Original Merger Agreement and the Stock Option Agreement on September 12, 1993, Paramount and Viacom

announced their proposed merger. In a number of public statements, the
parties indicated that the pending transaction was a virtual certainty.
Redstone described it as a "marriage" that would "never be torn asunder"
and stated that only a "nuclear attack" could break the deal. Redstone
also called Diller and John Malone of Tele-Communications Inc., a major
stockholder of QVC, to dissuade them from making a competing bid.

Despite these attempts to discourage a competing bid, Diller sent a letter
to Davis on September 20, 1993, proposing a merger in which QVC would
acquire Paramount for approximately $80 per share, consisting of 0.893
shares of QVC common stock and $30 in cash. QVC also expressed its
eagerness to meet with Paramount to negotiate the details of a
transaction. When the Paramount Board met on September 27, it was
advised by Davis that the Original Merger Agreement prohibited
Paramount from having discussions with QVC (or anyone else) unless
certain conditions were satisfied. In particular, QVC had to supply
evidence that its proposal was not subject to financing contingencies. The
Paramount Board was also provided information from Lazard describing
QVC and its proposal.

On October 5, 1993, QVC provided Paramount with evidence of QVC's
financing. The Paramount Board then held another meeting on October
11, and decided to authorize management to meet with QVC. Davis also
informed the Paramount Board that Booz-Allen & Hamilton ("Booz-
Allen"), a management consulting firm, had been retained to assess, *inter
alia*, the incremental earnings potential from a Paramount-Viacom
merger and a Paramount-QVC merger. Discussions proceeded slowly,
however, due to a delay in Paramount signing a confidentiality
agreement. In response to Paramount's request for information, QVC
provided two binders of documents to Paramount on October 20.

On October 21, 1993, QVC filed this action and publicly announced an
$80 cash tender offer for 51 percent of Paramount's outstanding shares
(the "QVC tender offer"). Each remaining share of Paramount common
stock would be converted into 1.42857 shares of QVC common stock in a
second-step merger. The tender offer was conditioned on, among other
things, the invalidation of the Stock Option Agreement, which was worth
over $200 million by that point. QVC contends that it had to commence
a tender offer because of the slow pace of the merger discussions and the
need to begin seeking clearance under federal antitrust laws.

Confronted by QVC's hostile bid, which on its face offered over $10 per
share more than the consideration provided by the Original Merger
Agreement, Viacom realized that it would need to raise its bid in order to
remain competitive. Within hours after QVC's tender offer was
announced, Viacom entered into discussions with Paramount concerning
a revised transaction. These discussions led to serious negotiations
concerning a comprehensive amendment to the original Paramount-
Viacom transaction. In effect, the opportunity for a "new deal" with
Viacom was at hand for the Paramount Board. With the QVC hostile bid

offering greater value to the Paramount stockholders, the Paramount Board had considerable leverage with Viacom.

At a special meeting on October 24, 1993, the Paramount Board approved the Amended Merger Agreement and an amendment to the Stock Option Agreement. The Amended Merger Agreement was, however, essentially the same as the Original Merger Agreement, except that it included a few new provisions. One provision related to an $80 per share cash tender offer by Viacom for 51 percent of Paramount's stock, and another changed the merger consideration so that each share of Paramount would be converted into 0.20408 shares of Viacom Class A voting stock, 1.08317 shares of Viacom Class B nonvoting stock, and 0.20408 shares of a new series of Viacom convertible preferred stock. The Amended Merger Agreement also added a provision giving Paramount the right not to amend its Rights Agreement to exempt Viacom if the Paramount Board determined that such an amendment would be inconsistent with its fiduciary duties because another offer constituted a "better alternative." Finally, the Paramount Board was given the power to terminate the Amended Merger Agreement if it withdrew its recommendation of the Viacom transaction or recommended a competing transaction.

Although the Amended Merger Agreement offered more consideration to the Paramount stockholders and somewhat more flexibility to the Paramount Board than did the Original Merger Agreement, the defensive measures designed to make a competing bid more difficult were not removed or modified. In particular, there is no evidence in the record that Paramount sought to use its newly-acquired leverage to eliminate or modify the No-Shop Provision, the Termination Fee, or the Stock Option Agreement when the subject of amending the Original Merger Agreement was on the table.

Viacom's tender offer commenced on October 25, 1993, and QVC's tender offer was formally launched on October 27, 1993. Diller sent a letter to the Paramount Board on October 28 requesting an opportunity to negotiate with Paramount, and Oresman responded the following day by agreeing to meet. The meeting, held on November 1, was not very fruitful, however, after QVC's proposed guidelines for a "fair bidding process" were rejected by Paramount on the ground that "auction procedures" were inappropriate and contrary to Paramount's contractual obligations to Viacom.

On November 6, 1993, Viacom unilaterally raised its tender offer price to $85 per share in cash and offered a comparable increase in the value of the securities being proposed in the second-step merger. At a telephonic meeting held later that day, the Paramount Board agreed to recommend Viacom's higher bid to Paramount's stockholders.

QVC responded to Viacom's higher bid on November 12 by increasing its tender offer to $90 per share and by increasing the securities for its second-step merger by a similar amount. In response to QVC's latest offer, the Paramount Board scheduled a meeting for November 15, 1993.

Prior to the meeting, Oresman sent the members of the Paramount Board a document summarizing the "conditions and uncertainties" of QVC's offer. One director testified that this document gave him a very negative impression of the QVC bid.

At its meeting on November 15, 1993, the Paramount Board determined that the new QVC offer was not in the best interests of the stockholders. The purported basis for this conclusion was that QVC's bid was excessively conditional. The Paramount Board did not communicate with QVC regarding the status of the conditions because it believed that the No-Shop Provision prevented such communication in the absence of firm financing. Several Paramount directors also testified that they believed the Viacom transaction would be more advantageous to Paramount's future business prospects than a QVC transaction. Although a number of materials were distributed to the Paramount Board describing the Viacom and QVC transactions, the only quantitative analysis of the consideration to be received by the stockholders under each proposal was based on then-current market prices of the securities involved, not on the anticipated value of such securities at the time when the stockholders would receive them.

The preliminary injunction hearing in this case took place on November 16, 1993. On November 19, Diller wrote to the Paramount Board to inform it that QVC had obtained financing commitments for its tender offer and that there was no antitrust obstacle to the offer. On November 24, 1993, the Court of Chancery issued its decision granting a preliminary injunction in favor of QVC and the plaintiff stockholders. This appeal followed.

II. APPLICABLE PRINCIPLES OF ESTABLISHED DELAWARE LAW

The General Corporation Law of the State of Delaware (the "General Corporation Law") and the decisions of this Court have repeatedly recognized the fundamental principle that the management of the business and affairs of a Delaware corporation is entrusted to its directors, who are the duly elected and authorized representatives of the stockholders. 8 *Del.C.* § 141(a); *Aronson v. Lewis*; *Pogostin v. Rice*. Under normal circumstances, neither the courts nor the stockholders should interfere with the managerial decisions of the directors. The business judgment rule embodies the deference to which such decisions are entitled. *Aronson.*

Nevertheless, there are rare situations which mandate that a court take a more direct and active role in overseeing the decisions made and actions taken by directors. In these situations, a court subjects the directors' conduct to enhanced scrutiny to ensure that it is reasonable. [. . .] The case at bar implicates two such circumstances: (1) the approval of a transaction resulting in a sale of control, and (2) the adoption of defensive measures in response to a threat to corporate control.

A. The Significance of a Sale or Change of Control

When a majority of a corporation's voting shares are acquired by a single person or entity, or by a cohesive group acting together, there is a significant diminution in the voting power of those who thereby become minority stockholders. Under the statutory framework of the General Corporation Law, many of the most fundamental corporate changes can be implemented only if they are approved by a majority vote of the stockholders. Such actions include elections of directors, amendments to the certificate of incorporation, mergers, consolidations, sales of all or substantially all of the assets of the corporation, and dissolution. 8 *Del.C.* §§ 211, 242, 251–258, 263, 271, 275. Because of the overriding importance of voting rights, this Court and the Court of Chancery have consistently acted to protect stockholders from unwarranted interference with such rights.

In the absence of devices protecting the minority stockholders, stockholder votes are likely to become mere formalities where there is a majority stockholder. For example, minority stockholders can be deprived of a continuing equity interest in their corporation by means of a cash-out merger. *Weinberger v. UOP.* Absent effective protective provisions, minority stockholders must rely for protection solely on the fiduciary duties owed to them by the directors and the majority stockholder, since the minority stockholders have lost the power to influence corporate direction through the ballot. The acquisition of majority status and the consequent privilege of exerting the powers of majority ownership come at a price. That price is usually a control premium which recognizes not only the value of a control block of shares, but also compensates the minority stockholders for their resulting loss of voting power.

In the case before us, the public stockholders (in the aggregate) currently own a majority of Paramount's voting stock. Control of the corporation is not vested in a single person, entity, or group, but vested in the fluid aggregation of unaffiliated stockholders. In the event the Paramount-Viacom transaction is consummated, the public stockholders will receive cash and a minority equity voting position in the surviving corporation. Following such consummation, there will be a controlling stockholder who will have the voting power to: (a) elect directors; (b) cause a break-up of the corporation; (c) merge it with another company; (d) cash-out the public stockholders; (e) amend the certificate of incorporation; (f) sell all or substantially all of the corporate assets; or (g) otherwise alter materially the nature of the corporation and the public stockholders' interests. Irrespective of the present Paramount Board's vision of a long-term strategic alliance with Viacom, the proposed sale of control would provide the new controlling stockholder with the power to alter that vision.

Because of the intended sale of control, the Paramount-Viacom transaction has economic consequences of considerable significance to

the Paramount stockholders. Once control has shifted, the current
Paramount stockholders will have no leverage in the future to demand
another control premium. As a result, the Paramount stockholders are
entitled to receive, and should receive, a control premium and/or
protective devices of significant value. There being no such protective
provisions in the Viacom-Paramount transaction, the Paramount
directors had an obligation to take the maximum advantage of the
current opportunity to realize for the stockholders the best value
reasonably available.

B. The Obligations of Directors in a Sale or Change of Control Transaction

The consequences of a sale of control impose special obligations on the
directors of a corporation. In particular, they have the obligation of acting
reasonably to seek the transaction offering the best value reasonably
available to the stockholders. The courts will apply enhanced scrutiny to
ensure that the directors have acted reasonably. The obligations of the
directors and the enhanced scrutiny of the courts are well-established by
the decisions of this Court. The directors' fiduciary duties in a sale of
control context are those which generally attach. In short, "the directors
must act in accordance with their fundamental duties of care and
loyalty." *Barkan v. Amsted Indus., Inc.* As we held in *Macmillan:*

> It is basic to our law that the board of directors has the ultimate
> responsibility for managing the business and affairs of a
> corporation. In discharging this function, the directors owe
> fiduciary duties of care and loyalty to the corporation and its
> shareholders. **This unremitting obligation extends equally
> to board conduct in a sale of corporate control.** *Macmillan*
> (emphasis supplied).

In the sale of control context, the directors must focus on one primary
objective—to secure the transaction offering the best value reasonably
available for the stockholders—and they must exercise their fiduciary
duties to further that end. [. . .]

In pursuing this objective, the directors must be especially diligent. *See
Citron v. Fairchild Camera and Instrument Corp.* (discussing "a board's
active and direct role in the sale process"). In particular, this Court has
stressed the importance of the board being adequately informed in
negotiating a sale of control: "The need for adequate information is
central to the enlightened evaluation of a transaction that a board must
make." *Barkan.* This requirement is consistent with the general principle
that "directors have a duty to inform themselves, prior to making a
business decision, of all material information reasonably available to
them." *Aronson. See also Cede & Co. v. Technicolor, Inc.; Smith v. Van
Gorkom.* Moreover, the role of outside, independent directors becomes
particularly important because of the magnitude of a sale of control
transaction and the possibility, in certain cases, that management may

not necessarily be impartial. *See Macmillan* (requiring "the intense scrutiny and participation of the independent directors").

Barkan teaches some of the methods by which a board can fulfill its obligation to seek the best value reasonably available to the stockholders. *Barkan v. Amsted Indus., Inc.* These methods are designed to determine the existence and viability of possible alternatives. They include conducting an auction, canvassing the market, etc. Delaware law recognizes that there is "no single blueprint" that directors must follow. *Id.*; *Citron*; *Macmillan*.

In determining which alternative provides the best value for the stockholders, a board of directors is not limited to considering only the amount of cash involved, and is not required to ignore totally its view of the future value of a strategic alliance. *See Macmillan.* Instead, the directors should analyze the entire situation and evaluate in a disciplined manner the consideration being offered. Where stock or other non-cash consideration is involved, the board should try to quantify its value, if feasible, to achieve an objective comparison of the alternatives. In addition, the board may assess a variety of practical considerations relating to each alternative, including:

> [an offer's] fairness and feasibility; the proposed or actual financing for the offer, and the consequences of that financing; questions of illegality; . . . the risk of non-consum[m]ation; . . . the bidder's identity, prior background and other business venture experiences; and the bidder's business plans for the corporation and their effects on stockholder interests. *Macmillan.*

These considerations are important because the selection of one alternative may permanently foreclose other opportunities. While the assessment of these factors may be complex, the board's goal is straightforward: Having informed themselves of all material information reasonably available, the directors must decide which alternative is most likely to offer the best value reasonably available to the stockholders.

C. Enhanced Judicial Scrutiny of a Sale or Change of Control Transaction

Board action in the circumstances presented here is subject to enhanced scrutiny. Such scrutiny is mandated by: (a) the threatened diminution of the current stockholders' voting power; (b) the fact that an asset belonging to public stockholders (a control premium) is being sold and may never be available again; and (c) the traditional concern of Delaware courts for actions which impair or impede stockholder voting rights [. . .]. In *Macmillan,* this Court held:

> When *Revlon* duties devolve upon directors, this Court will continue to exact an enhanced judicial scrutiny at the threshold, as in *Unocal,* before the normal presumptions of the business judgment rule will apply. *Macmillan.* [. . .]

The key features of an enhanced scrutiny test are: (a) a judicial determination regarding the adequacy of the decisionmaking process employed by the directors, including the information on which the directors based their decision; and (b) a judicial examination of the reasonableness of the directors' action in light of the circumstances then existing. The directors have the burden of proving that they were adequately informed and acted reasonably.

Although an enhanced scrutiny test involves a review of the reasonableness of the substantive merits of a board's actions, a court should not ignore the complexity of the directors' task in a sale of control. There are many business and financial considerations implicated in investigating and selecting the best value reasonably available. The board of directors is the corporate decisionmaking body best equipped to make these judgments. Accordingly, a court applying enhanced judicial scrutiny should be deciding whether the directors made **a reasonable** decision, not **a perfect** decision. If a board selected one of several reasonable alternatives, a court should not second-guess that choice even though it might have decided otherwise or subsequent events may have cast doubt on the board's determination. Thus, courts will not substitute their business judgment for that of the directors, but will determine if the directors' decision was, on balance, within a range of reasonableness. *See Unocal; Macmillan; Nixon v. Blackwell.*

D. *Revlon* and *Time-Warner* Distinguished

The Paramount defendants and Viacom assert that the fiduciary obligations and the enhanced judicial scrutiny discussed above are not implicated in this case in the absence of a "break-up" of the corporation, and that the order granting the preliminary injunction should be reversed. This argument is based on their erroneous interpretation of our decisions in *Revlon* and *Time-Warner*.

In *Revlon,* we reviewed the actions of the board of directors of Revlon, Inc. ("Revlon"), which had rebuffed the overtures of Pantry Pride, Inc. and had instead entered into an agreement with Forstmann Little & Co. ("Forstmann") providing for the acquisition of 100 percent of Revlon's outstanding stock by Forstmann and the subsequent break-up of Revlon. Based on the facts and circumstances present in *Revlon,* we held that "[t]he directors' role changed from defenders of the corporate bastion to auctioneers charged with getting the best price for the stockholders at a sale of the company." *Revlon.* We further held that "when a board ends an intense bidding contest on an insubstantial basis, . . . [that] action cannot withstand the enhanced scrutiny which *Unocal* requires of director conduct." *Id.*

It is true that one of the circumstances bearing on these holdings was the fact that "the break-up of the company . . . had become a reality which even the directors embraced." *Id.* It does not follow, however, that a "break-up" must be present and "inevitable" before directors are subject to enhanced judicial scrutiny and are required to pursue a transaction that is calculated to produce the best value reasonably available to the stockholders. In fact, we stated in *Revlon* that "when bidders make relatively similar offers, or dissolution of the company becomes inevitable, the directors cannot fulfill their enhanced *Unocal* duties by playing favorites with the contending factions." *Id. Revlon* thus does not hold that an inevitable dissolution or "break-up" is necessary.

The decisions of this Court following *Revlon* reinforced the applicability of enhanced scrutiny and the directors' obligation to seek the best value reasonably available for the stockholders where there is a pending sale of control, regardless of whether or not there is to be a break-up of the corporation. In *Macmillan,* this Court held:

> We stated in *Revlon,* and again here, that **in a sale of corporate control** the responsibility of the directors is to get the highest value reasonably attainable for the shareholders. *Macmillan* (emphasis added). In *Barkan,* we observed further:

> We believe that the general principles announced in *Revlon,* in *Unocal Corp. v. Mesa Petroleum Co.,* and in *Moran v. Household International, Inc.,* govern this case and every case in which a **fundamental change of corporate control** occurs or is contemplated. *Barkan* (emphasis added).

Although *Macmillan* and *Barkan* are clear in holding that a change of control imposes on directors the obligation to obtain the best value reasonably available to the stockholders, the Paramount defendants have interpreted our decision in *Time-Warner* as requiring a corporate break-up in order for that obligation to apply. The facts in *Time-Warner,* however, were quite different from the facts of this case, and refute Paramount's position here. In *Time-Warner,* the Chancellor held that there was no change of control in the original stock-for-stock merger between Time and Warner because Time would be owned by a fluid aggregation of unaffiliated stockholders both before and after the merger:

> If the appropriate inquiry is whether a change in control is contemplated, the answer must be sought in the specific circumstances surrounding the transaction. Surely under some circumstances a stock for stock merger could reflect a transfer of corporate control. That would, for example, plainly be the case here if Warner were a private company. But where, as here, the shares of both constituent corporations are widely held, corporate control can be expected to remain unaffected by a stock for stock merger. [. . .] **Control of both remained in a large, fluid, changeable and changing market.**

The existence of a control block of stock in the hands of a single shareholder or a group with loyalty to each other does have real consequences to the financial value of "minority" stock. The law offers some protection to such shares through the imposition of a fiduciary duty upon controlling shareholders. **But here,**

effectuation of the merger would not have subjected Time shareholders to the risks and consequences of holders of minority shares. This is a reflection of the fact that no control passed to anyone in the transaction contemplated. The shareholders of Time would have "suffered" dilution, of course, but they would suffer the same type of dilution upon the public distribution of new stock. *Paramount Communications Inc. v. Time Inc.* (emphasis added).

Moreover, the transaction actually consummated in *Time-Warner* was not a merger, as originally planned, but a sale of Warner's stock to Time. [. . .] Nevertheless, the Paramount defendants here have argued that a break-up is a requirement and have focused on the following language in our *Time-Warner* decision: [. . .]

Under Delaware law there are, generally speaking and **without excluding other possibilities,** two circumstances which may implicate *Revlon* duties. The first, and clearer one, is when a corporation **initiates an active bidding process seeking to sell itself** or to effect a business reorganization involving a clear break-up of the company. However, *Revlon* duties may also be triggered where, in response to a bidder's offer, a target abandons its long-term strategy and seeks an alternative transaction involving the breakup of the company. *Id.* (emphasis added).

The Paramount defendants have misread the holding of *Time-Warner*. Contrary to their argument, our decision in *Time-Warner* expressly states that the two general scenarios discussed in the above-quoted paragraph are not the **only** instances where "*Revlon* duties" may be implicated. The Paramount defendants' argument totally ignores the phrase "without excluding other possibilities." Moreover, the instant case is clearly within the first general scenario set forth in *Time-Warner*. The Paramount Board, albeit unintentionally, had "initiate[d] an active bidding process seeking to sell itself" by agreeing to sell control of the corporation to Viacom in circumstances where another potential acquiror (QVC) was equally interested in being a bidder.

The Paramount defendants' position that **both** a change of control **and** a break-up are **required** must be rejected. Such a holding would unduly restrict the application of *Revlon,* is inconsistent with this Court's decisions in *Barkan* and *Macmillan,* and has no basis in policy. There are few events that have a more significant impact on the stockholders than a sale of control or a corporate break-up. Each event represents a fundamental (and perhaps irrevocable) change in the nature of the corporate enterprise from a practical standpoint. It is the significance of **each** of these events that justifies: (a) focusing on the directors' obligation to seek the best value reasonably available to the stockholders; and (b) requiring a close scrutiny of board action which could be contrary to the stockholders' interests.

Accordingly, when a corporation undertakes a transaction which will cause: (a) a change in corporate control; **or** (b) a break-up of the corporate entity, the directors' obligation is to seek the best value reasonably available to the stockholders. This obligation arises because the effect of the Viacom-Paramount transaction, if consummated, is to shift control of Paramount from the public stockholders to a controlling stockholder, Viacom. Neither *Time-Warner* nor any other decision of this Court holds that a "break-up" of the company is essential to give rise to this obligation where there is a sale of control.

III. BREACH OF FIDUCIARY DUTIES BY PARAMOUNT BOARD

We now turn to duties of the Paramount Board under the facts of this case and our conclusions as to the breaches of those duties which warrant injunctive relief.

A.   The Specific Obligations of the Paramount Board

Under the facts of this case, the Paramount directors had the obligation: (a) to be diligent and vigilant in examining critically the Paramount-Viacom transaction and the QVC tender offers; (b) to act in good faith; (c) to obtain, and act with due care on, all material information reasonably available, including information necessary to compare the two offers to determine which of these transactions, or an alternative course of action, would provide the best value reasonably available to the stockholders; and (d) to negotiate actively and in good faith with both Viacom and QVC to that end.

Having decided to sell control of the corporation, the Paramount directors were required to evaluate critically whether or not all material aspects of the Paramount-Viacom transaction (separately and in the aggregate) were reasonable and in the best interests of the Paramount stockholders in light of current circumstances, including: the change of control premium, the Stock Option Agreement, the Termination Fee, the coercive nature of both the Viacom and QVC tender offers, the No-Shop Provision, and the proposed disparate use of the Rights Agreement as to the Viacom and QVC tender offers, respectively.

These obligations necessarily implicated various issues, including the questions of whether or not those provisions and other aspects of the Paramount-Viacom transaction (separately and in the aggregate): (a) adversely affected the value provided to the Paramount stockholders; (b) inhibited or encouraged alternative bids; (c) were enforceable contractual obligations in light of the directors' fiduciary duties; and (d) in the end would advance or retard the Paramount directors' obligation to secure for the Paramount stockholders the best value reasonably available under the circumstances.

The Paramount defendants contend that they were precluded by certain contractual provisions, including the No-Shop Provision, from negotiating with QVC or seeking alternatives. Such provisions, whether or not they are presumptively valid in the abstract, may not validly define or limit the directors' fiduciary duties under Delaware law or prevent the Paramount directors from carrying out their fiduciary duties under Delaware law. To the extent such provisions are inconsistent with those duties, they are invalid and unenforceable. *See Revlon.*

Since the Paramount directors had already decided to sell control, they had an obligation to continue their search for the best value reasonably available to the stockholders. This continuing obligation included the responsibility, at the October 24 board meeting and thereafter, to evaluate critically both the QVC tender offers and the Paramount-Viacom transaction to determine if: (a) the QVC tender offer was, or would continue to be, conditional; (b) the QVC tender offer could be improved; (c) the Viacom tender offer or other aspects of the Paramount-Viacom transaction could be improved; (d) each of the respective offers would be reasonably likely to come to closure, and under what circumstances; (e) other material information was reasonably available for consideration by the Paramount directors; (f) there were viable and realistic alternative courses of action; and (g) the timing constraints could be managed so the directors could consider these matters carefully and deliberately.

B. The Breaches of Fiduciary Duty by the Paramount Board

The Paramount directors made the decision on September 12, 1993, that, in their judgment, a strategic merger with Viacom on the economic terms of the Original Merger Agreement was in the best interests of Paramount and its stockholders. Those terms provided a modest change of control premium to the stockholders. The directors also decided at that time that it was appropriate to agree to certain defensive measures (the Stock Option Agreement, the Termination Fee, and the No-Shop Provision) insisted upon by Viacom as part of that economic transaction. Those defensive measures, coupled with the sale of control and subsequent disparate treatment of competing bidders, implicated the judicial scrutiny of *Unocal, Revlon, Macmillan,* and their progeny. We conclude that the Paramount directors' process was not reasonable, and the result achieved for the stockholders was not reasonable under the circumstances.

When entering into the Original Merger Agreement, and thereafter, the Paramount Board clearly gave insufficient attention to the potential consequences of the defensive measures demanded by Viacom. The Stock Option Agreement had a number of unusual and potentially "draconian" provisions, including the Note Feature and the Put Feature. Furthermore, the Termination Fee, whether or not unreasonable by itself, clearly made Paramount less attractive to other bidders, when coupled with the Stock Option Agreement. Finally, the No-Shop Provision inhibited the Paramount Board's ability to negotiate with other potential bidders, particularly QVC which had already expressed an interest in Paramount.

Throughout the applicable time period, and especially from the first QVC merger proposal on September 20 through the Paramount Board meeting on November 15, QVC's interest in Paramount provided the **opportunity** for the Paramount Board to seek significantly higher value for the Paramount stockholders than that being offered by Viacom. QVC persistently demonstrated its intention to meet and exceed the Viacom offers, and frequently expressed its willingness to negotiate possible further increases.

The Paramount directors had the opportunity in the October 23–24 time frame, when the Original Merger Agreement was renegotiated, to take appropriate action to modify the improper defensive measures as well as to improve the economic terms of the Paramount-Viacom transaction. Under the circumstances existing at that time, it should have been clear to the Paramount Board that the Stock Option Agreement, coupled with the Termination Fee and the No-Shop Clause, were impeding the realization of the best value reasonably available to the Paramount stockholders. Nevertheless, the Paramount Board made no effort to eliminate or modify these counterproductive devices, and instead continued to cling to its vision of a strategic alliance with Viacom. Moreover, based on advice from the Paramount management, the Paramount directors considered the QVC offer to be "conditional" and asserted that they were precluded by the No-Shop Provision from seeking more information from, or negotiating with, QVC.

By November 12, 1993, the value of the revised QVC offer on its face exceeded that of the Viacom offer by over $1 billion at then current values. This significant disparity of value cannot be justified on the basis of the directors' vision of future strategy, primarily because the change of control would supplant the authority of the current Paramount Board to continue to hold and implement their strategic vision in any meaningful way. Moreover, their uninformed process had deprived their strategic vision of much of its credibility. *See Van Gorkom; Cede v. Technicolor; Hanson Trust PLC v. ML SCM Acquisition Inc.*

When the Paramount directors met on November 15 to consider QVC's increased tender offer, they remained prisoners of their own misconceptions and missed opportunities to eliminate the restrictions they had imposed on themselves. Yet, it was not "too late" to reconsider negotiating with QVC. The circumstances existing on November 15 made it clear that the defensive measures, taken as a whole, were problematic: (a) the No-Shop Provision could not define or limit their fiduciary duties; (b) the Stock Option Agreement had become "draconian"; and (c) the Termination Fee, in context with all the circumstances, was similarly deterring the realization of possibly higher bids. Nevertheless, the Paramount directors remained paralyzed by their uninformed belief that the QVC offer was "illusory." This final opportunity to negotiate on the stockholders' behalf and to fulfill their obligation to seek the best value reasonably available was thereby squandered. [. . .]

V. CONCLUSION

The realization of the best value reasonably available to the stockholders became the Paramount directors' primary obligation under these facts in light of the change of control. That obligation was not satisfied, and the Paramount Board's process was deficient. The directors' initial hope and expectation for a strategic alliance with Viacom was allowed to dominate their decisionmaking process to the point where the arsenal of defensive measures established at the outset was perpetuated (not modified or eliminated) when the situation was dramatically altered. QVC's unsolicited bid presented the opportunity for significantly greater value for the stockholders and enhanced negotiating leverage for the directors. Rather than seizing those opportunities, the Paramount directors chose to wall themselves off from material information which was reasonably available and to hide behind the defensive measures as a rationalization for refusing to negotiate with QVC or seeking other alternatives. Their view of the strategic alliance likewise became an empty rationalization as the opportunities for higher value for the stockholders continued to develop.

It is the nature of the judicial process that we decide only the case before us—a case which, on its facts, is clearly controlled by established Delaware law. Here, the proposed change of control and the implications thereof were crystal clear. In other cases they may be less clear. The holding of this case on its facts, coupled with the holdings of the principal cases discussed herein where the issue of sale of control is implicated, should provide a workable precedent against which to measure future cases.

For the reasons set forth herein, the November 24, 1993, Order of the Court of Chancery has been AFFIRMED, and this matter has been REMANDED for proceedings consistent herewith, as set forth in the December 9, 1993, Order of this Court. [. . .]

Corwin v. KKR Financial Holdings LLC

125 A.3d 304 (Del. 2015)

■ STRINE, CHIEF JUSTICE:

[. . .]

I. The Court Of Chancery Properly Held That The Complaint Did Not Plead Facts Supporting An Inference That KKR Was A Controlling Stockholder of Financial Holdings

The plaintiffs filed a challenge in the Court of Chancery to a stock-for-stock merger between KKR & Co. L.P. ("KKR") and KKR Financial Holdings LLC ("Financial Holdings") in which KKR acquired each share of Financial Holdings's stock for 0.51 of a share of KKR stock, a 35% premium to the unaffected market price. Below, the plaintiffs' primary argument was that the transaction was presumptively subject to the entire fairness standard of review because Financial Holdings's primary business was financing KKR's leveraged buyout activities, and instead of having employees manage the company's day-to-day operations, Financial Holdings was managed by KKR Financial Advisors, an affiliate of KKR, under a contractual management agreement that could only be terminated by Financial Holdings if it paid a termination fee. As a result, the plaintiffs alleged that KKR was a controlling stockholder of Financial Holdings, which was an LLC, not a corporation.

The defendants filed a motion to dismiss, taking issue with that argument. In a thoughtful and thorough decision, the Chancellor found that the defendants were correct that the plaintiffs' complaint did not plead facts supporting an inference that KKR was Financial Holdings's controlling stockholder. Among other things, the Chancellor noted that KKR owned less than 1% of Financial Holdings's stock, had no right to appoint any directors, and had no contractual right to veto any board action. Although the Chancellor acknowledged the unusual existential circumstances the plaintiffs cited, he noted that those were known at all relevant times by investors, and that Financial Holdings had real assets its independent board controlled and had the option of pursuing any path its directors chose.

In addressing whether KKR was a controlling stockholder, the Chancellor was focused on the reality that in cases where a party that did not have majority control of the entity's voting stock was found to be a controlling stockholder, the Court of Chancery, consistent with the instructions of this Court, looked for a combination of potent voting power and management control such that the stockholder could be deemed to have effective control of the board without actually owning a majority of stock. Not finding that combination here, the Chancellor noted:

> Plaintiffs' real grievance, as I see it, is that [Financial Holdings] was structured from its inception in a way that limited its value-maximizing options. According to plaintiffs, [Financial Holdings] serves as little more than a public vehicle for financing KKR-sponsored transactions and the terms of the Management Agreement make [Financial Holdings] unattractive as an acquisition target to anyone other than KKR because of [Financial Holdings]'s operational dependence on KKR and because of the significant cost that would be incurred to terminate the Management Agreement. I assume all that is true. But, every contractual obligation of a corporation constrains the corporation's freedom to operate to some degree and, in this particular case, the stockholders cannot claim to be surprised. Every stockholder of [Financial Holdings] knew about the limitations the Management Agreement imposed on [Financial Holdings]'s business when he, she or it acquired shares in [Financial Holdings]. They also knew that the business and affairs of [Financial Holdings] would be managed

> by a board of directors that would be subject to annual stockholder elections.
>
> At bottom, plaintiffs ask the Court to impose fiduciary obligations on a relatively nominal stockholder, not because of any coercive power that stockholder could wield over the board's ability to independently decide whether or not to approve the merger, but because of pre-existing contractual obligations with that stockholder that constrain the business or strategic options available to the corporation. Plaintiffs have cited no legal authority for that novel proposition, and I decline to create such a rule.

After carefully analyzing the pled facts and the relevant precedent, the Chancellor held:

> [T]here are no well-pled facts from which it is reasonable to infer that KKR could prevent the [Financial Holdings] board from freely exercising its independent judgment in considering the proposed merger or, put differently, that KKR had the power to exact retribution by removing the [Financial Holdings] directors from their offices if they did not bend to KKR's will in their consideration of the proposed merger.

Although the plaintiffs reiterate their position on appeal, the Chancellor correctly applied the law and we see no reason to repeat his lucid analysis of this question.

II. The Court of Chancery Correctly Held That The Fully Informed, Uncoerced Vote Of The Disinterested Stockholders Invoked The Business Judgment Rule Standard Of Review

On appeal, the plaintiffs further contend that, even if the Chancellor was correct in determining that KKR was not a controlling stockholder, he was wrong to dismiss the complaint because they contend that if the entire fairness standard did not apply, Revlon did, and the plaintiffs argue that they pled a Revlon claim against the defendant directors. But, as the defendants point out, the plaintiffs did not fairly argue below that Revlon applied and even if they did, they ignore the reality that Financial Holdings had in place an exculpatory charter provision, and that the transaction was approved by an independent board majority and by a fully informed, uncoerced stockholder vote. Therefore, the defendants argue, the plaintiffs failed to state a non-exculpated claim for breach of fiduciary duty. [. . .]

But we need not delve into whether the Court of Chancery's determination that *Revlon* did not apply to the merger is correct for a single reason: it does not matter. Because the Chancellor was correct in determining that the entire fairness standard did not apply to the merger, the Chancellor's analysis of the effect of the uncoerced, informed stockholder vote is outcome-determinative, even if *Revlon* applied to the merger.

[T]he Court of Chancery noted, and the defendants point out on appeal, that the plaintiffs did not contest the defendants' argument below that if the merger was not subject to the entire fairness standard, the business judgment standard of review was invoked because the merger was approved by a disinterested stockholder majority. The Chancellor agreed with that argument below, and adhered to precedent supporting the proposition that when a transaction not subject to the entire fairness standard is approved by a fully informed, uncoerced vote of the disinterested stockholders, the business judgment rule applies. [. . .]

[On appeal] [. . .], although the plaintiffs argue that adhering to the proposition that a fully informed, uncoerced stockholder vote invokes the business judgment rule would impair the operation of *Unocal* and *Revlon*, or expose stockholders to unfair action by directors without protection, the plaintiffs ignore several factors. First, *Unocal* and *Revlon* are primarily designed to give stockholders and the Court of Chancery the tool of injunctive relief to address important M & A decisions in real time, before closing. They were not tools designed with post-closing money damages claims in mind, the standards they articulate do not match the gross negligence standard for director due care liability under *Van Gorkom*, and with the prevalence of exculpatory charter provisions, due care liability is rarely even available. Second and most important, the doctrine applies only to fully informed, uncoerced stockholder votes, and if troubling facts regarding director behavior were not disclosed that would have been material to a voting stockholder, then the business judgment rule is not invoked. Here, however, all of the objective facts regarding the board's interests, KKR's interests, and the negotiation process, were fully disclosed.

Finally, when a transaction is not subject to the entire fairness standard, the long-standing policy of our law has been to avoid the uncertainties and costs of judicial second-guessing when the disinterested stockholders have had the free and informed chance to decide on the economic merits of a transaction for themselves. There are sound reasons for this policy. When the real parties in interest—the disinterested equity owners—can easily protect themselves at the ballot box by simply voting no, the utility of a litigation-intrusive standard of review promises more costs to stockholders in the form of litigation rents and inhibitions on risk-taking than it promises in terms of benefits to them. The reason for that is tied to the core rationale of the business judgment rule, which is that judges are poorly positioned to evaluate the wisdom of business decisions and there is little utility to having them second-guess the determination of impartial decision-makers with more information (in the case of directors) or an actual economic stake in the outcome (in the case of informed, disinterested stockholders). In circumstances, therefore, where the stockholders have had the voluntary choice to accept or reject a transaction, the business judgment rule standard of review is the presumptively correct one and best facilitates wealth creation through the corporate form.

For these reasons, therefore, we affirm the Court of Chancery's judgment on the basis of its well-reasoned decision.

F. APPRAISAL RIGHTS

Verition Partners Master Fund Ltd. v. Aruba Networks, Inc.

210 A.3d 128 (Del. 2019)

In this statutory appraisal case, the Court of Chancery found that the fair value of Aruba Networks, Inc., as defined by 8 *Del. C.* § 262, was $ 17.13 per share, which was the thirty-day average market price at which its shares traded before the media reported news of the transaction that gave rise to the appellants' appraisal rights. In its post-trial opinion, the Court of Chancery engaged in a wide-ranging discussion of its view on the evolution of our State's appraisal law and how certain recent decisions have affected the relevance of market-based evidence to determining fair value. For purposes of this appeal, we need not respond in full to the dicta and instead focus on the key issue before us: whether the Court of Chancery abused its discretion, based on this record, in arriving at Aruba's thirty-day average unaffected market price as the fair value of the appellants' shares. Because the Court of Chancery's decision to use Aruba's stock price instead of the deal price minus synergies was rooted in an erroneous factual finding that lacked record support, we answer that in the positive and reverse the Court of Chancery's judgment. On remand, the Court of Chancery shall enter a final judgment for the petitioners awarding them $ 19.10 per share, which reflects the deal price minus the portion of synergies left with the seller as estimated by the respondent in this case, Aruba.

I.

In August 2014, Hewlett-Packard Company ("HP"), a publicly traded company, approached Aruba, another publicly traded company, about a potential combination. Aruba hired professionals and, in addition to negotiating with HP, began to shop the deal. Five other logical strategic bidders were approached, but none of them showed any interest. The petitioners did not argue below that private equity bidders could compete given the synergies a combination with HP or another strategic buyer could garner.

After several months of negotiations between the two companies, the Aruba board decided to accept HP's offer of $ 24.67 per share. News of the deal leaked to the press about two weeks later, causing Aruba's stock price to jump from $ 18.37 to $ 22.24. The next day, after the market closed, Aruba released its quarterly results, which beat analyst expectations. Aruba's stock price rose by 9.7% the following day on the strength of its earnings to close at $ 24.81 per share, just above the deal price.

Not long after the deal leaked, both companies' boards approved the transaction, and Aruba and HP formally announced the merger at a price of $ 24.67 per share. The final merger agreement allowed for another passive market check. However, no superior bid emerged, and the deal closed on May 18, 2015.

II.

On August 28, 2015, the appellants and petitioners below, Verition Partners Master Fund Ltd. and Verition Multi-Strategy Master Fund Ltd. (collectively, "Verition"), filed this appraisal proceeding in the Court of Chancery, asking the court to appraise the "fair value" of their shares under § 262. The respondent was Aruba, albeit an Aruba now 100% controlled by HP. In its pretrial and initial post-trial briefing, Verition maintained that Aruba's fair value was $ 32.57 per share, and Aruba contended that its fair value was either $ 19.45 per share (before trial) or $ 19.75 per share (after trial). In its post-trial answering brief, Aruba contended that its "deal price less synergies" value was $ 19.10 per share. Neither party claimed that Aruba's preannouncement stock price was the best measure of fair value at the time of the merger.

Post-trial argument was scheduled for May 17, 2017, but the Court of Chancery postponed the hearing "once it became clear that the Delaware Supreme Court's forthcoming decision in *DFC* [*Global Corp. v. Muirfield Value Partners, L.P.*] likely would have a significant effect on the legal landscape." After this Court issued its opinion in *DFC*, the Court of Chancery allowed the parties to submit supplemental briefing on the opinion's implications, and the parties submitted simultaneous briefs on September 15, 2017. Both parties continued to argue for their preferred fair value calculation, and neither party advocated for the adoption of the stock price, though Aruba did contend that the stock price was now "informative" of fair value and lent support to its argument that fair value as of the time of the merger was in the $ 19 to $ 20 per share range. And the parties hewed to these positions during post-trial oral argument.

On December 14, 2017, this Court issued its opinion in *Dell, Inc. v. Magnetar Global Event Driven Master Fund Ltd.*, reversing the Court of Chancery's appraisal decision in that case. Six days later, the Vice Chancellor in this case—who was also the trial judge in *Dell*—sent the parties a letter on his own motion. In the letter, the Vice Chancellor requested supplemental briefing on "the market attributes of Aruba's stock" in part because he "learned how many errors [he] made in the *Dell* matter."

The parties submitted simultaneous briefs in response to the Vice Chancellor's *sua sponte* request on January 26, 2018. In its brief, Aruba abandoned deal price minus synergies as its main benchmark and argued for the first time that its preannouncement stock price was "the single most important mark of its fair value." Accordingly, Aruba asked the Court of Chancery to award the thirty-day unaffected market price of $ 17.13 per share. Aruba's brief focused mainly on how the market for its stock was efficient.

On February 15, 2018, the Court of Chancery issued its post-trial opinion finding that the fair value under § 262 was $ 17.13 per share. In its opinion, the Court of Chancery considered three different valuation measures: first, the "unaffected market price" of Aruba's stock before news of the merger leaked; second, the deal price minus the portion of synergies left with the seller; and third, the two expert witnesses' valuations, which were based primarily on discounted cash flow ("DCF") models.

In weighing the valuation methodologies, the Court of Chancery gave no weight to the parties' DCF models. The Court of Chancery also determined, based on its own analysis, that the appropriate deal price minus synergies value was $ 18.20. In reaching that conclusion, the Court of Chancery started with an estimate of the total amount of synergies HP expected to realize. To determine how much of those synergies Aruba's stockholders received in the deal price, the Court of Chancery took the midpoint of a study suggesting that "on average, sellers collect 31% of the capitalized value of synergies, with the seller's share varying widely from 6% to 51%." This resulted in a deal price minus synergies value of $ 18.20 per share, $ 0.90 lower than Aruba's own estimate of deal price minus synergies. And although the Vice Chancellor was "inclined to think that Aruba's representatives bargained less effectively than they might have," "indicat[ing] that [Aruba] obtained fewer synergies than the midpoint range and imply[ing] value *north* of $ 18.20 per share," he failed to explain why his estimate of $ 18.20 per share was more reliable than Aruba's own estimate of $ 19.10 per share.

However, the Vice Chancellor did not adopt his deal price minus synergies value, in part because he believed that his "deal-price-less-synergies figure continues to incorporate an element of value resulting from the merger" in the form of "reduced agency costs that result from unitary (or controlling) ownership." To remedy this, the Vice Chancellor elected to rely exclusively on the stock price because he thought he would need to estimate and back out these theoretical "reduced agency costs" from the deal price to arrive at a figure that reflected Aruba's value as a going concern. According to the Court of Chancery, using the "unaffected market price" of Aruba's publicly traded shares "provide[d] a direct estimate" of that endpoint, which led him to find the sole indicator of fair value to be that "unaffected market price" of $ 17.13 per share. Although § 262 requires the Court of Chancery to assess Aruba's fair value as of "the effective date of the merger," the Court of Chancery arrived at the unaffected market price by averaging the trading price of Aruba's stock during the thirty days before news of the merger leaked, which was three to four months prior to closing.

III.

We reverse the trial court's fair value determination. Under *Cavalier Oil Corp. v. Hartnett*, the Court of Chancery's task in an appraisal case is "to value what has been taken from the shareholder: 'viz. his proportionate interest in a going concern.' " That is, the court must value the company "as an operating entity . . . but without regard to post-merger events or other possible business combinations." *Cavalier Oil* draws this requirement from § 262's command that the court determine fair value "exclusive of any element of value arising from the accomplishment or expectation of the merger or consolidation," which this Court has interpreted as ruling out consideration of not just the gains that the particular merger will produce, but also the gains that might be obtained from any other merger. As a result, fair value "is more properly described as the value of the company to the stockholder as a going concern, rather than its value to a third party as an acquisition." Under this reading of § 262, the Court of Chancery must "exclude from any appraisal award the amount of any value that the selling company's shareholders would receive because a buyer intends to operate the subject company, not as a stand-alone going concern, but as a part of a larger enterprise, from which synergistic gains can be extracted." For this reason, in cases where the Court of Chancery has used the price at which a company is sold in a third-party transaction, it has excised a reasonable estimate of whatever share of synergy or other value the buyer expects from changes it plans to make to the company's "going concern" business plan that has been included in the purchase price as an inducement to the sale. No party in this proceeding argued to us that the long-standing use of going-concern value, or its concomitant requirement to excise synergy gains, should be revisited.

Applying the going-concern standard, we hold that the Court of Chancery abused its discretion in using Aruba's "unaffected market price" because it did so on the inapt theory that it needed to make an additional deduction from the deal price for unspecified "reduced agency costs." It appears to us that the Court of Chancery would have given weight to the deal price minus synergies absent its view that it also had to deduct unspecified agency costs to adhere to *Cavalier Oil*'s going-concern standard. As Verition points out, this aspect of the decision is not grounded in the record. Judging by the law review articles cited by the Court of Chancery, the theory underlying the court's decision appears to be that the acquisition would reduce agency costs essentially because the resulting consolidation of ownership and control would align the interests of Aruba's managers and its public stockholders. In other words, the theory goes, replacing a dispersed group of owners with a concentrated group of owners can be expected to add value because the new owners are more capable of making sure management isn't shirking or diverting the company's profits, and that added value must be excluded under § 262 as "arising from the accomplishment or expectation of the merger or consolidation." However, unlike a private equity deal, the merger at issue in this case would not replace Aruba's public stockholders with a concentrated group of owners; rather, it would swap out one set of public stockholders for another: HP's.

Indeed, neither party presented any evidence to suggest that any part of the deal price paid by HP, a strategic buyer, involved the potential for agency cost reductions that were not already captured by its synergies estimate. Synergies do not just involve the benefits when, for example, two symbiotic product lines can be sold together. They also classically involve cost reductions that arise because, for example, a strategic buyer believes it can produce the same or greater profits with fewer employees—in English terms, rendering some of the existing employees "redundant." Private equity firms often expect to improve performance and squeeze costs too, including by reducing "agency costs." Here, the Court of Chancery's belief that it had to deduct for agency costs ignores the reality that HP's synergies case likely already priced any agency cost reductions it may have expected. In short, the Court of Chancery acknowledged that there were estimates of the synergies expected by HP, and the record provides no reason to believe that those estimates omitted any other added value HP thought it could achieve because of the combination. For this reason, Aruba itself presented a deal price minus synergies value of $ 19.10 per share as one of its suggested outcomes.

As to this issue, Aruba never argued that its deal price minus synergies case did not fully account for all the "agency cost" reductions it expected, and the Court of Chancery's view that some measure of agency costs had to be accounted for finds no basis in the record. Nor does it find any basis in the corporate finance literature; given that all the cost reductions HP expected as a widely held, strategic buyer were likely to be fully accounted for by its expected synergies. Theory here tracks the facts, and there was no reasonable basis to infer that Aruba was cheating itself out of extra agency cost reductions by using only the cost reductions that were anticipated in commercial reality. However, instead of at least awarding Verition the deal price minus HP's estimate of its expected synergies left with the seller, which generated a value that was corroborated by the standalone DCF models used by Aruba's and HP's boards in agreeing to the transaction, the Court of Chancery gave exclusive weight to the thirty-day average unaffected market price of $ 17.13 per share.

In addition to believing that it had to account for unspecified agency costs, the Court of Chancery also seemed to suggest that rote reliance on market prices was compelled based on its reading of *DFC* and *Dell*. Like any human perspective, the trial judge's broader reading of *Dell* and *DFC* is arguable, but the trial judge's sense that those decisions somehow compelled him to make the decision he did was not supported by any reasonable reading of those decisions or grounded in any direct citation to them. Among other things, the trial judge seemed to find it novel that *DFC* and *Dell* recognized that when a public company with a deep trading market is sold at a substantial premium to the preannouncement price, after a process in which interested buyers all had a fair and viable opportunity to bid, the deal price is a strong indicator of fair value, as a matter of economic reality and theory. The apparent novelty the trial judge perceived is surprising, given the long history of giving important weight to market-tested deal prices in the Court of Chancery and this Court, a history that long predated the trial judge's contrary determination in *Dell.*

For example, the Court of Chancery equated the view that the deal price can serve as reliable evidence of fair value when a buyer pays the highest price, after other logical buyers have been given access to confidential information and a fair chance to present a superior offer, with being one that "discount[s] the importance of competition." Of course, when there is an open opportunity for many buyers to buy and only a few bid (or even just one bids), that does not necessarily mean that there is a failure of competition; it may just mean that the target's value is not sufficiently enticing to buyers to engender a bidding war above the winning price. In this case, for instance, Aruba approached other logical strategic buyers prior to signing the deal with HP, and none of those potential buyers were interested. Then, after signing and the announcement of the deal, still no other buyer emerged even though the merger agreement allowed for superior bids. It cannot be that an open chance for buyers to bid signals a market failure simply because buyers do not believe the asset on sale is sufficiently valuable for them to engage in a bidding contest against each other. If that were the jurisprudential conclusion, then the judiciary would itself infuse assets with extra value by virtue of the fact that no actual market participants saw enough value to pay a higher price. That sort of alchemy has no rational basis in economics.

In fact, encouraged by *Weinberger v. UOP, Inc.,* our courts have for years applied corporate finance principles such as the capital asset pricing model to value companies in appraisal proceedings in ways that depend on market efficiency. The reliable application of valuation methods used in appraisal proceedings, such as DCF and comparable companies analysis, often depends on market data and the efficiency of the markets from which that data is derived. For example, it is difficult to come up with a reliable beta if the subject company's shares do not trade in an efficient market, and the reliability of a comparable companies or transactions analysis depends on the underlying efficiency of the markets from which the multiples used in the analysis are derived.

Even before this Court's seminal opinion in *Weinberger*, the old Delaware "block" method used market prices in one of its three prongs. In forsaking the Delaware block method as a rigid basis to determine fair value, *Weinberger* did not hold that market value was no longer relevant; in fact,

Weinberger explicitly condoned its use. Extending this basic point, *DFC* and *Dell* merely recognized that a buyer in possession of material nonpublic information about the seller is in a strong position (and is uniquely incentivized) to properly value the seller when agreeing to buy the company at a particular deal price, and that view of value should be given considerable weight by the Court of Chancery absent deficiencies in the deal process.

Likewise, assuming an efficient market, the unaffected market price and that price as adjusted upward by a competitive bidding process leading to a sale of the entire company was likely to be strong evidence of fair value. By asserting that *Dell* and *DFC* "indicate[ ] that Aruba's unaffected market price is entitled to substantial weight," the Vice Chancellor seemed to suggest that this Court signaled in both cases that trading prices should be treated as exclusive indicators of fair value. However, *Dell* and *DFC* did not imply that the market price of a stock was necessarily the best estimate of the stock's so-called fundamental value at any particular time. Rather, they did recognize that when a market was informationally efficient in the sense that "the market's digestion and assessment of all publicly available information concerning [the Company] [is] quickly impounded into the Company's stock price," the market price is likely to be more informative of fundamental value. In fact, *Dell*'s references to market efficiency focused on informational efficiency—the idea that markets quickly reflect publicly available information and can be a proxy for fair value—not the idea that an informationally efficient market price invariably reflects the company's fair value in an appraisal or fundamental value in economic terms. Nonetheless, to the extent the Court of Chancery read *DFC* and *Dell* as reaffirming the traditional Delaware view, which is accepted in corporate finance, that the price a stock trades at in an efficient market is an important indicator of its economic value that should be given weight, it was correct. And to the extent that the Court of Chancery also read *DFC* and *Dell* as reaffirming the view that when that market price is further informed by the efforts of arm's length buyers of the entire company to learn more through due diligence, involving confidential non-public information, and with the keener incentives of someone considering taking the non-diversifiable risk of buying the entire entity, the price that results from that process is even more likely to be indicative of so-called fundamental value, it was correct.

Here, the price that HP paid could be seen as reflecting a better assessment of Aruba's going-concern value for reasons consistent with corporate finance theory. For starters, the unaffected market price was a measurement from three to four months prior to the valuation date, a time period during which it is possible for new, material information relevant to a company's future earnings to emerge. Even more important, HP had more incentive to study Aruba closely than ordinary traders in small blocks of Aruba shares, and also had material, nonpublic information that, by definition, could not have been baked into the public trading price. For example, HP knew about Aruba's strong quarterly earnings before the market did, and likely took that information into account when pricing the deal. Based on the record evidence, the Court of Chancery could easily have found that HP and Aruba's back and forth over price, HP's access to nonpublic information to supplement its consideration of the public information available to stock market buyers, and the currency of the information that they had at the time of striking a bargain had improved the parties' ability to estimate Aruba's going-concern value over that of the market as a whole. In particular, HP had better insight into Aruba's future prospects than the market because it was aware that Aruba expected its quarterly results to exceed analysts' expectations. When those strong quarterly results were finally reported—after the close of the period that the Court of Chancery used to measure the "unaffected market price"—Aruba's stock price jumped 9.7%. Indeed, after the market learned about the strong quarter and the likelihood of a strategic deal with HP, Aruba's stock traded at $ 24.81, $ 0.14 away from the actual price HP paid. Of course, despite expressing concern about the fact that no other bidder emerged to compete with HP at the $ 24-plus price range, the Court of Chancery then awarded Verition $ 7.54 per share less than the $ 24.67 deal price.

By relying exclusively on the thirty-day average market price, the Court of Chancery not only abused its discretion by double counting agency costs but also injected due process and fairness problems into the proceedings. As Verition argued, the Vice Chancellor's desire not to award deal price minus synergies could be seen—in light of his letter to the parties and the overall tone of his opinion and reargument decision— as a results-oriented move to generate an odd result compelled by his personal frustration at being reversed in *Dell*. Indeed, the idea of awarding the stock price came into the proceedings from the Vice Chancellor himself after requesting supplemental post-trial briefing on the matter. Prior to that point, neither party argued for that figure as the fair value under § 262. Because the Vice Chancellor introduced this issue late in the proceedings, the extent to which the market price approximated fair value was never subjected to the crucible of pretrial discovery, expert depositions, cross-expert rebuttal, expert testimony at trial, and cross examination at trial. Instead, the Vice Chancellor surfaced Aruba's stock price as an appropriate measure of fair value in a way that is antithetical to the traditional hallmarks of a Court of Chancery appraisal proceeding. The lack of a developed record on whether the stock price was an adequate proxy for fair value buttresses our holding that the Court of Chancery abused its discretion by awarding the thirty-day average unaffected market price of $ 17.13 per share.

These procedural issues relate to substance in an important way. The reason for pretrial discovery and trial is for parties to have a chance to test each other's evidence and to give the fact-finder a reliable basis to make an ultimate determination after each side has a fair chance to develop a record and to comment upon it. The lack of that process here as to the Vice Chancellor's ultimate remedy is troubling. The Vice Chancellor slighted several important factors in choosing to give exclusive weight to the unaffected market price. Under the semi-strong form of the efficient capital markets hypothesis, the unaffected market price is not assumed to factor in nonpublic information. In this case, however, HP had signed a confidentiality agreement, done exclusive due diligence, gotten access to material nonpublic information, and had a much sharper incentive to engage in price discovery than an ordinary trader because it was seeking to acquire all shares. Moreover, its information base was more current as of the time of the deal than the trading price used by the Vice Chancellor. Compounding these issues was the reality that Aruba was set to release strong earnings that HP knew about in the final negotiations, but that the market did not. As previously noted, Aruba's stock price jumped 9.7% once those earnings were finally reported to the public. None of these issues were illuminated in the traditional way, and none of them were discussed by the Court of Chancery in a reasoned way in giving exclusive weight to a prior trading price that was $ 7.54 below what HP agreed to pay, and well below what Aruba had previously argued was fair value.

This multitude of concerns gives us pause, as does the evident plausibility of Verition's concern that the trial judge was bent on using the thirty-day average market price as a personal reaction to being reversed in a different case. In a reargument decision addressing the petitioner's argument to this effect, the Vice Chancellor denied that this was the case. We take him at his word. However, so too do we take him at his word that he viewed an estimate of deal price minus synergies as compelling evidence of fair value on this record but that he could not come up with a reliable estimate of his own because he wanted to double count agency costs, and also lacked confidence in his underlying synergy deduction. Nevertheless, fixing the double counting problem and hewing to the record developed by the parties themselves leaves a reliable estimate of deal price minus synergies, which is the one that Aruba advanced until the Vice Chancellor himself injected the thirty-day average market price as his own speculative idea. Of course, estimating synergies and allocating a reasonable portion to the seller certainly involves imprecision, but no more than other valuation methods, like a DCF analysis that involves estimating (i) future free cash flows; (ii) the weighted average cost of capital (including the stock's beta); and (iii) the perpetuity growth rate. But here there is no basis to think Aruba was being generous in its evaluation of deal price minus synergies. And, as any measure of value should be, Aruba's $ 19.10 deal price minus synergies value is corroborated by abundant record evidence.

The Vice Chancellor himself concluded that because the HP-Aruba transaction involved enormous synergies, "the deal price . . . operates as a ceiling for fair value." That conclusion was abundantly supported by the record. Aruba's estimate of $ 19.10 resulting from that method was corroborated by HP's and Aruba's real-time considerations and Aruba's DCF, comparable companies, and comparable transactions analyses.

Rather than burden the parties with further proceedings, we order that a final judgment be entered for the petitioners in the amount of $ 19.10 per share plus any interest to which the petitioners are entitled.

G. REGULATORY IMPACTS

Ralls Corporation v. CFIUS

758 F.3d 296 (D.C. Cir. 2014)

■ KAREN LeCRAFT HENDERSON, CIRCUIT JUDGE.

I. BACKGROUND

A. Statutory Regulatory Framework

This case involves Executive Branch review of a business transaction under section 721 of the DPA, also known as the "Exon-Florio Amendment." As amended, section 721 of the DPA [Defense Production Act of 1950] directs "the President, acting through [the Committee on Foreign Investment in the United States, or CFIUS]," to review a "covered transaction to determine the effects of the transaction on the national security of the United States." Section 721 defines a covered transaction as "any merger, acquisition, or takeover . . ., by or with any foreign person which could result in foreign control of any person engaged in interstate commerce in the United States."

Review of covered transactions under section 721 begins with CFIUS. As noted, CFIUS is chaired by the Treasury Secretary and its members include the heads of various federal agencies and other high-ranking Government officials with foreign policy, national security and economic responsibilities. CFIUS review is initiated in one of two ways. First, any party to a covered transaction may initiate review, either before or after the transaction is completed, by submitting a written notice to the CFIUS chairman. Alternatively, CFIUS may initiate review *sua sponte*. The CFIUS review period lasts thirty days, during which CFIUS considers the eleven factors set forth in 50 U.S.C. app. § 2170(f) to assess the transaction's effect on national security.

During its review, if CFIUS determines that "the transaction threatens to impair the national security of the United States and that threat has not been mitigated," it must "immediately conduct an investigation of the effects of [the] covered transaction on the national security . . . and take any necessary actions in connection with the transaction to protect the national security." CFIUS is given express authority to "negotiate, enter into or impose, and enforce any agreement or condition with any party to the covered transaction in order to mitigate any threat to the national security of the United States that arises as a result of the covered transaction." The investigation period lasts no more than forty-five days. If CFIUS determines at the end of an investigation that the national security effects of the transaction have been mitigated and that the transaction need not be prohibited, action under section 721 terminates and CFIUS submits a final investigation report to the Congress.

If CFIUS concludes at the end of its investigation that a covered transaction should be suspended or prohibited, it must "send a report to the President requesting the President's decision," which report includes, *inter alia,* information regarding the transaction's effect on national security and CFIUS's recommendation. Once CFIUS's report is submitted to the President, he has fifteen days to "take such action for such time as the President considers appropriate to suspend or prohibit any covered transaction that threatens to impair the national security of the United States." The President may exercise his authority under section 721 only if he finds that

> there is credible evidence that leads [him] to believe that the foreign interest exercising control might take action that threatens to impair the national security; and . . . provisions of law, other than [section 721] and the International Emergency Economic Powers Act, do not, in the judgment of the President, provide adequate and appropriate authority for the President to protect the national security in the matter before the President.

Significantly, the statute provides that "[t]he actions of the President under paragraph (1) of subsection (d) of this section and the findings of the President under paragraph (4) of subsection (d) of this section shall not be subject to judicial review."

B. Factual Background

Ralls is an American company incorporated in Delaware with its principal place of business in Georgia. Ralls is owned by two Chinese nationals, Dawei Duan and Jialiang Wu. Duan is the chief financial officer of Sany Group (Sany), a Chinese manufacturing company, and, at the time of the transaction at issue, Wu was a Sany vice-president and the general manager of Sany Electric Company, Ltd. (Sany Electric). Ralls's amended complaint asserts that "Ralls is in the business of identifying U.S. opportunities for the construction of windfarms in which the wind turbines of Sany Electric, its affiliate, can be used and their quality and reliability demonstrated to the U.S. wind industry in comparison to competitor products."

In March 2012, Ralls purchased the Project Companies, which are four American-owned, limited liability companies: Pine City Windfarm, LLC; Mule Hollow Windfarm, LLC; High Plateau Windfarm, LLC; and Lower Ridge Windfarm, LLC. The Project Companies were originally created by an Oregon entity (Oregon Windfarms, LLC) owned by American citizens to develop four windfarms in north-central Oregon (collectively, Butter Creek projects). [. . .]

The Butter Creek project sites are located in and around the eastern region of a restricted airspace and bombing zone maintained by the United States Navy (Navy). Three of the windfarm sites are located within seven miles of the restricted airspace while the fourth—Lower Ridge—is located within the restricted airspace. After the Navy urged Ralls to move the Lower Ridge site "to reduce airspace conflicts between the Lower Ridge wind turbines and low-level military aircraft training," Ralls relocated the windfarm but it remains within the restricted airspace.

Ralls's complaint alleges that Oregon Windfarms, LLC, has developed nine other windfarm projects (Echo Projects) in the same general vicinity as the Butter Creek projects and that all nine use foreign-made wind turbines. According to Ralls, seven turbines used by the Echo Projects are located within the restricted airspace and one of the nine Echo Projects—Pacific Canyon—is currently owned by foreign investors. In addition, Ralls claims that there are "dozens if not hundreds of existing turbines in or near the western region of the restricted airspace" that "are foreign-made and foreign-owned." The Appellees conceded at oral argument that there are other foreign-owned wind turbines near the restricted airspace.

On June 28, 2012, Ralls submitted a twenty-five-page notice to CFIUS informing it of Ralls's March acquisition of the Project Companies. The notice explained why Ralls believed the transaction did not pose a national security threat. CFIUS initiated its review pursuant to 50 U.S.C. app. § 2170(b)(1). [. . .] Ralls contends that CFIUS did not apprise Ralls of the gravamen of its concern with the transaction and did not, during the presentation or at any other time, disclose to Ralls the information it reviewed.

CFIUS determined that Ralls's acquisition of the Project Companies posed a national security threat and on July 25 it issued an Order Establishing Interim Mitigation Measures (July Order) to mitigate the threat. The July Order required Ralls to (1) cease all construction and operations at the Butter Creek project sites, (2) "remove all stockpiled or stored items from the [project sites] no later than July 30, 2012, and shall not deposit, stockpile, or store any new items at the [project sites]" and (3) cease all access to the project sites. Five days later, July 30, CFIUS launched an investigation under 50 U.S.C. app. § 2170(b)(2).

Three days into its investigation, August 2, CFIUS issued an Amended Order Establishing Interim Mitigation Measures (CFIUS Order). In addition to the July Order restrictions, the CFIUS Order prohibited Ralls from completing any sale of the Project Companies or their assets without first removing all items (including concrete foundations) from the Butter Creek project sites, notifying CFIUS of the sale and giving CFIUS ten business days to object to the sale. The CFIUS Order remained in effect "until CFIUS concludes action or the President takes action under section 721" or until express "revocation by CFIUS or the President." Neither the July Order nor the CFIUS Order disclosed the nature of the national security threat the transaction posed or the evidence on which CFIUS relied in issuing the orders. On September 13, the investigation period ended and CFIUS submitted its report (including its recommendation) to the President, requesting his decision.

On September 28, the President issued an "Order Regarding the Acquisition of Four U.S. Wind Farm Project Companies by Ralls Corporation" (Presidential Order). The Presidential Order stated that "[t]here is credible evidence that leads [the President] to believe that Ralls . . . might take action that threatens to impair the national security of the United States" and that "[p]rovisions of law, other than section 721 and the International Emergency Economic Powers Act . . . do not, in [the President's] judgment, provide adequate and appropriate authority for [the President] to protect the national security in this matter." In light of the findings, the Presidential Order directed that the transaction be prohibited. "In order to effectuate" the prohibition, the Presidential Order required Ralls to, *inter alia*, (1) divest itself of all interests in the Project Companies, their assets and their operations within ninety days of the Order, (2) remove all items from the project sites "stockpiled, stored, deposited, installed, or affixed thereon," (3) cease access to the project sites, (4) refrain from selling, transferring or facilitating the sale or transfer of "any items made or otherwise produced by the Sany Group to any third party for use or installation at the [project sites]" and (5) adhere to restrictions on the sale of the Project Companies and their assets to third parties. JA 89–91. The Presidential Order also "revoked" both orders issued by CFIUS.

It is undisputed that neither CFIUS nor the President gave Ralls notice of the evidence on which they respectively relied nor an opportunity to rebut that evidence.

C. District Court Proceedings

Approximately two weeks before the Presidential Order issued, Ralls filed suit against CFIUS and its then-chairman, Treasury Secretary Timothy Geithner, in district court. Ralls sought to invalidate the CFIUS Order and to enjoin its enforcement, claiming that CFIUS exceeded its statutory authority and acted arbitrarily and capriciously in issuing the Order in violation of the Administrative Procedure Act (APA), and that the Order deprived Ralls of its constitutionally protected property interests in violation of the Due Process Clause of the Fifth Amendment to the United States Constitution [. . .]

In dismissing Ralls's [ ] due process claim, [the court] first determined that the Presidential Order did not deprive Ralls of a constitutionally protected property interest. Although the court acknowledged that Ralls had "entered into a transaction in March 2012 through which it obtained certain property rights under state law," it nonetheless found that Ralls had no constitutionally protected interest because Ralls "voluntarily acquired those state property rights subject to the known risk of a Presidential veto" and "waived the opportunity ... to obtain a determination from CFIUS and the President before it entered into the transaction." The court then concluded that, even if Ralls had a constitutionally protected property interest, the Appellees provided Ralls with due process. According to the court, CFIUS informed Ralls in June 2012 that the transaction had to be reviewed and gave Ralls the opportunity to submit evidence in its favor in its notice filing and during follow-up conversations with—and a presentation to—CFIUS officials.

Ralls timely appealed the district court's Rule 12(b)(6) dismissal of its due process challenge to the Presidential Order and the Rule 12(b)(1) dismissal of its five CFIUS Order claims. [. . .]

II. DUE PROCESS CLAIM

[. . .]

2. What Process is Due?

"[U]nlike some legal rules," due process "is not a technical conception with a fixed content unrelated to time, place and circumstances." To the contrary, "due process is flexible and calls for such procedural protections as the particular situation demands." In the seminal case of *Mathews v. Eldridge*, the United States Supreme Court established a three-factor balancing test to determine the

> "specific dictates of due process"

First, the private interest that will be affected by the official action; second, the risk of an erroneous deprivation of such interest through the procedures used, and the probable value, if any, of additional or substitute procedural safeguards; and finally, the Government's interest, including the function involved and the fiscal and administrative burdens that the additional or substitute procedural requirement would entail.

Due process ordinarily requires that procedures provide notice of the proposed official action and "the opportunity to be heard at a meaningful time and in a meaningful manner." Both the Supreme Court and this Court have recognized that the right to know the factual basis for the action and the opportunity to rebut the evidence supporting that action are essential components of due process. [. . .]

We conclude that the Presidential Order deprived Ralls of its constitutionally protected property interests without due process of law. [. . .] [D]ue process requires, at the least, that an affected party be informed of the official action, be given access to the unclassified evidence on which the official actor relied and be afforded an opportunity to rebut that evidence. Although the Presidential Order deprived Ralls of significant property interests—interests, according to the district court record, valued at $6 million—Ralls was not given any of these procedural protections at any point. Under our [Foreign Terrorist Organization][34] precedent, this lack of process constitutes a clear constitutional violation, notwithstanding the Appellees' substantial interest in national security and despite our uncertainty that more process would have led to a different presidential decision. As the FTO cases make plain, a substantial interest in national security supports withholding only the *classified* information but does not excuse the failure to provide notice of, and access to, the unclassified information used to prohibit the transaction. That Ralls had the opportunity to present evidence to CFIUS and to interact with it, then, is plainly not enough to satisfy due process because Ralls never had the opportunity to tailor its submission to the Appellees' concerns or rebut the factual premises underlying the President's action.

[. . .] The Appellees' argument that we should refrain from requiring disclosure of the President's thinking on sensitive questions is off-base. Our conclusion that the procedure followed in issuing the Presidential Order violates due process does not mean the President must, in the future, disclose his thinking on sensitive questions related to national security in reviewing a covered transaction. We hold only that Ralls must receive the procedural protections we have spelled out before the Presidential Order prohibits the transaction. The DPA expressly provides that CFIUS acts on behalf of the President in reviewing covered transactions, and the procedure makes clear that the President acts only after reviewing the record compiled by CFIUS and CFIUS's recommendation. Adequate process at the CFIUS stage, we believe, would also satisfy the President's due process obligation. As for the Appellees' belated assertion of executive privilege, this argument was not raised in the Appellees' brief and we leave it to the district court on remand to consider whether the executive privilege shields the ordered disclosure.

In sum, we conclude that the Presidential Order deprived Ralls of constitutionally protected property interests without due process of law. We remand to the district court with instructions that Ralls be provided the requisite process set forth herein, which should include access to the unclassified evidence on which the President relied and an opportunity to respond thereto. *See NCRI,* 251 F.3d at 209 (leaving FTO designation in place and ordering Secretary of State to provide designated entity with access to unclassified evidence supporting designation and opportunity to respond). Should disputes arise on remand—such as an executive privilege claim—the district court is well-positioned to resolve them. Finally, because the CFIUS Order claims were dismissed on a jurisdictional ground, and given the scant merits briefing, we leave it to

---

[34] The Secretary of State can designate certain organizations as FTO if the Secretary finds that (1) the organization is foreign, (2) the organization engages in "terrorist activity" as that term is defined in AEDPA and (3) the terrorist activity of the organization threatens national security or U.S. nationals.

the district court to address the merits of Ralls's remaining claims in the first instance. *So ordered.*

United States v. AT&T Inc.

310 F.Supp.3d 161 (D.D.C. 2018)

■ RICHARD J. LEON, UNITED STATES DISTRICT JUDGE.

If there ever were an antitrust case where the parties had a dramatically different assessment of the current state of the relevant market and a fundamentally different vision of its future development, this is the one. Small wonder it had to go to trial!

November 20, 2017, the U.S. Department of Justice's Antitrust Division brought this suit, on behalf of the United States of America ("the Government" or "the plaintiff"), to block the merger of AT&T Inc. ("AT&T") and Time Warner Inc. ("Time Warner") as a violation of Section 7 of the Clayton Act, 15 U.S.C. § 18. The Government claims, in essence, that permitting AT&T to acquire Time Warner is likely to substantially lessen competition in the video programming and distribution market nationwide by enabling AT&T to use Time Warner's "must have" television content to either raise its rivals' video programming costs or, by way of a "blackout," drive those same rivals' customers to its subsidiary, DirecTV. Thus, according to the Government, consumers nationwide will be harmed by increased prices for access to Turner networks, notwithstanding the Government's concession that this vertical merger would result in hundreds of millions of dollars in annual cost savings to AT&T's customers and notwithstanding the fact that (unlike in "horizontal" mergers) no competitor will be eliminated by the merger's proposed vertical integration.

Not surprisingly, the defendants, AT&T, Time Warner, and DirecTV, strongly disagree. Their vision couldn't be more different. The video programming and distribution market, they point out, has been, and is, in the middle of a revolution where high-speed internet access has facilitated a "veritable explosion" of new, innovative video content and advertising offerings over the past five years. Vertically integrated entities like Netflix, Hulu, and Amazon have achieved remarkable success in creating and providing affordable, on-demand video content directly to viewers over the internet. Meanwhile, web giants Facebook and Google have developed new ways to use data to create effective—and lucrative—digital advertisements tailored to the individual consumer.

As a result of these "tectonic changes" brought on by the proliferation of high-speed internet access, video programmers such as Time Warner and video distributors such as AT&T find themselves facing two stark realities: declining video subscriptions and flatlining television advertising revenues. Indeed, cost-conscious consumers increasingly choose to "cut" or "shave" the cord, abandoning their traditional cable- or satellite- TV packages for cheaper content alternatives available over the internet. At the same time, Facebook's and Google's dominant digital advertising platforms have surpassed television advertising in revenue. Watching vertically integrated, data-informed entities thrive as television subscriptions and advertising revenues declined, AT&T and Time Warner concluded that each had a problem that the other could solve: Time Warner could provide AT&T with the ability to experiment with and develop innovative video content and advertising offerings for AT&T's many video and wireless customers, and AT&T could afford Time Warner access to customer relationships and valuable data about its programming. Together, AT&T and Time Warner concluded that both companies could stop "chasing taillights" and catch up with the competition. Those were the circumstances that drove AT&T, a distributor of content, and Time Warner, a content creator and programmer, to announce their historic $108 billion merger in October 2016 (the "proposed merger" or "challenged merger"). Those are the circumstances that cause them to claim today that their merger will increase not only innovation, but competition in this marketplace for years to come.

Section 7 of the Clayton Act assigns this Court the "uncertain task" of weighing the parties' competing visions of the future of the relevant market and the challenged merger's place within it. Nothing less than a comprehensive inquiry into future competitive conditions in that market is expected. And the Government has the burden of proof to demonstrate that the merger is likely to lessen competition substantially in that uncertain future.

Since announcing the transaction in late October 2016, defendants have delayed closing on the merger agreement for about 18 months as a result of the Government's investigation and suit. The deal is now set to expire if not consummated on or before June 21, 2018—a turn of events that would require AT&T to pay Time Warner a "break-up fee" of $500 million [. . .]

The following is the Court's Opinion. [. . .] Ultimately, I conclude that the Government has failed to meet its burden to establish that the proposed "transaction is likely to lessen competition substantially."

I.   Background

AT&T is a "leading provider of communications and digital entertainment services in the United States and the world." AT&T has two traditional MVPD [multi-channel video programming distributors] products: DirecTV and U-verse. Despite that substantial traditional MVPD subscriber base, AT&T witnesses testified that they believe the company's future lies in the use of online and mobile wireless connections to access premium video. As John Stankey, the AT&T executive who will be tasked with running Time Warner should the merger proceed, explained, AT&T acquired DirecTV in 2015 not in an effort to double down on the satellite business—a concededly mature and indeed declining asset—but to "pick up a lot of new customers that we could work on migrating" to new, innovative products necessary to compete in the future.

Time Warner, by contrast, is in the entertainment business. It has three distinct units: Warner Bros., Turner, and HBO. Turner operates, among other things, ten linear cable networks that televise scheduled video programming around the clock. HBO is a premium, subscription-based video service that offers movie and television shows, including a significant amount of original content. Unlike Turner, which collects both programming fees and advertising revenue, HBO relies solely on subscription payments to operate. Warner Bros. operates a studio that creates movies, television programs, and other kinds of video content that are licensed both to Time Warner's other businesses and to third parties.

On October 22, 2016, AT&T announced its plan to acquire Time Warner. Inclusive of debt, the transaction is valued at approximately $108 billion.

At trial, the evidence showed that defendants view the proposed merger as an essential response to the [changing] industry dynamics . . . —that is, the increasing importance of web- and mobile-based content offerings; the explosion in targeted, digital advertising; and the limitations attendant with AT&T's and Time Warner's respective business models. The proposed merger would do so, defendants' executives asserted, through vertical integration of the companies' complementary assets: Time Warner's popular content and significant advertising inventory, and AT&T's consumer relationships, customer data, and large wireless business.

The Government seeks to enjoin the proposed merger on the basis that it violates Section 7 of the Clayton Act, 15 U.S.C. § 18. As relevant here, Section 7 "prohibits acquisitions, including mergers, 'where in any line of commerce or in any activity affecting commerce in any section of the country, the effect of such acquisition may be substantially to lessen competition.'" The Government "has the ultimate burden of proving a Section 7 violation by a preponderance of the evidence."

By using "the words 'may be substantially to lessen competition'" in Section 7, Congress indicated "that its concern was with probabilities, not certainties." Although certainty of harm is not necessary to prove a Section 7 violation, neither is the "mere possibility" of harm sufficient. Rather, to grant injunctive relief under the Clayton Act, the Court *must* conclude that the Government has introduced evidence sufficient to show that the challenged "transaction is likely to lessen competition substantially."

In assessing the Government's Section 7 case, the court must engage in a "'comprehensive inquiry' into the 'future competitive conditions in a given market,'" keeping in mind that "the Clayton Act protects 'competition,' rather than any particular competitor." "[O]nly . . . examination of the particular market—its structure, history and probable future—can provide the appropriate setting for judging the probable anticompetitive effect of the merger."

II.   Analysis

In the typical horizontal merger case under Section 7, the Government's path to carrying its prima facie burden is clear: by putting forward statistics to show that the proposed "merger would produce a firm controlling an undue percentage share of the relevant market, and would result in a significant increase in the concentration of firms in that market," the Government triggers a " 'presumption' that the merger will substantially lessen competition." In this case, however, the "familiar" horizontal merger playbook is of little use. That is, of course, because the proposed transaction between AT&T and Time Warner is a vertical merger—*i.e.*, one that involves "firms that do not operate in the same market" and thus "produce[s] no immediate change in the level of concentration in any relevant market." The parties therefore agree that in this case "there is no short-cut way to establish anticompetitive effects, as there is with horizontal mergers." Further complicating the Government's challenge is the recognition among academics, courts, and antitrust enforcement authorities alike that "many vertical mergers create vertical integration efficiencies between purchasers and sellers."

As the Government also notes, the "principal objective of antitrust policy is to maximize consumer welfare by encouraging firms to behave competitively." As such, any proper assessment of a proposed merger, [government expert] Professor Shapiro testified, must consider both the positive and negative "impact[s] on consumers" by "balancing" the proconsumer, "positive elements" of the merger against the asserted anticompetitive harms.

The challenged vertical merger here would unite Time Warner, a creator and supplier of popular video content, with AT&T, a large downstream purchaser and distributor of video content. The Government concedes that the challenged merger, like most vertical mergers, will result in significant benefits to customers of the merged company. Specifically, the Government's lead expert, Professor Carl Shapiro, estimates that the merger will cause AT&T to lower the price of DirecTV, resulting in $352 million in annual savings for DirecTV's customers.

Notwithstanding those conceded consumer benefits, the Government contends that the challenged merger is "likely to lessen competition substantially." The challenged merger would likely result in a substantial lessening of competition, according to the Government, in three "mutually reinforcing" ways.

First and foremost, the Government argues that the challenged merger would enable Turner to charge AT&T's rival distributors—and ultimately consumers—higher prices for its content on account of its post-merger relationship with AT&T. *Second*, the Government contends that the challenged merger will substantially lessen competition by creating an increased risk that the merged firm will act, either unilaterally or in coordination with Comcast-NBCU, to thwart the rise of the lower-cost, consumer-friendly virtual MVPDs that are threatening the traditional pay-TV model. *Finally*, the Government alleges that the merged entity could harm competition by preventing AT&T's rival distributors from using HBO as a promotional tool to attract and retain customers.

In the remainder of this section, I will analyze each of those theories of harm to competition. Initially, I will set forth the relevant market definition, which incorporates the Government's proposed product and geographic markets. Next, I will discuss the conceded consumer benefits associated with the proposed merger. Mindful of those conceded benefits, and the need to balance them against the Government's allegations of consumer harm, I will then evaluate whether the Government has carried its burden to show a likelihood that the challenged merger will result in a substantial lessening of competition. For the reasons discussed in detail below, I have concluded that the answer to that question is no!

A. Market Definition

Typically, "[m]erger analysis starts with defining the relevant market" in which to assess the alleged anticompetitive harms. The relevant market comprises two parts: a product market and a geographic market. Here, the Government defines the primary relevant product market as the "Multichannel Video Distribution" market, and the relevant geographic markets as the approximately 1,200 local markets in which residents have access to video offerings from the same set of multichannel video programming distributors.

Horizontal merger cases often "to a great extent. . . hinge[ ] on" market definition because such definition affects the ultimate market concentration statistics associated with a proposed transaction. For that reason, market definition is often heavily contested in horizontal merger cases, turning on fine-grained economic analyses of "SSNIPs" and cross-elasticity of demand. Happily, I need not delve deeply into those concepts here.

B. Conceded Consumer Benefits of Proposed Merger

Vertical mergers often generate efficiencies and other procompetitive effects. The proposed merger is no exception. Indeed, the Government concedes that this case implicates one "standard benefit" associated with vertical mergers: the elimination of double marginalization ("EDM"). As relevant here (and at the risk of oversimplifying things), double marginalization refers to the situation in which two different firms in the same industry, but at different levels in the supply chain, each apply their own markups (reflecting their own margins) in pricing their products. Those "stacked" margins are both incorporated into the final price that consumers have to pay for the end product. By vertically integrating two such firms into one, the merged company is able to "shrink that total margin so there's one instead of two," leading to lower prices for consumers. EDM is, therefore, procompetitive.

[EDS. The court goes on to parse each of the government's arguments for enjoining the merger in technical detail, and shoots down each argument. I have omitted these ~165 pages of technical analysis for your sanity.]

III.   Conclusion

The parties have waged an epic battle, under extremely restricted deadlines, to litigate and try this historic vertical merger case. [. . .] The Court has now spoken and the defendants have won. But, the process is not quite over yet!

There is a grave and understandable fear on the part of the defendants that the Government will now seek to do *indirectly* what it couldn't accomplish directly by seeking a stay of this Court's order pending an appeal to our Circuit Court.

The consequences of receiving such a stay would cause irreparable harm to the defendants in general and AT&T in specific. First, it would effectively prevent the consummation of the merger by the June 21, 2018 break-up date for the deal. Second, it would cause AT&T to have to pay the $500 million break-up fee it will owe to Time Warner if the deal is not consummated by that date. Those two consequences, of course, would occur regardless of whether this Court's decision were later upheld following appellate review. In this Court's judgment, a stay pending appeal would be a manifestly unjust outcome in this case.

The Government has had this merger on hold now since October of 2016 when it launched its investigation. In that 18-plus month period, the companies have twice extended the break-up date to accommodate the Government's litigation of this case. During that same period, the video programming and distribution industry has continued to evolve at a breakneck pace. The cost to the defendants and the Government to investigate, litigate, and try this case has undoubtedly been staggering— easily in the tens of millions of dollars.

If the Government were to ask me to stay this Court's ruling, I would, under the law, have to weigh whether the Government has a strong likelihood of success on the merits and would suffer irreparable harm should the stay be denied, among other things. Well, suffice it to say—as my 170-plus page opinion makes clear—I do not believe that the Government has a likelihood of success on the merits of an appeal. And in my judgment, given that our Circuit Court has never hesitated to unwind an unblocked merger if the law and facts warrant doing so, there would be no irreparable harm to the Government—only to the defendants—if my ruling were stayed. As such, I could not, and would not, grant such a stay in the first instance.

That of course is not to suggest in any way that the Government should not consider seeking appellate review of the merits of this Court's decision. That is, by any standard, fair game. But the temptation by some to view this decision as being something more than a resolution of this specific case should be resisted by one and all!

The Government here has taken its best shot to block the merger based on the law and facts, and within the time allowed. The defendants did their best to oppose it. The Court has spoken. To use a stay to accomplish *indirectly* what could not be done directly—especially when it would cause certain irreparable harm to the defendants—simply would be unjust. I hope and trust that the Government will have the good judgment, wisdom, and courage to avoid such a manifest injustice. To do otherwise, I fear, would undermine the faith in our system of justice of not only the defendants, but their millions of shareholders and the business community at large.

* * *

Thus, for all of the foregoing reasons, the Government's request to enjoin the proposed merger is **DENIED.**

H. REVIEW PROBLEMS

1. Martial Arts Tea, a bubble tea giant, has decided that it wishes to purchase boutique bubble tea company Slowly Cup. Both are public companies. Martial Arts wishes to merge with Slowly, but both wish to avoid the costly process of obtaining a vote from Slowly's stockholders. How might the parties design such a transaction? Consider DGCL § 251(h). If the original Soda Pop shareholders sue, should the court give them appraisal rights?[35]

2. ACo, Inc. is a company that produces steel drums. ACo, Inc. has several subsidiaries, including one in Quebec, Canada called CanadaCo. Over the course of six months, ACo's board of directors sold off several of its unprofitable subsidiaries. ACo's CEO then began negotiating the sale of CanadaCo, its Canadian subsidiary, to raise funds and improve ACo's balance sheets. CanadaCo had been the only ACo subsidiary producing income in the past four years, and it accounted for between approximately 35 percent (in the first of four years) and 52 percent (in the most recent year) of ACo's pre-tax income. Moreover, CanadaCo represented 51 percent of ACo's total assets and 45 percent of its net revenue. After ACo entered into an agreement to sell CanadaCo to BCo, Inc., one of ACo's shareholders, Mr. Dogz, filed a lawsuit in the Delaware Court to block the sale. Mr. Dogz argued that the sale of CanadaCo constituted a sale of "all or substantially all" of ACo's assets. Is Mr. Dogz correct that this sale constituted a sale of "all or substantially all" of ACo's assets, which would require a majority vote of the shareholders under § 271?[36]

3. JournalismGalore, Inc. owned several groups of newspaper publishers and other journalistic ventures, both in the United States and in the

---

[35] *See* City of N. Miami Beach Gen. Employees' Ret. Plan v. Dr Pepper Snapple Grp., Inc., 189 A.3d 188 (Del. Ch. 2018).

[36] *See* Katz v. Bregman, 431 A.2d 1274 (Del. Ch. 1981).

United Kingdom. USGroupCo. and UKGroupCo., together, are very valuable to JournalismGalore. Individually, each group was similarly important to JournalismGalore in terms of financials and prestige, although UKGroupCo. may have been slightly more valuable than USGroupCo. UKGroupCo. accounted for 49% of revenues, 36% book value of assets, and produced 57% of EBITDA, and it owned JournalismGalore's most prestigious asset, a very popular newspaper within the UK. Nevertheless, JournalismGalore agreed to sell UKGroupCo. to a third party. The controlling shareholder of JournalismGalore, Inc. objected to the sale on the grounds that it amounted to a sale of "all or substantially all" of JournalismGalore's assets and thus required shareholder approval. Will the objecting shareholder be successful in its argument?[37]

---

37   *See* Hollinger Inc. v. Hollinger Int'l, Inc., 858 A.2d 342 (Del. Ch. 2004).

CHAPTER VII

CLOSELY HELD CORPORATIONS

A. CLOSELY HELD CORPORATIONS DEFINED

Delaware General Corporation Law
Section 342. Close corporation defined; contents of certificate of incorporation.

(a) A close corporation is a corporation organized under this chapter whose certificate of incorporation contains the provisions required by § 102 of this title and, in addition, provides that:

(1) All of the corporation's issued stock of all classes, exclusive of treasury shares, shall be represented by certificates and shall be held of record by not more than a specified number of persons, not exceeding 30; and

(2) All of the issued stock of all classes shall be subject to 1 or more of the restrictions on transfer permitted by § 202 of this title; and

(3) The corporation shall make no offering of any of its stock of any class which would constitute a "public offering" within the meaning of the United States Securities Act of 1933 [15 U.S.C. § 77a et seq.] as it may be amended from time to time.

(b) The certificate of incorporation of a close corporation may set forth the qualifications of stockholders, either by specifying classes of persons who shall be entitled to be holders of record of stock of any class, or by specifying classes of persons who shall not be entitled to be holders of stock of any class or both.

(c) For purposes of determining the number of holders of record of the stock of a close corporation, stock which is held in joint or common tenancy or by the entireties shall be treated as held by 1 stockholder.

Section 343. Formation of a close corporation.

A close corporation shall be formed in accordance with §§ 101, 102 and 103 of this title, except that:

(1) Its certificate of incorporation shall contain a heading stating the name of the corporation and that it is a close corporation; and

(2) Its certificate of incorporation shall contain the provisions required by § 342 of this title.

Section 344. Election of existing corporation to become a close corporation.

Any corporation organized under this chapter may become a close corporation under this subchapter by executing, acknowledging and filing, in accordance with § 103 of this title, a certificate of amendment of its certificate of incorporation which shall contain a statement that it elects to become a close corporation, the provisions required by § 342 of this title to appear in the certificate of incorporation of a close corporation, and a heading stating the name of the corporation and that it is a close corporation. Such amendment shall be adopted in accordance with the requirements of § 241 or 242 of this title, except that it must be approved by a vote of the holders of record of at least ⅔ of the shares of each class of stock of the corporation which are outstanding.

Section 350. Agreements restricting discretion of directors.

A written agreement among the stockholders of a close corporation holding a majority of the outstanding stock entitled to vote, whether solely among themselves or with a party not a stockholder, is not invalid, as between the parties to the agreement, on the ground that it so relates to the conduct of the business and affairs of the corporation as to restrict or interfere with the discretion or powers of the board of directors. The effect of any such agreement shall be to relieve the directors and impose upon the stockholders who are parties to the agreement the liability for managerial acts or omissions which is imposed on directors to the extent and so long as the discretion or powers of the board in its management of corporate affairs is controlled by such agreement.

Section 351. Management by stockholders.

The certificate of incorporation of a close corporation may provide that the business of the corporation shall be managed by the stockholders of the corporation rather than by a board of directors. So long as this provision continues in effect:

(1) No meeting of stockholders need be called to elect directors;

(2) Unless the context clearly requires otherwise, the stockholders of the corporation shall be deemed to be directors for purposes of applying provisions of this chapter; and

(3) The stockholders of the corporation shall be subject to all liabilities of directors.

Such a provision may be inserted in the certificate of incorporation by amendment if all incorporators and subscribers or all holders of record of all of the outstanding stock, whether or not having voting power, authorize such a provision. An amendment to the certificate of incorporation to delete such a provision shall be adopted by a vote of the holders of a majority of all outstanding stock of the corporation, whether or not otherwise entitled to vote. If the certificate of incorporation contains a provision authorized by this section, the existence of such provision shall be noted conspicuously on the face or back of every stock certificate issued by such corporation.

Section 352. Appointment of custodian for close corporation.

(a) In addition to § 226 of this title respecting the appointment of a custodian for any corporation, the Court of Chancery, upon application of any stockholder, may appoint 1 or more persons to be custodians, and, if the corporation is insolvent, to be receivers, of any close corporation when:

(1) Pursuant to § 351 of this title the business and affairs of the corporation are managed by the stockholders and they are so divided that the business of the corporation is suffering or is threatened with irreparable injury and any remedy with respect to such deadlock provided in the certificate of incorporation or bylaws or in any written agreement of the stockholders has failed; or

(2) The petitioning stockholder has the right to the dissolution of the corporation under a provision of the certificate of incorporation permitted by § 355 of this title.

(b) In lieu of appointing a custodian for a close corporation under this section or § 226 of this title the Court of Chancery may appoint a provisional director, whose powers and status shall be as provided in § 353 of this title if the Court determines that it would be in the best interest of the corporation. Such appointment shall not preclude any subsequent order of the Court appointing a custodian for such corporation.

Section 353. Appointment of a provisional director in certain cases.

(a) Notwithstanding any contrary provision of the certificate of incorporation or the bylaws or agreement of the stockholders, the Court of Chancery may appoint a provisional director for a close corporation if the directors are so divided respecting the management of the corporation's business and affairs that the votes required for action by the board of directors cannot be obtained with the consequence that the business and affairs of the corporation can no longer be conducted to the advantage of the stockholders generally. [. . .]

B. FIDUCIARY DUTIES

Nixon v. Blackwell

626 A.2d 1366 (Del. 1993)

■ VEASEY, CHIEF JUSTICE:

In this action we review a decision of the Court of Chancery holding that the defendant directors of a closely-held corporation breached their fiduciary duties to the plaintiffs by maintaining a discriminatory policy that unfairly favors employee stockholders over plaintiffs. The Vice Chancellor found that the directors treated the plaintiffs unfairly by establishing an employee stock ownership plan ("ESOP") and by purchasing key man life insurance policies to provide liquidity for defendants and other corporate employees to enable them to sell their stock while providing no comparable liquidity for minority stockholders. We conclude that the Court of Chancery applied erroneous legal standards and made findings of fact which were not the product of an orderly and logical deductive reasoning process. Accordingly, we REVERSE and REMAND to the Court of Chancery for proceedings not inconsistent with this opinion.

I. FACTS

[. . .]

A. The Parties

Plaintiffs are 14 minority stockholders of Class B, non-voting, stock of E.C. Barton & Co. (the "Corporation"). The individual defendants are the members of the board of directors (the "Board" or the "directors"). The Corporation is also a defendant. Plaintiffs collectively own only Class B stock, and own no Class A stock. Their total holdings comprise approximately 25 percent of all the common stock outstanding as of the end of fiscal year 1989.

At all relevant times, the Board consisted of ten individuals who either are currently employed, or were once employed, by the Corporation. At the time this suit was filed, these directors collectively owned approximately 47.5 percent of all the outstanding Class A shares. The remaining Class A shares were held by certain other present and former employees of the Corporation.

B. Mr. Barton's Testamentary Plan

The Corporation is a non-public, closely-held Delaware corporation headquartered in Arkansas. It is engaged in the business of selling wholesale and retail lumber in the Mississippi Delta. The Corporation was formed in 1928 by E.C. Barton ("Mr. Barton") and has two classes of common stock: Class A voting stock and Class B non-voting stock. [. . .]

[EDS.—After the death of Mr. Barton, 49 percent of the Class A voting stock was bequeathed outright to eight of his loyal employees. The remaining 51 percent, along with 14 percent of the Class B non-voting stock, was placed into an independently managed 15-year trust for the same eight people. Mrs. Barton, Mr. Barton's second wife, received outright 61 percent of Class B non-voting stock. The non-voting Class B shares Mr. Barton bequeathed to his family represented 75 percent of the Corporation's total equity. In the 1970s, the Corporation bought back from Mrs. Barton and from the trust 45 percent of the non-voting Class B shares at a price of $45 per share, leaving Mrs. Barton's three children collectively with 30 percent of the outstanding Class B non-voting stock. The children have no voting rights despite their substantial equity interest in the Corporation. The children are also the only non-employee Class B stockholders.]

There is no public market for, or trading in, either class of the Corporation's stock. This creates problems for stockholders, particularly the Class B minority stockholders, who wish to sell or otherwise realize the value of their shares. The corporation purported to address this problem in several ways over the years.

C.   The Self-Tenders

The Corporation occasionally offered to purchase the Class B stock of the non-employee stockholders through a series of self-tender offers. [. . .]

D.   The Employee Stock Ownership Plan ("ESOP")

In November 1975 the Corporation established an ESOP designed to hold Class B non-voting stock for the benefit of eligible employees of the Corporation. The ESOP is a tax-qualified profit-sharing plan whereby employees of the Corporation are allocated a share of the assets held by the plan in proportion to their annual compensation, subject to certain vesting requirements. The ESOP is funded by annual cash contributions from the Corporation. Under the plan, terminating and retiring employees are entitled to receive their interest in the ESOP by taking Class B stock or cash in lieu of stock. It appears from the record that most terminating employees and retirees elect to receive cash in lieu of stock. The Corporation commissions an annual appraisal of the Corporation to determine the value of its stock for ESOP purposes. Thus, the ESOP provides employee Class B stockholders with a substantial measure of liquidity not available to non-employee stockholders. The Corporation had the option of repurchasing Class A stock from the employees upon their retirement or death. [. . .]

E.   The Key Man Insurance Policies

The Corporation also purchased certain key man life insurance policies with death benefits payable to the Corporation. [. . .] In 1982 the Corporation purchased additional key man policies in connection with agreements entered into between the Corporation and nine key officers and directors. Each executive executed an agreement giving the Corporation a call option to substitute Class B non-voting stock for their Class A voting stock upon the occurrence of certain events, including death and termination of employment, so that the voting shares could be reissued to new key personnel. In return, the Board adopted a resolution creating a non-binding recommendation that a portion of the key man life insurance proceeds be used to repurchase the exchanged Class B stock from the executives' estates at a price at least equal to 80 percent of their ESOP value. [. . .]

Despite the strong recommendation, the ultimate decision on the use of insurance proceeds for this purpose was left to the discretion of the Corporation's management or the Board. [. . .]

The record and the findings of the trial court are not precisely clear on the issue of corporate benefit compared with individual benefit to the defendants with respect to the proceeds of the key man insurance policies. [. . .] The analysis of this issue would seem to call for a disciplined balancing test by a court reviewing the matter for entire fairness. [. . .]

F. Dividend Policy and Compensation

The Board from time to time paid modest dividends. Because the earnings were solid in many years and dividends relatively low, the retained earnings of the Corporation continued to increase at a relatively high level. Plaintiffs challenged these corporate decisions as unfair to the minority. [. . .]

II. PROCEEDINGS IN THE COURT OF CHANCERY

[. . .] At trial, the plaintiffs charged the defendants with (1) attempting to force the minority stockholders to sell their shares at a discount by embarking on a scheme to pay negligible dividends, (2) breaching their fiduciary duties by authorizing excessive compensation for themselves and other employees of the Corporation, and (3) breaching their fiduciary duties by pursuing a discriminatory liquidity policy that favors employee stockholders over non-employee stockholders through the ESOP and key man life insurance policies. [. . .]

The Vice Chancellor held that the Corporation's low-dividend policy was within the bounds of business judgment, that the executive compensation levels were not excessive, and ruled in favor of defendants on these issues. The Vice Chancellor further held, however, that the defendant directors had breached their fiduciary duties to the minority. The basis for this ruling was that it was "inherently unfair" for the defendants to establish the ESOP and to purchase key man life insurance to provide liquidity for themselves while providing no comparable method by which the non-employee Class B stockholders may liquidate their stock at fair value. Holding that the "needs of all stockholders must be considered and addressed when providing liquidity," the court ruled that the directors breached their fiduciary duties, and granted relief to plaintiffs. [. . .] The trial court ruled

[. . .] 4. On the claim of the plaintiffs presented at trial that the individual defendants breached their fiduciary duty as directors and treated the plaintiffs unfairly as the non-employee, minority Class B stockholders of the Company by providing no method by which plaintiffs might liquidate their stock at fair value while providing a means through the ESOP and key-man life insurance whereby the stock of terminating employees could be purchased from them, judgment is entered in favor of the plaintiffs.

5.   Pursuant to the judgment entered in paragraph 4 above, defendants shall take the following steps in order to remedy the unfair treatment of Class B stockholders:

> a.   An amount equal to the total of all key man life insurance premiums paid to date, together with interest from the date of payment shall be used to repurchase Class B stock other than shares held by the ESOP or defendants, at a price to be set by an independent appraiser.

> b.   Hereafter, neither the ESOP nor the company shall purchase or repurchase any stock without offering to purchase the same number of shares, on the same terms and conditions, from the Class B stockholders other than defendants and the ESOP. [. . .]

III. RATIONALE OF THE VICE CHANCELLOR'S DECISION

[. . .] The only issue before this Court is the ruling by the trial court as implemented in its judgment and final order that the defendants breached their fiduciary duties by failing to provide a parity of liquidity. The theory of the trial court on this issue is based upon the fact that, as directors, defendants approved the ESOP and the key man life insurance program, both of which had the effect of benefiting them as employees, with no corresponding benefit to plaintiffs. Thus, the trial court reasoned, defendants are on both sides of the transaction and the business judgment rule does not apply. Therefore, defendants have the burden of showing the entire fairness of their actions on these issues, which burden the Vice Chancellor held they had not carried.

> The following portions of the opinion of the trial court are crucial to the determination of the issues on appeal: [. . .] All Barton stockholders face the same liquidity problem. If they are to sell their shares, they must persuade defendants to authorize a repurchase by the company. The stockholders have no bargaining power and must accept whatever terms are dictated by defendants or retain their stock. If the stockholder is pressed for cash to pay estate taxes, for example, as has happened more than once, the stockholder is entirely at defendants' mercy. Defendants recognized their employee stockholders' liquidity needs when they established the ESOP. As noted previously, employees have the option of taking cash in lieu of the shares allocated to their accounts. Moreover, the disparity in

bargaining position is eliminated for employee stockholders because the cash payment is determined on the basis of an annual valuation made by an independent party. *No similar plan or arrangement has been put into place with respect to the Class B stockholders. There is no point in time at which they can be assured of receiving cash for all or any portion of their holdings at a price determined by an independent appraiser.*

Defendants have gone one step farther in addressing their own liquidity problems. [. . .] *In order to solve defendants' own liquidity problem, the company has been purchasing key man life insurance since at least 1982. The proceeds will help assure that Barton is in a position to purchase all of defendants' stock at the time of death.* In 1989, the premium cost for the key man insurance was slightly higher than the total amount paid in dividends for the year.

While the purchase of key man life insurance may be a relatively small corporate expenditure, it is concrete evidence that defendants have favored their own interests as stockholders over plaintiffs. It also makes one wonder whether the decisions to accumulate large amounts of cash and pay low dividends were not also at least partially motivated by self-interest. The law is settled that fiduciaries may not benefit themselves at the expense of the corporation, *Guth v. Loft, Inc*, and that, when directors make self-interested decisions, they must establish the entire fairness of those decisions. *Weinberger v. UOP, Inc.*

I find it inherently unfair for defendants to be purchasing key man life insurance in order to provide liquidity for themselves while providing no method by which plaintiffs may liquidate their stock at fair value. By this ruling, I am not suggesting that there is some generalized duty to purchase illiquid stock at any particular price. However, the needs of all stockholders must be considered and addressed when decisions are made to provide some form of liquidity. Both the ESOP and the key man insurance provide some measure of liquidity, but only for a select group of stockholders. Accordingly, I find that relief is warranted. Blackwell v. Nixon. [. . .]

V. APPLICABLE PRINCIPLES OF SUBSTANTIVE LAW

[. . .] [W]e agree with the trial court that the entire fairness test applies to this aspect of the case. Accordingly, defendants have the burden of showing the entire fairness of those transactions. *Sinclair Oil Corp. v. Levien; Weinberger v. UOP, Inc.*

When directors of a Delaware corporation are on both sides of a transaction, they are required to demonstrate their utmost good faith and the most scrupulous inherent fairness of the bargain. . . . The requirement of fairness is unflinching in its demand that where one stands on both sides of a transaction, he has the burden of establishing its entire fairness, sufficient to pass the test of careful scrutiny by the courts. *Weinberger.*

Weinberger explains further the two aspects of entire fairness, fair price and fair dealing:

> The concept of fairness has two basic aspects: fair dealing and fair price. The former embraces questions of when the transaction was timed, how it was initiated, structured, negotiated, disclosed to the directors, and how the approvals of the directors and the stockholders were obtained. The latter aspect of fairness relates to the economic and financial considerations of the proposed merger, including all relevant factors: assets, market value, earnings, future prospects, and any other elements that affect the intrinsic or inherent value of a company's stock. . . . All aspects of the issue must be examined as a whole since the question is one of entire fairness. *Weinberger.*

[. . .] It is often of critical importance whether a particular decision is one to which the business judgment rule applies or the entire fairness rule applies. [. . .]

> [B]ecause the effect of the proper invocation of the business judgment rule is so powerful and the standard of entire fairness so exacting, the determination of the appropriate standard of judicial review frequently is determinative of the outcome of derivative litigation. *Mills Acquisition Co. v. MacMillan, Inc.*

[. . .] Application of the entire fairness rule does not, however, always implicate liability of the conflicted corporate decisionmaker, nor does it necessarily render the decision void.

The entire fairness analysis essentially requires "judicial scrutiny." *Weinberger.* In business judgment rule cases, an essential element is the fact that there has been a business decision made by a disinterested and independent corporate decisionmaker. *Aronson v. Lewis*; *Smith v. Van Gorkom.* When there is no independent corporate decisionmaker, the court may become the objective arbiter. [. . .]

The trial court in this case, however, appears to have adopted the novel legal principle that Class B stockholders had a right to "liquidity" equal to that which the court found to be available to the defendants. It is well established in our jurisprudence that stockholders need not always be treated equally for all purposes. *Unocal Corp. v. Mesa Petroleum Co.* (discriminatory exchange offer held valid); and *Cheff v. Mathes* (selective stock repurchase held valid).

[. . .] This holding of the trial court overlooks the significant facts that the minority stockholders were not: (a) employees of the Corporation; (b) entitled to share in an ESOP; (c) qualified for key man insurance; or (d) protected by specific provisions in the certificate of incorporation, by-laws, or a stockholders' agreement.

There is support in this record for the fact that the ESOP is a corporate benefit and was established, at least in part, to benefit the Corporation. Generally speaking, the creation of ESOPs is a normal corporate practice and is generally thought to benefit the corporation. The same is true generally with respect to key man insurance programs. If such corporate practices were necessarily to require equal treatment for non-employee stockholders, that would be a matter for legislative determination in Delaware. There is no such legislation to that effect. If we were to adopt such a rule, our decision would border on judicial legislation. *See Providence & Worcester Co. v. Baker.*

Accordingly, we hold that the Vice Chancellor erred as a matter of law in concluding that the liquidity afforded to the employee stockholders by the ESOP and the key man insurance required substantially equal treatment for the non-employee stockholders. Moreover, the Vice Chancellor failed to evaluate and articulate, for example, whether or not and to what extent (a) corporate benefits flowed from the ESOP and the key man insurance; (b) the ESOP and key man insurance plans are novel, extraordinary, or relatively routine business practices; (c) the dividend policy was even relevant; (d) Mr. Barton's plan for employee management and benefits should be honored; and (e) the self-tenders showed defendants' willingness to provide an exit opportunity for the plaintiffs.

In a case where the court is scrutinizing the fairness of a self-interested corporate transaction the court should articulate the standards which it is applying in its scrutiny of the transactions. These standards are not carved in stone for all cases because a court of equity must necessarily have the flexibility to deal with varying circumstances and issues. Yet, the standards must be reasonable, articulable, and articulated. [. . .] The court's decision should not be the product solely of subjective, reflexive impressions based primarily on suspicion or what has sometimes been called the "smell test."

We hold on this record that defendants have met their burden of establishing the entire fairness of their dealings with the non-employee Class B stockholders, and are entitled to judgment. The record is sufficient to conclude that plaintiffs' claim that the defendant directors have maintained a discriminatory policy of favoring Class A employee stockholders over Class B non-employee stockholders is without merit. The directors have followed a consistent policy originally established by Mr. Barton, the founder of the Corporation, whose intent from the formation of the Corporation was to use the Class A stock as the vehicle for the Corporation's continuity through employee management and ownership.

Mr. Barton established the Corporation in 1928 by creating two classes of stock, not one, and by holding 100 percent of the Class A stock and 82 percent of the Class B stock. Mr. Barton himself established the practice of purchasing key man life insurance with funds of the Corporation to retain in the employ of the Corporation valuable employees by assuring them that, following their retirement or death, the Corporation will have liquid assets which could be used to repurchase the shares acquired by the employee, which shares may otherwise constitute an illiquid and unsalable asset of his or her estate. Another rational purpose is to prevent the stock from passing out of the control of the employees of the Corporation into the hands of family or descendants of the employee.

The directors' actions following Mr. Barton's death are consistent with Mr. Barton's plan. An ESOP, for example, is normally established for employees. Accordingly, there is no inequity in limiting ESOP benefits to the employee stockholders. Indeed, it makes no sense to include non-employees in ESOP benefits. The fact that the Class B stock represented 75 percent of the Corporation's total equity is irrelevant to the issue of fair dealing. The Class B stock was given no voting rights because those stockholders were not intended to have a direct voice in the management and operation of the Corporation. They were simply passive investors— entitled to be treated fairly but not necessarily to be treated equally. The fortunes of the Corporation rested with the Class A employee stockholders and the Class B stockholders benefited from the multiple increases in value of their Class B stock. Moreover, the Board made continuing efforts to buy back the Class B stock.

We hold that paragraphs 4 and 5 of the March 10, 1992 order of the trial court and the order of May 20, 1992, awarding fees and costs to plaintiffs, are reversed and remanded with instructions to conform the judgment to the findings and conclusions in this opinion.

VI. NO SPECIAL RULES FOR A "CLOSELY-HELD CORPORATION" NOT QUALIFIED AS A "CLOSE CORPORATION" UNDER SUBCHAPTER XIV OF THE DELAWARE GENERAL CORPORATION LAW.

We wish to address one further matter which was raised at oral argument before this Court: Whether there should be any special, judicially-created rules to "protect" minority stockholders of closely-held Delaware corporations.

The case at bar points up the basic dilemma of minority stockholders in receiving fair value for their stock as to which there is no market and no market valuation. It is not difficult to be sympathetic, in the abstract, to a stockholder who finds himself or herself in that position. A stockholder who bargains for stock in a closely-held corporation and who pays for those shares (unlike the plaintiffs in this case who acquired their stock through gift) can make a business judgment whether to buy into such a minority position, and if so on what terms. One could bargain for definitive provisions of self-ordering permitted to a Delaware corporation through the certificate of incorporation or by-laws by reason of the provisions in 8 *Del.C.* §§ 102, 109, and 141(a). Moreover, in addition to such mechanisms, a stockholder intending to buy into a minority position in a Delaware corporation may enter into definitive stockholder agreements, and such agreements may provide for elaborate earnings tests, buy-out provisions, voting trusts, or other voting agreements. *See, e.g.,* 8 *Del.C.* § 218[.] [. . .]

The tools of good corporate practice are designed to give a purchasing minority stockholder the opportunity to bargain for protection before parting with consideration. It would do violence to normal corporate practice and our corporation law to fashion an ad hoc ruling which would result in a court-imposed stockholder buy-out for which the parties had not contracted.

In 1967, when the Delaware General Corporation Law was significantly revised, a new Subchapter XIV entitled "Close Corporations; Special Provisions," became a part of that law for the first time. [. . .] Subchapter XIV is a narrowly constructed statute which applies only to a corporation which is designated as a "close corporation" in its certificate of incorporation, and which fulfills other requirements, including a limitation to 30 on the number of stockholders, that all classes of stock have to have at least one restriction on transfer, and that there be no "public offering." 8 *Del.C.* § 342. Accordingly, subchapter XIV applies only to "close corporations," as defined in section 342. "Unless a corporation elects to become a close corporation under this subchapter in the manner prescribed in this subchapter, it shall be subject in all respects to this chapter, except this subchapter." 8 *Del.C.* § 341. The corporation before the Court in this matter, is not a "close corporation." Therefore it is not governed by the provisions of Subchapter XIV.

One cannot read into the situation presented in the case at bar any special relief for the minority stockholders in this closely-held, but not statutory "close corporation" because the provisions of Subchapter XIV relating to close corporations and other statutory schemes preempt the field in their respective areas. It would run counter to the spirit of the doctrine of independent legal significance, and would be inappropriate judicial legislation for this Court to fashion a special judicially-created rule for minority investors when the entity does not fall within those statutes, or when there are no negotiated special provisions in the certificate of incorporation, by-laws, or stockholder agreements. The entire fairness test, correctly applied and articulated, is the proper judicial approach.

VII. CONCLUSION

We hold that the Court of Chancery correctly determined that the entire fairness test is applicable in reviewing the actions of the defendants in establishing and implementing the ESOP and the key man life insurance program. The Vice Chancellor erred, however, as a matter of law in concluding on this record that the defendants had not carried their burden of showing entire fairness. [. . .]

Riblet Products Corp. v. Nagy

683 A.2d 37 (Del. 1996)

■ VEASEY, CHIEF JUSTICE:

[. . .] We consider whether or not majority stockholders of a closely-held Delaware corporation can be found to have breached a fiduciary duty owing to a minority stockholder who is also the chief executive officer ("CEO") of the corporation and thus an employee of the corporation under written contract when the dispute arises solely with respect to that employment contract. [. . .]

Facts

[. . .] Riblet Products Corporation ("Riblet") is a closely-held Delaware corporation with its principal place of business in Indiana. It manufactures components of "site-built" homes and recreational vehicles. In 1981, Riblet entered into an employment contract (the "1981 contract") with Ernest J. Nagy ("Nagy"), then Chairman, President, and CEO of Riblet. Nagy was also the owner of 14% of Riblet's stock. The 1981 contract stated in relevant part that if Nagy should be "discharged for any reason other than theft, disclosure of trade secrets, or 'similar dishonest acts,' he would receive 60 percent of his regular salary until he turned 62." [. . .]

In 1986, David Bistricer, Nachum Stein, and their relatives (collectively the "Majority Stockholders") acquired an 85% interest in Riblet by means of a leveraged buy out. The new group of investors paid Nagy more than $3 million for his previous 14% interest, and Nagy acquired a 15% interest in the new corporation, the RPC Holding Corporation (the new "Riblet"). The Majority Stockholders also entered into a new employment contract (the "1986 Contract") with Nagy.

The terms of the 1986 Contract provide in relevant part that if Riblet terminated Nagy's employment for "cause" all benefits of the 1986 Contract would cease. The 1986 Contract defines "cause" as "conviction of a felony, fraud, dishonesty, illegal use of federally controlled substances, and/or misappropriation of [Riblet's] funds." The 1986 Contract further provides that if Riblet terminated Nagy's employment "other than for cause as defined herein" Nagy would receive "all salaries, benefits, bonuses, and other direct and indirect forms of compensation" for the remainder of his five-year term.

In 1990, Riblet fired Nagy, allegedly "because Nagy engaged in a series of self-dealing transactions with the firm (for example, he was an undisclosed principal in the group buying Riblet's headquarters building) and refused to follow explicit instructions issued by the board of directors (he wrote checks without the required approval, and he kept his personal secretary on the payroll after the board discharged her.)" [. . .]

Nagy challenged the dismissal [. . .] alleging [among others] [. . .] a claim against the Majority Stockholders for breach of their fiduciary duties as majority stockholders to Nagy, a minority stockholder.

[In the U.S. District Court for the Northern District of Indiana,] [t]he jury found that [. . .] the Majority Stockholders breached their fiduciary duties to Nagy, and held them jointly and severally liable with Riblet for the compensatory damages award and assessed $375,000 in punitive damages against each of them.

The defendants appealed the verdict on both grounds. The Seventh Circuit [. . .] [f]inding that Delaware law applied to the breach of fiduciary duty claim, [. . .] certified the following question of law to this Court pursuant to Delaware Supreme Court Rule 41(a)(ii):

> [. . .]

In view of the invitation by the Seventh Circuit to reformulate the question, we respectfully suggest that it would be preferable if the question were to be restated as follows:

> Whether majority stockholders of a Delaware corporation may be held liable for violation of a fiduciary duty to a minority stockholder who is an employee of the corporation under an employment contract with respect to issues involving that employment. [. . .]

Analysis

[. . .] The Seventh Circuited noted:

> The Supreme Court of Delaware has never addressed the question. *Ueltzhoffer v. Fox Fire Development Co.* [. . .] marks its closest approach to the subject. . . . [. . .]

In *Ueltzhoffer*, a minority stockholder and employee of a closely-held corporation brought a breach of fiduciary duty claim against the majority stockholders based on his termination. Ueltzhoffer alleged that "his termination amounted to a wrongful freeze out of his stock interest in Drummond and Fox Fire Co." [. . .] Significantly, Ueltzhoffer did not have an employment contract with the corporation.

The Court of Chancery rejected Ueltzhoffer's arguments "that in close corporations profits frequently are taken out as salary and that termination of a minority stockholder's employment without a valid business purpose has been recognized as a breach of fiduciary duties in other jurisdictions" and should be recognized in Delaware. [. . .] The Court of Chancery reasoned:

> There are two problems with the plaintiffs' argument. First, to the extent that there is some sort of "business purpose" test associated with the determination as to whether Ueltzhoffer's termination was wrongful, I find that defendants have established one. . . . Thus, I am not prepared to conclude that

the Martas terminated Ueltzhoffer for the sole and improper purpose of freezing him out of the corporate entities.

[Second,] [a]s a matter of law, I am aware of no Delaware authority following [*Wilkes v. Springside Nursing Home, Inc.*] or applying *Wilkes* outside of the context of a close corporation. [. . .]

In *Wilkes*, the Supreme Court of Massachusetts held that majority stockholders of a closely-held corporation breached their fiduciary duty to a minority stockholder when they terminated his employment and refused to reelect him as a salaried officer and director. [. . .] *Wilkes* has not been adopted as Delaware law.

This is a case governed by an employment contract. Nagy actively and successfully pursued his contractual rights as an employee. These contractual rights are separate from his rights as a stockholder. *See Shaw v. Agri-Mark, Inc.* (distinguishing between rights arising from contract and "the rights exclusively reserved for 'stockholders' under either Delaware common law or the Delaware General Corporation Law.").

This is not a case of breach of fiduciary duty to Nagy *qua* stockholder. To be sure, the Majority Stockholders may well owe fiduciary duties to Nagy as a minority stockholder. But that is not the issue here. Nagy does not allege that his termination amounted to a wrongful freeze out of his stock interest in Riblet, nor does he contend that he was harmed as a stockholder by being terminated. Moreover, this is not an attempt to bring a derivative suit by Nagy as a stockholder on behalf of the corporation for actionable injury to it arising out of the termination of the employment agreement.

Conclusion

The certified question is therefore answered in the **NEGATIVE**.

Blaustein v. Lord Baltimore Capital Corporation

84 A.3d 954 (Del. 2014)

■ BERGER, JUSTICE:

In this appeal we consider whether a minority stockholder in a closely held corporation has a right to a non-conflicted board decision on whether to repurchase her shares. The stockholder argues that such a right exists, both under common law fiduciary duty principles and under the implied covenant of good faith and fair dealing. [. . .]

FACTUAL AND PROCEDURAL BACKGROUND

This dispute arises from Susan M. Blaustein's unsuccessful attempts to sell her stock in Lord Baltimore Capital Corporation, a closely held Delaware corporation that was created by members of the Thalheimer family in 1998. The Thalheimer stockholders are Louis Thalheimer

("Louis"), Marjorie Thalheimer Coleman ("Marjorie"), and Elizabeth Thalheimer Wachs ("Elizabeth").

On January 1, 1999, Blaustein and her sister, Jeanne, became stockholders pursuant to the Lord Baltimore Capital Corporation Shareholders' Agreement. Paragraph 7(d) of the Shareholders' Agreement addresses repurchases of stock from minority stockholders. That provision states:

> Notwithstanding any other provision of this Agreement, the Company may repurchase Shares upon terms and conditions agreeable to the Company and the Shareholder who owns the Shares to be repurchased provided that the repurchase is approved either (i) by a majority, being at least four, of all of the Directors of the Company then authorized (regardless of the number attending the meeting of the Board of Directors) at a duly called meeting of the Board of Directors or (ii) in writing by Shareholders who, in the aggregate, own of record or beneficially 70% or more of all Shares then issued and outstanding.

Despite the existence of this provision, Blaustein alleges that she bought into Lord Baltimore with the understanding that, after a ten-year waiting period, she would be guaranteed the opportunity to sell her stock for full value. This understanding allegedly was based on several oral promises from Louis, who explained to her that he could not put the promises into writing because "doing so might jeopardize the 'S' corporation tax status of Lord Baltimore and possibly jeopardize as well the Section 355 tax-free treatment of the transactions that had resulted in . . . the formation of Lord Baltimore."

When Blaustein attempted to sell her stock, after the ten-year period had expired, Louis refused to offer her anything better than a 52% discount from the net asset value of her shares. Blaustein tried to negotiate, and made several proposals for a buyout at a less severe discount. Louis presented some of Blaustein's proposals to the Lord Baltimore board, and the board discussed them at several board meetings, but Louis and the board did not deviate from their requirement of a 52% discount. [EDS.— At that time, the board was comprised of two groups: the four "Thalheimer directors" and the three "Blaustein directors." The Thalheimer directors included Louis, Elizabeth, William Coleman (Marjorie's husband), and Donald Kilpatrick. Kilpatrick was an independent director appointed by the Thalheimer stockholders. The Blaustein directors included Susan Blaustein, her sister Jeanne, and a third independent director appointed by Susan and Jeanne.] Not surprisingly, the parties dispute the board's motivation. Louis argues that he and the other Thalheimer directors have acted at all times in Lord Baltimore's best interests. Blaustein argues that a majority of Lord Baltimore's seven directors (i.e., all four Thalheimer directors) are conflicted and that they rejected her proposals in order to preserve personal tax benefits that might have been jeopardized were they to allow Blaustein to cash out at a reasonable price.

Blaustein filed a complaint in the Court of Chancery against Louis and Lord Baltimore (collectively, "Louis," unless the context requires otherwise) alleging promissory estoppel, breach of fiduciary duty, and breach of the implied covenant of good faith and fair dealing. In its May 31, 2012 Memorandum Opinion, the Court of Chancery dismissed that complaint except as to the implied covenant claim. Louis then moved for summary judgment on the implied covenant claim, and Blaustein sought leave to amend her complaint to allege a new fiduciary duty claim and a new implied covenant claim. In its April 30, 2013 Memorandum Opinion, the Court of Chancery granted Louis's motion for summary judgment and denied Blaustein's request to amend her complaint. This appeal followed.

DISCUSSION

Blaustein appeals from the Court of Chancery's rejection of two proposed new claims she sought to add by amending her complaint—one for breach of fiduciary duty, and one for breach of the implied covenant of good faith and fair dealing. Blaustein does not challenge the dismissal of her other claims. As explained below, we find that the Court of Chancery correctly rejected both proposed new claims.

I.   *Fiduciary Duty Claims*

Blaustein moved to amend her complaint to add a claim for breach of fiduciary duty against the Thalheimer directors. In her proposed Amended and Supplemented Verified Complaint, Blaustein alleges that the Thalheimer directors breached their fiduciary duties by failing to consider and negotiate, free of conflict, a repurchase of her shares. This breach, Blaustein alleges, has directly harmed her by depriving her of liquidity and control over her asset portfolio. Blaustein also appears to allege that the Thalheimer directors' failure to accept her repurchase proposals amounted to a breach that harmed "Lord Baltimore and its shareholders as a whole." Thus, Blaustein's breach of fiduciary duty claim actually contains two separate claims—one direct and one derivative.

A.   Direct Claim

Blaustein alleges that the Thalheimer directors acted out of self-interest when they refused to negotiate a repurchase of her shares at anything less than a 52% discount. She argues that these allegations of self-interest are sufficient to trigger entire fairness review because Blaustein has a "right to a non-conflicted corporate decision" on whether her shares should be repurchased and at what price. Blaustein relies on both common law fiduciary duty principles and Paragraph 7(d) of the Shareholders' Agreement in support of her claim.

Under common law, the directors of a closely held corporation have no general fiduciary duty to repurchase the stock of a minority stockholder. An investor must rely on contractual protections if liquidity is a matter of concern. Blaustein has no inherent right to sell her stock to the company at "full value," or any other price. It follows that she has no right to insist on the formation of an independent board committee to negotiate with her.

The Shareholders' Agreement provides the only protection available to Blaustein. But the relevant provision, Paragraph 7(d), gives the stockholder and the company discretion as to whether to engage in a transaction, and as to the price. It does not impose any affirmative duty on either party to consider or negotiate any repurchase proposal. In sum, Blaustein's direct fiduciary duty claim would be subject to dismissal under Rule 12(b)(6), and the trial court correctly denied her motion to amend the complaint to add that claim.

B. Derivative Claim

The trial court noted that Blaustein's proposed amended complaint could be read to allege a derivative claim. Blaustein alleges that her repurchase proposal created an investment opportunity for Lord Baltimore that the Thalheimer directors failed faithfully to consider because they were concerned with preserving their personal tax planning interests. This allegation implicates the directors' duty to act at all times in good faith and in the furtherance of the corporation's bests interests. A failure to do so would harm Lord Baltimore directly, and all of its stockholders derivatively.

To maintain a derivative claim, a stockholder must allege that the company wrongfully refused a demand to address the alleged wrong, or that a demand on the board would have been futile. The mere allegation that there is a control group within the board is insufficient to excuse demand. Rather, a plaintiff must allege with particularity that a majority of the board lacks independence or is otherwise incapable of validly exercising its business judgment.

Blaustein made no demand, and her futility allegations are conclusory. At best, the allegations create a reasonable doubt as to the independence of three of the seven Lord Baltimore directors: Elizabeth, Coleman and Louis. The complaint challenges Kilpatrick's independence only by alleging that he was appointed by the Thalheimer stockholders and that he has voted with them in the past. Such allegations, without more, are insufficient to demonstrate a lack of independence. Because a majority of the directors are independent, demand is not excused. Thus, the derivative claim also would be subject to dismissal, and the Court of Chancery properly denied leave to amend.

II. Implied Covenant Claim

Blaustein argues that the Court of Chancery erred by rejecting her proposed new claim for breach of the implied covenant of good faith and fair dealing. The proposed complaint alleges that Paragraph 7(d) of the Shareholder Agreement contains an implied contractual right to good-faith negotiation of stockholder redemption proposals. But the plain language of Paragraph 7(d) gives both parties complete discretion in deciding whether, and at what price, to execute a redemption transaction. Paragraph 7(d) states that "the Company [Lord Baltimore] *may* repurchase Shares upon terms and conditions agreeable to the Company and the Shareholder who owns the Shares to be repurchased...." This provision is permissive. The remainder of Paragraph 7(d) requires that any repurchase be approved by a majority of the directors or 70% of the stockholders. The approval requirement protects Lord Baltimore and the non-selling stockholders from a stock repurchase that is not in their best interest.

The implied covenant of good faith and fair dealing cannot be employed to impose new contract terms that could have been bargained for but were not. Rather, the implied covenant is used in limited circumstances to include "what the parties would have agreed to themselves had they considered the issue in their original bargaining positions at the time of contracting." Here, the parties did consider whether, and on what terms, minority stockholders would be able to have their stock repurchased. Paragraph 7(d) does not contain any promise of a "full value" price or independent negotiators. Because the implied covenant does not give parties the right to renegotiate their contracts, the trial court correctly denied Blaustein's proposed new claim. [...]

CONCLUSION

Based on the foregoing, the judgment of the Court of Chancery is hereby AFFIRMED.

CHAPTER VIII

LIMITED LIABILITY COMPANIES

A. FORMATION

A Guy Named Moe LLC v. Chipotle Mexican Grill of Colorado LLC

447 Md. 425 (Md. 2016)

In this case we are asked to determine whether A Guy Named Moe, LLC, the Petitioner, a foreign limited liability company doing business in Maryland, having filed a civil action in the Circuit Court for Anne Arundel County, although not registered to do business in Maryland, can continue to pursue its claims, once Chipotle Mexican Grill of Colorado, LLC, the Respondent, moved to dismiss the case because of Moe's failure to register. [. . .]

The parties to this case are two foreign limited liability companies: A Guy Named Moe, LLC and Chipotle Mexican Grill of Colorado, LLC. Both companies operate a chain of restaurants, which are respectively known as "Moe's Southwest Grill" and "Chipotle Mexican Grill." The dispute between the parties, which underlies this appeal, began in 2012, when Chipotle applied for a "special exception" to build a restaurant at 36 Market Space in Annapolis, Maryland, which is approximately 425 feet from Moe's Southwest Grill at 122 Dock Street. The Department of Planning and Zoning for the City of Annapolis recommended that the City's Board of Appeals approve Chipotle's application, but Moe opposed that recommendation during Board proceedings. The Board, though, unanimously approved Chipotle's request in the Spring of 2013.

Moe subsequently filed a petition for judicial review, pursuant to Maryland Rule 7–201 *et seq.*, asking that the Circuit Court for Anne Arundel County review the Board's decision. Chipotle then filed a Motion to Dismiss in which it argued that Moe was unable to file a petition for judicial review because its right to do business had been forfeited, and, thus, could not "maintain" suit under Section 4A–1007(a) of the Corporations and Associations Article of the Maryland Code. [. . .]

Moe, in response, filed an Amended Petition for Judicial Review and attached a "Certificate of Good Standing" issued by the State Department of Assessments and Taxation on September 24, 2013. Moe argued that, while it was not registered to do business in Maryland when it had filed its petition, it could still "maintain" the action under Section 4A–1007 of

685

the Corporations and Associations Article because it had subsequently successfully registered and paid the associated penalty. [. . .]

It is undisputed that prior to filing suit, Moe's right to do business in Maryland was forfeited by the State Department of Assessments and Taxation pursuant to Section 4A–1013(a) of the Corporations and Associations Article, Maryland Code:

> The Department may forfeit the right of any foreign limited liability company to do business in this State if the limited liability company fails to file with the Department any report or fails to pay any late filing penalties required by law.

Upon forfeiture of the right to do business a foreign limited liability company is treated as if it never registered.

> On forfeiture of its right to do business in this State, the foreign limited liability company is subject to the same rules, legal provisions, and sanctions as if it had never qualified or been licensed to do business in this State.

Under Section 4A–1009(a)(1) of the Corporations and Associations Article Maryland Code, "doing business," however, does not include "maintaining suit[.]"

[. . .] "Unless the [foreign] limited liability company shows to the satisfaction of the court" that it has paid a penalty for noncompliance and complied with the registration requirements, it cannot "maintain" suit[.] [. . .]

The issue, thus, is queued up: If a foreign limited liability company had filed a judicial review action after it had forfeited its right to do business, could it then "maintain" the suit, after it cured the infirmity? [. . .]

Moe argues that the prohibition on *maintaining* suit does not prohibit it from *filing* suit and that its subsequent registration efforts would allow the suit to continue. Moe asserts that not only is such an interpretation of "maintain" warranted by a plain meaning interpretation, but also that we concluded as much in *Kendrick & Roberts v. Warren Bros. Co.* Chipotle argues that the prohibition on "maintaining" suit includes a prohibition on commencing suit.

The statute does not answer the question, but embraces an ambiguity that has permitted the two varying interpretations developed by the Circuit Court and our intermediate appellate court. Section 4A–1007(a) of the Corporations and Associations Article admonishes that a foreign limited liability company "may not maintain suit in any court of this State" if it is noncompliant, but this prohibition is subject to the proviso, "[u]nless the [foreign] limited liability company shows to the satisfaction of the court" that it has paid a penalty for noncompliance and complied with the registration requirements.

"Maintain," used in Section 4A–1007(a), means "to continue" something already in existence, and coupled with "unless the limited liability company shows to the satisfaction of the court," indicates that the Legislature intended to permit a noncompliant foreign limited liability to "cure" its failure to comply with registration requirements, even though having failed to register before filing suit. The history of Section 4A–1007(a) after our decision in *Kendrick,* and the *Kendrick* case itself, as well as out of state cases interpreting the words "maintain" and "unless" or "until" in similar statutes support this analysis.

In *Kendrick* we analyzed an iteration of our foreign corporation statute, [. . .] which stated that, "No such foreign corporation shall be permitted to maintain any action, either at law or equity, in the courts of this state, until the provisions of this Act shall have been complied with." In the case, Kendrick & Roberts Inc., a West Virginia corporation, had sued Warren Bros. Co., which in response stated that, "at the time of the institution of this suit in this Court the said foreign corporation had not filed in the office of the Secretary of the State of Maryland." Kendrick & Roberts Inc. alleged, thereafter "by way of replication," that two months after filing suit, "the plaintiff fully complied with all the requirements of the law of the state of Maryland relating to foreign corporations". The trial court allowed the action to proceed, and Kendrick & Roberts Inc. prevailed.

We affirmed and held that, "The statute does not forbid the institution or bringing of the action, but prevents the maintaining of such action until the provisions of the law shall have been complied with." We recognized that, "The meaning of the word 'maintain' has been defined 'in pleading, to support what has already been brought into existence.' " We concluded that, "omission on the part of the plaintiff does not operate to end a suit otherwise regularly instituted, or to destroy a right in other respects validly existing, and the greatest effect ... would be to suspend the prosecution of such suit until compliance was had with statute." [. . .]

Both the foreign corporation statute and the statute governing foreign limited liability companies embody identical "may not maintain suit" language that we interpreted in *Kendrick*. Foreign limited liability companies and foreign corporations also suffer identical consequences upon failure "to file with the Department any report or fail[ure] to pay any late filing penalties required by law" such that the Department of Assessments and Taxation may forfeit the entities's right "to do business in this State." Upon forfeiture of the right to do business, a foreign limited liability company and a foreign corporation are "subject to the same rules, legal provisions, and sanctions as if [they] had never qualified or been licensed to do business in this State."

Our analysis that a foreign limited liability company may cure the infirmity of failure to register from the time of filing suit also finds support in our sister jurisdictions interpreting the words "maintain" and "unless" or "until" in statutes similar to ours.

In *Nolte v. MT Tech. Enterprises, LLC,* MT filed suit when it was not registered to transact business in Virginia. Under the Virginia Code

§ 13.1–1057(A) "[a] foreign limited liability company transacting business in the Commonwealth may not *maintain* any action, suit, or proceeding in any court of the Commonwealth until it has registered in the Commonwealth." While MT was not registered when it initiated suit, it registered "before the trial court entered its final order" granting judgment in its favor.

The Supreme Court of Virginia affirmed and concluded that MT could maintain its suit after registering. The court interpreted the statutory language in Virginia Code § 13.1–1057(A) of "maintain" as " 'to continue (something),' not to start or commence." [. . .]

A similar result was reached by the Delaware Supreme Court in interpreting its foreign corporation statute. In *Hudson Farms, Inc. v. McGrellis*, Hudson Farms Inc., a Pennsylvania corporation, filed a mechanic's lien against John McGrellis in Delaware at a time when Hudson Farms was not licensed to do business there. McGrellis filed a motion for summary judgment asserting that Hudson Farms was a foreign corporation not licensed to do business in Delaware, and was, therefore, barred from initiating the action. The trial court determined that Hudson Farms was not licensed at the time it filed the action and dismissed the action without prejudice, although, "the practical effect of the [trial court's] ruling was to defeat Hudson Farms' cause of action because the period for filing a mechanic's lien had expired." Hudson Farms, in a motion for reargument, asserted that, between McGrellis's filing of the motion for summary judgment and the date of the hearing on the motion, it had properly registered to do business in Delaware. The trial court denied reargument, "ruling, in effect, the Hudson Farms registration efforts were unavailing since its nonregistered status at the time of filing suit was an uncorrectable defect."

The Supreme Court of Delaware reversed [. . .] and stated that, "The great majority of courts which have construed such statutes have concluded that a court may stay a suit commenced by a non-qualified foreign corporation until the foreign corporation obtains the requisite authority." [. . .]

The court determined that Delaware's statute as well as those in other states was similar to Section 117 of the Model Business Corporation Act (1960), which stated, in part, that "[n]o foreign corporation transacting business in this State without a certificate of authority shall be permitted to maintain any action, suit or proceeding in any court of this State, until such corporation shall have obtained a certificate of authority." The court reasoned that, "It is not unreasonable to assume, as most courts do, that the word "until," as used in § 117, provides an inference that a proceeding may be stayed until compliance occurs." [. . .]

In the case *sub judice*, we shall hold that a foreign limited liability company can "cure" its failure to comply with registration requirements and continue its suit even though not registered at the time of filing suit. What was true in *Kendrick* remains true today with respect to a foreign limited liability company: "omission on the part of the plaintiff does not operate to end a suit otherwise regularly instituted." Thus, once a foreign limited liability company comes into compliance with the statute, it may maintain its action even though not registered when initiating the suit. [. . .]

B. LIMITED LIABILITY

Duray Development, LLC v. Perrin
288 Mich. App. 143, 792 N.W.2d 749 (2010)

[. . .]

I.   BASIC FACTS AND PROCEDURAL HISTORY

Duray Development is a residential development company whose sole member is Robert Munger. Munger's responsibilities were to locate and purchase property, and then work with engineering companies and municipalities to have the property zoned and fully developed for residential living. In 2004, Duray Development purchased 40 acres of undeveloped property called "Copper Corners," located at the intersection of 76th Street and Craft Avenue in Caledonia Township, Michigan.

On September 30, 2004, Duray Development entered into a contract with Perrin, Perrin Excavating, and KDM Excavating for excavating at Copper Corners. In that contract, Munger signed on Duray Development's behalf, Perrin signed on behalf of himself and Perrin Excavating, and Dan Vining signed on behalf of KDM Excavating.

On October 27, 2004, Duray Development and Perrin entered into a new contract, intended to supersede the September 30, 2004 contract. The new contract contained the same language and provisions as the earlier contract. However, the new contract was between Duray Development and Outlaw only, and Perrin, Perrin Excavating, and KDM Excavating were not parties. Outlaw was an excavation company that Perrin and Vining had recently formed. Perrin and Vining signed the new contract on behalf of Outlaw, and both held themselves out to Duray Development as the owners and persons in charge of the company. Although the parties did not execute the second contract until October 27, 2004, it was drafted on September 30, 2004, the same day the parties signed the first contract. Once signed, all parties proceeded under the contract as if Outlaw were the contractor for the Copper Corners development.

Two contracts were drafted because Perrin had not yet formed Outlaw at the time of the first contract. However, Duray Development did not want to wait for Perrin to finish forming the company before starting the excavation of Copper Corners. Therefore, the parties entered into the first contract on September 30, 2004, and then entered into the second contract once the parties thought Outlaw was a valid limited liability company.

Defendants began excavation and grading work pursuant to the contracts, but did not perform satisfactorily or on time. Duray Development then sued defendants for breach of contract. Defendants answered and filed a counterclaim against Duray Development, alleging that they performed the work according to the terms of the contracts and that Duray Development owed defendants approximately $35,000. Duray Development later learned through discovery that Outlaw did not obtain a "filed" status as a limited liability company until November 29, 2004, and therefore Outlaw was not a valid limited liability company at the time the parties executed the second contract.

[. . .] After trial, the trial court ruled in favor of Duray Development, finding that Perrin was in breach of contract and owed $96,367.68 in damages to Duray Development.

In a posttrial memorandum, Perrin argued that he was not personally liable for Duray Development's damages. He asserted that, although Outlaw was not a valid limited liability company at the time of the execution of the second contract, Outlaw was nevertheless liable to Duray Development under the doctrine of de facto corporation. The trial court opined that if Outlaw were a corporation, then the de facto corporation doctrine most likely would have applied. However, the trial court concluded that the Limited Liability Company Act "clearly and specifically provides for the time that a limited liability company comes into existence and has powers to contract" and therefore superseded the de facto corporation doctrine and made it inapplicable to limited liability companies altogether. Perrin now appeals.

II. PERRIN'S PERSONAL LIABILITY

A. Standard of Review

Perrin argues that he was not personally liable because he signed the second contract on behalf of Outlaw. According to Perrin, even though Outlaw was not yet a properly formed limited liability company, the parties all treated the contract as though Outlaw was a properly formed limited liability company and, therefore, the doctrine of de facto corporation shielded Perrin from personal liability. He further argues that the doctrine of corporation by estoppel precluded Duray Development from arguing that he is personally liable.

The issue whether the doctrine of de facto corporation applies to Perrin requires us to consider the Limited Liability Company Act and the Business Corporation Act. [. . .]

Despite his contention on appeal, Perrin did not preserve the issue of corporation by estoppel. [. . .]

B. The Limited Liability Company Act

The Limited Liability Company Act provides precisely when a limited liability company comes into existence. [It] provides that "[t]he existence of the limited liability company begins on the effective date of the articles of organization [. . .]." MCL 450.4104(1) requires that the articles of organization be delivered to the administrator of the Michigan Department of Energy, Labor and Economic Growth (DELEG). Under MCL 450.4104(2), after delivery of the articles of organization, "the administrator shall endorse upon it the word 'filed' with his or her official title and the date of receipt and of filing[.]" And under MCL 450.4104(6), "[a] document filed under [MCL 450.4104(2)] is effective at the time it is endorsed[.]"

Once a limited liability company comes into existence, limited liability applies, and a member or manager is not liable for the acts, debts, or obligations of the company. In contrast, a person who signs a contract on behalf of a company that is not yet in existence generally becomes personally liable on that contract. However, a company can become liable if, (1) after the company comes into existence, it either ratifies or adopts that contract, (2) a court determines that a de facto corporation existed at the time of the contract, or (3) a court orders that corporation by estoppel prevented the opposing party from arguing against the existence of a corporation.

In this case, Perrin signed the articles of organization for Outlaw on the same day as the second contract, October 27, 2004. Perrin then signed the October 27, 2004 contract on behalf of Outlaw. However, the DELEG administrator did not endorse the articles of organization until November 29, 2004. Therefore, pursuant to the Limited Liability Company Act, Outlaw was not in existence on October 27, 2004. And Outlaw did not adopt or ratify the second contract. Therefore, Perrin became personally liable for Outlaw's obligations *unless* a de facto limited liability company existed or limited liability company by estoppel applied.

C. De Facto Corporation and Corporation By Estoppel

De facto corporation and corporation by estoppel are separate and distinct doctrines that warrant individual treatment. The de facto corporation doctrine provides that a defectively formed corporation—that is, one that fails to meet the technical requirements for forming a de jure corporation—may attain the legal status of a de facto corporation if certain requirements are met, as discussed later in this opinion. The most important aspect of a de facto corporation is that courts perceive and treat it in all respects as if it were a properly formed de jure corporation. For example, it can sue and be sued. Often, as in this case, the status of the company is crucial to determine whether the parties forming the corporation are individually liable.

Corporation by estoppel, on the other hand, is an equitable remedy and does not concern legal status. The general rule is: "Where a body assumes to be a corporation and acts under a particular name, a third party dealing with it under such assumed name is estopped to deny its corporate existence." Like the de facto corporation doctrine, corporation by estoppel often arises in the context of assessing individual versus corporate liability. The purpose of the doctrine is so "that one who contracts with an association as a corporation is estopped to deny its corporate existence . . . so as to prevent one from maintaining an action on the contract against the associates, or against the officers making the contract, as individuals or partners."

In sum, the de facto corporation doctrine allows a defectively formed corporation to attain the legal status of a corporation. The corporation by estoppel doctrine prevents a party who dealt with an association as though it were a corporation from denying its existence. Stated another way, the de facto corporation doctrine establishes the legal existence of the corporation. By contrast, the corporation by estoppel doctrine merely prevents one from arguing against it, and does nothing to establish its actual existence in the eyes of the rest of the world. [. . .]

D.　The De Facto Corporation Doctrine

The Michigan Supreme Court established the four elements for a de facto corporation long ago:

> "When incorporators have [1] proceeded in good faith, [2] under a valid statute, [3] for an authorized purpose, and [4] have executed and acknowledged articles of association pursuant to that purpose, a corporation *de facto* instantly comes into being. A *de facto* corporation is an actual corporation. As to all the world, except the State, it enjoys the status and powers of a *de jure* corporation." *Tisch Auto Supply Co. V. Nelson.*

Here, there is no question that elements (2), (3), and (4) were satisfied. First, the Limited Liability Company Act is a valid statute that allows for limited liability companies in Michigan. Second, Perrin and Vining presumably formed Outlaw for the purpose of starting a new excavation company, which is an authorized purpose. Third, Perrin executed the articles of organization on October 27, 2004, the same day the parties executed the second contract.

It is less obvious whether the first element of the doctrine—good faith—was satisfied. There is little guidance in Michigan caselaw for a definition, or application, of this specific element. But in *Newcomb-Endicott Co. v. Fee,* the Michigan Supreme Court, although applying a different set of elements, did state that in the absence of a claim or evidence of fraud or false representation on the part of the incorporators, and in light of a bona fide attempt to incorporate, there was no reason to deny a company the status of a *de facto* corporation.

Here, Duray Development does not allege that Perrin set up the corporation through fraud or false representations; that is, Duray Development does not allege that Perrin set up the corporation as a sham, for fraudulent purposes, or as a mere instrumentality under a theory of piercing the corporate veil. Rather, as the record indicates, Duray Development did not learn until after filing the complaint in this case that Outlaw was not a valid limited liability company on October 27,

2004. Duray Development at all times dealt with Outlaw as a valid corporation with which it contracted. Duray Development's sole member, Munger, testified that once the second contract took effect, Duray Development no longer considered Perrin or Perrin Excavating as parties to the contract, but instead considered Outlaw to be the new "contractor." There is no evidence whatsoever to suggest that Perrin formed Outlaw in anything other than good faith. Accordingly, the trial court was correct to conclude that, had Outlaw been formed as a corporation instead of a limited liability company, it would have been a de facto corporation for purposes of liability on the October 27, 2004 contract. Thus, all elements of a de facto corporation were present in this case.

The trial court, however, concluded that the de facto *corporation* doctrine does not apply to *limited liability companies* and therefore did not apply to Outlaw. It reasoned that the plain reading of the Limited Liability Company Act "clearly and specifically provides for the time that a limited liability company comes into existence and has powers to contract." [. . .]

That is not to say, however, that the doctrine *cannot* be applied to a limited liability company. [. . .]

The Supreme Court's conclusion in *Newcomb-Endicott Co.,* that statutes contemplating complete organization of an association do not preclude application of the de facto corporation doctrine, contradicts the idea that the de facto corporation doctrine perished on enactment of the Business Corporation Act and the Limited Liability Company Act. Although *Newcomb-Endicott Co.* dealt with a corporation rather than a limited liability company, it would be arbitrary to conclude, without any precedent to the contrary, that the de facto corporation doctrine applies to corporations but not to limited liability companies.

Indeed, the similarities between the Business Corporation Act and the Limited Liability Company Act support the conclusion that the de facto corporation doctrine applies to both. The purposes for forming a limited liability company and a corporation are similar. [. . .]

Accordingly, we conclude that the de facto corporation doctrine applies to Outlaw, a limited liability company. As a result, Outlaw, and not Perrin, individually, is liable for the breach of the October 27, 2004 contract.

E.   Corporation By Estoppel

As stated previously, generally, a person who signs a contract on behalf of a company that is not yet in existence becomes personally liable on that contract. However, a court can order that the company is instead liable if it finds that corporation by estoppel prevented the opposing party from arguing against the existence of a corporation. The Supreme Court in *Estey Mfg. Co. v. Runnells,* summarized the principle of corporation by estoppel as follows: "Where a body assumes to be a corporation and acts under a particular name, a third party dealing with it under such assumed name is estopped to deny its corporate existence."

As with the doctrine of de facto corporation, this Court has not addressed whether corporation by estoppel can be applied to limited liability companies. However, corporation by estoppel is an equitable remedy, and its purpose is to prevent one who contracts with a corporation from later denying its existence in order to hold the individual officers or partners liable. The doctrine has come up on numerous occasions in conjunction with de facto corporations. In that setting, the rule is:

> In the case of the associates in the corporation *de facto,* and those who have had dealings with it, there is a mutual estoppel, resting upon broad grounds of right, justice and equity. The first class are not suffered to deny their incorporation, nor the second to dispute the validity of their assertions of corporate powers. *Swartwout v. Michigan Air Line R. Co.*

With this in mind, and in light of the purpose of corporation by estoppel, the corporate structure has little impact on the equitable principles at stake. In other words, there is no reason or purpose to draw a distinction on the basis of corporate form. Furthermore, like *de facto* corporation, because corporation by estoppel coexists with the Business Corporation Act, so too can it coexist with the Limited Liability Company Act.

[. . .] [W]e conclude that the doctrine of corporation by estoppel may reasonably be extended to limited liability companies.

Moreover, here, the record clearly supports a finding of "limited liability company by estoppel" through the extension of the corporation by estoppel doctrine. Perrin was an individual party to the first contract, as was his limited liability company, Perrin Excavating. However, only Outlaw became a party to the second contract, which superseded the first. And all parties dealt with the second contract as though Outlaw were a party. After the second contract, Duray Development received billings from Outlaw, and not from Perrin. Duray Development also received a certificate of liability insurance for Outlaw. Munger testified that he dealt with Perrin, Perrin Excavating, and KDM Excavating before the second contract and only dealt with Outlaw after. Duray Development continued to assume Outlaw was a valid limited liability company after filing the lawsuit and only learned of the filing and contract discrepancies once litigation began in July 2006.

However, we cannot find plain error requiring reversal on the doctrine of limited liability company by estoppel. Perrin did not raise the issue in the trial court, and the trial court did not err by not raising it for him. "Trial courts are not the research assistants of the litigants; the parties have a duty to fully present their legal arguments to the court for its resolution of their dispute." "[A] party may not remain silent in the trial court, only to prevail on an issue that was not called to the trial court's attention." Accordingly, it was not the trial court's responsibility to raise an argument for Perrin that he did not raise for himself. And, as indicated above, corporation by estoppel, like de facto corporation, has never been applied to limited liability companies in the past. Thus, we cannot conclude that the trial court made a clear and obvious mistake by not applying the corporation by estoppel doctrine when there is no precedent indicating that the trial court should have applied the doctrine. Accordingly, we conclude that no plain error occurred requiring reversal on this issue. [. . .]

In Re Coinmint, LLC

261 A.3d 867 (Del. 2021)

■ ZURN, VICE CHANCELLOR.

[. . .]

I.   BACKGROUND

[. . .] Nominal Respondent Coinmint, LLC [. . .] is a private bitcoin mining firm that operates one of the largest digital currency centers in the world. It was founded by two childhood friends, nonparties Prieur Leary and Ashton Soniat. Leary and Soniat formed Coinmint as a Delaware limited liability company in August 2016. Leary and Soniat hold their interests in Coinmint via their respective entities: Petitioner Mintvest Capital Ltd. [. . .] and Respondent Coinmint Living Trust [. . .]. Mintvest and CLT are and always have been Coinmint's only Members [. . .].

At the time of formation, the parties agreed Leary would run Coinmint's day-to-day operations, contributing labor and know-how, while Soniat would fund those operations. Leary and Soniat agreed that Mintvest and CLT would be Coinmint's 50% owners, that the friends would "work together agreeing on all material decisions and expenditures," and that Soniat would eventually contribute more capital and Leary would be diluted [EDS.—in a manner that is directly related to the capital put in]. [. . .]

As agreed, Leary operated Coinmint and Soniat bankrolled those operations via CLT. The parties now dispute how certain of CLT's cash infusions should be classified (*i.e.*, whether they are capital contributions or loans under the Operating Agreement) and whether those cash infusions diluted Mintvest's stake in the Company. Leary maintains that Mintvest was never diluted, but instead maintained its 50% equity interest notwithstanding CLT's nearly continuous funding. CLT contends that Mintvest was significantly diluted to the point that its interest in the Company was under 5%, but then Leary and Soniat renegotiated and increased Mintvest's stake to 18.2%. The facts presented at trial support CLT's position.

A.   The Parties Memorialize Their Understanding In The Operating Agreement, But Eschew Its Formalities.

Under the Operating Agreement, Coinmint is manager-managed with a Board of Managers [. . .], and all Company actions and decisions flow through the Board. While Members retain the right to vote on certain major decisions, like effectuating a merger, they have no "authority or power to act for or on behalf of the Company." Section 4.3(f) of the Operating Agreement states that "any Board action shall require the approval of a Majority of the Managers then serving on the Board." Sections 4.3 through 4.6 of the Operating Agreement describe (1) how the Managers may take action on the Company's behalf, including at a formal meeting or by written consent, and (2) what vote is required to take such action, including when majority Board approval and majority Member approval are needed.

Under Section 4.1(b), Mintvest appointed Leary to serve as a Manager and its Board designee; CLT appointed itself to serve as a Manager and Board designee. Under Section 4.2(a), those Managers could be removed "with or without cause, only by the Member who designated such Manager to serve on the Board."

Each Manager's voting power is determined by its appointing Member's respective equity stake. Each Manager shall have the voting power equivalent to the Sharing Ratio of the Member that appointed such Manager and, unless otherwise expressly stated in this Agreement, all actions by or requiring the consent or approval of the Board shall require the consent or approval of a Majority of the Board.

The Member's Sharing Ratio, or equity interest, and its correlating voting power may be increased or diluted via cash infusion. The Operating Agreement contemplates that cash infusions may take the form of either a loan or capital contribution. Cash infusions in the form of loans are not contributions; they cannot increase a Member's equity stake, and do not have dilutive effect. Capital contributions affect voting power of the Members and their appointed Managers.

Section 3.2(a) of the Operating Agreement contemplates that if there are "insufficient Available Funds to cover operating deficits or other capital needs of the Company, the Board shall notify the Members in writing of such deficits and other cash needs," after which each Member is required to make an additional capital contribution to the Company. In other words, the Board must determine that a capital call is required, vote to make the capital call, and approve written notice to the Members. The Board must do so in compliance with the Operating Agreement's procedural requirements. Thereafter, the Board must send advance written notice of the call to the Members.

Each Member has the right to match its counterpart's capital contributions to avoid dilutive effect. If a Member fails to make a required capital contribution, the other Member may make that contribution, and the parties' respective equity percentages will be immediately adjusted to reflect the disparate contributions. Such adjustments shall be "effective as of the date the amount requested under [Section 3.2(a)] was due," and "shall be made by the Board in good faith." The Board should provide notice of any adjustment to the diluted Member, but failure to do so does not nullify the dilution.

The parties did not follow the Operating Agreement's formalities, and instead mutually pursued a fast-and-loose course of operations and documentation. As Leary explained, "our meetings were . . . like this[:] Ashton and I would get together and agree on certain things and then do them." Soniat corroborated this statement:

> I think it's pretty clear how things were run. It was run casually. And we had to act very quickly, as displayed in the WhatsApp messages, where he was on the ground, either in China or Upstate New York, and would tell me that, you know, "we need money fast. Sorry for the last notice, but, you know, I can buy $500,000, a million dollars' worth of machines, but if we don't wire the money tomorrow they may not be there."

> And so it was a very fluid process, quick, where we had to act. And, as I said, we were on the phone hours and hours per day. So I mean, if he ever wanted to have an official meeting, I would probably find that bizarre, but I would have agreed, for sure.

Leary never complained about Coinmint's internal lack of formal process, and instead advocated for eschewing formalities and praised the outcomes. It is undisputed that the Company has had no formal Board meetings where minutes were created. And except for written consents executed in November and December 2019 (the validity of which Mintvest disputes), the Board never executed a written consent in lieu of a meeting to authorize Company action.

B. CLT Dilutes Mintvest; Leary Negotiates To Increase Mintvest's Diluted Position To 18.2 Percent.

As contemplated at formation, Leary requested from Soniat, and Soniat provided, funds to support the Company's operations; neither Mintvest nor Leary provided funds aside from an initial contribution. Some of the funds Soniat provided on CLT's behalf were loans, and others were treated as capital contributions.

By the end of 2016, Soniat's capital contributions diluted Mintvest's interest to 5.5%. By early 2017, it was reduced even further. But consistent with the Company's internal practice of disavowing formal procedures, Coinmint does not have any Board minutes reflecting a capital call vote; any written consent authorizing a capital call; or any capital call notice sent to Members. Leary never objected on Mintvest's behalf to characterizing Soniat's cash infusions as CLT capital contributions—until he filed this suit.

Throughout 2017, Leary and Soniat negotiated Mintvest's equity stake. Leary did not contest that Mintvest was diluted by Soniat's cash contributions, but felt that Mintvest should not have been diluted so significantly because Leary had contributed significant "sweat equity." Soniat agreed, and the parties discussed an adjustment over the next several months.

In October 2017, the parties agreed to "peg" Mintvest's interest at a higher percentage. [. . .] Leary and Soniat agreed to peg Mintvest's equity stake at 18.2%, and Soniat agreed that he would only fund the Company with loans going forward, so as to avoid Mintvest's further dilution.[. . .]

[. . .] [T]he parties memorialized this agreed-to equity split in a Statement of Changes in Partners' Equity backdated to August 31, 2017 (the "October 2017 Agreement"). Leary signed the October 2017 Agreement, and did not suggest or demand that a Board meeting was required to make the 18.2% equity split official. Thus, as with every other Company decision, the October 2017 Agreement was not effectuated through any formal board meeting or written consent.

A series of documents executed after the October 2017 Agreement reflect the agreed-to 81.8% to 18.2% equity split. Leary admits he received these documents and did not protest Mintvest's equity pegged at 18.2%. Mintvest's 18.2% ownership was also confirmed through the Company's 2018 financial statements. [. . .]

On August 9, 2019, Leary once more confirmed that he was "100% comfortable with" Mintvest's equity pegged at 18.2%. [. . .] Yet, in this litigation Mintvest seeks equitable relief in this Court based on the assertion that Mintvest continues to hold 50% of the Company.

As promised, Soniat funded the Company's ongoing operations via loans so that Mintvest would not be further diluted. As Soniat testified at trial and as corroborated by the paper record, after October 2017, he loaned tens of millions of dollars to the Company to help keep it afloat, even when it was extremely risky to do so and collapse of bitcoin prices otherwise would have resulted in a bankruptcy. By 2019, he had loaned over $20 million to the Company on CLT's behalf, but had not received any interest payments on those loans. Soniat credibly testified that he would never have put this capital at risk if Leary had not agreed with him that CLT was the 81.8% owner of the Company. CLT does not contend any of these loan infusions were or are dilutive.

C.   Coinmint Is Converted To A Puerto Rican Entity.

On or about January 19, 2018, the Company filed a Certificate of Conversion with the Delaware Secretary of State and the Secretary of State (the "Conversion"). On January 25, Coinmint domesticated in Puerto Rico. As of that date, Coinmint became and was thereafter operated as a Puerto Rican entity. [. . .] The record demonstrates that although the Managers did not formally authorize the Conversion via vote or written consent, Leary was fully aware of the Conversion, supported it, and participated in it on Mintvest's behalf, alongside CLT. [. . .] [EDS.—From 2017–2019, Leary took various actions relating to Coinmint's Puerto Rican domicile, such as filing SEC documents listing Puerto Rico as the "jurisdiction of incorporation/organization."]

D. Leary And Soniat's Relationship Deteriorates.

Leary and Soniat's relationship deteriorated over time, taking its toll on Coinmint. By 2019, Leary and Soniat disagreed as to how the Company should be run and managed.[. . .] [O]n December 2, 2019, CLT, as Coinmint's 81.8% Manager and 81.8% Member, approved resolutions (i) amending the Operating Agreement to provide that "[a] majority of the members shall determine the composition of the Board, and that "[a]ny Manager may be removed from the Board with or without cause by a Majority Vote of the Members"; (ii) removing Leary from the Board under those amended terms; and (iii) designating CLT as Coinmint's sole Manager. CLT and Mintvest, via Leary and Soniat, are not able to continue working together on day-to-day tasks going forward.

E. This Action Follows.

Mintvest filed this action against CLT in December 2019. [. . .] Count I seeks to nullify the Conversion. [. . .]

II. ANALYSIS

[. . .] When CLT and Mintvest executed the Operating Agreement, they mutually understood that they would be Coinmint's equal equity holders, and that either could be diluted by the other's capital contribution. [. . .]

Mintvest maintains that it was not properly diluted because CLT's cash infusions did not adhere to Section 3.2's formalities for facilitating dilution via capital contribution and Leary did not agree to dilution, so CLT's cash infusions should therefore be treated as loans. Specifically, Mintvest argues that the Court must enforce the Operating Agreement's terms as written because (1) it provides that Mintvest owns 50% of Coinmint, (2) Mintvest bargained for its protections against dilution, and (3) CLT cannot excuse its failure to comply with the Operating Agreement's formalities, as the Operating Agreement contains integration and "no waiver" provisions. As a result, Mintvest maintains that Leary's removal as Manager and the Company's Conversion are invalid, and the Company should be dissolved.

CLT maintains that Mintvest was diluted notwithstanding the Operating Agreement's terms because Leary and Mintvest set those terms aside through waiver, estoppel, and acquiescence. CLT asserts Leary not only agreed that Mintvest would be an 18.2% owner, but also advocated for it and confirmed it on multiple occasions. On that basis, CLT presses that the Court should treat the October 2017 Agreement as a written amendment to the Sharing Ratios set forth on Schedule I of the Operating Agreement. CLT also relies on the equitable defenses of quasi-estoppel and laches.

The parties do not dispute the Operating Agreement's meaning and mandate, nor that they did not follow it. This matter hinges on whether CLT has carried its burden on its affirmative defenses to determine whether Mintvest was diluted to a minority position. I am satisfied that the greater weight of the evidence rests on CLT's side of the scale. Under the doctrines of waiver, estoppel, and acquiescence, I conclude that CLT's cash infusions were capital contributions, and that Mintvest agreed to dilution notwithstanding the Operating Agreement's requirements and is therefore an 18.2% Member. Under those same doctrines, and in view of CLT's majority voting power, Mintvest's claim that the Conversion was invalid because it was effectuated without its vote or consent also fails.

These determinations resolve Count I in CLT's favor. [. . .]

A. Based On Its Equitable Defenses, CLT Has Demonstrated That Mintvest Was Diluted To 18.2% And Coinmint Was Converted To A Puerto Rican Entity.

Limited liability companies are creatures of contract. The Delaware Limited Liability Company Act (the "Act") rests on the fundamental policy of freedom of contract. As an enabling statute, "[t]he Act is replete with fundamental provisions made subject to modification in the [a]greement," and therefore "leaves latitude for substantial private ordering," provided that statutory and judicially imposed parameters are honored. The Act contains relatively few mandates, and it explicitly assures that contractual arrangements will be given effect to the fullest permissible extent.

Although the Act provides default and gap-filling provisions, the limited liability company agreement serves as the primary source of rules governing the "affairs of a limited liability company and the conduct of its business." "[S]uch agreements operate to displace otherwise applicable default provisions in [the] Act." Delaware's LLC law is therefore "explicitly contractarian," and fundamentally regards and enforces the limited liability company agreement as a contract. Our Courts construe such agreements as any other contract, by "effectuat[ing] the parties' intent based on the parties' words and the plain meaning of those words." *Zimmerman v. Crothall.*

Actions that do not comport with an operating agreement's terms may be void or voidable.

Void acts are those the entity itself has no implicit or explicit authority to undertake or those acts that are fundamentally contrary to public policy. Stated differently, they are acts that the entity lacks the power or capacity to effectuate. Voidable acts are within the power or capacity of an entity, but were not properly authorized or effectuated by the representatives of the entity. *CompoSecure, L.L.C. v. CardUX.*

Action that is otherwise permissible, but fails to adhere to provisions of a limited liability company agreement, is voidable, not void, and so can be "validated in equity." *In re Oxbow Carbon LLC Unitholder Litig.,* "[V]oidable acts are ratifiable because the [entity] can lawfully accomplish them if it does so in the appropriate manner." Where "disputed corporate actions . . . lawfully could have been accomplished by the Defendants had they done them in the appropriate manner, i.e., had they given proper notice of the [action]," and where those "actions were in the interest of [the corporation] and did not constitute *ultra vires* acts, fraud or corporate waste," they are "voidable actions susceptible to cure by" equitable defenses. Drafters of operating agreements are also free to use their flexibility in contracting to agree that failure to follow certain procedures means an otherwise voidable action is void. "[T]he contractual imposition of voidness trumps the common law." Thus, where (1) the Act enables the entity or its representatives to take certain action as distilled in the operating agreement; (2) the operating agreement implements that grant of authority and prescribes certain approvals for effectuating it; and (3) the operating agreement does not expressly deem the action void for failure to obtain those approvals, that action will be "voidable, not void," as the entity and its representatives could have carried out the action had "the proper approvals had been obtained." *CompoSecure I.* Such voidable breaches of LLC agreements are subject to equitable defenses, including waiver, estoppel, and laches.

1. Mintvest Was Diluted To 18.2%.

The Company's Delaware Operating Agreement is a contract governed by the Act. The drafters included certain terms governing capital contributions and their dilutive effect: the Board must notify Members in writing of cash needs, each Member's share, and the date the capital contribution is due; a nonpaying Member is deemed non-contributing; and the Board adjusts the Sharing Ratios accordingly. In turn, Board action requires the approval of a majority of the Managers, and all Board action is to be taken at a minuted meeting or by written consent. The Operating Agreement does not specify that bilateral noncompliance with those terms would void any action, although a Manager acting unilaterally has no power or authority to bind the Company.

Mintvest claims that CLT and Mintvest failed to adhere to those terms in diluting Mintvest's Sharing Ratio (and ultimately leveraging Mintvest's diluted position to cause the Conversion). This series of actions was a voidable breach of the Operating Agreement. CLT [. . .] asserts that failure is excused under well-established equitable defenses [. . .].

a. Mintvest Waived The Operating Agreement's Dilution Requirements.

"It is well settled in Delaware that contractual requirements or conditions may be waived." "Waiver is the voluntary and intentional relinquishment of a known right" either conferred by statute or secured by contract. It implies knowledge of all material facts and an intent to waive, together with a willingness to refrain from enforcing those contractual rights. "Waiver is a unilateral action and depends on what one party intended to do, rather than upon what he induced his adversary to do, as in estoppel." "Unlike estoppel, waiver does not necessarily imply that one party to the controversy has been misled to his detriment in reliance on the conduct of the other party." A party asserting waiver must demonstrate that (1) there is a requirement or condition to be waived; (2) the waiving party knew of the requirement or condition; and (3) the waiving party intended to waive that requirement or condition. "The facts relied upon to prove waiver must be unequivocal." If a waiver occurs, "[a] waiving party typically is prohibited from retracting its waiver if the non-waiving party has suffered prejudice or has relied to his detriment on the waiver." *Amirsaleh v. Bd.of Trade of City of N.Y., Inc.*

This exacting standard has been met here. Section 3.2 includes requirements or conditions that must be satisfied for a dilutive capital contribution. Leary was aware of Mintvest's right to invoke those provisions; nothing in the credible record indicates that he was unaware of Section 3.2's mandate. Nonetheless, the preponderance of the evidence supports the conclusion that Leary unequivocally waived Section 3.2's requirements by negotiating for and agreeing to "peg" his ownership interest at 18.2% in view of CLT's capital contributions.

Between 2016 and 2017, Leary repeatedly and informally requested capital from CLT, and CLT provided that capital without insisting on formalities. Leary acknowledged that Mintvest's ownership interest had been significantly diluted to below 5%. Believing Mintvest deserved a greater stake in the Company because of Leary's "sweat equity," Leary requested and Soniat agreed to increase and "peg" Mintvest's interest at 18.2%. Leary never objected that CLT's capital contributions did not follow Section 3.2's requirements and should therefore be treated as non-dilutive loans. This was consistent with Leary's insistence that Soniat forego formal processes, Soniat's agreement, and the resultant lack of formal board meetings, written consents, or any similar processes.

In fact, after pegging Mintvest's equity at 18.2%, Leary again tried to avoid formalities, saying that the new 18.2% interest agreement did not need to be documented. But Soniat insisted, and the parties memorialized the agreed-to equity split in the October 2017 Agreement, which Leary executed without suggesting or demanding that a Board meeting was required to make the 18.2% equity split official. And a series of documents Leary received and executed without protest after the October 2017 Agreement reflects the agreed-to 81.8% to 18.2% equity split.[. . . .]On August 9, Leary once more confirmed that he was "100% comfortable with" Mintvest's equity pegged at 18.2%. Twelve days later, Leary again recognized Mintvest's 18.2% stake attempting to use it as leverage to support that he be given an option to exit his position as "a minority equity holder." The preponderance of the evidence demonstrates that Mintvest unequivocally waived the formalities set forth in Section 3.2. [. . .]

b. Mintvest Is Estopped From Invoking The Operating Agreement's Dilution Requirements.

[. . .]The doctrine of equitable estoppel arises when, by its conduct, a party intentionally or unintentionally leads another, in reliance on that conduct, to change position to his detriment," and will only be found where "one who has been induced to alter his line of conduct, with respect to the subject matter in controversy, so as to have subjected himself to some liability, he would not otherwise have incurred, or to have foregone some right or remedy which he otherwise would have taken."

As with waiver, the preponderance of the evidence supports a finding of estoppel[.] [. . .] First, because Leary regularly contested formalities, Soniat did not invoke Section 3.2's procedures despite his preference for documentation and bookkeeping. Rather, he followed Leary's lead, providing capital when Leary requested it to fund Coinmint's operations, but testified that he would have held formal meetings and solicited formal consents.

Second, Soniat infused the Company with significant funds from CLT. Consistent with their early understanding as consummated in the Operating Agreement that CLT would provide capital and Mintvest could consequently be diluted, and as a result of Leary's failure to object or demand otherwise, Soniat continued to fund Coinmint's operations while believing that those funds were categorized as dilutive capital contributions and that CLT was accruing a greater equity stake in the Company.

Soniat's belief was affirmed and reinforced by his negotiations with Leary and their mutual acknowledgement that CLT's contributions were, in fact, dilutive. Throughout 2017, Leary was aware of and acted on Soniat's belief that dilution was mutually accepted. When Leary agreed that Mintvest had been diluted and pressed his belief that it should be diluted no further than 18.2%, notwithstanding CLT's significant contributions, Soniat agreed that Mintvest's equity would be pegged at that percentage. CLT therefore agreed to categorize all future cash infusions as loans in order to preserve Mintvest's equity, and relied on Mintvest's agreement to the 81.8%–18.2% equity split in advancing tens of millions of dollars to Coinmint in the form of loans. As Soniat testified without contradiction or cross-examination, he never would have done that had there not been agreement that CLT was the 81.8% owner of Coinmint (as opposed to 50%), nor would it have made economic sense for him to do so. Accordingly, all of the elements of estoppel have been met.

c. *Mintvest Acquiesced In Being Diluted To 18.2%, Despite Section 3.2's Protections.*

As recognized by Vice Chancellor Glasscock, "[t]he doctrine of acquiescence effectively works an estoppel: where a plaintiff has remained silent with knowledge of her rights, and the defendant has knowledge of the plaintiff's silence and relies on that silence to the defendant's detriment, the plaintiff will be estopped from seeking protection of those rights." *Lehman Bros Hldgs, Inc. v. Spanish Broad Sys., Inc.* In order to prevail on an acquiescence defense, a defendant must show that (1) the plaintiff remained silent (2) with knowledge of her rights (3) and with the knowledge or expectation that the defendant would likely rely on her silence, (4) the defendant knew of the plaintiff's silence, and (5) the defendant in fact relied to her detriment on the plaintiff's silence. *Id.*

[. . .] These elements are satisfied here. Mintvest concedes as much, contesting only one element: that Mintvest had knowledge of its rights. [. . .] But as noted above, Leary was aware of the Operating Agreement's terms, and nothing indicates that Soniat or CLT acted to obscure Leary's right to invoke its protections. Instead, Leary actively solicited Soniat's funds, with objecting to their form or injection process, to quickly purchase equipment Leary ordered and believed was necessary for Coinmint's business. Leary knew that Mintvest had been diluted down to around 5.5% by the end of 2016, signing a capital statement reflecting that dilution.[. . .] Mintvest does not identify a single fact of which it was unaware, and therefore its sole defense to the application of the doctrine of acquiescence [. . .] fails. [. . .]

2. The Conversion Was Valid, And Coinmint Is A Puerto Rican Entity.

Mintvest challenges the Conversion on the basis that it "took place with neither the formal vote nor written consent of Mintvest['] [. . .] But Mintvest was diluted to an 18.2% Member, such that CLT's majority consent and correlating majority Manager vote could have effectuated the Conversion even over Mintvest's formal objection. Accordingly, the Conversion is a voidable act, and the same equitable principles that foreclose Mintvest from contesting its dilution also foreclose it from challenging the Conversion on the basis that it was not conducted in accordance with the Operating Agreement's procedural requirements.

A. The Conversion Is Voidable And Can Be Cured In Equity.

"The first step when analyzing a case involving the internal affairs of an LLC is . . . to examine the LLC agreement to determine whether it addresses the issue." If the agreement covers the issue, the agreement controls unless it violates one of the Act's mandatory provisions. If the agreement is silent, then the Court must look to the Act to see if one of its default provisions apply. If neither the agreement nor the Act addresses the matter, "the rules of law and equity shall govern." *Godden v. Franco.* [. . .]

Coinmint's Operating Agreement does not specify a manner of authorizing a conversion, so I turn to the Act. Section 18–216 of the Act governs conversion of a Delaware limited liability company. Section 18–216(b) supplies a default rule that is subject to contractual variation, not a mandatory rule. It provides:

> If the limited liability company agreement specifies the manner of authorizing a conversion of the limited liability company, the conversion shall be authorized as specified in the limited liability company agreement. *If the limited liability company agreement does not specify the manner of authorizing a conversion of the limited liability company and does not prohibit*

a conversion of the limited liability company, the conversion shall be authorized in the same manner as is specified in the limited liability company agreement for authorizing a merger or consolidation that involves the limited liability company as a constituent party to the merger or consolidation.

"The statute does not mandate that the company's conversion must be implemented pursuant to an agreement," and "[t]he omission of such a directive, and the concurrent absence of any statutory requirements . . . provide flexibility." *Symonds v. O'Toole.* Here, the parties availed themselves of Section 18–216's flexibility by subjecting conversion to the Operating Agreement's merger provisions. The Operating Agreement's relevant terms require two steps: majority Member consent under Section 4.6, followed by formal Board approval via meeting or written consent, under Sections 4.3(f) and 4.4. It is undisputed that the Managers did not approve the Conversion at a board meeting or secure written consents. But in view of CLT's majority stake and the interplay of Sections 4.3(f), 4.4, and 4.6, that failure renders the Conversion voidable under the Operating Agreement, rather than void.

Section 4.6 conditions the Board's power to effectuate a conversion on the consent of a "Majority of Members" who "in the aggregate, own more than fifty percent (50%) of the Sharing Ratios owned by all of the Members:"

> Notwithstanding anything to the contrary contained in this Agreement, without the consent of Majority of Members, neither the Board nor any Manager or Officer shall have the power or authority . . . . [t]o effect a merger or plan of exchange of the Company . . . .

[. . .] Mintvest's basis for voiding the Conversion is its unfounded position that it owned 50% of the Company in January 2018, and that CLT effectuated the Conversion without Leary's consent. But as stated, Mintvest was diluted to 18.2%, and CLT held 81.8%. CLT alone "own[ed] more than fifty percent (50%) of the Sharing Ratios owned by all of the Members," so CLT alone could give consent of the "Majority of Members." CLT did so. As a result, the Board retained the power to authorize the Conversion.

With majority Member consent, conversion must then follow Section 4.4, which provides that "all actions of the Board provided for here in shall be taken either at a meeting and evidenced by written minutes thereof . . . or by written consent without a meeting." And actions taken at a meeting or by written consent must comply with Section 4.3(f), which provides that "any Board action shall require the approval of a Majority of the Managers then serving on the Board," as keyed to the appointing Member's Sharing Ratio. Sections 4.3(f) and 4.4 do not include voiding language. If a conversion is challenged because the Board did not formally authorize it under Sections 4.3(f) and 4.4, that failure is voidable and subject to equitable defenses. CLT and Mintvest's failure to comply with Section 4.3 and 4.4's formalities on Coinmint's behalf is ratifiable because the Company could lawfully accomplish it "if it d[id] so in the appropriate manner." [. . .]

* * * * *

Because Mintvest waived Section 3.2's requirements, acquiesced in its dilution, and is estopped from asserting otherwise, I conclude that CLT's cash infusions were dilutive capital contributions, and that Mintvest's Sharing Ratio was pegged at 18.2% as of October 2017. With its voting power diluted, Mintvest also acquiesced to and is estopped from challenging the Conversion, which Mintvest participated in and CLT effectuated with its majority voting power, albeit without approving it by holding a formal vote or acting by written consent. Judgment is entered in CLT's favor on Count I.

C. REVERSE PIERCING THE CORPORATE VEIL

<h2 style="text-align:center">Manichaean Capital, LLC v.
Excela Technologies, Inc.</h2>

251 A.3d 694 (Del. Ch. 2021)

■ SLIGHTS, VICE CHANCELLOR. [. . .]

I.   BACKGROUND [. . .]

A.   Parties

Plaintiff, Manichaean Capital, LLC, a Delaware LLC, along with individual plaintiffs, [. . .] were equity holders in SourceHOV Holdings prior to its acquisition by Exela in a merger consummated on July 12, 2017.

Defendant, Exela, a Delaware corporation, sits atop a network of "resident and non-resident direct and indirect subsidiaries," many of which have been named as defendants here (the "Exela Subsidiaries"). Exela operates in the business process automation space. [. . . .]

The Exela network is depicted in the chart below:

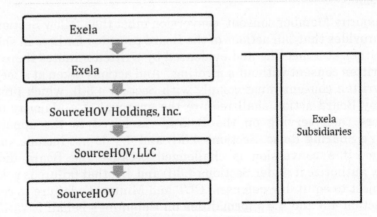

B.   The Merger

On July 12, 2017, SourceHOV Holdings merged with [a special purpose vehicle (SVP LLC) created by Exela to complete the acquisition of SourceHOV] [. . .] in a transaction whereby each share of SourceHOV Holdings common stock was converted into a right to receive one membership unit of [SPV] LLC (the "Merger"). Prior to the Merger, Plaintiffs held 10,304 shares of common stock in SourceHOV Holdings. [. . .]

[The Merger Agreement] declared that if a stockholder sought appraisal, [SPV] LLC would send that stockholder's equity interests in SourceHOV Holdings to Exela.

C.   The Appraisal Action

Plaintiffs expressly dissented with respect to the Merger and, on September 27, 2017, filed an appraisal action in this court (the "Appraisal Action"). [. . .] The Court entered its final judgment [in favor of the plaintiffs and valued their stake at $57,684,471 plus interest, significantly above the consideration they would have received in the Merger]. [. . .]

While the appeal was pending, Plaintiffs sent a demand letter to SourceHOV Holdings requesting immediate payment of the Appraisal Judgment. As of the filing of this lawsuit, none of that judgment had been paid. [. . .]

D.   The Charging Order

On July 15, 2020, Plaintiffs filed a Motion for Charging Order against SourceHOV Holding's membership interest in SourceHOV, LLC. The Court granted the Motion on August 15, 2020. The charging order mandated that "[a]ny and all distributions made by SourceHOV, LLC and payable to SourceHOV Holdings, Inc. in respect of SourceHOV Holdings, Inc.'s membership interest in SourceHOV, LLC shall be paid to [Plaintiffs]" (the "Charging Order"). In other words, to the extent Exela, as parent of SourceHOV Holdings, wishes to receive distributions from its subsidiaries below SourceHOV Holdings, any money that flows through SourceHOV Holdings must first be paid to Plaintiffs as SourceHOV Holdings' judgment creditors before it reaches Exela.

E.   The A/R Facility

On January 10, 2020, mere weeks before this Court's decision in the Appraisal Action, Exela, through its subsidiaries, entered into a $160 million accounts receivable securitization facility (the "A/R Facility"). [. . .] The A/R Facility permitted value once held by the SourceHOV Subsidiaries to be held by Exela's indirect subsidiary, allowing a diversion of funds around SourceHOV Holdings and directly into the coffers of Exela.

On January 10, 2020, mere weeks before this Court's decision in the Appraisal Action, Exela, through its subsidiaries, entered into a $160 million accounts receivable securitization facility (the "A/R Facility"). To facilitate the transaction, Exela created two entities, Exela Receivables Holdco LLC ("Receivables Holdco") and Exela Receivables I LLC ("Receivables I"). Under the First Tier Purchase and Sale Agreement, thirteen of the SourceHOV Subsidiaries sold their accounts receivable to Receivables Holdco. Then, under the Second Tier Purchase Agreement, Receivables Holdco sold those receivables to Receivables I. Under the Loan and Security Agreement, Receivables I then pledged the receivables as collateral for loans and letters of credit to be issued to Receivables I. More specifically, Receivables I pledged certain collection accounts, including sixteen "Interim Collection Accounts," all but three of which were accounts owned directly by the SourceHOV Subsidiaries. The A/R Facility permitted value once held by the SourceHOV Subsidiaries to be held by Exela's indirect subsidiary, allowing a diversion of funds around SourceHOV Holdings and directly into the coffers of Exela.

II. ANALYSIS

[. . .]

A. The Rationale for Statutory Appraisal

The creation of a statutory appraisal right was a significant step forward in the development of our corporate law. [. . .] The appraisal right granted under 8 *Del. C.* § 262 is a "statutory right . . . given [to] the shareholder as compensation for the abrogation of the common law rule that a single shareholder could block a merger." The right is significant and reflects the reality that our law now allows a corporation's majority owners to force a sale of the corporation, and the minority's equity in the corporation, without minority consent and even when the price paid in the transaction may be deemed by the minority to be inadequate. For this result to make sense, the dissenting shareholders must have a means to secure fair value through a proper appraisal of their shares. And, importantly, the dissenting shareholder should, absent compelling circumstances, actually *get paid* the fair value of "that which has been taken from him." Anything less frustrates the origin and purpose of the statutory appraisal remedy.

In the ordinary course, when judgment debtors fail to pay, the legal remedies of a charging order against a judgment debtor's LLC interests or a writ of execution against the judgment debtor's assets are available as tools for collection. This Opinion considers what options are available to the judgment debtor in an appraisal action if, after a plaintiff receives a writ of execution or charging order, an appraisal judgment is still left unpaid. In considering the question, it is useful to remember that in appraisal actions, it is the acquirer, not the target, who is "the real party in interest on the respondent's side of the case." [. . .]

C. Traditional Veil-Piercing

Plaintiffs allege that Exela's undercapitalization of its subsidiary (SourceHOV Holdings), lack of corporate separateness and subsequent attempts to divert funds away from SourceHOV Holdings to avoid the claims of its creditors provide ample bases to pierce SourceHOV Holdings' corporate veil to reach up the chain to Exela. "Delaware public policy disfavors disregarding the separate legal existence of business entities." With that said, in "exceptional case[s]," corporate veil-piercing is necessary and appropriate.

Delaware courts consider a number of factors in determining whether to disregard the corporate form and pierce the corporate veil, including: "(1) whether the company was adequately capitalized for the undertaking; (2) whether the company was solvent; (3) whether corporate formalities were observed; (4) whether the dominant shareholder siphoned company funds; and (5) whether, in general, the company simply functioned as a facade for the dominant shareholder." *Doberstein v. G-P. Indus., Inc.* While these factors are useful, any single one of them is not determinative. An ultimate decision regarding veil-piercing is largely based on some combination of these factors, in addition to "an overall element of injustice or unfairness." *Id.*

As to the specific factors, Plaintiffs make a compelling case in their Complaint that Exela and SourceHOV Holdings "operate[ ] as a single economic entity such that it would be inequitable for this Court to uphold a legal distinction between them." First, accepting the allegations in the Complaint as true, it is reasonably conceivable that SourceHOV Holdings is insolvent and that its insolvency, at least in part, is the result of Exela's undercapitalization of SourceHOV Holdings. Insolvency is adequately pled if a plaintiff's allegations allow a reasonable inference of either "(1) a deficiency of assets below liabilities with no reasonable prospect that the business can be successfully continued in the face thereof or (2) an inability to meet maturing obligations as they fall due in the ordinary course of business." SourceHOV Holdings is a holding company with no direct operating assets. In fact, its only asset is its membership interest in SourceHOV, LLC, which in turn holds interests in its solvent subsidiaries. SourceHOV Holdings has no bank account, money market account or brokerage account. With those facts as background, the Complaint alleges funds that once flowed up from the SourceHOV Subsidiaries to SourceHOV Holdings as a matter of course, are now bypassing SourceHOV Holdings and flowing directly to Exela. According to Plaintiffs, this arrangement was put in place by Exela and others while the likelihood that SourceHOV Holdings would face a substantial appraisal judgment was well known to all involved in the A/R Facility. Now that SourceHOV Holdings has no funds, and no prospect of securing funds, it is unable to meet its obligations as they become due, and it is at least reasonably conceivable that it will never be able to do so. The fact that certain of the SourceHOV Subsidiaries might be profitable, say Plaintiffs, does not suggest that SourceHOV Holdings itself is solvent, absent evidence that such money flows through SourceHOV Holdings, which, according to the Complaint, is not and may never again be the case.

The Complaint's case for veil-piercing does not rest on insolvency alone. It alleges that Exela was aware of SourceHOV Holdings' potential liability long ago and yet made a deliberate decision to undercapitalize the entity. Exela knew at the time it acquired SourceHOV Holdings that dissenting shareholders would be entitled to the fair value of their shares. Indeed, Exela recognized in its Form 10-K, filed on March 16, 2018, that there was a risk of a significant loss associated with the Appraisal Action. [. . .] Yet, notwithstanding its recognition of substantial exposure to the appraisal petitioners, Exela made the deliberate decision to avoid flowing funds through SourceHOV Holdings. With funds either remaining at the subsidiary level or potentially flowing around SourceHOV Holdings to Exela, there is no way for Plaintiffs to enforce their judgment against SourceHOV Holdings.

Beyond the apparently deliberate effort to starve SourceHOV Holdings of cash, Plaintiffs further allege that Exela failed to observe certain corporate formalities. Specifically, Plaintiffs allege that Exela: (1) is headquartered at the same address as SourceHOV Holdings, (2) has failed to maintain proper business registrations for SourceHOV Holdings, (3) has significantly overlapping personnel with SourceHOV Holdings, (4) has referred to Exela and its subsidiaries as one combined enterprise in SEC filings and (5) requires SourceHOV Holdings to obtain Exela's consent before SourceHOV Holdings may pay its own creditors.

With concerns about insolvency, undercapitalization and corporate formalities well pled, Plaintiffs turn next to the fraud and injustice associated with the A/R Facility. "Acts intended to leave a debtor judgment proof are sufficient to show fraud and injustice." Plaintiffs compellingly allege that fraud and injustice has resulted and will result from the diversion of funds from SourceHOV Holdings to Exela in an explicit attempt to avoid payment of the Appraisal Judgment. As mentioned, Exela knew that SourceHOV Holdings would be required to pay a judgment of some amount, at the latest, when Plaintiffs sent their appraisal demand in September 2017. The extent of that exposure became all too clear as the appraisal petitioners developed evidence, including expert valuation evidence, that the fair value of SourceHOV Holdings was exponentially greater than the price paid in the Merger. This evidence was presented at trial in June 2019, summarized in post-trial oral arguments in October 2019, then relied upon in the Court's post-trial decision issued on January 30, 2020. Yet, mere weeks before entry of the judgment, on January 10, 2020, Defendants entered into the A/R Facility.

[. . .] According to Plaintiffs' well-pled allegations, the receivables pledged were not Exela's to pledge and yet, as a result of the pledge, accounts receivable income that should flow up to SourceHOV Holdings no longer does.

[. . .] Taking Plaintiffs' well-pled characterization as fact, it is reasonably conceivable the A/R Facility was created in order deliberately to prevent funds from flowing through SourceHOV Holdings and to enable SourceHOV Holdings to avoid its obligations to creditors, including, and perhaps especially, Plaintiffs. Assuming the pled facts are true, it is reasonably conceivable that it is necessary to pierce the SourceHOV Holdings corporate veil to avoid fraud and injustice.

D. Reverse Veil-Piercing

[. . .] Delaware law allows for reverse veil-piercing in limited circumstances and in circumscribed execution.

1. The Mechanics of Reverse Veil-Piercing and its Proper Application

At its most basic level, reverse veil-piercing involves the imposition of liability on a business organization for the liabilities of its owners. In the parent/subsidiary context, "where the subsidiary is a mere alter ego of the parent . . . the Court [will] treat the assets of the subsidiary as those of the parent." *Spring Real Estate, LLC v. Echo/RT Hldgs., LLC.* As the doctrine has evolved, courts now recognize two variants of reverse veil-piercing: insider and outsider reverse veil-piercing. Insider reverse veil-piercing is implicated where "the controlling [member] urges the court to disregard the corporate entity that otherwise separates the [member] from the corporation." *SkyCable.* Outsider reverse veil-piercing is implicated where "an outside third party, frequently a creditor, urges a court to render a company liable on a judgment against its member." *Id.* Given Plaintiffs are creditors of SourceHOV Holdings, the single member and 100% owner of SourceHOV LLC, which in turn is the single member and owner of the SourceHOV Subsidiaries, and Plaintiffs seek to hold the subsidiaries liable for a judgment held against the member, this case concerns outsider veil-piercing. [. . .]

Courts declining to allow reverse veil-piercing have relied primarily, and understandably, on a desire to protect innocent parties. [. . .]

To start, reverse veil-piercing has the potential to bypass normal judgment collection procedures by permitting the judgment creditor of a parent to jump in front of the subsidiary's creditors. For obvious reasons, this dynamic would "unsettle the expectations of corporate creditors who understand their loans to be secured . . . by corporate assets" and could lead to corporate creditors "insist[ing] on being compensated for the increased risk of default posed by outside reverse-piercing claims." *Flyod v. I.R.S. U.S.* As (if not more) important, "to the extent that the corporation has other non-culpable shareholders, they obviously will be prejudiced if the corporation's assets can be attached directly." *Cascade Energy & Materials Corp. v. Banks.* Courts rejecting reverse veil-piercing have emphasized that the risk of harm to innocent stakeholders is often avoidable because judgment creditors can invoke other claims and remedies to achieve the same outcome. [. . .]

[. . .] In the traditional veil-piercing context, Delaware courts have forcefully stated that "Delaware has a powerful interest of its own in preventing the entities that it charters from being used as vehicles for fraud. Delaware's legitimacy as a chartering jurisdiction depends on it." *SkyCable, LLC v. DIRECTV, Inc.* [. . .]

Delaware embraces and will protect "corporate separateness;" but Delaware will not countenance the use of the corporate form as a means to facilitate fraud or injustice. Mindful of the need to balance these important policies [. . .], I am satisfied there is a place for a carefully circumscribed reverse veil-piercing rule within Delaware law.

In defining the rule, I begin by stressing that I am not endorsing "insider" reverse veil-piercing. The rule stated here applies only to "outsider" reverse veil-piercing. Also at the threshold, it must be emphasized that, just like with traditional veil-piercing, reverse veil-piercing should be sanctioned only in the most "exceptional circumstances." The framework outlined here to evaluate reverse veil-piercing claims comes with an express recognition that such claims, if not guided by appropriate standards, can threaten innocent third-party creditors and shareholders and lead to a host of unpredictable outcomes for these constituencies.

Only in cases alleging egregious facts, coupled with the lack of real and substantial prejudice to third parties, should the court even consider utilizing the reverse veil-piercing doctrine. With prejudice to third-parties in mind and a framework designed to deal with such concerns, however, reverse veil-piercing can act as a deterrent to owners of companies, particularly those that are closely held, from shuffling their assets among their controlled entities with the express purpose of avoiding a judgment.

The natural starting place when reviewing a claim for reverse veil-piercing are the traditional factors Delaware courts consider when reviewing a traditional veil-piercing claim—the so-called "alter ego" factors that include insolvency, undercapitalization, commingling of corporate and personal funds, the absence of corporate formalities, and whether the subsidiary is simply a facade for the owner.

The court should then ask whether the owner is utilizing the corporate form to perpetuate fraud or an injustice. This inquiry should focus on additional factors, including "(1) the degree to which allowing a reverse pierce would impair the legitimate expectations of any adversely affected shareholders who are not responsible for the conduct of the insider that gave rise to the reverse pierce claim, and the degree to which allowing a reverse pierce would establish a precedent troubling to shareholders generally; (2) the degree to which the corporate entity whose disregard is sought has exercised dominion and control over the insider who is subject to the claim by the party seeking a reverse pierce; (3) the degree to which the injury alleged by the person seeking a reverse pierce is related to the corporate entity's dominion and control of the insider, or to that person's reasonable reliance upon a lack of separate entity status between the insider and the corporate entity; (4) the degree to which the public convenience, as articulated by [the Delaware General Corporation Law and Delaware's common law], would be served by allowing a reverse pierce; (5) the extent and severity of the wrongful conduct, if any, engaged in by the corporate entity whose disregard is sought by the insider; (6) the possibility that the person seeking the reverse pierce is himself guilty of wrongful conduct sufficient to bar him from obtaining equitable relief;" (7) the extent to which the reverse pierce will harm innocent third-party creditors of the entity the plaintiff seeks to reach; and (8) the extent to which other claims or remedies are practically available to the creditor at law or in equity to recover the debt. Crespi, *The Reverse Perice Doctrine: Applying Appropriate Standards.* Fundamentally, reverse veil-piercing, like traditional veil-piercing, is rooted in equity, and the court must consider all relevant factors, including those just noted, to reach an equitable result.

Applying this framework, Delaware courts will be well-equipped to handle the varying concerns courts and commentators have rightfully expressed regarding reverse veil-piercing. The expectations of third-party creditors and investors will be well-protected. And the "public convenience" factor will require "the balancing of the social value of upholding the legitimate expectations of the affected corporate creditors or debtors, applying a rebuttable presumption in favor of assuring such expectations, against the importance of the policies served by allowing a reverse pierce under the particular circumstances involved." Crespi.

2. Plaintiffs' Reverse Veil-Piercing Claim Is Well-Pled

After carefully reviewing the Complaint, I am satisfied this is one of those "exceptional circumstances" where a plaintiff has well pled a basis for reverse veil-piercing. It is at least reasonably conceivable that the SourceHOV Subsidiaries are alter egos of SourceHOV Holdings and that the subsidiaries have actively participated in a scheme to defraud or work an injustice against SourceHOV Holdings creditors, like Plaintiffs, by diverting funds that would normally flow to SourceHOV Holdings away from that entity to Exela. At this stage, from the well pled allegations in the Complaint, I see no innocent shareholders or creditors of the SourceHOV Subsidiaries that would be harmed by reverse veil-piercing, nor any potential alternative claims at law or in equity, as against the SourceHOV Subsidiaries or SourceHOV Holdings itself, that would for certain remedy the harm.

Beginning with the "alter ego" factors, as previously discussed, the Complaint well-pleads facts that allow a reasonable inference that SourceHOV Holdings is insolvent and that it is undercapitalized. The Complaint also pleads a reasonably conceivable basis to conclude that corporate formalities have not been maintained since the Merger. As alleged, all of the Exela entities, including SourceHOV Holdings and the SourceHOV Subsidiaries, have overlapping personnel and directors and share the same offices; many of the SourceHOV Subsidiaries do not have updated corporate registrations; the entities have failed to maintain accurate or complete corporate records; Exela must give its approval before SourceHOV Holdings can pay debts; and all Exela-related entities have been collectively referred to as one Exela-controlled enterprise in SEC filings.

Turning to the broader fraud or injustice inquiry, the question here is whether the subsidiaries are being used to perpetuate fraud or injustice against a judgment creditor of their parent. Certain of the SourceHOV Subsidiaries' active participation in a potential fraudulent or unjust scheme, as pled, is evident with a glance at the First Tier Purchase and Sale Agreement associated with the A/R Facility. Under this agreement, thirteen of the SourceHOV Subsidiaries sold their receivables to another one of Exela's indirect subsidiaries. The Complaint alleges that the managers of these SourceHOV Subsidiaries knew about SourceHOV Holdings' inadequate capitalization and, knowing that certain of their proceeds would otherwise go to the judgment creditors of SourceHOV Holdings, they actively "divert[ed] assets away from SourceHOV by pledging certain accounts receivable as collateral for a $160 million accounts receivable security facility." As mentioned in the discussion of traditional veil-piercing, discovery will bear out whether (or not) Plaintiffs accurately describe the mechanics and purpose of the A/R Facility in the Complaint. For now, accepting those allegations as true, it is reasonably conceivable that certain SourceHOV Subsidiaries used the A/R Facility to prevent their proceeds from going to SourceHOV Holdings' judgment creditors. Specific allegations of intentional acts aimed at avoiding judgments through the use of legal constructs are sufficient to well plead fraud under traditional veil-piercing, and the review of such pled facts in support of a reverse veil-piercing claim is no different.

Finally, the Complaint well pleads a basis to infer that Plaintiffs will be able to satisfy the additional elements to sustain a reverse veil-piercing claim. [. . .]

Impairment of expectations of adversely affected shareholders. The Complaint pleads no basis to infer that other owners of SourceHOV Holdings or the SourceHOV Subsidiaries will be adversely affected by reverse veil-piercing. The SourceHOV Subsidiaries indirectly are wholly owned by SourceHOV Holdings, which in turn is wholly-owned by Exela. Thus, all entities involved in the alleged scheme to starve SourceHOV Holdings of funds are connected by unified ownership.

The exercise of dominion and control and degree to which that caused Plaintiffs' injury. According to the Complaint, Exela and certain of the SourceHOV Subsidiaries agreed to the A/R Facility without the involvement or consent, and to the detriment of, the dormant SourceHOV Holdings. This allows a pleading-stage inference of dominion and control causing injury to Plaintiffs sufficient to justify reverse veil-piercing.

The public convenience as articulated by the DGCL and Delaware Common Law. [. . .] Plaintiffs allege, "Exela and SourceHOV have retained all of the benefits of the [Merger] at issue in the Appraisal Action without paying compensation for Plaintiffs' dissenting shares and are using their corporate structure as a sham in an attempt to render SourceHOV 'judgment proof.' [. . .]" Reverse veil-piercing, in this circumstance, would serve the public convenience as expressed in Delaware's appraisal statute.

The extent of the wrongful activity. The Complaint well-pleads that Exela and the SourceHOV Subsidiaries (with SourceHOV Holdings' acquiescence) have initiated a scheme to ensure that Exela retains the significant value of Plaintiffs' ownership in pre-Merger SourceHOV Holdings, interest taken over Plaintiffs' dissent to the Merger, without paying a nickel for that equity. If true, this is the sort of wrongful conduct that justifies reverse veil-piercing.

Plaintiffs' wrongful conduct. [no evidence] [. . .]

Harm to innocent third-party creditors. [no evidence] [. . .]

III. CONCLUSION

For the foregoing reasons, the Motion to Dismiss [. . .] is DENIED. [. . .]Fiduciary Duties

Stephen Bushi, M.D. v. Sage Health Care, PLLC

203 P.3d 694 (Idaho 2009)

[. . .]

Factual Background and Procedural Background

In 1994, licensed psychiatrists, Charles C. Novak, Stephen T. Bushi, David A. Kent, and Cantril T. Nielsen, formed [Sage Health Care, PLLC], under the Idaho Limited Liability Act [. . .]. [. . .] Each of the original members contributed $2,000 and held a 25% interest in the LLC. Dr. Nielsen subsequently withdrew from Sage, and Dr. Roberto Negron acquired a 25% ownership interest in Sage.

All the members of Sage were signatories to the operating agreement, including amendments. The agreement vested equal management rights in the members. It provided that to amend its terms, consent of all but one of the members was required. It also addressed the grounds for dissociation of its members. Mandatory dissociation would occur if a member withdrew with the consent of the majority of the remaining members or with the death or decree of incompetency of a member. A member could be dissociated by a majority vote of the other members upon the happening of the following: bankruptcy of the member; attachment or levy upon the member's interest; the member's loss of professional license; a finding by the member's professional society that the member is guilty of an ethical violation; the member's inability to obtain professional liability insurance; or the member's conviction for a felony. The operating agreement also provided a calculation for determining the value of a member's interest upon dissociation.

Starting around 2002, Bushi began to date a nurse practitioner employed at Sage. This was not prohibited under the terms of the operating agreement; however, because the other members had concerns about potential liability stemming from the relationship, Sage arranged for Bushi to have no role in supervising the nurse practitioner.

In July 2003, Sage obtained a business line of credit loan from Wells Fargo Bank, which was intended to serve as a source of liquidity for Sage if and when it was needed. Sage never used the line of credit and never approved its use by any member. In October 2005, Respondents received correspondence from Wells Fargo indicating that nearly $45,000 had been borrowed on the line of credit at 15.5% interest. Respondents learned that Bushi had applied for and received funds on Sage's line of credit based solely on his signature; Respondents had not consented to or known about this extension of credit. The name on the line of credit account was listed as "Sage Health Care, PLLC Stephen Bushi," and Bushi maintains that he believed that this line of credit was his personal line of credit, not a business line of credit. After Respondents confronted him, Bushi admitted he had borrowed the funds on the line of credit and used them for his personal expenses. Respondents demanded he repay the funds to Wells Fargo.

At a members' meeting on October 27, 2005, Respondents, according to Bushi, informed him they wanted him out as a member of Sage because he was dating the nurse practitioner. [. . .] After this meeting, concerned about his future with Sage, Bushi joined another psychiatry group in November 2005. Bushi thought he was within his rights under the operating agreement to join the competing group. The minutes from a December 8, 2005 members' meeting reflect that Respondents voted to deny Bushi profit sharing in 2006, and that "one reason for him not being involved with the profit sharing was due to his connection with [Sage's] competitor." At this time, Respondents stopped scheduling Bushi to provide services for various Sage contracts in which he had previously been participating.

At that same December 8, 2005 meeting, Respondents also offered to buy out Bushi's share in Sage for a figure prepared by Sage's accountant and told Bushi he needed to decide whether to accept the offer by January 2006. Bushi thought the offer was "ridiculous" and told Respondents he would not comment on any amount until he had spoken to his attorney.

At a members' meeting on January 17, 2006, Respondents presented Bushi with a non-compete agreement that would have prohibited him from participating in any practice competing against them. In return, Bushi would be paid $15,000 for his withdrawal and dissociation from Sage and relinquishment of any and all rights of ownership in Sage. Following this meeting, Bushi's counsel wrote a letter to Respondents rejecting their offer and explaining that Bushi would continue as a member and retain his rights, including his right to a share in the profits of Sage, until a mutually satisfactory agreement had been reached.

On January 24, 2006, Respondents served Bushi notice that a members' meeting would be held on January 30, 2006. The notice stated that three items were on the agenda: an amendment to the operating agreement; following the amendment, the termination of the membership of a member pursuant to the operating agreement as amended; and continuation of the business. Bushi's counsel appeared at the meeting by proxy in Bushi's absence. At the meeting, Respondents voted to amend the operating agreement to require mandatory dissociation of a member upon an affirmative vote by all but one of the members. Following the amendment, Respondents voted—with Bushi dissenting—to dissociate Bushi, effective immediately. Applying the formula in the operating agreement, Sage's accountant determined that the value of Bushi's membership interest as of January 30, 2006 was $11,245.

In a letter dated July 11, 2006, Respondents sent two checks to Bushi, one for $11,245 (for his membership interest) and one for $5,138.27 (for his 2006 profit share and for the remainder of his 2005 profit share, the first part of which Bushi had directed be put towards paying off the Wells Fargo credit line). These were tendered as full payment upon Bushi's dissociation. By letter dated July 18, 2006, Bushi's attorney refused tender of the two checks and returned them.

As of June 6, 2006, Bushi had not paid off the Wells Fargo credit line and Sage continued to be liable for that loan. Respondents filed a civil action against Bushi in the Fourth Judicial District. After the suit was filed, Bushi paid all amounts due and owing to Wells Fargo, and Respondents dismissed the lawsuit.

Bushi filed the instant case on October 19, 2006, asserting claims for breach of fiduciary duty [. . .] and seeking declaratory relief and an equitable accounting. [. . .]

[. . .] Respondents asked the court to grant summary judgment as follows: declaring that Bushi's membership in Sage was properly terminated under the terms of the operating agreement as amended and the Idaho Limited Liability Company Act; declaring that the value of Bushi's membership was properly determined under the terms of the operating agreement and in compliance with the terms of the Idaho Limited Liability Company Act; declaring that the profits of Sage were properly determined and distributed among the members in accordance with the signed written agreements of the members regarding distribution of profits [. . .].

The district court granted Respondents' motion for summary judgment. [. . .]

Bushi timely appealed the district court's decision. [. . .]

Analysis

Bushi challenges the district court's grant of summary judgment as to his [. . .] breach of fiduciary duty. [. . .]

In order "[t]o establish a claim for breach of fiduciary duty, [a] plaintiff must establish that defendants owed plaintiff a fiduciary duty and that the fiduciary duty was breached." *Tolley v. THI Co.* Respondents do not contend that they did not owe Bushi fiduciary duties; rather, they assert that they did not breach those duties. Although this is not a disputed point of law, this Court has not yet directly addressed the question of whether members of a limited liability company owe each other fiduciary duties. Accordingly, we address this threshold question before considering whether there is a genuine issue of material fact whether there was a breach of Respondents' fiduciary duties to Bushi. [. . .]

Idaho's original act governing limited liability companies, the Idaho Limited Liability Company Act [. . .] identifies certain specific duties that members of an LLC owe to one another; however, it does not use the term "fiduciary," does not state that it is an exhaustive list of duties members owe one another, and does not address the conduct at issue in this case. In 2008, the legislature enacted comprehensive amendments to the statutory scheme through the Idaho Uniform Limited Liability Company Act. The new act states unequivocally that members of an LLC owe each other the fiduciary duties of loyalty and care. Until July 1, 2010, the original act governs all limited liability companies formed prior to July 1, 2008 that do not elect to be subject to the new act. Sage was formed prior to July 1, 2008, and this litigation began prior to the enactment of the new act. Thus, the original act governs this case.

While the original act does not expressly state that members of an LLC owe one another fiduciary duties, it does state that "[u]nless displaced by particular provisions of this chapter, the principles of law and equity supplement the provisions of this chapter." Idaho Code § 53–668(2). It appears that the majority of courts considering the issue have concluded that members of an LLC owe one another the fiduciary duties of trust and loyalty. *See* NTS Am.Jur.2d Limited Liability Companies § 11 (2008) (citing *McConnell v. Hunt Sports Ent.* (holding a limited liability company, like a partnership, involves a fiduciary relationship); *Purcell v. Southern Hills Investments, LLC* (holding that common law fiduciary duties, similar to the ones imposed on partnerships and closely-held corporations, are applicable to Indiana LLCs)). We conclude that, under Idaho's original LLC act, members of an LLC owe one another fiduciary duties.

Generally, whether a fiduciary has breached his duty is a question of fact. [. . .]

In addressing Bushi's claim for breach of fiduciary duty, the district court stated: Whether the other Sage Health Care Members owed a fiduciary duty to Bushi *under these circumstances and with respect to the buy-out offers* is debatable. By this statement, the district court seems to have been acknowledging that the question of whether Respondents breached their fiduciary duties to Bushi is a question of fact and that the facts surrounding Bushi's termination are disputed. The court went on to state however that breach of fiduciary duty is a tort claim and Bushi failed to introduce any case law that stands for the proposition that a breach of fiduciary duty precludes enforcement of a contract. This latter statement appears to reflect the trial courts view that summary judgment on this issue was appropriate as a matter of law, despite the existence of disputed facts, because those facts were not material in light of the legal conclusion. This was error.

While it is true that generally a member of an LLC is not liable to the LLC or any other member for actions taken in compliance with the operating agreement, the member must have relied on the provisions of the agreement in good faith. In *Schafer [v. RMS Realty]*, the Court of Appeals of Ohio considered whether Schafer, a minority partner in a realty partnership, had a claim for breach of fiduciary duty against the partnership and the other partners when, in compliance with the partnership agreement, the other partners issued a capital call that Schafer could not meet. Schafer's failure to meet the call triggered a provision in the partnership agreement that diluted the interest of any partner who could not meet a call. Schafer's interest decreased from twenty-five to nineteen percent pursuant to the dilution provision, and this result was, Schafer claimed, the true motivation for the call.

Like Respondents, the partners in *Schafer* urged that no breach of fiduciary duty had occurred since their actions were taken in compliance with the partnership agreement. [. . .] [However,] the *Schafer* court affirmed the jury's finding that the other partners breached their fiduciary duties to Schafer when they caused his ownership interest to be diluted:

> [W]hile the partnership agreement allowed the partners to vote for capital calls "as required for the purposes of the partnership," the majority's ability in this regard was "encumbered by [the] supreme fiduciary duty of fairness, honesty, good faith, and loyalty" to their minority partner. *Labovitz v. Dolan.*

Similarly, even if Respondents' actions in dissociating Bushi were technically in compliance with the terms of the operating agreement, this does not necessarily bar Bushi's claim for breach of fiduciary duty if those actions were improperly motivated.

Respondents offer a number of reasons why they terminated Bushi, including: their concern that Bushi's romance could subject them to potential liability under federal law; their view that Bushi's association with a competitor of Sage breached the operating agreement; and, finally, the fact that Bushi ran up approximately $60,000 in debt on Sage's line of credit without the knowledge or authorization of the other members of

Sage, also in breach of the operating agreement. Bushi, however, alleges that Respondents were motivated by financial gain. He points out that each member of Sage, in applying for the line of credit with Wells Fargo, valued his membership interest at $250,000. In contrast, Sage's accountant determined that Bushi's interest in Sage was $11,245 under the terms of the operating agreement governing dissociation of a member.

Drawing all reasonable inferences in Bushi's favor, this Court cannot conclude that there is no genuine issue of material fact as to Respondents' motivation in dissociating Bushi. A reasonable person could infer that Respondents acted in bad faith by removing Bushi from the LLC in order to advance their personal financial interests. If that were the case, Respondents would be liable to Bushi despite their technical compliance with the operating agreement. Accordingly, we vacate the district court's grant of summary judgment with respect to this issue and remand to the district court for further proceedings. [. . .]

D. DISSOLUTION

In re GR BURGR, LLC
C.A. No. 12825-VCS (Del. Ch. 2017)

■ SLIGHTS, VICE CHANCELLOR.

[. . .]

I. BACKGROUND

[. . .]

A. The Creation, Governance and Business of GRB

GRB is a Delaware limited liability company formed in December 2012 by [Gordon] Ramsay (through his entity GRUS) and Seibel [to develop and operate first-class burger-themes restaurants]. GRUS and Seibel each own a 50% membership interest in GRB. Each is entitled to designate one manager of GRB; GRUS appointed non-party Stuart Gillies and Seibel designated himself. The LLC Agreement gives the managers the "full and exclusive right, power and authority to manage all of the business and affairs of the Company." All decisions made by the managers require a majority vote—meaning the two managers must act unanimously. If the two managers cannot reach unanimous agreement, the LLC Agreement offers no mechanism by which to break that deadlock. The LLC Agreement provides that GRB will be dissolved upon or under the following events or circumstances: "(a) the LLC ceases its business operations on a permanent basis; (b) the sale or transfer of all or substantially all of the assets of the LLC; (a) [sic] the entry of a decree of judicial dissolution; or (b) [sic] as otherwise determined by the Managers."

[. . .]Along with the execution of the LLC Agreement, GRB and GRUS executed an agreement whereby GRUS licensed to GRB the trademark "BURGR Gordon Ramsay" (the "License Agreement"). [. . .]On December 13, 2012, GRB entered into the Caesars Agreement with Caesars, pursuant to which GRB provided to Caesars a sublicense to use the name "BURGR Gordon Ramsay," and a license to use certain recipes, menus and other trade property developed by GRB, for use in the "BURGR Gordon Ramsay" restaurant in Planet Hollywood. In exchange for the sublicense and license, Caesars agreed to pay GRB license fees based on a percentage of gross restaurant sales and gross retail sales. Since its formation, GRB has engaged in no other revenue-generating business aside from the Caesars Agreement and the corresponding BURGR Gordon Ramsay restaurant in Planet Hollywood. [. . .]

Caesars's businesses are subject to "privileged licenses," including those issued by the Nevada Gaming Commission. Due to certain requirements associated with these licenses, Caesars conditioned the rights and obligations of each party under the Caesars Agreement upon Caesars's satisfaction that GRB and its members, managers and affiliates are not (and do not become) "Unsuitable Person[s]." As defined in the Caesars Agreement, "Unsuitable Person" includes any person "whose affiliation with [Caesars] or its [a]ffiliates could be anticipated to result in a disciplinary action relating to, or the loss of, inability to reinstate or failure to obtain" the gaming and alcohol licenses held by Caesars or "who is or might be engaged or about to be engaged in any activity which could adversely impact the business or reputation of [Caesars] or its [a]ffiliates." The Caesars Agreement further provides that Caesars may make the determination that any person associated with GRB, its members, managers and affiliates is an "Unsuitable Person" in its "sole and exclusive judgment." Upon a determination of unsuitability,

> (a) Gordon Ramsay and/or GRB shall terminate any relationship with the [p]erson who is the source of such issue, (b) Gordon Ramsay and/or GRB shall cease the activity or relationship creating the issue to [Caesars's] satisfaction, in [Caesars's] sole judgment, or (c) if such activity or relationship is not subject to cure as set forth in the foregoing clauses (a) and (b), as determined by [Caesars] in its sole discretion, [Caesars] shall, without prejudice to any other rights or remedies of [Caesars] including at law or in equity, have the right to terminate [the Caesars Agreement] and its relationship with Gordon Ramsay and GRB.

B. Seibel is Convicted of Impeding the Administration of the Internal Revenue Code, Causing Caesars to Terminate the Caesars Agreement

[. . .][In 2016, Seibel was convicted of a felony tax-rated offense]. Following the sentencing, on September 2, 2016, Caesars sent a letter to GRB, Seibel and Ramsay stating that Seibel's felony conviction rendered him an "Unsuitable Person," and demanding, therefore, that "GRB, [ ] within 10 business days of the receipt of this letter, terminate any relationship with Mr. Seibel and provide Caesars with written evidence of such terminated relationship." The letter went on to state that "[i]f GRB fails to terminate the relationship with Mr. Seibel, Caesars will be required to terminate the [Caesars] Agreement pursuant to Section 4.2.5 of the [Caesars] Agreement."

Following receipt of the September 2 letter from Caesars, on September 6, 2016, GRUS sent a letter to Seibel's attorney requesting that Seibel "terminate *any* relationship" with GRB and "sign all necessary documents to confirm such termination." In response, Seibel proposed to transfer his interest in GRB to a family trust. Caesars, however, rejected the proposal on September 12, 2016, after it "determined that because the proposed assignees have direct and/or indirect relationships with Mr. Seibel, the proposed assignees are Unsuitable Persons," as defined in the Caesars Agreement. In a letter dated September 12, 2016, GRUS renewed its demand that Seibel completely disassociate from GRB and "fully comply with Caesars' requirements within their timeline." Seibel did not do so.

By letter dated September 21, 2016, Caesars terminated the Caesars Agreement because "[a]s of 11:59 p.m. on September 20, 2016, Caesars had not received any evidence that GRB had disassociated with Rowen Seibel, an individual who is an Unsuitable Person, pursuant to the [Caesars] Agreement." Based on the termination of the Caesars Agreement, GRUS sent GRB notice of its termination of the License Agreement on September 22, 2016.

C. Procedural Posture

GRUS filed its Petition [. . .] seeking the judicial dissolution and winding up of GRB pursuant to the terms of the LLC Agreement and Section 18–802. [. . .]

II. ANALYSIS

GRUS's motion for judgment on the pleadings requires the Court to determine whether the uncontested facts as admitted by Seibel in his Answer entitle GRUS to judicial dissolution of GRB as a matter of law. For the reasons that follow, I find that the deadlock between the parties, as evidenced by the undisputed facts, has rendered it no longer reasonably practicable for GRB to operate in accordance with its LLC Agreement. I also find no basis in equity to deny dissolution. [. . .]

B. Judicial Dissolution of an LLC Pursuant to 6 *Del. C.* § 18–802

GRB's LLC Agreement allows for dissolution of the Company pursuant to a judicial decree of dissolution under Section 18–802 which, in turn, provides that "[o]n application by or for a member or manager the Court of Chancery may decree dissolution of a limited liability company whenever it is not reasonably practicable to carry on the business in conformity with a limited liability company agreement." *6 Del. C. § 18–802.*

The "not reasonably practicable" standard does not require a petitioner to "show that the purpose of the limited liability company has been 'completely frustrated.'" *Fisk Ventures, LLC v. Segal.* Rather, "[t]he standard is whether it is reasonably practicable for [the company] to continue to operate its business in conformity with its LLC Agreement." *Id.* Our law provides no blueprint for determining whether it is "not reasonably practicable" for an LLC to continue, but "several convincing factual circumstances have pervaded the case law: (1) the members' vote is deadlocked at the Board level; (2) the operating agreement gives no means of navigating around the deadlock; and (3) due to the financial condition of the company, there is effectively no business to operate." *Id.* None of these factors are "individually dispositive; nor must they all exist for a court to find it no longer reasonably practicable for a business to continue operating." *Id.* While judicial dissolution of an LLC is a "discretionary remedy" that is "granted sparingly," "it has been granted 'in situations where there was 'deadlock' that prevented the [entity] from operating and where the defined purpose of the entity was . . . impossible to carry out.'" *Meyer Natural Foods LLC v. Duff.*

In setting up his argument that dissolution should not be ordered in this case, Seibel relies on this court's opinion in *In re Arrow Investment Advisors, LLC,* and argues that "[i]n applying only the undisputed facts to the law, the Court should also bear in mind that dissolution is an 'extreme' remedy of 'last resort' and that the Court's statutory power to order dissolution is 'limited.'" In doing so, he has only partially set the table because, while he quotes *Arrow Investment* correctly, he has not quoted it completely. After discussing the "limited" nature of the court's power to dissolve a Delaware entity, the court went on to explain the impact of management dysfunction and deadlock on the dissolution analysis:

> The court will not dissolve an LLC merely because the LLC has not experienced a smooth glide to profitability or because events have not turned out exactly as the LLC's owners originally envisioned; such events are, of course, common in the risk-laden process of birthing new entities in the hope that they will become mature, profitable ventures. In part because a hair-trigger dissolution standard would ignore this market reality and thwart the expectations of reasonable investors that entities will not be judicially terminated simply because of some market turbulence, *dissolution is reserved for situations in which the LLC's management has become so dysfunctional or its business purpose so thwarted that it is no longer practicable to operate the business, such as in the case of a voting deadlock or where the defined purpose of the entity has become impossible to fulfill. Id.*

As discussed below, Seibel has failed to account for the fact that he and Ramsay no longer speak and no longer make decisions for GRB. This dysfunction and voting deadlock has left the Company in a petrified state with no means in the LLC Agreement to break free.

Seibel also argues that equity should step in to prevent the dissolution of GRB even if the Court finds that it is "not reasonably practicable" for the Company to carry on its business in conformity with the LLC Agreement because "where one LLC member pursues dissolution to usurp a business opportunity or where he seeks to disenfranchise other LLC members for his personal and sole benefit, the requested dissolution should be denied." Seibel's appeal to equity to prevent a dissolution of GRB rings hollow, however, because the circumstance that has created the deadlock and the resulting need for dissolution is of his own making.

C. Insurmountable Deadlock at GRB Justifies Judicial Dissolution

GRUS's "primary legal argument supporting [its] request for judicial dissolution of GRB . . . is that the two 50% owners of GRB—GRUS and Seibel—are deadlocked as to the management of the Company and the Company's LLC Agreement provides no means for resolving that deadlock." In the context of judicial dissolution, "[d]eadlock refers to the inability to make decisions and take action, such as when an LLC agreement requires an unattainable voting threshold." Where there are two 50% owners of a company, an unbreakable deadlock can form a basis for dissolution even if the company is still engaged in marginal operations. In this regard, the decision in *Haley v. Talcott* is instructive. There, on a motion for summary judgment, the court ordered judicial dissolution of a LLC pursuant to Section 18–802 upon concluding that there was "deadlock between the parties about the business strategy and future of the LLC" with no reasonable exit mechanism, rendering the LLC unable to "function[ ] as provided for in the LLC Agreement." The company's only asset was a piece of real estate leased to a restaurant, and the parties could not agree about what to do with that land—one wanted to continue the lease with the restaurant and the other wanted to end the lease and sell the property. The two members had not interacted since a falling out and were engaged in other litigation relating to the LLC.

In analyzing the dispute, the court drew parallels between Section 18–802 and 8 *Del. C.* § 273 ("Section 273"), which governs the dissolution of joint venture corporations with two 50% owners. Section 273 "sets forth three pre-requisites for a judicial order of dissolution: 1) the corporation must have two 50% stockholders, 2) those stockholders must be engaged in a joint venture, and 3) they must be unable to agree upon whether to discontinue the business or how to dispose of its assets." *Haley v. Talcott.* The court found, by analogy, that all three of these pre-requisites were met where the parties were 50% members of the LLC, the parties intended to be and were engaged in a joint venture and the parties were at an impasse regarding how best to manage the LLC's lone asset. In so holding, the court noted that while the business was "technically functioning, this operation is purely a residual inertial status quo," *id.* and further noted that it was "not credible that the LLC could, if necessary, take any important action that required a vote of the members." *Id.* Therefore, after determining that the exit provision in the LLC agreement was not an adequate remedy in lieu of judicial dissolution, the court granted dissolution pursuant to Section 18–802 because it was "not reasonably practicable for the LLC to continue to carry on business in conformity with the LLC Agreement." *Id.*

Here, GRUS and Seibel are both 50% owners of GRB, each is entitled to appoint one manager, all decisions of the managers must be unanimous besides those relating to the License Agreement, and the LLC Agreement does not provide any mechanism to break a voting deadlock. The undisputed facts reveal that the relationship between GRUS and Seibel is, at best, acrimonious, as evidenced by the Counterclaims here, the Nevada Action and the litigation proceedings in New York stemming back to 2014. While the working relationship between the parties arguably had broken down prior to Seibel's felony conviction in 2016, the facts as admitted in the pleadings show clearly that whatever deadlock may have arisen prior to Seibel's conviction solidified to igneous rock thereafter.

Seibel was convicted and sentenced for impeding the administration of the Internal Revenue Code. Then, Caesars declared Seibel an "Unsuitable Person" and ordered GRB and GRUS to disassociate from him. When GRUS sought to comply with Caesars's direction by having Seibel voluntarily separate from GRB, Seibel refused. When Seibel proposed, as a compromise, that he would transfer his interest in GRB to a family trust, GRUS and Caesars both indicated that this was inadequate to cure the "Unsuitable Person" problem. When Caesars learned that Seibel remained at GRB after its disassociation deadline passed, it terminated the Caesars Agreement. It is difficult to imagine how GRB could be any more dysfunctional or deadlocked.

Given these undisputed facts, the notion that the deadlock might somehow be broken in the future is simply not reasonably conceivable. Ramsay, and his entity GRUS, no longer want to be associated with Seibel due to his felony tax-related conviction and the reputational damage that will flow from their continued connection with him. This circumstance will not change as future events unfold. It also distinguishes this case from the legion Delaware authority cited by Seibel to the effect that a party cannot seek dissolution simply to extricate himself from what he considers to a "bad deal." Here, GRUS and Seibel elected to do business together in the form of GRB, each presuming that the other was an honorable actor. This presumption was shattered when Seibel was convicted of a felony, especially one involving dishonesty. Tax fraud is not a Las Vegas moment. It should come as no surprise to Seibel that his conduct leading to that conviction will have consequences (here, as relates to GRB) that extend beyond his conviction and sentencing. This is especially so given that GRB's only revenue-generating business was in a casino, an enterprise that GRUS, Seibel and GRB knew was highly regulated.

Whether right or wrong, Caesars has determined in its "sole judgment" that Seibel is an "Unsuitable Person," a consequence from GRUS and GRB's perspective that is entirely of Seibel's own doing. GRUS finds itself in a lifeless joint venture that does not resemble the one it bargained for. The undisputed facts reveal that the parties will remain deadlocked without a mechanism in the LLC Agreement to break through. It is, therefore, "not reasonably practicable" for GRUS and Seibel to carry on GRB "in conformity with [the] limited liability company agreement." *6 Del. C. § 18–802. Fisk Ventures, LLC v. Segal.*

D. Equitable Principles do not Override the fact that Judicial Dissolution is Warranted

Seibel argues that even if GRUS has satisfied the "not reasonably practicable" standard for dissolution, the Court should decline to order dissolution at this pleadings stage as a matter of equity. He correctly points out that Section 18–802 provides that the court "may" grant dissolution where it is no longer reasonably practicable for the company to continue to operate in accordance with its operating agreement; the General Assembly appears deliberately to have chosen not to mandate that result. According to Seibel, the Court should invoke equity to deny the Petition because the dissolution is "being exploited tactically for an ulterior and inequitable purpose . . . [because GRUS is] pursu[ing] dissolution to usurp a business opportunity . . . [and] seeks to disenfranchise [the] other LLC member[ ] for [Ramsay's] personal and sole benefit." Specifically, Seibel alleges that:

> Ramsay's currently undisputed plan, which includes dissolution of GRB, is expressly designed to usurp GRB's entire BURGR Restaurant business by interfering with GRB's ability to pursue its business purpose. . . . Ramsay and Petitioner refused to consider additional corporate opportunities for GRB, or to meet with Seibel to discuss the potential opportunities, beginning in 2013. [. . .]

> Ramsay then colluded with [Caesars] to terminate the [Caesars Agreement], which then permitted Ramsay to terminate the License Agreement, thereby depriving GRB of two of its three principal assets: the [Caesars Agreement] under which the BURGR Restaurant operated in the Planet Hollywood hotel, and the License Agreement under which the BURGR Restaurant was marketed under the Gordon Ramsay name. Viewed in the light most favorable to Seibel, and prior to any discovery, the pleadings establish that Ramsay and [Caesars] decided to enable Ramsay to obtain the full profits of the

BURGR Restaurant by contriving an unsubstantiated finding that Seibel was an 'unsuitable' person. Ramsay and [Caesars] then rejected all efforts by Seibel to ameliorate and cure any perceived basis for an unsuitable person finding. And then based upon the contrived unsuitable person determination, the [Caesars Agreement] and, in turn, the License [Agreement] were terminated. GRB was deprived of these valuable assets without remuneration, but without depriving Ramsay or [Caesars] from continuing to market and operate the BURGR Restaurant in the Planet Hollywood hotel—which they have done and which has remained profitable.

Given this history, Seibel maintains that "[e]quity 'should not stand idle' . . . where the purpose of the dissolution is to aid the Petitioner in exploiting GRB's entire business for itself (or for its principal), and thus dissolution should be denied at this stage of the proceedings."

Seibel relies primarily upon this court's decision[ ] in *In re Mobilactive Media, LLC* [. . .] as support for the proposition that "equity" should step in to prevent the dissolution of GRB. In *Mobilactive Media*, the court rendered a post-trial decision finding the defendant liable for breach of fiduciary duties. The court then addressed defendant's petition for dissolution and summarily denied it upon concluding that the defendant was proffering the consequences of its own breach of fiduciary duty (the usurpation of corporate opportunities) as the primary basis for its argument that the business could no longer fulfill its designated purpose. Specifically, the court held that the defendant "should not be permitted to use its inequitable conduct to extricate itself from what it has long considered to be a bad deal with [plaintiff] and [the company] and simultaneously hinder [plaintiff] from recovering the damages he is due." Importantly, the court was concerned that the defendant was seeking to dissolve the entity before the defendant had paid the damages to the entity that the court had just ordered the defendant to pay for breaching his fiduciary duty. Needless to say, no such concern exists here. [. . .]

Seibel has pointed to nothing that would suggest that GRUS sought to dissolve or walk away from GRB prior to Seibel's conviction for tax fraud and Caesar's subsequent termination of the Caesar's Agreement. [. . .][T]he Petition at issue here is not the latest act in a long-playing drama where one member of a joint venture gins up any excuse imaginable to separate from the other. The deadlock here is temporally related to a series of events, caused by Seibel, that have rendered GRB no longer able to function.

A case not cited by Seibel, *In re Data Processing Consultants, Ltd.*, is especially informative in its discussion of the scope and utility of the court's equitable powers in the dissolution context. There, the court acknowledged that Section 273 allows the court to decline to order dissolution on equitable grounds even when the petitioner satisfies the statutory criteria for dissolution, but only in "narrow" circumstances where the petitioner has engaged in demonstrable "bad faith in the seeking of [ ] dissolution." The court emphasized that "such [equitable] power should be sparingly exercised." Citing *Data Processing*, this court has since illustrated the limited reach of the bad faith exception, ordering dissolution and the appointment of a receiver under Section 273 even in the face of allegations that the petitioner had engaged in past instances of usurpation of corporate opportunities because such instances did not adequately portend "specific future" harm that would justify perpetuating a dysfunctional joint venture.

Here, Seibel has failed to point to any "specific future" business opportunity that GRUS or Ramsay are seeking to exploit or any specific harm that will arise from the dissolution. This is unsurprising since Seibel has admitted that the only revenue-generating business that GRB has ever engaged in—the Caesars Agreement—was initiated in late 2012 when the Company was founded. Beyond referencing an opportunity that has now been terminated by the other party, Seibel has not identified any "specific future business opportunity" that rightfully belongs to GRB that GRUS is attempting to take for itself through the use of this dissolution proceeding. It is not enough for Seibel merely to state that Ramsay may, at some point in the future, engage in some other burger venture that uses his name and likeness to capitalize on the celebrity and status Ramsay has spent his career building. Seibel cannot reasonably expect that this court would indefinitely lock Ramsay in a failed joint venture and thereby preclude him from ever engaging in a business that bears resemblance to GRB—a restaurant business that exploits Ramsay's celebrity to sell one of the most popular and beloved food preparations in all of history. Any such result would be the antithesis of equitable.

Even if GRUS, Ramsay and Caesars have engaged in a scheme to usurp corporate opportunities from GRB and Seibel, as Seibel alleges, the scheme has already run its course—Caesars has terminated the Caesars Agreement and GRUS has terminated the License Agreement. Claims relating to these alleged harms can be prosecuted either individually by Seibel or derivatively by a receiver on behalf of GRB as appropriate. Given that this court will allow a dissolution to proceed even when there are first-filed derivative claims pending, there is no principled basis upon which to conclude that *later-filed* derivative claims alleging past harms should stand in the way of an otherwise properly supported petition for dissolution. Unlike in *Mobilactive*, Seibel has not alleged any facts that would allow a reasonable inference that he would not be able to recover fully any damages he is owed if dissolution is granted. Therefore, because Seibel has failed to allege bad faith in the bringing of the dissolution, but rather points only to prior bad acts that predate the Petition and were allegedly undertaken separate and apart from the Petition, equity will not preclude the entry of an otherwise justified decree of dissolution.

III. CONCLUSION

For the foregoing reasons, Petitioner's Motion for Judgment on the Pleadings is GRANTED and judicial dissolution is ordered pursuant to 6 *Del. C.* § 18–802. [. . .]

CHAPTER IX

SECURITIES LAW

A. SECURITIES DEFINED

Securities Act of 1933
Section 2(a)(1)

[. . .] The term "security" means any note, stock, treasury stock, security future, security-based swap, bond, debenture, evidence of indebtedness, certificate of interest or participation in any profit-sharing agreement, collateral-trust certificate, preorganization certificate or subscription, transferable share, investment contract, voting-trust certificate, certificate of deposit for a security, fractional undivided interest in oil, gas, or other mineral rights, any put, call, straddle, option, or privilege on any security, certificate of deposit, or group or index of securities (including any interest therein or based on the value thereof), or any put, call, straddle, option, or privilege entered into on a national securities exchange relating to foreign currency, or, in general, any interest or instrument commonly known as a "security", or any certificate of interest or participation in, temporary or interim certificate for, receipt for, guarantee of, or warrant or right to subscribe to or purchase, any of the foregoing.

Securities Exchange Act of 1934
Section 3(a)(10)

The term "security" means any note, stock, treasury stock, security future, security-based swap, bond, debenture, certificate of interest or participation in any profit-sharing agreement or in any oil, gas, or other mineral royalty or lease, any collateral-trust certificate, preorganization certificate or subscription, transferable share, investment contract, voting-trust certificate, certificate of deposit for a security, any put, call, straddle, option, or privilege on any security, certificate of deposit, or group or index of securities (including any interest therein or based on the value thereof), or any put, call, straddle, option, or privilege entered into on a national securities exchange relating to foreign currency, or in general, any instrument commonly known as a "security"; or any certificate of interest or participation in, temporary or interim certificate for, receipt for, or warrant or right to subscribe to or purchase, any of the foregoing; but shall not include currency or any note, draft, bill of exchange, or banker's acceptance which has a maturity at the time of issuance of not exceeding nine months, exclusive of days of grace, or any renewal thereof the maturity of which is likewise limited.

Kemmerer v. Weaver

445 F.2d 76 (7th Cir. 1971)

This suit was brought under the Securities and Exchange Act of 1933 and the Securities and Exchange Act of 1934 and Rule 10B–5 promulgated pursuant thereto. Plaintiffs claimed defendants offered for sale certain investment contracts wherein there was not a full, complete and fair disclosure of all the material facts.

Plaintiffs filed their complaint against the individual defendants together with defendant Weavers' Beaver Association, an agricultural cooperative, and American-Canadian Beavers Company, Inc., a Utah corporation, alleging that the plaintiffs were sold their investment contracts involving live, breeding beaver as a result of certain material misrepresentations and omissions upon which the plaintiffs relied.

[. . .] The trial court made findings of fact and conclusions of law and entered judgment holding that the Beaver contracts were investment contracts as defined by Section 3(a)(10) of the Securities and Exchange Act of 1934, and that material misrepresentations and omissions of fact were made in the sale of these securities to plaintiffs.

Defendants Mark Weaver, Ted Weaver, Van Weaver, Elizabeth Weaver Milligan, Jerry Milligan and Sally Weaver were judged to be liable to plaintiff Harold Kemmerer in the amount of $50,675.00 and to plaintiff Gordon Gregory in the amount of $9,300.00. Defendants Mark Weaver and Lawrence Milligan were judged to be liable to plaintiff Robert Albrecht in the amount of $12,200.00.

The record herein is voluminous consisting of five volumes of transcript plus many exhibits. A summary discloses that the Weavers' Beaver Association was organized as a Utah non-profit agricultural cooperative in 1957. Until late in 1964, the Weaver family had a majority of the directors of the Association. The Court dismissed this Association for lack of jurisdiction in that service of process had never been obtained. The trial court also found that defendant, American-Canadian Beaver Co., Inc., had no liability to plaintiffs and held that the individual appellants were the controlling persons of Weavers' Beaver Association.

The investment contracts were for the sale, care and resale of domestic breeding beaver which were claimed to have a large value in the fur industry. Defendants sold these beaver to plaintiffs and others for prices up to $1,200 each, representing that they were seventh generation domestic beaver, and further, representing that there existed a ready market for the resale of these animals.

Pursuant to the terms of the agreement, defendants were to have complete control in the care and feeding of the beaver, and were to select an appropriate market for resale. Due to the hoped for reproduction of the beaver, a 100% return within one year was guaranteed.

Instead of selling exclusively domestic beaver, defendants actually sold to plaintiffs and others, certain wild-trapped beaver which ranged in actual market value of from $20 to $75 each. Furthermore, there was no immediate market for resale as had been promised by defendants. Many purchasers were placed upon a one-year waiting list.

[. . .] We consider the most important issue in this case to be whether the contracts for the sale, care, feeding and ultimate resale of the beaver were investment contracts within the meaning of the Securities and Exchange Act.

This question already has been answered affirmatively in another suit against these same defendants for the same kind of an operation as hereinbefore described, and we agree with the holding and reasoning of that case. *Continental Marketing Corporation v. S.E.C.* The Court, in *Continental Marketing*, found that such contracts were investment contracts because the role of the investor was to supply capital with the hopes of a favorable return, and that, as such, they fit within the United States Supreme Court's definition of an investment contract in *S.E.C. v. W. J. Howey Co.* as "[. . .] a contract, transaction or scheme whereby a person invests his money in a common enterprise and is led to expect profits solely from the efforts of the promoter or a third party."

The *Howey* court further stated, in language most relevant to the present case, that the concept of an investment contract "embodies a flexible rather than a static principle, one that is capable of adaptation to meet the countless and variable schemes devised by those who seek the use of the money of others on the promise of profits." *Id.*

The investment scheme involved in the present case clearly qualified as an "investment contract" and hence a "security" as those terms have been construed by the United States Supreme Court in *Howey* and in *Tcherepnin et al. v. Knight.* The whole underlying format of the arrangement was that the purchaser of individual beavers was to put up the money and then "sit back and let nature take its course" or, more precisely, to "let things ride while (his) herd builds up and up and up", hoping ultimately to "sell the herd (or part of it), bank the profits and enjoy long-term capital gains." *Quotations from Sales Literature.* The words of the contracts and the duties set forth therein clearly contemplate an investment relationship, whereby the individual investors placed their money in the expertise of the defendants who would provide everything to make that investment grow. And, of course, as a practical matter, it would have been physically impossible for the average purchaser of live breeding beaver to take absolute possession of his animals. He would not have had the secret food formula, the special pen design, nor would he have known anything of the sexing and breeding of the beaver, all of which was to be provided by the Association. In short, the "investment by members of the public was a profit-making venture in a common enterprise, the success of which was inescapably tied to the efforts of the ranchers and the other defendants and not to the efforts of the investors." *Continental Marketing Corp. v. S.E.C.*

[. . .] [W]e [also] conclude that the record overwhelmingly supports the District Judge's conclusion that material misrepresentations occurred. Specifically, the Court found that Mark Weaver was purchasing wild trapped beaver at prices ranging from $20 to $75 each; that between 1950 and 1965 approximately 11,000 such wild beaver were purchased by defendants of which approximately one half were introduced into the herd; that there was no ready resale market for the beaver. These, and other facts, were not disclosed to or known by the plaintiffs in the present case when they purchased their beaver at prices ranging up to $2400 per pair. Nor did the plaintiffs have any way of knowing which beaver were domesticated and which were wild, that fact being known only to the defendants by means of a special tattoo mark which was not revealed until an SEC investigation of this operation began in 1966. We conclude that these and other misrepresentations and nondisclosures were clearly material, for they certainly prevented the present plaintiffs from knowing that the true value of their investment was considerably less than they had bargained for.

The judgment in favor of the plaintiffs is affirmed. [. . .]

B. REGISTRATION

Doran v. Petroleum Management Corp.
545 F.2d 893 (5th Cir. 1977)

[. . .]

I.   Facts

Prior to July 1970, Petroleum Management Corporation (PMC) organized a California limited partnership for the purpose of drilling and operating four wells in Wyoming. The limited partnership agreement provided for both "participants," whose capital contributions were to be used first to pay all intangible expenses incurred by the partnership, and "special participants," whose capital contributions were to be applied first to pay tangible drilling expenses.

[. . .] As found by the district court, PMC contacted only four other persons with respect to possible participation in the partnership. All but the plaintiff declined.

During the late summer of 1970, plaintiff William H. Doran, Jr., received a telephone call from a California securities broker previously known to him. The broker, Phillip Kendrick, advised Doran of the opportunity to become a "special participant" in the partnership. [. . .] PMC informed Doran that two of the proposed four wells had already been completed. Doran agreed to become a "special participant" in the Wyoming drilling program. In consideration for his partnership share, Doran agreed to contribute $125,000 toward the partnership. Doran was to discharge this obligation by paying PMC $25,000 down and in addition assuming responsibility for the payment of a $113,643 note owed by PMC to Mid-Continent Supply Co. Doran's share in the production payments from the wells was to be used to make the installment payments on the Mid-Continent note.

[. . .] During 1970 and 1971, PMC periodically sent Doran production information on the completed wells of the limited partnership. Throughout this period, however, the wells were deliberately overproduced in violation of the production allowances established by the Wyoming Oil and Gas Conservation Commission. As a consequence, on November 16, 1971, the Commission ordered the partnership's wells sealed for a period of 338 days. On May 1, 1972, the Commission notified PMC that production from the wells could resume on August 9, 1972. After August 9, the wells yielded a production income level below that obtained prior to the Commission's order.

Following the cessation of production payments between November 1971 and August 1972 and the decreased yields thereafter, the Mid-Continent note upon which Doran was primarily liable went into default. Mid-Continent subsequently obtained a state court judgment against Doran, PMC, and the two signatory officers of PMC for $50,815.50 plus interest and attorney's fees.

On October 16, 1972, Doran filed this suit in federal district court seeking damages for breach of contract, rescission of the contract based on violations of the Securities Acts of 1933 and 1934, and a judgment declaring the defendants liable for payment of the state judgment obtained by Mid-Continent.

The court below found that the offer and sale of the "special participant" interest was a private offering because Doran was a sophisticated investor who did not need the protection of the Securities Acts. The court also found that there was no evidence that PMC, its officers, or Kendrick made any misrepresentation or omissions of material facts to Doran. Finally, the court found that the overproduction of the wells was not a breach of the partnership agreement, but in any event there was no evidence that Doran suffered any losses as a result of the overproduction. The court concluded that all relief requested by Doran should be denied. Doran filed this appeal.

II. The Private Offering Exemption

No registration statement was filed with any federal or state regulatory body in connection with the defendants' offering of securities. Along with two other factors that we may take as established that the defendants sold or offered to sell these securities, and that the defendants used interstate transportation or communication in connection with the sale or offer of sale the plaintiff thus states a prima facie case for a violation of the federal securities laws.

The defendants do not contest the existence of the elements of plaintiff's prima facie case but raise an affirmative defense that the relevant transactions came within the exemption from registration found in § 4(2), 15 U.S.C. § 177d(2). Specifically, they contend that the offering of securities was not a public offering. The defendants, who of course bear the burden of proving this affirmative defense, must therefore show that the offering was private.

This court has in the past identified four factors relevant to whether an offering qualifies for the exemption. The consideration of these factors, along with the policies embodied in the 1933 Act, structure the inquiry. The relevant factors include the number of offerees and their relationship to each other and the issuer, the number of units offered, the size of the offering, and the manner of the offering. Consideration of these factors need not exhaust the inquiry, nor is one factor's weighing heavily in favor of the private status of the offering sufficient to ensure the availability of the exemption. Rather, these factors serve as guideposts to the court in attempting to determine whether subjecting the offering to registration requirements would further the purposes of the 1933 Act.

The term, "private offering," is not defined in the Securities Act of 1933. The scope of the § 4(2) private offering exemption must therefore be determined by reference to the legislative purposes of the Act. In *SEC v. Ralston Purina Co.*, *supra*, the SEC had sought to enjoin a corporation's offer of unregistered stock to its employees, and the Court grappled with the corporation's defense that the offering came within the private placement exemption. The Court began by looking to the statutory purpose:

> Since exempt transactions are those as to which "there is no practical need for . . . (the bill's) application," the applicability of (§ 4(2)) should turn on whether the particular class of persons affected need the protection of the Act. An offering to those who are shown to be able to fend for themselves is a transaction "not involving any public offering." 346 U.S. at 124.

According to the Court, the purpose of the Act was "to protect investors by promoting full disclosure of information thought necessary to informed investment decisions." *Id.* It therefore followed that "the exemption question turns on the knowledge of the offerees." *Id.* at 126–27. That formulation remains the touchstone of the inquiry into the scope of the private offering exemption. It is most nearly reflected in the first of the four factors: the number of offerees and their relationship to each other and to the issuer.

In the case at bar, the defendants may have demonstrated the presence of the latter three factors. [. . .]

Nevertheless, with respect to the first, most critical, and conceptually most problematic factor, the record does not permit us to agree that the defendants have proved that they are entitled to the limited sanctuary afforded by § 4(2). We must examine more closely the importance of demonstrating both the number of offerees and their relationship to the issuer in order to see why the defendants have not yet gained the § 4(2) exemption.

A.   The Number of Offerees

Establishing the number of persons involved in an offering is important both in order to ascertain the magnitude of the offering and in order to determine the characteristics and knowledge of the persons thus identified.

The number of offerees, not the number of purchasers, is the relevant figure in considering the number of persons involved in an offering. A private placement claimant's failure to adduce any evidence regarding the number of offerees will be fatal to the claim. The number of offerees is not itself a decisive factor in determining the availability of the private offering exemption. Just as an offering to few may be public, so an offering to many may be private. Nevertheless, "the more offerees, the more likelihood that the offering is public." *Hill York Corp. v. Amer. Int'l Franchies, Inc.* In the case at bar, the record indicates that eight investors were offered limited partnership shares in the drilling program a total that would be entirely consistent with a finding that the offering was private.

The defendants attempt to limit the number of offerees even further, however. They argue that Doran was the sole offeree because all others contacted by PMC were offered "participant" rather than "special participant" interests. The district court, which did not issue a finding of fact or conclusion of law with respect to this argument, appears to have assumed that there were eight offerees.

The argument is, in any event, unsupported by the record. [. . .]

In considering the number of offerees solely as indicative of the magnitude or scope of an offering, the difference between one and eight offerees is relatively unimportant. Rejecting the argument that Doran was the sole offeree is significant, however, because it means that in considering the need of the offerees for the protection that registration would have afforded we must look beyond Doran's interests to those of all his fellow offerees. Even the offeree-plaintiff's 20–20 vision with respect to the facts underlying the security would not save the exemption if any one of his fellow offerees was in a blind.

B.   The Offerees' Relationship to the Issuer

Since *SEC v. Ralston, supra,* courts have sought to determine the need of offerees for the protections afforded by registration by focusing on the relationship between offerees and issuer and more particularly on the information available to the offerees by virtue of that relationship. [. . .]

1. The role of investment sophistication

The lower court's finding that Doran was a sophisticated investor is amply supported by the record, as is the sophistication of the other offerees. Doran holds a petroleum engineering degree from Texas A&M University. His net worth is in excess of $1,000,000. His holdings of approximately twenty-six oil and gas properties are valued at $850,000.

Nevertheless, evidence of a high degree of business or legal sophistication on the part of all offerees does not suffice to bring the offering within the private placement exemption. We clearly established that proposition in *Hill York Corp.* We reasoned that "if the plaintiffs did not possess the information requisite for a registration statement, they could not bring their sophisticated knowledge of business affairs to bear in deciding whether or not to invest . . . ." Sophistication is not a substitute for access to the information that registration would disclose. [. . .]

[T]here must be sufficient basis of accurate information upon which the sophisticated investor may exercise his skills. Just as a scientist cannot be without his specimens, so the shrewdest investor's acuity will be blunted without specifications about the issuer. For an investor to be invested with exemptive status he must have the required data for judgment.

2. The requirement of available information

[. . .] The requirement that all offerees have available the information registration would provide has been firmly established by this court as a necessary condition of gaining the private offering exemption. [. . .]

[W]e shall require on remand that the defendants demonstrate that all offerees, whatever their expertise, had available the information a registration statement would have afforded a prospective investor in a public offering. Such a showing is not independently sufficient to establish that the offering qualified for the private placement exemption, but it is necessary to gain the exemption and is to be weighed along with the sophistication and number of the offerees, the number of units offered, and the size and manner of the offering. Because in this case these latter factors weigh heavily in favor of the private offering exemption, satisfaction of the necessary condition regarding the availability of relevant information to the offerees would compel the conclusion that this offering fell within the exemption. [. . .]

C. On Remand: The Issuer-Offeree Relationship

In determining on remand the extent of the information available to the offerees, the district court must keep in mind that the "availability" of information means either disclosure of or effective access to the relevant information. The relationship between issuer and offeree is most critical when the issuer relies on the latter route.

[. . .] [I]f the defendants could prove that all offerees were actually furnished the information a registration statement would have provided, whether the offerees occupied a position of access pre-existing such disclosure would not be dispositive of the status of the offering. [. . .]

Alternatively it might be shown that the offeree had access to the files and record of the company that contained the relevant information. Such access might be afforded merely by the position of the offeree or by the issuer's promise to open appropriate files and records to the offeree as well as to answer inquiries regarding material information. In either case, the relationship between offeree and issuer now becomes critical, for it must be shown that the offeree could realistically have been expected to take advantage of his access to ascertain the relevant information. Similarly the investment sophistication of the offeree assumes added importance, for it is important that he could have been expected to ask the right questions and seek out the relevant information.

In sum, both the relationship between issuer and offeree and the latter's investment sophistication are critical when the issuer or another relies on the offeree's "access" rather than the issuer's "disclosure" to come within the exemption. We shall first show that this formulation is consistent with the current state of private offering law in this and other circuits. Second, we shall examine the misconception that our cases require a privileged or "insider" relationship between issuer and offeree as a necessary condition of coming within the § 4(2) exemption. Once the distinction between "access" and "disclosure" is fully recognized, our caselaw should not be construed to embody such a requirement. [. . .]

IV. Conclusion

An examination of the record and the district court's opinion in this case leaves unanswered the central question in all cases that turn on the availability of the § 4(2) exemption. Did the offerees know or have a realistic opportunity to learn facts essential to an investment judgment? We remand so that the trial court can answer that question. [. . .]

We are conscious of the difficulty of formulating black letter law in this area in light of the multiplicity of security transactions and their multifarious natures. Securities regulation is often a matter of the hound chasing the hare as issuers devise new ways to issue their securities and the definition of a security itself expands. We do not want the private offering exemption to swallow the Securities Act, and we must resolve doubtful cases against the private placement claimant and in favor of the Act's paramount value of disclosure. By the same token, we must heed the existence and purposes of the exemption, and be cautious lest we discourage private avenues for raising capital. Our present emphasis on the availability of information as the sine qua non of the private offering is an attempt to steer a middle course.

We must reverse in part the judgment of the district court and remand for proceedings not inconsistent with this opinion. [. . .]

Escott v. BarChris Construction Corporation

283 F.Supp. 643 (S.D.N.Y. 1968)

This is an action by purchasers of 5 1/2 per cent convertible subordinated fifteen-year debentures of BarChris Construction Corporation (BarChris). Plaintiffs purport to sue on their own behalf and "on behalf of all other and present and former holders" of the debentures.

The action is brought under Section 11 of the Securities Act of 1933. Plaintiffs allege that the registration statement with respect to these debentures filed with the Securities and Exchange Commission [. . .] contained material false statements and material omissions.

Defendants fall into three categories: (1) the persons who signed the registration statement; (2) the underwriters, consisting of eight investment banking firms, led by Drexel & Co. (Drexel); and (3) BarChris's auditors, Peat, Marwick, Mitchell & Co. (Peat, Marwick).

The signers, in addition to BarChris itself, were the nine directors of BarChris, plus its controller, defendant Trilling, who was not a director. Of the nine directors, five were officers of BarChris, i.e., defendants Vitolo, president; Russo, executive vice president; Pugliese, vice president; Kircher, treasurer; and Birnbaum, secretary. Of the remaining four, defendant Grant was a member of the firm of Perkins, Daniels, McCormack & Collins, BarChris's attorneys. He became a director in October 1960. Defendant Coleman, a partner in Drexel, became a director on April 17, 1961, as did [. . .] Auslander [. . .] who [was] not otherwise connected with BarChris.

Defendants, in addition to denying that the registration statement was false, have pleaded the defenses open to them under Section 11 of the Act [. . .].

[. . .] On the main issue of liability, the questions to be decided are (1) did the registration statement contain false statements of fact, or did it omit to state facts which should have been stated in order to prevent it from being misleading; (2) if so, were the facts which were falsely stated or omitted "material" within the meaning of the Act; (3) if so, have defendants established their affirmative defenses? [. . .]

At the time relevant here, BarChris was engaged primarily in the construction of bowling alleys, somewhat euphemistically referred to as "bowling centers." [. . .] They contained not only a number of alleys or "lanes," but also, in most cases, bar and restaurant facilities.

[. . .] BarChris benefited from [an] increased interest in bowling [throughout the nation in the early 1950s]. Its construction operations expanded rapidly. It is estimated that in 1960 BarChris installed approximately three per cent of all lanes built in the United States. [. . .].

BarChris's sales increased dramatically from 1956 to 1960. According to the prospectus, net sales, in round figures, in 1956 were some $800,000, in 1957 $1,300,000, in 1958 $1,700,000. In 1959 they increased to over $3,300,000, and by 1960 they had leaped to over $9,165,000.

For some years the business had exceeded the managerial capacity of its founders. [Founders] Vitolo and Pugliese are each men of limited education. [. . .]

Rather early in their career they enlisted the aid of Russo, who was trained as an accountant. [. . .] He eventually became executive vice president of BarChris. In that capacity he handled many of the transactions which figure in this case.

In 1959 BarChris hired Kircher, a certified public accountant who had been employed by Peat, Marwick. He started as controller and became treasurer in 1960. In October of that year, another ex-Peat, Marwick employee, Trilling, succeeded Kircher as controller. At approximately the same time Birnbaum, a young attorney, was hired as house counsel. He became secretary on April 17, 1961.

In general, BarChris's method of operation was to enter into a contract with a customer, receive from him at that time a comparatively small down payment on the purchase price, and proceed to construct and equip the bowling alley. When the work was finished and the building delivered, the customer paid the balance of the contract price in notes, payable in installments over a period of years. [. . .]

[This strategy meant] BarChris was in constant need of cash to finance its operations, a need which grew more pressing as operations expanded.

In December 1959, BarChris sold 560,000 shares of common stock to the public at $3.00 per share. This issue was underwritten by Peter Morgan & Company, one of the present defendants.

By early 1961, BarChris needed additional working capital. The proceeds of the sale of the debentures involved in this action were to be devoted, in part at least, to fill that need. [. . .] [BarChris filed its registration statement for the debentures with the SEC on March 30, 1961.]

[By the time the company received the proceeds from its initial round of financing in May 1961,] BarChris was experiencing difficulties in collecting amounts due from some of its customers.

[. . .] In October 1962 BarChris came to the end of the road. On October 29, 1962, it filed in this court a petition for an arrangement under Chapter XI of the Bankruptcy Act. BarChris defaulted in the payment of the interest due on November 1, 1962 on the debentures.

A. The Debenture Registration Statement

In preparing the registration statement for the debentures, Grant acted for BarChris. [. . .]

Grant used [. . .] old registration statements as a model in preparing the new one, making the changes which he considered necessary in order to meet the new situation. The underwriters were represented by the

Philadelphia law firm of Drinker, Biddle & Reath. John A. Ballard, a member of that firm, was in charge of that work, assisted by a young associate named Stanton.

Peat, Marwick, BarChris's auditors, who had previously audited BarChris's annual balance sheet and earnings figures for 1958 and 1959, did the same for 1960. These figures were set forth in the registration statement. In addition, Peat, Marwick undertook a so-called "S-1 review," the proper scope of which is one of the matters debated here.

The registration statement in its final form contained a prospectus as well as other information. Plaintiffs' claims of falsities and omissions pertain solely to the prospectus [. . .].

The prospectus contained, among other things, a description of BarChris's business, a description of its real property, some material pertaining to certain of its subsidiaries, and remarks about various other aspects of its affairs. It also contained financial information. It included a consolidated balance sheet as of December 31, 1960, with elaborate explanatory notes. These figures had been audited by Peat, Marwick. It also contained unaudited figures as to net sales, gross profit and net earnings for the first quarter ended March 31, 1961, as compared with the similar quarter for 1960. [. . .]

Plaintiffs challenge the accuracy of a number of these figures. They also charge that the text of the prospectus, apart from the figures, was false in a number of respects, and that material information was omitted. [. . .]

[. . .] I find that the 1960 sales figure of $9,165,320, as stated in [. . .] the prospectus, was inaccurate in that it included [$653,900 worth of sales] which should not have been included. [. . .]

The total figure, instead of $9,165,320, should have been $8,511,420. [. . .]

The net operating income, instead of $1,742,801, should have been $1,496,196.

Since the net operating income figure was incorrect, it necessarily follows that [. . .] the earnings per share figure was incorrect. [. . .]

B. Materiality

It is a prerequisite to liability under Section 11 of the Act that the fact which is falsely stated in a registration statement, or the fact that is omitted when it should have been stated to avoid misleading, be "material." The regulations of the Securities and Exchange Commission pertaining to the registration of securities define the word as follows: "The term 'material' [. . .] limits the information required to those matters as to which an average prudent investor ought reasonably to be informed before purchasing the security registered."

What are "matters as to which an average prudent investor ought reasonably to be informed"? It seems obvious that they are matters which such an investor needs to know before he can make an intelligent, informed decision whether or not to buy the security. [. . .]

The average prudent investor is not concerned with minor inaccuracies or with errors as to matters which are of no interest to him. The facts which tend to deter him from purchasing a security are facts which have an important bearing upon the nature or condition of the issuing corporation or its business.

Judged by this test, there is no doubt that many of the misstatements and omissions in this prospectus were material. This is true of all of them which relate to the state of affairs in 1961, i.e., the overstatement of sales and gross profit for the first quarter, the understatement of contingent liabilities as of April 30, the overstatement of orders on hand and the failure to disclose the true facts with respect to officers' loans, customers' delinquencies, application of proceeds and the prospective operation of several alleys.

The misstatements and omissions pertaining to BarChris's status as of December 31, 1960, however, present a much closer question. The 1960 earnings figures, the 1960 balance sheet and the contingent liabilities as of December 31, 1960 were not nearly as erroneous as plaintiffs have claimed. But they were wrong to some extent, as we have seen. Would it have deterred the average prudent investor from purchasing these debentures if he had been informed that the 1960 sales were $8,511,420 rather than $9,165,320, that the net operating income was $1,496,196 rather than $1,742,801 and that the earnings per share in 1960 were approximately 65¢ rather than 75¢? According to the unchallenged figures, sales in 1959 were $3,320,121, net operating income was $441,103, and earnings per share were 33¢. Would it have made a difference to an average prudent investor if he had known that in 1960 sales were only 256 per cent of 1959 sales, not 276 per cent; that net operating income was up by only $1,055,093, not by $1,301,698, and that earnings per share, while still approximately twice those of 1959, were not something more than twice?

These debentures were rated "B" by the investment rating services. They were thus characterized as speculative, as any prudent investor must have realized. It would seem that anyone interested in buying these convertible debentures would have been attracted primarily by the conversion feature, by the growth potential of the stock. The growth which the company enjoyed in 1960 over prior years was striking, even on the correct figures. It is hard to see how a prospective purchaser of this type of investment would have been deterred from buying if he had been advised of these comparatively minor errors in reporting 1960 sales and earnings.

Since no one knows what moves or does not move the mythical "average prudent investor," it comes down to a question of judgment, to be exercised by the trier of the fact as best he can in the light of all the circumstances. It is my best judgment that the average prudent investor would not have cared about these errors in the 1960 sales and earnings figures, regrettable though they may be. I therefore find that they were not material within the meaning of Section 11.

The same is true of the understatement of contingent liabilities [. . .] by approximately $375,000. [. . .]

This leaves for consideration the errors in the 1960 balance sheet figures [. . .]. Current assets were overstated by approximately $600,000. Liabilities were understated by approximately $325,000 by the failure to treat the liability [on one of BarChris's construction projects] as a direct liability of BarChris on a consolidated basis. Of this $325,000 approximately $65,000, the amount payable on [that construction project] within one year, should have been treated as a current liability.

As per balance sheet, cash was $285,482. In fact, $145,000 of this had been borrowed temporarily from Talcott and was to be returned by January 16, 1961 so that realistically, cash was only $140,482. Trade accounts receivable were overstated by $150,000 by including [. . .] an alley which was not sold to an outside buyer.

As per balance sheet, total current assets were $4,524,021, and total current liabilities were $2,413,867, a ratio of approximately 1.9 to 1. This was bad enough, but on the true facts, the ratio was worse. As corrected, current assets, as near as one can tell, were approximately $3,924,000, and current liabilities approximately $2,478,000, a ratio of approximately 1.6 to 1.

Would it have made any difference if a prospective purchaser of these debentures had been advised of these facts? There must be some point at which errors in disclosing a company's balance sheet position become material, even to a growth-oriented investor. On all the evidence I find that these balance sheet errors were material within the meaning of Section 11.

Since there was an abundance of material misstatements pertaining to 1961 affairs, whether or not the errors in the 1960 figures were material does not affect the outcome of this case except to the extent that it bears upon the liability of Peat, Marwick. That subject will be discussed hereinafter.

C. The "Due Diligence" Defenses

Section 11(b) of the Act provides that:

> [. . .] no person, other than the issuer, shall be liable [. . .] who shall sustain the burden of proof—
>
> (3) that (A) as regards any part of the registration statement not purporting to be made on the authority of an expert [. . .] he had, after reasonable investigation, reasonable ground to believe and did believe, at the time such part of the registration statement became effective, that the statements therein were true and that there was no omission to state a material fact required to be stated therein or necessary to make the

statements therein not misleading; [. . .] and (C) as regards any part of the registration statement purporting to be made on the authority of an expert (other than himself) [. . .] he had no reasonable ground to believe and did not believe, at the time such part of the registration statement became effective, that the statements therein were untrue or that there was an omission to state a material fact required to be stated therein or necessary to make the statements therein not misleading [. . .].

Section 11(c) defines "reasonable investigation" [under the above provision] as follows: "[. . .] the standard of reasonableness shall be that required of a prudent man in the management of his own property."

Every defendant, except BarChris itself, to whom, as the issuer, these defenses are not available, and except Peat, Marwick, whose position rests on a different statutory provision, has pleaded these affirmative defenses. Each claims that (1) as to the part of the registration statement purporting to be made on the authority of an expert (which, for convenience, I shall refer to as the "expertised portion"), he had no reasonable ground to believe and did not believe that there were any untrue statements or material omissions, and (2) as to the other parts of the registration statement, he made a reasonable investigation, as a result of which he had reasonable ground to believe and did believe that the registration statement was true and that no material fact was omitted. As to each defendant, the question is whether he has sustained the burden of proving these defenses. Surprising enough, there is little or no judicial authority on this question. No decisions directly in point under Section 11 have been found.

Before considering the evidence, a preliminary matter should be disposed of. The defendants do not agree among themselves as to who the "experts" were or as to the parts of the registration statement which were expertised. [. . .] To say that the entire registration statement is expertised because some lawyer prepared it would be an unreasonable construction of the statute. Neither the lawyer for the company nor the lawyer for the underwriters is an expert within the meaning of Section 11. The only expert, in the statutory sense, was Peat, Marwick, and the only parts of the registration statement which purported to be made upon the authority of an expert were the portions which purported to be made on Peat, Marwick's authority.

The parties also disagree as to what those portions were. [. . .] The registration statement contains a report of Peat, Marwick as independent public accountants dated February 23, 1961. This relates only to the consolidated balance sheet of BarChris and consolidated subsidiaries as of December 31, 1960, and the related statement of earnings and retained earnings for the five years then ended. This is all that Peat, Marwick purported to certify. It is perfectly clear that it did not purport to certify the 1961 figures, some of which are expressly stated in the prospectus to have been unaudited. [. . .]

I turn now to the question of whether defendants have proved their due diligence defenses. [. . .]

1. Russo

Russo was [. . .] the chief executive officer of BarChris. He was a member of the executive committee. He was familiar with all aspects of the business. [. . .]

[. . .] It was Russo who arranged for the temporary increase in BarChris's cash in banks on December 31, 1960, a transaction which borders on the fraudulent. He was thoroughly aware of BarChris's stringent financial condition in May 1961. He had personally advanced large sums to BarChris of which $175,000 remained unpaid as of May 16.

In short, Russo knew all the relevant facts. He could not have believed that there were no untrue statements or material omissions in the prospectus. Russo has no due diligence defenses.

2. Vitolo and Pugliese

They were the founders of the business who stuck with it to the end. Vitolo was president, and Pugliese was vice president. Despite their titles, their field of responsibility in the administration of BarChris's affairs during the period in question seems to have been less all-embracing than Russo's. [.]

Vitolo and Pugliese are each men of limited education. It is not hard to believe that for them the prospectus was difficult reading, if indeed they read it at all.

But whether it was or not is irrelevant. The liability of a director who signs a registration statement does not depend upon whether or not he read it or, if he did, whether or not he understood what he was reading.

[. . .] All in all, the position of Vitolo and Pugliese is not significantly different [. . .] from Russo's. They could not have believed that the registration statement was wholly true and that no material facts had been omitted. And in any case, there is nothing to show that they made any investigation of anything which they may not have known about or understood. They have not proved their due diligence defenses.

3. Kircher

Kircher was treasurer of BarChris and its chief financial officer. He is a certified public accountant and an intelligent man. He was thoroughly familiar with BarChris's financial affairs. [. . .]

Moreover, as a member of the executive committee, Kircher was kept informed as to those branches of the business of which he did not have direct charge. He knew about the operation of alleys, present and prospective. [. . .] In brief, Kircher knew all the relevant facts.

Kircher worked on the preparation of the registration statement. He conferred with Grant and on occasion with Ballard. He supplied information to them about the company's business. He read the prospectus and understood it. [. . .]

Kircher's contention is that he had never before dealt with a registration statement, that he did not know what it should contain, and that he relied wholly on Grant, Ballard and Peat, Marwick to guide him. He claims that it was their fault, not his, if there was anything wrong with it. He says that all the facts were recorded in BarChris's books where these "experts" could have seen them if they had looked. He says that he truthfully answered all their questions. In effect, he says that if they did not know enough to ask the right questions and to give him the proper instructions, that is not his responsibility.

There is an issue of credibility here. In fact, Kircher was not frank in dealing with Grant and Ballard. He withheld information from them. But even if he had told them all the facts, this would not have constituted the due diligence contemplated by the statute. Knowing the facts, Kircher had reason to believe that the expertised portion of the prospectus, i.e., the 1960 figures, was in part incorrect. He could not shut his eyes to the facts and rely on Peat, Marwick for that portion.

As to the rest of the prospectus, knowing the facts, he did not have a reasonable ground to believe it to be true. On the contrary, he must have known that in part it was untrue. Under these circumstances, he was not entitled to sit back and place the blame on the lawyers for not advising him about it.

Kircher has not proved his due diligence defenses.

4. Trilling

Trilling's position is somewhat different from Kircher's. He was BarChris's controller. He signed the registration statement in that capacity, although he was not a director.

Trilling entered BarChris's employ in October 1960. He was Kircher's subordinate. When Kircher asked him for information, he furnished it. On at least one occasion he got it wrong.

Trilling was not a member of the executive committee. He was a comparatively minor figure in BarChris. [. . .]

Trilling may well have been unaware of several of the inaccuracies in the prospectus. But he must have known of some of them. As a financial officer, he was familiar with BarChris's finances and with its books of account. [. . .] I cannot find that Trilling believed the entire prospectus to be true.

But even if he did, he still did not establish his due diligence defenses. He did not prove that as to the parts of the prospectus expertised by Peat, Marwick he had no reasonable ground to believe that it was untrue. He also failed to prove, as to the parts of the prospectus not expertised by

Peat, Marwick, that he made a reasonable investigation which afforded him a reasonable ground to believe that it was true. As far as appears, he made no investigation. He did what was asked of him and assumed that others would properly take care of supplying accurate data as to the other aspects of the company's business. This would have been well enough but for the fact that he signed the registration statement. As a signer, he could not avoid responsibility by leaving it up to others to make it accurate. Trilling did not sustain the burden of proving his due diligence defenses.

5. Birnbaum

Birnbaum was a young lawyer, admitted to the bar in 1957, who [. . .] was employed by BarChris as house counsel and assistant secretary in October 1960. Unfortunately for him, he became secretary and a director of BarChris on April 17, 1961, after the first version of the registration statement had been filed with the Securities and Exchange Commission. He signed the later amendments, thereby becoming responsible for the accuracy of the prospectus in its final form.

Although the prospectus, in its description of "management," lists Birnbaum among the "executive officers" and devotes several sentences to a recital of his career, the fact seems to be that he was not an executive officer in any real sense. He did not participate in the management of the company. As house counsel, he attended to legal matters of a routine nature. [. . .]

One of Birnbaum's more important duties [. . .] was to keep the corporate minutes of BarChris and its subsidiaries. This necessarily informed him to a considerable extent about the company's affairs. [. . .]

It seems probable that Birnbaum did not know of many of the inaccuracies in the prospectus. He must, however, have appreciated some of them. In any case, he made no investigation and relied on the others to get it right. Unlike Trilling, he was entitled to rely upon Peat, Marwick for the 1960 figures, for as far as appears, he had no personal knowledge of the company's books of account or financial transactions. But he was not entitled to rely upon Kircher, Grant and Ballard for the other portions of the prospectus. As a lawyer, he should have known his obligations under the statute. He should have known that he was required to make a reasonable investigation of the truth of all the statements in the unexpertised portion of the document which he signed. Having failed to make such an investigation, he did not have reasonable ground to believe that all these statements were true. Birnbaum has not established his due diligence defenses except as to the audited 1960 figures.

6. Auslander

Auslander was an "outside" director, i.e., one who was not an officer of BarChris. [. . .] In February 1961 Vitolo asked him to become a director of BarChris. Vitolo gave him an enthusiastic account of BarChris's progress and prospects.

In February and early March 1961, before accepting Vitolo's invitation, Auslander made some investigation of BarChris. He obtained Dun & Bradstreet reports which contained sales and earnings figures for periods earlier than December 31, 1960. He caused inquiry to be made of certain of BarChris's banks and was advised that they regarded BarChris favorably. [. . .]

On March 3, 1961, Auslander indicated his willingness to accept a place on the board. Shortly thereafter, on March 14, Kircher sent him a copy of BarChris's annual report for 1960. Auslander observed that BarChris's auditors were Peat, Marwick. [. . .] He thought well of them.

Auslander was elected a director on April 17, 1961. The registration statement in its original form had already been filed, of course without his signature. On May 10, 1961, he signed a signature page for the first amendment to the registration statement which was filed on May 11, 1961. This was a separate sheet without any document attached. Auslander did not know that it was a signature page for a registration statement. He vaguely understood that it was something "for the SEC."

Auslander attended a meeting of BarChris's directors on May 15, 1961. At that meeting he, along with the other directors, signed the signature sheet for the second amendment which constituted the registration statement in its final form. Again, this was only a separate sheet without any document attached. Auslander never saw a copy of the registration statement in its final form.

At the May 15 directors' meeting, however, Auslander did realize that what he was signing was a signature sheet to a registration statement. This was the first time that he had appreciated that fact. A copy of the registration statement in its earlier form as amended on May 11, 1961 was passed around at the meeting. Auslander glanced at it briefly. He did not read it thoroughly.

At the May 15 meeting, Russo and Vitolo stated that everything was in order and that the prospectus was correct. Auslander believed this statement.

In considering Auslander's due diligence defenses, a distinction is to be drawn between the expertised and non-expertised portions of the prospectus. As to the former, Auslander knew that Peat, Marwick had audited the 1960 figures. He believed them to be correct because he had confidence in Peat, Marwick. He had no reasonable ground to believe otherwise.

As to the non-expertised portions, however, Auslander is in a different position. He seems to have been under the impression that Peat, Marwick was responsible for all the figures. This impression was not correct, as he would have realized if he had read the prospectus carefully. Auslander made no investigation of the accuracy of the prospectus. He relied on the assurance of Vitolo and Russo and upon the information he had received in answer to his inquiries back in February and early March. These inquiries were general ones, in the nature of a credit check. The information which he received in answer to them was also general, without specific reference to the statements in the prospectus, which was not prepared until some time thereafter.

It is true that Auslander became a director on the eve of the financing. He had little opportunity to familiarize himself with the company's affairs. The question is whether, under such circumstances, Auslander did enough to establish his due diligence defense with respect to the non-expertised portions of the prospectus.

Section 11 imposes liability in the first instance upon a director, no matter how new he is. He is presumed to know his responsibility when he becomes a director. He can escape liability only by using that reasonable care to investigate the facts which a prudent man would employ in the management of his own property. In my opinion, a prudent man would not act in an important matter without any knowledge of the relevant facts, in sole reliance upon representations of persons who are comparative strangers and upon general information which does not purport to cover the particular case. To say that such minimal conduct measures up to the statutory standard would, to all intents and purposes, absolve new directors from responsibility merely because they are new. This is not a sensible construction of Section 11, when one bears in mind its fundamental purpose of requiring full and truthful disclosure for the protection of investors.

I find and conclude that Auslander has not established his due diligence defense with respect to the misstatements and omissions in those portions of the prospectus other than the audited 1960 figures. [. . .]

8. Grant

Grant became a director of BarChris in October 1960. His law firm was counsel to BarChris in matters pertaining to the registration of securities. Grant drafted the registration statement for the stock issue in 1959 and for the warrants in January 1961. He also drafted the registration statement for the debentures. In the preliminary division of work between him and Ballard, the underwriters' counsel, Grant took initial responsibility for preparing the registration statement, while Ballard devoted his efforts in the first instance to preparing the indenture.

Grant is sued as a director and as a signer of the registration statement. This is not an action against him for malpractice in his capacity as a lawyer. Nevertheless, in considering Grant's due diligence defenses, the unique position which he occupied cannot be disregarded. As the director most directly concerned with writing the registration statement and assuring its accuracy, more was required of him in the way of reasonable investigation than could fairly be expected of a director who had no connection with this work.

There is no valid basis for plaintiffs' accusation that Grant knew that the prospectus was false in some respects and incomplete and misleading in others. Having seen him testify at length, I am satisfied as to his integrity. I find that Grant honestly believed that the registration statement was true and that no material facts had been omitted from it.

In this belief he was mistaken, and the fact is that for all his work, he never discovered any of the errors or omissions which have been recounted at length in this opinion, with the single exception of [one of BarChris's construction projects]. [. . .]

Grant contends that a finding that he did not make a reasonable investigation would be equivalent to a holding that a lawyer for an issuing company, in order to show due diligence, must make an independent audit of the figures supplied to him by his client. I do not consider this to be a realistic statement of the issue. There were errors and omissions here which could have been detected without an audit. The question is whether, despite his failure to detect them, Grant made a reasonable effort to that end.

Much of this registration statement is a scissors and paste-pot job. Grant lifted large portions from the earlier prospectuses, modifying them in some instances to the extent that he considered necessary. But BarChris's affairs had changed for the worse by May 1961. Statements that were accurate in January were no longer accurate in May. Grant never discovered this. He accepted the assurances of Kircher and Russo that any change which might have occurred had been for the better, rather than the contrary.

It is claimed that a lawyer is entitled to rely on the statements of his client and that to require him to verify their accuracy would set an unreasonably high standard. This is too broad a generalization. It is all a matter of degree. To require an audit would obviously be unreasonable. On the other hand, to require a check of matters easily verifiable is not unreasonable. Even honest clients can make mistakes. The statute imposes liability for untrue statements regardless of whether they are intentionally untrue. The way to prevent mistakes is to test oral information by examining the original written record.

There were things which Grant could readily have checked which he did not check. For example, he was unaware of the provisions of [some of BarChris's key] agreements. He never read them. [. . .]

[. . .] On the subject of minutes, Grant knew that minutes of certain meetings of the BarChris executive committee held in 1961 had not been written up. Kircher, who had acted as secretary at those meetings, had complete notes of them. Kircher told Grant that there was no point in writing up the minutes because the matters discussed at those meetings were purely routine. Grant did not insist that the minutes be written up, nor did he look at Kircher's notes. [. . .]

He knew that BarChris was short of cash, but he had no idea how short. He did not know that BarChris was withholding delivery of checks already drawn and signed because there was not enough money in the bank to pay them. He did not know that the officers of the company intended to use immediately approximately one-third of the financing proceeds in a manner not disclosed in the prospectus, including approximately $1,000,000 in paying old debts. [. . .]

Grant was entitled to rely on Peat, Marwick for the 1960 figures. He had no reasonable ground to believe them to be inaccurate. But the matters which I have mentioned were not within the expertised portion of the prospectus. As to this, Grant, was obliged to make a reasonable investigation. I am forced to find that he did not make one. After making all due allowances for the fact that Bar Chris's officers misled him, there are too many instances in which Grant failed to make an inquiry which he could easily have made which, if pursued, would have put him on his guard. In my opinion, this finding on the evidence in this case does not establish an unreasonably high standard in other cases for company counsel who are also directors. Each case must rest on its own facts. I conclude that Grant has not established his due diligence defenses except as to the audited 1960 figures.

9. The Underwriters

The underwriters other than Drexel made no investigation of the accuracy of the prospectus. [. . .] They all relied upon Drexel as the "lead" underwriter. Drexel did make an investigation. [. . .] Drexel's attorneys acted as attorneys for the entire group of underwriters. [. . .]

Like Grant, Ballard, without checking, relied on the information which he got from Kircher. He also relied on Grant who, as company counsel, presumably was familiar with its affairs.

[. . .] Coleman testified that Drexel had an understanding with its attorneys that "we expect them to inspect on our behalf the corporate records of the company [. . .]." Ballard manifested his awareness of this understanding by sending Stanton to read the minutes and the major contracts. It is difficult to square this understanding with the formal opinion of Ballard's firm which expressly disclaimed any attempt to verify information supplied by the company and its counsel.

In any event, it is clear that no effectual attempt at verification was made. The question is whether due diligence required that it be made. [. . .]

I have already held that this procedure is not sufficient in Grant's case. Are underwriters in a different position, as far as due diligence is concerned?

The underwriters say that the prospectus is the company's prospectus, not theirs. Doubtless this is the way they customarily regard it. But the Securities Act makes no such distinction. The underwriters are just as responsible as the company if the prospectus is false. And prospective investors rely upon the reputation of the underwriters in deciding whether to purchase the securities.

[. . .] The purpose of Section 11 is to protect investors. To that end the underwriters are made responsible for the truth of the prospectus. [. . .] To effectuate the statute's purpose, the phrase "reasonable investigation" must be construed to require more effort on the part of the underwriters than the mere accurate reporting in the prospectus of "date presented" to them by the company. [. . .] In order to make the underwriters' participation in this enterprise of any value to the investors, the underwriters must make some reasonable attempt to verify the data submitted to them. They may not rely solely on the company's officers or on the company's counsel. [. . .]

It is impossible to lay down a rigid rule suitable for every case defining the extent to which such verification must go. It is a question of degree, a matter of judgment in each case. In the present case, the underwriters' counsel made almost no attempt to verify management's representations. I hold that that was insufficient.

On the evidence in this case, I find that the underwriters' counsel did not make a reasonable investigation of the truth of those portions of the prospectus which were not made on the authority of Peat, Marwick as an expert. Drexel is bound by their failure. It is not a matter of relying upon counsel for legal advice. Here the attorneys were dealing with matters of fact. Drexel delegated to them, as its agent, the business of examining the corporate minutes and contracts. It must bear the consequences of their failure to make an adequate examination.

The other underwriters, who did nothing and relied solely on Drexel and on the lawyers, are also bound by it. It follows that although Drexel and the other underwriters believed that those portions of the prospectus were true, they had no reasonable ground for that belief, within the meaning of the statute. Hence, they have not established their due diligence defense, except as to the 1960 audited figures.

10. Peat, Marwick

[. . .] The part of the registration statement purporting to be made upon the authority of Peat, Marwick as an expert was [. . .] the 1960 figures. But because the statute requires the court to determine Peat, Marwick's belief, and the grounds thereof, "at the time such part of the registration statement became effective," for the purposes of this affirmative defense, the matter must be viewed as of May 16, 1961, and the question is whether at that time Peat, Marwick, after reasonable investigation, had reasonable ground to believe and did believe that the 1960 figures were true and that no material fact had been omitted from the registration statement which should have been included in order to make the 1960 figures not misleading.

It may be noted that we are concerned at this point only with the question of Peat, Marwick's liability to plaintiffs. [. . .]

11. The 1960 Audit

[. . .] Most of the actual work [to prepare the audit] was performed by a senior accountant, Berardi [. . .].

Berardi was then about thirty years old. He was not yet a C.P.A. He had had no previous experience with the bowling industry. This was his first job as a senior accountant. He could hardly have been given a more difficult assignment. [. . .]

It is unnecessary to recount everything that Berardi did in the course of the audit. We are concerned only with the evidence relating to what Berardi did or did not do with respect to those items which I have found to have been incorrectly reported in the 1960 figures in the prospectus. More narrowly, we are directly concerned only with such of those items as I have found to be material.

a. Capitol Lanes

First and foremost is Berardi's failure to discover that [Capitol Lanes, one of BarChris's construction projects] had not been sold. This error affected both the sales figure and the liability side of the balance sheet. [. . .] [EDS.—The court found that Berardi failed to realize that Capital Lanes was previously known as Heavenly Lanes. Berardi included Heavenly Lanes in a list of jobs that BarChris had completed. However, BarChris was still operating the location under the name Capitol Lanes, so no sale had actually occurred.]

[Berardi] never identified [the] mysterious [Capitol Lanes] with the Heavenly Lanes which he had included in his sales and profit figures. The vital question is whether he failed to make a reasonable investigation which, if he had made it, would have revealed the truth. [. . .]

The burden of proof on this issue is on Peat, Marwick. Although the question is a rather close one, I find that Peat, Marwick has not sustained that burden. [EDS.—The court concluded that Berardi did not adequately investigate certain records that suggested Heavenly Lanes and Capitol Lanes were the same location.] Peat, Marwick has not proved that Berardi made a reasonable investigation as far as Capitol Lanes was concerned and that his ignorance of the true facts was justified.

[. . .] Accountants should not be held to a standard higher than that recognized in their profession. I do not do so here. Berardi's review did not come up to that standard. He did not take some of the steps which Peat, Marwick's written program prescribed. He did not spend an adequate amount of time on a task of this magnitude. Most important of all, he was too easily satisfied with glib answers to his inquiries.

[. . .] [T]he burden of proof is on Peat, Marwick. I find that that burden has not been satisfied. I conclude that Peat, Marwick has not established its due diligence defense.

[. . .] Defendants' motions to dismiss this action [. . .] are denied.

C. FRAUD

Securities Exchange Act of 1934
Section 10(b)

It shall be unlawful for any person, directly or indirectly, by the use of any means or instrumentality of interstate commerce or of the mails, or of any facility of any national securities exchange—

(a) (1) To effect a short sale, or to use or employ any stop-loss order in connection with the purchase or sale, of any security other than a government security, in contravention of such rules and regulations as the Commission may prescribe as necessary or appropriate in the public interest or for the protection of investors. [. . .]

(b) To use or employ, in connection with the purchase or sale of any security registered on a national securities exchange or any security not so registered, [. . .] any manipulative or deceptive device or contrivance in contravention of such rules and regulations as the Commission may prescribe as necessary or appropriate in the public interest or for the protection of investors. [. . .]

Rules and Regulations Under the Securities Exchange Act of 1934
Rule 10b–5: Employment of manipulative and deceptive devices.

It shall be unlawful for any person, directly or indirectly, by the use of any means or instrumentality of interstate commerce, or of the mails or of any facility of any national securities exchange,

(a) To employ any device, scheme, or artifice to defraud,

(b) To make any untrue statement of a material fact or to omit to state a material fact necessary in order to make the statements made, in the light of the circumstances under which they were made, not misleading, or

(c) To engage in any act, practice, or course of business which operates or would operate as a fraud or deceit upon any person, in connection with the purchase or sale of any security.

Halliburton Co. v. Erica P. John Fund, Inc.
573 U.S. 258 (2014)

■ CHIEF JUSTICE ROBERTS delivered the opinion of the Court.

Investors can recover damages in a private securities fraud action only if they prove that they relied on the defendant's misrepresentation in deciding to buy or sell a company's stock. In *Basic Inc. v. Levinson*, we held that investors could satisfy this reliance requirement by invoking a presumption that the price of stock traded in an efficient market reflects all public, material information—including material misstatements. In such a case, we concluded, anyone who buys or sells the stock at the market price may be considered to have relied on those misstatements.

We also held, however, that a defendant could rebut this presumption in a number of ways, including by showing that the alleged misrepresentation did not actually affect the stock's price—that is, that the misrepresentation had no "price impact." The questions presented are whether we should overrule or modify *Basic*'s presumption of reliance and, if not, whether defendants should nonetheless be afforded an opportunity in securities class action cases to rebut the presumption at the class certification stage, by showing a lack of price impact.

I

Respondent Erica P. John Fund, Inc. (EPJ Fund), is the lead plaintiff in a putative class action against Halliburton and one of its executives (collectively Halliburton) alleging violations of section 10(b) of the Securities Exchange Act of 1934 and Securities and Exchange Commission Rule 10b–5. According to EPJ Fund, between June 3, 1999, and December 7, 2001, Halliburton made a series of misrepresentations regarding its potential liability in asbestos litigation, its expected revenue from certain construction contracts, and the anticipated benefits of its merger with another company—all in an attempt to inflate the price of its stock. Halliburton subsequently made a number of corrective disclosures, which, EPJ Fund contends, caused the company's stock price to drop and investors to lose money.

EPJ Fund moved to certify a class comprising all investors who purchased Halliburton common stock during the class period. The District Court found that the proposed class satisfied all the threshold requirements of Federal Rule of Civil Procedure 23(a): It was sufficiently numerous, there were common questions of law or fact, the representative parties' claims were typical of the class claims, and the representatives could fairly and adequately protect the interests of the class. And except for one difficulty, the court would have also concluded that the class satisfied the requirement of Rule 23(b)(3) that "the questions of law or fact common to class members predominate over any questions affecting only individual members." The difficulty was that Circuit precedent required securities fraud plaintiffs to prove "loss causation"—a causal connection between the defendants' alleged misrepresentations and the plaintiffs' economic losses—in order to invoke *Basic*'s presumption of reliance and obtain class certification. [. . .]

II

Halliburton urges us to overrule *Basic*'s presumption of reliance and to instead require every securities fraud plaintiff to prove that he actually relied on the defendant's misrepresentation in deciding to buy or sell a company's stock. Before overturning a long-settled precedent, however, we require "special justification," not just an argument that the precedent was wrongly decided. Halliburton has failed to make that showing.

A

Section 10(b) of the Securities Exchange Act of 1934 and the Securities and Exchange Commission's Rule 10b–5 prohibit making any material misstatement or omission in connection with the purchase or sale of any security. Although section 10(b) does not create an express private cause of action, we have long recognized an implied private cause of action to enforce the provision and its implementing regulation. To recover damages for violations of section 10(b) and Rule 10b–5, a plaintiff must prove "(1) a material misrepresentation or omission by the defendant; (2) scienter; (3) a connection between the misrepresentation or omission and the purchase or sale of a security; (4) reliance upon the misrepresentation or omission; (5) economic loss; and (6) loss causation." *Amgen Inc. v. Connecticut Retirement Plans & Trust Funds.*

The reliance element "ensures that there is a proper connection between a defendant's misrepresentation and a plaintiff's injury." *Id.* "The traditional (and most direct) way a plaintiff can demonstrate reliance is by showing that he was aware of a company's statement and engaged in a relevant transaction—*e.g.*, purchasing common stock—based on that specific misrepresentation." *Id.*

In *Basic*, however, we recognized that requiring such direct proof of reliance "would place an unnecessarily unrealistic evidentiary burden on the Rule 10b–5 plaintiff who has traded on an impersonal market." That is because, even assuming an investor could prove that he was aware of the misrepresentation, he would still have to "show a speculative state of facts, *i.e.*, how he would have acted . . . if the misrepresentation had not been made."

We also noted that "[r]equiring proof of individualized reliance" from every securities fraud plaintiff "effectively would . . . prevent [ ] [plaintiffs] from proceeding with a class action" in Rule 10b–5 suits. If every plaintiff had to prove direct reliance on the defendant's misrepresentation, "individual issues then would . . . overwhelm[ ] the common ones," making certification under Rule 23(b)(3) inappropriate.

To address these concerns, *Basic* held that securities fraud plaintiffs can in certain circumstances satisfy the reliance element of a Rule 10b–5 action by invoking a rebuttable presumption of reliance, rather than proving direct reliance on a misrepresentation. The Court based that presumption on what is known as the "fraud-on-the-market" theory, which holds that "the market price of shares traded on well-developed markets reflects all publicly available information, and, hence, any material misrepresentations." The Court also noted that, rather than scrutinize every piece of public information about a company for himself, the typical "investor who buys or sells stock at the price set by the market does so in reliance on the integrity of that price"—the belief that it reflects all public, material information. As a result, whenever the investor buys or sells stock at the market price, his "reliance on any public material misrepresentations . . . may be presumed for purposes of a Rule 10b–5 action."

Based on this theory, a plaintiff must make the following showings to demonstrate that the presumption of reliance applies in a given case: (1) that the alleged misrepresentations were publicly known, (2) that they were material, (3) that the stock traded in an efficient market, and (4) that the plaintiff traded the stock between the time the misrepresentations were made and when the truth was revealed.

At the same time, *Basic* emphasized that the presumption of reliance was rebuttable rather than conclusive. Specifically, "[a]ny showing that severs the link between the alleged misrepresentation and either the price received (or paid) by the plaintiff, or his decision to trade at a fair market price, will be sufficient to rebut the presumption of reliance." So for example, if a defendant could show that the alleged misrepresentation did not, for whatever reason, actually affect the market price, or that a plaintiff would have bought or sold the stock even had he been aware that the stock's price was tainted by fraud, then the presumption of reliance would not apply. In either of those cases, a plaintiff would have to prove that he directly relied on the defendant's misrepresentation in buying or selling the stock.

B

Halliburton contends that securities fraud plaintiffs should *always* have to prove direct reliance and that the *Basic* Court erred in allowing them to invoke a presumption of reliance instead. According to Halliburton, the *Basic* presumption contravenes congressional intent and has been undermined by subsequent developments in economic theory. Neither argument, however, so discredits *Basic* as to constitute "special justification" for overruling the decision. [. . .]

Halliburton's primary argument for overruling *Basic* is that the decision rested on two premises that can no longer withstand scrutiny. The first premise concerns what is known as the "efficient capital markets hypothesis." *Basic* stated that "the market price of shares traded on well-developed markets reflects all publicly available information, and, hence, any material misrepresentations." From that statement, Halliburton concludes that the *Basic* Court espoused "a robust view of market efficiency" that is no longer tenable, for "overwhelming empirical evidence [now] suggests that capital markets are not fundamentally efficient." To support this contention, Halliburton cites studies purporting to show that "public information is often not incorporated immediately (much less rationally) into market prices." [. . .]

Halliburton's criticisms fail to take *Basic* on its own terms. Halliburton focuses on the debate among economists about the degree to which the market price of a company's stock reflects public information about the company—and thus the degree to which an investor can earn an abnormal, above-market return by trading on such information. That debate is not new. Indeed, the *Basic* Court acknowledged it and declined to enter the fray, declaring that "[w]e need not determine by adjudication what economists and social scientists have debated through the use of sophisticated statistical analysis and the application of economic theory." To recognize the presumption of reliance, the Court explained, was not "conclusively to adopt any particular theory of how quickly and completely publicly available information is reflected in market price." The Court instead based the presumption on the fairly modest premise that "market professionals generally consider most publicly announced material statements about companies, thereby affecting stock market prices." *Basic*'s presumption of reliance thus does not rest on a "binary" view of market efficiency. Indeed, in making the presumption rebuttable, *Basic* recognized that market efficiency is a matter of degree and accordingly made it a matter of proof.

The academic debates discussed by Halliburton have not refuted the modest premise underlying the presumption of reliance. Even the foremost critics of the efficient-capital-markets hypothesis acknowledge that public information generally affects stock prices. Halliburton also conceded as much in its reply brief and at oral argument. Debates about the precise *degree* to which stock prices accurately reflect public information are thus largely beside the point. "That the . . . price [of a stock] may be inaccurate does not detract from the fact that false statements affect it, and cause loss," which is "all that *Basic* requires." Even though the efficient capital markets hypothesis may have "garnered substantial criticism since *Basic*," Halliburton has not identified the kind of fundamental shift in economic theory that could justify overruling a precedent on the ground that it misunderstood, or has since been overtaken by, economic realities. [. . .]

C

[. . .] Halliburton and its *amici* [also] contend that, by facilitating securities class actions, the *Basic* presumption produces a number of serious and harmful consequences. Such class actions, they say, allow plaintiffs to extort large settlements from defendants for meritless claims; punish innocent shareholders, who end up having to pay settlements and judgments; impose excessive costs on businesses; and consume a disproportionately large share of judicial resources.

These concerns are more appropriately addressed to Congress, which has in fact responded, to some extent, to many of the issues raised by Halliburton and its *amici*. Congress has, for example, enacted the Private Securities Litigation Reform Act of 1995 (PSLRA), which sought to combat perceived abuses in securities litigation with heightened pleading requirements, limits on damages and attorney's fees, a "safe harbor" for certain kinds of statements, restrictions on the selection of lead plaintiffs in securities class actions, sanctions for frivolous litigation, and stays of discovery pending motions to dismiss. [. . .]

III

[. . .] As noted, to invoke the *Basic* presumption, a plaintiff must prove that: (1) the alleged misrepresentations were publicly known, (2) they were material, (3) the stock traded in an efficient market, and (4) the plaintiff traded the stock between when the misrepresentations were made and when the truth was revealed. Each of these requirements follows from the fraud-on-the-market theory underlying the presumption. If the misrepresentation was not publicly known, then it could not have distorted the stock's market price. So too if the misrepresentation was immaterial[. . .] or if the market in which the stock traded was inefficient. And if the plaintiff did not buy or sell the stock after the misrepresentation was made but before the truth was revealed, then he could not be said to have acted in reliance on a fraud-tainted price.

The first three prerequisites are directed at price impact—"whether the alleged misrepresentations affected the market price in the first place." [. . .]

Halliburton argues that since the *Basic* presumption hinges on price impact, plaintiffs should be required to prove it directly in order to invoke the presumption. Proving the presumption's prerequisites, which are at best an imperfect proxy for price impact, should not suffice.

Far from a modest refinement of the *Basic* presumption, this proposal would radically alter the required showing for the reliance element of the Rule 10b–5 cause of action. What is called the *Basic* presumption actually incorporates two constituent presumptions: First, if a plaintiff shows that the defendant's misrepresentation was public and material and that the stock traded in a generally efficient market, he is entitled to a presumption that the misrepresentation affected the stock price. Second, if the plaintiff also shows that he purchased the stock at the market price during the relevant period, he is entitled to a further presumption that he purchased the stock in reliance on the defendant's misrepresentation.

By requiring plaintiffs to prove price impact directly, Halliburton's proposal would take away the first constituent presumption. Halliburton's argument for doing so is the same as its primary argument for overruling the *Basic* presumption altogether: Because market efficiency is not a yes-or-no proposition, a public, material misrepresentation might not affect a stock's price even in a generally efficient market. But as explained, *Basic* never suggested otherwise; that is why it affords defendants an opportunity to rebut the presumption by showing, among other things, that the particular misrepresentation at issue did not affect the stock's market price. For the same reasons we declined to completely jettison the *Basic* presumption, we decline to effectively jettison half of it by revising the prerequisites for invoking it. [. . .]

Even if plaintiffs need not directly prove price impact to invoke the *Basic* presumption, Halliburton contends that defendants should at least be allowed to defeat the presumption at the class certification stage through evidence that the misrepresentation did not in fact affect the stock price. We agree. [. . .]

There is no dispute that defendants may introduce such evidence at the merits stage to rebut the *Basic* presumption. *Basic* itself "made clear that the presumption was just that, and could be rebutted by appropriate evidence," including evidence that the asserted misrepresentation (or its correction) did not affect the market price of the defendant's stock.

Nor is there any dispute that defendants may introduce price impact evidence at the class certification stage, so long as it is for the purpose of countering a plaintiff's showing of market efficiency, rather than directly rebutting the presumption. [. . .]

Defendants—like plaintiffs—may accordingly submit price impact evidence prior to class certification. [. . .]

* * *

More than 25 years ago, we held that plaintiffs could satisfy the reliance element of the Rule 10b–5 cause of action by invoking a presumption that a public, material misrepresentation will distort the price of stock traded in an efficient market, and that anyone who purchases the stock at the market price may be considered to have done so in reliance on the misrepresentation. We adhere to that decision and decline to modify the prerequisites for invoking the presumption of reliance. But to maintain the consistency of the presumption with the class certification requirements of Federal Rule of Civil Procedure 23, defendants must be afforded an opportunity before class certification to defeat the presumption through evidence that an alleged misrepresentation did not actually affect the market price of the stock.

Because the courts below denied Halliburton that opportunity, we vacate the judgment of the Court of Appeals for the Fifth Circuit and remand the case for further proceedings consistent with this opinion.

West v. Prudential Securities, Inc.
282 F.3d 935 (7th Cir. 2002)

■ EASTERBROOK, CIRCUIT JUDGE.

According to the complaint in this securities-fraud action, James Hofman, a stockbroker working for Prudential Securities, told 11 of his customers that Jefferson Savings Bancorp was "certain" to be acquired, at a big premium, in the near future. Hofman continued making this statement for seven months (repeating it to some clients); it was a lie, for no acquisition was impending. And if the statement had been the truth, then Hofman was inviting unlawful trading on the basis of material non-public information. [. . .] What we must decide is whether the action may proceed, not on behalf of those who received Hofman's "news" in person but on behalf of *everyone* who bought Jefferson stock during the months when Hofman was misbehaving. The district judge certified such a class, invoking the fraud-on-the-market doctrine of *Basic, Inc. v. Levinson.* Prudential asks us to entertain an interlocutory appeal under Fed.R.Civ.P. 23(f). For two reasons, this is an appropriate case for such an appeal, which we now accept.

First, the district court's order marks a substantial extension of the fraud-on-the-market approach. *Basic* held that "[b]ecause most publicly available information is reflected in market price, an investor's reliance on any public material misrepresentations, therefore, may be presumed for purposes of a Rule 10b–5 action." The theme of *Basic* and other fraud-on-the-market decisions is that *public* information reaches professional investors, whose evaluations of that information and trades quickly influence securities prices. But Hofman did not release information to the public, and his clients thought that they were receiving and acting on non-public information; its value (if any) lay precisely in the fact that other traders did not know the news. No newspaper or other organ of general circulation reported that Jefferson was soon to be acquired. As plaintiffs summarize their position, their "argument in a nutshell is that it is unimportant for purposes of the fraud-on-the-market doctrine whether the information was "publicly available" in the . . . sense that . . . the information was disseminated through a press release, or prospectus or other written format". Yet extending the fraud-on-the-market doctrine in this way requires not only a departure from *Basic* but also a novelty in fraud cases as a class—as another court of appeals remarked only recently in another securities suit, oral frauds have not been allowed to proceed as class actions, for the details of the deceit differ from victim to victim, and the nature of the loss also may be statement-specific. The appeal thus presents a novel and potentially important question of law.

Second, very few securities class actions are litigated to conclusion, so review of this novel and important legal issue may be possible only through the Rule 23(f) device. [. . .]

Because the parties' papers have developed their positions fully, and the district court has set a trial date less than two months away, we think it best to resolve the appeal promptly, and thus we turn to the merits.

Causation is the shortcoming in this class certification. *Basic* describes a mechanism by which public information affects stock prices, and thus may affect traders who did not know about that information. Professional investors monitor news about many firms; good news implies higher dividends and other benefits, which induces these investors to value the stock more highly, and they continue buying until the gains are exhausted. With many professional investors alert to news, markets are efficient in the sense that they rapidly adjust to all public information; if some of this information is false, the price will reach an incorrect level, staying there until the truth emerges. This approach has the support of financial economics as well as the imprimatur of the Justices: few propositions in economics are better established than the quick adjustment of securities prices to public information.

No similar mechanism explains how prices would respond to non-public information, such as statements made by Hofman to a handful of his clients. These do not come to the attention of professional investors or money managers, so the price-adjustment mechanism just described does not operate. Sometimes full-time market watchers can infer important news from the identity of a trader (when the corporation's CEO goes on a buying spree, this implies good news) or from the sheer volume of trades (an unprecedented buying volume may suggest that a bidder is accumulating stock in anticipation of a tender offer), but neither the identity of Hofman's customers nor the volume of their trades would have conveyed information to the market in this fashion. No one these days accepts the strongest version of the efficient capital market hypothesis, under which non-public information automatically affects prices. That version is empirically false: the public announcement of news (good and bad) has big effects on stock prices, which could not happen if prices already incorporated the effect of non-public information. Thus it is hard to see how Hofman's non-public statements could have caused changes in the price of Jefferson Savings stock. *Basic* founded the fraud-on-the-market doctrine on a causal mechanism with both theoretical and empirical power; for non-public information there is nothing comparable.

The district court did not identify any causal link between non-public information and securities prices, let alone show that the link is as strong as the one deemed sufficient (by a bare majority) in *Basic* (only four of the six Justices who participated in that case endorsed the fraud-on-the-market doctrine). [. . .]

Because the record here does not demonstrate that non-public information affected the price of Jefferson Savings' stock, a remand is unnecessary. What the plaintiffs have going for them is that Jefferson's stock *did* rise in price (by about $5, or 20% of its trading price) during the months when Hofman was touting an impending acquisition, plus a model of demand-pull price increases offered by their expert. Barclay[, a reputable financial economist for the plaintiffs,] started with a model devised by another economist, [Joel Hasbrouck,] in which trades themselves convey information to the market and thus affect price. Hasbrouck's model assumes that some trades are by informed traders and some by uninformed traders, and that the market may be able to draw inferences about which is which. The model has not been verified empirically. Barclay approached the issue differently, assuming that *all* trades affect prices by raising demand even if no trader is well informed—as if there were an economic market in "Jefferson Savings stock" as there is in dill pickles or fluffy towels. Hofman's tips raised the demand for Jefferson Savings stock and curtailed the supply (for the tippees were less likely to sell their own shares); that combination of effects raised the stock's price. Yet investors do not want Jefferson Savings *stock* (as if they sought to paper their walls with beautiful certificates); they want monetary returns (at given risk levels), returns that are available from many financial instruments. One fundamental attribute of efficient markets is that *information,* not demand in the abstract, determines stock prices. There are so many substitutes for any one firm's stock that the effective demand curve is horizontal. It may shift up or down with new information but is not sloped like the demand curve for physical products. That is why institutional purchases (which can be large in relation to normal trading volume) do not elevate prices, while relatively small trades by insiders can have substantial effects; the latter trades convey information, and the former do not. Barclay, who took the view that the market for Jefferson Savings securities is efficient, did not explain why he departed from the normal understanding that information rather than raw demand determines securities prices.

Data may upset theory, and if Barclay had demonstrated that demand by itself elevates securities prices, then the courts would be required to attend closely. What Barclay did is inquire whether the price of Jefferson Savings stock rose during the period of additional demand by Hofman's customers. He gave an affirmative answer and stopped. Yet it is not possible to prove a relation between demand and price without considering *other* potential reasons. Was there perhaps some truthful Jefferson-specific information released to the market at the time? Did Jefferson perhaps move *with* the market? It rose relative to a basket of all financial institutions, but (according to Cox's report) not relative to a portfolio of Midwestern financial intermediaries. Several Missouri banks and thrifts similar to Jefferson Savings were acquired during the months in question, and these transactions conveyed some information about the probability of a deal involving Jefferson Savings. If the price of Jefferson Savings was doing just what one would have expected in the presence of this changing probability of acquisition, and the absence of any Hofman-induced trades, then the causal link between Hofman's statements and price has not been made out. By failing to test for and exclude other potential sources of price movement, Barclay undercut the power of the inference that he advanced.

Indeed, Barclay's report calls into question his belief that the market for Jefferson Savings stock is efficient, the foundation of the fraud-on-the-market doctrine. In an efficient market, how could *one* ignorant outsider's lie cause a long-term rise in price? Professional investors would notice the inexplicable rise and either investigate for themselves (discovering the truth) or sell short immediately, driving the price back down. In an efficient market, a lie told by someone with nothing to back up the statement (no professional would have thought Hofman a person "in the know") will self-destruct long before eight months have passed. Hofman asserted that an acquisition was imminent. That statement might gull people for a month, but after two or three months have passed the lack of a merger or tender offer puts the lie to the assertion; professional investors then draw more astute inferences and the price effect disappears. That this did not occur implies either that Jefferson Savings was not closely followed by professional investors (and that the market therefore does not satisfy *Basic*'s efficiency requirement) or that something other than Hofman's statements explains these price changes.

The record thus does not support extension of the fraud-on-the-market doctrine to the non-public statements Hofman is alleged to have made about Jefferson Savings Bancorp. The order certifying a class is REVERSED.

Santa Fe Industries, Inc. v. Green
430 U.S. 462 (1977)

■ MR. JUSTICE WHITE, delivered the opinion of the Court.

[. . .] In 1936, petitioner Santa Fe Industries, Inc. (Santa Fe), acquired control of 60% of the stock of Kirby Lumber Corp. (Kirby), a Delaware corporation. Through a series of purchases over the succeeding years, Santa Fe increased its control of Kirby's stock to 95%; the purchase prices during the period 1968–1973 ranged from $65 to $92.50 per share. In 1974, wishing to acquire 100% ownership of Kirby, Santa Fe availed itself of § 253 of the Delaware Corporation Law, known as the "short-form merger" statute. Section 253 permits a parent corporation owning at least 90% of the stock of a subsidiary to merge with that subsidiary, upon approval by the parent's board of directors, and to make payment in cash for the shares of the minority stockholders. The statute does not require the consent of, or advance notice to, the minority stockholders. However, notice of the merger must be given within 10 days after its effective date, and any stockholder who is dissatisfied with the terms of the merger may petition the Delaware Court of Chancery for a decree ordering the surviving corporation to pay him the fair value of his shares, as determined by a court-appointed appraiser subject to review by the court.

Santa Fe obtained independent appraisals of the physical assets of Kirby land, timber, buildings, and machinery and of Kirby's oil, gas, and mineral interests. These appraisals, together with other financial information, were submitted to Morgan Stanley & Co. (Morgan Stanley), an investment banking firm retained to appraise the fair market value of Kirby stock. Kirby's physical assets were appraised at $320 million (amounting to $640 for each of the 500,000 shares); Kirby's stock was valued by Morgan Stanley at $125 per share. Under the terms of the merger, minority stockholders were offered $150 per share.

The provisions of the short-form merger statute were fully complied with. The minority stockholders of Kirby were notified the day after the merger became effective and were advised of their right to obtain an appraisal in Delaware court if dissatisfied with the offer of $150 per share. They also received an information statement containing, in addition to the relevant financial data about Kirby, the appraisals of the value of Kirby's assets and the Morgan Stanley appraisal concluding that the fair market value of the stock was $125 per share.

Respondents, minority stockholders of Kirby, objected to the terms of the merger, but did not pursue their appraisal remedy in the Delaware Court of Chancery. Instead, they brought this action in federal court on behalf of the corporation and other minority stockholders, seeking to set aside the merger or to recover what they claimed to be the fair value of their shares. The amended complaint asserted that, based on the fair market value of Kirby's physical assets as revealed by the appraisal included in the information statement sent to minority shareholders, Kirby's stock was worth at least $772 per share. The complaint alleged further that the merger took place without prior notice to minority stockholders; that the purpose of the merger was to appropriate the difference between the "conceded pro rata value of the physical assets," and the offer of $150 per share to "freez(e) out the minority stockholders at a wholly inadequate price," and that Santa Fe, knowing the appraised value of the physical assets, obtained a "fraudulent appraisal" of the stock from Morgan Stanley and offered $25 above that appraisal "in order to lull the minority stockholders into erroneously believing that [Santa Fe was] generous." This course of conduct was alleged to be "a violation of Rule 10b–5 because defendants employed a 'device, scheme, or artifice to defraud' and engaged in an 'act, practice or course of business which operates or would operate as a fraud or deceit upon any person, in connection with the purchase or sale of any security." Morgan Stanley assertedly participated in the fraud as an accessory by submitting its appraisal of $125 per share although knowing the appraised value of the physical assets.

The District Court dismissed the complaint for failure to state a claim upon which relief could be granted. As the District Court understood the complaint, respondents' case rested on two distinct grounds. First, federal law was assertedly violated because the merger was for the sole purpose of eliminating the minority from the company, therefore lacking any justifiable business purpose, and because the merger was undertaken without prior notice to the minority shareholders. Second, the low valuation placed on the shares in the cash-exchange offer was itself said to be a fraud actionable under Rule 10b–5. In rejecting the first ground for recovery, the District Court reasoned that Delaware law required neither a business purpose for a short-form merger nor prior notice to the minority shareholders who the statute contemplated would be removed from the company, and that Rule 10b–5 did not override these provisions of state corporate law by independently placing a duty on the majority not to merge without prior notice and without a justifiable business purpose.

As for the claim that actionable fraud inhered in the allegedly gross undervaluation of the minority shares, the District Court observed that respondents valued their shares at a minimum of $772 per share, "basing this figure on the pro rata value of Kirby's physical assets." Accepting this valuation for purposes of the motion to dismiss, the District Court further noted that, as revealed by the complaint, the physical asset appraisal, along with other information relevant to Morgan Stanley's valuation of the shares, had been included with the information statement sent to respondents within the time required by state law. It thought that if "full and fair disclosure is made, transactions eliminating minority interests are beyond the purview of Rule 10b–5," and concluded that the "complaint fail[ed] to allege an omission, misstatement or fraudulent course of conduct that would have impeded a shareholder's judgment of the value of the offer." The complaint therefore failed to state a claim and was dismissed.

A divided Court of Appeals for the Second Circuit reversed. [. . .] [T]he Court of Appeals did not disturb the District Court's conclusion that the complaint did not allege a material misrepresentation or nondisclosure with respect to the value of the stock; and the court declined to rule that a claim of gross undervaluation itself would suffice to make out a Rule 10b–5 case. [. . .] [H]owever, the court fundamentally disagreed with the District Court as to the reach and coverage of Rule 10b–5. The Court of Appeals' view was that, although the Rule plainly reached material misrepresentations and nondisclosures in connection with the purchase or sale of securities, neither misrepresentation nor nondisclosure was a necessary element of a Rule 10b–5 action; the Rule reached "breaches of fiduciary duty by a majority against minority shareholders without any charge of misrepresentation or lack of disclosure." [. . .]

We granted the petition for certiorari challenging this holding because of the importance of the issue involved to the administration of the federal securities laws. We reverse.

II

Section 10(b) of the 1934 Act makes it "unlawful for any person . . . to use or employ . . . any manipulative or deceptive device or contrivance in contravention of [Securities and Exchange Commission rules]"; Rule 10b–5, promulgated by the SEC under § 10(b), prohibits, in addition to nondisclosure and misrepresentation, any "artifice to defraud" or any act "which operates or would operate as a fraud or deceit." The court below construed the term "fraud" in Rule 10b–5 by adverting to the use of the term in several of this Court's decisions in contexts other than the 1934 Act and the related Securities Act of 1933. The Court of Appeals' approach to the interpretation of Rule 10b–5 is inconsistent with that taken by the Court last Term in *Ernst & Ernst v. Hochfelder.*

Ernst & Ernst makes clear that in deciding whether a complaint states a cause of action for "fraud" under Rule 10b–5, "we turn first to the language of s 10(b), for '(t)he starting point in every case involving construction of a statute is the language itself.'" In holding that a cause of action under Rule 10b–5 does not lie for mere negligence, the Court began with the principle that "(a)scertainment of congressional intent with respect to the standard of liability created by a particular section of the (1933 and 1934) Acts must . . . rest primarily on the language of that section," and then focused on the statutory language of § 10(b) "(t)he words 'manipulative or deceptive' used in conjunction with 'device or contrivance.'" The same language and the same principle apply to this case.

To the extent that the Court of Appeals would rely on the use of the term "fraud" in Rule 10b–5 to bring within the ambit of the Rule all breaches of fiduciary duty in connection with a securities transaction, its interpretation would, like the interpretation rejected by the Court in *Ernst & Ernst,* "add a gloss to the operative language of the statute quite different from its commonly accepted meaning." But, as the Court there held, the language of the statute must control the interpretation of the Rule. [. . .]

The language of § 10(b) gives no indication that Congress meant to prohibit any conduct not involving manipulation or deception. Nor have we been cited to any evidence in the legislative history that would support a departure from the language of the statute. [. . .] Thus the claim of fraud and fiduciary breach in this complaint states a cause of action under any part of Rule 10b–5 only if the conduct alleged can be fairly viewed as "manipulative or deceptive" within the meaning of the statute.

III

It is our judgment that the transaction, if carried out as alleged in the complaint, was neither deceptive nor manipulative and therefore did not violate either § 10(b) of the Act or Rule 10b–5.

As we have indicated, the case comes to us on the premise that the complaint failed to allege a material misrepresentation or material failure to disclose. The finding of the District Court, undisturbed by the Court of Appeals, was that there was no "omission" or "misstatement" in the information statement accompanying the notice of merger. On the basis of the information provided, minority shareholders could either accept the price offered or reject it and seek an appraisal in the Delaware Court of Chancery. Their choice was fairly presented, and they were furnished with all relevant information on which to base their decision.

We therefore find inapposite the cases relied upon by respondents and the court below, in which the breaches of fiduciary duty held violative of Rule 10b–5 included some element of deception. Those cases forcefully reflect the principle that "[§] 10(b) must be read flexibly, not technically and restrictively" and that the statute provides a cause of action for any plaintiff who "suffer(s) an injury as a result of deceptive practices touching its sale (or purchase) of securities . . . ." *Superintendent of Insurance v. Bankers Life & Ca. Co.* But the cases do not support the proposition, adopted by the Court of Appeals below and urged by respondents here, that a breach of fiduciary duty by majority stockholders, without any deception, misrepresentation, or nondisclosure, violates the statute and the Rule.

It is also readily apparent that the conduct alleged in the complaint was not "manipulative" within the meaning of the statute. "Manipulation" is "virtually a term of art when used in connection with securities markets." *Ernst & Ernst.* The term refers generally to practices, such as wash sales, matched orders, or rigged prices, that are intended to mislead investors by artificially affecting market activity. [. . .] Indeed, nondisclosure is usually essential to the success of a manipulative scheme. No doubt Congress meant to prohibit the full range of ingenious devices that might be used to manipulate securities prices. But we do not think it would have chosen this "term of art" if it had meant to bring within the scope of § 10(b) instances of corporate mismanagement such as this, in which the essence of the complaint is that shareholders were treated unfairly by a fiduciary.

IV

[. . .] [T]here are additional considerations that weigh heavily against permitting a cause of action under Rule 10b–5 for the breach of corporate fiduciary duty alleged in this complaint. Congress did not expressly provide a private cause of action for violations of § 10(b). Although we have recognized an implied cause of action under that section in some circumstances, we have also recognized that a private cause of action under the antifraud provisions of the Securities Exchange Act should not be implied where it is "unnecessary to ensure the fulfillment of Congress' purposes" in adopting that Act. *Piper v. Chris-Craft Industries.* As we noted earlier, the Court repeatedly has described the "fundamental purpose" of the Act as implementing a "philosophy of full disclosure"; once full and fair disclosure has occurred, the fairness of the terms of the transaction is at most a tangential concern of the statute. [W]e are reluctant to recognize a cause of action here to serve what is "at best a subsidiary purpose" of the federal legislation.

A second factor in determining whether Congress intended to create a federal cause of action in these circumstances is "whether 'the cause of action (is) one traditionally relegated to state law . . .' " *Piper v. Chris-Craft Industries.* The Delaware Legislature has supplied minority shareholders with a cause of action in the Delaware Court of Chancery to recover the fair value of shares allegedly undervalued in a short-form merger. Of course, the existence of a particular state-law remedy is not dispositive of the question whether Congress meant of provide a similar federal remedy, but as in [. . .] *Piper*, we conclude that "it is entirely appropriate in this instance to relegate respondent and others in his situation to whatever remedy is created by state law."

The reasoning behind a holding that the complaint in this case alleged fraud under Rule 10b–5 could not be easily contained. It is difficult to imagine how a court could distinguish, for purposes of Rule 10b–5 fraud, between a majority stockholder's use of a short-form merger to eliminate the minority at an unfair price and the use of some other device, such as a long-form merger, tender offer, or liquidation, to achieve the same result; or indeed how a court could distinguish the alleged abuses in these going private transactions from other types of fiduciary self-dealing involving transactions in [securities]. [. . .] In addition to posing a "danger of vexatious litigation which could result from a widely expanded class of plaintiffs under Rule 10b–5," this extension of the federal securities laws would overlap and quite possibly interfere with state corporate law. *Blue Chip Stamps v. Manor Drug Stores.* [. . .]

We thus adhere to the position that "Congress by [§] 10(b) did not seek to regulate transactions which constitute no more than internal corporate mismanagement." There may well be a need for uniform federal fiduciary standards to govern mergers such as that challenged in this complaint. But those standards should not be supplied by judicial extension of § 10(b) and Rule 10b–5 to "cover the corporate universe."

The judgment of the Court of Appeals is reversed, and the case is remanded for further proceedings consistent with this opinion. [. . .]

D. INSIDER TRADING

Securities Exchange Act of 1934
Section 20A

(a) PRIVATE RIGHTS OF ACTION BASED ON CONTEMPORANEOUS TRADING

Any person who violates any provision of this chapter or the rules or regulations thereunder by purchasing or selling a security while in possession of material, nonpublic information shall be liable in an action in any court of competent jurisdiction to any person who, contemporaneously with the purchase or sale of securities that is the subject of such violation, has purchased (where such violation is based on a sale of securities) or sold (where such violation is based on a purchase of securities) securities of the same class.

(b) LIMITATIONS ON LIABILITY

(1) Contemporaneous trading actions limited to profit gained or loss avoided

The total amount of damages imposed under subsection (a) shall not exceed the profit gained or loss avoided in the transaction or transactions that are the subject of the violation.

(2) Offsetting disgorgements against liability

The total amount of damages imposed against any person under subsection (a) shall be diminished by the amounts, if any, that such person may be required to disgorge, pursuant to a court order [. . .].

(3) Controlling person liability

No person shall be liable under this section solely by reason of employing another person who is liable under this section [. . .].

(4) Statute of limitations

No action may be brought under this section more than 5 years after the date of the last transaction that is the subject of the violation.

(c) JOINT AND SEVERAL LIABILITY FOR COMMUNICATING

Any person who violates any provision of this chapter or the rules or regulations thereunder by communicating material, nonpublic information shall be jointly and severally liable under subsection (a) with, and to the same extent as, any person or persons liable under subsection (a) to whom the communication was directed. [. . .]

Rules and Regulations Under the Securities Exchange Act of 1934

Rule 10b5–1: Trading "on the basis of" material nonpublic information in insider trading cases.

(a) *Manipulative or deceptive devices.* The "manipulative or deceptive device[s] or contrivance[s]" prohibited by Section 10(b) of the Act [. . .] and [. . .] Rule 10b–5 [. . .] include, among other things, the purchase or sale of a security of any issuer, on the basis of material nonpublic information about that security or issuer, in breach of a duty of trust or confidence that is owed directly, indirectly, or derivatively, to the issuer of that security or the shareholders of that issuer, or to any other person who is the source of the material nonpublic information.

(b) *Awareness of material nonpublic information.* Subject to the affirmative defenses in paragraph (c) of this section, a purchase or sale of a security of an issuer is on the basis of material nonpublic information for purposes of Section 10(b) and Rule 10b–5 if the person making the purchase or sale was aware of the material nonpublic information when the person made the purchase or sale. The law of insider trading is otherwise defined by judicial opinions construing Rule 10b–5, and Rule 10b5–1 does not modify the scope of insider trading law in any other respect.

(c) *Affirmative defenses.* (1)(i) Subject to paragraph (1)(ii) of this section, a person's purchase or sale is not on the basis of material nonpublic information if the person making the purchase or sale demonstrates that:

(A) Before becoming aware of the information, the person had:

(1) Entered into a binding contract to purchase or sell the security,

(2) Instructed another person to purchase or sell the security for the instructing person's account, or

(3) Adopted a written plan for trading securities;

(B) The contract, instruction, or plan described in paragraph (c)(1)(i)(A) of this section:

(1) Specified the amount of securities to be purchased or sold and the price at which and the date on which the securities were to be purchased or sold;

(2) Included a written formula or algorithm, or computer program, for determining the amount of securities to be purchased or sold and the price at which and the date on which the securities were to be purchased or sold; or

(3) Did not permit the person to exercise any subsequent influence over how, when, or whether to effect purchases or sales; provided, in addition, that any other person who, pursuant to the contract, instruction, or plan, did exercise such influence must not have been aware of the material nonpublic information when doing so; and

(C) The purchase or sale that occurred was pursuant to the contract, instruction, or plan. [. . .]

(ii) Paragraph (c)(1)(i) of this section is applicable only when:

(A) The contract, instruction, or plan to purchase or sell securities was given or entered into in good faith and not as part of a plan or scheme to evade the prohibitions of this section, and the person who entered into the contract, instruction, or plan has acted in good faith with respect to the contract, instruction or plan;

(B) If the person who entered into the contract, instruction, or plan is:

(1) A director or officer [. . .] of the issuer, no purchases or sales occur until expiration of a cooling-off period consisting of the later of:

(i) Ninety days after the adoption of the contract, instruction, or plan or

(ii) Two business days following the disclosure of the issuer's financial results [. . .]; or

(2)   Not the issuer and not a director or officer [. . .] of the issuer, no purchases or sales occur until the expiration of a cooling-off period that is 30 days after the adoption of the contract, instruction or plan;

(C)   If the person who entered into a plan [. . .] is a director or officer [. . .] of the issuer of the securities, such director or officer included a representation in the plan certifying that, on the date of adoption of the plan:

(1)   The individual director or officer is not aware of any material nonpublic information about the security or issuer; and

(2)   The individual director or officer is adopting the plan in good faith and not as part of a plan or scheme to evade the prohibitions of this section; [. . .]

(2)   A person other than a natural person also may demonstrate that a purchase or sale of securities is not "on the basis of" material nonpublic information if the person demonstrates that:

(i)   The individual making the investment decision on behalf of the person to purchase or sell the securities was not aware of the information; and

(ii) The person had implemented reasonable policies and procedures, taking into consideration the nature of the person's business, to ensure that individuals making investment decisions would not violate the laws prohibiting trading on the basis of material nonpublic information. These policies and procedures may include those that restrict any purchase, sale, and causing any purchase or sale of any security as to which the person has material nonpublic information, or those that prevent such individuals from becoming aware of such information.

Rule 10b5–2: Duties of trust or confidence in misappropriation insider trading cases.

This section provides a non-exclusive definition of circumstances in which a person has a duty of trust or confidence for purposes of the "misappropriation" theory of insider trading under Section 10(b) of the Act and Rule 10b–5. [. . .]

(a)   *Scope of Rule.* This section shall apply to any violation of Section 10(b) of the Act (15 U.S.C. 78j(b)) and § 240.10b–5 thereunder that is based on the purchase or sale of securities on the basis of, or the communication of, material nonpublic information misappropriated in breach of a duty of trust or confidence.

(b)   *Enumerated "duties of trust or confidence."* For purposes of this section, a "duty of trust or confidence" exists in the following circumstances, among others:

(1) Whenever a person agrees to maintain information in confidence;

(2) Whenever the person communicating the material nonpublic information and the person to whom it is communicated have a history, pattern, or practice of sharing confidences, such that the recipient of the information knows or reasonably should know that the person communicating the material nonpublic information expects that the recipient will maintain its confidentiality; or

(3) Whenever a person receives or obtains material nonpublic information from his or her spouse, parent, child, or sibling; provided, however, that the person receiving or obtaining the information may demonstrate that no duty of trust or confidence existed with respect to the information, by establishing that he or she neither knew nor reasonably should have known that the person who was the source of the information expected that the person would keep the information confidential, because of the parties' history, pattern, or practice of sharing and maintaining confidences, and because there was no agreement or understanding to maintain the confidentiality of the information.

1. DISCLOSE OR ABSTAIN

Chiarella v. United States
445 U.S. 222 (1980)

■ POWELL, JUSTICE, for the majority.

The question in this case is whether a person who learns from the confidential documents of one corporation that it is planning an attempt to secure control of a second corporation violates § 10(b) of the Securities Exchange Act of 1934 if he fails to disclose the impending takeover before trading in the target company's securities.

I

Petitioner is a printer by trade. In 1975 and 1976, he worked as a "markup man" in the New York composing room of Pandick Press, a financial printer. Among documents that petitioner handled were five announcements of corporate takeover bids. When these documents were delivered to the printer, the identities of the acquiring and target corporations were concealed by blank spaces or false names. The true names were sent to the printer on the night of the final printing.

The petitioner, however, was able to deduce the names of the target companies before the final printing from other information contained in the documents. Without disclosing his knowledge, petitioner purchased stock in the target companies and sold the shares immediately after the takeover attempts were made public. By this method, petitioner realized a gain of slightly more than $30,000 in the course of 14 months.

Subsequently, the Securities and Exchange Commission [. . .] began an investigation of his trading activities. In May 1977, petitioner entered into a consent decree with the Commission in which he agreed to return his profits to the sellers of the shares. On the same day, he was discharged by Pandick Press.

In January 1978, petitioner was indicted on 17 counts of violating § 10(b) of the Securities Exchange Act of 1934 (1934 Act) and SEC Rule 10b–5. After petitioner unsuccessfully moved to dismiss the indictment, he was brought to trial and convicted on all counts.

The Court of Appeals for the Second Circuit affirmed petitioner's conviction. We granted certiorari, and we now reverse.

II

Section 10(b) of the 1934 Act, [. . .] prohibits the use "in connection with the purchase or sale of any security . . . [of] any manipulative or deceptive device or contrivance in contravention of such rules and regulations as the Commission may prescribe." Pursuant to this section, the SEC promulgated Rule 10b–5 which provides in pertinent part:

> It shall be unlawful for any person, directly or indirectly, by the use of any means or instrumentality of interstate commerce, or of the mails or of any facility of any national securities exchange,
>
> (a) To employ any device, scheme, or artifice to defraud, [or] [. . .]
>
> (c) To engage in any act, practice, or course of business which operates or would operate as a fraud or deceit upon any person, in connection with the purchase or sale of any security.

This case concerns the legal effect of the petitioner's silence. The District Court's charge permitted the jury to convict the petitioner if it found that he willfully failed to inform sellers of target company securities that he knew of a forthcoming takeover bid that would make their shares more valuable. In order to decide whether silence in such circumstances violates § 10(b), it is necessary to review the language and legislative history of that statute as well as its interpretation by the Commission and the federal courts.

Although the starting point of our inquiry is the language of the statute, § 10(b) does not state whether silence may constitute a manipulative or deceptive device. Section 10(b) was designed as a catch-all clause to prevent fraudulent practices. But neither the legislative history nor the statute itself affords specific guidance for the resolution of this case. When Rule 10b–5 was promulgated in 1942, the SEC did not discuss the possibility that failure to provide information might run afoul of § 10(b).

[. . .] In *Cady, Roberts & Co.,* the Commission decided that a corporate insider must abstain from trading in the shares of his corporation unless he has first disclosed all material inside information known to him. The obligation to disclose or abstain derives from

[a]n affirmative duty to disclose material information[, which] has been traditionally imposed on corporate 'insiders,' particular officers, directors, or controlling stockholders. We, and the courts have consistently held that insiders must disclose material facts which are known to them by virtue of their position but which are not known to persons with whom they deal and which, if known, would affect their investment judgment.

The Commission emphasized that the duty arose from (i) the existence of a relationship affording access to inside information intended to be available only for a corporate purpose, and (ii) the unfairness of allowing a corporate insider to take advantage of that information by trading without disclosure.

That the relationship between a corporate insider and the stockholders of his corporation gives rise to a disclosure obligation is not a novel twist of the law. At common law, misrepresentation made for the purpose of inducing reliance upon the false statement is fraudulent. But one who fails to disclose material information prior to the consummation of a transaction commits fraud only when he is under a duty to do so. And the duty to disclose arises when one party has information "that the other [party] is entitled to know because of a fiduciary or other similar relation of trust and confidence between them." In its *Cady, Roberts* decision, the Commission recognized a relationship of trust and confidence between the shareholders of a corporation and those insiders who have obtained confidential information by reason of their position with that corporation. This relationship gives rise to a duty to disclose because of the "necessity of preventing a corporate insider from . . . tak[ing] unfair advantage of the uninformed minority stockholders." *Speed v. Transamerica Corp.*

The federal courts have found violations of § 10(b) where corporate insiders used undisclosed information for their own benefit. The cases also have emphasized, in accordance with the common-law rule, that "[t]he party charged with failing to disclose market information must be under a duty to disclose it." *Frigitemp Corp. v. Financial Dynamics Fund, Inc.* Accordingly, a purchaser of stock who has no duty to a prospective seller because he is neither an insider nor a fiduciary has been held to have no obligation to reveal material facts. [. . .]

Thus, administrative and judicial interpretations have established that silence in connection with the purchase or sale of securities may operate as a fraud actionable under § 10(b) despite the absence of statutory language or legislative history specifically addressing the legality of nondisclosure. But such liability is premised upon a duty to disclose arising from a relationship of trust and confidence between parties to a transaction. Application of a duty to disclose prior to trading guarantees that corporate insiders, who have an obligation to place the shareholder's welfare before their own, will not benefit personally through fraudulent use of material, nonpublic information.

III

In this case, the petitioner was convicted of violating § 10(b) although he was not a corporate insider and he received no confidential information from the target company. Moreover, the "market information" upon which he relied did not concern the earning power or operations of the target company, but only the plans of the acquiring company. Petitioner's use of that information was not a fraud under § 10(b) unless he was subject to an affirmative duty to disclose it before trading. In this case, the jury instructions failed to specify any such duty. In effect, the trial court instructed the jury that petitioner owed a duty to everyone; to all sellers, indeed, to the market as a whole. The jury simply was told to decide whether petitioner used material, nonpublic information at a time when "he knew other people trading in the securities market did not have access to the same information."

The Court of Appeals affirmed the conviction by holding that "*[a]nyone—* corporate insider or not—who regularly receives material nonpublic information may not use that information to trade in securities without incurring an affirmative duty to disclose." Although the court said that its test would include only persons who regularly receive material, nonpublic information, its rationale for that limitation is unrelated to the existence of a duty to disclose. The Court of Appeals, like the trial court, failed to identify a relationship between petitioner and the sellers that could give rise to a duty. Its decision thus rested solely upon its belief that the federal securities laws have "created a system providing equal access to information necessary for reasoned and intelligent investment decisions." The use by anyone of material information not generally available is fraudulent, this theory suggests, because such information gives certain buyers or sellers an unfair advantage over less informed buyers and sellers.

This reasoning suffers from two defects. First, not every instance of financial unfairness constitutes fraudulent activity under § 10(b). Second, the element required to make silence fraudulent—a duty to disclose—is absent in this case. No duty could arise from petitioner's relationship with the sellers of the target company's securities, for petitioner had no prior dealings with them. He was not their agent, he was not a fiduciary, he was not a person in whom the sellers had placed their trust and confidence. He was, in fact, a complete stranger who dealt with the sellers only through impersonal market transactions.

We cannot affirm petitioner's conviction without recognizing a general duty between all participants in market transactions to forgo actions based on material, nonpublic information. Formulation of such a broad duty, which departs radically from the established doctrine that duty arises from a specific relationship between two parties should not be undertaken absent some explicit evidence of congressional intent.

As we have seen, no such evidence emerges from the language or legislative history of § 10(b). Moreover, neither the Congress nor the Commission ever has adopted a parity-of-information rule.

[. . .] Section 10(b) is aptly described as a catchall provision, but what it catches must be fraud. When an allegation of fraud is based upon nondisclosure, there can be no fraud absent a duty to speak. We hold that a duty to disclose under § 10(b) does not arise from the mere possession of nonpublic market information. The contrary result is without support in the legislative history of § 10(b) and would be inconsistent with the careful plan that Congress has enacted for regulation of the securities markets. [. . .]

The judgment of the Court of Appeals is reversed.

■ BURGER, CHIEF JUSTICE, dissenting.

[. . .] I would affirm the conviction. [. . .]

I would read § 10(b) and Rule 10b–5 to encompass and build on this principle: to mean that a person who has misappropriated nonpublic information has an absolute duty to disclose that information or to refrain from trading. [. . .]

Here, Chiarella, himself, testified that he obtained his informational advantage by decoding confidential material entrusted to his employer by its customers. He admitted that the information he traded on was "confidential," not "to be use[d] . . . for personal gain." [. . .] Even more telling perhaps is Chiarella's counsel's statement in closing argument:

> Let me say right up front, too, Mr. Chiarella got on the stand and he conceded, he said candidly, "I used clues I got while I was at work. I looked at these various documents and I deciphered them and I decoded them and I used that information as a basis for purchasing stock." There is no question about that. We don't have to go through a hullabaloo about that. It is something he concedes. There is no mystery about that.

In this Court, counsel similarly conceded that "[w]e do not dispute the proposition that Chiarella *violated his duty as an agent of the offeror corporations not to use their confidential information for personal profit.*" These statements are tantamount to a formal stipulation that Chiarella's informational advantage was unlawfully obtained. [. . .]

In sum, the evidence shows beyond all doubt that Chiarella, working literally in the shadows of the warning signs in the printshop misappropriated—stole to put it bluntly—valuable nonpublic information entrusted to him in the utmost confidence. He then exploited his ill-gotten informational advantage by purchasing securities in the market. In my view, such conduct plainly violates § 10(b) and Rule 10b–5. Accordingly, I would affirm the judgment of the Court of Appeals.

■ BLACKMUN, JUSTICE, joined by MARSHALL, JUSTICE, dissenting.

[. . .] I write separately because, in my view, it is unnecessary to rest petitioner's conviction on a "misappropriation" theory. The fact that petitioner Chiarella purloined, or [. . .] "stole," information concerning pending tender offers certainly is the most dramatic evidence that petitioner was guilty of fraud. He has conceded that he knew it was wrong, and he and his co-workers in the printshop were specifically warned by their employer that actions of this kind were improper and forbidden. But I also would find petitioner's conduct fraudulent within the meaning of § 10(b) of the Securities Exchange Act of 1934, and the Securities and Exchange Commission's Rule 10b–5, even if he had obtained the blessing of his employer's principals before embarking on his profiteering scheme. Indeed, I think petitioner's brand of manipulative trading, with or without such approval, lies close to the heart of what the securities laws are intended to prohibit.

[. . .] I, of course, agree with the Court that a relationship of trust can establish a duty to disclose under § 10(b) and Rule 10b–5. But I do not agree that a failure to disclose violates the Rule only when the responsibilities of a relationship of that kind have been breached. As applied to this case, the Court's approach unduly minimizes the importance of petitioner's *access* to confidential information that the honest investor no matter how diligently he tried, could not legally obtain. In doing so, it further advances an interpretation of § 10(b) and Rule 10b–5 that stops short of their full implications. [. . .]

Whatever the outer limits of the Rule, petitioner Chiarella's case fits neatly near the center of its analytical framework. He occupied a relationship to the takeover companies giving him intimate access to concededly material information that was sedulously guarded from public access. The information, in the words of *Cady, Roberts & Co.*, was "intended to be available only for a corporate purpose and not for the personal benefit of anyone." Petitioner, moreover, knew that the information was unavailable to those with whom he dealt. And he took full, virtually riskless advantage of this artificial information gap by selling the stocks shortly after each takeover bid was announced. By any reasonable definition, his trading was "inherent[ly] unfai[r]." *Id.* [. . .]

2. INSIDER TIPS

Dirks v. Securities and Exchange Commission
463 U.S. 646 (1983)

■ POWELL, JUSTICE, for the majority.

Petitioner Raymond Dirks received material nonpublic information from "insiders" of a corporation with which he had no connection. He disclosed this information to investors who relied on it in trading in the shares of the corporation. The question is whether Dirks violated the antifraud provisions of the federal securities laws by this disclosure.

I

In 1973, Dirks was an officer of a New York broker-dealer firm who specialized in providing investment analysis of insurance company securities to institutional investors. On March 6, Dirks received information from Ronald Secrist, a former officer of Equity Funding of America. Secrist alleged that the assets of Equity Funding, a diversified corporation primarily engaged in selling life insurance and mutual funds, were vastly overstated as the result of fraudulent corporate practices. Secrist also stated that various regulatory agencies had failed to act on similar charges made by Equity Funding employees. He urged Dirks to verify the fraud and disclose it publicly.

Dirks decided to investigate the allegations. [. . .] Neither Dirks nor his firm owned or traded any Equity Funding stock, but throughout his investigation he openly discussed the information he had obtained with a number of clients and investors. Some of these persons sold their holdings of Equity Funding securities, including five investment advisers who liquidated holdings of more than $16 million.

While Dirks was in Los Angeles, he was in touch regularly with William Blundell, the *Wall Street Journal*'s Los Angeles bureau chief. Dirks urged Blundell to write a story on the fraud allegations. [. . .]

During the two-week period in which Dirks pursued his investigation and spread word of Secrist's charges, the price of Equity Funding stock fell from $26 per share to less than $15 per share. This led the New York Stock Exchange to halt trading on March 27. Shortly thereafter California insurance authorities impounded Equity Funding's records and uncovered evidence of the fraud. Only then did the Securities and Exchange Commission (SEC) file a complaint against Equity Funding and only then, on April 2, did the *Wall Street Journal* publish a front-page story based largely on information assembled by Dirks. Equity Funding immediately went into receivership.

The SEC began an investigation into Dirks' role in the exposure of the fraud. After a hearing by an administrative law judge, the SEC found that Dirks had aided and abetted violations of § 17(a) of the Securities Act of 1933, § 10(b) of the Securities Exchange Act of 1934, and SEC Rule 10b–5, by repeating the allegations of fraud to members of the investment community who later sold their Equity Funding stock. The SEC concluded: "Where 'tippees'—regardless of their motivation or occupation—come into possession of material 'information that they know is confidential and know or should know came from a corporate insider,' they must either publicly disclose that information or refrain from trading." Recognizing, however, that Dirks "played an important role in bringing [Equity Funding's] massive fraud to light," the SEC only censured him.

Dirks sought review in the Court of Appeals for the District of Columbia Circuit. The court entered judgment against Dirks "for the reasons stated by the Commission in its opinion." [. . .]

II

In the seminal case of *In re Cady, Roberts & Co.*, the SEC recognized that the common law in some jurisdictions imposes on "corporate 'insiders,' particularly officers, directors, or controlling stockholders" an "affirmative duty of disclosure . . . when dealing in securities." *Id.* The SEC found that not only did breach of this common-law duty also establish the elements of a Rule 10b–5 violation, but that individuals other than corporate insiders could be obligated either to disclose material nonpublic information before trading or to abstain from trading altogether. In *Chiarella* [*v. United States*], we accepted the two elements set out in *Cady Roberts* for establishing a Rule 10b–5 violation: "(i) the existence of a relationship affording access to inside information intended to be available only for a corporate purpose, and (ii) the unfairness of allowing a corporate insider to take advantage of that information by trading without disclosure." In examining whether Chiarella had an obligation to disclose or abstain, the Court found that there is no general duty to disclose before trading on material nonpublic information, and held that "a duty to disclose under § 10(b) does not arise from the mere possession of nonpublic market information." *Chiarella v. United States*. Such a duty arises rather from the existence of a fiduciary relationship.

Not "all breaches of fiduciary duty in connection with a securities transaction," however, come within the ambit of Rule 10b–5. *Santa Fe Industries, Inc. v. Green*. There must also be "manipulation or deception." *Id.* In an inside-trading case this fraud derives from the "inherent unfairness involved where one takes advantage" of "information intended to be available only for a corporate purpose and not for the personal benefit of anyone." *In re Merrill Lynch, Pierce, Fenner & Smith, Inc.* Thus, an insider will be liable under Rule 10b–5 for inside trading only where he fails to disclose material nonpublic information before trading on it and thus makes "secret profits." *In re Cady, Roberts & Co.*

III

We were explicit in *Chiarella* [*v. United States*] in saying that there can be no duty to disclose where the person who has traded on inside information "was not [the corporation's] agent, . . . was not a fiduciary, [or] was not a person in whom the sellers [of the securities] had placed their trust and confidence." Not to require such a fiduciary relationship, we recognized, would "depar[t] radically from the established doctrine that duty arises from a specific relationship between two parties" and would amount to "recognizing a general duty between all participants in market transactions to forgo actions based on material, nonpublic information." *Id.* This requirement of a specific relationship between the shareholders and the individual trading on inside information has created analytical difficulties for the SEC and courts in policing tippees

who trade on inside information. Unlike insiders who have independent
fiduciary duties to both the corporation and its shareholders, the typical
tippee has no such relationships. In view of this absence, it has been
unclear how a tippee acquires the *Cady, Roberts* duty to refrain from
trading on inside information.

A

The SEC's position [. . .] is that a tippee "inherits" the *Cady, Roberts*
obligation to shareholders whenever he receives inside information from
an insider:

> In tipping potential traders, Dirks breached a duty which he had
> assumed as a result of knowingly receiving confidential
> information from [Equity Funding] insiders. Tippees such as
> Dirks who receive non-public material information from
> insiders become "subject to the same duty as [the] insiders."
> *Shapiro v. Merrill Lynch, Pierce, Fenner & Smith, Inc.* [. . .]
> Dirks—standing in their shoes—committed a breach of the
> fiduciary duty which he had assumed in dealing with them,
> when he passed the information on to traders.

[. . .] In effect, the SEC's theory of tippee liability [. . .] appears rooted in
the idea that the antifraud provisions require equal information among
all traders. This conflicts with the principle set forth in *Chiarella* that
only some persons, under some circumstances, will be barred from
trading while in possession of material nonpublic information. [. . .] [O]ur
opinion in *Chiarella* [repudiates] any notion that all traders must enjoy
equal information before trading[.] [. . .] We reaffirm today that "[a] duty
[to disclose] arises from the relationship between parties . . .and not
merely from one's ability to acquire information because of his position
in the market." *Chiarella v. United States.*

Imposing a duty to disclose or abstain solely because a person knowingly
receives material nonpublic information from an insider and trades on it
could have an inhibiting influence on the role of market analysts, which
the SEC itself recognizes is necessary to the preservation of a healthy
market. [As the SEC notes], [i]t is commonplace for analysts to "ferret
out and analyze information," and this often is done by meeting with and
questioning corporate officers and others who are insiders. And
information that the analysts obtain normally may be the basis for
judgments as to the market worth of a corporation's securities. The
analyst's judgment in this respect is made available in market letters or
otherwise to clients of the firm. It is the nature of this type of information,
and indeed of the markets themselves, that such information cannot be
made simultaneously available to all of the corporation's stockholders or
the public generally.

B

The conclusion that recipients of inside information do not invariably
acquire a duty to disclose or abstain does not mean that such tippees

always are free to trade on the information. [. . .] [S]ome tippees must assume an insider's duty to the shareholders not because they receive inside information, but rather because it has been made available to them *improperly*. And for Rule 10b–5 purposes, the insider's disclosure is improper only where it would violate his *Cady, Roberts* duty. Thus, a tippee assumes a fiduciary duty to the shareholders of a corporation not to trade on material nonpublic information only when the insider has breached his fiduciary duty to the shareholders by disclosing the information to the tippee and the tippee knows or should know that there has been a breach. [. . .] Tipping thus properly is viewed only as a means of indirectly violating the *Cady, Roberts* disclose-or-abstain rule.

C

In determining whether a tippee is under an obligation to disclose or abstain, it thus is necessary to determine whether the insider's "tip" constituted a breach of the insider's fiduciary duty. All disclosures of confidential corporate information are not inconsistent with the duty insiders owe to shareholders. [. . .] In some situations, the insider will act consistently with his fiduciary duty to shareholders, and yet release of the information may affect the market. For example, it may not be clear—either to the corporate insider or to the recipient analyst— whether the information will be viewed as material nonpublic information. Corporate officials may mistakenly think the information already has been disclosed or that it is not material enough to affect the market. Whether disclosure is a breach of duty therefore depends in large part on the purpose of the disclosure. This standard was identified by the SEC itself in [*In re*] *Cady, Roberts:* a purpose of the securities laws was to eliminate "use of inside information for personal advantage." [. . .] Absent some personal gain, there has been no breach of duty to stockholders. And absent a breach by the insider, there is no derivative breach. As [the concurrence] stated in [*In re*] *Investors Management Co.*: "It is important in this type of case to focus on policing insiders and what they do . . . rather than on policing information *per se* and its possession . . . ." [. . .]

IV

Under the inside-trading and tipping rules set forth above, we find that there was no actionable violation by Dirks. It is undisputed that Dirks himself was a stranger to Equity Funding, with no pre-existing fiduciary duty to its shareholders. He took no action, directly or indirectly, that induced the shareholders or officers of Equity Funding to repose trust or confidence in him. There was no expectation by Dirk's sources that he would keep their information in confidence. Nor did Dirks misappropriate or illegally obtain the information about Equity Funding. Unless the insiders breached their *Cady, Roberts* duty to shareholders in disclosing the nonpublic information to Dirks, he breached no duty when he passed it on to investors as well as to the *Wall Street Journal*.

It is clear that neither Secrist nor the other Equity Funding employees violated their *Cady, Roberts* duty to the corporation's shareholders by providing information to Dirks. The tippers received no monetary or personal benefit for revealing Equity Funding's secrets, nor was their purpose to make a gift of valuable information to Dirks. As the facts of this case clearly indicate, the tippers were motivated by a desire to expose the fraud. In the absence of a breach of duty to shareholders by the insiders, there was no derivative breach by Dirks. Dirks therefore could not have been "a participant after the fact in [an] insider's breach of a fiduciary duty." *Chiarella v. United States.*

V

We conclude that Dirks, in the circumstances of this case, had no duty to abstain from use of the inside information that he obtained. The judgment of the Court of Appeals therefore is

Reversed.

■ JUSTICE BLACKMUN, with whom JUSTICE BRENNAN and JUSTICE MARSHALL join, dissenting.

The Court today takes still another step to limit the protections provided investors by § 10(b) of the Securities Exchange Act of 1934.The device employed in this case engrafts a special motivational requirement on the fiduciary duty doctrine. This innovation excuses a knowing and intentional violation of an insider's duty to shareholders if the insider does not act from a motive of personal gain. [. . .]

The fact that the insider himself does not benefit from the breach does not eradicate the shareholder's injury. It makes no difference to the shareholder whether the corporate insider gained or intended to gain personally from the transaction; the shareholder still has lost because of the insider's misuse of nonpublic information. The duty is addressed not to the insider's motives, but to his actions and their consequences on the shareholder. Personal gain is not an element of the breach of this duty. [. . .]

Although Secrist's general motive to expose the Equity Funding fraud was laudable, the means he chose were not. Moreover, even assuming that Dirks played a substantial role in exposing the fraud, he and his clients should not profit from the information they obtained from Secrist. [. . .] The Court's holding is deficient in policy terms not because it fails to create a legal norm out of that ethical norm [. . .] but because it actually rewards Dirks for his aiding and abetting. [. . .]

In my view, Secrist violated his duty to Equity Funding shareholders by transmitting material nonpublic information to Dirks with the intention that Dirks would cause his clients to trade on that information. Dirks, therefore, was under a duty to make the information publicly available or to refrain from actions that he knew would lead to trading. Because Dirks caused his clients to trade, he violated § 10(b) and Rule 10b–5. Any other result is a disservice to this country's attempt to provide fair and efficient capital markets. I dissent.

United States v. Newman
773 F.3d 438 (2d Cir. 2014)

BACKGROUND

This case arises from the Government's ongoing investigation into suspected insider trading activity at hedge funds. [. . .] [The government] charged Newman [and] Chiasson with conspiracy to commit securities fraud, in violation of 18 U.S.C. § 371 [. . .] [and] [. . .] with securities fraud, in violation of sections 10(b) and 32 of the 1934 Act, SEC Rules 10b–5 and 105b–2, and 18 U.S.C. § 2. [. . .]

At trial, the Government presented evidence that a group of financial analysts exchanged information they obtained from company insiders [. . .]. Specifically, the Government alleged that these analysts received information from insiders at Dell and NVIDIA disclosing those companies' earnings numbers before they were publicly released [. . .]. These analysts then passed the inside information to their portfolio managers, including Newman and Chiasson, who, in turn, executed trades in Dell and NVIDIA stock, earning approximately $4 million and $68 million, respectively, in profits for their respective funds.

Newman and Chiasson were several steps removed from the corporate insiders and there was no evidence that either was aware of the source of the inside information. With respect to the Dell tipping chain, the evidence established that Rob Ray of Dell's investor relations department tipped information regarding Dell's consolidated earnings numbers to Sandy Goyal, an analyst at Neuberger Berman. Goyal in turn gave the information to Diamondback analyst Jesse Tortora. Tortora in turn relayed the information to his manager Newman as well as to other analysts including Level Global analyst Spyridon "Sam" Adondakis. Adondakis then passed along the Dell information to Chiasson, making Newman and Chiasson three and four levels removed from the inside tipper, respectively.

With respect to the NVIDIA tipping chain, the evidence established that Chris Choi of NVIDIA's finance unit tipped inside information to Hyung Lim, a former executive at technology companies Broadcom Corp. and Altera Corp. [. . .]. Lim passed the information to co-defendant Danny Kuo, an analyst at Whittier Trust. Kuo circulated the information to the group of analyst friends, including Tortora and Adondakis, who in turn gave the information to Newman and Chiasson, making Newman and Chiasson four levels removed from the inside tippers.

[. . .] [T]he Government charged that Newman and Chiasson were criminally liable for insider trading because, as sophisticated traders, they must have known that information was disclosed by insiders in breach of a fiduciary duty, and not for any legitimate corporate purpose.

At the close of evidence, Newman and Chiasson moved for a judgment of acquittal [. . .]. They argued that there was no evidence that the corporate insiders provided inside information in exchange for a personal benefit which is required to establish tipper liability under *Dirks v. S.E.C.* Because a tippee's liability derives from the liability of the tipper, Newman and Chiasson argued that they could not be found guilty of insider trading. Newman and Chiasson also argued that, even if the corporate insiders had received a personal benefit in exchange for the inside information, there was no evidence that they knew about any such benefit. Absent such knowledge, appellants argued, they were not aware of, or participants in, the tippers' fraudulent breaches of fiduciary duties to Dell or NVIDIA, and could not be convicted of insider trading under Dirks. In the alternative, appellants requested that the court instruct the jury that it must find that Newman and Chiasson knew that the corporate insiders had disclosed confidential information for personal benefit in order to find them guilty.

[. . .] [T]he district court did not give Newman and Chiasson's proposed jury instruction. Instead, the district court gave the following instructions on the tippers' intent and the personal benefit requirement:

> Now, if you find that Mr. Ray and/or Mr. Choi had a fiduciary or other relationship of trust and confidence with their employers, then you must next consider whether the [G]overnment has proven beyond a reasonable doubt that they intentionally breached that duty of trust and confidence by disclosing material[,] nonpublic information for their own benefit.

On the issue of the appellants' knowledge, the district court instructed the jury:

> To meet its burden, the [G]overnment must also prove beyond a reasonable doubt that the defendant [. . .] knew that the material, nonpublic information had been disclosed by the insider in breach of a duty of trust and confidence. The mere receipt of material, nonpublic information by a defendant, and even trading on that information, is not sufficient; he must have known that it was originally disclosed by the insider in violation of a duty of confidentiality.

[T]he jury returned a verdict of guilty on all counts. [. . .]

This appeal followed.

DISCUSSION

Newman and Chiasson raise a number of arguments on appeal. [. . .]

I.   The Law of Insider Trading

Section 10(b) of the 1934 Act, prohibits the use "in connection with the purchase or sale of any security . . . [of] any manipulative or deceptive device or contrivance in contravention of such rules and regulations as the Commission may prescribe . . . ." [. . .]

A. The "Classical" and "Misappropriation" Theories of Insider Trading

The classical theory holds that a corporate insider (such as an officer or director) violates Section 10(b) and Rule 10b–5 by trading in the corporation's securities on the basis of material, nonpublic information about the corporation. Under this theory, there is a special "relationship of trust and confidence between the shareholders of a corporation and those insiders who have obtained confidential information by reason of their position within that corporation." *Chiarella v. United States*. As a result of this relationship, corporate insiders that possess material, nonpublic information have "a duty to disclose [or to abstain from trading] because of the 'necessity of preventing a corporate insider from . . . tak[ing] unfair advantage of . . . uninformed . . . stockholders.' " *Id.*

In accepting this theory of insider trading, the Supreme Court explicitly rejected the notion of "a general duty between all participants in market transactions to forgo actions based on material, nonpublic information." *Id.* Instead, the Court limited the scope of insider trading liability to situations where the insider had "a duty to disclose arising from a relationship of trust and confidence between parties to a transaction," such as that between corporate officers and shareholders. *Id.*

An alternative, but overlapping, theory of insider trading liability, commonly called the "misappropriation" theory, expands the scope of insider trading liability to certain other "outsiders," who do not have any fiduciary or other relationship to a corporation or its shareholders. Liability may attach where an "outsider" possesses material non-public information about a corporation and another person uses that information to trade in breach of a duty owed to the owner. [. . .]

B. Tipping Liability

[. . .] Courts have expanded insider trading liability to reach situations where the insider or misappropriator in possession of material nonpublic information (the "tipper") does not himself trade but discloses the information to an outsider (a "tippee") who then trades on the basis of the information before it is publicly disclosed. The elements of tipping liability are the same, regardless of whether the tipper's duty arises under the "classical" or the "misappropriation" theory.

[. . .] [In *Dirks*, the Court articulated the general principle of tipping liability: "Not only are insiders forbidden by their fiduciary relationship from personally using undisclosed corporate information to their advantage, but they may not give such information to an outsider for the same improper purpose of exploiting the information for their personal gain." *Dirks v. S.E.C.* The test for determining whether the corporate insider has breached his fiduciary duty "is whether the insider personally will benefit, directly or indirectly, from his disclosure. Absent some personal gain, there has been no breach of duty . . . ." *Id.*

The Supreme Court rejected the SEC's theory that a recipient of confidential information (i.e. the "tippee") must refrain from trading "whenever he receives inside information from an insider." Id. Instead, the Court held that "[t]he tippee's duty to disclose or abstain is derivative from that of the insider's duty." Id. Because the tipper's breach of fiduciary duty requires that he "personally will benefit, directly or indirectly, from his disclosure," a tippee may not be held liable in the absence of such benefit. Moreover, the Supreme Court held that a tippee may be found liable "only when the insider has breached his fiduciary duty . . . and the tippee knows or should know that there has been a breach." *Id.* [. . .]

E. Mens Rea

Liability for securities fraud also requires proof that the defendant acted with [. . .] "a mental state embracing intent to deceive, manipulate or defraud." *Ernst & Ernst v. Hochfelder.* In order to establish a criminal violation of the securities laws, the Government must show that the defendant acted "willfully." 15 U.S.C. § 78ff(a). We have defined willfulness in this context "as a realization on the defendant's part that he was doing a wrongful act under the securities laws." *United States v. Cassese.* [. . .]

II. The Requirements of Tippee Liability

The Government concedes that tippee liability requires proof of a personal benefit to the insider. However, the Government argues that it was not required to prove that Newman and Chiasson knew that the insiders at Dell and NVIDIA received a personal benefit in order to be found guilty of insider trading. Instead, the Government contends [. . .] that it merely needed to prove that the "defendants traded on material, nonpublic information they knew insiders had disclosed in breach of a duty of confidentiality . . . ."

In support of this position, the Government cites *Dirks* for the proposition that the Supreme Court only required that the "tippee know that the tipper disclosed information in breach of a duty." In addition, the Government relies on dicta in a number of our decisions post-*Dirks*, in which we have described the elements of tippee liability without specifically stating that the Government must prove that the tippee knew that the corporate insider who disclosed confidential information did so for his own personal benefit. By selectively parsing this dictum, the Government seeks to revive the absolute bar on tippee trading that the Supreme Court explicitly rejected in *Dirks*.

[However,] the Supreme Court was quite clear in *Dirks*. First, the tippee's liability derives only from the tipper's breach of a fiduciary duty, not from trading on material, non-public information. [. . .] Second, the corporate insider has committed no breach of fiduciary duty unless he receives a personal benefit in exchange for the disclosure. Third, even in the presence of a tipper's breach, a tippee is liable only if he knows or should have known of the breach.

While we have not yet been presented with the question of whether the tippee's knowledge of a tipper's breach requires knowledge of the tipper's personal benefit, the answer follows naturally from *Dirks*. *Dirks* counsels us that the exchange of confidential information for personal benefit is not separate from an insider's fiduciary breach; it is the fiduciary breach that triggers liability for securities fraud under Rule 10b–5. For purposes of insider trading liability, the insider's disclosure of confidential information, standing alone, is not a breach. Thus, without establishing that the tippee knows of the personal benefit received by the insider in exchange for the disclosure, the Government cannot meet its burden of showing that the tippee knew of a breach.

[. . .] We note that the Government has not cited, nor have we found, a single case in which tippees as remote as Newman and Chiasson have been held *criminally* liable for insider trading. [. . .]

In light of Dirks, we find no support for the Government's contention that knowledge of a breach of the duty of confidentiality without knowledge of the personal benefit is sufficient to impose criminal liability. [. . .] [N]othing in the law requires a symmetry of information in the nation's securities markets.

[. . .] [W]e conclude that a tippee's knowledge of the insider's breach necessarily requires knowledge that the insider disclosed confidential information in exchange for personal benefit. [. . .]

In sum, we hold that to sustain an insider trading conviction against a tippee, the Government must prove each of the following elements beyond a reasonable doubt: that (1) the corporate insider was entrusted with a fiduciary duty; (2) the corporate insider breached his fiduciary duty by (a) disclosing confidential information to a tippee (b) in exchange for a personal benefit; (3) the tippee knew of the tipper's breach, that is, he knew the information was confidential and divulged for personal benefit; and (4) the tippee still used that information to trade in a security or tip another individual for personal benefit.

In view of this conclusion, we find [. . .] that the district court's instruction failed to accurately advise the jury of the law. [. . .]

III. Insufficiency of the Evidence

[. . .] The circumstantial evidence in this case was simply too thin to warrant the inference that the corporate insiders received any personal benefit in exchange for their tips. As to the Dell tips, the Government established that Goyal and Ray were not "close" friends, but had known each other for years, having both attended business school and worked at Dell together. Further, Ray, who wanted to become a Wall Street analyst like Goyal, sought career advice and assistance from Goyal. The evidence further showed that Goyal advised Ray on a range of topics, from discussing the qualifying examination in order to become a financial analyst to editing Ray's résumé and sending it to a Wall Street recruiter, and that some of this assistance began before Ray began to provide tips about Dell's earnings. The evidence also established that Lim and Choi were "family friends" that had met through church and occasionally socialized together. The Government argues that these facts were sufficient to prove that the tippers derived some benefit from the tip. We disagree. If this was a "benefit," practically anything would qualify.

We have observed that "[p]ersonal benefit is broadly defined to include not only pecuniary gain, but also [. . .] any reputational benefit that will translate into future earnings and the benefit one would obtain from simply making a gift of confidential information to a trading relative or friend." *United States v. Jiau*. This standard, although permissive, does not suggest that the Government may prove the receipt of a personal benefit by the mere fact of a friendship, particularly of a casual or social nature. [. . .] [The burden of proof] requires evidence of "a relationship between the insider and the recipient that suggests a quid pro quo from the latter, or an intention to benefit the [latter]." *United States v. Jiau*.

[. . .] Here the "career advice" that Goyal gave Ray, the Dell tipper, was little more than the encouragement one would generally expect of a fellow alumnus or casual acquaintance. Crucially, Goyal testified that he would have given Ray advice without receiving information because he routinely did so for industry colleagues. Although the Government argues that the jury could have reasonably inferred from the evidence that Ray and Goyal swapped career advice for inside information, Ray himself disavowed that any such quid pro quo existed. Further, the evidence showed Goyal began giving Ray "career advice" over a year before Ray began providing any insider information. Thus, it would not be possible under the circumstances for a jury in a criminal trial to find beyond a reasonable doubt that Ray received a personal benefit in exchange for the disclosure of confidential information.

The evidence of personal benefit was even more scant in the NVIDIA chain. [EDS.—The court concluded there was insufficient evidence to support an inference of personal benefit. The court also held that the Government did not present any evidence that Newman or Chiasson knew the insiders received a personal benefit in exchange for sharing the confidential information.]

It is largely uncontroverted that Chiasson and Newman, and even their analysts, [. . .] knew next to nothing about the insiders and nothing about what, if any, personal benefit had been provided to them. Adondakis said that he did not know what the relationship between the insider and the first-level tippee was, nor was he aware of any personal benefits exchanged for the information, nor did he communicate any such information to Chiasson. Adondakis testified that he merely told Chiasson that Goyal "was talking to someone within Dell," and that a friend of a friend of Tortora's would be getting NVIDIA information.

Adondakis further testified that he did not specifically tell Chiasson that the source of the NVIDIA information worked at NVIDIA. Similarly, Tortora testified that, while he was aware Goyal received information from someone at Dell who had access to "overall" financial numbers, he was not aware of the insider's name, or position, or the circumstances of how Goyal obtained the information. Tortora further testified that he did not know whether Choi received a personal benefit for disclosing inside information regarding NVIDIA.

The Government now invites us to conclude that the jury could have found that the appellants knew the insiders disclosed the information "for some personal reason rather than for no reason at all." But the Supreme Court affirmatively rejected the premise that a tipper who discloses confidential information necessarily does so to receive a personal benefit. *See Dirks v. S.E.C.* Moreover, it is inconceivable that a jury could conclude, beyond a reasonable doubt, that Newman and Chiasson were aware of a personal benefit, when Adondakis and Tortora, who were more intimately involved in the insider trading scheme as part of the "corrupt" analyst group, disavowed any such knowledge. [. . .]

In short, the bare facts in support of the Government's theory of the case are as consistent with an inference of innocence as one of guilt. [. . .] Because the Government failed to demonstrate that Newman and Chiasson had the intent to commit insider trading, it cannot sustain the convictions on either the substantive insider trading counts or the conspiracy count. Consequently, we reverse Newman and Chiasson's convictions and remand with instructions to dismiss the indictment [with prejudice] as it pertains to them. [. . .]

Salman v. United States
137 S. Ct. 420 (2016)

■ ALITO, JUSTICE, for the unanimous Court.

Section 10(b) of the Securities Exchange Act of 1934 and the Securities and Exchange Commission's Rule 10b–5 prohibit undisclosed trading on inside corporate information by individuals who are under a duty of trust and confidence that prohibits them from secretly using such information for their personal advantage. Individuals under this duty may face criminal and civil liability for trading on inside information (unless they make appropriate disclosures ahead of time).

These persons also may not tip inside information to others for trading. The tippee acquires the tipper's duty to disclose or abstain from trading if the tippee knows the information was disclosed in breach of the tipper's duty, and the tippee may commit securities fraud by trading in disregard of that knowledge. In *Dirks v. SEC*, this Court explained that a tippee's liability for trading on inside information hinges on whether the tipper breached a fiduciary duty by disclosing the information. A tipper breaches such a fiduciary duty, we held, when the tipper discloses the inside information for a personal benefit. And, we went on to say, a jury can infer a personal benefit—and thus a breach of the tipper's duty— where the tipper receives something of value in exchange for the tip or "makes a gift of confidential information to a trading relative or friend." *Id.* [. . .]

I

Maher Kara was an investment banker in Citigroup's healthcare investment banking group. He dealt with highly confidential information about mergers and acquisitions involving Citigroup's clients. Maher enjoyed a close relationship with his older brother, Mounir Kara (known as Michael). After Maher started at Citigroup, he began discussing aspects of his job with Michael. At first, he relied on Michael's chemistry background to help him grasp scientific concepts relevant to his new job. [. . .] Michael began to trade on the information Maher shared with him. At first, Maher was unaware of his brother's trading activity, but eventually he began to suspect that it was taking place.

Ultimately, Maher began to assist Michael's trading by sharing inside information with his brother about pending mergers and acquisitions. Maher sometimes used code words to communicate corporate information to his brother. Other times, he shared inside information about deals he was not working on in order to avoid detection. Without his younger brother's knowledge, Michael fed the information to others— including Salman, Michael's friend and Maher's brother-in-law. By the time the authorities caught on, Salman had made over $1.5 million in profits that he split with another relative who executed trades via a brokerage account on Salman's behalf.

Salman was indicted on one count of conspiracy to commit securities fraud and four counts of securities fraud. Facing charges of their own, both Maher and Michael pleaded guilty and testified at Salman's trial.

The evidence at trial established that Maher and Michael enjoyed a "very close relationship." Maher "love[d] [his] brother very much," Michael was like "a second father to Maher," and Michael was the best man at Maher's wedding to Salman's sister. Maher testified that he shared inside information with his brother to benefit him and with the expectation that his brother would trade on it. While Maher explained that he disclosed the information in large part to appease Michael (who pestered him incessantly for it), he also testified that he tipped his brother to "help him" and to "fulfil[l] whatever needs he had." For instance, Michael once called Maher and told him that "he needed a favor." Maher offered his brother money but Michael asked for information instead. Maher then disclosed an upcoming acquisition. Although he instantly regretted the tip and called his brother back to implore him not to trade, Maher expected his brother to do so anyway.

For his part, Michael told the jury that his brother's tips gave him "timely information that the average person does not have access to" and "access to stocks, options, and what have you, that I can capitalize on, that the average person would never have or dream of." Michael testified that he became friends with Salman when Maher was courting Salman's sister and later began sharing Maher's tips with Salman. As he explained at trial, "any time a major deal came in, [Salman] was the first on my phone list." Michael also testified that he told Salman that the information was coming from Maher.

After a jury trial in the Northern District of California, Salman was convicted on all counts. He was sentenced to 36 months of imprisonment, three years of supervised release, and over $730,000 in restitution. After his motion for a new trial was denied, Salman appealed to the Ninth Circuit. [. . .] The court acknowledged that *Dirks* and [the] Second Circuit [*United States v. Newman*] allow a factfinder to infer a personal benefit to the tipper from a gift of confidential information to a trading relative or friend. But the court concluded that, "[t]o the extent" *Dirks* permits "such an inference," the inference "is impermissible in the absence of proof of a meaningfully close personal relationship that generates an exchange that is objective, consequential, and represents at least a potential gain of a pecuniary or similarly valuable nature."

Pointing to *Newman,* Salman argued that his conviction should be reversed. While the evidence established that Maher made a gift of trading information to Michael and that Salman knew it, there was no evidence that Maher received anything of "a pecuniary or similarly valuable nature" in exchange—or that Salman knew of any such benefit. The Ninth Circuit disagreed and affirmed Salman's conviction. The court reasoned that the case was governed by *Dirks*'s holding that a tipper benefits personally by making a gift of confidential information to a trading relative or friend. Indeed, Maher's disclosures to Michael were "precisely the gift of confidential information to a trading relative that *Dirks* envisioned." To the extent *Newman* went further and required additional gain to the tipper in cases involving gifts of confidential information to family and friends, the Ninth Circuit "decline[d] to follow it."

We granted certiorari to resolve the tension between the Second Circuit's *Newman* decision and the Ninth Circuit's decision in this case.

II

A

In this case, Salman contends that an insider's "gift of confidential information to a trading relative or friend," *Dirks v. SEC,* is not enough to establish securities fraud. Instead, Salman argues, a tipper does not personally benefit unless the tipper's goal in disclosing inside information is to obtain money, property, or something of tangible value. He claims that our insider-trading precedents, and the cases those precedents cite, involve situations in which the insider exploited confidential information for the insider's own "tangible monetary profit."

He suggests that his position is reinforced by our criminal-fraud precedents outside of the insider-trading context, because those cases confirm that a fraudster must personally obtain money or property. More broadly, Salman urges that defining a gift as a personal benefit renders the insider-trading offense indeterminate and overbroad: indeterminate, because liability may turn on facts such as the closeness of the relationship between tipper and tippee and the tipper's purpose for disclosure; and overbroad, because the Government may avoid having to prove a concrete personal benefit by simply arguing that the tipper meant to give a gift to the tippee. He also argues that we should interpret *Dirks'* standard narrowly so as to avoid constitutional concerns. Finally, Salman contends that gift situations create especially troubling problems for remote tippees—that is, tippees who receive inside information from another tippee, rather than the tipper—who may have no knowledge of the relationship between the original tipper and tippee and thus may not know why the tipper made the disclosure.

The Government disagrees and argues that a gift of confidential information to anyone, not just a "trading relative or friend," is enough to prove securities fraud. Under the Government's view, a tipper personally benefits whenever the tipper discloses confidential trading information for a noncorporate purpose. Accordingly, a gift to a friend, a family member, or anyone else would support the inference that the tipper exploited the trading value of inside information for personal purposes and thus personally benefited from the disclosure. The Government claims to find support for this reading in *Dirks* and the precedents on which *Dirks* relied.

The Government also argues that Salman's concerns about unlimited and indeterminate liability for remote tippees are significantly alleviated by other statutory elements that prosecutors must satisfy to convict a tippee for insider trading. The Government observes that, in order to establish a defendant's criminal liability as a tippee, it must prove beyond a reasonable doubt that the tipper expected that the information being disclosed would be used in securities trading. The Government also notes that, to establish a defendant's criminal liability as a tippee, it must prove that the tippee knew that the tipper breached a duty—in other words, that the tippee knew that the tipper disclosed the information for a personal benefit and that the tipper expected trading to ensue.

B

We adhere to *Dirks*, which easily resolves the narrow issue presented here.

In *Dirks*, we explained that a tippee is exposed to liability for trading on inside information only if the tippee participates in a breach of the tipper's fiduciary duty. Whether the tipper breached that duty depends "in large part on the purpose of the disclosure" to the tippee. *Dirks v. SEC.* "[T]he test," we explained, "is whether the insider personally will benefit, directly or indirectly, from his disclosure." *Id.* Thus, the disclosure of confidential information without personal benefit is not enough. In determining whether a tipper derived a personal benefit, we instructed courts to "focus on objective criteria, *i.e.*, whether the insider receives a direct or indirect personal benefit from the disclosure, such as a pecuniary gain or a reputational benefit that will translate into future earnings." *Id.* This personal benefit can "often" be inferred "from objective facts and circumstances," we explained, such as "a relationship between the insider and the recipient that suggests a *quid pro quo* from the latter, or an intention to benefit the particular recipient." *Id.* In particular, we held that "[t]he elements of fiduciary duty and exploitation of nonpublic information also exist *when an insider makes a gift of confidential information to a trading relative or friend.*" *Id.* In such cases, "[t]he tip and trade resemble trading by the insider followed by a gift of the profits to the recipient." *Id.* We then applied this gift-giving principle to resolve *Dirks* itself, finding it dispositive that the tippers "received no monetary or personal benefit" from their tips to Dirks, "*nor was their purpose to make a gift of valuable information to Dirks.*" *Id.*

Our discussion of gift giving resolves this case. Maher, the tipper, provided inside information to a close relative, his brother Michael. *Dirks* makes clear that a tipper breaches a fiduciary duty by making a gift of confidential information to "a trading relative," and that rule is sufficient to resolve the case at hand. As Salman's counsel acknowledged at oral argument, Maher would have breached his duty had he personally traded on the information here himself then given the proceeds as a gift to his brother. It is obvious that Maher would personally benefit in that situation. But Maher effectively achieved the same result by disclosing the information to Michael, and allowing him to trade on it. *Dirks* appropriately prohibits that approach, as well. *Dirks* specifies that when a tipper gives inside information to "a trading relative or friend," the jury can infer that the tipper meant to provide the equivalent of a cash gift. In such situations, the tipper benefits personally because giving a gift of trading information is the same thing as trading by the tipper followed by a gift of the proceeds. Here, by disclosing confidential information as a gift to his brother with the expectation that he would trade on it, Maher breached his duty of trust and confidence to Citigroup and its clients—a duty Salman acquired, and breached himself, by trading on the information with full knowledge that it had been improperly disclosed.

To the extent *Newman* held that the tipper must also receive something of a "pecuniary or similarly valuable nature" in exchange for a gift to family or friends, we agree with the Ninth Circuit that this requirement is inconsistent with *Dirks*.

C

[. . .] Making a gift of inside information to a relative like Michael is little different from trading on the information, obtaining the profits, and doling them out to the trading relative. The tipper benefits either way. The facts of this case illustrate the point: In one of their tipper-tippee interactions, Michael asked Maher for a favor, declined Maher's offer of money, and instead requested and received lucrative trading information.

[. . .] Salman's conduct is in the heartland of *Dirks'* rule concerning gifts. It remains the case that "[d]etermining whether an insider personally benefits from a particular disclosure, a question of fact, will not always be easy for courts." *Dirks v. SEC*. But there is no need for us to address those difficult cases today, because [as the Ninth Circuit concluded,] this case involves "precisely the 'gift of confidential information to a trading relative' that *Dirks* envisioned."

[. . .] Accordingly, the Ninth Circuit's judgment is affirmed.

3. MISAPPROPRIATION

United States v. O'Hagan
521 U.S. 642 (1997)

■ GINSBURG, JUSTICE, for the majority.

This case concerns the interpretation and enforcement of § 10(b) and § 14(e) of the Securities Exchange Act of 1934, and rules made by the Securities and Exchange Commission pursuant to these provisions, Rule 10b–5 and Rule 14e–3(a). Two prime questions are presented. [. . .] (1) Is a person who trades in securities for personal profit, using confidential information misappropriated in breach of a fiduciary duty to the source of the information, guilty of violating § 10(b) and Rule 10b–5? (2) Did the Commission exceed its rulemaking authority by adopting Rule 14e–3(a), which proscribes trading on undisclosed information in the tender offer setting, even in the absence of a duty to disclose? [. . .]

I

Respondent James Herman O'Hagan was a partner in the law firm of Dorsey & Whitney in Minneapolis, Minnesota. In July 1988, Grand Metropolitan PLC (Grand Met), a company based in London, England, retained Dorsey & Whitney as local counsel to represent Grand Met regarding a potential tender offer for the common stock of the Pillsbury Company, headquartered in Minneapolis. Both Grand Met and Dorsey & Whitney took precautions to protect the confidentiality of Grand Met's tender offer plans. O'Hagan did no work on the Grand Met representation. [. . .]

On August 18, 1988, while Dorsey & Whitney was still representing Grand Met, O'Hagan began purchasing call options for Pillsbury stock. Each option gave him the right to purchase 100 shares of Pillsbury stock by a specified date in September 1988. [. . .] By the end of September, he owned 2,500 unexpired Pillsbury options, apparently more than any other individual investor. O'Hagan also purchased, in September 1988, some 5,000 shares of Pillsbury common stock, at a price just under $39 per share. When Grand Met announced its tender offer in October, the price of Pillsbury stock rose to nearly $60 per share. O'Hagan then sold his Pillsbury call options and common stock, making a profit of more than $4.3 million.

The Securities and Exchange Commission (SEC or Commission) initiated an investigation into O'Hagan's transactions, culminating in a 57-count indictment. The indictment alleged that O'Hagan defrauded his law firm and its client, Grand Met, by using for his own trading purposes material, nonpublic information regarding Grand Met's planned tender offer. According to the indictment, O'Hagan used the profits he gained through this trading to conceal his previous embezzlement and conversion of unrelated client trust funds. [Among other charges,] O'Hagan was charged with [. . .] 17 counts of securities fraud, in violation of § 10(b) of the Securities Exchange Act of 1934 (Exchange Act) and SEC Rule 10b–5; [and] 17 counts of fraudulent trading in connection with a tender offer, in violation of § 14(e) of the Exchange Act, and SEC Rule 14e–3(a). A jury convicted O'Hagan on all 57 counts, and he was sentenced to a 41-month term of imprisonment.

A divided panel of the Court of Appeals for the Eighth Circuit reversed all of O'Hagan's convictions. Liability under § 10(b) and Rule 10b–5, the Eighth Circuit held, may not be grounded on the "misappropriation theory" of securities fraud on which the prosecution relied. The Court of Appeals also held that Rule 14e–3(a)—which prohibits trading while in possession of material, nonpublic information relating to a tender offer— exceeds the SEC's § 14(e) rulemaking authority because the Rule contains no breach of fiduciary duty requirement. [. . .]

Decisions of the Courts of Appeals are in conflict on the propriety of the misappropriation theory under § 10(b) and Rule 10b–5, and on the legitimacy of Rule 14e–3(a) under § 14(e). We granted certiorari and now reverse the Eighth Circuit's judgment.

II

We address first the Court of Appeals' reversal of O'Hagan's convictions under § 10(b) and Rule 10b–5. [. . .] [T]he Eighth Circuit rejected the misappropriation theory as a basis for § 10(b) liability. We hold, in accord with several other Courts of Appeals, that criminal liability under § 10(b) may be predicated on the misappropriation theory.

A

[. . .] Under the "traditional" or "classical theory" of insider trading liability, § 10(b) and Rule 10b–5 are violated when a corporate insider trades in the securities of his corporation on the basis of material, nonpublic information. Trading on such information qualifies as a "deceptive device" under § 10(b), we have affirmed, because "a relationship of trust and confidence [exists] between the shareholders of a corporation and those insiders who have obtained confidential information by reason of their position with that corporation." *Chiarella v. United States.* That relationship, we recognized, "gives rise to a duty to disclose [or to abstain from trading] because of the 'necessity of preventing a corporate insider from . . . tak[ing] unfair advantage of . . . uninformed . . . stockholders.' " *Id.* The classical theory applies not only to officers, directors, and other permanent insiders of a corporation, but also to attorneys, accountants, consultants, and others who temporarily become fiduciaries of a corporation.

The "misappropriation theory" holds that a person commits fraud "in connection with" a securities transaction, and thereby violates § 10(b) and Rule 10b–5, when he misappropriates confidential information for securities trading purposes, in breach of a duty owed to the source of the information. Under this theory, a fiduciary's undisclosed, self-serving use of a principal's information to purchase or sell securities, in breach of a duty of loyalty and confidentiality, defrauds the principal of the exclusive use of that information. In lieu of premising liability on a fiduciary relationship between company insider and purchaser or seller of the company's stock, the misappropriation theory premises liability on a fiduciary-turned-trader's deception of those who entrusted him with access to confidential information.

The two theories are complementary, each addressing efforts to capitalize on nonpublic information through the purchase or sale of securities. The classical theory targets a corporate insider's breach of duty to shareholders with whom the insider transacts; the misappropriation theory outlaws trading on the basis of nonpublic information by a corporate "outsider" in breach of a duty owed not to a trading party, but to the source of the information. [As the Government explains in its brief,] the misappropriation theory is thus designed to "protec[t] the integrity of the securities markets against abuses by 'outsiders' to a corporation who have access to confidential information that will affect th[e] corporation's security price when revealed, but who owe no fiduciary or other duty to that corporation's shareholders."

In this case, the indictment alleged that O'Hagan, in breach of a duty of trust and confidence he owed to his law firm, Dorsey & Whitney, and to its client, Grand Met, traded on the basis of nonpublic information regarding Grand Met's planned tender offer for Pillsbury common stock. This conduct, the Government charged, constituted a fraudulent device in connection with the purchase and sale of securities.[5]

B

We agree with the Government that misappropriation, as just defined, satisfies § 10(b)'s requirement that chargeable conduct involve a

---

[5]	The Government could not have prosecuted O'Hagan under the classical theory, for O'Hagan was not an "insider" of Pillsbury, the corporation in whose stock he traded. Although an "outsider" with respect to Pillsbury, O'Hagan had an intimate association with, and was found to have traded on confidential information from, Dorsey & Whitney, counsel to tender offeror Grand Met. Under the misappropriation theory, O'Hagan's securities trading does not escape Exchange Act sanction [. . .] simply because he was associated with, and gained nonpublic information from, the bidder, rather than the target.

"deceptive device or contrivance" used "in connection with" the purchase or sale of securities. We observe, first, that misappropriators, as the Government describes them, deal in deception. [As the Government notes in its brief,] [a] fiduciary who "[pretends] loyalty to the principal while secretly converting the principal's information for personal gain," defrauds the principal. [. . .]

Deception through nondisclosure is central to the theory of liability for which the Government seeks recognition. As counsel for the Government stated in explanation of the theory at oral argument: "[. . .] To satisfy the requirement of the Securities Act that there be no deception, there would only have to be disclosure."

The misappropriation theory advanced by the Government is consistent with *Santa Fe Industries, Inc. v. Green,* a decision underscoring that § 10(b) is not an all-purpose breach of fiduciary duty ban; rather, it trains on conduct involving manipulation or deception. In contrast to the Government's allegations in this case, in *Santa Fe Industries,* all pertinent facts were disclosed by the persons charged with violating § 10(b) and Rule 10b–5 therefore, there was no deception through nondisclosure to which liability under those provisions could attach. Similarly, full disclosure forecloses liability under the misappropriation theory: Because the deception essential to the misappropriation theory involves feigning fidelity to the source of information, if the fiduciary discloses to the source that he plans to trade on the nonpublic information, there is no "deceptive device" and thus no § 10(b) violation— although the fiduciary-turned-trader may remain liable under state law for breach of a duty of loyalty.

We turn next to the § 10(b) requirement that the misappropriator's deceptive use of information be "in connection with the purchase or sale of [a] security." This element is satisfied because the fiduciary's fraud is consummated, not when the fiduciary gains the confidential information, but when, without disclosure to his principal, he uses the information to purchase or sell securities. The securities transaction and the breach of duty thus coincide. This is so even though the person or entity defrauded is not the other party to the trade, but is, instead, the source of the nonpublic information. A misappropriator who trades on the basis of material, nonpublic information, in short, gains his advantageous market position through deception; he deceives the source of the information and simultaneously harms members of the investing public.

[. . .] The misappropriation theory comports with § 10(b)'s language, which requires deception "in connection with the purchase or sale of any security," not deception of an identifiable purchaser or seller. The theory is also well tuned to an animating purpose of the Exchange Act: to insure honest securities markets and thereby promote investor confidence. Although informational disparity is inevitable in the securities markets, investors likely would hesitate to venture their capital in a market where trading based on misappropriated nonpublic information is unchecked by law. An investor's informational disadvantage vis-á-vis a misappropriator with material, nonpublic information stems from contrivance, not luck; it is a disadvantage that cannot be overcome with research or skill.

In sum, considering the inhibiting impact on market participation of trading on misappropriated information, and the congressional purposes underlying § 10(b), it makes scant sense to hold a lawyer like O'Hagan a § 10(b) violator if he works for a law firm representing the target of a tender offer, but not if he works for a law firm representing the bidder. The text of the statute requires no such result. The misappropriation at issue here was properly made the subject of a § 10(b) charge because it meets the statutory requirement that there be "deceptive" conduct "in connection with" securities transactions. [. . .]

III

We consider next the ground on which the Court of Appeals reversed O'Hagan's convictions for fraudulent trading in connection with a tender offer, in violation of § 14(e) of the Exchange Act and SEC Rule 14e–3(a). A sole question is before us as to these convictions: Did the Commission, as the Court of Appeals held, exceed its rulemaking authority under § 14(e) when it adopted Rule 14e–3(a) without requiring a showing that the trading at issue entailed a breach of fiduciary duty? We hold that the Commission, in this regard and to the extent relevant to this case, did not exceed its authority.

The governing statutory provision, § 14(e) of the Exchange Act, reads in relevant part:

> It shall be unlawful for any person . . . to engage in any fraudulent, deceptive, or manipulative acts or practices, in connection with any tender offer . . . .The [SEC] shall, for the purposes of this subsection, by rules and regulations define, and prescribe means reasonably designed to prevent, such acts and practices as are fraudulent, deceptive, or manipulative.

Section 14(e)'s first sentence prohibits fraudulent acts in connection with a tender offer. This self-operating proscription was one of several provisions added to the Exchange Act in 1968 by the Williams Act. The section's second sentence delegates definitional and prophylactic rulemaking authority to the Commission. Congress added this rulemaking delegation to § 14(e) in 1970 amendments to the Williams Act.

Through § 14(e) and other provisions on disclosure in the Williams Act, Congress sought to ensure that shareholders "confronted by a cash tender offer for their stock [would] not be required to respond without adequate information." *Rondeau v. Mosinee Paper Corp.* [. . .]

Relying on § 14(e)'s rulemaking authorization, the Commission, in 1980, promulgated Rule 14e–3(a). That measure provides:

> (a) If any person has taken a substantial step or steps to commence, or has commenced, a tender offer (the 'offering person'), it shall constitute a fraudulent, deceptive or manipulative act or practice within the meaning of section 14(e) of the [Exchange] Act for any other person who is in possession of material information relating to such tender offer which information he knows or has reason to know is nonpublic and which he knows or has reason to know has been acquired directly or indirectly from:
>
> > (1) The offering person,
> >
> > (2) The issuer of the securities sought or to be sought by such tender offer, or
> >
> > (3) Any officer, director, partner or employee or any other person acting on behalf of the offering person or such issuer, to purchase or sell or cause to be purchased or sold any of such securities or any securities convertible into or exchangeable for any such securities or any option or right to obtain or to dispose of any of the foregoing securities, unless within a reasonable time prior to any purchase or sale such information and its source are publicly disclosed by press release or otherwise."

As characterized by the Commission, Rule 14e–3(a) is a "disclose or abstain from trading" requirement. The Second Circuit concisely described the Rule's thrust:

> One violates Rule 14e–3(a) if he trades on the basis of material nonpublic information concerning a pending tender offer that he knows or has reason to know has been acquired 'directly or indirectly' from an insider of the offeror or issuer, or someone working on their behalf. Rule 14e–3(a) is a disclosure provision. It creates a duty in those traders who fall within its ambit to abstain or disclose, *without regard to whether the trader owes a pre-existing fiduciary duty* to respect the confidentiality of the information." *United States v. Chestman.*

In the Eighth Circuit's view, because Rule 14e–3(a) applies whether or not the trading in question breaches a fiduciary duty, the regulation exceeds the SEC's § 14(e) rulemaking authority. [. . .]

The Eighth Circuit homed in on the essence of § 14(e)'s rulemaking authorization: "[T]he statute empowers the SEC to 'define' and 'prescribe means reasonably designed to prevent' 'acts and practices' which are 'fraudulent.'" All that means, the Eighth Circuit found plain, is that the SEC may "identify and regulate," in the tender offer context, "acts and practices" the law already defines as "fraudulent"; but, the Eighth Circuit maintained, the SEC may not "create its own definition of fraud." [. . .]

We need not resolve in this case whether the Commission's authority under § 14(e) to "define . . . such acts and practices as are fraudulent" is broader than the Commission's fraud-defining authority under § 10(b), for we agree with the United States that Rule 14e–3(a), as applied to cases of this genre, qualifies under § 14(e) as a "means reasonably designed to prevent" fraudulent trading on material, nonpublic information in the tender offer context. A prophylactic measure, because its mission is to prevent, typically encompasses more than the core activity prohibited. [. . .] We hold, accordingly, that under § 14(e), the Commission may prohibit acts not themselves fraudulent under the common law or § 10(b), if the prohibition is "reasonably designed to prevent . . . acts and practices [that] are fraudulent."

Because Congress has authorized the Commission, in § 14(e), to prescribe legislative rules, we owe the Commission's judgment "more than mere deference or weight." *Batterton v. Francis.* Therefore, in determining whether Rule 14e–3(a)'s "disclose or abstain from trading" requirement is reasonably designed to prevent fraudulent acts, we must accord the Commission's assessment "controlling weight unless [it is] arbitrary, capricious, or manifestly contrary to the statute." *Chevron U.S.A. Inc. v. Natural Resources Defense Council, Inc.* In this case, we conclude, the Commission's assessment is none of these.

The United States emphasizes that Rule 14e–3(a) reaches trading in which "a breach of duty is likely but difficult to prove." "Particularly in the context of a tender offer," as the Tenth Circuit recognized, "there is a fairly wide circle of people with confidential information," notably, the attorneys, investment bankers, and accountants involved in structuring the transaction. *SEC v. Peters.* The availability of that information may lead to abuse, for "even a hint of an upcoming tender offer may send the price of the target company's stock soaring." *SEC v. Materia.* Individuals entrusted with nonpublic information, particularly if they have no long-term loyalty to the issuer, may find the temptation to trade on that information hard to resist in view of "the very large short-term profits potentially available [to them]." *SEC v. Peters.*

"[I]t may be possible to prove circumstantially that a person [traded on the basis of material, nonpublic information], but almost impossible to prove that the trader obtained such information in breach of a fiduciary duty owed either by the trader or by the ultimate insider source of the information." *Id.* [. . .] The SEC, cognizant of the proof problem that could enable sophisticated traders to escape responsibility, placed in Rule 14e–3(a) a "disclose or abstain from trading" command that does not require specific proof of a breach of fiduciary duty. That prescription, we are satisfied, applied to this case, is a "means reasonably designed to prevent" fraudulent trading on material, nonpublic information in the tender offer context. *See United States v. Chestman.* Therefore, insofar as it serves to prevent the type of misappropriation charged against

O'Hagan, Rule 14e–3(a) is a proper exercise of the Commission's prophylactic power under § 14(e). [. . .]

The judgment of the Court of Appeals for the Eighth Circuit is reversed, and the case is remanded for further proceedings consistent with this opinion. [. . .]

4. CIVIL LIABILITY

Morgan Stanley v. Skowron
989 F.Supp.2d 356 (2013)

I. Introduction

Morgan Stanley brings this action against Joseph F. "Chip" Skowron III seeking compensatory and punitive damages, disgorgement, reimbursement, contribution, and attorneys' fees in connection with Skowron's acts of insider trading while employed at Morgan Stanley. [. . .]

Morgan Stanley now moves for partial summary judgement on its faithless servant claim [. . .].

II. Background

In December 2006, Morgan Stanley acquired a hedge-fund management company called FrontPoint Partners LLC. Skowron was employed as a co-portfolio manager at FrontPoint at the time of the acquisition. By letter dated October 31, 2006 (the "Offer Letter"), Morgan Stanley offered Skowron a position as Managing Director and Senior Portfolio Manager. The Offer Letter states that Skowron will receive an annual base salary of $1.5 million, plus Management Fees and Incentive Fees to be calculated based on the overall size and performance of the investment funds managed by Skowron and his co-portfolio managers.

[. . .] [T]he Offer Letter [. . .] require[s] Skowron to comply with Morgan Stanley's Code of Conduct. The Code of Conduct prohibits insider trading and requires employees to safeguard confidential information and cooperate fully with governmental and internal investigations. The Code of Conduct also requires employees to promptly notify Morgan Stanley if they may have violated the law or the firm's policies.

Between April 12, 2007 and December 1, 2010, Morgan Stanley paid Skowron $31,067,356.76 in compensation. On August 15, 2011, Skowron pled guilty to conspiracy to commit insider trading from at least April 2007 through November 2010. In his plea colloquy, Skowron admitted to selling stocks held by Morgan Stanley's portfolios on the basis of material non-public information and then lying to the SEC under oath regarding his receipt of such information. The above actions took place during his tenure as a Morgan Stanley employee.

At the sentencing hearing, Judge Denise Cote sentenced Skowron to five years in prison and awarded Morgan Stanley restitution of twenty percent of Skowron's compensation during the period of the conspiracy. Morgan Stanley then brought this civil case against Skowron seeking forfeiture of the remaining compensation paid during the conspiracy period, among other remedies. [. . .]

IV. Applicable Review

A. New York Faithless Servant Doctrine

New York courts "continue to apply two alternative standards for determining whether an employee's conduct warrants forfeiture under the faithless servant doctrine." *Carco Grp., Inc. v. Maconachy*. Despite the persistence of conflicting standards, "New York courts have not reconciled any differences between them, or defined the circumstances, if any, in which one standard should apply rather than the other." *Phansalkar v. Andersen Weinroth & Co., L.P.*

The first standard is met when "the misconduct and unfaithfulness . . . substantially violates the contract of service" *Id.* such that it "permeate[s] [the employee's] service in its most material and substantial part." *Id.* The second standard requires only "misconduct [ ] that rises to the level of a breach of a duty of loyalty or good faith." *Id.* In other words, it is sufficient that the employee "acts adversely to his employer in any part of the transaction, or omits to disclose any interest which would naturally influence his conduct in dealing with the subject of the employment." *Id.*

An employee who is found to be faithless normally forfeits all compensation received during the period of disloyalty, regardless of whether the employer suffered any damages. However, the Second Circuit has carved out a limited exception where compensation is expressly allocated among discrete tasks, such as commissions. In such cases, the employee may keep compensation derived from any transactions that were separate from and untainted by the disloyalty. [. . .]

V. Discussion

[. . .]

B. Skowron Is a Faithless Servant Under Either Standard

It is not necessary to decide which New York standard applies, because Skowron is a faithless servant under even the more stringent standard. Skowron does not contest that his behavior constituted a breach of the duty of loyalty and good faith. Instead, he argues that his misconduct did not substantially violate the terms of his employment contract such that it permeated his service as an employee.

Morgan Stanley's Code of Conduct, which was made a condition of Skowron's employment, expressly prohibits insider trading and emphasizes the importance of preserving confidentiality. It states in bold italicized letters: "You may never, under any circumstances, trade, encourage others to trade, or recommend securities or other financial instruments based on, and in some circumstances, while in possession of, inside information." The Code requires employees to know and comply with all applicable securities laws, and states that "confidential information generated and gathered in our business is a valuable asset . . . [that] must be protected from the time of its creation or receipt until its authorized disposal." Indeed, several full pages of the Code are devoted to protecting confidential information and preventing the "misuse of inside information." The Code also requires employees to cooperate fully with governmental and internal investigations, and to promptly self-report any possible violation of law or company policy to their superiors.

Skowron argues that his breach of the above provisions was limited and did not permeate his service in substantial part. This argument lacks any merit. Insider trading is the ultimate abuse of a portfolio manager's position and privileges because it goes to the heart of his "primary areas of responsibility." *Phansalkar v. Andersen Weinroth & Co., L.P.* Indeed, "[t]he duty of an employee not to use or divulge confidential knowledge acquired during his employment is implicit in the employer-employee relation, is an absolute, and not a relative duty." *Schanfield v. Sojitz Corp. of Am.* That duty is all the more crucial for a portfolio manager who is "entrusted to lawfully invest hundreds of millions of dollars and to safeguard the Firm's reputation." Plaintiff's Br. In addition to exposing Morgan Stanley to government investigations and direct financial losses, Skowron's behavior damaged the firm's reputation, a valuable corporate asset.

Although Skowron only admitted to one instance of insider trading, he admittedly lied and covered up his involvement for years afterwards. Thus, Skowron's acts of disloyalty "occurred repeatedly," "lasted for many months," "persisted boldly through an opportunity to correct them," and occurred in his "primary areas of responsibility." *Phansalkar v. Andersen Weinroth & Co., L.P.* Under these circumstances, it is patently clear that Skowron's actions substantially violated the terms of his employment contract and permeated his service. [. . .]

It is sufficient that Skowron knowingly committed insider trading, explicitly lied to the SEC under oath, and failed to disclose his participation to Morgan Stanley over the course of several years. This is especially true given that Morgan Stanley's Code of Conduct imposed on Skowron an affirmative duty to disclose any wrongdoing. No reasonable jury could conclude that Skowron's insider trading and subsequent cover-up did not substantially violate the terms of his employment and permeate his service. Because Skowron has raised no genuine issue of material fact for trial, Morgan Stanley is entitled to summary judgment on its faithless servant claim. [. . .]

VI. Conclusion

For the foregoing reasons, Morgan Stanley's motion for partial summary judgment on its faithless servant claim is GRANTED. Skowron must forfeit the full measure of compensation he received from Morgan Stanley during the damages period, namely $31,067,356.76, offset by the amount ordered to be paid as restitution in the criminal proceeding. [. . .]

E. REVIEW PROBLEMS

1. Chris is interested in investing in a safe, liquid commodity. Lori, the owner of Love Galleries, promises that purchasing 12 Impressionist paintings from Love Galleries would produce a safe profit. Lori promises that she will create a market for the 12 paintings, and that Chris can resell the paintings if he wishes. Chris purchases 12 paintings for $1.5 million, and those paintings are accompanied by authentication documents and a "guaranteed repurchase allowance" document. The latter document gives Chris "the right to trade the painting back into the defendant Galleries' Naive American Impressionism fund for a fund painting which had greater profit potential, and a share of the fund's profits when plaintiff, along with other investors, invested for profit in the defendant Galleries' Naive American Impressionism school of art fund." Is the sale of a painting, along with its attendance guaranteed repurchase allowance document, the sale of a security?[1]

2. Juliet, an associate at a major law firm, is representing Big Pharma, a public company, in its acquisition of a Little Pharma, another public company. The deal is set to close in several weeks, at which time Little Pharma will be acquired for three times its trading price. One night, Juliet's boyfriend, who has a key to her apartment, lets himself into the apartment to cook her a surprise dinner before she gets home. Romeo also decides to snoop around Juliet's apartment to figure out her ring size, as he is about to propose marriage to her. While snooping, Romeo, an FBI trainee, comes across some deal documents relating to the Big Pharma/Little Pharma deal. When he learns that Little Pharma will be sold for three times its trading price, he immediately purchases Little Pharma stock (after all, he is a mere trainee and needs to pay for many anticipated engagement- and wedding-related expenses). He also tips several of his friends and family. Under what theory, if any, could Romeo be prosecuted for insider trading?[2]

3. Sven is a former member of Congress who served on committees that oversee the telecommunications industry. He now makes a living as a regulatory consultant. On a routine golf outing with potential consulting clients, Sven is told by the CEO of Telegiant that it plans to purchase Sprightly. Both are public companies. The next day, Sven purchases Sprightly stock through his own account and his spouse's account. When Telegiant acquires Sprightly, Sprightly's stock soars in value and Sven profits to the tune of $1 million. Under what theory, if any, could Sven be prosecuted for insider trading?[3]

---

[1] *See* Stenger v. R.H. Love Galleries, Inc., 741 F.2d. 144 (1984).

[2] *See* https://www.justice.gov/usao-sdny/press-release/file/1521706/download.

[3] *See* https://www.sec.gov/news/press-release/2022-128.

INDEX

References are to Pages

Loss of capacity, principal's, 66
Manifestation terminating actual authority, 66
Restatement provisions, 65–67
Third parties, principal's liability in tort, 43–44
Tort liability. Liability in tort, principal's, above
Undisclosed principal's liability, 35

Mergers and acquisitions, 535–536, 642–651

CLOSELY HELD CORPORATIONS
Certificate of incorporation, 665
Custodian, appointment of, 667
Discretion, agreements restricting, 666
Provisional director, appointment of, 667
Discriminatory policy favoring employee stockholders, 668–676
Election of existing corporation, 666
Fiduciary duties, breach of
Discriminatory policy favoring employee stockholders, 668–676
Minority stockholder, repurchase of shares, 679–683
Minority stockholder/employee, liability to, 677–679
Management by stockholders, 666–667
Minority stockholder, repurchase of shares, 679–683
Minority stockholder/employee, liability to, 677–679
Provisional director, appointment of, 667

CONFLICTS OF INTEREST
Corporate directors and officers, 455–461

Liability in contract. Agency, this index

Authority of officers, 232–238
Forum selection provisions, 224–231
Candor, duty of, 468–474
Certificate of incorporation, 209–211
Classes and series of stock, 213
Closely Held Corporations, this index
Conflicts of interest, directors and officers, 455–461
Corporate opportunity doctrine, 461–468

Corporate purpose
Generally, 244–258
Business Roundtable statement, 257–258
De facto corporations and corporations by estoppel, 691–695
Definitions
Generally, 201–214
Delaware law, 209–214
Statutory terminology, 203
Derivative actions. Shareholders, this index
Directors and officers
Authority of officers, 232–238
Conflicts of interest, 455–461
Demands and duties, intersection of, 495–503
Duty of loyalty, below
Fiduciary duties, below
Indemnification, 421–422
Independence of directors, 410–415
Settlement agreement, entering into, 232–238
Dominant shareholders. Duty of loyalty, below
Duties and demands, intersection of, 495–503
Duty of candor, 468–474
Duty of care
Generally, 423–454
Business judgment rule, 432–442
Demand futility, 442–450
Dividend in kind as waste of corporate assets, 423–427
Duty of loyalty
Generally, 454–474
Conflicts of interest, 455–461
Controlling shareholders
Generally, 503–528
Exercise of control over business, 513–516
Parent and subsidiary, 503–507
Performance awards, standard of review, 516–528
Corporate opportunity doctrine, 461–468
Delaware law, 454
Intrinsic fairness test, 503–507
Parent and subsidiary, 503–507
Fiduciary duties of directors and officers
Generally, 419–531
Conflicts of interest, 455–461
Corporate opportunity doctrine, 461–468
Demands and duties, intersection of, 495–503
Duty of candor, 468–474
Duty of care, above
Duty of loyalty, above
Good faith obligation
Generally, 474–489
Caremark duties, 489–495
Review problems, 528–531
Roles of directors and officers, Delaware law, 419–423